The Almanac of British Politics

'A really useful guide to our rulers, a fountain of arcana and attitude.'

Jeremy Paxman

Praise for previous editions:

'The political equivalent of Wisden.'

Martin Kettle, *The Sunday Times*

'Quite simply, this is the bible, certainly as far as reporters of electoral politics are concerned ... It is Waller's encyclopaedic knowledge of the electoral map coupled with ... Criddle's idiosyncratic pen portraits that make the *Almanac* what it is today.'

Professor Michael Thrasher, University of Plymouth, *Representation*

'An essential guide for political journalists, a mine of information for enthusiasts, useful for everyone else and a bargain.'

Professor David Denver, Lancaster University

The Almanac of British Politics has established itself over nearly twenty years as the definitive guide to the electoral map of Great Britain. This new edition has been thoroughly revised and updated following Labour's historic election victory in 2001. Its comprehensive coverage provides a witty and informative biographical profile of every Member of Parliament and a detailed social, demographic, economic and political analysis of each constituency. In addition it contains a wealth of maps, tables and statistics to give the clearest picture of the British social and political landscape in the twenty-first century.

Robert Waller is Head of History at Greenacre School, Banstead, and a former Fellow and Lecturer in Politics and History at Oxford University.

Byron Criddle is Reader in Politics at the University of Aberdeen.

The Almanac of British Politics

Seventh Edition

Robert Waller and Byron Criddle

London and New York

First edition published 1983
Second edition 1985
Third edition 1987
by Croom Helm Ltd

Fourth edition published 1991
Fifth edition 1996
Sixth edition 1999
Seventh edition 2002
by Routledge
11 New Fetter Lane, London EC4P 4EE

Simultaneously published in the USA and Canada
by Routledge
29 West 35th Street, New York, NY 10001

Routledge is an imprint of the Taylor & Francis Group

© 1983, 1985, 1987, 1991 Robert Waller
© 1996, 1999, 2002 Robert Waller and Byron Criddle

Typeset in Times by
HWA Text and Data Management, Tunbridge Wells
Printed and bound in Great Britain by
TJ International Ltd, Padstow, Cornwall

British Library Cataloguing in Publication Data
A catalogue record for this book is available from
the British Library

Library of Congress Cataloging in Publication Data
A catalog record has been requested

ISBN 0–415–26833–8 (hbk)
ISBN 0–415–26834–6 (pbk)

Contents

List of maps

Introduction

This is the seventh edition of a book which has for nearly 20 years now attempted to describe the political geography or electoral anatomy of the United Kingdom. By means of individual constituency profiles, an assessment is made of what influences the various parts of the country to vote as they do. How do social and economic characteristics affect political behaviour and preference? What are the local and national determinants of voting patterns? What makes each parliamentary seat 'tick'? How strong are regional factors, or the personal votes of MPs and candidates? The title of the book, and its approach and format, owe much to Michael Barone's illuminating, enjoyable and unique *Almanac of American Politics*, of which the 2002 volume is the 15th biennial edition, to which a great debt must be acknowledged.

It is indeed in the spirit of attempting to replicate the service provided by that American *Almanac* that in the most recent three editions of this book pen portraits of MPs and candidates have been added to those of the constituencies. Essentially Byron Criddle has been responsible for writing the descriptions of politicians: he is the 'people person', as it were, while Robert Waller has continued to undertake the description and analysis of places.

In the latter, constituency, section certain national themes are illustrated. Those parts of the country which have a concentration of middle-class residents – those who work in non-manual occupations – tend to produce constituencies supporting the Conservative party, while those with a higher proportion of working-class manual employees have long harboured Labour seats.

Although dramatic changes in housing tenure patterns in recent years have obscured the once stark differences between local authority housing and owner-occupation, neighbourhoods dominated by council-built housing, now frequently called 'social housing', a usage which will be found in this edition, are still regarded as producing a political ambience strongly favourable to Labour, or indeed in 2001 to abstention – MORI polling during the 2001 campaign found that only 52% of the remaining council tenants voted.

Districts favoured by non-white residents, whether Asian or Afro-Caribbean in origin, usually provide a reliable source of support for the Labour party. The heaviest concentrations of Asians and black people are to be found in various parts of London (such as Ealing Southall, Brent, Hounslow, Newham, Haringey, Lambeth, Hackney and parts of Tower Hamlets), in Birmingham and other parts of the West Midlands, and in the cities of Manchester, Bradford, Leeds and Leicester and in the towns of Blackburn and Slough.

Agricultural areas are traditionally very poor ground for Labour. They are much more fertile territory for the Conservatives, and in some parts of Britain (particularly the 'Celtic fringe') for the Liberal Democrats. It should be remembered that the 2001 General Election was not merely affected by but actually postponed from its original intended date of 3 May because of the perception of a crisis in the countryside. In the end, however, little electoral impact can be detected, even in the rural areas most affected.

Certain types of industry, such as coal-mining, nurture Labour strongholds – which can outlast the destruction of the activity which first brought workers to the area. A high proportion of voters in the armed services, such as are found at Aldershot and Gosport in Hampshire, skew the political characteristics of a constituency to the Tories.

These variable indicators, and others too, are incorporated in the text describing each seat, or the statistics associated with it. In the text, any features of specific interest relating to a constituency and its history are recorded. These short essays are inevitably impressionistic; they try to point out the individuality of each locality. The electoral histories of British constituencies reveal changing trends and developments since the Second World War.

The Conservatives at first did increasingly well in the South of England, although 'New' Labour have made a very significant recovery in their landslide years of 1997 and 2001, while maintaining their grip on the North, thus raising the spectre of 'Two Nations' once again in British politics. Unemployment has also varied greatly between North and South, between depressed and affluent districts. Several cities have swung to Labour as the population has dropped, as the middle classes have fled to the suburbs or beyond, as ethnic minority communities have grown, or where old religious cleavages have declined in importance, as in the case of the end of the working-class Orange Protestant Tory vote in Liverpool and Glasgow. Other constituencies trended towards the Tories, especially in the 1980s, for example those based on New Towns (in the south of England at least), but have swung back to Labour after 18 years of Conservative government since 1997. Such long-term patterns superimpose themselves upon more uniform and regular swings between the political parties which are to be found at each general election.

It is likely that a thorough local knowledge will aid in predicting and understanding the results of the next general election as well. But it is hoped that this *Almanac* will be more than a guide to the political and electoral map of Britain. It is hoped that electoral evidence, together with the social and economic information, will help to produce a series of thumbnail sketches which build up to a characterisation of the United Kingdom and what makes it behave as it does. Elections offer a mass of evidence relating to the history and traditions of each part of the country. The *Almanac* should be able to tell the reader where the leafy residential areas of a town are to be found, where the council estates are, where one can discern that divide between 'the right and wrong sides of the tracks', the 'east and west ends of town'. All kinds of political cleavage are illustrated: between North and South, England and

Scotland, urban and rural areas. There are electorally significant distinctions of class and tenure, race and language. The *Almanac* aims to be more than a handbook for elections. The political topography of the nation should have a wider relevance. Elections inform social and economic history and sociology. British society should not be analysed as if it were of secondary importance, offering clues to election results, and to the reasons behind the short-term success and failure of mere political parties.

The Almanac of British Politics is a personal description of the country and its elected politicians. The authors fully realise that they cannot know as much about each district as the inhabitants themselves, and may have made judgments about personalities which are in error. They welcome corrections and improvements which might be incorporated in future editions, which will strive for an ever more accurate understanding of the electoral reflection of the character of the United Kingdom.

Acknowledgements

Many individuals have assisted the authors in putting together this *Almanac*, and indeed in making it at all possible to do so. Not all can be named here, but we are most grateful for each and every contribution.

We would like to thank Craig Fowlie, Jennifer Lovel, and the staff at Routledge for their continued faith in backing this project, now completing its second decade. John Hodgson and HWA Text and Data Management managed the project of overseeing the preparation of the book with admirable speed, thoroughness, flexibility and all-round efficiency.

Particular thanks should go to several individuals who gave generously of their expertise and advice during the preparation of this edition.

Leslie Raphael performed an invaluable and essential task as compiler of the statistics and results sections of the constituency pages, with great enthusiasm, speed and accuracy as well as diligence, and made several important suggestions which shaped their content.

Gary Haley of PCS Mapping and DTP drew the maps of constituencies under the 1997 boundaries.

Professor Colin Rallings and Professor Michael Thrasher of Plymouth University's Local Government Elections Centre once again kindly allowed us early access to the data included in their excellent annual handbook of local election results, a unique resource. Philip Cowley of Hull University shared his invaluable research on dissident MPs.

Without the help of Mark Barker and Janet Askham the word processing of the constituency and candidate profiles could not have been completed.

1991 Census statistics for the new seats were published in the OPCS Census Monitor series.

A cornucopia of up-to-date statistical material was provided by Simon Atkinson, Roger Mortimore and other colleagues at MORI (Market and Opinion Research International); by Professor Danny Dorling and Heather Eyre of the Department of Geography at Leeds University; by Chris Squire of the Royal College of Radiologists; and by Richard Heller of Age Concern and the *Mail on Sunday*.

The authors would also like to thank the *Daily Telegraph* for the opportunity to undertake substantial preliminary work for the seventh edition under the aegis of that newspaper's 2001 Election web site. Help is particularly owed to Kim Fletcher, Derek Bishton, Charles Moore, and all those who inputted and corrected; also to

Adrian Tear of Lead Hat productions, Fin Fahey of Albedo Systems Ltd and those others who designed and managed the site.

Valuable information was again supplied by numerous kind and informed sources, such as Colin Startup, Graham Thomson, David Denver, John Austen, Peter Golds, Adam Gray, Kevin Harper, Chris Rennard, Peter Andrews and Mike Steele.

Robert Waller would like to thank colleagues and pupils at Haileybury, Hertford and Greenacre School for Girls, Banstead for their valued assistance and forbearance during the production of this edition.

Byron Criddle acknowledges the advice of Andrew Roth, with whom he co-writes *Parliamentary Profiles*.

The 2001 Parliament

The June 2001 General Election result

The Conservatives did not suffer a second successive overwhelming defeat on 7 June 2001 because of a poor campaign. Nor did they lose as a result of tactical voting, the turnout, their policy on Europe – or because of the leadership of William Hague.

Certainly the party struggled through the four weeks of the election campaign, but it might be suggested that the stridency, divisions and changes of direction noticed by pundits, opponents and voters alike were more due to their being in a losing position than the cause of it.

Not only the seeds but also the growth and completed form of their defeat date from months or even years before the mauling of 7 June.

Put simply, the New Labour government was re-elected because in 2001 it was not time for a change.

Given the general prosperity as evidenced by property values, low mortgage rates, relatively low and declining unemployment, and low and stable inflation, the electorate perceived no reason to evict their government as they had with such decisiveness in 1997. The critical open-minded voters felt it was an occasion to 'let the good times roll'.

Labour may not deserve all the credit for this 'feelgood' factor in an age of international economic determinants, but at least they did not wreck things this time. MORI opinion polling results during the campaign found only 3% of voters considered Labour's image to be extreme, a far cry from the ideological decades of the 1970s and 1980s, and a quarter of the level considering the Conservative party to have abandoned the centre ground.

What is more, 30% considered the Tories to be divided, nearly three times the figure for Labour; the electorate always looks askance at parties which cannot agree within themselves.

On all the issues deemed critical by voters, Labour's position was far stronger than that of their chief opposition, and importantly the government was trusted with the future stewardship of the nation's health and education – 53% thinking that NHS services will improve under a second term, compared with only 31% think that these will get worse, and 60% believing that standards in schools will improve: a formidable expectation to live up to.

Labour has long been ahead on these 'caring and spending' issues, but this time they also won on taxation and managing the economy, both national and for the voters' own families. NOP found a 21% lead among all voters trusting them as the party 'to make you and your family better off', possibly the single key polling question.

Pensions were nominated as a vital issue by around 30% of voters, and it should be remembered that the grey vote will have proved decisive in many constituencies. Gallup found during the campaign that 80% of over-65s said they would certainly vote, while less than half of those with a first opportunity of voting failed to cast a ballot. Whether this is a life-cycle choice or whether it betokens a further decline in turnout remains to be seen.

Arguably, turnout was so low in 2001 largely because of the inevitability of the Labour victory and the lack of any movement during an exceptionally flat campaign. It is not yet proven that low turnout is an unhealthy sign for democracy rather than an indication of a temporary lack of interest; the exceptionally high turnout figures for strife-torn seats in Northern Ireland such as West Tyrone should be examined before any such conclusion is made.

Although a majority of the electorate remained clearly opposed to a single currency, Labour had a 12% opinion poll lead on giving Britain a strong voice in Europe, reflecting a fatalism that it is in this direction that Britain's future lies; and the promise of a referendum on the euro effectively kicked this issue into touch for the time being for most voters.

A Gallup poll for the *Daily Telegraph* in mid-campaign found that only 5% of respondents cited any aspect of Europe as 'the most urgent problem facing the country at the present time'. The highest figure was 38% nominating the ever-important NHS, a clear sign that it was felt that Britain is not currently facing any particular crisis, as it was for example during the fuel tax protests in September 2000.

It is still the case that policies and performance matter more than leaders, and although Tony Blair clearly ran ahead of his party and William Hague's ratings were poor, there is no evidence that any other Conservative leader would have done better; indeed ICM evidence in the last week of the June 2001 campaign suggested that Ann Widdecombe, Kenneth Clarke and Michael Portillo would all have done worse, regardless of the effect of the bitter contest needed to bring any of them into the top party post.

Lest the Conservatives descend into a vicious spiral of panic, they should realise that in fact it has usually been the case in modern British politics that governments are given a second term. It is only Labour that historically has had a poor record in this respect, with a reputation for economic incompetence, ideological extremism and crippling disunity. It must now be recognised that the party has fundamentally changed in the post-Thatcher era, due to the three-time general election winner's ideological and electoral triumphs. Labour's damaging associations with the unions, inflation, inefficient spending, and high direct taxation must now be seen as a thing of the past.

A MORI poll for *The Economist* taken just before the election found that 29% defined 'New Labour' as closest to their own political views, compared with 12% Old Labour, 11% One Nation Tory, 9% Thatcherite Tory, 12% Liberal and 7% Social Democrat. For the time being a new consensus appeared to be in vogue.

The Conservatives should no longer consider themselves the natural party of government, and therefore the need to agonise over each defeat is, paradoxically, reduced. It is well nigh inevitable that Labour will hit hard times in due course, in the most likely form of economic recession or the unravelling of the European project, at which time this fundamental constitutional issue will become very real to the British voter.

STATE OF THE PARTIES

MPs BY PARTY

	2001 General Election	1997 General Election
Labour	412	418
Conservative	166	165
Liberal Democrats	52	46
Ulster Unionists	6	10
Scottish National Party	5	6
Democratic Unionist	5	2
Plaid Cymru	4	4
Sinn Fein	4	2
Social Democratic and Labour Party	3	3
Independent	1	1
Speaker	1	1

VOTES CAST IN THE UK GENERAL ELECTION 2001

	Votes	%	% change	Votes 1997
Labour	10,724,895	40.7	-2.5	13,541,891
Conservative	8,357,622	31.7	+1.0	9,590,720
Liberal Democrat	4,812,833	18.3	+1.5	5,243,012
Scottish National Party	464,305	1.8	-0.2	626,154
UK Independence Party	390,575	1.5	+1.1	106,028
Ulster Unionist	216,839	0.8	-0.0	258,349
Plaid Cymru	195,892	0.7	+0.2	62,565
Democratic Unionist	181,999	0.7	+0.3	107,348
Sinn Fein	175,933	0.7	+0.3	126,921
SDLP	169,865	0.6	+0.0	190,814
Green	166,487	0.6	+0.4	65,996
Independent	127,590	0.5		
Scottish Socialist Party	72,279	0.3		
Socialist Alliance	60,496	0.2		
Socialist Labour Party	57,536	0.2		
British National Party	47,129	0.2		
Alliance Party	28,999	0.1		
Speaker	16,053	0.1		
UK Unionist	13,509	0.1		
Others	88,262	0.3		
Total votes	26,368,798			31,182,348
Turnout	59.4 %			71.4 %

Regional survey

THE SOUTH WEST

The south-western peninsula has long been considered relatively poor ground for the Conservatives despite its predominantly rural nature and its dependence on tourism and agriculture to a greater degree than most English regions. Indeed despite the attempts the Tories made to corral the 'countryside vote' after the debates on fox hunting during the 1997 Parliament, and also the impact of foot and mouth disease in this area in 2001, they did fall back further in the general election, though they are still the largest party in the region, holding 20 of its 51 constituencies. As the Liberal Democrats advanced one to 15 seats, and Labour also added one to reach 16, this is the one region of Britain which can truly be described as an arena for three-party competition.

There is a historic tendency to Liberalism based on the region's strong Non-conformist tradition, and a distinct distance is felt from London as a metropolitan centre and the seat of government, which has usually militated against the Conservatives, the overall champion governing party of the twentieth century; while in the last two Labour landslide elections they too have performed very strongly in the region's urban areas: Bristol, Plymouth, Swindon, Exeter and Gloucester, and even holding semi-rural seats like Stroud and the Forest of Dean and re-establishing a toehold in Cornwall at Falmouth and Camborne.

The region's results were proportionately more marginal and volatile than the others in England too in 2001. Four seats changed hands. The only Labour gain from the Conservatives anywhere in Britain was registered at Dorset South, based on Weymouth and Portland, which they had briefly previously held after a by-election in the early 1960s in which the Conservative vote had been split (over the issue of Europe). This may well have been assisted by the publicity given to the tactical voting campaign in the county of Dorset led by the left-wing singer Billy Bragg, for the Liberal Democrat share did slip markedly in the constituency, although a reciprocal squeeze on the Labour vote was scarcely evident in Mid Dorset and Poole, which the Tories lost to the Lib Dems.

Elsewhere in the region, Jackie Ballard's loss of Taunton was almost certainly brought about by a vigorous campaign, particularly at the Exmoor end of the seat, against her personal opposition to hunting. This Conservative gain from the Liberal Democrats was offset in Devon by the victory of Richard Younger-Ross over the controversial MP Patrick Nicholls at Teignbridge, while the Liberal Democrats' failed to take the neighbouring Totnes from Anthony Steen after a campaign dominated by negative remarks about his age and appearance.

Despite the blight of foot and mouth, Liberal Democrat members held on in Torridge/West Devon and North Devon, and Labour easily held all their 1997 gains. Perhaps the most difficult of these were at Gloucester, where Tess Kingham retired after one term, finding Commons life less than amenable, to be succeeded as candidate by a young Asian candidate, Parmjit Dhanda; and the Forest of Dean, also affected by foot and mouth, where Diana Organ held on after a spirited defence.

Most sitting members held on easily, and in Torbay Adrian Sanders confounded many predictions by substantially strengthening his personal grip despite the Liberal Democrats' disastrous performance in the council elections of the previous year. There do however remain many marginals which should provide interesting contests next time.

A Conservative revival would see the Liberal Democrats under renewed threat in the Somerset seats of Weston and Somerton/Frome. South Dorset is the site of Labour's smallest majority anywhere, 153 votes. Finally, in the event of a Conservative meltdown, a number of their seats remain vulnerable: West and North Dorset, Taunton and Wells in Somerset, and North Wiltshire all remain prime targets. Dorset, which until 2001 was one of only two all-Conservative counties (the other being Surrey, where they now also no longer have a monopoly), now finds that at least half its constituencies are marginal. Such is the scope and scale of the Conservatives' decline in British politics.

THE SOUTH OF ENGLAND (SOUTH OF THE THAMES)

Although still the most Conservative region of the United Kingdom, with just under two-thirds of its seats in their hands, the South of England nevertheless saw the Tories' weakest change of share outside London, as they increased by just 1% – nowhere near enough to become competitive nationally again. Specifically, Labour lost no seats here, not even any of their eight 1997 gains in the county of Kent, even though it was the part of the country most affected by the influx of asylum seekers in the last few years.

Indeed, the Tories suffered a net loss since 1997. Although they regained the Isle of Wight, a highly unusual seat whose politics are, literally, insular (they had also regained control of the local council after years of Liberal dominance), they could not win Romsey, which they had lost to the Liberal Democrats in a by-election in May 2000, and even more surprisingly, their redoubt of Surrey underwent its first breach as Guildford was won by that party's candidate Sue Doughty.

The Liberal Democrats hold a string of seats in the so-called M3 corridor: Winchester and Eastleigh as well as Romsey, although this is less due to any connection with the motorway than the coincidence of a series of by-election campaigns (like Newbury, only just retained for a third time by David Rendel). Once elected, though, Liberal Democrat MPs are hard to shift: MORI research has found that over 70% of voters are satisfied with their performance, compared with under 50% for both Labour and Conservative representatives. The Liberal Democrats also came within 5% of the vote of winning Surrey South West and Eastbourne as well, and within 10% of ousting Julian Lewis in New Forest East.

Still more significant, though, was the new Labour (and New Labour) government's ability to hold on in seats lost in the Thatcher years, such as Dartford, Medway and Brighton Kemptown, and those never won before 1997, like Hove, Gillingham and Thanet South. Indeed, they strengthened their position in many of these gains and regains. Reading, for example, awarded its two first-term MPs among the highest pro-Labour swings in the country. The resorts of the south coast, with their social problems and down-at-heel air, look as if they have undergone a long-term shift in character and allegiance. Tactical voting, as clearly in play at Hastings and Rye, harms the Conservatives further.

With their established weakness in so many points north and outside England, the Tories must secure almost a clean sweep of southern English seats in order to form a government again. Currently, this looks unlikely. The region remains a critical battleground in determining the political colour of the nation's leadership.

GREATER LONDON

The capital and seat of government, with its 74 seats (still an over-representation compared with the rest of England) supplies many vital contests in general elections. It was therefore more than symbolic of the renewed dominance of the Labour administration that it was the Conservatives' weakest region in June 2001. Even though they gained two seats to increase their representation to 13, and predicted losses in Uxbridge and Chipping Barnet failed to occur, the overall Tory share dropped here alone in Britain. Labour increased their grip on most of their 1997 gains, as indeed did the Liberal Democrats in the five seats they had taken from the Conservatives in 1997. A Tory revival in Greater London is at the same time vital and unlikely.

One of the reasons for this must be the prosperity of the conurbation as a whole. Its pockets of serious and severe deprivation are certainly causes for concern, but these areas have not voted Conservatives into Parliament for many decades. Even in poorer seats though, the boom in property values over the four years before 2001, recorded in the constituency statistics throughout the body of this book, are at their most striking in Greater London. A combination of this increase, lower interest and hence mortgage rates, and relatively low unemployment and inflation levels, mean that for many (not all) Londoners they truly have 'never had it so good'.

Another factor which may add to Labour's increased strength in 2001 was their strong performance in seats with a large proportion of non-white voters. According to the early results from the 2001 Census, ethnic minorities now form over 25% of the population in the capital, and a breakdown of opinion poll data suggests that around three-quarters of those who voted supported Labour. Although many reside in safe Labour seats, and fewer than half of Afro-Caribbeans voted, the substantial middle-class Asian blocs in places such as Brent North, Harrow and Enfield Southgate were probably major contributors to the large further swings to Labour in 2001, due to the incumbency factor of the government as a whole in addition to that of the first-term MPs for these constituencies.

Labour's two losses, in Havering borough on the outer eastern fringe of Greater London, owe much to unusual local Conservative activism, especially on the part of the new Romford MP Andrew Rosindell, who appears to have replicated a degree of community politics associated much more with the Liberal Democrats. The ethnic and social nature of this area, which has much in common with the historic and now neighbouring county of Essex also may be relevant: this is the part of Greater London with the fewest non-white voters.

The palm for the most dramatic improvement anywhere in Britain, though, should go to Edward Davey, the Liberal Democrat MP for Kingston and Surbiton, who increased his majority after a bruising contest with the abrasive David Shaw, former Conservative member for Dover, from 56 to 15,676. The Liberal Democrats also held on in inner-city Southwark and Bermondsey with an increased majority over Labour, and moved forward strongly in Hornsey & Wood Green and Holborn & St Pancras. Together with a renewed challenge in Orpington, scene of one of their most famous by-election victories (in 1962), the third-largest party can look forward to further advances in a variety of boroughs, especially should the Labour government meet less kind fortune in its second term.

London will lose a seat in the next boundary review, on the north side of the river, but these changes are not due to come into effect until after the next General Election in 2005 or 2006.

THE SOUTH OF ENGLAND (NORTH OF THE THAMES)

Prior to the 2001 Election, the Conservatives nurtured high hopes in the counties of Bedfordshire, Berkshire, Buckinghamshire, Hertfordshire and Oxfordshire, with nine seats as targets required for victory with an overall majority in the United Kingdom – five in Hertfordshire alone (all Labour gains in 1997). In the end, the only gain they made was a purely technical one, as their new candidate David Cameron replaced Shaun Woodward in Witney, west Oxfordshire, after he had defected to Labour in mid term and found a safe seat in St Helens South in the industrial north of England.

Even Milton Keynes North East, Labour's third most vulnerable seat of all, was held, and the pattern of New Town retentions was maintained in Hemel Hempstead, Stevenage and (most narrowly) Welwyn Hatfield as well. These modern communities, still growing though now with exclusively private housing development, represent an archetypal face of Britain as it enters the twenty-first century: privatised in a social sense, not class conscious, instrumental, where people vote according to what is perceived as best for them and their families over the next four years rather than due to ancestral or deeply felt loyalties. In June 2001 New Labour clearly fitted that bill after their successful stewardship of the economy in their first term.

That volatility also means that these marginals cannot be taken for granted in the long run, however, and a keen fight is sure to be re-engaged next time. This is not in general strong ground for the Liberal Democrats, but in addition to their easy win in the intellectual Oxford West and Abingdon division (there is a movement towards the party in the seats in ancient university towns, as they advanced to second place ahead of the Conservatives in Oxford East and Cambridge), they surprised many by cutting the Tory lead in affluent Maidenhead to just over 3,000.

EAST ANGLIA

The flatlands of eastern England (including Essex) offered the Conservatives their most improved regional results in the 2001 General Election, though that is saying very little given the deeply disappointing lack of overall progress they made: just two gains, in Norfolk North West and in Castle Point in Essex.

They did at least hold on to a number of rural seats left marginal after 1997, and closed the gap in Braintree, Peterborough and Harlow, but their failure to regain Harwich, say, must be regarded as disastrous, and they lost one seat, Norfolk North, to a Liberal Democrat campaign heavily targeted and using both community activist politics and a tactical voting squeeze on Labour to the utmost effect.

The Liberal Democrat Bob Russell strengthened his hold on Colchester, which no longer looks like a three-way marginal as the Liberal Democrats appear to be locking up the anti-Conservative vote, as in many other seats around the country, which bodes well for their long-term prospects.

In this most rapidly growing of regions Labour's share fell by less than 2%, and as long as they win most of the urban seats in the east of England they are likely to form the government at Westminster.

One more rather odd result needs to be mentioned. Martin Bell, after winning triumphantly in Tatton in Cheshire on an anti-sleaze platform against Neil Hamilton in 1997, was mindful of his promise not to seek a second term in that seat; but rather than retiring undefeated, he instead contested Brentwood & Ongar in Essex against the relatively blameless Eric Pickles after allegations that the local Conservative party had been infiltrated by a right-wing religious sect. As Labour and the Liberal Democrats did not on this occasion withdraw in his favour, his defeat was almost inevitable – but in a way his resulting share of nearly 32% was as creditable as it had been inTatton for a non-party candidate in the circumstances.

EAST MIDLANDS

The East Midlands is one of the critical electoral battlegrounds in England, just as important as the neighbouring West Midlands, which is more often under the spotlight as a political cockpit. In their *annus mirabilis* of 1997 Labour made no fewer than 18 gains in the region's five counties (Derbyshire, Leicestershire, Lincolnshire, Northamptonshire and Nottinghamshire), and their dominance was confimed in 2001 when they held all but one of these. That was Newark, where the party and its MP Fiona Jones had been beset by particular difficulties which cannot be ascribed to regional factors – indeed the other gains in Nottinghamshire were held with increased margins. Most impressive of all was the retention of all five gains in Northamptonshire, including the three super-marginals of Kettering, Wellingborough and Northampton South.

Labour suffered one blow only, although possibly not one which will bring too many tears to the leaders of the modernising party. Chesterfield, Tony Benn's sanctuary for the last 17 years, did not return his sometime left-wing 'Old Labour' successor Reg Race, but gave the Liberal Democrats their first foothold in the East Midlands for well over 60 years.

The Conservatives must hope to do much better in the region next time, as their target list – and the magnitude of their task – will remain pretty much identical to that of 2001.

WEST MIDLANDS

There were a number of unlikely Labour gains in 1997 in the West Midlands, and hence top Conservative targets: Rugby/Kenilworth, Shrewsbury/Atcham, Warwick/ Leamington, and The Wrekin led these. Every single one was held by their first-term Labour MP, and in every one there was a larger majority as a result of a further swing to the governing party. This would have been partly a result of effective campaign targeting of resources, but also of the incumbency and indeed double incumbency effect; that is, the replacement of a sitting Tory MP by a Labour member who used assiduous methods of publicity to trumpet energetic constituency services. This will make it hard to dislodge these MPs next time too, magnifying the mountain facing the Conservatives as they attempt to move nearer to taking office.

The only Labour loss did come in a seat they had taken from the Tories in 1997, but it was not a regain. Dr Richard Taylor, fighting as an Independent on the issue of saving the Kidderminster Hospital, won in Wyre Forest, a victory every bit as striking and convincing as that of Martin Bell against Neil Hamilton four years before, although in this case little could be laid at the door of the ousted MP, David Lock. The victory came after a series of victories for hospital campaigners in local elections in the area.

What will happen in Wyre Forest next time is a moot point: it may be that, like Martin Bell, Dr Taylor will only serve for one term, although it is unlikely that he will fight again and lose, as Bell did – certainly not in a different constituency on a different issue.

One other seat changed hands, and that probably more of a surprise than Wyre Forest in the end. Ludlow, which had not featured on the national radar screen as a potential gain, fell to the Liberal Democrat Matthew Green, over a new Tory candidate following Christopher Gill's disgruntled and 11th hour retirement, offering a tasty morsel to the third party (in national terms) in a south Shropshire seat named after a small town known for its almost perfectly preserved medieval street plan and its glut of gourmet restaurants. The Conservatives will hope to gobble it up again, along with its fellow Welsh Marcher Lib Dem seat Hereford, where they slashed the majority, and hope for better fortune against Labour in the main course of the battle in the West Midlands region.

YORKSHIRE

Along with the much smaller north of England region, the broad acres of Yorkshire saw no changes of hand at all in the 2001 Election – a situation which was eminently satisfactory in the view of the Labour government, returned after a full first term for another full term for the first time ever, but politically fatal for the leader of the Conservative party, born and still with a residence in the county.

Scant compensation it would surely have been, but William Hague did at least see his own majority in Richmond leap to become the largest and safest of any Conservative in the country, just as John Major's had been in Huntingdon in the two previous general elections. However, all the party's targets evaded defeat: the youngest MP elected in 1997, Christopher Leslie of Shipley; John Grogan in Selby, one of the most rural seats held by Labour; both middle class seats in Leeds, North West and North East; and the Sikh Marsha Singh held his seat against a Conservative from the far more populous Muslim community in Bradford West. It was an impressively solid display.

Nor could any impact be made on the Liberal Democrats' Richard Allan in Sheffield Hallam or Phil Willis in Harrogate/Knaresborough. Both increased their margins substantially after their first term to demonstrate the power of incumbency and are now ranked among the safest dozen of the 52 Liberal Democrat seats. The success in Harrogate suggests an affinity for the party among voters resident in the nation's largest spa towns, parallelling that now well established further south and west in Bath and Cheltenham.

THE NORTH WEST

The north west of England, together with Greater London, formed the Conservatives' worst regions in 1992 and 1997, as a long-term trend to Labour was exacerbated by substantial deteriorations in their national position. In Merseyside for example, the Tories, who actually held a majority of the seats in the city of Liverpool as recently as 1959, lost not only all the urban constituencies but also their traditional suburban strongholds in the Wirral, Crosby and Southport. Their last redoubt in the city of Manchester (Withington) had fallen in 1987, and in 1997 they retained only two seats in the Greater Manchester conurbation, Cheadle and Altrincham and Sale. In that latter year they also lost their two seats in each of the towns of Bury, Bolton and Blackpool. Finally, the classic swing marginals covering former textile mill towns in Lancashire on the west side of the Pennines, such as Pendle, Hyndburn and Rossendale/Darwen, were lost in 1992 after the imposition of the council tax which particularly affected their small terraced housing stock, and Labour built up their leads there to five-figure margins in 1997. A major recovery effort was necessary in a region which has always been one of the most competitive and decisive in British electoral history, going back to the days when contests were decided on issues such as free trade and tariff reform, and education policy for Nonconformist and Established Church schools.

The issues in the North West in 2001 appeared similar to those in the rest of Britain, though, and the result was the same too. The Conservatives managed to make no net gains at all, and they suffered another loss in Cheadle, taking a famous name in Liberal history (it was held by Dr Michael Winstanley in 1966, when they only won 12 seats) back into the hands of the third and formerly centre party – formerly because by most measures the Liberal Democrats now stand to the left of New Labour. Indeed, the Tories only 'broke even' in the region because of their wholly expected regain of

Tatton, won in extraordinary circumstances by the Independent Martin Bell in 1997 but not defended by him in 2001.

Across the North West the Conservatives managed a positive two-party swing of just 2.3% against Labour, but the Liberal Democrats increased their share of the vote by more than they did. One should finally, on a rather alarming note, mention the unexpected success of the far-right and racist British National Party (BNP) in the towns of Oldham and Burnley, fought in a background of tension between poor white and Muslim communities which brought riots and violent clashes in the year of 2001 – and this before the appalling events of 11 September of that year in the United States and their protracted aftermath.

THE NORTH OF ENGLAND

The smallest of the standard regions of England, the far North is not without electoral interest. The large predominantly rural constituency of Hexham in Northumberland, for example, was the third top Conservative target for Labour after the 1997 Election. It was also the seat in which the foot and mouth epidemic of 2001 was first identified. As a result of the perceived inappropriateness and impracticality of holding an election before the disease was under control, the General Election was itself postponed by five weeks from its intended date. The effect in Hexham is unclear: there was an above average 6% increase in the Conservative share of votes cast, and rather interestingly the second highest turnout in England, at 71%, which was also one of the ten lowest drops recorded. The worst affected seat in terms of cases of foot and mouth of all, Penrith and the Border, showed an even larger Conservative share improvement.

No seats actually changed hands, but there were some notable figures returned: the Liberal Democrat Deputy Leader Alan Beith won Berwick upon Tweed, the most northerly seat in England, for the ninth time; Tony Blair himself represents Sedgefield in Durham, of course, where his personal result in a very safe seat was not strikingly good; once again Sunderland South easily won the race to declare first on the night, giving the first solid evidence of the dramatic story of turnout decline as fewer than half its voters needed counting; and more entertainingly, Peter Mandelson held on at Hartlepool against a variety of opponents including Arthur Scargill, and delivered the defiant speech of the night in triumphal acceptance. His result was substantially better compared with 1997 than the Prime Minister's.

The traditional marginals in the region now all look fairly safe for Labour: Darlington, Stockton South, even Tynemouth, despite a good Tory local government showing in May 2000 and the Tories must wait for happier times and circumstances, and possibly the enactment of boundary changes in Cumbria already well on in the redistribution cycle, to add gains to their present three rural divisions.

WALES

The Conservatives still have no seats at all in Wales, having failed to regain Monmouth by just 384 votes. Yet this conceals one of the lesser-known aspects of the June 2001 results: Wales was actually Labour's worst region of Britain in terms of change since 1997, as their share of the votes cast fell by over 6%, and their share of the electorate as a whole by more because of the very substantial drop in turnout. Although they lost no South Welsh ex-mining valley seats as they had in their disastrous 1999 initial Welsh Assembly elections (when, astonishingly, Plaid Cymru won Llanelli, Islwyn – Neil Kinnock's former seat – and Rhondda), the aftermath of the central party's misguided and ultimately unsuccessful attempt to keep Rhodri Morgan from the leadership of the devolved body was still apparent. They did lose the rural west Wales (and Welsh-speaking) Carmarthen East and Dinefwr seat to the nationalists, and their compensatory regain of Ynys Mon had much to do with the retirement of the abrasive Plaid Cymru leader Ieuan Wyn Jones – substantial swings were also recorded where other Nationalists and party leaders did not contest in 2001.

This did however mark a break in the pattern of the Plaid's successful concentration of its vote in the Welsh-speaking north-west corner of what they would not like to call the Principality. Labour will remain the dominant party in Wales, but it must look over its shoulder very warily next time against the nationalists, the Conservatives in Monmouth and perhaps the Vale of Glamorgan, and the Liberal Democrats in the very heart of the Welsh capital at Cardiff Central. Wales has shown that its favours cannot be taken for granted.

NORTHERN IRELAND

Although there were only 20 changes of hand between parties in the 641 parliamentary contests in England, Scotland and Wales in 2001, there were no fewer than seven in Northern Ireland's 18 seats, by far the highest in living memory. The mainland parties do not contest Northern Irish constituencies, and politics is run on a completely different basis due to the unique history and continuing cleavages in the politics of the province, but the churning in 2001 demonstrated a clear and new pattern of movement from the more moderate to the more extreme wings of both nationalist and unionist electoral politics.

Sinn Fein won West Tyrone from the Ulster Unionist William Thompson, and Fermanagh and South Tyrone following the retirement of the same party's Ken Maginnis, thus doubling their representation from two (Gerry Adams and Martin McGuinness) to four. Meanwhile, Ian Paisley's Democratic Unionist Party also took seats from David Trimble's larger Ulster Unionists in Strangford, Belfast North and East Londonderry. The one seat which travelled in the other direction merely reversed William McCrea's Antrim South by-election gain in 2000. Finally, the Ulster Unionist Lady Hermon did take North Down from the independent Robert McCartney, but even this was achieved largely due to the withdrawal of the Alliance Party.

Nine of the 18 Northern Irish seats are now in the hands of either Sinn Fein or the DUP, and the polarisation of politics in this troubled part of the world suggested no easy solutions to its manifold and manifest problems.

SCOTLAND

Much of the attention in the 2001 Election campaign relating to the question of whether the Conservatives could break their duck by returning an MP north of the border for the first time since 1992 was concentrated on the former Foreign Secretary Malcolm Rifkind, as he tried to regain Edinburgh Pentlands. Some commentators even thought that if he won he would be a serious contender for the party leadership, missing the point that if the Conservatives had done that well under William Hague they probably would not have needed a new leader. Rifkind lost anyway, but a much less heralded Tory did become their lone Scottish MP, Peter Duncan of Galloway and Upper Nithsdale.

Galloway is a rural seat and was heavily affected by the foot and mouth scourge, though not as much so as Dumfries next door where there was scarcely a dent in the Labour majority. More relevantly, perhaps, the SNP MP Alasdair Morgan had migrated to the newly established Scottish Parliament and did not defend the Westminster seat; as in almost all the other seats where this happened, the nationalist share went down. Clearly in Scotland, at least, there is a significant feeling among the electorate that Westminster may no longer be as important as it was before devolution.

A number of other points may be made about the 2001 general election in Scotland, despite the overall lack of gains and losses. The Liberal Democrats did well, holding all their seats, even in the three cases where the sitting member had retired and increasing their share by nearly 4% overall. Charles Kennedy's own result was as rewarding as his leadership of the party had been adjudged impressive by the electorate. Labour held all their 1997 gains comfortably, and benefited from one of their largest share increases anywhere on the highest turnout in Scotland in Eastwood, after a vigorous local campaign.

Five members of the new Cabinet held seats in Scotland (and the Lord Chancellor is a Scot too) and the party is still boosted by its powerful 'delegation' from north Britain. On 7 February 2002 the Scottish Boundary Commission published provisional recommendations which suggested that Scotland should lose 13 seats in the House of Commons at Westminster. This was due to the equalisation of constituency sizes with England following the establishment of the Scottish Parliament in Edinburgh; with an assembly of their own it is felt that Scots no longer need over-representation in London. (Interestingly, the same principle has not been applied in Wales, where the seats are still on average over 10,000 votes smaller than in the rest of the United Kingdom – perhaps a reflection of the admitted relative weakness of the Welsh Assembly.)

Although the Scottish Commission's proposals have to go through an extensive review procedure, which can be expected to give rise to some changes both of boundaries and names, and must then be confirmed by the UK Parliament, it was stated to be fully intended to have the new constituencies north of the border ready for the next General Election in 2005 or 2006, even though this will lead to a substantial loss for the ruling Labour party and a consequent embarrassing game of musical chairs as MPs wishing to remain at Westminster scramble for fewer seats.

Although it is not always clear exactly which can be described as the 13 seats which disappear, at least 11 of them were clearly held by the dominant Labour party in 2001: two in Glasgow, one each in Aberdeen and Dundee, and one in each of Rutherglen/North Lanarkshire, South Lanarkshire, Ayrshire, Fife, the former Central region around Falkirk, Dunbartonshire, and Renfrewshire.

The losers of the other two are not so clear. North Tayside appears to vanish, but the changes in the Tayside area actually pleased the SNP, who perceived improved chances in both Dundee East and a new Ochil, both currently targets of their's held by Labour. On the southern border, a new seat has been suggested called Peebles, Clydesdale and Annandale which includes substantial elements not only of the former Liberal Democrat Tweeddale, once held by David Steel, but also of Dumfries, a Labour seat in 1997 and 2001; Dumfries town is proposed to join Galloway, which would convert that seat into a three-way marginal, further threatening the single Tory MP in Scotland, Peter Duncan, as well as its own member, Russell Brown.

Other members will also find their task of being returned harder, although there are clear opportunities for the big hitters Gordon Brown, John Reid and Alistair Darling to move into safe new seats; among those with a harder task are the left-wing Labour rebel George Galloway (currently Glasgow Kelvin) and the Muslim MP Mohammed Sarwar (Glasgow Govan), George Foulkes in Ayrshire, Frank Doran in Aberdeen, and Lewis Moonie in Fife. The Liberal Democrat John Barrett may have a harder task in a newly redrawn Edinburgh North West.

If their commitment to the Commons is such that they wish to stand again, the boundary changes may even call into question the position of two of its most Honourable members: the Father of the House Tam Dalyell (Linlithgow, merged with Falkirk East) and the Speaker of the House Michael Martin (Glasgow Springburn). It all adds a considerable dose of spice to a region long dominated by a single party.

New Scottish constituencies
Provisional recommendations, February 2002

Old seat	New seat	Political effect
Aberdeen Central	Split between Aberdeen N and S	Lab loss
Aberdeen N	Aberdeen N	Lab hold
Aberdeen S	Aberdeen S	Lab hold
Aberdeens W/Kincardine	Aberdeens W/Kincardine	LD hold
Airdrie/Shotts	Airdrie/Shotts	Lab hold
Angus	Angus	SNP hold
Argyll/Bute	Argyll/Bute	LD hold
Ayr	Ayr, New Cumnock and Carrick	Lab hold
Banff and Buchan	Banff, Buchan and Huntly	SNP hold
Caithness/Sutherland/ Easter Ross	Caithness/Sutherland/Easter Ross	LD hold
Carrick/Cumnock/Doon Valley	Split between Ayr and Kilmarnock	Lab loss
Clydebank/Milngavie	Split, mostly to Dunbartonshire West	Lab loss
Clydesdale	Lanark and Hamilton East	Lab hold
Coatbridge/Chryston	Coatbridge/Chryston/Bellshill	Lab hold
Cumbernauld/Kilsyth	Cumbernauld/Kilsyth/Kirkintilloch E	Lab hold
Cunninghame N	Ayrshire N/Isle of Arran	Lab hold
Cunninghame S	Irvine, Troon and Prestwick	Lab hold
Dumbarton	Dunbartonshire West	Lab hold
Dumfries	Split between Galloway and Peebles	Lab loss
Dundee E	Dundee E	Lab hold
Dundee W	Dundee W	Lab hold
Dunfermline E	Split, Dunfermline and Kirkcaldy	Lab loss
Dunfermline West	Dunfermline and West Fife	Lab hold
East Kilbride	East Kilbride/Strathaven/ Lesmahagow	Lab hold
East Lothian	East Lothian	Lab hold
*Eastwood	Eastwood	Lab hold
Edinburgh Central	Split	Lab loss
Edinburgh E/Mussleburgh	Edinburgh SE	Lab hold
Edinburgh N/Leith	Edinburgh NE	Lab hold
Edinburgh Pentlands	Edinburgh W	Lab hold
Edinburgh S	Edinburgh S	Lab hold
Edinburgh W	Edinburgh NW	LD hold
Falkirk E	Split between Falkirk and Linlithgow	Lab loss
Falkirk W	Falkirk	Lab hold
Fife Central	Glenrothes	Lab hold

Old seat	New seat	Political effect
Fife NE	Fife NE	LD hold
Galloway/Upper Nithsdale	Dumfries and Galloway	three-way marginal(C)
Glasgow Anniesland	Glasgow NW	Lab hold
Glasgow Baillieston	Glasgow E	Lab hold
Glasgow Cathcart	Glasgow S	Lab hold
Glasgow Govan	Split	Lab loss
Glasgow Kelvin	Glasgow C	Lab hold
Glasgow Maryhill	Glasgow N	Lab hold
Glasgow Pollok	Glasgow SW	Lab hold
Glasgow Rutherglen	Rutherglen and Hamilton W	Lab hold
Glasgow Shettleston	Split between Glasgow E, C, NE	Lab loss
Glasgow Springburn	Glasgow NE	Speaker hold
Gordon	Gordon	LD hold
Greenock and Inverclyde	Inverclyde	Lab hold
Hamilton N/Bellshill	Split	Lab loss
Hamilton S	Split	Lab loss
Inverness E/Nairn/Lochaber	Inverness/Badenoch	Lab hold
Kilmarnock/Loudoun	Kilmarnock/Stewarton/Cumnock	Lab hold
Kirkcaldy	Kirkcaldy/Cowdenbeath	Lab hold
Linlithgow	Linlithgow	Lab hold
Livingston	Livingston	Lab hold
Midlothian	Midlothian	Lab hold
Moray	Moray	SNP hold
Motherwell/Wishaw	Motherwell/Wishaw	Lab hold
Ochil	Strathearn and Ochil	Lab hold
*Orkney/Shetland	Orkney/Shetland	LD hold
Paisley N	Renfrewshire N/Paisley N	Lab hold
Paisley S	Renfrewshire S/Paisley S	Lab hold
Perth	Perth/Atholl	SNP hold
Renfrewshire W	Split between Paisley N/S	Lab loss
Ross/Skye/Inverness W	Ross/Skye/Lochaber	LD hold
Roxburgh/Berwickshire	Berwickshire/Roxburgh/Selkirk	LD hold
Stirling	Stirling	Lab hold
Strathkelvin/Bearsden	Bearsden /Bishopbriggs/Kirkintilloch W	Lab hold
Tayside North	Split between Perth and Angus	SNP loss
Tweeddale/Ettrick/ Lauderdale	Peebles/Clydesdale/Annandale	three-way marginal
*Western Isles	Na h-Eileanan An Iar	Lab hold

* Boundaries unchanged

Please note that 'political effect' does not represent a prediction for the next general election, but an assessment of how the 2001 Election might have been represented on new constituency boundaries.

These names and boundaries are provisional, announced in February 2002 but subject to a thorough inquiry process and to being ratified by the Westminster Parliament.

Members of Parliament

The Election of 2001 produced 99 new MPs (or 15% of the Commons, a much lower figure than the 260 – 40% – in 1997): 38 Labour, 33 Conservative (of whom seven were former MPs returning after being defeated in 1997), 14 Liberal Democrat, two Sinn Fein, three DUP, two UUP, two Plaid Cymru, four SNP and one Independent. Labour's new intake comprised only 9% of the PLP, the Conservatives' 20% of their parliamentary strength and the Liberal Democrats' 26%. Only 27 of the new MPs were coming as victors in seats where the occupancy had changed hands at the Election, the lowest number of inter-party exchanges in any election since 1955. Of the remainder of the 99 new MPs, 72 were replacements for retiring members, of whom 17 had not retired on grounds of age but had left Westminster to concentrate on membership of the devolved Scottish or Welsh Parliaments.

The 38 new Labour MPs seemed likely to make little difference to the cohesion of the 412-strong PLP. Labour candidates post-1997 had been carefully screened by Millbank before being allowed to apply to Constituency Labour Parties for selection. Scrutiny for Labour's approved bank of potential candidates – or 'National Parliamentary Panel' – formed part of the process instilling into the PLP a culture of government by weeding out the unconventional or unreliable – or in the sub-Orwellian language of one of the senior MPs involved in the screening process, excluding those who 'appeared not to have a pragmatic line on policy disagreements' or who could 'not avoid sounding divisive and combative if disagreeing with party policy' or – more bluntly – showed 'an unpreparedness to listen to the Whips'. Given that Labour's 38 new MPs had emerged from this scrutinising grid, few seemed likely to be disruptive. About a third of them were professional politicians, party staffers who had worked as ministerial advisers or for MPs; three from Downing Street, one the former head of the No 10 Policy Unit, and could be taken to be reliable. Another fifth were similarly high-ranking union officials from the AEEU, GMBU, MSF or UNISON, a number of whom were believed to have acquired their safe Labour seats under unofficial inter-union pacts to ensure the unions did not cancel each other out in any one selection contest. Union-derived candidates, being a similar sort of professional politician to the party staffers already mentioned, could also be expected to conform – unless the government adopted a policy of public service privatisation that threatened the interests of the public sector unions. Finally, around a third of Labour's new MPs were municipal politicians, a number of whom council leaders who, on past evidence of former council leaders elected to the PLP, were unlikely to behave rebelliously.

Not that there was much cause for concern about the loyalty of the PLP on the evidence of the 1997 to 2001 Parliament, in which fewer MPs of the governing party had rebelled than in any Parliament since 1955. Research by Philip Cowley of Hull University has shown that whilst some 133 Labour MPs cast dissident votes at least once against the government between 1997 and 2001, of these only 53 did so more than ten times, and of these 53, only 25 did so more than 20 times. These latter 25 MPs constituted the hard core of Labour dissidents and were virtually the same people as were members of the left-wing Campaign Group, the top three leading rebels being Jeremy Corbyn with 64 dissident votes, John McDonnell 59, and Dennis Skinner 41. But even in the case of these more regular rebels, their level of dissent had been toned down from the previous Parliament when, for example, Jeremy Corbyn had cast 72 rebellious votes, Dennis Skinner 121, and other leading rebels, such as Lynne Jones and Alan Simpson, had voted more often against the Whips in opposition than they did in government. Moreover, the more recent the MP, the less likely the rebel – only five of the 183-strong 1997 intake (40% of the PLP) being amongst the top 25 rebels. Furthermore, by 2001 over half of all Labour MPs had no experience of Westminster other than as Government-supporting MPs. The fratricidal strife of the 1980s was a distant memory. From the earliest rebellions of the new 2001 House it was unclear if the same, reduced, scale of revolt was to characterise the new Parliament as it did that of 1997–2001, but the initial rebellions involved mostly the same – usually Campaign Group-linked – MPs.

The 33-strong Conservative intake of 2001 was characterised, as had been the intake of 1997, by right-of-centre Eurosceptic credentials. In the July 2001 third leadership ballot, of those of the 33 whose votes were revealed, 14 voted for Iain Duncan Smith, ten for Michael Portillo, and four for Kenneth Clarke. The three-way division of the 166 Conservative MPs in that final ballot – 59 for Clarke, 54 for Duncan Smith, 53 for Portillo – implied a 2:1 Eurosceptic predominance, though at the first ballot, in a field of five candidates, Clarke – the only committed Europhile – polled only 36 votes. On another salient dimension dividing the party, that of social libertarians versus traditionalists, with some of the One Nation tradition with the social libertarians in the disparate Portillo camp, it would seem that, Europe aside, the Eurosceptic Duncan Smith leadership was vulnerable to the large number of Portillo-voting former senior shadow spokesmen who went to the back benches in 2001; a total of 11 of Hague's Shadow Cabinet were not part of Duncan Smith's front bench team.

Some attention has been paid to the fact that fewer women were elected to the Commons in 2001 (118) than in 1997 (120, but augmented by a subsequent 1997 by-election to 121). The large increase in the number of women MPs in 1997 had been the consequence of Labour's introduction of all-women shortlists from which 35 of Labour's 65 new women MPs of 1997 had benefited (comprising a third of all new Labour MPs in that year). In contrast, in 2001 only four of Labour's 38 new MPs were women. This was because the practice of all-women shortlisting had been dropped in 1996, and because the number of seats available to be filled by new women candidates was effectively limited in 2001 to those where MPs were retiring, it being assumed that Labour would not win any seats in addition to its large 418 total in 1997. Labour's net loss of six women MPs (from 101 to 95 – 23% of the PLP) was thus largely responsible for the fall in the total number of women – which was sustained, rather fortuitously, by the election of three new women MPs by parties in Northern Ireland. But with Labour poised in 2002 to legislate to reintroduce all-women shortlists and the Conservatives (with only 14 women MPs) under pressure to override the traditional hostility to such discrimination among the Party's grass roots, it seemed possible that the upward trend in the number of women MPs would resume at the next general election, unless Labour suffered substantial seat losses..

Apart from sex and race (Labour being the only party in the Commons with non-white ethnic minority MPs – 12 by 2001) it is often claimed that the parties in the Commons are virtually indistinguishable – comprised of middle-aged, middle-class men. The claim to 'middle-class' uniformity is the most misleading. In 2001 similar proportions of Labour (43%) and Conservative MPs (39%) came from professional occupations, but the professions from which Labour MPs were drawn were public sector ones such as the civil service or teaching whilst Conservative professionals were overwhelmingly lawyers or army officers (the latter being in the public sector but atypical of it). Very small proportions of Labour MPs came from a business background – 8%, compared to the Conservatives' 36%. So by these two measures alone it is evident that there is a clear sectoral divide between Labour and Conservative 'middle-class' MPs, Labour drawing on the public sector and the Conservatives the private sector. Moreover, another occupational category that still separates the parties is manual work, with 51 (12%) Labour MPs – as against 1 Conservative MP – having come from manual employment. But Labour's proletarian base, though shrinking, remains in many more cases a generation removed, with MPs in 'professional' occupations, but with their parents in manual ones. The category of previous employment which is growing in both parties, however, is that of the professional politician. Upwards of 130 of Labour's 412 MPs have some form of political employment in their c.v.s, but at least 10% of each party's MPs can be categorised as professional politicians per se. The Liberal Democrats somewhat straddle the divide between Labour and the Tories, with their 52 MPs comprising 15 teachers or lecturers, or civil servants (i.e. public sector), and 14 private sector business people and 12 private sector professionals.

The social dissimilarities between the parties are more marked when educational background is analysed. Of Conservative MPs, 64% attended public schools, as compared to 17% of Labour and 35% of Liberal Democrats. As revealing of social background is the possession of a public school and Oxbridge educational pedigree, and if such a test is applied to the three parties, significant differences emerge. Whereas 36% (60) of the 166 Conservative MPs attended a public school and Oxford or Cambridge, only 7% (30) of Labour's 412 MPs had a similar background, and in Labour's case this included a number whose 'public schools' were merely former direct grant grammar schools. Of the Liberal Democrats' 52 MPs, 19% (10) had a public school and Oxbridge background. Clearly the social profiles of the parties, as thus measured, are still quite distinct. This is notwithstanding the continued decline in the number of Conservative MPs from the grander public schools such as Eton, which provided between a quarter and a fifth of all Conservative MPs for the first six decades of the last century, but by 2001 was providing a mere 8%, or 14 MPs out of 166. This decline symbolises the retreat of the upper and upper middle class from political careers, now become more arduous because full-time, lower in status, and badly paid relative to other professions. Thus a certain levelling process is at work, but important social distinctions remain and it was not impossible that in an age of collapsed deference the Conservative Party's contemporary electoral decline owed something to perceptions of its social elitism.

Commons divisions 2001–2002

1. REFERENDUM ON THE EU NICE TREATY

19 July 2001

Labour MPs voting for (4):
Denzil Davies
Frank Field
John McDonnell
Alan Simpson

2. THE DISMISSAL OF THE SPECIAL ADVISER TO TRANSPORT SECRETARY STEPHEN BYERS

22 October 2001

Labour MPs voting for (3):
Jeremy Corbyn
Tam Dalyell
Paul Marsden

3. REGULAR HEALTH CHECKS FOR INCAPACITY BENEFIT CLAIMANTS

26 October 2001

Labour MPs voting against (5):
Harry Barnes
Lynne Jones
John McDonnell
Dennis Skinner
David Winnick

4. THE BOMBING OF AFGHANISTAN

1 November 2001

Labour MPs voting against (11, including 3 tellers):

Diane Abbott	Lynne Jones	Tellers: Paul Marsden
Jeremy Corbyn	Robert Marshall-Andrews	Kerry Pollard
Tam Dalyell	Alan Simpson	John McDonnell
George Galloway	Mike Wood	

5. TERRORISM, CRIME & SECURITY BILL

21 November 2001

Labour MPs voting against (32):

Diane Abbott	Fabian Hamilton	Robert Marshall-Andrews
John Austin	Kelvin Hopkins	Brian Sedgemore
Harry Barnes	Lynne Jones	Alan Simpson
Andrew Bennett	Peter Kilfoyle	Dennis Skinner
Richard Burden	Terry Lewis	Llew Smith
Jeremy Corbyn	Tony Lloyd	David Taylor
Ann Cryer	Christine McCafferty	Robert Wareing
Tam Dalyell	John McDonnell	David Winnick
Mark Fisher	Kevin McNamara	Jimmy Wray
George Galloway	Alice Mahon	Dr Tony Wright
Neil Gerrard	Jim Marshall	

6. TERRORISM, CRIME & SECURITY BILL: BAN ON INCITEMENT TO RELIGIOUS HATRED

27 November 2001

Labour MPs voting against (21):

Diane Abbott	Denzil Davies	Gordon Prentice
Harry Barnes	Neil Gerrard	Brian Sedgemore
Andrew Bennett	Kelvin Hopkins	Alan Simpson
Harry Best	Lynne Jones	Dennis Skinner
Ronnie Campbell	Tony McWalter	Llew Smith
Jeremy Corbyn	Alice Mahon	Jon Trickett
John Cryer	Robert Marshall-Andrews	David Taylor

7. REQUIREMENT FOR RELIGIOUS SCHOOLS TO ADMIT 25% OF PUPILS FROM FAMILIES OF OTHER FAITHS OR NO FAITH

6 February 2002

Labour MPs voting for (46 including teller):

John Austin	Janet Dean	John McDonnell
Andrew Bennett	Frank Dobson	John McWilliam
Roger Berry	Gwyneth Dunwoody	Alice Mahon
Harold Best	Clive Efford	Chris Mullin
Martin Caton	Paul Flynn	Martin O'Neill
Colin Challen	Neil Gerrard	Gordon Prentice
David Chaytor	Ian Gibson	Gwyn Prosser
Michael Clapham	Jane Griffiths	Brian Sedgemore
David Clelland	David Hinchliffe	Alan Simpson
Ann Clwyd	Kelvin Hopkins	Dennis Skinner
Harry Cohen	Eric Illsley	Chris Smith
Jeremy Corbyn	Glenda Jackson	Clive Soley
Ann Cryer	Lynne Jones	Gerry Steinberg
Tam Dalyell	Terry Lewis	Robert Wareing
Valerie Davey	Christine McCafferty	Dr Tony Wright
		Teller: Jon Owen Jones

8. HUNTING WITH HOUNDS

18 March 2002

Labour MPs voting against a complete ban (4):

Kate Hoey	Jack Straw	Gareth Thomas
Huw Irranca-Davis		

Liberal Democrat MPs voting against a complete ban (13):

Alan Beith	Archy Kirkwood	Sir Robert Smith
Matthew Green	Norman Lamb	John Thurso
Evan Harris	Lembit Opik	Paul Tyler
Nick Harvey	Alan Reid	Roger Williams
Paul Keetch		

Conservative MPs voting for a complete ban (7):

David Amess	John Randall	Sir Teddy Taylor
David Atkinson	John Taylor	Ann Widdecombe
Roger Gale		

GUARDIAN LETTER DESCRIBING THE EURO AS A 'COSTLY DISTRACTION'

22 January 2002

Labour MP signatories (28):

Harold Best	Terry Davis	Alice Mahon
Ronnie Campbell	Hilton Dawson	John McDonnell
Harry Cohen	David Drew	Austin Mitchell
Jeremy Corbyn	Bill Etherington	Alan Simpson
Michael Clapham	Ian Gibson	Dennis Skinner
Jon Cruddas	Tom Harris	Llew Smith
Ann Cryer	Kelvin Hopkins	David Taylor
John Cryer	Alan Howarth	Mike Wood
Ian Davidson	Terry Lewis	Jimmy Wray
Denzil Davies		

LABOUR PARTY CAMPAIGN GROUP MEMBERSHIP (22)

November 2001

Diane Abbott	John Cryer	Austin Mitchell
John Austin	Bill Etherington	John McDonnell
Harry Barnes	Neil Gerrard	Phil Sawford
Ronnie Campbell	Kelvin Hopkins	Alan Simpson
Michael Clapham	Lynne Jones	Dennis Skinner
Harry Cohen	Terry Lewis	Llew Smith
Jeremy Corbyn	Alice Mahon	Mike Wood
Ann Cryer		

2001 Parliament: oldest MPs

Labour

Piara Khabra	Nov 1922
*Sir Ray Powell	Jun 1928
Bill O'Brien	Jan 1929
Tom Cox	Jan 1930
Gerald Kaufman	Jun 1930
Robert Wareing	Aug 1930
Alan Williams	Oct 1930
Gwyneth Dunwoody	Dec 1930
Dennis Skinner	Feb 1932
Tam Dalyell	Aug 1932
David Winnick	Jun 1933
Joe Benton	Sep 1933
Kevin McNamara	5 Sep 1934
Austin Mitchell	19 Sep 1934
Paul Flynn	Feb 1935
Frank Cook	Nov 1935
Terence Lewis	Dec 1935
Glenda Jackson	May 1936
Harry Barnes	Jul 1936
Nigel Beard	Oct 1936
Brian Sedgemore	17 Mar 1937
Ann Clwyd	21 Mar 1937
Derek Foster	25 Jun 1937
Peter Pike	26 Jun 1937
Alice Mahon	Sep 1937
Eddie O'Hara	Oct 1937
Alan Keen	Nov 1937
Harold Best	Dec 1937
Terry Davis	Jan 1938
Jimmy Wray	Apr 1938
Stuart Bell	16 May 1938
Geoffrey Robinson	25 May 1938
John Prescott	31 May 1938
George Stevenson	Aug 1938
Ian Gibson	Sep 1938
Denzil Davies	Oct 1938
Ken Purchase	Jan 1939
Andrew Bennett	Mar 1939
Clive Soley	7 May 1939
Helen Jackson	19 May 1939
Donald Anderson	Jun 1939
Desmond Turner	July 1939
Jack Cunningham	Aug 1939
Michael Meacher	Nov 1939
Ann Cryer	Dec 1939
Frank Dobson	Mar 1940
Anne Campbell	6 Apr 1940
Valerie Davey	10 Apr 1940
Brian Iddon	5 Jul 1940
Ben Chapman	8 Jul 1940
Barry Sheerman	17 Aug 1940
Bill Tynan	18 Aug 1940

* Deceased Dec 2001

Conservative

Sir Peter Tapsell	Feb 1930
Michael Mates	Jun 1934
Sir Sydney Chapman	Oct 1935
Marion Roe	Jul 1936
Sir Teddy Taylor	Apr 1937
Sir Alan Haselhurst	Jun 1937
Peter Viggers	13 Mar 1938
Nicholas Winterton	31 Mar 1938
Sir Michael Lord	Oct 1938
John Horam	Mar 1939
Sir Patrick Cormack	May 1939
Anthony Steen	Jul 1939
John Gummer	Nov 1939
Gillian Shephard	Jan 1940
David Atkinson	Mar 1940
Bill Cash	May 1940
Kenneth Clarke	2 Jul 1940
Sir Brian Mawhinney	26 Jul 1940
John Wilkinson	Sep 1940

Liberal Democrat

Brian Cotter   Aug 1938

Other

Revd Ian Paisley	DUP	Apr 1926	Roy Beggs	UU	Feb 1936
Revd Martin Smyth	UU	Jun 1931	Seamus Mallon	SDLP	Aug 1936
Richard Taylor	Ind	Jul 1934	John Hume	SDLP	Jan 1937
Eddie McGrady	SDLP	Jun 1935			

2001 Parliament: longest (continuously) serving MPs

Tam Dalyell	Lab	1962	Peter Bottomley	C	1975
Alan Williams	Lab	1964	Geoffrey Robinson	Lab	1976
Kevin McNamara	Lab	1966	Sir Alan Haselhurst	C	1977
Sir Peter Tapsell	C	1966	David Atkinson	C	1977
Tom Cox	Lab	1970	Austin Mitchell	Lab	1977
Revd Ian Paisley	DUP	1970	Michael Martin	Speaker	1979
Sir Patrick Cormack	C	1970	Terry Davis	Lab	1979
Gavin Strang	Lab	1970	David Winnick	Lab	1979
John Prescott	Lab	1970	Derek Foster	Lab	1979
Gerald Kaufman	Lab	1970	David Marshall	Lab	1979
Jack Cunningham	Lab	1970	Ernie Ross	Lab	1979
Denzil Davies	Lab	1970	Martin O'Neill	Lab	1979
Kenneth Clarke	C	1970	George Foulkes	Lab	1979
Michael Meacher	Lab	1970	Barry Sheerman	Lab	1979
Dennis Skinner	Lab	1970	Douglas Hogg	C	1979
Nicholas Winterton	C	1971	Frank Field	Lab	1979
Alan Beith	LD	1973	Clive Soley	Lab	1979
Sir George Young	C	1974(F)	Frank Dobson	Lab	1979
Bruce George	Lab	1974(F)	John Gummer	C	1979
Robin Cook	Lab	1974(F)	Brian Mawhinney	C	1979
Sir John Stanley	C	1974(F)	Sir Sydney Chapman	C	1979
Gwyneth Dunwoody	Lab	1974(F)	Richard Shepherd	C	1979
Andrew Bennett	Lab	1974(F)	John McWilliam	Lab	1979
Peter Viggers	C	1974(F)	*Sir Ray Powell	Lab	1979
Sir Michael Spicer	C	1974(F)	Stephen Dorrell	C	1979
Anthony Steen	C	1974(F)	John Wilkinson	C	1979
Michael Mates	C	1974(O)	Jack Straw	Lab	1979
Donald Anderson	Lab	1974(O)	Peter Robinson	DUP	1979
			Richard Page	C	1979(D)

* Deceased Dec 2001

2001 Parliament: youngest MPs

Labour

David Lammy	Jul 72
Christopher Leslie	Jun 72
Claire Ward	May 72
Parmjit Dhanda	Sep 71
James Purnell	Mar 70
Andy Burnham	Jan 70
Yvette Cooper	Mar 69
Sion Simon	Dec 68
Ruth Kelly	May 68
Paul Marsden	Mar 68
Douglas Alexander	Oct 67
Oona King	Oct 67
Jim Murphy	Aug 67
Lorna Fitzsimons	Aug 67
Gareth R Thomas	Jul 67
Ivan Lewis	Mar 67
Tom Watson	Jan 67
Stephen Twigg	Dec 66
David Wright	Dec 66
David Cairns	Aug 66
Jonathan Shaw	Jun 66
David Miliband	Jul 65
Jim Knight	Mar 65

Conservative

George Osborne	May 71
Graham Brady	May 67
David Cameron	Oct 66
Bill Wiggin	Jun 66
Gregory Barker	Mar 66
Andrew Rosindell	Mar 66
Mark Francois	Aug 65
Peter Duncan	Jul 65
Jonathan Djanogly	Mar 65

Liberal Democrat

Matthew Green	Apr 70
Richard Allan	Feb 66
Edward Davey	Dec 65
David Laws	Nov 65
Evan Harris	Oct 65
Alistair Carmichael	Jul 65
Steven Webb	Jul 65
Michael Moore	Jun 65
Lembit Opik	Mar 65

Other

Michelle Gildernew (SF)	Jan 70
Angus Robertson (SNP)	Sep 69
Adam Price (PC)	Sep 68

Seats ranked by marginality and safety

Labour

		%Maj	Second
1	Dorset South	0.3	C
2	Braintree	0.7	C
3	Monmouth	0.9	C
4	Lancaster and Wyre	0.9	C
5	Kettering	1.2	C
6	Northampton South	1.7	C
7	Cardiff Central	1.9	LD
8	Ynys Mon	2.4	PC
9	Welwyn Hatfield	2.8	C
10	Shipley	3.1	C
11	Clwyd West	3.2	C
12	Bexleyheath and Crayford	3.6	C
13	Milton Keynes North East	3.9	C
14	Hornchurch	4.2	C
15	Selby	4.3	C
16	Edinburgh Pentlands	4.5	C
17	Hammersmith and Fulham	4.5	C
18	Thanet South	4.5	C
19	Forest of Dean	4.6	C
20	Wellingborough	4.6	C
21	Ilford North	5.3	C
22	Rugby and Kenilworth	5.3	C
23	Gillingham	5.4	C
24	Harwich	5.4	C
25	Enfield North	6.0	C
26	Oldham East and Saddleworth	6.0	LD
27	Calder Valley	6.5	C
28	Ayr	6.6	C
29	Redditch	6.7	C
30	Peterborough	7.2	C
31	Shrewsbury and Atcham	7.2	C
32	Dartford	7.4	C
33	Scarborough and Whitby	7.5	C
34	Hove	7.6	C
35	Bristol West	8.0	LD
36	Preseli Pembrokeshire	8.0	C
37	Gloucester	8.0	C
38	Putney	8.1	C
39	Hemel Hempstead	8.2	C
40	Western Isles	8.2	SNP
41	South Ribble	8.2	C
42	Finchley and Golders Green	8.5	C
43	Wolverhampton South West	8.5	C
44	Birmingham Yardley	8.6	LD
45	The Wrekin	8.6	C
46	Croydon Central	8.7	C
47	Elmet	9.1	C
48	Wimbledon	9.1	C
49	Stroud	9.1	C
50	Keighley	9.2	C
51	Sittingbourne and Sheppey	9.3	C
52	High Peak	9.3	C
53	Stourbridge	9.5	C
54	Brigg and Goole	9.6	C
55	Falmouth and Camborne	9.7	C
56	Medway	9.8	C
57	Colne Valley	9.9	C
58	Wirral West	10.0	C
59	St Albans	10.2	C
60	Vale of Glamorgan	10.4	C
61	Burton	10.4	C
62	Wandsyke	10.4	C
63	Hastings and Rye	10.5	C
64	Pendle	10.8	C
65	Bradford West	10.9	C
66	Chatham and Aylesford	10.9	C
67	Inverness East, Nairn and Lochaber	11.1	SNP
68	Warwick and Leamington	11.1	C
60	Gravesham	11.1	C
70	Great Yarmouth	11.3	C
71	Stafford	11.3	C
72	Tamworth	11.4	C
73	Dover	11.6	C

	%Maj	Second		%Maj	Second
74 Aberdeen South	11.9	LD	123 Chorley	17.6	C
75 Watford	12.0	C	124 Dudley North	17.6	C
76 Broxtowe	12.0	C	125 Llanelli	17.7	PC
77 Corby	12.1	C	126 Vale of Clwyd	17.8	C
78 Morecambe and Lunesdale	12.2	C	127 Leeds North East	17.8	C
79 Carmarthen West and			128 Conwy	18.1	C
South Pembrokeshire	12.3	C	129 Leicestershire North West	18.1	C
80 Leeds North West	12.3	C	130 Waveney	18.1	C
81 Birmingham Edgbaston	12.4	C	131 Hendon	18.2	C
82 Pudsey	12.5	C	132 Halesowen and		
83 Brighton Kemptown	12.6	C	Rowley Regis	18.7	C
84 Rossendale and Darwen	12.6	C	133 Dudley South	18.8	C
85 Wirral South	12.7	C	134 Eastwood	18.9	C
86 Gedling	12.8	C	135 Basildon	18.9	C
87 Reading East	12.8	C	136 Northampton North	19.0	C
88 Norwich North	12.9	C	137 Swindon North	19.1	C
89 Harlow	13.0	C	138 Plymouth Sutton	19.2	C
90 Worcester	13.0	C	139 Wakefield	19.3	C
91 Batley and Spen	13.1	C	140 Tynemouth	19.8	C
92 Harrow West	13.2	C	141 Gower	19.8	C
93 Enfield Southgate	13.2	C	142 Cambridge	20.0	LD
94 Cleethorpes	13.2	C	143 Birmingham Hall Green	20.1	C
95 Bolton West	13.4	C	144 Stevenage	20.2	C
96 Blackpool North and			145 Dewsbury	20.3	C
Fleetwood	13.4	C	146 Clydesdale	20.4	SNP
97 Staffordshire Moorlands	13.7	C	147 Sherwood	20.4	C
98 Battersea	13.7	C	148 Stockton South	20.6	C
99 Dundee East	13.8	SNP	149 Coventry South	20.6	C
100 Portsmouth North	13.9	C	150 Norwich South	20.7	C
101 Cardiff North	14.3	C	151 Eltham	20.7	C
102 Erewash	14.3	C	152 Dumfries	20.7	C
103 Copeland	14.3	C	153 Ipswich	20.8	C
104 Rochdale	14.3	LD	154 Blaydon	21.1	LD
105 Loughborough	14.4	C	155 Reading West	21.1	C
106 Bury North	14.6	C	156 Middlesbrough South and		
107 Aberdeen North	14.7	SNP	East Cleveland	21.3	C
108 Edinburgh South	14.8	LD	157 Blackpool South	21.3	C
109 Derbyshire South	15.1	C	158 Hyndburn	21.5	C
110 Ochil	15.2	SNP	159 Bolton North East	21.6	C
111 Bedford	15.2	C	160 Warwickshire North	21.7	C
112 Halifax	15.2	C	161 Hampstead and Highgate	22.2	C
113 City of Chester	15.4	C	162 Exeter	22.3	C
114 Milton Keynes South West	15.4	C	163 Lancashire West	22.4	C
115 Derby North	15.8	C	164 Crosby	22.7	C
116 Amber Valley	16.2	C	165 Lincoln	22.7	C
117 Warrington South	16.3	C	166 Blackburn	22.8	C
118 Carlisle	16.3	C	167 Harrow East	23.1	C
119 Swindon South	16.9	C	168 Brentford and Isleworth	23.2	C
120 Crawley	17.1	C	169 Dundee West	23.3	SNP
121 Nuneaton	17.4	C	170 Birmingham Perry Barr	23.4	C
122 Stirling	17.5	C	171 Darlington	23.4	C

	%Maj	Second
172 Bristol North West	23.7	C
173 Edinburgh Central	23.7	LD
174 Brighton Pavilion	23.7	C
175 Crewe and Nantwich	23.8	C
176 Hornsey and Wood Green	24.1	LD
177 Weaver Vale	24.5	C
178 Cunninghame North	24.8	SNP
179 Delyn	24.8	C
180 Bassetlaw	25.1	C
181 Aberdeen Central	25.1	SNP
182 Glasgow Govan	25.3	SNP
183 Cumbernauld and Kilsyth	25.3	SNP
184 Barrow and Furness	25.3	C
185 Luton North	25.5	C
186 Coventry NW	25.6	C
187 Renfrewshire West	25.6	SNP
188 Bradford North	25.6	C
189 Luton South	25.8	C
190 Birmingham Selly Oak	25.8	C
191 Islington South and Finsbury	25.8	LD
192 Newcastle under Lyme	25.8	C
193 Workington	25.9	C
194 Oxford East	26.0	LD
195 Don Valley	26.0	C
196 Alyn and Deeside	26.0	C
197 Cannock Chase	26.1	C
198 Bethnal Green and Bow	26.1	C
199 Ellesmere Port and Neston	26.2	C
200 Ealing North	26.3	C
201 Birmingham Northfield	26.4	C
202 Kingswood	26.5	C
203 Edinburgh North and Leith	26.5	LD
204 Newport West	26.5	C
205 Clwyd South	26.6	C
206 St Helens South	26.6	LD
207 Thurrock	26.8	C
208 Southampton Test	27.0	C
209 Glasgow Kelvin	27.1	LD
210 Southampton Itchen	27.1	C
211 Telford	27.2	C
212 Bridgend	27.2	C
213 Nottingham South	27.3	C
214 Kilmarnock and Loudoun	27.4	SNP
215 Bradford South	27.5	C
216 Falkirk West	27.6	SNP
217 Stalybridge and Hyde	27.6	C
218 Tooting	27.7	C
219 Regent's Park and Kensington North	27.7	C

	%Maj	Second
220 Edmonton	28.1	C
221 Dumbarton	28.2	SNP
222 Strathkelvin and Bearsden	28.2	LD
223 Huddersfield	28.4	C
224 Walsall South	28.5	C
225 Burnley	28.5	C
226 City of York	28.7	C
227 Linlithgow	28.8	SNP
228 Ealing Acton and Shepherd's Bush	29.0	C
229 Leicester West	29.0	C
230 Walsall North	29.1	C
231 Normanton	29.1	C
232 Derbyshire NE	29.1	C
233 Stoke on Trent South	29.1	C
234 Ealing Southall	29.2	C
235 East Lothian	29.4	C
236 Livingston	29.5	SNP
237 Swansea West	29.8	C
238 Lewisham East	29.8	C
239 West Bromwich East	29.9	C
240 Mansfield	30.0	C
241 Brent North	30.1	C
242 Heywood and Middleton	30.1	C
243 Wrexham	30.6	C
244 East Kilbride	30.6	SNP
245 Scunthorpe	30.8	C
246 Fife Central	31.0	SNP
247 Plymouth Devonport	31.2	C
248 Midlothian	31.4	SNP
249 Leicester South	31.4	C
250 Morley and Rothwell	31.4	C
251 Dagenham	31.5	C
252 Newport East	31.6	C
253 Wolverhampton North East	31.7	C
254 Falkirk East	31.8	SNP
255 Kirkcaldy	31.8	SNP
256 Slough	32.1	C
257 Derby South	32.2	C
258 Dulwich and West Norwood	32.2	C
259 Bury South	32.3	C
260 City of Durham	32.4	LD
261 Birmingham Erdington	32.6	C
262 Stockport	32.7	C
263 Wallasey	32.9	C
264 Manchester Withington	32.9	LD
265 Clydebank and Milngavie	33.0	SNP
266 Leicester East	33.1	C
267 Bristol East	33.2	C
268 Cardiff West	33.2	C

	%Maj	Second		%Maj	Second
269 Newcastle upon Tyne			315 Paisley South	39.0	SNP
Central	33.3	LD	316 Stoke on Trent North	39.1	C
270 Worsley	33.3	C	317 Glasgow Cathcart	39.5	SNP
271 Oldham West and Royton	33.4	C	318 Newcastle upon Tyne North	39.7	C
272 Erith and Thamesmead	33.5	C	319 Cunninghame South	40.1	SNP
273 Ashfield	33.7	C	320 Croydon North	40.3	C
274 Ilford South	33.9	C	321 Hamilton South	40.3	SNP
275 Stretford and Urmston	34.0	C	322 Rother Valley	40.4	C
276 Preston	34.0	C	323 Nottingham North	40.7	C
277 Sheffield Hillsborough	34.3	LD	324 Wigan	40.9	C
278 Sheffield Heeley	34.3	LD	325 Greenwich and Woolwich	41.3	C
279 Paisley North	34.3	SNP	326 Stockton North	41.3	C
280 Cardiff South and Penarth	34.4	C	327 Glasgow Anniesland	41.4	SNP
281 Bristol South	34.6	C	328 Poplar and Canning Town	41.4	C
282 Nottingham East	34.7	C	329 Manchester Gorton	41.5	LD
283 Great Grimsby	34.8	C	330 Hayes and Harlington	41.6	C
284 Greenock and Inverclyde	34.8	LD	331 Durham North West	41.6	C
285 Feltham and Heston	35.0	C	332 Sheffield Central	41.7	LD
286 Wansbeck	35.0	LD	333 Stoke on Trent Central	41.9	C
287 Redcar	35.2	C	334 Coventry North East	42.3	C
288 Blyth Valley	35.3	LD	335 St Helens North	42.3	C
289 Edinburgh East and			336 Glasgow Baillieston	42.3	SNP
Musselburgh	35.3	SNP	337 Neath	42.3	PC
290 Doncaster Central	35.4	C	338 Islington North	42.9	LD
291 Dunfermline West	35.4	SNP	339 Glasgow Rutherglen	43.2	SNP
292 West Bromwich West	35.7	C	340 Ashton under Lyne	43.4	C
293 Barnsley W and Penistone	35.7	C	341 Newcastle upon Tyne East		
294 Holborn and St Pancras	35.9	LD	and Wallsend	43.5	LD
295 Wythenshawe and			342 Leeds East	43.5	C
Sale East	36.0	C	343 Eccles	43.8	C
296 Bishop Auckland	36.1	C	344 Sunderland South	43.8	C
297 Mitcham and Morden	36.3	C	345 Birmingham Hodge Hill	43.9	C
298 Motherwell and Wishaw	36.9	SNP	346 Sedgefield	44.0	C
299 Carrick, Cumnock and			347 Walthamstow	44.1	C
Doon Valley	37.0	C	348 Birmingham Sparkbrook		
300 Caerphilly	37.2	PC	and Small Heath	44.3	LD
301 Kingston upon Hull North	37.4	LD	349 Hemsworth	44.4	C
302 Bolton South East	37.7	C	350 Glasgow Maryhill	44.5	SNP
303 Warley	37.7	C	351 Rotherham	44.5	C
304 Kingston upon Hull			352 Glasgow Pollok	44.6	SNP
West and Hessle	37.9	C	353 Hamilton N and Bellshill	44.6	SNP
305 Barking	37.9	C	354 Sunderland North	44.8	C
306 Liverpool Garston	38.3	LD	355 Brent East	45.0	C
307 Leyton and Wanstead	38.3	C	356 Denton and Reddish	45.6	C
308 Hartlepool	38.3	C	357 Wolverhampton		
309 Liverpool Wavertree	38.3	LD	South East	45.7	C
310 Streatham	38.6	LD	358 Hackney North and		
311 Lewisham West	38.7	C	Stoke Newington	46.1	C
312 Airdrie and Shotts	38.9	SNP	359 Pontypridd	46.2	PC
313 Warrington North	39.0	C	360 Torfaen	46.2	C
314 Vauxhall	39.0	LD	361 South Shields	46.3	C

	%Maj	Second
362 Leigh	46.4	C
363 Leeds West	46.5	C
364 Merthyr Tydfil and Rhymney	47.1	PC
365 Rhondda	47.2	PC
366 Glasgow Shettleston	48.0	SNP
367 Ogmore	48.0	PC
368 Cynon Valley	48.2	PC
369 Islwyn	48.3	LD
370 Doncaster North	48.4	C
371 Middlesbrough	48.4	C
372 Durham North	48.4	C
373 Wentworth	48.7	C
374 Salford	48.9	LD
375 Bolsover	49.1	C
376 Hackney South and Shoreditch	49.6	LD
377 Kingston upon Hull East	49.6	LD
378 Dunfermline East	50.1	SNP
379 Knowsley North and Sefton East	50.4	C
380 Coatbridge and Chryston	50.5	SNP
381 Halton	50.6	C
382 Makerfield	50.9	C
383 Jarrow	51.0	LD
384 Liverpool West Derby	51.3	Lib
385 Barnsley East and Mexborough	51.6	LD
386 Pontefract and Castleford	52.2	C
387 Lewisham Deptford	52.5	C
388 Sheffield Attercliffe	52.6	C
389 Leeds Central	52.7	C
390 Manchester Central	53.0	LD
391 Gateshead East and Washington West	53.3	LD
392 Aberavon	53.4	PC
393 West Ham	53.4	C
394 Tottenham	53.5	C
395 Swansea East	53.7	PC
396 Birkenhead	53.8	C
397 Manchester Blackley	54.5	C
398 Liverpool Riverside	54.7	LD
399 Barnsley Central	54.9	LD
400 Tyneside North	55.0	C
401 Camberwell and Peckham	56.3	LD
402 East Ham	56.4	C
403 Tyne Bridge	57.2	C
404 Birmingham Ladywood	57.6	C
405 Knowsley South	58.3	LD

	%Maj	Second
406 Houghton and Washington East	58.9	C
407 Brent South	60.7	C
408 Blaenau Gwent	60.9	PC
409 Liverpool Walton	63.2	LD
410 Easington	66.5	C
411 Sheffield Brightside	66.7	C
412 Bootle	69.0	LD

Conservative

	%Maj	Second
1 Galloway and Upper Nithsdale	0.2	SNP
2 Taunton	0.4	LD
3 Orpington	0.5	LD
4 Boston and Skegness	1.3	Lab
5 Beverley and Holderness	1.7	Lab
6 Surrey South West	1.7	LD
7 Bedfordshire South West	1.8	Lab
8 Basingstoke	1.8	Lab
9 Castle Point	2.5	Lab
10 Dorset West	2.9	LD
11 Upminster	3.7	Lab
12 Haltemprice and Howden	4.3	LD
13 Isle of Wight	4.5	LD
14 Canterbury	4.6	Lab
15 Eastbourne	4.8	LD
16 Bury St Edmunds	5.0	Lab
17 Bosworth	5.1	Lab
18 Wells	5.4	LD
19 Hexham	6.0	Lab
20 Uxbridge	6.3	Lab
21 Chipping Barnet	6.4	Lab
22 Brentwood and Ongar	6.5	IndBell
23 Westmorland and Lonsdale	6.6	LD
24 Gosport	6.6	Lab
25 Altrincham and Sale West	6.8	Lab
26 Norfolk North West	6.8	Lab
27 Wycombe	7.0	Lab
28 Totnes	7.3	LD
29 Wiltshire North	7.3	LD
30 Suffolk Central and Ipswich North	7.4	Lab
31 Maidenhead	7.6	LD
32 Hertfordshire North East	7.7	Lab
33 Spelthorne	7.8	Lab
34 Old Bexley and Sidcup	7.9	Lab
35 Dorset North	7.9	LD
36 Meriden	8.5	Lab
37 Suffolk Coastal	8.6	Lab

		%Maj	Second			%Maj	Second
38	Norfolk Mid	8.7	Lab	85	Woking	15.8	LD
39	Newark	9.0	Lab	86	Macclesfield	15.8	Lab
40	New Forest East	9.1	LD	87	Congleton	15.8	Lab
41	Bournemouth East	9.6	LD	88	Thanet North	15.9	Lab
42	Grantham and Stamford	9.8	Lab	89	Essex North	16.0	Lab
43	Aldridge-Brownhills	10.0	Lab	90	Charnwood	16.0	Lab
44	Suffolk West	10.1	Lab	91	Witney	16.2	Lab
45	Banbury	10.1	Lab	92	Staffordshire South	16.3	Lab
46	Faversham and Mid Kent	10.2	Lab	93	Salisbury	16.5	LD
47	Eddisbury	10.3	Lab	94	Romford	16.7	Lab
48	Havant	10.4	Lab	95	Louth and Horncastle	17.0	Lab
49	Bridgwater	10.4	LD	96	Daventry	17.0	Lab
50	Westbury	10.5	LD	97	Devon East	17.1	LD
51	Lichfield	10.6	Lab	98	Bedfordshire Mid	17.3	Lab
52	Yorkshire East	10.8	Lab	99	Hertfordshire South West	17.3	Lab
53	Beckenham	10.9	Lab	100	Cambridgeshire South East	17.3	LD
54	Billericay	11.0	Lab	101	Cambridgeshire South	17.4	LD
55	Ryedale	11.1	LD	102	Hampshire East	17.7	LD
56	Suffolk South	11.2	Lab	103	Norfolk South West	17.7	Lab
57	Tiverton and Honiton	11.3	LD	104	Sleaford and North		
58	Harborough	11.3	LD		Hykeham	17.7	Lab
59	Wantage	11.4	Lab	105	Bromsgrove	17.8	Lab
60	Hertsmere	11.8	Lab	106	Woodspring	18.0	Lab
61	Hertford and Stortford	11.9	Lab	107	Poole	18.3	Lab
62	Worcestershire West	12.0	LD	108	Rutland and Melton	18.3	Lab
63	Norfolk South	12.3	Lab	109	Cambridgeshire		
64	Folkestone and Hythe	12.9	LD		North West	18.4	Lab
65	Chelmsford West	13.0	Lab	110	Rochford and Southend		
66	Blaby	13.0	Lab		East	18.8	Lab
67	Stone	13.2	Lab	111	Bedfordshire North East	19.0	Lab
68	Cities of London and			112	Henley	19.0	LD
	Westminster	13.2	Lab	113	Gainsborough	19.1	Lab
69	Cambridgeshire North East	13.3	Lab	114	Tewkesbury	19.2	Lab
70	Shropshire North	13.4	Lab	115	Maldon and Chelmsford		
71	Rushcliffe	13.5	Lab		East	19.2	Lab
72	Bracknell	13.6	Lab	116	Croydon South	19.3	Lab
73	Wokingham	13.7	LD	117	Rayleigh	19.4	Lab
74	Bournemouth West	14.0	Lab	118	Tonbridge and Malling	19.4	Lab
75	Worthing East and			119	Solihull	19.5	LD
	Shoreham	14.3	Lab	120	Runnymede and Weybridge	19.7	Lab
76	Bognor Regis and			121	Epping Forest	19.9	Lab
	Littlehampton	14.5	Lab	122	Ruislip-Northwood	20.3	Lab
77	Aldershot	14.5	Lab	123	Reigate	20.3	Lab
78	Derbyshire West	14.6	Lab	124	Aylesbury	20.4	Lab
79	Hitchin and Harpenden	14.8	Lab	125	Tatton	20.9	Lab
80	Chingford and Woodford			126	Bromley and Chislehurst	20.9	Lab
	Green	14.8	Lab	127	Worthing West	20.9	LD
81	Sussex Mid	15.1	LD	128	Windsor	21.1	LD
82	Devon South West	15.2	Lab	129	Southend West	21.2	Lab
83	Ashford	15.4	Lab	130	Fylde	21.5	Lab
84	Fareham	15.4	Lab	131	Stratford on Avon	21.5	LD

		%Maj	Second
132	Mole Valley	21.6	LD
133	Epsom and Ewell	21.6	Lab
134	Leominster	22.2	LD
135	Devizes	22.3	Lab
136	Maidstone and the Weald	22.6	Lab
137	Ribble Valley	22.9	LD
138	Chichester	22.9	LD
139	Sutton Coldfield	23.3	Lab
140	Bexhill and Battle	23.5	LD
141	Worcestershire Mid	23.7	Lab
142	Broxbourne	23.8	Lab
143	Sevenoaks	23.8	Lab
144	Surrey Heath	24.0	LD
145	Saffron Walden	24.0	LD
146	South Holland and the Deepings	24.0	Lab
147	Tunbridge Wells	24.2	LD
148	Hampshire North West	24.7	Lab
149	Esher and Walton	25.3	Lab
150	Vale of York	25.8	Lab
151	Huntingdon	26.1	LD
152	Cotswold	26.1	LD
153	Wealden	26.1	LD
154	Chesham and Amersham	26.2	LD
155	Skipton and Ripon	26.3	LD
156	Horsham	26.9	LD
157	Christchurch	27.3	LD
158	Beaconsfield	27.6	Lab
159	Surrey East	28.1	LD
160	Buckingham	29.4	Lab
161	Arundel and South Downs	29.9	LD
162	New Forest West	29.9	LD
163	Hampshire North East	30.2	LD
164	Kensington and Chelsea	31.3	Lab
165	Penrith and the Border	33.2	LD
166	Richmond (Yorkshire)	37.1	Lab

Liberal Democrat

		%Maj	Second
1	Cheadle	0.1	C
2	Weston super Mare	0.7	C
3	Norfolk North	0.9	C
4	Dorset Mid and Poole North	0.9	C
5	Guildford	1.1	C
6	Somerton and Frome	1.3	C
7	Brecon and Radnorshire	2.0	C
8	Torridge and Devon West	2.1	C
9	Hereford	2.2	C

		%Maj	Second
10	Ludlow	3.8	C
11	Newbury	4.8	C
12	Romsey	4.9	C
13	Teignbridge	5.1	C
14	Argyll and Bute	5.3	Lab
15	Chesterfield	5.8	Lab
16	Devon North	6.1	C
17	Eastleigh	6.4	C
18	Southport	7.3	C
19	Yeovil	8.2	C
20	Richmond Park	10.1	C
21	Cornwall South East	10.4	C
22	Sutton and Cheam	10.8	C
23	Caithness, Sutherland and Easter Ross	11.0	Lab
24	Carshalton and Wallington	11.2	C
25	Cheltenham	12.6	C
26	Colchester	12.7	C
27	Aberdeenshire West and Deeside	12.7	C
28	Torbay	14.1	C
29	Twickenham	15.3	C
30	Tweeddale, Ettrick and Lauderdale	15.5	Lab
31	Portsmouth South	15.5	C
32	Truro and St Austell	16.0	C
33	Winchester	16.3	C
34	Northavon	17.7	C
35	Oxford West and Abingdon	17.8	C
36	Cornwall North	18.2	C
37	Edinburgh West	19.2	Lab
38	St Ives	20.4	C
39	Orkney and Shetland	20.8	Lab
40	Harrogate and Knaresborough	21.0	C
41	Bath	21.4	C
42	Lewes	21.4	C
43	Montgomeryshire	21.5	C
44	Hazel Grove	21.9	C
45	Gordon	22.5	C
46	Berwick upon Tweed	23.3	C
47	Sheffield Hallam	24.4	C
48	Roxburgh and Berwickshire	26.1	C
49	Southwark North and Bermondsey	26.1	Lab
50	Fife North East	28.1	C
51	Kingston and Surbiton	31.9	C
52	Ross, Skye and Inverness West	37.2	Lab

Ulster Unionist

	%Maj	Second
1 Antrim East	0.4	DUP
2 Antrim South	2.3	DUP
3 Upper Bann	4.0	DUP
4 Belfast South	14.2	SDLP
5 Down North	19.7	UKUP
6 Lagan Valley	39.9	APNI

Democratic Unionist

	%Maj	Second
1 Strangford	2.6	UUP
2 Londonderry East	4.8	UUP
3 Belfast North	15.6	SF
4 Belfast East	19.3	UUP
5 Antrim North	28.9	UUP

Sinn Fein

	%Maj	Second
1 Fermanagh and South Tyrone	0.1	UUP
2 Tyrone West	10.4	UUP
3 Ulster Mid	19.9	DUP
4 Belfast West	47.2	SDLP

Social Democratic and Labour

	%Maj	Second
1 Newry and Armagh	6.4	SF
2 Foyle	23.6	SF
3 Down South	26.6	SF

Scottish National

	%Maj	Second
1 Perth	0.1	C
2 Moray	5.2	Lab
3 Tayside North	8.5	C
4 Angus	10.3	C
5 Banff and Buchan	34.1	C

Plaid Cymru

	%Maj	Second
1 Carmarthen East and Dinefwr	6.8	Lab
2 Ceredigion	11.4	LD
3 Caernarfon	12.1	Lab
4 Meirionnydd nant Conwy	27.0	Lab

Other

	%Maj	Second
1 Wyre Forest (Independent)	35.9	Lab
2 Glasgow Springburn (Speaker)	47.2	SNP

Statistical tables: constituencies

The 20 seats with the most pensioner voters (England and Wales)

		%	Winning party 2001
1	Worthing West	45.1	C
2	Bexhill and Battle	44.2	C
3	Devon East	43.8	C
4	Harwich	43.7	Lab
5	Christchurch	43.5	C
6	Eastbourne	42.2	C
7	New Forest West	40.8	C
8	Thanet North	39.0	C
9	Bognor Regis and Littlehampton	39.0	C
10	Bournemouth West	37.8	C
11	Lewes	36.3	LD
12	Torbay	36.3	LD
13	Norfolk North	36.0	LD
14	Dorset West	35.9	C
15	Clwyd West	35.5	Lab
16	Totnes	35.5	C
17	Chichester	35.1	C
18	Hove	35.1	Lab
19	Isle of Wight	35.0	C
20	Blackpool North and Fleetwood	34.8	Lab

The 20 seats with the highest proportion of electors in financial hardship (Britain)

		%	Winning party 2001
1	Birmingham Ladywood	71.6	Lab
2	Glasgow Springburn	66.6	Speaker
3	Glasgow Shettleston	64.9	Lab
4	Birmingham Sparkbrook and Small Heath	62.8	Lab
5	Poplar and Canning Town	60.2	Lab
6	Bethnal Green and Bow	57.6	Lab
7	Glasgow Maryhill	57.1	Lab
8	Camberwell and Peckham	56.5	Lab
9	Southwark North and Bermondsey	55.1	LD
10	Glasgow Baillieston	54.2	Lab
11	Hackney South and Shoreditch	53.9	Lab
12	Glasgow Pollok	53.5	Lab
13	Glasgow Anniesland	51.5	Lab
14	Manchester Central	51.2	Lab
15	Wolverhampton South East	50.7	Lab
16	Birmingham Hodge Hill	49.4	Lab
17	Sheffield Brightside	48.8	Lab
18	Glasgow Govan	48.8	Lab
19	Airdrie and Shotts	48.6	Lab
20	Motherwell and Wishaw	48.6	Lab

The 20 seats with the lowest proportion of electors in financial hardship (Britain)

		%	Winning party 2001
1	Wokingham	2.6	C
2	Surrey Heath	2.7	C
3	Woodspring	2.8	C
4	Buckingham	3.0	C
5	Devon South West	3.0	C
6	Saffron Walden	3.2	C
7	Beaconsfield	3.3	C
8	Ceredigion	3.5	PC
9	Surrey East	3.5	C
10	Esher and Walton	3.6	C
11	Henley	3.6	C
12	Hampshire North East	3.7	C
13	Rayleigh	3.8	C
14	Sussex Mid	3.9	C
15	Bedfordshire Mid	3.9	C
16	Epsom and Ewell	4.0	C
17	Wantage	4.1	C
18	Castle Point	4.2	C
19	Mole Valley	4.4	C
20	Sheffield Hallam	4.4	LD

The 20 most rural seats (Britain)

		% Living in Rural Census Enumeration Districts	*Winning party 2001*
1	Ceredigion	69.9	PC
2	Montgomeryshire	64.3	LD
3	Orkney and Shetland	62.5	LD
4	Leominster	60.7	C
5	Penrith and the Border	60.2	C
6	Carmarthen East and Dinefwr	55.8	PC
7	Galloway and Upper Nithsdale	52.5	C
8	Brecon and Radnorshire	51.8	LD
9	Torridge and Devon West	51.5	LD
10	Ludlow	50.3	LD
11	Meirionnydd nant Conwy	49.2	PC
12	South Holland and the Deepings	48.7	C
13	Vale of York	47.4	C
14	Tiverton and Honiton	47.2	C
15	Norfolk North	46.2	LD
16	Louth and Horncastle	45.8	C
17	Caithness, Sutherland and Easter Ross	45.8	LD
18	Carmarthen West and South Pembrokeshire	45.3	Lab
19	Preseli Pembrokeshire	45.2	Lab
20	Caernarfon	44.1	PC

The 20 seats with the highest proportion of agricultural workers

		%	*Winning party 2001*
1	Galloway and Upper Nithsdale	16.9	C
2	Montgomeryshire	15.5	LD
3	Ceredigion	14.0	PC
4	Carmarthen East and Dinefwr	13.7	PC
5	Orkney and Shetland	13.6	LD
6	Brecon and Radnorshire	12.8	LD
7	Leominster	12.7	C
8	Penrith and the Border	12.6	C
9	Argyll and Bute	12.3	LD
	South Holland and the Deepings	12.3	C
11	Torridge and West Devon	12.0	LD
12	Fermanagh and South Tyrone	11.9	SF
13	Roxburgh and Berwickshire	11.8	LD
14	Banff and Buchan	11.5	SNP
15	Preseli Pembrokeshire	11.3	Lab
16	Ludlow	11.1	LD
	Meirionnydd nant Conwy	11.1	PC
18	Tyrone West	10.6	SF
19	Louth and Horncastle	10.4	C
20	Tiverton and Honiton	10.3	C

Highest property values 2000 (England and Wales)

		£	Winning party 2001
1	Kensington and Chelsea	555,835	C
2	Cities of London and Westminster	373,403	C
3	Hampstead and Highgate	344,238	Lab
4	Hammersmith and Fulham	304,542	Lab
5	Richmond Park	303,186	LD
6	Regent's Park and Kensington North	296,425	Lab
7	Esher and Walton	278,681	C
8	Holborn and St Pancras	276,760	Lab
9	Islington South and Finsbury	274,282	Lab
10	Beaconsfield	265,637	C
11	Battersea	262,775	Lab
12	Wimbledon	250,527	Lab
13	Putney	244,545	Lab
14	Ealing Acton and Shepherd's Bush	241,314	Lab
15	Mole Valley	236,700	C
16	Chesham and Amersham	230,356	C
17	Finchley and Golders Green	227,818	Lab
18	Twickenham	226,990	LD
19	Windsor	226,804	C
20	Runnymede and Weybridge	226,017	C

Lowest property values 2000 (England and Wales)

		£	Winning party 2001
1	Rhondda	27,300	Lab
2	Manchester Blackley	30,838	Lab
3	Cynon Valley	33,854	Lab
4	Liverpool Walton	34,917	Lab
5	Blaenau Gwent	35,175	Lab
6	Sheffield Brightside	35,592	Lab
7	Stoke on Trent Central	36,975	Lab
8	Hull East	37,685	Lab
9	Manchester Gorton	37,686	Lab
10	Middlesbrough	38,280	Lab
11	Hull North	38,873	Lab
12	Merthyr Tydfil and Rhymney	38,883	Lab
13	Bolton South East	39,225	Lab
14	Hyndburn	39,557	Lab
15	Bootle	40,210	Lab
16	Great Grimsby	40,981	Lab
17	Easington	41,288	Lab
18	Burnley	41,767	Lab
19	Llanelli	42,133	Lab
20	Scunthorpe	42,404	Lab

Highest unemployment rate, June 2001

		%	Winnning party 2001
1	Birmingham Ladywood	12.8	Lab
2	Belfast West	11.5	SF
3	Birmingham Sparkbrook and Small Heath	11.2	Lab
4	Foyle	10.8	SDLP
5	Liverpool Riverside	10.3	Lab
6	Manchester Central	10.2	Lab
7	Camberwell and Peckham	10.1	Lab
8	Bethnal Green and Bow	10.0	Lab
9	Poplar and Canning Town	9.9	Lab
10	Middlesbrough	9.1	Lab
11	South Shields	9.0	Lab
12	Hackney South and Shoreditch	8.9	Lab
	Tottenham	8.9	Lab
14	Glasgow Springburn	8.7	Speaker
	Liverpool Walton	8.7	Lab
16	Belfast North	8.5	DUP
	Bootle	8.5	Lab
18	Liverpool West Derby	8.4	Lab
19	Birkenhead	8.2	Lab
	Sheffield Central	8.2	Lab

Lowest unemployment rate, June 2001

		%	Winning party 2001
1	Mole Valley	0.5	C
	Surrey Heath	0.5	C
	Witney	0.5	C
4	Hampshire North East	0.6	C
	Reigate	0.6	C
	Surrey East	0.6	C
	Woking	0.6	C
	Wokingham	0.6	C
9	Buckingham	0.7	C
	Epsom and Ewell	0.7	C
	Hertford and Stortford	0.7	C
	Romsey	0.7	C
	Runnymede and Weybridge	0.7	C
	St Albans	0.7	Lab
	Surrey South West	0.7	C
	Sussex Mid	0.7	C
	Wantage	0.7	C

Highest proportion of professional and managerial workers

		%	Winning party 2001
1	Kensington and Chelsea	62.9	C
2	Hampstead and Highgate	60.6	Lab
3	Sheffield Hallam	59.3	LD
4	Bristol West	57.9	Lab
5	Richmond Park	57.8	LD
6	Hornsey and Wood Green	54.4	Lab
7	Finchley and Golders Green	53.9	Lab
8	Twickenham	53.2	LD
9	Wimbledon	51.6	Lab
10	Hammersmith and Fulham	50.8	Lab
11	Cities of London and Westminster	49.7	C
12	Esher and Walton	49.5	C
	Putney	49.5	Lab
14	Maidenhead	49.2	C
15	Chesham and Amersham	48.7	C
	Chipping Barnet	48.7	C
	Wokingham	48.7	C
18	Epsom and Ewell	48.2	C
19	Battersea	48.0	Lab
	St Albans	48.0	Lab

Lowest proportion of professional and managerial workers

		%	Winning party 2001
1	West Bromwich West	15.9	Lab
2	Birmingham Hodge Hill	16.6	Lab
	Sheffield Brightside	16.6	Lab
4	Wolverhampton South East	17.0	Lab
5	Nottingham North	17.4	Lab
	Stoke on Trent North	17.4	Lab
7	Plymouth Devonport	17.7	Lab
8	Bootle	18.0	Lab
	Dagenham	18.0	Lab
10	Walsall North	18.1	Lab
11	Liverpool Walton	18.4	Lab
12	Belfast West	18.6	SF
13	Pontefract and Castleford	18.8	Lab
14	Hull East	18.9	Lab
15	Glasgow Springburn	19.5	Speaker
	Wolverhampton North East	19.5	Lab
17	Stoke on Trent Central	19.6	Lab
	Tyne Bridge	19.6	Lab
19	Easington	19.7	Lab
20	Barking	19.8	Lab
	Glasgow Shettleston	19.8	Lab

Highest proportion of non-manual workers

		%	Winning party 2001
1	Sheffield Hallam	80.1	LD
2	Kensington and Chelsea	79.9	C
3	Bristol West	79.5	Lab
4	Hampstead and Highgate	79.2	Lab
5	Richmond Park	78.9	LD
6	Wimbledon	77.1	Lab
7	Finchley and Golders Green	76.7	Lab
8	Twickenham	76.2	LD
9	Cheadle	75.3	LD
10	Chipping Barnet	75.1	C
	Croydon	75.1	C
12	Epsom and Ewell	75.0	C
	Hornsey and Wood Green	75.0	Lab
14	Eastwood	74.9	Lab
15	Beckenham	74.5	C
16	Hammersmith and Fulham	74.2	Lab
17	Esher and Walton	74.1	C
18	Bromley and Chislehurst	73.8	C
19	Harrow West	73.2	Lab
20	Sutton Coldfield	73.0	C

Lowest proportion of non-manual workers

		%	Winning party 2001
1	Stoke on Trent North	35.5	Lab
2	Blaenau Gwent	36.7	Lab
3	Wolverhampton South East	36.8	Lab
4	Sheffield Brightside	37.3	Lab
5	West Bromwich West	37.5	Lab
6	Stoke on Trent Central	38.0	Lab
7	Walsall North	38.1	Lab
8	Ogmore	38.2	Lab
	Plymouth Devonport	38.2	Lab
10	Easington	38.6	Lab
	Pontefract and Castleford	38.6	Lab
12	Birmingham Ladywood	38.7	Lab
13	Nottingham North	38.9	Lab
14	Stoke on Trent South	39.0	Lab
15	Ashfield	39.3	Lab
16	Birmingham Hodge Hill	39.5	Lab
	Leicester East	39.5	Lab
18	Wolverhampton North East	40.3	Lab
19	Birmingham Sparkbrook and Small Heath	40.7	Lab
20	Moray	40.9	SNP

University admissions (England) 1998: most students entering university

Home constituency	Number of students	Winning party 2001
Harrow East	940	Lab
Ealing Southall	870	Lab
Hendon	830	Lab
Harrow West	790	Lab
Finchley and Golders Green	785	Lab
Ilford South	760	Lab
Brent North	735	Lab
Brentford and Isleworth	735	Lab
Richmond Park	730	LD
Chipping Barnet	715	C
East Ham	700	Lab
Chesham and Amersham	690	C
Sutton Coldfield	685	C
Enfield Southgate	680	Lab
Winchester	675	LD
Twickenham	670	LD
Cheadle	670	LD
Croydon South	670	C
Cambridgeshire South	665	C
Hornsey and Wood Green	655	Lab
Bristol West	650	Lab
Hertfordshire South West	645	C
Esher and Walton	645	C
Surrey South West	640	C
Ealing North	640	Lab

University admissions (England) 1998: fewest students entering university

Home constituency	Number of students	Winning party 2001
Nottingham North	115	Lab
Sheffield Brightside	130	Lab
Sheffield Attercliffe	135	Lab
Hull East	165	Lab
Sheffield Hillsborough	165	Lab
Dagenham	165	Lab
Rother Valley	175	Lab
Salford	175	Lab
Bristol South	175	Lab
Birmingham Hodge Hill	180	Lab
Leeds Central	180	Lab
Thurrock	185	Lab
Hull North	190	Lab
Barnsley East/Mexborough	190	Lab
Leeds East	195	Lab
Derbyshire North East	195	Lab
Pontefract/Castleford	195	Lab
Bootle	200	Lab
Birmingham Yardley	200	Lab

Highest proportion of non-white residents

		%	Winning party 2001
1	Brent South	55.4	Lab
2	Birmingham Ladywood	53.6	Lab
3	Birmingham Sparkbrook/Small Heath	52.1	Lab
4	East Ham	48.7	Lab
5	Ealing Southall	47.3	Lab
6	West Ham	43.1	Lab
7	Brent North	41.6	Lab
8	Tottenham	38.3	Lab
9	Bethnal Green and Bow	38.1	Lab
10	Leicester East	38.0	Lab
11	Birmingham Perry Barr	37.6	Lab
12	Brent East	36.7	Lab
13	Bradford West	36.6	Lab
14	Ilford South	35.5	Lab
15	Hackney North and Stoke Newington	34.9	Lab
16	Vauxhall	34.3	Lab
17	Camberwell and Peckham	33.7	Lab
18	Leicester South	32.3	Lab
19	Hackney South and Shoreditch	32.2	Lab
20	Lewisham Deptford	32.1	Lab

Most cases of foot and mouth (to 12 July 2001)

	Number of cases	Winning party 2001
Penrith and the Border	602	C
Dumfries	131	Lab
Torridge and West Devon	120	LD
Carlisle	74	Lab
Skipton and Ripon	56	C
Forest of Dean	47	Lab
Bishop Auckland	44	Lab
Devon North	41	LD
Durham North West	37	Lab
Ribble Valley	36	C
Richmond (Yorkshire)	35	C
Galloway and Upper Nithsdale	35	C
Hexham	32	C
Hereford	31	LD
Brecon and Radnorshire	27	LD
Montgomeryshire	27	LD
Berwick upon Tweed	20	LD
Burton	20	Lab

Most Incapacity Benefit claimants (August 1999)

		Number of claimants	Winning party 2001
1	Liverpool Riverside	10510	Lab
2	Glasgow Shettleston	9640	Lab
3	Merthyr Tydfil and Rhymney	9520	Lab
4	Rhondda	9330	Lab
5	Liverpool Walton	9220	Lab
6	Manchester Central	9195	Lab
7	Glasgow Springburn	8865	Speaker
8	Liverpool West Derby	8405	Lab
9	Manchester Blackley	8290	Lab
10	Caerphilly	8205	Lab
11	Knowsley South	8070	Lab
12	Tyne Bridge	7930	Lab
13	Knowsley North	7870	Lab
14	Birkenhead	7855	Lab
15	Glasgow Maryhill	7720	Lab
16	Glasgow Baillieston	7600	Lab
17	Airdrie and Shotts	7575	Lab
18	Blaenau Gwent	7485	Lab
19	Liverpool Wavertree	7350	Lab
20	Barnsley East/Mexborough	7250	Lab

Fewest Incapacity Benefit claimants (August 1999)

		Number of claimants	Winning party 2001
1	Wokingham	935	C
2	Western Isles	995	Lab
3	Buckingham	1025	C
4	Henley	1030	C
5	Orkney and Shetland	1075	LD
6	Beaconsfield	1114	C
7	Maidenhead	1120	C
8	Mole Valley	1125	C
9	Chesham and Amersham	1140	C
10	Surrey Heath	1220	C
11	Windsor	1243	C
12	Horsham	1290	C
13	Aberdeenshire West/Kincardine	1315	LD
14	Cambridgeshire South	1330	C
15	Surrey South West	1355	C
16	Arundel and South Downs	1370	C
	Rutland and Melton	1370	C
	Wantage	1370	C
19	Esher and Walton	1380	C
	Bedfordshire Mid	1380	C

Highest number of Income Support claimants (August 1998)

		Number of claimants	Winning party 2001
1	Liverpool Riverside	17200	Lab
2	Birmingham Ladywood	16360	Lab
3	Manchester Central	16125	Lab
4	Tottenham	16085	Lab
5	Poplar and Canning Town	15290	Lab
6	Birmingham Sparkbrook/Small Heath	15215	Lab
7	Hackney South/Shoreditch	14925	Lab
8	Regent's Park/Kensington North	14865	Lab
9	Bethnal Green/Bow	14510	Lab
10	Liverpool West Derby	14120	Lab
11	Liverpool Walton	13830	Lab
12	Glasgow Springburn	13720	Speaker
13	Manchester Blackley	13600	Lab
14	Glasgow Shettleston	13460	Lab
15	Hackney North/Stoke Newington	13455	Lab
16	Vauxhall	13070	Lab
17	East Ham	12815	Lab
18	Tyne Bridge	12490	Lab
19	Birkenhead	12420	Lab
20	Holborn and St Pancras	12075	Lab

Lowest number of Income Support claimants (August 1998)

		Number of claimants	Winning party 2001
1	Orkney and Shetland	1825	LD
2	Wokingham	2050	C
3	Buckingham	2065	C
4	Chesham and Amersham	2200	C
5	Henley	2295	C
6	Aberdeenshire West/Kincardine	2300	LD
7	Sheffield Hallam	2500	LD
8	Gordon	2550	LD
9	Romsey	2595	LD
10	Beaconsfield	2655	C
11	Maidenhead	2675	C
12	Western Isles	2685	Lab
13	Horsham	2720	C
14	Vale of York	2754	C
15	Hexham	2765	C
16	Surrey Heath	2785	C
17	Haltemprice	2789	C
18	Arundel and South Downs	2795	C
19	Epsom and Ewell	2825	C
20	Montgomeryshire	2850	LD

The 20 seats with the highest turnout 2001

		%	Winning party 2001
1	Ulster Mid	81.3	SF
2	Tyrone West	79.9	SF
3	Fermanagh and South Tyrone	78.0	SF
4	Newry and Armagh	76.8	SDLP
5	Belfast West	74.3	SF
6	Winchester	72.3	LD
7	Brecon and Radnorshire	71.8	LD
8	Monmouth	71.5	Lab
9	Down South	70.8	SDLP
10	Hexham	70.8	C
11	Eastwood	70.7	Lab
12	Northavon	70.7	LD
13	Foyle	70.7	SDLP
14	Torridge and West Devon	70.5	LD
15	Carmarthen East and Dinefwr	70.4	PC
16	Somerton and Frome	70.3	LD
17	Upper Bann	70.3	UUP
18	Norfolk North	70.2	LD
19	Norfolk Mid	70.1	C
20	Wandsyke	70.1	Lab

The 20 seats with the lowest turnout 2001

		%	Winning party 2001
1	Liverpool Riverside	34.8	Lab
2	Manchester Central	39.1	Lab
3	Glasgow Shettleston	39.7	Lab
4	Glasgow Maryhill	40.1	Lab
5	Salford	41.6	Lab
6	Leeds Central	41.7	Lab
7	Manchester Gorton	42.7	Lab
8	Glasgow Kelvin	43.6	Lab
9	Glasgow Springburn	43.7	Speaker
10	Liverpool Walton	43.8	Lab
11	Tyne Bridge	44.2	Lab
12	Birmingham Ladywood	44.3	Lab
13	Liverpool Wavertree	44.3	Lab
14	Vauxhall	44.8	Lab
15	Manchester Blackley	44.9	Lab
16	Kensington and Chelsea	45.2	C
17	Poplar and Canning Town	45.4	Lab
18	Hull North	45.4	Lab
19	Barking	45.5	Lab
20	Liverpool West Derby	45.5	Lab

Explanation of statistical terms

The statistics for socio-economic class, non-white residents, and Welsh and Irish speaking, are taken from the Parliamentary Constituency Monitors for the 1991 Census, published in 1996 by the Office of National Statistics. Figures from the 2001 Census were not yet available at constituency level at the time this edition of the *Almanac* went to press.

SOCIO-ECONOMIC CLASS

The two socio-economic variables included are 'per cent Prof/Man' and 'per cent Non-Manual'. The first refers to those employed in professional and managerial occupations, essentially 'ABs' in market research terms. These are the middle and upper-middle classes, traditionally the bedrock of Conservative support in the era of class voting, but increasingly open to the appeal of the New Labour and Liberal Democrat parties in recent years. These include not only senior private sector managers but also professional groups often employed in the public sector and open to the intellectual and instrumental appeal of the left and centre-left. MORI opinion polling taken throughout the 2001 General Election suggested that 39% of professional and managerial voters opted for the Conservatives, 30% for Labour, and an above-average 25% for the Liberal Democrats. Approximate turnout at 68% was almost 10% higher than the national norm.

'Non-manual' includes all these and adds the junior non-manual workers, often white-collar, clerical and management included in the 'lower middle class'. This group seems to have broken evenly between Conservative and Labour in 2001, with the Liberal Democrats polling around 20%. The remainder not included in these figures consist of manual workers, whether skilled, semi-skilled or unskilled: traditionally defined, the working class. Over half of those (in market research terms, C2DEs) who voted chose Labour, with the Conservatives and Liberal Democrats both substantially below their national figures, but turnout is estimated at just under 55%.

Owing to the nature of their economies, the non-manual and professional and managerial figures are higher in urban areas, especially the capital cities of London, Edinburgh and Cardiff, and lower in rural constituencies.

The national baseline with which to compare the constituency figures is as follows: 33.2% of those in work were employed in professional and managerial occupations in 1991, plus another 23.2% in junior non-manual jobs, making a total of 56.4% in all non-manual occupations.

NON-WHITE

The statistic '% Non-white' refers to the percentage of residents in each seat who categorised themselves in an ethnic group other than white in the 1991 Census. This was the first time that a direct racial question was asked in a decennial Census in Britain. Figures published by the Office of National Statistics in the autumn 2001 issue of *Population Trends* suggested that the total numbers in ethnic minority groups in Britain had increased from 5.5% in 1991 to 7.1% in 2000, but these figures are not yet available at constituency level.

Non-white people, of both Asian and Afro-Caribbean ethnic origin, have tended to be strong supporters of the Labour party regardless of their occupation. MORI opinion polling during the 2001 General Election campaign suggested that 73% of non-white respondents indicated a Labour voting preference, compared with 13% Liberal Democrat and only 12% Conservative. However, turnout among this segment of British society was estimated at only 47%.

WELSH AND IRISH SPEAKING

In all Welsh seats there is also a figure published in the 1991 Census for the percentage of residents who can speak Welsh (not necessarily as their preferred or main language). This is generally an accurate indicator of support for the Welsh national party, Plaid Cymru, who hold four of the five seats with a majority of Welsh-speakers in the west of the principality; the remaining seat, Ynys Mon, was held by their former parliamentary leader, Ieuan Wyn Jones, until his retirement from the Commons in 2001, when it was regained by Labour.

Irish Gaelic speakers are also included for the 18 Northern Irish seats. Although in each case a minority within the constituency, Irish speaking is associated with nationalist and republican, rather than unionist support.

UNEMPLOYMENT

The unemployment figures included in the statistical tables for each constituency are taken from the House of Commons Library Research Paper 01/65 (18 July 2001) which includes the percentage of unemployed claimants of Job Seekers Allowance resident in each seat in the UK in June 2001, together with comparisons in the levels for June 1997, at the time of the previous general election.

In all cases these figures have fallen, which may indicate one reason why the government was re-elected with an overwhelming majority in 2001.

It may be noted that the figures refer to allowance claimants; a higher proportion of people consider themselves to be unemployed but for a variety of reasons do not or are not eligible to claim jobseekers' benefits.

INCOME SUPPORT CLAIMANTS

The numbers of Income Support claimants were provided by the Office of National Statistics at ward level for 1998 and aggregated to constituencies by the Department of Geography at Leeds University. Income Support (IS) is a non-contributory benefit. From October 1996 the Jobseeker's Allowance replaced IS for unemployed people. In general IS is now only available to people who are not required to be available for work such as pensioners, lone parents and sick and disabled people.

INCAPACITY BENEFIT

The numbers of Incapacity Benefit claimants per constituency were supplied by the Office of National Statistics at 1999 ward level and aggregated by the Department of Geography at Leeds University. Incapacity benefit replaced Sickness Benefit and Invalidity Benefit from 13 April 1995. It is paid to people who are assessed as being incapable of work and who meet the same contribution conditions as for Sickness Benefit.

A high level of Incapacity Benefit claimants in a constituency is an indicator of poor health and a multiply-deprived environment.

UNIVERSITY ADMISSIONS

The data for university admissions in 1998 were calculated by the Department of Geography, Leeds University, from statistics supplied by the University and College Admissions Service (UCAS) for applicants' home postcode, and aggregated to parliamentary constituency. Data was excluded if the postcode proved to be an institution such as a school or college (5% of the whole) or which was not adequately postcoded to flag up to 1998 wards (2.6%). Mature students and those who applied to higher education directly were picked up by UCAS 'backcoding'.

RURAL SEATS

The list of the most rural seats in Britain was calculated from the Census Enumeration district (ED) statistics provided by the government Office of National Statistics and aggregated to constituency level by Dr Roger Mortimore of MORI (Market and Opinion Research International). These are not indicators of employment but rather of the geographic nature of these EDs. In the case of Scotland, some people are employed in agriculture but live in EDs not classified as rural because of their high proportion of social housing. For agricultural employment, see the list of the 20 most agricultural seats described below.

As will be seen from the list of the top 20 rural seats in Britain, relatively few are currently represented by a Labour MP, and indeed not many more by a Conservative. Rural seats are most likely to be held by either a Liberal Democrat or a Scottish or Welsh Nationalist.

AGRICULTURAL SEATS

While wide tracts of the country remain rural in aspect, a mere 2% of the workforce was employed in farming, fishing and forestry at the time of the 1991 Census. Of the 20 most agricultural seats, 12 constituencies (or their predecessor seats) were in Conservative hands in 1979, but by 2001 that figure had fallen to six, all but one in England, and that one a narrow regain in that year (Galloway and Upper Nithsdale). Of the seats, all but two (both in Lincolnshire) are in the Celtic fringe, including the south-western peninsula and Welsh Marcher areas of England, regions which since the 1970s have seen strong Liberal Democrat and Nationalist advances.

FOOT AND MOUTH CASES

The number of foot and mouth cases in each constituency up to 12 July 2001 was supplied by the DEFRA website http://www.maff.gov.uk.

PENSIONERS

The percentage of pensioner voters per constituency in England and Wales were supplied by Age Concern, Appendix to General Election Paper 2001, with data calculated by Professor Paul Whiteley, University of Sheffield.

PREMATURE MORTALITY

The index for premature mortality and rank order of all 641 British constituencies was based on the standard mortality rates (SMRs) for deaths under 65. The index for premature mortality or avoidable deaths refers to the percentage of deaths which would not have occurred had that constituency had the mortality rate of the best off health million. The figures are taken from *The Widening Gap: Health Inequalities and Policy in Britain*, by M. Shaw, D. Dorling, D. Gordon and G. Davey Smith (Policy Press, Bristol, 1999) and supplied by Christopher Squire of the Royal College of Radiologists.

FINANCIAL HARDSHIP

The percentage of households in financial hardship and their rank order were calculated by Experian, the property research company, from the ward statistics provided by the National Statistical Office, and their standard Indices of Deprivation based on household income and claimancy.

PROPERTY VALUES

Average property values for 2000 and change 1997–2000 were based on sales price figures compiled by the property research company Experian and placed on their website experian.co.uk in 2001.

These replace the housing tenure figures used in previous editions of this *Almanac* due to the rapid and major changes in housing tenure in recent years which have seen the replacement of the separate category of local authority or council housing by the notion of social housing, figures for which are not yet available.

Within the text in the constituency entries of the book, however, extensive reference is still made to council-built housing and estates, for there remains a strong political association of Labour voting with housing which is other than owner-occupied, and particularly with neighbourhoods with a concentration or even a tradition of such developments, which have created an environment usually associated not only with social and economic deprivation and a hostility to the Conservative party, but, in recent years, with non-voting. MORI polling figures estimate that among those who still classify themselves as council or housing association tenants, Labour held a 42-point lead over the Conservatives in the 2001 General Election, but that barely over half (52%) actually turned out to vote in the election.

List of abbreviations

ACAS	Advisory Conciliation and Arbitration Service	COHSE	Confederation of Health Service Employees (now UNISON)
AEEU	Amalgamated Engineering and Electrical Union	Coop	Co-operative Party
		CP	Communist Party
AEU	Amalgamated Engineering Union	CPGB	Communist Party of Great Britain
AIDS	acquired immune deficiency syndrome	CPSA	Civil and Public Staffs Association
AL	Asian League	CSA	Child Support Agency
ALDC	Association of Liberal Democrat Councillors	CV	curriculum vitae
		CWU	Communications Workers Union
ANU	Australian National University		
APNI	Alliance Party of Northern Ireland	DEFRA	Department for Environment, Food and Rural Affairs
APEX	Association of Professional, Executive, Clerical and Computer Staff	DHSS	Department of Health and Social Security
		DTI	Department of Trade and Industry
ASLEF	Associated Society of Locomotive Engineers and Firemen	DUP	Democratic Unionist Party
		EEC	European Economic Community
AUEW	Amalgamated Union of Engineering Workers	EETPU	Electrical, Electronic Telecommunications and Plumbing Union
AWOL	absent without official leave		
Av prop val	Average property value	Elect	electorate
B & B	bed and breakfast	EMS	European Monetary System
BBC	British Broadcasting Corporation	EMU	economic and monetary union
		ERM	Exchange Rate Mechanism
BNP	British National Party	ETA	Basque Homeland and Freedom (Euzkadi ta Askatasuna)
BSE	bovine spongiform encephalopathy	ETU	Electrical Trades Union
C	Conservative	FBU	Fire Brigades Union
CAP	Common Agricultural Policy	FC	football club
CBI	Confederation of British Industry	FE	further education
		FCO	Foreign and Commonwealth Office
CEGB	Central Electricity Generating Board	Fin hard	financial hardship
CLP	Constituency Labour Party	Gaelic sp	Gaelic speaking
CND	Campaign for Nuclear Disarmament	GCHQ	Government Communications Headquarters

Gen	General
GKN	Guest, Keen and Nettlefolds
GLC	Greater London Council
GM	genetically modified
GMBU	General, Municipal and Boilermakers Union
GPMU	Graphical, Paper and Media Union
Grn	Green
HMI	Her Majesty's Inspector
ICI	Imperial Chemical Industries
ILEA	Inner London Education Authority
ILP	Independent Labour Party
Ind	Independent
Ind C	Independent Conservative
Ind Lab	Independent Labour
INSEAD	European Institute of Business Administration
IOD	Institute of Directors
IPPR	Institute for Public Policy Research
IRA	Irish Republican Army
Irish sp	Irish speaking
IT	information technology
ITN	Independent Television News
JP	Justice Party
KCVO	Knight Commander, the Royal Victorian Order
LA	Left Alliance
Lab	Labour
Lab/Coop	Labour and Cooperative Party
L/C	Labour and Cooperative
LCA	Legalise Cannabis Alliance
LCC	London County Council
L Ch	Labour Change
LD	Liberal Democrat
LEA	local education authority
Lib	Liberal
Lib Dem	Liberal Democrat
Loc Auth	local authority
Loc C	Local Conservative
Loy C	Loyal Conservative
LSE	London School of Economics
LWT	London Weekend Television
MAFF	Ministry of Agriculture, Fisheries and Food
Maj	majority
Marx	Marxist Party
ME	myalgic encephalomyelitis

MIT	Massachusetts Institute of Technology
MK	Mebyon Kernow (Cornish nationalist)
MLA	Member of the London Assembly
MMR	measles, mumps and rubella
MOD	Ministry of Defence
MOSAIC	Neighbourhood classification based on census data
MP	Member of Parliament
MRLP	Monster Raving Loony Party
MSF	Manufacturing, Science and Finance Union
MSP	Member of the Scottish Parliament
Mus	Muslim Party
NACRO	National Association for the Care and Resettlement of Offenders
NAFTA	North American Free Trade Agreement
NALGO	National Association of Local Government Officers (now UNISON)
Nat Dem	National Democratic Party
NATO	North Atlantic Treaty Organisation
NBP	New Britain Party
NCB	National Coal Board
NCCL	National Council for Civil Liberties
NCU	National Communications Union
NE	north east
NEC	National Executive Committee
NEDO	National Economic Development Organisation
NF	National Front
NHS	National Health Service
NIMBY	'not in my back yard'
NIWC	Northern Ireland Women's Coalition
N Lab	New Labour
NLP	Natural Law Party
NUM	National Union of Mineworkers
NUPE	National Union of Public Employees (now UNISON)
NUR	National Union of Railwaymen
NUS	National Union of Students
NUT	National Union of Teachers

NW	north west
OMOV	one member one vote
OSM	Orkney and Shetland Movement
Oth	other(s)
OU	Open University
OUP	Official Unionist Party
Own Occ	owner occupied
PA	personal assistant
PA	ProLife Alliance
PC	'political correctness' / 'politically correct'
PC	Plaid Cymru (Welsh Nationalist)
PE	physical education
PECP	Pro Euro Conservative Party
PFI	Private Finance Initiative
PJP	People's Justice Party
P Lab	Popular Labour
PLP	Parliamentary Labour Party
PM	Prime Minister
POW	Prisoner of war
POEU	Post Office Engineering Union
Pop	population
PPS	parliamentary private secretary
PR	proportional representation or public relations
Prem mort	Premature mortality
Prof/Man	professional and managerial
Prog U	Progressive Unionist
PUP	Popular Unionist Party
QC	Queen's Counsel
RADA	Royal Academy of Dramatic Arts
RAF	Royal Air Force
RC	Roman Catholic
Ref	Referendum Party
Revd	Reverend
RIBA	Royal Institute of British Architects
RMT	National Union of Rail, Maritime and Transport Workers
RNC	Royal Naval College
RP	'received pronunciation'
RUC	Royal Ulster Constabulary
SA	Socialist Alliance
SAS	Special Air Service
SDLP	Social, Democratic and Labour Party
SDP	Social Democratic Party
SE	south east

SF	Sinn Fein
SLD	Social and Liberal Democrats
SLP	Socialist Labour Party
SMR	standard mortality rate
SNP	Scottish National Party
Soc Lab	Socialist Labour Party
SOGAT	Society of Graphical and Allied Trades (now GPMU)
SPGB	Socialist Party of Great Britain
Spkr	Speaker
SPUC	Society for the Protection of the Unborn Child
SSA	Scottish Socialist Alliance
SSP	Scottish Socialist Party
SUP	Scottish Unionist Party
SW	south west
SWP	Socialist Workers Party
TA	Territorial Army
TASS	Technical Administrative and Supervisory Staffs
TGWU	Transport and General workers Union
TUC	Trades Union Congress
TW	Third Way
UCAS	Universities and Colleges Admissions Service
UCATT	Union of Construction, Allied Trades and Technicians
UCW	Union of Communication Workers
UDM	Union of Democratic Mineworkers
UEFA	European Football Association
UKIP	United Kingdom Independence Party
UKUP	United Kingdom Unionist Party
UNISON	See COHSE, NUPE, NALGO
USAF	United States Air Force
USDAW	Union of Shop, Distributive and Allied Workers
UU	Ulster Unionist
UUP	Ulster Unionist Party
VAT	Value Added Tax
WEA	Workers Educational Association
Welsh sp	Welsh speaking
WFLOE	Women for Life on Earth
WI	Women's Institute
WP	Workers' Party
WR	Wessex Regionalist
WRP	Workers' Revolutionary Party

Constituencies and
Members of Parliament

ABERAVON

For long the mighty steelworks of Abbey and Margam, near Port Talbot, dominated the constituency of Aberavon, which lies behind the sand dunes between the Bristol Channel and the South Wales valleys and mountains. British Steel once employed 12,500 workers here but Port Talbot has suffered like other areas dependent on 'traditional' industries, and after reorganisation only a fraction of that number still have jobs in the steel industry. The area was featured in the national press in July 2000 when Corus, the Anglo-Dutch company which has taken over the plants, announced further reductions in employment here.

Port Talbot is situated at the mouth ('Aber') of the river Afan, but this is an English-speaking constituency, full of the descendants of immigrants from further east who came to work at the industry of Port Talbot from the eighteenth century onwards. Less than one-tenth of the inhabitants of the Aberavon seat can speak Welsh. This fact was recognised in the 1980s when the name of the local government district covering the area was changed from Afan to Port Talbot. The retention of the name Aberavon for the parliamentary constituency does at least make the seat first in the national alphabetical list. That is, however, one of its only electoral distinctions, for it returned Labour's former Welsh Secretary John Morris with extremely safe margins for nearly four decades before his retirement in June 2001.

Essentially the Aberavon seat is centred on the coastal strip near the steelworks, and Port Talbot is far and away its largest community. Port Talbot does have a beach and some of the characteristics of a seaside resort, but none of the wards here elect Conservative councillors. The seat also extends west across the river Neath to Skewen and Jersey Marine, and reaches into the hills to take in the old mining town of Glyncorrwg at the top of its blind valley near Maesteg. It is, however, difficult to argue that this is truly a 'Welsh valley constituency'.

It is, though, extremely strongly Labour. Aberavon is one of the most working-class seats in Wales, ranking along with Blaenau Gwent, Ogmore and Rhondda; Morris's successor Hywel Francis won a majority over the Tories in 2001 that was over 16,000, which is more than 50% of those who voted, making it the 21st safest Labour seat in Britain and the third in Wales. Plaid Cymru pose little threat; although they moved forward from fourth to second, they still polled a single figure percentage vote.

One new feature in 2001 though was the relatively high vote given to minor party candidates, who together did achieve over 10%. Besides a local character standing as Captain Beany of the Bean Party, a local Ratepayer candidate, one of five elected to Neath-Port Talbot unitary authority in 1999 (Andrew Dutton of Port Talbot ward) did actually save his deposit. There is quite a scattering of opposition to Labour in local government in this constituency (there are also Ratepayer councillors in Margam and Social Democrats in Aberavon).

However in parliamentary terms Aberavon remains as before, a Labour stronghold in a gaunt landscape which betokens the physical and mental scars caused by the rise and fall of heavy industry in the hills and on the plain.

Social indices:			2001 Gen. Election:			
% Non-white	0.8		Lab	19,063	63.1	−8.2
% Welsh sp	8.7		PC	2,955	9.8	+4.0
% Prof/Man	21.5		LD	2,933	9.7	−1.6
% Non-manual	43.2		C	2,296	7.6	−0.3
£ Av prop val 2000	43 K		Ind	1,960	6.5	
% Increase 97–00	20.5		Ind	727	2.4	+1.5
% Unemployed 2001	4.3		SA	256	0.8	
% Decrease 97–01	2.0		Lab maj	16,108	53.4	
% Fin hard/Rank	32.4	109	Turnout		60.8	−11.1
% Pensioners	29.0		Elect	49,660		
% Prem mort/Rank	41	159				

Member of Parliament

Hywel Francis, son of the former Welsh miners' leader and founding chairman of the Wales TUC, Dai Francis, was elected in 2001. A former adviser to Welsh Secretary Paul Murphy, he was born in 1946, and educated at secondary schools in Neath and Cardiff, Whitchurch Grammar School, Cardiff and Swansea University, obtaining a doctorate in History. Professor of Continuing Education at Swansea, after more than three decades at the University, he is Vice President of the Welsh Labour History Society, Chairman of the Paul Robeson Cymru Committee and a Trustee of the Bevan Foundation. Rather more than just a typical example of a Welsh Labour candidate reflecting the transition from mining to teaching – from the coal face to the chalk face – he comes from the top drawer of the Welsh Labour establishment, with links to virtually everyone in the Labour Taffia, though too late at the age of 55 to entertain ministerial ambitions despite having headed the Welsh devolution referendum campaign (won by a whisker) in 1997. A dour, deliberate speaker, his maiden speech urged work for the disabled.

ABERDEEN CENTRAL

Having been given a third and extra seat in the last United Kingdom-wide redistribution of Westminster seats as recently in 1997, the granite city of Aberdeen, Scotland's third largest after Glasgow and Edinburgh, seems set to lose representational influence in London, 450 miles to the south, now the number of Scottish seats is reduced by 13 following the creation of the devolved Parliament at Holyrood. With barely 50,000 electors in 2001, Aberdeen Central was one of the smaller constituencies in urban Scotland, and was in a very vulnerable position – nearly 20,000 voters short of the UK average.

Its results in June 2001 looked even thinner on the ground due to a turnout of just 52.75%, the lowest in Scotland outside Glasgow and Edinburgh Central. Labour's winning figure of 12,025 votes cast was the fourth smallest of their 412 victories. Having said that, Central was clearly the safest of their three wins in Aberdeen, as there were serious challenges from the SNP in North and the Liberal Democrats in South. Central comprises territory from both the north and south sides of the city, capturing some council estates from the NW Aberdeen bloc, such as Hilton and Stockethill, but also some very middle-class areas such as Rosemount, Queen's

Cross, Harlaw and Rubislaw (near but not encompassing the massive defunct quarry) in the fashionable south-western sector of the city. Central also includes some poorish inner-city territory such as Pittodrie (home of Aberdeen's proud football club), the university neighbourhood in Old Aberdeen and St Machar's Cathedral, and, as might be expected, the very heart of the commercial and business centre of a conurbation to which the discovery of North Sea oil brought so much change.

Although Central is divided, there was little in the way of a contest in 2001. The Tories slipped to fourth while both the SNP and the Liberal Democrats improved their position by 4% apiece, but the main threat to Frank Doran's continuing tenure of an Aberdeen seat lies in the hands of the Boundary Commissioners for Scotland, as this seat will be split up between South and North.

Social indices:			2001 Gen. Election:			
% Non-white	2.6		Lab	12,025	45.5	−4.3
% Prof/Man	38.1		SNP	5,379	20.4	+4.2
% Non-manual	60.5		LD	4,547	17.2	+4.0
% Unemployed 2001	2.9		C	3,761	14.2	−5.3
% Decrease 97–01	2.0		SSP	717	2.7	
% Fin hard/Rank	32.8	108	Lab maj	6,646	25.1	
% Prem mort/Rank	47	67	Turnout		52.8	−12.9
			Elect	50,098		

Member of Parliament

Frank Doran won this seat in 1997, having represented Aberdeen South from 1987 to 1992 and been the only Labour MP (apart from by-election entrants) to be beaten in 1992. A Dundee-born (1949) solicitor, educated at Leith Academy and Dundee University, he is a former member, with his partner of ten years, Joan Ruddock MP, of the left-wing Supper Club, which resisted the Gulf War. Although an Energy spokesman in Opposition, partly whilst Tony Blair was chief Energy spokesman, he received no government post under Tony Blair, other than PPS to Ian McCartney (1997–2001), a sidelining also experienced by Joan Ruddock who was dropped as a minister after only a year. His selection in 1995 for Aberdeen Central was locally divisive, ending as it did the parliamentary career of the popular local man and MP of 25 years, Bob Hughes, and with the Boundary Commissioners dealing with Scotland's over-representation at Westminster, he could well be competing with his neighbour, Malcolm Savidge, as Labour's three Aberdeen seats are reduced to two.

ABERDEEN NORTH

In general the Scottish National Party were very disappointed by their showing in the 2001 General Election, failing to make any gains and slipping back in their six existing seats, losing one, Galloway and Upper Nithsdale. However, their very best showing, an increase from 1997 of nearly 7% of the share of the vote (though it might be noted, of only a little over 300 actual votes) occurred in Aberdeen North. Even this, however, must be counted as something of a let-down, as they trailed Labour by over 4,000 compared with just 398 in the same seat in the inaugural Scottish Parliament contests of May 1999. Perhaps their appeal is perceived by the electors as not quite so appropriate when choosing a government sitting in London for the whole United Kingdom, now that some powers at least have been transferred to Edinburgh, to a body which though scarcely sovereign receives the lion's share of attention in the Scottish press. If one of the purposes of the central Labour government's devolution measures was to blunt the force of the SNP, it seems to have worked so far.

Aberdeen North does include the very heavily Labour council estates of Northfield and Mastrick on the north-west edge of the city. However, in 1997 well over 20,000 voters came in from the Gordon constituency, which has been held by Malcolm Bruce for the Liberal Democrats (and their predecessors) since its creation in 1983. Gordon included many of the rapidly growing suburbs of Aberdeen, whose growth was stimulated by the oil boom of the 1970s – Aberdeen is acknowledged as the official centre for North Sea oil exploration and exploitation. The private housing estates around Bridge of Don and Dyce, conveniently placed for the airport, had been within the Aberdeen city boundaries for a couple of decades, but this situation was not recognised by the Scottish Boundary Commission until the 1990s when they at last allocated them to an Aberdeen seat.

More changes are on the way, as the Aberdeen area is particularly affected by the redistribution consequent on the creation of an Edinburgh parliament, which means that the number of Scottish seats will be reduced as their smaller electorates are expanded to the UK average. However this happens in detail, it cannot help the SNP, as the North division is surrounded by territory which is strong for Labour and the Liberal Democrats and weaker for them, thus further reducing their chances of any gains in Greater Aberdeen, at least at Westminster.

Social indices:			2001 Gen. Election:			
% Non-white	0.8		Lab	13,157	43.3	–4.5
% Prof/Man	24.3		SNP	8,708	28.7	+6.9
% Non-manual	50.0		LD	4,991	16.4	+2.3
% Unemployed 2001	1.9		C	3,047	10.0	–5.0
% Decrease 97–01	1.6		SSP	454	1.5	
% Fin hard/Rank	29.1	142	Lab maj	4,449	14.7	
% Prem mort/Rank	40	181	Turnout		57.6	–13.2
			Elect	52,746		

Member of Parliament

Malcolm Savidge is in the exposed position of being one of four English-born Labour MPs in Scottish seats, potentially vulnerable to any post-devolution upsurge of Anglophobia stoked up by the SNP, especially after the very tight result in this seat in the Scottish Parliament election in 1999, which was part-confirmed by the comparatively large pro-SNP swing here in 2001. Claiming descent from a medieval Commons Speaker, he was born in Surrey in 1946, attended Wallington County Grammar School for Boys and Aberdeen University, and spent 24 years as a Maths teacher in Aberdeen schools. A bespectacled, broad-grinning Blairite loyalist unkindly dubbed 'one of the government's loyal nonentities' as the bowler of soft Prime Ministerial questions, and a strong backer of the government on Iraq, Kosovo and Sierra Leone, he broke ranks to call for direct election of the Lords by PR, and, more importantly, has been prominent in opposing British support for the American proposed anti-ballistic missile programme. He faces a fight for one of a reduced number of Aberdeen seats in the next Parliament.

ABERDEEN SOUTH

The constituency of Aberdeen South was fought very hard indeed by the Liberal Democrats in 2001. They had good reason to hope that this might be the site of a rare gain on top of their existing 47 seats, as Nicol Stephen, a former MP for Kincardine and Deeside (1991–92) had won in the coterminous Scottish Parliament seat in 1999. He was barred by the strictures against dual mandates from standing again in Aberdeen South this time, as he had in 1997 – and this may have cost some personal votes, very important to Lib Dems, as his successor Ian Yuill fell short by over 4,000 votes. However it should also be seen as a strong endorsement for Labour's Anne Begg, who increased her share of the vote from 35% to nearly 40%, the third best improvement of any of her Scottish colleagues except Jim Murphy (Eastwood) and Mohammed Sarwar (Glasgow Govan).

South consists of territory on both sides of the river Dee, and electors who were formerly in both the very different South which existed up to 1992 and in the old Kincardine and Deeside. The former South seat was a Conservative–Labour marginal, while Kincardine and Deeside was won by the Liberal Democrats at a by-election in November 1991, although recovered by the Tories five months later. The new South looked very like a three-way marginal, but the Conservatives have now finished third twice, and may well have been squeezed tactically in 2001. Labour have long had strong areas here, notably in Torry on the south side of the harbour, and in the nearby council estate wards of Kincorth and Nigg, though they used to be in Kincardine/Deeside and must have voted tactically to a large extent before. However the critical factor in 1997 and 2001 was almost certainly Labour's massively strong national performance. Should Mr Blair's government become unpopular, either throughout Britain or just in Scotland, Aberdeen South cannot be regarded as permanently safe for Labour. The Liberal Democrats do very well in the affluent suburbs along the Dee inland, such as Cults and Peterculter; and unlikely though it looks immediately after their second disaster of 2001, even the Conservatives cannot be written off here forever. As comfortably the largest of the three current Aberdeen seats, South is the least significantly affected by the forthcoming Westminster parliamentary boundary changes, and bordered by Aberdeen Central (strongly Labour) and Aberdeenshire West and Kincardine (Liberal Democrat) it should remain a rare Labour–Lib Dem marginal.

Social indices:			2001 Gen. Election:			
% Non-white	1.1		Lab	14,696	39.8	+4.6
% Prof/Man	38.0		LD	10,308	27.9	+0.3
% Non-manual	61.8		C	7,098	19.2	−7.1
% Unemployed 2001	1.8		SNP	4,293	11.6	+1.9
% Decrease 97–01	1.1		SSP	495	1.3	
% Fin hard/Rank	18.4	301	Lab maj	4,388	11.9	
% Prem mort/Rank	31	330	Turnout		62.6	−10.2
			Elect	58,907		

Member of Parliament

Anne Begg, a former teacher, born in 1955 and educated at Brechin High School and Aberdeen University, was elected in 1997, following an *Observer* poll showing Labour ahead of the Liberal Democrats in what was a three-way Tory-held marginal seat. Toothy, small and wheelchair-bound as a victim of a degenerative brittle bone disease, she angered other disabled people by advising them to work rather than rely on benefits (though later campaigned for embryonic stem cell research into degenerative diseases), before spending a year as a Whips' nominee on Labour's NEC as an orthodox replacement for Dennis Skinner. The beneficiary of an all-women shortlist in 1995, she emerged with enhanced credibility in 2001 by doing well against a potentially threatening Liberal Democrat candidate, in one of the few Labour and Liberal marginal seats. Her wheelchair has taken her to the frontbench – if no more than physically.

ABERDEENSHIRE WEST AND KINCARDINE

The major redistribution of seats in 1997 in north-eastern Scotland threw together some very interesting and marginal constituencies, usually with some internally conflicting political traditions. One such example is Aberdeenshire West and Kincardine.

West Aberdeenshire has an interesting recent electoral history involving some colourful figures. In 1966 the seat of that name was gained from the Tories by James Davidson, a Liberal who, unusually, decided to retire after just one term in the Commons. In his absence the seat was defended in 1970 by Jo Grimond's wife, Laura, but she was beaten by the eccentric 'hero of Aden', Colonel Colin 'Mad Mitch' Mitchell, who was most interested in campaigning to save the Argyll and Sutherland Highlanders. Then he too gave up after just one term. Russell Fairgrieve took over West Aberdeenshire for the Conservatives, and he didn't retire for nine years, until 1983. In that year the seat was broken up. Part of it went into Gordon, which was seized by Malcolm Bruce of the Liberal Alliance. The other was placed with Kincardine, an area which is much more Conservative to this day, in a seat called Kincardine and Deeside.

All the same, Kincardine and Deeside was won by the Liberal Democrat Nicol Stephen in a by-election in November 1991 caused by the death of Alick Buchanan-Smith. The Conservatives recaptured it fairly easily five months later when the government of the country was at stake, but both geographical elements in the new constituency have now shown a capability of rebelling in favour of Liberals. It was therefore no great surprise when Sir Robert Smith gained Aberdeenshire West and Kincardine for the Liberal Democrats on 1 May 1997, with a notional swing of 8% from the Conservative defender, George Kynoch.

The West Aberdeenshire part includes the communities around Westhill, Kemnay and Alford formerly in Gordon; Royal Deeside around Braemar and Ballater; and Mid Deeside around prosperous little communities like Aboyne and Banchory. The Kincardine section includes the rapidly growing commuter community – almost 'New Town' – of Portlethen, one rail stop south of Aberdeen; the port of Stonehaven; and the farmland of the Mearns, the setting for Lewis Grassic Gibbon's classic novel *Cloud Howe*. Much of this territory is ancestrally Conservative, and Aberdeenshire West and Kincardine featured high on the list of Conservative targets in 2001 – but in the event, their solitary gain was rather unexpectedly Galloway/Upper Nithsdale, at the expense of the SNP rather than either Labour or the Liberal Democrats, and Sir Robert – or Bob Smith – benefited from four years of incumbency to double his majority.

Social indices:			2001 Gen. Election:			
% Non-white	0.7		LD	16,507	43.5	+2.5
% Prof/Man	37.1		C	11,686	30.8	–4.1
% Non-manual	57.9		Lab	4,669	12.3	+3.2
% Unemployed 2001	1.3		SNP	4,634	12.2	–0.9
% Decrease 97–01	0.9		SSP	418	1.1	
% Fin hard/Rank	6.0	583	LD maj	4,821	12.7	
% Prem mort/Rank	17	519	Turnout		62.0	–11.1
			Elect	61,180		

Member of Parliament

Big, affable, diffident **Sir Robert Smith**, born in 1958, educated at Merchant Taylors', Northwood, and Aberdeen University, a local farmer and third baronet, is a Lib Dem MP with usefully dispersed political antecedents. He is a former leading local figure in the SDP, but his grandfather, Sir William Smith, the first baronet, was the local Conservative MP (for Central Aberdeenshire) between the Wars, and the late Alick Buchanan-Smith, Tory MP for Kincardine until 1991, was a distant cousin. These Conservative roots mingle well with his own cautious votes on gun control and hunting while his urban colleagues vote the more politically correct ticket. He reflects the fact that in Scotland the Liberal Democrats partly double up as an acceptable version of the Tory Party, as confirmed in 2001, when he was joined on the Lib Dem benches by John Thurso, the new MP for Caithness, Sutherland and Easter Ross, the bearer of a much older baronetcy. A spokesman on Scotland and a Whip from 1999, in 2001 he was made Deputy Chief Whip, a suitable berth for a relatively reticent Commons performer.

AIRDRIE AND SHOTTS

It is quite likely that John Smith would have become a Labour Prime Minister but for his tragic death at the age of 55 early in 1994. He was member for Monklands East, but he would have assumed the Premiership (presuming Labour would still have won the election) while representing the seat to be known as Airdrie and Shotts.

A little over two-thirds of this seat came from the pre-1997 Monklands East, centred on the town of Airdrie, north of the A8/M8 roads about a dozen miles east of Glasgow; the remainder consists of a group of small industrial communities south of that motorway and formerly in the Motherwell North division: Shotts, Stane, Dykehead, Newmains, Cleland and Bonkle. Motherwell North was every bit as strongly Labour as Monklands East, and this will remain a solid seat for Helen Liddell, John Smith's successor.

Now Secretary of State for Scotland, Helen Liddell had an initial tough fight against the SNP in the 1994 by-election, but she has now won Airdrie and Shotts twice very easily and is set fair for the continuation of her career. Airdrie is even more working class in make-up than its 'twin' to the west, Coatbridge. The local Labour Party has been riven by internal dissension over the question of whether councillors from Coatbridge (who all happen to be Catholics) have denied influence in the local council to representatives from Airdrie, which, by (exaggerated) tradition is a Protestant town. Whatever the truth of the matter, the dispute has not so far affected Labour in parliamentary contests in either a Coatbridge- or an Airdrie-based constituency, although there may be a faint shadow of sectarianism in the near deposit-saving 1,439 votes polled by the only 'Scottish Unionist' candidate contesting a seat in the 2001 General Election, actually pipping the Scottish Socialist in the battle for fifth and sixth place.

Social indices:			2001 Gen. Election:			
% Non-white	0.7		Lab	18,478	58.2	−3.6
% Prof/Man	26.6		SNP	6,138	19.3	−5.1
% Non-manual	46.1		LD	2,376	7.5	+3.3
% Unemployed 2001	5.6		C	1,960	6.2	−2.7
% Decrease 97–01	3.1		SUP	1,439	4.5	
% Fin hard/Rank	48.6	19	SSP	1,171	3.7	
% Prem mort/Rank	54	23	SLP	174	0.5	
			Lab maj	12,340	38.9	
			Turnout		54.4	−17.0
			Elect	58,349		

Member of Parliament

The career of Labour's **Helen Liddell**, promoted to the Cabinet as Scottish Secretary in the wake of Peter Mandelson's second going in January 2001 (after having held a succession of jobs in the Treasury, Scottish Office, Transport and the DTI), had been somewhat becalmed following her earlier failure to land the Scottish job. Variously dubbed 'a cross between Miss Jean Brodie and Lulu' and 'Stalin's Granny', she is a tough party apparatchik with a reputation as a hammer of the SNP, which ran her close in the sectarian Monklands by-election following the death of John Smith in 1994. A bus-driver's daughter, born in 1950, educated at St Patrick's (RC) High School, Coatbridge and Strathclyde University, she ran the Scottish Labour Party for 11 years after lasting only one year as economic correspondent on BBC Scotland, where her strong Lanarkshire accent did not meet with universal approval. Controversially she spent four years as Robert Maxwell's PR chief in Scotland, and wrote a bodice-ripping novel, *Elite*, in 1990. Presiding over a post-devolution Scotland Office of drastically reduced competence, but with a good election result in Scotland behind her – an SNP vote cut back to 20% (despite their 28% in the 1999 Scottish election) – her presence in Cabinet maintains a generous over-representation of (six) Scots.

ALDERSHOT

There are only a few constituencies in the country which have traditionally been influenced by the armed services vote, and most of them seem to be in Hampshire. It is known that Portsmouth and Gosport are more Conservative than their class make-up would suggest because of the interests of the Royal Navy and associated defence trades and industries. Since the establishment of the army camp in 1854 the name of Aldershot has been linked with the idea of square-bashing and basic training by generations of soldiers, and others besides. There are now fewer units based in Aldershot than in times past, but the military town is still a prominent and symbolic landmark. Aldershot still advertises itself proudly as 'The Home of the British Army' on its 'Welcome to …' roadside boards. The constituency also includes Farnborough, which claims to be the birthplace of aeronautical research and development, and thousands of visitors are attracted to its autumn air show.

The seat is squeezed into a compact area in the far north-east of Hampshire, and it has usually lost territory in recent boundary reviews. The reason for this is that its population is still expanding, not in Aldershot or Farnborough but in the third population centre in the constituency, Yateley. Yateley parish has reached a population of over 21,000; it is 90% owner-occupied, close enough to the M3 to be a major commuting base, and Conservative in general elections even if Liberal Democrat in local contests. In fact places like Yateley and Farnborough actually decide the destiny of the Aldershot seat, not the Army vote. An illustration of this lies in the fact that the Queens ward of Aldershot, at the heart of the military town, consistently produces one of the lowest turnouts of any ward in local elections in Britain: 14.0% in the Rushmoor District May elections in 2000, for example. The reasons for this are, presumably, a high turnover of residents leading to an inaccurate register, voters absent on duty elsewhere, and a lack of feeling that municipal government is relevant to Army voters. Turnout in general elections is low, too. It is the civilian Conservatism of the Aldershot division that ultimately guarantees its safety for the Tory Party.

There was little change in the share of vote among the main parties in 2001, but a rather curious pair of candidatures. Alan Hope, the landlord of the Dog and Partridge pub in Yateley and joint leader (with his cat, Mandu) of the Official Monster Raving Loony Party, was actually beaten into last place by the druid Arthur Pendragon. Only partially due to this split in the loony vote, Gerald Howarth should have a seat for a long term of service in Aldershot.

Social indices:			2001 Gen. Election:			
% Non-white	2.3		C	19,106	42.2	−0.5
% Prof/Man	32.8		LD	12,542	27.7	−2.8
% Non-manual	56.7		Lab	11,391	25.1	+1.0
£ Av prop val 2000	125 K		UKIP	797	1.8	+0.3
% Increase 97–00	50.1		Grn	630	1.4	
% Unemployed 2001	0.9		Ind	459	1.0	+0.3
% Decrease 97–01	0.9		MRLP	390	0.9	
% Fin hard/Rank	8.7	497	C maj	6,564	14.5	
% Pensioners	16.9		Turnout		57.9	−13.2
% Prem mort/Rank	18	502	Elect	78,262		

Member of Parliament

Gerald Howarth was elected for Aldershot in 1997, having earlier sat for Cannock and Burntwood from 1983 to 1992. The succession of this hard-right Thatcherite to the seat previously held by the 'One Nation' MP Sir Julian Critchley (who had dubbed him 'PPS to the handbag over the water' – as Margaret Thatcher's last parliamentary aide), graphically underscored the virtual elimination of the moderate wing of the Conservative parliamentary party. Born in 1947 and educated at Bloxham School and Southampton University, he worked in merchant banking before becoming an MP, and in Lord Parkinson's lobbying company (with Sir James Goldsmith as its major client) whilst out of the House after 1992. Of the Thatcherite 'No Turning Back' Group, he covered the full range of right-wing causes from white South Africa, through birching, immigration and Pinochet, to Europhobia. A small man of staring gaze, and a friend of tobacco companies, he defended to the last ditch his long-time friend Neil Hamilton against all allegations of 'cash for questions', claiming him to be the victim of a 'vicious' media witchhunt and of a miscarriage of justice. He voted for Iain Duncan Smith in all the leadership ballots in 2001, and was appointed a Defence spokesman in 2002.

ALDRIDGE-BROWNHILLS

When Aldridge-Brownhills was created in 1974, it was regarded as an ultra-marginal seat; and indeed its first contest, in February of that year, produced a victory by only 366 votes for Labour's Geoffrey Edge over the Conservative Dame Patricia Hornsby-Smith. Edge increased his majority in October 1974, but lost in 1979 by over 5,000 to Richard Shepherd, who increased that lead in the three subsequent elections to between 10,000 and 12,000. Even in the twin catastrophes of 1997 and 2001 Shepherd held on (albeit by only 2,500 and 3,750 respectively). This might be due to the MP's own well-known independence and energy, but it probably helped too in both the last two elections that this Maastricht rebel was not opposed by the Referendum Party, the UK Independence Party, or any fringe candidates who might have split his potential vote. In the 1999 European Parliament elections, the Conservatives held their 1997 share here while the UK Independence Party tapped a solid well of feeling by polling over 6%, above the regional average.

Aldridge-Brownhills is a seat of two distinct parts. Brownhills is an ex-mining town which almost always returns a Labour councillor to Walsall Metropolitan

Borough Council. Before 1974 it was included in the safely Labour Walsall North seat. Aldridge is much more middle class, with largely private post-war housing, and it was largely responsible for the Conservative character of the Walsall South constituency which existed before 1974, when Aldridge-Brownhills was incorporated as the eastern end of the enlarged West Midlands Borough of Walsall.

The two elements of the seat are not equal in size: Aldridge has grown much more quickly than Brownhills. The Conservatives have usually led in Walsall Wood, Hatherton Rushall, and Streetly, the best residential area in the seat, which, like many other districts on the edge of Sutton Park, houses some of the wealthiest West Midlanders. Over 47% of the households in Streetly ward have at least two cars. The Conservatives polled 79.5% of the vote there in a straight fight with Labour in the Walsall borough elections in May 2000.

Aldridge-Brownhills seems to have swung to the right to become another all-white (98%) Tory residential district on the edge of the West Midlands conurbation, and, having survived the last two general elections, its individualistic member will continue to plough his furrow in the Commons.

Social indices:			2001 Gen. Election:			
% Non-white	2.0		C	18,974	50.2	+3.0
% Prof/Man	29.6		Lab	15,206	40.2	−1.5
% Non-manual	53.5		LD	3,251	8.6	−2.6
£ Av prop val 2000	95 K		SA	379	1.0	
% Increase 97–00	23.5		C maj	3,768	10.0	
% Unemployed 2001	2.6		Turnout		60.6	−13.7
% Decrease 97–01	1.4		Elect	62,388		
% Fin hard/Rank	16.8	321				
% Pensioners	24.1					
% Prem mort/Rank	23	446				

Member of Parliament

Born in 1942, educated at Isleworth Grammar School and the LSE, **Richard Shepherd**, a former Lloyd's underwriter and owner of a small chain of up-market grocers shops, is a respected, sensitive, libertarian bachelor, and one of the Conservatives' most uncompromising Europhobes – stripped of the Whip for five months in 1994–95. MP here since 1979, an advocate of open government who rebelled against the Scott Report, and who campaigns incessantly for radical freedom of information legislation, he ran for Speaker in 2000 with the cross-party backing of Martin Bell and Labour's Dr Tony Wright and polled 136 votes. Seen (by the *Guardian*) as having 'antediluvian views on many things, such as foreigners' but 'very nice in a schoolboyish sort of way', in 2000 he was one of only two Tories to join Labour rebels in opposing part privatisation of air traffic control. The antithesis of the Tory yes-man, he has disdain for the Whips, whom he sees as treating MPs like 'a chorus of Tiller girls', and voted for Iain Duncan Smith in all the leadership ballots in 2001.

ALTRINCHAM AND SALE WEST

This is part of Cheshire's middle-class belt, south of Manchester. Altrincham and Sale, however, are large enough towns to be more than dormitories. They have a life and character of their own, and can act as minor economic counter-attractions to Manchester. Altrincham includes the neighbourhood of Timperley and the ward of Broadheath. All this is not, in general, Rolls-Royce or stockbroker country as can be found in some of the smaller communities further out. But the seat also continues to include Hale and Bowdon, which when last individually measured by the Census were found to be two of the five highest-status small towns in the country: each reached a level of 69% non-manual workers way back in 1971. This figure was exceeded in England only by Harpenden and Chorleywood in Hertfordshire and by Formby in Shirley Williams's one-time Crosby seat. In the 1991 Census it was revealed that over 49% of the households in Hale and Bowdon ward had at least two cars, the highest figure in the whole of Greater Manchester (pipping the desirable and exclusive Bramhall neighbourhood of Cheadle constituency). There really are millionaires in Hale, secluded in leafy private roads and luxury houses, especially out in Halebarns.

It need hardly be said that Hale and Bowdon are Tory, as are most of the less rich wards in this seat. Trafford was the only metropolitan borough in England to remain under Conservative control after their disastrous May 1994 local elections, and mostly this was due to this constituency. There is a Labour ward at Sale St Martin's, which still has a large minority of council-built housing, and the Lib Dems usually win Timperley Village. In their disastrous year of 1997, the Conservative share of the vote fell by over 11% in Altrincham and Sale West, and Labour reduced the majority to almost exactly one-tenth of its previous level of 15,600. In 2001 in a rare three-cornered fight, though, the still-youthful Graham Brady doubled his lead to 3,000 and now seems to be past the worst of the slump to continue his role in opposition, probably for a considerable time to come.

Social indices:			2001 Gen. Election:			
% Non-white	2.7		C	20,113	46.2	+3.0
% Prof/Man	44.6		Lab	17,172	39.4	−0.8
% Non-manual	70.7		LD	6,283	14.4	+1.8
£ Av prop val 2000	154 K		C maj	2,941	6.8	
% Increase 97–00	55.8		Turnout		60.7	−12.7
% Unemployed 2001	1.6		Elect	71,820		
% Decrease 97–01	1.4					
% Fin hard/Rank	9.3	480				
% Pensioners	25.8					
% Prem mort/Rank	23	444				

Member of Parliament

A Conservative education spokesman, **Graham Brady** was the youngest Tory MP (born in 1967) elected in 1997, and remained only the second youngest in 2001. One of only two Conservatives elected in either the Manchester or Liverpool conurbations in 1997, by 2001 he was the sole standard-bearer of Toryism in the area. A PR man, who was educated locally at Altrincham Grammar School, and at Durham University, and specialises in defending grammar schools, he is hostile to the euro, voted for Michael Howard for leader in 1997 and, initially, for David Davis in 2001. He has also voted for homosexual sex at 16, and bears some resemblance, with a big mouth full of teeth, to Prince Andrew.

ALYN AND DEESIDE

Alyn and Deeside is a compact constituency set at the head of the Dee estuary, on the very border with Cheshire and England. The main centres of population lie along the west bank of the Dee in the industrial areas of Connah's Quay, Shotton, Queensferry and Sandycroft, and in the inland town of Buckley. A contrast is provided by the more physically attractive villages of Hawarden, Ewloe, Hope and Caergwrle, and the seat extends west into the Clwydian hills.

Despite the historical connection between Hawarden and Liberalism (this was the site of Gladstone's country house), this is a safe Labour constituency, the successor to the East Flintshire division which had been held by just two MPs, Eirene White and Barry Jones, from 1950 to 1983, with the Tories second. In the latter year, Labour's majority was reduced to just 1,368, but subsequently it has been built up again to over 9,000 in 2001, even after a decrease in their share of 9.5% between 1997 and 2001, when the turnout dropped even more than the UK norm.

This is in the main a heavily industrial area, once dependent on the giant steelworks at Shotton whose closure afflicted Alyn and Deeside with a near 20% unemployment rate, and economic decline and depression through much of the 1980s. By the mid-1990s, however, diversification had helped to improve the situation considerably and the unemployment rate was below the national average. This was unlikely to help the Conservatives though, who led only in the villages and more rural areas. Despite the Gladstonian link the Liberal Democrats could attain just one-eighth of the vote here, and the Welsh Nationalists have even more of a problem, scraping together just 3% in a seat which reaches across the Dee to include suburbs of Chester such as Sealand. This is the only seat in Wales where a minority (47.5%) of the inhabitants were born inside the principality.

Social indices:			2001 Gen. Election:			
% Non-white	0.6		Lab	18,525	52.3	−9.6
% Welsh sp	9.6		C	9,303	26.3	+3.5
% Prof/Man	26.2		LD	4,585	12.9	+3.2
% Non-manual	49.7		PC	1,182	3.3	+1.6
£ Av prop val 2000	64 K		Grn	881	2.5	
% Increase 97–00	25.1		UKIP	481	1.4	
% Unemployed 2001	2.8		Ind	253	0.7	
% Decrease 97–01	0.9		CPGB	211	0.6	
% Fin hard/Rank	12.3	411	Lab maj	9,222	26.0	
% Pensioners	22.9		Turnout		58.6	−13.6
% Prem mort/Rank	32	305	Elect	60,478		

Member of Parliament

Mark Tami was elected in 2001 following allegations that he had been parachuted into the seat as an AEEU favourite son in place of the deliberately late-retiring MP Barry Jones. The allegation of John Marek – also retiring as MP for neighbouring Wrexham – that this was an example of 'Blairite poodles' being inserted by way of NEC-imposed shortlists, was denied by AEEU leader Sir Ken Jackson. Born in 1962 and educated at Enfield Grammar School and Swansea University, Mark Tami is one of a clutch of union apparatchiks inheriting safe Labour seats – many like him late in the day – in 2001. A campaigner for the retention of jobs in the local aerospace industry, he also follows his union's lead in fiercely opposing PR voting systems, as in his co-authored Fabian Society pamphlet *Votes For All* in 2000.

AMBER VALLEY

Amber Valley is an industrial area in mid-Derbyshire, centred on three towns of some 20,000 souls each, Alfreton, Heanor and Ripley, together with surrounding villages like Ambergate, where the Amber flows into Derbyshire's main river, the Derwent. It always seemed something of an aberration that Amber Valley was held by the Conservative Phillip Oppenheim from its creation in 1983, and indeed he perished by over 11,500 votes in the Labour landslide of 1997, suffering a 13% decline in his share of vote.

This is in fact a gritty, ordinary East Midland seat, nowhere near as beautiful as its name. It was once a coal-mining area, but the seams were relatively exposed to the surface and therefore more rapidly worked out, and the coalfield declined rapidly after the First World War. The last pits closed in the late 1960s. Now light industrial estates form the economic base, and there is much hope advanced for Amber Valley's future. It is well connected by spur roads to the nearby M1, and the terraced Victorian houses (mainly owner-occupied) have been brightened up with colourful touches of individuality.

These economic changes may well have been largely responsible for the swing to the right in the area's politics up to 1987. Had Oppenheim achieved the miracle of creating a safe Tory seat in mid-Derbyshire?

If he thought he had, he received a rude awakening. In April 1992 the swing back to Labour was 8%, one of the highest in any target seat. Oppenheim's majority was cut to 712. There was an even greater movement of opinion in 1997, as his talents were diverted into a thoughtful and independently minded national newspaper column and Judy Mallaber joined 100 Labour women colleagues in the Commons, and like all but three (defeated) and six (retired) she was returned to Westminster in 2001, though after a 16% decline in turnout. Like several neighbouring seats, Amber Valley has now been restored to its safe Labour heritage.

Social indices:			2001 Gen. Election:			
% Non-white	0.7		Lab	23,101	51.9	−2.8
% Prof/Man	27.2		C	15,874	35.7	+2.2
% Non-manual	45.5		LD	5,538	12.4	+4.7
£ Av prop val 2000	59 K		Lab maj	7,227	16.2	
% Increase 97–00	24.5		Turnout		60.3	−15.8
% Unemployed 2001	2.8		Elect	73,798		
% Decrease 97–01	1.1					
% Fin hard/Rank	16.8	318				
% Pensioners	26.0					
% Prem mort/Rank	33	295				

Member of Parliament

Judy Mallaber, elected in 1997, belies a sectarian past including Communist Party membership and chairmanship of the left-wing independent Labour Research Department, as a witty, fluent Blairite loyalist. Born in 1951 and with the impeccably elitist academic pedigree of North London Collegiate and St Anne's College, Oxford, she worked for ten years as research officer for NUPE, whose commitment to a national minimum wage she has duly reflected in Commons interventions, and for eight years ran the Labour-linked Local Government Information Unit. Frizzy-haired and wire-rimmed spectacled, her lack of ministerial preferment is odd given her loyalism and diligence as a constituency MP, but may well be linked to her advancing years. In November 2001 she posed a planted-sounding question to Tony Blair on school performance to the accompaniment of Tory jeers.

ANGUS

For many years, until 1974, the county of Angus formed some of the Conservatives' best territory in rural Scotland. The historic county stretched from the edge of the Highlands and the fringes of the Grampians to the outskirts of Dundee. The mainstay of the economy is agriculture, with some textile industry. There are also some coastal ports, well known for fishing, and tourist resorts. The communities of the constituency are bleak ground for Labour. Montrose and Arbroath are ancient and highly respectable burghs. The golfing town of Carnoustie, struggling to regain its status as an Open Championship site, and Monifieth near Dundee are fashionable residential areas and resorts. It was not Labour that shocked the Tories in 1974, and have troubled them ever since, but the Scottish Nationalists.

Mrs Thatcher's friend and confidant Jock Bruce-Gardyne was defeated in Angus South (as it then was) by the SNP's Andrew Welsh in October 1974. Peter Fraser (now Lord Fraser of Carmyllie) recovered it narrowly in 1979, but the Angus seat was regained by Welsh in 1987. In 1997, the Conservatives lost all their remaining seats in Scotland and Welsh was able to increase his lead to over 10,000, making Angus the second safest of the SNP's constituencies. It still is, but after Welsh transferred to the Edinburgh Parliament along with four of the other five SNP MPs, his successor Michael Weir held on with a majority cut by two-thirds. This was not because of an increase in the Tory share though, for it remained static, but rather a transfer to Labour (up 8%), Liberal Democrats (up five), and to not voting at all – the turnout fell by 13 points, as did the SNP figure. This pattern was repeated in all the seats the SNP was defending except for Banff and Buchan, where Alex Salmond stayed on, his loyalty rewarded with a renewal of personal support.

Social indices:			2001 Gen. Election:			
% Non-white	0.5		SNP	12,347	35.3	−13.0
% Prof/Man	33.1		C	8,736	25.0	+0.3
% Non-manual	53.7		Lab	8,183	23.4	+7.7
% Unemployed 2001	5.1		LD	5,015	14.3	+4.9
% Decrease 97–01	1.8		SSP	732	2.1	
% Fin hard/Rank	26.4	185	SNP maj	3,611	10.3	
% Prem mort/Rank	35	247	Turnout		59.3	−12.8
			Elect	59,004		

Member of Parliament

With the retreat to the Scottish Parliament of Andrew Welsh, the SNP's MP of 20 years, his party turned to **Michael Weir**, a locally born (1947), bred and based solicitor and former councillor, educated at the local Arbroath High School, and at Aberdeen University. He is of the generation which came of age politically during the SNP's first upsurge, when the uncharismatic Andrew Welsh was one of the SNPs 'First Eleven' elected in October 1974. As a third party MP and a Scottish Nationalist he combines the roles traditionally expected of each: assiduous raising of local grievances – such as the 'rock-bottom' morale in the Tayside NHS, with calls for 'full fiscal autonomy' for the Scottish Parliament – in other words Scottish independence. His elevation from his party's 'B' team to the Commons benches did not preclude, in fringe party fashion, his immediate appointment to shadow no fewer than four departments of state.

ANTRIM EAST

The seat of Antrim East contains the whole of two Northern Irish district areas, Larne and Carrickfergus, together with four wards of Newtownabbey, lying between the M2 motorway and Belfast Lough. This is essentially a coastal division lying between the Antrim hills and the sea. The northern part of the seat consists of headlands and glens and picturesque villages. In the centre is Larne, a very busy sea ferry port with some heavy engineering industry and a power-station. But the south, from Carrickfergus to Belfast, is almost continuously urban. The political balance of the constituency is controlled by this latter section. In the 1980s Carrickfergus suffered severely from the closure of ICI and Courtaulds, the makers of man-made fibres, and several related industries. Although an overwhelmingly Protestant district, Antrim East has by no means escaped the dire effects of the recession and the decimation of the artificial fibre industry in the province.

The seat will always return a unionist member of Parliament, but the question is – of what variety? As part of Ian Paisley's old North Antrim citadel, it was originally expected that Antrim East would elect a Democratic Unionist. However, the Official

Unionist Roy Beggs pulled off a genuine surprise in the first contest here, in 1983, to beat the DUP by 367 votes. Beggs benefited from the truce between the unionist parties to win easily in 1986 and 1987, and by the time the Paisleyites re-entered the fray in 1992 he had built up his position to such an extent that he won by a clear 7,000 plus over Nigel Dodds, Lord Mayor of Belfast. In 1997 the result was almost an exact replay of 1992, with the exception that (helped by minor boundary changes) the Alliance Party moved ahead of the DUP into second place. In 2001, however, although Antrim East was one of only 11 out of 18 Northern Irish seats not to change hands, it very nearly provided a fourth gain for the DUP from the Ulster Unionists as the province dramatically polarised under the strain affecting the Belfast or Good Friday Agreement.

Social indices:		2001 Gen. Election:			
% Prof/Man	27.8	UUP	13,101	36.4	−2.4
% Non-manual	52.0	DUP	12,973	36.0	+16.6
% RC	12.9	APNI	4,483	12.5	−7.7
% Irish sp	2.1	SDLP	2,641	7.3	+2.7
% Unemployed 2001	4.3	Ind	1,092	3.0	−0.3
% Decrease 97–01	2.1	SF	903	2.5	+0.9
		C	807	2.2	−4.6
		UUP maj	128	0.4	
		Turnout		59.1	+0.9
		Elect	60,897		

Member of Parliament

Ulster Unionist Whip, **Roy Beggs**, who was once arrested and fined for inciting an Orange road blockade, is one of the few remaining lower-flying members of his reduced parliamentary contingent of six MPs, following the electoral demise of some of the colleagues once dubbed by David Trimble as the 'Woodentops'. An ex-teacher and sometime Paisleyite, he deserted Trimble in 1998 to vote with five of his then nine MP colleagues against the Good Friday Agreement. A tall, burly, square-faced Protestant Ulsterman, who is pro-caning, anti-smoking, and Europhobic, he was born in 1936, educated at Ballyclare High School and Stranmillis Teacher Training College, Belfast, and taught for 25 years before going into first a coachworks, then a farming business. First elected in 1983, he now sits on the Commons' fifth smallest majority.

ANTRIM NORTH

The Antrim North seat is deeply and strongly associated with the *éminence grise* of the Northern Irish scene for over 25 years, the Reverend Ian Paisley, the founder and leader of the Democratic Unionist Party. This brooding giant has been returned to Westminster with consistently massive majorities since he ousted Official Unionist Henry Clark at the 1970 General Election. In 1992 Paisley obtained a 15,000 majority and an absolute majority of the vote even against Ulster Unionist Party opposition. In 1997 there were signs that Paisley's popularity might be waning slightly, as the Ulster

Unionists improved a little, and his own share slipped below 50%. This scarcely represented a serious dent in the Paisleyite position, though, and in 2001 this was one of the few constituencies in Northern Ireland where the balance of the parties did not change perceptibly from four years before.

The constituency consists of the whole of three district council areas: Ballymena, Ballymoney and Moyle. It is largely rural and agricultural and very scenic. The northern or Atlantic coast has attractive beaches and the renowned Giant's Causeway. The east coast has a narrow coastal road opening into the glens. The Antrim hills fall away towards the river Bann to the west. The main urban centres are Ballymena, Ballymoney and Ballycastle. There is some industry, both of an agriculturally based kind and of more modern types.

There is a one-in-four Catholic minority community, including that on Rathlin Island in the North Channel, to which Ian Paisley is said to give good constituency service. However, their votes cannot influence the destiny of the seat, so long utterly locked in the hands of the big fellow from Ballymena.

Social indices:		2001 Gen. Election:			
% Prof/Man	31.6	DUP	24,539	49.9	+3.3
% Non-manual	48.9	UUP	10,315	21.0	−2.7
% RC	26.6	SDLP	8,283	16.8	+1.0
% Irish sp	5.1	SF	4,822	9.8	+3.5
% Unemployed 2001	4.4	APNI	1,258	2.6	−3.6
% Decrease 97–01	2.8	DUP maj	14,224	28.9	
		Turnout		66.1	+2.3
		Elect	74,451		

Member of Parliament

The **Revd Dr Ian Paisley**, one of the Commons' most bizarre embellishments, has been MP here since 1970, when he ousted an MP representing the old Ulster Unionist establishment, Henry Clark. Paisley is *sui generis* – founder both of his own party, the Democratic Unionist Party, and of his own denomination, the Free Presbyterian Church of Ulster, numbering a mere 12,363 souls spread over 67 churches, one of them – oddly enough – in Lowestoft and presided over by Paisley's son. Now the second oldest MP, born in 1926, educated at schools in Ballymena and at sundry fundamentalist bible colleges, and described variously as a bellicose, paranoid, bigoted sectarian, he represents working-class Protestants against the middle-class Unionists. Though his doctorate is honorary and from Bob Jones University, South Carolina, he is no mean biblical scholar, but inevitably is seen as an anachronism in a secular age. Representing at least half the Protestant electorate in Northern Ireland, he is no joke there and in opposing all power-sharing damagingly split the Unionist vote in 2001. He liked his *Spitting Image* puppet.

ANTRIM SOUTH

Seven of Northern Ireland's 18 seats changed hands on 7 June 2001, and another two nearly did (Antrim East and Upper Bann). Mostly this represented movements to the parties generally held to be on the more extreme wings of unionism and nationalism, but in South Antrim the Ulster Unionists' David Burnside gained the seat from the DUP's William McCrea by just over 1,000 votes. This does in fact represent a regain, as McCrea had defeated Burnside in the November 2000 by-election caused by the death of the Ulster Unionists' Clifford Forsythe. As Burnside is on the hard-line agreement-sceptic wing of his party this reverse in the re-run should perhaps be regarded as more a choice between personalities than policies, but it all added to the impression of mayhem gathering pace in 2001 in the north-eastern corner of Ireland.

The constituency of South Antrim held for many years more than one electoral record. In the House of Commons before the 1983 boundary changes it was the largest seat in population and electorate, with over 132,000 voters in 1982. Thus it offered the clearest justification for the award of five extra seats to Northern Ireland, to bring the total to 17. South Antrim also frequently produced the largest majority in the House: over 50,000 for Knox Cunningham in 1959, when he polled 95.1% of the vote as a Unionist candidate; and the highest majority in the 1979 General Election, 38,868 for the Official Unionist James Molyneaux.

The seat includes the whole of Antrim district and some wards from Newtownabbey. It stretches from Lough Neagh and the river Bann to the west to the borders of Belfast and Antrim East. The seat is mainly rural, but with the M2 motorway running westwards it has excellent communications between the urban and industrial areas. These are Antrim, Randalstown and Ballyclare and Glengormley on the fringes of Belfast. The seat has been affected by the sharp decline in the man-made fibre industry in the past 30 years. It has a very important agricultural sector and a valuable eel fishing industry based at Toone. It also contains Aldergrove airport and the service industries associated with it. In recent years this rather befits a seat of departures and bumpy landings.

Social indices:		2001 Gen. Election:			
% Prof/Man	28.8	UUP	16,366	37.1	−20.4
% Non-manual	53.9	DUP	15,355	34.8	
% RC	22.9	SDLP	5,336	12.1	−4.1
% Irish sp	4.3	SF	4,160	9.4	+3.9
% Unemployed 2001	2.9	APNI	1,969	4.5	−7.2
% Decrease 97–01	1.5	Ind	972	2.2	
		UUP maj	1,011	2.3	
		Turnout		62.5	+4.6
		Elect	70,651		

Member of Parliament

David Burnside narrowly recaptured this seat in 2001 having narrowly failed to retain it for the Ulster Unionists at the by-election in June 2000. Coming with a reputation as a hardliner on power-sharing – an electoral necessity when pitted against a Paisleyite opponent – he has however demonstrated the suppleness of the public relations man in balancing his cautious response to the announcement of IRA decommissioning in October 2001, with a challenge to Tony Blair about the 'deep-seated republicanism at the heart of his government' in November. Born in

1951 and educated at Coleraine Academical Institution and at Queen's University Belfast, he has unusually for an Ulster Unionist spent most of his professional career outside Northern Ireland, handling PR at the Institute of Directors, or at British Airways, and as a director of Robert Maxwell's newspaper, *The European* – a metropolitan career unmatched by his more parochial colleagues. Parting company with British Airways after running its campaign against rival Virgin Airways, he also insists that he is 'not a career politician'.

ARGYLL AND BUTE

As recently as the 1970s, the vast constituency of Argyll was usually the last in Britain to declare its result, often on the Saturday after the election, as votes were conveyed by boat from Mull, Jura and Islay, as well as smaller and even more remote islands like Coll, Tiree and Colonsay. Argyll also includes vast tracts of moorland on the mainland, divided by deep sea lochs which make communications within the seat very difficult. The seat includes the long Kintyre peninsula. The only towns of any size are Oban and Dunoon (where the late John Smith, a native of Argyll, went to school). Since 1983 another island has been added, Bute near the mouth of the Clyde. This is the fourth largest seat in Britain, nearly two million acres in area, and its difficult terrain and thinly scattered population make for individual and personal politics as in the other huge Highland seats further up the west coast.

Argyll was one of the hearts of laird paternalism, and it was safely Tory until February 1974 when, after the retirement of Conservative frontbencher Michael Noble, it was gained by Scottish Nationalist Iain MacCormick in a surprise late result. MacCormick held on until 1979, when Argyll was recovered for the Tories by John Mackay. Then in 1987, not generally regarded as a good year for the centrist Alliance parties, Mrs Ray Michie benefited from the Conservative decline in Scotland and notched up one of the two Liberal gains of the General Election north of the border. As is often the way in very rural seats, she managed to consolidate her position in 1992 and 1997, but on her retirement in 2001 it was not regarded as a safe handover to a Liberal Democrat successor, especially as their first candidate selected by the party withdrew after a court case involving alleged sexual offences. Some felt that the main threat would come from the SNP, but the Nationalists performed poorly across Scotland in 2001 and slipped to fourth here, and it was Labour who slashed the Lib Dem lead to around a quarter of its previous figure, and four parties are still in long-term contention in this beautiful, fascinating and individual constituency, especially if proposals are confirmed expanding its electorate by the remaining 20,000 council area voters around Helensburgh, now in Dumbarton.

The region of Strathclyde, abolished in the mid-1990s, was generally thought of as heavily urban and industrial. Argyll and Bute, which made up half its acreage, gave the lie to that. All the parties will have to canvass vigorously, by boat and on foot as well as by more conventional means, if they are to win what is effectively a Highland seat.

Social indices:			2001 Gen. Election:			
% Non-white	1.0		LD	9,245	29.9	−10.3
% Prof/Man	32.1		Lab	7,592	24.5	+8.9
% Non-manual	50.4		C	6,436	20.8	+1.8
% Unemployed 2001	4.1		SNP	6,433	20.8	−2.4
% Decrease 97–01	1.7		SSP	1,251	4.0	
% Fin hard/Rank	16.5	328	LD maj	1,653	5.3	
% Prem mort/Rank	48	62	Turnout		63.0	−9.3
			Elect	49,175		

Member of Parliament

Alan Reid, a chess-playing computer programmer at Glasgow University, was elected in 2001 in place of the retiring Liberal Democrat MP, Mrs Ray Michie. He was not, however, his party's first choice, having replaced Paul Coleshill, a homosexual law reform campaigner (in a way that Mrs Michie had certainly not been), who withdrew as candidate early in 2001. Formerly on Renfrewshire Council, Alan Reid was born in 1954 and educated lengthily at Prestwick, then Ayr, Academies, Strathclyde University, Jordanhill Teacher Training College, and Bell College (where he studied computing). Firmly in his party's Europhile tradition, he backs euro entry as a supposed means of reviving local farming, fishing and tourist industries, and seeks to emulate Mrs Michie's defence of Gaelic culture. Reputedly Parliament's most accomplished chess-player, if with some competition from his party colleague Evan Harris, he will need to use his mathematical skills to enhance his significantly depleted majority before the next election.

ARUNDEL AND SOUTH DOWNS

The sixth safest Conservative seat after the 2001 General Election, Arundel and South Downs is one of only a handful of places where a Tory MP obtained an absolute majority of over 50% of all votes cast. None at all obtained over half the eligible electorate, of course; with a turnout of 64.7% Howard Flight barely convinced one-third of all voters even in this 'Tory heartland'. This figure may surprise a visitor to this douce segment of deep southern England.

This is the eighth and additional seat created in West Sussex by the 1995 Boundary Commission report. Only about 12,500 voters from the former Arundel are to be found here. They come from Aldingbourne, Barnham, Walberton and the little town of Arundel itself, perched on a hill and dominated by the Roman Catholic cathedral and even more by the vast castle of the Duke of Norfolk, the premier Catholic peer in the realm – and one of the closest to the throne to declare a party political allegiance: he sits in the House of Lords on the Conservative benches. In that preference he is in line with most of the more plebeian residents of his home area.

Arundel and South Downs draws upon territory which was previously in no fewer than five different seats. It is a ragbag created to reduce the electorates of a number of previously oversized constituencies, covering pretty much the central geographic section of the county of West Sussex. The largest single donation came from the Horsham seat, with over 30,000 electors in places such as Pulborough and Steyning,

Storrington and Sullington, Henfield and West Grinstead. Some 12,500 voters were imported from Mid Sussex, in Hurstpierpoint and Keymer, and Bolney and Clayton. Finally smaller portions arrived from Shoreham and Chichester constituencies. There are no towns of even as much as 10,000 souls, and at one stage the Boundary Commission suggested calling this seat 'Chanctonbury' after the ancient hill fort at its heart on the Downs. However, although Arundel does have a population of only 3,000, its historical claims won it continued mention in a constituency title.

This may be an artificially created seat, but it brings together communities which have much in common. This is prosperous, middle-class, small town and village, Tory England. It offers Howard Flight a custom-built constituency as an utterly secure base from which to pursue a long parliamentary career.

Social indices:			2001 Gen. Election			
% Non-white	0.7		C	23,969	52.2	−0.9
% Prof/Man	42.2		LD	10,265	22.4	−3.4
% Non-manual	62.9		Lab	9,488	20.7	+2.4
£ Av prop val 2000	180 K		UKIP	2,167	4.7	+1.8
% Increase 97–00	64.6		C maj	13,704	29.9	
% Unemployed 2001	0.8		Turnout		64.7	−11.2
% Decrease 97–01	1.0		Elect	70,956		
% Fin hard/Rank	4.5	618				
% Pensioners	32.3					
% Prem mort/Rank	6	622				

Member of Parliament

Howard Flight, a big and breezy merchant banker, son of a regional Westminster Bank official, and grandson of 'a rampant socialist' whose effect on him was to think 'it was all rubbish from an early age', became a Treasury spokesman in 2001, having been elected in 1997. Misleadingly self-described as 'Essex Man', he comes with rather more traditional accoutrements than most of the Romford-born, as a plummy-voiced public school (albeit Brentwood) and Cambridge (Magdalene)-and-Michigan-educated investment manager, initially with Rothschild's Bank, but eventually with his own Guinness-Flight company, and whose wife works at Sotheby's. His political pedigree is right wing with links to the Freedom Association and the Selsdon Group, a keen advocate of welfare privatisation and a backer of Redwood in 1997 even into the last ditch with Kenneth Clarke. A defender of capitalism as redolent of a Bach fugue, he prefers its unregulated American to its European version and has opposed the EU's withholding tax. He dismissed Labour's total handgun ban as 'political correctness', and voted the slightly racy Portillo option in the 2001 leadership stakes.

ASHFIELD

The west Nottinghamshire ex-mining constituency of Ashfield has a habit of springing surprises in the form of larger than average and expected swings. In 1977 it produced one of the most dramatic results in the history of British by-elections. On the same day that Labour held a much more marginal seat at Grimsby, they lost a 23,000 majority to Conservative Tim Smith. The seat was regained for Labour by Frank Haynes in 1979, but an explanation of the by-election reverse was still sought. Was it a specific response to the departure of David Marquand to join Roy Jenkins at the EEC, and his replacement with another non-miner candidate? Or was it a result of some drastic change in the political nature and anatomy of Ashfield?

At that time Ashfield consisted of a slice of the older part of the Notts coalfield, set back to back with the Derbyshire border, over which lies Dennis Skinner's Bolsover fiefdom. Its three main towns were Sutton-in-Ashfield, Kirkby-in-Ashfield and Hucknall. In 1983 Hucknall was moved into the new seat of Sherwood, and replaced by D.H. Lawrence's Eastwood, smaller than Hucknall but at least as inclined to vote Labour. All the same, Ashfield was changing: the percentage of owner-occupiers rose from 50% in 1971 to 58% in 1981 and 70% in 1991. Labour's majority was cut to 6,000 in 1983 and 4,000 in 1987 and it still looked marginal. Then in 1992 the (new) Labour candidate Geoff Hoon secured a positive swing of over 7%, triple the national average, and the majority shot up to 13,000. In 1997 the pro-Labour swing was even larger, at over 11%, and the lead reached 23,000. It was reduced by 10,000 in 2001, but more as a result of a massive 17% drop in turnout than a 5.5% swing to the Tories. What can account for such a series of transformations?

Apart from the usual disruptive effects of a by-election, which causes ripples for some elections subsequently, the answer in Ashfield's case lies in the history and tribulations of the Nottinghamshire coalfield. Always associated with moderation rather than militancy, compared with the Yorkshire field, say, and even with Derbyshire next door, most Notts miners rejected Arthur Scargill's call for a strike in 1984, and carried on working, founding their own breakaway union, the UDM. The bitter wrangles between pickets and working miners caused a legacy of resentment in Nottinghamshire that pushed several seats towards the right and the Tories: in 1987 Mansfield was nearly lost and Sherwood, site of the most pits of all, saw an increased Tory majority. Then the pendulum swung the other way. Despite the protestations of gratitude and loyalty from Mrs Thatcher and other Conservative ministers to the working Notts miners and the UDM, the axe still fell on most Nottinghamshire pits in a frighteningly short time. Faced with the bitter prospect that Scargill's arguments might have been correct after all, and feeling betrayed by the Tories, the swing back to Labour in the Nottinghamshire coalfield was among the highest anywhere in Britain. Ashfield's Labour resurgence was following the same trend, but the 2001 drop in turnout suggests a lack of warm positive enthusiasm for New Labour and its untraditional leader. It must now be regarded as an ex-mining seat with a rich if chequered political and industrial history.

Social indices:			2001 Gen. Election:			
% Non-white	0.7		Lab	22,875	58.1	−7.0
% Prof/Man	21.0		C	9,607	24.4	+4.2
% Non-manual	39.3		LD	4,428	11.3	+1.6
£ Av prop val 2000	50 K		Ind	1,471	3.7	
% Increase 97–00	28.5		SA	589	1.5	
% Unemployed 2001	4.5		SLP	380	1.0	
% Decrease 97–01	1.5		Lab maj	13,268	33.7	
% Fin hard/Rank	25.8	193	Turnout		53.6	−16.4
% Pensioners	25.1		Elect	73,428		
% Prem mort/Rank	31	314				

Member of Parliament

Geoff Hoon, Secretary of State for Defence from 1999, a clever Europhile barrister and former MEP, is one of Tony Blair's blandly rising technocrats. Limitlessly confident if in a rather unmemorable way, an orthodox, impassive, career politician par excellence, he has conformed with fellow New Labour modernisers Darling, Mandelson and Byers in the removal of all facial hair – in his case a moustache. A Derby railwayman's son, born in 1953 and educated at Nottingham High School and Jesus College, Cambridge, elected MP in 1992, after ten years as the local representative in the European Parliament, he was soon a Whip (1994) and DTI spokesman (1995–97) and rose quickly in government under the patronage of Tony Blair's mentor, the Lord Chancellor, Lord Irvine – ambitious lawyers all, even, in his case, to the extent of advocating wigless barristers, cuts in legal aid, and conditional fees, an orthodox meld of populism and Treasury-driven expediency. As Defence Secretary, the Afghanistan bombing lent him some prominence but essentially in a walk-on part scripted by the Pentagon.

ASHFORD

The Ashford seat may be split fairly neatly into four sections. The prosperous northern suburbs such as Kennington provide the Conservatives' greatest strength within the town, and they managed to hold Ashford North in the county council elections even in their *annus terribilis* of 1997. On the other hand the London overspill estates around Stanhope in west Ashford returned a complete set of Labour councillors and quite a few of the 15,380 voters that party convinced in the 2001 General Election. Thirdly, the fastest-growing part of the town of Ashford lies in the private residential housing estates of Willesborough on its southern borders; here the Liberal Democrats dominate at local level. These three urban areas account for about half of the total population of the Ashford constituency, and almost suggest a three-way marginal (at least in a poor Tory year). However, the fourth and final area consists of the vast rural hinterland, extending through the hilly Weald to the prosperous and attractive town of Tenterden near the Sussex border. This is all solidly Conservative apart from an oasis of Lib Dem support around Pluckley (setting for the TV series *The Darling Buds of May* based on H.E. Bates's tales of rural idyll) and Smarden. This area on the western fringe of the seat may be affected by the proposed high-speed rail link to the Channel Tunnel, which has caused development disputes in the area.

Nevertheless, the rural area, the largest single element in the constituency, seems likely to continue to tip Ashford decisively to the Conservative interest. Damian Green managed to hold on by over 5,000 even in 1997, and his opposition locally is divided. There are high hopes for the expansion of Ashford's economy due to the opening of the Channel Tunnel, with an international rail passenger station and inland freight clearance depot, office and hotel development, and an expansion in employment. Ashford likes to claim that it is, or will be, 'the light at the end of the Tunnel'. Not, it might be thought, for Liberal Democrat or Labour though.

Social indices:			2001 Gen. Election:			
% Non-white	1.5		C	22,739	47.4	+6.0
% Prof/Man	34.3		Lab	15,380	32.1	+0.4
% Non-manual	56.7		LD	7,236	15.1	−4.6
£ Av prop val 2000	118 K		Grn	1,353	2.8	+1.6
% Increase 97–00	51.4		UKIP	1,229	2.6	
% Unemployed 2001	1.7		C maj	7,359	15.4	
% Decrease 97–01	2.2		Turnout		62.5	−12.1
% Fin hard/Rank	14.1	373	Elect	76,699		
% Pensioners	25.8					
% Prem mort/Rank	19	489				

Member of Parliament

Damian Green, Shadow Education Secretary from 2001, and previously a spokesman on Education and Environment under William Hague, was one of a handful of Kenneth Clarke-supporting One Nation Conservatives elected in 1997, who switched to the temporising and unorthodox Portillo candidacy in 2001 but returned to endorse Clarke in the final membership ballot. Born in 1958 and educated at a primary school in Barry, South Wales, Reading School and Balliol College, Oxford, he was a financial journalist with the BBC and Channel 4 before working as a speech writer for John Major (1993–94) and a member of the Downing Street policy unit. An evolving, out-of-time Europhile, he has urged his Tory Reform Group colleagues to resist the right-wing obsession with cutting public spending and pitch for higher standards in public services, but his trimming away from Kenneth Clarke in 2001 doubtless ensured his Shadow Cabinet post under Iain Duncan Smith. His membership of SPUC reflects his Catholic background.

ASHTON-UNDER-LYNE

The Boundary Commission is becoming more and more willing to create cross-borough constituencies in the metropolitan areas to ensure more equal electorates. In their most recent review they crossed London borough lines for the first time. All the other former metropolitan counties see paired boroughs, and in Greater Manchester there are now five sets: Salford/Wigan, Manchester/Trafford, Oldham/Rochdale, Tameside/Stockport and now, for the first time, Oldham/Tameside. This means that the borough of Tameside, east of Manchester, is the only one paired with two other boroughs – and it is not one of the larger units in Greater Manchester, either. The seat which crosses the line between Tameside and Oldham for the first time is Ashton-under-Lyne.

Ashton-under-Lyne used to consist essentially of that part of Tameside north of the river Tame – the old textile-working communities of Ashton, Droylsden and Mossley, all of which used to be in Lancashire (Stalybridge and Hyde south of the river were in Cheshire). This is a compact seat. There is little countryside here, but a chain of built-up valley communities, with plenty of terraced housing, and a significant Asian minority in Ashton, though not in Droylsden. In the 1997 boundary changes the furthest community to the east, Mossley, was switched to Stalybridge/ Hyde. Mossley only had some 8,000 electors, mainly Labour. However it was not to be missed, as over 23,000 voters came in from Oldham borough. These are situated in the two wards of the community of Failsworth, and in Hollinwood ward further towards the centre of Oldham. These are all strongly Labour, although Hollinwood sees Liberal Democrat activity in local elections. This was decidedly not reflected in the 2001 General Election results, although the fact that the seat approaches the troubled centre of Oldham quite closely accounts for one of the higher BNP shares in that summer of racial troubles in former Lancashire textile towns.

Social indices:			2001 Gen. Election:			
% Non-white	5.6		Lab	22,340	62.5	−5.0
% Prof/Man	21.5		C	6,822	19.1	+0.1
% Non-manual	45.3		LD	4,237	11.8	+2.1
£ Av prop val 2000	46 K		BNP	1,617	4.5	
% Increase 97–00	19.2		Grn	748	2.1	
% Unemployed 2001	3.3		Lab maj	15,518	43.4	
% Decrease 97–01	1.9		Turnout		49.1	−16.4
% Fin hard/Rank	28.2	156	Elect	72,820		
% Pensioners	25.1					
% Prem mort/Rank	47	70				

Member of Parliament

David Heyes replaced the veteran Labour MP Robert Sheldon who retired in 2001. A Tameside councillor who beat a Millbank-favoured candidate for the nomination, he sought selection as one committed to sustaining Labour's 'vital' union link and, as a former NALGO shop steward, urged the provision of public service by directly employed public sector workers on 'decent rates of pay'. Born in 1946 and educated at Blackley Technical High School, Manchester, and the Open University, he spent 25 years as a local government officer before first running his own computer graphic design business, and then managing a Citizens' Advice Bureau. Rising politically through activism in nearby Oldham as a councillor and party campaigner, he was, at the time of his selection, vice-chairman of Ashton-under-Lyne CLP, and reflects the importance of local roots under the OMOV selection system.

AYLESBURY

In the late 1980s Aylesbury was one of the affluent 'country' towns which was picked out as a site for 'designer' violence inflicted on Friday and Saturday nights by lager-swilling youths who could hardly be described as deprived (financially at least).

During the unwelcome attention that town gained at the time its troubles were variously seen as the product of boredom verging on nihilism, and even as the consequence of the amoral materialism of 'Thatcher's Britain'. In the 1990s under the gentler regime of John Major there was still danger in Aylesbury, with the occasional murder in the town centre streets. However, be that as it may – and Aylesbury's resemblance to the old 'wild' West has certainly been exaggerated – this constituency posed no threat to the party of Mrs Thatcher and Mr Major.

This seat is set in mid-Buckinghamshire. Only about a half of the electorate are in the town of Aylesbury itself, and these are certainly capable of menacing the Tories in local elections; five of the six Aylesbury town wards were won by the Liberal Democrats in the 2001 county council contests. The town's rapid expansion in the 1950s and 1960s did involve council housing (particularly on the northern side of town) and dreary private 'starter' homes, as well as some more upmarket development. The other half of the constituency is a very different kettle of fish. Here we have some of the most Tory territory in England, which remained loyal in the 1990s even as almost every other district council area (and actually every single other county council) rejected Conservative rule at municipal level. This includes Great Missenden, Princes Risborough, Stokenchurch and Wendover, and numerous villages.

In 2001, unsurprisingly, Aylesbury still returned a Tory MP. David Lidington's majority was slightly increased, from 8,000 to 10,000, and the Lib Dems in second place failed to squeeze Labour's support at all, which went up for the second successive election. Unless there is a move to tactical voting, Aylesbury will remain safe for the Conservatives next time.

Social indices:			2001 Gen. Election:			
% Non-white	5.0		C	23,230	47.3	+3.1
% Prof/Man	36.5		LD	13,221	26.9	−2.6
% Non-manual	60.5		Lab	11,388	23.2	+1.0
£ Av prop val 2000	137 K		UKIP	1,248	2.5	
% Increase 97–00	44.1		C maj	10,009	20.4	
% Unemployed 2001	1.1		Turnout		61.4	−11.5
% Decrease 97–01	1.1		Elect	80,002		
% Fin hard/Rank	10.2	462				
% Pensioners	20.7					
% Prem mort/Rank	16	521				

Member of Parliament

David Lidington, a Treasury spokesman from 2001, elected in 1992, is a mildly Eurosceptic orthodox loyalist who has served a variety of masters. He was on Hague's frontbench as part of the Home Affairs team (1999–2001), having been for two years Hague's PPS (1997–99). As a former Home Office adviser to Douglas

Hurd (1987–89), he had made a guarded defence of the Maastricht Treaty, favouring a Europe of 'variable geometry'. His Hurd connection did not preclude his signing the new-Thatcherite 'Raising the Standard' tract in 1991 calling for social cohesion but not without selling off health, welfare and pensions. Born in 1956, and educated at Haberdashers' Aske's and Sidney Sussex College, Cambridge (acquiring a doctorate in History, which he decently ignores in his mode of address), he was previously a PR man with RTZ and BP. Sensing the mood, and as his former PPS (1994–97, again at the Home Office), he voted for Michael Howard as leader in 1997, then prudently switched to Hague in the final ballots. He voted in 2001 for the racier trimming Portillo ticket, but unlike the hard-core Portillistas retained his frontbench post again under Michael Howard as Shadow Chancellor. Hurd/Hague/Howard/Portillo – pretty well a man for all factions.

AYR

The Conservative Party has been both fortunate and unlucky in Ayr in recent elections. On a couple of occasions they held the seat very narrowly in general elections; then in 1997 they suffered from a boundary change which removed one of their strongest areas and lost despite incurring one of the smallest pro-Labour swings anywhere in Britain – just 5%. In the inaugural contests for the Scottish Parliament in May 1999 they lost to Labour by just 25 votes, the closest of the 73 constituency battles; then in a by-election for that body in March 2000 the Tories gained it, with Labour falling to third behind the SNP, igniting hopes that Phil Gallie might repeat the result for them and return to Westminster the next year. However, he did not. The 2000 upset had been very much fuelled by the campaign against the Labour-led Scottish executive's decision to repeal the section of the Local Government Act forbidding the promotion of homosexuality, backed by such diverse elements as the wealthy Stagecoach company and Cardinal Winning of Glasgow; in 2001 a broader and quieter choice was made endorsing Labour's second term in office in Westminster.

Ayr is a divided town politically. The northern half contains most of the council estates and the commercial harbour. It is very strong Labour territory. The ward of Braehead, for example, produced an 88% vote for Labour in the district elections of May 1992 (just a month after their great disappointment in the General Election when they lost by 85 votes), Whitletts one of 89%.

On the other hand southern Ayr is a fashionable residential area and seaside resort. The constituency does still include Conservative sections. For 2001 it stretched up the coast, which is dotted with famous golf links, to include the seaside resort towns of Prestwick and Troon. Only parts of southern Ayr (a place once described as the 'Bournemouth of the north') were still in the seat. Boundary changes announced in February 2002, however, move the centre of gravity of the seat southwards, as Troon and Prestwick will be lost and replaced by New Cumnock and Carrick from George Foulkes's safe Labour seat. The era of Ayr close contests may be over.

Social indices:			2001 Gen. Election:			
% Non-white	0.5		Lab	16,801	43.6	−4.9
% Prof/Man	36.3		C	14,256	37.0	+3.2
% Non-manual	58.9		SNP	4,621	12.0	−0.6
% Unemployed 2001	5.2		LD	2,089	5.4	+0.7
% Decrease 97–01	2.2		SSP	692	1.8	
% Fin hard/Rank	28.4	153	UKIP	101	0.3	
% Prem mort/Rank	42	144	Lab maj	2,545	6.6	
			Turnout		69.3	−10.9
			Elect	55,630		

Member of Parliament

Sandra Osborne won Ayr in 1997 after seven years as a local councillor and selection from an all-women shortlist which duly excluded her husband, the candidate in 1992, from the running. Diminutive, bespectacled, snub-nosed and mousey, and PPS to Scottish Office Ministers Brian Wilson (1999–2001) and George Foulkes (2001–), she has followed a safely loyalist path, if unhappy about air traffic control privatisation, against which she (worried that privatisation would jeopardise plans for a new air traffic centre at Prestwick) made an impassioned speech in May 2000, but without – as a PPS – joining the 46 rebels who voted against the government. Daughter of a labourer, born in 1956 and educated at Camphill Senior Secondary School, Paisley, Jordanhill Teacher Training College and Strathclyde University, she formerly worked as a 'women's aid worker' with battered women. She was one of 36 beneficiaries of all-women shortlists elected in 1997 – and one of ten women Labour MPs returned for Scottish seats in 2001.

BANBURY

The electorate of this north Oxfordshire constituency is drawn mainly from the expanding towns of Banbury and Bicester (whose North electoral division was by far the most populous in the county in the June 2001 Elections, with 15,472 on the roll, having doubled in 20 years), the remainder being made up of the villages of north-east Oxfordshire. It might be thought that this is an identikit Tory seat in the comfortable south Midlands, but both Bicester and, especially, Banbury have large council estates and modern industrial development. Banbury is a Labour-voting town in an even year, at least in local elections, as wards like Neithrop, Ruscote and the newer Hardwick estate turn out heavily for them. Labour reduced the Tory majority in the constituency to around 5,000 in both the 1964 and 1966 General Elections. After many very lean years they at least re-established themselves in second place ahead of the Liberal Democrats in 1992; but this was at a distance of 16,720 votes behind the Conservative MP Tony Baldry. Then in 1997 they won a General Election again, and did slightly better even than they had in the 1960s, cutting Baldry's majority to 4,737 on a 10% swing. In 2001 the result was almost identical to that four years previously – very pleasing for New Labour nationally, of course, as they fulfilled Tony Blair's dream of the party's first ever second full term in office, but probably indicating that even at this high-water mark Banbury is beyond their reach. We are back in the 1964–66 situation, and the precedent of 1970 is rather ominous on all counts.

All of the new housing in the constituency is private, of course. The proportion of owner-occupiers in the seat has risen from less than half in 1971 to 55% in 1981 and 67% in 1991. There is still a strong armed forces presence around Bicester, and despite the closure of the USAF base at Upper Heyford the percentage of men employed in the services is higher than in any other seat in the south-east of England north of the Thames. There is also plenty of prosperous farming and some tourism, although most of the stone-cottaged villages on the edge of the Cotswolds are relatively undiscovered. Average house prices grew from £74,000 in 1997 to £120,000 at the turn of the new century.

With this economic base, it seems that the constituency will remain favourable to Tony Baldry and the Conservative Party. In a way that implies that it is somewhat misnamed, as Banbury itself continues to be outvoted by Bicester and the villages. A more accurate title might be Cherwell, after the district council area in which the whole seat is set; or, if the future of local government arrangements is uncertain, the prosaic but descriptive North Oxfordshire.

Social indices:			2001 Gen. Election:			
% Non-white	3.7		C	23,271	45.2	+2.3
% Prof/Man	30.5		Lab	18,052	35.0	+0.2
% Non-manual	51.9		LD	8,216	15.9	−0.8
£ Av prop val 2000	121 K		Grn	1,281	2.5	+1.6
% Increase 97–00	62.9		UKIP	695	1.3	+0.7
% Unemployed 2001	0.8		C maj	5,219	10.1	
% Decrease 97–01	1.1		Turnout		61.8	−13.7
% Fin hard/Rank	11.7	420	Elect	83,392		
% Pensioners	21.0					
% Prem mort/Rank	13	556				

Member of Parliament

Barrister and Freemason **Tony Baldry** became Conservative MP here in 1983, and served as a minister from 1990 to 1997, severally at Energy (1990), Environment (1990–94), Foreign and Commonwealth Office (1994–95) and ultimately as Fisheries Minister (1995–97), a post which tested his customary Europhilia, but not sufficiently to ensure his inclusion in William Hague's frontbench team following his three-ballot backing for Ken Clarke in 1997, a kamikaze strategy he repeated in the 2001 ballots. Born in 1950 and educated at the Quaker public school, Leighton Park, Reading, and at Sussex University, an engagingly pragmatic Wet, he graces the Tory Reform Group and the Bow Group. He was known as 'Baldrick' to his civil servants, one of whom on being asked by him which department was responsible for the decay of the West Pier at Brighton, replied 'Yours, Minister'. The demise of his ministerial career was duly iced in 2001 by his appointment to the chairmanship of the Select Committee on International Development where he was surrounded by a cluster of similar put-out-to-grass, sacked Labour ministers.

BANFF AND BUCHAN

From 1990 to 2000 the leader of the Scottish National Party was Alex Salmond, the honourable member for the division of Banff and Buchan, now comfortably his party's safest at Westminster. Salmond originally decided to give up this constituency in favour of the Scottish Parliament seat he won in May 1999, along with all the other five SNP MPs, but his mind was changed when it was apparent that this would leave the party's representatives in London without any experience at all in this arena, and their narrow victories in June 2001 suggest that he will add much needed weight to the new team.

This seat is fairly similar to the old East Aberdeenshire, which existed before 1983, and which is probably still best known as the constituency of the colourful and independent Conservative, Robert Boothby, from 1924 to 1958. In fact this part of Scotland has always been as inclined to the SNP as any, as Moray/Nairn, Banff and East Aberdeenshire were all held by their candidates between 1974 and 1979, and the two seats which succeeded these three after the 1983 redistribution were regained from the Tories in 1987. Salmond increased his majority to nearly 13,000 in 1997 and, alone suffering no real adverse swing in 2001, seems to have solved any problems the SNP ever had in Banff and Buchan.

The two largest towns in the seat are Fraserburgh and Peterhead, which expanded through North Sea oil in the 1970s; but both have their difficulties, with the fishing crisis in the North Sea and a major heroin dependency problem, particularly in Fraserburgh, rare for relatively small communities. There are several other small burghs on the northern coast and inland: Banff, Macduff, Portsoy, Rosehearty and Aberchirder.

Social indices:			2001 Gen. Election:			
% Non-white	0.3		SNP	16,710	54.2	−1.5
% Prof/Man	25.0		C	6,207	20.1	−3.7
% Non-manual	41.8		Lab	4,363	14.2	+2.3
% Unemployed 2001	2.1		LD	2,769	9.0	+3.0
% Decrease 97–01	1.0		SSP	447	1.5	
% Fin hard/Rank	20.8	258	UKIP	310	1.0	
% Prem mort/Rank	34	266	SNP maj	10,503	34.1	
			Turnout		54.5	−14.2
			Elect	56,496		

Member of Parliament

Alex Salmond, SNP Leader 1990–2000, decided to reverse his decision to join his five Westminster colleagues in ditching the Commons for the Scottish Parliament, so as to give effective leadership to the team of SNP novices elected in their place in 2001. Born in 1954, an electrician's son and adenoidal product of a Linlithgow council estate, he attended Linlithgow Academy and St Andrews University, where, prompted by its heavily Anglicised culture, he joined the SNP. Elected MP in 1987 and Leader by 1990, he set the party on a supposedly 'social democratic' trajectory in order to break into Labour's industrial heartlands and rid the SNP of its 'Tartan Tory' tag, despite its reliance in its rural small-town heartland on a petty bourgeois electorate. Sardonic in the manner of many Nationalist politicians, his claim to be 'one of the few practising Anglophiles in Scottish politics' belies a nascent Anglophobia in Scotland. Seen as 'quite a nasty piece of work' (Ian Aitken, the *Guardian*), 'with an instinct for the lower blow' (Matthew Parris, *The Times*), he described NATO bombing of Kosovo in March 1999 as 'unpardonable folly' – annoying Foreign Secretary Robin Cook from whom he had taken over as a racing tipster on the Glasgow Herald.

BARKING

In the 'Thatcher decade' of the 1980s, the former Labour strongholds of Dagenham and Barking in outer east London demonstrated a dramatic swing to the Conservatives, never before associated with this working-class environment. In Barking, formerly the seat of the colourful if scarcely typical MP Tom Driberg, Labour's majority in 1987 was reduced to just 3,400.

How had this haemorrhage of support come about? Barking is very much the older half of this Thames-side borough, once a fishing village growing up around its eponymous creek, later known for grittier but still worthy ventures, as the home of Joe Coral bookmakers and the East Anglian scrap metal company. The housing stock of this working-class town is still based on council estates and older terraces; there is little social change evident in the Census figures.

The explanation of Barking/Dagenham's unaccustomed marginal status in the 1980s lies more in the fact that the borough lies in the centre of that wedge north-east of London which demonstrated the largest swings away from Labour in the Thatcher years. The almost all-white skilled manual working-class areas such as those to a large extent employed by the Ford motor works at Dagenham abandoned their traditional allegiance to Labour, maybe as the party stressed its more ideological and dogmatic policies, such as those supportive of the rights of minorities. Barking and Dagenham are still close to the heart of the Cockney world, while areas to the west have become part of the multiracial 'inner city'. In order to recover here Labour have had to present a more attractive and electable image to the local voters. The first sign that they could do this came in 1992, when Jo Richardson's majority in Barking nearly doubled to 6,200. Then came walkover by-elections in June 1994, caused by Jo Richardson's death, and former leadership candidate Bryan Gould's re-emigration to New Zealand from Dagenham, which saw two potent women enter Parliament, Barking choosing Margaret Hodge. New Labour clearly assuaged all of the fears of the Barking electorate about their competence and moderation in government, as they re-elected Ms Hodge with a thumping 16,000 majority at the 1997 General Election.

There are signs though that not all Barking voters are convinced, even as Labour has changed its spots. In 2001 there was a 5% swing back to the Conservatives; and Barking was one of only five seats where the British National Party saved its deposit; one hopes that this evidence of right-wing sentiment does not betoken racial strife as in the other main areas of BNP success in that year, Oldham and Burnley.

Social indices:			2001 Gen. Election:			
% Non-white	9.4		Lab	15,302	60.9	−4.9
% Prof/Man	19.8		C	5,768	23.0	+5.4
% Non-manual	49.3		LD	2,450	9.8	+0.3
£ Av prop val 2000	81 K		BNP	1,606	6.4	+3.7
% Increase 97–00	43.3		Lab maj	9,534	37.9	
% Unemployed 2001	4.0		Turnout		45.5	−15.9
% Decrease 97–01	3.4		Elect	55,229		
% Fin hard/Rank	44.2	28				
% Pensioners	27.9					
% Prem mort/Rank	42	136				

Member of Parliament

Margaret Hodge, an MP since 1994 and an Education (and Employment) Minister since 1998, was a modishly left-wing Islington Council leader for ten years (1982–92), before emerging as a £50,000 consultant with Price Waterhouse and a Blairite moderniser. Born in 1944, small and animated, with a doll-like appearance belying her 57 years, she is the daughter of a German Jewish steel trader, was educated (privately) at Bromley High School for Girls, Oxford High School and the LSE, and worked as a market researcher until becoming a fulltime politician in Islington. To Quentin Letts (*Daily Telegraph*) she 'personifies privileged north London Labour'; to others, her bossy abrasiveness earns her the nickname 'Enver', recalling the late Albanian dictator Enver Hoxha (pronounced 'Hodga'). Made a minister in 1998 as reward for her very on-message chairmanship of the Education Select Committee (backing school league tables, scrapping student tuition grants, paying teachers by results and defending public schools), her career by 2001 was becalmed – still at Education – but too old to rise further.

BARNSLEY CENTRAL

Barnsley is one of those towns which are usually regarded as stereotypes of heavy industry and gritty northern popular culture. It used to be surrounded by pits and slag heaps, the headquarters of the once-powerful Yorkshire NUM, for so long the seat of the court of 'King' Arthur Scargill. However, Barnsley was the centre of the older western coalfield in South Yorkshire – the handful of more prosperous and modern pits which have so far survived the swingeing closure programme are to be found further east, around Doncaster. Barnsley Central is no longer a coal-mining constituency. But all around the town the debris of mining and other industry dominates a landscape which enjoys fewer redeeming features than most of the working-class stereotypes. There really are no leafy suburbs; no Conservative wards here.

For 34 years Barnsley was represented by a Labour MP with very different views from Arthur Scargill. Roy Mason was a staunch and tough right-winger, himself a miner at the age of 14. He held the seat from 1953 to 1987. The only serious opposition came from within his own party, and he faced a long series of threats to his candidacy. When he finally decided to retire voluntarily, in 1986, rumours were momentarily sparked that Arthur Scargill himself might bid for the succession. In fact the nomination was won by the chief administrative officer of the Yorkshire area NUM, Eric Illsley. No Labour candidate has many worries in Barnsley. At local level there are very few Conservative candidates, the burden of opposition (where there is any) often being taken by Ratepayers. The Liberal Democrats have no tradition here and little appeal. In 2001 Illsley's majority was ranked as the 13th safest for Labour in Britain, seven places down on 1997 due to a 6% movement to the Lib Dems, now in (a very distant) second place.

Like the two other Barnsley constituencies, Central is still slightly smaller than average which means that Barnsley is somewhat over-represented in Parliament. Given that its male unemployment rate, and percentage of persons with a limiting long-term illness, are both about 50% higher than the national average, and that it has a plethora of other social and economic problems, this can scarcely be resented.

Social indices:			2001 Gen. Election:			
% Non-white	0.8		Lab	19,181	69.6	−7.4
% Prof/Man	22.4		LD	4,051	14.7	+5.2
% Non-manual	42.0		C	3,608	13.1	+3.3
£ Av prop val 2000	43 K		SA	703	2.6	
% Increase 97–00	16.5		Lab maj	15,130	54.9	
% Unemployed 2001	4.4		Turnout		45.8	−13.8
% Decrease 97–01	2.9		Elect	60,086		
% Fin hard/Rank	30.8	124				
% Pensioners	24.4					
% Prem mort/Rank	43	126				

Member of Parliament

Eric Illsley is one of 15 frontbenchers dropped by Tony Blair on forming his government in 1997, despite having previously been a Northern Ireland spokesman and Whip. He is also one of nine MPs out of a PLP of 412 who were previously sponsored by the Miners Union, though he came from behind an NUM desk rather than from a coal face. Born in 1955, educated at Barnsley Holgate Grammar School, Barnsley Technical College, and Leeds University, he was elected in 1987. Without a frontbench role after 1997, he was parked on the Foreign Affairs Select Committee and piloted a Bill concerning the Lloyds TSB merger and its effect on employees, all the while filling out as backmost bench ballast for the Whips. He rebelled on cuts in Incapacity Benefit in 1999.

BARNSLEY EAST AND MEXBOROUGH

Back in the 1950s and 1960s, if one was to inquire which was the safest Labour seat in England, a fair bet would have been that the reply would have been Hemsworth. This was the seat at the heart of the Yorkshire coalfield where it was reputed that the Labour votes were weighed and not counted. When the metropolitan counties of West and South Yorkshire were created, though, the seat of Hemsworth was split in two. The eponymous town is itself in West Yorkshire, and has taken its electorally famous name with it. But in many ways its true successor was Barnsley East, to which half its electorate was assigned, and which was the safest Labour seat in the whole of Britain in percentage majority terms in 1983 and 1987.

The reason for these record performances is not hard to divine. The constituency consists of one-class towns which were almost all created by and for one industry – coal. With the decline and indeed virtual extinction of the coal industry these battered communities have fought hard to make a living and unemployment has dropped from 15% to under 6% between 1991 and 2001. The towns are too small to sustain a middle class of any size and prosperous residential areas, and they are all overwhelmingly Labour: Thurnscoe, Goldthorpe, Bolton upon Dearne, Darfield, Wombwell, Mexborough (added for the 1997 Election). They look old-fashioned, with unmodernised shopping facilities and housing spruced up with no other innovations than the rash of satellite dishes which always betokens a working-class environment. The constituency is 99.5% white and in many ways lies in the very depths of England.

This seat has slipped down the list of the very safest for Labour in the last couple of elections although Jeff Ennis won in 2001 by nearly 17,000 votes. Here, as in several other areas of Labour hegemony, the Liberal Democrats have made a marked if limited advance, from less than 10% to nearly 16% between 1992 and 2001. New Labour, though, can hardly be unhappy with a share of 67%; there was not exactly an electoral earthquake east of Barnsley.

Social indices:			2001 Gen. Election:			
% Non-white	0.5		Lab	21,945	67.5	–5.6
% Prof/Man	22.4		LD	5,156	15.9	+5.5
% Non-manual	42.6		C	4,024	12.4	+1.0
£ Av prop val 2000	46 K		SLP	722	2.2	–0.6
% Increase 97–00	17.7		UKIP	662	2.0	
% Unemployed 2001	4.5		Lab maj	16,789	51.6	
% Decrease 97–01	3.2		Turnout		49.5	–14.4
% Fin hard/Rank	28.9	145	Elect	65,655		
% Pensioners	25.4					
% Prem mort/Rank	39	199				

Member of Parliament

Jeff Ennis, elected at a 1996 by-election, is a former teacher, born in 1952, educated at Hemsworth Grammar School and Redland College, Bristol. With only four former miners left as MPs on the dying Yorkshire coalfield, the best he can do is evoke his miner father and both miner grandfathers. A very big and burly moustached loyalist, he managed to stop himself resigning as Tessa Jowell's PPS over lone parent benefit cuts in 1997, but as her ex-PPS in 2001 was assigned to the Education Select Committee.

BARNSLEY WEST AND PENISTONE

This seat was created in 1983 when just over half of the former Penistone constituency was moved into the Sheffield Hillsborough seat. The remainder was placed together with three wards from the former Barnsley seat: the towns of Darton and Worsbrough and the western ward of Park in Barnsley itself. The two elements are almost equally balanced, which justifies the name of the seat; and the Commission must have felt they got their borders right in this part of South Yorkshire, for no further changes were proposed in their most recent report, in 1995.

The constituency rolls down from sheep-farming moorland at the north end of the Peak District through the small towns of Penistone, Dodworth and Hoyland to the outskirts of Barnsley. It is not as monolithically Labour as the other two Barnsley divisions, for both Penistone wards, East and West, have been won by Tories even as recently as May 2000 when their national ratings were in a deep and long trough, and the Conservatives have at least bothered to contest most of the other wards – which is far from universal in local elections in Barnsley until very recently, when a concerted effort has been made, although it has led to abysmal showings such as the 28 votes and 43 votes polled successively in 1999 and 2000 in Wombwell North ward (East and Mexborough constituency) by a Ms Grace and a Ms Cuss respectively.

Despite this, and despite the aberrant Lib Dem increase in share in 1997 (but not in 2001), Barnsley West and Penistone must be classed as a totally safe Labour seat.

Social indices:			2001 Gen. Election:			
% Non-white	0.5		Lab	20,244	58.6	–0.7
% Prof/Man	29.2		C	7,892	22.8	+4.5
% Non-manual	48.2		LD	6,428	18.6	+0.6
£ Av prop val 2000	62 K		Lab maj	12,352	35.7	
% Increase 97–00	26.4		Turnout		52.9	–12.1
% Unemployed 2001	3.6		Elect	65,291		
% Decrease 97–01	2.0					
% Fin hard/Rank	22.2	240				
% Pensioners	25.8					
% Prem mort/Rank	34	275				

Member of Parliament

Mick Clapham, an ex-miner, born in 1943 and educated at Barnsley Technical College, Leeds Poly and Bradford University, was elected in 1992. As a Campaign Grouper he was actively rebellious against the government, resigning as Alan Millburn's PPS over lone parent child benefit cuts, and voting against the Whips on military action against Iraq, the Prime Minister's right to nominate life peers, curbing jury trials, cutting disability benefit, restoring the link between pensions and average earnings, and air traffic control privatisation. An ex-Scargill ally who has since attacked his former patron's 'Stalinist' excesses, his strikingly arched eyebrows give him a quizzical look, for some recalling a character out of 'Sons and Lovers'. In a PLP of 412 MPs he is one of 10 ex-coalminers.

BARROW AND FURNESS

Tucked away beyond the Lake District in west Cumbria lies one of Britain's least known and most remote industrial districts. The largest of the towns here is

Barrow-in-Furness, a port and shipbuilding centre strongly associated with the name of Vickers. Britain's nuclear submarines are constructed in the harbour here, but the economy has suffered all the threats and alarms to which single-industry towns are subject. Its recent political response has been iconoclastic and widely variable.

The Barrow-in-Furness constituency had been fairly safely Labour from the war until 1983, electing for the last 17 of those years a man who reached Cabinet rank, Albert Booth. Then came one of the biggest upsets of the 1983 Election, as Booth was ousted really rather easily by a swing of about 10% to a Conservative imported from Manchester, Cecil Franks. The core of the Tory success in the constituency in 1983 lay in Barrow itself. Many seats with a strong defence establishment presence did well for the Conservatives in 1983: Portsmouth North, Newbury, Aldershot and others. It could well be that Labour – and Albert Booth – suffered from the feeling abroad in the nation that they might indulge in anti-defence policies and specifically anti-nuclear aspirations.

In 1987, assisted for the first time by his incumbency vote, Franks suffered very little in the way of an anti-government swing, and it seemed that if Barrow retained its faith in the Conservatives' ability to maintain the 'home industry' he would be the favourite to retain it in 1992. But Barrow sprung another unpleasant surprise on its MP in 1992. Another large swing, 6.8%, replaced Franks with Labour's John Hutton. It was one of their best performances in a key target constituency, and it was out of line with other swings in Cumbria.

Then in 1997 the Conservative vote dropped by 14%, higher even than the national or regional north-western averages. In 2001 the result closely reflected the national changes, including a turnout drop of 12%, but Hutton retained a majority of nigh on 10,000, and Barrow, although apparently unpredictable, looks safe for Labour for the foreseeable future.

Its wards demonstrate an array of political characteristics. The Labour vote is very heavy in the low-cost private housing around the docks, and on Barrow Island and Walney Island. However, there are relatively few council estates in Barrow, and the owner-occupation rate surpassed 85% in the 1991 Census. There are good Tory wards in west and north Barrow, most notably Hawcoat; and the 'Furness' part of the seat, including the small towns of Dalton and Ulverston, leans to the right as well. This mixture has shown it can elect either main party, and the present position owes much to New Labour's appeal as Britain enters a new century.

Social indices:			2001 Gen. Election:			
% Non-white	0.5		Lab	21,724	55.7	−1.6
% Prof/Man	24.6		C	11,835	30.3	+3.1
% Non-manual	45.5		LD	4,750	12.2	+3.3
£ Av prop val 2000	47 K		UKIP	711	1.8	
% Increase 97–00	20.2		Lab maj	9,889	25.3	
% Unemployed 2001	3.6		Turnout		60.3	−11.8
% Decrease 97–01	2.5		Elect	64,746		
% Fin hard/Rank	24.2	210				
% Pensioners	26.0					
% Prem mort/Rank	39	197				

Member of Parliament

A staunch Blairite elected in 1992, **John Hutton**, a Health Minister from 1998, after a year as Margaret Beckett's PPS, is a slight, gaunt-looking introvert, who as MP for Barrow prudently defends the local defence industry by urging more Trident nuclear submarines. A former law lecturer at Newcastle Polytechnic (1981–92), he was born in London in 1955, son of a salesman and labourer, and educated at Westcliff High School, Southend, and Magdalen College, Oxford. His boss at Health, Alan Milburn, is his former flatmate, and another rising Blairite; Stephen Byers is a former colleague from Newcastle Poly.

BASILDON

There is a great myth about Basildon. It derives from the fact that this Essex New Town seat reported its result earlier than any other marginal on the night of the April 1992 General Election. The Conservative David Amess held on, with a huge grin, and it has subsequently become widely accepted that this was the point at which the Tories' fourth successive General Election victory became clear, confounding the predictions of the pollsters and the pundits. Basildon also came to be seen as some kind of a political weathervane, the seat that Labour must win if they were ever to form another government. Both these perceptions were untrue. Basildon was untypical on the night of 9 April 1992, and it is a very untypical seat in general.

The swing to Labour in Basildon between the 1987 and 1992 results was just 1.3%, little more than a third of that in all Conservative–Labour marginals (3.5%). If the whole country had behaved like Basildon the Tories would have been back with an overall majority of over 70, not 21; taking Basildon as the guide would have produced more inaccurate predictions than were actually made. What is more, it is known that Basildon had been relatively poor ground for Labour for some years. Basildon actually swung to the Conservatives in 1987. It is clear that people who move to English New Towns often see themselves in a different way from those who remain in traditional working-class communities, and they vote differently as a result. Basildon, like other New Towns in Essex and Hertfordshire, saw a long-term swing to the right.

Then in 1997 Labour did indeed win Basildon, and very easily too. David Amess had signalled his lack of confidence by deserting the site of his famous triumph for the safer Southend West. His successor as Tory candidate, John Baron, suffered a disastrous 14% drop in share of vote, and Labour's Angela Smith won by over 13,000 votes. Yet Basildon was still untypical, this time recording a higher than average swing to Labour. This was in line with other south-eastern New Towns like Harlow and Hemel Hempstead – whose instrumental voters had suffered from the slump under John Major's government. Many returned to their ancestral loyalties, over-compensating for the defections of the 1980s. In 2001 Basildon swung back markedly to the Tories, although not by so much as other south Essex divisions.

Basildon is the largest of the batch of New Towns which were designated by the Reith Committee immediately after the Second World War, and this seat consists mainly of its planned neighbourhoods: Fryerns, Lee Chapel North, Nethermayne, Pitsea, Langdon Hills and Vange. Both New Towns and the county of Essex have tended towards exaggerated electoral swings reflecting changes of political mood and fashion and it should still not be assumed that its results have a much wider significance for the country as a whole beyond the domain of Essex New Town man and woman.

Social indices:			2001 Gen. Election:			
% Non-white	2.1		Lab/Coop	21,551	52.7	−3.1
% Prof/Man	24.5		C	13,813	33.8	+3.0
% Non-manual	54.1		LD	3,691	9.0	+0.3
£ Av prop val 2000	80 K		UKIP	1,397	3.4	
% Increase 97–00	36.1		SA	423	1.0	
% Unemployed 2001	2.7		L/C maj	7,738	18.9	
% Decrease 97–01	2.7		Turnout		55.1	−16.6
% Fin hard/Rank	23.1	224	Elect	74,121		
% Pensioners	20.4					
% Prem mort/Rank	25	426				

Member of Parliament

Angela Smith, reaching the frontbench as an Assistant Whip from 2001, and previously (1999–2001) Paul Boateng's PPS, won Basildon in 1997 after being selected from an all-women shortlist. A personable, short-tongued, toothy, little-girl-voiced animal rights campaigner – who ran PR for the League Against Cruel Sports from 1983 to 1995, before working as Alan Michael's research assistant from 1995 to 1997, she represents in her commitment to fox hunting bans a leading preoccupation among contemporary Labour activists, and speaks regularly at vegetarian-catered animal welfare fringe meetings at Labour Party conferences. The daughter of a Ford car factory worker, she was born in 1959 and educated locally at Chalvedon School, and at Leicester Polytechnic, married her history teacher, served eight years on Essex County Council, three as Chief Whip, and backs 'Cuba Solidarity'.

BASINGSTOKE

The originators of the Almanacs of American and British Politics motored down the M3 to Basingstoke on 7 June 2001, choosing this seat as a worthy benchmark of modern British electoral opinion to observe it participating (rather unenthusiastically) in the democratic process. The seat did not change hands that day, but the fact that it was indeed close implied that Labour had won another historic landslide overall majority and a second full term of government for the first time in the party's history.

The Conservatives only won Basingstoke by some 800 votes, although Andrew Hunter had had a notional majority of nearly 18,000 five years previously. In fact Labour's Jon Hartley was even closer to prevailing than his predecessors had been in previous landslide years like 1945, 1966 and even 1997; there have, however, been great changes in this area over these years.

Basingstoke has been one of the most rapidly expanding towns in Britain in the post-war epoch. In 1951 it was a north Hampshire country town of 16,000 souls. By

1961 it had reached 26,000, and then the population doubled in ten years. The massive private and council housing developments continued to burgeon on the north and west sides of the town, and population increase was noted even in the 1991 Census in areas such as Chineham (population 977 in 1981 and 5,745 in 1991). Safely Conservative even in 1945, it was felt by some that the element of 'London overspill' might create chances for Labour or for the centre parties here.

This was not, however, initially to prove the case. Labour could win some of the 'council estate' wards at local levels, such as South Ham and Norden, and did indeed manage to recover second place in the 1992 General Election, but the recent development in Basingstoke has been private. Chineham, mentioned above, does not have a single council-built house. The remaining villages are also very Conservative. This is a prosperous and booming area. Situated just off the M3 motorway, it is not only popular among commuters to south-west London but for companies, especially those in modern high-tech industries, moving their headquarters out of the capital. On leaving the M3, the visitor will observe the most recent signs of further expansion of office space reminiscent of an American 'edge city' in Orange County California, or Fairfax County Virginia, near Washington DC's Dulles International Airport.

As in so many New Towns in southern England, demographics and economics both seemed to favour the Conservative Party in the 1970s, 1980s and early 1990s – but then to swing massively towards New Labour. It now has marginal status, with Labour needing a further 1% swing to win for the first time ever.

Social indices:			2001 Gen. Election:			
% Non-white	2.7		C	20,490	42.7	–0.6
% Prof/Man	35.3		Lab	19,610	40.9	+1.7
% Non-manual	61.4		LD	6,693	13.9	–3.1
£ Av prop val 2000	131 K		UKIP	1,202	2.5	
% Increase 97–00	54.9		C maj	880	1.8	
% Unemployed 2001	0.8		Turnout		60.7	–13.5
% Decrease 97–01	1.3		Elect	79,110		
% Fin hard/Rank	13.4	387				
% Pensioners	17.8					
% Prem mort/Rank	18	503				

Member of Parliament

Tall and burly pipesmoking **Andrew Hunter** has been MP here since 1983. He is a hard right-winger as a former defender of white South Africa and as one – as he sees it – 'of a handful of mainland (Tory) MPs who have consistently opposed the sell-out to terrorism in Northern Ireland' (i.e. voted with hardline Unionists against all power-sharing). Born in 1943, the son of an RAF squadron leader, and educated at St George's School, Harpenden, Jesus College, Cambridge, and (ecclesiastically but inconclusively) at Westcott House, Cambridge, he was a Classics master at Harrow for 12 years. The demise of white South Africa leaving him with Northern Ireland as his leading preoccupation, he was nonetheless denied the Northern Ireland Select Committee chairmanship on account of his hard-line reputation. In 2001, as an Iain

Duncan Smith supporter, he was told to drop his membership of the voluntary-repatriation-advocating Monday Club.

BASSETLAW

There is no town or village called 'Bassetlaw'. This seat in the far north of Nottinghamshire is named after a medieval 'hundred', or group of parishes. The chief town, however, is undoubtedly Worksop. Worksop, as its unglamorous and down-to-earth name seems to imply, is an industrial centre, long dependent on mining. Until recently it boasted three working pits – Manton, Streetly and Shireoaks. The constituency has, of course, suffered from the destruction of the coal-mining industry which has hit Nottinghamshire particularly hard in recent years. There remains a Labour majority in Worksop's council estates and internal pit villages, like Manton and Rhodesia. There are other pit towns and villages in the seat outside Worksop, like Warsop in the Meden valley and Harworth, where there was a famous strike in 1936 which signalled the end of the schism between the official and breakaway unions which had followed the 1926 strike, in a pungent precursor of the events in the county after the great conflict of 1984–85. Although most of these pits were first sunk in the twentieth century, that epoch also encompassed the death of all mining in the Bassetlaw division except for at Harworth.

The resentment felt by the Notts miners against the Conservative government which apparently has turned its back on them, seems likely to keep Bassetlaw safely Labour, although it does include Tory areas. Worksop's hilly South ward is an attractive residential area, heading out towards the public school, Worksop College, and the remnants of Sherwood Forest and the Dukeries. It also includes swathes of villages which have few Labour voters and are often left unopposed to the Tories in local contests: places like Blyth on the A1, and Clayworth, Everton, Rampton with its high-security hospital, Ranskill, Sturton and Sutton.

This far north-eastern segment of Nottinghamshire, the part of the seat beneath which coal has never been mined, is socially and politically much more like the flatlands of Lincolnshire just over the county boundary towards Gainsborough – where Labour only just hold on to second place. However, the rural and agricultural element of Bassetlaw should continue to be outvoted by its mining – or ex-mining – western half. In 2001 the Labour vote went down by nearly 8,000 while those for the Conservatives and Liberal Democrats remained almost identical to 1997 – hardly a ringing endorsement of Tony Blair's first four years in office.

Social indices:			2001 Gen. Election:			
% Non-white	0.9		Lab	21,506	55.3	−5.7
% Prof/Man	27.1		C	11,758	30.2	+5.3
% Non-manual	44.7		LD	4,942	12.7	+2.5
£ Av prop val 2000	61 K		SLP	689	1.8	
% Increase 97–00	30.4		Lab maj	9,748	25.1	
% Unemployed 2001	4.2		Turnout		56.9	−13.4
% Decrease 97–01	1.8		Elect	68,302		
% Fin hard/Rank	21.0	253				
% Pensioners	24.1					
% Prem mort/Rank	33	284				

Member of Parliament

John Mann, elected as a replacement for the retiring Joe Ashton, is one of a clutch of political union apparatchiks elected in 2001, having worked for five years as head of research at AEEU, five more as a National Training Officer at the TUC, and from 1995 to 2000 at Millbank as Labour Party Trade Union Liaison Officer – with a spell of four years on Lambeth Council. Full-faced and bombastic, born in 1960 and educated at Bradford Grammar School and Manchester University, the selection process for the seat was not universally approved – with even his own union having encouraged him to bid for the nomination in the Chesterfield seat being vacated by Tony Benn, and with allegations of postal vote irregularities (with a third of the votes having been cast postally). With business interests in East-West trade, he favours EU enlargement, but otherwise comes to Westminster with a reputation as a Millbank 'fixer' and has been described by the left-wing paper, *Red Pepper*, as an 'anti-left machinator', from his time in the National Association of Labour Students. Author of a Fabian pamphlet entitled 'Labour Youth: The Missing Generation' (1986), he stresses his scholarship- boy status at the fee-paying Bradford Grammar School.

BATH

Don Foster, the Liberal Democrat MP for Bath, seems to get stronger and stronger, in his constituency at least. In 2001, for the first time, he obtained over 50% of the vote here for the first time, and his third victory. He is now more solidly established than his distinguished predecessor ever was.

The Conservative Party emerged triumphant from the General Election of 1992; but its chairman, who had headed the national organisation through the campaign, lost his own seat. Many would consider Chris Patten to be a severe loss to British politics as well as to his party, as he decided to migrate to take on the thorny and inscrutable problems of the Governorship of Hong Kong, followed by the equally complex international issues of the European Commission.

In many ways Bath seemed to be a suitable seat for the civilised, cultured, moderate, thoughtful Patten. It is one of the most attractive cities in England, a major spa town known best for its Royal Crescent, the Roman baths and the abbey. There are many delightful residential neighbourhoods lining the bowl of hills surrounding the city. Yet despite the apparent elegance and affluence of Bath, it had not in recent years been a Tory stronghold. Labour came within 800 votes of winning the seat in 1966, and in the 1974 Elections Bath looked like a strong three-way marginal as the Liberal Christopher Mayhew forced his way into a strong second place. In 1983 the *Guardian* journalist Malcolm Dean took 36% of the vote in the SDP's first contest, and in 1987 he did even better – nearly 43%, less than 1,500 votes behind Chris Patten. In 1992 a new candidate from another new party, Don Foster of the Liberal Democrats, ousted Patten by 3,768 – really rather easily.

What was the problem? Patten's absence from his local front line cannot have helped – either during the last three or four weeks of intensive battle, when he had to commute to and from Central Office in London, or indeed during his years as a Cabinet Minister holding a marginal seat. The local Liberal Democrats were free to campaign tirelessly in one of their top target seats. What is more, they could squeeze the large residual anti-Tory vote in the less charming parts of the city, such as Southdown and Twerton in west and south-west Bath. Finally there was the regional element: the south-west is the Liberal Democrats' strongest area. As in the other great western spa, Cheltenham, a combination of special and regional factors finished off the Tory defence.

Social indices:			2001 Gen. Election:			
% Non-white	2.4		LD	23,372	50.5	+2.0
% Prof/Man	41.9		C	13,478	29.1	−2.1
% Non-manual	63.5		Lab	7,269	15.7	−0.7
£ Av prop val 2000	157 K		Grn	1,469	3.2	+2.1
% Increase 97–00	73.2		UKIP	708	1.5	+0.9
% Unemployed 2001	1.7		LD maj	9,894	21.4	
% Decrease 97–01	3.7		Turnout		64.9	−11.4
% Fin hard/Rank	12.3	410	Elect	71,372		
% Pensioners	31.2					
% Prem mort/Rank	19	486				

Member of Parliament

Don Foster, who won the seat in 1992 by ousting the Tory Party chairman, Chris Patten, in 2001 became Liberal Democrat Transport spokesman, having previously been Shadow Education (1992–99) and Environment (1999–2001) spokesman. An ambitious and abrasive public school science teacher (at Sevenoaks for six years), he was born in 1947, the son of a policeman-turned-parson, and educated at Lancaster Royal Grammar School and Keele University, and reached Bath via educational research at Bristol University. He takes an urban politically correct line against rural interests such as gun control and hunting, and a suburban line against 'the scourge of leylandii', and backs Lib-Lab tactical voting. He thought better of running – without hope – for the Lib Dem leadership in 1999.

BATLEY AND SPEN

The Times newspaper's list of the June 2001 Election results recorded a swing to the Conservatives in Batley and Spen of 0.03%. This did of course mask a considerable number of changes of electoral mind and behaviour, not least a reduction in turnout of 8,453 voters, but it nevertheless represented no progress for the Conservatives in a target seat in one of the regions which had shown the most hopeful signs of recovery for them between 1997 and 2001. It must have been especially disappointing for their returning candidate, Elizabeth Peacock.

Known as an active, feisty and independent local MP, Mrs Peacock managed to achieve one of the better results among defending Conservatives in 1997. She only lost by 6,141 votes. In previous years, this would have been regarded as a terrible result for an incumbent, but actually her share was one of the half dozen to drop least in seats won by Labour. She had also done well to suffer no adverse swing at all in her previous defence in 1992.

Batley and Spen is a predominantly working-class seat. It includes the decidedly Labour town of Batley, whose eastern ward is home for a large Asian minority (a third of its whole population), and whose western half has extensive council housing. The Conservatives fight back in the smaller, semi-rural communities such as Birstall and Birkenshaw, Gomersal and Oakenshaw, and Cleckheaton. Before the creation of the metropolitan borough of Kirklees in the 1970s most of these communities were already lumped together for local government purposes in the borough of Spenborough, created in 1955 and named after the river Spen. The Spen element in this constituency is almost all-white, strongly owner-occupied, and possessed of conservative cultural values.

Perhaps one of the consequences of this distrust of change is an unwillingness to move against an incumbent MP, which seems already to be assisting Mike Wood as it did Elizabeth Peacock, and it will be interesting to see how he fares in his own third contest here in 2005 or 2006.

Social indices:			2001 Gen. Election:			
% Non-white	10.9		Lab	19,224	49.9	+0.5
% Prof/Man	27.1		C	14,160	36.7	+0.4
% Non-manual	48.1		LD	3,989	10.3	+1.5
£ Av prop val 2000	55 K		Grn	595	1.5	+0.7
% Increase 97–00	22.9		UKIP	574	1.5	
% Unemployed 2001	2.8		Lab maj	5,064	13.1	
% Decrease 97–01	2.0		Turnout		60.5	−12.6
% Fin hard/Rank	27.8	161	Elect	63,665		
% Pensioners	23.0					
% Prem mort/Rank	35	262				

Member of Parliament

Labour's **Mike Wood** is one of a handful of the huge 1997 intake who joined the Campaign Group and has rebelled regularly against the government, in his case 20 times, making him the 25th most rebellious Labour MP in the 1997–2001 House. A bearded social worker for 32 years, son of a foundry worker, he was born in 1946 and educated elongatedly, and in part ecclesiastically, at Nantwich and Acton Grammar School, Nantwich, Salisbury and Wells Theological College, Leeds University and Leeds Polytechnic. He has kicked over the Blairite traces on lone parent benefit cuts, disability benefits, linking pensions to average earnings, freedom of information, and air traffic control sell-off. Only four of Labour's 183-strong 1997 new intake were more rebellious than he, but oddly all this has been done quietly, with few questions or interventions to his name. In the new House in 2001 he was part of an 11-strong Labour rebellion against the bombing of Afghanistan, and in January 2002 co-signed an anti-Euro letter to the *Guardian*.

BATTERSEA

In 1997, when Labour's Martin Linton gained Battersea on a 10% swing from the Conservative MP John Bowis, he put an end to what is surely the Conservative

Party's greatest success story in modern British electoral politics. What was once the inner-city, deprived site of two Labour constituencies was still one of the most reliable Tory-voting places in the country in local elections; and Battersea had appeared to be attaining the status of a safe Conservative parliamentary seat too. This was the 'Wandsworth effect', named after the London borough which contains Battersea and also the Putney and Tooting divisions.

Wandsworth is often referred to as the 'model' of Conservative local government, the party's 'flagship' authority, and a source of much pride and joy for Central Office. When we attempt the task of explaining the remarkable swing of Battersea to the right in parliamentary elections, we should indeed start with the recent history of the borough of Wandsworth. In May 1986, before the days of the poll tax, the Conservatives only held on to the borough by the narrowest of margins, 31 seats to 30. Then came the privatising, cost-cutting, and tax-reducing regime led by Sir Paul Beresford, the New Zealand-born dentist who now sits in Parliament as MP for Mole Valley. With some assistance from central government, the Wandsworth Tories managed to reduce the local community charge level to a derisory figure. Faced with the relatively vast sums levied in neighbouring Labour councils like Lambeth, the voters opted for self-interest in May 1990 and returned the Tories with a much increased majority of 35–48 councillors to 13 for Labour. Only one ward within the Battersea constituency resisted the landslide. The habit of voting Conservative locally stuck, and even outlasted the poll tax; in May 1994 the Tories never looked like losing Wandsworth and held on with a comfortable majority of 29. There had only been a 2% swing against them.

There is certainly an association between the success of the Tories in local government in Wandsworth and their positive swings in Battersea. However, there is another critical factor too: the change in the socio-economic nature of the constituency over recent years. Inner-city Battersea contains some of London's best-known, if unglamorous, landmarks: the shell of the Battersea power-station, the Dogs' Home, Clapham Junction, the new Covent Garden Market, the former *Observer* newspaper building on Queenstown Road. It includes the rather seedy Balham: in the words of the late Peter Sellers, the Gateway to the South. Wandsworth itself is still dominated by the John Young brewery. Most of Clapham is in the seat. Yet all this territory has been gentrifying since the 1970s. Young urban professionals invested in terraced housing on the unfashionable side of the river. There were jokes about 'South Chelsea' and 'Cla'ham'. Wine bars sprouted on Battersea High Street.

The raw figures amply sustain such subjective evidence. In the period between the 1981 and 1991 Censuses, the proportion of owner-occupied housing in the Battersea constituency rose from 29% to 49%, that of council housing fell from 39% to 23%. Even more strikingly, the proportion of non-white residents actually fell, from 21.6% to 21.1% – this is the only seat in the country with an ethnic minority presence of over one-fifth where this is true. The percentage of households with pensioners living alone is now among the lowest in London. Nearly half of all employees were in professional and managerial occupations by 1991, and the manual working-class proportion was lower than average for London.

These social changes assisted the Conservatives in the 1980s and early 1990s, but New Labour in prospect and in office has not threatened the prosperity which underpins the lifestyles of Battersea residents, and indeed with average house values rising by no less than 72% to £263,000 in the period of the first Blair government, while mortgage interest rates fell substantially along with unemployment and inflation, it is scarcely surprising that Battersea swung even further towards the incumbent government in June 2001.

Social indices:			2001 Gen. Election:			
% Non-white	21.1		Lab	18,498	50.3	−0.5
% Prof/Man	48.0		C	13,445	36.5	−2.9
% Non-manual	70.7		LD	4,450	12.1	+4.7
£ Av prop val 2000	263 K		Ind	411	1.1	
% Increase 97–00	72.0		Lab maj	5,053	13.7	
% Unemployed 2001	3.5		Turnout		54.5	−16.3
% Decrease 97–01	3.3		Elect	67,495		
% Fin hard/Rank	26.4	182				
% Pensioners	18.2					
% Prem mort/Rank	43	128				

Member of Parliament

Martin Linton, Labour's 1997 victor, a tall, half-Swedish journalist, was Stockholm-born in 1944, son of an Anglican parson, and educated at Christ's Hospital and Pembroke College, Oxford, and worked – from 1966 – successively on the *Mail*, *Financial Times*, *Labour Weekly*, *Daily Star*, and the *Guardian*. Known mainly as an advocate of PR and transparent party funding, and for a rather earnest mien, he is also an accomplished tickler-of-the-ivories at Battersea Labour Party soirees at the annual party conference, and thinks he's done far more as an MP than as a *Guardian* journalist. PPS to Baroness Blackstone from 2001, he is interested in speculating about the 'Third Way' and has written about 'the Swedish Road to Socialism'.

BEACONSFIELD

South Buckinghamshire is the most Conservative part of the most Conservative county in England – the only one of which the party retained overall control in the 1993 county council elections – and in 2001 they won every county division within the district. The constituency which covers the southern tip of Bucks is Beaconsfield, and it will come as no surprise to discover that it is one of the very safest Conservative seats in the land – its percentage majority was the seventh largest in the 2001 Election. Even after its MP Tim Smith felt he had to resign over 'sleaze' charges at the last minute before the 1997 General Election, his replacement Dominic Grieve held on by a comfortable 14,000 over a scarcely-advancing Liberal Democrat, and although it is true that the Tory share of the vote dipped below 50% for the first time in Beaconsfield, it is back as an absolute majority of votes cast now.

The reason for this monolithic commitment to the right is clear; this is one of the most comfortable and affluent corners of the Home Counties. Property values are very high (the average in 2000 of £265,000 was the second highest outside Greater

London after Esher and Walton), as commuters and those who can afford not to enjoy a touch of quasi-rural existence are conveniently wedged near the M4 and M40 motorways, not too far from Heathrow Airport or west London. The largest town is Beaconsfield, from which the great Tory Prime Minister Benjamin Disraeli took the title of his earldom (his country house at Hughenden was in the vicinity). The other communities are bywords for wealth and conservatism: Gerrards Cross, with its detached modern mansions; Denham, known for its production of movies, and Burnham Beeches where so many of them have been filmed; Iver, from which the vitriolic red-headed right-wing (once left-wing) columnist Paul Johnson has fulminated; Stoke Poges; Dorney, the 'unspoilt' village occupied by many celebrities who felt threatened by Eton College's plans to build a rowing trench; and Taplow, nearest village to Cliveden, the palatial home of the Astors and the pre-war Cliveden set, who included sympathisers with Nazi Germany. It is all a far cry from the Durham Gala.

There will be no further excitement in Beaconsfield at the next general election. There was scarcely any even when the Conservatives had to defend it in a by-election while in office, in 1982, when Tim Smith retained it with a comfy majority. Some observers did, however, take note of the Labour candidate who polled just 3,886 votes. He was a young barrister by the name of Tony Blair, trying for the first time to enter Parliament.

Social indices:			2001 Gen. Election:			
% Non-white	2.9		C	20,233	50.4	+1.2
% Prof/Man	36.5		Lab	9,168	22.8	+2.8
% Non-manual	61.2		LD	9,117	22.7	+1.4
£ Av prop val 2000	266 K		UKIP	1,626	4.1	+3.2
% Increase 97–00	51.7		C maj	11,065	27.6	
% Unemployed 2001	0.9		Turnout		58.7	−14.1
% Decrease 97–01	0.8		Elect	68,378		
% Fin hard/Rank	3.3	635				
% Pensioners	23.7					
% Prem mort/Rank	6	623				

Member of Parliament

Dominic Grieve, first elected in 1997, a half-French, bilingual, Churchy barrister, is, as the son of Percy Grieve QC, MP for Solihull 1964–83 (for whom he distributed leaflets from the age of six), one of 18 sons or daughters of MPs elected to the Commons in 2001. Born in 1956 and educated at Westminster School and Magdalen College, Oxford, and called to the Bar in 1980, he has opposed Scottish devolution, called for a directly elected House of Lords and expressed concern at traffic congestion on the three motorways that traverse his constituency. Beaky-nosed, with plastered-down hair and a precise manner, his Scottish roots landed him with a Scottish frontbench spokesmanship in 1999 (having voted for William Hague in 1997). In 2001 he became part of the Shadow Home Office team, having voted for Iain Duncan Smith in the third ballot, but for David Davis before that. He doggedly pursued Henry McLeish over his sub-letting of his constituency office until McLeish duly resigned as Scottish First Minister in November 2001.

BECKENHAM

Although in the end Jacqui Lait retained Beckenham for the Conservatives in 2001 with a six-vote larger majority than the party had in 1997, that it was seriously discussed as another possible Labour gain in Greater London indicates the extent of that party's ambitions in the south-east, not only renewed but reaching hitherto uncharted ground.

Bromley in outer south-east London (many residents would still say Kent) is the largest of the capital's boroughs in terms of area and the second most populous, after Croydon. Beckenham is the most compact of the Bromley borough seats. It is tucked in the north-west corner of the borough, the closest of the seats to inner London. This does have a slight effect on its political make-up. The communities on the inner edge towards Crystal Palace, Penge and Anerley, and to a certain extent Clock House, have few Conservative voters. There is an ethnic minority population here, and terraced Victorian and Edwardian housing rather than inter-war semis and detached. In local elections Labour usually win Penge, and are competitive in Lawrie Park and Kent House too, while the Liberal Democrats are strongest in Anerley and Clock House. But as one proceeds further out into suburbia, the terrain becomes very Tory: central Beckenham, Shortlands, Kelsey Park, Copers Cope.

The Conservative MP Piers Merchant won by 15,000 in 1992 but with newspaper suggestions of an extra-marital dalliance and the huge London-wide swing from the Tories, Labour's strength in the inner part of the seat was reflected in 1997 by their ability to garner 18,000 votes. They finished less than 5,000 behind Merchant in a seat in which the Conservative Party had always previously been able to rely on a five-figure majority. Nor had the Tories bottomed out. In the autumn after the General Election it was shown that the allegations against Merchant were in fact true, and he resigned to cause a by-election which took place in November 1997. By then Labour were even higher in the polls than they had been in May, and they cut the Conservative lead to just 1,227, admittedly on a 44% turnout. This now looks like the closest they will come to an astonishing gain in Bromley borough, but Beckenham will still be treated as a marginal for at least one more general election.

Social indices:			2001 Gen. Election:			
% Non-white	7.1		C	20,618	45.3	+2.8
% Prof/Man	46.0		Lab	15,659	34.4	+1.0
% Non-manual	74.9		LD	7,308	16.0	−2.1
£ Av prop val 2000	151 K		Grn	961	2.1	
% Increase 97–00	65.4		UKIP	782	1.7	+0.8
% Unemployed 2001	2.6		Lib	234	0.5	−0.8
% Decrease 97–01	2.3		C maj	4,959	10.9	
% Fin hard/Rank	9.9	469	Turnout		63.1	−11.6
% Pensioners	25.2		Elect	72,241		
% Prem mort/Rank	20	478				

Member of Parliament

Jacqui Lait, one of a number of ambitious Scots Tories who have had to take the high road South to winnable seats, held Hastings for only one Parliament (1992–97) and then was returned for Beckenham in the 1997 by-election. Big and residually Scots-accented, she was born in 1947, and educated at Paisley Grammar School and Strathclyde University, and despite her Europhilia, William Hague, whose PPS she had been (1995–96), made her a Whip in 1999 and a Social Security spokesman in 2000, and despite her backing for Kenneth Clarke in 2001 she became one of a small clutch of token left Europhiles on Iain Duncan Smith's frontbench team. But in getting her post-devolution job of shadowing the hollowed-out Scottish Office she was proving that you can run (from Scotland) but you might as well not have bothered. A former lobbyist who became the first female Tory Whip in the Major government (1996–97), her election for Beckenham upped the number of Conservative women MPs to 14, where it stayed after 2001. A past campaigner for separate married women's taxation and against alcohol and tobacco smuggling, she has latterly trimmed to scepticism on a common currency.

BEDFORD

It used to be widely believed that parliamentary boundary changes always hurt the Labour Party. However, this was certainly not true of those that came into force before the 1997 General Election, and Bedford, which their candidate Patrick Hall won by 8,300 votes, is one example of a redrawn seat which could for the foreseeable future be regarded as an extra safe addition to their representation in the Commons.

The creation of a sixth and extra seat in Bedfordshire by the Boundary Commission had significant knock-on effects in the rest of the county. One of these involved the reduction of the former North Bedfordshire seat to its compact urban core around the county town of Bedford itself. As elsewhere in the country (and indeed the county) this type of revision offered opportunities for the Labour Party. Labour had only ever won Bedford before in their landslide years, 1945 and 1966. Stripped of the extremely Conservative villages wedged in the northern tip of Bedfordshire, this renamed borough constituency would have returned Patrick Hall with a swing of less than 5%. In the event, in line with the regional pattern, he achieved 13% in 1997, and in line with most gainers in that year, held on with no significant weakening of his position in 2001.

Bedford is a mixed and interesting town. It has stood out as the centre for its sub-region since at least the ninth century (when it resisted marauding Scandinavians) and retains the commercial, service and educational facilities for its generally prosperous hinterland. It has industry and brewing interests too, and has long been a major administrative centre. There are good residential areas in the town, along the banks of the Ouse in Newnham ward, and in the north of the town in De Parys and (newer) Brickhill, although the Liberal Democrats are successful in local elections in a few carefully targeted wards. On June 7, 2001, the Liberal Democrats obtained 29.1% of the vote in the council elections, but only 15.8% in the General Election on the same day – one of the biggest variations anywhere.

Bedford has also been a major centre of post-war immigration. Some of this is Asian: Queen's Park ward in the west of the town is 39% non-white, Cauldwell along the A6 to the south 30%, Harpur along the A6 to the north 17%. More unusual is Bedford's large Italian community, attracted initially largely by employment in the brickfields of north Bedfordshire. Bilingual signs and leaflets in local government buildings surprise the uninitiated visitor.

The Italian community does not vote as a bloc, but the redrawn Bedford's character as a compact and mixed urban unit suggests that it should now be regarded as a likely Labour seat even in a year of Conservative recovery.

Social indices:			2001 Gen. Election:			
% Non-white	14.4		Lab	19,454	47.9	−2.7
% Prof/Man	34.6		C	13,297	32.8	−0.9
% Non-manual	58.5		LD	6,425	15.8	+3.5
£ Av prop val 2000	88 K		Ind	973	2.4	
% Increase 97–00	44.6		UKIP	430	1.1	
% Unemployed 2001	3.8		Lab maj	6,157	15.2	
% Decrease 97–01	1.6		Turnout		59.9	−13.7
% Fin hard/Rank	18.7	292	Elect	67,763		
% Pensioners	23.4					
% Prem mort/Rank	28	371				

Member of Parliament

Elected in 1997, **Patrick Hall**, a half-Belgian bachelor, is Labour's third MP for Bedford since 1945. A former town planner and Bedfordshire County Councillor, and as an MP a very unobtrusive Blairite loyalist, he was born in 1951 and educated at the local public school, Bedford Modern, and at Birmingham University. The pitcher of on-message questions, to Tory laughter he has claimed many of his constituents supported 'the government's commitment to the flexible and speedy implementation of the heavily-indebted poor countries initiative'. Though tabling only six written questions in his first year, he favours electoral reform, more accountable banks, the east of England as a separate region, and planning advice to avoid building on flood plains, none of which counted against him as he became in 2001 the first ever Labour MP for Bedford to win a second term. But return of a 'New' Labour MP in Bedford in 2001 should not be mistaken for a revival of a radical dissenting tradition personified by Bedford's most famous son, John Bunyan.

BEDFORDSHIRE MID

The creation of the new seat of North East Bedfordshire in time for the May 1997 Election meant that the constituency of Bedfordshire Mid was made up of a somewhat different part of the middle of the county from before. The neighbouring small towns of Biggleswade and Sandy have been lost to NE Bedfordshire, as was the ward of Arlesey. Kempston, which is really part of the Bedford built-up area, was donated to the new seat named after the county town. In exchange the division received such non-Luton territory as Flitwick and Toddington from Luton North, which was pared down to an urban core. Mid Bedfordshire is still a safely Conservative seat, although their numerical majority has been reduced since 1992 by the loss of 20,000 voters in boundary changes and 6,000 in turnout.

Flitwick is a rapidly expanding town, conveniently situated on the main London railway line, where no concessions were made to rural history when the brash new shopping centres were opened. The substantial part of the seat that has passed through those revisions undisturbed is also extremely Conservative: prosperous farmland studded by small market towns like Ampthill. If it were not for the presence of brickfields among the more conventional type of fields, Bedfordshire Mid would be almost entirely non-industrial. Jonathan Sayeed beat his Labour challenger by over 8,000 in the dark Conservative days of 2001, which suggests that it will remain a Tory citadel, too solid a structure for Labour or the centre parties to demolish.

Social indices:			2001 Gen. Election:			
% Non-white	2.2		C	22,109	47.4	+1.4
% Prof/Man	40.9		Lab	14,043	30.1	−2.4
% Non-manual	62.4		LD	9,205	19.7	+2.9
£ Av prop val 2000	130 K		UKIP	1,281	2.7	
% Increase 97–00	59.5		C maj	8,066	17.3	
% Unemployed 2001	1.1		Turnout		66.1	−12.3
% Decrease 97–01	0.8		Elect	70,594		
% Fin hard/Rank	3.9	627				
% Pensioners	23.4					
% Prem mort/Rank	9	603				

Member of Parliament

Jonathan Sayeed, the Conservatives' only non-white MP (since the defeat in 1992 of Nirj Deva), but who does not – as half-Indian – wish to be so categorised, was elected here in 1997, having earlier made his name as the Tory who beat Tony Benn at Bristol South East in 1983 (and so quashed Benn's leadership hopes against Neil Kinnock), a seat he retained until 1992. Born in 1948 and educated at Woolverstone Hall School and Dartmouth Naval College, he served in the Navy for seven years before founding a shipping company, and – after his 1992 defeat – a PR business. Ranked among the Eurosceptics, especially on the single currency, he took a cautious stance on military intervention in Iraq and Kosovo, is concerned about the vulnerability to terrorists of the former Soviet Union's nuclear arsenal, and sought voluntary disclosure of religious affiliation in the 2001 Census. Having backed Hague for leader in 1997 (offering him office space), he was an Ancram voter in 2001 until his man dropped out, and with his vote in the final ballot undisclosed, joined the frontbench Shadow DEFRA team in 2001, as the only example of multiculturalism available to Iain Duncan Smith.

BEDFORDSHIRE NORTH EAST

In 1997 the new seat of North East Bedfordshire took very Tory territory from a number of formerly oversized seats. From North Bedfordshire came the rural and true-blue northern tip of the county, along with some commuting villages for Bedford, such as Clapham and the very affluent Bromham. The northern section of Mid Bedfordshire is also included, based on the small towns of Biggleswade (pop. 13,000) and Sandy (9,000) along the A1 Great North Road, and Stotfold (6,000) and Potton (4,000). All this is massively Tory, without even a substantial Liberal

Democrat presence as in so many of the more rural parts of southern England. It should have provided a safe haven for any aspiring Conservative.

In fact the result in 1997 was closer than predicted. Nicholas Lyell did indeed win but by less than 6,000 compared with the estimated 20,000 had the seat existed in 1992. The Labour vote increased by over 12%, close to the national average; but Lyell must also have been hampered by the presence of not only a Referendum Party candidate but also an Independent Conservative, who between them took over 8.5% of the total vote. In 2001, although these presences were removed, the Conservative vote remained static as the turnout slipped from 78% to 65%, and the new candidate Alastair Burt scarcely increased his numerical majority, which remains only in four figures even in the seat with the 564th greatest financial hardship in Britain, according to the 2001 Experian Information Solutions index.

Social indices:			2001 Gen. Election:			
% Non-white	1.5		C	22,586	49.9	+5.6
% Prof/Man	40.1		Lab	14,009	31.0	−1.6
% Non-manual	62.1		LD	7,409	16.4	+2.1
£ Av prop val 2000	108 K		UKIP	1,242	2.7	
% Increase 97–00	48.9		C maj	8,577	19.0	
% Unemployed 2001	1.3		Turnout		65.1	−12.7
% Decrease 97–01	0.8		Elect	69,451		
% Fin hard/Rank	6.8	564				
% Pensioners	23.4					
% Prem mort/Rank	22	458				

Member of Parliament

Alistair Burt, solicitor and former MP for marginal Bury North, replaced the departing former Attorney General Sir Nicholas Lyell as Conservative MP here in 2001. Though first elected in the Thatcherite flood of 1983, he is a One Nation Tory, and yet one of a handful of the bloodied infantry of the 1997 campaign to be selected for a safe seat, despite the advice from Central Office to defeated MPs not to chicken run, but 'to stay in your infantry trenches'. He had to wait for Margaret Thatcher's fall before getting a government post, and by the end of the Major government was Social Security Minister responsible for the disabled and for the Child Support Agency. An active Christian who has opposed Sunday trading, embryo research and abortion, he was born in 1955, and educated at Bury Grammar School and St John's College, Oxford. His record as a Tory Reform Grouper and as one of only four MPs known to have voted for Kenneth Clarke among the 33-strong Tory intake of 2001, ought to have ensured his exclusion from preferment under Iain Duncan Smith, but he was appointed a junior Education spokesman in the new leader's frontbench team as a gesture toward inclusivity.

BEDFORDSHIRE SOUTH WEST

The south-western strip of Bedfordshire, along the Buckinghamshire border, might on initial inspection appear to be a long-established Conservative constituency in the south-east of England. In 1992 it returned David Madel, its Tory MP of 22 years, with a majority of 21,273 over Labour. Yet over 85% of it came from the old South Beds seat, which was actually held by Gwilym Roberts for Labour between 1966 and 1970. In 1997, Madel's majority very nearly evaporated, as Labour closed the gap to just 132 votes, on a 15% swing. This left it as Labour's No. 2 target seat in the 2001 General Election, and they failed to take it by another bare three-figure margin. Why has this area turned twice so violently?

The largest town in the constituency is Dunstable, which houses many skilled workers – the Dunstable/Luton 'conurbation' is, or rather used to be, the General Motors (Vauxhall) metropolis in England. There are, however, differences between the two towns which are deeper than the untutored outsider might suspect. Dunstable is nearly all-white, unlike it larger neighbour, and it is dominated by owner-occupied semi-detached housing. Despite its frequently drab and dreary appearance it has usually returned a large Conservative majority. Dunstable and other parts of south Bedfordshire do not seem to like Luton: in a survey for the Banham Commission in 1994 no fewer than 40% of South Beds respondents volunteered Luton as a place that they specifically disliked. This was the highest figure recorded anywhere in the country for such negative feelings. It reflected a strong wish not to be merged with Luton and thus 'taken over'.

Most of the rest of the constituency shares Dunstable's political predilections and prejudices. A second major population centre lies in the twin towns of Leighton Buzzard and Linslade, which between them have nearly 32,000 residents, almost as many as Dunstable. There is also a strip of housing developments, largely council originally, on the edge of Luton, principally at Houghton Regis. Until very recently we can observe the increasingly Conservative preference of the skilled manual class. This group, now often known as 'C2s', were studied back in the 1960s by the sociological team led by John Goldthorpe which considered the phenomenon of the 'affluent worker'; their fieldwork was largely conducted in the Greater Luton area. Among the many findings of their survey was that although these workers could still by no means be considered 'bourgeois', they were becoming increasingly 'instrumental' in their political behaviour, ready to choose whichever option seems best at the time for themselves and their families, rather than maintaining a solid loyalty to their 'class' and the traditional party thereof, Labour.

In 1979 this very often led to an individual decision to reject Mr Callaghan's government, and in 1983 and 1987 to support Mrs Thatcher's approach. In 1992 Mr Major's Conservative Party were once again decisively judged to have 'delivered the goods' to the voters of South West Bedfordshire. In 1997 it was not. The mid 1990s recession, and the perceived economic incompetence of the government, did not appeal to the instrumental instincts and judgments of the skilled workers and other voters of constituencies over much of England, decisively including areas of modern semi-urban middle England such as Bedfordshire South West. In 2001 the economically prudent, and lucky, New Labour government had not yet alienated this type of constituency to suffer a significant adverse swing, and Bedfordshire South West remains a knife-edge marginal. No one can take the allegiance of these electors for granted.

Social indices:			2001 Gen. Election:			
% Non-white	2.1		C	18,477	42.1	+1.4
% Prof/Man	33.7		Lab	17,701	40.4	−0.1
% Non-manual	57.8		LD	6,473	14.8	+0.5
£ Av prop val 2000	102 K		UKIP	1,203	2.7	+1.9
% Increase 97–00	47.0		C maj	776	1.8	
% Unemployed 2001	1.5		Turnout		60.8	−15.0
% Decrease 97–01	1.1		Elect	72,126		
% Fin hard/Rank	12.6	404				
% Pensioners	19.5					
% Prem mort/Rank	19	494				

Member of Parliament

Andrew Selous, a reinsurance underwriter and former director of a family electronics business, replaced the retiring MP Sir David Madel in 2001. An LSE graduate, born in 1962, he has as part of his political backdrop activism in the Battersea part of the Tory flagship borough of Wandsworth, and family links through his mother to the former Australian Foreign Minister and Governor General, the late Lord Casey. The Antipodean roots may well colour his preference for 'the UK being internationally competitive worldwide as well as within Europe', and his strong support for NATO. He has also declared that his motivation for aspiring to become an MP was his Christian faith – wishing 'to see the Conservative Party become the party for the poor and disadvantaged'. He duly backed Iain Duncan Smith's election as the leader who could 'unite the party on Europe'.

BELFAST EAST

If west Belfast is generally regarded as the centre of that troubled city's Catholic nationalism and republicanism, east Belfast has a strong claim to be a citadel of Orange Protestant 'loyalism'. Only just over 5% voted for SDLP or Sinn Fein candidates in the 2001 General Election, and this is a fairly reliable guide to the proportion of Roman Catholics in the electorate.

The residential areas are in fact more varied than some would think, stretching out from inner-city terraces in places such as Ballymacarrett to attractive tree-lined suburbia in Knock and Belmont. Stormont Castle is also to be found in this outer, middle-class part of the city.

This is somewhat ironic, for East has returned in its last five elections one of the stronger Protestant opponents of the British government's attempts at power-sharing between the Northern Irish communities and with the Irish Republic. Peter Robinson, the deputy leader of the Democratic Unionist Party, won his first election here when he beat William Craig, the former Vanguard leader and Official Unionist candidate, by just 64 votes; a more moderate politician, Oliver Napier of the Alliance Party, was also within a thousand votes of victory. Since then, though, Robinson has won easily, although the middle-class areas still provide a reasonable level of support for the Alliance, whose leader John Alderdice received 30% in 1992, but only half that by the more polarised year of 2001.

Robinson also faces opposition from the main loyalist party, the Ulster Unionists, but he has won by around seven thousand votes in the last two elections. His 20-plus years of service clearly count for much in this Protestant heartland.

Social indices:		2001 Gen. Election:			
% Prof/Man	30.2	DUP	15,667	42.5	−0.1
% Non-manual	58.7	UUP	8,550	23.2	−2.1
% RC	5.9	APNI	5,832	15.8	−8.0
% Irish sp	1.5	PUP	3,669	10.0	
% Unemployed 2001	4.4	SF	1,237	3.4	+1.3
% Decrease 97–01	2.9	SDLP	880	2.4	+0.8
		C	800	2.2	−0.2
		WP	123	0.3	−0.3
		Ind	71	0.2	
		DUP maj	7,117	19.3	
		Turnout		63.0	−0.2
		Elect	58,455		

Member of Parliament

Peter Robinson won this seat for the Paisleyites in 1979, making him second only to his leader (elected in 1970) as the longest-serving Ulster MP. Inappropriately dubbed 'an altar boy to the Revd Ian Paisley' (Simon Hoggart, the *Guardian*), while he mirrors Paisley's intransigent hostility to power sharing, he currently sits in the Northern Ireland Executive as Regional Development Minister, and could well come to balance the UUP's David Trimble as his party's more deft, cerebral and pragmatic equivalent. A slight, uncharismatic man who neither smokes nor drinks, but likes Diet Coke and breeding Koi carp, he was briefly an estate agent until running Paisley's party, having been propelled into hardline Loyalist politics as a teenager by the killing of a friend by an IRA bomb. Born in 1948 and educated at Annadale Grammar School and Castlereagh College of Further Education, he votes progressively with Labour on social and economic issues (if not on homosexuality) and with the Conservatives on foreign and defence policy, but claims to be 'a traditional Carson-style Unionist', with his politics 'based on conviction not expediency'. Such rhetoric is the obligatory stuff of Ulster politics, and Carson's defiant statue stands symbolically at Stormont in his constituency. With his equally astringent wife, Iris, joining him in the Commons in 2001, the House has never known so tough and political a married couple since the much less hardline duo of Nye Bevan and Jennie Lee.

BELFAST NORTH

The heaviest defeat for a sitting member in 2001 was suffered by Cecil Walker, the Ulster Unionist MP for Belfast North, who finished fourth with only 12% of the vote behind DUP, Sinn Fein and SDLP candidates. He received 21,500 votes in 1997, less than 5,000 just four years later – and he did not lose the official backing of his party – indeed it is said that he wished to retire but was persuaded to stand by UUP leaders. He was, however, left cruelly exposed: 76 years old and severely affected by deafness, he was even more handicapped by his support for the Good Friday

Agreement in one of the most bitterly divided and strife-ridden parts of Northern Ireland.

The wards which make up the Belfast North seat bear names containing some grim reminders of the tragic and turbulent recent history of the Northern Irish capital: Ardoyne (the site of the school access stand-off of summer 2001), New Lodge, Crumlin and Woodvale. There is a substantial and growing Catholic minority in the constituency, often concentrated in intensely Nationalist enclaves such as the Ardoyne and New Lodge; the predominant tone, though, is still Unionist. The seat extends from beyond the edge of the city through a pleasant residential area along the Antrim Road to the battered slums which form part of the cockpit of the UK's greatest civil strife in recent years. The Shankill Road is known as the heart of Belfast working-class loyalism; its proximity to the Catholic Falls Road which also leads out to the west from the city centre had caused the erection of the Belfast version of the Berlin Wall, the ironically named Peace Line, between them. Berlin no longer requires such a stark reminder of division; it remains to be seen for how long Belfast will.

Although there was a remarkable seven-way contest in Belfast North in 1979, which resulted in a win for the DUP's John McQuade with just 27% of the vote, the seat was held for 18 years from 1983 for the Official Unionists by the quiet figure of Cecil Walker. In 1997 there were again no fewer than seven candidates, but Walker achieved more than twice the vote of his nearest rival, although significantly without DUP opposition. In 2001 though, the more hardline DUP not only stood, but put forward a very strong candidate in the form of 42-year-old Nigel Dodds, who immediately became the favourite to oust Walker easily. It might be noted that Sinn Fein also increased its vote to 25%, surpassing the SDLP and bringing the total Nationalist share in Belfast North to over 46%. This suggests that demographic shifts in the area are occurring which mean that it will not for ever be counted in any unionist camp.

Social indices:		2001 Gen. Election:			
% Prof/Man	22.8	DUP	16,718	40.8	
% Non-manual	46.9	SF	10,331	25.2	+5.0
% RC	36.6	SDLP	8,592	21.0	+0.6
% Irish sp	7.6	UUP	4,904	12.0	−39.8
% Unemployed 2001	8.5	WP	253	0.6	−0.1
% Decrease 97–01	4.3	Ind	134	0.3	
		DUP maj	6,387	15.6	
		Turnout		67.2	+3.0
		Elect	60,941		

Member of Parliament

Although **Nigel Dodds**, who was elected DUP MP here in 2001, was one of seven new Northern Ireland MPs capturing seats from other parties (in his case from the Ulster Unionists), there is much that is atypical about this new Ulster MP. Born in 1958 and educated at Portora Royal School, Enniskillen, at St John's College, Cambridge and at Queen's University Belfast, he is a barrister who has also worked for 12 years in the Secretariat of the European Parliament. A cosmopolitan background of Cambridge, the Bar and Strasbourg is not normally associated with the socially modest Paisleyite tradition of Unionism. A former Lord Mayor of Belfast, and initially a Minister in the Northern Ireland Executive after 1999, his victory came at the expense of the septuagenarian Unionist Cecil Walker, an MP so low profile at Westminster as to have made only one speech in four years and to have survived at the 1997 Election only by courtesy of Nigel Dodds' standing aside to allow him a free run against the Nationalists. But with Walker as one of only three Unionist MPs to back David Trimble's support for the Good Friday Agreement on power sharing, Dodds won this seat in the Northern Ireland Assembly elections of 1998 and cemented his victory by pushing Cecil Walker into fourth place in 2001. An articulate and respected voice of hard-line Loyalism, he kept out of the limelight during the ugly Protestant haranguing of Catholic schoolchildren in the Ardoyne district of his constituency during September 2001.

BELFAST SOUTH

South Belfast is traditionally regarded as the most affluent and middle-class part of the city. Here is to be found the Queen's University campus, and many of the most select residential areas of the Northern Irish capital such as the Malone Road. It was held to be relatively isolated from the worst of the 'Troubles', but that no part of Belfast is immune from violence was brutally shown by the assassination in 1981 of South's Official Unionist MP Robert Bradford, at one of his advice centres.

The subsequent by-election was won convincingly by the Grand Master of the Orange Order of Northern Ireland, Martin Smyth, a minister of religion as Bradford was. Smyth stood in the Official Unionist interest, and remains MP to this day, although the label under which he campaigns does tend to change from time to time – currently he is an Ulster Unionist.

He has traditionally enjoyed one of the safer seats in Northern Ireland, but in a ten-way contest in 1997 his majority was dramatically reduced from 16,000 to 4,600, and in an eight-sided battle in 2001 his lead was 5,400. Among this remarkably high number of opponents are to be found many different facets of the complex political and unique political landscape of Belfast: to name but those parties who saved their deposit either in 1997 or 2001 are David Ervine of the Popular Unionists, regarded as an unusually able leader of a party which speaks for a significant brand of Protestant paramilitarism, the SDLP and Sinn Fein as the two chief wings of Catholic nationalism and republicanism; the non-sectarian Alliance Party (not to be confused with the defunct British Liberal-SDP alliance but nevertheless with informal links to the Liberal Democrats); and last but not least the Women's Coalition, whose Monica McWilliams had won a peace award (Frank Cousins, 1996) two years before John Hume and David Trimble took the Nobel Prize after the Good Friday Agreement. Many might wish that she had herself received more, perhaps far more, than 7.8% of the vote here in Belfast South in 2001, which was yet another year of divisiveness in this shattered city.

Social indices:		2001 Gen. Election:			
% Prof/Man	44.3	UUP	17,008	44.8	+8.8
% Non-manual	68.1	SDLP	11,609	30.6	+6.3
% RC	26.1	NIWC	2,968	7.8	+4.8
% Irish sp	6.9	SF	2,894	7.6	+2.5
% Unemployed 2001	4.8	APNI	2,042	5.4	–7.6
% Decrease 97–01	4.4	PUP	1,112	2.9	–11.5
		WP	204	0.5	–0.2
		Ind	115	0.3	
		UUP maj	5,399	14.2	
		Turnout		63.9	+1.6
		Elect	59,436		

Member of Parliament

Revd Martin Smyth, who quit as UUP Whip over his opposition to the power-sharing Good Friday Agreement in 1998, when he found himself in a dissident majority of six MPs against the three MPs backing Trimble (by 2001 all these pro-Agreement MPs had gone), has been MP here since 1982, when he succeeded the murdered Revd Robert Bradford. In March 2000 he ran David Trimble close in a UUP leadership challenge, polling 43%. An uncharismatic, soft-spoken hardliner, he was born in 1931, educated at Methodist College, Belfast, Magee University, Londonderry, and Trinity College, Dublin, and was a Presbyterian minister for 25 years. In 2000 he welcomed his own Party's defeat by Paisleyite Revd William McCrea in the South Antrim by-election, a sign of the inevitable polarisation of Ulster politics in the election run-up over the IRA's refusal to surrender its arms. A past Grand Master of the Grand Orange Lodge of Ireland for 24 years, he rejected Trimble's call in April 2000 to break the Orange Lodge's historic link with Ulster Unionism. Transposing his preoccupation with insularity to Indonesia, he has spoken up for Christian Moluccan Islanders threatened by Islamic extremists.

BELFAST WEST

West Belfast is in many ways the most distinctive part of the United Kingdom, of which most of its residents do not wish to be part.

This is the stronghold of Belfast's Catholic, Nationalist/Republican community. There used to be a considerable Protestant population too, but this has been much diminished by residential segregation and flight since the Troubles began. West Belfast is an area which has long been cursed with considerable unemployment (the rate among men in June 2001 was 17%, the highest of any of the 659 constituencies) and shocking social and housing problems in addition to the all-too-familiar violence associated with the names of parts of the seat such as the Falls Road, the Divis Flats, Ballymurphy and Andersonstown. No other Westminster constituency looks so degraded, so war-torn.

From 1945 to 1983 the competition for the representation of Belfast West was between Unionists and some brand of Labour candidate such as Jack Beattie (Irish Labour Party) and Gerry Fitt, who held it for 17 years with great popularity and showing much bravery, despite the enmity of Protestants and some more extreme Nationalists.

In 1983 the General Election campaign in Belfast West must have been the most bitter and fraught in the UK. Gerry Fitt stood as an Independent, opposed (that seems too mild a word) by his former SDLP colleagues and by Provisional Sinn Fein's leading figure, Gerry Adams. Adams, an ex-internee, clearly won a majority of the Catholic vote and, although Fitt clearly picked up some Protestant votes, the split in the more moderate Nationalist vote let Adams in.

Gerry Adams did not take his seat at Westminster, but increased his stature as the leading republican politician in Northern Ireland, and held on against the SDLP's Dr Joe Hendron in 1987, assisted by a reappearance of the 20% Unionist vote. In 1992, though, the tables were turned as Hendron beat Adams by just 589, almost certainly votes provided by Protestants voting tactically against Adams, a man they identified closely with the IRA and its campaign of violence.

In 1997 and 2001, though, Adams increased his share of the vote by a total of no less than 25%, and in the latter year he received the support of the highest proportion of the electorate of any politician contesting the General Election (45.45%). Whatever is thought of his apparent and real position, it cannot be denied that he has become an extremely successful democratically elected politician, and that Sinn Fein has continued to grow both relative to the SDLP and in absolute terms, and it is far from inconceivable that Gerry Adams will lead his party to his stated ambition of the largest in the Northern Ireland 'statelet'.

Social indices:		2001 Gen. Election:			
% Prof/Man	18.6	SF	27,096	66.1	+10.2
% Non-manual	43.5	SDLP	7,754	18.9	−19.8
% RC	76.9	DUP	2,641	6.4	
% Irish sp	19.9	UUP	2,541	6.2	+2.8
% Unemployed 2001	11.5	WP	736	1.8	+0.2
% Decrease 97–01	4.3	TW	116	0.3	
		Ind	98	0.2	
		SF maj	19,342	47.2	
		Turnout		68.7	−5.5
		Elect	59,617		

Member of Parliament

Sinn Fein President **Gerry Adams** has been MP here from 1983 to 1992 and since 1997, and for the same seat in the Northern Ireland Assembly from 1998. Born in 1948 into a family of republican veterans, he attended St Mary's (Christian Brothers) Grammar School, and has had no discernible occupation outside republican politics since working as a barman in Belfast pubs in the early 1970s. A pious Catholic who has served as guard of honour at over 200 IRA funerals – allegedly at 23 an IRA commanding officer in Belfast, tall, black-bearded and with reconstructed teeth, he cuts, for Unionists, a most sinister figure. Not taking the Oath, he does not take his Commons seat, yet he and his colleague Martin McGuinness are said to represent that faction in the Republican movement who see the armed struggle as over – and not just in Ireland; in January 2001 he advised the Basque Nationalists, ETA, to end their violence. Having taken the parliamentary road, he finds himself in the paradoxical position of having to sustain Trimble as Unionist leader, without whom the power-sharing strategy would collapse. Asked (by the *Guardian*) if he had ever put a gun to anyone's head his answer was 'No'. Though Catholic fecundity may be on his side, he does not believe that 'out-breeding Unionists ([which] may be an enjoyable pastime for those who have the energy) amounts to a political strategy' – 'we can't give up the task of winning Unionists over'. Going moderate has reaped dividends with younger Catholics and by October 2001 he was reported as 'asking the IRA to disarm'.

BERWICK-UPON-TWEED

For many years the Liberal deputy leader Alan Beith performed a skilful balancing act in Berwick-upon-Tweed. When he won the seat from the Tories in a by-election in November 1973 the Liberal revival of the early 1970s was already petering out into disappointment, and Beith only crept home by 57 votes. In the General Election of February 1974 his majority rose to a princely 443, but in October that same year it was reduced to double figures again, to 73 this time. After all this brinkmanship it was a genuine surprise when he romped home by over 5,000 in 1979, when the Tories actually won the General Election. Since then his lead has never slipped below 5,000 although it was halved in 1992 as both the Conservatives and Labour increased their share. The main item of interest in the 1997 result was that Labour narrowly overtook the sinking Tories to move into second place. Something superficially rather odd happened in 2001: Labour dropped by 9%, much more than the national or regional average, and back to third again. One explanation might be that the rural parts of the seat were affected in that year by foot and mouth, and the governing party did not in general do well in such places.

However, Beith has always been able when necessary to place a squeeze on the considerable potential Labour vote, for the Berwick constituency includes some ex-mining villages like Ellington as well as the mixed-class small towns of Berwick, Alnwick and Amble. The Conservative vote is of a traditional and even deferential kind, given the long-term influence of the Percy family of Alnwick Castle. Besides farming, there is a substantial tourist industry attracted by the dramatic coastline: the constituency includes the castles at Warkworth, Bamburgh and Dunstanburgh on the cliffs, as well as Holy Island and the Farne Islands.

Before Beith, Berwick did have something of a Liberal tradition – Sir Edward Grey was the member from 1885 to 1916, and Sir William Beveridge was briefly MP here at the end of the Second World War. But modern Liberalism here in England's northernmost constituency owes much to the present incumbent, now approaching his fourth decade in the Commons. Like a high proportion of centrist MPs, having managed to enter Parliament at a by-election, he has been able to capitalise on his personal vote and to provide exceptional constituency services.

Social indices:			2001 Gen. Election:			
% Non-white	0.2		LD	18,651	51.4	+5.9
% Prof/Man	29.6		C	10,193	28.1	+4.0
% Non-manual	48.9		Lab	6,435	17.7	−8.5
£ Av prop val 2000	75 K		UKIP	1,029	2.8	+2.0
% Increase 97–00	32.6		LD maj	8,458	23.3	
% Unemployed 2001	3.4		Turnout		63.8	−10.3
% Decrease 97–01	1.9		Elect	56,918		
% Fin hard/Rank	18.7	291				
% Pensioners	29.2					
% Prem mort/Rank	29	351				

Member of Parliament

The Liberal Democrats' perennial Deputy Leader, **Alan Beith**, won this seat on the back of a Tory call-girl scandal in 1973 and has subsequently converted it into a relatively safe seat, making him by 2001 the longest serving Lib Dem MP. An uncharismatic Methodist of conservative views on tobacco, Sunday trading, abortion, embryo research and pornography, he also, with other rural Lib Dem MPs, shuns politically correct lines on gun bans and hunting, there being three hunts operating in his constituency. Born into a working-class Tory family in 1943 and educated at King's School, Macclesfield and Balliol and Nuffield Colleges, Oxford, he was a Politics lecturer at Newcastle University for seven years. A disappointed candidate for Speaker in 2000, polling the second lowest total of 83 votes in a field of 12 candidates – all of whom were voted on separately, in 2001 he married (as a widower) the former Lib Dem MP, Diana (now Baroness) Maddock. Being around so long as to have held all the shadow high offices of state – Treasury, Home Office, Foreign Office, Chief Whip – everything bar Shadow PM, and denied the Speakership, his peerage in 2001 seemed a little overdue.

BETHNAL GREEN AND BOW

Poverty and unemployment, massive council housing developments following the destruction of the Second World War and slum clearance, vibrant popular culture, a cosmopolitan mix of communities, racial tension and violence, a heartland of the Labour Party which has seen vigorous and even alarming challenges at local level – all these elements should be included in a thumbnail sketch of the borough of Tower Hamlets, which can still do scant justice to the heartland of London's East End.

The Bethnal Green and Bow seat produced one of the most unusual results at the 1997 General Election. At the time of Labour's greatest ever national triumph, their share of the vote actually declined by over 7%, their second worst result in Britain. Conversely, the Conservative vote actually went up by nearly 5%. This extraordinary result can only be accounted for by the racial politics of the East End.

In a constituency where most of the electors are either white or Muslim, Labour chose as its candidate Oona King, who has one Afro-Caribbean and one Jewish parent. Meanwhile the Tories picked an Asian, Dr Kabir Choudhury. This clearly rallied more of the largely Bangladeshi ethnic minority vote, while another temptation to some sections of the white communities was the presence of a British National Party candidate, who gleaned 3,350 votes. Labour won the seat fairly easily in the end, of course, but the individual nature of Bethnal Green and Bow suggests that its future will remain unpredictable. That is always possible in such a riven series of neighbourhoods, where old traditions meet new and none.

The seat consists roughly of the northern, inland half of the inner East London borough of Tower Hamlets, so named on its creation in 1965 because of the number of tight working-class communities that have historically existed there. It does reach the Thames at St Katherine's Dock and Wapping. Further north are to be found Whitechapel, Spitalfields with its Bangladeshi majority (the local Tower Hamlets ward has been renamed as Spitalfields and Banglatown), Bethnal Green itself, still mainly white, Old Ford on the south side of Victoria Park, and Bow.

There was less of a fray in 2001 without the participation of Socialist Labour, Real Labour and independent Liberal candidates, and the BNP did not save their deposit (although they may have shared some ground with the New Britain Party's sole national candidate, City of London activist Dennis Delderfield) and there were signs that most of the electorate had accepted Oona King – she polled just over 50% of the vote – but further ructions and alarums can always be expected in this heterogeneous melting-pot in the inner East End.

Social indices:			2001 Gen. Election:			
% Non-white	38.1		Lab	19,380	50.5	+4.1
% Prof/Man	32.4		C	9,323	24.3	+3.2
% Non-manual	54.9		LD	5,946	15.5	+3.5
£ Av prop val 2000	182 K		Grn	1,666	4.3	+2.5
% Increase 97–00	72.5		BNP	1,267	3.2	–4.2
% Unemployed 2001	10.0		NBP	888	2.3	
% Decrease 97–01	3.6		Lab maj	10,057	26.1	
% Fin hard/Rank	57.6	6	Turnout		48.6	–12.6
% Pensioners	23.5		Elect	79,192		
% Prem mort/Rank	52	35				

Member of Parliament

Oona King, one of Labour's – by 2001 – 12 non-white MPs, brings to the Commons a café-au-lait complexion and sexual chemistry born of the multi-cultural union between her African-American civil rights émigré father Professor Preston King, and her Jewish-Geordie mother, Hazel Stern (sister of Miriam Stoppard) – a melange somewhat at variance with the Bengali origins of most of her non-white constituents. With a singular extemporaneous oratorical style, accompanied by gentle swaying, she was born in 1967, educated at Haverstock School, Hampstead and York University, before working for Labour MEPs, including Glenys Kinnock. A backer of PR, and dubbed Labour's answer to Whoopi Goldberg, she is seen as tenacious, talented, sharp and tough, as well as exuding immense charm. In 2001 she was ranked in the Top 10 of MPs by the youth-circulating magazine *Mixmag*, for 'exhibiting cool vibes on legalising cannabis'. Only the second black woman MP (but with a history of awkward relations with the other – Diane Abbott) and trailed as a rising star, she was still waiting in 2001 for the Downing Street call.

BEVERLEY AND HOLDERNESS

It is one of the clearest signs of the extent of the Conservative defeat at the 2001 General Election that they won the Beverley and Holderness constituency – by only 781 votes. All the predictions about the political complexion of this new seat on its creation before 1997 were that it would be very safely Conservative. The notional majority had it existed in 1992 was calculated to be 16,000, and this over the Liberal Democrats. In the event Labour's vote shot up in 1997 in its first contest by about 19%, and James Cran was nearly defeated; and he did not strengthen this position four years later.

One should not be misled by the name. This constituency contains only a minority of the seat of Beverley which existed from 1983–97, that portion around the county town (of the East Riding of Yorkshire, and while it existed of Humberside) itself. Indeed most of the electors in this division, 41,000 in all, reside in Holderness, which formerly constituted a borough and was included in the Bridlington constituency. Holderness is a remote and little-known part of England, including the southernmost section of the Yorkshire coast, from Hornsea down through Withernsea to Spurn Head, the spit of land projecting into the North Sea at the mouth of the Humber which is a birdwatchers' paradise.

All these areas clearly voted Conservative in all general elections since the war. In 2001 the urban wards of Beverley itself must have supported Labour strongly, and there is evidence from the elections for the new unitary authority of the East Riding that they performed competitively in most of Holderness too. Truly this seat has turned up the book and confounded the experts.

Social indices:			2001 Gen. Election:			
% Non-white	0.4		C	19,168	41.3	+0.2
% Prof/Man	36.5		Lab	18,387	39.6	+0.8
% Non-manual	59.5		LD	7,356	15.9	−2.6
£ Av prop val 2000	64 K		UKIP	1,464	3.2	+1.8
% Increase 97–00	18.5		C maj	781	1.7	
% Unemployed 2001	2.8		Turnout		61.7	−11.9
% Decrease 97–01	0.9		Elect	75,146		
% Fin hard/Rank	7.8	530				
% Pensioners	25.4					
% Prem mort/Rank	17	517				

Member of Parliament

James Cran, a flinty Aberdonian law-and-order traditionalist, Eurosceptic and Opposition Whip, has been MP here since 1987. Born in 1944 and educated at Ruthrieston School, Aberdeen, and Aberdeen University, he worked originally for the National Association of Pension Funds and then the CBI. He was 'Chief Whip' to the Maastricht rebels, though denying he was a natural rebel, and hesitating to bring down Major if the alternative was Heseltine. In 1997 he voted for Howard, then Redwood, then Hague – rejecting Redwood's pact with Clarke, because of Clarke's Europhilia, and was a Whip from 1997 to 2001, when, after not revealing his leadership choice, he was briefly Deputy Shadow Leader of the Commons until resigning in October, reportedly unhappy with his job even though – like Shadow Commons Leader, Eric Forth – he had refused to sign the Commission for Racial Equality's call for a non-racist election campaign in April.

BEXHILL AND BATTLE

There were unexpected perturbations in the apparently tranquil and mature East Sussex seat of Bexhill and Battle in the run-up to the 2001 General Election. Most of these stemmed from the departure of the MP since 1983, Charles Wardle, who having announced his retirement endorsed the UK Independence Party candidate for the seat, its leader and also an MEP, Nigel Farage, rather than Greg Barker. The last named had already suffered from a split in the local party after he was accused of embellishing his business experience and credentials before selection. Barker has indeed taken his seat in the Commons, scarcely surprising in what was one of the Tories' 20 safest seats in 1997. Farage did poll comfortably the highest UKIP vote in 2001, 3,474 or nearly 8%, but it can hardly be said that this adversely affected Barker's position: his share of the vote was actually 0.02% up on that Wardle achieved in 1997!

This East Sussex constituency was created in 1983 as essentially the former Rye county division minus the Cinque Port towns of Rye and Winchelsea, which are now placed in Hastings and Rye. Bexhill and Battle consists of a coastal strip between Hastings and Eastbourne, together with the fertile and wooded countryside behind. This is the area most associated with the Norman conquest of England of 1066, for William I landed at Pevensey and defeated the army of the Anglo-Saxon regime at Battle, the heart of the inland part of the seat. Despite this history of conflict, in future the seat is more likely to settle down and reflect the peaceful image of Bexhill rather than that of battle.

The reasons for this are not hard to fathom. Its residents are white – or at least 99% of them are. Fewer than one in ten live in council-built housing. The main sources of employment are tourism and agriculture. Above all, according to Age Concern research this is the seat in the country with the second highest proportion of pensioners, after Worthing West. Thirty-five per cent of the electorate are of pensionable age, which may well mean that around half of all votes in the Bexhill and Battle constituency were cast by the elderly in 2001, who have a strikingly better turnout rate than younger groups. In parts of Bexhill itself the figures are even more dramatic: 65% of all the households in Sackville ward consist only of pensioners, and 59% do in Collington ward. The support of 'grey voters' cannot be taken for granted, but the stability of the result here suggests that Greg Barker can hope for a long run after his initial election at the age of 35.

The constituency is based largely on the local government district of Rother. The river Rother flows into the Channel at Rye, and forms the Kent–East Sussex border for part of its length. The environment could not be more different from that other constituency of Rother Valley and the town of Rotherham. If that is in the Socialist Republic of South Yorkshire, Bexhill and Battle is the Tory citadel of deep south England.

Social indices:			2001 Gen. Election:			
% Non-white	1.0		C	21,555	48.1	+0.0
% Prof/Man	40.9		LD	11,052	24.7	−0.8
% Non-manual	62.0		Lab	8,702	19.4	+1.3
£ Av prop val 2000	121 K		UKIP	3,474	7.8	+6.2
% Increase 97–00	52.6		C maj	10,503	23.5	
% Unemployed 2001	1.5		Turnout		64.9	−9.8
% Decrease 97–01	1.7		Elect	69,010		
% Fin hard/Rank	4.8	607				
% Pensioners	44.2					
% Prem mort/Rank	15	539				

Member of Parliament

In 2001 **Gregory Barker** replaced as Conservative MP the quit-before-pushed MP Charles Wardle, who had lost local party support over his paid consultancy with Mohamed Al-Fayed. Barker, born in 1966 and educated at Steyning Grammar School, Lancing College, Royal Holloway College London University, and the London Business School, came well-connected to the Tory right as an adviser to David Willetts and Chairman of the Centre for Policy Studies policy group, Agenda 2000. However, his impressive portfolio of past and present business activities, covering advertising, oil and banking, became a source of dispute within the Constituency Association, with allegations of 'exaggeration'. He nonetheless triumphed despite the candidacy of the UKIP leader Nigel Farage, who was backed by Charles Wardle, and after attacking the decision to drop plans for the Bexhill and Hastings bypass, declared his support for Michael Portillo in the leadership race.

BEXLEYHEATH AND CRAYFORD

Before the 2001 Election, pundits predicted that Bexleyheath and Crayford was one of Labour's most vulnerable seats in Greater London. Indeed it was, and it now stands as the Conservatives' no.1 target for a gain in the capital next time; but in many ways the fact that Nigel Beard won any kind of victory here, even though it was by a margin of just 1,472, was an even more remarkable feat than his first in 1997.

In time for that election, the Boundary Commission moved the Crayford section of the former Erith and Crayford constituency to join Bexleyheath. The new seat produced a surprise result. Erith and Crayford was a marginal, with the Tories holding it by just 2,339 votes in 1992. Bexleyheath, on the other hand, was a safe Conservative seat, retained by Cyril Townsend the previous time with a very comfortable 14,000 lead over Labour. This is a very heavily owner-occupied, suburban, commuting area. The percentage of professionals and those in higher managerial occupations is not particularly high, nor is there a large percentage of adults with higher educational qualifications, but this is very far from a radical section of outer London.

Labour required an unprecedented swing of 12% to take Bexleyheath and Crayford in 1997; they achieved 15%, making the 61-year-old Nigel Beard one of the more unexpected additions to the Commons. To win the seat for a second time,

Labour needed to pull off another massive victory, when they had never before achieved two in succession with adequate working majorities for full parliaments. Their unprecedented achievement in avoiding the rejection of the electorate is most clearly reflected in results in apparently natural Tory seats like Bexleyheath and Crayford. Or perhaps, on a more cynical view, the turnout, 13% down here, suggests the voters were disillusioned – but not just by the government.

Social indices:			2001 Gen. Election:			
% Non-white	3.7		Lab	17,593	43.6	–1.9
% Prof/Man	30.1		C	16,121	39.9	+1.5
% Non-manual	62.3		LD	4,476	11.1	–0.1
£ Av prop val 2000	108 K		BNP	1,408	3.5	+2.6
% Increase 97–00	43.3		UKIP	780	1.9	+1.1
% Unemployed 2001	2.0		Lab maj	1,472	3.6	
% Decrease 97–01	2.4		Turnout		63.5	–12.6
% Fin hard/Rank	9.2	484	Elect	63,580		
% Pensioners	24.7					
% Prem mort/Rank	18	500				

Member of Parliament

Labour's **Nigel Beard** won this seat from the Conservatives in 1997. An industrial manager who has specialised in science and technology, he was the oldest Labour entrant in 1997, backs greater industrial democracy, government support for high-tech industries, EU control of the arms trade and electoral reform. Son of a railway porter, he was born in Leeds in 1936 and educated at Castleford Grammar School and University College, London, before working variously as a scientific officer in the civil service and as a manager with ICI – making him one of the few Labour MPs with private sector experience – and sits on the Treasury Select Committee.

BILLERICAY

The county of Essex declared some of the best results in the country for the Conservatives in the 2001 Election. In Billericay John Baron must have heaved a sigh of relief as he put behind him his failure to hold Basildon in 1997 and increase the majority he inherited here from Teresa Gorman from 1,256 to over 5,000. With a rare Tory gain in Castle Point – and arguably Romford and Upminster can be counted as Essex still as well – and the move away from marginality of this seat and Southend West where the Liberal Democrats had challenged strongly in 1997, the Party could point to a distinct revival in the county. Yet in fact this would mask the true decline here since the happier days of Conservative government, and any self-congratulation should have rung hollow. That Billericay should ever have been close was a sign of the depths to which the Conservatives have sunk in Essex and in the nation.

Although the well-publicised MP Teresa Gorman held her seat in 1997, her majority was slashed from a notional 20,998 to just 1,356. This represented a swing of no less than 17.6% to Labour, one of the highest figures in the land. A 'local Conservative' obtained 3,377 votes and held his deposit, having surpassed the threshold of one-twentieth of the total votes cast, and these presumably largely returned to their labelled party allegiance in 2001. It was a shock that Teresa Gorman nearly lost what had seemed to be an extremely safe Tory constituency.

When in 1983 the Boundary Commissioners separated the New Town of Basildon from the more owner-occupied, middle-class communities of Billericay and Wickford they recreated a famous constituency name in British politics. In the 1950s and 1960s Billericay was consistently among the first seats to declare a result on General Election night, despite the fact that it had one of the largest electorates in England and was often a knife-edge marginal. The Billericay returns were an early pointer to the likely outcome of the election itself, and, as such, eagerly awaited.

The current Billericay, though, has none of these features. Its announcement is not especially speedy, its electorate only a little larger than average, its political character until 1997 very safely Conservative. Only Pitsea of the Basildon New Town neighbourhoods is included in this seat. Although Billericay had been a safe seat since its revival in 1983, its name has not ceased to be associated with controversy and 'news value'. The extreme right-wing Conservative MP for Basildon, Harvey Proctor, gained the nomination for the new seat and won easily in 1983. More than any other Tory member, Proctor had been named as having connections with extra-parliamentary Nationalist and racist organisations. Yet it was not this that led to his removal as Conservative candidate just before the 1987 Election, but his connection in a court case involving teenage 'rent boys'. This was too much for the previously loyal Billericay Conservative Association, and he was replaced at the 11th hour by Teresa Gorman. If they expected this to produce an MP less prone to publicity they were mistaken; it remains to be seen whether John Baron will make waves as his two predecessors did, in their distinct ways.

Social indices:			2001 Gen. Election:			
% Non-white	1.9		C	21,608	47.4	+7.6
% Prof/Man	34.5		Lab	16,595	36.4	−0.9
% Non-manual	63.9		LD	6,323	13.9	−1.9
£ Av prop val 2000	121 K		UKIP	1,072	2.4	
% Increase 97–00	47.7		C maj	5,013	11.0	
% Unemployed 2001	1.9		Turnout		58.1	−14.3
% Decrease 97–01	2.0		Elect	78,528		
% Fin hard/Rank	12.4	406				
% Pensioners	21.1					
% Prem mort/Rank	17	514				

Member of Parliament

John Baron replaced the retiring Teresa Gorman here in 2001, having failed in 1997 to retain for the Conservatives the emblematic next-door seat of Basildon. Born in 1959 and educated variously but ultimately at Queen's College, Taunton, and Jesus College, Cambridge, and RMA Sandhurst, he spent four years in the Royal Regiment of Fusiliers, serving in Ulster, Cyprus and Germany, before heading for merchant banking with Rothschilds. A right-wing Eurosceptic of conventional mode and a targeter of the burden of tax and regulation on small businesses, and of the climate change levy, he voted for David Davis in the 2001 leadership ballots.

BIRKENHEAD

The centre of Birkenhead is only a little over a mile through the Mersey tunnel from the city centre of Liverpool. Birkenhead is therefore a closer constituency physically to inner Liverpool than some of the peripheral Liverpool seats like Garston and West Derby, and very much part of the heart of Merseyside. Its politics also reflect the strongly pro-Labour bias of this colourful, dramatic part of the world.

The seat includes, for example, the modern Ford council estate in the Bidston ward, which has a ferocious reputation for crime and drug abuse, every bit as severe as peripheral Liverpool estates like Croxteth, Netherley and Stockbridge Village. Bidston is a Labour stronghold of course, as are the wards in the central industrial areas of the town, long dependent on the threatened and insecure shipbuilding industry. This is also an area of multiple deprivation, with a mixture of decaying terraces and poor-quality modern council blocks. The wards of Birkenhead itself and Tranmere, which includes the community of Rock Ferry, are overwhelmingly Labour. The only substantial middle-class presence is to be found in Claughton ward, which includes Birkenhead Park, and Oxton. This is the old classic west end of Birkenhead, with many handsome Victorian mansions in leafy residential roads, and proud institutions like Birkenhead School. Nevertheless, it is the Liberal Democrats, not the Conservatives, who do best in local elections in these wards, although they have never been able to transfer this achievement to parliamentary elections. Indeed in 2001 the Lib Dems finished third again in Birkenhead, as the Labour MP Frank Field won by over 15,000 from the Conservatives on a turnout of just 47%, down 18% from 1997, a degree of change mirroring that over the river in Liverpool Riverside, where the lowest proportion anywhere in the UK went to the polls.

Electoral politics in Birkenhead have held plenty of interest in recent years, but this has mainly centred on the internal problems of the Labour Party and the travails of Frank Field. Strongly – if independently – associated with the right of the party, Field was opposed by 'Socialist Labour' in 1997, but they were brushed aside with 1,168 votes and did not stand in 2001 despite the higher-profile national campaign of the Far Left. Liverpool's twin town across the Mersey in this economically and socially battered region offers scant comfort to the supporters of any party other than Labour, but also nowadays little enthusiasm for any party at all.

Social indices:			2001 Gen. Election:			
% Non-white	1.5		Lab	20,418	70.5	−0.3
% Prof/Man	28.6		C	4,827	16.7	+1.5
% Non-manual	51.2		LD	3,722	12.8	+3.8
£ Av prop val 2000	46 K		Lab maj	15,591	53.8	
% Increase 97–00	18.9		Turnout		47.7	−18.1
% Unemployed 2001	8.2		Elect	60,726		
% Decrease 97–01	4.6					
% Fin hard/Rank	32.2	114				
% Pensioners	25.2					
% Prem mort/Rank	53	27				

Member of Parliament

Frank Field, an uptight, ascetic, cadaverous bachelor, is one of a clutch of dropped and disaffected Labour ex-ministers. As a Social Security minister for 15 months he was supposed to think the unthinkable on welfare reform (in effect to move rightwards away from the Beveridge principle of universality), came up with proposals for self-help and compulsory private pensions, and was blocked both by his boss Harriet Harman and by Gordon Brown's Treasury, where his proposals clashed with Treasury ideas about targeted benefits and tax incentives. A lone operator, incapable of being a team player, and a political outsider, he nonetheless blazed a few trails in his time – for OMOV, council house sales and Lib-Labbery. Born in 1942 and suffering a violent father, he attended Clement Danes Grammar School and Hull University and, initially a teacher, rose politically by running the Child Poverty Action Group and the Low Pay Unit until being elected for Birkenhead in 1979, and then spent 12 years fending off would-be Trotskyist deselectors during Labour's worst years. A Germanophobic Eurosceptic and a High Anglican defender of the 1662 Prayer Book, he rebelled 21 times against the government after being dropped from it, during the remainder of the 1997–2001 Parliament, often on his own, as over benefit fraudsters in May 2001, and in the new House in July 2001 he rebelled to demand a referendum on the Nice Treaty, and in November called on the Prime Minister to sack Gordon Brown.

BIRMINGHAM EDGBASTON

The constituency of Birmingham Edgbaston provided one of the most memorable moments of General Election night in 1997, when the presentable Gisela Stuart notched up the first of many gains for New Labour. It was a significant omen, for Labour had never won this seat before. In 2001 it was a key target marginal again scheduled to be declared early, and the Conservatives looked to Edgbaston for an early sign of the revival which was not to come, as their unfortunate candidate Nigel Hastilow, the butt of running jokes in the *Independent* newspaper's diary column, slipped even further behind.

Edgbaston is probably the best-known middle-class residential area in England's second largest city. Situated just south-west of the city centre, it still contains large mansions, many of which are converted to institutional use, but some of which are still occupied by single families. Edgbaston ward has leafy parks, the Warwickshire and Test cricket ground, and ranks as the educational centre of the city, harbouring Birmingham University, and King Edward's Grammar School. Despite all these marks of distinction, it must now be considered a Labour seat. Although the centre of gravity of the Edgbaston seat has gradually been moved out towards the suburbs in boundary changes, the latest addition being Bartley Green in 1997, Gisela Stuart's triumphs have shown that Labour can now appeal across the board, from the edge of the inner city through areas of considerable affluence to peripheral council estates and new private housing.

Social indices:			2001 Gen. Election:			
% Non-white	11.0		Lab	18,517	49.1	+0.5
% Prof/Man	39.9		C	13,819	36.6	−2.0
% Non-manual	61.4		LD	4,528	12.0	+2.3
£ Av prop val 2000	100 K		PECP	454	1.2	
% Increase 97–00	32.0		SLP	431	1.1	
% Unemployed 2001	5.4		Lab maj	4,698	12.4	
% Decrease 97–01	2.2		Turnout		56.0	−13.0
% Fin hard/Rank	30.3	127	Elect	67,405		
% Pensioners	28.2					
% Prem mort/Rank	38	208				

Member of Parliament

Gisela Stuart, born (1955) Gisela Gschaider in Bavaria, is a rare German in British politics, and in view of the threat to Rover's Longbridge plant by the pull-out of BMW, it may not have been prudent of her to venture the joke that 'born in Munich, I have ended up inheriting Neville Chamberlain's seat by purely democratic means'. After secondary schooling in Germany she studied at Manchester Polytechnic and London University, becoming a college law lecturer. By 1999 after achingly loyal support for the Blair government, she joined it as a Junior Health Minister. But in 2001 her fledgling ministerial career imploded following an incident in the election campaign, which provided – with John Prescott's scuffle in Rhyl – one of the more damaging (for Labour) visual images of the campaign, in which she stood quietly by as an irate girlfriend of a cancer patient berated Tony Blair outside a Birmingham hospital. But parked on the Foreign Affairs Select Committee she reverted to the role of on-message defender of government policy on Afghanistan.

BIRMINGHAM ERDINGTON

By the time Robin Corbett retired at very short notice before the 2001 General Election, to be replaced by the *Daily Telegraph* and *Spectator*'s tame-ish New Labour columnist Sion Simon, Erdington had come to be regarded as a safe Labour seat ripe for inheritance, and it was hard to remember that it had seen the closest contest in Birmingham in 1983 and 1987, and that when the veteran MP Julius Silverman, who had sat in Parliament for nearly 40 years, retired in 1983, his majority in 1979 had been just 680 votes. The next Labour candidate Robin Corbett did very well to hold on by just 231 in 1983, the peak of Thatcherite success. Corbett increased his majority to 2,500 in 1987 and to 4,700 in 1992, but the seat remained marginal in appearance. However, the advent of Kingstanding ward from Perry Barr constituency already made Erdington safe enough, even before the (slightly less than average) swing from the Conservatives in 1997, which was in no way reversed in 2001.

Erdington is a mixed constituency in the north-eastern corner of Birmingham. It includes a good residential area in Erdington ward itself, up against the border with affluent Sutton Coldfield, but as one progresses further into the city the Labour vote strengthens. Here is Kingsbury ward, which includes the large ultra-modern tower-block estate of Castle Vale; and two historic landmarks from different eras, the old tyre works of Fort Dunlop and the 'Spaghetti Junction' motorway intersection at Gravelly Hill. Even Erdington ward was held by Labour though, in their poor May 2000 local elections in Birmingham, as was Kingsbury, as was Kingstanding.

Kingstanding is basically a large semi-detached council estate, still half in the hands of the local authority at the time of the 1991 Census, its streets laid out in neat geometric patterns. Fewer than one-tenth of the voters in the ward are non-white, and its continued allegiance to Labour gives the lie to any who might think that racial polarisation is the sole key to the complex politics of Birmingham; indeed the Erdington constituency as a whole now counts, uniquely, as a largely peripheral, largely white, safe Labour seat in the second city.

Social indices:			2001 Gen. Election:			
% Non-white	9.2		Lab	17,375	56.8	−2.0
% Prof/Man	21.2		C	7,413	24.2	−3.3
% Non-manual	44.5		LD	3,602	11.8	+1.6
£ Av prop val 2000	55 K		NF	681	2.2	
% Increase 97–00	19.8		SA	669	2.2	
% Unemployed 2001	6.2		UKIP	521	1.7	
% Decrease 97–01	2.8		SLP	343	1.1	
% Fin hard/Rank	40.8	46	Lab maj	9,962	32.6	
% Pensioners	27.3		Turnout		46.6	−14.3
% Prem mort/Rank	52	37	Elect	65,668		

Member of Parliament

Sion Simon, a journalist who came to notice as a Blairite apologist in Conservative publications such as the *Spectator* and the *Daily Telegraph*, and whose column in the latter he self-dubbed as 'a notoriously craven and complicit mouthpiece of the Blairist conspiracy', inherited this safe seat in 2001. A realist who sees the problem of 'a society with high welfare and service expectations, but which doesn't want to pay tax', he sees Blair's task as 'to pull down the rusting structure of twentieth century collectivism and replace it with something more modern'. A one-time aide to George Robertson MP, and a Walworth Road/Millbank officer during the 1992 and 1997 Elections, and a former manager with Guinness plc, he was born in 1968 and educated at Handsworth Grammar School and Magdalen College, Oxford – whose admission procedures he defended against Gordon Brown's 'bizarre onslaught' in 2000. With modishly narrow spectacles and of slight build, having slimmed down from (in his own words) 'grossly fat', he has defended Labour candidate selections against Harriet Harman's call for more women, dismissed Lord Hattersley's assault on 'New Labour' as outdated, blamed Trotskyists for stirring up race riots in Bradford, and described the 2001 foot-and-mouth outbreak as 'just a crisis in one small industry'. His Corsican grandfather fought with De Gaulle's Free French.

BIRMINGHAM HALL GREEN

Like so many other cities, Britain's second largest centre of population, Birmingham, now sends not a single Conservative to Parliament. One of the last two seats to crack to the Labour onslaught, in 1997, was Hall Green.

It is not so much a classic old upper-class district like Edgbaston, the other perpetually Tory division; rather it is a peripheral constituency on the south and south-eastern edge of Birmingham. Billesley and Brandwood wards contain a complex mixture of council housing and owner-occupied dwellings, but Hall Green ward itself is 84% owner-occupied with only 8% local authority tenants. One thing that the wards do have in common is that they are very largely composed of white residents; the seat as a whole was over 90% white at the last published Census, in a cosmopolitan city which was over a fifth non-white as a whole.

The political characteristics reflect these other indicators. Billesley and Brandwood are historically regarded as marginal, with Billesley usually electing Labour councillors (like the city council leader Theresa Stewart), largely because of the tower block cluster at Highter's Heath on the very southern edge of Birmingham, and Brandwood Tory more often than not. Hall Green is one of the most middle-class wards in the city, very different in every way from neighbouring Sparkhill; the trees seem to start to grow as soon as one passes the 'Hall Green' sign on the A34 travelling south towards the edge of the city. In many ways this suburban constituency is far removed from the turmoil and tensions of Birmingham city centre, five miles to the north; in others its politics are shaped by them.

There only needed to be a 4% swing to Labour to dislodge Andrew Hargreaves in 1997 – and they achieved an extra 10%, their best performance in Birmingham. Stephen McCabe won by over 8,000 in an undersized seat, probably benefiting from a squeeze on the Liberal Democrats, who polled less than a tenth of the vote despite local government successes in the constituency's eponymous ward. The turnout dropped by 14% in 2001, but there was no significant movement between the major parties, and Hall Green, like all the other seats prefixed by the name of Birmingham, seems likely to remain in Labour hands for the foreseeable future.

Social indices:			2001 Gen. Election:			
% Non-white	9.3		Lab	18,049	54.6	+1.1
% Prof/Man	27.8		C	11,401	34.5	+1.1
% Non-manual	54.0		LD	2,926	8.8	–0.8
£ Av prop val 2000	76 K		UKIP	708	2.1	
% Increase 97–00	29.3		Lab maj	6,648	20.1	
% Unemployed 2001	4.8		Turnout		57.5	–13.7
% Decrease 97–01	2.3		Elect	57,563		
% Fin hard/Rank	26.8	178				
% Pensioners	27.9					
% Prem mort/Rank	35	254				

Member of Parliament

Strongly Scots-accented former social worker **Steve McCabe**, who won this seat in 1997, is one of a score of migrant Scots occupying Labour seats in England. Born in 1955, educated at Port Glasgow Senior Secondary School, Moray House College of Education, and Bradford University, he has done little to earn his self-description as a 'socialist Blairite', unless that is implied in his call for the RUC to cease being a 'colonial police force' (having been appointed to the Northern Ireland Select

Committee in 1998) and his urging the police to make more use of 'anti-social behaviour orders' in November 2001. His background as a city councillor for eight years and a social worker for 20 years is typical of many of Labour's municipal public-sector-derived MPs.

BIRMINGHAM HODGE HILL

Hodge Hill, east Birmingham, is effectively the successor to the Stechford seat, which achieved note when it elected a Conservative in the 1977 by-election caused by its long-term and then Labour MP Roy Jenkins's move to EEC headquarters in Brussels. At the 1979 General Election, Labour's by-election loser, Terry Davis, regained the seat, but by only 1,649 votes. In 1983 Stechford was metamorphosed into Hodge Hill, and Terry Davis is still the MP for the area. He has gradually built up his majority, to reach a comfortable 11,618 in 2001, on a turnout of under 50% and with seven opponents of very varied persuasions including the BNP, Justice for Kashmiris and Socialist Labour. Hodge Hill has a substantial number of both owner-occupiers and council tenants. Less than in most parts of the country, however, can the political tastes of Hodge Hill be predicted from tenure. The council estates on the eastern edge of Birmingham, in Shard End and Hodge Hill wards, are full of white skilled workers, who have shown an inclination to prefer the Tories in several recent years. On the other hand a considerable proportion of the owner-occupiers are to be found in Washwood Heath nearer the city centre, which is heavily non-white, mainly Pakistani, and Justice for Kashmiri and other Asian independent candidates have usually beaten Labour there in recent years. Washwood Heath is actually part of the huge east Birmingham Asian (and mainly Muslim) neighbourhood, which is centred on the Sparkbrook and Small Heath seat.

This eastern wedge of Birmingham demonstrates a range of attributes, from Asian owner-occupiers of the inner city to Tory working-class voters in the peripheral council estates. Both stereotypes are far from perfect, of course, and with the return of the Labour Party to the political centre, wards like Shard End were quite happy to return a Labour councillor to the city council in May 2000, and despite the prominence of ethnic issues here none of the minor candidates came near to saving their deposit in 2001. The veteran Davis was returned to Westminster very comfortably for a sixth full term.

Social indices:			2001 Gen. Election:			
% Non-white	17.0		Lab	16,901	63.9	−1.7
% Prof/Man	16.6		C	5,283	20.0	−4.0
% Non-manual	39.5		LD	2,147	8.1	−0.4
£ Av prop val 2000	50 K		BNP	889	3.4	
% Increase 97–00	19.0		PJP	561	2.1	
% Unemployed 2001	8.1		SLP	284	1.1	
% Decrease 97–01	2.6		UKIP	275	1.0	−0.9
% Fin hard/Rank	49.4	16	Mus	125	0.5	
% Pensioners	29.3		Lab maj	11,618	43.9	
% Prem mort/Rank	45	88	Turnout		47.9	−13.0
			Elect	55,254		

Member of Parliament

The career of **Terry Davis**, now a crumpled bear-like veteran West Midlands MP, began as a then-rare Labour by-election-winning-MP at Bromsgrove in 1971. Losing the seat in 1974 he returned in 1979 for Stechford – later resprayed as Hodge Hill. Born in 1938, the son of a Conservative-voting insurance man, educated at King Edward VI Grammar School, Stourbridge, University College, London and Michigan University, and a former motor industry manager, he is a Eurosceptic from the centre-right of the party, if occasionally joining the left before 1997 to oppose the Defence estimates, anti-terrorism legislation, and the Gulf War. Dropped as a frontbench spokesman as long ago as 1987, and from the Public Accounts Committee in 1994, he was by 1997 too old and too disorderly (with 37 rebellious votes between 1992 and 1997) for office, and has latterly grazed innocuously as a delegate to the Council of Europe and the Western European Union.

BIRMINGHAM LADYWOOD

Ladywood, in Birmingham's inner city, has had a complex and fascinating electoral history. There was a time in the 1920s when it was the constituency of the future Conservative Prime Minister Neville Chamberlain. In 1924 Chamberlain beat the Labour candidate, one Oswald Mosley, by 77 votes. In 1929 Labour captured Ladywood by 11 votes (Chamberlain had departed to safe pastures at Edgbaston). After the Second World War Ladywood seemed like a safe Labour seat, owing to residential and population decline and the end of the business vote. However, in a 1969 by-election the Liberal Wallace Lawler swept home. His stewardship of the seat lasted only a year before the seat returned to Labour. John Sever did well to hold Ladywood for Labour in another by-election in 1977, caused by the resignation of Brian Walden to present the ITV programme *Weekend World*; but Sever was not reselected for 1983 and replaced by Clare Short.

Clare Short still holds Ladywood, which can be considered a safe Labour seat in all but the most exceptional circumstances. The constituency includes the city centre – which Americans would call the 'downtown': the Bull Ring, New Street Station, Paradise Circus, and so on. It also includes some of the most heavily non-white areas in the whole of Britain: Soho ward, over two-thirds non-white; and now, following the reduction of Birmingham's allocation of parliamentary seats by one, two wards from the former Small Heath seat. Aston and Nechells are both multicultural inner-city wards with a high proportion of council housing, largely in purpose-built modern flats. Overall Ladywood now covers northern and eastern parts of Birmingham's inner city, and may truly be described as the central seat. Nowhere in the United Kingdom was there a higher unemployment rate than in central Birmingham in June 2001, and Ladywood pipped Belfast West for the unenviable title of number one constituency in this regard, with 12.8%. Overall its proportion of non-white residents reaches approximately 55%, one of two white minority seats in the city.

In 2001 Clare Short was faced by seven opponents, and the Kashmiri People's Justice Party saved its deposit in fourth place, but she still scored more than six times as many votes as her closest opponent, the Conservative, although only half as many as the number of abstentions. It's all a far cry from the days of Neville Chamberlain.

Social indices:			2001 Gen. Election:			
% Non-white	53.6		Lab	21,694	68.9	−5.2
% Prof/Man	21.9		C	3,551	11.3	−2.0
% Non-manual	38.7		LD	2,586	8.2	+0.3
£ Av prop val 2000	47 K		PJP	2,112	6.7	
% Increase 97–00	29.6		SLP	443	1.4	
% Unemployed 2001	12.8		Mus	432	1.4	
% Decrease 97–01	3.3		PA	392	1.2	
% Fin hard/Rank	71.6	1	UKIP	283	0.9	
% Pensioners	20.2		Lab maj	18,143	57.6	
% Prem mort/Rank	54	22	Turnout		44.3	−10.0
			Elect	71,113		

Member of Parliament

Potentially the Blair Cabinet's stormiest petrel, **Clare Short** – in the marginal post of International Development Secretary – is the least conventional of Labour's senior women politicians, with two frontbench resignations in Opposition (over terrorism legislation in 1988 and the Gulf War in 1991), and occasional off-message utterances as a Cabinet Minister, such as her call to close the Dome, criticism of the US record on aid, and an attack on 'toadying' loyalist backbenchers. She has also never voted for the winner in any Labour leadership or deputy leadership election. But on a long leash from Tony Blair, she has repaid his tolerance by loyally backing the bombing of Kosovo and Belgrade, and – albeit seated alongside the PM as a grim-faced, tortured conscience – the bombing of Afghanistan as well. She also took on the hard left by defending before a party conference the blocking in 1995 of Liz Davies as a Labour candidate, so inviting the accusation of being an authoritarian careerist. Big, strapping, emotional and abrasive, she was Birmingham-born in 1946, into an Irish Republican family, educated at St Paul's (RC) Girls' Grammar School, Keele and Leeds Universities, and was reunited in 1996 with her by then adult City-lawyer son, whom she had given up for adoption as a baby. Originally concerned about images of under-clothed women in tabloid newspapers, in 2001 she was keen to liberate over-clothed women in Afghanistan.

BIRMINGHAM NORTHFIELD

The West Midlands' 'capital city' has traditionally had several critical marginal seats whose allegiances help to decide the identity of the nation's government, but there is little doubt which has swung most often with the tide. The seat of Northfield, in the south-western corner of Birmingham, changed hands four times between 1979 and 1992, three times with a majority of less than 1,000, lastly when the Tory MP Roger King was beaten by Richard Burden by 630 votes.

Northfield has traditionally been a working-class seat, with a high proportion of council tenants and skilled workers – the long-troubled Longbridge motor factory, once Austin, then Rover, lies within its boundaries. However, changes in housing tenure and Britain's manufacturing industrial base both strongly challenge this characterisation, and with a preponderance of owner occupiers and a more mixed occupational pattern Northfield is open to the pressures of most of the national aspirations and threats which affect our increasingly instrumental and less class-conscious electorate.

In 1997 Burden achieved a swing of no less than 13% over the Conservatives and increased his majority to nearly 11,500. In 2001 his lead fell to less than 8,000, more due to the slump in turnout than to a very modest drop in his share. Does this mean that Northfield has finally lost its marginal status? Oddly enough, arguably not. This is the kind of seat in which the Conservatives will have to be competitive if they are ever to form a majority government again. It is still crucial to the outcome of a general election. That is a measure of just how far the Tories are away from power at the moment.

Social indices:			2001 Gen. Election:			
% Non-white	4.1		Lab	16,528	56.0	−1.5
% Prof/Man	25.1		C	8,730	29.6	+1.6
% Non-manual	47.6		LD	3,322	11.2	+0.8
£ Av prop val 2000	63 K		UKIP	550	1.9	
% Increase 97–00	24.0		SA	193	0.7	
% Unemployed 2001	5.7		SLP	151	0.5	
% Decrease 97–01	1.7		CPGB	60	0.2	
% Fin hard/Rank	38.7	60	Lab maj	7,798	26.4	
% Pensioners	26.9		Turnout		52.8	−15.5
% Prem mort/Rank	37	212	Elect	55,922		

Member of Parliament

Richard Burden, Labour MP here since 1992, is an ex-NALGO officer who favours PR, and achieved brief fame in 1995 for attacking Tony Blair's conversion of Labour into 'a US-style, ruthlessly-effective machine', after Peter Mandelson's orchestration of a dirty campaign against the winning Liberal Democrats in the Littleborough and Saddleworth by-election. Himself an ex-Liberal he was born in 1954 and educated at Wallasey Technical Grammar School, Bramhall Technical Grammar, St John's College of Further Education, Manchester, and York and Warwick Universities. He was PPS to Jeff Rooker 1997–2001, opposed water privatisation as a union official, and is a supporter of the Palestinian Arabs. Inevitably he has had to fight hard to save 20,000 Longbridge car plant jobs.

BIRMINGHAM PERRY BARR

Perry Barr saw one of the most bitterly disputed and damaging of handovers caused by the retirement of a Labour MP in 2001, all the more so for not being brought about at the last minute like Gerry Bermingham's much-publicised departure in favour of Shaun Woodward in St Helens South. Jeff Rooker, though a lively 60 years old and certainly not ready for departure from active politics, as indicated by his immediate reappointment to government office as a Minister of State in the Home Office with a seat in the Lords, nevertheless announced in January 2000 that he would not stand again. Eventually Khalid Mahmood was selected as his Labour replacement, but not without the active and public opposition of many local activists particularly in Perry Barr ward. This led directly to a spectacularly bad result for Labour, with their vote dropping by 16.5% in a turnout of only just over half of those on the register. The main beneficiaries were the Liberal Democrats, as in St Helens, who more than doubled their share. Like Woodward, though, Mahmood did take his place in the Commons, where at least he is not likely to start as unpopular with his colleagues.

The north-west Birmingham seat of Perry Barr is divided into two distinct and very different parts. In the 1960s and 1970s, the Perry Barr constituency was a predominantly white, working-class peripheral seat, and a genuine marginal, changing hands with (or sometimes against) the national tide. The Conservatives gained it, somehow against the tide, in 1964 and again in 1970, in each case for just one term. Then in 1983 and again in 1997 Labour received great boosts as the heavily non-white wards of Handsworth and Sandwell were added. Handsworth is much closer to the centre of the city, and a neighbourhood which was known and notorious for giving its name to the riots a couple of years earlier. The other majority non-white ward, Sandwell, named after Sandwell Park, the Birmingham section of which is within its bounds, is a different kind of neighbourhood. It was originally strongly Conservative and middle class, with large houses and leafy roads. It is also part of the general Handsworth area, including Handsworth Wood, and was part of the old Handsworth seat of the liberal Conservative Sir Edward Boyle, which gradually became occupied by West Indian and Asian immigrants until it fell to Labour in February 1974. There is still a middle-class Tory vote in Sandwell, although it is 57% non-white, and much of it still looks the part of an attractive suburb. The ethnic mix in these wards is a complex mix of Indian, Pakistani and Caribbean in origin.

There are two other wards, Oscott and Perry Barr. These are majority owner-occupied, almost all white, and far less solidly Labour; Perry Barr was won by the Liberal Democrats in 2000 although this particular success predates the quarrel over Rooker's successor. Overall, Perry Barr should return Mahmood again, but it cannot be safely predicted that this will be without further incident or dispute.

Social indices:			2001 Gen. Election:			
% Non-white	37.6		Lab	17,415	46.5	−16.5
% Prof/Man	24.4		C	8,662	23.1	+1.4
% Non-manual	48.5		LD	8,566	22.9	+13.0
£ Av prop val 2000	55 K		SLP	1,544	4.1	
% Increase 97–00	19.7		SA	465	1.2	
% Unemployed 2001	6.6		UKIP	352	0.9	
% Decrease 97–01	2.0		Marx	221	0.6	
% Fin hard/Rank	29.1	141	Mus	192	0.5	
% Pensioners	24.7		Lab maj	8,753	23.4	
% Prem mort/Rank	37	217	Turnout		52.6	−12.0
			Elect	71,121		

Member of Parliament

Khalid Mahmood inherited this seat in 2001 with a very depleted majority, after a protracted selection process delayed by intense ethnic rivalries within the local non-white population, and allegations of postal vote ballot-rigging. Succeeding Jeff Rooker, who did not support his selection, he was born in 1961 and educated at Golden Hillock Comprehensive in Sparkbrook, Garrets Green College, Birmingham, and Birmingham Polytechnic. A lightly Birmingham-accented Kashmiri, formerly an engineer, and a one-time Birmingham City Councillor (1990–93), he was, as the Commons' only other Muslim MP (after Mohammed Sarwar), inevitably drawn into the limelight after the terrorist attack on the World Trade Center in September 2001. He sought to deflect attacks on Muslims in general by claiming essential similarities between Islam, Judaism and Christianity, and expressed his concern about third-generation Muslim youths in Britain whose poor education and ignorance of their religion made them prey to Muslim fanatics and targets of the BNP. In November 2001 he admitted his *Observer* article, declaring British Muslims' support for the bombing of Afghanistan, was drafted with the help of Foreign Office Minister Denis MacShane.

BIRMINGHAM SELLY OAK

Selly Oak is one of those urban seats which has slipped away from the Conservatives owing to social change as well as shorter-term preference over the past 50 years. Originally this south Birmingham seat was typified by some of the best housing areas in the city, similar in standard to the neighbouring Edgbaston. Then the proportion of non-white immigrants increased at the northern end of the seat, in Moseley ward, which by 1991 was one-quarter Asian or Afro-Caribbean and usually returned a Labour candidate to Birmingham city council. Meanwhile council estates were built near the southern edge of the city, at King's Norton, which also moved towards Labour.

The Conservatives held Selly Oak from its creation in 1955 right up to October 1974, a period in which it had withstood three Labour General Election victories, including one landslide. Anthony Beaumont-Dark regained it for the Tories in 1979 and retained the seat through the Thatcher years. But by now the Tories could only keep Selly Oak in a year when they won a landslide, and it was won by Labour's Lynne Jones in 1992. In 1997 she benefited from a typical swing of 12% to increase her majority to 14,000, the highest in the constituency's history.

The profile of the Selly Oak seat (which also includes Selly Park and the former Cadbury model community of Bournville in addition to Moseley and King's Norton) is fairly typical of the city as a whole, which swung strongly (and usefully) to Labour in both 1992 and 1997 and held steady in 2001 with the exception of two unconnected swings to the Liberal Democrats, in Yardley and Perry Barr. Although they did quite well in the council elections in May 2000, they were still 8% behind in the wards within Selly Oak constituency, and it is hard seeing the Tories winning any seats in the second city in the foreseeable future, unless one counts Sutton Coldfield as a Birmingham seat.

Social indices:			2001 Gen. Election:			
% Non-white	11.7		Lab	21,015	52.4	–3.2
% Prof/Man	39.1		C	10,676	26.6	–1.1
% Non-manual	60.6		LD	6,532	16.3	+4.2
£ Av prop val 2000	82 K		Grn	1,309	3.3	
% Increase 97–00	38.7		UKIP	568	1.4	
% Unemployed 2001	4.7		Lab maj	10,339	25.8	
% Decrease 97–01	1.9		Turnout		56.3	–13.9
% Fin hard/Rank	21.9	245	Elect	71,237		
% Pensioners	25.8					
% Prem mort/Rank	39	193				

Member of Parliament

Lynne Jones, MP here since 1992, has replaced Clare Short as Birmingham's most left-wing Labour MP. A Campaign Group member (by 2001 one of only four Labour women MPs in the Group), she has been active in all the main revolts against the Blair government on lone parent benefit cuts, university tuition fees, predatory newspaper pricing, Incapacity Benefits, legal aid reform, pensions linked to earnings, jury trials, freedom of information, and air traffic control privatisation. In all, during the 1997–2001 Parliament she was the fourth most rebellious Labour MP, with 38 dissentient votes, compared with her 34 rebellions between 1992 and 1997. A smart, tiny, winsomely attractive former Birmingham City Councillor, she was born in 1951, raised on a council estate, daughter of an unemployed schizophrenic father (an unhappy experience which lies behind her interest in mental health), and educated at Bartley Green Girls Grammar School and Birmingham University, acquiring a doctorate (which she uses) in biochemistry, and Birmingham Polytechnic. Her deceptively mild-looking appearance belies the tough idealism of a committed radical, who favoured Livingstone for leader in 1994, but was only able to vote for Beckett. In the 2001 House she quickly rebelled over health checks for disability benefit claimants and in the various divisions on the Terrorism, Crime and Security Bill.

BIRMINGHAM SPARKBROOK AND SMALL HEATH

The Sparkbrook and Small Heath seat, the creation of a merger before the 1997 General Election, has a majority of Asian residents, although that is not the same as a majority of voters, and this has led to strong demands for the dominant Labour Party to select a Muslim candidate. Although there have been voluble rows and rifts, and the suspension of the local party, the former Small Heath MP Roger Godsiff still sits for this constituency. Apart from the aberrant Fox Hollies ward, which is essentially a peripheral white working-class area, all of this territory is homogeneous. It is inner south-east Birmingham, with small Victorian terraces and more modern council housing. It is poor (fourth in the national ranking of financial hardship provided by Experian in 2001), it had the second highest unemployment rate of any constituency in England in June 2001, it is working-class and it is predominantly Asian – particularly the Islamic communities of Pakistani and Bangladeshi origin, which contrasts with the Hindu and Sikh concentration further north-west.

Six of Godsiff's seven opponents in 2001 were Asian Muslims (the exception being the UK Independence candidate). The People's Justice Party, a predominantly Kashmiri movement, obtained by far their highest performance here, 13%, which would have held their deposit even under the old rules when it was one eighth of the vote, and came third ahead of the Conservatives. Nevertheless, Godsiff still won by a very large margin, which will reinforce the defence that MPs should not be chosen on racial or religious grounds. It is more likely that a Muslim MP will take over here through internal Labour Party decision-making than that there will be a change of hands at the ballot.

Social indices:			2001 Gen. Election:			
% Non-white	52.1		Lab	21,087	57.5	–6.7
% Prof/Man	21.2		LD	4,841	13.2	+3.9
% Non-manual	40.7		PJP	4,770	13.0	
£ Av prop val 2000	47 K		C	3,948	10.8	–6.7
% Increase 97–00	24.1		Ind	662	1.8	
% Unemployed 2001	11.2		UKIP	634	1.7	
% Decrease 97–01	3.7		Mus	401	1.1	
% Fin hard/Rank	62.8	4	SA	304	0.8	
% Pensioners	20.4		Lab maj	16,246	44.3	
% Prem mort/Rank	53	28	Turnout		49.3	–7.8
			Elect	74,358		

Member of Parliament

Roger Godsiff, MP here since 1992, is the last Birmingham Labour MP to emerge from the union (APEX-GMB) school for right-wing fixers. A very low-profile ex-union official who inherited the Small Heath seat in 1992 from his union leader Dennis Howell, in disputed circumstances, he eventually prevailed over self-cancelling rivals from the majority Asian community. Selection for the new Sparkbrook and Small Heath seat in 1996 was also disputed and required NEC intervention. A Londoner, born in 1946, he attended Catford Comprehensive School, but sends his own children to private schools. Tall, moon-faced, bushy eyebrowed and bland, he cuts an elusive figure, balancing exceedingly rare Commons appearances with intensive ward-heeling in his constituency, where his tenure requires continuing factionalism within the non-white population.

BIRMINGHAM YARDLEY

A moment of rare excitement during the BBC TV coverage of the 2001 General Election results was provided by the airing of a report that Labour was in trouble in Birmingham Yardley, threatened by a potential Liberal Democrat gain. This was particularly newsworthy as the MP here, Estelle Morris, was strongly tipped to be nominated as the new Secretary of State for Education in the reshuffled Cabinet. This latter speculation at least was well-founded, after she had in fact been returned, repulsing John Hemming's challenge by a little over 2,500 votes.

Nevertheless, there was really a story here, even if not quite as dramatic as depicted on the TV. The West Midlands is one of the weakest areas in the whole country for the Liberal Democrats, and the city of Birmingham is in general no exception. The Lib Dems really have little strength in any of the parliamentary constituencies in the city – except this one.

Yardley is situated on the south-eastern edge of Birmingham, up against the border with Solihull. It is one of the least non-white of all the Birmingham seats, with no inner-city characteristics and consisting largely of skilled working-class voters, in the main owner-occupiers but with few professionals and higher managers and few with advanced educational qualifications. Its three wards are Acock's Green, Sheldon and Yardley itself. Before the 1990s the constituency was a classic Labour–Conservative marginal, which changed hands regularly with the ebb and flow of electoral fortune. The Conservatives gained it in 1959, 1970 and 1979; Labour in 1945, 1964 and 1974. In 1992 Labour's Estelle Morris seized the seat from the sitting Tory MP David Gilroy Bevan by just 162 votes; another close major party contest, one might think – nothing unusual for Yardley.

A closer glance at the 1992 result, however, reveals that it was actually a three-party cliffhanger. The Liberal Democrat John Hemming finished third, but with 30% of the vote and less than 2,000 votes behind Morris. Their share of the vote had advanced by nearly 10% since 1987. This is a reflection of their utter dominance of the city council politics of this constituency since the 1990s. Having started to impress themselves in Yardley ward some time before, the Liberal Democrats swept all opposition out of the way in the other two wards, and now win all three with large majorities in the regular local elections in May. John Hemming himself was elected to the city council by gaining an Acock's Green seat in 1990. It is not always possible for the Liberal Democrats to exploit such success based on local activism, especially where the two other parties are both competitive. The achievement in Yardley in 1992 can therefore hardly be understated, and it might have been even greater had there not be a misleading local poll during the campaign which suggested that Hemming had no chance of winning and was being heavily squeezed by the major-party battle.

Since then Hemming's share of the vote has increased again, to 33% in 1997 and 38% in 2001, and although Labour's dominance of the last two General Elections has enabled them to withstand this dynamic thrust he is now in a very clear second place, and should the Labour government become unpopular, Estelle Morris will probably be the most likely Cabinet Minister to lose her seat next time.

Social indices:			2001 Gen. Election:			
% Non-white	7.5		Lab	14,085	46.9	−0.1
% Prof/Man	20.6		LD	11,507	38.3	+5.4
% Non-manual	45.9		C	3,941	13.1	−4.7
£ Av prop val 2000	63 K		UKIP	329	1.1	+0.7
% Increase 97–00	28.4		SLP	151	0.5	
% Unemployed 2001	5.3		Lab maj	2,578	8.6	
% Decrease 97–01	1.6		Turnout		57.2	−14.0
% Fin hard/Rank	27.3	167	Elect	52,444		
% Pensioners	29.9					
% Prem mort/Rank	37	209				

Member of Parliament

Labour's **Estelle Morris**, an intense, cadaverous, Mancunian-accented Education Minister from 1997, who was promoted to Secretary of State for Education in 2001, a daughter and niece of two former Manchester MPs (Charles Morris MP for Openshaw 1963–83 and Alf – now Lord – Morris, MP for Wythenshaw 1964–92), has held this seat since 1992. A dogged performer from Labour's chalk face, she was born in 1952, educated at Whalley Range High School, Manchester, and – as she disclosed in 2001 – 'A'-level-less, but with seven 'O' levels, at Coventry College of Education and Warwick University, and was a teacher for 18 years and a Warwick district councillor for 12. A monotonous, monochrome orator who knows how to intone the jargon, after 2001 it was her task to ignore the prejudices of the school teachers over grammar, 'charter' and 'faith-based' schools. Her presence in the Cabinet helped maintain a quota of seven women (only three of whom – herself, Hewitt and Beckett – in important departments).

BISHOP AUCKLAND

County Durham is usually regarded as a citadel of heavy industry and embedded Labour Party strength. But in fact west Durham is mainly rural, with farmland in the valleys between the high moors. This south-westerly Durham seat includes Teesdale, with Barnard Castle and Startforth, and the Wear valley, with Bishop Auckland itself. All this is fairly Conservative; the Bishops of Durham have sat in their palace at Bishop Auckland for centuries, and they have not always been as associated with the left as the most famous recent incumbent, David Jenkins. In recent General Elections before 1997 the Tories were able to poll around 18,000 votes, comfortably higher than in any Durham constituency except the marginal Darlington.

However, this is not enough. Bishop Auckland has been won by Labour continuously since 1935, when it was regained by the Etonian economics expert Hugh Dalton, Chancellor of the Exchequer in the Attlee government after the war. Labour's strength lies in the east end of the seat, on the old Durham coalfield, around Spennymoor, Coundon and Shildon. Derek Foster's share of the vote dipped by over 7% in 2001, but this should not be held against the former Chief Whip personally; after all, his next door neighbour, Tony Blair of Sedgefield, actually did just about as badly in a rather disappointing regional result for Labour, overshadowed by their unique second landslide nationally.

Social indices:			2001 Gen. Election:			
% Non-white	0.5		Lab	22,680	58.8	−7.1
% Prof/Man	25.5		C	8,754	22.7	+2.5
% Non-manual	45.0		LD	6,073	15.7	+6.4
£ Av prop val 2000	55 K		Grn	1,052	2.7	
% Increase 97–00	23.4		Lab maj	13,926	36.1	
% Unemployed 2001	4.4		Turnout		57.2	−11.7
% Decrease 97–01	1.5		Elect	67,377		
% Fin hard/Rank	27.0	174				
% Pensioners	27.2					
% Prem mort/Rank	40	174				

Member of Parliament

Once an orthodox authority figure as Labour's Chief Whip (1985–95), **Derek Foster**, MP since 1979, was the quickest to join the ranks of the disaffected, having resigned after two days as a minister, on realising he was not getting the Cabinet post promised in return for standing down as the elected Chief Whip to enable Tony Blair to appoint Donald Dewar and all future occupants rather than (as was customary) have them elected by the PLP. Born in 1937, son of a long-unemployed shipyard worker, and educated at Bede Grammar School, Sunderland and St Catherine's College, Oxford, he has been described as 'a Salvationist who does not blow his own trumpet', yet he certainly blasted the Blair government in 1999 as 'not fit to polish the boots of the post-war Attlee government' and praised the 'awkward squad' rebels as more valuable than those on the government benches. This showed how gamekeepers can turn poacher and how relations between Durham-based Labour leaders in the 1990s – Blair, Foster, Mandelson, Clark – were as acrimonious as in the 1940s between Dalton, Shinwell, Chuter Ede and Whiteley. Otherwise his appearance has been likened (by Simon Hoggart of the *Guardian*) to that of a snooker referee.

BLABY

All three seats in Leicester were won by Labour in 2001. Rather like other all-Labour cities such as Hull, Birmingham and Nottingham, this is due to the fact that a large proportion of the middle-class suburbs lie outside the city boundaries. Even with the creation in 1997 of an all-suburban seat outside Leicester in the shape of Charnwood, the suburbs still play a major role in two other Leicestershire divisions, Harborough and Blaby.

The safe Conservative constituency of Blaby wraps itself round the south-west of Leicester in a kidney shape, taking in Blaby itself and several population centres which are actually equally or more populous: Braunstone, Narborough, Countesthorpe, Glen Parva. It then extends through the open countryside of south Leicestershire to the small town of Lutterworth just off the M1 motorway. Blaby is perhaps still best known as the seat of the former Chancellor Nigel Lawson (1974–92). Although the swing to Labour in 1997 was actually higher than that in any of the three Leicester seats, Lawson's successor Andrew Robathan still held on by a relatively comfortable majority of rather over 6,000 in both 1997 and 2001. Labour does best in the neighbourhoods closest to the city at Braunstone and Enderby, but could only win the former in the county council elections on the same day as the general. Ranking 621st out of 641 in the Experian index of financial hardship in 2001, and also ranking in the top 20 owner-occupied seats with well over 80%, this 97% white seat shares very little of the characteristics of inner Leicester, including its political history and preferences.

Social indices:			2001 Gen. Election:			
% Non-white	2.7		C	22,104	46.4	+0.6
% Prof/Man	35.7		Lab	15,895	33.4	−0.4
% Non-manual	58.6		LD	8,286	17.4	+2.5
£ Av prop val 2000	85 K		BNP	1,357	2.8	+1.9
% Increase 97–00	37.2		C maj	6,209	13.0	
% Unemployed 2001	1.3		Turnout		64.5	−11.6
% Decrease 97–01	0.5		Elect	73,907		
% Fin hard/Rank	4.4	621				
% Pensioners	21.3					
% Prem mort/Rank	10	598				

Member of Parliament

Andrew Robathan, born in 1951, a pink-faced former Coldstream Guards officer for 15 years after a public school and Oxford (Merchant Taylors' and Oriel) and Sandhurst education, won this seat in 1992. A contributor to the 'Bearing the Standard' call in 1991 for social cohesion, but with private health, welfare and prisons, he was a Redwood-supporting Eurosceptic, an opponent of the politically correct inclusion of women in combative Army roles, and speaks against homosexual sex at 16 by evoking Oscar Wilde's penchant for under-aged boys. Though not obviously a sporter of open-toed sandals he is a member of Friends of the Earth and the Woodland Trust, cycles and recycles and also urges defence of the threatened water vole ('Ratty' in *Wind in the Willows*) from its predator, the feral mink. He voted the racily pragmatic – but failed – Portillo option in 2001 and returned with the Portillistas to the backbenches, from where he had only been semi-released from 1995 to 1997 as PPS to another doomed species, Sports Minister Iain Sproat.

BLACKBURN

The Lancashire textile town of Blackburn is still associated, particularly by senior citizens, with the redoubtable Labour politician Barbara Castle, who represented it in Parliament from 1945 to 1979, even though the MP for over 22 years has been another prominent figure, Jack Straw, Home Secretary from 1997 and Foreign Secretary since 2001. One might think that any constituency which sends successive leading Labour figures to the Commons must always have been a very safe seat, but that is not quite the case. Although no Conservative has been elected by Blackburn for many decades, Jack Straw's majority fell to 3,000 in 1983 and it was still barely 6,000 in 1992. In 2001 he won by less than 10,000 again, with the support of just 30% of all registered electors, although a higher proportion was represented, as it were, only by non-voters (45%); the pair of left socialist opponents he attracted scarcely scraped a thousand votes between them despite his rather illiberal approach to his first senior Cabinet post.

Blackburn is a starkly divided town, and not without its problems. Some 20% of the population is non-white, mainly Asian, concentrated in the nineteenth-century terraces of the 'inner-city', in wards like Brookhouse north-west of the town centre. Brookhouse, in which eight out of every ten residents is non-white, has both Indian and Pakistani communities and has seen fighting, rioting and other disturbances in the past few years. There has also been some white reaction to the growing ethnic minority population; back in the 1970s the far right National Party led by John Kingsley Read actually won a couple of seats on the local council. Labour can generally rely on the white working-class vote in council estates wards on the edge of town like Higher Croft and Shadsworth, although there is a danger of low turnout (16% in Higher Croft in May 2000, for example). On the other hand there are some fine residential areas in Blackburn which provide a basis for a Conservative vote. The Tories fight back in outer north-west Blackburn with Darwen unitary authority wards such as Beardwood with Lammack, and the mansions which once belonged to mill owners still stand around Corporation Park, itself a monument to the civic pride of a town of independence and some wealth. Blackburn is an educational and sporting centre too, with one of the leading soccer teams of the Premiership years. It is in many ways all very impressive for a town of little over 100,000 souls.

Social indices:			2001 Gen. Election:			
% Non-white	20.2		Lab	21,808	53.9	−1.2
% Prof/Man	26.4		C	12,559	31.0	+6.4
% Non-manual	46.0		LD	3,264	8.1	−2.5
£ Av prop val 2000	46 K		UKIP	1,185	2.9	
% Increase 97–00	25.0		Ind	577	1.4	
% Unemployed 2001	4.9		SLP	559	1.4	+0.0
% Decrease 97–01	1.3		Ind	532	1.3	
% Fin hard/Rank	35.7	84	Lab maj	9,249	22.8	
% Pensioners	25.1		Turnout		55.7	−9.3
% Prem mort/Rank	48	59	Elect	72,621		

Member of Parliament

Jack Straw – MP since 1979 – is one of Labour's most successful professional politicians. Born in 1946, son of an insurance clerk, educated at Brentwood School and Leeds University, and nominally a lawyer, he has actually been a full-time politician virtually since student days, running the NUS and bag-carrying for Peter Shore and Barbara Castle until taking over her Blackburn seat in 1979, and shadowing in turn Education, Environment and the Home Office in opposition from 1987 to 1997. As part of the Blairite strategy of outflanking the Tories in policy areas once owned by them (in this case law and order), as Home Secretary (1997–2001) he fell foul of the civil libertarians on freedom of information, jury trials and asylum seekers, prompting backbench revolts, but hopefully playing well with an electorate casting rather more than the 40 votes of the PLP's hardcore rebels. He skilfully played the Pinochet case when Spain tried to extradite the former Chilean leader whilst in hospital in London in 2000, bouncing him around the appeal courts for months to please the Left, but then letting him go to please the rest, and so preserve his own leadership hopes. His pinched poker face, small wire-rimmed spectacles, austere demeanour and intense style recall Sir Stafford Cripps rather than Ernie Bevin, into whose shoes he was lowered as Foreign Secretary in 2001, where the job involved waiting to see what the Americans did in Afghanistan. Only the Chancellorship remains for him, and No.10.

BLACKPOOL NORTH AND FLEETWOOD

It was no surprise that Labour's Gordon Marsden gained Blackpool South in 1997 – he had a notional majority of only 394 to overcome. Jane Humble's triumph was much less expected. She secured a swing of over 14% to remove the sitting Tory MP Harold Elletson from Blackpool North and Fleetwood, a seat made up of territory from two previous constituencies which had never elected a Labour MP before; and Ms Humble won by nearly 9,000!

This seat includes over half of the former Wyre division, the compact, urban coastal strip north of Blackpool. The main communities are Thornton Cleveleys, a residential and holiday community, and Fleetwood, best known as a fishing and container port. It was logical enough to pair this area with the northern end of Blackpool, with which it is contiguous; there is no break to the built-up area, and the famous trams come up this far too. Nevertheless, it was felt that Blackpool North and Fleetwood would remain Conservative in all but the most disastrous circumstances – which have duly repeated themselves, as in 2001 little happened except that over 14% fewer voters turned out. The Liberal Democrats do only about half as well as the national average, and the gap between the two main parties is a little more than across Britain as a whole.

Social indices:			2001 Gen. Election:			
% Non-white	0.7		Lab	21,610	50.8	−1.4
% Prof/Man	27.5		C	15,889	37.3	+1.8
% Non-manual	55.3		LD	4,132	9.7	+1.1
£ Av prop val 2000	57 K		UKIP	950		
% Increase 97–00	15.9		Lab maj	5,721	13.4	
% Unemployed 2001	3.5		Turnout		57.2	−14.5
% Decrease 97–01	1.5		Elect	74,456		
% Fin hard/Rank	11.4	428				
% Pensioners	34.8					
% Prem mort/Rank	43	114				

Member of Parliament

Joan Humble has indeed led a parliamentary life of blameless humility since arriving in 1997 on the Labour flood tide. Born (1951) Jovanka Piplica, her father a Slav-born bus driver, and educated at Greenhead Grammar School, Keighley and Lancaster University, she was a DHSS clerk and tax officer for five years before becoming a housewife for eight years and a full-time Lancashire county councillor for 12. A very locally focused MP (tourism, fishing) she is – deviantly – technophobic. Otherwise, she is an identikit Labour backbencher: public sector, councillor, female, loyal.

BLACKPOOL SOUTH

It might be thought that Blackpool, traditionally the mecca of the northern working classes, would all the same be one of the safest Conservative towns in the country. Its economy is dependent on tourism, scarcely 10% of its housing is council-owned; this, together with the image of the seaside landlady, scarcely seems promising for the left.

Yet in fact there are hardly any overwhelmingly Tory wards, and after the 1997 General Election Labour won both of the town's constituencies – their first ever parliamentary success in Blackpool. What is more, it wasn't even close.

South contains the lion's share of the town of Blackpool, 15 of its 22 wards. In addition to the Labour strongholds which were already in South – Clifton, Foxhall, Hawes Side and Victoria – great help was received from the ex-North territory in 1997. Three of the four wards donated are clearly Labour-supporting (Brunswick, Park and Talbot) and the fourth, Layton, is won by Labour in local elections. The famous Golden Mile and almost all of the centre of the town are situated in South; the boundary with North/Fleetwood runs along the line of the North station and the northernmost of Blackpool's unique three piers.

As expected Gordon Marsden gained South in 1997, but the editor of *History Today*, with his knowledge of Blackpool's hitherto all-Tory electoral tradition, can hardly have expected a majority of over 11,500. Despite the fears of the MP and others that Labour's abandonment of Blackpool as a conference centre might be resented, and a well-matched vote total in the latest unitary authority elections in May 2000, there was almost no movement in party shares in 2001, but turnout fell to an unprecedentedly poor 52%, unusual outside inner cities. Blackpool now seems as solid for Labour as it was through most of the last century for the Conservatives. The historian can look forward to the future with optimism.

Social indices:			2001 Gen. Election:			
% Non-white	0.8		Lab	21,060	54.3	−2.7
% Prof/Man	27.5		C	12,798	33.0	−1.4
% Non-manual	52.2		LD	4,115	10.6	+2.1
£ Av prop val 2000	50 K		UKIP	819	2.1	
% Increase 97–00	13.8		Lab maj	8,262	21.3	
% Unemployed 2001	4.2		Turnout		52.2	−15.6
% Decrease 97–01	2.2		Elect	74,311		
% Fin hard/Rank	17.6	310				
% Pensioners	29.9					
% Prem mort/Rank	49	50				

Member of Parliament

Gordon Marsden, born in 1953, son of a refrigeration engineer, educated at Stockport Grammar School and New College, Oxford, the Warburg Institute, London University and Harvard, was the sixth Labour MP to declare himself homosexual. Elected here in 1997, a loyal Blairite – at least publicly – ex-Editor of *History Today* (1985–97), he knows as a professional historian how rarely Labour has won workable majorities. Self-assured, absorbed, discerning and cerebral with closely-cropped peroxide-looking hair and matinée idol features, he retains his Brighton home, handier now for more party conferences than his address in unfashionable Blackpool, whose declining interests he inevitably defends as an MP. In 2001 he became joint PPS to the Lord Chancellor, but has been sagely described as 'too lively and interesting to become a minister' (Simon Hoggart, the *Guardian*).

BLAENAU GWENT

Ebbw Vale was one of the most famous of all constituency names. From 1929 to 1960 Ebbw Vale was represented by Aneurin Bevan, long regarded as the leading figure on the left of the Labour Party. Then it was held for 23 years by Bevan's friend and biographer Michael Foot – who did become party leader. But the name of Ebbw Vale is no longer found in Parliament. In 1983 one of the three valley head towns of the constituency, Rhymney, was transferred to join Merthyr Tydfil. The other towns, Tredegar and Ebbw Vale, were included in Blaenau Gwent ('blaenau' means 'uplands' in Welsh). There they were joined by Brynmawr and the northern half of the old Abertillery division.

Foot had no worries about his renamed constituency. Coal-mining and steel production, which had formed the core of employment in Ebbw Vale, have ceased and given way to a variety of lighter industries, and male unemployment was only a little higher than the Welsh average in the early 1990s. All the same, the essential characteristics of these working-class communities remain, and both, in 1983, with the added boost of Foot as party leader, and in 1992 after he had retired and handed over to Llewellyn Smith, Blaenau Gwent produced the largest and safest majority of any Labour seat.

In 1992 Labour polled 79% of the vote in Blaenau Gwent, the highest share of any party in any seat in the United Kingdom. The same could be said of Llewellyn Smith's percentage lead, 69.2%. His numerical majority was 30,067, surpassed only by John Major's in Huntingdon. By 2001 these records were lost, and Llew Smith's numerical majority had dropped by over ten thousand. This was mainly due to the reduction in turnout to under 60%, and although this still ranks as Labour's fifth safest seat, for the first time under half the electorate in Blaenau Gwent remained loyal to the decades of tradition of overwhelming Labour support established so notably by Ebbw Vale.

Social indices:			2001 Gen. Election:			
% Non-white	0.5		Lab	22,855	72.0	−7.4
% Welsh sp	2.2		PC	3,542	11.2	+5.9
% Prof/Man	20.8		LD	2,945	9.3	+0.6
% Non-manual	36.7		C	2,383	7.5	+0.9
£ Av prop val 2000	35 K		Lab maj	19,313	60.9	
% Increase 97–00	18.8		Turnout		59.5	−12.9
% Unemployed 2001	6.2		Elect	53,353		
% Decrease 97–01	1.9					
% Fin hard/Rank	40.0	51				
% Pensioners	27.6					
% Prem mort/Rank	41	165				

Member of Parliament

Llew Smith, a stocky, trim-bearded Walter Ulbricht look-alike, was elected here in 1992, as the less famous, but equally rebellious, successor to two Labour icons: Aneurin Bevan and Michael Foot. Born in 1944, son of a miner, and educated at Greenfield Secondary Modern School, Newbridge and – via Coleg Harlech – Cardiff University, he worked as a labourer at Pilkington Glass and George Wimpeys, before following Neil Kinnock as South Wales WEA organiser and being MEP for SE Wales for ten years. Ostensibly – as the only Campaign Group member in Wales – the most left-wing Welsh Labour MP, he has missed none of the major rebellions: lone parent benefit cuts, threat of military action against Iraq, university tuition fees, the Prime Minister's power to nominate life peers, NATO bombing of Kosovo, Incapacity Benefits, legal aid reform, pensions linked to earnings, curbs on jury trials, freedom of information, air traffic control privatisation, and he publicly fell out with the leadership over his opposition to Welsh devolution. In all, he voted 26 times against the government in the 1997 to 2001 Parliament (making him the 11th most rebellious backbencher), compared to his 30 rebellions in the 1992–97 House, when he also opposed Blair on Clause Four. In 2001 he joined the rebellion against the Terrorism, Crime and Security Bill.

BLAYDON

Sometimes the Liberal Democrats and their predecessors – at least those in the Liberal rather than the Social Democrat tradition – can use activism and success in local government as a springboard in parliamentary elections, but often they have not been able to, particularly when the main opposition is to Labour in predominantly working-class areas. Liverpool forms a notable example. It is too early to say what will happen in the Blaydon division of Gateshead, where the Lib Dems' rather rapid advance in metropolitan borough elections meant that Labour were left with only two of the nine wards within the constituency in May 2000, and 47% of the total vote. In the General Election the next year, John McWilliam did at least hold on, but his majority was more than halved, and the LD share went up exactly10%. By no stretch of the imagination could this now be described as a monolithic Labour seat; there really is a race on now in Blaydon.

The Metropolitan Borough of Gateshead lies on the south bank of the Tyne, facing Newcastle. At the western end of the borough can be found the constituency of Blaydon, whose name has become renowned in north-eastern folklore (and well beyond) through the popular traditional song about working people trekking to see the 'Blaydon Races'. The seat consists mainly of the small towns of Blaydon, Ryton and Whickham. Here too can be found the old mining village of Chopwell, which achieved a reputation as one of the nation's red 'Little Moscows' in the 1920s and almost alone stood out against the Liberal Democrat tide in 2000. Whether in the twenty-first century this will increasingly be seen as an aberration from the tradition of coal mining and Labour and socialist solidarity will be interesting to observe.

Social indices:			2001 Gen. Election:			
% Non-white	0.5		Lab	20,340	54.8	–5.1
% Prof/Man	28.5		LD	12,531	33.8	+10.0
% Non-manual	55.9		C	4,215	11.4	–1.8
£ Av prop val 2000	60 K		Lab maj	7,809	21.1	
% Increase 97–00	17.7		Turnout		57.4	–13.6
% Unemployed 2001	3.1		Elect	64,574		
% Decrease 97–01	2.4					
% Fin hard/Rank	22.7	232				
% Pensioners	26.1					
% Prem mort/Rank	33	289				

Member of Parliament

John McWilliam, one of a score of Labour Scots in English seats, was elected here in 1979. Born in 1941, educated at Leith Academy, Heriot Watt and Napier Colleges, and a former telephone engineer (and son of one), he was a Whip for three years in the 1980s before disappearing into the obscurity of committee chairmanships. Cocky and loquacious, he is a soft Eurosceptic who introduced a Bill to tighten rules on phone tapping and defends defence industry jobs. One of the 1979 intake whose career was blighted by the ensuing 18 years of Tory government, his bid for the Speakership in 2000 netted the lowest tally of any of the 12 contenders: 32 votes.

BLYTH VALLEY

Blyth is one of those constituencies which became well known because of a close fight by an MP at odds with his party to keep his seat. The independently minded Eddie Milne was dropped by the local party before the February 1974 Election in favour of a right-winger, Ivor Richard. Standing as an Independent Labour candidate Milne beat Richard that February, but lost to a Labour QC, John Ryman, in October. Milne's vote did not fade rapidly, as has happened to some ex-MPs who have persisted in seeking election. In 1979 he still polled 18,000 votes to take second place, but he died before the 1983 General Election. Blyth Valley was again looking like a marginal of an unusual variety, not between Labour and Conservative but between Labour and SDP. In 1983 the latter party had got within 3,000 votes of victory, and in 1987 it was closer still – just 853 votes. The reasons for this were multiple. Perhaps there was a partial inheritance of Eddie Milne's 'Independent Labour' tradition. Tory tactical voting played its part. So did the personality factor: John Ryman's behaviour became increasingly eccentric and he announced his retirement in 1986 after forsaking the Labour Whip in the Commons. His successor, Ronnie Campbell, was thought by some to have far-left Militant connections. Finally the seat has undergone significant demographic change.

Blyth itself is one of those gritty northern towns of resolute and remorselessly industrial aspect. The skyline is overshadowed by the power station, by the former coal mine, and by the dockyards. Bare council estates ring the town, which has very few middle-class roads. The constituency, compactly tucked into the south-eastern corner of Northumberland, also includes ex-mining villages like Seghill and Seaton

Delaval. But the most rapidly growing area in recent decades has been the private housing 'New Town' of Cramlington. Opinions about Cramlington are mixed, but it has played an important role in the politics of the Blyth Valley constituency, providing the core of the SDP and Liberal Democrat vote.

The Liberal Democrats do still have a number of councillors on Blyth Valley district council, but only 9 out of 50 in the last all-out elections of May 1999, and Ronnie Campbell has now won twice easily enough. In 2001 for the first time almost in memory, there was no significant swing in Blyth Valley, although turnout fell by 14%. This was close to the regional average. After so many controversial characters and upheavals, the politics of Blyth Valley seem to be returning to 'normality'.

Social indices:			2001 Gen. Election:			
% Non-white	0.6		Lab	20,627	59.7	−4.5
% Prof/Man	26.0		LD	8,439	24.4	+2.0
% Non-manual	52.2		C	5,484	15.9	+2.5
£ Av prop val 2000	53 K		Lab maj	12,188	35.3	
% Increase 97–00	22.3		Turnout		54.6	−14.2
% Unemployed 2001	4.4		Elect	63,274		
% Decrease 97–01	1.8					
% Fin hard/Rank	23.7	214				
% Pensioners	21.9					
% Prem mort/Rank	34	273				

Member of Parliament

In 1918 the Parliamentary Labour Party was dubbed 'a committee of check-weighmen', nearly half of the PLP (25 out of 57) being miners. By 2001 in a PLP of 412 the total was 11 (ex-miners or NUM officials) and of these 11 collectors' items one is **Ronnie Campbell**, MP here since 1987. Facially birthmarked and with a Geordie accent which has been described as making Gazza sound like Brian Sewell, he was born in 1943, and after secondary modern schooling was a miner for 27 years until made redundant a year before he became an MP. He fairly regularly rebels with other Campaign Groupers, notably on lone parent benefit cuts, university tuition fees, Incapacity Benefits, pensions linked to earnings and freedom of information, his belligerent verbal outbursts symbolising the eclipse of a proletarian culture and the mining industry's terminal decay. In November 2001 he called for British Muslims who had gone to fight for the Taliban in Afghanistan 'never to set foot back in this country again'. Earlier in the year he received tabloid exposure following an altercation in an Indian restaurant.

BOGNOR REGIS AND LITTLEHAMPTON

The Bognor Regis and Littlehampton division covers a coastal strip of West Sussex. In the west we have retirement and resort country, from Pagham through Aldwick, Bognor itself, Felpham and Middleton-on-Sea. The eastern half is more industrial, around the old port of Littlehampton, stopping just short of Rustington, which is in a Worthing constituency.

Labour can elect some local councillors in parts of Littlehampton, six in 1999, and the Liberal Democrats do very well next door in Adur district (at municipal level only). However, this is still a Conservative seat, although Nick Gibb's majority was cut to little over 5,000 in 2001 as Labour moved clearly into second place, which is likely to be part of the party's strength on the Sussex coast, spreading westwards from Brighton and Hove. This is a relatively new phenomenon. The population is generally elderly (among the ten highest proportion of pensioners voting according to Age Concern/ Essex University figures), white, middle class and in the top third of affluent seats. There is virtually no council housing. However, only 58% of voters bothered to turn out in 2001. It is rumoured that the dying words of King George V were not very complimentary about the central town of this constituency. Did the electorate, this time, decide to echo him after a lacklustre campaign: 'Bugger Bognor ...'.

Social indices:			2001 Gen. Election:			
% Non-white	1.1		C	17,602	45.2	+1.0
% Prof/Man	29.2		Lab	11,959	30.7	+2.2
% Non-manual	53.3		LD	6,846	17.6	−6.4
£ Av prop val 2000	97 K		UKIP	1,779	4.6	+1.3
% Increase 97–00	46.4		Grn	782	2.0	
% Unemployed 2001	1.6		C maj	5,643	14.5	
% Decrease 97–01	1.3		Turnout		58.2	−11.6
% Fin hard/Rank	11.4	427	Elect	66,903		
% Pensioners	39.0					
% Prem mort/Rank	33	294				

Member of Parliament

Nick Gibb won this new seat for the Conservatives in 1997. A former Peat Marwick tax accountant, he was born in 1960, educated at Maidstone Grammar School, Roundhay School, Leeds, Thornes House School, Wakefield and Durham University. An 'arch right-winger' (according to Julie Kirkbride MP) since student days, linked to the Adam Smith Institute, in 1999 he was forced to withdraw for calling Treasury Minister Dawn Primarolo 'a stupid woman'. He has sought tax relief on BUPA premiums for his many elderly constituents. Reputedly voting for Lilley then Hague in 1997, he was a Treasury (1998–99) then DTI (1999–2001) spokesman; as an 'impassioned Portillista' (Hwyel Williams) he backed the Portillo candidacy in 2001, briefly took a frontbench job as Transport and the Regions spokesman but quit to join the rest of the backbench Portillistas in October 2001.

BOLSOVER

One of the most well-known parliamentary constituency names is Bolsover, an east Derbyshire division whose political cast has been created by coal-mining. This is not because it enjoys marginal status or notably close contests but because of the fame of its highly active and visible (some would say aggressive) Labour MP, Dennis Skinner, who is sometimes (affectionately) described as 'The Beast of Bolsover'.

Skinner's reputation in the House and outside as a diehard scourge of Conservatives serves well the taste of his constituency, which is dominated by large ex-mining villages like Shirebrook, Temple Normanton, Clowne and Scarcliffe. The town of Bolsover itself, perched on its crag, nestling around its castle, overlooks the industrial valley which housed British Coal's North Derbyshire headquarters. This seat used, in the days of mining, to rank among the top two or three in the proportion of workers employed in the coal industry. Now there are no deep pits left.

The Conservative and Liberal Democrat parties often fail to put forward candidates for local elections in this district, and they may as well, one feels, throw in the towel similarly in parliamentary contests. Skinner's majority, long the largest in Derbyshire, remained so in 2001 at nearly 19,000, although it fell by over 8,000 due to the reluctance of electors to visit the ballot booths after the quietest campaign since the 1950s at least. Skinner remains, apparently as hard and immovable as stone, even after the near neighbouring Chesterfield seat abandoned socialism to elect a Liberal Democrat.

Social indices:			2001 Gen. Election:			
% Non-white	0.5		Lab	26,249	68.6	−5.4
% Prof/Man	23.0		C	7,472	19.5	+2.8
% Non-manual	41.7		LD	4,550	11.9	+2.6
£ Av prop val 2000	50 K		Lab maj	18,777	49.1	
% Increase 97–00	27.3		Turnout		56.7	−14.7
% Unemployed 2001	4.6		Elect	67,537		
% Decrease 97–01	1.3					
% Fin hard/Rank	23.6	215				
% Pensioners	26.6					
% Prem mort/Rank	36	231				

Member of Parliament

Dennis Skinner, the proletarian conscience of the hard Left, a miner's son born in 1932 and educated at Tupton Hall Grammar School, is one of the PLP's 11 ex-miners and has represented Bolsover since 1970. He was Labour's most rebellious backbencher between 1992 and 1997 with 121 defiant votes, but has been more deferential to Labour in power with 41 rebellious votes during the 1997–2001 Parliament, making him third in the peck order of 'usual suspects'. Tolerated by Blair, even re-elected to Labour's NEC, grudgingly accepted by the Tories, as a caricature of a bitter class warrior, his role as 'Her Majesty's Heckler-in-Chief' extends to shouted abuse during moments of high ceremony, as to Black Rod during the 2000 State Opening, to tell the Queen to read the (republican) *Guardian*. Tall, straight-backed with a swaggering gait, an MP who will not pair and who avoids the boredom of unpublicised committee work for the greater exposure of the Chamber, he is one of Parliament's best carved embellishments, and few complain he has twice now evaded an earlier promise to retire at 65. In his old age he has developed the art of kicking the Whips in the groin at every given opportunity whilst bowling underarm Tory-bashing 'questions' at Tony Blair. Having supped so long at the well of dissent, little scope remains to surprise or shock.

BOLTON NORTH EAST

Bolton, an industrial town in the north-west sector of Greater Manchester's built-up sprawl, has long been identified with unglamorous grit: it has been known as the home of Fred Dibnah, television's steeplejack and a professional 'character'; of a ringful of stage wrestlers; and the setting for Bill Naughton's treatments of working-class life, *Spring and Port Wine* and *The Family Way*. It has also long been known for its political marginality. From 1950 to 1979 the Bolton East constituency fell in each case to the party which actually won the General Election as a whole, establishing it as one of a select band of 'weather-vane' seats which typified the electoral behaviour of the nation. In 1983 there were major boundary changes consequent upon the enlargement of Bolton's bounds on becoming a metropolitan borough some years before, and none of the new seats were very similar to any previous Bolton division, but North East has carried on the tradition of marginality.

There were three close contests in Bolton NE, all won by the Conservatives – but a further boundary change made their position weaker, and they were not helped when the sitting MP Peter Thurnham, frustrated on being denied shortlisting at the safe Westmorland seat, defected to the Liberal Democrats before retiring. In 1997 David Crausby rode the tidal wave of national Labour success to record a 12,000 majority.

The seat is almost evenly balanced, socially, politically, and geographically. It possesses a Conservative northern half, which consists of the well-established middle-class ward of Astley Bridge on the road towards Blackburn, and, even further north, the rapidly growing private estates and improved cottages of Bradshaw and Bromley Cross. This contrasts sharply with the Labour-supporting inner-city terraces of the central wards of Halliwell, Tonge and Central, and the eastern peripheral council estate of Breightmet. For example, at the time of the 1991 Census 35% of the population of Central ward was non-white, and only 33% of households owned a car; in Bradshaw the non-white figure was 1%, and 76% owned a car – indeed 33% owned two cars or more. In 2001 the inner Labour wards again predominated, but future contests will probably be considerably closer in this traditionally marginal town.

Social indices:			2001 Gen. Election:			
% Non-white	8.4		Lab	21,166	54.3	−1.8
% Prof/Man	30.2		C	12,744	32.7	+2.3
% Non-manual	54.2		LD	4,004	10.3	+0.4
£ Av prop val 2000	57 K		Grn	629	1.6	
% Increase 97–00	23.9		SLP	407	1.0	−0.3
% Unemployed 2001	3.7		Lab maj	8,422	21.6	
% Decrease 97–01	1.4		Turnout		56.0	−16.4
% Fin hard/Rank	25.4	195	Elect	69,514		
% Pensioners	25.3					
% Prem mort/Rank	43	122				

Member of Parliament

David Crausby, a rare blue-collar worker in Labour's 1997 intake, sank into the green leather benches as a low-profile loyalist. A dark and sallow complexioned engineer (for 20 years an AEEU works convenor), born in 1946 and educated at

Derby Grammar School, Bury, and Bury Technical College, he has concentrated on the local issues of jobs, crime and education. Having fought two close contests – 1987 and 1992 – to reach the Commons, once there he has been eclipsed by his two Bolton colleagues.

BOLTON SOUTH EAST

From 1983 to 1997 Labour only occupied one of the three seats in the borough of Bolton. One reason for this is that a disproportionate amount of Labour's support has been packed into a single safe seat, Bolton South East, leaving the other two to be won by the Tories in 1983, 1987 and 1992. In the last two landslides Labour did win all three seats, but the basic pattern remains: South East is by far their strongest among the three, although in 2001 Brian Iddon's majority was cut substantially as his share fell by 7% and the turnout by 15% to a bare half of the electorate.

Actually only about half the SE constituency lies within traditional Bolton boundaries, and the outlying communities of Farnworth, Little Lever and Kearsley are also included. They were previously part of the Farnworth seat of SDP defector John Roper, which was irretrievably split asunder in 1983. Roper did not contest Bolton South East in 1983, preferring to contest Worsley, where he was defeated, setting him off on a journey through the political wilderness which ended in the Conservative Party. In Bolton itself Harper Green is essentially a peripheral council estate. Derby and Burnden are inner city wards, which harbour a high proportion of privately rented housing and ethnic variety: 46% of the population of Derby ward were from groups other than white in the latest official figures, the highest proportion in the borough. In May 2000 Derby was taken by an Asian Muslim Tory candidate, a reminder that Labour should not take anyone for granted.

Social indices:			2001 Gen. Election:			
% Non-white	13.4		Lab	21,129	61.9	−7.0
% Prof/Man	22.0		C	8,258	24.2	+4.5
% Non-manual	44.7		LD	3,941	11.5	+2.8
£ Av prop val 2000	39 K		SLP	826	2.4	
% Increase 97–00	16.6		Lab maj	12,871	37.7	
% Unemployed 2001	4.6		Turnout		50.1	−15.1
% Decrease 97–01	0.7		Elect	68,140		
% Fin hard/Rank	34.6	96				
% Pensioners	24.7					
% Prem mort/Rank	49	54				

Member of Parliament

Dr Brian Iddon, a former Salford University chemistry lecturer for 31 years, son of a market gardener and butcher, born in 1940, and educated, after failing the 11-plus, at Christ Church (Secondary Modern) School, Southport, Southport Technical College and Hull University, held the seat for Labour in 1997 as the replacement for the deselected MP David Young, and soon built a reputation as a campaigner for cannabis decriminalisation. Coming late to the Commons (at 56) and with a shopping list of utilities he wanted to renationalise, he settled instead for a limited portfolio of rebellions on lone parent benefit cuts, disability benefit cuts, and the linking of pensions to average earnings. In October 2001, in a frisson of anxiety, he asked whose advice the government valued most – 'special advisers' or 'all its backbenchers'.

BOLTON WEST

West Bolton includes some very fine residential areas. In Deane-cum-Heaton ward, around Bolton School and along the A673 Chorley New Road, the nineteenth-century mansions of Bolton's textile magnates can still be seen, some still in use as family homes. Bolton's wealth derived from its mills, and there was a classic west/east divide between those who profited from them and those who formed the bulk of the work force. Yet Bolton West has not always elected a Conservative MP. From 1951 to 1964 there was a curious electoral pact between the Liberals and the Conservatives in Bolton, rather like that in another textile town over the Pennines – Huddersfield. The Tories gave Liberal MP Arthur Holt a free run in Bolton West, while the Liberals stood down in turn in East. In 1964 the pact ended. Labour won both seats, and Arthur Holt finished bottom of the poll in West. Between 1964 and 1983 Labour only lost the seat twice, in 1970 and February 1974.

In Thatcher's decade of the 1980s, the Conservative Thomas Sackville was able to hold West reasonably comfortably twice. Then in 1992 his majority was slashed to 1,079, and despite the removal of the Labour Halliwell ward (which was not named after one of Bolton's sons, Leslie Halliwell, the author of film guides) Labour's Ruth Kelly gained West in 1997 with a majority of 7,000, had three children in quick succession and held it with scarcely a negative swing in 2001. This is still the least strongly Labour Bolton seat though, and should there ever be another close contest between the two currently biggest parties, it will still rank as a crucial marginal.

Social indices:			2001 Gen. Election:			
% Non-white	2.5		Lab	19,381	47.0	–2.5
% Prof/Man	38.1		C	13,863	33.6	–1.5
% Non-manual	61.9		LD	7,573	18.4	+7.6
£ Av prop val 2000	74 K		SA	397	1.0	
% Increase 97–00	34.8		Lab maj	5,518	13.4	
% Unemployed 2001	1.9		Turnout		62.4	–15.0
% Decrease 97–01	0.8		Elect	66,033		
% Fin hard/Rank	16.9	317				
% Pensioners	24.7					
% Prem mort/Rank	26	409				

Member of Parliament

Ruth Kelly, elected in 1997, belatedly became Economic Secretary to the Treasury in 2001. A pharmacist's daughter, with an attractive, somewhat androgynous look, a low-registered voice and the elitist pedigree of (eventually) Westminster School, Queen's College, Oxford and the LSE, a Bank of England economist and former *Guardian* financial journalist, she was supposed to be one of the highfliers of

Labour's 1997 intake, but instead settled initially, as a good Catholic, for motherhood (thrice) and the small job of PPS to hapless Nick Brown (1998–2001), after having been substituted as a more loyal and more specialist Treasury Select Committee member in place of Diane Abbott (1997–98). One of 12 1997 intake MPs to be brought into government in 2001, she came with the highest intellectual reputation.

BOOTLE

Bootle has been the safest seat of all in the last two general elections. Of the 412 they won in June 2001, it gave Labour its largest percentage majority, 69.01, technically requiring a 35% swing to the second placed party, the Liberal Democrats, to bring about a change of hands. The MP Joe Benton amassed 78% of the vote, the runner-up 8.5%. No other party even comes near having such a margin. This is as close to one-party hegemony as can currently be found in the United Kingdom.

Bootle is a town not unfamiliar with tragedy, and reminders seem to recur. It was in its shopping centre that Jamie Bulger was abducted by his two child murderers in 1993, and their release under new identities stoked further national newspaper stories in the summer of 2001. The poverty and deprivations of the inner city generate many problems for those whose names never reach the headlines.

Bootle is part of the metropolitan borough of Sefton, but it has very little in common with the middle-class commuting and seaside communities of Crosby, Maghull, Formby and Southport. This tough and depressed dockland town is far more similar to the neighbouring districts of working-class north Liverpool. The Linacre ward, for example, borders Liverpool Riverside's Vauxhall and shares its overwhelmingly Labour voting patterns. All the wards are very safely Labour, whether they are situated in the inner city or consist of peripheral council estates like Netherton: in May 2000, for example, Labour obtained 87% of votes cast in Netherton and Orrell ward, against solitary Socialist Alternative opposition on a 16% turnout.

Two far-left candidates did manage 6% of the vote between them in the parliamentary election of 2001, while no other options to the three main parties were offered – no Green (in this environment overshadowed by the docks which created it, many now silent), no UK Independence (Europe is not thought to be a relevant threat), nobody from the far right in this over 99% white seat (one of the highest figures in the whole of England), no Loony or trivial candidate. There is not perhaps that much to laugh about in Bootle politics.

Social indices:			2001 Gen. Election:			
% Non-white	0.6		Lab	21,400	77.6	−5.3
% Prof/Man	18.0		LD	2,357	8.5	+2.8
% Non-manual	48.4		C	2,194	8.0	−0.5
£ Av prop val 2000	40 K		SLP	971	3.5	
% Increase 97–00	20.1		SA	672	2.4	+1.3
% Unemployed 2001	8.5		Lab maj	19,043	69.0	
% Decrease 97–01	4.3		Turnout		49.0	−17.7
% Fin hard/Rank	43.2	34	Elect	56,320		
% Pensioners	25.4					
% Prem mort/Rank	52	31				

Member of Parliament

Joe Benton, a former Labour whip from a classic working-class Liverpool Catholic background, who was elected here in 1990, was born in 1933 and, after St Monica's (RC) School and Bootle Technical College, worked successively as a clerk in a shipping company and a personnel officer with Girobank. He defends Liverpool pools firms against the National Lottery and as a Catholic opposes abortion, embryo research, homosexuality and euthanasia. He was dropped as a Whip on the morrow of victory in 1997.

BOSTON AND SKEGNESS

Boston – the largest town in the constituency and famed for its notable landmark, the Stump, a church tower which can be seen for miles in this low country by the Wash – and its hinterland were formerly associated with the flatlands of Holland in the south-east of the county, and makes up the more populous element in this seat. The remainder consists of electors taken from East Lindsey, abolished before the 1997 Election. Skegness is the premier resort of Lincolnshire's east coast. Its sands and renowned bracing air have traditionally proved a magnet for the workers of the East Midlands coalfield and of industrial towns like Nottingham.

Labour has now twice pushed the Conservatives to the limit in Boston and Skegness, failing by just 647 in 1997 and 515 in 2001. In such a tight two-party race, the Liberal Democrats were clearly squeezed on the second occasion, suffering a rare loss of over 4% in their share. Clearly this seat must now be regarded as an exceptionally tight two-way marginal, even though this part of mid-east Lincolnshire has never elected a Labour MP. They can win council wards in Boston itself such as Skirbeck and Witham with their council estates, and in Skegness, especially in its northern half; the Liberal Democrats do well in Burgh le Marsh and Wainfleet; and the Conservatives fight back in smaller villages on the coast and on the low land. With over 26,000 people living in Boston and 16,000 in Skegness, the urban portion makes up about half of the constituency, and overall a competitive and tense balance is struck in this distinctive part of the east country, apparently rather remote but visited more often than one might imagine by incomers ranging from working-class Midlanders taking the breeze to Americans from New England, seeking their heritage in the original Boston.

Social indices:			2001 Gen. Election:			
% Non-white	0.7		C	17,298	42.9	+0.5
% Prof/Man	27.6		Lab	16,783	41.6	+0.6
% Non-manual	47.6		LD	4,994	12.4	−4.2
£ Av prop val 2000	57 K		UKIP	717	1.8	
% Increase 97–00	25.6		Grn	521	1.3	
% Unemployed 2001	2.1		C maj	515	1.3	
% Decrease 97–01	1.6		Turnout		58.4	−10.5
% Fin hard/Rank	12.4	407	Elect	69,010		
% Pensioners	30.8					
% Prem mort/Rank	35	253				

Member of Parliament

Mark Simmonds replaced the veteran eccentric Europhobic MP Sir Richard Body as Tory MP here in 2001. A Nottingham-born but London-based estate agent, originally with Savills and Strutt & Parker, he now runs his own company. Born in 1964, educated at Worksop College and Trent Polytechnic, he is yet another product – among rising Conservative candidates – of his party's flagship borough of Wandsworth, where he ran the housing committee, which pioneered huge council house sales, and where he privatised the borough valuers' department. A supporter of Iain Duncan Smith's successful leadership bid, he has opposed EU enlargement as threatening local farmers with cheap and inferior imported agricultural produce.

BOSWORTH

As seems fitting for the site of one of the decisive battles of British history, when Henry VII (exploiting a rather weakly legitimate claim) established the mighty Tudor dynasty by defeating and killing Richard III on Bosworth Field in 1485, this is one of those constituencies which has seen tight and hard-fought contests, dashed hopes and seized opportunities in recent decades. Labour held the seat right through the years of the Tory governments of 1951 to 1964, but lost it in 1970 to Adam Butler (son of Rab). For much of this time (1959–70) the MP was the well-known right-wing warrior Woodrow Wyatt, still opining in the Sunday press nearly three decades after he lost his seat in the Commons until his death during the last parliament. They have never quite recaptured it. Much of the decline of the Labour vote can probably be ascribed to the reduction of the influence of the old Leicestershire coalfield, and the growth of new private housing in the Leicester suburban belt and around Hinckley. Boundary changes have further strengthened the Conservative position. Before 1983 the best area for Labour had always been Coalville, which was the mining centre its name implied, but which is now in the North West Leicestershire seat, with Bosworth reduced to just about the same boundaries as the local authority of Hinckley and Bosworth.

Labour slipped to third place in the redrawn Bosworth in 1983 and 1987, but recovered to take second place in 1992, still 19,000 votes behind the Conservatives. In the 1995 boundary changes some 14,000 voters in the white Leicester suburbs (Groby, Ratby – good Nordic names!) were lost to the newly created Charnwood division, but the Conservatives remained (over-)confident. Labour's only consistent ward had been Earl Shilton; Hinckley is a growing, middle-class town and continues to increase its influence in this constituency named after a smaller town. Then in 1997 Labour achieved an unprecedented 12% swing and lost by barely over a thousand votes and in 2001 David Tredinnick held on by just 2,000. There has been clear evidence of Liberal Democrat tactical voting in Labour's favour in the last two General Elections (they did distinctly better in the county council contests on the same days, by winning with 24% to Labour's 16% in the 2001 General Election). There may well yet be more close battles in Bosworth.

Social indices:			2001 Gen. Election:			
% Non-white	1.0		C	20,030	44.4	+3.8
% Prof/Man	31.1		Lab	17,750	39.4	+0.7
% Non-manual	52.2		LD	7,326	16.2	−1.6
£ Av prop val 2000	78 K		C maj	2,280	5.1	
% Increase 97–00	28.8		Turnout		64.4	−12.1
% Unemployed 2001	2.0		Elect	69,992		
% Fin hard/Rank	10.3	459				
% Pensioners	23.8					
% Prem mort/Rank	19	490				

Member of Parliament

David Tredinnick, a tall, angular, stiff-necked, red-faced ex-Guards officer and loss-making hereditary member of Lloyd's, born in 1950, son of a Lloyd's underwriter, and educated at Eton, Cape Town University and St John's College, Oxford, was one of the few sleaze-tainted – in his case cash-for-questions – Conservative MPs to survive the 1997 Tory wipe-out. He reportedly backed Hague in the 1997 leadership ballots but did not disclose his preference in 2001. Unkindly dubbed (by Andrew Rawnsley) 'memorably forgettable', and never closer to office than as PPS to a junior Welsh Office minister for three years in the early 1990s, he is keen on complementary medicine being available on the NHS since damaging his spine on falling from a horse. In 2001 there were only 13 other Old Etonian Conservative MPs.

BOURNEMOUTH EAST

The balmy south coast resort of Bournemouth is a monument to the Victorian love affair with the seaside. Attracted by the pine-clad slopes of the Bourne Valley, people came here to retire, or just to visit; they still do. It is even yet a highly successful and rather genteel retreat.

The East division lost the centre of the town and the East Cliff ward to its neighbour, Bournemouth West, in the most recent boundary changes. Its centre of gravity is now well to the east of the heart of the Bournemouth–Poole 'conurbation', including the communities of Boscombe and Southbourne. Both Bournemouth and Poole, like other English south coast districts, give considerable support to the Liberal Democrats in local elections – in Bournemouth East wards in the unitary authority elections of May 1999, for example, they returned 14 councillors, the Tories 11. Yet general elections are a different matter. All three seats in Poole and Bournemouth survived the Conservative debâcle in 2001, although East was the closest for the second time in a row, with a majority over the Lib Dems of just 3,434, or 9.6% of the total vote.

East has one of the lowest proportions of council-built housing anywhere in Britain. It has, as one might expect, a very high proportion of pensioners, substantially over a third of those who cast their ballots on 7 June 2001. The voters here might vote against the party in local elections and by-elections (Christchurch is just next door to the east) but they are Conservative folk when it comes to a priced general election vote. Bournemouth East has a tradition of electing well-known Conservative names, and indeed sometimes of losing them in less than desirable circumstances: as well as being the seat of Churchill's mercurial friend Brendan Bracken, it was represented by Suez rebel Nigel Nicolson, who was denied renomination by the local party in 1959, and also of John Cordle, whose political career was ended in 1977 by the Poulson fraud scandals. But the voters of Bournemouth East have yet to remove a Conservative MP.

Social indices:			2001 Gen. Election:			
% Non-white	1.4		C	15,501	43.3	+1.9
% Prof/Man	36.2		LD	12,067	33.7	+2.3
% Non-manual	63.1		Lab	7,107	19.9	−1.3
£ Av prop val 2000	106 K		UKIP	1,124	3.1	+1.3
% Increase 97–00	49.8		C maj	3,434	9.6	
% Unemployed 2001	2.8		Turnout		59.2	−11.0
% Decrease 97–01	2.6		Elect	60,454		
% Fin hard/Rank	7.6	536				
% Pensioners	34.3					
% Prem mort/Rank	33	287				

Member of Parliament

David Atkinson, MP here since 1977, (and so the 11th-longest-serving Tory MP) is of the Conservative Party's garagiste tendency, having inherited a car dealership before moving into PR. With an interest in complementary medicine – in his case chiropractice, and computers (as Matthew Parris has put it, 'every Parliament needs a techno-nerd'), he was born in 1940, attended St George's (RC) College, Weybridge, Southend College of Technology and the College of Automobile and Aeronautical Engineering, Chelsea, and takes a Catholic line on embryo research, and a deviant non-Tory line against hunting, being one of eight Tories to vote for a ban in January 2001. He also favours resettlement of displaced Palestinians, an unusual position for a seat with Jewish voters. A Hague voter in 1997, he was circumspect in the 2001 ballots, and his time as PPS to (fellow Catholic) Paul Channon 1979–87 was the nearest he got to office.

BOURNEMOUTH WEST

For many resorts of the British coast the last decades have seen economic decline, social changes, and political transformation. The Conservatives have lost their MPs in places such as Brighton, Hove, Torbay, Margate, Clacton and even Frinton; and further north in Scarborough and Whitby, Morecambe, Blackpool and Southport, never mind Rhyl and Colwyn Bay in Wales and Ayrshire in Scotland. In 2001 Weymouth in South Dorset joined this throng. Yet they held both Bournemouth divisions, and this town seems far less affected by the malaise of declining holiday preferences and increasing numbers of small hotels turning to the DSS for new clients. Symbolically, Bournemouth has become more popular as a venue for party conferences, while Blackpool has become less.

In 2001 Labour did clearly establish themselves in second place in Bournemouth West, while the Liberal Democrats were runners-up in East. West contains the two most working-class wards in Bournemouth, with large council estates and Labour councillors: Wallisdown and Kinson. Nevertheless, John Butterfill has held on by nearly 5,000, and the seat is more typified by Bournemouth's prospering town centre, all of which is included in West, with its new offices and even corporate headquarters especially in banking, finance and insurance (the Portman Building Society, Abbey Life, Chase Manhattan, McCarthy and Stone sheltered housing): it gleams on a sunny day, a far remove from the dowdy and shabby rivals elsewhere. In local government terms the Tories are stronger here than in East or in Poole, the seats which bracket West. They do best of all in East Cliff and West Cliff, and it might be said that the opposition have, if not a mountain to climb, at least a cliff or two to scale.

Social indices:			2001 Gen. Election:			
% Non-white	1.7		C	14,417	42.8	+1.2
% Prof/Man	33.7		Lab	9,699	28.8	+4.3
% Non-manual	58.6		LD	8,468	25.2	−2.6
£ Av prop val 2000	106 K		UKIP	1,064	3.2	+2.5
% Increase 97–00	47.8		C maj	4,718	14.0	
% Unemployed 2001	2.7		Turnout		54.2	−12.0
% Decrease 97–01	3.9		Elect	62,038		
% Fin hard/Rank	13.9	381				
% Pensioners	37.8					
% Prem mort/Rank	29	364				

Member of Parliament

John Butterfill, a pudgy-faced chartered surveyor, born in 1941 and educated at Caterham and a college of estate management, was elected here in 1983, having lost Croydon NW to the Liberals at a by-election two years earlier, and helped later (in 1993) to lose the neighbouring Christchurch seat, also to the Liberals. He is a Europhile whose attempt in 1995 to align the UK with Continental double-summer time predictably had the SNP leader Alex Salmond attacking him for 'threatening Scotland with daylight robbery'. He voted for Kenneth Clarke in all ballots in 1997 and for Portillo in 2001. He ran for the chairmanship of the 1922 Committee Executive in 2001, garnering the votes of 11 of the 166 Conservative MPs. A sometime complainer against incursion of Liverpool dropouts into Bournemouth, he could at least be thankful that the town had not suffered the downward mobility that had handed other seaside resorts to the Labour Party.

BRACKNELL

In 1992 the Conservative frontbencher Andrew Mackay had a majority of 28,680, the party's third highest. In 2001 he was returned to the Commons, but by just 6,713. This precipitous drop was caused by three factors. His oversized East Berkshire constituency has been reduced to a somewhat less strongly Conservative core, named after Bracknell. There has been a massive swing of over 13% to Labour over two general elections even taking account of the boundary changes. Finally, the turnout has plummeted from over 81% to under 61%.

The seat is closely based on Bracknell New Town, although extraneous wards do remain, such as Sandhurst (home of the Royal Military Academy) and Crowthorne (where the Broadmoor secure mental hospital is located). Bracknell's population has now stabilised at around 50,000, but it has finally achieved the feat of having a constituency named after it. Bracknell can be politically marginal. It voted almost evenly Labour and Conservative in 1979, when local elections took place on the same day as a general election. The New Town wards returned a full slate of Labour county councillors in May 1981. But then disaster struck the Labour Party in Bracknell. They could not elect a single councillor in the District elections of 1983 and 1987. Even in 1991, by when 12 years of Tory national rule had savagely depleted the Conservative ranks of local councillors, Bracknell Forest Borough returned 32 Conservatives to seven Labour representatives (and a lone Liberal Democrat).

Perhaps this is not too surprising. Bracknell is one of the more recently designated New Towns (1949), and was one of the last to complete its development as new neighbourhoods were carved out of the piney woods. It is one of the centres for high-technology industries such as computing, and as part of England's 'Silicon Valley' along the M4 corridor west from London it has welcomed the new headquarters of many large companies. If it once took 'overspill' families, they are now largely subsumed among highly paid professional workers – and who is to say that the earlier migrants have not themselves changed their minds in their new environment? Bracknell has been one of the most successful New Towns socially and above all economically. This is not Skelmersdale. Average house prices in 2000 were £62,000 in West Lancashire and £159,000 here. That economic reality is reflected in Bracknell's general allegiance to the Conservative Party; but also it must be remembered that this area has boomed under New Labour in the last few years too, those property values rising by 53% during the period of their first term, and voters here clearly felt the good times were rolling here in 2001, and they did not need to change course in the light of perceived stormy weather, at the heart of our national meteorological forecasting network.

Social indices:			2001 Gen. Election:			
% Non-white	2.5		C	22,962	46.6	−0.7
% Prof/Man	41.9		Lab	16,249	33.0	+3.2
% Non-manual	65.2		LD	8,424	17.1	+1.7
£ Av prop val 2000	159 K		UKIP	1,266	2.6	+1.6
% Increase 97–00	52.9		PA	324	0.7	+0.2
% Unemployed 2001	0.9		C maj	6,713	13.6	
% Decrease 97–01	0.8		Turnout		60.7	−13.8
% Fin hard/Rank	6.6	573	Elect	81,118		
% Pensioners	17.8					
% Prem mort/Rank	11	584				

Member of Parliament

Andrew Mackay, Shadow Northern Ireland Secretary (1997–2001) and formerly a government Whip (1992–97) – eventually Deputy Chief Whip under Major – was born in 1949 and educated at Solihull School, and as an estate agent personifies his party's retreat from the ownership of vast tracts of land to the marketing of small parcels of it. He snatched Roy Jenkins' former Birmingham Stechford seat for two years in the 1970s before resurfacing here (as 'Berkshire East') in 1983. Right wing on law and order and immigration, he is libertarian on abortion and on homosexuality at 16. Dalek-voiced, slant-eyed, permanently-tanned and expensively-tailored, he is second-married to vivacious former Press-Gallery-starlet-turned-MP Julie Kirkbride, with whom he fathered his third child in 2000. A Hague voter in 1997, he opted for the racier Portillo option in 2001 (though backed Clarke in the conclusive membership ballot) and followed Portillo onto the backbenches.

BRADFORD NORTH

Despite its name, Bradford North is in fact a kidney-shaped seat nestling around the eastern side of the old textile city. Why it is not called Bradford East remains a mystery. It does not have many council estates, but a considerable quantity of old private housing, ranging from near-slum terraces to substantial Victorian houses at the north end of the city. There is a large Asian population in the inner part of the seat; Bradford has become known as one of the chief recipient areas of immigrants from the Indian subcontinent, particularly from Pakistan. Bradford Moor ward, along the main road to Pudsey and Leeds directly east of the town centre, is now majority white; also strongly Labour is Bowling to its south. Further north, the pattern is more mixed: the cricketing ward of Undercliffe is almost always Labour, and the almost all-white Eccleshill usually; but Bolton has been Lib Dem in recent years and Idle, stretching out into the Yorkshire villages and countryside, also returns Liberal Democrats to the metropolitan borough council.

At parliamentary level Bradford North has had a chequered history, featuring a Labour MP who defected to the SDP (Ben Ford), a Conservative taking advantage of the subsequent brouhaha (Geoffrey Lawler), a far-left member who died in office (Pat Wall), and the country's first Mormon member, Terry Rooney. Despite allegations that the new and laxer rules for postal voting (which signally failed to increase the turnout in 2001) were being abused by gangs forcibly collecting batches of completed application forms, the results showed no signs of unusual or undue influence and a drop in completed votes of near the national average.

Social indices:			2001 Gen. Election:				
% Non-white	20.7		Lab	17,419	49.7	−6.3	
% Prof/Man	23.9		C	8,450	24.1	−1.5	
% Non-manual	47.0		LD	6,924	19.8	+5.3	
£ Av prop val 2000	47 K		BNP	1,613	4.6		
% Increase 97–00	22.5		Grn	611	1.7		
% Unemployed 2001	6.2		Lab maj	8,969	25.6		
% Decrease 97–01	2.3		Turnout		52.7	−10.6	
% Fin hard/Rank	37.1	74	Elect	66,454			
% Pensioners	23.9						
% Prem mort/Rank	46	75					

Member of Parliament

Terry Rooney, a dour-looking Catholic who turned Mormon at his wife's instigation, is a loyalist – as PPS to Michael Meacher (from 1997) – and was dubbed a 'Walworth Road puppet' after replacing in 1990 the dead Militant-linked MP Pat Wall, whose local Trotskyist associates he had helped purge. Son of a labourer, born in 1950 and educated at Buttershaw Comprehensive and Bradford and Ilkley Community College, he was a welfare rights advice worker for nine years after ten years as an insurance broker. A former Bradford councillor for eight years, his experience of badly-funded welfare makes him a supporter of the 'welfare to work' strategy, though he voted for Beckett, not Blair, in 1994.

BRADFORD SOUTH

Something always seems to be happening in Bradford politics. Unlike the other two seats the South constituency has always been won by Labour, but only by 110 votes in 1983 and by 309 in 1987. As in the case of Bradford North, South saw a by-election as a result of a tragic death in the 1990s. Yet curiously its electoral history has been if anything the least dramatic of the three Bradford constituencies over the last 15 years. Here there was no complication caused by a defecting MP like Edward Lyons of West or a deselected MP like Ben Ford of North. It has simply been a close and competitive two-party battle. That this should seem almost dull by Bradford standards is an eloquent testament to the colourful complexity of politics in the textile city below the eastern Pennines.

South is the Bradford seat with the fewest Asian voters and the most council housing. These indicators are linked, for few immigrants from the New Common-wealth have found their way onto council estates in most parts of Britain. Here in Bradford South are the grim inter-war estate of Buttershaw, in the south-west of the city (site of the early plays of Andrea Dunbar, who wrote from personal experience and died in her 20s), and the more modern developments in Tong ward in the south-east. The best ward for the Tories is Queensbury, perched on top of a hill outside the old city limits, but long included in a Bradford seat. The wards of Great Horton, Odsal, Wibsey and Wyke are all fairly marginal historically and were close in May 2000, the last council contests before Tony Blair asked for a verdict on his first term. Just over a year later, though, Bradford South gave the Prime Minister the go-ahead he so yearned for.

The former Labour council leader, Gerry Sutcliffe, easily took over in the 1994 by-election caused by the death of the active left-winger Bob Cryer in a car crash. His majority slipped from 13,000 in 1997 to 9,662 in 2001, but this was almost entirely due to a very poor turnout of 51%, the lowest of a Bradford seat.

Social indices:			2001 Gen. Election:			
% Non-white	8.0		Lab	19,603	55.8	−0.9
% Prof/Man	24.4		C	9,941	28.3	+0.3
% Non-manual	48.3		LD	3,717	10.6	−0.7
£ Av prop val 2000	46 K		UKIP	783	2.2	
% Increase 97–00	18.7		SLP	571	1.6	
% Unemployed 2001	4.4		SA	302	0.9	
% Decrease 97–01	1.7		Ind	220	0.6	
% Fin hard/Rank	33.7	104	Lab maj	9,662	27.5	
% Pensioners	23.6		Turnout		51.3	−14.6
% Prem mort/Rank	42	142	Elect	68,450		

Member of Parliament

Gerry Sutcliffe, MP here since 1994, was made a Labour Whip in 1999, by 2001 ranking fourth in the Whips' Office as Vice Chamberlain of the Household. Previously he was PPS to the hapless Harriet Harman (1997–98), and Stephen Byers (1998–99). Though a Blairite loyalist, his print union (originally SOGAT) background explained his hard lobbying during the legislation to restore union workplace negotiation rights in 1998. Born in 1953 and educated at Cardinal Hinsley (RC) Grammar School, Bradford, he worked initially as a shop assistant in a men's outfitter's for two years before becoming a printer and from 1980 to 1994 a union official. He rose locally to lead Bradford Council as an opponent of the left-wing 'trendy Wendys and Nigels' and the Militant left, and having failed to replace Militant-linked MP Pat Wall in Bradford North, he was preparing a similar challenge to hard left-winger Bob Cryer in Bradford South when Cryer was killed in a car crash, so creating the vacancy he filled. The hard core of the Labour Whips' Office is traditionally drawn from the unfashionable heavy metal union wing of the party, as evident in his case as ever.

BRADFORD WEST

Something very odd indeed happened in Bradford West in 1997. Labour returned their very worst result anywhere in Britain, as their share dropped by nearly 12%, and the Labour majority over the Conservatives went down from 9,500 to under 4,000. The result almost reversed the massive pro-Labour national trend. What on earth happened?

The answer seem to lie in candidature and the complex racial and religious politics of Bradford. Labour did not re-select the sitting member, Max Madden, but chose instead Marsha Singh – of Sikh origin. The majority of the 37% non-white residents are Muslims, like the Conservative candidate Mohammed Riaz. This must have helped Mr Riaz to hold the Tory vote steady, while reducing that of Mr Singh – who seems also to have suffered from a loss of some white votes; the Liberal Democrats' Helen Wright actually increased their share in third place.

Bradford West is a constituency of complexity and even contradictions. It contains much of the large Asian population of inner-city Bradford, but also western communities like Clayton and Thornton which are almost outside the built-up area of the city. It includes some of the poorest parts of Bradford and indeed of West Yorkshire, but also the best residential areas. It is the most middle-class of the three Bradford seats, but until 1997 the most strongly Labour. Before that election Labour held the vast majority of the votes in the Asian 'ghetto', centred on Manningham, once the fashionable west end of the city, but whose wool merchants' mansions are now often faded, often multi-occupied. West also includes Heaton, long considered the best leafy middle-class area, site of such elite institutions as Bradford Grammar School.

Labour's fortunes in Bradford West must be dependent largely on their ability to win the support of the burgeoning Asian – largely Muslim – community. University ward was 74% non-white at the time of the 1991 Census, and the neighbouring Toller 53%. Overall, over 36% of the population was from the ethnic minority groups, up from about 27% in 1981.

Pundits both in and outside Bradford predicted a further advance for the Tories and their articulate candidate Mohammed Riaz in 2001, but in fact little changed from 1997 except for one rather bizarre thing: the Green Party increased their vote by 368% and took third place ahead of the Liberal Democrats, whose share went down from 15% to 6%. Why? It is impossible to prove, but it might be noted that the Green candidate's name was Robinson, whereas all the other six offering themselves possessed distinctive Asian names.

Social indices:			2001 Gen. Election:			
% Non-white	36.6		Lab	18,401	48.0	+6.4
% Prof/Man	30.1		C	14,236	37.1	+4.1
% Non-manual	52.5		Grn	2,672	7.0	+5.1
£ Av prop val 2000	46 K		LD	2,437	6.4	−8.4
% Increase 97–00	12.2		UKIP	427	1.1	
% Unemployed 2001	7.8		AL	197	0.5	
% Decrease 97–01	2.5		Lab maj	4,165	10.9	
% Fin hard/Rank	37.8	70	Turnout		53.6	−9.8
% Pensioners	22.8		Elect	71,620		
% Prem mort/Rank	49	53				

Member of Parliament

Marsha Singh is one of Labour's 12 non-white MPs, in his case a secular Sikh (born in the Punjab in 1954, educated at Bellevue Boys Upper School, Bradford and Loughborough University), who finds himself representing a large local population of Pakistani Muslims, and so exposed to the 'ethnic factionalism' he deplores. Such ethnic complexities explain the anti-Labour swing he suffered when elected here in 1997. Inevitably required to articulate Kashmiri grievances, he has sought to focus on non-racial issues such as the means-testing of applications for local authority residential accommodation, and on pensions linking to average earnings, on which he rebelled in 2000.

BRAINTREE

Without wishing to adopt a cyclical theory of electoral history, the case study of Braintree constituency in Essex does bear close scrutiny.

When created in 1974, it was thought likely to be a marginal. Indeed its first two contests did result in very narrow Tory victories over Labour, by 2,000 in February and 1,000 in October, but it should be remembered that Labour actually won nationally. Tony Newton increased his majority by steps to 17,500 votes in 1992, having entered the Cabinet in 1988. Then in 1997 there was a most dramatic return to marginal status: and this time Labour finally were victorious, and Alan Hurst became one of the most unexpected of the new MPs. In many ways it was even more surprising when he held of the challenge of the American-born Conservative Brooks Newmark to win again, by 358, in 2001. Four close fights thus sandwich four easy Tory victories.

The Braintree seat lies in the very heart and geographical centre of Essex. It is an extensive division of over 40,000 hectares in area, but it does not touch the county boundary at any point. In local elections Labour can win a number of wards in the urban parts of the seat, in Braintree itself and its working-class suburb of Bocking, and in the town of Witham, which grew rapidly in the 1960s and 1970s. However, the Conservatives fight back in the prosperous villages and small towns which make up the balance of the constituency: in the Brain Valley at Black Notley and White Notley, along the A12 road and main railway line to Colchester at Hatfield Peverel and Kelvedon, along the Roman road of Stane Street at Coggeshall, and in the Colne Valley. It might be noted that this is one of the fastest growing constituencies in the country, having increased by over 6,000 electors between 1997 and 2001, notably in the 'new village' of Great Notley to the south-west of Braintree, which endeavours to be a fully formed community of 2,000 houses. Both of the tumescent Braintree county council divisions were gained by Conservatives on the same day as the June 2001 General Election. This is not a good omen for the Labour Party in this constituency.

Hurst's achievement seems even more striking when it is compared with Labour's performance elsewhere in the Essex sub-region, where they lost three of the four sitting members to be ousted, though the Conservatives did worse in the north and east of the county, also failing to regain Harwich or Colchester. No one can know how the patterns will develop in the first quarter of the new century.

Social indices:			2001 Gen. Election:			
% Non-white	1.4		Lab	21,123	42.0	−0.7
% Prof/Man	31.7		C	20,765	41.3	+1.2
% Non-manual	57.1		LD	5,664	11.3	−0.3
£ Av prop val 2000	103 K		Grn	1,241	2.5	+1.2
% Increase 97–00	61.2		LCA	774	1.5	
% Unemployed 2001	1.6		UKIP	748	1.5	
% Decrease 97–01	1.7		Lab maj	358	0.7	
% Fin hard/Rank	13.9	380	Turnout		63.6	−12.8
% Pensioners	23.7		Elect	79,157		
% Prem mort/Rank	10	592				

Member of Parliament

Alan Hurst, a very unexpected Labour MP, who spent 16 years on Southend Borough Council and five on Essex County Council, born in 1945 and educated at Westcliff High School and Liverpool University swept in on the 1997 floodtide, is a mild-mannered Southend solicitor. Initially he adopted the mode of diligent constituency MP dealing with local concerns on cottage hospitals, school buses and beef farming, and as a defender of the traditional single Member first-past-the-post voting system. But latterly he upped his profile with revolts on linking pensions to average earnings, curbing jury trials, and the right of the Prime Minister to nominate life peers, so establishing a mix of diligence and dissent which translated in his case into a majority of 358 – Labour's second smallest.

BRECON AND RADNORSHIRE

The Brecon and Radnor seat (it has been renamed but the boundaries have not altered) has been the site of a see-saw battle between Liberal Democrat and Conservative for over a decade. Four times out of the last five, the decisive majority has been less than 1,000, most recently as two new contenders battled it out, Roger Williams pipping Felix Aubel by 751 votes. Only in 1997 has a losing candidate been plunged into the depths, as the Liberal Democrat Richard Livsey seized the airy heights with an unusually large majority, for this seat, of just over 5,000 against the incumbent Tory MP Jonathan Evans.

In the two previous General Elections, there is no doubt that the Welsh seat of Brecon and Radnor had the closest results of any in Britain, although Ayr in Scotland and Portsmouth South in England are worthy contenders. In 1987 Richard Livsey, who had gained the seat in a very exciting by-election in 1985 by 556, held off the Tory challenge by just 56 votes. Five years later the positions were reversed as Jonathan Evans regained Brecon and Radnor by a margin of 130. What is more, the Labour Party were also seen as credible contenders on both occasions. What causes these cliffhanging results in this mid-Wales seat?

One element is the very diversity of the division. It is the largest seat in area in Wales, and one of the top ten in this respect in Britain. It contains the whole of the two traditional counties of Brecon and Radnor – or Brecknock and Radnorshire, or whatever: there are several variations of the names and the Boundary Commission chose a different combination for the 1997 Election. Most of the extensive terrain is agricultural, given to farming and forestry in the hills; but there is also a corner around Ystradgynlais where the economy was shaped by coal mining, and this provides the kernel of the Labour vote that gave that party control of the seat's representation from 1945 to 1979, and has made them competitive since. Elsewhere, though, the rural ambience provides a suitable setting for a super-tight Liberal–Conservative battle, although this was sparked in the first place by one of those accidents of history: a by-election.

On the death of the sitting Tory MP Tom Hooson in 1985, the Liberals leapt forward from third place to seize the seat in a thrilling three-way contest. They had not previously had a record of success in Brecon and Radnor, but they are formidable by-election campaigners the breadth of the land. Richard Livsey worked hard to try to build up a personal vote in this seat of small and tight-knit communities – Brecon, Builth Wells, Llandrindod Wells, Hay on Wye – and outlying farms. This failed to save him or the next sitting member though, in 1992 or 1997, and Roger Williams cannot rely on incumbency next time.

Social indices:			2001 Gen. Election:			
% Non-white	0.6		LD	13,824	36.8	−4.0
% Welsh sp	17.7		C	13,073	34.8	+5.9
% Prof/Man	35.3		Lab	8,024	21.4	−5.3
% Non-manual	52.9		PC	1,301	3.5	+2.0
£ Av prop val 2000	81 K		Ind	762	2.0	
% Increase 97–00	39.3		UKIP	452	1.2	
% Unemployed 2001	3.2		Ind	80	0.2	
% Decrease 97–01	0.6		LD maj	751	2.0	
% Fin hard/Rank	6.8	565	Turnout		71.8	−10.4
% Pensioners	30.8		Elect	52,247		
% Prem mort/Rank	30	341				

Member of Parliament

Roger Williams replaced the retiring Liberal Democrat MP Richard Livsey here in 2001, one local farmer succeeding another in the UK's sixth most agricultural seat. With the characteristically craggy features of the Welsh hill farmer, and a Powys County councillor from 1981, who joined the Liberal Democrats from the SDP in 1989, he was born in 1948 into a farming family at Talgarth. But whilst described as having 'his feet in the soil of Brecon and Radnor', he nonetheless experienced a somewhat elitist education at Christ's College, Brecon and Selwyn College, Cambridge – coincidentally the same as his parliamentary colleague Simon Hughes. Despite his strong local roots and the fact that he was to become one of only two working farmers among his party's 52 MPs after the 2001 Election, he saw his inherited majority of 5,000 virtually decimated and in his maiden speech spoke of the constituency's dire economic prospects both in its declining industrial strip at Ystradgynlais and with the impact of foot-and-mouth on farming and tourism.

BRENT EAST

Although their recommendations are almost certainly not going to be ready for implementation by the time of the next General Election, the parliamentary Boundary Commission has already decided to reduce the number of seats allocated to the North London Borough of Brent from the three it has possessed since 1974; by the commencement of the review in progress, in 2000, Brent's electorate reached just 2.41 seat quotas. It will be combined with northern wards of the City of Westminster, but the final implementation of the changes will not be until 2006 or 2007 at the earliest, so Brent East will continue for one more election in its present form, and the borough will remain over-represented for the time being: a borough whose municipal politics have been colourful, troubled and conflictual, with more than a hint of scandal – so much so that the magazine *Private Eye* rechristened it 'Bent'.

Brent East is best known nowadays as the former seat of the London Mayor, the independent and on critical occasions Independent left-wing but media-friendly Ken Livingstone who retired in 2001 and handed it over to an official Labour candidate, Paul Daisley. But it was not always a safe seat. When Livingstone entered Parliament in 1987 he scraped home over the feisty Conservative candidate Harriet Crawley (pregnant and unwed) by only 1,653 votes. He increased his majority to nearly 16,000 in 1997, but then courted and accepted expulsion from the party as he opposed and humiliated the official Labour machine and its candidate for mayor Frank Dobson in 2000, after himself being excluded from the nomination by decidedly undemocratic New Labour machinations.

Among Brent East's distinctive neighbourhoods are Kilburn, long known as one of the most heavily Irish neighbourhoods in London, and Cricklewood, just about the nation's leading centre for middle-class Irish immigration in recent years. In 1991, half the population in Church End and Brentwater wards was non-white. The Labour stronghold was Carlton ward, which largely consisted of council tower blocks, with its massive population density (121 residents per hectare) and 30% Afro-Caribbean population. Brent East is truly one of the melting-pots of London.

Social indices:			2001 Gen. Election:			
% Non-white	36.7		Lab	18,325	63.2	−4.1
% Prof/Man	36.4		C	5,278	18.2	−4.1
% Non-manual	62.6		LD	3,065	10.6	+2.8
£ Av prop val 2000	185 K		Grn	1,361	4.7	
% Increase 97–00	60.7		PA	392	1.4	+0.7
% Unemployed 2001	5.9		SLP	383	1.3	−0.0
% Decrease 97–01	5.9		UKIP	188	0.6	
% Fin hard/Rank	21.8	247	Lab maj	13,047	45.0	
% Pensioners	19.3		Turnout		49.9	−16.0
% Prem mort/Rank	42	146	Elect	58,095		

Member of Parliament

Paul Daisley, elected here in 2001, replaced Ken Livingstone as Labour's local standard-bearer following Livingstone's expulsion from the party for running against Labour's official London mayoral candidate, Frank Dobson, and – of course – defeating him. Daisley, owner of his own PR company, was born in 1957 and educated at Littlemore School, Oxfordshire and Abingdon College. With a local base as a Brent councillor from 1990, and as Council Leader from 1996, and seen as a Blairite, he bills himself as 'the council leader responsible for transforming Brent into a model Labour authority', it having previously been a much publicised example of municipal mayhem, with splits in the Labour Party handing power to the Conservatives. But his selection was highly contested – not least by members of the Black Socialist Society, who criticised selection of yet another white candidate in a seat comprising 37% non-white residents. As Council Leader he has taken a stand against black gangsters in Harlesden, whilst calling for Labour nationally to be 'grown-up' and to readmit Livingstone to membership in acknowledgement of the

London Mayor's 'conciliatory' stance – this before Livingstone's legal moves to block the government's plans for part-privatisation of the tube.

BRENT NORTH

Few electoral observers will be able to answer this question: in which constituency did the Labour Party increase its share of the vote by the greatest percentage in the June 2001 General Election? The answer is surprising for a number of reasons. One is that Labour had already posted one of its very best performances in Brent North in 1997, when Barry Gardiner took the seat from the veteran Conservative incumbent, the former headmaster Sir Rhodes Boyson, with a phenomenal swing of 19%. Surely there would be a movement back to the Conservatives in this part of outer north-west London, which had also seen the huge swings that had taken the most unlikely Conservative seats such as Harrow West and Michael Portillo's Enfield Southgate. More specifically, Barry Gardiner had been mentioned as a possible target because of his pro-Israeli stance, particularly in a seat where it was felt that the balance of the large Asian population in the seat was moving from Hindu to Muslim religious groups. It was not just in his own old school that there were fears for the continued Commons career of the Haileyburian first-term MP.

Yet in fact Gardiner's share increased by another 9%, making an increase over two elections and nine years of very nearly 30%, doubling to 60%. What explains this remarkable continued transformation? Partly one can point to the further pro-Labour swings in nearby seats like the aforementioned in the boroughs of Brent and Enfield. Outer London had done well economically under the New Labour government, with property value rises, mortgage reductions, and a strict control of unemployment and inflation. Yet this was no more apparent in Brent North than elsewhere. The threat of a Muslim candidacy or organised boycott clearly came to nothing. Finally, it may well be that Gardiner benefited exceptionally strongly from the factor of double incumbency, indeed quadruple incumbency. It has been said that Asian communities are especially inclined to support the winning side, and now the national Labour government had replaced the Tories after their 18-year spell, and Gardiner himself had taken over from Boyson. Asians in Brent North are both numerous and relatively prosperous, established in business and education. Had much of their support for the Conservatives previously been instrumental and conditional? This would be far from culpable, but instead impeccably rational.

Rhodes Boyson had been securely established in his seat for over 23 years. Brent North had looked like an aberration: a strongly Conservative seat which was over 40% non-white. Perhaps too Brent North is yet another demonstration of another transformation, that of New Labour, which has put far behind it the image of incompetence, ideology and extremism and disunity which so dogged previous incarnations, not least in this borough of Brent.

Social indices:			2001 Gen. Election:			
% Non-white	41.6		Lab	20,149	59.4	+8.7
% Prof/Man	40.0		C	9,944	29.3	−10.8
% Non-manual	68.3		LD	3,846	11.3	+3.2
£ Av prop val 2000	149 K		Lab maj	10,205	30.1	
% Increase 97–00	55.2		Turnout		57.7	−12.8
% Unemployed 2001	2.8		Elect	58,789		
% Decrease 97–01	2.8					
% Fin hard/Rank	10.7	447				
% Pensioners	22.8					
% Prem mort/Rank	21	465				

Member of Parliament

Barry Gardiner, MP here since 1997, is one of Labour's most ponderous orators, to whom a bored parliamentary colleague mockingly sought to set fire during one of his laboriously-delivered Commons speeches. Somewhat excessively educated at Glasgow High School, Haileybury, St Andrews University, Harvard, and Corpus Christi College, Cambridge, he was Glasgow-born in 1957, is a shipping arbitrator by trade, and in 1997 contributed to the PLP's pool of 43 beards – since 2001 raised to 49. A contributor to *The Philosophical Quarterly*, he has more prosaically campaigned for local leaseholders against landlords, backed attempts to license dangerous mini cab drivers, and profited from the ethnic diversity of a constituency in which, he claims, 61% speak English only as their second language.

BRENT SOUTH

Brent South is one of the three seats in Britain where it is the white residents who are in a minority. The 1991 Census showed it as the most heavily non-white seat in Britain (55.4%). Both of the main non-white groups identified by the Census are present in force in Brent South: about a quarter of all residents are Afro-Caribbean and about a quarter are Asian.

The constituency is a long strip on the southern border of Brent, from Alperton and Barham in the west to Kensal Rise in the east. The heaviest concentration of Asians is to be found in the west and central parts of the seat, around the major shopping area in Wembley. Afro-Caribbeans predominate further east, around Harlesden and the Stonebridge estate just off the A406 North Circular Road. Much of this latter territory suffers from poor housing conditions and high crime rates, with well over one-tenth of all households consisting of a single-parent family. Not surprisingly, all the wards in the east of the constituency are Labour strongholds.

The mainly Asian areas have a different story to tell, though. The Liberal Democrats are active locally and long ago made sure of taking Alperton and Barham in Brent Council elections. Tokyngton ward, though 62% non-white, is a pleasant residential area of semi-detached housing and elected one Conservative in May 1998. All this is pretty close to being outdated though, for after the next General Election Brent South will cease to exist, as a new seat crossing the boundaries of Brent and Westminster will be created to right the over-representation of Brent borough. In any case the representation here at parliamentary level is safely Labour. In 2001 Brent South became the safest Labour seat in London, and shot up into the top ten of large percentage majorities. Paul Boateng's base is becoming even more secure as his ministerial prospects appear to brighten further.

Social indices:			2001 Gen. Election:			
% Non-white	55.4		Lab	20,984	73.3	+0.3
% Prof/Man	26.5		C	3,604	12.6	−3.3
% Non-manual	51.0		LD	3,098	10.8	+3.1
£ Av prop val 2000	125 K		SA	491	1.7	
% Increase 97–00	72.6		Ind	460	1.6	
% Unemployed 2001	5.6		Lab maj	17,380	60.7	
% Decrease 97–01	6.4		Turnout		51.2	−13.2
% Fin hard/Rank	34.3	98	Elect	55,891		
% Pensioners	17.6					
% Prem mort/Rank	42	150				

Member of Parliament

Paul Boateng Financial Secretary to the Treasury from 2001, was Britain's first non-white (in his case half-black) minister in the Commons (an Asian peer was a minister in Lloyd George's coalition). Greeting his victory here in 1987 (as one of the Commons' first four post-war non-white Labour MPs) with the rhetorically radical shout of 'Today Brent South, tomorrow Soweto!', his modishly-tailored rise has been relentless since his swift entry to the frontbench within two years of reaching the Commons, and postings in government at Health and the Home Office. A solicitor-turned-barrister of mixed Scots-Ghanaian parentage, born in 1951 and educated at Accra Academy, Apsley Grammar School and Bristol University, he is a smoothly self-confident performer, and because less accident-prone than the excessively smooth Asian ex-minister Keith Vaz, ought to be the first non-white Cabinet Minister. He is by far the most successful of the clutch of (originally) left-wing MPs to have emerged from Ken Livingstone's GLC of the early 1980s, as a listing of the rest of them will confirm – Tony Banks, John McDonnell, and Livingstone himself. Unlike them he has not been reduced to arguing about pigeons in Trafalgar Square or turning up for Campaign Group reunions in the 'Noe' lobby.

BRENTFORD AND ISLEWORTH

Brentford and Isleworth is now very safely in Labour hands and it is hard to believe that only in 1997 it still had a Conservative MP, Nirj Deva, now a member of the European Parliament. In 2001 Ann Keen posted her second successive five-figure majority, and is clearly well established in this long, thin, varied constituency in west London. It can no longer be classed as a marginal.

When the seat was first contested in 1974 two sitting MPs battled it out – Barney Hayhoe, Conservative member for Heston and Isleworth, and Michael Barnes, the Labour MP for Brentford and Chiswick. Hayhoe won both of the two General Elections of that year, but in each case by a hair's breadth: his majorities were 726 in

February and 232 in October. Then came three comfortable Conservative General Election victories, and Brentford and Isleworth was held easily. In 1992 however, Sir Barney Hayhoe retired and the new Tory candidate Nirj Deva saw his party's majority slashed to just over 2,000. With an unhelpful boundary change, the Conservatives were in grave danger of losing the seat for the first time; Nirj Deva was totally swamped by the national swing of 1997, losing by no fewer than 14,424 votes to Ann Keen, who joined her husband as a Hounslow MP.

Brentford and Isleworth is the eastern half of the borough of Hounslow. For much of its length the seat hugs the north bank of the Thames as the river curves round past Kew Gardens, the Old Deer Park and Syon Park. The housing is very mixed. There are some owner-occupied Tory areas like Spring Grove and Hounslow South. Council estates tip neighbourhoodss like Gunnersbury and Isleworth South to Labour. Chiswick has a large number of liberal urban professionals. There is oldish private housing of poorer quality in the centres of Brentford and Hounslow. The population is mixed too: there are not quite so many Asians as in the other Hounslow seat, Feltham and Heston, but it includes the central Hounslow neighbourhood. It will now take a swing of 12% back to the Conservatives for them to retake Brentford and Isleworth. This seems an unlikely eventuality – at least in one go.

Social indices:			2001 Gen. Election:			
% Non-white	22.4		Lab	23,275	52.3	−5.2
% Prof/Man	43.3		C	12,957	29.1	−2.6
% Non-manual	68.5		LD	5,994	13.5	+5.2
£ Av prop val 2000	204 K		Grn	1,324	3.0	+1.8
% Increase 97–00	71.8		UKIP	412	0.9	−0.2
% Unemployed 2001	1.6		SA	408	0.9	
% Decrease 97–01	3.3		Ind	144	0.3	
% Fin hard/Rank	16.4	330	Lab maj	10,318	23.2	
% Pensioners	21.5		Turnout		53.0	−18.0
% Prem mort/Rank	32	298	Elect	84,049		

Member of Parliament

For Labour's **Ann Keen**, elected here in 1997 after two previous attempts, the Commons is home-from-home, with her husband as MP for the next-door seat of Feltham and Heston, and her sister Sylvia Heal as a Deputy Speaker. With her rediscovery in 1995 of her by then 28-year-old homosexual son whom she had given up for adoption as a baby, she has become a leader of the campaign to lower the homosexual age of consent to 16. A steelworker's daughter and a former nurse, born in 1948 and educated at Elfed Secondary Modern School, Flint, and eventually at Surrey University, she rose in Labour politics as a friend of Neil and Glenys Kinnock, and mirrored their political journey away from the unilateralist left, if not as far as the sunlit uplands of Brussels and Strasbourg. But her role as PPS to Gordon Brown from 2000 (and previously to Frank Dobson) will doubtless feature in her CV a little more prominently than that of liaising with the defecting Tory MP Shaun Woodward during his Damascene conversion in 1999.

BRENTWOOD AND ONGAR

This superficially unexceptionable Essex constituency received a disproportionate amount of attention in the 2001 General Election, for one reason only. The only independent MP in the Commons, Martin Bell, fulfilling a pledge he made when elected on an anti-sleaze campaign against Neil Hamilton at Tatton in 1997 to serve there for one term only, decided to accept invitations to transfer his attentions and services to Brentwood and Ongar, citing the alleged excessive influence in the local Conservative Party of the controversial sect, the Peniel Church, led by 'Bishop' Michael Reid. Clearly Martin Bell felt that he still had much to offer the Commons, a theatre he treated with all the seriousness of the war zones where he had made his name with the BBC.

Yet there was much which made his candidacy at Brentwood weaker than it had been at Tatton. There was no evidence that the amiable and moderate MP, Eric Pickles, has succumbed to the wiles of Peniel or done anything improper. Labour and the Liberal Democrats had no intention of withdrawing, and not only giving Bell a clear run but helping considerably with his campaign, as they had in the Cheshire seat. Bell looked uncomfortably like a man hawking his conscience around the country in a bid to retain a place in the comfortable club of Westminster – and surely there were more appropriate causes to fight among Labour MPs – Geoffrey Robinson, Keith Vaz, even Peter Mandelson? Most outside observers predicted humiliation, fourth place, even a lost deposit.

Martin Bell proved these prophets wrong. If Dr Richard Taylor of Wyre Forest did indeed take his place to become the Independent hero of 2001, Bell still polled over 31%, massively more than any other fringe candidate, and would clearly have won if both the Labour and Liberal Democrats had withdrawn, or indeed just the latter, as they had at Wyre Forest. It should be said that Eric Pickles did hold on with a drop in his own vote of just 7% – less than Keith Vaz, for example, and far less than the 24% suffered by Neil Hamilton four years before. Nevertheless, the British public does seem increasingly to be articulating some demand for truly non-party characters, which should shake up the established parties to no ill effect. The turnout here was nearly 10% higher than the national average too.

Brentwood is situated just beyond the north-eastern fringe of Greater London, near the boundary of the London Borough of Havering on the road to the Essex capital of Chelmsford. It is a modern town of mainly middle-class owner-occupiers, and forms a substantial population centre of over 50,000 souls when the contiguous neighbourhoods of Pilgrims Hatch, Hutton, Shenfield and Warley are included. The seat also includes a number of villages and the small town of Chipping Ongar in the Epping Forest district. Barring further revelations of a religious or other nature, Martin Bell is unlikely to intervene here again and the seat should revert to safety for Eric Pickles, who has appeared to behave with dignity under the spotlight.

Social indices:			2001 Gen. Election:			
% Non-white	1.8		C	16,558	38.0	−7.4
% Prof/Man	43.3		Ind	13,737	31.5	
% Non-manual	70.6		LD	6,772	15.6	−10.7
£ Av prop val 2000	172 K		Lab	5,505	12.6	−9.5
% Increase 97–00	53.4		UKIP	611	1.4	+0.5
% Unemployed 2001	0.9		Ind	239	0.5	
% Decrease 97–01	1.5		Ind	68	0.2	
% Fin hard/Rank	5.8	586	Ind	52	0.1	
% Pensioners	25.3		C maj	2,821	6.5	
% Prem mort/Rank	13	562	Turnout		67.3	−9.6
			Elect	64,695		

Member of Parliament

Elected here in 1992, **Eric Pickles**, a shrewd and affable, porcine stage Yorkshireman, had been parachuted into this safe Essex fastness as reward for having 'done a Wandsworth' as Leader of Bradford Council during the 18 months of Tory control. Awkwardly poised as one whose gut Thatcherism is balanced by pro-European instincts, he was born in 1952 in Keighley where his father had a shop on a council estate, and attended Greenhead Grammar School and Leeds Polytechnic. Essex's other working-class Tory (see also Robert Spink in Castle Point), a vice chairman of the Party under John Major (1993–97), he is thought to have voted in 1997 for Kenneth Clarke, but in 2001 backed Iain Duncan Smith and moved from being a Social Security spokesman (1998–2001) to Shadow Transport Minister in 2001, following his albeit close defeat of Martin Bell.

BRIDGEND

The nearest thing to a marginal, let alone a Conservative, seat, in the county of Mid Glamorgan in Labour's South Wales heartland is Bridgend; and Win Griffiths held a majority of over 10,000 for Labour in that constituency in 2001. Yet it was won by the Tories once, in 1983, when the seat was first contested. The creation of a separate seat of Bridgend gave the Conservatives some hope in this most forbidding of areas. They are competitive in the market and commercial centre of Bridgend itself, which has never been a coal-mining town but belongs to the more fertile Vale of Glamorgan. There are Tory votes in wards within the town like Newcastle and Brackla and nearby in attractive residential communities such as Coity and Coychurch. Pencoed and Laleston do not have 'valley' type voting patterns either, but a significant Conservative minority. The seat also passes through prosperous Vale farmland, and Conservative villages like St Brides Major, to the coast. The Tories also hope to build up a lead in the seaside resorts like Ogmore-by-Sea and Porthcawl, the home base of the first (and so far only) Conservative MP for Bridgend, Peter Hubbard-Miles.

All so far described is more than a little reminiscent of the neighbouring seat to the east, Vale of Glamorgan, which was won by Labour in a by-election in 1989 but often held by the Conservatives in General Elections. However, Win Griffiths gained Bridgend fairly easily in 1987, by over 4,000, and increased his margin subsequently as noted above. The balance was shifted by the industrial areas that exist within the constituency. It does not stretch right up into the valleys, but it includes two patches of very heavy Labour support. One is the Cornelly/Pyle/Kenfig area over towards Margam, Port Talbot and their steelworks. The other is north of Bridgend, at the foot of the valleys: Tondu, Aberkenfig, Bryncethin and Sarn.

Bridgend has a higher proportion of professional and managerial workers than any of the valley seats and the same as Vale of Glamorgan. If a seat were of this profile in England, it would be regarded as marginal; in Wales, however, it must now be regarded as safely Labour for the foreseeable future.

Social indices:			2001 Gen. Election:			
% Non-white	1.1		Lab	19,422	52.5	−5.6
% Welsh sp	8.2		C	9,377	25.3	+2.5
% Prof/Man	35.0		LD	5,330	14.4	+2.9
% Non-manual	56.7		PC	2,652	7.2	+3.4
£ Av prop val 2000	72 K		PA	223	0.6	
% Increase 97–00	20.3		Lab maj	10,045	27.2	
% Unemployed 2001	3.2		Turnout		60.2	−12.3
% Decrease 97–01	1.5		Elect	61,496		
% Fin hard/Rank	14.3	366				
% Pensioners	27.9					
% Prem mort/Rank	31	317				

Member of Parliament

Win Griffiths, a quiet wiry Welsh chalk-face worker, taught for 11 years before becoming an MEP for ten years (1979–89, South Wales) until his election here in 1987, when he went straight onto the Education Select Committee before being a spokesman on Environment, then Education, for Wales. A Methodist lay preacher with attendant reservations on smoking, euthanasia and homosexuality, he was born in 1943, educated at Brecon Boys Grammar School and Cardiff University (where he was a Socialist Society contemporary of Neil Kinnock, a connection later helping him get the Bridgend seat), and served for 12 months as a junior Welsh Office Minister before being sacked on age grounds in 1998 – a sacking publicly disapproved by Paul Flynn MP.

BRIDGWATER

After the Liberal Democrats swept through Somerset in local and county council elections in the 1990s there were predictions that they could win all the parliamentary constituencies in the county too, but these have proved to be distinctly over-optimistic. In 2001 they lost Taunton and nearly Somerton and Frome as well, saw their majority reduced in Yeovil on Paddy Ashdown's retirement, and went backwards in Wells and Bridgwater. In the last named they clearly suffered from a strong Labour performance in third place, but it should also be noted that the Tory share went up by nearly 4% despite the departure of the 30-year incumbent MP, Tom King.

The town of Bridgwater itself has a remarkable tradition of loyalty to the Labour Party. The former Bridgwater Borough Council was one of very few local authorities in the nation which remained under Labour control even in the late 1960s, in the darkest days of Harold Wilson's government. Now the town is only part of Sedgemoor District, but the residual Labour vote is hard to crack; in 2001, for example, in the County Council Elections on the same day as the General, four of Labour's five wins were in the wards in Bridgwater itself. The constituency stretches north-westward through the beautiful Quantock Hills to the cliffs of the Somerset coastline at Minehead and Watchet, taking in 15 wards from West Somerset district to add to the 20 in Sedgemoor. This is traditional Tory territory, in more senses than one; just as in the case of Jackie Ballard in neighbouring Taunton, the Lib Dems may well have suffered from the topicality of hunting and other 'countryside' issues. It is not beyond the bounds of possibility that they might even lose their second place to Labour here, and the historical evidence suggests they will not conquer the Labour redoubt in Bridgwater town itself. On the same day as the 2001 General Election the Liberal Democrats lost control of Somerset county, gains being made by both the Conservatives and Labour. Ashdown's departure reflects an end to its status as a Lib Dem model.

Social indices:			2001 Gen. Election:			
% Non-white	0.5		C	19,354	40.4	+3.5
% Prof/Man	28.1		LD	14,367	30.0	−3.6
% Non-manual	48.5		Lab	12,803	26.8	+2.0
£ Av prop val 2000	81 K		UKIP	1,323	2.8	
% Increase 97–00	38.6		C maj	4,987	10.4	
% Unemployed 2001	2.7		Turnout		64.6	−10.2
% Decrease 97–01	2.3		Elect	74,079		
% Fin hard/Rank	13.1	394				
% Pensioners	30.4					
% Prem mort/Rank	20	477				

Member of Parliament

Ian Liddell-Grainger inherited this seat from the retiring Tom King in 2001, becoming only the third Conservative MP for Bridgwater since 1950. Born in 1959 and educated at Millfield School and the South of Scotland Agricultural College in Edinburgh, he farmed in Berwickshire before diversifying into running Newcastle-based property investment and office furniture companies. A political victim of Liberal Democrat success in the West Country, he lost Tory-held Torridge and West Devon in 1997, but saw off another expected Lib-Dem assault at Bridgwater in 2001. A critic of Labour spin-doctors, and a defender of farming interests recalled for his brandishing a leg of lamb at the 1999 Conservative Party Conference with an accompanying claim that Labour's agricultural policy had not 'got a leg to stand on', he comes to the Commons the bearer of royal blood as a great, great, great grandson of Queen Victoria (via Victoria's son Leopold, Duke of Albany) and thus is approximately 283rd in line of succession to the Throne. Balding and puckish-looking with a toothy smile and receding both in hair and chin, his interest in his royal inheritance emerged in his maiden speech when he referred to the local Battle of Sedgemore of 1685 as 'the last time republicanism raised its ugly head' in battle. His accession to the Throne would occasion the third by-election in Bridgwater since 1938.

BRIGG AND GOOLE

This is a divided seat socially and politically, not one of the Boundary Commission's more logical creations in 1997, a throwback to the now abolished county of Humberside. Brigg is a small and conservative Lincolnshire market town, as evinced by the folk song 'Brigg Fair', whereas Goole is an industrial, working-class and Labour stronghold, in history and in sympathy part of the Yorkshire coalfield. There have been many redrawings of constituency boundary in this area and it will not survive for long in its present form, as the seat will be split due to local government reform: the Brigg section is now in North Lincolnshire unitary authority and Goole sits, still uncomfortably, in the East Riding of Yorkshire (it was never there before; before the creation of Humberside in 1974 it was in the West Riding).

Goole (population 18,000) is considerably larger than Brigg (5,000) and in 1997 the gritty inland port on the river Ouse has won the battles of the main towns and propelled a Labour member to Parliament, as Ian Cawsey has twice defeated the Isle of Axholme's Donald Stewart, by just under 4,000 votes. In an even year between the two main parties, Brigg and Goole would tend to favour the Conservatives. Indeed some over-subtle observers predicted a Tory gain in 2001, on the grounds that the rural section (this is one of only a handful of Labour-held seats in England with over 2,000 employed in agriculture) would turn out more heavily than the urban vote in Goole. In fact turnout overall dropped less than average, and the theory appears to have been disproved. Labour clearly treated it as a key vulnerable marginal and must do so again as this Trentside division is contested probably for the last time in 2005 or 2006.

Social indices:			2001 Gen. Election:			
% Non-white	0.6		Lab	20,066	48.9	−1.3
% Prof/Man	26.8		C	16,105	39.2	+2.7
% Non-manual	45.8		LD	3,796	9.2	−0.8
£ Av prop val 2000	57 K		UKIP	688	1.7	
% Increase 97–00	19.6		SLP	399	1.0	
% Unemployed 2001	3.1		Lab maj	3,961	9.6	
% Decrease 97–01	1.8		Turnout		64.6	−8.9
% Fin hard/Rank	10.6	450	Elect	63,536		
% Pensioners	25.9					
% Prem mort/Rank	35	255				

Member of Parliament

Labour's **Ian Cawsey**, PPS to Lord Williams of Mostyn, leader of the House of Lords from 2001, cheery and burly, won the seat in 1997. Born in 1960, educated at Wintringham School, an ex-local council leader, originally an IT worker, he worked for ten years as researcher for neighbouring MP Elliot Morley, whose interest in animal welfare he shares. Between them they have kept the fox hunting issue on the boil so as to mobilise the voters in a second general election.

BRIGHTON KEMPTOWN

There are parts of the country which are clearly swinging on a long-term pattern towards Labour, quite apart from the factors lying behind their two successive huge national victories, and for differing reasons too. One of these is the newly elevated city of Brighton and Hove, and its eastern seat, Kemptown, which registered a further movement away from the Tories in 2001.

Brighton Kemptown was the first seat that Labour ever won in Sussex, and the only one in the county they had won before 1997. It was something of a shock when Dennis Hobden seized the constituency in 1964 – and he swept in by a margin of fully seven votes. Hobden had the temerity to win again in 1966, but in 1970 the seat reverted to the Tory fold, where it remained until 1997, in the hands of Andrew Bowden. In the boundary changes which came into force before that election, the seat was expanded to bring in over 15,000 voters from the Lewes constituency, from the bungaloid coast around Peacehaven and Telscombe, a development which was felt to improve the Conservatives' chances of holding Kemptown. It probably did, but in a year like 1997 when not only the other Brighton seat, Pavilion, fell, but Hove did as well, Sir Andrew Bowden went down by over 3,500.

Kemptown is the 'east end' of Brighton, not only geographically but sociologically too. Here is the more plebeian, less fashionable side of the south coast's most famous seaside resort, beyond the East or Palace Pier. Well behind the front, council estates climb into the South Downs, such as Whitehawk just below the racecourse and Moulsecoomb, where there have been youth riots and one or two horrific crimes. Here Labour can also count on success in the Falmer ward and they also have a lot going for them in the central wards too, including the presence of one of the nation's largest gay communities.

The seat also includes the Conservative strongholds of Rottingdean and Woodingdean, and it is ironic that the elite girls private school, Roedean, and the fast-rising independent Brighton College, whose dynamic headmaster is Anthony Seldon, a renowned historian and initiator of the book *Conservative Century*, should now find themselves in a Labour constituency. Kemptown may swing yet further to Labour, and in any case should now be regarded as normally a Labour seat, if perhaps an exceptional rather than a normal constituency.

Social indices:			2001 Gen. Election:			
% Non-white	2.1		Lab	18,745	47.8	+1.3
% Prof/Man	33.4		C	13,823	35.3	−3.6
% Non-manual	59.2		LD	4,064	10.4	+0.7
£ Av prop val 2000	110K		Grn	1,290	3.3	
% Increase 97–00	63.2		UKIP	543	1.4	
% Unemployed 2001	4.0		SLP	364	0.9	+0.2
% Decrease 97–01	4.3		Ind	227	0.6	
% Fin hard/Rank	16.4	331	PA	147	0.4	
% Pensioners	31.5		Lab maj	4,922	12.6	
% Prem mort/Rank	42	153	Turnout		58.0	−12.8
			Elect	67,621		

Member of Parliament

Desmond Turner, a sonorous-voiced question reader, who won the seat for Labour in 1997, has been a mix of fawning Blairite and moderate rebel over disability benefit cuts and – of local concern given the nearby flight path into Gatwick – air traffic control privatisation. Born in 1939 and educated at Luton Grammar School and Imperial College, London, a biochemist with a doctorate, he highlights the poverty of Brighton behind the Regency facades, which has accounted for the Tory decline. He has also fought a successful campaign against expanding the Portobello sewage works, and lobbied to retain the Newhaven/Dieppe ferry.

BRIGHTON PAVILION

It came as little surprise when Labour won Brighton Pavilion for the first time in May 1997, although few expected David Lepper's majority to be as much as 13,000, as he polled nearly twice as many votes as his defeated adversary, the solicitor-general Sir Derek Spencer. Lepper held his seat easily in 2001, but Pavilion's ability to stand out took another new form, as the Green Party secured its best result anywhere in the UK: saving its deposit with over 9% of the vote. This had been presaged and prepared by local government activity, including 12.5% in the all-out Brighton and Hove unitary council elections in 1999 – achieving an astonishing 49%, electing three councillors – in the north central St Peter's ward including Brighton's 'cathedral' parish church itself, and the station.

This western division centres on the traditionally more elegant end of the seafront, towards once genteel Hove; in few other towns could there be a ward named Regency. Inland there are comfortable suburbs with a high proportion of London commuters, like Preston and Patcham.

Even in 1945 and 1966 (when the Conservatives won by over 6,000) Labour could get nowhere near to victory in Brighton Pavilion. Yet after 1992 for the first time Pavilion looked like a marginal, as a swing of over 6% slashed the Tory majority to just over 3,500. Pavilion is now a much better bet for Labour than Kemptown, its next-door neighbour to the east. What has happened in the western half of Brighton?

There is no doubt that the town of Brighton has moved to the left in recent decades. It always had a somewhat raffish reputation: as the setting for Graham Greene's then shocking tale of juvenile crime and intractability, *Brighton Rock*; and as the destination for adulterous and other sinful Londoners anxious not to foul their own nests. Now, though, Brighton is the home of a large and relatively confident gay community, which has been given no reason to favour the Conservative Party. There are also a large number of social security claimants, few of whom will vote, and of seasonally unemployed casual workers, some of whom might. The radical concrete and plate-glass of Sussex University is set in the constituency, in Stanmer ward. Brighton Council has for several years been controlled by a Labour local council which has simultaneously managed to be both left-wing and popular – at least it has consistently been re-elected. The Green vote shows that Brighton Pavilion remains determinedly counter-cultural, though, and more surprises may be on the way.

Social indices:			2001 Gen. Election:			
% Non-white	3.7		Lab/Coop	19,846	48.7	−5.9
% Prof/Man	43.4		C	10,203	25.1	−2.6
% Non-manual	67.3		LD	5,348	13.1	+3.6
£ Av prop val 2000	120 K		Grn	3,806	9.3	+6.8
% Increase 97–00	72.3		SLP	573	1.4	
% Unemployed 2001	4.6		Ind	409	1.0	+0.7
% Decrease 97–01	5.2		UKIP	361	0.9	+0.5
% Fin hard/Rank	11.1	436	PA	177	0.4	
% Pensioners	27.3		L/C maj	9,643	23.7	
% Prem mort/Rank	36	236	Turnout		58.8	−14.8
			Elect	69,200		

Member of Parliament

David Lepper, one of Labour's 1997 intake, bald and beaky and of Huguenot origin, born in 1945, a lorry driver's son, educated at secondary modern schools in Richmond and Wimbledon and at Kent and Sussex Universities, is a standard issue Labour MP: a schoolteacher for 27 years and local councillor for 17 – eventually as leader of Brighton council – and as a reflection of his town's downward mobility, he campaigns against its poverty and homelessness. One is here reminded of the London Labour MP and government Whip who when hearing a constituent complain at how her area had deteriorated, replied 'Well, why else do you think you've got a Labour MP?' As Brighton goes, so goes the nation.

BRISTOL EAST

Bristol East, which had removed Tony Benn in 1983 after over 30 years representing part of the largest of West Country cities, returned to the Labour fold in 1992, five years before they recaptured national government. In 1997 the Labour majority increased to over 16,000, although the changes in the share of votes were close to the national average. In the most recent General Election, as in the country as a whole, there was little change in the main parties' share of the vote: both Labour and Conservatives down a little, Lib Dems up but still clearly third. Labour's Jean Corston was 33% ahead, compared with a national figure of 9%. It is now clear that Benn's defeat and the Conservative victories of the 1980s were quite exceptional in Bristol East.

The neighbourhoods which make up the constituency – Brislington East and West, Easton, Eastville, Lawrence Hill and Stockwood – constitute a mixture along the eastern fringe of the city which adds up to a microcosm of 'middle England', typified most of all perhaps by the skilled working-class owner-occupiers of Brislington. It might be summed up as a seat which is generally supportive of Labour, and heavily so in their landslide years, but which was capable of being attracted by the Conservatives' economic appeal in Labour's very dark period of 1983 and 1987.

Social indices:			2001 Gen. Election:			
% Non-white	8.0		Lab	22,180	55.0	−1.9
% Prof/Man	26.9		C	8,788	21.8	−1.6
% Non-manual	54.4		LD	6,915	17.1	+2.4
£ Av prop val 2000	64 K		Grn	1,110	2.8	
% Increase 97–00	49.1		UKIP	572	1.4	
% Unemployed 2001	3.8		SLP	438	1.1	−0.5
% Decrease 97–01	3.1		SA	331	0.8	
% Fin hard/Rank	24.9	202	Lab maj	13,392	33.2	
% Pensioners	27.0		Turnout		57.4	−12.5
% Prem mort/Rank	33	281	Elect	70,279		

Member of Parliament

Jean Corston, Chairman of the PLP from July 2001, elected here in 1992, was previously (1997–2001) PPS to David Blunkett, and a former Labour Party regional organiser, in Bristol (1976–85) and London (1985–86) – a background which serves to keep her out of the rebellions to which her left-wing feminist inclinations – and second marriage to the radical sociologist Peter Townsend – might otherwise tempt her. Residually Somerset-brogued, she was born Jean Parkin, daughter of a union official, in 1942, educated at Yeovil Girls' High School, Somerset College of Art and Technology and – much later – graduating in law at the LSE aged 47, before practising briefly as a barrister. Her past is not Blairite (she voted for Beckett as leader in 1994) and ageism being what it is, could expect no further advancement as she approached her 60th year. But in July 2001 the decision of Clive Soley to give up the Chairmanship of the PLP opened a door and she beat Tony Lloyd for the job, soon relishing her role in presciently recommending that Labour MPs needed therapy, especially no doubt those attacking Blunkett's emergency anti-terrorist measures which she publicly backed in November 2001.

BRISTOL NORTH WEST

As in the case of Lorenz's climatic theories, sometimes related (by subsequent writers) to butterflies flapping their wings, seemingly minor boundary changes can have dramatic political effects. Bristol North West is a case in point. This extremely marginal seat produced the second closest result in the 1992 General Election – the Conservative MP Michael Stern held on by just 45 votes. However, his task was made very significantly harder in 1997 by the fact that the Boundary Commission removed just one Bristol ward. That ward is the mightily Conservative Westbury-on-Trym. An example of its allegiances may be taken from the May 1992 Bristol City elections, just one month after the General. Some 72% of the Westbury-on-Trym voters opted for the Conservative candidate, and only 12% for Labour. Without doubt the removal of that ward would have tipped the balance in North West in an even year like 1992. This is disguised by the fact that there have been no even years since the boundary changes, but rather two Labour landslides. Bristol NW is certainly a Labour banker now, for more than one reason.

Currently it includes communities from outside the city: Patchway, Filton and Stoke Gifford. This is the neighbourhood around the Rolls-Royce aero engine factory and has a considerable and growing population. For this reason boundary changes are in the offing which will remove the extraneous territory into a new seat, named Filton and Bradley Stoke – two places never previously dignified in a constituency title – and Westbury on Trym returned to Bristol North West; but this will not happen until after the next election.

The rest of NW is classic marginal territory: a Conservative owner-occupied middle-class vote in Horfield battling against Labour's port of Avonmouth and council estates like Southmead, Kingsweston and Sea Mills. North-West Bristol has traditionally been politically the most marginal part of the city. Since the Second World War the representation has changed hands between the two major parties in 1955, 1959, 1966, 1970, October 1974, 1979 and 1997. There have been eight different MPs since 1950. Doug Naysmith is likely to have a longer tenure than most.

Social indices:			2001 Gen. Election:			
% Non-white	2.9		Lab/Coop	24,436	52.3	+2.4
% Prof/Man	26.5		C	13,349	28.6	–0.7
% Non-manual	53.2		LD	7,387	15.8	+2.7
£ Av prop val 2000	82 K		UKIP	1,149	2.5	
% Increase 97–00	43.7		SLP	371	0.8	–0.1
% Unemployed 2001	2.4		L/C maj	11,087	23.7	
% Decrease 97–01	2.3		Turnout		60.8	–12.8
% Fin hard/Rank	20.0	280	Elect	76,756		
% Pensioners	26.7					
% Prem mort/Rank	31	327				

Member of Parliament

Doug Naysmith finally won here in 1997 – a seasoned campaigner from earlier election campaigns, and one of them in this seat in 1992. A grey-bearded immunologist at Bristol University, with a doctorate from Edinburgh University, he was born in 1941 and educated at George Heriot School, Edinburgh, and at Edinburgh and Yale Universities. Arriving late (aged 56) after 17 years on Bristol City Council, with no prospect of advancement, he has been an unobtrusive backbencher, his Leftist (CND) past airbrushed by the culture of loyalism pervading the post-1997 PLP. In 2000 he introduced a bill about recycling newspapers.

BRISTOL SOUTH

South is the most working-class seat in Bristol, with the highest unemployment and council housing content. It stretches from inner-city Bedminster with its cheap B&Bs and ageing housing through mixed Knowle to the massive modern developments on the southern edge of the seat at Bishopsworth, Filwood and Whitchurch Park, where around half the voters still live in council-owned accommodation. This was the spiritual heartland of Labour's former Chief Whip the late Michael Cocks, who represented South in the Commons for 17 years, and took his seat in the upper house as Lord Cocks of Hartcliffe – another working-class council estate.

Cocks was deselected in favour of a left-winger, Dawn Primarolo, before the 1987 Election. This, the outcome of a long and bitter faction-fight in the Bristol South party, may have been partly responsible for the slashing of the majority in South to 1,400 in 1987 – a terrible result in what should be a safe Labour seat. However, Dawn Primarolo has established herself subsequently, and with her incumbency vote and the general swing to Labour in the Bristol area she increased her majority to a comfortable 14,000 in 2001. It would seem that her moments of danger in Bristol South are over.

Social indices:			2001 Gen. Election:			
% Non-white	2.1		Lab	23,299	56.9	−3.1
% Prof/Man	20.9		C	9,118	22.3	+1.1
% Non-manual	49.1		LD	6,078	14.8	+1.4
£ Av prop val 2000	76 K		Grn	1,233	3.0	+1.6
% Increase 97–00	53.8		SA	496	1.2	+0.5
% Unemployed 2001	3.1		UKIP	496	1.2	
% Decrease 97–01	3.6		SLP	250	0.6	
% Fin hard/Rank	26.6	181	Lab maj	14,181	34.6	
% Pensioners	25.2		Turnout		56.5	−12.4
% Prem mort/Rank	35	261	Elect	72,490		

Member of Parliament

Dawn Primarolo, MP here since 1987, and Paymaster General from 1999, is one of the surprise ministerial successes of the Blair government. Born in 1954 in London, daughter of an electrician, she was brought up in Crawley, attending Thomas Bennett Comprehensive School, Bristol Polytechnic and Bristol University, and worked for Avon County Council as an education researcher. Originally – but no longer (since 2000) – listed as a Campaign Grouper (in 1997 she was one of three Campaign Group MPs in government) and thus on paper one of the most left-wing members, with a background of poll tax non-payment, Gulf War rebellion, resister of OMOV, and – as Tony Benn's deaconess-on-earth – toppler of Benn's Bristol nemesis, the right-wing Chief Whip, Michael Cocks, who had in turn ousted Benn from his redrawn seat in 1983. A Treasury minister since 1997, she has transmuted from 'Red Dawn' to 'Rosy Pink', but doesn't think she's sold out, claiming that being in government 'certainly beats Opposition'. Her initially primary school teacher deliberate mode of speech doubtless lay behind the soubriquet 'Dumb Spice', and the barb of a former Tory MP, Angela Knight, that 'her backside is so much more appealing than her mind'. Her name more redolent of the circus ring than the Treasury, she retained her first husband's surname in preference to her own surname of 'Gasson' – believed damaging for a politician.

BRISTOL WEST

In 2001 the Tories came third in Bristol West, although only just, in an exciting and well contested three-way marginal among one of the UK's best informed and largest electorates. Nevertheless, it was the first time they had sunk so low, and it requires a deal of explanation.

Bristol West was always considered as the city's Conservative heartland. In 1966, for example, or even as late as October 1974, it was the single Tory seat in Bristol. Unlike in many British towns, the classic West End has survived in the West Country's capital – an attractive residential area close to the city centre, rising up the hills to the north and west of the downtown area which was itself largely rebuilt after the Second World War. Here we find the green parks and elegant eighteenth- and nineteenth-century housing of Clifton, with its chic shops and restaurants, Clifton College and Bristol Zoo, the expensive modern Roman Catholic cathedral, and the university. Many of the famous schools of Bristol, once direct grant and now independent, are to be found in the constituency, in Cotham and Redland as well as in Clifton. Even more wealthy is the Stoke Bishop ward across the Downs, which includes the exclusive Sneyd Park neighbourhood. Bristol West is, overall, by far the most middle-class of the city's constituencies, and has never had any significant council housing. Yet in 1997 Labour leapt from third place to first, and the Chief Secretary to the Treasury William Waldegrave was beaten by 1,500 votes. The Liberal Democrats have maintained a 28% share twice now, and the seat clearly is one of the closest three-way contests in Britain. Where does all this non-Tory support come from?

First, it should be remembered that West includes most of the central city area, in wards like Cabot and Ashley, which contains most of the troubled St Paul's district where there were serious riots in 1981. Ashley is 30% non-white, the highest figure for any Bristol ward. Second, Bristol West has a high proportion of intellectuals, ranking in the top handful of seats in the nation when it comes to the proportion of students and of those with professional qualifications. These 'progressive' middle-class voters can by no means be counted as reliable supporters of the Conservative Party, certainly not in the era of New Labour government and Tory slump. The Liberal Democrats do even better in local elections than in parliamentary contests, and Bristol West is likely to see another close three-sided battle, certainly the most watchable in the city, at the next General Election.

Social indices:			2001 Gen. Election:				
% Non-white	7.0		Lab	20,505	36.8	+1.6	
% Prof/Man	57.9		LD	16,079	28.9	+0.9	
% Non-manual	79.5		C	16,040	28.8	-4.0	
£ Av prop val 2000	145 K		Grn	1,961	3.5	+2.2	
% Increase 97–00	56.3		SLP	590	1.1	+0.7	
% Unemployed 2001	2.8		UKIP	490	0.9		
% Decrease 97–01	2.8		Lab maj	4,426	8.0		
% Fin hard/Rank	9.1	487	Turnout		65.6	-8.2	
% Pensioners	24.2		Elect	84,821			
% Prem mort/Rank	28	382					

Member of Parliament

Valerie Davey, surprise Labour victor here in 1997 following a favourable *Observer* opinion poll of which she made much use, was an unobtrusive backbencher posing seven written questions in her first year. A standard issue Labour MP as a former teacher turned full-time councillor, she was an Avon County Councillor for 15 years, its leader for four. Born in 1940 in the Surrey suburbs, educated at persistently undisclosed schools and at Birmingham and London Universities, she is of serious blue-stocking appearance and Methodist affiliation. She was placed on the Education Select Committee in 1997 and remained there four years on (still without her own schooling identified).

BROMLEY AND CHISLEHURST

This is still a very safe Conservative seat, which returned the right-winger Eric Forth in 2001 in an almost identical result to four years before, a lead of 9,000 or 20% of votes cast over Labour, and this at a time when the Tories were suffering their second successive crushing defeat nationally. There is one aberrant Labour area, Mottingham, which has the highest proportion of council housing of any in the borough, and consists of a planned inter-war estate with a geometrical street layout. Mottingham is right on the boundary with the boroughs of Lewisham and Greenwich, and almost looks out of place in Bromley. There are some working-class voters in central Bromley too, but most wards here consist of affluent and strongly Conservative neighbourhoods: Bickley, Hayes, Plaistow and Sundridge, Chislehurst itself.

However the Liberal Democrats make little impact in this seat in outer south-east London, just as they do in general on Bromley council, unlike the battery of five seats they have in equally middle-class outer south-west Greater London, where they have five MPs and control of Richmond upon Thames and Sutton councils. It is not easy to explain this difference. Certainly there is a more intellectual cast to Richmond at least, but this applies less to Sutton or Surbiton, say. Perhaps the place to look is local government activism, image and performance (three different things, though often confused). The Lib Dems and their predecessors have been operating and building up support through community politics in the south-western boroughs since the 1970s, whereas the Tories in Bromley were best known for defending residents' interests, for example over transport matters, even before the abolition of Ken Livingstone's GLC in 1986. The Liberal Democrats have never become municipally successful, nor built up habits of Labour tactical voting in local or, by extension, parliamentary politics.

Social indices:			2001 Gen. Election:			
% Non-white	4.6		C	21,412	49.5	+3.2
% Prof/Man	44.3		Lab	12,375	28.6	+3.4
% Non-manual	73.8		LD	8,180	18.9	−4.8
£ Av prop val 2000	181 K		UKIP	1,264	2.9	+0.7
% Increase 97–00	55.3		C maj	9,037	20.9	
% Unemployed 2001	1.7		Turnout		62.9	−11.3
% Decrease 97–01	1.6		Elect	68,763		
% Fin hard/Rank	11.2	433				
% Pensioners	28.2					
% Prem mort/Rank	18	505				

Member of Parliament

Eric Forth, Shadow Leader of the Commons from 2001, and a Thatcherite Glaswegian who migrated even further from his former Mid-Worcestershire seat to this one in 1997, has developed an unpopular reputation as a saboteur of Private Members' Bills including even the saintly Sir George Young's attempt to curb the danger of London mini cab drivers, doing so ostensibly because he sees such bills as proxy government legislation and subject to inadequate scrutiny. Born in 1944 and educated at Jordanhill College School and Glasgow University, he sold business machines and computers before becoming an MEP for Birmingham (1979–84) and then coming in on the Thatcher tide of 1983. A root-and-branch Eurosceptic, as an abrasive Trade, then Education, minister before 1997, as the latter he extolled the virtues of the 5 'Rs' – 'reading, riting, rithmetic, right and rong'. A David Davis, then Iain Duncan Smith, backer in 2001, he was doubtless one of the 'nutters' to whom the Labour Party Chairman alluded when reviewing Duncan Smith's frontbench appointments. His three-piece, pin-stripe suits would be redolent of a lost age were they not more 'Arthur Daley' than 'Peter Tapsell', and accompanied by garish kipper ties and a fair amount of jewellery. With his fellow bill-wrecking accomplice David Maclean now seated alongside him on the frontbench as Chief Whip, they make an abrasive Caledonian duo, the Burke and Hare of the graveyard of legislation.

BROMSGROVE

Bromsgrove was associated with Redditch in a seat that Labour managed to win in a by-election in 1971 – which was to prove their last parliamentary by-election gain from the Tories for 11 years. This area has seen great population growth, however, and there are now two seats, one each for Bromsgrove and Redditch. Each was defended by a bright and well-thought-of female MP in 2001, and each was retained, although while Jacqui Smith of Redditch saw her majority for Labour nearly halved, that of the Conservative member for Bromsgrove, Julie Kirkbride, was nearly doubled.

There has been substantial development in the Bromsgrove district, principally of middle-class private estates. The town of Bromsgrove itself has strong Labour wards, in its southern and western section, at the densely populated Charford council estate, Whitford and Sidemoor; and also further north near Hagley at Waseford and the most socially deprived ward according to most indicators, Uffdown. The Conservatives, however, do well in other parts of Bromsgrove, and, critically, in a number of communities which serve as affluent commuting bases for the West Midlands conurbation. These include Cofton Hackett, Alvechurch, Wythall and the most well-off of all, Barnt Green. This is an attractive neighbourhood, set near to the Clent Hills, and some of the villages offer a touch of rural calm despite their handy location within a few minutes drive of, say, the Rover car factory on the Birmingham borders. These wards are almost all-white, almost all owner-occupied, and predominantly middle class.

The Liberal Democrats are not very active here, with 11.89% in 2001 (a leap forward from 11.88 in 1997?); and Labour slipped back by 4% in second place. It is a far cry from the days of the 1971 by-election. The poet A.E. Housman hailed from Fockbury near Bromsgrove; as he might put it, Bromsgrove is Labour's 'land of lost content', the happy highways where (just) once they went, and cannot come again.

Social indices:			2001 Gen. Election:			
% Non-white	1.4		C	23,640	51.7	+4.6
% Prof/Man	38.9		Lab	15,502	33.9	−3.9
% Non-manual	61.1		LD	5,430	11.9	+0.0
£ Av prop val 2000	116 K		UKIP	1,112	2.4	+2.0
% Increase 97–00	40.0		C maj	8,138	17.8	
% Unemployed 2001	2.0		Turnout		67.1	−10.0
% Decrease 97–01	1.4		Elect	68,115		
% Fin hard/Rank	15.4	346				
% Pensioners	24.1					
% Prem mort/Rank	16	528				

Member of Parliament

Julie Kirkbride, the Conservatives' fake blonde bombshell, won here in 1997, one of a mere handful of new Tory women MPs. A standard orthodox right-wing Eurosceptic, she hails from a working-class Yorkshire background, born in 1960, and rising via Highfields Grammar School, Halifax to Girton College, Cambridge and then jobs in TV and on the *Telegraph* as a much-admired Press Gallery journalist. Variously seen as 'toothsome and buxom' and as 'fiery, forthright and fetching', she married in 1997, as his second wife, fellow MP Andrew Mackay, and has rivalled five of Blair's babes in also producing a babe of her own, Angus, in 2000. Latterly she has worried about the safety of single-dose MMR vaccine for babies. A Hague voter in 1997, she and her husband backed Portillo in all three ballots in July 2001.

BROXBOURNE

This constituency, which is based on a local government borough of the same name, clings to the western side of the River Lea on the Essex border, and shares a boundary with the London Borough of Enfield to the south. It incorporates a chain of suburban communities bypassed by the A10 road – from south to north: Waltham Cross, Cheshunt, Turnford, Wormley, the small community of Broxbourne itself, and

Hoddesdon. These are almost without exception affluent and very Conservative, though with a lower than national average of educational qualifications: the proportion with degrees or other higher qualifications is less than that in, say, Watford or Milton Keynes or Stevenage. In some ways Broxbourne is similar to the haunts of 'Essex Man' just across the border. Many successful Spurs and Arsenal footballers live here, conveniently close to the clubs' training pitches.

Only one ward, Waltham Cross South, right on the London border, has been consistently Labour, even in the many mid-terms of Conservative government. Two others have a significant Labour minority presence, one in the middle of the seat (Bury Green) and one at the north end (Rye Park, Hoddesdon). One of the reasons the Conservatives have quite such a large majority here is that the Liberal Democrats are not successful even in local politics; Broxbourne does not seem to be a Liberal-minded neck of the woods.

In 2001 Marion Roe increased her numerical majority despite a bigger slump in the turnout than the national average, to a figure even lower than average for England, under 55%. Perhaps even New Labour in government proved too left-wing for local tastes.

Social indices:			2001 Gen. Election:			
% Non-white	1.8		C	20,487	54.1	+5.3
% Prof/Man	30.5		Lab	11,494	30.4	–4.3
% Non-manual	60.9		LD	4,158	11.0	–0.3
£ Av prop val 2000	144 K		UKIP	858	2.3	
% Increase 97–00	53.3		BNP	848	2.2	+0.9
% Unemployed 2001	1.7		C maj	8,993	23.8	
% Decrease 97–01	1.8		Turnout		54.9	–15.6
% Fin hard/Rank	10.3	456	Elect	68,982		
% Pensioners	21.3					
% Prem mort/Rank	16	532				

Member of Parliament

Marion Roe, chairman of the Administration Select Committee, a dry-as-dust right-wing loyalist, was elected here in 1983 and was briefly (1987–88) a junior Environment minister. Inserted into the Health Select Committee chair in 1992 as a replacement for unreliable maverick Nick Winterton, she backed Redwood in 1997 – even unto his last-ditch pact with Ken Clarke, but kept her counsel in the leadership ballots in 2001. Born in 1936 and educated at Bromley and Croydon High Schools, she married a Rothschild banker. A campaigner on women's issues such as cancer screening and equal tax treatment for married women, she is traditionalist on working mothers, seeing them as taking out insurance against divorce, and opposes 'abortion on demand'. Latterly she has opposed mobile phone masts. Somewhat of brassy aspect she is known for her very big hair – a luxuriating bouffant, beehive job held in gravity-defying suspension which (according to Andrew Rawnsley) last saw service on the late Dusty Springfield.

BROXTOWE

Nottingham city elected three Labour MPs in 1992, even though the Conservatives won the General Election with an overall majority. This is because Nottingham's three main middle-class – and Tory – residential areas lie outside the city boundaries: West Bridgford in Rushcliffe constituency, Carlton and Arnold in Gedling, and Beeston and its associated neighbourhoods in Broxtowe. In 1992 these neighbourhoods returned a trio of Conservative members; in 1997 only Kenneth Clarke of Rushcliffe survived, as both Gedling and Broxtowe fell to Labour on 13% swings, and in 2001 these two actually swung further still to Labour, in stark contrast with the nearby Nottinghamshire seat of Newark, which they also gained in 1997. Clearly both Vernon Coaker of Gedling and Nick Palmer here were deemed to have done a very respectable job of representing their party and their constituencies.

The name of this seat sometimes causes confusion. There is no town or community called Broxtowe, at least not within the constituency; there is a council estate called Broxtowe in Nottingham North. Nor is this seat similar to that of the same name which existed before 1955; that has effectively been replaced by the Ashfield division. The constituency under discussion was in essence the former Beeston, renamed in 1983 to take account of the title of the borough council, which had been created in the early 1970s. It consists of a number of suburban communities to the west of Nottingham and in the main part of that city's built-up area: Beeston, Stapleford, Chilwell, Toton, Attenborough, Bramcote, and Kimberley, and a few villages.

The constituency is largely comprised of twentieth-century owner-occupied dwellings, largely occupied by white middle-class voters, with a strong commuting element. There are traditional Labour wards in central Beeston, Stapleford North and Stapleford West; however, some of the other wards include some of the best residential property in the whole of Greater Nottingham, such as in Bramcote Hills and Chilwell, but Labour did well here too in 2001, as the county council elections on the same day show. This is the sort of seat the Conservatives must recapture if they are to regain office, its result closely reflecting the national picture – a seat well worth keeping an eye on.

Social indices:			2001 Gen. Election:			
% Non-white	2.5		Lab	23,836	48.6	+1.6
% Prof/Man	36.4		C	17,963	36.7	−0.8
% Non-manual	59.5		LD	7,205	14.7	+2.8
£ Av prop val 2000	73 K		Lab maj	5,873	12.0	
% Increase 97–00	32.7		Turnout		66.5	−11.9
% Unemployed 2001	2.1		Elect	73,675		
% Decrease 97–01	1.4					
% Fin hard/Rank	12.8	401				
% Pensioners	24.0					
% Prem mort/Rank	16	522				

Member of Parliament

Nick Palmer, a quiet Labour loyalist elected on the 1997 floodtide, is a computer scientist (previously with Ciba-Geigy) who is keen on animal welfare, mandatory bells on bikes, same-day acknowledgement of business letters and – inevitably – more internet use. Born in 1950, educated in Denmark and Austria and with a Maths doctorate from London University, he is probably – as a member of the Cleft Palate Association – the first MP to overcome such a disability.

BUCKINGHAM

Buckingham is one of the ten safest Tory seats. The lively Conservative MP John Bercow won by over 13,300 votes in 2001, more than in 1997, partly because of a turnout of almost 70%, also in the top ten in England; he obtained more support than his two main opponents put together.

This is a rural seat containing the small town of Buckingham itself and a large number of villages, many affluent rather than agricultural. Overall it is a seat with relatively little deprivation, few of its citizens needing to seek the assistance of state benefits: it is among the three with the fewest claiming Incapacity Benefit, or Income Support, their numbers exceeding only those in Scottish rural seats with small populations and that paragon of comfort and affluence, John Redwood's Wokingham. It is by far the physically largest seat in the county, covering all of the land of its northern half except for that submerged beneath Milton Keynes. Buckingham itself, as befits the site of Britain's first private university, is strongly Conservative; the villages even more so: Brill with its windmill, Great Brickhill, Great Horwood and Grendon Underwood, Long Crendon and Marsh Gibbon and Newton Longville, Quainton, Wing and Wingrave and Winslow. It sounds like a list from Flanders and Swann's, *The Slow Train* and indeed some sleepy railway lines do still operate in this peaceful neck of the woods. It is unlikely that John Bercow will be leaving on a one-way ticket in the foreseeable future.

Social indices:			2001 Gen. Election:			
% Non-white	1.3		C	24,296	53.7	+3.9
% Prof/Man	44.5		Lab	10,971	24.2	–0.5
% Non-manual	66.3		LD	9,037	20.0	–4.7
£ Av prop val 2000	162 K		UKIP	968	2.1	
% Increase 97–00	55.8		C maj	13,325	29.4	
% Unemployed 2001	0.7		Turnout		69.4	–9.1
% Decrease 97–01	0.6		Elect	65,270		
% Fin hard/Rank	3.0	638				
% Pensioners	20.8					
% Prem mort/Rank	4	629				

Member of Parliament

John Bercow, who was elected here in 1997, after two earlier contests on the forlorn council estates of Motherwell South (1987) and Bristol South (1992), became Shadow Chief Secretary to the Treasury in 2001 after shadowing Education and

Home Affairs (1999–2001). A sallow-skinned, pint-sized, partisan son of a Jewish taxi driver and car salesman, he was born in 1963 and educated at Finchley Manorhill School and Essex University. A former party staffer as adviser to Jonathan Aitken and Virginia Bottomley (1995–96), a political consultant with Saatchi and a very Eurosceptic Thatcherite from the disbanded right-wing Federation of Conservative Students, his reputation was originally for having only his hair parted in the centre. Seen by Lord Parkinson as a 'tremendous street fighter', he is one of the few Tories who vote for homosexual sex at 16, has a highly accomplished, fluent style as a Commons debater and questioner – yet for all his abrasiveness, voted the temporising Portillo ticket in 2001 in the quest for more electable terrain, and described the Conservative Party as 'racist, sexist and homophobic' in January 2002.

BURNLEY

Immediately after the General Election on 7 June 2001, very few outside the East Lancashire town of Burnley noticed that its result was in any way unusual. The veteran Labour MP, Peter Pike, had been returned for a fifth term. Burnley had not attracted national attention during the campaign, unlike another former Pennine textile town a few miles away, Oldham, where there had been racially charged riots. On the night, and afterwards, much publicity was given to the very large British National Party vote recorded in both Oldham constituencies. The question of whether the BNP's electoral success had been generated by the riots, or whether their longer-term activism had caused it – and perhaps the riots too – was debated. Yet relevant evidence was in fact present in Burnley, where the BNP had obtained over 11%, their second best anywhere and actually more than in Oldham East and Saddleworth where the centre of the disturbances had been located. A couple of weeks later Burnley too was aflame, and it was clear that the tension was far from confined to Oldham, and that BNP votes were not a short-term response to street disturbance.

As the focus shifted to Burnley in the summer of 2001, it became clear that both poor-white and Asian, predominantly Muslim, communities felt hard done by economically and politically, excluded from regenerative resources and mutually distrustful to the point of enmity. Many people in white working-class areas like Burnley Wood in the south-east of the town felt that their position was unheeded by politicians of all established parties, and for each person who voted for the BNP (4,151 in all) there may have been more who did not vote at all (the turnout was 55%). No one is suggesting that the BNP will win in Burnley or places like it, but the underlying problems, not all racial in nature, will have to be addressed more effectively if the answers are to lie within the compass of democratic politics.

Burnley itself is not without its middle-class districts, north-east towards Nelson and Pendle and up Rose Hill to the south towards Rossendale. It is a town of owner-occupiers, who hold nearly three-quarters of all dwellings – only in Brunshaw and Coal Clough wards do council tenants approach half of the whole. Many of the little terraced cottages survive from Burnley's cotton-industry period, not necessarily gentrified. It is a local tradition that newly-marrieds buy their own inexpensive homes, and it does not imply affluence. Some of the white working-class areas have streets with many boarded up houses and multiple social deprivations. The Asian population of about 5,000, almost all of Pakistani origin, is concentrated in the central Calder and Daneshouse wards, and although this is much fewer than in nearby towns it is not going to go away, nor would the town as a whole benefit if it did. A more satisfactory *modus vivendi* must clearly be established.

Social indices:			2001 Gen. Election:			
% Non-white	5.5		Lab	18,195	49.3	−8.6
% Prof/Man	25.9		C	7,697	20.9	+0.6
% Non-manual	45.5		LD	5,975	16.2	−1.2
£ Av prop val 2000	42 K		BNP	4,151	11.3	
% Increase 97–00	11.6		UKIP	866	2.3	
% Unemployed 2001	2.8		Lab maj	10,498	28.5	
% Decrease 97–01	0.7		Turnout		55.6	−11.4
% Fin hard/Rank	29.6	136	Elect	66,393		
% Pensioners	25.9					
% Prem mort/Rank	46	80				

Member of Parliament

Peter Pike, a big, shambling, bucolic-looking man, who makes discursive interruptions from the backmost bench, has been Labour MP here since 1983, but looks as if he could just as easily be mucking out a pigsty somewhere in Wessex. Born in 1937 and educated at secondary modern schools in Morden and Hinchley Wood in the Surrey suburbs and at Kingston technical college, he worked variously as a bank clerk (for eight years), Labour Party agent in Burnley (for four years) and inspector at Mullards factory in Burnley, to which he had been evacuated in the War. A Worzel Gummidge lookalike, he backed the Eurosceptic Gould for leader in 1992 and Beckett not Blair in 1994, and exited promptly from the frontbench, where he had shadowed rural affairs and housing since 1990. He was passed over in 1997 even for the non-job of Second Church Estates Commissioner, allegedly on account of the disapproval of the style consultants. He has chaired the Deregulation and Regulatory Reform Select Committee since 1997, and has criticised air traffic control privatisation, and intends to retire at the next election.

BURTON

Labour had only won Burton once before 1997, in another landslide year, 1945. Even in 1966 they fell short, by 277 votes, and the Conservatives held the seat continuously from 1950 to 1997. This is surprising. The Burton constituency is substantially more working class than average, and the centre of Burton, with its terraces of small nineteenth-century houses, looks like Labour territory – and indeed is, in local elections. Labour wins almost all of the wards within the town of Burton on Trent, many with massive majorities – in May 1999, for example, they polled 76% in Burton ward, 78% in Waterside, 67% in Winshil, and so on. There is a significant Asian presence in the town, mainly Pakistani: the Broadway, Uxbridge and Victoria wards are all over one-fifth non-white. In municipal contests Labour also polls well in the constituency's second town and only other urban community, Uttoxeter. Why then have they gone for a Burton so often here, as one might say?

Burton is one of Britain's great brewing towns, and the traditional connection between the Tory Party and the brewing trade may affect the constituency's politics. More crucial though, is the fact that the seat contains almost the whole of the East Staffordshire district, which stretches way beyond the limits of the town of Burton. Stapenhill, on a hill across the Trent from Burton, is a Tory ward. So are Tutbury and Hanbury, and Branston, and Outwoods, and the Needwood Forest, and the growing Stretton, and many others. Indeed the rural section of the constituency is every bit as much Conservative as the town is Labour, and accounts for a majority of the voters – Burton itself has only about 30,000 electors in a seat of over 72,000. The Liberal Democrats are badly squeezed out as the two disparate parts of the constituency battle it out.

The prominent Conservative backbencher Sir Ivan Lawrence held a majority of almost exactly 6,000 in 1992. In 1997, although the pro-Labour swing was slightly below average, this was almost exactly reversed, as Janet Dean beat Lawrence by 6,330, and she held on by 4,849 in 2001. In the event of an even election, though, Burton will now be a knife-edge marginal, the kind of seat which will be won by whoever gets the most votes across Britain as a whole – which is not, at the moment, the same thing as who actually wins the election, due to the heavy inbuilt bias of the electoral system against the Conservatives.

Social indices:			2001 Gen. Election:			
% Non-white	4.3		Lab	22,783	49.0	–2.0
% Prof/Man	28.1		C	17,934	38.6	–0.8
% Non-manual	48.7		LD	4,468	9.6	+1.1
£ Av prop val 2000	70 K		UKIP	984	2.1	
% Increase 97–00	35.4		PA	288	0.6	
% Unemployed 2001	2.8		Lab maj	4,849	10.4	
% Decrease 97–01	2.0		Turnout		61.8	–13.3
% Fin hard/Rank	16.6	325	Elect	75,194		
% Pensioners	24.6					
% Prem mort/Rank	31	329				

Member of Parliament

Janet Dean, Labour's winner here in 1997 and a first-time parliamentary candidate, was one of 35 beneficiaries of an all-women's shortlist. Born in 1949 and educated at Winsford Verdin County Grammar School, she had nevertheless 16 years' experience on Derbyshire County Council and six years on the local District Council. A bank clerk before her marriage at the age of 19, less a Blair's Babe than a Blair's Granny, she has not much troubled the scorers in four years – but did rebel in 2000 over the proposed sell-off of air traffic control, a matter of some local concern given the proximity of East Midlands Airport. She was on the Home Affairs Select Committee from 2001.

BURY NORTH

Alistair Burt held Bury North for the Conservatives from 1983 to 1997, apparently building up a personal vote of generous proportions; but this was not enough to prevent a crushing defeat by nearly 8,000 votes at the hands of Labour's David Chaytor in 1997. There was a swing of 11% from Conservative to Labour. There was no swing in 2001, except to abstentions, which accounted for 37% of those on the register. Among those who do vote, this is a two-party battle, and the Liberal Democrats are stuck in a lowly third place, with just 12% of preferences.

Bury itself, the heart of this seat, was always one of the more prosperous of the Lancashire textile towns. There are low-status and strongly Labour wards, with terraced housing and a small non-white community such as at Redvales, which covers Bury town centre, and East ward. However there are very few council estates of any size, and overall the seat is about 80% owner-occupied. There are strongly Conservative wards at Church in the west of the town of Bury and in the independent communities of Ramsbottom and particularly Tottington.

The Conservatives will probably have to win an overall majority in a general election if they are ever to regain Bury North. In that sense it is still a critical marginal, but it is hard to see David Chaytor being removed, next time at least; he might well represent Bury longer than Alistair Burt, who has himself returned, translated to Bedfordshire North East.

Social indices:			2001 Gen. Election:			
% Non-white	4.2		Lab	22,945	51.2	–0.6
% Prof/Man	35.1		C	16,413	36.6	–0.9
% Non-manual	58.2		LD	5,430	12.1	+3.9
£ Av prop val 2000	64 K		Lab maj	6,532	14.6	
% Increase 97–00	24.4		Turnout		63.0	–15.1
% Unemployed 2001	2.0		Elect	71,108		
% Decrease 97–01	0.5					
% Fin hard/Rank	17.8	309				
% Pensioners	23.2					
% Prem mort/Rank	30	337				

Member of Parliament

David Chaytor – a rugged lantern-jawed further education lecturer for 24 years, eventually at Manchester College of Arts and Technology (1990–97), born in 1949, locally educated at Bury Grammar School, Huddersfield Polytechnic and Bradford University, won here in 1997, having been forced by an all-women shortlist out of Calder Valley, which as a Calderdale councillor since 1982 he had fought twice in 1987 and 1992, ceding the candidacy to a novice local woman councillor of six years' experience. Ambitious as a dumbed down unilateralist, though still a campaigner agianst nuclear power arriving too old for office, he joined – as one of 14 of the 183 new Labour MPs – the first rebellion against lone parent benefit cuts in December 1997 and turned up again for the later revolts on means testing disability benefits and air traffic control part-privatisation. In 2001 he achieved the solace of the Education

Select Committee. Prompted by the West Lothian question, he wants devolution to the English regions.

BURY SOUTH

Only the Liberal Democrats received more votes in 2001 than in 1997 in Bury South, and that was from a base of one of their worst performances anywhere in England. There was a huge 17% drop in turnout. Labour's vote went down in absolute terms from over 28,500 to under 23,500, and the Tories fell proportionately even more, by nearly 6,000 to just over 10,000. This is only about 40% of their winning total as recently as 1992, and a powerful demonstration of the way that the voters cannot be taken for granted nowadays. The proportion of people committed to voting for any party is far less than politicians would like to believe.

When this critical marginal division was created in 1983 only about a third of it came from the former seat called Bury and Radcliffe, and it contains none of the historic community of Bury itself. The bulk actually originated in the Middleton and Prestwich constituency. Prestwich has a reputation as a desirable residential area, and is also said to be very Jewish in population and character. Neither of these stereotyped views is quite correct, although it is true that many members of the Manchester Jewish community (the second largest in Britain after London's) did do well, and moved up and out and north of the original Cheetham Hill ghetto. Prestwich is pleasantly situated on the edge of Heaton Park, but there has always been a large Labour-voting minority there. Ivan Lewis is himself from a local and Jewish background, and now has a very safe base.

Bury South also includes Radcliffe, which is mixed but usually slightly favourable towards Labour, Whitefield, more Conservative, and the quaintly named ward of Besses o' the Barn.

Social indices:			2001 Gen. Election:			
% Non-white	3.1		Lab	23,406	59.2	+2.3
% Prof/Man	34.1		C	10,634	26.9	−5.4
% Non-manual	58.4		LD	5,499	13.9	+5.5
£ Av prop val 2000	58 K		Lab maj	12,772	32.3	
% Increase 97–00	16.0		Turnout		58.8	−16.8
% Unemployed 2001	2.2		Elect	67,276		
% Decrease 97–01	1.3					
% Fin hard/Rank	16.5	327				
% Pensioners	25.3					
% Prem mort/Rank	35	252				

Member of Parliament

Ivan Lewis, one of a small number of the 1997 entrants to be made Junior Ministers in 2001 – in his case at Education – is a former PPS to Stephen Byers (1999–2001), whose emerging career balances that of his less on-message Bury North neighbour, David Chaytor, as an ultra-loyalist Blairite, displaying, according to one observer, 'glutinous fealty' with his 'robotic' interjections. Prestwich-born (1967) – and a leading Zionist – and educated at William Hulme's Grammar School (until his parents ran out of cash), Stand Sixth Form College and Bury FE College, he worked for a Jewish welfare organisation in Manchester. With his wife working for the Leeds-based kosher food firm, Rakusens, and with the retirement of Greville Janner in 1997, he is the highest-profile Zionist MP, with assistance from Louise Ellman.

BURY ST EDMUNDS

Unlike the neighbouring East Anglian county of Norfolk, rural and small-town Suffolk has always resisted the temptation to elect a Labour MP. The political landscape, like the appearance of the countryside, is different here; agricultural trade unionism never flourished, and landowners and their church and party traditionally had a greater grip on the county. Yet during the 2001 General Election campaign, especially as most published opinion polls gave Labour an even bigger lead than in 1997, there were predictions of more than one Labour gain in Suffolk seats outside Ipswich and Lowestoft (Waveney), and biographies of candidates like Mark Ereira here, hastily sought. In the end, the Conservatives held Suffolk South and West and Coastal and Central, all with swings from Labour, small but sufficient. Yet they had a fright. If the turnout had held at traditional levels at 70+%, rather than falling, the story may have been different.

There always were Labour votes in the towns, in the overspill council estates of north Bury, for example, and in Stowmarket where Labour has won every local council contest in recent years. The Labour-supporting element was outvoted by the numerous villages of the seat where the turnout held up better.

Most of Bury St Edmunds looks like a centre of Conservatism, with its cathedral and old abbey grounds, its old narrow streets and named gates a legacy of Scandinavian invasion many centuries ago, and its fifteenth-century Angel hotel, covered in Virginia creeper. As well as such grandeur, it boasts the smallest pub in England, the Nutshell, another product of antiquity. Appearances are not always deceptive, either, and Bury St Edmunds is likely to continue to return a Conservative MP to Westminster, assuming they do not decline even further.

Social indices:			2001 Gen. Election:			
% Non-white	1.0		C	21,850	43.5	+5.1
% Prof/Man	32.1		Lab	19,347	38.5	+0.8
% Non-manual	53.4		LD	6,998	13.9	−4.3
£ Av prop val 2000	98 K		UKIP	831	1.7	
% Increase 97–00	44.7		Ind	651	1.3	
% Unemployed 2001	1.5		SLP	580	1.2	
% Decrease 97–01	1.1		C maj	2,503	5.0	
% Fin hard/Rank	9.4	479	Turnout		66.0	−9.0
% Pensioners	26.1		Elect	76,146		
% Prem mort/Rank	8	613				

Member of Parliament

David Ruffley, dubbed by ex-MP Michael Brown 'a new Tory rottweiler, shaping up to be the rudest MP', with an instinct for the jugular, narrowly won here in 1997.

Politically ecumenical as Ken Clarke's former right-wing conscience, he served Clarke as special adviser at Education, Home Office and Treasury over five years up to 1996, but voted for Hague in 1997. Born in 1962, a Bolton solicitor's son, educated at Bolton School and Queen's College, Cambridge, he was originally with the City law firm of Clifford Chance for six years. He has enjoyed baiting Chancellor Brown on tax levels and Geoffrey Robinson, and the self-styled Cardinal Wolsey, Lord Chancellor Irvine, on wallpaper. A single currency opponent, he strongly defends first-past-the-post voting and though pencilled-in for Cabinet office by 2015, was still off the frontbench in 2001 having voted for Portillo. His consolation was in membership of the Treasury Select Committee (1998–) but former political advisers are supposed to rise faster than this.

CAERNARFON

One of the features concealed in the details of the 2001 General Election results was the manner in which seats vacated by former party leaders swung away from their parties. This happened in John Major's Huntingdon, Paddy Ashdown's Yeovil – and the constituency of Dafydd Wigley, who gave up Caernarfon after over 27 years. All these three were held (see below for Ynys Mon), but here Plaid Cymru's vote dropped by 7%, and their majority was reduced to half Wigley's lead in 1997. Incidentally this pattern was not repeated in the one seat where a current party leader retired: the SNP's John Swinney of Tayside North.

There is no more purely 'Welsh' constituency than Caernarfon. Some 79% of the population speak Welsh, which is the prime language in many parts of the seat – this is the highest proportion of any division. It is scarcely surprising that it has also been one of the Welsh Nationalists' strongest seats; all four of the party's MPs represent seats with a majority of Welsh speakers, and the fifth and other such constituency is Ynys Mon, where another former parliamentary leader Ieuan Wyn Jones actually failed to hand over to a Plaid successor after 14 years. The relationship between language and electoral favour is undeniable.

The Welsh nationalism of Caernarfon is clearly much more than a flash in the pan. One of the previous members for this area was the Welsh wizard David Lloyd George, who represented the Carnarvon (as spelt then) district of boroughs from 1890 to 1945 without a break. This Liberal tradition gave way to Labour, in the person of Goronwy Roberts, who represented the seat from 1945 to February 1974, before being defeated by Wigley.

Caernarfon includes the Lleyn peninsula, much of it wild and remote but incorporating a district popular with holidaymakers around Portmadoc, Criccieth and Pwllheli. The main town of Caernarfon is predominantly Welsh-speaking as well, but rather incongruously it boasts a great Norman castle and was the site of the investiture of the (very English) Prince of Wales.

The Conservatives are too English a party ever to have a chance in this land of nonconformist radicalism, the Welsh language, and the memory of Lloyd George. However, the example of Ynys Mon suggests that Labour cannot be written off completely and for all time in Welsh-speaking Wales, and for the first time in a quarter of century Caernarfon must again be treated as a marginal.

Social indices:			2001 Gen. Election:			
% Non-white	0.5		PC	12,894	44.4	−7.4
% Welsh sp	79.0		Lab	9,383	32.3	+3.9
% Prof/Man	32.9		C	4,403	15.2	+2.7
% Non-manual	53.3		LD	1,823	6.3	+1.3
£ Av prop val 2000	59 K		UKIP	550	1.9	
% Increase 97–00	23.4		PC maj	3,511	12.1	
% Unemployed 2001	4.4		Turnout		61.4	−11.3
% Decrease 97–01	3.3		Elect	47,354		
% Fin hard/Rank	9.1	486				
% Pensioners	31.0					
% Prem mort/Rank	32	303				

Member of Parliament

Hywel Williams, elected in 2001 in place of the retiring, ailing Welsh Nationalist former leader Dafydd Wigley, was locally-born (1953) in Pwllheli, the birthplace of Plaid Cymru. A shopkeeper's son, educated at Ysgol Glan y Mor, Pwllheli, and Cardiff and Bangor Universities, he is a former social worker in Glamorgan and Gwynedd, who became a social work lecturer at Bangor University in 1984 and headed its Social Work Practice Centre for two years until 1994, before becoming a freelance lecturer and consultant. With his Party contesting Anglicised South Wales seats with non-Welsh-speaking candidates, he sounds a more exclusive note by listing 'language policy' among his interests, and in his maiden speech described his constituency as 'one of the heartlands of the Welsh language'. He sounds radical in his attack on private finance initiatives (PFI) in the NHS, and on the bombing of Afghanistan in October 2001.

CAERPHILLY

This constituency is certainly characterised by the letter 'C'. Caerphilly might be most widely known through its castle and its cheese, but it is coal that has shaped its political and electoral culture.

Deep coal-mining is basically extinct in South Wales now, but the Labour legacy lives on. From virtually the beginning of the century the miners in the valleys took to the new party, and have sustained it ever since: there is to this day no greater stronghold or concentration of safe Labour seats. The South Wales miners were noted for many decades, both before and after the Great War, to be at the cutting edge of the trade union movement. Bitter and sometimes violent conflicts arose between the union and the owners – and indeed the forces of the government. The remoteness of the valley communities, and their one-industry nature, assisted them in becoming virtually one-party no-contests in general elections, even in 1931. Even now none of the true valley seats, of which there are 11, is even close to being marginal. They form quite a team for Labour.

The Caerphilly seat consists of the lower Rhymney Valley. Caerphilly itself, and Bedwas and Machen, not far from Cardiff in the first valley fold north of the capital. The constituency edges up the valley through ex-mining communities like Ystrad Mynach and Hengoed towards Bargoed. All this has voted fairly solidly Labour in general elections, but Plaid Cymru have been sporadically active, coming closest in a 1968 by-election (1,874 votes), and more than doubling its share in 2001. However victory seems beyond their grasp in a seat where less than one tenth of the voters speak Welsh. Second place is another matter. Meanwhile, one 'C' that definitely does not typify Caerphilly is that which stands for Conservative.

Social indices:			2001 Gen. Election:			
% Non-white	0.8		Lab	22,597	58.2	−9.6
% Welsh sp	8.0		PC	8,172	21.0	+11.4
% Prof/Man	25.7		C	4,413	11.4	+0.6
% Non-manual	50.7		LD	3,649	9.4	+1.2
£ Av prop val 2000	54 K		Lab maj	14,425	37.2	
% Increase 97–00	22.5		Turnout		57.4	−12.6
% Unemployed 2001	4.3		Elect	67,593		
% Decrease 97–01	2.6					
% Fin hard/Rank	25.4	194				
% Pensioners	22.3					
% Prem mort/Rank	35	244				

Member of Parliament

Wayne David, elected here in 2001, is a former (1989–99) MEP. His profile is very familiar as the grandson (not even *son*) of miners, the son of a teacher, and himself an ex-WEA tutor organiser – in the steps of Neil Kinnock and Ron Davies, his beleaguered predecessor as MP. Born in 1957 and educated at Cynffig Comprehensive, Kenfig Hill Bridgend, and at Swansea and Cardiff Universities, he was latterly a policy adviser for the Youth Service. He lists devolution as one of his interests but already bears its scars, having been sensationally beaten by Plaid Cymru in the Welsh Assembly Election in 1999 in the Rhondda, the first ever loss by Labour of the area since capturing it in 1910. With a reputation as a Europhile after ten years as an MEP, he quit the Tribune Group over its hostility to Maastricht, and disowned a revolt among MEPs against Tony Blair's dropping of Clause 4, saying 'it was part of making Labour acceptable to the City and to industry'.

CAITHNESS, SUTHERLAND AND EASTER ROSS

By 1979, Caithness and Sutherland, the northernmost constituency on the mainland of Great Britain, already had the unique distinction of having been represented by MPs of four different affiliations since 1945. Then Robert Maclennan, the Labour MP, made it five different parties by deserting to the SDP in 1981. It is arguable that his subsequent allegiance to the SLD and then the Liberal Democrats might even qualify as representation by still yet more new parties.

The first of the many shocks administered in Caithness and Sutherland came in 1945, when E.L. Gandar-Dower was elected as a Tory by six votes over Labour, with the leader of the Liberal Party, Sir Archibald Sinclair, losing his seat in third place, another 55 votes behind. Gandar-Dower later became an Independent, and so did Sir David Robertson who succeeded him in 1950. In 1964 the seat was gained by a Liberal, George Mackie, and in 1966 Maclennan took over – with a majority of 64.

It is a tribute to the way that politics is treated on an individual basis here that Caithness and Sutherland stayed loyal to Bob Maclennan through his various changes of party, though there were times in the 1970s when the SNP threatened to add yet another name to the list of parties winning in Caithness and Sutherland.

Caithness and Sutherland has always been a vast seat, of varying landscape. Caithness is in general relatively flat and prosperous farmland in the far north-eastern corner of Scotland, stretching to John O'Groats. Its two main towns are the grey granite port of Wick and Thurso, near to the Dounreay nuclear reactor. It is smaller than Sutherland but it has the bulk of the population of the seat. Sutherland is a wild and untamed world, with a population of 13,000 spread amongst a million acres of inaccessible moorland and weirdly shaped mountains like Suilven and Quinag. In the 1997 boundary changes, another 10,000 electors were added in Easter Ross, on the east coast just south of the Sutherland border near Dornoch, around the seaside towns of Invergordon and Tain; this was new territory for Maclennan, but it was used to voting Liberal Democrat (and indeed ex-SDP): previously it was in Charles Kennedy's seat.

With this multifarious history, many wondered what dramatic twist would occur when the one fixed point, Robert Maclennan, retired after 35 years in 2001. Yet in fact there was no significant change in any of the major parties' vote share, and (Viscount) John Thurso took over for the Liberal Democrats with a surprising lack of fuss, probably assisted by his family's long and close political associations with this seat.

Social indices:			2001 Gen. Election:			
% Non-white	0.6		LD	9,041	36.4	+0.8
% Prof/Man	30.8		Lab	6,297	25.3	−2.5
% Non-manual	48.4		SNP	5,273	21.2	−1.8
% Unemployed 2001	5.2		C	3,513	14.1	+3.3
% Decrease 97–01	3.0		SSP	544	2.2	
% Fin hard/Rank	16.5	329	Ind	199	0.8	
% Prem mort/Rank	44	105	LD maj	2,744	11.0	
			Turnout		60.3	−9.9
			Elect	41,225		

Member of Parliament

John Thurso – actually, 'Sir John Archibald Sinclair, sixth baronet, and third Viscount Thurso' – was one of the more exotic of the 99-strong new intake of MPs in 2001. Self-dubbed 'a hereditary Liberal and a Liberal hereditary', he is the fourth generation of his family to represent this constituency in the Liberal interest, beginning with his great, great, great grandfather Sir George Sinclair in 1811, and down to his grandfather Sir Archibald Sinclair (first Viscount Thurso) who held the seat from 1922 to 1945, was leader of the Liberal Party, and served as Air Minister in the Wartime Coalition. Drawn ineluctably into politics in the Lords by inheriting the Viscountcy in 1995, he became the first ejected hereditary peer to stand and win a Commons seat in 2001. A company director with interests in hotels, catering and banking, but known currently for his ownership of the fashionable health farm, Champney's, he was born in 1953, and educated at Eton and Westminster Technical

College (for day-release hotel courses). He has excoriated Thatcherism for wreaking havoc in the countryside with the loss of shops, pubs, post offices and cottage hospitals, warned that the hunting issue is one that could 'inflame the countryside', and called for a completion of Lords reform to either a fully- or part-elected Chamber. A chatelain with a Victorian melodrama-style waxed moustache, a 'Winchester drawl and a fondness for tweed capes' (*Sunday Times*) and a penchant for chopping up trees ('shades of Gladstone, except I have a chainsaw'), he cuts a dash amongst the otherwise somewhat suburban personnel on the Liberal Democrat benches, doubling the Party's complement both of Old Etonians and of baronets to two.

CALDER VALLEY

As the fast-moving streams rush down the eastern slope of the Pennines into Yorkshire they forge a landscape of valleys which were transformed in the earliest days of the Industrial Revolution. The damp climate and the easy water power made this rugged district suitable for the manufacture of woollen textiles, and little industrial communities hug the valley bottoms and the steep-sided hills. This constituency follows the river Calder and its tributaries as it winds south of Halifax, from the topmost town of Todmorden amongst the moors, as far as Brighouse.

The Calder Valley division was created in 1983. It consists of the former Sowerby seat, which since the war had always been Labour, but always narrowly, plus Brighouse and Rastrick from the old Brighouse and Spenborough seat, which was super-marginal: for example Labour won by 47 votes in 1959, Conservative, by 59 in 1970, five changes of party allegiance in 30 years. This sounded like the recipe for a new seat which would see very close contests, especially as the Liberal Democrats do well in contests for the local metropolitan borough, Calderdale. Yet there have been no photo-finishes in Calder Valley. The Conservative Donald Thompson won its first three contests fairly easily, but in 1997 there was a 9.5% swing to Labour, which put their candidate Christine McCafferty in by over 6,000 votes. Her Herculean efforts were recorded in an account of the campaign by Pete Davies, *This England*.

Each of the small communities in the Calder and Ryburn valleys has its own distinctive character: precipitous Hebden Bridge with its tourism and elements of counter-culture, remote Todmorden, with its high unemployment, where Labour is strongest, while Elland and Brighouse with its famous brass band are on flatter country nearer the heart and big towns of West Yorkshire. Three-quarters of householders are owner-occupiers and over 98% of residents are white. Calder Valley was a hard nut for Labour to crack. Now she is in, it has so far proved hard to loosen Christine McCafferty's grip on the seat, as in 2001 Sue Robson-Catling increased the Tory share by just 1%, although Labour's numerical majority was halved as the total vote slumped by 9,000.

Social indices:			2001 Gen. Election:			
% Non-white	1.4		Lab	20,244	42.7	−3.4
% Prof/Man	34.7		C	17,150	36.2	+1.1
% Non-manual	55.8		LD	7,596	16.0	+1.3
£ Av prop val 2000	63 K		Grn	1,034	2.2	+1.3
% Increase 97–00	20.9		UKIP	729	1.5	
% Unemployed 2001	2.6		LCA	672	1.4	
% Decrease 97–01	1.3		Lab maj	3,094	6.5	
% Fin hard/Rank	19.0	289	Turnout		63.0	−12.4
% Pensioners	25.8		Elect	75,298		
% Prem mort/Rank	31	311				

Member of Parliament

Christine McCafferty was elected in 1997 – a standard-issue Labour candidate with no previous general election candidacy, launched by an all-women shortlist with a background as a local councillor (for six years) and as a social worker – in her case as manager of a Well Woman centre for eight years. Born in 1945, educated at Whalley Range Grammar School and in Australia, she has been mocked by Tory MPs for worrying about endangered bird life. A tabler of a mere eight written questions in her first year, preoccupied with women's health issues, she is a keen advocate of family planning overseas, of availability of abortion in this country, a campaigner for lowered VAT on sanitary products, and helped block Tory MP Edward Leigh's election to the chairmanship of the International Development Select Committee on account of his Catholic views on abortion and contraception. She thus reflects at least some feminists' requirement that women MPs should specifically represent women and women's concerns. In 1999 she rebelled on Incapacity Benefit cuts.

CAMBERWELL AND PECKHAM

This constituency holds several records.

Some of these would not arouse pride in residents. This is a contender for the title of London's poorest seat, and certainly tops the list of financial hardship in the Experian index published in 2001, although this is of course only one way of measuring such a concept. It is set half-way down the long thin south London borough of Southwark, between Simon Hughes's Southwark (North) and Bermondsey to the north and Dulwich to the south, but it is truly part of the inner city. It had the highest proportion of council housing of any London constituency at the time of the 1991 Census, the latest official figures (64%), and it included the individual ward with the highest percentage thereof (87) – Liddle. Liddle ward, which covered the fearsome North Peckham housing estates, demonstrated a number of other extremes: highest proportion of single-parent families in the borough, lowest level of car ownership, and a horrific crime rate, brought brutally to national attention by the murder of 10-year-old Damilola Taylor in 2000.

It is scarcely surprising that Camberwell and Peckham was held by Labour by a majority of 56% in 2001, on a turnout of less than half of those on the electoral roll. It has one of the highest proportions in the nation of residents who described themselves in the 1991 Census as black (over a quarter of the whole) and certainly the highest of those who said they were of black African origin (over a tenth). The housing conditions for recent newcomers are often very poor, and the state schools have to cope with as wide a variety of languages as any in the country. Camberwell and Peckham also has a range of social and economic problems, typical of the inner city, which continue to require urgent attention.

Social indices:			2001 Gen. Election:			
% Non-white	33.7		Lab	17,473	69.6	+0.1
% Prof/Man	26.2		LD	3,350	13.3	+2.1
% Non-manual	51.0		C	2,740	10.9	−0.7
£ Av prop val 2000	130 K		Grn	805	3.2	
% Increase 97–00	68.7		SA	478	1.9	+1.1
% Unemployed 2001	10.1		SLP	188	0.7	−1.7
% Decrease 97–01	5.1		WRP	70	0.3	−0.1
% Fin hard/Rank	56.5	8	Lab maj	14,123	56.3	
% Pensioners	21.0		Turnout		46.8	−10.0
% Prem mort/Rank	51	40	Elect	53,694		

Member of Parliament

Harriet Harman, surprisingly resurrected as Solicitor General in 2001, had been one of the Blair government's most senior Cabinet casualties, when she was sacked after a year at Social Security. Previously a rising star since her election here in 1982, she is the daughter of a Harley Street consultant and a niece of the Countess of Longford, was expensively educated at St Paul's Girls' School, before attending York University, worked as a solicitor for the NCCL for four years up to her election as an MP, and married the ex-Communist TGWU official and Greenwich picket line organiser, Jack Dromey. She was damaged politically by having to carry through the Tory policy of lone parent benefit cuts, generating Labour's first big backbench revolt in 1997, and adding to her earlier conflict with the Party activists over the selective schooling of her children. Cruelly seen as arrogant, icy and an air-head, she was (according to Simon Hoggart) 'not born but assembled in a lab by Peter Mandelson'. Her return as a law officer confirms the absence of lawyers in the PLP, and doubtless required on her part some swotting up from long-discarded legal textbooks for a professional politician whose career was unusually being given the kiss of life.

CAMBRIDGE

The ancient university cities of England no longer smile on the Conservative Party with kind favour. Oxford East is now safely Labour, while Oxford West and Abingdon fell to the Liberal Democrats in 1997 and in 2001. Cambridge has been represented by Labour's Anne Campbell since 1992, but the stars of the 2001 show here were the Liberal Democrats, who advanced by nearly 9%, and took second place while Labour fell back by almost the same amount. While speculation might commence as to whether in due course the Lib Dems may emulate the success of their counterparts in the university half of Oxford, especially if the Labour government should come to be deemed intellectually inefficient, the future for the Conservatives seems far more bleak in the long term as well as the short.

The academic world did not respond well to Thatcherite Conservatism, with its cutbacks in funding and in grants, and its allegedly reactionary social policies. The university and other academic institutions do not completely dominate the city, of course, especially as the high-tech science park and many related disciplines including advanced medical research have flourished in the past ten years, but as in Oxford this does not help the Conservatives either. They have long performed poorly in local elections and can rely on few wards, winning only Cherry Hinton in 2000 (actually one of their better recent years) and none at all in the coterminous county council elections on 7 June 2001. It does not help them either that the two affluent residential areas on the southern edge of the city wards, Queen Edith's and Trumpington, are placed in the South Cambridgeshire constituency.

Labour win in the council estates like Abbey and King's Hedges in north Cambridge, and in terraced working-class wards like Petersfield and Coleridge. The Liberal Democrats have tended to come top in the central 'university' wards such as Market and Newnham for over two decades, but have extended their range far beyond in the city council contests in recent years, taking nine out of 14 wards in 2000 for example. In 2001 they did as well as any 'centre' party has since Shirley Williams's last attempt to re-enter the Commons, in 1983, as an SDP candidate. No one would be better pleased than she if they were to do even better next time, especially from a distinctly left-of-centre position.

Social indices:			2001 Gen. Election:			
% Non-white	6.1		Lab	19,316	45.1	−8.3
% Prof/Man	43.9		LD	10,737	25.1	+8.9
% Non-manual	63.5		C	9,829	22.9	−3.0
£ Av prop val 2000	144 K		Grn	1,413	3.3	+2.0
% Increase 97–00	54.1		SA	716	1.7	
% Unemployed 2001	1.8		UKIP	532	1.2	
% Decrease 97–01	1.9		PA	232	0.5	+0.2
% Fin hard/Rank	15.0	354	WRP	61	0.1	−0.1
% Pensioners	25.0		Lab maj	8,579	20.0	
% Prem mort/Rank	12	575	Turnout		60.6	−11.0
			Elect	70,663		

Member of Parliament

Anne Campbell, a steely blonde, serenely smiling statistician, has held Cambridge since 1992 – the first ever Labour MP for the city to win it more than once. As PPS to John Battle (at the DTI, 1997–99) and Patricia Hewitt (from 1999), she has been a safe Blairite pair of hands, and apolitically keen on IT. Born in 1940 and educated at Penistone Grammar School and Newnham College, Cambridge (reading Maths), she taught for eight years, lectured in statistics for 13, became chief statistician at the National Institute of Agricultural Botany for nine, and is appropriately keen on cycling. She salts her defence of Cambridge's unfashionably elitist University by reminding Labour Party populists of its 69 Nobel Prize winners, whilst seeking wider 'access'. In 2001 she safely criticised asylum seekers' vouchers – which the government had decided to scrap – still enjoying the link, at 61, as PPS to her fellow Newnham alumnus, Patricia Hewitt.

CAMBRIDGESHIRE NORTH EAST

For 14 years, the MP for the heart of the Fens was one of the best-known personalities in the Commons. Clement Freud was elected for the Isle of Ely in a 'surprise' by-election gain in 1973, and subsequently returned for North East Cambridgeshire after the cathedral city of Ely was transferred out of the constituency in 1983. Freud had been a Liberal, a chef, a gourmet, a TV and radio personality, a sometime director of the Playboy Club, and a class winner in the *Daily Mail* London/New York air race of 1969. Despite his often spiky individualism few seriously expected him to lose his seat in 1987 – it was widely believed that the Fenland people felt they had benefited from having a distinctive representative, one of the few recognised far beyond the confines of the House of Commons itself. Yet the Conservatives' new candidate, Malcolm Moss, himself based in Wisbech, secured a 6% swing from the Alliance, which was enough to unseat Freud by nearly 1,500 votes.

In 1992, with Moss's incumbency and Freud's absence, NE Cambridgeshire reverted to its original status of a safe Tory seat, as a further swing of over 10% increased the numerical majority to 15,093. In 1997 Labour increased their share by fully 20%, although this was more at the expense of the Liberal Democrats than the Tories, who still won by over 5,000. For the first time for over 30 years, little note-worthy happened in 2001, apart from the lowest turnout in the county, barely 60%.

Although the bleak scenery of Fenland, its altitude hovering around zero, doesn't look very prosperous to the untrained eye, this is essentially Tory country, with relatively little Liberal Democrat activity in local politics or Labour tradition, even in the towns of Wisbech, March, Whittlesey and Chatteris. The electoral history of this constituency demonstrates the potentially disruptive effect of a by-election, especially when won by a powerful 'character'. North East Cambridgeshire has now abandoned the experiment, and returned to a pre-Freudian way of thinking.

Social indices:			2001 Gen. Election:				
% Non-white	0.8		C	23,132	48.1	+5.1	
% Prof/Man	25.8		Lab	16,759	34.9	+1.0	
% Non-manual	46.0		LD	6,733	14.0	–2.4	
£ Av prop val 2000	69 K		UKIP	1,189	2.5		
% Increase 97–00	33.9		PA	238	0.5		
% Unemployed 2001	2.0		C maj	6,373	13.3		
% Decrease 97–01	2.1		Turnout		60.1	–12.7	
% Fin hard/Rank	10.5	453	Elect	79,891			
% Prem mort/Rank	32	309					

Member of Parliament

Malcolm Moss, former Northern Ireland minister from 1994 to 1997, was first elected in 1987 when he ended the 14-year tenure of the exotic Liberal MP Clement

Freud. Born in 1943, son of an insurance agent, educated at Audenshaw Grammar School and St John's College, Cambridge, he was a public schoolmaster for four years before turning to insurance, eventually with his own locally (Wisbech) based company. A big affable man of rightist hue, he has been low-profiled in opposition by his Europhilia, though he backed Hague in the leadership ballots, and continued as a spokesman on Northern Ireland (1997–99), moving to Shadow Agriculture (1999–2001) and, after backing the centre-right candidate, Michael Ancram, in 2001, Transport and Local Government. He piloted through legislation on the registration of osteopaths in 1993.

CAMBRIDGESHIRE NORTH WEST

Effectively this is the seventh, extra and new seat allocated to Cambridgeshire by the 1995 Boundary Commission. Most of its electorate came from John Major's formerly swollen Huntingdon constituency, which boasted 93,000 electors in 1992. In addition to the 40,000 voters from the former Huntingdon, NW Cambridgeshire was given the four wards of the Peterborough seat south of the River Nene. It is indeed strongly influenced by that large town, for the old Huntingdon stretched far north to curl round Peterborough taking in some of its southern, western and northern suburbs.

This did not threaten the Tories' certain grip on the seat. Those outlying parts of the unitary authority of Peterborough which were in Huntingdon are every bit as Conservative as the elements in Huntingdon District. For example, in the council elections of May 1999, a poor year for the Conservatives, the Tory share of the vote in Glinton ward was 82% and in Northborough 81%. The new arrivals, the four wards of Peterborough city south of the Nene, also favour the Conservatives on balance, especially Orton Waterville, though Labour usually takes Fletton.

The Tories have had a very bad trot since autumn 1992, but there are islands of optimism in the despair. Cambridgeshire's population growth in the past three decades has been based on prosperity and private house building, and remains highly fertile ground for the blue party.

Social indices:			2001 Gen. Election:			
% Non-white	2.3		C	21,895	49.8	+1.7
% Prof/Man	32.5		Lab	13,794	31.4	−0.8
% Non-manual	54.9		LD	6,957	15.8	+0.7
£ Av prop val 2000	86 K		UKIP	881	2.0	+1.5
% Increase 97–00	38.6		Ind	429	1.0	
% Unemployed 2001	1.5		C maj	8,101	18.4	
% Decrease 97–01	1.5		Turnout		62.3	−11.9
% Fin hard/Rank	10.9	442	Elect	70,569		
% Prem mort/Rank	16	527				

Member of Parliament

A rare case of an Ulsterman in mainland politics, **Sir Brian Mawhinney**, who moved from Peterborough to this safer seat in 1997, comes with an oddly mirthless smile and a reputation as something of a martinet. A hapless Tory Party chairman (1995–97) under Major, by relocating here he at least got into a lifeboat as the rest went down with the sliding deckchairs in May 1997 in the worst Tory sinking in 150 years – and has oddly lingered in the Commons since. Entering the House in 1979, he rose through posts in Ulster, Health and Transport. Born in 1940, he attended Royal Belfast Academical Institution and Queen's University Belfast, Michigan University and London University (where he obtained a doctorate in radiation biology), and lectured in medical physics at London University for 14 years. Until knighted by the exiting Major in 1997, he was one of only two Tory MPs to employ his academic doctorate in his title. An Anglican, but with Plymouth Brethren origins, his civil servants reputedly greeted his arrival with 'the Ego has landed'.

CAMBRIDGESHIRE SOUTH

At first sight the South Cambridgeshire division seems almost to be drawn to be very safely Conservative. Anomalously it includes the two most affluent wards within Cambridge city, Queen Edith's and Trumpington, lopped off its southern edge because it is a little too large for one whole seat. The rest of the South Cambridgeshire seat essentially consists of villages and very small towns. Most of the few wards which Labour usually win in the annual South Cambridgeshire council elections are in fact in the neighbouring SE Cambridgeshire constituency: Fulbourn, Teversham, Histon, Cottenham. Bassingbourn is their best area, but even it has only 3,000 electors and was won by the Tories in May 2000. So was Sawston, the largest single community, boasting a population of just 7,000. On the other hand the smaller agricultural villages are very poor ground for Labour: in Arrington ward in 2000 they garnered but 21 votes or 3%.

Yet the Conservative strength is to some extent illusory. In the 2001 General Election, Andrew Lansley obtained only 44%, well short of an absolute majority, and his comfortable-looking lead of 8,000 was ensured by the continued almost even division of opposition between Labour and the Liberal Democrats – making tactical voting very difficult as there was no agreement about who was the stronger challenger. The Lib Dems tend to win Queen Edith's and Trumpington in Cambridge city elections too nowadays.

An unusually picturesque example of the predominantly rural tone is Grantchester, whose vicarage, originally made famous by Rupert Brooke's poetry, is now home to South Cambridgeshire's most famous resident, Lord (Jeffrey) Archer. Peers, like prisoners and lunatics, are not allowed a vote in parliamentary elections. The Conservatives, however, do not suffer from Lord Archer's disqualification in this particular seat.

Social indices:			2001 Gen. Election:			
% Non-white	1.8		C	21,387	44.2	+2.2
% Prof/Man	45.5		LD	12,984	26.9	+1.0
% Non-manual	65.7		Lab	11,737	24.3	−0.8
£ Av prop val 2000	147 K		Grn	1,182	2.4	
% Increase 97–00	51.2		UKIP	875	1.8	+1.3
% Unemployed 2001	0.8		PA	176	0.4	
% Decrease 97–01	0.9		C maj	8,403	17.4	
% Fin hard/Rank	4.8	610	Turnout		67.1	−9.8
% Pensioners	23.6		Elect	72,095		
% Prem mort/Rank	−2	637				

Member of Parliament

Elected in 1997, **Andrew Lansley**, one of 11 Shadow Cabinet members who went to the backbenches following the election of Iain Duncan Smith in 2001, had, under William Hague, been Shadow Cabinet Office minister responsible for policy review (1999–2001) and for running the 2001 Election campaign. A former party apparatchik who as Conservative Research Director (1990–95) co-authored the 'Double Whammy' slogan attacking Labour's tax plans in 1992 and ran the equally successful – if on a low turnout – Euro-election campaign of 1999, he was previously a civil servant for eight years, serving as Norman Tebbit's principal private secretary. Born in 1956 and educated at Brentwood School and Exeter University, he initially backed Michael Howard in the 1997 ballot, but in 2001 supported Kenneth Clarke, now believing that the Conservatives – contrary to the rightward slant of the recent election campaign – 'have to build a coalition from the centre to the right' and that 'there's an enormous constituency for social liberalism'. With the shrewd look of a career politician about him and with fashionably classless speech, he is taken to be a potential future leader, but in 2001 eschewed repeating Hague's presumptuousness of 1997.

CAMBRIDGESHIRE SOUTH EAST

SE Cambridgeshire is made up of dozens of villages, the small town of Soham, and the little cathedral city of Ely. As in the next door seat of South Cambridgeshire, opposition to the Conservatives, who polled 44% here too, is very evenly divided between Liberal Democrat and Labour. This is due to a considerable extent to the fact that in local government no clear or consistent challenger has emerged either. The Lib Dems do very well in East Cambridgeshire district elections (particularly in Ely itself, part of a constituency they held from 1973 to 1987). This district has been in their control from 1999, but that is only partly in this seat and does not comprise the whole of it. In the South Cambridgeshire council area included here Labour have several councillors in wards such as Teversham and Cottenham. Finally, in the General Election of 2001 the UK Independence Party could actually put forward a local councillor here, Mr Scarr of Fulbourn ward, re-elected in 2000 after having defected from the Liberal Democrats, of all parties – it takes all sorts to make the democratic world, one is glad to observe. This made no difference to the overall political picture;

the varied opposition to the Tories ruffled them about as much as the tiny Gog Magog Hills disturb the landscape of the Cambridgeshire flatlands.

Social indices:			2001 Gen. Election:			
% Non-white	1.2		C	22,927	44.2	+1.2
% Prof/Man	38.6		LD	13,937	26.9	+1.8
% Non-manual	60.4		Lab	13,714	26.4	−0.1
£ Av prop val 2000	125 K		UKIP	1,308	2.5	
% Increase 97–00	47.7		C maj	8,990	17.3	
% Unemployed 2001	1.0		Turnout		63.5	−11.5
% Decrease 97–01	0.8		Elect	81,663		
% Fin hard/Rank	5.7	591				
% Prem mort/Rank	9	602				

Member of Parliament

James Paice, a Home Office spokesman, and former Employment minister (1994–97) and Agriculture spokesman (under William Hague, 1997–2001), was elected here in 1987. A farmer, tall, blond, balding and with classless-to-estuarial speech, born in 1949 and educated at Framlingham College and Writtle College of Agriculture, and a protégé of John Selwyn Gummer whose PPS he was (1990–94), he is out of step as one who has said that 'the European ideal was the reason I originally came into politics' and for backing Maastricht as an 'unashamed supporter'. But he prudently backed Hague in the 1997 leadership ballots, and initially David Davis in 2001, before switching to Clarke and becoming one of ten of Clarke's supporters to be given frontbench jobs under Iain Duncan Smith. He rejects right-to-roam legislation as 'totally socialist' and though he doesn't hunt he strongly defends his important local blood-stock industry.

CANNOCK CHASE

Cannock Chase is an area of rough and hilly woodland, a playground for the urban dwellers nearby. But the communities that surround it and make up the constituency that now bears its name have a long working-class and Labour tradition. Their economies were based on coal: the old pits at Cannock and Hednesford, and the post-war colliery at Lea Hall, Rugeley. There are also two massive power-stations at Rugeley, and this background of heavy industry makes Cannock Chase a very plausible Labour seat. From 1945 to 1970 Cannock was the seat of Jennie Lee, not just Aneurin Bevan's wife and widow but a formidable minister in her own right in Harold Wilson's government.

Boundary changes and the massive problems of Labour which allowed Mrs Thatcher's dominance kept the party out here in the 1970s and 1980s, but the 1990s brought a strong recovery as Tony Wright ousted Gerald Howarth, now safer in far more traditional Conservative territory in Aldershot, in 1992 and winning by nearly ten times as much in 1997. In 2001 there was no significant change in Tony Wright's percentage majority, but two developments of note. The turnout dropped by over 18%, the sixth greatest in the UK. The Liberal Democrats improved their share and absolute numbers, but this may have been a 'neither of the above' factor: there were four fewer candidates this time, and those who disappeared had accounted for an unusually high 9% in 1997. All in all, less interest was shown in the Cannock Chase election in 2001, by electors and aspirants alike.

Social indices:			2001 Gen. Election:			
% Non-white	0.8		Lab	23,049	56.1	+1.3
% Prof/Man	24.2		C	12,345	30.1	+2.9
% Non-manual	45.2		LD	5,670	13.8	+5.1
£ Av prop val 2000	63 K		Lab maj	10,704	26.1	
% Increase 97–00	22.6		Turnout		55.9	−16.4
% Unemployed 2001	2.8		Elect	73,423		
% Decrease 97–01	1.3					
% Fin hard/Rank	19.6	282				
% Pensioners	20.6					
% Prem mort/Rank	33	285				

Member of Parliament

Dr Tony Wright, elected here in 1992, is an academic maverick ignored for office after a short spell as PPS to the Lord Chancellor, and an increasingly vocal critic of New Labour's 'theoretical vapidity'. Born in 1948, educated at Kettering Grammar School, LSE, Harvard, and Balliol College, Oxford, he taught Politics for 17 years at Birmingham University. With his cheeky-chappy mien reflecting the detachment and lack of earnest self-belief of the career politician, and equally disengaged from his former academic life, where he sees people 'writing more and more about less and less', he has settled for the role of gadfly on radical freedom of information legislation and on Lib-Lab tactical voting. Reflecting academic Labourites' strange obsession with constitutional tinkering, he wants fixed term parliaments, has called for a new national anthem, wants a smaller, leaner monarchy but is happy for Prince Charles to marry Mrs Parker Bowles. His call for all England footballers who score a hat trick of goals to be knighted was regarded by Quentin Letts (late of the *Telegraph*) as an example of how embarrassing it is to see 'a clever man trying to be so feebly populist'. Having settled for chairing the Public Administration Select Committee, he used it in November 2001 to attack UNISON leader Dave Prentis's defence of the public sector. He rebelled against the anti-terrorism legislation in 2001.

CANTERBURY

One of the dogs which didn't bark in 2001 was a widely predicted movement away from the governing Labour Party in the county of Kent, due to its exposure to the alleged wave of asylum seekers in the previous two or three years. In fact Kent saw a further increase in the Labour share, one of ten counties to do so. They lost none of their eight seats, seven of them gains in 1997, and indeed here in Canterbury they halved Julian Brazier's majority from 4,000 to 2,000. Admittedly, this was clearly a result of a tactical squeeze on the Liberal Democrats, as Brazier's vote went up too (about as much as that of anti-European Union candidates went down). Nevertheless, the result was not expected by many outside the constituency, or, one suspects, many within.

It might be thought that the home of the chief luminary of the Church of England in the heart of prosperous Kent would be a Tory citadel, but actually Canterbury itself is the least strongly Conservative part of the seat. There are Labour voters – and councillors – in those wards where there is a substantial minority of council-built housing, Northgate and Sturry North; and the Liberal Democrats usually win the other wards within the cathedral city. Traditionally the Tories do pile up their vote in the many villages included in the constituency and in most of the seaside resort and fishing port of Whitstable, especially Tankerton.

It is natural to think still of the Conservatives as suffering from aberrant results in the last two general elections. After all, they were in office for most of the twentieth century and have won four of the last six national contests for government. Yet they have it all to do to recover the ground lost since the 1990s, and even this symbolic heart of the establishment must be treated as a genuine marginal next time.

Social indices:			2001 Gen. Election:			
% Non-white	1.9		C	18,711	41.5	+2.8
% Prof/Man	38.5		Lab	16,642	36.9	+5.6
% Non-manual	61.4		LD	8,056	17.8	−5.9
£ Av prop val 2000	112 K		Grn	920	2.0	+1.0
% Increase 97–00	52.8		UKIP	803	1.8	+1.3
% Unemployed 2001	2.1		C maj	2,069	4.6	
% Decrease 97–01	2.0		Turnout		60.9	−11.7
% Fin hard/Rank	11.3	432	Elect	74,159		
% Pensioners	31.2					
% Prem mort/Rank	18	504				

Member of Parliament

Julian Brazier, a former soldier-turned-management-consultant, MP here since 1987, and rather unflatteringly seen as having 'two brains fewer than David Willetts' (David McKie), is as close as the Commons comes to a spitting image of the comic actor, Hugh Laurie. Very tall, born in 1953 into a military family and appropriately educated at the soldiers' public school, Wellington, and then at Brasenose College, Oxford, he was a Redwood-backing Eurosceptic in 1995 and 1997, and voted in 2001 for Iain Duncan Smith with whom he had earlier shared an office for three years, and as a Catholic opposes embryo research and abortion. He was for three years (1990–93) PPS to Gillian Shepherd. His faintly loopy air evokes the boyish enthusiasm of a character from Enid Blyton, but in 2001 he suffered the traumatic experience of involvement in a driving accident in Italy in which a motor cyclist was killed.

CARDIFF CENTRAL

The Central division of Cardiff is by any measure one of the most interesting constituencies in the principality – indeed, in Britain. It is socially diverse, physically dramatic, and politically and electorally unusual. It stands at the heart of a proud nation's capital city, and rightly forms one of the keenest centres of interest in general elections in Wales. It was, however, probably not as widely noticed nationally that Labour actually came close to losing Cardiff Central, to the Liberal Democrats, in 2001. It now has one of their five smallest majorities.

This should not have come as a surprise, as the 2001 result was preceded two years earlier by a Liberal Democrat victory in the constituency section of the inaugural Welsh Assembly elections. Since its creation in 1983, Central has been held by the Conservatives as well as Labour, although they have declined both absolutely and tactically here. As its marginal history may indicate, Cardiff Central is a very mixed seat. It includes part of the northern Cardiff middle-class belt, in the affluent shape of Cyncoed ward. The ward of Pentwyn includes modern private estates of originally designed housing set on windy hills north-east of the centre. Central also takes in the community of Roath, which includes Plasnewydd ward; here the housing is more likely to be terraced, and occupied by students and a more transient population. The Adamsdown ward is part of the old inner city, and used to be overwhelmingly Labour. However, as in all of the aforementioned wards, the Liberal Democrats are not merely competitive but usually victorious in unitary city council elections. Finally there is the centre of the city, with the castle and the fine civic buildings and University of Wales. There are very few council tenants in the seat, and the proportion of professional workers is very high, as one would expect in a seat which contains a centre of bureaucracy and government: the percentage of those with higher academic qualifications is the highest of any seat in Wales. However, public sector middle-class workers may well be less inclined to support the Conservative Party than those in the private sector. It might also be noted that Cardiff Central contains the highest percentage of non-white residents in Wales, although this does not approach the figures recorded in many urban seats in England.

The Liberal Democrats' local – and indeed now devolved – government strength in the varied and colourful communities of this fascinating seat should not be underestimated, and is unlikely to disappear. If anything, the chances are that Labour's second term in national government will bring greater electoral difficulties than the first, and the Lib Dems seem very well placed to pick up this seat at the topmost, parliamentary, level in 2005 or 2006.

Social indices:			2001 Gen. Election:				
% Non-white	6.8		Lab/Coop	13,451	38.6	−5.1	
% Welsh sp	10.3		LD	12,792	36.7	+11.8	
% Prof/Man	40.1		C	5,537	15.9	−4.2	
% Non-manual	67.8		PC	1,680	4.8	+1.3	
£ Av prop val 2000	87 K		Grn	661	1.9		
% Increase 97–00	38.6		SA	283	0.8		
% Unemployed 2001	3.4		UKIP	221	0.6		
% Decrease 97–01	3.1		PA	217	0.6		
% Fin hard/Rank	11.7	419	L/C maj	659	1.9		
% Pensioners	21.8		Turnout		58.3	−11.7	
% Prem mort/Rank	27	387	Elect	59,785			

Member of Parliament

Jon Owen Jones, a bearded and rare – in South Wales – Welsh-speaking, biology teacher before winning here in 1992, joined the ranks of Blair's discarded ministers in 1999, when dropped from the slimmed-down post-devolution Welsh Office where he had served for a year, after five years as a Whip. Born in 1954 in the Rhondda, a former miner's son, and educated at Ysgol Cymraeg, Pontygwaith, and at East Anglia University, he has campaigned for more public lavatories for women and for prompt payment of debts to small businesses, but in 2000 belied his five years as a Labour Whip by rebelling on the Freedom of Information bill, and in 2002 rebelled over faith schools. He backs legalisation of cannabis.

CARDIFF NORTH

The north side of Cardiff has long been its most desirable residential quarter, and the parliamentary constituency of Cardiff North is the most middle class in the whole of Wales. Over 83% of the housing was owner-occupied at the time of the last published Census, also a record for the principality. This seat, and its predecessors, used to be regarded as Tory bankers; a Cardiff North with somewhat different boundaries was won by Labour in 1966, but even then only by 672 votes in a landslide year. Then in 1997 the Conservatives lost every seat they held in Wales, most of them by considerable margins, and Labour's Julie Morgan joined her husband Rhodri, also a Cardiff MP, in the Commons with a thumping majority of over 8,000, and she held on with little change apart from an 11% decline in turnout (though it was still 10% higher than the UK average) in 2001.

The essence of Cardiff North consists of a swathe of middle-class owner-occupied neighbourhoods which traditionally voted Tory: Heath Park, Llanishen, Whitchurch and the most Conservative of all, Rhiwbina and Lisvane, these last the only ones still Conservative in the 1999 all-out unitary city council elections. The main centres of Labour strength lie in the former council estate of Llandaff North and in Gabalfa, nearer to the centre of the city. However, overall North does not look the part of a marginal, still less a Labour seat.

Labour's fine performances in recent years must have something to do with the larger than average regional, and national, swing against the Conservatives. Like Scotland, Wales is less inclined to the Conservatives than England, even controlling for social class, and there is often resentment at the amount of power wielded in London. It should be noted, though, that in 2001 Wales was Labour's worst area, as their share of the vote declined by 6%, although it must be said that this was mainly due to the rise of Plaid Cymru (and abstentions) at their expense further west in south Wales, and not in the English-speaking capital. There is also a high proportion of public sector workers in Cardiff North's middle classes – lecturers and teachers as well as those working for local government and the Welsh Office. These groups have been less likely to support the Conservatives than their opposite numbers in the private sector, and appear to have swung quite strongly towards Tony Blair's party in 1997/2001. Whether this will last after the public sector policy changes threatened by

Labour for their second term is one of the bigger and most important questions in the politics of the early twenty-first century.

Social indices:			2001 Gen. Election:			
% Non-white	2.5		Lab	19,845	45.9	−4.6
% Welsh sp	8.3		C	13,680	31.6	−2.0
% Prof/Man	43.4		LD	6,631	15.3	+4.4
% Non-manual	71.6		PC	2,471	5.7	+3.2
£ Av prop val 2000	93 K		UKIP	613	1.4	
% Increase 97–00	28.1		Lab maj	6,165	14.3	
% Unemployed 2001	1.4		Turnout		69.0	−11.2
% Decrease 97–01	1.7		Elect	62,634		
% Fin hard/Rank	8.7	494				
% Pensioners	31.1					
% Prem mort/Rank	26	400				

Member of Parliament

Julie Morgan, elected in 1997, was part of five Commons husband-and-wife pairs, until she was politically separated from her husband Rhodri when he departed full-time for the Welsh Assembly as First Minister in 2001. Selected here on an all women shortlist, she has persistently campaigned on women's issues and, preoccupied with race and gender balance in the new Welsh Assembly, welcomed the selection of a black woman candidate in the first Assembly election (in 1999) at Monmouth, a seat the party duly lost. Born in 1944 and educated at Howells School, Llandaff (a private school) and at King's College, London, and Manchester and Cardiff Universities, she was a social worker, eventually with Dr Barnardos. Abstaining in 1997 on lone parent benefit cuts, in 1999 and 2000 she upped her profile by voting against the government on disability benefit cuts, pensions linked to average earnings, and freedom of information, registering a total of 14 rebellious votes during the 1997–2001 Parliament, making her the third most dissenting of the 65-strong 1997 intake of Labour women.

CARDIFF SOUTH AND PENARTH

James Callaghan represented a southern Cardiff seat for 42 years, becoming Labour Prime Minister in 1976 and in due course Father of the House (longest continuous membership). Twice during that time his constituency changed in name and character, latterly in 1983, when the seaside resort of Penarth was added to south Cardiff to create a seat of rare social and economic variety, which could even be regarded as marginal in a very good Tory year. Callaghan's majority in 1983 was only 2,276, and when he retired before the 1987 contest some thought he might have a sufficient personal vote to make life difficult for the new Labour candidate, Alun Michael. In fact Michael, despite his chequered history during the 1997–2001 Parliament (imposed as Tony Blair's choice as First Secretary in the new Welsh Assembly, but subsequently resigning and returning to the Westminster scene) has now managed to increase the Labour majority, to reach a highly satisfactory 12,000. There were no electoral signs whatsoever of increased unpopularity here, although it might be said that his 1997 share had probably been affected adversely by the 3,942 votes cast for a candidate running independently as New Labour. Clearly Alun Michael had established his own more formal credentials in that regard by 2001.

The basis of James Callaghan's vote, and now of Alun Michael's, was always situated in the docklands of the Welsh capital, in the Labour strongholds of Grangetown, Splott and Bute Town, the somewhat seedy, disreputable 'Tiger Bay' of literature, and the home area of singer Shirley Bassey. This is the location of a large non-white population, long-established through Cardiff's role as a port with African and Caribbean connections; unusually, the black population outnumbers the Asian. This should not be exaggerated, though: the population of Bute Town is now very small, only around 3,000, and overall the seat is only a little over 6% non-white.

Another source of Labour strength lies well to the north-east, in the massive and troubled peripheral council estates of Llanrumney and Trowbridge. There is nothing 'southern' about these, although they do at least lie towards the coast. However, the outlying Penarth is a different matter, and the Conservatives are probably still competitive there in a general election. Penarth is comfortably outvoted nowadays by the Cardiff element of the seat, which must now again be regarded as safe for Labour.

Social indices:			2001 Gen. Election:			
% Non-white	6.4		Lab/Coop	20,094	56.2	+2.8
% Welsh sp	4.1		C	7,807	21.8	+1.1
% Prof/Man	27.5		LD	4,572	12.8	+3.4
% Non-manual	54.1		PC	1,983	5.5	+2.4
£ Av prop val 2000	74 K		UKIP	501	1.4	
% Increase 97–00	37.1		SA	427	1.2	+0.4
% Unemployed 2001	4.5		PA	367	1.0	
% Decrease 97–01	3.1		L/C maj	12,287	34.4	
% Fin hard/Rank	27.2	169	Turnout		57.5	–11.0
% Pensioners	27.0		Elect	62,125		
% Prem mort/Rank	43	120				

Member of Parliament

Alun Michael, a community worker and local city councillor, was elected here as Lord Callaghan's successor in 1987, and enjoyed a successful career first as a Home Office minister and then as Welsh Secretary (1998–99), until asked by Tony Blair to contest the election for Welsh First Minister in 1999 against the unreliable maverick, Rhodri Morgan, and though he won, did so in a controversially weighted electoral college and was eventually replaced by Morgan anyway in February 2000. His election and leadership had not been popular and were blamed for Labour's weak performance in the first Assembly elections in May 1999. Born in 1943, a shopkeeper's son, and educated at Colwyn Bay Grammar School and at Keele University, where he was not politically involved, lacking charisma, and seen by his son Geraint as 'boring', his stalled career was fanned back into life at Westminster in 2001 – but only at Minister of State level, in the new DEFRA Ministry, and with unenviable responsibility for the political football of fox hunting legislation.

CARDIFF WEST

Cardiff West was the constituency of a famous Speaker of the House of Commons, George Thomas. It has on occasion been suggested that the Speaker should not represent a full-scale seat like other members, for it is impossible for him or her to offer certain constituency services or to ask questions in the House. Speakers are also forbidden from campaigning at election time, but the Conservatives and Liberals at least have rarely opposed the Speaker, as a matter of principle. George Thomas was re-elected with a massive majority in 1979 against Plaid Cymru and National Front candidates, whose vote was only slightly inflated by the lack of competition. Then when George Thomas retired from the Speakership and the Commons in 1983 Cardiff West fell to a very distinctive Conservative, Stefan Terlezki, who had been born in the Ukraine and retained a virulent anti-communism. Terlezki only served one term, for Cardiff West is the sort of seat that could only fall to the Tories in a year of Labour disaster, and by 1997 Rhodri Morgan had increased his majority to over 15,000. This was higher than any of George Thomas's margins as a Labour MP. Morgan is very popular in this seat, as his outstanding personal performance in the 1999 Welsh Assembly elections showed. The constituency element of this Additional Member System election was fought on exactly the same boundaries as Westminster, and Morgan swept in with the biggest Labour majority in Wales, boosted by Tony Blair's reluctance to appoint him as First Secretary designate, a position to which he has succeeded subsequently. His successor as this seat's representative in London, Kevin Brennan, could not quite match Rhodri Morgan's 1999 share of 62%, but still has a safe enough seat.

West has real problems. These centre on the massive Ely-Caerau council estate on the south-west edge of the city, which has seen riots, racial violence and general lawlessness as a minority of the population has come to see the police as an enemy. This is white, working-class territory, where Asian shopkeepers have been terrorised and burnt out, and middle-aged residents kicked to death by youth gangs. Closer to the centre of the city are to be found the bohemian area of Canton, and the mixed-race Riverside. The only Conservative neighbourhoods lie in Llandaff ward, near Cardiff's cathedral, which is a residential area of real charm and convenience, and untypical in political terms too of the rest of the constituency.

Social indices:			2001 Gen. Election:			
% Non-white	6.2		Lab	18,594	54.6	−5.8
% Welsh sp	6.9		C	7,273	21.3	−0.2
% Prof/Man	34.7		LD	4,458	13.1	+2.2
% Non-manual	58.9		PC	3,296	9.7	+4.8
£ Av prop val 2000	76 K		UKIP	462	1.4	
% Increase 97–00	29.8		Lab maj	11,321	33.2	
% Unemployed 2001	4.3		Turnout		58.4	−10.8
% Decrease 97–01	3.4		Elect	58,348		
% Fin hard/Rank	27.7	162				
% Pensioners	25.8					
% Prem mort/Rank	41	161				

Member of Parliament

With the departure to the Welsh Assembly of the tousled Blair-disapproved Welsh First Minister, Rhodri Morgan, **Kevin Brennan** is Labour's unsurprising new shoo-in here, having carried Rhodri Morgan's bags as his adviser for five years, and organised both of his 1997 and 1998 leadership campaigns, been chairman of the local CLP for two years, and a Cardiff councillor for nine years. Yet another Welshman of Irish origins, to join Paul Murphy, Don Touhig, and Paul Flynn, he was born in 1959, educated at St Albans (RC) Comprehensive School, Pontypool, Pembroke College, Oxford, and at the Universities of Cardiff and Glamorgan. A teacher for nine years, he is the son of a steel worker and a retired dinner lady, and reflects the now common background of Labour candidates in Wales: teachers who are one or two generations away from pit or steelworks. He was also typically one of eight new Labour MPs in 2001 to have risen on an MP's or minister's coat-tails as a party staffer, and – in his case – stepping straight into his employer's vacated seat. In the Young Communist League as a youthful dalliance in 1975, he was President of the Oxford Union the term after William Hague in 1982, and campaigned for PR for the Welsh Assembly elections.

CARLISLE

Rather like Barrow-in-Furness at the other end of Cumbria, Carlisle is a working-class and industrial town tucked away in predominantly rural and remote countryside. Labour have not lost Carlisle since 1964, but at the height of Thatcherism and in the depths of Old Labour, they held on by just 71 votes in 1983 and by only 916 in 1987. Although urban itself, with only a few more rural wards tacked on by the Boundary Commission in 1997 (some thought there should have been more, as the seat is smaller than the national average), the result in 2001 was undoubtedly affected by discontent with the way the government handled the foot-and-mouth crisis of that year, which had caused the postponement of the elections and which was at its very worst in north Cumbria. Labour's vote dropped by over 6%, and that of the Conservatives in second place increased by almost the same amount. Turnout fell by over 13% and as a consequence of these two developments Eric Martlew's vote went down from 25,000 in 1997 to under 18,000.

Unlike Barrow, the city has a high proportion of council-built estates, which ring this isolated city in Scottish border country. There is a variety of industry, but the largest employer is probably still Courtaulds Textiles. For a long time it was the only part of England which boasted state pubs. This still looks fairly safe for Labour, but they should not take success for granted. Carlisle remains a slightly eccentric seat in a far corner of England, but it demands and deserves equal attention with more metropolitan centres.

Social indices:			2001 Gen. Election:			
% Non-white	0.7		Lab	17,856	51.2	−6.3
% Prof/Man	24.0		C	12,154	34.8	+5.8
% Non-manual	47.5		LD	4,076	11.7	+1.2
£ Av prop val 2000	53 K		LCA	554	1.6	
% Increase 97–00	12.2		SA	269	0.8	
% Unemployed 2001	3.6		Lab maj	5,702	16.3	
% Decrease 97–01	2.2		Turnout		59.4	−13.4
% Fin hard/Rank	22.9	227	Elect	58,811		
% Pensioners	27.3					
% Prem mort/Rank	42	151				

Member of Parliament

Eric Martlew, elected here in 1987 and a Labour Whip in Opposition, was dropped in 1997, but made a PPS, first to David Clark and then to Baroness Jay after Clark was sacked in 1998. A burly man, he came with solid local credentials. Born in 1949, educated locally at Harraby Secondary School and at technical college, he worked as a lab technician and then personnel manager at the local Nestlé's factory for 21 years, sat on the local County Council for 14 years, and was Chairman of Carlisle Labour Party for six years. Reasonably enough a campaigner for an upgraded West Coast Main Line, he served as a rather plodding Defence spokesman in Opposition, under the equally lacklustre and hapless David Clark. He was critical of the handling of the foot-and-mouth crisis in 2001, and an advocate of vaccination against the disease. His career as a PPS ended with Lady Jay's departure from government in 2001.

CARMARTHEN EAST AND DINEFWR

The Welsh Nationalists met mixed fortune in 2001. Their hopes were buoyant. Plaid Cymru had done very well in the Welsh Assembly elections of May 1999, breaking out of their Welsh-speaking west Wales fastness to take Labour strongholds in the industrial valleys, including even Neil Kinnock's former Islwyn. They expected to return more than four MPs two years later; but they failed to do so. Not only did they not manage to repeat their valley successes, but they could not even hold Ynys Mon (Anglesey) where their party leader Ieuan Wyn Jones retired to concentrate on the Cardiff Assembly. However, as expected, they did repeat their 1999 gain from Labour of Carmarthen East and Dinefwr.

   Although this seat contains no part of the town of Carmarthen, it does include the bulk of the former seat of that name, which existed before 1997. It is therefore fair to describe it as the successor to the old Carmarthen division, which had a complex electoral history, and a rich Nationalist tradition. The seat was won on two occasions (1966 and October 1974) by Gwynfor Evans, then leader of Plaid Cymru: and on another, in February 1974, he lost to Labour by just three votes. The Conservatives surged remarkably from a mere 5.7% of the vote in October 1974 to come within a thousand votes of victory in 1983, but have slipped far back since. The Liberal Democrats held the Carmarthen seat until 1957, but obtained well under a tenth of the vote in 2001.

This is one of only five majority Welsh-speaking seats. Besides the eastern half of the Carmarthen district, it includes Dinefwr. There are no communities larger than the size of a village in the Carmarthen section, which is very heavily devoted to agriculture. Dinefwr is also largely rural, and contains some beautiful scenery around the market towns of Llandeilo and Llandovery, but also the old anthracite-mining towns of Ammanford and Brynamman on the very edge of the south Welsh coalfield. The extraction of coal is part of the history of the constituency, but not of its future, and Labour must now worry that they may go the same way.

Social indices:			2001 Gen. Election:			
% Non-white	0.5		PC	16,130	42.4	+7.7
% Welsh sp	66.4		Lab	13,540	35.6	−7.3
% Prof/Man	35.6		C	4,912	12.9	+0.9
% Non-manual	53.3		LD	2,815	7.4	−0.2
£ Av prop val 2000	61 K		UKIP	656	1.7	
% Increase 97–00	35.8		PC maj	2,590	6.8	
% Unemployed 2001	2.9		Turnout		70.4	−8.2
% Decrease 97–01	2.1		Elect	54,035		
% Fin hard/Rank	7.4	544				
% Pensioners	30.4					
% Prem mort/Rank	37	222				

Member of Parliament

Adam Price ousted Labour MP Dr Alan Williams from this seat, which has been a Labour-Welsh Nationalist marginal since the death of Labour's Lady Megan Lloyd George in 1966. Atypically for a Plaid Cymru MP, Price comes from a south Welsh working-class mining background, claims to have been politicised by the 1984 miners' strike, and was born locally (in 1968), within the only constituency that combines a mining tradition with a majority Welsh-speaking population. He was educated at Amman Valley Comprehensive, Saarland University, Cardiff University, and the North East Wales Institute, Wrexham, set up his own economic development consultancy, and worked with Welsh Secretary Ron Davies to achieve EU Objective 1 funding for West Wales and the Valleys. But in September 2001 he only narrowly failed, as a 'reluctant Eurosceptic', to get his party to reject UK membership of the euro on the grounds of the Central Bank's insistence on recession-inducing low budget deficits enforced by fines. The youngest Welsh MP, he articulates – in the manner of all Nationalist MPs – a spread of locally-pertinent grievances on student tuition fees, the NHS, rural banking and renewable energy, and – as has become fashionable among at least Welsh, if not Scottish, Nationalists – the description of himself as a 'democratic socialist'. His capture of this seat – whilst his party was failing to take other mining seats – confirmed, however, that the Plaid's attempt to penetrate the old south Welsh mining valleys with a 'socialist' pitch, still fails unless there is a local Welsh-speaking majority, Welsh nationalism not having escaped its cultural lager. Of half-English parentage, and self-described as 'an out gay man', he angered Labour by exposing Tony Blair's 2001 backing for an Indian tycoon's takeover of the Romanian steel industry during the 2002 Ogmore by-election.

CARMARTHEN WEST AND SOUTH PEMBROKESHIRE

Two extra seats were created in Wales in time for the 1997 General Election, despite the fact that Wales was over-represented already: its seats are officially set to be smaller in electorate than those in England, and unlike in Scotland there are no plans to correct this following the establishment of a devolved assembly and executive.

The two newcomers are at opposite ends of the country. One is in north-east Wales, in the Vale of Clwyd. The other is down in the south-west, where this seat has been formed from minority parts of two old seats, Carmarthen and Pembroke. Its name locates it fairly clearly. The bulk of the old Pembroke is now in Preseli Pembrokeshire; most of the former Carmarthen is now in Carmarthen East and Dinefwr.

South Pembrokeshire provides over 30,000 of the electors. At the 1992 General Election, Labour regained the Pembroke seat from the Conservatives after a 22-year break, but only by 755 votes; and it is generally believed that Pembrokeshire south of Milford Haven is the better part for the Tories. Although the industrial Pembroke Dock is the largest community here, it also includes the genteel coast which was known as 'Little England Beyond Wales': Tenby, Saundersfoot, Manorbier and many other villages which have large numbers of retirees, many English. The Conservatives may have polled more votes than Labour in South Pembrokeshire in 2001, after halving the Labour majority compared with 1997; however, the Carmarthen West section is a different matter. Carmarthen was a Labour-Plaid Cymru marginal for years, with the Conservatives in a distant third place. The territory included in this seat takes in the whole of the county town of Carmarthen itself, and the rural territory along the historic border between Carmarthenshire and Pembrokeshire. This is Welsh-speaking country, with the single exception of the township of Laugharne, best known as a residence of Dylan Thomas.

Although it is Labour who have benefited from the generosity of the electoral system in providing this extra constituency so far, they might not be so comfortable in a year when they do not win a national landslide, and it is possible that one day a Tory recovery might bring this divided seat within their grasp for the first time, although it was Plaid Cymru who made the greater advance, presumably in the Carmarthen West section, in 2001.

Social indices:			2001 Gen. Election:			
% Non-white	0.6		Lab	15,349	41.6	−7.6
% Welsh sp	24.6		C	10,811	29.3	+2.7
% Prof/Man	35.4		PC	6,893	18.7	+6.0
% Non-manual	54.7		LD	3,248	8.8	+0.6
£ Av prop val 2000	62 K		UKIP	537	1.5	
% Increase 97–00	20.6		Ind	78	0.2	
% Unemployed 2001	3.9		Lab maj	4,538	12.3	
% Decrease 97–01	3.1		Turnout		65.3	−11.2
% Fin hard/Rank	8.5	504	Elect	56,518		
% Pensioners	29.5					
% Prem mort/Rank	29	358				

Member of Parliament

Becoming the first Labour MP here for 22 years in 1992, tall, bald and bearded, **Nick Ainger** – a Whip from 2001 – cuts a dash as another English import into Wales. Born in Sheffield in 1947 and educated at Netherthorpe Grammar School, Staveley, Derbyshire, he moved to Milford Haven in the 1970s as a marine rigger. A Dyfed county councillor for 12 years from 1981, his careful nursing of constituency interests such as oil tanker safety, local military installations and threats to fishing and farming, were after 1997 accompanied by his job as PPS to Welsh Secretaries, originally to the benighted Ron Davies, who resigned in 1998, and then Alun Michael (1998–99), and finally Paul Murphy (1999–2001).

CARRICK, CUMNOCK AND DOON VALLEY

Carrick, Cumnock and Doon Valley is a rather lengthy but somewhat romantic-sounding name for the southern part of the old county of Ayrshire. It does do justice to the disparate nature of the seat. Carrick is in general soft coastal country, with Conservative predominance in the seaside resort of Girvan and in the farmland inland (though not in the small town of Maybole). This section is heavily outvoted by Cumnock and Doon Valley, the heart of the former South Ayrshire coalfield, where stark communities like Dalmellington and New Cumnock lie isolated among the rugged moors, offering as bleak an industrial scene as any in Britain. The seat also includes another ex-mining area, the Mauchline basin, and essentially it is a very safe Labour seat, awarding George Foulkes a majority of nearly 15,000 even on 2001's turnout of just 62%.

George Foulkes did have difficulty once, though, when he first contested this constituency's predecessor, South Ayrshire, in 1979. In October 1974 the largest numerical majority in Scotland was obtained by South Ayrshire's Labour MP, Jim Sillars. Sillars was then regarded as a bright young prospect in the party, with a liveliness and intellectual acumen not always (then, at least) associated with Labour MPs for Scottish seats. But he became disaffected with the Labour Party, particularly over lack of progress towards devolution, and resigned the whip in 1976 to become one of the two 'Scottish Labour Party' MPs. In 1979 Sillars held the official Labour candidate Foulkes to a majority of just over 1,500, but then retired from the Ayrshire scene (he became a Scottish Nationalist and held Glasgow Govan for the SNP from the 1988 by-election to 1992). Foulkes has had no significant trouble since.

However, this seat is effectively one of those slated for distruction in the Scottish Boundary Commission changes which reduce the number of constituencies from 72 to 59.

Social indices:			2001 Gen. Election:			
% Non-white	0.5		Lab/Coop	22,174	55.3	−4.5
% Prof/Man	29.6		C	7,318	18.2	+1.3
% Non-manual	48.6		SNP	6,258	15.6	−1.1
% Unemployed 2001	5.4		LD	2,932	7.3	+2.0
% Decrease 97–01	2.0		SSP	1,058	2.6	
% Fin hard/Rank	33.9	101	SLP	367	0.9	
% Prem mort/Rank	43	131	L/C maj	14,856	37.0	
			Turnout		61.8	−13.2
			Elect	64,919		

Member of Parliament

George Foulkes, elected in 1979, when he retrieved the seat from the ex-Labour MP, Jim Sillars, who had defected to the Nationalists, a minister for four years from 1997 at International Development with Clare Short, until moved to form part of a two-minister team at the rump Scottish Office in January 2001, was born in 1942, educated at Keith Grammar School, Haberdashers' Aske's, and Edinburgh University. Chubby and convivial, he was off the Opposition frontbench for a while in the early 1990s after a drunken incident, and must have wondered, as the clock ticks on, how he survived – albeit in marginal posts – the post-victory reshuffle of 2001. Meanwhile his 'proudest achievement is to have played a little part in the return of democracy to Chile', by monitoring free elections and seeing the return of a socialist president to 'avenge the coup that ousted Salvador Allende'.

CARSHALTON AND WALLINGTON

Despite the semi-comic reputation of Carshalton Beeches as a fashionable ex-Surrey top residential area, the Carshalton and Wallington constituency is far from iron-clad Conservative territory in either local government or parliamentary representation, has not been for a goodly number of years, and will not be in the foreseeable future.

The Beeches are not socially typical of the division as a whole. For a start it includes part of the giant inter-war council estate of St Helier, shared with the Mitcham and Morden seat in the borough of Merton. This provides two reliably Labour wards. There is another large council estate in Roundshaw, south Beddington, the site of the former Croydon Airport. Much more significantly, it should be borne in mind that Carshalton and Wallington forms one of the two seats in the London Borough of Sutton. Sutton has stepwise, as the Americans might say, become one of the strongest Liberal Democrat fortresses in England over the past decade or so. After taking minority control of the council in 1986, and an overall majority four years later, in 1998 the Liberal Democrats won 46 seats there (including Carshalton Beeches, easily), the Conservatives and Labour just five apiece. The Sutton councillor (Carshalton Central ward) Tom Brake ousted the Conservative MP Nigel Forman in one of five Liberal Democrat gains in outer south-west London in the 1997 General Election as the Tories lost no less than 16% of the share of the vote. As in the borough elections, the Lib Dems are showing that they can build on success, and in 2001 Brake doubled his lead. Who is to say that he will not still be established 10 or 15 years on, like his municipal colleagues?

Social indices:			2001 Gen. Election:			
% Non-white	5.6		LD	18,289	45.0	+6.8
% Prof/Man	33.9		C	13,742	33.8	+0.3
% Non-manual	63.2		Lab	7,466	18.4	−5.5
£ Av prop val 2000	136 K		Grn	614	1.5	+0.7
% Increase 97–00	59.4		UKIP	501	1.2	+0.8
% Unemployed 2001	1.8		LD maj	4,547	11.2	
% Decrease 97–01	2.0		Turnout		60.3	−13.0
% Fin hard/Rank	19.1	288	Elect	67,337		
% Pensioners	24.6					
% Prem mort/Rank	25	423				

Member of Parliament

Tom Brake, a young (born in 1962) computer software consultant, educated at the Lycée International in Paris and Imperial College, London, won here for the Liberal Democrats in 1997. Tall, lean, an Environment spokesman and Whip, he has the easy job of complaining about awful rail services and road congestion on behalf of his suburban audience. In common with three of his five colleagues who captured seats in the south-west London suburbs in 1997, a local councillor (Sutton) who had also fought the seat before – in 1992 – before winning in 1997, his local roots were effective, as was his youth, in dealing with the Tory fight-back in the form of a 56-year-old imported marketing director, Ken Andrew.

CASTLE POINT

In 2001 the Conservatives only reversed five of their 120-plus losses to Labour in 1997, but Castle Point was one of them. It had certainly been one of the most unlikely changes of hands, for Robert Spink had won by 17,000 votes in 1992, and all that was overturned by Labour's Christine Butler, who increased her party's share of the vote by over 18%. Castle Point was the fourth safest Conservative seat to fall in 1997. It was comfortably the seat Labour won in 1997 which had the fewest electors in financial hardship according to the Experian/national statistics index, ranking at 18th lowest with just over 4% in economic difficulties. It had all the attributes of a non-marginal.

The Castle Point constituency had the third highest proportion of owner-occupiers in the United Kingdom in 1991 – 89.4%. It consists of the towns of Benfleet and Canvey Island. It was created in 1983 when the rapidly growing South East Essex division was reduced in size, losing Rayleigh to the Rochford seat.

Castle Point is not an overwhelmingly middle-class seat – indeed the percentages of professional, managerial and even junior non-manual and clerical workers are less than the national average. The flat Canvey Island itself, dominated by its oil refinery, is far from wealthy or glamorous. Castle Point is remarkably homogeneous; until 1995 the Conservatives almost always won every ward in local elections. Then the remarkable swing to Labour began. In May 1995 Labour gained 31 seats on Castle Point council, increasing their representation from three to 34 out of the total of 39. Almost nobody believed that this could be translated to a general election victory, but in the exceptional year of 1997 it certainly was. Christine Butler was far from humiliated in 2001, and her result would have been regarded as excellent should her colleagues defending seats have not done quite so well; her share of the vote scarcely declined, but the Liberal Democrats were reduced to under 8%, one of their worst showings in England.

Social indices:			2001 Gen. Election:				
% Non-white	1.2		C	17,738	44.6	+4.5	
% Prof/Man	29.6		Lab	16,753	42.1	−0.3	
% Non-manual	60.9		LD	3,116	7.8	−1.4	
£ Av prop val 2000	99 K		UKIP	1,273	3.2		
% Increase 97–00	42.1		Ind	663	1.7		
% Unemployed 2001	1.7		Ind	220	0.6		
% Decrease 97–01	2.5		C maj	985	2.5		
% Fin hard/Rank	4.2	624	Turnout		58.4	−14.0	
% Pensioners	22.8		Elect	68,108			
% Prem mort/Rank	14	554					

Member of Parliament

Dr Robert Spink, a Yorkshire-born (1948) and -accented former mill boy and electronics apprentice who eventually acquired a Manchester University doctorate in management economics, was one of two former Tory MPs who obeyed Central Office instructions to stay and fight in their old seats and managed to win them back in 2001. An engineer with EMI for 11 years who became a management consultant, eventually running Bournemouth Airport, he held the seat from 1992 to 1997, establishing a reputation as a keen privatiser and deregulator, if conservative on Sunday trading. He was Ann Widdecombe's PPS for three years, is homophobic and anti-abortion, favours capital punishment for child and police murders, and has, in the past, voted for bans on fox hunting. His re-election in 2001 followed an eve-of-election attempt by members of the local Conservative Association to deselect him as candidate.

CEREDIGION

This individualistic part of west Wales produces a rather surprising development at each general election. One of the most dramatic, and, to outsiders at least, surprising results anywhere in the United Kingdom in 1992 occurred in the constituency of Ceredigion and Pembroke North. The apparently well-established Liberal Democrat MP Geraint Howells, who had held the seat and its predecessor Cardigan since 1974, was ousted as his vote fell by over 11%. However, he was not overtaken by the Conservatives, who had finished second in 1987, or even by Labour, who had been third. Instead, leaping from fourth place to first, the victor was the Plaid Cymru candidate Cynog Dafis. The Nationalists almost doubled their share of the vote, from

16% to 31%. In 1997, Dafis strengthened his position further, increasing his share to 41%, and securing a majority of nigh on 7,000 votes over Labour, who advanced into second place. Then in 2001 the position changed again, as the Liberal Democrats bounced back up by about 10% to retake second, at least, while Labour dropped a similar amount and into fourth and last. The explanation for this last change is easier than some: it was merely confirming the order established in the by-election held in February 2000, when Cynog Dafis rather nobly gave up his Westminster seat (unlike any of his colleagues in Scotland or Wales) on election to a devolved body in 1999. He was succeeded by Simon Thomas.

This always was one of the strongest Welsh-speaking parts of Celtic rural west Wales. Ceredigion is a district of hill farms and little Welsh-speaking towns like Tregaron and Newcastle Emlyn. It boasts wild moors and one of the largest bogs in Britain. It ranks as the seat with the highest proportion of residents living in Census enumeration districts classified as rural under the MOSAIC categorisation, very nearly 70%. The support of the 'English' parties' is concentrated on the superb holiday coast of Cardigan Bay, and in the university town of Aberystwyth. In the 1997 boundary changes the seat was reduced to the traditional boundaries of Cardiganshire, and the Pembroke North section removed to the new Preseli Pembrokeshire seat. It now looks again as if the battle will be joined between Plaid and the Liberal Democrats, and such is the unpredictable history and nature of the seat that Simon Thomas can never regard it as safe.

Social indices:			2001 Gen. Election:			
% Non-white	1.3		PC	13,241	38.3	−3.4
% Welsh sp	59.1		LD	9,297	26.9	+10.4
% Prof/Man	40.7		C	6,730	19.4	+4.6
% Non-manual	58.9		Lab	5,338	15.4	−8.9
£ Av prop val 2000	74 K		PC maj	3,944	11.4	
% Increase 97–00	31.4		Turnout		61.7	−12.2
% Unemployed 2001	3.1		Elect	56,118		
% Decrease 97–01	1.7					
% Fin hard/Rank	3.5	634				
% Pensioners	30.7					
% Prem mort/Rank	30	340				

Member of Parliament

Simon Thomas retained this seat for Plaid Cymru at the 2000 by-election following the retreat to the Welsh Assembly of the former Plaid MP Cynog Dafis, whose preoccupation with environmentalism he shares. The complete Welsh Nationalist apparatchik, born in 1964 and educated at Aberdare Boys' School and Aberystwyth University, he has worked for the party in some form for at least eight years, latterly writing its election manifesto whilst doubling up as a 'community development officer' stimulating rural development through public-private-voluntary sector partnerships. Wire-rimmed spectacled, slim, with short, dark, retreating hair, he is the first male MP known to have worn studs in his ear. South Wales-accented, he learnt Welsh as a young adult, has a zealous air, and cycles.

CHARNWOOD

Leicestershire was awarded a tenth and extra seat by the Parliamentary Boundary Commission which reported in 1995. It was named after the local government district and ancient forest of Charnwood. By any standards it is a safe Conservative seat. So, a piece of thoroughly good news for the Conservative Party then? Actually, no. They were in fact extremely disappointed with the Commission's work.

How can this apparent paradox be explained? The answer is that the 20,000-plus extra Tory voters must have come from somewhere, and in practice the Tory majorities in no fewer than five other seats in Leicestershire have been reduced. In particular, the newly drawn Loughborough became vulnerable to Labour, who duly gained it in 1997. The Conservatives would prefer Charnwood to be less safe for them. It corrals too many Conservative voters into one seat, rather than spreading them efficiently to safeguard a number of constituencies.

Charnwood took voters from four former Leicestershire seats. About 20,000 voters came from Loughborough's Soar valley in the suburbs immediately north of Leicester, chiefly in Birstall but also in Thurcaston and Mountsorrel. Another 22,000 came from the other bank of the Soar, north-east of Leicester, at Six Hills, East Goscote, Queniborough, Syston and Thurmaston. These were formerly in the Rutland and Melton constituency. Charnwood then curls round through the outside Leicester suburbs, wrapping itself round the city in a kidney shape, taking 15,000 voters from a third seat, Blaby: these are in the communities of Glenfields, Kirby Muxloe and Leicester Forest East, familiar to many for its M1 motorway service station. Finally 14,000 electors were taken from Bosworth, in the almost all-white suburbs of Groby, Ratby and Bradgate wards. The Tory position in all the seats from which territory and population is drawn has been weakened: by about 3,000 votes in Rutland and Melton, 6,000 in Blaby, 5,000 in Bosworth, 2,000 in Harborough (through consequent changes) and, worst of all, by as much as 8,000 in Loughborough – which Labour won by 6,400 in 2001.

Charnwood is a logical creation, however much the Conservatives may dislike it. It consists of middle-class, white, owner-occupied outer suburbs of Leicester, a city which now has 80,000 non-white residents, mainly Asians. This all adds to a recipe for a safely Conservative seat, even in 1997 and 2001.

Social indices:			2001 Gen. Election:			
% Non-white	4.4		C	23,283	48.2	+1.8
% Prof/Man	33.7		Lab	15,544	32.2	–3.8
% Non-manual	56.9		LD	7,835	16.2	+3.4
£ Av prop val 2000	83 K		UKIP	1,603	3.3	
% Increase 97–00	29.8		C maj	7,739	16.0	
% Unemployed 2001	1.4		Turnout		64.5	–12.8
% Decrease 97–01	0.6		Elect	74,836		
% Fin hard/Rank	6.6	572				
% Pensioners	23.6					
% Prem mort/Rank	12	572				

Member of Parliament

Stephen Dorrell moved here from vulnerable Loughborough (a seat he won in 1979) in 1997, after serving in a series of government posts, eventually as Health Secretary. Born in 1952, and Uppingham and Brasenose College, Oxford-educated, he was and is again a director of his family's industrial clothing company. A man whose rise was slow until after Mrs Thatcher's exit, he reached the Cabinet in 1994 as National Heritage Secretary and moved to Health in 1995 as a more voter-friendly face than Virginia Bottomley. A One Nation Europhile, and protégé of Peter Walker, he trimmed in a Eurosceptic direction, but without helping his leadership prospects in 1997, and quit the frontbench in 1998 after a year as Education spokesman. With his career politically stalled and only restorable under an unlikely comeback by Kenneth Clarke, whom he backed after dropping his own leadership bid in 1997, he supported the more viable-seeming Portillo candidacy in 2001 (though returned to back Clarke in the conclusive membership ballot), but unlike a number of Portillo voters did not return to the frontbench under Iain Duncan Smith.

CHATHAM AND AYLESFORD

This is an 'odd coupling' of a seat. Chatham is a tough, working-class town with long connections with the Royal Navy and some Labour-voting wards, while the small town of Aylesford (population 9,000) and the rest of the constituency is of a different hue. These wards are essentially rural, containing large villages and small towns like Larkfield and Snodland, and amount to some 26,000 voters in all. When Chatham and Aylesford was first contested in 1997 most pundits predicted that the Conservatives would win, but that was not to take into account the swing to Labour in Kent and England as a whole that year. Jonathan Shaw increased his party's share of the vote by over 16% (if the notional estimates for 1992 are to be trusted), and defeated the Conservative candidate Richard Knox-Johnston by nearly 3,000 votes.

The same – and other – observers were over-quick to write Shaw off again in 2001. It was a logical call, though. Not only was another crushing Labour victory against all precedent, but it seemed likely that the issue of asylum seekers, legal and otherwise, mixed up with immigration in general, would play particularly strongly against Labour in the county most affected as a first port of entry. It did not, despite the Conservatives' attempts to raise the profile of the issue – yet another cause for post mortems among the defeated party after the campaign. Indeed Jonathan Shaw, like many Labour first-term incumbents seeking re-election, actually increased his lead and his share of the votes cast – by over 5% in fact, a well above-average performance in all respects, except for the 14% drop in turnout. It would be foolish to discount this Labour candidate's chances for a third time.

Social indices:			2001 Gen. Election:				
% Non-white	3.1		Lab	19,180	48.3	+5.2
% Prof/Man	29.1		C	14,840	37.3	−0.1
% Non-manual	56.5		LD	4,705	11.8	−3.2
£ Av prop val 2000	76 K		UKIP	1,010	2.5	+1.5
% Increase 97–00	31.0		Lab maj	4,340	10.9	
% Unemployed 2001	2.3		Turnout		57.0	−14.1
% Decrease 97–01	2.2		Elect	69,759		
% Fin hard/Rank	11.5	425				
% Pensioners	17.7					
% Prem mort/Rank	27	395				

Member of Parliament

Jonathan Shaw, one of Labour's surprise winners in 1997, came with the standard pedigree of local councillor and social worker. Born locally in 1966 and educated at Vintners' Boys' School, Maidstone and at colleges of further education, he has concentrated on local concerns such as radiation from nuclear submarines at Chatham, Tory-controlled Kent County Council's school spending cuts, Channel Tunnel safety, 'filthy and dilapidated commuter trains', and Kent's pressure from asylum seekers. He was one of only 14 new Labour MPs who rebelled on lone parent benefit cuts in 1997 and again in 2000 over air traffic control privatisation, but in March 2001 earned sketch-writers' headlines for a scripted intervention urging Blair to 'save the pounds' of Tory spending cuts. He favours electoral reform which retains the MP's constituency link, with his own activity as a constituency MP doubtless assisting his survival in 2001.

CHEADLE

The closest margin recorded in the 2001 General Election was in Cheadle. At 33 votes, this was not one of the very smallest winning majorities in modern times, certainly not compared with two in Winchester in 1997, which effectively necessitated a re-run after the discovery of irregularities in a handful of ballots; and one has to go back to 1987, when two seats (Mansfield and Brecon/Radnor) shared the smallest lead of 56 votes to find a higher lowest, as it were. Nevertheless it must have felt quite tight enough to those concerned here, especially the victorious Liberal Democrat Patsy Calton, and the defeated Conservative MP, Stephen Day.

Cheadle is the most socially upmarket constituency in Greater Manchester. It has the highest proportion of professional and managerial workers (and not far off the most of these in the whole of the United Kingdom), the highest proportion of owner-occupiers (88%, the second highest anywhere), and clearly the highest proportion of detached housing (37%) of an urban seat in the north of England. Cheadle is a solid suburban bloc in the south-western corner of Stockport borough. It consists of a variety of communities with a distinct pecking order. Bramhall is the most desirable, followed by Cheadle itself with Gatley, Cheadle Hulme and finally by the more modern private housing estates of Heald Green. All distinguish themselves very strongly from the troubled city of Manchester to their north, which nevertheless still provides much of the economic propulsion in the area.

Yet this seat has a very respectable non-Conservative tradition, and is not held by a Tory now. The seat also named Cheadle, but including in addition the territory included in the Hazel Grove division since 1974, was held for the Liberals by Dr Michael Winstanley from 1966 to 1970, when there were far fewer third-party MPs. Winstanley went with Hazel Grove, which was a very hotly contested Conservative marginal until 1997, when it was regained by Andrew Stunell. Now Patsy Calton has recreated the full Liberal heritage in the South Manchester suburbs, strongly based too on local government activity and success, and influenced from a variety of liberalisms ranging from the nineteenth-century Manchester School to the *Guardian* newspaper, which do not necessarily fit well together but proved just enough to edge out Conservatism at its weakest point, perhaps for over a century.

Social indices:			2001 Gen. Election:			
% Non-white	3.1		LD	18,477	42.4	+4.7
% Prof/Man	47.4		C	18,444	42.3	−1.4
% Non-manual	75.3		Lab	6,086	14.0	−1.8
£ Av prop val 2000	117 K		UKIP	599	1.4	
% Increase 97–00	34.6		LD maj	33	0.1	
% Unemployed 2001	1.1		Turnout		63.2	−14.4
% Decrease 97–01	0.8		Elect	69,002		
% Fin hard/Rank	4.7	614				
% Pensioners	24.5					
% Prem mort/Rank	5	625				

Member of Parliament

Patsy Calton, a locally rooted schoolteacher, was elected here in 2001 on her third attempt to capture the seat. Born in 1948 and educated at Wymondham College, Norfolk and University of Manchester Institute of Science and Technology, and a science teacher for 30 years, she has all the accoutrements of the traditional Liberal Democrat MP, including a local Stockport council base, and a propensity to articulate purely local concerns such as the incomplete state of a link road to Manchester Airport, high council tax, inadequate local government and educational grants, and disproportionate spending on refuse disposal – standard issue pavement politics. And of the eight Liberal Democrat MPs with majorities under 1,000 votes, hers is the most perilous at 33 – the Commons' lowest majority.

CHELMSFORD WEST

Rather like God, the Boundary Commission sometimes works in mysterious ways. Until the 1992 Election the whole of the Essex county town of Chelmsford was contained in one seat, but its neighbour Colchester was split in two and each half was diluted with rural territory. Now Colchester has been united as a single urban seat – while Chelmsford borough has been divided, and its eastern section linked for parliamentary purposes with Maldon (formerly tied to Colchester South!).

In fact, the picture is not quite as confusing as it might be. The Maldon and Chelmsford East seat actually only contains villages and suburbs (such as Great

Baddow) associated with Chelmsford. The whole of the centre of the county town is in Chelmsford West. There is quite a lot of extraneous rural territory too, of course, and the affluent suburban village of Writtle, and some 14,000 voters have been picked up around Great Waltham and Roxwell from the Braintree seat, but essentially this is the successor to the old unified Chelmsford.

This long-established town in central Essex is undeniably predominantly middle class and well-off. The unemployment rate is well below average. 'Essex Man' is not known for his left-wing or even liberal views. Yet for some years in the 1970s and 1980s the Conservative hold on Chelmsford was shaky in the extreme. The MP until 1987 was a nationally known figure, Norman St John-Stevas, a suave and civilised aesthete who was sacked from Mrs Thatcher's Cabinet in 1981, two years into the life of her first government. Yet Stevas's majority in 1983 was a mere 378, as the perennial Liberal candidate Stuart Mole gathered over 29,000 votes against him. Chelmsford marked one of the Liberals' strongest challenges anywhere in Britain, and most certainly in Essex.

It was felt that this lack of security was one of the influences which led Norman St John-Stevas to accept a peerage, as Lord St John of Fawsley, and move to 'another place' rather than contest the 1987 Election. However, the Liberals did not inherit Chelmsford; quite the reverse, in fact. The new Tory candidate, Simon Burns, increased the margin to nearly 8,000 in 1987 and enjoyed a further massive swing as the Lib Dem challenge fell apart in 1992. Their share dropped from 40% to 29%, the Labour vote more than doubled, and Burns acquired a majority of over 18,000. In the Tories' disastrous years of 1997 and 2001, Burns's majority dropped to under 7,000, but this was because the Labour share rose twice, and the Liberal Democrats have now slipped clearly into third place.

Chelmsford West remains at least as safe as the old Chelmsford. Perhaps the Essex men and women who make up the electorate here prefer the more conventional character and style of Simon Burns to the flamboyant Stevas; perhaps indeed that they came close to rejecting him several times was a reflection of right-wing, rather than liberal (or Liberal), attitudes.

Social indices:			2001 Gen. Election:			
% Non-white	2.3		C	20,446	42.5	+1.9
% Prof/Man	38.9		Lab	14,185	29.5	+3.1
% Non-manual	66.9		LD	11,197	23.3	−5.9
£ Av prop val 2000	113 K		Grn	837	1.7	+1.0
% Increase 97–00	50.9		UKIP	785	1.6	+1.1
% Unemployed 2001	1.3		LCA	693	1.4	
% Decrease 97–01	1.7		C maj	6,261	13.0	
% Fin hard/Rank	8.4	511	Turnout		61.5	−15.5
% Pensioners	22.0		Elect	78,291		
% Prem mort/Rank	2	634				

Member of Parliament

Simon Burns – a Tory Health spokesman since 2001 and MP here since 1997 – was originally elected for Chelmsford in 1987, a seat he rebuilt into a safe one following its decay into a tight Conservative-Liberal marginal during the incumbency of Norman St John Stevas. A Junior Health Minister under John Major (1996–97), having previously spent two years in the Whips' Office, he was dropped as an Opposition spokesman, on Social Security, then Environment, under William Hague in 1999. Born in 1952 and educated at Stamford School and Worcester College, Oxford, he worked for Sally Oppenheim MP and for the IOD before becoming an MP. His political leanings have wobbled from Thatcherite zealot to a Major loyalist over Maastricht, but he was discreet about his leadership preferences in 1997 and 2001. Tall, with front-combed centrally parted hair, he has sought to stop the run down of the local Marconi factories, and campaigned against football hooligans.

CHELTENHAM

The Liberal Democrat MP for Cheltenham, Nigel Jones, had a busy and over-dramatic term between 1997 and 2001, which included being seriously injured in a sword-wielding attack by a constituent at his surgery in January 2000 in which his agent, Councillor Andrew Pennington, was killed; the assailant's defence lawyer actually stood against Jones in the 2001 General Election, but came last of the eight candidates. However, the results were far from exciting, indeed almost a re-run of 1997 on a 12% lower turnout.

Cheltenham has long been perhaps the largest and most fashionable inland spa in the country. Set in a bowl of hills in the Gloucestershire Cotswolds, it is an artistic, cultural and educational centre – the site of such well-known establishments as Cheltenham College, Cheltenham Ladies' College, Cheltenham Grammar School and Dean Close School. It also has a booming economy. It has increasingly been favoured as a headquarters (re)location for firms moving out of London, such as Eagle Star insurance, with its incongruous town centre tower block. Cheltenham is conveniently sited on the A40 and near the M5 motorway. Another major employer in the town is the government secret communications centre, GCHQ. With its capacity for adapting to modern technology, and the streets of large, elegant houses dating from previous centuries, one would think that Cheltenham would be a Tory stronghold. Yet in fact Cheltenham was one of the four seats that the Conservatives lost to the Liberal Democrats in the April 1992 General Election and now appears safely in Nigel Jones's hands. How has this come to happen?

Many observers would give just one clear explanation. The Conservatives picked as their new candidate in 1992 a black barrister from Birmingham, John Taylor. Cheltenham is less than 2% non-white, and is if anything associated with imperial memories. There may even exist some of the retired colonels from the Raj and elsewhere with whom Cheltenham's image is sometimes (mis)identified. Certainly elements in the local Conservative Party received widespread publicity for opposing John Taylor's selection. Mr Taylor suffered an adverse swing of over 5% to the Liberal Democrats, and Nigel Jones, a local computer consultant, took the seat. Ergo, Cheltenham strikes a blow in the face of anti-racism.

It should be argued, though, that the picture is more complex than this. For a start, Cheltenham has long been at the top end of the list of national Liberal targets. The Liberal Democrats have controlled the borough council for a number of years, including the whole of the 1990s. In many ways Cheltenham has been a Liberal town for decades, and perhaps only the popular and deeply rooted MP from 1974 to 1992, Charles Irving, could have held on as long as the Tories did. Irving had been a member of the council since 1948, and twice Mayor of Cheltenham. Anyone attempting to succeed him on his retirement through ill health would have faced an uphill battle, and a non-local candidate had even less of a chance, whatever his colour. John Taylor, now in the Lords, surfaced again in the controversy over racism in the Conservative Party after the retiring East Yorkshire MP John Townend's remarks in April 2001. Meanwhile Nigel Jones seems set fair for a long career in the lower house.

Social indices:			2001 Gen. Election:			
% Non-white	1.9		LD	19,970	47.7	−1.7
% Prof/Man	37.0		C	14,715	35.2	−1.1
% Non-manual	62.9		Lab	5,041	12.0	+1.9
£ Av prop val 2000	125 K		Grn	735	1.8	
% Increase 97–00	57.2		MRLP	513	1.2	+0.5
% Unemployed 2001	2.6		UKIP	482	1.2	+0.6
% Decrease 97–01	2.1		PA	272	0.7	+0.2
% Fin hard/Rank	14.0	378	Ind	107	0.3	
% Pensioners	28.5		LD maj	5,255	12.6	
% Prem mort/Rank	27	393	Turnout		61.9	−12.1
			Elect	67,563		

Member of Parliament

Bearded former ICL computer consultant **Nigel Jones** won the seat for the Liberal Democrats in 1992 on the back of white resentment of the black Conservative candidate, John Taylor, held it in 1997, and narrowly missed being killed in January 1998 by a crazed samurai sword-wielding constituent, who did however manage to kill a Liberal Democrat councillor during the attack. Son of a farm worker, locally born in 1944 and educated at Prince Henry's Grammar School, Evesham, it took this dreadful incident to bring an uncharismatic MP to national public attention, though he had long been an effective ward heeler in his constituency, especially on the big local issue of union rights at GCHQ. With a life immersed in computers, from his first job at Westminster Bank, he has covered – in his party's mode – a number of spokesman-ships, notably Sport, but since the big influx of younger MPs in 1997 and 2001, has been somewhat eclipsed.

CHESHAM AND AMERSHAM

Even in 2001 the Conservative MP for Chesham and Amersham Cheryl Gillan won a majority of nearly 12,000 over the Liberal Democrats, and took an absolute majority of all votes cast. Chesham and Amersham is composed of pleasant leafy towns and villages set in the Chiltern hills – close enough to London to rank as a desirable commuter base, far enough out to give at least the illusion of pastoral peace. There are some very Conservative communities here: Amersham, Chesham (especially the aptly named Chesham Bois), the Chalfonts, Hazlemere from the district of Wycombe and many secluded villages, including the Quaker settlement of Jordans. On most demographic indicators it is one of the most middle-class seats even in the south-east of England; it has the most detached housing in the region and the lowest proportion of local authority stock. In local government terms Buckinghamshire is the most historically Conservative of all counties, remaining under their overall control even in disastrous years like 1993, before the removal of Milton Keynes to form a unitary authority; and there are no Labour councillors whatsoever on Chiltern district council, easily held by the Tories in 1999. It really is a blueprint for a Tory stronghold.

Social indices:			2001 Gen. Election:			
% Non-white	2.4		C	22,867	50.5	+0.1
% Prof/Man	48.7		LD	10,985	24.3	+0.4
% Non-manual	72.2		Lab	8,497	18.8	−0.9
£ Av prop val 2000	230 K		UKIP	1,367	3.0	+1.8
% Increase 97–00	60.9		Grn	1,114	2.5	
% Unemployed 2001	0.8		PA	453	1.0	
% Decrease 97–01	0.6		C maj	11,882	26.2	
% Fin hard/Rank	4.9	605	Turnout		64.7	−10.7
% Pensioners	23.1		Elect	70,021		
% Prem mort/Rank	0	636				

Member of Parliament

Cheryl Gillan, a Whip from 2001, a jolly hockeysticks but partisan and occasionally petulant spokesman, formerly on Trade, Foreign Affairs and International Development, is one of only 14 Tory women MPs, only six of whom are frontbenchers. Elected in 1992, she was born in 1952, educated at Cheltenham Ladies College and at law college, but worked in accountancy marketing. A Junior Minister at Education and Employment at the end of the Major government (1995–97), she is one of several MPs to have experienced mugging (in 1997), bravely chasing her assailant for several hundred yards in stockinged feet. She has been in and out of the Positive Europe Group and was pressed by her constituency party in 1996 to lobby John Major against his European policy. She voted for William Hague in 1997 and for the raffish Portillo option in 2001 and retained her frontbench status under Iain Duncan Smith, as a rare-for-the-Tories female Whip.

CHESTER, CITY OF

If one were to consult the Parliamentary Boundary Commission's own literature documenting their recommendations for Chester, one would be directed to 'City of Chester' – and then it is somewhat surprising to find that it is designated as a county, not a borough constituency! The City of Chester seat does indeed contain rural areas outside the historic city itself, and it was these that saved it for the Tories, and their 'celebrity' candidate Gyles Brandreth, at the 1992 General Election. They only just won, though, by 1,101 votes, and there was to be no salvation in 1997: Christine Russell defeated Brandreth by over 10,500 on a 78% turnout. By 2001 Brandreth had returned to his other interests, which include guest appearances in Dictionary Corner on Channel 4's weekday afternoon quiz Countdown and his Teddy Bear museum in

Stratford on Avon (which appears in the index of his excellent whip's diary, *Breaking the Code*, between Norman Tebbit and Dame Kiri Te Kanawa). The turnout in Chester went down to 64% and Christine Russell's majority to under 7,000.

Despite the appearance of Chester as a prosperous and historic market centre, which draws tourists to its cathedral, its walls, its zoo and its 'Rows' of elevated arcades of shops, it now for the first time has the status of a semi-safe Labour seat. Labour piles up the votes in wards such as Blacon, the huge council estate in the north-west of the city, in Dee Point and in Sealand, and are competitive in several of the suburbs such as Upton and Hoole. The Liberal Democrats also do fairly well in local elections but are squeezed out by the tight two-party situation in general elections.

Labour did not win Chester in either 1945 or 1966; why are they so strong now? The answer must have much to do with regionality. Although a proud and independent city in its own right, Chester is part of the North West, and it is within the distant orbit of Merseyside, set as it is on the verge of the Wirral. The Conservatives have lost all their seats in Liverpool, where they did hold two even in 1966; in 1992 they lost Wallasey on the Wirral for the first time, and in 1997 and 2001 Wirral South and Wirral West too. Chester is thought by many to be a cut or two above any part of Merseyside, but in fact is not far away, in any real sense.

Social indices:			2001 Gen. Election:			
% Non-white	1.2		Lab	21,760	48.5	−4.5
% Prof/Man	37.1		C	14,866	33.1	−1.1
% Non-manual	62.5		LD	6,589	14.7	+5.2
£ Av prop val 2000	97 K		UKIP	899	2.0	
% Increase 97–00	40.0		Ind	763	1.7	
% Unemployed 2001	2.2		Lab maj	6,894	15.4	
% Decrease 97–01	2.4		Turnout		63.8	−14.7
% Fin hard/Rank	13.7	384	Elect	70,382		
% Pensioners	27.1					
% Prem mort/Rank	31	320				

Member of Parliament

Christine Russell, a former librarian and PA to Labour MEPs, won here for Labour in 1997, so depriving the Commons of the slight but amusingly camp persona of Gyles Brandreth. A farmer's daughter, born in 1945 and educated at Spalding High School and Northwest London Polytechnic, she has been a loyal, unobtrusive, locally focused MP, who tabled a mere eight written questions in her first year. Selected initially from an all-women shortlist, she had to submit to an open selection after the suspension of the practice in 1996, but otherwise owes her rise to 17 years on Chester council.

CHESTERFIELD

One of the most generally unexpected turn-ups of the 2001 General Election was the victory of the Liberal Democrat Paul Holmes in Chesterfield, a constituency famous as the base since 1984 of the Labour left-wing's veteran spiritual leader, Tony Benn, who had declared that he was leaving Westminster after over 50 years in order to continue his political career, deeming the Commons to be sadly and undemocratically bypassed. Indeed, north Derbyshire used to be something of a paradise for socialists in the Labour Party, and Dennis Skinner is still MP for Bolsover, next door to Chesterfield. Benn's selected replacement was an ex left-winger Reg Race, the member for Wood Green (1979–83), but he lost by over 2,500. Whether Labour would have done better with a more centrist, Blairite candidate – or indeed whether Benn himself might have been removed again from the institution he loved – can never be proven.

However, the change of party here should not have come as a complete surprise. Tony Benn had never had a huge majority in Chesterfield, reaching a peak of 8,577 in 1987. Two points should be made. Benn was not to everybody's taste, even in Chesterfield, and the Liberals, having established themselves in second place in 1984, have tactically squeezed the Tory vote subsequently: it fell as low as 8% in 2001. Secondly, the Liberal Democrats have a strong base in local government in the town. In May 1999 they won 19 out of the 47 seats on the borough council, in ex-Labour wards like Brockwell, Holmebrook, New Whittington and Newbold as well as among the historic middle-class Conservative minority in Walton and West on the fringes of the Peak District countryside; in fact they actually obtained more votes than Labour in those council elections. On the same day as the General Election in June 2001 the Lib Dems made two further gains on Derbyshire county council in the electoral divisions within the town, in Moor/St Helen's and North electoral divisions. 'Liberal Democracy' is alive and well in Chesterfield.

Social indices:			2001 Gen. Election:			
% Non-white	1.3		LD	21,249	47.8	+8.3
% Prof/Man	28.1		Lab	18,663	42.0	–8.8
% Non-manual	49.2		C	3,613	8.1	–1.1
£ Av prop val 2000	56 K		SA	437	1.0	
% Increase 97–00	19.8		SLP	295	0.7	
% Unemployed 2001	4.9		Ind	184	0.4	
% Decrease 97–01	1.4		LD maj	2,586	5.8	
% Fin hard/Rank	23.1	223	Turnout		60.7	–10.2
% Pensioners	27.5		Elect	73,252		
% Prem mort/Rank	37	210				

Member of Parliament

Paul Holmes, one of nine schoolteachers amongst the Liberal Democrats' 52 MPs (and one of four in the 14-strong intake of 2001), won the seat from Labour, so blocking the political resurrection of the would-be retread, Reg Race, who was MP for Wood Green from 1979 to 1983, and who duly reacted gracelessly in defeat at the count. Unusually for a Liberal Democrat MP, from a working-class background, he was born in 1957 in Sheffield, the son of a plumber and caretaker, and attended Firth Park School Sheffield and York and Sheffield Universities and taught for 12 years. His concerns about yet more changes to the structure of school examinations, as voiced in his maiden speech, will doubtless be pursued through his membership of the Education Select Committee to which he was appropriately consigned. Less parochially he has opposed the suggested American national missile defence system. Unlike most Liberal Democrat MPs who have won by ousting Conservatives and so rely on a Lib-Lab tactical vote crafted by-election leaflet bar-charts declaring 'Labour cannot win here', Holmes campaigned against this alignment, his bar-charts declaring 'The Conservatives cannot win here' and his election literature targeting the failings of the Labour government and branding Labour's Reg Race a carpet-bagger for trailing his coat all round the country looking for seats until 'eventually coming to Chesterfield'. The famous twisted spire of the town's church is a not inappropriate symbol of the variable geometry of the Liberal Democrats' campaign strategy.

CHICHESTER

West Sussex's Chichester seat runs along the Hampshire border, from the Channel coast at Selsey Bill at its southern end; it seems fitting that the veteran TV astronomer Sir Patrick Moore, who observes the sky at night from his home and observatory at Selsey, is a staunch Conservative. The seat includes the creek territory of Bosham and the Witterings, a millionaires' playground, and passes through the Roman town of Chichester itself on low-lying and easily flooded land up through the beautiful South Downs to the douce little towns of Petworth and Midhurst, petering out at the village of Fernhurst just south of Haslemere (SW Surrey). The aristocratic influence is strong in this attractive neck of the woods – the stately homes include Cowdray Park at Midhurst, Petworth House and the Goodwood House of the Dukes of Richmond and Gordon, famed also for the nearby racecourse.

In 2001 Andrew Tyrie's task of holding on, easy enough in all honesty to start with, was made even more of a piece of cake by divided opposition in 2001, as the Liberal Democrats slipped back by nearly 5% in second place and Labour advanced by almost the same amount in third. This will help next time too, as any anti-Tory tactical voting decision will be made more difficult to assess – who is in the best position to oust Tyrie? The truth might be – no-one. It might be said in jest that Chichester will be in the hands of the Conservative Party until the revolution. But it seems quite probable that even after the revolution the workers' soviet for Chichester would be Tory.

Social indices:			2001 Gen. Election:			
% Non-white	0.9		C	23,320	47.1	+0.7
% Prof/Man	37.7		LD	11,965	24.2	−4.8
% Non-manual	58.3		Lab	10,627	21.5	+4.2
£ Av prop val 2000	160 K		UKIP	2,308	4.7	+3.2
% Increase 97–00	52.3		Grn	1,292	2.6	
% Unemployed 2001	1.2		C maj	11,355	22.9	
% Decrease 97–01	1.1		Turnout		63.7	−11.2
% Fin hard/Rank	7.3	551	Elect	77,703		
% Pensioners	35.1					
% Prem mort/Rank	19	487				

Member of Parliament

Andrew Tyrie, another professional politician as a former special adviser to a string of Conservative ministers including John Major when PM, inherited the seat in 1997. Born in 1957, able, shrewd and patronising, and educated at Felsted School and Trinity College, Oxford, the College of Europe, Bruges, and Wolfson College, Oxford, he came without the orthodox line on Europe, where he is not opposed to monetary union on principle. In 2001 he ran Kenneth Clarke's leadership campaign and – in defeat – was made an offer he was expected to refuse (and did) – of deputy to the right-winger Tim Collins, shadowing the Cabinet Office. Reflecting the fact that politicians say odd things in Opposition (as Lord Hailsham did when attacking an 'elected dictatorship') he favours bi-cameralism made legitimate by election of the Lords, and targets – as a gamekeeper-turned-poacher – Labour's sprawl of special advisers, especially Alistair Campbell. In November 2001 he attacked Tony Blair's 'messianic rhetoric' about a 'new world order' as 'naïve, confused and dangerous'.

CHINGFORD AND WOODFORD GREEN

Although since 1997 the boundaries of the outer north-east London boroughs of Waltham Forest and Redbridge have been crossed to create this newly drawn and named constituency, Chingford is the core of this seat, supplying 48,000 of its 63,000 voters. All of Chingford's wards are Tory, even in generally disastrous local elections like those of May 1998: Chingford Green, Endlebury, Hale End, Hatch Lane, Larkswood and Valley. The Woodford section has a distinguished Conservative pedigree too, going back to the seat of that name which was the last of Winston Churchill's many ports of call in the Commons, which may have started in 1900 in Oldham but which ended in 1964 here. Chingford and Woodford Green is not upper-class territory. The proportions of professional and managerial workers, and adults with higher educational qualifications, are actually lower than the national average. There are far more junior non-manual (lower middle-class) workers than average, though, and critically the seat is heavily owner-occupied and over 90% white.

The MP for Chingford since 1992, and for the renamed seat since 1997, has been Iain Duncan Smith, who has achievements of note as a successful party leadership contender himself, but the seat will also forever be associated with another prominent right-winger, Norman Tebbit, that brusque, articulate partisan who was for many years Mrs Thatcher's iron-knuckled lieutenant, and who earned the image of a leather-jacketed bruiser on satirical TV programmes and a variety of nicknames including that of the 'Chingford Skinhead'.

Social indices:			2001 Gen. Election:			
% Non-white	7.0		C	17,834	48.2	+0.7
% Prof/Man	37.4		Lab	12,347	33.4	−1.2
% Non-manual	67.3		LD	5,739	15.5	+0.0
£ Av prop val 2000	149 K		BNP	1,062	2.9	+0.5
% Increase 97–00	48.0		C maj	5,487	14.8	
% Unemployed 2001	2.4		Turnout		58.5	−12.2
% Decrease 97–01	2.0		Elect	63,252		
% Fin hard/Rank	10.3	460				
% Pensioners	27.7					
% Prem mort/Rank	14	549				

Member of Parliament

Iain Duncan Smith, MP here since 1992 – originally as 'Chingford' – became leader of the Conservative Party in September 2001, after beating Kenneth Clarke by a margin of two to one in a ballot of the party membership. Earlier – in July – he had polled the support of 54 MPs to Clarke's 59 and Portillo's 53 in the final of three ballots of MPs, in the first of which he had had the support of 39 (or 24%) of the 166 Tory MPs. The least experienced Conservative leader since Bonar Law in 1911, he had been an MP for only nine years, never been a minister, and had only held shadow spokesmanships for four years (on Social Security, 1997–99, and Defence, 1999–2001). His personal CV was also slight, educated not at public school and Oxbridge – nor yet at the other extreme, the 'university of life'. He attended HMS Conway, a training ship for merchant seamen, took a course at a language school in Perugia, Italy, and spent one year at Sandhurst, before joining the Scots Guards for six years (serving in Rhodesia and Ulster), then working for seven years with Marconi, briefly at a property company where he was made redundant, and finally at Jane's Military Books. Explaining his surprising victory in 2001 lay in knowing less who he was than who he wasn't. He was not Michael Portillo, mistrusted for his trimming to the centre and for his social libertarianism, nor was he Ken Clarke, mistrusted for his uncompromising Europhilia. What he was, was the son, born in 1954, of a Second World War RAF fighter ace with 19 'kills' to his name, had a recent record of Eurosceptic rebellion (with 11 votes against the Maastricht Bill and 47 abstentions), and was a family man with a decorous, high-born wife (daughter of the fifth Lord Cottesloe), all of great importance to the elderly Conservative membership for whom the War, Germanophobia, and a settled social order had meaning. Leading campaigner for the most right-wing leadership contender, Redwood, in 1997, he was in turn the most right-wing option on offer in 2001, if masked by some 'One Nation' rhetoric. Seen by supporters as 'a decent, middle-ranking, old fashioned 50s human being', to others he was a dull uncharismatic man with the script-dependent debating skills of the average army officer, and with many of his party's most experienced and ambitious figures brooding on the Commons benches behind him. He is his party's first Catholic leader.

CHIPPING BARNET

The north London borough of Barnet lost one of it four seats in the boundary review before the 1997 General Election, but this scarcely affected Chipping Barnet; in fact, if anything it made its boundaries more regular and its composition more logical. In many ways it is now truly not just a, but the, Barnet seat.

Previously this constituency on the very outermost northern fringe of London contained the communities of High Barnet and Chipping Barnet, New Barnet and East Barnet; but a curious salient jutted into it, consisting of the Finchley constituency's ward of Friern Barnet. In the only boundary change to affect the seat, Chipping Barnet was given Friern, thus uniting all the Barnets at last. The rest of the borough bearing Barnet's name is contained in the Hendon and Finchley and Golders Green divisions.

The other communities in Chipping Barnet besides the abundance of Barnets are in the main solidly middle-class expensive residential areas with scarcely any industry: Totteridge with its mansions lining the green and the road, Hadley, Brunswick Park and part of Cockfosters over towards Southgate and the Enfield border, and Arkley, which has a council estate and is usually won by Labour in local elections. In 1997 Sir Sydney Chapman only just held on in the teeth of a 14% swing to Labour. At least he did win though; both the other Tory seats in Barnet were lost. As Chipping Barnet was the second closest Tory-held seat in London, and as opinion polls suggested that the capital would be Labour's best region, many felt that the seat would fall to a renewed assault in 2001. In fact no Conservative seats were lost in London, and Chapman held on with a positive swing of just over 2%. The Tories are still in a parlous state, though, if they must claim this as one of their greater triumphs in a general election.

Social indices:			2001 Gen. Election:			
% Non-white	11.0		C	19,702	46.4	+3.4
% Prof/Man	48.7		Lab	17,001	40.0	−0.9
% Non-manual	75.1		LD	5,753	13.6	+1.2
£ Av prop val 2000	187 K		C maj	2,701	6.4	
% Increase 97–00	56.1		Turnout		60.5	−11.3
% Unemployed 2001	2.2		Elect	70,217		
% Decrease 97–01	1.4					
% Fin hard/Rank	8.2	515				
% Pensioners	25.6					
% Prem mort/Rank	9	608				

Member of Parliament

Fading after 22 years as Reggie Maudling's successor here in 1979 (but earlier – 1970–74 – MP for Birmingham Handsworth), **Sir Sydney Chapman**, a former architect, latterly with parliamentary responsibility for the architecturally-challenged Portcullis House, born in 1935, educated at Rugby and Manchester University, was silenced by long years – up to 1997 – in the Whips' Office. He now emerges as a genial non-partisan figure, keen on tree-planting in the green belt, a liberal minded environmentalist and a Europhile. The third oldest Tory MP, out of time and out of place, he survives as one of the few remaining knights of the shire (or more appropriately, suburbs) now down to single figures with the demise of Conservative governments under which six 'Ks' a year were routinely sprinkled over the backbenches.

CHORLEY

In the 1970s, Chorley was one of a group of Lancashire marginals which tended to swing with the tide at General Elections. It was won by the Conservatives in 1970 and by Labour in 1974. Following boundary changes in 1983, the seat was somewhat more favourable to the Tories, without being finally out of Labour's reach: it was still the sort of seat which Labour had to win to form a national government. They fell just over 4,000 votes short in 1992, when they did of course fail to win the General Election. They were about the same distance behind the Conservatives in Chorley in 1992 as they were across the country as a whole (though the Liberal Democrats were considerably weaker). Assisted by favourable boundary changes, Labour's Lindsay Hoyle, the son of the former Warrington MP Doug Hoyle, ousted the Conservative MP Den Dover by fully 9,870 in 1997 and held it just as comfortably in 2001.

The seat is divided between its more urban and more rural sections. Chorley town is solidly Labour in local elections, most of all in the East and South West wards. The most upper-class residential area in the town is the North West ward. Outside Chorley itself, Euxton, Withnell, Clayton-le-Woods and Whittle-le-Woods are inclined to the Conservatives; Coppull sees a rare Labour-Liberal Democrat battle. Overall, this constituency is now inclined to Labour in an even year; and one wonders when one of those will come along again, given the dominance of Tony Blair's New Labour and the disarray of the Tories in the aftermath of their unprecedented back to back disasters.

Social indices:			2001 Gen. Election:			
% Non-white	1.0		Lab	25,088	52.3	−0.7
% Prof/Man	35.1		C	16,644	34.7	−1.2
% Non-manual	58.0		LD	5,372	11.2	+2.7
£ Av prop val 2000	71 K		UKIP	848	1.8	
% Increase 97–00	28.2		Lab maj	8,444	17.6	
% Unemployed 2001	2.0		Turnout		62.2	−15.3
% Decrease 97–01	1.2		Elect	77,036		
% Fin hard/Rank	14.0	376				
% Pensioners	22.4					
% Prem mort/Rank	23	442				

Member of Parliament

Born into a life of politics as an MP's son, if bearing little physical resemblance to his father Doug (later Lord) Hoyle (MP for Nelson and Colne 1974–79 and Warrington 1981–97), **Lindsay Hoyle** won Chorley for Labour in 1997 and proceeded to act as a local ambassador on job protection in aerospace, textiles and Royal Ordnance and defence of north-western regionalist interests. Chubby-faced and beaky-nosed with a partly poshed-up version of his father's voice, he was born in 1957, educated at

Bolton School and FE college, owned a printing business, and spent 18 years on Chorley Council. His ambivalent name is to be blamed on his father who was of the generation who knew of the Australian cricket captain, Lindsay Hassett. In the wake of Princess Diana's death he called for Heathrow Airport to be named after her. His parliamentary career comprised membership of the Trade and Industry Select Committee from 1998.

CHRISTCHURCH

The fifth largest increase in the Conservative share of the vote between 1997 and 2001 was recorded in the Christchurch division of Dorset. This was nothing to do with tactical voting or regional swing, both of which had featured as stories during that rather flat campaign: indeed Dorset was Labour's best county statistically, not their's. All that was happening was that Christchurch was returning to type after having results distorted for several years by the happenstance of a dramatic by-election.

Christchurch, previously one of the ten safest Conservative seats in Britain, made its mark on electoral history in the by-election on 29 July 1993 in which a Tory majority of 23,000 was turned into a Liberal Democrat victory by over 16,000 votes. The swing was 35%, among the three highest in modern political times. Coming on the heels of another cataclysmic reverse for the government at the Newbury by-election, and also the disastrous county council results on the same day in May 1993, the Christchurch result raised the possibility of the destruction of the long-term Tory hegemony in its heartland of southern England.

The Conservative government was shocked by both the location and the scale of their defeat. How could they lose Christchurch, of all places? This constituency east and north of Bournemouth seemed to be made in heaven for them, as demography went. It was not the constituency with the most pensioners, as some ill-informed reporters wrote; but it was in the national top ten on this score. It was the seat with the highest proportion of detached houses in the United Kingdom, 55% in all. Most of its wards had re-elected Conservative councillors even on the *dies terribilis* of the county council elections that May. The Conservative candidate was no greenhorn but the experienced and able former Kingswood MP, Rob Hayward. Yet the Liberal Democrats' Diana Maddock swept in by a landslide to raise her party's total representation at Westminster to 22. How could this transformation happen?

The fact of an anti-government swing was unsurprising, given the unpopularity of Mr Major's administration at the time; the scale should perhaps be seen in the light of the British electorate's ever-increasing willingness to put aside traditional loyalties in 'unpriced' mid-term elections and opinion polls. Swings get ever larger as more and more voters realise that they can express a protest against their previous favourites without actually putting the government out of office immediately. The Conservative candidate also suffered through a very large degree of tactical voting by anti-government party supporters: Labour was reduced to a paltry total of 1,453 votes in July 1993. Maybe the record size of anti-Conservative swings are more a matter of the 'devaluation of the currency' of mid-term votes; after all, the Conservatives suffered some whopping losses between 1987 and 1992, and managed to reverse them all and win the ensuing General Election.

In 1997 this did not happen again, as the Conservatives failed to regain seats like Newbury and Eastleigh – but they did win Christchurch, as Christopher Chope beat Diana Maddock by 2,000. It was always going to be a hard place for the Lib Dems to retain in a general election. The seat contains the small seaside borough of Christchurch and the owner-occupied, affluent, modern, growing estates of the east Dorset Bournemouth suburbs around Hurn Airport: Verwood, Ferndown, West Moors, St Leonards and St Ives, West Parley. It is scarcely surprising that it has now finally reverted to the status of a safe Tory hold.

Social indices:			2001 Gen. Election:			
% Non-white	0.6		C	27,306	55.1	+8.7
% Prof/Man	37.0		LD	13,762	27.8	−14.8
% Non-manual	62.6		Lab	7,506	15.1	+8.2
£ Av prop val 2000	150 K		UKIP	993	2.0	+0.9
% Increase 97–00	50.3		C maj	13,544	27.3	
% Unemployed 2001	1.3		Turnout		67.4	−11.2
% Decrease 97–01	1.4		Elect	73,503		
% Fin hard/Rank	4.8	609				
% Pensioners	43.5					
% Prem mort/Rank	10	589				

Member of Parliament

Christopher Chope, a judge's son with a down-turned mouth and a Treasury spokesman from 2001, was returned here in 1997 ousting the Liberal by-election winner, Diana Maddock. A hardline Thatcherite, who was a barrister in Peter Rawlinson's chambers, he was born in 1947, and educated at Marlborough and St Andrew's University and helped create the Tories' iconic borough of Wandsworth, where as its leader (1979–83) he pioneered the selling-off of council houses and services, before becoming MP for Southampton Itchen in the Thatcher landslide of 1983. With a stiff boy scout manner and a taste for rottweilers, as Junior Local Government Minister (1986–90) he piloted through compulsory competitive tendering, and the poll tax, whose later abolition he tried to stop in 1991. From 1990 to 1992 he was a Junior Transport Minister. In 1997 he backed Michael Howard as leader but was still brought to the frontbench for two years, as spokesman on the Environment, then Trade and Industry. In 2001 he backed the winner in all the ballots and returned to the frontbench.

CITIES OF LONDON AND WESTMINSTER

It could fairly be said that the very heart of the nation lies in this constituency, the Cities of London and Westminster. Only 5,500 electors live in the square mile of the City of London proper (although it had two MPs until 1950), but it is the hub of the British economic and financial empire. The seat also includes the West End, with its retail shopping centre of the capital, and the meccas of entertainment. Here are most of the tourist 'sights' of London – St Paul's Cathedral and Westminster Abbey, the Tower and Buckingham Place, Piccadilly Circus and Trafalgar Square. Finally, in

Westminster itself can be found the legislative and executive pinnacle of the British constitution – the Houses of Parliament and Whitehall.

It might be thought that few people would live in this pulsating vortex of British affairs. Yet in fact the seat is a populous one, of 72,000 resident voters as well as the millions of commuters and visitors. In 1997 it absorbed three wards from the old Westminster North seat: the mixed and cosmopolitan Bayswater, with its almost Middle Eastern atmosphere along Queensway, the Labour council estate ward of Church Street around Lisson Grove, and the strongly Conservative Lancaster Gate. These additions more or less cancel themselves out, but the seat is safely Conservative anyway.

There have long been some Labour-voting areas here: there is council housing in Millbank and in the post-war tower-block Churchill estate, but these are overwhelmed by some of the most strongly Tory wards in Britain. Here are the super-rich neighbourhoods of Mayfair, Knightsbridge and Belgravia. Areas such as Pimlico and Victoria may appear more mixed on the surface, but the voting patterns of those who are resident, eligible, on the register, and go to the polling stations are solidly Conservative. This last point became particularly topical in June 2001. Only 47% of the voters in the Cities of London and Westminster actually cast votes. This must be counted as evidence that low turnout is not necessarily associated with depressed or squalid areas, and thus as a rejection of democracy through alienation, anomie and apathy. Here it is more correlated with the rapidly changing population and low accuracy of registration found in inner urban areas – rich and poor alike.

Social indices:			2001 Gen. Election:			
% Non-white	17.6		C	15,737	46.3	–0.9
% Prof/Man	49.7		Lab	11,238	33.1	–2.0
% Non-manual	69.8		LD	5,218	15.4	+3.1
£ Av prop val 2000	375 K		Grn	1,318	3.9	
% Increase 97–00	52.4		UKIP	464	1.4	+0.8
% Unemployed 2001	2.9		C maj	4,499	13.2	
% Decrease 97–01	1.5		Turnout		47.2	–10.9
% Fin hard/Rank	20.3	274	Elect	71,935		
% Pensioners	22.0					
% Prem mort/Rank	29	362				

Member of Parliament

Mark Field, elected in 2001 to replace the datedly patrician figure of Peter Brooke, was born in 1964, educated at Reading School, St Edmund Hall, Oxford and Chester College of Law, worked initially as a solicitor, but then set up his own employment agency. A sometime opponent of AIDS-combating charitable trusts as 'little more than gay rights fronts', he helped, as a local councillor, Michael Portillo to secure the Kensington and Chelsea by-election nomination in 1999 in preference to any Europhile (even though he had earlier backed tentative negotiations on entry to the Euro), and voted for Portillo in all three leadership ballots in July 2001. Of half-German parentage, he opposes the 'upset of equilibrium' caused by devolution in the UK, and rejects tight rules on MPs' outside earnings as a disincentive to City high earners becoming MPs on £55,000 a year.

CLEETHORPES

In retrospect, Labour's gain of Cleethorpes in 1997 was unsurprising. It did not achieve national attention, but the result in the constituency of Brigg and Cleethorpes in 1992 was one of the best in the country for Labour. In 1987 they had languished in third place, with under 23% of the vote, well behind the Liberal Alliance who were themselves over 12,000 votes behind the Conservative victor, Michael Brown. Then Labour's candidate Ian Cawsey, research assistant to Elliot Morley, the MP for Scunthorpe (also in South Humberside/North Lincolnshire), surged forward to achieve a share of 35%. This was entirely at the expense of the Liberal Democrats, for they dropped back by no less than 14% while Brown actually slightly increased his share of the vote. In 1997, Labour's new candidate Shona McIsaac was assisted by favourable boundary changes as well as a huge 15% swing from the Conservatives. In 2001 there was a small swing back to the Conservatives, nowhere near enough to change the essential local or national balance of power.

As the change in name implies, the seat has lost the small and Conservative market town of Brigg, together with its surrounding villages, as the new Brigg and Goole division has been created. The seat is now based on the seaside resort of Cleethorpes, which also serves as a favoured residential area for its larger neighbour Grimsby. However, it does contain heavy industry at the deep-sea port of Immingham, whose oil refineries darken the North Sea shore's skyline; and it continues west into Glanford borough to take in Barton upon Humber, at the southern end of the Humber Bridge. The seat curls round Grimsby in a kidney shape, completely surrounding it on the landward side. There are some very Tory Wold villages, but overall Labour must be favourites to retain the seat for a third time.

Social indices:			2001 Gen. Election:			
% Non-white	0.7		Lab	21,032	49.6	−2.0
% Prof/Man	26.5		C	15,412	36.3	+2.9
% Non-manual	48.2		LD	5,080	12.0	+0.6
£ Av prop val 2000	55 K		UKIP	894	2.1	
% Increase 97–00	17.1		Lab maj	5,620	13.2	
% Unemployed 2001	4.0		Turnout		62.0	−11.4
% Decrease 97–01	2.1		Elect	68,392		
% Fin hard/Rank	14.0	377				
% Pensioners	24.8					
% Prem mort/Rank	33	293				

Member of Parliament

Shona McIsaac, a former journalist on women's magazines, and one of the 35 products of all-women shortlists, won here in her first parliamentary contest in 1997 after heavily targeting Tory MP Michael Brown's links with the lobbyist Ian Greer. A staunch Blairite loyalist who pitches stooge questions, she focuses hard on constituency issues. Daughter of a Royal Navy cook and chief petty officer, Scots born in 1960, and educated at military schools, secondary schools in Plymouth, and Durham University, she cut her political teeth with eight years on the right-wing-dominated Tory-controlled Wandsworth Council, takes a class-war line on the House of Lords, and loyally defended closed lists in the Euro elections, claiming that people only voted for the party, not individual candidates, and that she wouldn't even vote for herself without the party label, an unlikely piece of self-abnegation. Her good behaviour led to appointment in 2000 as PPS to Northern Ireland ministers Adam Ingram and then from 2001 to Jane Kennedy.

CLWYD SOUTH

Clwyd South is an extensive, rural seat in North Wales. There are no large towns, and quite a bit of rugged countryside, including the dramatic mountains around Llangollen. At first sight, this would not seem to be ideal terrain to harbour a Labour seat. But this is Wales; the Conservative Party cannot rely on the rural vote here. Two other factors hamper them too. This area has a high proportion of Welsh speakers for Clwyd, about a fifth of the total; and these individuals, often with a nonconformist and Nationalist background, are not usually well disposed to a Conservative Party which is seen as English and elitist. Finally, there is industry here too, in the hinterland around Wrexham which was once dominated by coal-mining and brickmaking, and which is now diversifying: there is a large chemical works at Cefn-mawr, for example.

There are some voters in the villages and hill farms in the picturesque scenery around Llangollen, Corwen and Llanrhaeadr-ym-Mochnant, which is just about in mid Wales. More are to be found, however, in a compact industrial area around Chirk and Ruabon, which includes the Pontcysyllte aqueduct, which is one of the most impressive features of the British canal system (the Shropshire Union canal manages to penetrate through the mountains all the way to Llangollen). This is Labour country. The Plas Madoc ward, for example, near Cefn-mawr still has over 90% of its housing in council hands, a rare figure even for an inner-city area nowadays. Labour won Clwyd South by nearly 9,000 votes in 2001, even though they suffered a typical loss of 7% in share, mainly to Plaid Cymru, in their worst region in Britain that year. There is however no reason why Martyn Jones should not have a secure future here.

Social indices:			2001 Gen. Election:			
% Non-white	0.4		Lab	17,217	51.4	−6.7
% Welsh sp	22.0		C	8,319	24.8	+1.8
% Prof/Man	28.7		PC	3,982	11.9	+5.5
% Non-manual	45.5		LD	3,426	10.2	+0.9
£ Av prop val 2000	61 K		UKIP	552	1.6	
% Increase 97–00	25.7		Lab maj	8,898	26.6	
% Unemployed 2001	2.8		Turnout		62.4	−11.2
% Decrease 97–01	1.3		Elect	53,680		
% Fin hard/Rank	23.2	222				
% Pensioners	27.0					
% Prem mort/Rank	33	280				

Member of Parliament

Labour's **Martyn Jones**, MP here since 1987, and chairman of the Welsh Affairs Select Committee from 1997, is shaggy-haired, bearded and floppy bow-tied, more in the manner of a President of the Royal Academy than of backbench lobby fodder. A one-time Whip (1988–92) and Agriculture spokesman who was tipped off the frontbench in 1995 after voting for Prescott, not Blair, in 1994, he claims – as a former microbiologist in the brewing industry for 18 years – to have identified the cause of BSE in 1990, and offends against political correctness as a Commons opponent of gun control. Born in 1947, the son of an engine driver, educated at Grove Park Grammar School, Wrexham, and a host of polytechnics, he speaks 'schoolboy Welsh' in a seat where one in four claim to speak it properly. This may be more however than Boris Johnson, his Tory opponent in 1997, who – passing through on his way to Henley – knew little more than the Welsh for 'fish and chips'.

CLWYD WEST

The North Wales holiday coast is one of the most Conservative parts of the Principality, not that this is saying much when they have not actually won any seats at all since 1992. The seat of Clwyd North West returned Rod Richards with the largest majority of any of the six Tory MPs elected in Wales in that year. This was the seat which had become nationally known as the constituency of Sir Anthony Meyer, the somewhat eccentric and liberal figure who acted as a 'stalking horse' by opposing Margaret Thatcher for the leadership of the party in autumn 1989. Sir Anthony's action probably helped to precipitate the successful coup against Mrs Thatcher a year later, but he was resoundingly deselected by the loyalists of Clwyd North West, and failed to appear even as an independent candidate in 1992. His activities clearly had little effect on the Conservative vote in Clwyd NW, although Labour advanced at the expense of the Liberal Democrats and almost halved the Tory lead from nearly 12,000 to 6,000.

Then in major boundary changes effected in 1997 Clwyd was awarded an extra seat by the Welsh parliamentary Boundary Commission (they were unable to take account of the local government structural review which recommended the abolition of the county tier in Wales). The new Clwyd West includes the coastal resorts of Colwyn Bay, Abergele, Towyn and Kinmel Bay on the Foryd estuary, together with a large but sparsely populated rural hinterland stretching as far as the Llyn Brenig reservoir and the town of Ruthin.

Most of the voters, however, are situated on the coastal strip, from the elegant sweep of wooded and hilly Colwyn Bay to the flatter caravan and camping resorts further east. This seat, like the old Clwyd NW, contains the most elderly population of any in Wales. If it were in England, there would be little doubt that it would be a safe Conservative seat. The Tories have always done worse in Wales than England, though, and in 2001, as in 1997, they lost in every Welsh constituency. The best that could be said is that at least they only fell 1,115 votes short in Clwyd West – fewer than anywhere else – and should they reappear on the parliamentary map west of the border, it would be one of the first two, along with Monmouth, to fall. The best outlook – but scarcely a triumphant one. It is hypothetical, and as far as we know, could be pie in the sky too.

Social indices:			2001 Gen. Election:			
% Non-white	0.6		Lab	13,426	38.8	+1.7
% Welsh sp	29.3		C	12,311	35.6	+3.1
% Prof/Man	36.6		PC	4,453	12.9	−0.6
% Non-manual	57.8		LD	3,934	11.4	−1.4
£ Av prop val 2000	63 K		UKIP	476	1.4	
% Increase 97–00	20.5		Lab maj	1,115	3.2	
% Unemployed 2001	3.3		Turnout		64.1	−11.2
% Decrease 97–01	1.3		Elect	53,960		
% Fin hard/Rank	8.2	516				
% Pensioners	35.5					
% Prem mort/Rank	30	343				

Member of Parliament

Gareth Thomas (one of a pair of Labour MPs of that name elected in 1997) is a barrister, born in 1954, son of a toolmaker, educated at Rock Ferry High School, Birkenhead, and Aberystwyth University. Loyalist and pro-European, he favours devolution, but like the Eurosceptic MP, Denzil Davies, accepts the reality of Wales's financial dependence on England. That most of his interventions have been focused on local, and more broadly, Welsh affairs, is attributable to his ability as a Welsh speaker, a rare skill among Merseyside Welsh MPs, or indeed any Welsh Labour MPs, and to the linkage between a keenness for European integration and the regionalisation of UK government. As yet another Labour MP for a declining seaside resort, he has also backed local complaints over the incursion of dole tenants, thieves and prostitutes in once respectable, chapel-strewn Colwyn Bay. With a high approval rating, in 2001 he became PPS to Wales Secretary, Paul Murphy.

CLYDEBANK AND MILNGAVIE

Scotland seems to have harboured more bizarrely drawn seats than the rest of the United Kingdom put together. In particular, it specialises in combining very Conservative towns and very Labour towns in the same constituency. Before 1983 all three of the former Dunbartonshire seats were of this nature. Central Dunbartonshire contained Clydebank and Milngavie, an association continued since then with only minor boundary changes.

Clydebank is the epitome of a working-class town which was called into existence by shipbuilding, located down the river from Glasgow towards the Firth of Clyde. It has a large majority of council tenants and working-class residents, and apart from the Old Kilpatrick neighbourhood and one rural ward (Hardgate) has virtually no Tory voters. Milngavie, on the other hand, like its neighbour Bearsden, is one of the most desirable residential areas for Glasgow commuters, about 80% owner-occupied and mainly housing middle-class workers. Traditionally Milngavie was very Conservative, but in recent years the Liberal Democrats have proved extremely competitive in local council politics, and easily took its East Dunbartonshire unitary authority electoral divisions in May 1999.

The Conservatives had another problem too. Milngavie, even with the addition of 3,410 voters in Kilmardinny from the Strathkelvin/Bearsden constituency in the 1997 boundary changes, is much smaller than Clydebank. Labour have held this seat comfortably since 1983, as they did Central Dunbartonshire before. The opposition is very divided. There is a small Conservative core in Milngavie. The SNP advanced into second place in 1997, as in so many Scottish seats. Even the Liberal Democrats may hope that their local activism in part of the constituency offers some chance of a respectable vote. In 2001 the Scottish Socialist Party stood for the first time, perhaps hoping to tap the tradition of radicalism typified by the Upper Clyde Shipbuilders dispute of the 1970s, but they failed to attain the 5% threshold to save their deposit. Labour remained able to beat off opposition directed at them from any angle, except perhaps, from the Scottish Boundary Commission which proposes to split the seat next time, finally separating its disparate halves, as Clydebank goes into Dunbartonshire West and Milngavie heads east to join Bearsden.

Social indices:			2001 Gen. Election:			
% Non-white	1.1		Lab	17,249	53.1	−2.1
% Prof/Man	34.2		SNP	6,525	20.1	−1.1
% Non-manual	60.7		LD	3,909	12.0	+1.6
% Unemployed 2001	5.3		C	3,514	10.8	−1.7
% Decrease 97–01	2.6		SSP	1,294	4.0	
% Fin hard/Rank	41.4	41	Lab maj	10,724	33.0	
% Prem mort/Rank	47	72	Turnout		61.8	−13.2
			Elect	52,534		

Member of Parliament

Tony Worthington was elected in 1987 and by 2001 was one of four English-born Labour MPs in Scottish seats – a distinction which has in the past qualified him for the unwelcome attention of Scotland Watch, an extremist fringe of the Scottish Nationalist movement which targets 'settlers'. (Meanwhile some 20 Scots-born Labour MPs represent English seats without arousing similar interest south of the border.) Tall and grey, he was born in 1941, attended the City School, Lincoln, the LSE and a string of other universities, including Glasgow, before working as a sociology lecturer at Jordanhill Education College in Glasgow, and sitting for long enough – 17 years – on Strathclyde Council to qualify for a seat at Westminster. Having been an Opposition spokesman between 1989 and 1997 in a range of posts covering Scotland, Overseas Aid, Foreign Affairs and Northern Ireland (but with a glitch in 1994 when he was dropped for being AWOL – and temporarily held hostage by rebels – in Somalia) he was given a Junior Ministerial job in Northern Ireland, where after a year's workmanlike service he was dropped in the first reshuffle in 1998. In 1999 he was worthily assigned to the International Development Select Committee where by 2001 he was able to enjoy the company of an assortment of other sacked ministers and never-to-be-ministers.

CLYDESDALE

Jimmy Hood held on here in south Lanarkshire comfortably in his first three elections, enjoying a majority of 14,000 in 1997. However, Clydesdale is not quite the monolithic Labour citadel that so many Strathclyde seats have been, and Hood's Labour majority fell by over 6,000 in 2001. Although the SNP had a disappointing election across Scotland as a whole, dropping from 22% to 20%, they did improve here and closed the gap in a clear second place. They may have benefited from some squeeze on the Conservatives in third place, and from the presence of a left-wing Scottish Socialist, but they also have laid the ground with activity in South Lanarkshire unitary authority elections, for example gaining Douglas division from Labour on a remarkably high turnout of 71% in 1999. In the Scottish Parliament constituency election on the same day the SNP reduced Labour's lead to just under 10%.

Clydesdale is not really part of the central Scottish industrial belt. It does contain an ex-mining area around Lesmahagow, Douglas and Coalburn, which is Labour's strongest area. Carluke is also industrial, as is the Stonehouse/Larkhall section towards Hamilton. But Lanark itself is a county, almost a country town, and the constituency also includes over 100,000 hectares of countryside, including rolling moorland such as that of the Tinto hills. The seat stretches as far as Biggar, a rural SNP stronghold, and passes for many miles alongside the A74 trunk road, entry point to Scotland for so many visitors. Carstairs Junction, where the train lines from the south to Edinburgh and Glasgow diverge, is also in the seat – and was also won by the SNP in the 1999 locals.

The is likely to be split three ways next time, with only a small proportion of its electorate around Biggar following the name 'Clydesdale' to Peebles, with Lanark joining Hamilton East and Strathaven and Lesmahagow linking with East Kilbride.

Social indices:			2001 Gen. Election:			
% Non-white	0.6		Lab	17,822	46.6	−5.9
% Prof/Man	33.4		SNP	10,028	26.2	+4.1
% Non-manual	54.1		C	5,034	13.2	−3.1
% Unemployed 2001	4.0		LD	4,111	10.8	+2.4
% Decrease 97–01	1.5		SSP	974	2.5	
% Fin hard/Rank	29.6	134	UKIP	253	0.7	
% Prem mort/Rank	41	169	Lab maj	7,794	20.4	
			Turnout		59.3	−12.3
			Elect	64,423		

Member of Parliament

Jimmy Hood, elected here in 1987 in succession to Dame Judith Hart, low-slung, barrel-chested and built like a bouncer, is a collector's item as one of only 11 ex-mine workers or NUM-sponsored MPs in a PLP of 412. The son of a miner, born in 1948, and locally schooled at Lesmahagow and Motherwell Technical College (and later day-release at Nottingham University), he worked for 23 years as a mining engineer, mostly on the Nottinghamshire coalfield. This non-Scottish sojourn was used against him in 1987 by his, interestingly enough English-born, SNP opponent. With former links to Arthur Scargill whom he backed against the non-striking Notts miners during the 1984 strike, he was originally with the hard left Campaign Group, voting against the Gulf War in 1990 and the Defence Estimates in 1993, and was a Prescott, not

Blair, voter in 1994. Latterly mellowed as a pro-European Commons chairman he has allowed his Campaign Group membership to lapse, and trodden the path of respectable obscurity as chairman of the Select Committee on European Scrutiny.

COATBRIDGE AND CHRYSTON

Despite the change of name, this is very much the former Monklands West seat, held by Tom Clarke for Labour from 1983 to 1997. Most of the electorate is concentrated within the tough, heavy industrial town of Coatbridge. The local Labour Party completely dominates the political scene in Monklands, but spice has been added in recent years by bitter internal dissension. Monklands is based on two towns, Coatbridge and Airdrie, both of a similar size. Councillors from Airdrie have frequently alleged that power has been hogged by Coatbridge-based Labour politicians, chairing all committees and taking decisions in private caucuses. The apparent discord is made all the more tense by the suggestion that it may be connected with the historic preponderance of Roman Catholics in Coatbridge and of Protestants in Airdrie.

Whatever the internal problems of the Monklands Labour Party, they have no difficulty at all winning Coatbridge and Chryston, a seat with a majority of working-class residents and council tenants. In 2001 Tom Clarke obtained 65% of the vote, and a majority of 15,000 over the SNP, who lagged far behind with under 15%. The Liberal Democrats and Conservatives are exceptionally weak here, but the SSP saved its deposit in 2001, and may in due course advance to third place in Coatbridge and Chryston.

Social indices:			2001 Gen. Election:			
% Non-white	0.6		Lab	19,807	65.3	–3.0
% Prof/Man	26.2		SNP	4,493	14.8	–2.2
% Non-manual	49.4		LD	2,293	7.6	+2.1
% Unemployed 2001	4.9		C	2,171	7.2	–1.4
% Decrease 97–01	2.4		SSP	1,547	5.1	
% Fin hard/Rank	43.6	32	Lab maj	15,314	50.5	
% Prem mort/Rank	53	29	Turnout		58.1	–14.2
			Elect	52,178		

Member of Parliament

Tom Clarke, an MP in this neighbourhood since 1973, when he followed Jimmy Dempsey as MP for Coatbridge and Airdrie, was dropped from the government by Tony Blair after only one year as Film and Tourism Minister, his appointment in 1997 having been required under Labour's rule about appointing to government anyone with an elected place on the Shadow Cabinet. As a minister he published a report on the British film industry. A miner's son, born in 1941, educated at St Mary's (RC) Secondary School, Coatbridge, he worked originally as an office boy and clerk for ten years, and then for the Scottish Film Council, eventually as its director. He resented charges that he had been disloyal to Labour in the tricky Monklands East by-election in 1994 where traditional religious rivalries were mobilised. A moderate (Hattersley-

Smith-Blair) voter in leadership contests, he covered a range of spokesmanships in opposition – Scotland, Aid, Disability, Health. Coatbridge-born and a local councillor for 18 years and provost for eight years parallel with being an MP, he could scarcely be more local.

COLCHESTER

In 1997 Essex produced one of the nation's closest three-way political battles. All three major English parties obtained between 30% and 35% of the vote, and between 15,891 and 17,886 votes. Top of this congested pile was the Liberal Democrat, Bob Russell: a fine performance, especially given that he could not expect to benefit from any tactical voting in such competitive circumstances. Having made the break-through, though, he was the bookies' favourite to hold on in 2001, and indeed he strengthened his grip, winning by over 5,000 as both his rivals lost some share and more votes.

Russell's success story is based on at least three classical Liberal stratagems. His original win undoubtedly owed much to a long tradition of hard work in local politics and elections for Colchester borough council, in which he has been closely involved as a former councillor, leader and mayor. Although they do not control that body, it should be remembered that it contains many rural wards included since 1997 in the safely Conservative Essex North constituency; the core of urban Colchester has chosen Lib Dem councillors for years. Secondly, once elected, he like most other Liberal Democrat incumbents has worked hard, gleaning publicity and recognition for his independent and energetic efforts on the part of constituents and thus himself. Finally, he should now be established enough for the developing electoral statistics to commend him to tactical voters, as Labour supporters tend to vote to keep a Tory out, and vice versa. For all these reasons, Russell is already a hot tip for a third term in this historic town, with its tradition of political battles ever since the British tribes and the Romans contended two millennia ago.

Social indices:			2001 Gen. Election:			
% Non-white	2.9		LD	18,627	42.6	+8.2
% Prof/Man	31.6		C	13,074	29.9	–1.5
% Non-manual	55.8		Lab	10,925	25.0	–5.6
£ Av prop val 2000	86 K		UKIP	631	1.4	
% Increase 97–00	41.4		Ind	479	1.1	
% Unemployed 2001	1.7		LD maj	5,553	12.7	
% Decrease 97–01	2.0		Turnout		55.4	–14.2
% Fin hard/Rank	14.6	359	Elect	78,955		
% Pensioners	22.8					
% Prem mort/Rank	23	440				

Member of Parliament

Bob Russell, Liberal Democrat victor here in 1997, big-spectacled and with a white front-combed pudding basin haircut, somewhat resembles a cross between a scout master and the Milky Bar Kid 40 years on. A primary schoolteacher's son, born in

1946, Colchester localness exudes from every pore. Schooled here at St Helena's Secondary Modern, and at North East Essex Technical College, he has been in turn a local Labour, SDP and – still is – Lib Dem councillor (leading the Council 1987–91), and worked before 1997 for 11 years as press officer at the local Essex University, having started work in 1963 as a reporter on the local paper. He will also recount that Humpty Dumpty was a Royalist gun on Colchester Town wall, knocked out during the Civil War, with none of the King's horses or the King's men able to reassemble it. No Liberal MP since Cyril Smith has been this local. With St Helena the patron saint of Colchester and the person after whom his school was named, he has urged restoration of British citizenship for the inhabitants of the island of St Helena. Otherwise he likes Morris dancing, votes against homosexual sex at 16, wants darts given Olympic status, became a Whip in 1999 and speaks in the House on sport.

COLNE VALLEY

Colne Valley is one of the best known and historic of constituencies, the seat of Victor Grayson and Philip Snowden and Richard Wainwright. Grayson was elected as a socialist MP before the First World War, and enjoyed a meteoric career before physically disappearing in obscure circumstances. Snowden was the first Labour Chancellor of the Exchequer in the 1920s. But Richard Wainwright sat as a Liberal, and for many years Colne Valley was the only true Liberal/Labour marginal in the country. Small wonder that a former Labour MP for Colne Valley, David Clark, was able to write a book about the history of this one seat.

The storyline has been rewritten to tell another interesting tale since 1987. The Conservatives had not figured prominently in the tale of Colne Valley, but they were given a boost by boundary changes in 1983, which brought in three western wards of the town of Huddersfield to supplement the traditional valley communities. When Richard Wainwright retired from his second term as MP in 1987, the Liberals could not defend the seat, and it fell narrowly to the Tories' Graham Riddick. Labour remained competitive, and the 1987 Election in Colne Valley produced one of the closest three-way battles in the country. Few if any managed to predict the 1992 result accurately. To general surprise, Graham Riddick increased his vote substantially, at the expense of the Liberal Democrats' Nigel Priestley. Labour trod water, but by default took second place because of the Lib Dem decline. The upshot was that the Tory majority shot up: to over 7,000.

It should be remembered that for all its Liberal and Labour traditions, this is a prosperous constituency. It has a higher than average proportion of professional and managerial workers. Eight out of ten houses are owner-occupied. Unemployment is low. The old constituency which existed before 1983 is represented by the Colne and Holme valley communities of Holmfirth, Meltham, Golcar, Linthwaite, Slaithwaite and Marsden. This is the country in which the sentimental TV series *Last of the Summer Wine* was set and filmed. The western section of Huddersfield, Lindley and Crosland Moor wards have a strong Conservative element: in its textile industry days Huddersfield generated much wealth, and many of its better-off residents resided in solid gritstone houses on its western hills.

In 1997 Labour enjoyed a nationally average 11% increase in vote share and Kali Mountford gained the seat with a majority of just under 5,000. The Liberal Democrats fell back further in third place, but no party can be written off here: in 2001, in a generally undisturbed pattern, they were the only party to increase their share of vote. When the Labour government becomes unpopular, as eventually even it must, all three will again be in contention in this classic marginal.

Social indices:			2001 Gen. Election:			
% Non-white	5.6		Lab	18,967	40.4	−0.9
% Prof/Man	34.8		C	14,328	30.5	−2.2
% Non-manual	55.9		LD	11,694	24.9	+2.3
£ Av prop val 2000	64 K		Grn	1,081	2.3	+1.4
% Increase 97–00	25.8		UKIP	917	2.0	+1.1
% Unemployed 2001	2.6		Lab maj	4,639	9.9	
% Decrease 97–01	1.3		Turnout		63.3	−13.6
% Fin hard/Rank	16.8	320	Elect	74,192		
% Pensioners	24.8					
% Prem mort/Rank	28	378				

Member of Parliament

Kali Mountford, Labour victor here in 1997, though a loyal backbencher, had a bumpy ride, troubled by illness and upset by her suspension for leaking a Social Security Select Committee report to Chancellor Brown's PPS Don Touhig in 1999. Otherwise she is fairly standard issue: born in 1954, daughter of an engine driver, was educated at Crewe Grammar School for Girls and (as a mature student) Crewe and Alsager College, worked for 20 years as a civil service benefits clerk, was active in the civil servants' union (CPSA), spent four years on Sheffield City Council, was parachuted into the Commons first time out on an all-women shortlist, and is hostile to sexist comments about women MPs. Discharged from the Social Security Select Committee after a year, following her faux pas in 1999, in 2001 she was appointed to the Treasury Select Committee – an acknowledgement of her reliability.

CONGLETON

The Liberal Democrats suffered a second successive disappointment in Congleton constituency in 2001. This south-eastern Cheshire seat had the status of a genuine target about ten years ago. They enjoyed overall control of the borough council, whose boundaries were almost identical with the parliamentary seat. They (and their allies) had consistently polled more votes than any other party in the Cheshire county council elections in this area. Yet in the May 1997 General Election the Conservative Ann Winterton was returned with a majority of over 6,000 and the Liberal Democrats alone saw their share of the vote fall, as Labour nearly caught them after an advance of over 8%, and in 2001 they had one of their ten worst results in Britain, falling back by a further 8%. Nor was this tactical voting in Labour's favour, for Ann Winterton's Tory share went up more than anyone else's.

Congleton, which was only created in 1983, is made up of a number of small towns, along with villages set on the Cheshire plain. Congleton itself, its suburb of Buglawton, and the old salt-mining town of Middlewich, have had strong Labour elements in the past, although the Tories took both Congleton seats in the 2001 county council contests on general election day. Sandbach, Holmes Chapel, Alsager and the villages were traditionally Tory.

The Liberal Democrats could still take 38 of the 48 council seats in May 1999, but their parliamentary performances have been extremely poor over two elections when their number of MPs has risen to 52. One can only assume that here the voters felt that the Liberals might have a good chance of winning at municipal level, but not at Westminster, an increasingly outdated view. Ann Winterton, who shares some of the personal popularity and independence of her husband Nicholas, who sits for the neighbouring seat of Macclesfield, has done very well indeed individually at a dire time for the Conservative Party.

Social indices:			2001 Gen. Election:				
% Non-white	0.7		C	20,872	46.3	+5.1	
% Prof/Man	40.3		Lab	13,738	30.5	+2.9	
% Non-manual	60.6		LD	9,719	21.6	−8.2	
£ Av prop val 2000	90 K		UKIP	754	1.7	+0.2	
% Increase 97–00	30.2		C maj	7,134	15.8		
% Unemployed 2001	1.6		Turnout		62.7	−14.9	
% Decrease 97–01	0.9		Elect	71,941			
% Fin hard/Rank	8.1	522					
% Pensioners	24.1						
% Prem mort/Rank	20	475					

Member of Parliament

Ann Winterton, MP here since 1983, is a hard-right Thatcherite replica of her husband Nick, MP for the next-door seat of Macclesfield. Seen as 'Congleton's crusader for family values' (Hywel Williams), she is a proud and bloody-minded member of the awkward squad; a wholesale Eurosceptic deeply conservative on issues of abortion, embryo research, homosexuality and euthanasia. But, like her husband, she is not a routine free-marketeer, rebelling in a protectionist direction on Sunday trading, defence of the Royal Ordnance factories, and Heseltine's pit closures. Brought surprisingly to the frontbench by William Hague as a spokesman on drugs in 1998, having voted for John Redwood until he dropped out of the leadership race in 1997, her leadership preference was not disclosed in 2001, but she emerged promoted into the Shadow Cabinet as Shadow Minister of Agriculture (having served for ten years on the Agriculture Select Committee up to 1997). She was born in 1941, daughter of a Durham miner-turned-owner of a plant hire firm, was educated at Erdington Grammar School for Girls, Birmingham, and met Nick as his boss's daughter.

CONWY

Hidden by the fact that remarkably few seats underwent changes of hand in 2001, there were many interesting and surprising results. One of these was at Conwy. In 1999, in the first election for the Welsh Assembly, Plaid Cymru had won on these constituency boundaries, not Labour. Surely in a general election two years later when they were looking to make advances (and did in fact improve by over 10% compared with Labour in Wales-wide share: they went up 4.3%, Labour down 6.2%) they might hope to win again, and Labour's Betty Williams was thought to be in trouble. Yet on 7 June the Nationalists came fourth again, and Betty Williams won by over 6,000. It was not even close.

North-west Wales, formerly known as the county of Gwynedd, is often thought of as the most 'Welsh' part of the Principality, and indeed two of its four constituencies are currently held by Plaid Cymru. But not all of west Wales is dominated by Celtic influence. In the south-west, Pembroke behaves more like an English coastal constituency, and was held by the Tories from 1970 to 1992. The north Wales coast too is noted for its caravan parks and its dependence on tourism. Welsh speakers are in a minority in the seat of Conwy, and the 'English' parties still predominate, in general elections anyway. The seat contains the northern half of the old Caernarvonshire: the university town of Bangor, the large holiday resort of Llandudno, the walled and castellated town of Conwy, the smaller seaside resorts of Penmaenmawr and Llanfairfechan, and Bethesda on the way up towards Snowdon.

Perhaps the key to the superficially inexplicable result in 2001 was the collapse of the Liberal Democrat vote following the retirement from the fray of their veteran and persistent candidate, the Reverend Roger Roberts. He must have had a rare non-incumbent personal vote and, now he has moved on, Betty Williams seems to have a safe berth with divided opposition.

Social indices:			2001 Gen. Election:			
% Non-white	1.5		Lab	14,366	41.8	+6.8
% Welsh sp	41.2		C	8,147	23.7	−0.6
% Prof/Man	33.4		LD	5,800	16.9	−14.3
% Non-manual	54.5		PC	5,665	16.5	+9.6
£ Av prop val 2000	65 K		UKIP	388	1.1	
% Increase 97–00	15.7		Lab maj	6,219	18.1	
% Unemployed 2001	4.6		Turnout		62.8	−12.7
% Decrease 97–01	2.9		Elect	54,751		
% Fin hard/Rank	13.6	385				
% Pensioners	33.7					
% Prem mort/Rank	31	316				

Member of Parliament

Labour's **Betty Williams** was elected here to great surprise in 1997 and, after three years of unobtrusive loyalty apart from voting against disability benefit cuts (having a disabled son), she took to resisting more generally, rebelling on restoring the link between pensions and average earnings, exempting policy advice from the Freedom of Information Bill, and opposing air traffic control privatisation, and by the end of the Parliament in 2001 had voted against the government 16 times, so making her the most dissenting (tied with Anne Cryer) of the 65 new Labour women MPs elected in 1997. Such a record served no doubt to deflect the multiple opponents she faced in 2001 – but particularly the Welsh Nationalists who had captured the seat in the 1999 Welsh Assembly elections. She was locally (Bangor) born (1944) and educated at Ysgol Dyffryn Nantlle Secondary School, Penygroes, and Bangor Normal College.

COPELAND

After years of static election results in the Copeland division of Northumberland, a series of changes seems in train. Jack Cunningham's majority fell from 12,000 to under 5,000 in June 2001, and this was not primarily because of the turnout, which was higher than average, but because of a clear movement of support from Labour to Conservative. This is highly likely to be due to the proximity of the most severe outbreak of foot and mouth in Britain that year: although the epidemic made little national impact during the campaign, it was of course responsible for the postponement of the General Election by a month, which many locally felt was a gesture that did not make up for a tardy and ineffective government response to an economic catastrophe in north Cumbria and the western borders. The suspicion that Labour felt they could do without rural support did not help here on the fringe of the Lake District either. Cunningham is likely to retire before the next general election, but the long-term future of his party here is also threatened by proposed boundary changes.

Copeland has long had one of the smallest electorates in England, at around 53,000. After several reviews in which this situation was allowed to pass without successful challenge, in late June 2001 the Commission proposed after an enquiry that Keswick and the heart of Cumbrian lakeland should be transferred from Workington seat. This will not happen in time for the next election, or to pose problems for the former Cabinet minister; but in an even year it is expected to become a marginal in due course. Copeland does already include some of the most spectacular Lake District scenery: the quieter western lakes like Wastwater and Ennerdale Water and England's highest mountain, Scafell Pike. However, mountains and lakes do not have votes, and the majority of the population are concentrated on and near the economically depressed coast, which accounts for the fact that this constituency has been Labour since 1935. The largest town, Whitehaven, is a planned port of the eighteenth century, when it was created by the Lowther family. Haig Colliery, which overlooked Whitehaven harbour, was the last working pit in Cumbria; it was closed in 1986. There are also the former coal-mining towns like Cleator Moor and Egremont, rugged Frizington, and also the remote Millom, which once possessed ironworks, at the south end of the constituency beyond the Black Combe mountain. Like most of the towns of west Cumbria, these communities seem old-fashioned and unchanging. Unemployment has often been rife, and the memory of the 1930s is easily recalled. One stark exception to all this is the nuclear power station at Windscale ('Sellafield'), the first in the world, sitting on the coastal plain in the centre of the division; hypermodern scientific development here offers jobs, while infuriating environmentalists, and frequently placing the seat's Labour MP in an awkward position.

Social indices:			2001 Gen. Election:			
% Non-white	0.4		Lab	17,991	51.8	−6.4
% Prof/Man	26.7		C	13,027	37.5	+8.3
% Non-manual	42.7		LD	3,732	10.7	+1.5
£ Av prop val 2000	50 K		Lab maj	4,964	14.3	
% Increase 97–00	16.4		Turnout		64.9	−11.3
% Unemployed 2001	5.1		Elect	53,526		
% Decrease 97–01	2.4					
% Fin hard/Rank	23.5	221				
% Pensioners	24.1					
% Prem mort/Rank	39	192				

Member of Parliament

Dr Jack Cunningham (the doctorate being in chemistry from Durham University), dropped in 1999 as Cabinet Office Minister, remained in the Commons after 2001 at the age of 62 (born in 1939) three decades on from his first election in 1970. A beneficiary of the regionally important General and Municipal Workers' Union network in which his father was prominent, he became a Junior Minister in the 1970s – in the Callaghan government – after being Callaghan's PPS, and was given the Agriculture Ministry in 1997 where he had to mop up after the BSE crisis. Previously outclassed by Foreign Secretary, Douglas Hurd, when shadowing him in Opposition, known unflatteringly as 'Junket Jack' and (by Brian Sedgemore) as 'Alderman Vanity', he cuts a politically incorrect dash with ecologists for his constituency-linked advocacy of nuclear power (Sellafield) and his former consultancy with chemical industry interests. The somewhat nebulous Cabinet Office job was the end of his ministerial career, as it was of his successor, Mo Mowlam; in 2001 the post went to John Prescott.

CORBY

The county of Northamptonshire demonstrates a very clear example of how Labour managed to organise the location of their votes very efficiently in the 2001 General Election. In their three super-close marginals of Kettering, Northampton South and Wellingborough they increased their share of the vote, as they had to, and held on. In neighbouring Corby, Phil Hope suffered a 6% drop, but this ultimately did not matter: his margin could absorb the blow. This effective targeting shows awareness on the part of strategists and voters alike.

For many years Corby has seemed like a striking anomaly in the East Midland county of Northamptonshire. In the inter-war years the town boomed almost from nothing as steelworks were constructed to exploit the local resources of iron ore. Many workers came down from Scotland, migrating from the grime of Clydeside to rural Northants, not far from the ancient Rockingham Castle. In 2001 there was still a Glasgow Rangers Supporters clubhouse in the town. In 1950 Corby was designated as a government-sponsored New Town, and its population further expanded to its present level of over 50,000. More recently, however, Corby became submerged under the pall of a deep depression as the steelworks suffered decline and closure, and unemployment was running at 27% in 1981. It was said that Corby was in danger of becoming a ghost town.

It was at this moment that Corby was awarded a seat of its own – or more accurately, one named after it. It had been the Labour stronghold in Northamptonshire since the war, and had always kept the Kettering seat, in which it was included, in that party's hands, although by less than 1,500 votes in 1979. When the new Corby seat was first contested in 1983, most observers thought Labour must take it. Yet they did not do so until their national landslide of 1997. In 1983 they were in the depths of their internecine strife and unattractive image. Then in 1987 Mrs Thatcher's government won another overall majority in the Commons of over 100. The victor on each of these occasions was William Powell; but he never won easily, and would have fallen in 1992 had he not managed to restrict the swing to a mere 1.4%, thus clinging on for a third time, by just 342 votes.

There is Conservative territory in the seat, typified by small towns like Irthlingborough, Raunds, Thrapston and Oundle, site of a distinguished public school, and also by village wards like that of Margaret Beaufort, Fineshade and Prebendal, three (or four?) splendid names. This section managed to outvote the eponymous town three times. Corby returned to its more traditional Labour allegiance in 1997, though, and after two decades of marginality, this part of Northamptonshire now looks safely Labour again. No doubt if it should become very close, Labour would put the extra effort in, as they clearly did in its neighbours in 2001.

Social indices:			2001 Gen. Election:			
% Non-white	1.0		Lab/Coop	23,283	49.3	−6.1
% Prof/Man	23.6		C	17,583	37.2	+3.8
% Non-manual	43.7		LD	4,751	10.1	+2.6
£ Av prop val 2000	79 K		UKIP	855	1.8	+0.9
% Increase 97–00	44.2		SLP	750	1.6	
% Unemployed 2001	2.5		L/C maj	5,700	12.1	
% Decrease 97–01	1.1		Turnout		65.3	−12.6
% Fin hard/Rank	24.9	201	Elect	72,304		
% Pensioners	23.1					
% Prem mort/Rank	39	190				

Member of Parliament

Phil Hope, Labour victor here in 1997 at his second attempt, and PPS to Nick Raynsford from 1997 to 2001, is a loyalist bowler of stooge questions. Son of a Metropolitan Police Commander, born in 1955, educated at Wandsworth Comprehensive School and St Luke's College, Exeter, a former teacher, youth policy adviser and community worker, and local town and county councillor, he backs the European Union for its aid to the ex-steel town of Corby. A former tap dancer, he has yet to do so at Prime Minister's Question Time, where, more constructively, in December 2001 he raised with his leader the matter of street lighting in Corby.

CORNWALL NORTH

The Liberal Democrats attained their highest numerical majority in the Cornwall North division in 1997, as Paul Tyler won by 13,933. In 2001 that record was not repeated because of fine personal performances by Edward Davey and Charles Kennedy as well as a small swing to the Conservatives here and a larger turnout drop. Nevertheless victory was still somewhat more comfortable than Tyler's first ever victory, in Bodmin, in February 1974, when he won by just nine votes. Tyler was out of Parliament from October 1974 until he gained North Cornwall from Sir Gerry Neale in 1992. However, North Cornwall, like North Devon, their other gain in the West Country that year, has a tradition of Liberal success, having had prominent and long-serving Liberal MPs well within living memory.

In the case of North Cornwall, this was in the bulky shape of John Pardoe, who was MP from 1966 to 1979. Pardoe stood for the leadership of the party against David Steel in 1976, and undoubtedly ranked as the Liberal No.2 in Parliament for some years before his defeat by the Tory Gerry Neale, who is said to have mobilised the holiday home vote against him. But Neale, later Sir Gerry, himself lasted the same time as Pardoe, 13 years, before succumbing to a 6.5% swing.

The town of Bodmin, standing under its bleak moor (but nevertheless a somewhat unlikely recipient of London overspill population after the Second World War), was an addition to North Cornwall in the boundary changes of 1983, but there has been no redrawing of lines since. Other towns in this thinly populated seat, which relies heavily on tourism and agriculture, are Bude and Stratton, Launceston, and the large (for Cornwall) holiday resort of Newquay (usually the Tories' best area). Here too is Rock, the small resort fashionable among public school teenagers, accused by Tyler of an excess of noise and lack of consideration for others, especially local residents, that is voters.

As well as the period of Pardoe's tenure, the Liberals won North Cornwall at every election between 1929 and 1950. It must now be classed as a Liberal Democrat stronghold, with the Conservatives a distant second. It is one of Labour's weakest seats: they obtained less than one-tenth of the vote even in 1997 and 2001.

Social indices:			2001 Gen. Election:			
% Non-white	0.6		LD	28,082	52.0	−1.1
% Prof/Man	31.2		C	18,250	33.8	+4.3
% Non-manual	49.5		Lab	5,257	9.7	+0.3
£ Av prop val 2000	90 K		UKIP	2,394	4.4	
% Increase 97–00	40.5		LD maj	9,832	18.2	
% Unemployed 2001	2.9		Turnout		63.8	−9.4
% Decrease 97–01	1.9		Elect	84,662		
% Fin hard/Rank	8.7	499				
% Pensioners	30.6					
% Prem mort/Rank	23	449				

Member of Parliament

Paul Tyler, Liberal Democrat Shadow Leader of the House from 2001, but no longer Chief Whip as he had been (1997–2001), won here in 1992 after seven months as MP for Bodmin 18 years before in 1974. Born in 1941, churchy, public school and Oxford (Sherborne and Exeter College) educated, with datedly RP speech, and hair wrapped over a balding pate, he wisely pulled out from the standing-room-only Lib Dem leadership race in 2000 allowing his equally dated-seeming old Etonian colleague David Rendel to take a predictable drubbing. Inevitably in his Party's mode an assiduous constituency MP on fishing, farming and tourism, he can sound Eurosceptic, confronting as he does the contradiction between his party's uncritical Europhile stance nationally and its Eurosceptic electoral support in its south-western heartland. He votes against hunting bans, backing his Liberal Democrat colleague Lembit Opik's 'Middle Way' of licensed hunts.

CORNWALL SOUTH EAST

In 1997 the Conservatives lost their three remaining seats in Cornwall, Falmouth/ Camborne to Labour and St Ives and SE Cornwall to the Liberal Democrats. The latter was the biggest surprise and the best achievement. In 1992 Robert Hicks had resisted the regional swing from his party to the Liberal Democrats to produce a result which was almost a carbon copy of that in 1987, thus generating a majority of over 7,000 – larger than average for a West Country Conservative. Yet this unusually healthy Tory performance came in a seat which has indeed long enjoyed a Liberal tradition now clearly revived as Colin Breed held the Cornish seat nearest to the Devon border easily in 2001.

The main centres of population in the South East Cornwall seat are Fowey and Lostwithiel (both in Restormel District; most of the constituency is in Caradon); Saltash and Torpoint, just over the Tamar from Plymouth; the twin seaside resort ports of East and West Looe; and the inland town of Liskeard. The bijou fishing village of Polperro, now heavily commercialised and grievously crowded in the summer, is also in the division.

One issue which the Conservatives must hope raises its head is that of Europe. In the June 1999 European Parliament elections the Liberal Democrats did very badly within Cornwall. They did not poll the most votes within any Cornish division, and the anti-European 'fringe' parties did exceptionally well. Here, for example, the UK Independence Party received 14% of the votes cast (under the regional PR system). Added to those for the Tories, this made almost exactly half, admittedly on a 31% turnout and in a one-issue election – but also at a time of Conservative slump. One day they may be back in contention in SE Cornwall.

Social indices:			2001 Gen. Election:			
% Non-white	0.4		LD	23,756	45.9	−1.2
% Prof/Man	32.5		C	18,381	35.5	−0.3
% Non-manual	51.8		Lab	6,429	12.4	−0.4
£ Av prop val 2000	80 K		UKIP	1,978	3.8	+1.3
% Increase 97–00	36.6		MK	1,209	2.3	+1.3
% Unemployed 2001	2.3		LD maj	5,375	10.4	
% Decrease 97–01	2.1		Turnout		65.4	−10.3
% Fin hard/Rank	7.7	534	Elect	79,090		
% Pensioners	29.2					
% Prem mort/Rank	16	529				

Member of Parliament

Colin Breed, an uncharismatic, bearded former bank clerk-turned-self-employed small businessman, and Liberal Democrat Agriculture spokesman, won this seat in 1997, aided by the retirement of the moderate Tory MP, Sir Robert Hicks. Born in London in 1947, son of a chef, educated at Torquay Grammar School, he was a Midland Bank employee for 17 years before setting up his own finance and regional distribution businesses. A Methodist lay preacher who votes conservatively on guns, hunting and homosexuality, he represents a seat held (as 'Bodmin') for the Liberals in much of the inter-war period by Isaac Foot, father of Michael. As Agriculture spokesman he was put on the map during the foot-and-mouth crisis in 2001, drawing upon his reserves of sub-Churchillian oratory to claim at one stage that 'we are beginning to see some beginning of the end'. It was interesting also to note that amongst all the Liberal Democrat MPs representing rural seats, actual farmers were in such short supply on the Party's benches as to require this former London-born bank clerk – albeit appropriately surnamed – to carry the pitchfork.

COTSWOLD

Appropriately named, too, for this easternmost seat in Gloucestershire can more than any other parliamentary division truly be described as the heart of the Cotswolds. It includes many of the names most associated with those gentle hills: Bourton-on-the-Water, Chipping Campden, Fairford, Lechlade, Moreton-in-Marsh, Stow-on-the-Wold and Northleach, as well as its largest town, Cirencester, which no longer features in the constituency title. As in many of the most attractive parts of Britain, there is a double reason for Conservatism: simply that the residents have much that is pleasant to conserve (and here we think not just of environmental matters); and also that tourism tends to be a commercial pursuit carried on by private enterprise. This is a rural seat, too, with sheep farming in the more rugged uplands and dairy farmers elsewhere.

The Liberal Democrats do well in local elections, as in so many parts of western England, but seem to be able to run no more than a distant second in parliamentary elections – again, as in so many cases elsewhere. In 2001 they only just edged ahead of Labour in the Cotswold seat, and lagged nearly 12,000 votes behind the Conservatives, as they had in 1997 on a higher turnout. Mr Clifton-Brown has good cause to expect to be able to count on a long run, in this affluent and deeply conservative English heartland.

Social indices:			2001 Gen. Election:			
% Non-white	0.8		C	23,133	50.3	+4.0
% Prof/Man	38.6		LD	11,150	24.2	+1.3
% Non-manual	57.7		Lab	10,383	22.6	−0.1
£ Av prop val 2000	160 K		UKIP	1,315	2.9	
% Increase 97–00	52.1		C maj	11,983	26.1	
% Unemployed 2001	0.9		Turnout		67.5	−8.5
% Decrease 97–01	0.8		Elect	68,154		
% Fin hard/Rank	5.7	590				
% Pensioners	30.4					
% Prem mort/Rank	11	583				

Member of Parliament

A short, square-faced countryman, **Geoffrey Clifton-Brown**, an Agriculture spokesman since 2001 and previously a Whip under Hague, for whom he had voted in 1997, is part of a dying breed, as a scion of the wealthy political squirearchy and a parliamentary dynasty going back to the nineteenth century, which produced seven MPs, including two post-war Speakers, Colonel Douglas Clifton-Brown (1943–51) and his son-in-law, Sir Harry Hylton-Foster, Speaker from 1959 to 1965. He inherited the larger forerunner of this seat – Cirencester and Tewkesbury – from Nicholas Ridley in 1992. A 900-acre Norfolk farmer, born in 1953, one of his party's 14 Etonians in 2001, he attended the Royal Agricultural College, Cirencester, and is linked through his mother to the opulent Vestey meat trading family. More abrasive and partisan than his mild looks suggest, he is a whipper-in for the hunting, shooting and fishing brigade. He is also concerned about world population growth.

COVENTRY NORTH EAST

North East is the safest of the three Labour seats in Coventry, and is the successor to the old Coventry East division that sent Richard Crossman to Parliament from 1945 to 1974. Nevertheless it is not as monolithically constructed as are Labour fortresses in many other British cities. The six wards in NE vary in age and social character, and none of them were overwhelmingly Labour in the city elections of May 2000, a relatively good but not historically outstanding Tory year. Foleshill ward, which contains the massive Courtaulds works and proceeds along the Foleshill Road north of the city centre, is marked by 'inner-city' terraced housing and its residents are over 50% non-white, mainly of Indian origin. It saw a close contest between Asian Labour and Conservative candidates in 2000 – the Tory may have benefited from a distinctively Muslim name, that of the Labour standard bearer being of Indian origin. Henley, on the other hand, is a peripheral ward with Coventry's highest proportion of council housing (35% in 1991). The Liberal Democrats won Upper Stoke in 2000, and the Conservatives Wyken.

However, Coventry NE is united by its parliamentary politics. Bob Ainsworth won over 60% of the vote at the 2001 General Election even though he was opposed for the first time by the socialist former Coventry South East MP, Dave Nellist, expelled in 1991 for his Militant tendency connections and a strong contender in two other

Coventry constituencies since. Nellist saved his deposit again, but the memory of his diligent and sincere constituency service is inevitably fading, and Northth East is safe for Ainsworth. It is a mainly working-class, industrial, Labour stronghold on the unfashionable side of the city, the side to which the wind blows, in contrast to the favoured Conservative sector in the south-west. It is an example of the classic British pattern of social and electoral geography.

Social indices:			2001 Gen. Election:			
% Non-white	17.6		Lab	22,739	61.0	−5.2
% Prof/Man	24.0		C	6,988	18.8	−0.6
% Non-manual	45.1		LD	4,163	11.2	+3.1
£ Av prop val 2000	49 K		SA	2,638	7.1	
% Increase 97–00	29.8		BNP	737	2.0	
% Unemployed 2001	4.8		Lab maj	15,751	42.3	
% Decrease 97–01	2.7		Turnout		50.4	−14.4
% Fin hard/Rank	38.9	58	Elect	73,998		
% Pensioners	24.2					
% Prem mort/Rank	42	138				

Member of Parliament

Bob Ainsworth, a Labour Whip for five years until 2001, comes, as Labour Whips habitually do, from his party's proletarian core, as a former Jaguar sheet metal worker and shop steward. A former deputy leader of Coventry Council, born in 1952, educated at Foxford Comprehensive School, he was elected first here in 1992 as a safe replacement for the hard left Campaign Group rebel, John Hughes. In January 2001 he benefited from the reshuffle after the second going of Peter Mandelson by becoming a Junior Minister at the Department of Environment, Transport and the Regions, and moving again to the Home Office after the election.

COVENTRY NORTH WEST

The 2001 Election did show that individuals do carry personal votes, even in traditionally party-dominated Britain. Note for example the excellent showings by Charles Kennedy in Ross, Skye and Inverness West following his elevation to the Liberal Democrat Party leadership, and of William Hague for much the same reason, even in national defeat; personal votes certainly played a part in the positive results of Andrew Rosindell (Conservative, Romford), Martin Salter (Labour, Reading West) and Edward Davey (Lib Dem, Kingston and Surbiton). On the other hand, the assistance of John Major in Huntingdon, Paddy Ashdown in Yeovil, and Dafydd Wigley in Caernarfon was clearly missed. Shaun Woodward's translation to St Helens South led to a 19% drop in the Labour share there. Yet there were also stories which did not run. Keith Vaz did not suffer unduly in Leicester East for adverse national publicity. Nor did Peter Mandelson in Hartlepool. Nor did Geoffrey Robinson, despite a raft of allegations of financial impropriety, in Coventry North West, which has proved remarkably loyal to him for a quarter of a century.

Coventry was for much of the twentieth century the hub of Britain's motor industry. Many car manufacturers have been based in the motor city, ever since

Daimler and Humber were the first to be founded in 1896. In the inter-war years Coventry's population soared as it attracted migrants from the depressed districts such as south Wales. The city showed considerable resilience in recovering from the wartime devastation it suffered. But then Coventry's automobile industry went into decline. Native car manufacturing seems to be running out of steam in Britain, just as coal-mining, steel and textiles were in the 1930s.

Coventry NW is the home of Jaguar-Daimler cars, who have two large plants in the constituency. Rather appropriately it has been represented for over 25 years by an ex-chief executive of Jaguar, Geoffrey Robinson, who initially did very well to retain the seat in a 1976 by-election at a time of unpopular Labour government and to maintain a reasonably healthy majority ever since, even winning by over 3,000 in 1983. This is a considerable achievement if the social and economic character of Coventry North West is considered. About 85% of the housing is owner-occupied, and Bablake ward contains some of the best residential areas in the city. The percentage of non-white residents is lower than the city-wide average. In many ways NW's economic profile closely resembles that of Birmingham Northfield, another car manufacturing division, with a predominance of affluent, white, skilled workers. Yet Northfield has been a cliff-hanging marginal which was won by the Tories in the three Thatcher elections, while Coventry NW has demonstrated far less volatility, rather a loyalty to Labour, and to Geoffrey Robinson. In 2001 there was a small drop in the Labour share of the vote, but not significantly more than average in Coventry or in Britain. Nor was the fall in turnout exceptionally high. There was, in fact, no evidence at all of special disillusionment with the veteran MP.

Social indices:			2001 Gen. Election:			
% Non-white	8.1		Lab	21,892	51.4	−5.4
% Prof/Man	28.8		C	11,018	25.9	−0.4
% Non-manual	52.4		LD	5,832	13.7	+3.2
£ Av prop val 2000	65 K		Ind	3,159	7.4	
% Increase 97–00	31.9		UKIP	650	1.5	
% Unemployed 2001	3.1		Lab maj	10,874	25.6	
% Decrease 97–01	2.0		Turnout		55.5	−15.6
% Fin hard/Rank	22.9	225	Elect	76,652		
% Pensioners	27.0					
% Prem mort/Rank	36	238				

Member of Parliament

Few Labour MPs have a background in private business (only 33, or 8%, of the 412 MPs elected in 2001), but **Geoffrey Robinson**, the MP here since 1976, is the most conspicuous, and by millions the richest. Born in 1938, the son of a furniture manufacturer and educated at Emanuel School, Wandsworth, Clare College, Cambridge and at Yale, he was initially a Labour Party researcher in the Wilson years before moving into state-sponsored industrial management of a kind fashionable at that time, and leading him to becoming chief executive at Jaguar Cars, before setting up his own technology transfer company, Trans-Tec. Whence, it was assumed, came his millionaire lifestyle of two Lutyens mansions, a flat on Park Lane, a villa in

Tuscany (made available to Tony Blair), and an apartment in Cannes, until it was revealed that he owed much to the benefactions of a Belgian millionairess and a lucrative association with Robert Maxwell. Appointed Paymaster General in 1997 under Gordon Brown, whose private office he had helped fund in Opposition, he suffered a rocky 20 months in office until sacked in December 1998 following revelations that he had made an earlier undisclosed house-buying loan of £373,000 to Peter Mandelson, who by late 1998 as Secretary of State for Trade and Industry, was responsible for investigating various Tory allegations about Robinson. By October 2001, when he was barred from the Commons for three weeks, he had been the subject of four investigations by the Standards and Privileges Committee concerning *inter alia* an undisclosed offshore trust, and his financial links with Robert Maxwell. A mini-Maxwell who, like him, owned a football club (Coventry City) and was a publisher (in his case of the *New Statesman*), Robinson's Trans-Tec company collapsed in 1999. His fall from grace underscored the disadvantages of New Labour's increasing reliance on private finance – in this case that of a self-made millionaire – instead of less risky but now politically unfashionable dependence on trade union paymasters.

COVENTRY SOUTH

In 2001 Labour's Jim Cunningham won Coventry South by a comfortable 8,000 margin. It is true that the wards which make up this seat do include the two most affluent and Conservative in the whole city, Wainbody and Earlsdon. Wainbody includes the elegant avenue of trees and mansions of the A429 Kenilworth Road as it enters the city (and, less elegant, the University of Warwick campus), known as Gibbet Hill. Earlsdon also includes a golf course, parks, gardens, the King Henry VIII school, and lots of two-car owner-occupied middle-class households. This is the south-western sector of the city, here as so often the most desirable residential quarter.

However, these two wards, situated before 1997 in the Conservative-inclined marginal of Coventry South West, and the more Labour-inclined Westwood, are outvoted by the section included in a South East division before Coventry lost one of its four constituencies in that year. These include Binley and Willenhall, with its council estate presence, and the central ward, St Michael's. The city centre is almost entirely situated in St Michael's. The centre was largely destroyed in the war – the best known of the many works of reconstruction is the new cathedral, which was consecrated in 1962, having replaced the one burnt down in 1940. St Michael's also includes the second highest number of non-white residents of any ward in the city. It is a Labour stronghold, and its creation helped to tip the balance and eliminate the Conservative presence in Coventry's 'delegation' to the Commons.

Social indices:			2001 Gen. Election:			
% Non-white	9.4		Lab	20,125	50.2	−0.7
% Prof/Man	34.8		C	11,846	29.5	+0.5
% Non-manual	56.7		LD	5,672	14.1	+4.9
£ Av prop val 2000	76 K		SA	1,475	3.7	−2.8
% Increase 97–00	34.5		Ind	564	1.4	
% Unemployed 2001	4.0		SLP	414	1.0	
% Decrease 97–01	2.2		Lab maj	8,279	20.6	
% Fin hard/Rank	25.8	192	Turnout		55.3	−14.5
% Pensioners	27.2		Elect	72,527		
% Prem mort/Rank	39	189				

Member of Parliament

Dour-looking émigré Scot **Jim Cunningham**, one of Labour's blue-collar worker MPs (who accounted for some 51 of the 412-strong PLP in 2001), is an orthodox trade union loyalist, brought in as a prominent local council leader in 1992 to oust the deselected Militant-linked MP Dave Nellist. Born in 1941, the son of a miner-turned-steelworker, educated at St Columba (RC) High School, Coatbridge, he worked in Coventry as an engineer at Rolls-Royce for 20 years, and was a member, also for 20 years, and eventually leader of Coventry City Council. He has campaigned for airport safety following a local crash in 1995, formerly chaired the Tribune Group, and in November 2001 pitched a terse question at the Prime Minister about getting food aid through to the bombed Afghans.

CRAWLEY

The New Town of Crawley, designated in 1946, formed a red blot on the county landscape to many Sussex residents' minds. With its large London overspill population and predominance of local authority housing, it contrasted sharply with the affluent middle-class norms of Sussex. Its political impact, however, was for over 50 years limited because it did not yet truly have a seat of its own. Before 1983 the town was situated in Horsham constituency, and did not even earn a mention in the title. In that year a seat called Crawley was created, but it still contained some extraneous rural – and Conservative – elements. Then for 1997 the Boundary Commission at last granted the borough of Crawley a seat of its very own, and made it possible for Labour to win their first ever seat in West Sussex.

The five wards which were moved into Horsham constituency in the 1997 boundary changes – Balcombe, Copthorne and Worth, Crawley Down, Slaugham and Turners Hill – are all extremely Conservative and had undoubtedly accounted for more than half of Nicholas Soames's 7,765 majority in 1992. Their removal reduced that lead effectively by about 5,000 and made Crawley very vulnerable to any swing against the Conservative government. The sitting MP Nicholas Soames decamped to a much safer part of Sussex, and Labour's Laura Moffatt cruised home easily by nearly 12,000 votes, with a larger than average increase in vote share. This was reduced by 5,000 in 2001, alarming in some ways: it was mainly due to a very large drop in turnout, from an above average 73% in 1997 when Labour finally seized the seat, to just 55%, well below a dismal enough average. The Labour vote probably suffered from this more than that of their opponents, and Laura Moffatt must be concerned about any further decline, especially if Labour does not win a third landslide victory next time.

There are Tory middle-class residential neighbourhoods in the town itself, especially in the east and south quarters – Furnace Green and Pound Hill, especially Pound Hill North – and the party is competitive in local elections in wards such as Three Bridges and Southgate too. But Labour controls the borough council easily and has strongholds like Langley Green, Ifield, Tilgate, West Green and the newest residential area, Bewbush in the west of the town.

Crawley's growth has slowed down in recent years, and it has become far less of a stereotypical New Town. Its economic base is diverse and traditionally healthy, supporting a lower than average unemployment rate; Gatwick Airport is in the constituency, and provides many jobs. It has also seen a great change in housing tenure as the New Town Development Corporation homes have been sold off; in 1971 the borough had two-thirds of its housing stock in the public sector, in 1981 54%, and in 1991 just 30%. It will be far less now, as we do not need to await the figures from the 2001 Census to know that housing stock has continued to be transferred to other holders than local authorities, a permanent shift. The era of council and New Town authority housing is firmly in the past.

Social indices:			2001 Gen. Election:			
% Non-white	8.0		Lab	19,488	49.3	–5.7
% Prof/Man	28.0		C	12,718	32.2	+0.4
% Non-manual	55.7		LD	5,009	12.7	+4.5
£ Av prop val 2000	113 K		UKIP	1,137	2.9	+2.2
% Increase 97–00	61.9		MRLP	388	1.0	
% Unemployed 2001	1.2		JP	271	0.7	+0.2
% Decrease 97–01	1.3		SLP	260	0.7	
% Fin hard/Rank	15.3	348	SA	251	0.6	
% Pensioners	22.2		Lab maj	6,770	17.1	
% Prem mort/Rank	24	432	Turnout		55.2	–17.9
			Elect	71,626		

Member of Parliament

One of five Sussex Labour MPs elected in 1997, **Laura Moffatt**, a former nurse, was born in 1954 in London, daughter of a toolmaker, brought up in Crawley, and educated at Hazelwick Comprehensive School and Crawley College of Technology. A local councillor for 12 years, she was selected from an all-women shortlist. Detesting 'sexist terminology', she oddly opted in the Commons for assignment to the somewhat macho Defence Select Committee so that subsequently her interests ranged from the NHS to NATO, with some advocacy of equal opportunities in armed forces appointments. Her loyalty was acknowledged by her becoming PPS to the Lord Chancellor in 2001.

CREWE AND NANTWICH

This constituency is one of the most socially and politically divided in the country, and before Labour's landslide win in 1997, since its creation in 1983 it had always been a tightly fought Labour–Conservative marginal. Even the name reveals this. Crewe has always been a working-class island in comfy Cheshire, famed for its railway junction and marshalling yards and its manufacture of Rolls-Royce cars. Nantwich is a picturesque and affluent market town, with a centre typified by half-timbered buildings and antique shops; and the old Nantwich Rural District included many of the expanded villages which house Crewe's middle-class commuters – Willaston, Wistaston, Shavington, and others. Crewe has been the core of a Labour seat ever since the war; Nantwich, on the other hand, gave its name to a seat which always returned Conservatives. Crewe and Nantwich may be physically so close that their suburbs run into each other, yet they are worlds apart economically and electorally.

Gwyneth Dunwoody won the first three contests in Crewe and Nantwich narrowly, including by just 290 votes in 1983. For 1997, though, things were made substantially easier for Labour by boundary changes. The combined effect of these and Labour's unprecedented national strength enabled Dunwoody to win by a handsome margin in 1997 and again in 2001, and Crewe and Nantwich now looks like a safe seat.

Social indices:			2001 Gen. Election:			
% Non-white	1.2		Lab	22,556	54.3	−3.9
% Prof/Man	27.8		C	12,650	30.4	+3.5
% Non-manual	49.7		LD	5,595	13.5	+1.7
£ Av prop val 2000	66 K		UKIP	746	1.8	
% Increase 97–00	26.4		Lab maj	9,906	23.8	
% Unemployed 2001	2.4		Turnout		60.2	−13.5
% Decrease 97–01	1.5		Elect	69,040		
% Fin hard/Rank	16.2	334				
% Pensioners	25.9					
% Prem mort/Rank	29	361				

Member of Parliament

Gwyneth Dunwoody, grim-visaged, squarely-built and as hard-boiled as a 30-minute egg, was elected first here in 1974, after four years as MP for Exeter in the 1960s, when she was a Junior Trade Minister (1967–70). Born in 1930, she was educated at Fulham County Secondary School and Notre Dame Convent. Labour's longest-running woman MP among the 95 elected in 2001, she is decidedly not in tune with the 1997 intake of Blair's Babes, whom she mocks for their whingeing about sexism and Commons crèches, and scorns the ease with which they were dropped into the Commons on all-women shortlists without years of struggle first in hopeless seats. A tough, right-wing, union-backed member of the NEC in the faction-ridden 1980s, she is the daughter of Morgan Phillips, General Secretary of the Labour Party from 1944 to 1962, one of whose last acts was to launch 'Signposts For The Sixties', which promised 'an integrated transport system', for which she, as Transport Select Committee chairman, along with everyone else, was still waiting

40 years on. Confirming that one did not have to be left wing to vote against the Blair government, she was the tenth most rebellious MP in the 1997–2001 House, with 27 dissentient votes. In July 2001 a huge backbench revolt ensured she was not dropped as chairman of the Transport Select Committee, a position from which she had nagged ministers about the collapsing rail system. Nor did she take to the practice of dropping tame political apparatchiks into safe seats occupied by awkward people like herself, vowing 'I'm going to keep going until I'm 110 on sheer bile!' She ran for Speaker in 2000 and polled 170 votes.

CROSBY

One of Labour's best performances anywhere in the country in 1997 came in Crosby, Merseyside. Although they had never won the seat before, Clare Curtis-Tansley (as she then was) increased their share by an enormous 22% to oust the sitting Tory Sir Malcolm Thornton by over 7,000. Previously, apart from the brief interruption caused by the SDP's Shirley Williams after the famous by-election of 1981, Crosby had looked the part of a Tory stronghold. A large proportion of Merseyside's middle class live outside Liverpool and commute to work, either through the tunnels from the Wirral or from the constituency of Crosby, which is north of the city on the way to Southport. It includes the ultra middle-class town of Formby, which has its own 'Millionaire's Row' in the Freshfield neighbourhood, and Crosby itself has a very desirable residential area around Blundellsands and is home to a number of institutions which consider themselves elite: Merchant Taylors' School, Waterloo Rugby Club, Northern Cricket Club, and also the excellent non-league soccer team Marine FC.

It took some time for the effects of the 1991 by-election to wear off, and Labour did not regain even second place until 1992. They were then assisted considerably by boundary changes. Essentially the whole of the middle-class owner-occupied town of Maghull and some smaller communities such as Aintree, and villages on the west Lancashire plain like Ince Blundell, have been moved into a cross-border seat which pairs two metropolitan boroughs: Knowsley North and Sefton East. This removed over 30,000 electors from Crosby. In return the Church ward, which covers Seaforth to the south of Crosby towards the docks, was taken from Bootle. However, although the boundaries of the seat now more closely resemble those pertaining in the 1950s and 1960s, in the past Labour could never get closer than the 3,000-plus by which they lost in 1966; and it took an even bigger landslide for them actually to win Crosby in 1997.

After all this, it would have been reasonable to expect that Labour had peaked in 1997. Not a bit of it. In 2001 Claire Curtis-Thomas (she changed her name after becoming an MP) secured a further 4% increase in her vote share, and Crosby moved up the list of Labour safe seats. This can be put down to a combination of double incumbency and Merseyside regional long-term drift to Labour. It might be said that the memories of Shirley Williams and the SDP are even more distant than those of Conservative Party success here. The Liberal Democrat obtained only 11% here in 2001. However, with all due respect to the subsequent Lib Dem President, New Labour seem hardly a million miles away from Social Democracy themselves.

Social indices:			2001 Gen. Election:			
% Non-white	0.9		Lab	20,327	55.1	+4.1
% Prof/Man	41.1		C	11,974	32.5	−2.3
% Non-manual	71.8		LD	4,084	11.1	−0.4
£ Av prop val 2000	88 K		SLP	481	1.3	
% Increase 97–00	23.8		Lab maj	8,353	22.7	
% Unemployed 2001	3.5		Turnout		64.3	−12.9
% Decrease 97–01	2.6		Elect	57,375		
% Fin hard/Rank	9.0	490				
% Pensioners	27.7					
% Prem mort/Rank	30	331				

Member of Parliament

Very tall, Welsh-accented **Clare Curtis-Thomas**, a 'Blair's Babe' elected in 1997, quickly took six months off to bond with her own newborn babe. Elected originally as Clare Curtis-Tansley, she adopted her present name after her election, the various options being derived from her mother (Curtis) and two of her former husbands (Tansley and Thomas), but not her current husband whose name is 'Lewis'. Otherwise she is a rather rare Welsh-born (1958) female chartered mechanical engineer, educated at Mynyddbach Comprehensive School for Girls and Cardiff and Aston Universities, who doesn't rebel, claiming to be 'in the Centre, extremely rational and reasonable', though her name was originally on a Millbank blacklist of potentially disruptive unknown new MPs in 1997. The only trouble she appears to have been in was her initial absence as a nursing mother – which was disliked by the Whips.

CROYDON CENTRAL

Croydon is not just a major commuting base for the centre of London. It is also in its own right the commercial and shopping metropolis of outer south London, attracting daily its own influx of workers. It has an impressive cluster of skyscrapers at its heart, the district the Americans would call 'downtown'. It also has its own electoral anatomy, its own Labour council estates and Tory leafy suburbs, its own 'inner city' and periphery.

Croydon is the most populous borough in Greater London, with over 300,000 inhabitants. Nevertheless, it had to lose one of its four constituencies in time for the 1997 General Election. This means that the Croydon Central seat had to be expanded considerably. Logically enough, Central does include the 'downtown' area, but it spreads far and wide to the very edges of the borough and of London itself to include the giant New Addington council estate. New Addington, built in open fields in the 1950s, houses over 20,000 people and forms the main source of Labour support in the seat. It has historically been outvoted more often than not by the Conservative wards located between it and the centre of Croydon: Fairfield, Heathfield and Spring Park. This is middle-class, owner-occupied, suburban territory, not too dissimilar in nature from neighbouring outer London areas such as the borough of Bromley. In time for 1997, no fewer than 37,000 voters arrived in five wards from Croydon North East, which was abolished, bringing the total electorate to nearly 80,000, one of the largest anywhere in the United Kingdom.

Both sitting MPs, Sir Paul Beresford and David Congdon, had a claim on the new, big, Central. The local party opted for Congdon, but he ended up with the short straw. Beresford had to migrate to the super-safe Surrey seat of Mole Valley, where he duly won and which he still represents. Congdon suffered a swing of over 15% to Labour, and managed to lose Croydon Central to Labour's Geraint Davies. In 2001 Congdon came back for more, and was beaten again, by a similar 4,000 majority. It is still the sort of seat that the Tories would expect to win, and are likely to do so when (if?) they recover from their slough of despond.

Social indices:			2001 Gen. Election:			
% Non-white	12.7		Lab	21,643	47.2	+1.6
% Prof/Man	37.4		C	17,659	38.5	–0.1
% Non-manual	67.1		LD	5,156	11.2	+0.4
£ Av prop val 2000	116 K		UKIP	545	1.2	+0.7
% Increase 97–00	48.7		BNP	449	1.0	
% Unemployed 2001	3.4		MRLP	408	0.9	
% Decrease 97–01	2.5		Lab maj	3,984	8.7	
% Fin hard/Rank	18.4	298	Turnout		59.1	–10.5
% Pensioners	22.3		Elect	77,567		
% Prem mort/Rank	25	419				

Member of Parliament

Geraint Davies, son of a Welsh Office civil servant, born in 1960, educated at Llanishen Comprehensive School, Cardiff and Jesus College, Oxford, won the seat in 1997, after 11 years on Croydon Council, latterly as leader. He is an orthodox loyalist defender of the government's economic policy, with an earlier private sector background as a marketing manager with Colgate Palmolive and Unilever, before running his own 'green' travel company, Pure Crete. One of the small minority of 33 Labour MPs with private sector business experience, he was put on the Public Accounts Committee in 1997 and remained there after 2001.

CROYDON NORTH

Croydon North now looks like a very safe Labour seat. In 2001 Malcolm Wicks received three times as many preferences as his Conservative opponent, and was swept back to Westminster with a majority of over 18,000 – and this in a seat which he had gained as recently as nine years before. Clearly the bulk of the 20% increase in the Labour vote between 1992 and 2001 was due to the national swing to Tony Blair's party, which reached its peak in Outer London borough constituencies. However, Wicks has also been assisted by boundary redrawing, and social change. Around 30% of the residents of the constituency are black or Asian, these ethnic groups being approximately equal in number. Labour's strength in the seat is at its greatest in inner Croydon, in old terraces and newer council housing and in the gritty Thornton Heath, which looks more like inner than outer London. The Conservatives hope to fight back further north, in suburban Norbury and on the leafy slopes of Beulah Hill, but it now looks as if this seat has passed out of their range.

It is hard to believe that the Liberals actually won Croydon NW in a by-election as recently as 1981. This was at the height of the first flush of enthusiasm for the Alliance, and it was a short-lived peak. The by-election victor, Bill Pitt, was beaten in 1983 and by 2001 the Liberal Democrat share had slipped to a measly 10%.

Social indices:			2001 Gen. Election:			
% Non-white	30.9		Lab	26,610	63.5	+1.4
% Prof/Man	33.4		C	9,752	23.3	−3.9
% Non-manual	63.8		LD	4,375	10.4	+2.7
£ Av prop val 2000	107 K		UKIP	606	1.4	+0.7
% Increase 97–00	63.1		SA	539	1.3	
% Unemployed 2001	4.7		Lab maj	16,858	40.3	
% Decrease 97–01	3.4		Turnout		54.7	−13.5
% Fin hard/Rank	19.3	285	Elect	76,600		
% Pensioners	20.6					
% Prem mort/Rank	34	270				

Member of Parliament

Malcolm Wicks, a Work and Pensions Minister from 2001, and an Education Minister 1999–2000, is a former family policy specialist who delayed his arrival in government by saying for too long that benefits were a right of citizenship and not solely for the poor. Elected here in 1997, and for Croydon North West in 1992, and popular with women for his strong defence of the Child Support Agency, if not with the Serbs whose every action in the Balkans he excoriated, he was born in 1947, educated at Elizabeth College, Guernsey (fee paying), North West London Polytechnic, the LSE and York University. After academic posts he ran the Family Policy Studies Centre for nine years. As an Education minister his sardonic acceptance, in his party's populist way, that apprenticeship courses for 16 year olds may not lead straight to the Cambridge footlights, and his dubbing Oxford's selection procedures – in the wake of Gordon Brown's assault on them in 2000 – 'a scandal', served to confirm that a key element in the electoral success of Labour is the collapse of deference.

CROYDON SOUTH

Croydon South is one of the most middle-class seats in the country, with over three-quarters of residents in non-manual jobs. This largely determines its political preferences too. It is possible for a very socially upmarket constituency to be other than a safe Tory seat: examples would include Hampstead and Highgate, Richmond Park and Sheffield Hallam. But these have a very high proportion of adults with higher educational qualifications (to be blunt, intellectuals). Croydon South does not. Its neighbourhoods are solidly bourgeois, and proud of it. Their names are bywords for comfortable suburbia: Purley, Coulsdon, Sanderstead, and Selsdon, site of the famous hotel where Edward Heath's Conservatives held a conference that marked a right-wing turn in economic policy which coined the phrase 'Selsdon Man'.

This South has always been one of the safest Tory seats in the capital. It should not be confused with the seat of the same name which David Winnick won once for Labour, by 81 votes, in 1966. That constituency included central Croydon and the huge New Addington council estate. In 1974 large parts of the former East Surrey were renamed as an entirely new Croydon South. Even in 1997 South was won by Richard Ottaway for the Conservatives with a five-figure majority. Labour advanced into second place, but their vote share increased by little more than half as much as it did in their successful campaigns in the other two seats in Croydon. Their percentage share went up again in 2001, partly due perhaps to a 54% increase in house values in four years, but Ottaway remains utterly safe.

Social indices:			2001 Gen. Election:			
% Non-white	8.2		C	22,169	49.2	+1.9
% Prof/Man	46.7		Lab	13,472	29.9	+4.6
% Non-manual	75.1		LD	8,226	18.3	–2.9
£ Av prop val 2000	166 K		UKIP	998	2.2	+1.6
% Increase 97–00	54.2		Ind	195	0.4	+0.3
% Unemployed 2001	1.5		C maj	8,697	19.3	
% Decrease 97–01	1.3		Turnout		61.4	–12.1
% Fin hard/Rank	6.0	582	Elect	73,402		
% Pensioners	23.3					
% Prem mort/Rank	9	605				

Member of Parliament

Richard Ottaway, a slight, compact and puckish solicitor and former oil trader, was elected here in 1992, after four years at Nottingham North from 1983 to 1987. A government Whip form 1995 to 1997, in Opposition after 1997 he served as a Local Government, Defence and Treasury spokesman. He was earlier PPS to Michael Heseltine and voted for Ken Clarke in 1997, credentials unlikely to endear him to most of his current colleagues. Born in 1945, son of a Bristol academic, he attended Backwell Secondary Modern School and RNC Dartmouth and, after serving in the Navy for nine years, studied law at Bristol University. He led for the Tories on London government after 1997, accepting a mayor but not an assembly. He campaigns on abortion and world population control, but is quiet on Europe because he comes from the Positive Europe Group. He returned to the backbenches on the election of Iain Duncan Smith.

CUMBERNAULD AND KILSYTH

The New Town of Cumbernauld is set on a windy hill 15 miles north-east of Glasgow. To outsiders it is probably best known as the setting for Bill Forsyth's film Gregory's Girl. For parliamentary purposes it is linked with the smaller, older town of Kilsyth on the northern bank of the river Kelvin. This arrangement remained completely untouched in the round of boundary changes which came into force in 1997, but for 2005 or 2006 the Commission has suggested the addition of 18,000 electors and a name-and-a-half: Kirkintilloch East.

The reason why no further redrawing was needed after major changes in 1983 is that the population of the New Town has long since levelled off, and since 1981 only one ward (Balloch, Ravenswood and Seafar North) has grown. There has been one major statistical change, though, occasioned by the sale of the Development Corporation housing stock. In 1981 over 70% of all homes were local-authority owned, and only 28% were owner-occupied. By 1991 the proportion of owner-occupiers had more than doubled, to 57%, and only 39% were in council hands. This is one of the most dramatic examples of the spread of the 'property-owning democracy' anywhere in Britain.

There have been no significant electoral consequences, though. Cumbernauld and Kilsyth has remained a safe Labour seat. It is true that the SNP have been competitive in local elections in the New Town (but not Kilsyth) wards; but Labour won most of the contests here for the new North Lanarkshire unitary authority in 1995 and 1999, and the first Scottish Parliament contest in 1999. The Conservatives obtained less than 5% of the vote in Cumbernauld and Kilsyth in the 2001 Election and thus lost one of their only two forfeited deposits in Britain (Rhondda was the other; they also lost their three in Northern Ireland). The Liberal Democrats surged past them to finish fourth with 6.5%, an improvement on 1997's 3.8%.

Social indices:			2001 Gen. Election:			
% Non-white	1.2		Lab	16,144	54.4	−4.3
% Prof/Man	27.2		SNP	8,624	29.0	+1.2
% Non-manual	54.3		LD	1,934	6.5	+2.7
% Unemployed 2001	3.5		C	1,460	4.9	−1.9
% Decrease 97–01	1.7		SSP	1,287	4.3	+3.4
% Fin hard/Rank	38.4	62	Ind	250	0.8	
% Prem mort/Rank	43	125	Lab maj	7,520	25.3	
			Turnout		59.7	−15.3
			Elect	49,739		

Member of Parliament

Rose(mary) McKenna won here in 1997, having been a local councillor for 13 years, and part of Labour's Scottish quangocracy as a member of the Cumbernauld Development Corporation and of Scottish Enterprise. A Blairite moderniser in a Scottish Labour Party stuffed with Old Labour, she helped screen Labour's candidates for the Scottish Parliament and so helped create the Denis Canavan problem and a nearly-lost by-election at Falkirk, though another blocked Holyrood aspirant, Mark Lazarowicz, resurfaced alongside her in the PLP in 2001. A keen advocate of a devolved Parliament and of gender balance within it, she also backs 'welfare to work' from experience of her own impoverished childhood. Born in 1941, daughter of a pub-worker, educated at St Augustine's (RC) Comprehensive School and Notre Dame College of Education, she was a primary school teacher for 20 years, after seven years as a secretary, and is one of Blair's Scottish pit props. She was a PPS to Foreign Office ministers 1999–2001.

CUNNINGHAME NORTH

The Conservatives finished third in Cunninghame North in 2001, and it is hard to believe that when it was created 18 years before they had held the seat. It was based on the old North Ayrshire and Bute, which had been held safely by the Tories' John Corrie, and before him the writer, adventurer and explorer Sir Fitzroy Maclean. In the 1983 boundary changes Bute was transferred to join Argyll, but there are still islands in Cunninghame North – the large Arran and the small Cumbraes in the Firth of Clyde. These, together with the seaside resort of Largs, formed the Conservative strongholds in the division. But Labour could rely on the working-class coastal towns of Saltcoats and Ardrossan, and on the old mining district of the Garnock valley inland, centred on Beith, Dalry and Kilbirnie.

In 1987 Brian Wilson had gained Cunninghame North fairly easily, with a majority of well over 4,000. As in many Scottish seats, the Conservatives made a slight recovery in 1992, reducing Wilson's majority to less than 3,000, despite any incumbency effect that he might have built up. This was probably due to the realisation that Labour might actually form a national government that year, as well as somewhat greater favour being shown to John Major than Margaret Thatcher, whom many regarded as anti-Scottish. In 1997 though, as is well known, the Tories lost all their remaining seats in Scotland, and had to start at the very bottom by trying to regain some of those. In 2001 the SNP overtook them to finish second to Wilson. Conservative victory here is now not only a distant memory but a very remote possibility for the not-too-near future, although they will not be hurt by the re-drawing of the seat as Ayrshire North and Arran proposed by the Boundary Commission in 2002.

Social indices:			2001 Gen. Election:			
% Non-white	0.4		Lab	15,571	46.0	−4.2
% Prof/Man	35.1		SNP	7,173	21.2	+2.8
% Non-manual	54.8		C	6,666	19.7	−3.7
% Unemployed 2001	5.8		LD	3,060	9.0	+3.5
% Decrease 97–01	1.3		SSP	964	2.9	
% Fin hard/Rank	29.5	139	SLP	382	1.1	−0.1
% Prem mort/Rank	47	68	Lab maj	8,398	24.8	
			Turnout		61.5	−12.6
			Elect	54,993		

Member of Parliament

Former journalist **Brian Wilson**, MP here since 1987, born in 1948, educated at Dunoon Grammar School and Dundee University, is an anti-devolutionist and abrasive hammer of the SNP, factors which have blocked his advance into the Cabinet as Scottish Secretary. A perennial Minister of State, sequentially in the Scottish Office (1997–98), the DTI (1998–99), Scotland again (1999–2001), the Foreign Office (2001) and, after the election, the DTI again, with his political rise originally based on a romantic assault on Scottish lairds, his name in opposition was made on rail privatisation, where he displayed an off-message keenness for renationalisation. His unionist hostility to devolution, which derives from his conflation of Scottish nationalism with racism, led him to describe BBC TV's *Newsnight* Scottish opt-out as 'drivel' and a 'Mickey Mouse operation', a slur unlikely to endear him to the hugely pro-devolution Scottish media pack. The parent of a Downs syndrome child, he finds it 'grotesque that 95% of Downs children are eliminated as a result of amniocentesis'.

CUNNINGHAME SOUTH

Irvine in Ayrshire is the only one of Scotland's five New Towns to be sited on the coast; and indeed the only New Town in Britain next to the sea. It was scheduled to have an ultimate population of 100,000, but the only growth between 1981 and 1991 was recorded in the Girdle Toll ward, and Irvine still has fewer than 30,000 residents. Thus this parliamentary constituency is still very recognisable as the successor to the old Ayrshire Central, held safely by Labour since 1959, although the current seat is likely to give way to an Irvine, Troon and Prestwick division next time.

Besides Irvine, the Cunninghame South constituency contains the working-class towns of Stevenston and Kilwinning on the river Garnock. Labour wins almost all of the wards here in local district elections, even ousting Irvine Townhead's 'Moderate' in 1995 after two successive victories for moderation in that ward.

Since then little has stood in the way of Labour's sitting MP Brian Donohoe: not the SNP (down 6% over the last two elections); nor the Tories (down 7%); not the Liberal Democrats (lost deposit in 1997); nor Socialist Labour (fewer than 400 votes in 2001) or the Scottish Socialists (just over 1,200). No one has stood for Parliament as a Moderate. Perhaps New Labour and Tony Blair have cornered that particular market.

Social indices:			2001 Gen. Election:			
% Non-white	0.6		Lab	16,424	58.6	−4.1
% Prof/Man	25.0		SNP	5,194	18.5	−2.2
% Non-manual	43.4		C	2,682	9.6	−0.5
% Unemployed 2001	8.0		LD	2,094	7.5	+3.0
% Decrease 97–01	1.0		SSP	1,233	4.4	
% Fin hard/Rank	45.8	26	SLP	382	1.4	−0.0
% Prem mort/Rank	50	48	Lab maj	11,230	40.1	
			Turnout		56.0	−15.5
			Elect	49,982		

Member of Parliament

Labour MP **Brian Donohoe**'s fame-for-15-minutes, or rather as he puts it 'a minister of state for eight seconds', came in May 1997 when Tony Blair phoned to offer him a job as an Agriculture Minister before he realised he wasn't talking to Lord (Bernard) Donoughue. A former shipbuilding engineer and draughtsman and NALGO official, first elected here in 1992, he was born in 1948, educated at Irvine Royal Academy and Kilmarnock Technical College. A Transport Select Committee member since 1997, he has called for Scottish railways to be under the Scottish Parliament and for rail part-renationalisation.

CYNON VALLEY

Although they are still losing population, and although their electorates are much smaller than the average in the United Kingdom, the Boundary Commission left all the South Wales mining seats untouched in the 1997 redistribution, and there is no plan for Welsh seats to be reduced to a similar average size to those in England, as they already are in Northern Ireland and are scheduled to be in Scotland. The smallest of all the valley divisions is Cynon Valley, with just 48,500 voters. The reasons why this continued over-representation has been tolerated are that Wales as a whole is guaranteed at least 35 seats by Act of Parliament (in fact it has now been given 40) so its seats are on average considerably smaller than those in England or Northern Ireland; and that the topographical difficulties caused by the hills and valleys have made it hard to make minor adjustments to equalise electorates without greatly disturbing established local ties. Thus the electors of Cynon Valley have a vote which goes further towards electing a member of the Commons than most. The fact that Wales now has a devolved assembly is not regarded as sufficient to change the law, although the inauguration of the Scottish Parliament has. Perhaps this is an admission that Wales has not been deemed worthy of more than very limited self-government.

Cynon Valley is indeed a tight-knit and long-established unit. It is one of the most famous of the South Wales ex-mining valleys, set between Merthyr Tydfil and the Rhondda at the heart of the old coalfield. The seat used to be named after the main community, Aberdare, but since 1983 has taken the name of the local authority borough with which it has been coterminous. The communities along the 11-mile valley from Abercynon up through Mountain Ash, Aberaman, Aberdare, to the heads-of-the-valleys road at Hirwaun are all bedrock Labour territory. The percentage of Welsh speakers gradually rises the further up the valley one progresses, but it is always a small minority. Plaid Cymru are the opposition on the local council, with a respectable number of councillors, but they take a very distant second place in a general election.

Cynon Valley is a very working-class seat of overwhelming Labour history and traditions. It has never looked like springing any surprises. Perhaps the nearest it came to that was when it selected Ann Clwyd to fight the 1984 by-election caused by the death of Ioan Evans. She thus became the sole female representative of the Welsh valleys in the House of Commons, presaging by ten years Glenys Kinnock's massive Euro-victory in 1994.

Social indices:			2001 Gen. Election:			
% Non-white	0.7		Lab	17,685	65.6	−4.1
% Welsh sp	9.5		PC	4,687	17.4	+6.8
% Prof/Man	23.7		LD	2,541	9.4	−0.9
% Non-manual	44.8		C	2,045	7.6	+0.8
£ Av prop val 2000	34 K		Lab maj	12,998	48.2	
% Increase 97–00	17.7		Turnout		55.5	−13.7
% Unemployed 2001	4.2		Elect	48,591		
% Decrease 97–01	3.0					
% Fin hard/Rank	31.8	118				
% Pensioners	27.6					
% Prem mort/Rank	44	109				

Member of Parliament

Ann Clwyd, a deceptively smiling former journalist twice sacked from the frontbench, by Neil Kinnock in 1988 (after voting against the defence estimates), and by Tony Blair in 1995 (for going AWOL amongst the Kurds), was destined for the second dismissal anyway as an awkward squaddie, a sometimes vituperative third world human rights campaigner, on the Kurds and the East Timorese, and simply too old. Born in 1937 and educated at Queen's School Chester and Bangor University, she as a North Welsh woman was parachuted into the boyo culture of South Wales, where she was the first woman MP in a valleys mining seat, and was never on easy terms with the Whip Ray Powell, who secured her sacking in 1995. So under the Blair government she has been a woman-for-(nearly)-all-rebellions, on lone parent benefit cuts, Murdoch's predatory pricing, freedom of information, means testing of disability benefits, jury trial curbs, linking pensions to average earnings, and air traffic control privatisation. In total she cast 24 rebellious votes during the government's first term, making her the 18th most dissident Labour MP.

DAGENHAM

The largest council estate ever built in Britain – and one of the largest public housing developments in the world – was constructed on east London's Essex fringe in the 1920s. The vast and monotonous swathe of semi-detached and terraced houses for the working classes, originally named Becontree but later more usually known as Dagenham, had a population of 2,000 in 1922 but 103,000 in 1932. Dagenham is also known as the long-time seat of the main British factory of the Ford Motor Company, for most of that time and still now the nation's leading car manufacturer, although at times in the past two decades under heavy pressure from Vauxhall. As with that General Motors marque, international competition has been the prime cause of the cutbacks which have doomed their principal British factory, but as in other economic spheres the political and social legacy lives on.

Surely, then, Dagenham should always be a citadel of the Labour Party, created early in the century in the very bowels of the trade union movement, and for so long the mass party of the British working class. Indeed, for nearly 50 years, from the 1930s to the 1980s, this district was represented in Parliament by John Parker, who became the longest-serving member, the 'Father of the House of Commons'. What is more, Parker's successor as Labour MP was widely thought likely to play a major role in the party's future, and maybe in its revival, as the end of the century was to approach. Instead, Bryan Gould became increasingly semi-detached from the leadership of the party, and in 1994 announced his retirement from politics and his return to a senior academic post in his native New Zealand. Yet there have been some alarums. Indeed, at times in the 1980s this former socialist fortress had to be regarded as vulnerable to a Tory general election gain.

This was due to the massive regional swing against Labour in the outer East End in the Thatcher years, as the party lost its automatic grip on the loyalties of white working-class southern English voters. In 1987 Gould's majority had dropped to less than 2,500, a far cry from Parker's 24,500 in 1966 (or an even mightier 31,735 in

1950). Between these years it is arguable that the Labour Party had changed, moving to the left and being identified (especially in Greater London) with extreme and eccentric minority causes; it is interesting that the party locally retained its traditional image and remained in monolithic control of the Barking and Dagenham council right through the 1980s, as well as into the present century. It is also true that the electorate's philosophy changed, being exposed to alternatives to Labour hegemony through TV and Tory working-class tabloid newspapers, liking some aspects of Mrs Thatcher's leadership and distrusting the 'left' Labour Party. Ironically for its MP, the 1990s saw signs of modernisation in the party which increased its appeal in Dagenham. Bryan Gould was partially responsible for the change in image and substance, and his majority had already more than doubled in 1992.

Yet there appears to be something about Dagenham that breeds disillusionment in its MPs. Probably this is a coincidence, but like Bryan Gould, Judith Church announced her premature retirement, while still in her forties, not long into the 1997–2001 Parliament. She cited the frustrations of the Commons itself rather than anything to do with her specific seat. In 2001, her replacement and new hopeful Jon Cruddas suffered a fall in the Labour vote of nearly 8.5%. Of this, 5% went to the BNP, a doubling of their 1997 share, and the Conservatives increased by 7%: this was connected with their strongest showing in that election, in the neighbouring borough of Havering. Labour's grip in Dagenham has its uneasy aspects.

Social indices:			2001 Gen. Election:			
% Non-white	4.9		Lab	15,784	57.2	−8.5
% Prof/Man	18.0		C	7,091	25.7	+7.2
% Non-manual	48.4		LD	2,820	10.2	+2.7
£ Av prop val 2000	80 K		BNP	1,378	5.0	+2.5
% Increase 97–00	43.8		SA	262	0.9	
% Unemployed 2001	3.9		SLP	245	0.9	
% Decrease 97–01	2.2		Lab maj	8,693	31.5	
% Fin hard/Rank	35.8	83	Turnout		46.5	−15.3
% Pensioners	28.9		Elect	59,340		
% Prem mort/Rank	37	221				

Member of Parliament

Jon Cruddas replaced the disillusioned MP Judith Church, who in 2001 left the Commons after only six-and-a-half years, so belying her earlier reputation as a rising star on Labour's NEC. One of a clutch of senior political advisers who became MPs in 2001 (see also David Milliband, James Purnell and Andy Burnham), he was Deputy Political Secretary to Tony Blair from 1997 to 2001, and previously for three years chief assistant to Labour's General Secretary Larry Whitty. Son of a sailor, born in 1962, and educated at Oaklands (RC) Comprehensive, Portsmouth, and Warwick University (where he spent seven years, concluding with a doctorate), he has known no other life than that of a party staffer, having joined Labour's 'Policy Directorate' straight from university, and is married to another apparatchik, his wife having worked for Jack Cunningham, Mo Mowlam and Lord (Gus) Macdonald. Notwithstanding access to such networks of influence, he comes with a reputation for a certain independence, as confirmed by his insistence in July 2001 that his name should not be listed among London Labour MPs who supported the government's part-privatisation of the tube, claiming that he was 'still not very happy' about it. As Larry Whitty's PA in 1994 he implicitly helped with Tony Blair's successful leadership campaign against Beckett and Prescott, and yet is seen as close to Prescott's ally, Work and Pensions Minister, Ian McCartney, and to have strong union links to the TGWU, which he employed to secure the Dagenham nomination. In January 2002 he signed a *Guardian* letter describing the euro as 'a costly distraction' from repairing public services.

DARLINGTON

As recently as 1992 Darlington was regarded as a critical marginal seat. This comes as something of a surprise in County Durham. For most of the twentieth century Durham has been the very strongest Labour fortress in England. Its economy has been based on heavy industries, and in the main declining industries too – coal-mining, steel, shipbuilding, mechanical engineering. In local politics, many decades of unchallenged Labour control have not always been for the best, for the Labour Party or for the electorate, as office became a monopoly and corruption was not unknown.

In many ways, however, Darlington is untypical of the county, even though it is by some way the largest town. Unlike most Durham districts Darlington has never been a mining town, and it is not on the coast. Rather it was created by the railway revolution of the nineteenth century. In 1825 it formed the central station on the world's first passenger line, from Shildon to Stockton. Its railway works are now closed, but Darlington has developed a series of light industries and in the North East it seems a relatively prosperous town still. Under 25% of the population live in council estates, although there are still decaying Victorian terraces around the centre. As in the whole of County Durham there are only a very small number of non-white residents. Darlington is actually the shopping centre for a large part of North Yorkshire, as well as for the more rough-hewn communities of Durham. Around half of its population work in non-manual jobs. There is a large Conservative vote in the west and south-west of the town, in wards like College, Hummersknott, Mowden, Pierremont and Park West.

Labour may have held Darlington from 1964 until 9 June 1983, even retaining it in a by-election in March 1983 – the unfortunate Ossie O'Brien sat in the Commons for just three months, and has not returned to the Commons. But the Conservatives held it from 1951 to 1964, and from 1983 to 1992. Then Labour's Alan Milburn secured a swing of above average proportions – 5% – to oust the Thatcherite Michael Fallon. Following the New Labour landslide of 1997 Milburn's majority shot up to 16,000, and although the MP, now a Cabinet Minister and some people's tip for future leader of the Labour Party – suffered from the same regional swing as the current leader next door, it looks as if it will not stand in the way of his career and any future ambitions.

Social indices:			2001 Gen. Election:			
% Non-white	1.6		Lab	22,479	55.2	−6.4
% Prof/Man	27.2		C	12,950	31.8	+3.5
% Non-manual	51.5		LD	4,358	10.7	+3.5
£ Av prop val 2000	57 K		SA	469	1.2	
% Increase 97–00	18.6		Ind	269	0.7	
% Unemployed 2001	4.8		SLP	229	0.6	
% Decrease 97–01	2.7		Lab maj	9,529	23.4	
% Fin hard/Rank	22.0	242	Turnout		63.4	−10.6
% Pensioners	26.7		Elect	64,328		
% Prem mort/Rank	43	127				

Member of Parliament

Alan Milburn, elected in 1992, is an effortlessly-rising Blairite suit, if with a harder, chippier edge than is evident in the blander personas of other examples of the genre, such as Byers and Hoon. Pinched-faced, and abrasively Geordie-accented, he is a classic political apparatchik risen from trade union activism (campaigning against shipyard closure and running a 'Trade Union Studies Information Unit'). Son of a single mother, born in 1958, reared in the dead pit village of Tow Law, and educated at Stokesley Comprehensive School and Lancaster University, his earliest political affiliations were Trotskyist (IMG), and his earliest job in a left-wing bookshop. Currently Health Secretary, he has spent all his time in government either at Health (1997–98, and from 2000) or in the Treasury, as Chief Secretary 1998–2000, so he probably knows better than anyone the truth about NHS spending under a Labour government, as the customers struggle to work it out. Arguably the Department is not one in which an ambitious politician should linger.

DARTFORD

Bob Dunn was one of 19 Conservative MPs defeated in 1997 who tried to regain their former seats in 2001; only two of them succeeded (Robert Spink of Castle Point and Henry Bellingham of Norfolk North West). Like most of the 17 doubly defeated, Dunn made no significant impact in closing the gap. At least Dartford remains marginal, and a seat the Conservatives will win again when they return to office, or even close to it. This may however be too late for this particular former member, who turned 55 in 2001.

Dartford is the innermost constituency in Kent, nearest to south-east London, bordering Erith and Crayford in Bexley Borough – which is itself very much part of the 'Kentish' section of the capital. From its post-war creation in 1955 to 1983, Dartford was usually regarded as a Labour seat, although it was twice lost narrowly to the Conservatives in 1970 and 1979. On and off, Sydney Irving held it for Labour for 20 years and six elections. Then Dunn won it on the four consecutive occasions when the Conservative Party formed a government. It has now twice gone to Howard Stoate, and has a good claim to be a true bellwether, being won by whichever party forms a national government.

It always was the rural parts of the seat which gave the Conservatives a look-in. Dartford itself, and the smallish satellite town of Swanscombe, usually turn in a

Labour majority, at least in local elections. The northern wards of Dartford, towards the tunnel under the Thames to Essex, make up Labour's council estate stronghold, along with Swanscombe and Stone, the communities on the river between Dartford and Gravesend. This is industrial territory, led by the manufacture of pharmaceuticals, now overshadowed by the Dartford–Thurrock bridge, opened in 1991. The best residential area in Dartford itself is in the west of the town, generating some Tory wards like Maypole, but the Conservatives do better the further away from the Thames one goes, towards the North Downs or into the Darent valley.

Dartford remains a balanced seat, with urban and rural aspects, and Conservative and Labour elements, in competitive equilibrium.

Social indices:			2001 Gen. Election:			
% Non-white	3.8		Lab	21,466	48.0	−0.6
% Prof/Man	31.6		C	18,160	40.6	+0.3
% Non-manual	60.4		LD	3,781	8.5	−0.9
£ Av prop val 2000	107 K		UKIP	989	2.2	
% Increase 97–00	46.7		Ind	344	0.8	+0.2
% Unemployed 2001	1.6		Lab maj	3,306	7.4	
% Decrease 97–01	2.7		Turnout		61.9	−12.7
% Fin hard/Rank	13.0	396	Elect	72,258		
% Pensioners	23.3					
% Prem mort/Rank	26	403				

Member of Parliament

Dr Howard Stoate, a GP-turned-hospital tutor and medical journalist, won here for Labour in 1997. A model Blairite, he has been a one-club politician in his four-square defence of Labour's record on the NHS. Born in 1954, educated at Kingston Grammar School and King's College, London, he was a hospital doctor and tutor, and currently keeps his hand in with a little general practice. For ten years a Dartford councillor, he has a good – if loquacious – bedside manner. He talks fast and runs, and importantly for a Labour MP wanting to survive in a marginal seat in Kent, defends the county's existing grammar schools as used by his sons. Originally on the Health Select Committee, by 2001 he was PPS to John Denham at the Home Office.

DAVENTRY

When Reg Prentice, a recent Cabinet Minister, left the Labour Party during the 1974–79 Parliament he did not trifle with Liberals, Social Democrats or centrist notions of any kind – he crossed the floor to sit as a Conservative MP. Not surprisingly he declined to stand as a Tory in his Newham North East seat at the 1979 General Election, but managed to be offered a rock-solid Conservative constituency distant from east London in every way: Daventry, south Northants. He was duly elected with a majority of over 21,000, and joined Mrs Thatcher's frontbench team. But his ministerial career did not last long, and he returned to the backbenches, retaining his ironclad Conservative seat in hunting country in the shires until his retirement in 1987.

Labour won none of the six parliamentary seats in Northamptonshire in 1992. In 1997 they gained five of them, and in 2001 they held all five, under intense pressure: a certain indicator of another huge victory. The Tory exception was Daventry. Daventry has remained – and will remain – safe for Prentice's successor Tim Boswell. It is the most extensive and most rural seat in the county, curling round the county town of Northampton in addition to incorporating the southern half of the shire. There are few towns here, apart from Daventry itself which grew rapidly in the 1960s and 1970s, Brackley and Towcester. There are hundreds of villages like Silverstone where the British motor racing Grand Prix is held every year, and Thenford, where Michael Heseltine's country mansion is situated.

This is all Conservative country, and Northamptonshire is not one of the counties where the Liberal Democrats have been locally active; indeed they finished in third place, with half Labour's vote, in the 2001 Election.

Social indices:			2001 Gen. Election:			
% Non-white	1.3		C	27,911	49.2	+2.9
% Prof/Man	36.7		Lab	18,262	32.2	−2.2
% Non-manual	56.5		LD	9,130	16.1	+1.2
£ Av prop val 2000	117 K		UKIP	1,381	2.4	+1.7
% Increase 97–00	47.5		C maj	9,649	17.0	
% Unemployed 2001	1.4		Turnout		65.5	−11.5
% Decrease 97–01	0.5		Elect	86,537		
% Fin hard/Rank	7.6	538				
% Pensioners	21.5					
% Prem mort/Rank	9	606				

Member of Parliament

Bucolic and chubby-faced farmer's son **Tim Boswell**, Conservative spokesman for the disabled from 1999, is a One Nation Tory with a local 480-acre farm (with, he claims, a BSE-free herd) and a background in the Conservative Research Department and as a MAFF adviser. Born in 1942, educated at Marlborough and New College, Oxford, he stood aside in 1979 as a prominent Daventry Tory to let the Labour defector, Reg Prentice, have the seat for eight years before inheriting it himself in 1987. A Whip and Junior Minister throughout the Major years (1990–97), he campaigned for Clarke in 1997 as a long-time Europhile and remained a frontbencher under Hague. Deserting to back Ancram – until the final ballot in 2001, when he reverted to Clarke – he survived, with the same spokesmanship, under Iain Duncan Smith – a creditable negotiation of the currents. He votes with a small Tory minority in favour of 16 as the homosexual age of consent.

DELYN

The constituency of Delyn lies in the very north-eastern tip of Wales, including the Dee estuary and rounding the Point of Ayr to take in a little of the northern Irish Sea coast. On its creation in 1983, Delyn included sections of both the always Tory West Flintshire (retained even in 1966) and solidly Labour East Flintshire (held in 1959, say). It was felt that it was going to be very much a marginal seat. The west Flintshire section was larger, and the Conservative Keith Raffan won Delyn in 1983 and 1987; but on his retirement in 1992 Labour's David Hanson seized it by just over 2,000 votes, and he has won it by very much more comfortable margins twice more since.

It is easy to see why the seat was so finely balanced. Labour did best in Flint, which is an industrial centre and even boasts some tower blocks, and in the working-class town of Holywell. Mold, best known as the administrative and cultural headquarters of the county of Clwyd, is more mixed politically; and the Conservatives could rely on the seaside resort of Prestatyn and the rural hinterland, which included a number of villages amid the scenic Clwydian hills.

Then however the balance was shifted, as 12,000 voters were moved out of the constituency in 1997 into the new Vale of Clwyd seat, created as the Welsh Commission awarded an extra seat to north-east Wales. Crucially, most of these electors are in Prestatyn, along with its more Labour-voting suburb of Meliden. The reunification of Prestatyn, known to so many for its long-established Pontin's holiday camp, with its neighbouring north coast resort of Rhyl, is logical enough; both are in the Rhuddlan district. It did, however, ease Labour's task in holding Delyn, and it no longer can claim marginal status, not even should the Tories achieve the national improvement needed to remove the government.

Social indices:			2001 Gen. Election:			
% Non-white	0.4		Lab	17,825	51.5	−5.7
% Welsh sp	17.8		C	9,220	26.6	+0.6
% Prof/Man	30.6		LD	5,329	15.4	+5.2
% Non-manual	50.4		PC	2,262	6.5	+2.7
£ Av prop val 2000	69 K		Lab maj	8,605	24.8	
% Increase 97–00	29.6		Turnout		63.3	−10.7
% Unemployed 2001	2.4		Elect	54,732		
% Decrease 97–01	1.3					
% Fin hard/Rank	13.3	392				
% Pensioners	24.3					
% Prem mort/Rank	35	248				

Member of Parliament

David Hanson won this seat for Labour in 1992. Son of a fork-lift truck driver, he was born in Liverpool in 1957, attended Verdin Comprehensive School, Winsford, and Hull University, is a former worker for the Spastics Society and Re-Solv, and has campaigned on disability issues and solvent abuse. A loyalist, he was swiftly promoted in government via the Whips Office (1998–99), to the down-sized post-devolution Welsh Office where (1999–2000), in a two-man band, he was the one who represented the Merseyside end of the Principality. In 2001 he lost his job in the 'Wales' (ex-Welsh) Office, when the entire two-man team was comprised of South Walian Catholics from Pontypool, but he was compensated by being taken into Downing Street as the Prime Minister's PPS. His wife, Margaret, who had narrowly lost the 1999 Eddisbury by-election, also failed to be selected for the next-door seat of Alyn and Deeside in March 2001.

DENTON AND REDDISH

The second largest drop in turnout in 2001 occurred in the Greater Manchester seat of Denton and Reddish: over 18%, from 67% to 48.5%. The constituency combines almost all the elements adduced in explanation of the massive relative rejection of electoral participation which formed one of the biggest stories of that remarkable General Election. It is a safe Labour seat, a working-class area with no particularly pressing local issue, no crisis. Its small towns and industrial suburbs are not wealthy or even well off, though it is about a third of the way down the Experian financial hardship table: property values are exceptionally low, with an average house price in 2000 of less than £50,000. Finally, it ranked among the seats least visited on the *Daily Telegraph* constituency website during the campaign. There was very little interest in a contest in which there seemed very little point in voting.

The seat of Denton and Reddish was created almost from scratch in 1983, as the borough boundary between Stockport and Tameside in south-eastern Greater Manchester was breached for the first time. It may be worth detailing how the building blocks were put together, as essentially the structure has remained the same ever since. Before 1983 the town (not metro borough) of Stockport had two small seats of its own. As it has since been reduced to its current single core seat, territory on the edges such as Reddish was removed, and added to the Tameside towns of Denton, Audenshaw and Dukinfield in a cross-borough constituency. Its origins were even more complicated, though, for both Audenshaw and Denton were previously situated in a Manchester city division, Gorton.

One thing was certain among this mixed bag of a new seat – Denton and Reddish was safe for the Labour Party. In Tameside borough elections they can lose Audenshaw (to the Liberal Democrats) and even Denton West to the Conservatives in a bad year. Denton South, however, includes the large council overspill estate of Haughton Green, and the ex-Stockport element boosts Labour's lead too. In 2001 Andrew Bennett won his eighth term in the Commons with a lead of 15,000 – reduced from 20,000 solely by that drastic slump in enthusiasm for the democratic process in Denton and Reddish.

Social indices:			2001 Gen. Election:			
% Non-white	1.8		Lab	21,913	65.2	–0.2
% Prof/Man	22.3		C	6,583	19.6	–1.7
% Non-manual	48.8		LD	4,152	12.4	–0.9
£ Av prop val 2000	49 K		UKIP	945	2.8	
% Increase 97–00	17.1		Lab maj	15,330	45.6	
% Unemployed 2001	2.5		Turnout		48.5	–18.4
% Decrease 97–01	1.7		Elect	69,236		
% Fin hard/Rank	22.7	233				
% Pensioners	25.5					
% Prem mort/Rank	38	205				

Member of Parliament

Andrew Bennett entered the Commons in 1974 and has been MP here since 1983. With a greying full beard and a high-pitched voice, he is one of Labour's geography teachers with the associated accoutrements of rambling and right-to-roaming. Before 1997 he was one of his party's most rebellious backbenchers (ranked tenth with 41 dissentient votes, mostly on Defence and Europe) without actually being in the Campaign Group. In the 1997–2001 House he rebelled on military action against Iraq, jury trial curbs, the Prime Minister's right to nominate life peers, disability benefit cuts, and air traffic control sell-off. In the new Parliament elected in 2001 he voted against the Terrorism, Crime and Security Bill seven times in November 2001. Born in 1939, son of a local government officer, educated at Hulme Grammar School, Manchester and Birmingham University, he enjoyed 13 years at the chalk face before reaching the Commons, where, it has been said, one can almost hear the sandals in his voice.

DERBY NORTH

The northern division of Derby has been its more marginal seat, electing a Conservative, Greg Knight, on three occasions between 1983 and 1992, but these were the only times that Labour had failed in any Derby seat since before the Second World War. In 1997 Labour re-established their earlier supremacy, as Derby council leader Bob Laxton enjoyed a 13% swing, to bring about the end of Knight, and a new dawn for New Labour.

Most of the more favoured residential areas of Derby are to be found in this division. Allestree and Darley, off the A6 towards Belper, are safe Conservative wards. The seat also includes Spondon and Chaddesden, two eastern wards towards Nottingham of mixed political characteristics: they tend to swing with the tide in local elections, and must have backed Laxton last time, but Knight the three times before. Large-scale new private housing development has also swung Breadsall ward over from being a Labour banker to a Conservative gain in May 1992 (but not in the first elections for the new Derby unitary authority in 1996). Meanwhile most of the Labour strength in Derby North is concentrated in the northern inner city and in the council estates such as Mackworth. Derby North is the more middle-class half of the city, but it also contains more of Derby's council housing. After another comfortable Labour and Laxton victory in 2001, the Conservatives still need a swing of 10% to regain Derby North. It seems unlikely that they can do so at one attempt.

Social indices:			2001 Gen. Election:			
% Non-white	2.1		Lab	22,415	50.9	−2.3
% Prof/Man	31.0		C	15,433	35.0	+0.8
% Non-manual	53.3		LD	6,206	14.1	+5.1
£ Av prop val 2000	60 K		Lab maj	6,982	15.8	
% Increase 97–00	27.0		Turnout		57.6	−16.2
% Unemployed 2001	3.4		Elect	76,489		
% Decrease 97–01	2.1					
% Fin hard/Rank	22.2	241				
% Pensioners	27.2					
% Prem mort/Rank	35	258				

Member of Parliament

Bob Laxton came to the Commons in 1997 from Labour's depleted proletarian wing, Derby-born in 1944 and schooled at Allestree Woodlands Secondary Modern and at a local technical college and working as a telephone engineer for 36 years. On Derby council for 18 years, he led it for three. A loyalist, bearing one of the PLP's 49 beards, he is the complete local-boy made good with his job being to protect Derby's Rolls Royce and train-making factories. By 2001 he was PPS to another ex-union man – the former head of the Post Office Workers, Alan Johnson, Minister of State at the DTI, with responsibility for ACAS.

DERBY SOUTH

For several elections now, Derby South has ranked as by far the more favourable to Labour of the two seats in this dour Midland city. For many years it was held by the veteran peace campaigner Philip Noel-Baker, then from 1970 to 1983 by the right-winger Walter Johnson, who was noted for criticising Michael Foot's style of dress at the Cenotaph on Armistice Day 1981. On Johnson's retirement his more radical successor Margaret (Jackson) Beckett, the former Lincoln MP, almost lost to the Tories, as the majority was cut to a minimal 421. In 1987 she retained the seat with a still shaky lead of just over 1,500; but then her prospects became much more secure and indeed rosy. Margaret Beckett increased her majority to nigh on 7,000 at the 1992 General Election, and was subsequently elected as deputy leader of the Labour Party. She won by a very safe 14,000 in 2001, with no negative swing, although on the lowest turnout in Derby since the war, just 56%.

The sources of Labour's strength in the southern half of Derby are clear to see. It is in South that the city's famous railway works were to be found, the Rolls-Royce aero-engine factory, and Derby County Football Club's 'Baseball Ground', surrounded by dingy near-slum terraces, now replaced by a modern stadium with the hubristic name of Pride Park. Here too live most of the city's considerable minority of non-white residents, many of Asian extraction. There are council estates, in the Peartree area for example, and also Victorian terraces near the town centre. The best wards for the Conservatives are those containing newish private housing on the western edge of the city: Kingsway, Littleover and Mickleover. But the Tories have not won this Derby seat as a whole within memory and do not appear to be about to start now.

The announcement of severe redundancies at Rolls-Royce in October 2001, in the aftermath of but not necessarily due to the World Trade Center catastrophe, rocked the city of Derby, which had recently been named as one of the five most attractive in which to live in Britain. As the certainty of employment enjoyed by those known locally as 'Roycers' was sapped, just as the world as a whole seemed to become altogether more unstable and full of dangers, apparent and hidden, real and imagined.

Social indices:			2001 Gen. Election:			
% Non-white	18.0		Lab	24,310	56.4	+0.2
% Prof/Man	31.3		C	10,455	24.3	−0.9
% Non-manual	51.9		LD	8,310	19.3	+4.9
£ Av prop val 2000	57 K		Lab maj	13,855	32.2	
% Increase 97–00	32.2		Turnout		55.7	−12.2
% Unemployed 2001	5.7		Elect	77,366		
% Decrease 97–01	2.7					
% Fin hard/Rank	28.8	147				
% Pensioners	24.8					
% Prem mort/Rank	39	196				

Member of Parliament

Margaret Beckett, MP here since 1983 (and before that for Lincoln 1974–79) is Labour's longest-running female frontbencher, with all but two of her 24 years in the Commons spent as a spokesman, whip or minister. A professional politician, who has weaved amid the party's left-wing factions, and been out of step with Tony Blair on Clause 4, the minimum wage and union workplace recognition, she was nevertheless the Shadow Chief Secretary before 1992 who prefigured the tight-money regime of Chancellor Brown after 1997. Born in 1943, a carpenter's daughter, and educated at Catholic schools in Manchester and Norwich, she trained as a metallurgist at Manchester College of Science and Technology. Although she is Labour's senior woman figure – who bid for the leadership against Blair in 1994 – she lacks the charisma and warmth to make her a Barbara Castle, and her dourly impassive image alongside Blair on the Treasury bench as Leader of the House 1998–2001 conveyed the impression of less than unconditional support. At the DTI in the first year of the Blair government, in 2001 she was moved to the difficult Agriculture (renamed DEFRA) ministry, where foot-and-mouth had recently destroyed her predecessor, Nick Brown. By 2001 she and Michael Meacher (now in her department) were the last frontbench survivors of the 1976–79 Callaghan government.

DERBYSHIRE NORTH EAST

This constituency is now more socially mixed than it was in the 1950s and 1960s. There are still solidly Labour areas of North East Derbyshire: the ex-mining towns of Eckington and Killamarsh are situated only a few miles from Sheffield and look over the county boundary to the socially similar Labour fortresses of Attercliffe and Rother Valley. Clay Cross is south of Chesterfield, but it is of course still remembered for its Labour councillors who rebelled against the 1970–74 Conservative government and were held financially responsible for refusing to enact cuts; one of their leaders was the Bolsover MP Dennis Skinner's brother.

But this kidney-shaped constituency, which curls around Chesterfield, also contains some substantial pockets of Conservative middle-class commuters. After all, the Tories did amass over 22,500 votes in April 1992. The Dronfield area has seen massive new private housing development schemes, most notably at Gosforth Valley, where modern 'semis' and 'dets' spread up the Peak District foothills in the 1970s.

Many Dronfield residents work in Sheffield, and took the opportunity of avoiding that city's high rates for owner-occupiers by living in Derbyshire. Meanwhile, Holymoorside, Wingerworth and Brampton are stone Peak villages which have expanded to cater for affluent incomers as they have become the most fashionable commuting bases for the Chesterfield bourgeoisie. One man who moved on and up from Clay Cross to Wingerworth was the former world darts champion, John Lowe, although no one would accuse him of joining the bourgeois class. Labour can still hit the bullseye here, even if social change amounts to a moving of the oche.

Harry Barnes's majority has been changing in units of 6,000 in recent elections, from 6,000 in Labour's disappointing year of 1992 to 18,000 in 1997 and back down to 12,000 in 2001, when the turnout fell below 60%. The number of Conservative voters fell that year too, and North East has never quite approached marginal status.

Social indices:			2001 Gen. Election:			
% Non-white	0.6		Lab	23,437	55.6	−4.8
% Prof/Man	32.7		C	11,179	26.5	+1.3
% Non-manual	55.9		LD	7,508	17.8	+3.5
£ Av prop val 2000	71 K		Lab maj	12,258	29.1	
% Increase 97–00	24.8		Turnout		58.9	−13.7
% Unemployed 2001	3.9		Elect	71,527		
% Decrease 97–01	1.3					
% Fin hard/Rank	14.1	369				
% Pensioners	25.0					
% Prem mort/Rank	25	424				

Member of Parliament

Harry Barnes, MP since 1987, a Durham miner's son and railway clerk-turned-lecturer, got selected here on the back of his work in the extra-mural department at Sheffield University where his pupils included a number of miners who also became MPs in nearby coalfield seats. Born in 1936 and educated eventually at Ryhope Grammar School and Hull University, he has campaigned for Labour to organise and contest seats in Northern Ireland, for updated electoral registers, and for disability rights. Self-mockingly described as 'a little bald-headed 60-year-old man with glasses and false teeth and whose trousers do not match his jacket', his real claim to fame is as one of Labour's most rebellious backbenchers, second only to Skinner in Opposition 1992–97 with 80 dissentient votes, and in the 1997–2001 House joining his Campaign Group colleagues in all the major revolts against the government from lone parent benefit cuts in 1997 to air traffic control privatisation in 2000, if coming in only 13th with 25 votes of defiance. In the new 2001 Parliament he rebelled in the first months on Incapacity Benefits and the anti-terrorism legislation.

DERBYSHIRE SOUTH

The southern tip of Derbyshire has been through some political ups and downs, and elected some colourful and controversial characters, including from 1983 to 1992 Edwina Currie. Turning the clock back, for 25 years from 1945 the area (then named

Belper) offered a seat to the convivial Labour right-winger George Brown, who unsuccessfully contested his party's leadership against Harold Wilson in 1963. As the suburbs of Derby gradually encroached, Belper constituency swung steadily to the Tories, and Brown was defeated in 1970, declaring it was not the seat he had once known. Nor was it. The redistribution which came into force in February 1974 removed Brown's far-right successor, Geoffrey Stewart-Smith, and replaced him with a Labour member, Roderick MacFarquhar. In turn he was beaten in 1979 by a Conservative dentist, Sheila Faith; but in the face of further boundary changes she abandoned the area, unsuccessfully 'carpetbagging', offering herself for selection for new or vacant seats round the country. This was a piece of bad judgement. South Derbyshire was won by her replacement as Conservative candidate at the 1983 General Election, Edwina Currie, who held on for three elections, but was very soundly thrashed by Labour's Mark Todd in 1997. Although the scale of Mrs Currie's defeat – 13,967 votes – looked massive, in fact she suffered a swing close to the national and regional average.

Before 1983 the seat had been named after Belper, which is north of Derby and was never its geographical hub. In that year that town was moved into West Derbyshire. What remained was primarily the local government district of South Derbyshire, together with three southern wards of the city of Derby: Boulton, Chellaston and Mickleover. South Derbyshire was centred on Swadlincote, always the Labour stronghold in the Belper constituency: originally a mining town, Swadlincote was described by one famous son, the travel writer Rene Cutforth, as a 'hole in the ground'. However, he was referring to his childhood in the inter-war years, and Swadlincote is less bleak now. South Derbyshire also includes rural areas and small towns such as (the original) Melbourne and Repton, where there is a leading Midland boys' public school. Mark Todd's majority fell by 6,000 in 2001, as a result of a 4% reduction in the Labour share as well as a larger drop in turnout. If the Conservatives were to win South Derbyshire next time, they would probably take at least 100 seats from Labour, knocking out the government's overall majority without necessarily replacing it with one of their own.

Social indices:			2001 Gen. Election:			
% Non-white	2.1		Lab	26,338	50.7	−3.8
% Prof/Man	30.6		C	18,487	35.6	+4.3
% Non-manual	51.4		LD	5,233	10.1	+1.1
£ Av prop val 2000	74 K		UKIP	1,074	2.1	+1.0
% Increase 97–00	32.2		SLP	564	1.1	
% Unemployed 2001	1.8		Ind	249	0.5	
% Decrease 97–01	1.6		Lab maj	7,851	15.1	
% Fin hard/Rank	10.9	441	Turnout		64.1	−14.1
% Pensioners	24.9		Elect	81,010		
% Prem mort/Rank	25	418				

Member of Parliament

Mark Todd, winner here in 1997, is a big, burly, bushy-moustached man with a Tory-style educational pedigree of public school and Cambridge (Sherborne and

Emmanuel) and, indeed, a Tory MP grandfather, Alfred Todd who sat for Berwick-on-Tweed 1929–35. A former IT director in publishing, he cuts a common-sensical figure as a would-be reformer of the CAP and CSA, and has actually defended the government's part privatisation of air traffic control and opposed regulation of the use of dietary supplements (such as vitamin B6), believing individuals should make judgements for themselves. It has been said 'he expounds Labour policy with friendly gravitas' (*Observer*), and says of himself he is not 'by instinct a regulator', believing 'individual citizens should make judgements for themselves'.

DERBYSHIRE WEST

West Derbyshire has been for many years the one truly rural seat in the county, and has usually been considered the only true Conservative stronghold. In 2001 this was the only constituency the Tories could hold in Derbyshire, but there have been alarums even here.

Before the Second World War the constituency was often the possession of the Marquess of Hartington, the son and heir of the chief local aristocrat, the Duke of Devonshire of Chatsworth House. It did rebel to elect the populist Charlie White as a Common Wealther in 1944, and as the Labour candidate in 1945; and also in 1986 when the young Tory MP Matthew Parris resigned on taking over Brian Walden's job on *Weekend World*, and the Conservatives only won the ensuing by-election by a round 100 votes over the Liberal Alliance.

Win it they did, though, and with a rather surprising candidate. Patrick McLoughlin is a former (working) miner, still in his 20s when chosen: a refreshing choice for a rural, even aristocratic, seat. With the problematic by-election behind him, McLoughlin increased his majority to over 10,000 in 1987 and nearly 19,000 in 1992 as the residual Liberal Democrat support faded. In 1997 the Lib Dems fell back to third, and Labour advanced by 11% to cut McLoughlin's majority to just under 5,000, but he reinforced his position in 2001.

The West Derbyshire seat contains two towns of about 20,000 people: the spa of Matlock, which is Derbyshire's administrative capital; and Belper, transferred in 1983 from its own seat. Here too are three small towns of 5,000 souls apiece: Wirksworth, Ashbourne and Bakewell. Wirksworth is a quarrying town, often covered in white lime dust, and boasting some Labour voters: the Labour candidate in 2001 as in 1997 was Stephen Clamp, a Wirksworth town councillor, former town mayor, and Derbyshire Dales district representative. But Bakewell typifies the Conservatism of West Derbyshire. It is surrounded by soft White Peak scenery and the landed estates of Chatsworth and Haddon Hall. The local council changed its name from West Derbyshire to Derbyshire Dales, and this remains an excellent description of the area, although the Boundary Commission has not chosen to follow suit; included in the seat are the glorious tourist attractions of Dovedale and Lathkil Dale, Monsal Dale and Head, and countless others. There is much to conserve, here in the only remaining Conservative seat in Derbyshire.

Social indices:			2001 Gen. Election:			
% Non-white	0.5		C	24,280	48.0	+5.9
% Prof/Man	36.6		Lab	16,910	33.4	−0.1
% Non-manual	54.9		LD	7,922	15.7	−1.8
£ Av prop val 2000	96 K		UKIP	672	1.3	+0.5
% Increase 97–00	29.3		MRLP	472	0.9	+0.4
% Unemployed 2001	1.7		Ind	333	0.7	
% Decrease 97–01	0.9		C maj	7,370	14.6	
% Fin hard/Rank	8.7	495	Turnout		67.4	−10.8
% Pensioners	27.9		Elect	75,067		
% Prem mort/Rank	15	542				

Member of Parliament

Patrick McLoughlin, MP here since 1986, the Conservative Deputy Chief Whip since 1998, is both a collector's item and a rhetorical point, as a Tory MP who was a coal miner. The Tory working man has usually had at least one manifestation on the Commons benches: in the 1930s it was Gwilym Rowlands (Flint), in the 1950s Ray Mawby (Totnes), and – since the 1980s – Patrick McLoughlin, MP for a seat which once the Dukes of Devonshire traditionally reserved for their eldest son, the Marquess of Hartington. Dark, burly and not overly fluent, Staffordshire-accented with a lisp, he was born in 1957, a son and grandson of miners, and educated at Cardinal Griffin (RC) Secondary Modern, Cannock, and Staffordshire College of Agriculture, and initially worked as a farm labourer before spending six years at Littleton Colliery, Cannock. A Junior Minister at Transport, Employment and the DTI from 1989 to 1994, he became a Whip in 1995 and remained one thereafter under both changes of leadership, having voted for Michael Howard in 1997. To the snob Alan Clark he was: 'a nice man, but not a card of very high value'.

DEVIZES

Most of the 2001 Tory leadership contender and former Party Chairman Michael Ancram's Devizes constituency consists of rural and traditional Wiltshire territory in the district of Kennet. This was bolstered by two additions from outside Kennet in 1997: the town of Calne from North Wiltshire and the town of Melksham from West Wiltshire district and the Westbury division. More boundary changes are in the air as the county is scheduled to gain another seat in the Commission's next review, but this will not come into force by the next election, which will presumably take place in 2005 or 2006.

The small towns here are old boroughs and market centres for the agricultural terrain around, but they also have their own light industries. Devizes itself is the home of Wadworth's old-fashioned brewery, and Melksham's economy has long rested on its Avon Rubber Company tyre factory. Other centres of population include Marlborough, with its famous public school tucked under the Downs, and North Tidworth, with its army camp – a reminder that here we are not far away from Salisbury Plain, and the proportion employed in the armed services reaches the relatively high figure of 5%. Mostly, though, Devizes now consists of peaceful countryside, including the Vale of Pewsey and Savernake Forest, and a significant part of the rolling Wiltshire Downs.

Devizes is still safely Conservative. One 1997 change, the addition of Melksham, benefited Labour; but this had little significance, for that party is not a contender in these parts of Wiltshire, although they did move forward into second place in 2001. Indeed Labour's advance probably helped Michael Ancram to retain a majority of nearly 12,000, for the Liberal Democrats may ultimately have a better chance of ousting the Tories here in the long run, as they do in so many seats deeper into the west country.

Social indices:			2001 Gen. Election:			
% Non-white	1.0		C	25,159	47.2	+4.4
% Prof/Man	30.5		Lab	13,263	24.9	+0.7
% Non-manual	49.1		LD	11,756	22.1	−4.5
£ Av prop val 2000	129 K		UKIP	1,521	2.9	+1.8
% Increase 97–00	54.9		Ind	1,078	2.0	
% Unemployed 2001	1.1		MRLP	472	0.9	
% Decrease 97–01	1.0		C maj	11,896	22.3	
% Fin hard/Rank	9.9	467	Turnout		63.7	−11.0
% Pensioners	25.0		Elect	83,655		
% Prem mort/Rank	16	524				

Member of Parliament

Michael Ancram QC – actually 'Michael Kerr, Earl of Ancram, heir to the 12th Marquess of Lothian', has been MP for Devizes since 1992, having previously been MP for Berwick and East Lothian (February–October 1974) and for Edinburgh South (1979–87), the perambulations being symbolic of the decline of Scottish Conservatism. A Junior Scottish Office Minister in the 1980s and a middle-ranking Northern Ireland Minister under John Major, he was born in 1945, educated at Ampleforth, Christchurch, Oxford and Edinburgh University and is an advocate. An anglicised, Roman Catholic, Scottish aristocrat married to a daughter of the Duke of Norfolk, he is a One Nation Tory by instinct, but trimmed in 1997 by backing Hague, not Clarke, and was rewarded with the Party Chairmanship in 1998. In 2001, as one who 'always found it difficult to characterise myself', he made a leadership bid, securing the votes of 21 MPs in the first round and 17 in the second, whereafter he backed Iain Duncan Smith and became Shadow Foreign Secretary. Mild-mannered, pin-striped, and rather short and stocky for an aristocrat, he was clearly not the choice of his fellow MPs, and so never had the chance to test the appeal of an eventual 13th Marquess with the blue-rinsed matrons of Virginia Water.

DEVON EAST

Devon is a large and diverse county. The different districts have distinct individual characteristics. One can contrast the brash and lively appeal of the 'Devon Riviera' of Torbay with the undeveloped and unspoilt creek-indented coastline of the South Hams. The 'Golden Coast' of north Devon around Ilfracombe has yet a different nature, and its towering dark cliffs bear little resemblance to the gentler red cliffs of east Devon. The territory between the mouth of the Exe and the Dorset border was until the 1997 boundary changes in the Honiton constituency. Then the town of Honiton and two adjoining inland rural wards have been transferred to join Tiverton, and the seat renamed East Devon. The Tories lost two seats to Labour and two to the Liberal Democrats in the county in 1997, and only just held on to four of their remaining five with only East Devon a comfortable hold. However, in 2001, although they lost Teignbridge, they tightened their grip on all that remaining quartet, and East retained its ranking as the safest Conservative seat in the county.

One of the reasons for this is clear: over 34% of the population are of pensionable age, much the highest figure in Devon and third among the 'aged' seats in the country. Given the propensity of pensioners to see voting as a civic duty, it was estimated that nearly 44% of people who actually voted in 1997 in East Devon were senior citizens, and this figure would have been even nearer half in 2001. The coastal resorts of Sidmouth, Seaton and Budleigh Salterton are notably quiet, and tend not to cater for the tastes of the younger generation. Half of the population of the town of Budleigh Salterton are pensioners, and that means a higher proportion of the electorate, and a still higher proportion of voters. In the Town ward of Sidmouth the figure reaches the astonishing level of 61% of the population – there are scarcely any children here, only one in 20 residents being aged under 16. The largest town in the constituency, Exmouth, does have some light industry but overall this is very much a residential and resort area.

The Conservatism of East Devon is perhaps demonstrated by one of the most surprising of the defections that have taken place in recent years. In 1991 Stuart Hughes (subsequently Stuart Basil Fawlty Hughes) was elected to the East Devon District Council as a Raving Looney Jolly Green Giant candidate for Sidmouth Woolbrook ward. In May 1993 the Sidmouth Rural electoral division put him on to the County Council with a sweeping majority. Was staid old Sidmouth turning Looney? Apparently not, for Stuart Hughes, apparently changing his mind, joined the Conservative Party in time for the 1997 council elections. It was one of the few pieces of good news that they received that year. He was re-elected with a massive mandate, still as a Conservative, on the same day as the 2001 General Election. After their second successive national hammering, the party agonised about its reasons for failure and candidates for the leadership called for more inclusivity and a broader appeal. Perhaps the success of Stuart Hughes in Devon East might act as a shining light: in order to be successful, welcome and include more Loonies.

Social indices:			2001 Gen. Election:			
% Non-white	0.4		C	22,681	47.4	+4.0
% Prof/Man	32.7		LD	14,486	30.3	+1.2
% Non-manual	53.6		Lab	7,974	16.7	−1.0
£ Av prop val 2000	110 K		UKIP	2,696	5.6	+4.8
% Increase 97–00	39.3		C maj	8,195	17.1	
% Unemployed 2001	1.4		Turnout		68.1	−8.0
% Decrease 97–01	1.4		Elect	70,278		
% Fin hard/Rank	7.2	554				
% Pensioners	43.8					
% Prem mort/Rank	12	565				

Member of Parliament

The retirement of Sir Peter Emery in 2001 opened the way for **Hugo Swire** to inherit this safe Conservative seat as due reward for coming in bottom of the poll at Greenock and Inverclyde in 1997. Born in 1959 and with patrician good looks – if seen by his Labour opponent as an 'Alan B'Stard look-and-sound-alike', he comes with the near-impeccable credentials of Eton, St Andrews University, Sandhurst, the Guards (Grenadier), and Sotheby's – where he was Director from 1996. Only 'Oxbridge' is missing from such a trajectory, notwithstanding St Andrews' status as a fairly viable alternative. From a rich family of Hong Kong Taipans, one of five new Etonian MPs on the Tory benches in 2001, and married to the daughter of former Defence Minister Sir John Nott, he has called for aid for his constituency's foot-and-mouth-battered tourist industry, queried the relocation of the statue of Sir Walter Raleigh in Whitehall, and joined 13 other new Tory MPs in calling in a *Telegraph* letter for the election of Iain Duncan Smith as leader in August 2001, despite not having disclosed his vote in the parliamentary leadership ballots in July.

DEVON NORTH

In 1970 there were unofficial signs erected by roadsides at the borders of the North Devon constituency. They read: 'You are now entering Liberal country'. This was the seat of the Liberal Party leader at the time, Jeremy Thorpe. His career was ended in scandalous circumstances and the seat was lost in 1979 as the Tory Tony Speller romped home by a decisive 8,000 majority. Since the 1992 Election though, those signs can return, for North Devon again returns a Liberal (Democrat) MP.

The seat has a long-term radical tradition. It was held by Richard Acland as a Liberal and then a Common Wealth MP from 1935 to 1945. Then the young Jeremy Thorpe won the seat from the Conservatives at the 1959 General Election, one of only six victories anywhere in the country that year for the Liberals. Thorpe became leader in 1967, and presided over the Liberal revival of the early 1970s, and the disappointment of the two 1974 elections. Then disaster struck, as Norman Scott alleged that Thorpe had tried to have him killed after a homosexual affair between them. These charges were not substantiated in court, but some of the mud stuck, and the North Devon electorate decisively rejected their MP of 20 years at the next election.

Thorpe's six wins in North Devon obviously owed much to a personal vote, and Tony Speller held off the challenges of different candidates in 1983 and 1987. However, there is also a deep strand of Liberalism in this neck of the woods, which is successfully tapped by Nick Harvey, while in any case the Tories have been doing badly throughout the West Country. The seat is dependent on both agriculture and tourism, and there is a surprising amount of industry in Barnstaple, the unexpectedly tough and gritty working-class main town. Barnstaple has long been a Liberal stronghold in local elections, and it is not alone in the constituency. It is sometimes said that the native Devonians are more inclined to vote Liberal, the incomers and retirees Conservative, and indeed Harvey did well in the numerous rural villages and the small market town of South Molton. However, the Conservatives have struggled since the 1980s on the so-called 'Golden Coast' as well. The main holiday resort, Ilfracombe, has been racked by unemployment and economic decline as visitors seek more reliably sunny climes abroad, and this has been translated into disillusion with the government. In the latest local government elections, the Liberal Democrats have even managed to win too in happier seaside and retirement resorts such as Braunton and Combe Martin.

The inland parts of this seat suffered badly in the 2001 foot-and-mouth epidemic, and together with a general feeling that the Conservatives might be the true party of the countryside, Harvey did quite well to hold on. His majority was reduced, but the Conservative share fell too, while the former Stroud Conservative MP Roger Knapman held his deposit in the UK Independence Party's first contest here, and there were over 1,000 Green votes too. There may well be another tight and colourful contest next time in what most residents, and visitors, find to be a delightful corner of the land.

Social indices:			2001 Gen. Election:			
% Non-white	0.5		LD	21,784	44.2	−6.5
% Prof/Man	33.5		C	18,800	38.2	−1.3
% Non-manual	52.3		Lab	4,995	10.1	+0.4
£ Av prop val 2000	92 K		UKIP	2,484	5.0	
% Increase 97–00	47.9		Grn	1,191	2.4	
% Unemployed 2001	2.9		LD maj	2,984	6.1	
% Decrease 97–01	1.4		Turnout		68.3	−9.6
% Fin hard/Rank	10.7	446	Elect	72,100		
% Pensioners	30.5					
% Prem mort/Rank	23	447				

Member of Parliament

Nick Harvey, Culture, Media and Sports spokesman from 2001, having shadowed a good deal else in the past, has held this seat for the Liberal Democrats since 1992 when he avenged the 1979 defeat of the hapless Jeremy Thorpe. Tall, balding, genial and with a slight lisp, he was born in 1961, educated at Queen's College, Taunton and Middlesex Polytechnic, and worked in parliamentary consultancy. For long his party's sole Eurosceptic, as an anti-centralist, and voting against Maastricht, he was a good deal more representative of his Devonian electors than the Eurofanatics at the top of his party, though latterly has trimmed to accept the reality of the euro. Once tempted, he thought better of pitching for his Party's leadership in 1999 in a crowded field of five candidates, some of whom were palpably unelectable, and threw his weight behind Charles Kennedy.

DEVON SOUTH WEST

SW Devon is the second strongest Tory seat in the county after Devon East; indeed there are only two seats which can be called anything like safe. The seat contains a mixture of urban and rural. Plymstock and Plympton are effectively eastern middle-class and owner-occupied suburbs of Plymouth, lying across the river which mutually gives all these areas their name. On the other hand, a broad swathe of countryside is also included: the western part of the South Hams district, numbering around 23,000 voters, is also predominantly Conservative. This includes the affluent and attractive seaside and creekside communities of Newton Ferrers and Noss Mayo, and inland the small towns of Ivybridge, Modbury and South Brent and villages with deeply Devonian names like Yealmpton and Ugborough. One ward from West Devon is incorporated in the seat, Buckland Monachorum.

Both halves of the seat are inclined to the Conservative. Labour managed to beat the Liberal Democrats easily into second place in this seat in 2001, but the rural and suburban mixture allowed Gary Streeter to retain his place in the Commons by a relatively comfortable margin of over 7,000.

Social indices:			2001 Gen. Election:			
% Non-white	0.6		C	21,970	46.8	+3.9
% Prof/Man	32.9		Lab	14,826	31.6	+2.7
% Non-manual	58.2		LD	8,616	18.4	−5.4
£ Av prop val 2000	90 K		UKIP	1,492	3.2	+2.3
% Increase 97–00	35.6		C maj	7,144	15.2	
% Unemployed 2001	1.1		Turnout		66.1	−10.1
% Decrease 97–01	1.9		Elect	70,922		
% Fin hard/Rank	3.0	637				
% Pensioners	24.4					
% Prem mort/Rank	11	582				

Member of Parliament

Gary Streeter, a Conservative Party Vice-Chairman from 2001, was previously as Tory spokesman on International Development (1998–2001) a dispatch box sparring-partner-cum-punchbag for Clare Short. He came to Conservative politics via six years as an SDP councillor in Plymouth, where he denies he backed grammar school abolition, and followed Alan Clark as MP (for Plymouth Sutton) in 1992. Born in 1955, educated at Tiverton Grammar School and King's College, London, a solicitor in the Plymouth law firm founded by Michael Foot's father Isaac, as a self-confessed 'Christian Conservative' he rather unhelpfully predicted defeat in December 2000, by saying the Tories probably would not present themselves as 'the party of the poor' in time for the coming election. Alternately partisan and consensual, he backed Lilley, then Hague, in 1997, but grasped the more adventurous Portillo option in 2001.

DEWSBURY

Going into the 2001 Election, Ann Taylor, the Labour Party Chief Whip, was the Cabinet Minister with the smallest percentage majority and hence technically the most vulnerable seat. The good news for Ms Taylor was that she held on, easily, with no reduction in the safety of her seat. The bad news was that she was removed from the Cabinet on the day after the election. Ironically, one of the new female members of Tony Blair's second Cabinet, Estelle Morris, promoted to David Blunkett's former Education portfolio, nearly lost in her own constituency of Birmingham Yardley, and takes Ann Taylor's place, in the top table most marginal seat stakes at least.

Dewsbury was a very tightly contested seat between 1983 and 1992. In 1983 the Conservative John Whitfield was widely regarded as fortunate to gain this West Yorkshire constituency, for his party had not held it since the war, and he must have been assisted by the candidature of the sitting SDP MP, David Ginsburg, who had been elected under Labour colours. Indeed he was thought to have done quite well to lose to Ann Taylor in 1987 by only 445 votes. Then in 1992 Whitfield stood again, and for a second successive time held Taylor to a three-figure majority, 634.

The Conservatives' relatively strong showing in Dewsbury paralleled that in a neighbouring seat, Batley and Morley, which Elizabeth Peacock held from 1983 until 1997, apparently against the odds. The issues in both constituencies are similar, as are their social characteristics. Dewsbury consists of a group of towns which used to be dominated by the single industry of woollen weaving. There is a preponderance of owner-occupied housing, and a significant non-white minority of about 10%, which is concentrated in parts of Dewsbury. There have been bitter disputes about the state of education in schools with largely Asian rolls, and race relations could be considerably better. However, at least in 2001 the British National Party failed to save its deposit here, unlike in 1997, and also unlike in ex-textile towns on the Lancashire side of the Pennines.

Social indices:			2001 Gen. Election:			
% Non-white	13.5		Lab	18,524	50.5	+1.1
% Prof/Man	27.4		C	11,075	30.2	+0.1
% Non-manual	47.3		LD	4,382	12.0	+1.7
£ Av prop val 2000	58 K		BNP	1,632	4.5	–0.7
% Increase 97–00	24.4		Grn	560	1.5	+0.6
% Unemployed 2001	3.2		UKIP	478	1.3	
% Decrease 97–01	1.4		Lab maj	7,449	20.3	
% Fin hard/Rank	31.2	121	Turnout		58.8	–11.2
% Pensioners	24.1		Elect	62,344		
% Prem mort/Rank	36	233				

Member of Parliament

Ann Taylor, dropped by Tony Blair in 2001, having been Labour's first female Chief Whip (1998–2001), got her first post – as an Assistant Whip – from James Callaghan in 1977, aged 30. Elected for Bolton West (1974–83) and for Dewsbury in 1987, she was born in 1947, educated at Bolton School and Bradford and Sheffield Universities. From the party's old Right she has defended MPs working for lobbyists (as she did for Westminster Communications) and is conservative on homosexual law reform. Sporting a very severe short-back-and-sides-but-long-on-top hair cut and blessed with a somewhat metallic voice, under her rule she presided over a change of culture whereby MPs' performance and rebellions were reported on to local Labour parties (CLPs), a straight reversal of the reselection process in Opposition, in which the CLPs sacked the MPs for not rebelling. As Leader of the House (1997–98) she was taken to be less than keen on women-friendly changes to Westminster procedures.

DONCASTER CENTRAL

The 'Socialist Republic of South Yorkshire' has not always been as solidly Labour as it is now, with just one Liberal Democrat seat in the shape of Sheffield Hallam breaking the monopoly. From 1951 to 1964 the Doncaster constituency was held by Anthony Barber, a Conservative future Chancellor of the Exchequer. Even in 1970 and 1979 his successor Harold Walker, later a Deputy Speaker, enjoyed a Labour majority of only 3,000. Doncaster had for most of the twentieth century been surrounded by one of the most modern and productive coalfields in Britain, but it is itself a mixed town of many industries, as well as being a major shopping, service and transport and communications centre for the surrounding sub-region: it is well under two hours from London on the main east coast railway and situated very close to the motorway network in the shape of the M1 and M18. What is more, it possesses several middle-class residential areas of firm Tory persuasion, most notably to the south-east, beyond the famous racecourse. For much of the post-war period it has been a marginal seat.

Unfortunately for the Conservatives, though, boundary changes weakened their position substantially in 1983, and this handicap has been retained. The South East ward, which includes part of Bessacarr, the best Tory residential area in the town, was placed out in the Don Valley seat. Instead the mining village of Armthorpe, east of the town, has been included. Armthorpe is staunchly and militantly Labour, and the consequence of its inclusion was almost certainly to save Harold Walker's seat in 1983: he won by only 2,500.

Since then Labour have had little trouble holding Central, and its majority entered five figures in 1992. In 1997 Harold Walker retired, and Rosie Winterton has had no trouble in joining Don Valley's Caroline Flint as a female member of the Doncaster Borough's delegation to the Commons, previously an all-male preserve dominated by the mining tradition.

Social indices:			2001 Gen. Election:			
% Non-white	3.6		Lab	20,034	59.1	−3.0
% Prof/Man	26.8		C	8,035	23.7	+2.7
% Non-manual	47.8		LD	4,390	12.9	+3.5
£ Av prop val 2000	49 K		UKIP	926	2.7	+1.7
% Increase 97–00	13.9		SA	517	1.5	
% Unemployed 2001	5.2		Lab maj	11,999	35.4	
% Decrease 97–01	4.9		Turnout		52.1	−11.8
% Fin hard/Rank	22.3	236	Elect	65,087		
% Pensioners	27.3					
% Prem mort/Rank	37	214				

Member of Parliament

In so far as it helps in contemporary Labour politics to have the backing of the Deputy Prime Minister, **Rosie Winterton**, elected here in 1997, may be counted fortunate. One of three women inheriting safe Labour seats on the macho Yorkshire coalfield in 1997, she came with the stamp of John Prescott's approval as his PA at Westminster (and previously in Hull), and – belatedly – in 2001 was admitted into one of the government's rarefied inner sanctums as a parliamentary Secretary in the Lord Chancellor's Department. Born in 1958 and educated at Ackworth School (private), Doncaster Grammar School and Hull University, she has cheer-led for her mentor, diligently pursued local issues and worried about wheel-clamping. Her neighbour, Caroline Flint, conceded that not all Blair's Babes were Barbara Castles; this one has been likened to Barbara Windsor.

DONCASTER NORTH

Corruption and venality, major or minor, has fortunately played little role in British electoral politics, compared with almost any other democracy in the world. It was therefore unusual to find a number of related allegations and court cases afflicting the borough of Doncaster in South Yorkshire, particularly affecting the ruling Labour group, long in control, with resultant access to patronage and the distribution of contractual work. Legal matters may still arise, but we can say that the electoral consequences involve the candidature for a number of years now of Independents standing in safe Labour wards, particularly in the northern half of the borough, with some success, such as that of Martin Williams in Thorne ward in 1998. Councillor Williams stood in the 2001 General Election too, and obtained 9.3% of the vote, one of the half-dozen best Independent shares in a year featuring those of the much more nationally known Richard Taylor (Wyre Forest) and Martin Bell (Brentwood and Ongar). There had been an 'anti-sleaze' candidate here in the General Election in 1997, but this time Martin Williams almost trebled that vote. Perhaps the sleaze had got three times as bad.

Doncaster North is a constituency of communities shaped by coal-mining, although hardly any collieries survive in Britain into the twenty-first century. Nevertheless it has remained as a Labour stronghold into the post-coal age, carrying with it more than a vestige of South Yorkshire socialism bred by the close-knit Labour movement and the long local alliance between the Yorkshire NUM and the Labour Party.

The pits, and the villages and towns they created, are of different vintages in this seat set on the flat plain of the Don to the north and north-east of Doncaster. The oldest lie furthest to the west, at Bentley, Adwick-le-Street and Askern. More modern, and indeed largely opened up in the inter-war years, is the coalfield to the east, around Thorne and Stainforth, low-lying among the dykes, where the elevation reads remorselessly and monotonously in single figures. Only man-made excrescences, of varying kinds, vary the featureless landscape.

Social indices:			2001 Gen. Election:			
% Non-white	0.7		Lab	19,788	63.1	−6.7
% Prof/Man	20.8		C	4,601	14.7	−0.1
% Non-manual	41.0		LD	3,323	10.6	+2.1
£ Av prop val 2000	49 K		Ind	2,926	9.3	
% Increase 97–00	26.3		UKIP	725	2.3	
% Unemployed 2001	4.5		Lab maj	15,187	48.4	
% Decrease 97–01	4.0		Turnout		50.5	−12.8
% Fin hard/Rank	34.5	97	Elect	62,124		
% Pensioners	24.2					
% Prem mort/Rank	42	145				

Member of Parliament

Labour's **Kevin Hughes**, dropped from the Whips' Office in 2001 after five years, was elected here in 1992, and is one of only three ex-miners left in Yorkshire coalfield seats, three of his immediate neighbours by 1997 being women from London. A squarely-built miner's son, born in 1952, and educated at Duston Park Secondary Modern School and on day release at Sheffield University, as a miner for 20 years he has naturally spent much time opposing the closure of the coalfield, but compensated as a Whip by exhibiting a 'sense of discipline (which) makes Joe Stalin look like a primary school teacher' (Paul Routledge). Pronouncing himself 'a tad disappointed' at being dropped from the Whips' Office in 2001, he bit back by attacking unemployment and hospital waiting lists, but by November 2001 he was offering his Old Labourist support for David Blunkett's anti-terrorism legislation by caricaturing its opponents as 'yoghurt-eating, muesli-eating, *Guardian* readers'. An ex-Communist (until aged 20), his beard seems rather to go and come.

DON VALLEY

Before 1983 the former Don Valley seat completely surrounded Doncaster, a necklace of colliery villages which produced a massive majority for Labour. Since then, though, boundary changes and the decline of coal-mining have put a slightly different complexion on things. Though still no marginal, Don Valley has seen rather closer contests, and in 2001 there was a 4% swing from Labour to Conservative, which together with a drop in turnout to a very poor 55%, reduced Caroline Flint's majority to four figures – safe enough, but no uniform monolith.

The current seat named Don Valley still curls around the south side of Doncaster in a kidney shape, but its character is somewhat changed. Of its six Doncaster borough wards, two have usually been Conservative and a third marginal. The two Tory wards are South East, which includes part of Bessacarr, the most middle-class part of Doncaster itself, and a stretch of countryside down to Bawtry on the A1 and the Nottinghamshire border; and Southern Parks, which takes in a series of non-mining villages and small towns like Tickhill and Braithwell. In May 2000, the Conservatives outvoted Labour by between three and two to one in these two wards. The marginal is Hatfield, on the flatlands north-east of Doncaster, a close three-party outcome in that year. The other three wards are massively Labour: the old colliery communities of

New Edlington/Warmsworth and Conisbrough with its incongruous medieval castle set amidst industrial grime, and the more modern (1920s) pit village of New Rossington with its history of flirtation with communism and militancy in labour relations. This could hardly sound less up Tony Blair's street, but Don Valley does at least return a loyal supporter of his to the Commons.

Social indices:			2001 Gen. Election:			
% Non-white	0.7		Lab	20,009	54.6	−3.6
% Prof/Man	31.0		C	10,489	28.6	+4.0
% Non-manual	51.9		LD	4,089	11.2	+1.4
£ Av prop val 2000	56 K		Ind	800	2.2	
% Increase 97–00	15.2		UKIP	777	2.1	
% Unemployed 2001	3.3		SLP	466	1.3	−1.1
% Decrease 97–01	3.4		Lab maj	9,520	26.0	
% Fin hard/Rank	27.0	173	Turnout		55.3	−11.1
% Pensioners	22.9		Elect	66,244		
% Prem mort/Rank	31	321				

Member of Parliament

Caroline Flint, at last rewarded for her loyalty by becoming PPS to Peter Hain in 2001, represents the feminisation of the Yorkshire coalfield as one of three metropolitan women parachuted in 1997 into seats formerly reserved for miners since the dawn of time. A remarkably vivacious, gorblimey-accented, ultra-loyal bowler of stooge questions, an ex-GMB researcher and an equal opportunities officer, she was born in 1961 and educated at Twickenham Girls' School and East Anglia University. She concentrates on being a diligent constituency MP, and dislikes press attention on the loyalism of women Labour MPs as distinct from the equal toadyism of the men.

DORSET MID AND NORTH POOLE

The Liberal Democrats had high hopes of extending their tradition of parliamentary success in the west of England to make several gains in Dorset in 2001, particularly after the publicity given to local campaigns encouraging tactical 'vote swapping' between anti-Tory electors. Their most prominent target, Oliver Letwin of Dorset West, escaped though, as did Robert Walter of Dorset North. They did however win a seat given less national attention, Dorset Mid and North Poole, where Christopher Fraser was ousted in favour of Annette Brooke, giving the Lib Dems a toehold in the county again, following the Tories' recapture of Christchurch in 1997.

The wards which make up the constituency of Mid Dorset and North Poole, which was entirely new in 1997, came from no fewer than four former seats but only two genuinely different sources. One of these is the borough of Poole, which donated five wards and some 40,000 electors. These were previously in two different constituencies: Alderney and Canford Magna were in Bournemouth West, while Broadstone, Canford Heath and Creekmoor were in Poole itself. These wards are typical of the Bournemouth–Poole conurbation in their political make-up: affluent, attractive and suburban, they vote Conservative in general elections but tend to support the Liberal Democrats in municipal contests.

The second source of voters was 'Mid Dorset'. From the South Dorset seat came the small town of Wareham west of Poole Harbour, and the rural wards of Bere Regis and St Martin. This adds up to about 8,500 voters. From the old North Dorset came the communities of Lytchett Minster and Lytchett Matravers, and Corfe Mullen, constituting another 15,500 electors. This is not a far-flung constituency covering the geographical heart of the county, but a fairly compact semi-suburban seat curling round to the west and north of Poole. The housing is mainly modern and owner-occupied.

There are Liberal Democrats in all parts of the seat, and Annette Brooke was always going to give Christopher Fraser a close run for his money; in fact there was no evidence of a squeeze on the Labour vote, whether voluntary, assisted by high technology, deals between voters or any other new-fangled notion: the Labour share remained almost exactly constant. If any cause was damaged by the super-close two-party competition it was that of the anti-Europeans, who only did a third as well in 2001 as 1997.

Social indices:			2001 Gen. Election:			
% Non-white	0.8		LD	18,358	42.0	+2.7
% Prof/Man	32.3		C	17,974	41.1	+0.4
% Non-manual	59.1		Lab	6,765	15.5	−0.3
£ Av prop val 2000	111 K		UKIP	621	1.4	
% Increase 97–00	47.3		LD maj	384	0.9	
% Unemployed 2001	1.0		Turnout		65.6	−10.1
% Decrease 97–01	1.6		Elect	66,675		
% Fin hard/Rank	8.3	512				
% Pensioners	24.8					
% Prem mort/Rank	10	593				

Member of Parliament

Annette Brooke, one of three new women Liberal Democrat MPs who won seats from the Conservatives in 2001, contributes to her party's parliamentary pool of nine schoolteachers. With a birth-date-omitting CV but with her year of birth thought to be 1946 or 1947, she attended Romford County Technical School, the LSE and Hughes Hall, Cambridge (for a teaching diploma), and taught in Bournemouth for some 23 years, before becoming partner in a family business selling rocks and minerals. With her tenuous parliamentary career based on 15 years as a Poole councillor, eventually as Leader of the Council, she performs the expected role of Liberal Democrat MPs as an articulator of local grievances, which in 2001 involved opposing the sacking of 570 Marconi workers at a recently upgraded local plant. She immediately became a Liberal Democrat whip, confirming that in her party they also serve who simply stand and win.

DORSET NORTH

Dorset evokes the image of wild heaths and cliffs, especially to those who have read the novels of Thomas Hardy (or of a more recent author, John Fowles). But in fact six of Dorset's eight seats are predominantly urban or suburban; North Dorset is one of the other two, along with West. It is typified by small independent old market towns like Shaftesbury, Blandford Forum, Gillingham and Wimborne Minster, each with a population of a little over 6,000. There are also numerous rural parishes – over 80 in all. This covers the spectacular scenery of Cranborne Chase, the Blackmore Vale and the chalk downs. Like West Dorset, it is now a spacious and largely agricultural constituency of low population density.

The Liberals, in the person of Frank Byers, won North Dorset in 1945 and held it for five years; they have often secured a fairly strong second place since then, and in 1997 they came closest to victory so far, less than 3,000 votes behind the Conservative Robert Walter. After all, Paddy Ashdown's Yeovil citadel in south Somerset was nearby. In 2001 North Dorset was a prime target, but Walter actually increased his share and lead slightly. Despite talk of tactical voting, there was no squeeze on the Labour vote, and in fact that of anti-European candidates went down instead, which may have helped the Conservatives. There was almost certainly no significance in the disappearance of Ashdown from Yeovil and his replacement by a new leader from the distant Scottish Highlands.

Social indices:			2001 Gen. Election:				
% Non-white	0.5		C	22,314	46.7	+2.4	
% Prof/Man	35.1		LD	18,517	38.7	−0.4	
% Non-manual	55.3		Lab	5,334	11.2	+0.9	
£ Av prop val 2000	132 K		UKIP	1,019	2.1	+0.6	
% Increase 97–00	54.1		Ind	391	0.8		
% Unemployed 2001	0.9		Ind	246	0.5		
% Decrease 97–01	0.9		C maj	3,797	7.9		
% Fin hard/Rank	6.6	571	Turnout		66.3	−10.0	
% Pensioners	31.6		Elect	72,140			
% Prem mort/Rank	10	599					

Member of Parliament

Robert Walter, a Conservative frontbencher as a spokesman for Wales (1999–2001), is one of the rare Clarke supporters of the 1997 intake. A square-faced banker and sheep farmer, born in 1948 in Swansea, he attended Colston's School, Bristol, Lord Weymouth School, Warminster and Aston University, and in 1999 quit the Carlton Club after 18 years because it would not admit women, especially his girlfriend Barbara Nutt, and pursued the matter through a Private Member's Bill. Unfashionably Europhile, he backed Clarke in all three ballots in 2001 and returned to the backbenches.

DORSET SOUTH

The general consensus is that the opinion pollsters got it right in 2001, rather than suffering one of those periodic disasters which encourage newspaper proprietors and politicians to make foolish or mendacious statements that they will never pay any attention to polls again. However, critical observers point out that actually every published national poll during the four-week campaign reported a double-figure Labour lead, when in the end their lead was just 9%. Most polling projections suggested that Labour's majority would actually go up, and that they would gain seats from the Tories. In fact they took only one, Dorset South. The polls had all been affected, to varying degrees, by a number of factors which all conspired to exaggerate the Labour vote share prediction: once again, the reluctance of Conservatives to agree to answer questions; the underdog effect moderating huge winning margins; and the exceptionally low turnout, at its greatest among potential Labour voters. The *Sun*'s projection on 23 May 2001 of a Labour overall majority of over 330 based on a MORI survey was as far out as if they predicted no overall majority at all, in which case it would have been clear just how wrong they were.

As there was just the single Tory loss to Labour, it was not surprising that it occurred where it did. The narrowest Conservative majority anywhere in Britain in the 1997 General Election had come in Dorset South, where Ian Bruce held off Labour's Jim Knight by only 77 votes – their only double figure majority. Labour had actually come from third place, with a 15% increase in their share of the vote, easily their best in this part of the world. Oddly, however, this was not their best ever result in this constituency – on one occasion they managed to win it, after Guy Barnett (later the MP for Greenwich) had managed to take advantage of a split between pro- and anti-Common Market Conservatives (some things never change) in a 1962 by-election.

Despite its tradition of patrician representation (Viscount Hinchingbrooke 1945–62, Viscount Cranborne 1979–87), South Dorset is not primarily a rural seat of rolling acres. It is centred on the seaside resort of Weymouth, the Portland naval base and the Isle of Purbeck, famed for its marble quarries. It reaches as far as Swanage to the east (home town of David Mellor), but lost Wareham and Bere Regis in the recent boundary changes. There have always been pockets of Labour support in Weymouth and Portland, and two additional factors helped Jim Knight to reverse the 1997 result: the social and economic changes along the south coast of England which had seen the Tories lose previously in such other seats as Hastings, Hove, Thanet South and Torbay; and tactical voting, at its most publicly organised in Dorset (see also Dorset West). The Liberal Democrats fell by 6% here, and although Labour voters did not appear to reciprocate elsewhere in the county this probably tipped the balance in another extremely close contest.

Social indices:			2001 Gen. Election:			
% Non-white	0.8		Lab	19,027	42.0	+6.0
% Prof/Man	30.6		C	18,874	41.6	+5.5
% Non-manual	52.5		LD	6,531	14.4	−5.8
£ Av prop val 2000	101 K		UKIP	913	2.0	+0.3
% Increase 97–00	51.6		Lab maj	153	0.3	
% Unemployed 2001	1.8		Turnout		65.5	−8.7
% Decrease 97–01	2.5		Elect	69,233		
% Fin hard/Rank	10.1	464				
% Pensioners	30.2					
% Prem mort/Rank	27	394				

Member of Parliament

Jim Knight became, at his second attempt in the constituency, the first Labour MP to be elected for a Dorset seat at a general election, Guy Barnett (1962–64) having won this seat at a by-election aided by a split Tory vote. One of only two Labour gains in the 2001 Election, his victory was paid a good deal of attention at Labour's post-election party conference as a model of computer-based campaigning, which took the fight successfully to the Conservatives' Dorset heartland. An accountant's son, born in 1965 in Bexley, Kent and educated at the local Eltham College and at Fitzwilliam College, Cambridge, he was one of eight public-school-and-Oxbridge educated MPs in Labour's 38-strong 2001 intake, even if the famous old boy of his school, whom he cites as his political inspiration, Fenner Brockway, was hardly a typical public school product – the school having been founded to educate the sons of non-conformist missionaries. Modishly trim-bearded, and with a career encompassing theatre and arts centre management and publishing, he backs entry into the euro, and criticises Dorset's low standard spending assessment for education – an occupational hazard for Labour MPs representing ex-Tory rural seats unfavoured by a Labour government funnelling aid back to its industrial heartlands after years of Conservative neglect. As a reflection of residual local naval interests he was put on the Defence Select Committee in 2001. His majority of 153 is Labour's smallest.

DORSET WEST

It is scarcely surprising that the veteran left-wing pop singer Billy Bragg, a migrant to this attractive part of the countryside, decided that he could best direct his long-term and well-known political activism into organising and publicising tactical voting by Labour supporters, switching to the strong Liberal Democrat challengers against the Shadow Conservative Treasury Secretary Oliver Letwin. Methods ranged from setting up a sophisticated e-mail vote swap shop on the internet to dressing up as a Roman soldier, Tacticus, whose favoured Labour Party could not win here. True enough. The most rural of the Dorset seats, West Dorset includes Tolpuddle, whose early trade union martyrs have entered the annals of trade union hagiography. But it is as far as can be from a Labour stronghold.

Rather, entrenched Toryism has been the order of the day among these villages and small towns in Hardy country. Tolpuddle is just one of 132 civil parishes in this constituency, which covers over 103,000 hectares in area. The towns include Dorchester (Hardy's Casterbridge), Sherborne in the north of the county, the seaside resort of Lyme Regis, and slightly raffish Bridport, with its reputation for poaching and smuggling. It also includes one or two geographical features which have been the cause of some embarrassed smirks over the years, such as the Cerne Abbas Giant and the Piddle Valley. Until the arrival of the circus in 2001 there was little humour in the political contests in West Dorset, though. The Conservatives have always won within living memory. The Liberal Democrats have challenged strongly, cutting the Tory majority from 8,000 to under 2,000 in 1997. They would have had a good chance of winning had they indeed managed to squeeze the small Labour vote.

However, for all Bragg's efforts – and those of Tacticus – Letwin won again as 6,733 people resisted their blandishments and voted Labour again. Perhaps some of them just didn't like being told what to do.

Social indices:			2001 Gen. Election:			
% Non-white	0.5		C	22,126	44.6	+3.5
% Prof/Man	36.0		LD	20,712	41.8	+4.1
% Non-manual	55.9		Lab	6,733	13.6	−4.1
£ Av prop val 2000	123 K		C maj	1,414	2.9	
% Increase 97–00	49.8		Turnout		67.0	−9.1
% Unemployed 2001	1.1		Elect	74,016		
% Decrease 97–01	1.6					
% Fin hard/Rank	7.3	549				
% Pensioners	35.9					
% Prem mort/Rank	22	456				

Member of Parliament

Oliver Letwin, Shadow Home Secretary from 2001, elected in 1997 for the Dorset seat never lost by his party, is one of the most respected of Tory right-wing intellectuals, a rare Rolls Royce mind in politics. Born in 1956, son of the American Thatcherite political philosopher, Shirley Robin Letwin, educated at Eton, Trinity College, Cambridge (with a decently untouted doctorate in the philosophy of education), he ran the international privatisation unit at Rothschilds Bank. A sensitive Hampstead Jewish intellectual, now wading through Wessex mud in green wellies, he was, as part of Margaret Thatcher's Policy Unit (1983–86), a progenitor of the poll tax and of assisted places, is an unremitting opponent of Euro federalism, and followed Redwood all the way into the last ditch with Clarke in 1997. Brought to the frontbench in 1998, he was Shadow Chief Secretary by 2000. Voting in 2001 for the most potentially dynamic leadership option – Portillo, his intellectual penchant for blurting out the truth had been employed in the 2001 Election in his politically incredulous advocacy of £20 billion-worth of tax cuts, and later in the year was reflected in his naïve honesty in admitting the Tories probably couldn't win the next election, and with ever more disarming frankness, doubting if Iain Duncan Smith, elected two months earlier, would be leading the party into it.

DOVER

For many, Dover affords a first sight of England. It is one of only two English towns which the French dignify with their own version of its name (Douvres); the other is London/Londres. In the Second World War the famed cliffs of this major continental port became a symbol of bulldog patriotism and resistance, as well as sentiment. Yet its political preferences are not those of a stronghold of English Nationalistic Toryism, even after a very strong and even virulent campaign in Kent in 2001 centred on the issue of asylum seeking, which has undoubtedly grown in recent years and which clearly affects this classic south-eastern English port of entry more than anywhere else. Labour and their sitting MP Gwyn Prosser did not prove to be a soft touch, though, and held on by 5,000 despite the strongest adverse swing in Kent, 5% to the Conservatives.

This had been the most expected and ultimately easiest of Labour's eight gains in the county in 1997, all of which were retained in 2001 (against almost all predictions). It has a longer and stronger Labour tradition that almost any of the others. Besides the working-class population of Dover itself, torn by the long-running P&O/Sealink passenger ferry industrial dispute in the late 1980s and alarmed by the construction of the 'fixed-link' Channel Tunnel in the early 1990s, this constituency contains the remnants of the once-militant Kent coalfield. Opened up in the inter-war years, the Kent field never reached true prosperity. Owing to economic difficulties and its isolation from other mining areas, there was a shortage of labour and poor industrial relations which bred union militancy. There was an 'unpatriotic' strike during the Second World War only a few miles away from those white cliffs. Pit villages like Aylesham and the miners' Mill Hill district of Deal still maintain a strong Labour allegiance even though Betteshanger, the last colliery in Kent, was closed in August 1989. But this mixed constituency also includes very Conservative seaside spots like Walmer (the other face of Deal from Mill Hill), St Margaret's-at-Cliffe and Capel-le-Ferne.

Dover is a truly heterogeneous constituency: which other division could include coal-mining, seaside resorts, comfortable South of England villages and a major ferry port? It is certainly an exceptional seat in any terms, and it has become more so as new passions, hopes and fears have boiled in recent years, among both indigenous residents and newcomers.

Social indices:			2001 Gen. Election:			
% Non-white	0.9		Lab	21,943	48.8	−5.7
% Prof/Man	27.6		C	16,744	37.2	+4.4
% Non-manual	51.1		LD	5,131	11.4	+3.5
£ Av prop val 2000	78 K		UKIP	1,142	2.5	+1.7
% Increase 97–00	36.1		Lab maj	5,199	11.6	
% Unemployed 2001	3.1		Turnout		65.1	−13.8
% Decrease 97–01	3.7		Elect	69,025		
% Fin hard/Rank	13.3	389				
% Pensioners	29.0					
% Prem mort/Rank	33	291				

Member of Parliament

Stocky, bearded Welshman **Gwyn Prosser** has had a difficult job as MP for Dover since 1997, dealing from the front line with the difficult populist issue of illegal immigration and asylum seeking. Born in 1943 in Swansea where he attended Dunvant Secondary Modern and Swansea Technical Schools and Swansea College of Technology, he was a marine engineer, eventually on Dover Sealink ferries. He has fought against undermanning of the ferries, opposed the rival Channel Tunnel, protested the problems of ex-miners and joblessness on the defunct Kent coalfield, but more centrally, urged dispersal of asylum seekers away from Dover. The high adverse swing he suffered in 2001 underlined his problem on this issue.

DOWN NORTH

North Down is a very unusual seat in every way, and unusual for Northern Ireland too. In 2001 it offered a rare ray of hope, or consolation, for David Trimble as leader of the pro-Belfast Agreement Ulster Unionists, as they made their solitary gain compared with the 1997 General Election while an unprecedented number of parliamentary seats changed hands. This seat had not belonged to the largest Northern Irish party for over two decades.

For nearly 25 years until his death in early 1995 the MP was Sir James Kilfedder, latterly the leader and sole parliamentary representative (and candidate) of the Ulster Popular Unionist Party which he formed in 1980. It was the only seat won at the 1992 General Election by someone who was effectively an Independent, and in his last two contests Kilfedder had to hold off strong challenges from some very surprising quarters. In 1992 North Down was the setting for the only strong performance achieved by the Conservative Party, standing under their own colours in a general election in Northern Ireland for the first time: Dr Laurence Kennedy managed over 14,000 votes. This performance mirrored that of Robert McCartney, a prominent barrister, who, standing as a 'real Unionist', had cut Kilfedder's majority to less than 4,000 in 1987 making North Down uniquely a marginal between two Independents.

The tradition of independence was continued in the by-election of June 1995. It was widely regarded as a near-certainty that McCartney would win if he contested the seat this time, under whatever label he chose, and indeed he did defeat the Official Unionist on a low poll; the Conservatives, shorn of Dr Kennedy's candidature, plummeted from 32% to 2% of the vote. In 1997 McCartney continued the tradition of near-Independence in North Down, by again beating an Ulster Unionist, although by only 1,500 votes. The Conservatives again lost their deposit.

The reason for these unique results have much to do with the social and economic character of North Down. This is the most affluent seat in Northern Ireland, and in many ways the one which most closely resembles a British constituency. Much of the division is urban, with Bangor and Holywood among the larger communities. It is a popular dormitory area for Belfast, with some industry and public authority housing estates but also some very select areas favoured by the Northern Ireland Office for visiting civil servants.

Why did the long tradition of independence end in 2001? McCartney was as strong as ever, and his sceptical opposition to the form the Agreement had taken was indeed popular among Unionists in that year – both his share and his actual vote went up (turnout did not drop here), and he was again not opposed by Ian Paisley's advancing DUP. Trimble's party had a strong and attractive candidate in Lady (Sylvia) Hermon, the wife of the former RUC Chief Constable, Sir John. Most critically, though, the centrist and non-sectarian Alliance Party (not to be confused with the defunct British Liberal-SDP Alliance) withdrew, and almost all of their substantial share of the vote, over 20% in 1997, must have passed to Sylvia Hermon. The anti-agreement unionists harrumphed that she, and Trimble, had won with 'non-unionist' votes, but the fact is that in North Down at least enough voters do not see things in quite so narrow a way, as a perennial stand off between entrenched camps.

Social indices:		2001 Gen. Election:			
% Prof/Man	37.2	UUP	20,833	56.0	+24.9
% Non-manual	64.5	UKUP	13,509	36.3	+1.3
% RC	8.3	SDLP	1,275	3.4	−1.0
% Irish sp	1.7	C	815	2.2	−2.8
% Unemployed 2001	3.9	Ind	444	1.2	
% Decrease 97–01	1.7	SF	313	0.8	
		UUP maj	7,324	19.7	
		Turnout		58.8	+0.8
		Elect	63,212		

Member of Parliament

Lady Hermon, wife of the former Chief Constable of the Royal Ulster Constabulary (1980–89) Sir John Hermon, won this seat from the anti-Agreement UKUP MP Bob McCartney in 2001 – an odd case, in that election, of a Unionist seat being transferred from a hard-liner to a moderate and not vice-versa (as in Strangford or Londonderry East). She thus brought some unexpected comfort to her leader David Trimble, whose colleague she was (as Sylvia Paisley) in the law department at Queen's University Belfast, from 1978 to 1983, when one of their fellow lecturers Edgar Graham was shot by the IRA on the campus. An expert on the application of EU law to Northern Ireland, she was born into a farming family in 1955 and educated at Dungannon High School for Girls and the University of Wales, Aberystwyth. Author of her party's response to the Patten Report's proposals on reform of the RUC, her easy recapture of this seat was aided by the withdrawal of the Alliance Party whose vote in 1997 was as large as her majority in 2001. She is the first Ulster Unionist woman MP since Patricia McLaughlin vacated Belfast West in 1964.

DOWN SOUTH

South Down has an interesting electoral history. When the controversial figure of Enoch Powell returned to his spiritual home, Parliament, in October 1974 it was as Official Unionist MP for that constituency. Powell had long been associated with the Unionist cause, but it still surprised many that he should so quickly enter the maelstrom of Northern Irish politics after leaving the Conservative Party. Major boundary changes in 1983 made Powell's chances of retaining South Down much slimmer, and he held on by only 548 votes in that year, and by 1,842 in the 1986 by-election. In 1987 the axe finally fell as Eddie McGrady mobilised the Nationalist majority in the redrawn seat to inflict on Enoch Powell his second defeat in 13 parliamentary contests (he had lost his first, at the Normanton by-election in 1947).

The South Down seat is predominantly rural, with rolling countryside and a very important agricultural sector. It has a tourist industry based on the seaside town of Newcastle, the Mourne mountains and forest parks. Fishing is centred on Kilkeel, Annalong and Ardglass. The most important urban unit is Downpatrick, which is also an administrative centre for government services. On Carlingford Lough the port of Warrenpoint provides a roll-on/roll-off freight facility to serve Newry and its hinterland.

The man who beat Enoch Powell is still the MP for South Down, although in 2001 the political map changed more substantially than for several elections. Disputation regarding the implementation (or not) of the 1998 Good Friday Agreement weakened the more moderate parties in Northern Ireland across the province. On the unionist side, the DUP put up a candidate here in South Down for the first time, taking 15% almost directly from the UUP, whom they almost caught for third place. It is recognised that a unionist can no longer win here, and the more significant development was the further substantial advance of Sinn Fein, who are now in second place, and have the support of nearly 20% of the total vote compared with 3.6% in 1992. At this rate of advance, and with Eddie McGrady turning 70 at the time of the next general election, a further Sinn Fein gain on top of those achieved in 2001 must be regarded as distinctly possible.

Social indices:		2001 Gen. Election:			
% Prof/Man	31.4	SDLP	24,136	46.3	–6.6
% Non-manual	49.8	SF	10,278	19.7	+9.4
% RC	58.6	UUP	9,173	17.6	–15.2
% Irish sp	10.8	DUP	7,802	15.0	
% Unemployed 2001	4.7	APNI	685	1.3	–2.1
% Decrease 97–01	3.4	SDLP maj	13,858	26.6	
		Turnout		70.8	–0.0
		Elect	73,519		

Member of Parliament

Eddie McGrady, one of three SDLP MPs, has never really been more famous than for the man he beat in this seat at his fourth attempt in 1987 – Enoch Powell, so ending a long and singular political career. A bland retired accountant, born in 1935, educated at St Patrick's (RC) Grammar School, Downpatrick and Belfast College of Technology, he is the SDLP's Whip, an easy enough job when the three of them are not present for 90% of the Commons votes, he in particular working as a good constituency MP. Along with 11 other of Northern Ireland's 18 Westminster MPs, he also doubles-up as MLA (i.e. Member of the Northern Ireland Assembly) for his Westminster seat. Personifying the ageing face of moderate republicanism now challenged by Sinn Fein, and bland in a culture where blandness is uncommon, he has been likened in manner and appearance to Geoffrey Howe.

DUDLEY NORTH

Before 1997 the constituencies in Dudley on the western edge of the West Midlands conurbation were themselves divided on a north-south axis, with a marginal West and a Labour East seat. Now this has been twisted around 90 degrees, and Dudley North and South have been created.

Dudley North does actually contain more of East (five wards) than West, although the two wards taken from West are among the more strongly Conservative in that seat, especially the old market town of Sedgley. Sedgley, on the very north-western edge of the borough, contains some desirable private housing and is just about the most Tory ward in the whole of Dudley. The ex-East section of the constituency contains the semi-independent community of Coseley and the heart of the town of Dudley, including its castle on the hill. This is the only part of the whole borough which has a significant non-white minority, and generally does vote Labour, but not overwhelmingly so. Coseley tends to split on east–west lines, as a microcosm of the borough of Dudley as a whole – and indeed a microcosm of so many parts of Britain.

In its first contest in 1997, the Conservative vote is estimated to have dropped by 12 percent, and what was predicted to be a marginal seat was won easily by Labour's Ross Cranston, even though Arthur Scargill's Socialist Labour Party achieved one of their best results here, almost reaching the level required for return of their deposit. Perhaps they had benefited from the controversy lying behind Cranston's initial selection. It was confirmed (during the 2001 Election campaign, as it happened) by his predecessor John Gilbert that he had been offered a place in the Lords if he vacated North at the last moment in order to make room for Tony Blair's friend Charles Falconer – but he himself had to go to the Lords to make his appointment to the frontbench in the new government possible when his refusal to take his children out of private education aroused unquenchable objections to his candidature. Both Lords Falconer and Gilbert took immediate posts in Tony Blair's first government.

No one has suggested that Ross Cranston's position here was in any way illegitimately gained, although he succeeded Falconer as Solicitor General just a year after his entry to parliament. In 2001 he was not opposed by a left-wing socialist, but the BNP did even better than the Scargillites had done previously and nearly saved their deposit, while he held on again with over half of a total vote reduced by over 9,000 by the low turnout.

Social indices:			2001 Gen. Election:			
% Non-white	6.7		Lab	20,095	52.1	+0.9
% Prof/Man	24.9		C	13,295	34.5	+3.1
% Non-manual	46.1		LD	3,352	8.7	+0.5
£ Av prop val 2000	64 K		BNP	1,822	4.7	
% Increase 97–00	14.3		Lab maj	6,800	17.6	
% Unemployed 2001	5.0		Turnout		55.9	–13.5
% Decrease 97–01	1.6		Elect	68,964		
% Fin hard/Rank	30.3	128				
% Pensioners	25.2					
% Prem mort/Rank	35	259				

Member of Parliament

Ross Cranston QC, one of the few Australians in British politics, came from nowhere (or at least the LSE) in 1997, as a last-minute alternative to Tony Blair's friend, Charles Falconer – who was supposed to be parachuted-in to become Solicitor General, until his children's private schooling was exposed – and within a year, through his own insertion on an NEC-imposed shortlist, was himself Solicitor General. A dry, uncharismatic academic Blairite, he was born in 1948 in Brisbane and educated at the Universities of Queensland, Harvard and Oxford, and was replaced as Solicitor General in 2001 by the resurrected, sacked Cabinet Minister, Harriet Harman, but later in the year was loyally defending the rushed anti-terrorism legislation.

DUDLEY SOUTH

The majority (five) of the seven wards included in Dudley South in 1997 came from the former West, which had a Tory majority of nearly 6,000 in 1992, and not from the safe Labour Dudley East, which now constitutes the core of Dudley North. With this background, it is slightly surprising that Ian Pearson has held on just as easily as his colleague Ross Cranston in North, even after a larger fall in his vote share in 2001.

However, the two wards from East are strongly Labour, and the five from West mixed. These neighbourhoods include older, more industrial fringes of the Black Country such as Brierley Hill, Pensnett, Woodside and Netherton; and also more modern housing on the very edge of the West Midlands conurbation at Kingswinford and Wordsley. Also, in 1997 the Labour Party in Dudley South was still benefiting from the effects of the massive by-election win it secured after the death of the Tory MP for Dudley West, John Blackburn, in late 1994. Their locally born candidate Ian Pearson romped away with one of the largest swings ever recorded, and enjoyed a majority of over 20,000. A by-election usually influences the result of the following general election that constituency, and some part of Pearson's victory by 13,000 in 1997 may have derived from recent electoral history. However, Pearson's majority still outstripped Cranston's in 2001 (and he alone was opposed by Socialist Labour), and he should be the honourable member here for a long time to come.

Social indices:			2001 Gen. Election:			
% Non-white	3.8		Lab	18,109	49.8	−6.8
% Prof/Man	23.8		C	11,292	31.1	+1.6
% Non-manual	46.7		LD	5,421	14.9	+4.0
£ Av prop val 2000	67 K		UKIP	859	2.4	
% Increase 97–00	16.0		SA	663	1.8	
% Unemployed 2001	4.2		Lab maj	6,817	18.8	
% Decrease 97–01	0.8		Turnout		55.4	−16.4
% Fin hard/Rank	21.4	250	Elect	65,578		
% Pensioners	23.6					
% Prem mort/Rank	29	366				

Member of Parliament

Ian Pearson, a government Whip from 2001 and the monochrome victor in one of Labour's most thumping pre-1997 by-election successes, came in on a 60-year record 29% swing. Locally born in 1959, he attended Brierley Hill Grammar School, Balliol College, Oxford and Warwick University (where he gained a doctorate in industrial relations). A tall, hunch-shouldered suit, who urges West Midlands regionalism from his experience as a regional enterprise board executive, he was PPS to Geoffrey Robinson until the latter's fall from grace in 1998.

DULWICH AND WEST NORWOOD

The number of parliamentary seats within Greater London was reduced by ten by the 1995 Boundary Commission, and one of those abolished was Norwood. Or was it? The seat which John Fraser had held for Labour since 1966 has been split three ways, but most (30,000) of its 52,000 electors found themselves paired with most (45,000) of the Southwark borough constituency of Dulwich's 56,000 voters. In simple terms, Dulwich was divided almost as severely as Norwood.

In effect, the southern parts of both Dulwich and Norwood seats have been brought together, while their inner (and therefore more Labour) sections have been transferred to other seats. Before their national, and London-wide, disasters of 1997 and 2001 the Conservatives may have retained some hopes of winning this seat. It contains several attractive middle-class neighbourhoods. Within the Dulwich section are the College and Ruskin wards, which cover Dulwich Village, one of the most expensive and exclusive residential areas in south London, and an educational and cultural centre. Dulwich College, after which one of the wards is named, is among London's top independent schools. The areas which came from Norwood include the middle-class and Tory Thurlow Park, and Knight's Hill, Herne Hill and Gipsy Hill, all of which have some pleasant elevated roads, as their names imply.

There is now no question of this constituency being marginal, though. Tessa Jowell won the new seat by 61% to the Tories' 24% in 1997, and although her vote went down by 6% four years later, the Conservative share fell too, while the Liberal Democrats and the Greens did well and Socialist Labour also stood. The new Cabinet Minister could look forward with no real threat to her tenure of her constituency on the morrow of her triumph in June 2001.

Social indices:			2001 Gen. Election:			
% Non-white	23.0		Lab	20,999	54.9	−6.1
% Prof/Man	47.5		C	8,689	22.7	−1.5
% Non-manual	70.2		LD	5,806	15.2	+4.4
£ Av prop val 2000	166 K		Grn	1,914	5.0	
% Increase 97–00	72.9		SA	839	2.2	
% Unemployed 2001	5.9		Lab maj	12,310	32.2	
% Decrease 97–01	4.1		Turnout		54.3	−11.2
% Fin hard/Rank	22.9	226	Elect	70,497		
% Pensioners	22.0					
% Prem mort/Rank	43	133				

Member of Parliament

Tessa Jowell, promoted into the Cabinet in 2001 with responsibility for the Culture, Media and Sport Department Pandora's Box, first elected here in 1992, is an on-message identikit Blairite who defended Harriet Harman's choice of a selective school for her son, believing 'what she did was right as a mother', has Peter Mandelson as godfather to one of her own children, and slowed her rise by loyally carrying the can for exemption from the tobacco sponsorship ban in 1997 of Formula One, whose boss Bernie Ecclestone had given the Labour Party £1m. A doctor's daughter who became a social worker, she was educated at St Margaret's (private) School, Aberdeen and Edinburgh University. Though entering government in 1997, well up the order at Minister of State level, she remained stuck at Health and then at Education and Employment, until room was made in Cabinet with the removal of three women Cabinet members in 2001. Before 1997 her sweet nature was used to convince the Women's Institute about Labour, but not convincingly enough if their later barracking of the Prime Minister at the Albert Hall in 2000 was anything to go by.

DUMBARTON

The Dumbarton constituency is by no means socially homogeneous. The Firth of Clydeside town of Helensburgh has become popular as a dormitory for affluent commuters to Glasgow, and in 1999 its four local authority wards were equally shared between Conservative and Liberal Democrat. In the red corner is to be found the Vale of Leven, an old textile-working valley which was once known as one of Britain's 'Little Moscows', rare citadels of communism and militant working-class consciousness. The Vale includes the communities of Alexandria, Renton, Bonhill and Jamestown. The Tories obtained 6.5% of the vote in the Vale of Leven in the final Strathclyde regional elections of May 1994 and have not stood in subsequent west Dunbartonshire unitary authority contests. If Helensburgh and the Vale cancel each other out, the election is decided in the eponymous town of Dumbarton.

There are over 18,000 voters in this third section of the seat, and in recent years they have decisively rejected the Tories. Half of the housing in the town of Dumbarton is still council owned, and the Tories only put forward a candidate in one ward in May 1999, Dumbarton South, where they got just 77 votes, or a 4% share.

Dumbarton is not as monolithic a Labour seat as most in the central Scottish industrial belt, and John McFall's majority was only 9,500 in 2001; but the opposition was divided three ways, with the Liberal Democrats more than doubling their share while the other contenders fell back, the Tory into fourth place. Dumbarton is due to be included in a new West Dunbartonshire, which should be regarded as safe enough, at least while there is a popular Labour government in Westminster.

Social indices:			2001 Gen. Election:			
% Non-white	0.7		Lab/Coop	16,151	47.5	−2.1
% Prof/Man	28.5		SNP	6,576	19.3	−3.9
% Non-manual	52.0		LD	5,265	15.5	+7.9
% Unemployed 2001	5.5		C	4,648	13.7	−4.0
% Decrease 97–01	2.3		SSP	1,354	4.0	+3.3
% Fin hard/Rank	32.0	116	L/C maj	9,575	28.2	
% Prem mort/Rank	48	61	Turnout		60.4	−13.0
			Elect	56,267		

Member of Parliament

John McFall, chairman of the Treasury Select Committee from 2001, elected here in 1987, is one of Blair's discarded ministers, following a stint at the Northern Ireland Office and before that a government Whip. His political career launched as a unilateralist campaigner against the local Faslane Trident base, he was born in 1944, son of a school caretaker, educated at St Patrick's (RC) High School, Dumbarton, Paisley College of Technology and Strathclyde University, and spent 13 years teaching chemistry. A Gulf War rebel in 1991, by the mid-1990s he was confining himself to the more anodyne radicalism of fox hunting bans, with his Wild Animals (Protection) Bill – even with its hunting ban clause dropped – savaged by the House of Lords in 1995.

DUMFRIES

For the second time in a row the strength of Labour's performance in 2001 surprised most outside observers. Surely they would fall back, having seized this south-west Scottish seat by such a large margin four years before, especially after Dumfries had been the epicentre in Scotland of the foot-and-mouth outbreak that year, which had caused Tony Blair to postpone his long-nurtured plans to go the country in May? Next door in Galloway and Upper Nithsdale the Conservatives did indeed regain a toehold north of the border, by taking a seat from the SNP. Yet Russell Brown actually further increased his share. Whoever might have been held worthy of blame for the government's handling of the economic tragedy afflicting the countryside, it was not he.

It is well known that in 1997 the Conservatives lost all their parliamentary seats in Scotland. What surprised many is the very wide margins by which some previously safe strongholds fell. In none of these losses was the majority greater than the 9,643 by which Labour took Dumfries. Yet Dumfries and Dumfriesshire have formed one of the two or three safest Conservative seats in Scotland since the Second World War. In the Tories' dark days of the 1990s, Dumfries was one of the very few constituencies north of the border which they were considered certain to hold, along with Eastwood and, perhaps, Edinburgh Pentlands. This area never succumbed to the SNP surge of 1974, nor to the Liberal challenge which has been so successful in the neighbouring Borders seats. Sir Hector Monro retained a majority of over 6,000 over Labour in 1992 – the second largest margin among Tory seats in Scotland.

There have always been working-class and Labour voters in this division, in the council estates of its main town, for example, especially its suburb of Terregles. However until 1997 Dumfries had never fallen to Labour, and they needed a swing of 7% to take it. This was in fact close to the relative changes in share of the two parties across Scotland as a whole. In Dumfries, though, Labour did much better than they needed. Their share went up by no less than 18%, and the Conservatives' down by 15%. This was close to a straight exchange, as both Liberal Democrats and SNP remained static.

This is a division full of Scottish Lowland history and tradition. Besides Dumfries, the largest town in south-western Scotland, this seat contains the small town of Annan, and Annandale stretching far to the north into the hills and moors to Lockerbie and beyond. Here is Ecclefechan, birthplace of Thomas Carlyle, and Lochmaben, reputedly that of Robert the Bruce. It also meets the English border at probably its most famous crossing point: Gretna Green, renowned for its runaway marriages performed over blacksmiths' anvils.

In future Dumfries's town and county hinterland may well be split, although fierce resistance was promised to the Boundary Commission proposals to do so in early 2002, not least by the sitting Labour MP Russell Brown.

Social indices:			2001 Gen. Election:			
% Non-white	0.5		Lab	20,830	48.9	+1.4
% Prof/Man	28.5		C	11,996	28.2	+0.1
% Non-manual	48.1		LD	4,955	11.6	+0.6
% Unemployed 2001	4.1		SNP	4,103	9.6	−2.4
% Decrease 97–01	1.5		SSP	702	1.6	
% Fin hard/Rank	21.1	251	Lab maj	8,834	20.7	
% Prem mort/Rank	37	220	Turnout		67.7	−11.3
			Elect	62,931		

Member of Parliament

Russell Brown, who swept in on Labour's 1997 high tide, was helped here by the retirement of One Nation Tory Sir Hector Monro. As local as local gets, he was born locally in Annan in 1951, educated at Annan Academy, was a local or regional councillor for ten years, and worked for 18 years as a factory worker for ICI in Dumfries. Short, straight-backed and bearded (one of Labour's 49), and one of the PLP's 51 former manual workers, he campaigns on local issues such as arms dumps in the Beaufort Dyke and the Lockerbie bombing. Notwithstanding a serious outbreak of foot-and-mouth disease, and the Tory choice of a similarly One Nation candidate as Sir Hector Monro, he enjoyed a swing in Labour's direction in 2001, but then enjoyed less the (eventually dropped) allegations about sub-letting his constituency office to the local MSP (Scottish Parliament Member) whilst claiming full allowances.

DUNDEE EAST

Historically, Dundee East is the strongest ever Scottish Nationalist seat in industrial Scotland – and one of its two strongest seats anywhere (the other is the very individual Western Isles). However, the legacy of the past is rapidly falling away.

This was the constituency of Gordon Wilson, who became the SNP's parliamentary leader from 1974 to 1987. For much of this time it was the only Nationalist seat in industrial Scotland. How can this lengthy tenure be explained? The initial victories in the two 1974 Elections are not so surprising, for that year saw the zenith of the SNP's success (so far, anyway). They won seven seats in February and 11 in October. Almost all of these were lost in 1979, though, and it cannot but be suspected that Wilson was able to hold on because the Labour candidate was the ex-Communist Jimmy Reid, the Upper Clyde Shipbuilders work-in leader, whose policies and reputation must have frightened off some traditional Labour voters. Wilson's prominence grew in the 1980s, but in 1987 Labour performed extremely well in Scotland, and the party leader lost even as three new colleagues were elected against Tory MPs elsewhere: a severe blow at a moment of apparent advance.

With Gordon Wilson refraining from contesting Dundee East again in 1992, John McAllion was able to increase his Labour majority from 1,000 to over 4,500. It was the only seat in the country where the SNP share of the vote fell that year. There had been clearly a large personal vote for Wilson, which could no longer be mobilised, and the Nationalists slipped back another 6% in 1997, as Labour's majority increased to very nearly 10,000.

Dundee remains one of the Nationalists' strongest areas in industrial and urban Scotland, though. They very nearly won the Dundee West division in the inaugural Scottish Parliament contest in May 1999, but in 2001 they were still closer to winning East's seat at Westminster, increasing their share by 5% while that of the new Labour candidate Iain Luke fell by even more.

There are some middle-class residential areas, particularly to the east along the Tay at Broughty Ferry and Balgillo. These are heavily outnumbered though by the big, brooding council estates inland, including Fintry, Whitfield and Douglas and Angus. Dundee East is still a working-class seat, and Labour must start favourites next time, but an SNP revival is far from impossible should their rivals' governance at Westminster – or in Edinburgh – pall.

Social indices:			2001 Gen. Election:			
% Non-white	2.1		Lab	14,635	45.2	−5.9
% Prof/Man	28.3		SNP	10,160	31.4	+4.9
% Non-manual	52.9		C	3,900	12.1	−3.7
% Unemployed 2001	7.6		LD	2,784	8.6	+4.5
% Decrease 97–01	2.5		SSP	879	2.7	+2.2
% Fin hard/Rank	45.8	27	Lab maj	4,475	13.8	
% Prem mort/Rank	50	46	Turnout		57.2	−12.2
			Elect	56,535		

Member of Parliament

If **Iain Luke**, Labour's replacement here in 2001 for the retreated-to-Holyrood John McAllion, were a stick of rock, the word 'Dundee' would appear throughout. Born in the city in 1951, the son of a school caretaker and GMBU activist, he attended Stobswell Boys' Junior School and Harris Academy Dundee and, after five years as a tax collector, Dundee University; thence to 18 years as a local further education lecturer; paralleled by 17 years on Dundee City Council, including two years as Leader. For such a man was selection by OMOV invented and his maiden speech, larded with praise for his native city, came as second nature. A dour-looking, safer pair of hands than his Nationalist-leaning predecessor, McAllion, his anticipated conformism was recognised in appointment to the Broadcasting Select Committee in 2001.

DUNDEE WEST

In the 1999 Elections for the newly created devolved Scottish Parliament, the SNP's Calum Cashley finished only 121 votes behind the Labour victor, Kate Maclean. This was by far their best ever performance in the seat (the Edinburgh Parliament elections' constituencies are fought on the same boundaries as Westminster contests, although there is an additional member top-up system on a regional basis to ensure proportionality overall). Hopes were clearly raised that this would be followed up by a victory in the 2001 General Election; but they came nowhere near. Unlike Dundee East, West has avoided the temptation ever to elect a Nationalist MP, remaining loyal to Labour since its creation in 1950. Scotland's fourth city does have some middle-class and traditionally Tory residential districts, in both West and East. Winston Churchill was a Coalition Liberal MP for Dundee from 1918 to 1922, holding one of the two seats then fought for jointly; he was then beaten by Labour's E.D. Morel and the eccentric 'Labour Prohibitionist' Edwin Scrymgeour.

Dundee West does have a handful of Tory areas still, notably in the old 'West End' and the Riverside ward by the Tay, but the Conservatives' vote has crumbled in recent elections, and they have fallen back to third place with under a tenth of the vote in 2001. More typical politically and socially of Dundee West are the post-war council estates which climb the hills behind the city, away from the Tay beyond the Dundee Law (Dundee's central hill, an extinct volcano, its own version of Edinburgh's Arthur's Seat). The tower-block developments reinforce the impression of a working-class industrial city.

This image is correct. Dundee was once 'Juteopolis', the centre of the world's jute mill industry. The mills were particularly concentrated in the western working-class district of Lochee. But the jute industry was moved out to the Indian subcontinent in the early years of the twentieth century, and Dundee has had to look for ways of diversifying its economy. These include computers and electronics, publishing, tyre manufacture, food processing, carpets, heavy electrical engineering, greeting cards, oil-related marine engineering, instrument engineering, clothes manufacture, bio-technology and agri-technology – and Dundee is a major port for the offshore oil industry. Dundee is basically a Labour town, and the SNP obtained just 27% as the MP for over 20 years, Ernie Ross, held a majority of 6,800.

Social indices:			2001 Gen. Election:			
% Non-white	2.1		Lab	14,787	50.6	−3.2
% Prof/Man	28.1		SNP	7,987	27.3	+4.1
% Non-manual	50.5		C	2,656	9.1	−4.1
% Unemployed 2001	6.0		LD	2,620	9.0	+1.3
% Decrease 97–01	2.4		SSP	1,192	4.1	+3.0
% Fin hard/Rank	43.0	35	Lab maj	6,800	23.3	
% Prem mort/Rank	51	39	Turnout		54.4	−13.3
			Elect	53,760		

Member of Parliament

Ernie Ross was elected in 1979, a slight, dour, now cadaverous, and hauntedly poker-faced man, locally born in 1942, educated at St John's (RC) Junior Secondary School and employed as an engineer, first in a local shipyard and finally at the local Timex factory. For most of his career he has been so identified as a left-wing proponent of the Arab cause – specifically the Palestinians – as to be dubbed 'the MP for Nablus West' (the West Bank town with which Dundee was twinned). This one-club stance was modified with Labour forming a government in 1997, after which he set about blocking nationalist-inclined Labour MPs standing for the devolved Edinburgh parliament – driving one, Dennis Canavan, to stand as an independent and call him 'a government nark'. His new taste for loyalism led him in 1999, as a member of the Foreign Affairs Select Committee, to leak a draft report on Sierra Leone to Foreign Secretary Cook, an act for which he was dismissed from the Committee and suspended from the Commons for ten days, and thereafter known as 'the plumber' because of his ability to 'fix leaks'.

DUNFERMLINE EAST

Dunfermline East is a very suitable seat for one of the modern Labour Party's most prominent and powerful figures, Gordon Brown, the Chancellor of the Exchequer. He has held the seat since its creation in 1983, and: it is by any measure one of the safest Labour seats in Scotland, and, therefore, in Britain, although its proposed abolition in boundary changes may force Brown to follow some of its territory to join Kirkcaldy.

The left-wing tradition here is deep and goes back a long way into history. The seat does not include the town of Dunfermline nor is it mainly composed of the constituency named Dunfermline before 1983 – three-quarters of that seat went into Dunfermline West. East is in fact based on the heart of the old Fife coalfield, around towns such as Cowdenbeath and Lochgelly, where Gordon Brown's count was held in 2001, and Cardenden, home town of the crime writer Ian Rankin and his creation, Inspector Rebus. This area arguably has the strongest and most persistent Communist tradition of any in Britain. In the inter-war years some of the little mining communities here were once known as 'Little Moscows' – Lumphinnans, Kelty, Kinglassie and others. Willie Gallacher was Communist MP for West Fife from 1935 to 1950, at a time when there were at most two Communist members in Parliament (Phil Piratin represented Mile End in Stepney from 1945 to 1950). As late as 1990 a

Communist won the Ballingry/Lochore electoral division in the Fife regional council elections, defeating a Labour candidate.

The Communists have not posed a significant threat to Labour in a general election for a long time, though, and have not put up a candidate in the past decade (the changes associated with the end of the Cold War and the Iron Curtain have deeply split the former Communist Party ideologically and organisationally). Nor do the electors of Dunfermline East have much time for Scottish Nationalism, possibly seen as a deviation from socialist policy and practice. The SNP only obtained 15% of the vote in 2001, the Conservatives under 10%. Miles ahead was Gordon Brown, with 65% of the vote in a six-way contest, a figure exceeded in few seats in Scotland. Rebus notwithstanding, there are few puzzles or enigmas in electoral politics here.

Social indices:			2001 Gen. Election:			
% Non-white	0.7		Lab	19,487	64.8	−2.0
% Prof/Man	24.0		SNP	4,424	14.7	−0.8
% Non-manual	43.8		C	2,838	9.4	−0.6
% Unemployed 2001	4.8		LD	2,281	7.6	+1.7
% Decrease 97–01	2.0		SSP	770	2.6	
% Fin hard/Rank	38.2	66	UKIP	286	1.0	
% Prem mort/Rank	41	163	Lab maj	15,063	50.1	
			Turnout		57.0	−13.3
			Elect	52,811		

Member of Parliament

Gordon Brown, elected here in 1983, is the first of Labour's eight Chancellors (Snowden, Dalton, Cripps, Gaitskell, Callaghan, Jenkins and Healey) to enjoy liberally overflowing coffers, and so able to combine a Presbyterian devotion to 'prudence' with an allegedly massive investment in public services. A son of the Manse, born in 1951 and educated at Kirkcaldy High School (losing an eye), and with a History doctorate from Edinburgh University, he finally married in 2000. With his ambitions thwarted by Blair (and Mandelson) in 1994, his supporters in government marginalised in reshuffles since 1997, and as a man more spun against than spinning, he may yet, barring a major economic downturn, inherit the earth, whether sooner – in the wake of a shock election result scything down Labour's backbench foot soldiers and destabilising the Blair premiership, which would have to have happened but didn't in 2001 – or later, with the need for a Caledonian hero to save the Union after bad Scottish Parliament election results in 2003, in the manner that Canadian unity is saved by Prime Ministers from Quebec. A botched referendum on the euro seemed also likely to boost his career.

DUNFERMLINE WEST

For 500 years Dunfermline was Scotland's capital, and in its abbey is buried a national hero, Robert the Bruce, among eight kings, five queens, six princes and two princesses of the royal Scottish house. It was also the birthplace of the philanthropist Andrew Carnegie. As befits such an ancient and distinguished town, Dunfermline's politics are somewhat mixed, with some representation at local level for Labour, Liberal Democrat and SNP councillors. Dunfermline West, the seat which contains the whole of the eponymous town, is less overwhelmingly Labour than its neighbour to the east. However, the opposition is fairly evenly divided between the other three parties. The main town has its share of housing schemes with very much a plebeian, rather than royal, population. The seat extends west along the north bank of the Forth to the industrial towns of Torryburn, Culross and Kincardine, which are strongly Labour. Even inland villages like Saline are Labour bankers. With the opposition still split and Labour's share still over 50%, Rachel Squire's future in Dunfermline seems secure.

Social indices:			2001 Gen. Election:			
% Non-white	0.6		Lab	16,370	52.8	−0.2
% Prof/Man	29.8		SNP	5,390	17.4	−1.8
% Non-manual	53.5		LD	4,832	15.6	+2.0
% Unemployed 2001	5.0		C	3,166	10.2	−2.4
% Decrease 97–01	1.3		SSP	746	2.4	
% Fin hard/Rank	29.8	132	UKIP	471	1.5	
% Prem mort/Rank	44	111	Lab maj	10,980	35.4	
			Turnout		57.1	−12.4
			Elect	54,293		

Member of Parliament

Rachel Squire, PPS to Education and Employment Ministers, was elected in 1992 for this seat, having gained selection, despite her English birth (born in 1954 in Surrey) and private schooling (at Godolphin and Latimer, Hammersmith followed by Durham and Birmingham Universities) by her trade union background as UNISON's Scottish Region Education Officer for 10 years. Inevitably she has become, despite her earlier opposition to the defence estimates, a virtually one-club politician as campaigner for the threatened Rosyth Dockyard. With an angular countenance and deliberate mode of speech, slowed down by a brain tumour in 1993, and with a tendency to nod her head 'like an oil well' whenever a government minister is speaking, she seemed less vulnerable, with her English origins (as one of only four Labour MPs in Scotland who were English-born) and backbench status, given the suggestion that Gordon Brown would not contest the merged Dunfermline seat in the proposed reduction of Scottish constituencies.

DURHAM, CITY OF

Rather like the City of Chester, the City of Durham is a curiously named seat. Not only does it contain much other territory besides Durham itself, which had a population of under 30,000 in 1991, but it is designated as a county constituency. There are, of course, reasons for its title. The division was drawn to be identical to the 'City of Durham' local government unit; and it is as well to distinguish the seat from the six others in Durham county.

Despite its modest size, Durham really is one of England's most historic and distinguished cities. It is noted for its fine cathedral, set on a crag in a bend of the Wear – and the bishopric of Durham has long been one of the most senior in the country. Durham University was the first to be founded in England outside Oxbridge, and still operates on a collegiate system. The city houses the administrative headquarters of the county which bears its name, and many public servants as a result. It is close enough too to act as a commuting base for the North East's big city, Newcastle upon Tyne.

With the establishment presence (even granted the radicalism of a recent Bishop, David Jenkins), it might be thought that Durham would lean to the Conservatives in politics. Yet the seat has been Labour since 1935, and its character has been determined not so much by the church or the university as by the fact that Durham was also historically at the centre of the county's coalfield, and the site of the annual Miners' Gala, a celebration of working-class collectivism and the Labour Movement. Nonconformity has traditionally been strong in the outlying villages. Besides the city, the constituency contains the ex-mining areas of Brandon-Byshottles, Coxhoe, Sherburn and the Deerness valley to the west, all solidly Labour.

The centre challenged strongly in the City of Durham seat in 1983, the SDP coming within 2,000 votes of the Labour MP Dr Mark Hughes. However, with the decline and extinction of the SDP and the arrival of an energetic new Labour candidate in Gerry Steinberg, Labour's position was rapidly re-established. In 1997 he won by 22,500 over the Conservatives, with the Liberal Democrats back in third place. However, the Lib Dems revived in 2001, increasing their share of the vote by over 8%, almost entirely at Labour's expense. This was not unique in the county: they improved their share the most anywhere on average in Tyne and Wear (see Blaydon, for example, or most of the seats in Newcastle) and County Durham. This was usually an extension of council activism. In this constituency their greatest local government successes came in wards within the city itself such as Elvet and Framwelgate. They did manage to reach exactly one third of the total votes cast in the City elections of May 1999; they have not come close to matching that yet in parliamentary contests. But watch out, if Tony Blair's government should become nationally unpopular.

Social indices:			2001 Gen. Election:				
% Non-white	1.1		Lab	23,254	56.1	−7.2	
% Prof/Man	35.9		LD	9,813	23.7	+8.4	
% Non-manual	57.6		C	7,167	17.3	−0.2	
£ Av prop val 2000	68 K		UKIP	1,252	3.0		
% Increase 97–00	16.4		Lab maj	13,441	32.4		
% Unemployed 2001	2.8		Turnout		59.6	−11.3	
% Decrease 97–01	1.6		Elect	69,633			
% Fin hard/Rank	19.7	281					
% Pensioners	23.8						
% Prem mort/Rank	28	381					

Member of Parliament

Gerry Steinberg, MP here since 1987, is from Labour's chalk face. He was born in 1945, son of a commercial traveller, and traumatised by failure at the 11-plus, though later transferred from secondary modern school to Durham Johnstone Grammar School, trained as a teacher at Sheffield College of Education and taught in special schools for 20 years. He was duly outraged by Harriet Harman's use of selective schools for her children. A Eurosceptic, who nonetheless appreciates EU money for his dead coalfield, he is a staunch Zionist, whose likeness to Groucho Marx was seriously affected by the removal of his ample moustache.

DURHAM NORTH

North Durham was created in 1983 as an amalgamation of two former constituencies – Chester-le-Street without the New Town of Washington (in the county of Tyne and Wear) and Consett without the troubled town of Consett itself (transferred to North West Durham). The latter segment essentially consists of the working-class villages which made up the old Stanley Urban district, before coming under the aegis of Derwentside Council. In the 1995 Commission's report, far more minor changes were made: simply the uncontroversial removal of two wards (Burnopfield and Dipton) to NW Durham.

This did not alter the status of North Durham as a rock-solid Labour seat, in this most strongly Labour of all counties. The party had held Chester-le-Street since 1906, obtaining an 8,000 majority even in 1931 (when they scarcely won 50 seats in the whole country), and successfully withstood a Liberal by-election challenge even in 1973 when the Liberals were carrying all before them elsewhere. Chester-le-Street itself is quite a prosperous town on the original route from Newcastle to London, and there is something of a Conservative vote in the east of the town towards the stately grounds of Lambton Park, and the far more modern attractions of the purpose-built cricket ground, which has already staged internationals and whose facilities put those of ageing established Test stadia like Headingley (Leeds NW) to shame. But the town of Chester-le-Street is surrounded by old ex-mining villages, and with the Liberals quiescent even at local government level it can have surprised no one that the 1973 by-election victor Giles Radice held on to North Durham very easily four times then passed it on with no trouble whatever to Kevan Jones in 2001.

Social indices:			2001 Gen. Election:			
% Non-white	0.5		Lab	25,920	67.2	–3.1
% Prof/Man	25.7		C	7,237	18.8	+4.3
% Non-manual	52.3		LD	5,411	14.0	+3.0
£ Av prop val 2000	55 K		Lab maj	18,683	48.4	
% Increase 97–00	21.3		Turnout		57.0	–12.4
% Unemployed 2001	3.6		Elect	67,610		
% Decrease 97–01	2.2					
% Fin hard/Rank	27.5	165				
% Pensioners	24.2					
% Prem mort/Rank	32	300				

Member of Parliament

Continuing union influence in Labour safe seat selections was a feature of the 2001 Election, in which six former high-ranking union officials were numbered among

Labour's 38 new MPs – including the new MP here, **Kevan Jones**, a regional GMB official. He replaced the retiring Giles Radice, Labour's last Wykehamist MP, but also a former GMB research officer. A miner's son from the Nottinghamshire coalfield, he was born in 1964, educated at Portland Comprehensive Worksop, Newcastle Polytechnic and the University of Southern Maine, USA. As a former parliamentary aide to Nick Brown MP for four years, a regional GMB official for 12, a Newcastle city councillor (rising to Deputy Group Leader) for 11, and a leading figure in Labour's Northern Regional Party, his union, party and municipal connections were incapable of improvement. A north-east regional fixer credited with helping to insert Peter Mandelson at Hartlepool in 1992, he backs a north-eastern regional assembly, urges the retention of important local defence industry jobs, and joins on the train or plane to London an important nexus of north-east-based Labour Ministers and MPs.

DURHAM NORTH WEST

The North West Durham constituency contains some industrial scenery of an almost brutal nature. The seat of this name has always included several lonely little towns founded for coal-mining among the hills and moors around the upper Wear valley – Tow Law, Crook and Willington, Esh Winning. These isolated communities long ago bred a tight-knit spirit, of a determinedly working-class nature which often ensured unopposed Labour politics. Mining no longer takes place as the seams have been exhausted in the high country of west Durham, but many of the traditions, including the political loyalties, have remained. Since 1983 this territory has been joined by Consett, a town which suffered economic and social disaster in the early 1980s when its steelworks were closed. Consett was very much a one-industry town, and most of its male workers depended on the steel industry directly or indirectly. Consett is on Derwentside rather than in the Wear valley, but it is nevertheless remote and isolated. It is the highest town in County Durham, and the ruined site of the steelworks stood on the top of the hill, eerily dominating the redstone town like a kind of ghost.

For a time after the closure Consett took on some of the aspects of a boom town as the ex-steelworkers spent redundancy money; and most duly found new jobs, as Consett survived into the 1990s. However, the town stayed solidly Labour, and NW Durham has remained that rarity, a Labour seat with a low density of population and a large acreage. There was a shock in 1991 as the Liberal Democrats swept into power in the Wear Valley District Council, seizing 28 of the 40 seats as the local Labour Party possibly rested on its laurels after decades of domination. There was no echo of this whatsoever in the General Election the following year, though, as Hilary Armstrong increased her majority from 10,000 to 14,000 and the Liberal Democrats actually slipped 6% to a poor 14% and a distant third place. Unlike in several other north-eastern seats, the Liberal Democrats have made no discernible move forward in either local or parliamentary elections as the centuries have ticked over, and the NW Durham Armstrong dynasty carries on and on, with Hilary now organising all her colleagues as Chief Whip.

Social indices:			2001 Gen. Election:			
% Non-white	0.4		Lab	24,526	62.5	−6.2
% Prof/Man	29.6		C	8,193	20.9	+5.6
% Non-manual	50.0		LD	5,846	14.9	+4.1
£ Av prop val 2000	54 K		SLP	661	1.7	
% Increase 97–00	23.8		Lab maj	16,333	41.6	
% Unemployed 2001	3.9		Turnout		58.5	−10.5
% Decrease 97–01	2.2					
% Decrease 97–01	2.4		Elect	67,062		
% Fin hard/Rank	27.2	171				
% Pensioners	24.2					
% Prem mort/Rank	42	143				

Member of Parliament

Hilary Armstrong, a worthy and earnest lisping Methodist, was elected here in 1987 in succession to her father, who had held the seat since 1964. As an MP's daughter well-schooled in the political arts, she helped John Smith – as his PPS – secure union backing for his introduction of OMOV (one member one vote) in 1993. Born in 1945 and educated at Monkwearmouth Grammar School, West Ham College of Technology and Birmingham University, she was a social worker and then a lecturer at Sunderland Polytechnic, and spent four years in government after 1997, stuck as a Local Government and Housing Minister, trying to persuade reluctant Labour councillors to accept elected mayors. Dubbed 'a dull Harriet Harman', and with a rather relentless debating style, she was surprisingly promoted to Chief Whip without any previous experience of the Whips' Office, as became apparent in her publicised confrontation with the hitherto obscure backbencher Paul Marsden over his refusal to back the government's support for US bombing of Afghanistan in October 2001; in fact she became the first Labour Chief Whip in 20 years to lose an MP to the Opposition.

EALING, ACTON AND SHEPHERD'S BUSH

The Boundary Commission's decision, enacted for the first time in 1997, to create a cross-borough seat including wards from both Ealing and Hammersmith/Fulham caused great controversy and massive problems for the Conservatives, especially the sitting Acton MP Sir George Young. As in a number of other cases in London, the lines could hardly have been drawn in a better manner for Labour. The most Conservative wards from the former Acton seat, Pitshanger and Ealing Common, were not included, but the most strongly Labour bloc in north Hammersmith, around the White City and Wormwood Scrubs, were. It is easy to understand the Tories' rage at these changes. Ealing is classed by the Census as an Outer London borough, and it is a long way in a social and political sense from Hanger Lane to the inner-city terraces of Shepherd's Bush. The borough of Hammersmith and Fulham could have been paired with Kensington and Chelsea (where the Commission's work has been if anything even more disastrous for the Conservatives).

The result of the first contest in the new seat in 1997 was as expected. Sir George Young joined the 'chicken run' and found a safe seat in Hampshire (NW). Clive Soley won for Labour by 15,000 plus, in a ten-way contest in which seven of the combatants failed to attain a four -es also failed to make an impact. However, in the long term the fight is not over. The Boundary Commission has already decided that after their next review is passed into law, Ealing Borough will regain three seats of its very own and that Acton will be separated from the Hammersmith/Fulham section of this seat. This will not happen in time for the next general election – but it will happen.

Social indices:			2001 Gen. Election:				
% Non-white	24.2		Lab	20,144	54.1	–4.2	
% Prof/Man	45.7		C	9,355	25.1	–0.7	
% Non-manual	67.9		LD	6,171	16.6	+5.8	
£ Av prop val 2000	241 K		SA	529	1.4		
% Increase 97–00	69.3		UKIP	476	1.3	+0.5	
% Unemployed 2001	5.2		SLP	301	0.8	–0.5	
% Decrease 97–01	4.1		PA	225	0.6	+0.1	
% Fin hard/Rank	18.0	304	Lab maj	10,789	29.0		
% Pensioners	21.2		Turnout		52.6	–14.1	
% Prem mort/Rank	46	79	Elect	70,697			

Member of Parliament

Clive Soley, who was re-elected Chairman of the PLP by only six votes in November 2000, has been MP in this area since 1979, and is one of the MPs of that intake whose Opposition spokesmanships during the long Thatcher years never got exchanged for ministerial posts. Born in 1939 and educated at Downsall Secondary Modern, Ilford and later Newbattle Abbey College, Scotland and Strathclyde University, he worked as a probation officer for nine years. Originally a soft left-winger, keen on a united Ireland and a responsible press, he enjoyed more prominence after 1997 as Chairman of the PLP serving as a bridge between Blair and the large majority, as deviser of attempts to block Livingstone's mayoral candidacy, and as screener of would-be Labour parliamentary candidates. He ended up pleasing neither Downing Street nor the backbenchers, only narrowly held on to his job in November 2000, and after losing his NEC seat decided not to stand for re-election to the PLP chairmanship in 2001.

EALING NORTH

For decades now Ealing North has been a key constituency in London. Its percentages of owner-occupiers and council tenants, of working-class and middle-class residents, are all near to the average across the whole of the capital. It fell to the winning party in the great 'sea-change' General Elections of 1964, 1979 and 1997. It was long regarded as a vital and classic marginal, swinging with the tide. Then suddenly it started producing huge swings. In 1987 the Conservative MP Harry Greenway increased his majority from 6,000 to no less than 15,000, and benefited from a swing of very nearly 8%. Then in 1992 the situation was reversed and Greenway's lead was slashed to 6,000 again. In 1997 there was a further swing of no less than 16% to

Labour and Stephen Pound defeated Greenway by over 9,000. What accounts for this exceptional volatility?

The clue partially lies in the election in May 1986 of a Labour administration in Ealing borough. That regime immediately enacted a large rate rise, and Greenway's spectacular advance in 1987 was heavily influenced by public reaction against that and other unpopular policies – a rare example of local affairs impinging on a general election result. Labour was voted out of control of the council in May 1990, and by 1992 the factors which had produced the 1987 Tory landslide in Ealing North had all disappeared; politics returned to 'normal'. The huge swing of May 1997 was actually in line with the Outer London norm.

Most of the wards in Ealing North have been marginal. The Conservatives won almost all of them in 1990, and Labour gained several in 1994; in 1998 three of them actually split their council representation between Labour and Conservative: Costons, Mandeville and Wood End. This is 'middle' London; not Central London with its rapid pace of life and inner-city problems, nor the peripheral suburbs. Ealing North includes the communities of Greenford, Perivale and Northolt, and the area around Horsenden Hill. Some areas, like West End, Mandeville and Hobbayne, used to contain a majority of council housing, and are still more inclined to Labour than average.

London was a huge disappointment for the Conservatives in 2001. After four years of Tony Blair's government, their share of the vote in the capital actually fell, and in few places more than Ealing North, where it went down by 8%. Perhaps they were starved of the oxygen of publicity the hyperactive Harry Greenway had given them as an incumbent MP. The Liberal Democrats improved from a dismally low base. Whatever the reasons, Ealing North no longer looks marginal, which is very good news indeed for the prospect of an extended spell of Labour government – for the first time ever.

Social indices:			2001 Gen. Election:			
% Non-white	22.9		Lab	25,022	55.7	+2.0
% Prof/Man	37.9		C	13,185	29.3	−7.9
% Non-manual	64.5		LD	5,043	11.2	+4.2
£ Av prop val 2000	145 K		Grn	1,039	2.3	+1.4
% Increase 97–00	51.8		UKIP	668	1.5	+0.2
% Unemployed 2001	2.9		Lab maj	11,837	26.3	
% Decrease 97–01	2.6		Turnout		58.0	−13.3
% Fin hard/Rank	14.4	364	Elect	77,524		
% Pensioners	22.6					
% Prem mort/Rank	25	429				

Member of Parliament

Steve Pound, a bald and beaky Mr Punch lookalike, Labour victor here in 1997, is an off-message card, who plays to the gallery, as in his call at the Labour Party conference Tribune Rally in 1999 to 'put up two fingers to New Labour's authoritarian strain', or, starting the bidding at £1,250 when auctioning a Harrods hamper to raise funds for *Tribune*, asking, 'Where's Marshall-Andrews [radical, affluent Labour QC MP]? –That's only an hour's pay for him'. For 1960s nostalgics, he is the boy who bought the pills with which Stephen Ward committed suicide, his journalist father, Pelham Pound, having befriended and stood bail for the Profumo scandal's osteopath and pimp. The closest the PLP gets to having a stand-up comedian, he was born in 1948, educated at Hertford Grammar School and as a mature student, at LSE, and spent 15 years on Ealing council. Self-described as 'no slavish lickspittle of the frontbench' he is in fact more whimsical joker than actual rebel. Effortlessly sardonic, a politician's politician, he likes elected mayors, so long as they are not Ken Livingstone, for whom he recommends a poisoned tipped umbrella.

EALING SOUTHALL

The politics of Southall are dominated by the issues of race and religion. At the time of the most recently published Census in 1991, 51.2% of the population of this constituency classified themselves in ethnic groups other than white, mostly defining themselves as of Indian origin. Southall was one of the first two or three seats in Britain to become majority non-white. In 1992 it elected its first Asian MP, as the Labour Party selected Piara Khabra as their official candidate. This was resisted by the 75-year-old sitting MP, Sydney Bidwell, who stood in 1992 as 'True Labour' but obtained less than 10% of the vote as Khabra secured a lead of nearly 7,000 over his main challenger, the Conservative Professor Philip Treleaven. Bidwell had long resisted retirement; one of the reasons put forward for continued white representation of Southall was the occasional conflict between Hindus and Sikhs, the two largest Asian communities. It seems likely now that the MP for Southall for the foreseeable future will be Asian, and Piara Khabra, who was at least 67 years of age when first elected, has proved more permanent than some predicted, as he was re-elected in 2001 at 76-ish as the oldest MP.

Khabra has won three times by large margins, but Ealing Southall tends to attract large fields of candidates: eight in 2001, as in 1997. On this latest occasion one of the independents made a very serious effort. Avtar Lit, the proprietor of the Asian radio station, Sunrise, could call on the resources of finance, publicity and recognition. He proclaimed that he would win. Indeed he did obtain 5,764 votes and over 12% of the vote, a share apparently taken almost entirely from Khabra. This shows both the potential and the limitations of such a candidature. Southall remains dominated by the British party system, but Lit's intervention raised the electoral profile in this lively part of London.

Southall is the south-western part of the borough of Ealing. The community of Southall itself is overwhelmingly Asian. Northcote ward was 90% non-white in 1991, the highest figure recorded in any ward in the country; the proportion in Glebe ward was 81%, in Mount Pleasant 74%, in Dormers Wells 55%. Why has this corner of outer London become the most heavily Asian part of Britain? Partly the cause was the easy availability of inexpensive private housing; only about 13% of the housing is council-built. Southall is not too far from Heathrow airport, the major port of entry and a supplier of plentiful jobs. Once the district had initially become popular with Asian immigrants in the 1950s and 1960s, many others followed, to reunite with families, friends and neighbours. Many Asian businesses were started, and branches of Indian banks opened up. The commitment of British Asians to educational qualifications is demonstrated by the fact that Ealing Southall provided the second highest number of successful candidates for university admission, according to the latest UCAS figures based on home postcode (870 in 1998, exceeded only by Harrow East). Southall now presents the vivid picture of a Little India in West London.

Social indices:			2001 Gen. Election:			
% Non-white	47.3		Lab	22,239	47.5	−12.5
% Prof/Man	38.0		C	8,556	18.3	−2.5
% Non-manual	62.0		Ind	5,764	12.3	
£ Av prop val 2000	163 K		LD	4,680	10.0	−0.4
% Increase 97–00	56.0		Grn	2,119	4.5	+2.8
% Unemployed 2001	3.7		Ind	1,214	2.6	
% Decrease 97–01	2.2		Ind	1,166	2.5	
% Fin hard/Rank	29.4	140	SLP	921	2.0	−1.9
% Pensioners	18.9		Ind	169	0.4	
% Prem mort/Rank	40	178	Lab maj	13,683	29.2	
			Turnout		56.8	−10.0
			Elect	82,373		

Member of Parliament

Slight, balding and ungregarious **Piara Khabra**, Labour's oldest MP, born November 1922 in the Punjab, came to Britain in 1959 to work at the local Wolf's rubber factory which formed a magnet for the Asianisation of Southall at that time. An abrasive if mild-looking secular Sikh, he qualified as a teacher at Whitelands College, Putney, and taught for 14 years before concentrating on ward heeling among the Southall Indian community as a community worker, and eventually securing the deselection of the veteran white Labour MP Syd Bidwell. Elected in 1992, he is a rare Commons performer, and then strongly accented. A campaigner on euthanasia, he inevitably focuses on ease of immigration for his Indian voters' relatives.

EASINGTON

In 2001 the County Durham constituency of Easington returned the largest numerical majority of any of the 659 constituencies in the United Kingdom: 21,949, for Labour's John Cummings. This is not quite the safest seat in terms of percentage majority, a record held by Bootle where the total number of votes cast was considerably fewer. Nevertheless it still fits its image of the archetypal coalfield seat at the heart of the Labour Party's tradition, where it is said that votes are weighed rather than counted.

Easington is still associated by many with Manny Shinwell, the apparently indestructible Labour politician who first entered Parliament in 1922 and represented an east Durham constituency from 1935 to 1970, when he was well over 80 years of age. In the year of 1935 Shinwell defeated the ex-Labour leader Ramsay MacDonald at Seaham. Shinwell switched to Easington when that seat was created in 1950, and for the last 20 years of his life in the Commons he remained an active and prominent member – and similarly, even as a centenarian, in the Lords.

In the 1983 boundary changes Seaham was reunited with Easington, effectively recreating the scene of MacDonald's triumphs in 1929 and 1931, and his humiliation in 1935. It is characterised by the big ex-colliery villages near the coast: Horden, Murton, Easington itself; mining lasted longer here than anywhere else in Durham, as the deep seams which extend beneath the North Sea were tapped long after the reserves of west Durham were worked out. The two biggest population centres though are Seaham and the New Town of Peterlee. New Towns in Durham do not share the volatility of their southern counterparts, and this example, named after the Durham-born international miners' union leader, Peter Lee, remains appropriately loyal to Labour, who obtained very nearly ten times the vote of their Tory and Liberal Democrat rivals in 2001.

Social indices:			2001 Gen. Election:			
% Non-white	0.6		Lab	25,360	76.8	−3.4
% Prof/Man	19.7		C	3,411	10.3	+1.8
% Non-manual	38.6		LD	3,408	10.3	+3.1
£ Av prop val 2000	41 K		SLP	831	2.5	
% Increase 97–00	17.5		Lab maj	21,949	66.5	
% Unemployed 2001	4.8		Turnout		53.6	−13.4
% Decrease 97–01	1.8		Elect	61,532		
% Fin hard/Rank	39.9	52				
% Pensioners	25.1					
% Prem mort/Rank	50	47				

Member of Parliament

John Cummings, a fifth-generation child of the pits, is now one of only 11 remaining former mineworkers or NUM-sponsored MPs, having worked 30 years as a pit electrician before being elected here in 1987. Born in 1943 and locally educated at Murton schools and Easington Technical College, he spent 17 years on the local council, ten as leader, and was a Whip at Westminster for three years before being dropped by Blair on the morrow of victory in 1997. Though a left-wing defender of the dying coal industry and of a Palestinian state, he has rebelled only modestly against the Blair government, on the Prime Minister's power to nominate life peers and on disability benefit cuts. As a Catholic he backs curbs on abortion and embryo research.

EASTBOURNE

The resort of Eastbourne, nestling beneath the towering cliffs of Beachy Head, was founded in the eighteenth century, like Brighton, but it is decidedly quieter and more staid. Given its reputation as an upmarket and conservative retirement centre, and the fact that it has the sixth highest proportion of pensioners anywhere in Britain, it is surprising to be able to report that Eastbourne has recently had a dramatic and even violent electoral history.

The MP for Eastbourne for 16 years until 1990 was Ian Gow, an early Thatcher confidant, PPS when she became Prime Minister, and a robust but witty partisan on the right of the party. Mr Gow was noted for his vigorous support of the Unionist cause in Northern Ireland – indeed, he split from his leader over the Anglo-Irish agreement of 1985. In July 1990 the small village of Hankham was rocked by the car bomb explosion that killed Ian Gow, a victim of the tragic Troubles here in the heart of East Sussex.

Given the circumstances, few felt that the Conservatives would have much trouble holding Eastbourne in the ensuing by-election. In fact, some believed that it should not even be contested by the opposition parties. However, nothing can be taken for granted in by-elections, and in October 1990 the Liberal Democrat David Bellotti swept home by over 4,500 votes. There were a number of factors influencing this result, but above all there was the combination of the traditional mid-term protest vote and tactical voting behind the strongest challenger.

That challenger was undoubtedly David Bellotti, a well-established East Sussex county councillor and a regional leader of the Liberal Democrats. However, his tenure was always likely to be short-lived. An exit poll on by-election day suggested that had it been a General Election with the government of the country at stake the Conservatives would have held Eastbourne by 21%. When the crunch came, in April 1992, the new Conservative candidate Nigel Waterson regained the seat slightly less comfortably than that, but still with a margin of over 5,000.

Eastbourne might have seemed to be a likely Liberal Democrat gain in the great Conservative catastrophe of 1997, but Waterson held on by just under 2,000 votes. The main problem for the Lib Dems was that the Labour vote, presumably inspired by their national triumph, nearly tripled. In 2001 the Lib Dems targeted Eastbourne again, but despite a tremendous effort by Chris Berry and his team the Tory vote went up, perhaps helped by the disappearance of the Referendum Party. Labour's share increased again too. Given that the Conservative fortunes nationally may well have bottomed out, it is now quite likely that 1990 will mark the only Liberal victory in Eastbourne in a long lifetime.

Social indices:			2001 Gen. Election:			
% Non-white	1.7		C	19,738	44.1	+2.0
% Prof/Man	34.8		LD	17,584	39.3	+0.9
% Non-manual	60.1		Lab	5,967	13.3	+0.8
£ Av prop val 2000	98 K		UKIP	907	2.0	+1.5
% Increase 97–00	51.2		Lib	574	1.3	–0.1
% Unemployed 2001	2.4		C maj	2,154	4.8	
% Decrease 97–01	1.6		Turnout		60.7	–12.1
% Fin hard/Rank	12.6	405	Elect	73,784		
% Pensioners	42.2					
% Prem mort/Rank	26	413				

Member of Parliament

Burly, mild-looking solicitor, **Nigel Waterson**, a Conservative DTI spokesman from 2001, was born in 1950 and educated at Leeds Grammar School and Queen's College,

Oxford. A mainstream Eurosceptic loyalist, he campaigns against his town's downward mobility, as hotels convert to DSS hostels or berths for dispersed asylum seekers, and against the locally prominent Lib Dems, whose MP David Bellotti he ousted in 1992. His conventional rise in the Tory Party was via law-and-order conference speeches. He wavered in the leadership ballots in 1997 between Redwood and Hague, but voted for Lilley, then Hague, under whom he served as Whip, Home Office and Housing spokesman between 1997 and 2001. Though he backed the Portillo candidacy in all ballots in 2001, he retained a place on the frontbench.

EAST HAM

By-elections are held to be the most testing of occasions for whichever party is attempting to defend the seat. It is hardest for a candidate trying to defend the incumbent government's record, of course, but Opposition parties cannot rely on the loyalties of an electorate which knows that it is not choosing the identity of the national government. One thinks for example of the Liberal Alliance's challenge to Tony Benn at Chesterfield in 1984, for example, or of the little-noticed fact that Labour's Llin Golding almost lost Newcastle-under-Lyme to the same party in 1986.

However, Labour's utter dominance in the seat of Newham North East was demonstrated by the crushing victory of their candidate Stephen Timms in the 1994 by-election caused by the death of Ron Leighton. Not only did Timms win massively, but the Labour hegemony was somehow emphasised by the defection just before polling day of the Liberal Democrat candidate and sole local Lib Dem councillor Alec Kellaway, who announced that he was joining the Labour Party and recommending his erstwhile followers to do the same.

East Ham is effectively the old Newham NE plus one ward from Newham South. It is a densely populated, compact, very working-class seat which has a majority and growing non-white population. There are neighbourhoods composed of gridirons of long straight streets like Manor Park, Little Ilford, and those in the overwhelmingly Asian and black Kensington and Monega wards; in fact it had the highest proportion of terraced housing of any seat in London in 1991, over two-thirds of the total stock. There was little room for modern council estates.

The flavour of the seat is changed, though, by the one area that arrived in the 1997 boundary changes. It was South ward, which came from the constituency of the same name, which has been split in three. South was a large geographical area bordering the Thames, consisting largely of former docklands – the old King George V and Royal Albert docks were in the ward. The face of this area has changed dramatically in recent years. It is now the site of the new London City airport and of the private housing developments centred on Beckton. The population of the ward increased by 59% in the 1980s. What is more, the political flavour is different here. This is not an old-established Labour stronghold. The Conservatives challenged strongly in the old Newham South, and came close to winning South ward in the May 1990 and 1994 Elections. The residents are largely white, home-owning, car-owning, recent migrants. To the north the ward abutted the one in Newham NE which had a substantial Tory vote, Greatfield.

In the first contest in East Ham the only surprise was that the Socialist Labour candidate, Imran Khan (not the Pakistani cricketer), not only saved his deposit, but obtained the party's best performance anywhere by surpassing the Liberal Democrats and reaching third place. He did not fight East Ham again in 2001, which is the main reason why Labour's Stephen Timms managed to increase his vote share substantially to a massive 73% and even garner an increased majority in a turnout of just 52%. This was Labour's fourth best improvement anywhere, and East Ham is now their second safest seat in London, after Brent South.

Social indices:			2001 Gen. Election:			
% Non-white	48.7		Lab	27,241	73.1	+8.5
% Prof/Man	25.5		C	6,209	16.7	+0.6
% Non-manual	52.3		LD	2,600	7.0	+0.5
£ Av prop val 2000	91 K		SLP	783	2.1	−4.7
% Increase 97–00	58.0		UKIP	444	1.2	
% Unemployed 2001	7.2		Lab maj	21,032	56.4	
% Decrease 97–01	3.9		Turnout		52.3	−8.5
% Fin hard/Rank	40.6	49	Elect	71,255		
% Pensioners	20.4					
% Prem mort/Rank	42	139				

Member of Parliament

Stephen Timms, a tall, pudding-basin-haircut-sporting Europhile mathematician who spent 16 years in the computer industry, and a Christian Socialist (Baptist), won here in 1994, having run the local council for four years. Born in 1955, educated at Farnborough Grammar School and Emmanuel College, Cambridge, with his very long head and high forehead and fringe, he has the appearance of a grown-up Midwich Cuckoo. Mild, earnest, idealistic, uncharismatic, but above all orthodox, he has risen swiftly in government since 1998, in junior then middle-ranking posts at Social Security, the Treasury, and (since 2001) Education, without it seeming likely that he could expect to head a Department.

EAST KILBRIDE

This post-war New Town south of Glasgow was given its own seat in 1974. By the 1990s its population was a stable 70,000, and together with about 10,000 rural voters in 24,000 hectares of territory south of the New Town it could form the basis of a continuing constituency, unaltered in the boundary changes before the 1997 Election. It is a larger than average seat for Scotland, indeed not far below the UK-wide norm, and thus is unlikely to be much affected when the number of Scottish seats are reduced.

New Towns have a reputation for greater volatility than older communities, and there have been ups and downs – East Kilbride did see a rise in the SNP vote in 1974 and of the SDP share in 1983. In 1997 a Pro-Life (anti-abortion) candidate did exceptionally well in this rather Catholic constituency to take 1,170 votes.

However, all this took place a long way behind the winner, since 1987 Labour's Adam Ingram. East Kilbride now has a majority of owner-occupied housing. It has one of the lowest unemployment rates in urban central Scotland. Its economic structure reveals the seat to be almost exactly as middle class as average for Great Britain, which means that it is a little above that for Scotland. All the same, it is a safe Labour seat, which demonstrates the power of that party north of the border and the very different nature and history of Scottish New Towns from those in southern England.

Social indices:			2001 Gen. Election:			
% Non-white	0.6		Lab	22,205	53.3	−3.3
% Prof/Man	32.1		SNP	9,450	22.7	+1.8
% Non-manual	58.0		LD	4,278	10.3	+3.0
% Unemployed 2001	3.1		C	4,238	10.2	−1.8
% Decrease 97–01	1.6		SSP	1,519	3.6	
% Fin hard/Rank	30.8	123	Lab maj	12,755	30.6	
% Prem mort/Rank	40	176	Turnout		62.6	−12.2
			Elect	66,572		

Member of Parliament

Adam Ingram, elected here in 1987 and Minister of State for Defence from 2001, having previously served (1997–2001) at the Northern Ireland Office, and as a Whip and Social Security then DTI spokesman in Opposition (1988–97), rose originally as a protégé of Neil Kinnock, whose PPS he was from 1988 to 1992 and whose retreat from unilateralism he shared. Born in 1947, son of a fitter and educated at Cranhill Senior Secondary School and the Open University, he was an electricity board computer programmer for ten years before becoming a fulltime NALGO official, also for ten years, and served as an East Kilbride councillor from 1980 to 1987. Seen as something of a machine politician with a low public profile, he was, by 2001, one of 15 Scots out of a total of 88 MPs gracing the Treasury bench, that is 17% of Commons-based Ministers, compared to Scotland's 10% share of the population, and this nothwithstanding devolution. Nor could a future Brown premiership be expected to cut such generosity.

EASTLEIGH

The Hampshire constituency of Eastleigh came into the national limelight in bizarre circumstances in the early months of 1994. The first-term MP, the former journalist and economics expert Stephen Milligan, was found dead at his home in bizarre circumstances suggesting the tragic misfiring of a sexual fetish. The government could not hope to hold the seat – or indeed in all probability any seat – with the level of public disapprobation it was facing at the time, and the winner of the by-election was the Liberal Democrat David Chidgey, who had finished nearly 18,000 votes behind Milligan in 1992.

Eastleigh essentially takes in the suburban belt to the north and east of Southampton – Eastleigh itself, Hedge End, West End, Botley, Bursledon and Hound.

It lost nearly 25,000 voters before the 1997 Election, but the outcome was still more influenced by the 1994 by-election. The Conservatives had regained all their losses in the 1987–92 Parliament, but their fortunes had declined sadly since then, and David Chidgey surprised many by holding on by 754 votes. The Conservatives were second, but Labour was a close third. This is not without precedent. Back in 1966 Labour came within 701 votes of the Tories. Eastleigh itself is a railway town, and Labour even now wins its central wards in local elections.

In 2001 the three-way battle was less tight. Chidgey had three main advantages. As an incumbent MP of seven years' standing, he had been able to build up a formidable local machine, helping constituents and publicising this activity locally. Labour voters, realising that their candidate Sam Jaffa was unlikely to win, switched in some thousands to Chidgey to prevent a Tory regain. There was considerable energy expended on behalf of the Conservative candidate, Conor Burns, but his party scarcely recovered at all from its national slump and neither did his share of the vote in Eastleigh. Chidgey increased his majority more than fourfold, and secured another term – although it is doubtful whether Eastleigh will ever be a safe Lib Dem seat.

Social indices:			2001 Gen. Election:				
% Non-white	1.6		LD	19,360	40.7	+5.6	
% Prof/Man	33.3		C	16,302	34.3	+0.6	
% Non-manual	60.4		Lab	10,426	21.9	−4.9	
£ Av prop val 2000	114 K		UKIP	849	1.8	+1.0	
% Increase 97–00	54.6		Grn	636	1.3		
% Unemployed 2001	0.9		LD maj	3,058	6.4		
% Decrease 97–01	1.1		Turnout		63.8	−13.1	
% Fin hard/Rank	7.3	553	Elect	74,603			
% Pensioners	21.6						
% Prem mort/Rank	18	496					

Member of Parliament

Stocky and affable, **David Chidgey** won here at a by-election in 1994 and unexpectedly held on in 1997. A professional engineer, originally with the Admiralty, then for 20 years in a commercial practice, he was born in 1942 and educated at Brune Hill County High School, the Royal Naval College, Portsmouth and Portsmouth Polytechnic. In turn his party's Employment, Transport and Trade and Industry spokesman between 1994 and 1999, it was evidence of the party's new-found embarrassment of riches – with its expansion from a taxi-load of MPs to a substantial coach-full, that the new leader, Charles Kennedy, in 1999 was actually able to dispatch him to the backbenches (a concept meaningless when once Liberal MPs huddled for warmth on a single bench), and where he remained in 2001, his party's third oldest MP, with a dignified role as one of the panel of Commons chairmen.

EAST LOTHIAN

East Lothian has not always underpinned a safe Labour seat, but this has to some extent depended upon the policy adopted by the Boundary Commission. Before 1983 it was paired with Berwickshire in a highly marginal and quirky division which delighted in swimming against the tide. Berwick and East Lothian ousted Labour's John Mackintosh in February 1974 when Labour gained control of the government; he regained it in October of the same year, and it was held against all expectations by another Labour moderate, John Home Robertson, in the by-election caused by Mackintosh's premature death in 1978. In 1983 Berwickshire was removed into a Borders seat (which went Liberal) and the strongly Labour town of Musselburgh replaced it, having previously been in Edinburgh East. John Home Robertson held the new East Lothian safely until his migration to the Scottish Parliament meant that he gave way to Anne Picking in 2001. Without further decisive boundary changes being proposed for the next election, she should enjoy as comfortable a stint as her predecessor.

East Lothian becomes less Labour the further one moves away from Edinburgh. In its western section are to be found ex-coal-mining and solidly working-class communities like Tranent, Ormiston, Preston and Prestonpans. In the east are more Conservative farming and tourist areas like Cockenzie, Haddington, East Linton, Dirleton, North Berwick and Dunbar. This area is also the site of several fine golf courses, including the Open Championship location of Muirfield. The Labour-voting west still outvotes the Conservative and more scenic east.

Social indices:			2001 Gen. Election:				
% Non-white	0.4		Lab	17,407	47.2		−5.5
% Prof/Man	31.3		C	6,577	17.8		−2.1
% Non-manual	53.8		LD	6,506	17.6		+7.1
% Unemployed 2001	2.1		SNP	5,381	14.6		−1.1
% Decrease 97–01	2.1		SLP	624	1.7		
% Fin hard/Rank	27.2	170	SSP	376	1.0		
% Prem mort/Rank	32	302	Lab maj	10,830	29.4		
			Turnout		62.5		−13.1
			Elect	58,987			

Member of Parliament

Ann Picking, a Kent-based Scot returning to Scotland – to succeed departed-for-Holyrood MP John Home Robertson in 2001 – is a former nurse risen in the Labour Party via the union route, in her case UNISON which she has represented on Labour's NEC since 1997, as well as chairing the Party's Organisation Committee. Born in 1958 into the famous miners' union family of Moffats, and educated at Woodmill High School, Dunfermline, she became a nurse, joined COHSE in 1975 and rose through its ranks, eventually reaching COHSE/UNISON's NEC. Living in Kent from the mid-1980s she worked with management to save staff jobs in a switch from hospital to community care provision, and became an Ashford Borough Councillor in 1995. She claims to thrive on campaigning and taking on Tories, and to have addressed 10,000 people in Hyde Park. She has voiced veiled criticism of the PFI in the NHS, but as the reliable organisation-woman she is, gave firm backing from the platform of the 2001 Party Conference for international action in the wake of the terrorist attack on the World Trade Center.

EASTWOOD

One of Labour's very best performances anywhere in Britain in 2001 was to be found at Eastwood, where the first-term incumbent Jim Murphy further increased his share of the vote by 8%, making a total of 23.5% over the last two elections, while the Conservatives fell by another 5%, thus making what had been in all probability their strongest constituency north of the border into a safe Labour seat.

A large proportion of the Glaswegian middle class lives in the dormitory suburbs just outside the city boundaries – Bearsden and Milngavie in the north, and the district of Eastwood to the south-west. If these neighbourhoods were in England they might well be in Tory seats even yet. At least Bearsden and Milngavie are both included in seats with solidly Labour territory attached. That cannot be said of the predominantly affluent and owner-occupied Eastwood. The statistics show just how different Eastwood is from other parts of the Glasgow conurbation, of which it is an integral if suburban part. Some 80% of the housing is owner-occupied. Three-quarters of those in employment work in non-manual (middle-class) jobs. Over 80% of households own a car and over a third at least two. In the most affluent ward, Broom, over 95% have access to a vehicle and two-thirds to at least two. The Conservatives historically won massively in most of the neighbourhoods that make up this constituency (there is no place called Eastwood): Clarkston, Stamperland, Giffnock, Newton Mearns, Busby, Crookfur, Kirkhill, Eaglesham. Labour fought back in the small, detached, industrial town of Barrhead.

What happened here? It cannot have helped that the Conservatives have showed confusion and division while selecting candidates for Eastwood. First of all, in 1997 the sitting MP Allan Stewart suddenly announced his retirement on health grounds; then a possible replacement, Michael Hirst, ruled himself out in advance of publicity about a possible sexual scandal. Eventually the Tories chose Paul Cullen, the Solicitor-General for Scotland – but he went down on a 14% swing to Labour's Jim Murphy. Then in 2001 the next high-profile choice, the former Aberdeen South MP Raymond Robertson, also underperformed. Small wonder that in the immediate aftermath of this second national disaster the Scottish Conservative Party talked of a completely fresh start, with new leadership, and divorced from their colleagues in England. They need to do something very different to recover their position in Eastwood, and in Scotland as a whole.

Social indices:			2001 Gen. Election:			
% Non-white	2.4		Lab	23,036	47.6	+7.9
% Prof/Man	47.4		C	13,895	28.7	−4.8
% Non-manual	74.9		LD	6,239	12.9	+1.2
% Unemployed 2001	2.3		SNP	4,137	8.6	−4.5
% Decrease 97–01	1.3		SSP	814	1.7	
% Fin hard/Rank	18.4	300	Ind	247	0.5	
% Prem mort/Rank	22	462	Lab maj	9,141	18.9	
			Turnout		70.7	−7.6
			Elect	68,378		

Member of Parliament

Jim Murphy, tall, beaky and thin-faced, born in 1967, educated at secondary schools in Glasgow and Cape Town, and at Strathclyde University, and former National Union of Students president, won here in 1997. *Guardian*-described as 'so on-message that the message occasionally has to be surgically removed from his backside', he is a Blairite fixer who helped pull the Scottish Labour Party to the centre, but redeems himself with Old Labour by his skill as a Commons footballer. Unexpectedly winning this seat from the Tories in 1997, less unexpectedly he became a PPS, to Scotland Secretary Helen Liddell, in 2001 – only to face the allegation (of which he was cleared) in December of subletting his constituency office whilst claiming full allowances.

ECCLES

The central (in geographical terms) of the three seats in Greater Manchester's metropolitan borough of Salford is Eccles. Like the other two (Salford and Worsley) it is safely Labour. This is decidedly not middle-class commuting territory, even though it is situated pretty much due west of Manchester's city centre, which is normally a favourable compass point for residential areas in Britain. However, this is a working-class and industrial area, unified above all else by the Manchester Ship Canal along whose banks it lies – a monument to the greatness of Manchester's commercial history and traditions.

There are some middle-class and Conservative voting neighbourhoods. These lie within Eccles ward itself at Ellesmere Park and within Swinton South ward. These are not strong or large enough, however, even to win these wards in local council elections except in a very good Tory year, and the Conservative Party must resign itself to a distant second place in this constituency. The first-term Labour MP Ian Stewart saw his majority reduced by 7,500 in 2001, but this was principally due to a huge 17% drop in turnout, the product of a lacklustre election campaign with a certain result – the victory of a competent but unenthusing government – and something deeper: a lack of connection between citizens and politicians, and a lack of belief that voting for any party would really make a worthwhile difference. There were only three candidates in Eccles this time, and perhaps it was felt that even these offered little in the way of ideological variety or real choice.

Social indices:			2001 Gen. Election:			
% Non-white	1.8		Lab	21,395	64.5	−2.2
% Prof/Man	25.3		C	6,867	20.7	+2.0
% Non-manual	52.2		LD	4,920	14.8	+4.1
£ Av prop val 2000	49 K		Lab maj	14,528	43.8	
% Increase 97–00	19.4		Turnout		48.3	−17.4
% Unemployed 2001	3.0		Elect	68,764		
% Decrease 97–01	1.8					
% Fin hard/Rank	26.4	183				
% Pensioners	27.6					
% Prem mort/Rank	46	83				

Member of Parliament

Ian Stewart, elected in 1997, is a balding, bearded Scotsman, a labourer's son born in 1950 and educated at Calder Street Secondary School, Blantyre and at Alfred Turner Secondary Modern, Salford, and Irlam High School, and at Bolton Art College, Stretford Technical College, and Manchester Metropolitan University. Originally an electrician and Shell chemical plant worker, he was for nearly 20 years a TGWU official, this being his route to the Commons as his Union's influential North West Regional fixer for nine years up to 1997. He has been mildly rebellious against the Blair government, opposing lone parent benefit cuts and abolition of student maintenance grants, and calling for earnings-related pensions. Otherwise he is a staunch North Western regionalist, a pro-European and an IT enthusiast, whose mildly discordant record was seemingly overlooked when he was appointed PPS to DTI Minister and fellow Scot, Brian Wilson, in 2001.

EDDISBURY

The largest seat in area in Cheshire, by some way, is Eddisbury. Where, one may ask, is Eddisbury? There is no town or local government district of that name. In fact the constituency, which takes its name from Eddisbury Hill, near Delamere Forest, covers the south-western section of Cheshire. After fairly substantial boundary changes in 1997 Eddisbury lost about 12,000 voters net, but if anything actually increased still further in physical size. This gives the clue that it is predominantly rural. The seat still stretches far to the south-west, to reach the Welsh border, at Farndon for example, taking in Tarporley and Tarvin and Malpas and many other small communities. In addition, the western part of the Crewe and Nantwich constituency was added: places such as Audlem and Bunbury, Wrenbury, Acton and the Peckforton hills. This is all predominantly Conservative, even though it was previously in a Labour marginal seat.

The only political aberrance in Eddisbury will continue to come from its largest town. Winsford has expanded beyond recognition since beginning to accept Manchester overspill in the 1950s, and now has a population of over 27,000. All its wards are strongly Labour in local elections, and it still has a strong council-house and working-class presence. Winsford was originally famous for its rock salt mines and the area also produces most of Cheshire's sand from local quarries. There is even a Winsford ward called Gravel.

Gritty Winsford may be, but it has always been outvoted by the rural part of Eddisbury. This was true in the Labour landslide year of 1997, when the Conservative MP Alastair Goodlad held on by 1,185, and even in the by-election in July 1999 caused by Goodlad's translation (not transportation) to Australia as High Commissioner. If Labour could not win in such circumstances as these, it is unlikely that they ever will, and Stephen O'Brien increased his lead to over 4,500 in 2001, set for a long run in the soft Cheshire countryside.

Social indices:			2001 Gen. Election:			
% Non-white	0.7		C	20,556	46.3	+3.8
% Prof/Man	39.1		Lab	15,988	36.0	−4.1
% Non-manual	57.4		LD	6,975	15.7	+2.5
£ Av prop val 2000	100 K		UKIP	868	2.0	
% Increase 97–00	20.2		C maj	4,568	10.3	
% Unemployed 2001	2.2		Turnout		64.2	−11.6
% Decrease 97–01	1.1		Elect	69,181		
% Fin hard/Rank	12.9	399				
% Pensioners	22.9					
% Prem mort/Rank	27	391				

Member of Parliament

Mild-mannered former solicitor **Stephen O'Brien** won the Eddisbury by-election in 1999, after Sir Alistair Goodlad had, in A. A. Milne's words, 'gone out to govern New South Wales'. Tanzania-born in 1957, and educated at Loretto School, Kenya, and Sedbergh School, Emmanuel College, Cambridge, and Chester College of Law, his Tory roots are shallow: he has been a member since only 1995, and spent a period of seven years (in the 1980s) in the SDP in Wandsworth, when the local Tories were selling off the municipal furniture. An opponent of red tape choking business, his by-election victory on countryside issues killed Labour's hopes of being the first government for 17 years to take a seat from the Opposition at a by-election, with the attempt here to play the anti-fox hunting card. He backed the centre-right, traditionalist Ancram option in the first two ballots in 2001, then, with Ancram out of the running, voted for Iain Duncan Smith and joined the frontbench team as a Whip.

EDINBURGH CENTRAL

In 1983, when Edinburgh lost one of its seven seats in boundary changes, the New Town was placed together with the Old Town in a seat that united both types of the superb architecture of the heart of the Scottish capital. Here were to be found the Castle, the Royal Mile, St Giles' Cathedral, the older parts of Edinburgh University, the brooding tenements of the ancient walled city, Arthur's Seat and the drained loch in which Waverley station is to be found; and also the main shopping area, Princes Street, and the eighteenth-century terraces, squares, crescents and circuses of the New Town to its north. It was surely one of the most culturally and historically blessed constituencies in Britain.

In the changes passed by Parliament in 1995, the New Town (along with Stockbridge) was again separated from the Central seat, to be paired with Leith. In exchange, Central gained the Moat and Stenhouse wards from Edinburgh West. This was not a politically neutral swap. Although it has had periods and patches of decay and decline, the New Town is predominantly Conservative, and returned Tories to the city council right through the Thatcher years, when the Westminster government was deeply unpopular in Scotland. Stenhouse, though, is a Labour-voting council estate. It certainly contributed towards the increase in Alastair Darling's majority to 11,000 in 1997.

Although the Scottish Boundary Commission has proposed that it be split up again for the 2005/6 election, Edinburgh Central is a fascinating and diverse seat still; it continues to include one of the city's premier residential areas, around Ravelston Dykes in Murrayfield ward near the headquarters of Scotland's proud rugby union team. It holds several constituency records. It has the highest proportion of professional and managerial workers in Scotland, and also the highest number of residents born outside Scotland (mainly in England, though it also has the most non-white people in Edinburgh, mainly in the Tollcross/Haymarket area). In 2001 the Liberal Democrats advanced into second place and the Tories dropped to third. The loss of the New Town made a Conservative recovery very unlikely as well as the constituency somewhat less grand and elegant. Nevertheless, almost untouched by war bombing, the centre of Edinburgh remains an intriguing and colourful district, steeped in history and character, and containing relatively less built in the last century than almost any other seat in Britain. It is still a worthy seat of, and for, Scotland's capital.

Social indices:			2001 Gen. Election:			
% Non-white	3.6		Lab	14,495	42.1	−4.9
% Prof/Man	46.4		LD	6,353	18.5	+5.4
% Non-manual	71.3		C	5,643	16.4	−4.8
% Unemployed 2001	2.9		SNP	4,832	14.1	−1.7
% Decrease 97–01	2.3		Grn	1,809	5.3	+3.8
% Fin hard/Rank	21.6	249	SSP	1,258	3.7	
% Prem mort/Rank	50	43	Lab maj	8,142	23.7	
			Turnout		52.0	−15.1
			Elect	66,089		

Member of Parliament

Alistair Darling, a straight-faced Edinburgh lawyer after public school (Loretto) and Aberdeen University, was born in 1953 into a Tory-voting family, his great uncle being the Edinburgh Conservative MP, Sir William Darling, who sat for Edinburgh South from 1945 to 1957. A solicitor-turned-advocate, he rose politically on Lothian Regional Council in the 1980s. It has been noted that with his white hair and close-cropped beard (now removed), jet black eyebrows and penetrating eyes, his appearance seemed better suited to an Italian art-house movie than an Edinburgh courtroom. Employing his smoothly effective, if cold, unclubbable, technocratic manner in two key, not unrelated, Cabinet posts, bringing a thrifty Chief Secretary's eye to welfare reform as replacement in 1999 for the sacked Social Security Secretary, Harriet Harman, in 2001 he retained much of his responsibility in the new Work and Pensions ministry, risen under the patronage of Brown, not Blair.

EDINBURGH EAST AND MUSSELBURGH

In the 1997 boundary changes in the Lothian region, the status quo ante was more or less restored, as the town of Musselburgh once again joined the East division of the City of Edinburgh in a Westminster parliamentary constituency. It had been removed in the previous redistribution in 1983. Although clearly a Labour stronghold, fears that Musselburgh's disappearance actually threatened Labour's historic grip on East proved to be unfounded, and Gavin Strang won the redrawn seat comfortably three times between 1983 and 1992. In the latter year, despite some loss of support to the SNP, East provided Labour's largest margin of victory in the capital city. This was further reinforced in 1997, when the Tories slipped below the SNP into third place and Strang won by 14,500. In 2001 the Conservatives were overtaken again, this time by the Liberal Democrats, but little else happened – including much voting, as turnout fell from 70% to 58%.

Edinburgh East is a mixed seat, socially and politically. It consists of that part of the city to the east and south-east of Arthur's Seat. There are some good residential areas on the coast around Portobello, at Craigentinny and inland at Mountcastle and Jock's Lodge. But in the main the east side is, as in so many towns elsewhere in Britain, a working-class quarter. There are some grim council estates here, as at Craigmillar and Niddrie, though one of the worst, Bingham, was torn down and redeveloped in the 1980s. In the next boundary changes, Edinburgh loses a seat, and East will no longer exist in its current form, probably losing Musselburgh once again.

Social indices:			2001 Gen. Election:			
% Non-white	1.2		Lab	18,124	52.6	–1.0
% Prof/Man	29.6		SNP	5,956	17.3	–1.8
% Non-manual	60.8		LD	4,981	14.5	+3.7
% Unemployed 2001	2.6		C	3,906	11.3	–4.1
% Decrease 97–01	2.4		SSP	1,487	4.3	
% Fin hard/Rank	35.1	90	Lab maj	12,168	35.3	
% Prem mort/Rank	46	76	Turnout		58.2	–12.5
			Elect	59,241		

Member of Parliament

Dr Gavin Strang, one of Blair's most swiftly discarded Cabinet Ministers, originally included in government only because of his elected place on the Shadow Cabinet, spent one year as Transport Secretary (1997–98) after years typecast as an Opposition Agriculture spokesman, being one of a handful of Labour MPs from a farming background. With an over-earnest, rather untelegenic manner and throaty vowels, he was born in 1943 and educated at Morrison's Academy, Crieff, and Edinburgh University (where he obtained a doctorate he has proclaimed in his mode of address), and worked briefly as an agricultural research scientist before becoming MP here aged 27 in 1970. A former Falklands War and Gulf War rebel, after his sacking he led the revolt against air traffic control part-privatisation, and in 2002 called for renationalisation of the railways.

EDINBURGH NORTH AND LEITH

This seat, although renamed, is largely based on the Edinburgh Leith division which existed up to and including the 1992 General Election. It has always been won by Labour since 1945, and thus cannot be regarded as a marginal; at least not in normal circumstances. However times have been far from quiet in Leith, almost entirely due to the activities and antics of one man, Ron Brown.

Brown first engaged the national attention as a far-left-winger who endorsed Russian policy after the invasion of Afghanistan. In 1987 he seized the symbolic mace in the House (not without damage); in 1988 it was alleged that he was sharing Commons showers with a female assistant. In 1989 he was accused of damage to and theft from his mistress's flat. Ron Brown was certainly one of the most active of the 1979 intake to Parliament. In 1990 his local Leith party finally lost patience with him and replaced him as official candidate with Malcolm Chisholm.

Brown stood at the 1992 Election as Independent Labour but could finish no better than fifth, with just over 4,000 votes and a tenth share of the vote. Ahead of him were the Liberal Democrats (just), the Tories, and in second place the SNP, who more than doubled their vote. The Nationalists had never performed well in Edinburgh before 1992, but showed a promising improvement in most of the capital's seats in that year, none more so than in Leith. Malcolm Chisholm must have been hurt by Brown's candidature (and indeed by his tenure of office beforehand) and the expected five-figure Labour majority dropped to just under 5,000.

It increased in 1997, despite the boundary changes. The SNP moved past the Conservatives into second place, but their share of the vote did not increase; it was the Tories' which fell. In 2001 the news was made by the Liberal Democrats, who did well throughout Scotland (under their new Scottish leader, one of the few successes of the General Election) – but it was news about second place not first. There are some middle-class wards in the seat (which was originally going to be named 'Edinburgh Inverleith'): the New Town of course, and in a good year Stockbridge, Trinity and Newhaven. However these areas are outvoted by Labour strongholds. Leith is of course the port for Edinburgh, which though considerably brightened up with fashionable developments in recent years is still basically an industrial area of glowering dark stone tenements, warehouses and cobbled streets, featured in Irvine Welsh's 'Trainspotting', whose title reference involves Leith Central station, a 'barren desolate hangar'. The constituency also includes the grim council estate of Pilton, which became nationally notorious a few years ago for its drug problems and abandoned houses; there are virtually no Conservative voters in Pilton, where the social and economic profile matches that of any of Glasgow's most depressed neighbourhoods.

Although certain to be transformed by imminent boundary changes, Edinburgh North and Leith has been yet another of those fascinating constituencies in this most varied and visually exciting of cities, a paradise for the social and political geographer. It is a short distance physically from, say, Pilton to the New Town, but a vast chasm separates the two communities in most other ways. Labour has the task of representing the whole of the seat, but pockets within it have shown their favour to other parties, and to none – turnout in 2001 barely exceeded 50%. What were the others doing – trainspotting?

Social indices:			2001 Gen. Election:			
% Non-white	2.7		Lab	15,271	45.9	−1.0
% Prof/Man	39.5		LD	6,454	19.4	+6.4
% Non-manual	65.0		SNP	5,290	15.9	−4.2
% Unemployed 2001	3.9		C	4,626	13.9	−3.9
% Decrease 97–01	3.7		SSP	1,334	4.0	+3.2
% Fin hard/Rank	26.3	187	SLP	259	0.8	
% Prem mort/Rank	52	33	Lab maj	8,817	26.5	
			Turnout		53.2	−13.3
			Elect	62,475		

Member of Parliament

Mark Lazarowicz, a voluntary-sector-worker-turned-barrister, was elected here in 2001 in place of the departed-for-Holyrood MP Malcolm Chisholm. Born to Polish émigré parents in London in 1953, he attended the Catholic public school, St Benedict's Ealing, and St Andrew's University, before building a political career on Edinburgh City Council, where he spent seven years as leader from 1986 to 1993. A contemporary in Edinburgh local government of Alistair Darling and Nigel Griffiths, who both reached the Commons as Edinburgh MPs as early as 1987, he was unlucky in having to wait to reach Westminster at an age – almost 50 – precluding him from a ministerial career, dogged twice by having to fight the resistant Tory marginal Pentlands seat in 1987 and 1992, only to surrender it to a successful woman candidate in 1997. He suffered too the indignity of being blocked for selection for the Scottish Parliament elections of 1999. Grey-haired, straight-backed and straight-faced, and with all the appearance of a man who has missed the bus, he has however the consolation of the legal career for which he retrained in the 1990s.

EDINBURGH PENTLANDS

A number of observers, including *The Times* newspaper's political editor Philip Webster, constructed an interesting scenario whereby the Conservative candidate would regain Edinburgh Pentlands in the 2001 Election and return to lead his party out of its pit of despair. There was only one thing wrong with this original theory. If Pentlands were to be won, the Tories would have done well enough for their leader William Hague to be regarded as a success, and there would have been no vacancy. As things happened, there was a job opportunity, but Malcolm Rifkind was not eligible. He had again been beaten in Pentlands, in the second nationwide rout in a row.

The Pentland hills, southern enough to be regarded as Lowland but still often snow-capped in winter, overshadow the residential neighbourhoods of south-west Edinburgh. The constituency which is named after them is one of the most deeply divided socially and politically in the whole of Britain; yet it never returned a Labour MP before 1997, when every single Conservative was defeated, including the incumbent at Pentlands, the Secretary of State for Defence, Malcolm Rifkind.

It is hard to accept this when one is confronted by the massive 1970s development at Wester Hailes, a peripheral estate which is almost a concrete city in its own right, far removed in all senses from the elegance of central Edinburgh. The failure of many of the hopes for Wester Hailes has been acknowledged as much of it has already been torn down, with the intention of rebuilding in a friendlier style – Wester Hailes lost over 30% of its population in the 1980s. Pentlands also includes council estates of an earlier vintage, most notably at Sighthill, which also offer solid Labour support.

The Conservatives have fought back effectively in the owner-occupied and desirable residential districts which make up the rest of the seat though: the detached houses of Colinton, the bungalows of Fairmilehead, and the newer private housing estates stretching beyond the historic city borders to Currie and Balerno by the Water of Leith on the A70 road south-west towards Lanark, tight under the Pentlands themselves. This section is among the most middle-class, indeed professional and managerial, and affluent sections of urban Scotland.

It is difficult to know if electoral events will ever return to 'normal' in Scotland, whatever that is, but with a Labour government at Westminster likely to face the tests and trials any administration does, and with a solid Conservative base here they should be competitive in this area, probably renamed Edinburgh West. Surely though Rifkind will not have the patience to stand yet again. In hindsight it seems he should have sought a safe berth south of the border after his 1997 defeat; it was very noble of him not to, but was it in the long-term interest of his party?

Social indices:			2001 Gen. Election:			
% Non-white	1.8		Lab	15,797	40.6	–2.4
% Prof/Man	38.6		C	14,055	36.1	+3.7
% Non-manual	66.8		LD	4,210	10.8	+0.8
% Unemployed 2001	2.6		SNP	4,210	10.8	–2.2
% Decrease 97–01	1.9		SSP	555	1.4	
% Fin hard/Rank	20.4	270	UKIP	105	0.3	+0.1
% Prem mort/Rank	29	350	Lab maj	1,742	4.5	
			Turnout		65.1	–11.6
			Elect	59,841		

Member of Parliament

Lynda Clark QC, elected here in 1997, a small, snub-nosed, loud-voiced Edinburgh advocate from a working-class background in Dundee, was born in 1949, educated at Lawside Academy, Dundee, and at St Andrew's University and then at Edinburgh, where she obtained a doctorate. In 1999 she was given the seemingly intrinsically small job of 'Advocate General for Scotland' (albeit a post whose inflation into high significance would not lie beyond the capacities of even the most unimaginative legal mind) and in her January 2001 Question Time answered one question, on football. She owed her arrival at Westminster in 1997 to the self-sacrifice of the two-time Labour candidate for Pentlands, former Edinburgh City Council leader, Mark Lazarowicz, who withdrew in the face of local demand for a woman candidate. Dr Clark, duly won the seat Lazarowicz had been softening up for years. His reward was another Edinburgh seat in 2001.

EDINBURGH SOUTH

When the Labour Party gained Edinburgh South from the Conservatives in 1987 it was a historic achievement. The south side of Edinburgh is generally associated with the essence of the elegance and grace of bourgeois districts – Newington, Merchiston and Morningside. The Tories, though pressed as Labour support grew as peripheral council estates like Liberton and Gilmerton were constructed in the 1950s and 1960s, had never lost it, not even in 1945 or 1966. When South finally fell, it was a result not of continued demographic change, but of the massive unpopularity of Mrs Thatcher's government and party north of the border; the Scottish middle classes had become reluctant to vote Conservative. Thus this seat with one of the highest proportions of professional and managerial workers in the country voted in Nigel Griffiths, and returned him in 1992 and 1997 with increased majorities. It now looks (if not physically) like a safe Labour seat.

A threat has developed from a fresh quarter, though. The Liberal Democrats have advanced in just two general elections from 13% to over 27%. This doubling of the vote reflects a general advance in large cities throughout Britain, in Scotland in 2001, and specifically in Edinburgh city elections over some years in wards such as Merchiston, North Morningside, Marchmont and Sciennes. They outpolled Labour in the May 1999 Elections for example. However this success is patchy, confined to the more middle-class and less southern sections of South, and does not transfer to elections for parliaments – neither in London nor Edinburgh (where they came third, also in 1999).

Edinburgh South's electoral geography is the reverse of many big-city seats. It is the inner part of the wedge which harbours fine old middle-class housing, the outer part on the fringe of the city the massively Labour-supporting council developments. As in London and Cardiff professional jobs associated with government are thick on the ground in Edinburgh, and many such employed live in the northern portion of South. It also has one of the highest proportions of residents born outside Scotland, 20%, mainly English; Edinburgh Central has the highest of any Scottish constituency. In many ways South is the home of the Edinburgh Establishment. This no longer even approaches the implication that it is Conservative, although the Tories have hopes that in the imminent boundary changes more of the former Pentlands seat will be included in a re-drawn South.

Social indices:			2001 Gen. Election:			
% Non-white	3.2		Lab	15,671	42.2	–4.7
% Prof/Man	47.6		LD	10,172	27.4	+9.7
% Non-manual	70.8		C	6,172	16.6	–4.7
% Unemployed 2001	2.5		SNP	3,683	9.9	–3.0
% Decrease 97–01	2.8		SSP	933	2.5	
% Fin hard/Rank	20.3	273	LCA	535	1.4	
% Prem mort/Rank	37	219	Lab maj	5,499	14.8	
			Turnout		58.1	–13.7
			Elect	64,012		

Member of Parliament

Nigel Griffiths, a short, straight-backed man with a rather robotic style of oratory, was dropped as DTI Consumer Affairs minister from the government in Blair's first reshuffle in 1998, despite – or rather because of – close links to Chancellor Gordon Brown, whose researcher he once was. Yet, as evidence of the ebb and flow of the Brown–Blair dynamic, he was restored to the government, again at the DTI (with responsibility for small businesses) in the post-election reshuffle of 2001, one of only three ex-ministers (with Harriet Harman and Alan Michael) to be so reinstated. A former welfare rights officer and, as a frontbencher in opposition, campaigner on consumer issues, he was born in 1955, and educated at Hawick High School, Edinburgh University and Moray House College of Education. His election here in 1987 sent Tory MP Michael Ancram hurrying south to a safer perch at Devizes in 1992. As Consumer Affairs Minister his defence of the Murdoch press practice of predatory pricing sparked a backbench revolt in July 1998. In late 2001 allegations were made about his office-running expenses.

EDINBURGH WEST

After many years of knocking hard on the door which would open up Liberal Democrat representation in Edinburgh, Scotland's second party (in terms of both Westminster seats and Edinburgh government) turned West into a safe Lib Dem seat. On three occasions, the Conservative MP Lord James Douglas-Hamilton held on by a hair's breadth against a determined Liberal challenge. In 1983 his majority was 498. In 1987 it leapt to 1,234. In 1992 it sank to three figures again, at 879. In the debacle of 1997, it was scarcely surprising that Douglas-Hamilton perished, as the perennial Liberal Democrat candidate Donald Gorrie swept home by the biggest margin the seat had seen since 1979. Then in 1999 and 2001 the transformation was confirmed as Gorrie was able to hand the seat over respectively to Margaret Smith in the Edinburgh Parliament and John Barrett in the General Election. In the latter, the Conservatives slipped behind Labour into third, with Lord James no longer their candidate for the first time in 27 years.

Most of the Edinburgh West constituency still consists of solid bastions of the capital city's upper orders: the sought-after residential areas of Cramond and Barnton, Blackhall and Corstorphine (whose south-east ward is the base of the new MP John Barrett). Some of the best of Edinburgh's schools are to be found in this neighbourhood, including the catchment area of Edinburgh High School, long regarded as the best state school in the city – which pushes up residential values even higher. This is intellectual territory, and it is not surprising that the Liberal Democrats now seem very comfortable. The seat boundaries extend well to the west beyond the edge of the capital's built-up area to take in Queensferry from Linlithgow constituency and Kirkliston from Livingston. These wards include some miles of rural and open ground, and Edinburgh's airport. With the opposition now evenly divided between Labour and Conservative, the Liberal Democrats' soaring fortunes seemed unlikely to plummet to earth here, but they may be shot in the wing by the

Boundary Commission, whose proposed Edinburgh NW successor seat splits their Corstorphine stronghold.

Social indices:			2001 Gen. Election:			
% Non-white	1.4		LD	16,719	42.4	−0.9
% Prof/Man	37.9		Lab	9,130	23.1	+4.3
% Non-manual	66.2		C	8,894	22.5	−5.4
% Unemployed 2001	2.1		SNP	4,047	10.3	+1.4
% Decrease 97–01	1.9		SSP	688	1.7	
% Fin hard/Rank	22.7	230	LD maj	7,589	19.2	
% Prem mort/Rank	30	338	Turnout		63.8	−14.1
			Elect	61,895		

Member of Parliament

John Barrett, elected as the new Liberal Democrat MP here in 2001, is a municipal stand-in for the departing-for-Holyrood Donald Gorrie, whose origins had also been heavily municipal as a long-time local councillor. In John Barrett's case the municipal roots are shallower with only six years on Edinburgh City Council, but he has experience as Gorrie's election agent in 1997 and as an unsuccessful candidate in Linlithgow in the Scottish Parliament election of 1999. Born in 1953, he attended Forrester High School, Edinburgh, Telford College and Napier Polytechnic. Professionally he has strong involvement in the film industry, being on the board of the Edinburgh International Film Festival and the Edinburgh Filmhouse, and evinces additional routinely Liberal Democrat concern for the environment and conservation.

EDMONTON

There are few constituencies which produced such a dramatic result as Edmonton in 1997. Having lost five years earlier, Labour not only won, but won by a mile: they polled almost exactly twice as much as the defeated Conservative Ian Twinn. After little further change in 2001, they now hold a majority of nearly 30% of the total vote. By any standards, that counts as adding up to a safe seat.

Enfield is an outer London borough, on the northern edge of the capital bordering Hertfordshire, but this seat tucked in its south-eastern corner, Edmonton, has many of the characteristics of inner London. It includes a strip of wards on the west bank of the river Lea which are wedged between the strongly Labour Tottenham to the south and working-class Ponders End (where Norman Tebbit grew up) to the north. As one moves west away from the Lea it becomes more white, more Conservative, and more middle class – though there are few professional and managerial workers here. Both 'C1' (white-collar, clerical and junior non-manual) and 'C2' (skilled manual) occupational groups are heavily represented in Edmonton. Overall the seat is one-fifth non-white, mainly black Afro-Caribbean not Asian. These wards have a strong working-class presence, and one, Latymer, had by far the highest proportion (almost 50%) of council housing of any in the borough in 1991. All vote Labour in local elections and it comes as a surprise to find that the Conservatives won three parliamentary elections in Edmonton between 1983 and 1992, the middle one by 7,000 votes.

Edmonton does indeed have a long tradition of Labour voting, returning Labour MPs in every election from 1935 to 1979. The boundary changes in 1983 did not help Labour, but the real reason for their defeat was the massive unpopularity of the riven party under Michael Foot, which achieved less than 30% of the vote nationwide. Labour lost Edmonton during the slump of their popularity, but now they are successful again it has returned to traditional loyalties.

Social indices:			2001 Gen. Election:			
% Non-white	20.1		Lab/Coop	20,481	58.9	−1.4
% Prof/Man	27.4		C	10,709	30.8	+0.6
% Non-manual	55.1		LD	2,438	7.0	+0.7
£ Av prop val 2000	104 K		UKIP	406	1.2	+0.6
% Increase 97–00	44.6		Ind	344	1.0	
% Unemployed 2001	5.5		SA	296	0.9	
% Decrease 97–01	3.3		Ind	100	0.3	
% Fin hard/Rank	25.1	198	L/C maj	9,772	28.1	
% Pensioners	23.3		Turnout		55.8	−14.6
% Prem mort/Rank	29	352	Elect	62,294		

Member of Parliament

Amiable, dark-moustached, Scots-accented, and loyalist, **Andy Love**, by 2001 PPS to Health Minister Jacqui Smith, was born in 1949, educated at Greenock High School and Strathclyde University, and is one of a score of itinerant Scots holding seats for Labour in England. Winning here in 1997, having fought and lost it in 1992, he had risen in Labour politics via the Co-operative Party and movement and as a Haringey councillor. With a sizeable local Greek Cypriot minority, he makes regular visits to the island and prudently inveighs against Turkish occupation of its northern part.

ELLESMERE PORT AND NESTON

The division of Ellesmere Port and Neston is squeezed between the muddy, swampy estuary of the Dee and the Mersey. This is one of Britain's most functional, industrial landscapes. By the Mersey can be found the massive complex of the oil refinery at Stanlow, which became the centre of national attention during the combined farmers and truckers petrol tax protest blockades of September 2000, which briefly rattled Tony Blair and Gordon Brown's government. There is a power-station at Ince. Vauxhall Motors still have a major factory at the north end of Ellesmere Port, their main operational centre in Britain following the closures at Luton. There are docks, paper-works, oil depots, sewage works, fertiliser factories and many other concerns. Chimneys and flares overshadow the council estates of Ellesmere Port, a town created by the industrial revolution and the Manchester Ship Canal.

However, the south Wirral villages and the small town of Neston near the Dee marshes have a high proportion of commuters to Merseyside and Chester. Neston is essentially middle class, Ellesmere Port mainly working class; Neston over-whelmingly owner-occupied, Ellesmere Port substantially local-authority owned. Neston, especially its northern suburbs of Parkgate and Ness and Burton to the south, is inclined to the Conservatives; Ellesmere Port tips strongly to the Labour side, especially in the river-front wards; there is a more marginal owner-occupied section inland at Whitby and the more recently developed Groves ward.

Ellesmere Port and Neston started out in 1983 and 1987 as a Tory marginal, but Andrew Miller gained it for Labour in 1992, and won easily in 1997 and 2001, thus offering a reminder that although administratively in Cheshire this area is very much within the economic and political orbit of Merseyside, it is a disaster zone for the Tories.

Social indices:			2001 Gen. Election:			
% Non-white	0.6		Lab	22,964	55.3	−4.3
% Prof/Man	29.6		C	12,103	29.1	+0.1
% Non-manual	53.4		LD	4,828	11.6	+2.7
£ Av prop val 2000	77 K		UKIP	824	2.0	
% Increase 97–00	22.4		Grn	809	1.9	
% Unemployed 2001	2.5		Lab maj	10,861	26.2	
% Decrease 97–01	2.0		Turnout		60.9	−16.9
% Fin hard/Rank	20.7	261	Elect	68,147		
% Pensioners	22.3					
% Prem mort/Rank	34	264				

Member of Parliament

Ginger-bearded, if otherwise monochrome, **Andrew Miller**, an MSF (formerly ASTMS) trade union regional officer (1977–92), won this seat in 1992, and established a reputation as a keen advocate of e-commerce and as a defender of his constituent, the nanny Louise Woodward, accused of child-killing in the US in 1997. In 1993, as a Merseyside MP, he opposed creating the pools-threatening National Lottery. Born in 1949, son of a technician in the civil service, educated – after failing the 11-plus – at Hayling Island County Secondary School and taking a one-year diploma course at the LSE, he was originally a geology laboratory assistant at Portsmouth Polytechnic for nine years. A trade union politician, he helps swell the ranks of professional politicians in the PLP – about a third of the total – who have previously had some sort of paid political work, a professionalism which after nine years in the House saw him appointed a PPS at the DTI in 2001.

ELMET

Elmet was an entirely new constituency in 1983, but the Commission seems confident that they got it right then and no change at all has since been proposed. The name of the seat is a mystery to many. Elmet was the name of the last Celtic kingdom in England, but its exact borders do not appear to be known; there is a town called Sherburn-in-Elmet, but that is not in this seat. The late Poet Laureate Ted Hughes, himself a proud Yorkshireman, published a volume called *Remains of Elmet*, with accompanying photographs, but that was specifically set in the Calder Valley.

The boundaries of the Elmet constituency are at least clearly defined. It is made up of the far eastern wards of the city of Leeds, which was enlarged in the early 1970s to take in some neighbouring countryside and communities beyond the old city boundaries. Most of it is situated beyond the edge of the main built-up area: Wetherby, Barwick and Kippax, Garforth and Swillington. One ward from the periphery of Leeds itself is included, Whinmoor.

Elmet is a marginal seat. Whinmoor is part of the sprawl of vast council estates in east Leeds, and consistently returns Labour councillors. Both Barwick/Kippax and Garforth/Swillington are usually Labour wards. The south end of Garforth is a council estate where many ex-miners live, and votes Labour heavily. However, all of these areas were between 1983 and 1992 outvoted by Wetherby, the strongest Conservative ward in the whole of the city council. This market town ten miles north-east of Leeds has expanded since the war to take in many affluent commuters. It produced a 19% vote for Labour in the May 2000 local elections, but 69% for the Conservatives.

Wetherby will still have voted Conservative in 2001, but the whole of Elmet did not. Colin Burgon was returned for a second term, but with a reduced majority of 4,000 as the Conservatives improved a little from their depths of four years previously. They will have to increase their share by a greater increment next time if they are to win here, but it is not out of the question, as it seems to be in so many of the seats they held in the days when they could form governments.

Social indices:			2001 Gen. Election:			
% Non-white	1.1		Lab	22,038	48.0	−4.4
% Prof/Man	33.4		C	17,867	38.9	+2.7
% Non-manual	60.7		LD	5,001	10.9	+2.2
£ Av prop val 2000	98 K		UKIP	1,031	2.2	
% Increase 97–00	26.2		Lab maj	4,171	9.1	
% Unemployed 2001	1.7		Turnout		65.6	−11.2
% Decrease 97–01	1.4		Elect	70,041		
% Fin hard/Rank	15.2	350				
% Pensioners	24.4					
% Prem mort/Rank	22	460				

Member of Parliament

Colin Burgon, a Catholic-educated (St Michael's College, Leeds) warehouseman, clerk, teacher and finally local government officer, born in 1948, won this seat at his third attempt in 1997. An opponent of local opencast mining, he has, despite a forceful style, done little to trouble the scorers, tabling only five written questions in his first year, doubtless happy to have arrived at last and content to be loyal footsoldier.

ELTHAM

This is a seat in south-east London, roughly covering the southern half of the borough of Greenwich. It has ranked as a marginal since its creation in 1983, and indeed it bears a close resemblance to a seat which existed before then, Woolwich West, which Peter Bottomley won from Labour in a by-election in 1975 during the final period of unpopular Wilsonian Labour government. Bottomley consolidated his position in the three Thatcher victories, but his lead was sharply cut back from over 6,000 in 1987 to less than a third of that in the Major election. In 1997 Bottomley's decision to relocate in Worthing was fully justified as Labour's former London taxi driver Clive Efford seized the Eltham seat on a swing of over 13%, and in 2001 he held on easily as Labour notched up a second massive victory, although the turnout fell by an above average 17%, the Liberal Democrats being the only party to increase their number of votes, from a very low base indeed.

This is a patchy seat, with a mosaic of neighbourhoods of differing natures. The Conservatives do best in owner-occupied and middle-class parts such as those around the Palace and New Eltham; Labour fights back in former local authority estates like Shooters Hill and Well Hall. This is an almost all-white constituency, with relatively few working-class voters but a higher than average proportion of council and ex-council housing, and a history of Labour-controlled councils generally regarded as free of the 'loony left' type of criticism found elsewhere in London. It is just the sort of place which has given the greatest of favour to New Labour so far, and seems likely to do so next time unless they blot their copybook in a major way.

Social indices:			2001 Gen. Election:			
% Non-white	7.7		Lab	17,855	52.8	−1.8
% Prof/Man	32.2		C	10,859	32.1	+1.0
% Non-manual	62.5		LD	4,121	12.2	+3.7
£ Av prop val 2000	119 K		UKIP	706	2.1	
% Increase 97–00	52.3		Ind	251	0.7	
% Unemployed 2001	3.7		Lab maj	6,996	20.7	
% Decrease 97–01	3.0		Turnout		58.7	−17.0
% Fin hard/Rank	22.7	229	Elect	57,519		
% Pensioners	27.5					
% Prem mort/Rank	25	416				

Member of Parliament

Labour's bearded **Clive Efford**, elected in 1997, the Commons' first black-cab driver, has naturally-enough backed attempts to license rival rogue mini-cab drivers, with their reputation for personal menace, mechanical unreliability and geographical ignorance. Born in 1958 and educated at Walworth Comprehensive School, formerly working in his family's jeweller's shop, and a Greenwich councillor from 1989, he also backs energy efficiency, integrated transport, and vetting of private school staff 'to minimise the likelihood of further deranged individuals reaching the Tory benches'. In 1998 he met Eltham's most famous son, Bob Hope, in the United States. He is also a rare case of a Labour MP retaining his municipal political career alongside his parliamentary one.

ENFIELD NORTH

Labour gained all three seats in the north London borough of Enfield in 1997. Michael Portillo's defeat in Southgate took the most national headlines, but in its own way the result at Enfield North was at least as significant. Portillo's defeat was the icing on the cake as far as Labour was concerned: it meant that they had achieved a record-breaking landslide. Enfield North was just the kind of seat they needed to win to have an effective operational majority in the Commons.

The seats behaved somewhat differently in 2001. While Southgate swung even further towards Labour and Stephen Twigg strengthened his grip on his seat, the Conservatives made a substantial recovery in North and came within striking distance of winning, needing only another 3% swing at Labour's expense to nullify Joan Ryan's lead, reduced from nearly 7,000 to just over 2,000.

Enfield North looks on the surface like an archetypal marginal seat. Like its neighbour to the south, Edmonton, it ranges from the Conservative green belt in the west, to tower blocks and industry east of the Cambridge Road and up to the bank of the Lea. Enfield Town and Chase are Conservative, Ponders End and Enfield Lock and Wash are Labour. Like Edmonton, there are fewer professional and managerial workers than the national average, considerably fewer than the London norm, and considerably more junior non-manual and skilled manual.

However, there are factors which kept the seat Conservative until 1997, and which may bring it back more quickly than others lost in that year of utter disaster. There is plenty of pleasant suburban residential territory here, around the centre of the once independent town of Enfield. There is even open country around the Chase, still defined as within the borders of Greater London but physically indistinguishable from the Hertfordshire countryside. Less than one-tenth of the population is non-white, compared with one-fifth in Edmonton further in towards the centre of London. Finally this is not a haunt of intellectuals, with their liberal/left inclinations. Only 9.5% of adults have 'higher qualifications' as defined by the Census, well below the national average; compare it with Hampstead and Highgate with 35%, and that is a safe Labour seat – or Islington North with 22%.

Enfield North now ranks among Labour's most 25 vulnerable seats, and they could lose it and still be returned to government with a majority of over 100. To most people it counts as very marginal, but it is actually no longer the sort of seat which is won by whoever wins the general election. It is now more Conservative than that, just as it is now more Conservative than its neighbour, Enfield Southgate.

Social indices:			2001 Gen. Election:			
% Non-white	8.8		Lab	17,888	46.9	−3.8
% Prof/Man	28.6		C	15,597	40.9	+4.5
% Non-manual	55.9		LD	3,355	8.8	−0.2
£ Av prop val 2000	114 K		BNP	605	1.6	+0.4
% Increase 97–00	48.3		UKIP	247	0.6	−0.4
% Unemployed 2001	3.6		PA	241	0.6	
% Decrease 97–01	2.4		Ind	210	0.6	
% Fin hard/Rank	18.4	295	Lab maj	2,291	6.0	
% Pensioners	23.2		Turnout		56.3	−14.1
% Prem mort/Rank	22	450	Elect	67,756		

Member of Parliament

Joan Ryan, PPS to Chief Secretary to the Treasury Andrew Smith, won this seat in 1997. Initially (before the election) she sounded keen on renationalising public utilities, but as a backbencher has been ultra loyal, pitching on-message locally-focused questions, such as in October 2001 when on the day the government launched a campaign to remove abandoned cars from the streets, she posed a question on precisely that subject. A school teacher for 13 years, and a council deputy leader, she has been dubbed 'Junket Joan' for her trips to Cyprus where she backs the Greeks (a constituency interest) against the Turks. She backed the return of London government but without Livingstone as mayor. She was born in 1955, a painter and decorator's daughter, attended Catholic schools and the City of Liverpool College of Higher Education, South Bank Polytechnic and Avery Hill Teacher Training College.

ENFIELD SOUTHGATE

For many viewers, one the of highlights – if not the greatest – of General Election night in 1997 was the almost totally unexpected defeat of Defence Secretary Michael Portillo at Enfield Southgate. This star then associated with the Tory Right managed to lose a lead of 15,500 on a swing to Labour of 17.4%, elevating Stephen Twigg to instant prominence. This was indeed the third safest of all Tory seats to fall, although the swing was only slightly greater than the average in outer London, rather than a particularly vicious rebuke to Portillo. This northern fringe of London knocked the Conservatives back more than almost any other: note the results in the two Harrow seats and Brent North.

Southgate is the only truly middle-class suburban seat in Enfield. It is situated in the western section of the borough, and is almost entirely composed of owner-occupied private housing stock. Many of the neighbourhoods are well-known as comfortable commuting bases: Winchmore Hill, Oakwood, part of Cockfosters, Southgate itself. It also contains a semi-rural ward, which includes the attractive Trent Park. However, there were wards within the Southgate constituency which contributed to the triumph that Labour obtained against Michael Portillo in 1997. They had won Arnos and Bowes before, and in 1994 they added Palmers Green. The factor that these wards have in common, and which to a large extent explains their political preferences, is race. All have a significant non-white minority, principally Asian, plus a section of North London's Cypriot population; overall Enfield Southgate is about 14% non-white.

The notion that Stephen Twigg's 1997 triumph was but a flash in the pan should have been placed in doubt as early as May 1998, when Labour candidates finished only 2% behind Conservatives in the wards which make up the seat in the four-yearly Enfield London Borough elections, topping the polls in six out of the 11. Twigg proved an able and active member, and of course Portillo's charisma was missing too in 2001, when his replacement John Flack was unable to make any impact at all on the gap, which increased to over 5,500 after a further 10% change in the difference between party shares. Stephen Twigg may well have a long and successful career in the Commons even without moving from the seat in which he made such a spectacular start to his time in Parliament.

Social indices:			2001 Gen. Election:			
% Non-white	13.6		Lab	21,727	51.8	+7.6
% Prof/Man	45.4		C	16,181	38.6	−2.5
% Non-manual	72.0		LD	2,935	7.0	−3.7
£ Av prop val 2000	196 K		Grn	662	1.6	
% Increase 97–00	45.2		UKIP	298	0.7	
% Unemployed 2001	3.4		Ind	105	0.3	−0.2
% Decrease 97–01	2.0		Lab maj	5,546	13.2	
% Fin hard/Rank	7.4	545	Turnout		63.1	−7.6
% Pensioners	25.6		Elect	66,418		
% Prem mort/Rank	10	588				

Member of Parliament

Stephen Twigg was Labour's most emblematic winner in 1997 as the unexpected vanquisher of an unpopular Cabinet Minister, Michael Portillo, and as one of a clutch of known homosexual MPs. By the post-election reshuffle of 2001 he had, as parliamentary Secretary at the Privy Council Office (a grand title for Robin Cook's assistant), become one of 22 of the 183-strong 1997 intake of Labour MPs to have reached the frontbench. Born in 1966, son of a Communist insurance clerk, and educated at Southgate Comprehensive and Balliol College, Oxford, he rose as a protégé of Margaret Hodge on Islington council, as part of the clean-up team after a period of 'loony-leftism'. Very tall, sallow-skinned and blessed with a good deal of boyish charm, he has been dubbed 'New Labour's answer to Dale Winton', and likened by one woman MP to Tigger in *Winnie the Pooh*. Understandably backing PR, as one originally seeming unlikely to survive here without it, he also backs Israel and Greek Cyprus, and constituency interests explain that too. His homosexuality led him to heckle the overly heterosexual Labour MP Joe Ashton when Ashton opposed gay sex at 16 if it exposed boys to predatory teachers or children's home carers. His support for electoral reform involving the 'alternative vote' system is shared by his new boss, Robin Cook, if not obviously by the Prime Minister.

EPPING FOREST

Epping Forest has long been one of the playgrounds of north-east Londoners, and the communities attractively situated around its edges are desirable residential areas: Epping itself, Buckhurst Hill, Loughton, Theydon Bois and Chigwell, after which a very similar constituency was named before 1974. These are all solidly Conservative, and there are private streets of mansions and real wealth, in Chigwell in particular. In 2000 the value of the average house sale was close to £170,000, up 49% since 1997.

The only areas of Labour support are in the council-built estates; the large Broadway/Debden Green overspill development, the Paternoster ward of Waltham Abbey, and the Shelley ward of Epping. These were sufficient to push Labour into second place in the last three general elections. The true indication of the Tory strength here is that they actually held the seat both in the by-election in 1988, caused by the death of the veteran right-winger Sir John Biggs-Davison, when Steve Norris re-entered the Commons, and in the 1997 cataclysm, when Eleanor Laing took over with a 5,000 margin. She effectively doubled her lead in 2001, though this was partially disguised by a drop in turnout from 72% to 58%, both close to the national figure.

Social indices:			2001 Gen. Election:			
% Non-white	2.9		C	20,833	49.1	+3.6
% Prof/Man	36.6		Lab	12,407	29.3	−6.3
% Non-manual	65.6		LD	7,884	18.6	+5.2
£ Av prop val 2000	169 K		UKIP	1,290	3.0	
% Increase 97–00	49.4		C maj	8,426	19.9	
% Unemployed 2001	1.7		Turnout		58.4	−14.4
% Decrease 97–01	1.7		Elect	72,645		
% Fin hard/Rank	11.5	426				
% Pensioners	27.1					
% Prem mort/Rank	19	493				

Member of Parliament

Eleanor Laing, one of a mere handful of new Tory women MPs in 1997, backing William Hague was quickly onto the frontbench, first as a Whip in 1999, a spokesman on Scotland in 2000, and – after backing fellow Scot, Michael Ancram, then Iain Duncan Smith in 2001 – an Education spokesman. Itinerant, as all ambitious Scots Tories must be, she was born in 1958, and educated at St Columba's School, Kilmacolm and Edinburgh University, where she read law and, after practising it for four years, and lobbying for deregulated Sunday trading for two years, became a party apparatchik first as adviser to John MacGregor (1989–94), then at Central Office. Fluent and persuasive, with some courage she spoke and voted in 1998 for homosexual sex at 16, to the accompaniment of Nick Winterton's bullying interventions, and repeated her support in a further vote in 1999. She opposes Scottish devolution, abolition of grant-maintained schools, and positive discrimination in favour of women candidates and, in 2001, joined a handful of Labour's 1997 intake of women MPs, and her colleague Julie Kirkbride, in having a baby.

EPSOM AND EWELL

Chris Grayling retained the Surrey seat of Epsom and Ewell in 2001 with a majority of 10,000 over Labour, with the Liberal Democrats just behind in third place. This was about half the lead the party has had in an average year since the Second World War, but it was still one of the easiest 30 or so Conservative victories of their second consecutive disaster. This is an 'inner Surrey' seat, with little open countryside and very much within the commuting orbit of London. Indeed in some areas it is very hard to distinguish where the Greater London boundary lies; for example, the Worcester Park neighbourhood straddles the border with the London borough of Sutton, its relentless rows of semi-detached streets apparently recognising no such administrative distinction. Stoneleigh Park is similar. Ewell retains some aspects of an independent town, particularly in the old centre around its attractive lakes. Epsom, with its wells and downs and famous Derby racecourse, is the name most widely known and it does indeed have the most distinct identity. There is even a rather working-class area which votes Labour in north-west Epsom.

The local Epsom and Ewell Council is dominated by residents with a lively Liberal Democrat presence. However this masks a seat which demonstrates its underlying massive loyalty to the Conservative Party when it comes to the business of selecting a national government. In 2001 all the three main parties actually held their vote shares very well, the only real loser being the minor parties, whose sole representative, the former Conservative Family Campaign chairman Graham Webster-Gardiner, did not manage to equal the combined Referendum Party and UKIP total of 1997.

Social indices:			2001 Gen. Election:			
% Non-white	4.6		C	22,430	48.1	+2.5
% Prof/Man	48.2		Lab	12,350	26.5	+2.1
% Non-manual	75.0		LD	10,316	22.1	−0.7
£ Av prop val 2000	196 K		UKIP	1,547	3.3	+2.3
% Increase 97–00	54.4		C maj	10,080	21.6	
% Unemployed 2001	0.7		Turnout		62.8	−11.2
% Decrease 97–01	1.0		Elect	74,266		
% Fin hard/Rank	4.0	626				
% Pensioners	28.8					
% Prem mort/Rank	15	544				

Member of Parliament

The new Conservative MP here is **Chris Grayling**, an unpatrician-seeming balding international management consultant, and former television journalist and producer for BBC and Channel Four. Active in Wimbledon as a Merton Borough councillor since 1998, he was born in 1962, and educated at Royal Grammar School, High Wycombe and Sidney Sussex, Cambridge (reading History). He is the author of books on the Bridgewater Canal, the brewer Joseph Holt, English life in the 1920s, and Anglo-American relations since 1945; and claims he once hit Dennis Lillee for four. In his maiden speech he sounded like a Liberal Democrat, complaining about a downgraded Epsom hospital and a shortage of school places, but voted the full right-wing Eurosceptic ticket, backing Iain Duncan Smith in all three leadership ballots.

EREWASH

The constituency of Erewash, named after the river which flows from north to south through the seat and enters the Trent near Long Eaton, is an interesting amalgamation of the pre-1983 South East Derbyshire seat and the town of Ilkeston. South East Derbyshire usually returned a Labour member between 1950 and 1970, when it was seized by the Conservative Peter Rost, but it swung sharply to the right between 1970 and 1983. Ilkeston (D.H. Lawrence's 'Keston') was never the most Labour-inclined part of its eponymous constituency, which was also moving fairly dramatically towards the Tories in the late 1970s and early 1980s. It was scarcely surprising that Peter Rost won Erewash with an 11,000 majority when it was first fought in 1983.

Rost was a hard right-winger, and in many ways his views suited the temper of the Erewash constituency. It moved to the right for a number of reasons: the development of new owner-occupied estates, which is particularly noticeable in the lace town of Long Eaton, the chief community of the old SE Derbyshire, which rose from 50% owner-occupied to over 70% in just 20 years. There is no mining influence here now; we have moved a long way from Lawrence's era. Erewash is sandwiched between Derby and Nottingham, both of which have large ethnic minority populations; but Erewash is over 98% white, and most of its residents probably wish it to stay that way.

Nevertheless, although the reasons for the Conservative victories of the 1980s here are apparent, Labour's Liz Blackman was able to benefit from a 12% swing (huge but nationally and regionally typical) to oust Peter Rost's successor Angela Knight in May 1997. There was no significant movement between the major parties in 2001, and Erewash now lies very slightly on the more-Labour-than-average half of the political spectrum. The Monster Raving Loony candidate in this most recent election was RU Seerius, which sounds like a defeat for conventionality in orthography at least, but not necessarily a trivial point. After all, while 30% of Erewash's 78,000 electors voted for the returned MP Liz Blackman, 38% did not vote at all.

Social indices:			2001 Gen. Election:			
% Non-white	1.4		Lab	23,915	49.2	−2.5
% Prof/Man	26.3		C	16,983	34.9	−1.6
% Non-manual	47.4		LD	5,586	11.5	+2.9
£ Av prop val 2000	57 K		UKIP	692	1.4	
% Increase 97–00	20.3		BNP	591	1.2	
% Unemployed 2001	2.9		MRLP	428	0.9	
% Decrease 97–01	1.3		SLP	401	0.8	+0.0
% Fin hard/Rank	18.4	299	Lab maj	6,932	14.3	
% Pensioners	24.6		Turnout		61.9	−16.0
% Prem mort/Rank	29	367	Elect	78,484		

Member of Parliament

Elizabeth Blackman, born in 1949, educated at Carlisle County High School for Girls, Prince Henry's Grammar School, Otley, and Clifton College of Further Education, Nottingham, is a standard 1997-issue New Labour MP as a first time candidate, off an all-women short list, a former school teacher, local councillor, and a loyalist backbencher, who was rewarded in 2000 by being appointed PPS to Defence Secretary Geoff Hoon.

ERITH AND THAMESMEAD

The London boroughs of Bexley and Greenwich were merged to enable parliamentary constituencies with a greater equality of electorates to be drawn in time for the 1997 Election. This is the cross-borough border seat: Erith from Bexley is placed together with Thamesmead, formerly in the Woolwich section of Greenwich borough. The two boroughs contribute approximately equally to the new seat, each sending just over 30,000 voters. This constituency thus incorporates the major part of two old divisions, Erith/Crayford and Woolwich. The former was a Conservative marginal with a majority in 1992 of 2,339. The latter seat recorded a Labour majority of less than that, 2,225. So, a critical and very tight Conservative-Labour marginal, then? Indeed no; a safe Labour seat, held by Labour's John Austin with a majority of 11,000 or 33% of the total votes cast.

This apparent contradiction can be explained easily. The Erith section is indeed marginal; Erith and Crayford had been won by the Tories narrowly in 1983 after the Labour MP James Wellbeloved defected to the SDP, then easily in 1987 and narrowly again in 1992. Woolwich had an even more unusual history. Its MP also defected before 1983, but very unusually John Cartwright held on twice and, uniquely for a defector, nearly won as an Independent SDP candidate in 1992. It was he who was second to Labour's John Austin-Walker (as he then wished to be named), with the Tories way back in third place. There is not likely to be any impact from the Liberal Democrats, who polled just 11% in 2001, or any other centrist in the foreseeable future in this neck of the woods, and Labour will continue to sweep Thamesmead and this whole seat.

Thamesmead is a troubled new community, built on the edge of the Thames marshes. Housing conditions are far from ideal, and there is a paucity of recreational facilities. Worst of all, there are serious problems with gang crime, and racial conflict. Both Asian and Afro-Caribbean teenagers have been murdered in racist attacks in this area in the last few years, and there is far-right activism, counteracted by left-wing demonstrations. Unfortunately this seat on the Thames at the far east end of London shares some of the modern difficulties of boroughs such as Tower Hamlets further up the river that cut through the nation's capital.

Social indices:			2001 Gen. Election:			
% Non-white	15.4		Lab	19,769	59.3	−2.8
% Prof/Man	24.6		C	8,602	25.8	+5.6
% Non-manual	54.7		LD	3,800	11.4	−0.6
£ Av prop val 2000	84 K		SLP	1,180	3.5	
% Increase 97–00	53.0		Lab maj	11,167	33.5	
% Unemployed 2001	5.4		Turnout		50.2	−15.9
% Decrease 97–01	4.4		Elect	66,371		
% Fin hard/Rank	27.3	168				
% Pensioners	20.0					
% Prem mort/Rank	33	296				

Member of Parliament

John Austin (previously John Austin-Walker until deciding to drop his divorced wife's surname as part of his in 1997) has rebelled mildly against the Blair government on lone parent benefit cuts, predatory pricing of the Murdoch press, and on means testing Incapacity Benefit – a low strike rate for someone who was Chairman of the Campaign Group as recently as 1995, and who rebelled 24 times in the 1992–97 Parliament. An electrician's son, born in 1944, and educated at Glyn County Grammar School, Epsom, Goldsmith's College and Bristol University, he was a Labour Party organiser and community relations officer and has past links to the semi-Trotskyist Labour Herald. Pro-Kurds, pro-Arabs, anti-nuclear, anti-Serb and pro-Europe (but not a single currency), in March 1996 he apologised to the Chief Whip for speaking on a Sinn Fein platform. Elected here in 1992, he previously clashed as Greenwich Council leader with Neil Kinnock on opposition to rate capping. His recent demeanour has been much more accommodating, though he did join the main (32-strong) revolt against the Terrorism, Crime and Security Bill in November 2001.

ESHER AND WALTON

The rifts in the Conservative Party over the issue of the UK's relationship to the European Union were starkly illustrated by the very serious attempt to deselect the pro-European MP for Esher and Walton, Ian Taylor, towards the end of 2000. After receiving the backing of MPs, not all from his wing of the party, but no doubt all solely with his personal interests at heart, he was reselected by a far from comfortable margin. This was, however, the end of his worries about continuing as member for Esher and Walton, at least for the time being. Taylor had far more to fear from his own constituency membership than from Labour or Liberal Democrat opponents in the subsequent General Election.

This is an extremely middle-class and ultra-Conservative seat. There are many neighbourhoods in Surrey which are far from rich, despite the county's elite reputation. There are council estates and many working-class residents. However, Esher and Walton does have more than its fair share of exclusive neighbourhoods and private estates, and an exceptionally high proportion of professional and higher managerial workers even for this prosperous region of the Home Counties. Among them are Burwood Park in the Hersham South ward, and much of Esher itself, Oxshott and Cobham. Less grand but still very respectable are the Dittons, the Moleseys, Hinchley Wood, Stoke D'Abernon and Walton. Its average house prices are the highest of any constituency outside Greater London, at £279,000 in 2000.

The results of the 2001 General Election rather vindicate Ian Taylor's personal stance. He won very easily, helped by the closeness of the Labour and Lib Dem candidates to each other in second and third place. If there had been a huge groundswell of anti-European feeling, there was an opportunity to vote for the one other candidate, that of the UK Independence Party, which advocates British withdrawal from the EU itself. That candidate lost his deposit by failing to attain 5% of the total cast.

Social indices:			2001 Gen. Election:			
% Non-white	3.5		C	22,296	49.0	−0.9
% Prof/Man	49.5		Lab	10,758	23.6	+0.9
% Non-manual	74.1		LD	10,241	22.5	+2.1
£ Av prop val 2000	279 K		UKIP	2,236	4.9	+3.9
% Increase 97–00	60.6		C maj	11,538	25.3	
% Unemployed 2001	0.7		Turnout		61.9	−12.2
% Decrease 97–01	1.2		Elect	73,541		
% Fin hard/Rank	3.6	632				
% Pensioners	26.1					
% Prem mort/Rank	2	631				

Member of Parliament

Ian Taylor, elected for Esher in 1987, is a rare Clarke-supporting One Nation Europhile, who quit Hague's frontbench (as a Northern Ireland spokesman) after four months in 1997 over its increasingly Eurosceptic stance, and survived a deselection attempt in December 2000 with an intervention from Clarke who warned more extreme Eurosceptics in Esher of 'very severe consequences' if they dropped him. The stockbroker son of an educational welfare officer, and married to the daughter of the late Lord Alport (Tory MP for Colchester 1950–61), he was born in 1945, and educated at Whitley Abbey School, Coventry and Keele University, and as a DTI Minister (1994–97) in Major's government, was in charge of promoting IT. His votes for Clarke in 2001 reaffirmed his backbench exile where he could continue to favour GM organisms and stem cell therapy, whilst opposing the opening of a branch of McDonalds in Hinchley Wood.

ESSEX NORTH

In the major boundary changes affecting Essex as a result of the award of an extra seat to the county by the most recent Boundary Commission, which reported in 1995, the town of Colchester was given a single compact seat. Previously it had been divided into two along the line of the river Colne, and each half diluted with rural territory: Colchester North reached as far as the Suffolk border, while Colchester South was paired with the Maldon district. Now that arrangement has been dramatically reversed as Colchester is entirely surrounded by the new seat of Essex North. It looks just like the hole in the middle of a doughnut.

This was not good news for the Conservatives, who held both previous Colchester seats easily. Colchester itself was lost to the Liberal Democrats in 1997. The Conservative strength from much of the two former seats (which had majorities of 16,500 and 22,000 in 1992) is concentrated in Essex North, which is itself a plum that Bernard Jenkin held even in the dark days of 1997 and 2001; but they will be wishing they could have spread their vote around a little more widely and efficiently.

A majority, 41,000, of Essex North's electors came from the old Colchester North seat; 19,000 from Colchester South and Maldon; and fewer than 7,000 from Harwich. Essex North is a large, rural division. There are only four towns, each with a population of 6,000 or 7,000. These are Tiptree, known for its manufacture of jam and other preserves; Wivenhoe, site of the distinguished University of Essex; Brightlingsea, at the mouth of the river Colne; and West Mersea, on its island in the Blackwater. The seat runs from the Blackwater in the south all the way to the Stour and the Suffolk border, in 'Constable country' around Dedham. It contains numerous villages and a variety of types of countryside. There can be no doubt of its political colour: true blue.

Social indices:			2001 Gen. Election:			
% Non-white	0.9		C	21,325	47.4	+3.5
% Prof/Man	35.7		Lab	14,139	31.5	−1.7
% Non-manual	59.4		LD	7,867	17.5	−2.1
£ Av prop val 2000	107 K		UKIP	1,613	3.6	+1.2
% Increase 97–00	53.7		C maj	7,186	16.0	
% Unemployed 2001	1.3		Turnout		62.7	−12.6
% Decrease 97–01	1.0		Elect	71,680		
% Fin hard/Rank	4.5	615				
% Pensioners	26.6					
% Prem mort/Rank	11	580				

Member of Parliament

Bernard Jenkin, Shadow Defence Secretary from 2001, elected first in 1992, is son of former Thatcher Cabinet Minister, Patrick Jenkin, than whom he sees himself as less 'cautious' and 'more controversial'. Though of himself he says 'I used to be a wet but I'm all right now', to Tory wet Peter Bottomley his personal and political life is comparable to a large dead fish in a painting by Gail Lilley. Born in 1959 and educated at Highgate School, William Ellis School, and Corpus Christi College, Cambridge, he worked as a venture capital manager, and in 1998 voted to lower the homosexual age of consent to 16. As Transport spokesman (1998–2001) he wanted a full sell-off of the tube, and as Constitution spokesman (1997–98) he opposed devolution. Described as 'one of the cleverest young dicks on the Eurosceptic benches' (*New Statesman*), he backed Lilley, then Hague, in 1997, and Iain Duncan Smith all the way in 2001.

EXETER

One of the most bitter and distinctive political battles in the country was fought in Exeter in 1997. Defending the seat for the Conservatives was the director of the Conservative Family Campaign, Dr Adrian Rogers. His Labour opponent was a BBC journalist and open homosexual, Ben Bradshaw. Sexuality was indeed more than mentioned in the campaign. Nevertheless, Ben Bradshaw enjoyed a swing very close to the national average and won decisively, by over 11,700 votes. It was Labour's first win in Exeter since 1966.

Exeter is Devon's oldest city as well as its county town. Although much of the centre had to be rebuilt after the 'Baedeker' air raids of 1942, Exeter is still steeped in history. Geographically it is well sited at the heart of the large county of Devon; its strategic location also meant that it became over-familiar to thousands of motorists who were trapped over the years in its notorious traffic bottleneck, before the M5 motorway was completed. Exeter is an affluent market and commercial centre – well over half of its employed population work in non-manual occupations. This is usually a reliable indicator of Conservatism – but not always; Labour obtained a double-figure swing among the AB and C1 socio-economic groups as well as all other classes in 1997. The City of Exeter is not far from an ideal size to form a parliamentary seat on its own, and there have been no boundary changes since 1974. Labour are the strongest party in municipal elections, winning former council estate wards like Wonford, Whipton, Stoke Hill and Barton, and older working-class areas like Rougemont and Barton. The battle is closely joined, though, as the Conservatives fight back in the south in Countess Wear and Topsham along the Exe, and they can win marginal wards in the centre and north of the city too. Labour have only won Exeter in years in which they have achieved a national landslide. Sure enough, they did have another landslide in 2001, and Ben Bradshaw won again; but the fact that he increased his lead further in percentage terms, in academic parlance a swing to Labour even though his vote actually went down due to the lower turnout, suggests that his assiduous work as an active MP in his constituency and in the Commons means that he will probably survive if they don't make it three in a row.

Social indices:			2001 Gen. Election:				
% Non-white	1.3		Lab	26,194	49.8	+2.3	
% Prof/Man	30.7		C	14,435	27.4	−1.2	
% Non-manual	58.3		LD	6,512	12.4	−5.6	
£ Av prop val 2000	86 K		Lib	2,596	4.9	+1.6	
% Increase 97–00	40.6		Grn	1,240	2.4	+1.3	
% Unemployed 2001	2.4		UKIP	1,109	2.1	+1.1	
% Decrease 97–01	2.3		SA	530	1.0		
% Fin hard/Rank	14.5	362	Lab maj	11,759	22.3		
% Pensioners	27.1		Turnout		64.2	−14.0	
% Prem mort/Rank	29	354	Elect	81,942			

Member of Parliament

Former BBC journalist **Ben Bradshaw** won here in 1997, defeating the Conservatives' notoriously homophobic candidate Dr Adrian Rogers. A fluent and personable parted-down-the-middle Hugh Grant lookalike, he is a vicar's son, born in 1960, and educated at Thorpe St Andrew School, Norwich, and at Sussex University. Whilst he prefers to be known as 'a Labour MP who happens to be gay' he has inevitably been identified as one of seven Labour MPs who have declared their homosexuality, and, in his case, obtained a Commons 'spouses' pass for his partner. Having behaved as a very loyal Blairite, and favouring early entry to a European currency, he became one of the 1997 intake of MPs to be promoted into the government in 2001, as a Junior Foreign Office Minister with responsibility for the Middle East and Asia, and so was quickly tested at the despatch box after the Islamic terrorism in New York in September 2001.

FALKIRK EAST

Until 1983 there were still some Scottish constituencies that consisted of collections of towns or burghs, but which did not form a contiguous constituency but were associated for parliamentary purposes even though separated by several miles of countryside incorporated in other seats. This was a throwback to the days when there was a real distinction between county and borough (or burgh) constituencies. One such division was Stirling, Falkirk and Grangemouth. Then, however, the eastern part of the town of Falkirk was placed together with the oil refining community of Grangemouth and Bo'ness (a shortened form of Borrowstounness), in a compact seat at the inner end of the Firth of Forth. Labour have won Falkirk East comfortably in its first five contests.

This constituency's name is now even more confusing than before. After further boundary changes in 1997, the whole of the town of Falkirk is now in the Falkirk West division. East has gained several thousand voters around Carron, and the whole of Stenhousemuir is included in the seat too. The Conservatives have some isolated pockets of support, such as in the Park neighbourhood of Grangemouth and at Polmont near Linlithgow Bridge, but the seat is essentially working class and industrial and the Tories finished only third in 1997. The real opposition to the Labour hegemony comes from the Scottish National Party, who do well in local elections throughout the Falkirk district but finished over 10,000 votes behind Michael Connarty in 1997. This is a picture very common in central Scotland.

Falkirk is likely to be united as a single rather large constituency next time, based on West and with much of this East seat subsumed into Linlithgow.

Social indices:			2001 Gen. Election:			
% Non-white	0.5		Lab	18,536	55.0	–1.1
% Prof/Man	26.2		SNP	7,824	23.2	–0.7
% Non-manual	47.4		C	3,252	9.6	–4.3
% Unemployed 2001	3.7		LD	2,992	8.9	+3.7
% Decrease 97–01	1.2		SSP	725	2.2	
% Fin hard/Rank	37.3	72	SLP	373	1.1	
% Prem mort/Rank	36	237	Lab maj	10,712	31.8	
			Turnout		58.5	–14.8
			Elect	57,633		

Member of Parliament

Michael Connarty, a spiky if calmed-down former semi-hard-left kilted version of Ken Livingstone, was elected here in 1992, having been leader of Stirling Council for 10 years. PPS to Minister-for-only-a-year Tom Clarke, he was born an electrician's son in 1947 and educated at St Patrick's (RC) High School, Coatbridge, and Stirling University, and was a teacher of children with learning difficulties for 16 years. A strong devolutionist, he withdrew from his attempt to stand for the Scottish Parliament, unlike his neighbour Dennis Canavan who sought selection, was blocked, stood against Labour, and was expelled. Though a left-winger by instinct, he backs the Trident refit at nearby Rosyth where some of his voters work, and has steered clear of rebellion against the Blair government, constrained initially by his role as a PPS.

FALKIRK WEST

There has been plenty of drama in Falkirk West since 1997, although things seem to have quietened down now. The excitement all revolves around the controversial figure of Dennis Canavan, a left-wing Labour MP since 1974, who wished to enter the Scottish Parliament on its foundation in 1999. The New Labour establishment had other ideas, and excluded him from the shortlist for consideration, allegedly because of unsuitability; no-one had previously doubted his ability, although his views cast doubt on his loyalty to the leadership. Canavan stood anyway in the May 1999 Elections and swept to victory in Falkirk west as an independent, trouncing the official Labour candidate by 55% to 19%. Expelled from the parliamentary party, he continued to sit at Westminster until his resignation caused an awkward by-election just before Christmas 2000. It was widely thought that the SNP would take advantage of the dissension within Labour's forces, but Labour's standard bearer, Eric Joyce, who had come to national attention as an Army officer who campaigned, while serving, against class and racial prejudice, held on by just 705 votes.

Calm followed remarkable rapidly, as results returned to normal – and very similar to those in Falkirk West next door – in June 2001. Joyce now has a secure base from which to continue his forays, or perhaps rise through the ministerial ranks at least as long as he finds a seat as the two Falkirks are reduced to one by forthcoming boundary changes.

The whole of the town of Falkirk is now included within the Falkirk West division; Falkirk East consists of other towns and areas included within the local authority district named after its major population centre. Falkirk is a proud old burgh, an industrial centre in an old iron-founding area which has diversified to include light engineering, distilling, heavy vehicle assembly and a host of other manufacturing trades. Falkirk is the smallest town to boast two Scottish football league teams; among the pairs of rivals which number Celtic and Rangers, Hearts and Hibs, and Dundee and Dundee United must be added Falkirk and East Stirlingshire.

Among the other communities in the seat are the small (and very Labour) towns of Denny and Dunipace, Larbert and Bonnybridge. Apart from the Woodlands district of Falkirk, a favoured residential area, the Conservatives have little support here, and it will be left to the SNP to carry the standard of battle against Labour at both municipal and parliamentary levels.

Social indices:			2001 Gen. Election:			
% Non-white	0.8		Lab	16,022	51.9	−7.5
% Prof/Man	28.2		SNP	7,490	24.2	+0.8
% Non-manual	49.5		C	2,321	7.5	−4.6
% Unemployed 2001	5.1		LD	2,203	7.1	+2.0
% Decrease 97–01	1.9		Ind	1,464	4.7	
% Fin hard/Rank	35.6	86	SSP	707	2.3	
% Prem mort/Rank	46	87	Ind	490	1.6	
			SLP	194	0.6	
			Lab maj	8,532	27.6	
			Turnout		57.7	−15.0
			Elect	53,583		

Member of Parliament

Eric Joyce, who was born in 1960 and educated at Perth High School and at Stirling, Bath and Keele universities, replaced the disaffected, expelled and resigned Dennis Canavan as Labour MP here at the December 2000 by-election. Originally a private in the Black Watch for three years, he had made a name for himself as an Army major who published his complaints about alleged class and race prejudice in Army promotions whilst a serving officer, a breach of conduct for which he was dismissed. In his maiden speech in January 2001 he praised the local Alexanders bus factory for exporting buses to New York. He also favours American-style yellow school buses, presumably to be built locally. A rare, if atypically plebeian and unconventionally dissentient, military man in Labour ranks, he is also an active Fabian. In 2002 he welcomed the non-selection of the left-wing *Tribune* editor Mark Seddon for the Ogmore by-election in Wales, seeing him as a 'London-based' candidate in a seat 'where Nationalists are the main challengers'.

FALMOUTH AND CAMBORNE

In 1997 there was a titanic struggle in Falmouth and Camborne, but it was Labour's national strength which prevailed, even in this far corner of the land. Three parties entertained very real hopes of victory: the other two were the Conservatives, whose sitting member was the former Olympic quadruple gold medallist runner Sebastian Coe, later a member of the Lords and William Hague's close confidant and judo partner; and the Liberal Democrats, whose Terrye Jones hoped to build on a strong tradition of local activism in this most Liberal of all counties. Labour's Candy Atherton increased her party's share by nearly 5%, and ousted Coe by 2,688, with Jones in a close and competitive third. There were also substantial votes for the Referendum Party's Peter de Savary and a local Independent Labour candidate, who objected to the all women short-list imposed by the NEC.

The ex-athlete was up against a strong anti-Conservative tradition in this complex division. Within living memory Falmouth and Camborne was known as the single predominantly Labour seat in Cornwall – they held it from its creation in 1950 until 1970. Labour's traditional support was to be found at both ends of the seat, which extends from the Atlantic to the Channel coasts of Cornwall. The ports of Falmouth and Penryn in the south elected a Labour MP in 1945, and indeed the historian A.L. Rowse (then a left-winger) had finished a strong second for them in 1935. Meanwhile, the industrial belt around the twin towns of Camborne and Redruth to the north was once the centre of the Cornish tin-mining industry. Now, however, the mines have all closed, the last, at South Crofty, during the 1997–2001 parliament. Falmouth's economy relies more on its role as a holiday resort than as a working port, but this is hardly a secure platform, as the west country tourism industry has added short-term setbacks such as foot and mouth in 2001 to its longer-term difficulties created by increased consumer mobility in search of more fashionable leisure suppliers.

In 2001 there was another very lively contest, again won by Atherton with the former ITN journalist Nicholas Serpell second and the Liberal Democrats third, all a little more spread out than in 1997, and the minor parties did less well than that year, although the UKIP candidate was a former Conservative MP, John Browne of Winchester, who had previously tried to get back into the Commons as an anti-Federalist in his old seat in 1997, having tried as an independent Conservative on his deselection in 1992. He seems to be migrating south-westwards, and no nearer to regaining a place in the Commons; one wonders if he will end up contesting the Scilly Isles.

Social indices:			2001 Gen. Election:				
% Non-white	0.6		Lab	18,532	39.6	+5.7	
% Prof/Man	29.9		C	14,005	29.9	+1.1	
% Non-manual	52.4		LD	11,453	24.5	-0.7	
£ Av prop val 2000	82 K		UKIP	1,328	2.8	+2.2	
% Increase 97–00	47.3		MK	853	1.8	+1.4	
% Unemployed 2001	3.9		Lib	649	1.4	+0.4	
% Decrease 97–01	3.4		Lab maj	4,527	9.7		
% Fin hard/Rank	14.4	363	Turnout		64.3	-10.9	
% Pensioners	30.3		Elect	72,833			
% Prem mort/Rank	31	312					

Member of Parliament

The first of Labour's candidates picked from an all-women shortlist in 1994, **Candy Atherton**, elected here in 1997, uncomfortably represents an isolated red Labour outpost in a Cornish sea of Liberal Democrat yellow, and with a recent if now fading Lib Dem challenge in this seat, is no part of any tacit national Lib-Lab alliance against the Tories. Large and bespectacled, unlike her immediate Lib Dem MP neighbours she has shallow Cornish roots. She was born in Surrey in 1955, was educated at Sutton High School for Girls, Midhurst Grammar School and North London Polytechnic, worked as a researcher for left-wing MPs Judith Hart and Jo Richardson, served five years until 1991 on Islington council, and was a UNISON organiser, a probation officer and latterly a freelance journalist based in Wiltshire. Nor was she able to stop the closure of the last tin mine in her seat at South Crofty, but she still doubled her majority in 2001.

FAREHAM

Fareham constituency lines the Solent and Southampton Water, proceeding up the north-east bank thereof as far as the mouth of the river Hamble. This is affluent country, which was chosen as the location of the 1970s TV series *Howard's Way*, a melodrama set among the boating and yachting set. It includes the waterside communities of Warsash, Sarisbury and Locks Heath (which doubled its population in the 1980s) as well as the eponymous Fareham and, even further to the east, Portchester north of Portsmouth Harbour. The seat is over 85% owner-occupied and only 1% non-white.

In 2001 there was a new Conservative candidate for the first time since 1979, as Sir Peter Lloyd retired in favour of Mark Hoban. This did not alter its political complexion: Hoban held on by over 7,000 even though Labour further increased their vote by 5%, having nearly doubled it in 1997, and the Conservatives did not benefit from the collapse of the relatively large anti-EU vote. Labour are clearly the beneficiaries of a sub-regional electoral movement here, as they have advanced into a challenging position in Gosport next door and strengthened their grip on Portsmouth North. In due course this may be mean that Fareham achieves marginal status – but not yet.

Social indices:			2001 Gen. Election:			
% Non-white	1.0		C	21,389	47.1	+0.2
% Prof/Man	38.7		Lab	14,380	31.6	+4.7
% Non-manual	62.0		LD	8,503	18.7	–0.9
£ Av prop val 2000	123 K		UKIP	1,175	2.6	
% Increase 97–00	56.5		C maj	7,009	15.4	
% Unemployed 2001	0.9		Turnout		62.5	–13.3
% Decrease 97–01	1.3		Elect	72,678		
% Fin hard/Rank	5.6	594				
% Pensioners	23.6					
% Prem mort/Rank	14	551				

Member of Parliament

Mark Hoban, County Durham-born, but Guildford-based, is the new Conservative MP here. A chartered accountant, born in 1964, educated at St Leonard's (RC) Comprehensive, Durham and LSE, he has worked with Price Waterhouse Coopers or its predecessor companies since graduation, latterly advising banks and businesses on flotations and takeovers. In 1997 he fought the very safe Labour seat of South Shields, coming, as he engagingly puts it, 'second'. His Euroscepticism and strong belief in the free market, light regulation and low tax, sounds well to the right of retiring MP, Sir Peter Lloyd. In his maiden speech he spoke up for the local Vosper Thorneycroft shipyard and against the Treaty of Nice expanding the EU. He voted for the subtler option of Michael Portillo in the July 2001 leadership ballots.

FAVERSHAM AND MID KENT

Most of the shire counties of southern England received extra seats in the redistribution of parliamentary boundaries enacted after the Boundary Commission's report of 1995. The 'Garden of England', the south-easternmost county of Kent, was no exception. It was entitled to 17 seats, not the 16 it currently possessed. The main population growth had taken place at the centre of the county, and this is where an extra seat was created, essentially from the former divisions of Faversham, Mid Kent, Maidstone and Tonbridge and Malling, though consequential ripples have more minor effects in the western and eastern ends of this big county. It is not always easy to establish which individual seat has the best claim to be the additional one after boundary changes, but in this case it is fairly clear that the one which bears less resemblance to any previous division is Faversham and Mid Kent.

Do not be misled by the name. This constituency does not contain a majority of the voters of either of the former seats called Faversham or Mid Kent. Rather, it is made up of fairly equal portions of three old seats plus a minor contribution from a fourth: actually the largest single element comes from Maidstone (24,000 electors), which is not even mentioned in the seat's title; then come Faversham (20,000), Mid Kent (19,000) and Canterbury (3,000). It is more than something of a ragbag. The town of Faversham itself is detached from the bulk of the constituency formerly named after it, which is now called Sittingbourne and Sheppey. To it is added some of the lush rural countryside formerly in Mid Kent (most of which is now in Chatham and Aylesford). This is topped off with a couple of wards from the fringe of Canterbury constituency and a wedge of the eastern part of the county town of Maidstone. All of this is fairly solidly Conservative except for the last named, for eastern Maidstone includes three mainly council-estate wards, Park Wood, Shepway East and Shepway West, which are all Labour bankers in council elections.

In 1997, Labour polled over 17,000 votes in this new seat, but Andrew Rowe held on for the Conservatives by over 4,000. Although Labour did not go backwards in Kent in 2001, as most observers predicted, they did not cut the 4,000 majority further, even though Andrew Rowe had given way to a new candidate, Hugh Robertson. As it is surely unlikely that Labour will win three landslides in a row, this suggests that Labour may never be strong enough to win Faversham and Mid Kent.

Social indices:			2001 Gen. Election:			
% Non-white	1.1		C	18,739	45.6	+1.3
% Prof/Man	36.9		Lab	14,556	35.5	−0.5
% Non-manual	60.3		LD	5,529	13.5	+1.1
£ Av prop val 2000	126 K		UKIP	828	2.0	+1.1
% Increase 97–00	48.3		Grn	799	1.9	+1.2
% Unemployed 2001	1.4		Ind	600	1.5	
% Decrease 97–01	2.1		C maj	4,183	10.2	
% Fin hard/Rank	11.0	437	Turnout		60.4	−13.1
% Pensioners	23.8		Elect	67,995		
% Prem mort/Rank	12	573				

Member of Parliament

Hugh Robertson, as a former officer in the Life Guards (1985–95), elected in 2001, came with a traditional pedigree. Born in 1962, he attended King's School Canterbury and Sandhurst, and qualified in land management at Reading University. With service in Northern Ireland, the Gulf War, Bosnia and Cyprus, he quit the Army to find a parliamentary seat, joining the Tories in 1995. Latterly with Schroeder Investment Management, in 1993 he commanded the Household Cavalry at the Trooping of the Colour and at the State Opening of Parliament, and should make a suitable, soldierly chum for Julian Brazier next door in Canterbury. One of a clutch of ex-Army officers in the Tory intake of 2001, he spoke up for local apple-growing interests in his maiden speech, and voted for Michael Portillo in all three leadership ballots.

FELTHAM AND HESTON

The Conservatives won the Feltham and Heston constituency in the two general elections of the 1980s, but it never really looked like a Tory seat should the outcome of the national contest be anything other than a Conservative landslide. This is the western half of the borough of Hounslow, situated to the east of Heathrow airport. It covers the communities of East Bedfont, Hanworth and Cranford as well as those named in the title, and also Hounslow Heath ward, although Hounslow West has been moved into Brentford and Isleworth, which serves to make both Hounslow constituencies more marginal.

There are several reasons why this constituency is normally won by Labour. One important feature of Feltham and Heston is that it is the centre of one of London's largest Asian communities, predominantly Indian in origin, and including both Sikhs and Hindus. Several wards are around 50% non-white: Cranford, Hounslow Heath, and the three Heston wards; a majority of the 13 Labour councillors in these wards are themselves Asian in origin.

This is much the more working-class end of the borough, and it also has more council housing than Brentford and Isleworth. The Labour Party in the borough of Hounslow has never fallen foul of charges of being run by the 'loony left' and it has run the borough quietly enough for many years. There are now no Conservative councillors in the wards which make up Feltham and Heston, and while there has been some Liberal Democrat local success in wards such as Hanworth and Feltham South they are hopelessly squeezed out in general elections.

Labour has much going for it in the 1990s in Feltham and Heston, and it came as little surprise that Alan Keen increased his majority from 1,400 in 1992 to over 12,000 in 2001, even though the turnout dropped by 24%, to less than half, between these years. The west end of Hounslow looks safe for Labour for the foreseeable future.

Social indices:			2001 Gen. Election:			
% Non-white	27.0		Lab/Coop	21,406	59.2	−0.5
% Prof/Man	25.7		C	8,749	24.2	−2.8
% Non-manual	54.6		LD	4,998	13.8	+4.7
£ Av prop val 2000	114 K		SLP	651	1.8	
% Increase 97–00	55.2		Ind	204	0.6	
% Unemployed 2001	2.1		Ind	169	0.5	
% Decrease 97–01	3.2		L/C maj	12,657	35.0	
% Fin hard/Rank	20.7	263	Turnout		49.4	−16.2
% Pensioners	21.0		Elect	73,229		
% Prem mort/Rank	33	282				

Member of Parliament

Alan Keen, elected here in 1992, is part of five Commons husband-and-wife teams, his wife Ann being MP for the neighbouring seat of Brentford and Isleworth. Less high profile than his wife, he concentrates on local campaigning. Lewisham-born in 1937, but reared in his single mother's home town of Middlesbrough, whose accent he retains, he attended Sir William Turner's School, Redcar and was a football scout for Middlesbrough FC for nearly 30 years. Latterly a 'fire protection consultant', he has also worked as a systems analyst, accountant, and manager of various firms. One of the Commons' quieter MPs, he defends first-past-the-post voting, and said of the disregarded Jenkins Report on electoral reform in 1998 that he did not think 'Blair has any chance of getting this through Parliament'.

FERMANAGH AND SOUTH TYRONE

The Northern Irish seat of Fermanagh and South Tyrone is traditionally one of the cockpits of Unionist/Nationalist rivalry. For decades there has been a small Catholic majority, but as in neighbouring Mid Ulster the elections have often been decided by abstentionism and vote-splitting. The electoral history is convoluted and bitter. Among the Nationalist and Republican members here have been Frank McManus, Frank Maguire, the hunger striker Bobby Sands, and following his death his agent Owen Carron. Among the unionists have been the one-time party leader Harry West and from 1983 to 2001 Ken Maginnis. When Maginnis, at the same time a loyal pro-Belfast Agreement supporter of David Trimble and a man respected for his independence and courage, retired on health grounds there were predictions that his party would be unable to hold Fermanagh and South Tyrone in the polarised atmosphere prevalent at the time, and indeed his Ulster Unionist successor, his agent Jim Cooper, was hampered by the candidature of an independent loyalist, Jim Dixon, a victim of the Enniskillen bombing alleged to have DUP support. The Nationalist and Catholic vote was split too, and Sinn Fein's Michelle Gildernew was elected as her party's first female MP by just 53 votes. With suggestions of illegal electoral practices, there was talk of a challenge to her election. Once again, Fermanagh and South Tyrone had seen one of the most bitter and closely fought battles in a UK general election.

This is a border seat, sharing a long frontier with the Republic. It is rural and agricultural, with a significant tourist business based on the Erne lakes. The main urban centre is Enniskillen, site of one of the most-publicised bombings of the 1980s. The contrast between the peaceful beauty of the scenery and the vitriol and violence of politics makes Fermanagh and South Tyrone in many ways the setting for the most tragic form of drama in the UK politics, pursued by parliamentary and other means.

Social indices:		2001 Gen. Election:			
% Prof/Man	33.6	SF	17,739	34.1	+11.0
% Non-manual	42.4	UUP	17,686	34.0	−17.5
% RC	51.2	SDLP	9,706	18.7	−4.2
% Irish sp	11.5	Ind	6,843	13.2	
% Unemployed 2001	6.2	SF maj	53	0.1	
% Decrease 97–01	3.9	Turnout		78.0	+3.2
		Elect	66,640		

Member of Parliament

Michelle Gildernew, the first female Sinn Fein MP since Countess Markiewicz (aka Constance Gore-Booth) was elected as the first ever woman MP in 1918 (but by not taking her seat enabled Nancy, Viscountess Astor, to enjoy that distinction), won the seat in 2001 with the Commons' third smallest majority of 53 votes. With a reputation of being on the soft end of Sinn Fein without any IRA association, like the other three Sinn Fein MPs she boycotts Westminster and concentrates on her role in the Northern Ireland Assembly. Born in 1970 and educated at the University of Ulster, she became press officer for her party in 1997, was elected here to the Northern Ireland Assembly in 1998, declared on her selection for this seat that there would be 'no decommissioning in a partitionist Ireland', and on beating the Unionist James Cooper was inevitably met with accusations of ballot-rigging, in particular of a polling station accepting votes after 10 pm. As one of the youngest MPs, she personifies her party's claim to represent the aspirations of young Nationalist voters in contrast to the senescent SDLP.

FIFE CENTRAL

Fife Central is a seat with two distinguished and very distinct former MPs. For the first four years of its life, from 1983 to 1987, it was held by the veteran Labour member Willie Hamilton, known best as an anti-monarchist but in fact a right-winger within the party who was more than once threatened with deselection, and no Nationalist, as befits a man of County Durham coalmining origins. For the next 14 years the seat was held by Henry McLeish, now Scotland's second First Minister, rather narrowly elected by his party to succeed Donald Dewar in that important and symbolic role in 2000. McLeish had already announced his retirement from Westminster consequent on his decision to switch to Holyrood, and John MacDougall has inherited the seat with little fuss or fanfare. It will be an achievement if he can match the renown – or at least publicity – won by his predecessors.

Fife Central is different from the seat that Hamilton held for most of his 37 years in the Commons. It does not include most of the radical Fife coalfield, which has been in Gordon Brown's Dunfermline East since 1983, but is instead centred on the New Town of Glenrothes, designated in 1948. Its population grew from 1,150 then to 38,800 in 1991, providing 14,577 new houses by that date. The other population cluster is along the coast – not in seaside resorts but in the gritty industrial towns of Buckhaven, Methil and Leven. This is all solid Labour country. Scottish New Towns are not as volatile as those south of the border, and although the SNP secured a clear second place in 2001 MacDougall retained an absolute majority of the vote and a five-figure lead. The Tories took the 'bronze medal position'. This is one of the weaker seats in Britain for the Liberal Democrats, a far cry from their great strength next door in middle-class Fife NE. The seat will essentially be renamed Glenrothes in future contests.

Social indices:			2001 Gen. Election:			
% Non-white	0.8		Lab	18,310	56.3	−2.3
% Prof/Man	23.1		SNP	8,235	25.3	+0.3
% Non-manual	44.2		LD	2,775	8.5	+2.1
% Unemployed 2001	6.7		C	2,351	7.2	−1.8
% Decrease 97–01	1.2		SSP	841	2.6	
% Fin hard/Rank	40.9	44	Lab maj	10,075	31.0	
% Prem mort/Rank	43	134	Turnout		54.6	−15.4
			Elect	59,597		

Member of Parliament

John MacDougall replaced the retreated-to-Holyrood Henry McLeish here in 2001, every inch the product of the OMOV selection system which favours local worthies unless either the unions have organised to insert a favourite son of their's, or Millbank has managed by means of a sanitised shortlist to insert a metropolitan apparatchik (the latter being less likely in Scotland in the post-devolution climate). John MacDougall, born in 1947 and educated at Templehall Secondary Modern School, Kirkcaldy, and at Rosyth RN Dockyard College, Fife College and Glenrothes College, worked originally as a boilermaker, becoming GMB shop stewards' convenor at Methil oil rig yard, before leaving to pursue a career in local government as a councillor on Fife Regional Council, of which he was full-time leader from 1987 to 1996 and Convenor (of the revised Fife Council) from 1996 to 2001. The chairman of multifarious boards and quangos, he is every inch the local big-wig for whom late entry at the age of 53 to the Commons is the equivalent of elevation to the aldermanic bench.

FIFE NORTH EAST

University candidates and paparazzi may flock to St Andrews in Fife in the footsteps or pursuit of Prince William, but it is unlikely they will seek or find much excitement in the parliamentary politics in the constituency of his term-time residence. It is safely held for the Liberal Democrats by Menzies Campbell, who one would not say is the epitome of staidness, but rather of solidity.

Half of the acreage of Fife is contained within the Fife North East constituency, which is of a very different character from the rest of that ancient kingdom. The four other seats are all industrial working-class Labour strongholds. Fife NE is more typified by elegant tourist resorts and fishing villages, prosperous farming country between the Tay and the Forth, and the ancient university town of St Andrews. There are a large number of small, respectable burghs: there are 13 towns which have at some time earned burgh status in the constituency, some of them with a population of less than a thousand.

The politics of Fife North East could not be more different from those of the rest of the region either. Before 1987 it had been Conservative (or National Liberal, which was effectively the same thing) for many decades. Its views were, perhaps, eloquently represented by one of Auchtermuchty's most famous (self-proclaimed) sons, the eccentric and vituperative right-wing former *Sunday Express* editor and columnist, Sir John Junor. Auchtermuchty is but one of the old, stable, middle-class communities of north-east Fife – others include Cupar, Newport on Tay, Kilrenny and the Anstruthers, Crail, Elie/Earlsferry and Tayport. There is also Freuchie, with its superb village cricket team, and Falkland, with its former royal palace, both nestling under the Lomond hills, and of course St Andrews, a city of time-honoured Conservatism. If any single constituency can bear that honour, this is the true home of the game of golf.

The Conservative Party has been in steep decline in recent decades in Scotland, though, and succumbed to rivals on a number of fronts. In 1987 a strong challenge despatched the two-term sitting MP, Barry Henderson. This came not from Labour, but from the Liberals. Elsewhere in Fife the Liberal Democrats, as they now are, are very weak, finishing third or more usually fourth in the other four constituencies. Here they are mighty, holding most of the local council seats as well as the parliamentary representation in the shape of Menzies Campbell. Campbell has strengthened his grip on Fife NE in each of the last three elections, and now looks to be the firm favourite to retain it next time, even if the fortunes of the Lib Dems have peaked nationally.

Social indices:			2001 Gen. Election:			
% Non-white	0.7		LD	17,926	51.7	+0.4
% Prof/Man	35.6		C	8,190	23.6	−2.9
% Non-manual	55.1		Lab	3,950	11.4	+1.1
% Unemployed 2001	2.5		SNP	3,596	10.4	−0.5
% Decrease 97–01	1.2		SSP	610	1.8	
% Fin hard/Rank	15.1	351	LCA	420	1.2	
% Prem mort/Rank	28	376	LD maj	9,736	28.1	
			Turnout		56.0	−15.1
			Elect	61,900		

Member of Parliament

Here in the steps of H.H. Asquith (MP 1886–1918) comes the not-quite-so-grand figure of a Mr Speaker manqué, **Menzies Campbell** QC. Seeking the Speakership in 2000 as a consolation for eschewing a party leadership bid in 1999, he secured the third lowest vote (98) in a field of 12 candidates. Elected MP in 1987 after two earlier attempts, the Liberal Democrats' solemn and fastidiously-suited Foreign and previously Defence spokesman, is an Edinburgh lawyer who rose from Glasgow Labour-voting origins, as a debating and law student contemporary of John Smith, Donald Dewar and Derry Irvine. Born in 1941, and educated at Hillhead High School, and Glasgow University, his aloof and wooden style, marriage to a Major General's daughter, and votes against bans on fox hunting, make him a not-unsuitable MP for a seat containing Scotland's most upper-middle-class Anglicised university, and one playing host from 2001 to the Heir Presumptive. Once asked on *Any Questions*. 'What class are you?', he, a Glasgow joiner's son risen to the pinnacles of the Edinburgh legal establishment, responded in orthodox Caledonian fashion, 'I am no class, I am Scottish'. He would nevertheless have made an imposing Speaker.

FINCHLEY AND GOLDERS GREEN

The constituency name of Finchley will forever, one suspects, be associated with that of its most famous MP, now Lady Thatcher. Before she was removed as PM by her own party at the end of November 1990, Margaret Hilda Thatcher achieved many crushing victories. After displacing the three-time loser Edward Heath from the Conservative Party leadership in February 1975, she won a decisive victory at the General Election of May 1979, thus becoming the UK's first female Prime Minister. Further dramatic triumphs, securing three-figure overall majorities in the Commons, came in June 1983 and June 1987. Mrs Thatcher went on and on breaking records: three successive general election wins by the same party, the lengthiest premiership of the century, the longest-serving and perhaps the senior Western leader. She will be remembered as never having lost a general election (or indeed, a leadership contest). Yet for all this, and for her acknowledged influence on the agenda of British politics as well as the electoral scene, her home constituency of Finchley, north-west London, showed a bit less than total enthusiasm even when she was MP, and has now twice elected Labour representatives.

Mrs Thatcher did less well in Finchley than her party's average in London in 1979, 1983 and 1987. Finchley was by no means a Tory fortress. Odd occurrences like that of May 1986, when the Conservatives lost most of the council wards within the seat, opened up an intriguing long-shot which tantalised those millions of Britons who were not ranked among Mrs T's admirers.

She never did lose Finchley of course, although the seat she handed over to Hartley Booth in 1992 was no Tory stronghold but the least solid of the four seats in the borough of Barnet. Booth's majority over Labour was a less than totally convincing 6,000. The East Finchley, St Paul's and Woodhouse wards were normally won by Labour, and the off-chance opened up of a Labour gain. Despite boundary changes which brought in parts of Hendon South, with its distinctively Jewish flavour, this new seat could not withstand the huge pro-Labour swing in outer north London in 1997, and returned a most unexpected MP (not least for him), Rudolph Vis, in 1997. His re-election in 2001 was not quite as unexpected, although that he actually increased his percentage majority in a re-run against the former Hendon South member John Marshall was. Truly things have moved on: a Labour MP for Finchley. What would they have made of it in the 1980s?

Social indices:			2001 Gen. Election			
% Non-white	21.2		Lab	20,205	46.3	+0.2
% Prof/Man	53.9		C	16,489	37.8	−2.0
% Non-manual	76.7		LD	5,266	12.1	+0.8
£ Av prop val 2000	228 K		Grn	1,385	3.2	+2.0
% Increase 97–00	38.9		UKIP	330	0.8	+0.3
% Unemployed 2001	2.6		Lab maj	3,716	8.5	
% Decrease 97–01	2.2		Turnout		57.3	−12.3
% Fin hard/Rank	9.3	481	Elect	76,175		
% Pensioners	25.5					
% Prem mort/Rank	15	543				

Member of Parliament

Rudi Vis, one of two Dutchmen elected to the Commons in 1997 (the other being the Liberal Democrat Dr Peter Brand who was defeated in 2001) was so surprised to win that he asked how he was to deal with all the students who were waiting for him back at the ex-North East London Polytechnic now become University of East London, where he had been an economics lecturer for 26 years. Born in 1941, he attended High School in Alkmaar, Holland, the University of Maryland, US, the LSE and Brunel University, where he acquired a doctorate in economics. A former Barnet councillor for 12 years and a committed Europhile, he focuses on disparate local concerns, such as opposing nuclear waste transporting through his constituency, and sides with his Greek Cypriot minority against the Turks. More riskily he has backed the conversion of a highly-regarded local grammar school into a comprehensive, whilst not backing the controversial orthodox Jewish 'eruv' zone in Hampstead Garden Suburb, a stance which could have exposed him to his uncompromisingly pro-Jewish Tory opponent and former MP, John Marshall, in 2001.

FOLKESTONE AND HYTHE

The southernmost stretch of the Kent coast is probably its most attractive. The constituency includes two of the medieval Cinque Ports, Hythe and Romney, as well as the Romney Marsh country and Lydd, and the Elham valley inland. Two wildly contrasting individuals, both now passed away, who became known for their residence in the seat are Alan Clark, whose medieval Saltwood Castle lies just outside Hythe, and Derek Jarman, the gay film director who cultivated a unique rock garden at his cottage within sight of Dungeness power-station. Folkestone itself, second only to Dover as a continental ferry port, has more charm as a result than its functional rival seven miles north. It also feels, however, more threatened by the prospect of the Channel Tunnel's opening affecting its role as one end of a 'flexible link', and there was serious speculation before each of the last three elections that the position of its high-profile MP, the former Conservative Cabinet Minister Michael Howard, might be at risk to the Liberal Democrats.

In 1997 the Liberal Democrats lost almost as great a share of the vote as the Conservatives, while Labour improved their third place. The consequence was that Michael Howard won fairly easily, even in Kent, where the Conservatives lost nearly half of their seats that year. Howard did lose 13% of the vote, at least half of this to a particularly successful Referendum Party candidate, the gambler and zoo-keeper John Aspinall. In 2001, despite the adverse movements of the vote shares four years before, there were widespread suggestions once again that Howard was in trouble. These proved even more unfounded than before. Although there clearly was some tactical voting, as the Lib Dems advanced by around 5%, a similar amount to Labour's fall, Howard himself pushed his share up even more. This may well have been almost entirely due to the collapse of the Referendum Party's anti-European vote (Aspinall himself had also died, as had that party's founder James Goldsmith) but it was not inappropriate for the sceptical Michael Howard, who picked up 45% of the vote – just about enough to withstand any amount of tactically organised opposition.

Social indices:			2001 Gen. Election:			
% Non-white	1.1		C	20,645	45.0	+6.0
% Prof/Man	32.3		LD	14,738	32.1	+5.3
% Non-manual	55.1		Lab	9,260	20.2	–4.7
£ Av prop val 2000	89 K		UKIP	1,212	2.6	+1.9
% Increase 97–00	42.8		C maj	5,907	12.9	
% Unemployed 2001	3.1		Turnout		64.1	–9.0
% Decrease 97–01	4.0		Elect	71,503		
% Fin hard/Rank	10.3	457				
% Pensioners	33.1					
% Prem mort/Rank	26	398				

Member of Parliament

Michael Howard QC, self-retired to the backbenches in 1999 (after being a Minister from 1985, latterly in the Cabinet at Employment 1990–92, Environment 1992–93, Home Office 1993–97 and Shadow Foreign Secretary 1997–99), was restored as

Shadow Chancellor in 2001 by Iain Duncan Smith in order to 'give Gordon Brown a run for his money'. His leadership bid in 1997 had scored only 23 votes following Ann Widdecombe's character assassination of him. Born (1941) Michael Hecht, son of a Lithuanian Jewish dress-shop owner in Gorseinon in the Swansea Valley, he attended Llanelli Grammar School and Peterhouse, Cambridge. With a lawyer's deftness he introduced both the poll tax and, when required, its council tax replacement. The most Thatcherite among his Cambridge contemporaries of Clarke, Gummer, Brittan and Lamont, though waiting longer than they to land a seat (he was elected here in 1983), he has been seen as 'a dark, closed-up person who rarely relaxes and seldom shows warmth'. What he does show, however, are smoothly effective debating skills at the despatch box, unmatched by any other members of the 2001 Opposition frontbench, none of them, bar him, with Cabinet experience.

FOREST OF DEAN

As the successful defender of the constituency, Diana Organ, pointed out in her entry in the BBC2 engaging series of 'video diaries' of the 2001 General Election, *Campaign Confessions*, this seat is predominantly rural but with a Labour tradition based on its coal-mining heritage which all adds up to a fascinating and super-competitive marginal.

The Forest of Dean does have a tradition of supporting the Labour Party. But for the interruption of 1931–35, Labour held this seat (named successively Forest of Dean and, after 1950, West Gloucestershire) continuously from 1918 to 1979. Even in 1931, when Labour were reduced to but 50 seats in the whole of Britain, they lost the Forest of Dean by only 1,500 votes, and that to a National Labour candidate. This Labour history is not hard to explain. The Forest of Dean used to harbour an active coalfield, typified by little communities of miners around the tiny pits in the woods. The character of the Forest in those days is vividly captured in the plays of one of its most famous sons, Dennis Potter. The coal seams are now worked out, and the last colliery closed in 1965, although some open-cast mining continued, but stark towns like Coleford and Cinderford still stand as gaunt reminders of the forest's industrial past.

In recent years the Forest's continuing Labour support had been outvoted by the advance of the commuter suburbs around Gloucester, but things look different when they were largely excised in 1997. In that year Diana Organ defeated the former Tory MP for West Gloucestershire Paul Marland by over 6,000 votes. The rural elements remain, though, and in the foot-and-mouth year of 2001 Diana Organ was rightly worried, as her 'confessions' showed. In the end, though, came visible relief, and this hard-working and committed member was returned for a second term. It will be well worth watching again next time, though.

Social indices:			2001 Gen. Election:			
% Non-white	0.4		Lab	19,350	43.4	−4.8
% Prof/Man	33.4		C	17,301	38.8	+3.2
% Non-manual	52.6		LD	5,762	12.9	+0.6
£ Av prop val 2000	92 K		Grn	1,254	2.8	
% Increase 97–00	38.6		UKIP	661	1.5	
% Unemployed 2001	2.2		Ind	279	0.6	+0.2
% Decrease 97–01	1.0		Lab maj	2,049	4.6	
% Fin hard/Rank	9.0	491	Turnout		67.3	−11.7
% Pensioners	26.5		Elect	66,240		
% Prem mort/Rank	26	396				

Member of Parliament

Diana Organ, a lively, personable, short-white-haired schoolteacher, selected from an all-women shortlist, won here in 1997 after trying in 1992. Locally-focused on questions of transport, housing, fuel tax, opencast mining and beef farming, she was born in 1952, daughter of a GKN finance comptroller, and educated at Edgbaston Church of England fee-paying School for Girls, St Hugh's College, Oxford, and Bath and Bristol Universities. She has campaigned against unnecessary hysterectomies. Parked on the DEFRA Select Committee in 2001 (and earlier, 1997–99, on its predecessor the Agriculture Committee) her failure to 'advance' beyond a role as a diligent constituency MP is attributed more to age than her slight propensity to bridle – as on lone parent benefits and fuel tax rises.

FOYLE

For many decades the politics of the city of (London)Derry demonstrated the most stark example of gerrymandering in the United Kingdom. The ward boundaries were so drawn that Derry's Roman Catholic majority were confined to one of the city council's four divisions, thus maintaining permanent Protestant control. In parliamentary terms too, the Nationalists of the Bogside, the Creggan estate, were outvoted before 1983 owing to the inclusion of Unionist rural areas. In that year, however, a predominantly Catholic and Nationalist seat was created, and it is interesting to note that it was named Foyle, after the river, rather than 'Londonderry' with its English connotations.

Until the most recent redistribution, Foyle included seven wards of the Strabane local government authority, including the town itself, but these 10,000 or so voters have been removed and the constituency's boundaries are now identical to those of Derry Council's. Strabane was for a considerable time the most blighted unemployment blackspot in the United Kingdom, but Derry itself is far from free of this curse: in June 2001 it had the fourth highest jobseeker rate of any constituency, ahead for example of Liverpool Riverside, Manchester Central and any in London. There are some scenic areas bounded to the west by the river Foyle and Donegal beyond, to the north by Lough Foyle and to the east by the Sperrin mountains, but it is essentially a compact seat whose politics are dominated by those of the city of Derry, Northern Ireland's second largest urban unit. The MP for Foyle since its creation in

1983 has been John Hume, who has gradually improved his position even further from a strong base – some observers considered that Foyle had almost been drawn specifically for Hume, a native son of Derry who had not sat at Westminster before, and who served as deputy leader of his party from 1970 to 1979 and leader of 22 years from then until 2001. The roots of John Hume's success in holding Foyle are clear. Over 70% of the voters are Catholic and Nationalist, and in 2001 Hume received the support of about two-thirds of these, down from three-quarters in 1997. Mitchel McLaughlin of Sinn Fein could only take the votes of the other third, but should Hume retire from Westminster, as he has from most of his other elected positions, Sinn Fein are believed to have an excellent chance of taking the Foyle division. This is one reason why he may have decided not to run for the Presidency of the Republic of Ireland, which he had a very good chance of winning, in autumn 1997, and why he has maintained his Westminster seat, while relinquishing his party leadership and his responsibilities at Stormont.

Social indices:		2001 Gen. Election:			
% Prof/Man	28.2	SDLP	24,538	50.2	–2.3
% Non-manual	48.0	SF	12,988	26.6	+2.6
% RC	69.5	DUP	7,414	15.2	–6.4
% Irish sp	14.6	UUP	3,360	6.9	
% Unemployed 2001	10.8	APNI	579	1.2	–0.5
% Decrease 97–01	3.2	SDLP maj	11,550	23.6	
		Turnout		68.9	–1.8
		Elect	70,943		

Member of Parliament

John Hume, Nobel Prize-winning leader of the SDLP until 2001, was first elected here on the seat's creation in 1983. A veteran constitutional Nationalist, he retired in 2001 from the Northern Ireland Assembly as 30 years of stress dealing with tough opponents on both IRA and Unionist flanks took their toll. Seen by Edward Kennedy as 'the 101st Senator' for his ubiquity around the American Irish diaspora, he is less seen at Westminster than his less green SDLP colleagues. Co-author of the 1998 Good Friday Agreement and a 30-year-deliverer of his 'single transferable speech', he was born in 1934, educated at St Columb's (RC) College, Derry, St Patrick's Seminary, Maynooth (where he trained inconclusively as a priest) and the National University of Ireland, and was a school teacher for 10 years. An honest if uncharismatic man respected by opponents, the Ulster Unionists' ex-deputy leader John Taylor saw him as 'a first class politician who serves the Irish Nationalist cause well'. Maybe too well, for by 2001 his party had been overtaken by Sinn Fein, whose leader Gerry Adams he had drawn into mainstream politics. A victim of this success, he resigned as SDLP leader in September 2001.

FYLDE

The Fylde is the peninsula jutting into the Irish Sea about halfway up the coast of Lancashire. Its most well-known town is Blackpool. But South Fylde achieved political fame as a constituency too. In 1979, for example, it returned the largest Conservative majority, 32,247. This was also the largest majority on the mainland of Great Britain, exceeded only by the huge seats that were still permitted in Northern Ireland at that time. Nor was this an isolated achievement; South Fylde was consistently noted for producing the biggest Tory margin.

However, one of the reasons for this was that South Fylde's electorate was well above the quota – 94,000 in 1979. In 1983 around 30,000 electors from the Preston suburbs around Penwortham were moved into the South Ribble division, which leaves the core of the constituency as the local government borough of Fylde, basically Lytham St Anne's and Kirkham. The picture is completed by three other wards, two newly added in the 1995 redistribution: Preston Rural West is now joined by Ingol, a part of north-west Preston, and the village of Great Eccleston from Wyre.

Lytham St Anne's is a rather genteel seaside resort and residential area. It is south of bustling, plebeian Blackpool, and bears a calmer flavour. It has the kind of overwhelming Conservatism that Blackpool itself lacks. Even in the disastrous election years of 1997 and 2001 the Tories held all six electoral divisions within Fylde borough. It is solidly owner-occupied, has a high proportion of pensioners, and much new private housing development has taken place, inland in St Anne's especially.

The numerical Tory majorities in Fylde have dropped out of the record range since its truncation in 1983, but it is just as safe as before. In 2001 Michael Jack held a majority of 9,610 over Labour, at a time when the Conservatives were suffering their second worst general election result for nearly a century.

Social indices:			2001 Gen. Election:			
% Non-white	0.9		C	23,383	52.3	+3.4
% Prof/Man	39.2		Lab	13,773	30.8	−0.9
% Non-manual	64.8		LD	6,599	14.8	+0.1
£ Av prop val 2000	86 K		UKIP	982	2.2	
% Increase 97–00	25.8		C maj	9,610	21.5	
% Unemployed 2001	1.5		Turnout		62.0	−11.0
% Decrease 97–01	0.6		Elect	72,207		
% Fin hard/Rank	8.7	498				
% Pensioners	33.2					
% Prem mort/Rank	29	355				

Member of Parliament

Michael Jack, a minister in four different departments (Social Security, Home Office, Agriculture and Treasury) under John Major, and a Clarke-supporting Europhile now self-exiled to the backbenches, after shadowing Health in 1997 and Agriculture from 1997 to 1998 (when he resigned), was first elected here in 1987. Unpretentious, classless and a rare Tory wet, he was born, son of a clerk, in 1946, educated at Bradford Grammar School and Leicester University and was a food industry manager with Marks and Spencer and Northern Foods for 12 years.

GAINSBOROUGH

In the north-western corner of Lincolnshire are to be found the local government district of West Lindsey and the parliamentary constituency of Gainsborough. This, like much of Lincolnshire, seems rather a corner of England, off the beaten track and 'a long way round whichever way you go'. The seat hugs the east bank of the River Trent. The Trent is broad up here near its junction with the Humber, and with road bridges only every ten miles or so the West Lindsey area is decidedly cut off.

Remote it may be, but the politics of this seat have always been interesting. Back in the days before the Lib Dems had been so formed and named, the Liberals mounted a strong challenge over a number of elections, first to the fox hunting Sir Marcus Kimball and then to a younger right-winger, Edward Leigh. Their closest approach was to cut Leigh's majority to barely over 5,000 and 10% of the vote in 1983. Since then, however, their successors' position has considerably weakened. The Liberal (Alliance/Democrat) vote declined by 5% in 1987 and by a further 9% in 1992. In 1997 and equally in 2001 they slipped behind the resurgent Labour Party into third place, and the even distribution of votes opposing Edward Leigh allowed him to retain Gainsborough fairly easily even though his own share has dropped below 50% in the last two elections. He has also been assisted by the fact that the anti-EU parties have never put up a candidate against him, and with it still being far from obvious who an anti-Leigh tactical voter might support, his 8,000 majority is in effect even safer than it appears.

Social indices:			2001 Gen. Election:			
% Non-white	0.6		C	19,555	46.2	+3.1
% Prof/Man	32.6		Lab	11,484	27.1	−1.7
% Non-manual	52.6		LD	11,280	26.7	−1.5
£ Av prop val 2000	63 K		C maj	8,071	19.1	
% Increase 97–00	20.0		Turnout		64.2	−10.3
% Unemployed 2001	3.3		Elect	65,871		
% Decrease 97–01	1.2					
% Fin hard/Rank	12.7	402				
% Pensioners	26.7					
% Prem mort/Rank	27	390				

Member of Parliament

Edward Leigh, Chairman of the Public Accounts Committee from 2001, a non-practising barrister, Roman Catholic and right-wing Thatcherite, who was elected for Gainsborough and Horncastle in 1983 and for this successor seat in 1997, became a minister under Margaret Thatcher just before her exit, but was sacked in 1993 by John Major for encouraging Europhobic Tories to oppose the Maastricht Treaty. Born in 1950, son of Sir Neville Leigh KCVO, Clerk to the Privy Council, he attended the Oratory (RC) School, the French Lycée, London and Durham University. Of Margaret Thatcher he has said, 'I was with her from the beginning to the end, she has been a dominant influence in my life', even though he voted for Heseltine in 1990, preferring to back someone who had stabbed her in the front to those who had stabbed her in the back. Otherwise he voted for Redwood in 1995 and

1997, even following Redwood into his pact with the devil Clarke in the final ballot in 1997, and Iain Duncan Smith in all the ballots in 2001 – the most right-wing options one could sElect He is solidly Catholic on divorce, embryo research, contraception, abortion and homosexuality, some of which views led to Labour MPs blocking his election to the chairmanship of the International Development Select Committee in 2001.

GALLOWAY AND UPPER NITHSDALE

Most observers thought that the Conservative Party, which had won no seats at all in Scotland in 1997, would again draw a complete blank in 2001. Even the more optimistic who predicted that they would bounce off rock bottom talked up the chances of Malcolm Rifkind in Edinburgh Pentlands or Phil Gallie in Ayr; yet the sole Tory winner turned out to be a surprise, Peter Duncan, who took back Ian Lang's former Galloway and Upper Nithsdale seat from the SNP, by 74 votes.

There were two main reasons for this narrow, but much welcomed, gain. One was to do with foot-and-mouth disease, which had literally plagued this rural community, and which may have led to a mobilisation of support for the Conservatives, as the self-proclaimed party of the countryside: they did do distinctly well in some of the worst affected areas, such as just over the border in Penrith. Secondly, the SNP victor in Galloway in 1997, Alasdair Morgan, did not contest his Westminster seat, in order to concentrate on representing this area in the Scottish parliament, and it was felt by some that the Nationalists were paying less attention to the London assembly and placing their best and most experienced politicians in Edinburgh. Certainly their performance overall in the 2001 General Election was disappointing, and it remains to be seen if this is a long-term consequence of devolution.

Galloway is the far south-west corner of Scotland, the old counties of Kirkcudbright and Wigtown. Although in the Lowlands, Galloway has its mountains and lochs, glens and forests, and remains a quiet and accessible miniature version of the Highlands themselves. Its politics also resemble much of rural Scotland much further north: safely Conservative for many years until 1974, then falling to the SNP. Galloway crumbled in the second (October) Nationalist revolution of that year, and it returned to the Tory fold along with most of the others in 1979. However, it has always remained one of the SNP's brightest prospects, and it was one of the party's two gains in the 1997 Election, the other being North Tayside; Perth had already been gained in a by-election in 1995.

Labour and the Liberal Democrats are both very weak in an area which has little industry, but relies on farming and tourism, including that associated with the ferry port of Stranraer. The only solidly working-class areas currently are in the Upper Nithsdale section (formerly in Dumfriesshire) added on in 1983 – Sanquhar and Kirkconnel are ex-mining towns. However, the February 2002 provisional boundary proposals placed Dumfries town, with many more Labour votes, with Galloway, and three parties would have a chance in such an enlarged seat.

Social indices:			2001 Gen. Election:			
% Non-white	0.2		C	12,222	34.0	+3.5
% Prof/Man	29.6		SNP	12,148	33.8	−10.1
% Non-manual	46.7		Lab	7,258	20.2	+3.9
% Unemployed 2001	4.8		LD	3,698	10.3	+3.9
% Decrease 97–01	1.8		SSP	588	1.6	
% Fin hard/Rank	19.1	287	C maj	74	0.2	
% Prem mort/Rank	43	121	Turnout		68.1	−11.6
			Elect	52,756		

Member of Parliament

Whether the 'first shall be last' or 'the last first', **Peter Duncan** is the only Conservative MP in Scotland, having in 2001 ousted the SNP from a seat which it had only managed to take from the Conservatives twice in seven elections. A strapping, full-faced, Scots-accented, Ayrshire businessman, born in 1965 and educated at Ardrossan Academy and Birmingham University, for 12 years until his election he ran his family's 180-year-old textile business. Having been likened in physique to the world-famous belted Galloway bull, he looks the part in the United Kingdom's most agricultural constituency. Destined to install himself as a diligent constituency MP in the manner of Liberal and Nationalist MPs – calling for example for an upgrade of the road to the important job-sustaining ferry port of Stranraer – he was nonetheless spared the fate of novice third-party MPs of being promptly awarded an official spokesmanship. Not for him the Shadow Scottish Secretaryship as Scotland's sole Tory MP – that distinction went to an ex-pat Scots Tory with a London seat – but rather a seat on the superfluous post-devolution Scottish Affairs Select Committee, and time enough to augment his 74-vote majority, in the Commons' fourth most marginal seat.

GATESHEAD EAST AND WASHINGTON WEST

This is a seat which straddles the boundaries of the boroughs of Gateshead and Sunderland south of the Tyne, and between older and newer working-class areas; but this is not a significant political divide, for both parts of the seat are overwhelmingly Labour. The Gateshead wards are almost all socially and economically most typical of inner-city tightly packed nineteenth-century terraces; they have a low proportion of owner-occupiers and of council tenants, and a large number of privately rented houses, flats and bedsits for migrants. This being the North East, there are hardly any non-white residents as there undoubtedly would be in other cities. Washington New Town, unlike some of its counterparts in the South and Midlands, has always been solid for the Labour Party; most of its residents originated in older parts of the industrial North East. There is one middle-class ward, in Gateshead itself, Low Fell; but the Conservatives have not even been able to win Low Fell in recent years, and they slipped to third, although only by 29 votes, behind the Liberal Democrats in 2001; this paled in comparison with the 17,904 separating the latter from Labour's winner, Joyce Quin, although a couple of faint glimmers of light from their point of view were to be found in the Liberal Democrat gains of Low Fell and Pelaw/Heworth wards from Labour in May 2000.

Social indices:			2001 Gen. Election:			
% Non-white	0.9		Lab	22,903	68.1	−3.9
% Prof/Man	25.7		LD	4,999	14.9	+4.1
% Non-manual	51.9		C	4,970	14.8	+0.6
£ Av prop val 2000	59 K		UKIP	743	2.2	
% Increase 97–00	20.5		Lab maj	17,904	53.3	
% Unemployed 2001	3.6		Turnout		52.5	−14.7
% Decrease 97–01	2.3		Elect	64,041		
% Fin hard/Rank	36.0	82				
% Pensioners	22.8					
% Prem mort/Rank	40	186				

Member of Parliament

Joyce Quin, who was dropped in the post-election reshuffle of 2001, is an uncharismatic, hardworking, self-effacing Brown Owl in politics, as one of the Blair government's laterally-sliding middle-rank ministers, from Home Office, to Foreign Office, to Agriculture, and earlier serving for nine years as a frontbench spokesman before 1997. A teacher's daughter, born in 1944, the great niece of Durham's pre-war Labour MP Joshua Ritson, she was elected here in 1987 after education at Whitley Bay Grammar School, Newcastle University and the LSE, and a European Studies lecturing post at Bath University for four years, and another job teaching French and Politics at Durham for three years. This, and her time as an MEP for Tyne and Wear from 1979 to 1989, underscore the main theme of her political career, unqualified Europhilia, so staunch that initially she was kept out of the Foreign Office for fear of her excessive zeal for Brussels. Amazingly nice for a politician, it has been said 'her neatness and size put one in mind of Mrs Tittlemouse'. Even after removal from office she could be found gamely defending the government on television.

GEDLING

Labour gained two of the three suburban Nottingham seats in 1997, Gedling and Broxtowe; only Kenneth Clarke's Rushcliffe escaped Tony Blair's sweep of the county. This represented Labour's best ever result here in the East Midlands and indeed one which was not quite matched four years later, as the neighbouring county seat of Newark was a rare regain in 2001. The constituency of Gedling, compactly sited on the north-eastern fringe of Nottingham, is very similar to the old Carlton division which existed before 1983, which did not fall to Labour even in 1966. There is a small town called Gedling, but the seat's designation was chosen because of the existence of a local government borough of the same name. Gedling itself is an old mining district, but the political cast of the seat is shaped more by the middle-class towns of Carlton and Arnold within the economic orbit of Nottingham.

In fact Gedling is really a suburban middle-class commuting base for Nottingham, rather like Broxtowe diametrically across the city to the south-west and parts of

Rushcliffe across the river Trent to the south. Although largely part of the Greater Nottingham 'conurbation', these areas (and constituencies) are fiercely independent and determined to resist any expansion of Nottingham's boundaries or any other encroachment from the Labour-voting city. The differences are political, social and even racial; Nottingham has a large non-white minority but Gedling is over 97% white. As well as Carlton and Arnold, the seat ranges from wards like Porchester and Woodthorpe, which fringe the border next to relatively affluent Nottingham neighbourhoods like Mapperley, out to overgrown villages like Burton Joyce on the railway line to Newark and Lincoln, which offer the Tories some solace in a seat that has moved sharply against them in the last decade.

Gedling is the least upmarket of the three suburban Nottingham Conservative seats, and has Labour wards like Killisick and Oxclose in Arnold, and Netherfield, which includes Colwick near Holme Pierrepoint Country Park and Nottingham Racecourse. But in the main, modern private estates sprawl over the hills towards the Nottinghamshire countryside. Over 80% of the housing is owner-occupied. It was a fine achievement for the former Rushcliffe councillor Vernon Coaker to defeat the sitting Conservative MP Andrew Mitchell on a 13% swing in 1997, and an even finer one to hold on with an increased percentage and numerical majority in 2001.

Social indices:			2001 Gen. Election:			
% Non-white	2.6		Lab	22,383	51.1	+4.3
% Prof/Man	31.6		C	16,785	38.3	−1.2
% Non-manual	57.0		LD	4,648	10.6	+0.7
£ Av prop val 2000	67 K		Lab maj	5,598	12.8	
% Increase 97–00	23.3		Turnout		63.9	−11.9
% Unemployed 2001	2.5		Elect	68,540		
% Decrease 97–01	1.8					
% Fin hard/Rank	11.8	416				
% Pensioners	24.8					
% Prem mort/Rank	24	436				

Member of Parliament

Vernon Coaker was elected here on his second attempt in 1997 as a standard-issue Labour MP: a schoolteacher of 20 years standing and a local councillor for 14 years. Focused as an MP on teaching matters, he was born in 1953 in London – whose gorblimey brogue he retains – and educated at Drayton Manor Grammar School, Hanwell, Warwick University and Trent Polytechnic. A tall, burly policeman's son, routinely interested in such apolitical concerns as animal welfare, untidy gardens, football and juvenile crime, in late 2001 he asked the Prime Minister what could be done to get more young people to vote. His blameless loyalty saw him made PPS to Stephen Timms in 1999.

GILLINGHAM

In 2001, when the Liberal Democrats reversed the national decline in the share of their vote which had masked the dramatic increase in their number of MPs between

1992 and 1997, there were very few seats where their percentage actually went down compared with four years before, and usually clear explanations for the reason: the dissolution of the effects of a notable by-election (Christchurch), the retirement of a well-established MP (Orkney/Shetland, Argyll/Bute) or candidate (Conwy), the intervention of an independent (Brentwood/Ongar) or the replacement of the sole white candidate (Bradford West). Perhaps more significantly, there were some clear cases of tactical voting, usually though not always in favour of Labour in a tight two-horse race, such as here at Gillingham, where their share went down by over 5%, a similar figure to the increase in that of the first term Labour member, Paul Clark. The Conservatives, while actually increasing their proportion by more than the national average, gave the impression of further decline.

One of the most surprising of Labour's many gains in the 1997 General Election had been in this Kent division, a seat that they had not won since 1945; even in 1966 the Conservatives held it by over 3,000. This was not the only Labour triumph in the most south-eastern of counties. In 1992 they had not won a single seat. In 1997 they gained eight of the 17 Kent constituencies – and they held all of them in 2001.

Gillingham is the largest of the three main 'Medway towns', although probably the least known beyond the confines of the area. It is also the least industrial, although recently established employers like Akzo Chemie, Jubilee Hoseclips, CAV Lucas and Crest Packaging (a buy-out from Bowater Packaging) have been supplemented by the Gillingham Business Park, created in 1978. In fact Gillingham is largely residential, supplying workers for the renowned Chatham Navy Dockyard (on its borders) until its closure in 1984. It is not particularly high in status. It has no higher a proportion of professional and managerial workers than Gravesham or Dartford, and far lower than Canterbury or Maidstone. It has one of the lowest percentages of people with higher qualifications such as degrees anywhere in the home counties – fewer than one in ten. Yet it was regarded as a very safe Conservative seat until the revolution of 1997–2001. How may this contradictory information be reconciled?

First, some more social and demographic facts. In 1991 Gillingham had over 80% owner-occupiers and only 10% council tenants – half the national average, at a time when tenure and voting patterns were still strongly connected. It was also over 96% white at a time when politics were becoming more racially polarised, not less. We should also remember that constituencies with a historic connection with the armed services are skewed to the right compared with their class make-up – vide Gosport and Portsmouth North.

Second, the opposition to the Conservatives was previously evenly divided between Labour and Liberal Democrat. The Liberals posed a strong challenge in local government back in the 1970s, and were consistently the largest party on the former Gillingham borough council. Now, however, the parliamentary seat is clearly identifiable as a Labour–Tory two-party marginal, and the Lib Dems are third also on the new Medway Towns unitary authority. Nationally on the rise, Charles Kennedy's party has doubly gone backwards in Gillingham.

Social indices:			2001 Gen. Election:			
% Non-white	3.9		Lab	18,782	44.5	+4.7
% Prof/Man	29.8		C	16,510	39.1	+3.2
% Non-manual	58.6		LD	5,755	13.6	−5.4
£ Av prop val 2000	82 K		UKIP	933	2.2	+1.0
% Increase 97–00	36.5		SA	232	0.5	
% Unemployed 2001	2.2		Lab maj	2,272	5.4	
% Decrease 97–01	2.3		Turnout		59.5	−12.5
% Fin hard/Rank	11.9	415	Elect	70,898		
% Pensioners	20.6					
% Prem mort/Rank	18	497				

Member of Parliament

Paul Clark, a rather scrunch-faced, estuarially accented former AEEU apparatchik involved in TUC educational provision, won here in 1997 as a locally born (1957) former local councillor. One of Labour's 130 MPs to have had previous experience either as a party or union staffer or some other form of paid political activity, he was educated at Gillingham Grammar School and Keele University, and has naturally been preoccupied with Thames Corridor issues as one of a rash of Labour MPs who surprisingly swept through North Kent in 1997, in his case as Labour's seventh least expected new MP. In 2001 his surprising parliamentary career began to look up with his appointment as PPS to Lord Falconer, Minister for Housing, Planning and Regeneration, and a close friend of the Prime Minister.

GLASGOW ANNIESLAND

Although he only represented this constituency while it was named Anniesland for just over three years, it is associated with the name of Donald Dewar, the original First Minister of the Scottish Parliament established in 1999 by New Labour's policy of limited devolution, who died suddenly and in office in late 2000. He had previously for over 20 years represented this north-west Glasgow seat's linear predecessor, Garscadden, and was able to hand over a stronghold where the SNP proved much weaker than in the 1978 by-election which returned him to Westminster.

The old Garscadden was a homogeneous division. Glasgow has long had a reputation as one of the roughest, toughest and poorest cities in Western Europe. The working-class, industrial community on the Clyde was once known for its ferocious nineteenth-century tenement slums in the centre of the city. Now much of that inner city has been cleared, and the population dispersed to vast inter-war and post-war council estates on the various edges of Glasgow. Many of these are areas of multiple social and economic devastation, with inadequate social facilities and remote from the activity and life of the city to boot. Garscadden consisted of the north-western sector of such peripheral development, including the inter-war council estates of Knightswood and Yoker and the grim post-war squalor of Drumchapel under the Kilpatrick hills, six miles from the city centre. Drumchapel borders middle-class Bearsden, but they are light years apart socially. Two-thirds of Garscadden's housing was council built, and on the Drumchapel estates this figure rose to nearly 90%; only two households in ten owned a car. Not surprisingly, Garscadden was a Labour stronghold, with the SNP moving forward a little in second place in 1992 and the Tories barely able to muster one-tenth of the vote.

The small section of Hillhead which was added in 1997 as the seat took more of inner NW Glasgow is, by contrast, one of the poshest parts of the city. Kelvindale is part of Glasgow's classic west end, with fine residential terraces and crescents and distinguished institutions such as Glasgow High School. In the old days it was also strongly Conservative, but the whole of Glasgow has moved steadily to the left over the past couple of decades, and it came as no surprise that they polled only 11.5% in the new Anniesland seat in 1997, as Donald Dewar won very safely, and in 2000 and 2001 the story was more of the failure of the SNP to achieve even 20% of the vote in second place to Dewar's less renowned successor, John Robertson. After the 2001 Election, the publication of Dewar's will revealed wealth unsuspected by many; he bequeathed to Robertson the treasure of an utterly safe parliamentary inheritance. Anniesland will form the basis of a new Glasgow NW seat, as the city moves to compass point constituencies

Social indices:			2001 Gen. Election:			
% Non-white	1.7		Lab	15,102	56.5	−5.3
% Prof/Man	31.3		SNP	4,048	15.1	−2.0
% Non-manual	54.3		LD	3,244	12.1	+4.9
% Unemployed 2001	7.1		C	2,651	9.9	−1.5
% Decrease 97–01	3.2		SSP	1,486	5.6	+4.9
% Fin hard/Rank	51.5	13	SLP	191	0.7	
% Prem mort/Rank	63	5	Lab maj	11,054	41.4	
			Turnout		50.1	−13.8
			Elect	53,290		

Member of Parliament

John Robertson, a plump and square telephone engineer for 31 years before becoming an MP at the age of 48, succeeded Donald Dewar at a by-election in November 2000, having previously been Dewar's election agent and CLP chairman. Born in 1952 and educated at Shawlands Academy, Langside College and Stow College (at both of which taking electrical engineering courses) he rose politically through activity in the various unions covering the telecommunications industry over time, and was lucky to be in the right place as a local, reliable pair of hands to see off the SNP at the by-election after Donald Dewar's death. Having recently arrived, inevitably he dislikes the prospect of reducing Scotland's over-representation at Westminster, since any game of musical seats in Glasgow would potentially, on the basis of 'last in, first out', be to his disadvantage, but he has a base here.

GLASGOW BAILLIESTON

The former Glasgow seat of Provan held a large number of records, not all of them positive. It had the highest proportion of council housing of any constituency in Britain – 97% in 1971, still 74% after 20 years of sell-offs in 1991. It had the highest rates of male and female unemployment in Scotland. It had the lowest proportion of adults with higher educational qualifications in Scotland; and the highest proportion of one-parent families. It also had the most rapid rate of depopulation of any seat, and had dropped to just 36,500 electors in 1992. Clearly major boundary changes were necessary and the Provan name disappeared in 1997.

Most of Provan is included in the Glasgow Baillieston division. This is the 'outer east' Glasgow seat, taking in Baillieston itself, Carntyne and Mount Vernon from the old Shettleston, together with Easterhouse, Queenslie, Barlanark and Gartloch from Provan. Baillieston and Mount Vernon actually have a majority of owner-occupiers, a stark contrast to all the other neighbourhoods which are essentially massive post-war council developments of both low- and high-rise nature on either side of the M8 as it sweeps in from Edinburgh.

Many of these peripheral estates have had serious social problems. Housing conditions have been very poor, and few retail or entertainment facilities are provided. Easterhouse was built in fields several miles from the city centre, or from older neighbourhoods where the extended families of residents lived. These have not in the main been happy and stable communities. Despondency and desperation stalk the streets, and degradation seems only just around the corner. No wonder that the population has fallen so rapidly. Those who can, leave; and some of the worst housing erected in the 1950s and 1960s has already been knocked down.

Mount Vernon and Baillieston pull up the social statistics a little compared with the Provan base. Both wards have actually increased in population in recent decades, and appear relatively healthy communities. This is not to say that they are not strongly for Labour, though. Jim McVicar of the Scottish Socialist Party saved his deposit and finished between the Conservatives and Liberal Democrats in a near triple tie for third place in 2001, but Labour's battling boxing enthusiast Jimmy Wray defeated the SNP easily once again in the main event of the evening. He may have more difficulties knocking out Labour rivals for the new proposed Glasgow East division.

Social indices:			2001 Gen. Election:			
% Non-white	0.6		Lab	14,200	61.0	−4.6
% Prof/Man	20.6		SNP	4,361	18.7	−0.4
% Non-manual	46.0		C	1,580	6.8	−1.0
% Unemployed 2001	7.3		SSP	1,569	6.7	+3.7
% Decrease 97–01	4.4		LD	1,551	6.7	+2.8
% Fin hard/Rank	54.2	10	Lab maj	9,839	42.3	
% Prem mort/Rank	62	6	Turnout		47.2	−15.1
			Elect	49,268		

Member of Parliament

Labour's **Jimmy Wray**, a low-slung, double-breasted ex-lorry driver, coal man and (when slimmer) chimney sweep, who was brought up with ten people in one room and watched some of them die from tuberculosis, was a successful litigant against a former wife's allegation of domestic violence, and is proof positive of New Labour's still incomplete takeover by Islington-based polenta-eaters. Born in 1935 in the Gorbals, and retaining its distinctive burr, he attended St Bonaventure (RC)

Secondary School, and sat on Glasgow and Strathclyde Councils for a regulation 13 years until promoted to a seat in the Commons in 1987. Although a Campaign Group member, he is rarely rebellious except on the Middle East as when opposing the threat of military action against Iraq in 1998, and the anti-Islamic terrorist legislation of November 2001. Otherwise his Catholicism accounts for his resistance to homosexual law reform, and his intervention in the Monklands by-election of 1994 to rebut criticism of alleged Catholic nepotism on the local council. He also opposed Blair's Clause Four redraft. He has introduced legislation on knives and is known for selling watches and jewellery to fellow MPs.

GLASGOW CATHCART

Labour managed only one gain from the Conservatives anywhere in Britain at the 1979 General Election. But the Tory MP who lost his seat was Teddy Taylor, who would have probably have been Secretary of State for Scotland in Mrs Thatcher's new government. The seat concerned was the south Glasgow seat of Cathcart. Why did it fall to Labour? The answer is twofold. The Conservatives did not do nearly so well in Scotland as in the rest of Britain in that year, and there were many examples of pro-Labour swings north of the border. Also Cathcart had been moving towards Labour for many years, owing to the growth of the massive Castlemilk council estate in the southern half of the constituency.

Before Castlemilk began to spread up the slopes of the bowl of hills around Glasgow, Cathcart was a very safe Tory seat. In 1955, for example, they won it with a majority of 15,751, or over 45% of the total vote. Here are to be found the most respectable, owner-occupied residential districts within the city south of the Clyde – King's Park, Mount Florida, Cathcart, Newlands. The sturdy bungalows and semis used to turn in a reliable Conservative vote in general elections. Gradually, however, they were outnumbered, as the 1950s and 1960s passed, by the huge peripheral council development, which so transformed the politics of the Cathcart seat that it was said that Teddy Taylor held on only through his personal independent appeal. In 1979 he finally lost, to John Maxton – a nephew of Jimmy Maxton, the Clydeside ILP-er of the 1930s.

Maxton gradually increased his majority from 1979 to 1992, and Cathcart is no longer a possibility for the Tories, even though Castlemilk's population has now been shrinking for some years as people leave and sub-standard housing is demolished. Glenwood ward lost 44% of its population between 1981 and 1991, the sharpest decrease of any in Glasgow. In 1997 and 2001 the SNP have moved into second place, but very far behind Labour, for whom Tom Harris took over in the latter year.

Cahtcart forms the base for the provisionally proposed Glasgow South constituency, which would also be very safe for Labour.

Social indices:			2001 Gen. Election:			
% Non-white	2.6		Lab	14,902	54.4	−3.0
% Prof/Man	35.1		SNP	4,086	14.9	−3.6
% Non-manual	60.6		C	3,662	13.4	+0.6
% Unemployed 2001	5.1		LD	3,006	11.0	+4.1
% Decrease 97–01	2.6		SSP	1,730	6.3	+5.0
% Fin hard/Rank	39.9	54	Lab maj	10,816	39.5	
% Prem mort/Rank	55	19	Turnout		52.6	−16.6
			Elect	52,094		

Member of Parliament

Tom Harris was elected here in 2001, replacing a famous Glasgow political name, the retiring John Maxton – nephew of Jimmy. A journalist-turned-PR-man (latterly with Strathclyde Transport), his claim on the seat was helped by two years as Scottish Labour Party press officer in the early 1990s and as a spell (1998–2000) as the local CLP Chairman. Born in 1964, son of a lorry driver, he attended Garnock Academy in Ayrshire and Napier College, Edinburgh. He opposes electoral reform as a supposed remedy for low turnout, is concerned about misused air rifles causing blindness or brain damage, resists Paisleyite objections to reform of the RUC, and in January 2002 he co-signed a Eurosceptic letter to the *Guardian*, describing the euro as a 'costly distraction' from repairing public services. In a city of ageing Labour MPs facing a reduction in the number of seats, he is the youngest.

GLASGOW GOVAN

Govan is the Glasgow constituency most associated with shipbuilding, but over recent years the yards here on the south bank of the Clyde have gradually closed, while derricks still point skywards as mute reminders of Glasgow's great industrial past. It is also the Glasgow division most associated with Scottish National Party by-election gains. It was won by the charismatic Margo Macdonald in November 1973, but she found the Labour vote rock hard and resilient too, and held Govan for only four months. In 1988, in a by-election caused by the appointment of Labour's Bruce Millan to the EEC Commission, another powerful political personality took Govan by storm in the interests of the SNP.

Jim Sillars had already ruffled Labour's feathers in the late 1970s, when as the bright and promising MP for South Ayrshire he quit the Labour Party on the grounds that it was insufficiently committed to Scotland. He jointly founded the Scottish Labour Party but was defeated in 1979 as South Ayrshire reverted to Labour. In the 1980s he again changed party, and opposed Tam Dalyell for the SNP in 1987. He was a logical choice for the high-profile by-election the next year, when he seized Govan by over 3,500 votes. Many tipped that he would be able to hold on, but in 1992 Govan once again reverted to type, and elected Labour's Ian Davidson with a majority of over 4,000.

A new Labour candidate was needed due to major boundary changes in 1997, and he came not without controversy. Mohammed Sarwar was eventually elected as Britain's first Muslim MP after a spirited challenge from the SNP's Nicola Sturgeon, but he had to overcome repeated allegations of vote buying, both within the Labour selection process and the General Election, and looked vulnerable to disqualification or deselection at times; his resilience was demonstrated and rewarded not only by mere political survival but a much increased majority in 2001. Politics here continue to be well worth scrutinising for further surprises, not least to see whether Sarwar will survive the game of musical chairs as the city's number of MPs is reduced.

Social indices:			2001 Gen. Election:				
% Non-white	11.0		Lab	12,464	49.3	+5.2	
% Prof/Man	41.9		SNP	6,064	24.0	−11.1	
% Non-manual	64.3		LD	2,815	11.1	+5.2	
% Unemployed 2001	6.2		C	2,167	8.6	−0.2	
% Decrease 97–01	3.9		SSP	1,531	6.1	+3.7	
% Fin hard/Rank	48.8	18	CPGB	174	0.7		
% Prem mort/Rank	61	8	Ind	69	0.3	−0.7	
			Lab maj	6,400	25.3		
			Turnout		46.8	−17.9	
			Elect	54,068			

Member of Parliament

Mohammed Sarwar, Britain's first Muslim MP, was elected in 1997 in Scotland's most non-white (11%, mostly Pakistanis) constituency. Born in Pakistan in 1952, he was a Bhutto-supporting student activist before coming to Scotland aged 24, working as a street trader, eventually becoming a cash-and-carry millionaire. Selected for Govan after a hotly disputed process in 1995–96 and suspended when accused of election fraud immediately after his election in May 1997, he was acquitted in 1999. His Muslim background is reflected in his rebelling against the threat of military action against Iraq and vocal support of the NATO action against Serbia in defence of Kosovo Muslims. He calls also for a plebiscite in Kashmir and defends the beleaguered Govan shipyard.

GLASGOW KELVIN

Few parliamentary seats can be of more distinguished appearance, or have a more dramatic recent political history, than the Glasgow Kelvin division. The constituency includes the west end and the very heart of the city. Seven-eighths of it was contained in the former Hillhead, whose successor it is, in effect. Glasgow Hillhead became a famous name in British politics in the 1980s. Following his promising performance in the SDP's inaugural by-election at Warrington in July 1981, Roy Jenkins found a place in Parliament by winning Hillhead from the Conservatives on 25 March 1982. By the end of 1982 Jenkins had become leader of the Social Democratic Party and the Alliance's prospective candidate for Prime Minister. At first sight the rugged city of Glasgow might seem a surprising haven for a very English Welshman of notably sophisticated and intellectual tastes. But Hillhead was a very special part of Glasgow. Traditionally a Tory seat, and the last such left in Glasgow after the 1979 Election, Hillhead was one of the most middle-class seats in Britain. Its adult residents were more likely to have degrees than any other seat in Scotland. Here was to be found the University and many other established institutions, as well as mansions and fine domestic architecture in neighbourhoods like Kelvinside. In 1983 the seat was expanded to include the southern half of the abolished Kelvingrove, and Jenkins held on; Labour moved into second place. Then in 1987 Jenkins lost to George Galloway as a triumphant Labour Party swept every seat in Glasgow.

Kelvingrove had been a Labour seat since 1964, but Hillhead had also contained working-class areas, near the Clyde in Partick and Scotstoun. With the strength of Scottish favour for the Labour Party, even in predominantly middle-class seats, Galloway was able to increase his majority in Jenkins's absence in 1992, and despite his unorthodox policies and presentation remains the official Labour representative. In 2001 the Liberal Democrats overtook the SNP for second place, but this is in no way a reprise of the glorious days of Lord Jenkins of Hillhead.

It might be noted that with its extension to the east, this seat now includes almost the whole centre of Glasgow. Here are George Square and Queen Street Station, High Street and the cathedral. Here are the grand buildings which attest to Glasgow's great commercial success in the past, and many examples of the recent progressive developments in the city of culture. It is a sign of the devotion of Scotland to the Labour Party that the seat which contains so many of its elite institutions should have come to shun all other parties.

Like all the other Glasgow seats, Kelvin will effectively be split asunder in forthcoming boundary changes, setting problems for its highly controversial MP.

Social indices:			2001 Gen. Election:			
% Non-white	6.2		Lab	12,014	44.8	–6.1
% Prof/Man	52.2		LD	4,754	17.7	+3.6
% Non-manual	72.3		SNP	4,513	16.8	–4.5
% Unemployed 2001	5.0		C	2,388	8.9	–1.9
% Decrease 97–01	3.9		SSP	1,847	6.9	+5.7
% Fin hard/Rank	35.1	89	Grn	1,286	4.8	
% Prem mort/Rank	57	14	Lab maj	7,260	27.1	
			Turnout		43.6	–13.3
			Elect	61,534		

Member of Parliament

George Galloway, a deep-tanned, sharp-suited globe trotter and MP here (originally Hillhead) since beating Roy Jenkins in 1987, is essentially a one-club politician as a hitcher-on to any passing Arab camel train including that of Saddam Hussein, the PLO, Benazir Bhutto and Mohammed Sarwar, and opposed the bombing of Afghanistan following the destruction of the World Trade Center in September 2001, and the ensuing anti-terrorism legislation. Of his past dealings with the Iraqi regime it was said, 'if he had infuriated Saddam as much as he did his own party leader, he would now be in a Baghdad basement hanging off the end of a meat hook' (Andrew Rawnsley). Born in 1954, and educated at Harris Academy, Dundee, he was a manual worker before spending six years as a Scottish Labour Party organiser, and four years running War on Want. Currently with a PR company operating in the Middle East and

India, he strongly backed Scottish devolution, and continues to protest and get literally carried away at the Faslane submarine base. With ability and an impressively fluent and noteless debating style, his flaw as a career politician lies in his confrontational approach, though he denies that when he asked a fellow Labour MP 'why everyone takes an instant dislike to me', the reply was 'it saves time'. He is married to a Palestinian, and sees himself as a 'voice of the voiceless in the canyons of deprivation in the world'. In 2002 he threatened to run against the official Labour candidate if he was improperly deselected in the game of musical seats involved in cutting the number of constituencies in Glasgow.

GLASGOW MARYHILL

This is a predominantly working-class constituency in north Glasgow, stretching from the peripheral council estates of Milton, Possil and Summerston through the older neighbourhood of Maryhill itself to approach the old west end of the city at Woodside and North Kelvinside.

This latter section has a wider range of housing, and some mixture of races (including the largest concentration of Chinese in Scotland – still under one in a hundred of the whole population). It is within the orbit of influence of the universities, Glasgow and Strathclyde, and may account for a somewhat larger number of professional and managerial workers than, say, Springburn or Baillieston. However, most of the housing in Maryhill is still in public ownership, and all of the wards returned Labour candidates in the elections for the new unitary Glasgow city council in 1999 – even in the cosmopolitan Woodlands, where the Scottish Nationalist Party candidate's name was Khan.

One curious feature of the 1997 General Election in the Glasgow Maryhill division was that it supplied the best result anywhere for the yogic Natural Law Party. The only conceivable reason for this aberrant behaviour is the name of their candidate: Blair. Several hundred of Maryhill's electors must have thought they had a chance to vote directly for the leader and inspiration of New Labour. Even deprived of these misled individuals, the more famous Mr Blair could count on this very safe seat in that year as well as subsequently.

Maryhill is proposed to be subsumed in the new, larger Glasgow North and North East seats by the next General Election.

Social indices:			2001 Gen. Election:			
% Non-white	4.6		Lab	13,420	60.4	−4.6
% Prof/Man	28.0		SNP	3,532	15.9	−1.1
% Non-manual	49.4		LD	2,372	10.7	+3.5
% Unemployed 2001	7.3		SSP	1,745	7.8	+6.5
% Decrease 97–01	6.1		C	1,162	5.2	−0.7
% Fin hard/Rank	57.1	7	Lab maj	9,888	44.5	
% Prem mort/Rank	65	3	Turnout		40.1	−16.5
			Elect	55,431		

Member of Parliament

Ann McKechin followed the retiring Maria Fyfe as Labour MP here in 2001 – the only case where any of Labour's six retiring women MPs was replaced by another woman. Even then it was only by courtesy of an NEC-imposed all-women shortlist a few weeks before the election, as a last-minute effort by Labour to meet the complaint that the party had done nothing since 1997 to build on the large number of 101 women MPs elected in that year. She was born in 1961 into a classic West-of-Scotland Catholic Labour background, with her father a schoolteacher and councillor. She attended the Sacred Heart High School, Paisley, Paisley Grammar School, and Strathclyde University, and worked as a solicitor for 18 years before her election. Appropriately for a Scottish MP at Westminster shorn by devolution of much of the conventional domestic agenda, she lifts up her eyes to the hills of international aid and Third World debt relief. With Scotland set to lose seats at Westminster as part of a post-devolution adjustment, she, as the second youngest of Glasgow's ten Labour MPs, will have to hope there will be a seat left for her when the music stops. With gender on the agenda, doubtless her sex will be to her advantage.

GLASGOW POLLOK

Glasgow Pollok produced a unique result in the 1992 General Election. Tommy Sheridan, a well-known anti-poll-tax campaigner standing under the banner of Scottish Militant Labour, and campaigning from HM Prison Edinburgh (where he was serving a six-month sentence for disrupting warrant sales), obtained over 6,000 votes and finished in second place. Labour's vote declined by almost exactly the 19% that Sheridan secured. Just a month later, Tommy Sheridan actually won an election as he was returned to Glasgow City Council as the representative of Pollok ward, and one of his Scottish Militant Labour colleagues won the neighbouring ward of South Nitshill. What caused this phenomenon in the Pollok constituency?

Much must be credited to Sheridan's own dynamism and campaigning ability; he may have done well in whichever working-class Scottish seat he chose to contest. However, the Labour Party in Pollok did seem particularly open to the charges of inactivity and lack of colour. This is still the base of Tommy Sheridan, now the leader of the Scottish Socialist Party. He was elected to the Scottish Parliament on the regional list system, and did not contest a Westminster seat personally in the 2001 General Election, although led a dynamic Scotland-wide campaign, at once articulate and photogenic. He won the Pollok ward on Glasgow city council in May 1999, and in 2001 Keith Baldassara obtained the best SSP showing in Scotland, almost exactly 10% of the vote, and a clear third place ahead of the Liberal Democrats and Conservatives.

Boundary changes in 1997 brought in 25,000 voters from the old Govan – more than half of that seat. These are situated in the far south-west corner of Glasgow, in Hillington, Penilee, Cardonald and Mosspark. From the Pollok which existed in 1992 came the neighbourhoods of Cowglen, Arden, Nitshill and Pollok itself, all massive 1950s council estates set around Pollok Park and Pollok House. Finally, it might be noted that there is no 'c' in Pollok: its name is frequently inaccurately 'corrected' by proofreaders. This problem, at least, will be solved by its abolition as the individual neighbourhood names of Glasgow seats are to be replaced by compass points of less character, in this case, South West.

Social indices:			2001 Gen. Election:			
% Non-white	0.9		Lab/Coop	15,497	61.3	+1.4
% Prof/Man	23.7		SNP	4,229	16.7	−1.1
% Non-manual	49.4		SSP	2,522	10.0	−1.1
% Unemployed 2001	7.9		LD	1,612	6.4	+2.9
% Decrease 97–01	4.7		C	1,417	5.6	−0.4
% Fin hard/Rank	53.5	12	L/C maj	11,268	44.6	
% Prem mort/Rank	64	4	Turnout		51.4	−15.2
			Elect	49,201		

Member of Parliament

Bald, bushy-moustached **Ian Davidson**, who was elected as a Glasgow MP (for Govan) in 1992, when he ousted SNP's Jim Sillars, is a left-wing critic of Blairism who sought unsuccessfully to get onto the panel of approved candidates for the Scottish Parliament. A Eurosceptic who had worked for MEP Janey Buchan, he was an active rebel against Blair's leadership in Opposition, but has been rather more circumspect since 1997, voting against the government on means testing of Incapacity Benefits, linking pensions to average earnings, and air traffic control sell-off. But as evidence of the divisive potential in the PLP of the single European currency, he expressed his opposition in November 2001, and again in a letter to the *Guardian* in January 2002.

GLASGOW RUTHERGLEN

Until recently Rutherglen was an ancient burgh, independent of Glasgow in adminis-trative terms although more or less swallowed up by it physically. Rutherglen's first charter was granted in 1126, but in the local government reorganisation of the early 1970s the burgh was finally incorporated into the city of Glasgow, and its parliamentary constituency was perforce moved from the defunct Lanarkshire county to become a Glasgow city seat.

The Labour MP Gregor Mackenzie won Rutherglen from the Tories in a by-election in May 1964, and he held it seven times before handing over to Tommy McAvoy in 1987. Mackenzie's greatest challenge came from a possibly unexpected source: the Liberals. The Liberal Party had done badly in central Scotland for decades, and they rarely made news in Rutherglen until they suddenly trebled their vote in the 1979 General Election. They retained second place through the 1980s and won city council and regional seats. In the 1992 General Election though the Liberal Democrat vote was more than halved as they slumped from 24% to 11% in Rutherglen. There were slight improvements in 1997 and 2001, but they were still just in third place behind the SNP – and well behind Tommy McAvoy. Rutherglen still seems not fully integrated into Scotland's largest city, as evidenced for example by the fact that it has one of the lowest unemployment rates in Scotland, not one of the highest, and it was the only 'Glasgow' seat in 2001 where the Scottish Socialist Party did not recover its deposit; but otherwise its political profile is now not untypical. In the most recently proposed boundary changes, Rutherglen is released from Glasgow once more, to join part of a much smaller entity, Hamilton.

Social indices:			2001 Gen. Election:			
% Non-white	0.8		Lab/Coop	16,760	57.4	–0.1
% Prof/Man	27.9		SNP	4,135	14.2	–1.1
% Non-manual	55.4		LD	3,689	12.6	–1.9
% Unemployed 2001	3.5		C	3,301	11.3	+2.0
% Decrease 97–01	2.8		SSP	1,328	4.5	+3.8
% Fin hard/Rank	46.0	25	L/C maj	12,625	43.2	
% Prem mort/Rank	56	16	Turnout		56.3	–13.8
			Elect	51,855		

Member of Parliament

Tommy McAvoy is one of Labour's silent hewers of wood and drawers of water, as a Whip since 1991, by 1997 third in seniority as the Pairing Whip. A steelworker's son, born in 1943 and Catholic-secondary-school-educated, he was a sometime storeman, forklift truck driver, and AEU shop steward, who served a short five-year apprenticeship on Strathclyde Council before reaching Westminster in 1987, where, as a Catholic, he follows his church on low abortion limits, and voted in 1999 for devolving legislation on abortion to the Scottish Parliament where a higher proportion of fellow Catholics were likely to produce abortion curbs.

GLASGOW SHETTLESTON

In a publication entitled *The Widening Gap: Health Inequalities and Policy in Britain* in 1999, a group of distinguished academics identified a list of parliamentary constituencies in rank order of premature mortality, poverty and avoidable deaths. Of the 641 seats listed in Britain, Glasgow Shettleston had the very worst results, with a standard mortality rate (SMR) of 234 compared with an average of 100. The seats occupying the next five places in this grim table were also all in Glasgow; in order: Springburn, Maryhill, Pollok, Anniesland and Baillieston, followed only then by Manchester Central. Clearly this is a seat of multiple deprivations in a city racked by poverty and its associated ill health.

Shettleston covers the eastern and southern parts of Glasgow's inner city. Some of the neighbourhoods on the south bank have famous, historic names: Gorbals and Hutchesontown evoke memories of dark Victorian tenements and notorious and fearsome slums, but these areas are now almost entirely cleared. The seat extends well beyond the Clyde, as far as Crosshill and Queen's Park. North of the river is Glasgow's inner east end, with wards such as Parkhead, home of Celtic football club. All the wards within Shettleston are solidly Labour and David Marshall held it with consummate ease in 2001. The SNP were a distant second, the Conservatives and Liberal Democrats barely retained their deposits – and finished behind the Scottish Socialist Party. Together with the Socialist Labour vote, this made a total of 8% for the far left, one of the highest figures in Britain – the others also being in Glasgow – and given the figure quoted at the top of this entry some would wonder why that appeal is not even greater.

Shettleston is likely to be split three ways (between the new Central, East and North East) by the next election, but its problems will not thus be solved.

Social indices:			2001 Gen. Election:			
% Non-white	3.4		Lab	13,235	64.7	–8.5
% Prof/Man	19.8		SNP	3,417	16.7	+2.7
% Non-manual	42.6		SSP	1,396	6.8	+5.0
% Unemployed 2001	6.6		LD	1,105	5.4	+1.4
% Decrease 97–01	2.7		C	1,082	5.3	–0.2
% Fin hard/Rank	64.9	3	SLP	230	1.1	
% Prem mort/Rank	71	1	Lab maj	9,818	48.0	
			Turnout		39.7	–16.2
			Elect	51,557		

Member of Parliament

David Marshall is another low-profile Glaswegian Labour MP with all the usual accoutrements: a manual working past – in his case as a bus conductor – spells on the local Glasgow and Strathclyde councils, and a conservative (though in this case not Catholic driven) line on homosexuality and abortion. Disappeared into Commons committee chairmanships, he was born in 1941 and educated at various high schools in Larbert, Falkirk, and Glasgow and can be counted a safe pair of chins.

GLASGOW SPRINGBURN

To some controversially, the Speaker of the House of Commons remains a member with a fully sized seat, with 55,000 constituents to look after in the case of Michael Martin at Glasgow Springburn. The Speaker was not opposed here by Conservative or Liberal Democrat parties in 2001, but the SNP did put a candidate in the fray, as well as the Scottish Socialist Party, the Scottish Unionists, and one independent. Martin cannot as Speaker actually make speeches on the floor of the house, or ask questions of ministers, but complaints that they do not represent their own seat well are rare, and Michael Martin was re-elected in 2001 with almost as high a percentage of the vote as he had received as a Labour candidate in 1997, though on a very low turnout of less than 44%. His seat certainly needs representation too: it is one of the most poverty-stricken and deprived in Britain, with the second highest premature mortality rate and a male unemployment rate in mid 2001 of over 12%, the highest of any constituency in Scotland according to the House of Commons Library Research Papers.

Springburn is situated north of Glasgow's city centre and forms the majority of the North East seat proposed by the Boundary Commission in 2002. Like several other Glasgow constituencies, Springburn is dominated by housing schemes towards the edge of the city, to which residents were moved in the inter- and post-war years as a result of slum clearance in the inner city. The stark tower blocks of Balornock and

Barmulloch hang broodingly on their hills above the city centre, and the proportion of council housing in the more peripheral Lethamhill approaches 80%. The seat includes the grim and troubled neighbourhood of Sighthill, where a Kurdish asylum seeker was stabbed to death in the high summer of 2001; over 1,000 immigrants could not be assimilated into a development of only 5,000 inhabitants. There is a large amount of railway influence too, including the remains of the Cowlairs railyard, and in the inner part of the seat is the older and more mixed neighbourhood of Dennistoun, about half of which is owner-occupied.

Given that the SNP are the main challengers to Labour in almost all the other Glasgow seats, Michael Martin seems neither less nor more vulnerable to losing his seat as a result of standing as the Speaker rather than Labour, and his constituents have not indicated any significant changes of behaviour as a result of his elevation to the chairmanship of the House.

Social indices:			2001 Gen. Election:			
% Non-white	1.5		Spkr	16,053	66.6	
% Prof/Man	19.5		SNP	4,675	19.4	+2.9
% Non-manual	44.4		SSP	1,879	7.8	+6.5
% Unemployed 2001	8.7		SUP	1,289	5.3	
% Decrease 97–01	4.2		Ind	208	0.9	
% Fin hard/Rank	66.6	2	Spkr maj	11,378	47.2	
% Prem mort/Rank	69	2	Turnout		43.7	–15.4
			Elect	55,192		

Member of Parliament

Michael Martin, a hunched and pleasantly moon-faced Glaswegian, was propelled into the limelight after 21 years spent mostly in the anonymous role of a Commons chairman, by his buggins-turn-but-controversial election as Speaker in 2000. The first Catholic Speaker since the Reformation, and the first sheet metal worker to occupy the post, he was also the first Speaker whose Glasgow-accented instructions it was initially thought could for added clarity do with being displayed above the proscenium arch. He was born in 1945, attended St Patrick's (RC) Boys' School, Glasgow, reached the Commons in 1979 after an obligatory stint on Glasgow Council, habitually voted the Catholic ticket on abortion and homosexuality, and antagonised the press by ousting them from the Commons terrace. Semi-apologising in October 2001 for expressing a political opinion from the Chair on the subject of asylum seekers, his Speakership was met with a chorus of disdain. Dubbed 'a mediocrity who has never shown the potential to fulfil the demands of the Speakership' (Peter Riddell, the *Times*), he was disparaged by the *Telegraph* as 'temperamentally and intellectually unfit for the office'. Uniquely among recent Speakers he was not nominated for the post with cross-party support, is seen as a Labour Party placeman, and was elected in defiance of a post-1965 convention of alternating the Speakership between the two major parties. He struck a further discordant note in November 2001 by sacking his allegedly 'Sloane-Rangerish' secretary, and disappoints all traditionalists by wearing – unlike the last male Labour Speaker, George Thomas – neither the wig nor the tights.

GLOUCESTER

An argument could have been constructed for the likelihood of a change of hands in Gloucester in June 2001. The first-term Labour Blairite, Tess Kingham, had announced her disillusion with the Commons and departure from it while still in her thirties, and had been replaced as candidate by the even younger, 20-something Parmjit Dhanda, in a seat with no significant Asian population. Would the voters punish Labour? Dhanda did poll 7,000 votes less than Kingham had, but the Tories scarcely improved their figure, and he was elected with a majority of nearly 4,000.

Gloucestershire was a blackspot for the Conservatives in the 1997 General Election. The Liberal Democrats retained their grip on Cheltenham. The new Forest of Dean seat, replacing West Gloucestershire, easily fell to Labour. In the greatest shock, Labour also took the semi-rural Stroud constituency. Finally, the county town of Gloucester itself reverted to Labour for the first time since the Tories captured it in 1970.

Like West Gloucestershire, Gloucester itself was once a fairly safe Labour seat which had moved to the Conservatives on a long-term basis in the 1970s and 1980s. Labour had held it for a quarter of a century before Sally Oppenheim took it in 1970. Mrs Oppenheim rose rapidly to become Consumer Affairs Minister under Mrs Thatcher, and consolidated her hold on the seat, handing over a 12,000 majority safely to Douglas French in 1987.

It does not look so Tory now. The seat has been reduced to fit exactly the City of Gloucester local government boundaries. Labour usually win the largest share of votes in local elections in the city, and are dominant in Gloucester's largely two-party politics. Gloucester has always been a functional, commercial town, less elegant than its newer neighbour Cheltenham just a few miles away. It was the lowest crossing point of the Severn before the opening of the bridge, which accounts for its prominence in Roman and medieval times as one of the great towns of the west. It has always enjoyed a diversity of industry; once it was the home of Gloster aircraft, now it houses one of the greatest ice cream factories in the world.

There is still enough of a working-class population for Labour to do well in peripheral council estates like Matson, and further in towards the centre of the city. Gloucester possesses by far the largest proportion of non-white residents in the county, 6% in all, reaching 15% in Barton ward and 19% in Eastgate – and nearly half of these are Afro-Caribbean, a long-established community from which came the Gloucestershire and England cricketer, David 'Syd' Lawrence. The Conservatives fight back in private housing wards on the edge of the city, like Kingsholm and Longlevens, Hucclecote and Barnwood, but in recent years this has been nowhere near enough, and it looks as if Labour could be in for a lengthy period of success in Gloucester's variable political scene.

Social indices:			2001 Gen. Election:			
% Non-white	5.7		Lab	22,067	45.8	−4.2
% Prof/Man	28.8		C	18,187	37.7	+2.0
% Non-manual	56.0		LD	6,875	14.3	+3.8
£ Av prop val 2000	79 K		UKIP	822	1.7	+0.9
% Increase 97–00	42.2		SA	272	0.6	
% Unemployed 2001	3.6		Lab maj	3,880	8.0	
% Decrease 97–01	1.7		Turnout		59.4	−14.2
% Fin hard/Rank	15.7	338	Elect	81,144		
% Pensioners	24.1					
% Prem mort/Rank	32	306				

Member of Parliament

Parmjit Dhanda, London-based and of Sikh origins, replaced as Labour MP here the disillusioned Tess Kingham, who had come in on the Blairite flood of 1997, but soon became a vocal critic of 'bullying' Whips and Commons hours incompatible with her role as a nursing mother. Parmjit Dhanda found her exit after only four years a problem on the doorstep – one to add to his own problem, as orchestrated by the local press, of being a candidate of Sikh origin in a constituency with only 5% non-white residents, most of whom were Caribbean or Gujuratis. Tall, dark and London-declassé-accented, he was born in 1971 (making him Labour's fourth youngest MP, and the youngest of the 38-strong 2001 intake), and educated at Mellow Lane Comprehensive, Hayes, Middlesex and at Nottingham University. Trained as an electrical engineer, he worked as a national organiser with Connect, a union for IT professionals. He resisted Anne Cryer's controversial call for all Asian immigrants to learn English, but as one of two of Labour's non-white MPs representing seats with very small numbers of black or Asian voters, sought to paint on a broader canvas, and drew on his local government experience as a Hillingdon councillor to urge councils to drive harder bargains with out-of-town shopping centre developers to include community facilities such as health centres and polling stations in their plans. His election in 2001, with that of Khalid Mahmood, raised Labour's total of non-white MPs to 12.

GORDON

No constituency in Scotland increased in population so rapidly between the 1981 and 1991 Censuses as Gordon. This was very much connected with the effects of the oil boom radiating from the port of Aberdeen, Scotland's third largest city. Although this expansion created an extra constituency in the Grampian region in time for the 1997 Election, which took a substantial part of the more suburban section of Gordon into Aberdeen North, the Liberal Democrat member for Gordon since its creation in 1983, Malcolm Bruce, seems to have just become stronger and stronger.

Absorbing in 1997 with comfort 6,000 new rural voters from Moray around Keith and Strathisla and 8,000 from Banff/Buchan in Turriff and Upper Ythan (not a misprint), to join the villages, valleys and small burghs of Huntly and Oldmeldrum and Inverurie, Bruce has increased his lead over the Tories to an apparently impregnable 8,000. It would be amazing if there were to be a change of hands in Gordon in the foreseeable future.

Social indices:			2001 Gen. Election:			
% Non-white	0.4		LD	15,928	45.5	+2.9
% Prof/Man	35.5		C	8,049	23.0	−3.0
% Non-manual	55.6		SNP	5,760	16.5	−3.5
% Unemployed 2001	1.56		Lab	4,730	13.5	+3.2
% Decrease 97–01	0.9		SSP	534	1.5	
% Fin hard/Rank	11.2	434	LD maj	7,879	22.5	
% Prem mort/Rank	27	392	Turnout		58.3	−13.6
			Elect	59,996		

Member of Parliament

Malcolm Bruce, elected here in 1983, has been an MP in a small party long enough to shadow most of the major departments – Energy, Employment, Environment, Scotland, Trade and Industry, and Treasury and, from 2001, DEFRA. A short man with a Scottish name, he actually comes (born in 1944, the son of an agricultural merchant and hotelier) from Birkenhead and attended Wrekin College in Shropshire, before arriving in Scotland in order to attend St Andrews University. A former journalist, initially on the *Liverpool Daily Post* and then on oil-industry-related publications in Aberdeen, he retrained as a barrister in 1995 as an insurance against losing his sometimes wobbly seat. Wary of Ashdown's Lib-Labbery, from his own family's business background and understanding the conservative nature of Scottish Liberalism, he has voted against gun control and hunting bans, and enjoyed attacking Gordon Brown when Treasury spokesman.

GOSPORT

Gosport has one of the lowest percentages of professional and managerial workers of any Conservative constituency – only 25% at the time of the 1991 Census. This figure is a good indicator of how upper class a seat is, and usually of its political preferences. Yet it has so far withstood the tidal advance of New Labour. How is this apparent contradiction explained?

The main clue lies in Gosport's high armed services vote, for the town is but a mile across the water from Portsmouth, and Royal Navy bases abound. The services, like the defence and arms industries, have traditionally offered solid support to the Conservatives regardless of social class, seeing that party as by far the most likely to respect their role and guarantee their jobs. The constituency is also three-quarters owner-occupied and 99% white. It may be working class; it is not left-wing.

Gosport remains a compact seat, drawn to include the whole of Gosport borough and two wards from neighbouring Fareham, Hill Head and Stubbington. It is almost as densely populated as Portsmouth, which itself harbours some of the most tightly packed wards outside London. The Liberal Democrats have done well in local elections in Gosport in the last ten years, but have failed to make much impact in general elections. Perhaps that is when defence – and defence spending – issues come to the fore.

Gosport may still be Conservative – and may well remain so now, if Labour's popularity has peaked – but for the first time in living memory it no longer looks safe. In 2001 Peter Viggers's majority was reduced to 2,621, far and away his lowest ever. There could be no better illustration of the new appeal of Labour, no longer capable of being confused with a left-wing party or one which is soft on defence, or one which cannot appeal to the south of England. The old fears have been laid to rest, and a new electoral cartography charted.

Social indices:			2001 Gen. Election:			
% Non-white	1.0		C	17,364	43.6	+0.0
% Prof/Man	25.4		Lab	14,743	37.1	+6.4
% Non-manual	47.7		LD	6,011	15.1	–4.5
£ Av prop val 2000	85 K		UKIP	1,162	2.9	
% Increase 97–00	37.0		SLP	509	1.3	
% Unemployed 2001	1.3		C maj	2,621	6.6	
% Decrease 97–01	2.1		Turnout		57.1	–13.1
% Fin hard/Rank	13.4	386	Elect	69,626		
% Pensioners	24.7					
% Prem mort/Rank	24	433				

Member of Parliament

Peter Viggers, a fading, locally born (1938) company solicitor and Lloyd's underwriter, educated at Portsmouth Grammar School and Trinity College, Cambridge, who nearly drowned in a sailing accident in 1993 but thought of John Major, was elected here in 1974, and spent three years as a Northern Ireland Minister in the 1980s. Since then he has concentrated on defence-related issues without being gung-ho, for example on Serbia and Kosovo, where he feared British casualties. Paradoxically a Thatcherite who was also pro-European, he claims to have sung every part in Handel's Messiah and was overdue for a 'k' when the knighthood-distributing Tories lost office in 1997.

GOWER

Gower is a constituency of two very distinct and different parts. The Gower peninsula itself is well known for its holiday beaches, its chalets and bungalows, and the homes of wealthy commuters to nearby Swansea. But on the other side of Swansea are the Lliw and Swansea valleys, with stark working-class industrial communities like Gorseinon, Pontardulais and Pontardawe. The Labour votes piled up in this anthracite mining territory with a high proportion of Welsh speakers have usually easily outweighed the Gower peninsula's contribution.

Gareth Wardell's chances of holding Gower (which he had defended successfully in a by-election the year before) in 1983 were made substantially harder by a change in the balance of the seat. The 'peninsula' element of the seat was strengthened by the arrival of the Swansea city ward of Mumbles. The Mumbles are great rocks jutting out into Swansea Bay, and around them has grown an affluent residential area and popular seaside resort. The inclusion of Mumbles cut Labour's majority by about

3,000, and this effect was doubled by the removal of the Upper Swansea valley around Ystalyfera to the Neath constituency. Wardell scraped home in the 1983 General Election by just 1,205 votes over the Tories.

It now looks as if that was the low point for Labour in the Gower constituency. Wardell increased his lead to 7,000 by 1992, and the new Labour candidate Martin Caton won by 13,000 in 1997. In 2001 Labour did relatively badly in Wales, and the 6% of their share lost in 2001 was not untypical; nor was the decline in turnout of 12%. Between them these developments reduced the margin to the 1992 level. The influence of the Tory Gower peninsula in the seat which bears its name cannot entirely be discounted, but Labour can regard it as safe for the time being.

Social indices:			2001 Gen. Election:			
% Non-white	0.6		Lab	17,676	47.3	−6.5
% Welsh sp	20.4		C	10,281	27.5	+3.7
% Prof/Man	38.5		LD	4,507	12.1	−0.9
% Non-manual	61.2		PC	3,865	10.3	+5.2
£ Av prop val 2000	78 K		Grn	607	1.6	
% Increase 97–00	17.6		SLP	417	1.1	
% Unemployed 2001	3.0		Lab maj	7,395	19.8	
% Decrease 97–01	1.5		Turnout		63.4	−11.8
% Fin hard/Rank	9.6	476	Elect	58,943		
% Pensioners	30.0					
% Prem mort/Rank	26	401				

Member of Parliament

Martin Caton, a bearded former political assistant to a local MEP, and earlier a scientific officer at a plant breeding station in Aberystwyth, was elected here in 1997. English-born (1951) and educated at Newport Grammar School, Essex, and Norfolk School of Agriculture, he arrived in Wales as a student at Aberystwyth College of Further Education. Not without a certain wit, he wondered in a debate on sustainable development if there were 'theories at the bottom of your jargon', and perhaps dangerously dubbed his constituents as 'Jerks' for being half-way between people in Llanelli (known as 'Turks') and Swansea (known as 'Jacks'). He has been moderately rebellious on lone parent benefit cuts, the Prime Minister's power to nominate life peers, and pensions linked to average earnings and means testing of Incapacity Benefit, a record serving to insulate him from any risk of promotion.

GRANTHAM AND STAMFORD

In the boundary changes recommended by the Commission which reported in 1995, and which came into force for the first time at the 1997 Election, Lincolnshire was awarded an extra seat. This resulted in alterations to the boundaries of all the constituencies in the county, most of them major. This was certainly true in the case of the new seat of Grantham and Stamford. Both of these towns were detached from much or most of the divisions in which they were previously situated.

To take Stamford first. The residents of this profoundly beautiful old town (known as a film set, for example for the BBC's successful production of *Middlemarch*) must feel thoroughly disrupted by the Boundary Commission's work, for it seems to be placed with different territory at each review. Before 1983 it was in Rutland and Stamford, but then the Commission had to take note of the annexation of the tiniest county by Leicestershire in the 1970s; and from 1983 Stamford was associated with Spalding and other Fen country in the low-lying district of Holland. In 1997 the lines were completely redrawn again, to create a Grantham and Stamford seat which takes in the south-western corner of the county of Lincolnshire. Just over half of the former Stamford and Spalding seat is now in the constituency of South Holland and the Deepings. However, the 37,500 electors or so who stayed with Stamford form a clear majority of the Grantham and Stamford division. Despite the order of the two towns' names, it is the Grantham section which is in the minority.

Grantham made little impact on the national political scene until it achieved a kind of fame as Margaret Thatcher's home town. In a radio poll in the early 1980s it was voted (almost certainly unfairly) Britain's most boring town. In fact, despite the Thatcherite connections, there is a Labour vote in the more working-class parts of the semi-industrial Grantham: in the Earlesfield and Harrowby wards, for example. Apart from the eponymous town, little of the former Grantham seat is included in Grantham and Stamford; most of it is now in 'Sleaford and North Hykeham'.

Neither of the two seats which contributed to Grantham and Stamford had ever been won by Labour, although Grantham was represented by an Independent from the war years until 1951. In 1997 Labour did get close, but no closer than they had in 1966 in Grantham – between 2,000 and 3,000 votes in deficit. Quentin Davies nearly doubled his slender lead in 2001 and as in many seats in the east of England, it seems as if Labour peaked four years before, although even higher hopes were briefly raised by misleading polls pointing to a further advance.

Social indices:			2001 Gen. Election:			
% Non-white	1.0		C	21,329	46.1	+3.3
% Prof/Man	29.1		Lab	16,811	36.3	−1.4
% Non-manual	49.9		LD	6,665	14.4	+1.9
£ Av prop val 2000	79 K		UKIP	1,484	3.2	+2.2
% Increase 97–00	40.2		C maj	4,518	9.8	
% Unemployed 2001	1.9		Turnout		62.2	−11.1
% Decrease 97–01	1.3		Elect	74,459		
% Fin hard/Rank	13.2	393				
% Pensioners	26.3					
% Prem mort/Rank	26	404				

Member of Parliament

Quentin Davies, Shadow Northern Ireland Secretary from 2001, was elected here in 1987, but had to wait until the Conservatives were in Opposition to reach the frontbench, in 1998, successively as a Social Security, Treasury and Defence spokesman. A pin-striped merchant banker (and before that a diplomat) with a loud-voiced arrogant manner, seen by a former Commons clerk as 'a complete pain in the arse', he is a Thatcherite Europhile who, seeing Europe as the means of completing the Thatcherite revolution, disliked his heroine's Bruges speech, and upped his profile by savaging David Willetts' 'dissembling weasel words' over the Hamilton affair. A doctor's son, born in 1944, educated at Leighton Park School, Reading, Gonville and Caius College, Cambridge and Harvard, his Europhilia made him a Clarke-backer in 1997 and again in all three ballots in 2001, but this did not preclude his inclusion with nine other Clarke voters in Iain Duncan Smith's frontbench, albeit in his case in the salt mines of Ulster.

GRAVESHAM

This seat, which used to be named Gravesend, is one of the classic 'bellwether' seats, which has almost always backed whichever party forms the government. This happened as it changed hands four times between 1964 and 1979, and it happened again when the government next changed – 18 years later, in 1997.

Rather like Dartford, Gravesham constituency sees something of a battle between the Labour voters in the towns along the south bank of the river Thames and the Tories of the rural hinterland. North Gravesend and Northfleet, on the bank of the Thames, are the Labour strongholds in the seat, and Labour can also count on the support of council estate wards like those of Coldharbour, Westcourt and Singlewell on the southern edge of the town. Gravesend also has enough of a non-white population, almost all of Indian origin, concentrated in the central wards like Pelham, to give it easily the highest 'ethnic' proportion of any seat in Kent. The Conservative strength is greatest in the villages, like Meopham, Higham and Shorne.

Gravesham is still a bellwether in some ways. Although Chris Pond reversed Jacques Arnold's 5,000 majority in 1997, and there was no swing at all in 2001, except to abstentionism, which went up from 23% to over 37%, the Conservatives will certainly need to win it if they are ever to form a government again.

Social indices:			2001 Gen. Election:			
% Non-white	8.4		Lab	21,773	49.9	+0.2
% Prof/Man	30.6		C	16,911	38.8	–0.1
% Non-manual	56.7		LD	4,031	9.2	+1.5
£ Av prop val 2000	99 K		UKIP	924	2.1	
% Increase 97–00	41.2		Lab maj	4,862	11.1	
% Unemployed 2001	3.1		Turnout		62.7	–14.2
% Decrease 97–01	2.7		Elect	69,590		
% Fin hard/Rank	18.4	296				
% Pensioners	23.2					
% Prem mort/Rank	23	443				

Member of Parliament

Chris Pond, PPS to Paymaster General Dawn Primarolo from 1999, ought to have expected something better as a high-profile social policy expert who ran the Low Pay Unit before being elected in 1997, but may not have been well served by a soft-spoken, unpartisan manner. A milkman's son, born in 1952, educated at secondary schools in Palmers Green and Southgate, and Sussex University, he held various university research posts before spending 17 years at the Low Pay Unit. Now divorced from ex-MEP Carole Tongue, he has been dubbed a 'stomach-churning loyalist' by the *Independent*, and a government 'stooge' by Tory MP Julie Kirkbride.

GREAT GRIMSBY

Grimsby has usually been loyal to the Labour Party, and in some ways it has been unusually loyal to them. It was for 18 years the constituency of one of their most prominent theorists, Anthony Crosland. In the April 1977 by-election caused by Crosland's sudden death, the TV current affairs personality and former historian Austin Mitchell held the seat, on the same day as Labour were ousted by a 21% swing at Ashfield, Notts. In the 1979 General Election Mitchell increased his majority to over 6,000 – just about as large as Crosland had enjoyed in 1974, even at a time when Mrs Thatcher won the first of her three general election triumphs. In 1983 Grimsby did not fall to the Tory landslide. Then in 1987 Mitchell benefited from one of Labour's very best showings in England – a swing of nearly 8% from the Conservatives, and an increase in majority from 731 to 8,784. By 2001 Mitchell had become one of Labour's veterans, securing an easy seventh victory in Grimsby, as the locally based Liberal Democrat councillor Andrew De Freitas again challenged the Conservatives closely for second place.

Grimsby has long been known as a great fishing and container port. It has the largest accommodation capacity for frozen food in Europe. It has attempted to stave off depression by modernisation, and many Grimsby residents work in the petro-chemical complexes on the Humber bank. Grimsby's Labour preferences can be guessed from the sight of the Victorian terraced housing behind the docks, and peripheral council estates on the west and north-west sides of town. There is a large Conservative residential bloc in the south-east, around the People's Park, and towards the seaside resort of Cleethorpes: the wards of Scartho, Wintringham, Wellow, Weelsby, Springfield and Clee; but here Tories are in a minority, and they haven't won in a general election for nearly 70 years.

Social indices:			2001 Gen. Election:				
% Non-white	1.0		Lab	19,118	57.9	−1.9	
% Prof/Man	22.4		C	7,634	23.1	+1.0	
% Non-manual	42.2		LD	6,265	19.0	+0.9	
£ Av prop val 2000	41 K		Lab maj	11,484	34.8		
% Increase 97–00	8.8		Turnout		52.3	−14.0	
% Unemployed 2001	7.2		Elect	63,157			
% Decrease 97–01	2.6						
% Fin hard/Rank	28.8	148					
% Pensioners	25.6						
% Prem mort/Rank	45	89					

Member of Parliament

Austin Mitchell, an academic-turned-broadcaster-turned-MP, with a large self-amused laugh, is a big, burly tousle-haired lone operator, so fascinated by photography that he even photographed the applause he got when performing at the

Oxford Union. An iconoclastic, off-message MP who dubbed Labour's 1980s left-wing activists 'lunatics' and yet was ranked the 25th most rebellious Labour MP in the 1992–97 parliament, he also saw Margaret Thatcher as a destroyer of 'the flabby orthodoxies that had held sway for too long, including Labour's'; compared Tony Blair's policy-making style with Kim Il Sung's and yet, though eccentrically joining the Campaign Group in 1999, a collection of hard left-wingers who staff all the backbench rebellions, has barely whimpered against the Blair government, other than opposing student tuition fees and voting to block the Prime Minister's power to appoint life peers. Born in 1934, son of a dyer, he attended Bingley Grammar School, Manchester University and Nuffield College, Oxford (where he obtained a doctorate he doesn't cite), taught in New Zealand universities for eight years and worked in television for seven before replacing Tony Crosland here at the 1977 by-election. His politics are not dissimilar to his hero, Gaitskell's – right-of-centre but Eurosceptic (in his case because of what the EU has done to Grimsby's fishing industry), but too cynical to be fully engaged, he is at his best observing the passing scene, as in his description of the Whips' Office: 'Full of thugs and not to be seen as an annex of Balliol College'.

GREAT YARMOUTH

Great Yarmouth is the largest holiday resort and the largest working port in Norfolk. It is a ferry centre for travel to northern Europe and a base for North Sea oil and gas exploitation. Yarmouth itself is also known for a solid Labour vote. They won six county council seats in the town in 2001. Labour held the Yarmouth seat in the Commons from 1945 to 1951, and again from 1966 to 1970. In 1997 they continued the tradition of winning in landslide years, this time by a very comfortable margin after a swing even larger than the national average. Four years later, though, the Conservatives set out on what may be the road back, as they nearly halved Tony Wright's Labour lead. The Liberal Democrats are exceptionally weak for an English seat, and have no local government representation either; these two facts are connected.

It was not the town of Yarmouth itself which has kept the Conservatives in control of this seat at most times. The constituency also includes villages on the coast and in the rural hinterland. The former include Caister-on-Sea to the north of Great Yarmouth and Gorleston-on-Sea to the south; the latter include Bradwell, Hopton and Burgh Castle, which were once in Suffolk. These are all very Conservative areas, and in the past have proved sufficient to tip the balance in this seat in all but Labour's very best years.

Social indices:			2001 Gen. Election:			
% Non-white	0.9		Lab	20,344	50.4	–3.0
% Prof/Man	27.9		C	15,780	39.1	+3.5
% Non-manual	51.6		LD	3,392	8.4	–2.6
£ Av prop val 2000	61 K		UKIP	850	2.1	
% Increase 97–00	27.6		Lab maj	4,564	11.3	
% Unemployed 2001	5.8		Turnout		58.4	–12.8
% Decrease 97–01	2.6		Elect	69,131		
% Fin hard/Rank	18.0	305				
% Pensioners	29.7					
% Prem mort/Rank	32	299				

Member of Parliament

Labour's **Anthony Wright** is an unobtrusive loyalist namesake of the much more high-profile maverick MP for Cannock and Burntwood. A local man with a jowly face and heavy build, he led Yarmouth Council and ran the local Labour Party organisation. One of the PLP's dwindling minority (12%) of manual workers, originally an engineer, he was born in 1954 and was educated at a secondary modern school. As a foreign tripper he has taken up the cause of Greek Cyprus, and has set up an all party group on ME, which makes a change from urging the dualling of the A47. Of Labour's three Norfolk MPs, at least he sounds as if he comes from the county.

GREENOCK AND INVERCLYDE

Historically the town of Greenock and its environs on the south bank of the river Clyde have composed one of the rare examples of Labour/Liberal marginal political competition in Britain. In 1970 the Conservatives did not even put up a candidate, and Labour held off the Liberals by only 3,000 votes. The Liberal Party formed the main opposition in municipal politics too, and they were so strong that when the sitting right-wing Labour MP Dickson Mabon defected to the SDP before the 1983 Election, he had to go off to fight the neighbouring Renfrew West and Inverclyde seat, leaving Greenock to the Liberal partners in the Alliance. They did well again, too (in another year of great Labour weakness, it might be noted): the Labour candidate Norman Godman won by only 4,625.

The Liberal Democrats are still very competitive in local elections in the Greenock area, and in 2001 in a parallel result to that across Scotland as a whole, they improved their position compared with 1997 and took second place back from the SNP, who fell back in the parliamentary elections north of the border. It is safe enough for Labour, however, to have absorbed comfortably the loss in the 1997 boundary changes of the working-class shipbuilding town of Port Glasgow to the east of Greenock, and its replacement by the locally Liberal Democrat area of Inverclyde around Gourock and Wemyss Bay on the coast. Apart from the old west end of the town, Greenock is a very working-class industrial community sandwiched between the hills and moors and the Clyde. Industries and occupations associated with seafaring have declined, to be replaced with a specialisation in electronics and computing – both IBM and National Semi-Conductors have major plants in the town. Greenock and Inverclyde looks like remaining another of the battery of utterly safe Labour seats in west-central Scotland.

Social indices:			2001 Gen. Election:			
% Non-white	0.4		Lab	14,929	52.5	−3.6
% Prof/Man	27.8		LD	5,039	17.7	+3.9
% Non-manual	48.5		SNP	4,248	14.9	−3.6
% Unemployed 2001	4.9		C	3,000	10.6	−0.9
% Decrease 97–01	1.1		SSP	1,203	4.2	
% Fin hard/Rank	47.6	21	Lab maj	9,890	34.8	
% Prem mort/Rank	59	11	Turnout		59.3	−11.7
			Elect	47,884		

Member of Parliament

David Cairns, elected here in 2001, was already known for his campaign against the disqualification from sitting in Parliament of ex-Roman Catholic priests like himself, and for whom the law was changed in February 2001. Born in 1966 and educated at Notre Dame High School, Greenock, the Gregorian University, Rome, and the Franciscan Study Centre, Canterbury, he was a priest in Clapham for three years before becoming Director of the Christian Socialist Movement in 1994, and research assistant to fellow Catholic Siobhain McDonagh, MP for Mitcham and Morden (where he also served as a councillor and whip) and sister of Labour's General Secretary (1997–2001), Margaret McDonagh. Enjoying less than fulsome endorsement from his predecessor in this seat, Dr Norman Godman, who said he had wanted to be succeeded 'by a woman with good, honourable, Old Labour qualifications', he has about him the air of one too nice to be in politics and who, at a fringe meeting at the Labour Party Conference in 2001, invoked St Francis of Assisi in prayers for peace following the World Trade Center disaster. With his fellow Christian Socialist colleague, the ex-Anglican priest Chris Bryant, he was the first former clergyman to sit in the Commons since the sometime Baptist minister Sir Tom Williams retired in 1981.

GREENWICH AND WOOLWICH

Between them, the south-east London boroughs of Greenwich and Bexley lost a seat in the 1997 parliamentary boundary changes. Their electorates simply did not justify the continued allocation of six constituencies, and most of the seats had well below the average number of voters. This was certainly true of the Greenwich and Woolwich divisions, and at first it might be thought that the Greenwich and Woolwich constituency is an equal merger of the two. This is not true, however.

In fact the seat consists of the whole of the former Greenwich plus just four wards from Woolwich (adding up to only 15,000 electors) and one ward, Nightingale, from Eltham. Woolwich was split up between three seats, the others being Erith and Thamesmead, and Eltham. The section which is included in the Greenwich and Woolwich division is just the north-western corner, on the river front but upstream from Thamesmead: the Arsenal, Burrage, St Mary's and Woolwich Common wards.

Although Rosie Barnes had won Greenwich for the Social Democrats against a left-wing Labour candidate in a by-election in 1987, and John Cartwright had held Woolwich as an SDP defector until 1992, when both recorded strong second place performances, the underlying situation in Greenwich and (part of) Woolwich is essentially very strongly Labour. Apart from some isolated enclaves of affluence such as Blackheath Park this is a working-class – almost inner-city – seat, with a high non-white population in central Greenwich, massive tower blocks on the Ferrier estate, and industrial river frontage for some miles – the tourist attractions of the observatory and the Royal Naval College, and ships including the Cutty Sark, are an exception not the rule. After those historic social democratic diversions in both Greenwich and Woolwich, 'normal service' has now been resumed in the form of an easy win for Labour.

Social indices:			2001 Gen. Election:			
% Non-white	14.3		Lab	19,691	60.5	–2.9
% Prof/Man	36.9		C	6,258	19.2	+0.7
% Non-manual	60.0		LD	5,082	15.6	+3.1
£ Av prop val 2000	162 K		UKIP	672	2.1	
% Increase 97–00	61.8		SA	481	1.5	
% Unemployed 2001	6.8		SLP	352	1.1	
% Decrease 97–01	4.2		Lab maj	13,433	41.3	
% Fin hard/Rank	41.5	40	Turnout		52.0	–13.8
% Pensioners	24.2		Elect	62,530		
% Prem mort/Rank	43	118				

Member of Parliament

Nick Raynsford, born in 1945 and educated at public school and Cambridge (Repton and Sidney Sussex), is one of Labour's rare toffs, in his case from a family of Northamptonshire squires, traceable back to the fifteenth century, with his full name being 'Wyvill Richard Nicholls Raynsford'. A tall, balding, permanently smiling, vicarish, uncharismatic technocrat, he was elected for Greenwich in 1992 when he retrieved the seat from the SDP, having briefly sat for Fulham 1986–87 as one of Labour's false dawns. A perennial spokesman-turned-minister on Local Government, Housing and London, even making a brief pitch in 1999 to run for mayor, as a Minister he piloted through the legislation recreating both a London Assembly and Ken Livingstone. He also favours Labour campaigning in Northern Ireland, and in 2001 even sought to popularise the notion of elected mayors.

GUILDFORD

Surrey has long had a strong claim to be the most Conservative county. Every one of its seats remained Conservative even in 1997, a record shared only by Dorset; but Surrey has 11 constituencies and Dorset only seven. In 2001 it had the highest Tory share of the vote recorded in any English county, 47.6%. However, for the first time under its present boundaries since the creation of Greater London in 1965 removed its urban inner section, it does not have a full slate of Tory MPs. The reason for this lies in the Guildford constituency. Nick St Aubyn was defeated by the Liberal Democrat challenger Sue Doughty. This was to some extent predictable based on local government success: in the most recent Guildford borough elections of May 1999 the Liberal Democrats had returned 18 councillors in the wards within this seat to the Conservatives' four (Labour actually took six in two wards too). Yet this was not new, nor sufficient given the experience in so many other districts. Neither was the tactical squeeze which clearly operated against Labour. The fact was the Conservative share remained constant despite the near-disappearance of a significant anti-European party vote from 1997. The core of St Aubyn's problems lay in the failure of his party to mobilise its credibility or its message nationally and the Tories will have to do much better to overcome the incumbency that Sue Doughty is likely to exploit next time in this sophisticated seat.

The city of Guildford is not mainly a commuting base for London, although it is well connected as the A3 road runs through its centre. Like Reigate and Woking, it is big enough to act as a substantial commercial and employing centre of its own. It has a university (which is not a promoted polytechnic) and a modern Anglican cathedral atop a breezy hill. It also has extensive council estates in the north and west of the town, such as Park Barn, which have a long tradition of electing Labour local councillors, but which probably split their votes much more widely in general elections. There are also affluent and middle-class neighbourhoods in Guildford, such as Merrow and Burpham; but the Conservatives majority is really built up in the villages of mid-Surrey, such as Bramley, Cranleigh and Ewhurst. These are decidedly not agricultural communities, though their residents would like to think of them as rural. Guildford is a majority middle-class seat with a high proportion of professional and higher managerial workers, a very low unemployment rate, very high property values (the average house price in 2000 was £203,000), and a broad-based and resilient economy. That the Conservatives cannot be sure of winning such a constituency indicates the breadth and depth of their problems.

Social indices:			2001 Gen. Election:			
% Non-white	2.1		LD	20,358	42.6	+8.4
% Prof/Man	43.5		C	19,820	41.4	−1.1
% Non-manual	67.7		Lab	6,558	13.7	−3.8
£ Av prop val 2000	204 K		UKIP	736	1.5	+0.8
% Increase 97–00	67.9		Ind	370	0.8	+0.3
% Unemployed 2001	0.8		LD maj	538	1.1	
% Decrease 97–01	1.0		Turnout		62.9	−12.5
% Fin hard/Rank	6.7	567	Elect	76,046		
% Pensioners	25.6					
% Prem mort/Rank	9	610				

Member of Parliament

Sue Doughty, Guildford's first Liberal MP since that party's last landslide in 1906, won the seat in 2001 after campaigning on the sort of issues, such as debt-laden students and waste recycling (notably hostility to a proposed local waste incinerator), with appeal to the affluent middle class. Nor, unlike Liberal Democrats in their celtic fringe heartland, was her party's keenness for the euro incompatible with a dormitory town professional and managerial electorate put off – as she saw it – by 'Tory Euroscepticism'. Her defeated Tory opponent, Nick St Aubyn, attributed her success to an appeal to aspiring young professionals. With a background of employment in private (Norwich Union) and public sector (Thames Water) management, she was born in 1948, attended Mill Mount Grammar School, York and Northumberland College of Education and was initially a schoolteacher. One of three 50-something women in the Liberal Democrats' 14-strong 2001 intake, her election helped increase the total of Liberal Democrat women MPs to five, or 10% of the total (52).

HACKNEY NORTH AND STOKE NEWINGTON

Diane Abbott has had no difficulty holding Hackney North and Stoke Newington since 1987, increasing her vote by 9% in 1992 and another 6% in 1997, and she might have held her share in 2001 but for the fact that this inner urban seat produced the third biggest vote for the Greens anywhere in Britain, 7.4% for Councillor Chit Chong, who had topped the borough elections in North Defoe ward in 1998.

Hackney is by some standards the most deprived borough in London and indeed the country. Its northern half shares many of these characteristics, even though its proportion of council housing is somewhat lower than its southern partner. Overall the constituency is 35% non-white, more than half of these being Afro-Caribbeans. The relationship between the police and the black community has not been good, especially in the Stoke Newington area. Crime and drug use are relatively high for Britain. The seat also includes Stamford Hill, the home of a distinctive community of ultra-Orthodox Hasidic Jews, whose relationship with their neighbours has not always been without problems. One of the prominent members of that group is the long-term Conservative leader on Hackney council, Joe Lobenstein, who can bring two other Tories in on his coattails in Springfield ward, and there have been many other glitches in Labour's underwhelming performance in local elections in recent years, culminating in their failure to secure control in 1998, although those elections themselves were cast under a different pall when two councillors, one Conservative and one Liberal Democrat, were convicted of vote rigging and jailed three years later.

The complexity and roughness of Hackney's electoral politics are scarcely surprising in a borough in which many individuals and groups feel unhappy with their lot, and the conditions dealt to them. Squalor rubs shoulders with affluence, however, as homeowners in the constituency benefited from a rise in property values of nearly 70% between 1997 and 2000. This may well not have made relations between neighbours here more harmonious.

All this should not affect Diane Abbott's position. Freer from the threat of deselection than several of her predecessors, she can look forward to a long career in the House of Commons, representing a diverse and deprived part of inner London which is bound to throw up many cases for her to take, and causes for her to champion. One rare feature of the 2001 General Election here: all three major party candidates – Diane Abbott (Labour), Pauline (aka Molly) Dye (Conservative), and Meral Ece (Liberal Democrat) – were female.

Social indices:			2001 Gen. Election:			
% Non-white	34.9		Lab	18,081	61.0	−4.1
% Prof/Man	42.0		C	4,430	15.0	−2.0
% Non-manual	63.0		LD	4,170	14.1	+3.9
£ Av prop val 2000	159 K		Grn	2,184	7.4	+3.1
% Increase 97–00	68.2		SLP	756	2.6	
% Unemployed 2001	7.9		Lab maj	13,651	46.1	
% Decrease 97–01	8.8		Turnout		49.0	−3.9
% Fin hard/Rank	33.9	102	Elect	60,444		
% Pensioners	19.5					
% Prem mort/Rank	49	51				

Member of Parliament

Diane Abbott, one of Labour's 12 non-white MPs, won the seat in 1987 and joins her Campaign Group colleagues in most of the revolts against the Blair government. She rebelled 26 times in the 1997 to 2001 Parliament – the 11th most dissenting Labour MP, compared with 32 rebellions between 1992 and 1997. In the new House elected in 2001 she rebelled against the bombing of Afghanistan and, serially, against the anti-terrorism legislation. An intelligent but pugnacious and emotional extrovert who overstates and underprepares, she was born to Jamaican parents in 1953, educated at Harrow County Grammar School for Girls and Newnham College, Cambridge and worked as a Home Office civil servant, TV reporter and GLC press officer. Short and chubby, her black stretch velvet evoking for some an exploding mole, she was squeezed off the Treasury Select Committee in 1997 and the Foreign Affairs Select Committee in 2001. In early 2002 she raised the eyebrows of the politically correct by calling for black teachers in order to curb the cultural alienation of failing black schoolboys.

HACKNEY SOUTH AND SHOREDITCH

The multiple problems faced by the borough of Hackney are widely known: a very poor standard of housing exemplified by the notorious Holly Street estate, drug abuse, endemic truancy from school, theft and violent crime, a high degree of health problems and an overstrained health care system, more single-parent families than average and, equally with Tower Hamlets, the highest unemployment rate of any London borough. Hackney South and Shoreditch is a constituency with classic inner-city problems, similar to Bethnal Green and Bow to the east, or Camberwell and Peckham south of the river. Only half a dozen of London's 84 seats still had a majority of council housing in 1991, but this was one of them. All this would suggest that Hackney should be one of Labour's very safest areas. Yet in the 1998 borough elections they lost control. The Tories won the southernmost ward, Moorfields, and topped the poll in De Beauvoir; the Liberal Democrats won in Dalston, Queensbridge, Victoria, Wenlock and Wick wards. All these had traditionally given their preference to Labour. Yet the council's image of incompetence had led to suggestions of suspension and central government takeover.

This super-critical response to municipal administration has not, however, as yet affected Brian Sedgemore's iron grip on the parliamentary representation of the seat.

Indeed, in 2001 he increased his share of the vote by 5%, probably mainly because of the disappearance of the independent who stood as New Labour in 1997 and saved his deposit. The far left Socialist Alliance did better than in most of their forays in 2001, although they could hardly be said to live up to the rather politically inappropriate name of their candidate, Cecilia Prosper. When selecting a national government, Labour will continue to top the poll, as indeed they should in these Cockney heartlands of Haggerston and Homerton, Hoxton and Dalston, London Fields and Hackney Downs.

Social indices:			2001 Gen. Election:			
% Non-white	32.2		Lab	19,471	64.2	+4.8
% Prof/Man	32.6		LD	4,422	14.6	−0.4
% Non-manual	53.7		C	4,180	13.8	+0.5
£ Av prop val 2000	160 K		SA	1,401	4.6	
% Increase 97–00	78.1		Ind	471	1.6	
% Unemployed 2001	8.9		CPGB	259	0.9	−0.0
% Decrease 97–01	7.9		WRP	143	0.5	+0.1
% Fin hard/Rank	53.9	11	Lab maj	15,049	49.6	
% Pensioners	21.3		Turnout		47.4	−7.3
% Prem mort/Rank	51	41	Elect	63,990		

Member of Parliament

Elected here in 1983 after representing Luton West (1974–79), burly, Cro-Magnon featured **Brian Sedgemore**, born in 1937, educated at Heles School, Exeter, and Corpus Christi, Oxford, is one of Labour's iconoclastic loners who has never advanced further than being PPS to Tony Benn for two years in the 1970s. A quirkish left-winger who was alone on the Labour left in backing Maastricht, a seasoned parliamentary bruiser who likes to ridicule his Commons colleagues, and a sniffer-out of City fraud, he has rebelled against the Blair government on lone parent benefits, pensions, jury trials and disability benefit in the 1997–2001 House, and against the Terrorism, Crime and Security Bill in November 2001 which he dismissed as 'a rag-bag of the most coercive measures that the best mandarin minds from the Home Office can produce'. With past employment as barrister, civil servant and TV researcher, he has ridiculed Blair's Babes as 'Stepford Wives', and Ken Livingstone as 'arrogant and patronising', disputing his 'divine right to rule London'. To Margaret Hodge he is 'a disappointed man who has been around too long'. To the late Cranley Onslow he was 'the boil on the bottom of the Labour Party'.

HALESOWEN AND ROWLEY REGIS

The Boundary Commission which commenced work in 1991 and reported in mid 1995 noted that the borough of Dudley had three seats and was theoretically entitled to 3.5, while its neighbouring West Midlands borough to the east, Sandwell, had four seats but was only entitled to 3.28. Rather than consider the boroughs individually, and maybe give Dudley an extra seat while taking one away from Sandwell, it was decided to treat them as one, allocate seven seats in all, and draw a cross-borough constituency. This, Halesowen and Rowley Regis, is it.

It was thought at first that the Commission have managed to create another cliff-hanging marginal in this western part of the great urban sprawl of the West Midlands. It certainly appears divided. The Halesowen section came from the safely Conservative former division of Halesowen and Stourbridge: this supplies nearly 40,000 voters from Halesowen North and South, Belle Vale/Hasbury and Hayley Green wards. Halesowen is a prosperous town, with many of the attributes of its former county of Worcestershire, rather than looking to Birmingham. There are very few non-white residents and little council housing. The Tory majority in Halesowen/ Stourbridge was nearly 10,000 in 1992 and nearly half of this would have come from the part now linked with Sandwell wards. However, the other 30,000 electors in the new seat came from the former Warley West, which was a safe Labour division; admittedly its majority was smaller than that of Halesowen/Stourbridge but this southern area was the more strongly Labour: these are the staunchly industrial and working-class communities of Blackheath, Cradley Heath and Old Hill, and Rowley Regis. In each case about 40% of the housing was still in the hands of council tenants. Although there is no significant non-white community, this is reliably Labour territory.

Overall, the Tories might just have been ahead by a whisker had this new and divided seat been created in 1992, but it is impossible to prove. There is no doubt at all that in 1997 Labour romped to victory by 10,000, on a swing typical of the West Midlands average. In 2001 the turnout dropped by 14%, close to the English average, but there was very little change in the shares of the party vote. It will be very difficult to defeat Sylvia Heal; rather than Rowley Regis outvoting Halesowen, in all probability both halves of this new seat now vote for New Labour.

Social indices:			2001 Gen. Election:			
% Non-white	4.1		Lab	20,804	53.0	−1.1
% Prof/Man	27.3		C	13,445	34.2	+1.4
% Non-manual	51.6		LD	4,089	10.4	+1.9
£ Av prop val 2000	71 K		UKIP	936	2.4	
% Increase 97–00	26.6		Lab maj	7,359	18.7	
% Unemployed 2001	4.1		Turnout		59.8	−13.8
% Decrease 97–01	1.0		Elect	65,683		
% Fin hard/Rank	21.9	244				
% Pensioners	27.5					
% Prem mort/Rank	31	326				

Member of Parliament

Sylvia Heal, MP here since 1997 and before that only briefly (1990–92) for Mid Staffordshire, reached the Commons chair as a Deputy Speaker in 2000 faster than anyone in living memory or beyond, as much on a gender-balancing ticket (with the departure for the Lords of Speaker Betty Boothroyd) as any other. As part of a Commons pair of sisters (with Ann Keen), she was born in 1942, daughter of a Shotton steel worker, and educated at a local secondary modern school, worked as a hospital records clerk, then via Coleg Harlech went to Swansea University and became a social worker. Denying disloyalty over lone parent benefit cuts in 1997, she said as a PPS (to Defence Secretary George Robertson) she was unable to protest. To the late journalist and fellow Egham resident, George Gale (whose main preoccupation was waking up in time to get off the train at Egham after a hard day in Fleet Street pubs), she – with her immaculate blue-grey hair and pearl necklaces – 'actually looks like a Tory', almost a seamless reincarnation of past Conservative female Deputy Speakers, Dame Janet Fookes and Miss Betty Harvie Anderson.

HALIFAX

With its prominent mills and chimneys among dark terraces of housing, Halifax is one of those dramatically hilly Pennine towns whose industrial townscape betokens a Labour stronghold to the untutored observer. This impression is to a large extent misleading, for although Labour have indeed won Halifax in most elections since the war, losing only in disastrous years like 1955, 1959 and 1983, the contests have often been very narrow, in 1992, for example, when Alice Mahon's majority was actually reduced to under 500. The Elections of 1997 and 2001 mark historically unusual years for Halifax, as of course for the country as a whole; but the increase in the Labour vote since 1992 has if anything been less than the national average.

There are a number of reasons why Labour has not always been able to rely on Halifax's loyalties. There are solid gritstone houses in solid Tory wards like Northowram and Shelf, Warley to the west of the town, and the best residential area, Skerton, around Savile Park south of the town centre. Although there are council estates of varying vintage and condition in the northern wards of Illingworth and Mixenden, the Conservatives can win them in a good year; they are nearly all white, and there may be some resentment against Halifax's Asian minority population, mainly Pakistani, who are concentrated in the central wards like St John's. Labour can count on only one ward, Ovenden, in all local elections, and it was their sole victory in May 2000 – and that not overwhelming on a turnout of just 17%. Overall, the Tories were 8% ahead of Labour candidates within Halifax in those Calderdale elections, and they had led by a larger margin within the seat in the European contest of June 1999 too.

Alice Mahon was only 13% ahead for Labour in 2001's General Election. This sounds convincing, but her numerical majority was almost halved to 6,000; the seat would be on the Conservatives' list as a gain if they should ever form another government, and local election results here show clearly that they have the votes if they can mobilise their support – or if Labour's does not come out.

Social indices:			2001 Gen. Election:			
% Non-white	7.7		Lab	19,800	49.0	−5.3
% Prof/Man	26.8		C	13,671	33.8	+1.7
% Non-manual	49.1		LD	5,878	14.6	+2.6
£ Av prop val 2000	51 K		UKIP	1,041	2.6	+1.0
% Increase 97–00	19.4		Lab maj	6,129	15.2	
% Unemployed 2001	4.8		Turnout		57.8	−12.7
% Decrease 97–01	2.1		Elect	69,870		
% Fin hard/Rank	29.6	135				
% Pensioners	26.6					
% Prem mort/Rank	44	106				

Member of Parliament

Alice Mahon, a Campaign Grouper, voted against the government 25 times – including all the major revolts, from lone parent benefit cuts to air traffic control privatisation – between 1997 and 2001, making her the 13th most dissident Labour MP. From the Whips' perspective this was an improvement on her record in the 1992–97 Parliament when she rebelled 55 times and only three Labour MPs were more dissenting. A small, poker-faced, feminist class warrior, whose opposition to the bombing of Serbia earned from Clare Short a comparison with the appeasers of Hitler, she was born in 1937, educated at Halifax Grammar School and, as a mature student, Bradford University, and worked in manual jobs, as an auxiliary nurse and as a college lecturer before election for Halifax in 1987, when she retrieved the seat from the Conservatives. She briefly tried to conform as PPS to Chris Smith in 1997 but had to quit before the year was out after voting against 'punitive and cruel' lone parent benefit cuts. In 2001 she rebelled against the Terrorism, Crime and Security Bill.

HALTEMPRICE AND HOWDEN

East Yorkshire was extensively affected by the boundary redistribution which came into force at the 1997 Election, and in Haltemprice and Howden there was created a seat which combines the names of two constituencies that were abolished in the previous redrawing in 1983. It must be considered something of a long shot that Haltemprice and Howden ever resurfaced in a constituency title, as neither nowadays has a local government unit named after them, and neither is a nationally well-known name: Haltemprice is a suburb of Hull, and Howden a small rural town of scarcely 3,500 souls. This must rank as a concession to a historic and quaint tradition of constituency nomenclature, even perhaps a moment of sentimentality on behalf of the Commission.

Both Haltemprice and Howden divisions were solidly Conservative before 1983. This seat took over 45,000 voters from the Beverley seat which had existed since that year, and is effectively its successor, although the town of Beverley is now linked with Holderness on the coast. The roots of this area's Conservatism are not hard to identify. A town of 300,000 like Hull normally possesses enough of a middle-class professional or commercial element to produce sufficient Conservative votes to sustain at least one Tory parliamentary constituency. Where apparently there is no such regular Tory seat, as at Bradford, Leicester, Nottingham or Hull, one may surmise that the city boundaries have been so drawn that the most desirable residential areas are to be found outside. In this eventuality, Conservative dormitory seats do exist, if one looks for them – Blaby *et al.* for Leicester, Rushcliffe for Nottingham, and Beverley – now Haltemprice again – for Hull. In 2001, though, the last named no longer looked safe as there was one of the clearer examples of organised tactical voting against David Davis; the Labour vote fell by 8% and the Liberal Democrats rose by even more, cutting Davis's majority to just 1,903. His own share just about held up, though, and he was able to go forward to finish fourth in the bloody contest for his party leadership immediately thereafter.

Hull has three safe Labour divisions, but that is not to say that the big Humberside port has no wealthy or prosperous class of citizens. It is just that they tend to live in suburbs like Cottingham and Haltemprice, Kirk Ella and Anlaby and Willerby. This area has long sustained right-wing MPs of the independent and organising kind, from Major Sir Patrick Wall (1954 to 1987) to the subsequent Maastricht rebel James Cran. Cran has contested Beverley and Holderness since 1997, leaving this seat to David Davis, who had represented the Howden area, the middle of the three segments into which his former seat of Boothferry was split. This contains the flat land north of the Ouse but south of the Wolds, based on Howden itself and containing rural villages like Holme-on-Spalding-Moor; the Howden seat was also very safely Conservative, and provided a base for another knight of the shires, Sir Paul Bryan, who served for 32 years from 1955, just one year less than his neighbour Sir Patrick Wall. David Davis had already served for ten years as member for Boothferry when first elected here in 1997, and barring further disruption of boundaries or even more demonstrable tactical anti-voting may well be able to match the longevity of these two distinguished predecessors.

Social indices:			2001 Gen. Election:			
% Non-white	0.8		C	18,994	43.2	–0.8
% Prof/Man	39.2		LD	17,091	38.9	+10.1
% Non-manual	63.9		Lab	6,898	15.7	–7.9
£ Av prop val 2000	78 K		UKIP	945	2.2	+1.5
% Increase 97–00	9.3		C maj	1,903	4.3	
% Unemployed 2001	1.9		Turnout		65.5	–10.0
% Decrease 97–01	0.9		Elect	67,055		
% Fin hard/Rank	5.5	596				
% Pensioners	26.5					
% Prem mort/Rank	12	571				

Member of Parliament

David Davis, MP here since 1997 and before that for contiguous Boothferry from 1987, a former Whip (1990–93) and minister, eventually at the Foreign Office, was seen as a potential dark horse in any future Tory leadership race, despite his absence from the front line after 1997, as traditionally non-partisan chairman of the Public Accounts Committee, a post he deliberately sought away from the civil war among other would-be Tory leaders. But when he ran for the leadership in 2001 he was supported by only 21 MPs in the first ballot and 18 in the second. His consolation was the Chairmanship of the Conservative Party under Iain Duncan Smith's leadership from September 2001. The adopted son of a print worker, born in 1948 and educated at Bec Grammar School, Warwick University, London Business School and Harvard, he worked as a Tate and Lyle executive for 13 years. As whipper-in against the Maastricht rebels, he earned a reputation as a careerist sacrificing Eurosceptic principles, but memories fade and his classless manner, conventional good looks and humour do not count against him.

HALTON

Halton is Labour's truest stronghold in Cheshire, with a majority in 2001 of nearly 17,500 over the Tories. This is scarcely surprising given the social and economic history of the seat. Since Widnes was moved (by government decree) from Lancashire to Cheshire in the early 1970s, it has become possible for it to be united in a single parliamentary seat with the town on the opposite bank of the Mersey, Runcorn. Both are historically dependent on the chemical industry. Now linked by a major road bridge, there is no longer any need to take the ferry made famous by the music hall entertainer Stanley Holloway, which cost 'per 2d per person per trip'. The creation of the Widnes/Runcorn Borough Council, known as Halton, in 1974, made that of the constituency of the same name (in 1983) even more logical.

Both halves of the seat are strongly Labour. Widnes is one of the starker creations of the nineteenth-century industrial revolution, a stronghold of rugby league and of the working class, with the exception of one small favoured residential area at the north end of the town, Farnworth. Most of Runcorn is much newer (although it was developed as a port on the Manchester Ship Canal), for it was designated as a New Town in April 1964. Owing to overspill, largely from Liverpool, Runcorn is now larger than Widnes. Chemical manufacture is still paramount but diversification is taking place on a number of industrial estates, producing a wide range from pepper and spice to carpets and kidney machines. For all the modern development (such as Runcorn's Shopping City), there are still many poor housing areas on both sides of the Mersey – and many of them were not planned and built in Victorian times, either. There is no doubt that this seat will remain in the Labour column.

Social indices:			2001 Gen. Election:			
% Non-white	0.6		Lab	23,841	69.2	−1.7
% Prof/Man	23.4		C	6,413	18.6	+0.9
% Non-manual	46,3		LD	4,216	12.2	+4.9
£ Av prop val 2000	60 K		Lab maj	17,428	50.6	
% Increase 97–00	21.8		Turnout		54.1	−14.2
% Unemployed 2001	4.5		Elect	63,673		
% Decrease 97–01	3.0					
% Fin hard/Rank	28.7	150				
% Pensioners	23.1					
% Prem mort/Rank	41	162				

Member of Parliament

Derek Twigg, PPS to Helen Liddell (1999–2001) and then to Stephen Byers, is a model Blairite as a loyalist stooge questioner, one of a number 'jumping to their feet eager to ask Big Brother's questions, up and down like children on pogo sticks' (Quentin Letts, *Daily Telegraph*). A locally-born (1959) son of OMOV, he is as local as local gets, educated at Bankfield High School, Widnes, and at Halton FE College, and was a Halton district councillor for 14 years. He worked as a Department of Employment civil servant before election here in 1997, and as a witness of the Hillsborough football stadium disaster of 1989, in which friends died, he has sought a fuller investigation.

HAMILTON NORTH AND BELLSHILL

2001 may well have seen the second – and last – contest in this rather artificial constituency, as 2002 saw the Scottish Boundary Commission suggest dividing Cabinet Minister John Reid's seat, with Bellshill joining that of another, Helen Liddell, in Airdrie and Shotts, and Hamilton resplit, East and West.

This is an industrial constituency taking in largely working-class communities on both sides of the river Clyde about ten miles south-east of Glasgow. On the east bank of the Clyde came nearly 40,000 voters from Motherwell North. These are to be found not just in Bellshill, but in several other small towns and council estates: Mossend, Viewpark, Orbiston, Birkenshaw, New Stevenston, Holytown, Newarthill. These all have a majority of council-built housing; the one exception is the owner-occupied ward of Tannochside. This is ex-mining country, and it is also well within the orbit of the Ravenscraig steelworks. The traditions of Labour-voting are imbued with these heavy industries, and the only real opposition at both local and national level is supplied by the SNP, who have a handful of North Lanarkshire unitary authority councillors.

West of the Clyde lies the Hamilton North section of the seat, although this too is misnamed. It contains only a tiny part of the town of Hamilton, situated just north of the centre. There are only about 15,000 voters altogether, and these are mainly in the two small towns of Bothwell and Uddingston, now in the South Lanarkshire authority. Overall Hamilton North and Bellshill has been as safe as Motherwell North was, and a far from troublesome home base for the Northern Ireland Secretary, offering therefore a decided contrast with his main place of work.

Social indices:			2001 Gen. Election:			
% Non-white	1.0		Lab	18,786	61.8	–2.2
% Prof/Man	28.8		SNP	5,225	17.2	–1.9
% Non-manual	52.6		C	2,649	8.7	–1.7
% Unemployed 2001	5.1		LD	2,360	7.8	+2.7
% Decrease 97–01	2.4		SSP	1,189	3.9	
% Fin hard/Rank	44.0	30	SLP	195	0.6	
% Prem mort/Rank	55	20	Lab maj	13,561	44.6	
			Turnout		56.8	–14.1
			Elect	53,539		

Member of Parliament

Dr John Reid, as Northern Ireland Secretary after Peter Mandelson's exit in January 2001, was in his fourth government post, after Transport, Defence and Scotland, since 1997. A combative debater, well-versed in the political arts, he has shown himself a deft general spokesman for the government, especially whilst in the time-on-his-hands small post-devolution job of Scottish Secretary. Born in 1947, the first Catholic to be sent to the Ulster saltmines as Secretary of State, he says of his school, St Patrick's (RC) Secondary, Coatbridge, which also produced Labour MPs Helen Liddell and Michael Connarty, that 'it doesn't quite beat Eton, but we are ahead of Fettes'. First elected for Motherwell North from 1987 to 1997, his doctorate is in economic history from Stirling University. When Mandelson got the Northern Ireland job Reid said of the Unionists, 'They got the gay'. Well, now they've got the Catholic – though his father was a Presbyterian. He has rejected as 'unbalanced theorising' the parliamentary Standards Commissioner's report on his alleged misuse of parliamentary researchers for Labour Party work and alleged threatening of the witnesses involved.

HAMILTON SOUTH

This small seat of only 46,000 electors is ripe for heavy alteration as Scotland is reduced to a comparable level of representation at Westminster to the UK average, probably before the next general election. It contains the whole of the historic Hamilton constituency minus about 15,000 electors in Bothwell, Uddingston and a small north-east section of the town of Hamilton itself, which are now in Hamilton North and Bellshill. This now looks like a very safe Labour seat, but it has not always been so.

In 1967 Winnie Ewing became the first SNP MP for over 20 years when she seized the former Lanarkshire county town in a by-election caused by the retirement of the former Transport Minister Tom Fraser. Labour recaptured Hamilton at the subsequent General Election three years later, but in another by-election in 1978 they faced the former SNP MP for Glasgow Govan, Margo Macdonald. George Robertson did very well to vanquish her by over 6,000 votes. Robertson entered the Cabinet as Defence Secretary in 1997, but his translation to be NATO Secretary General caused yet another by-election in September 1999, when Labour's Bill Tynan held on by only 556 against another member of Scottish family Ewing, Annabel, daughter of Winnie. He only managed a paltry winning total here of 7,172 votes. The pattern continues, though, of Labour securing their position in general elections, away from that particular glare of publicity that Hamilton seems regularly to attract, and Tynan very easily beat a less well-known SNP name in one of the first handful of seats to be declared on 7 June 2001.

Social indices:			2001 Gen. Election:			
% Non-white	0.7		Lab	15,965	59.7	−5.9
% Prof/Man	26.2		SNP	5,190	19.4	+1.8
% Non-manual	51.8		LD	2,381	8.9	+3.8
% Unemployed 2001	4.7		C	1,876	7.0	−1.6
% Decrease 97–01	2.0		SSP	1,187	4.4	
% Fin hard/Rank	42.3	37	UKIP	151	0.6	
% Prem mort/Rank	52	34	Lab maj	10,775	40.3	
			Turnout		57.3	−13.8
			Elect	46,665		

Member of Parliament

Bill Tynan, with a reputation as an engineering union political 'fixer' and 'the kingmaker of Lanarkshire politics' (the *Herald*), narrowly squeaked in as George Robertson's successor here in 1999 when the Defence Secretary left to run NATO. A safe pair of union hands, as a toolmaker (of 27 years) who turned AEEU political officer for 11 years, he was born in 1940, educated at St Mungo's Academy, Glasgow, and Stow College where he trained as a mechanical engineer. Gnarled, dour-looking and austere, he loyally defends the Blair government's economic record and backs his Union boss Sir Ken Jackson's Europhile stance. Restoring his by-election-battered majority of 556 (over the SNP) to 10,775 in 2001, he had the satisfaction of seeing his erstwhile SNP challenger, Anabelle Ewing, similarly struggling at Perth, where she won by a mere 48 votes. He was allegedly about to back Wendy Alexander (a Brown-linked MSP) as next Scottish First Minister when she pulled out of the running in November 2001.

HAMMERSMITH AND FULHAM

This constituency, which contains most but not all of the borough of the same name (its five northernmost wards are currently in Ealing Acton and Shepherd's Bush) is a classic hard-fought marginal in west London. Fulham has been moving up the social scale for many years now, as middle-class home-buyers have been occupying the tight-packed narrow streets in the loop of the Thames conveniently situated just to the west of Chelsea. Palace ward was always a Tory stronghold; others moved that way, such as Town, Eel Brook, Sulivan and Colehill. There are many marginal wards of mixed characteristics, in neighbourhoods like Crabtree, Walham and Sherbrooke. Labour does best in areas with a substantial social housing presence, like Margravine, Gibbs Green and Sands End. The rest of the seat, around the centre of Hammersmith, also breaks fairly evenly. This section includes the pleasant leafy residential areas around the green spaces of Brook Green and Ravenscourt Park, as well as Labour wards like Hammersmith Broadway. What all this means is that the Conservatives would have a good chance of gaining the Hammersmith and Fulham constituency, should New Labour slip up in their second term of government.

Fulham is still gentrifying, and it is a mark of Labour's two utterly decisive national victories that Iain Coleman has been able to beat the former Fulham MP Matthew Carrington. In 2001 the margin was only 2,015, and a third tight contest seems very much on the cards in 2005 or 2006. Thereafter, though, all will change as the Boundary Commission has decided to pair boroughs a different way in that medium-term future, and a new heavily Tory Chelsea and Fulham seat will be created, leaving Hammersmith to reunite with Shepherds Bush, much safer for Labour than this constituency. This forcible divorce of Hammersmith and Fulham will mean less angst for politicians, less interest for pundits, and perhaps for voters too.

Social indices:			2001 Gen. Election:			
% Non-white	14.1		Lab	19,801	44.3	−2.5
% Prof/Man	50.8		C	17,786	39.8	+0.1
% Non-manual	74.2		LD	5,294	11.8	+3.1
£ Av prop val 2000	305 K		Grn	1,444	3.2	+2.2
% Increase 97–00	55.4		UKIP	375	0.8	+0.5
% Unemployed 2001	3.8		Lab maj	2,015	4.5	
% Decrease 97–01	3.8		Turnout		56.4	−12.3
% Fin hard/Rank	13.3	390	Elect	79,302		
% Pensioners	20.0					
% Prem mort/Rank	49	52				

Member of Parliament

Ian Coleman, one of the huge Labour intake of 1997, has left few footprints since. A former local government officer in Islington, he came with an earlier leftist reputation as leader of Hammersmith and Fulham Council, and opposition to the Clause 4 redraft. Posing only two written questions in his first year, he has not featured in lists of rebellious votes against the government. Born in 1958, he is one of Labour's 70 public-school-educated MPs, in his case Tonbridge. Once dubbed a 'Hainite' that would involve him, by 2001, being strong on European integration and the handing over of Gibraltar to Spain, but his recorded utterances are few.

HAMPSHIRE EAST

The seat of East Hampshire, first fought in 1997 after rapid population rise gave the county two extra seats, certainly looks like a ragbag. It is made up of territory from three previous divisions. About 32,000 voters were in the old East Hampshire, in the southern part of that constituency; the greatest population centres here are the country town of Petersfield and Horndean: both of these are home to around 12,000 souls. Also, three wards were detached from Havant constituency to join East Hampshire: Cowplain, Hart Plain and Waterloo; these are all very Conservative in general elections and amount to some 22,000 electors. Finally another 20,000 or so voters came in from the Winchester division, centred on Alton, which is actually the largest town in the new East Hampshire constituency.

The upshot of all this is a more compact seat, rather than the long strip down the eastern edge of the county that East Hampshire used to be. It is divided almost equally between suburbs in the Havant orbit of influence and country towns and villages further north. It was very safely Conservative even in 1997 and 2001, when Michael

Mates achieved a near five-figure majority despite the drop in turnout to under 64%. Over 80% of residents throughout the constituency are owner-occupiers; property prices rose on average by no less than 67% between 1997 and 2000, from a mean of £89,000 to £149,000. The voters are 99% white and 40% in professional and managerial occupations. It may be discerned that East Hampshire is not East Ham.

Social indices:			2001 Gen. Election:			
% Non-white	0.9		C	23,950	47.6	−0.4
% Prof/Man	39.9		LD	15,060	29.9	+1.8
% Non-manual	62.1		Lab	9,866	19.6	+2.5
£ Av prop val 2000	149 K		UKIP	1,413	2.8	+1.9
% Increase 97–00	67.3		C maj	8,890	17.7	
% Unemployed 2001	1.0		Turnout		63.8	−12.1
% Decrease 97–01	1.3		Elect	78,802		
% Fin hard/Rank	6.9	560				
% Pensioners	23.7					
% Prem mort/Rank	16	531				

Member of Parliament

The career of Colonel **Michael Mates** – elected for Petersfield in October 1974 and for the successor seat of Hampshire East in 1983 – has been stymied by his identity as a Heseltine- and Clarke-supporting One Nation Tory, and by his earlier disloyalty to Margaret Thatcher over poll tax banding, on which he led a serious revolt in 1988. A Queen's Dragoon Guards Officer for 20 years (1954–74), he was born in 1934, attended Blundell's School and, inconclusively, King's College, Cambridge. With his interest in defence and security issues reflected in his Chairmanship of the Defence (1987–92) and Northern Ireland (from 2001) Select Committees, his short 14-month ministerial career as a Northern Ireland Minister (1992–93) (which came as Major's reward to Heseletine whose failed 1990 leadership bid Mates had run) was ended by his association with the Turkish-Cypriot fugitive, fraudulent businessman and Tory Party donor, Asil Nadir, to whom he had given a watch inscribed 'Don't let the buggers get you down'. His backing of Kenneth Clarke in 1997 (as campaign manager) and again in 2001, iced the cake of his exclusion from the frontbench under both Hague and Duncan Smith without moreover the consolation of the once-customary knighthood for an elderly (by 2001 he was the second oldest) Conservative backbencher.

HAMPSHIRE NORTH EAST

It sounds as if this is one of the two extra and new seats allocated to the county of Hampshire by the 1995 report of the Boundary Commission. Certainly it is a new constituency name. Yet closer inspection reveals that North East Hampshire is really a pared-down version of the former East Hampshire constituency. All but 2,000 of North East Hampshire's 66,000 electors were formerly in East Hampshire (the minority in Eversley and Whitewater were in Aldershot). Indeed only one-third of the old East Hampshire is in the current seat bearing the same name, and it is that seat which is truly an additional newcomer.

East Hampshire returned a Conservative majority of over 29,000 in 1992, the second largest for that party (behind John Major's Huntingdon) and the fourth largest anywhere. Clearly this was partially due to its immense size (93,000 voters, the third largest in the UK), but it still counted as the 17th safest Conservative seat (in percentage terms), secure against a swing of up to 20% to the Liberal Democrats. North East Hampshire has proved equally reliable, offering James Arbuthnot a majority of over 13,000 in 2001, making it their fifth safest seat.

It consists of the northern half of the former East Hampshire, which was a long strip along the eastern edge of the county. The main population centres are Fleet, a rapidly growing town just off the M3 motorway, Whitehill with its military presence, Liss, Liphook and Hook, which was once proposed as a New Town; that plan was cancelled, but it didn't stop Hook doubling its population through private development in the 1980s. There are plenty of attractive villages to bolster the Tory majority. This area of Hampshire is both very Conservative and rapidly growing in population; all in all a delight for the right.

Social indices:			2001 Gen. Election:			
% Non-white	1.9		C	23,379	53.2	+2.3
% Prof/Man	43.4		LD	10,122	23.0	+0.3
% Non-manual	64.3		Lab	8,744	19.9	+3.8
£ Av prop val 2000	191 K		UKIP	1,702	3.9	+3.0
% Increase 97–00	62.6		C maj	13,257	30.2	
% Unemployed 2001	0.6		Turnout		61.6	−12.3
% Decrease 97–01	0.8		Elect	71,323		
% Fin hard/Rank	3.7	630				
% Pensioners	20.8					
% Prem mort/Rank	5	626				

Member of Parliament

James Arbuthnot, MP for this seat since 1997, when he 'chicken-ran' from the dismantled Wanstead and Woodford seat he had represented since 1987, is a Conservative MP of a species nearing extinction. The son of another Conservative MP, Sir John Arbuthnot, who sat for Dover from 1950 to 1964, he was educated at Eton and Trinity College, Cambridge, and earned a living at the Chancery Bar and as a (loss-making) Lloyd's underwriter. Though dry on economics as a poll tax rebel he was happier under John Major than Margaret Thatcher and did not enter the government until made a Whip by Major in 1992, and a Minister at Social Security (1994–95) and Defence (1995–97). An austere, desiccated man with a voice likened to that of a speaking clock, but with a patrician accent redolent of his party some decades ago, as William Hague's campaign manager in 1997 he became Chief Whip (1997–2001), but with his choice in 2001 somewhat obscure he left for the back-benches thereafter, in the company of a dozen of Hague's former Shadow Cabinet.

HAMPSHIRE NORTH WEST

North West Hampshire is made up of some rural parts of the western half of Basingstoke and Deane borough, now reaching almost to the town of Basingstoke itself with the addition of Sherborne St John; and the northern part of the Test Valley, centred on the town of Andover.

Andover was one of the communities chosen to expand to take in London overspill in the post-war years, and in the two decades after 1961 the population of this once sleepy town doubled to 32,000. The proportion of council houses trebled in the 1960s. Clearly there was a potential Labour vote in the newer northern half of Andover, but it never really materialised. Andover's population has stabilised, and a substantial amount of the council housing has been sold off. Labour moved up to second here in 2001, but they can never really challenge for the lead. Sir George Young has one of the Tories' 20 safest seats, in an attractive, comfortable and safe neck of the woods.

Premature mortality rates are only 73% of the national average, which amounts to a third of those recorded in the poorest parts of Glasgow. The percentage of electors defined by Experian as suffering financial hardship is 10, compared with 70 in Glasgow Springburn. Average house prices rose from £90,000 to £150,000 during the last parliament. Just over 5% voted Conservative in 2001 in Glasgow Shettleston or Glasgow Maryhill, just over 50% in North West Hampshire.

Social indices:			2001 Gen. Election:			
% Non-white	1.1		C	24,374	50.1	+4.9
% Prof/Man	34.6		Lab	12,365	25.4	+1.8
% Non-manual	58.1		LD	10,329	21.2	–2.9
£ Av prop val 2000	153 K		UKIP	1,563	3.2	+0.7
% Increase 97–00	67.2		C maj	12,009	24.7	
% Unemployed 2001	0.9		Turnout		63.7	–11.0
% Decrease 97–01	0.7		Elect	76,359		
% Fin hard/Rank	9.2	485				
% Pensioners	21.4					
% Prem mort/Rank	7	618				

Member of Parliament

Sir George Young, one of the Commons' four remaining baronets (in his case a sixth baronet) was elected originally as MP for Ealing Acton in 1974 but escaped its adversely redrawn seat in 1997 and relocated here. An immensely tall, bland, soft-spoken, patrician Tory, he was born in 1940 and educated at Eton and Christ Church, Oxford, but then worked, rather oddly for one with such cut class credentials, as an economist at 'Neddy' (the National Economic Development Organisation), a then-fashionable statist quango, before becoming an MP. With his wet One Nation Conservatism restricting his appeal to Margaret Thatcher, in her time he was never more than a Whip (1976–79 and 1990) or Junior Minister at Health or Environment (1979–86 – when he was dropped), and rose more steeply under Major to become Transport Secretary in 1995 – but at a price, in being given the dirty job of privatising the railways. Though a Clarke voter in 1997 he graced Hague's frontbench to give it balance, but mostly in the marginal post of Shadow Leader of the Commons, which he quit in 2000 to run as the party's man for the Speakership, winning the second highest tally of 241 votes, including many Labour MPs and some Cabinet ministers. Backing Clarke again in 2001 he retreated into one of the dignified recesses of Parliament as the Chairman of the Select Committee on Standards and Privileges.

HAMPSTEAD AND HIGHGATE

This constituency saw one of the most dramatic battles of the 1992 General Election – or at least, one of those which attracted the most media attention. A large part of the reason for the glare of publicity was that the Labour candidate, who gained the seat from the Tories, was a celebrity, the actress Glenda Jackson. Also, few parts of London have so clear or well-publicised an image as a haven of fashionable middle-class radicalism as this seat on the capital's northern heights.

In fact, Labour's results in Hampstead and Highgate since have been nothing to write home about. Celebrity candidates rarely achieve any special boost in general elections, and Miss Jackson did no better than the regional average in 1992 or 1997, and in 2001 the Labour vote slumped by 10%. Also, Hampstead and Highgate's legend of affluent left-wing attitudes is in danger of fostering several myths. It is true that the seat is more inclined to Labour than most seats of its economic composition, but it was a constituency of 65,000 electors in 2001, which spread far beyond the Hampstead Town district near the heath. In fact most of the Labour vote comes from less desirable residential areas – Kilburn, with its Irish and Afro-Caribbean flavour, West Hampstead, with its rapidly shifting population, and socially mixed Swiss Cottage, Fortune Green and Belsize Park are all in the seat. Hampstead Town actually voted Liberal Democrat in the most recent Camden borough elections, and the Lib Dems advanced by over 8% in 2001, shadowing an even larger rise at Labour's expense next door in Hornsey and Wood Green (although they were still third here). It was said by some that this was caused by a revolt of the intelligentsia against distasteful and illiberal Labour government policies, such as on asylum seekers. Has the lustre of the star faded?

Social indices:			2001 Gen. Election:			
% Non-white	15.4		Lab	16,601	46.9	−10.5
% Prof/Man	60.6		C	8,725	24.6	−2.6
% Non-manual	79.2		LD	7,273	20.5	+8.1
£ Av prop val 2000	344 K		Grn	1,654	4.7	
% Increase 97–00	65.2		SA	559	1.6	
% Unemployed 2001	4.0		UKIP	316	0.9	+0.6
% Decrease 97–01	3.9		Ind	144	0.4	
% Fin hard/Rank	16.3	332	PA	92	0.3	
% Pensioners	22.8		Ind	43	0.1	
% Prem mort/Rank	36	235	Lab maj	7,876	22.2	
			Turnout		54.2	−13.7
			Elect	65,309		

Member of Parliament

Glenda Jackson is a very rare example of an actor in politics, the combination being seen as an unnecessary excess of dissembling. Drawn into politics as an alternative to unsure prospects as a rising 60-year-old actress who, given the paucity of theatrical roles for ageing women, did not want to be typecast as the nurse in *Romeo and Juliet*, she won this seat from the Conservatives in 1992, and became a Transport Minister for two years in 1997 until dropped in 1999. A bricklayer's daughter, born in 1936, and educated at West Kirby County Grammar School for Girls and RADA, as a Transport Minister she conveyed a rather humourless image if without actressy vapourings. The official explanation of her being dropped, to run for London Mayor, held little water, since Frank Dobson was also sacked for that purpose as a 'Stop Ken'candidate. Like Dobson she failed to do so, and has had to accept that as in the theatre so in the Commons, the roles can run out.

HARBOROUGH

Harborough is the South East Leicestershire county division, and it has always been a safe Tory seat, including a mixture of Leicester suburban areas and rolling countryside. This formula of affluent Leicester suburbs – in this case the middle-class owner-occupied Oadby, and the rather more heterogeneous Wigston – and rural areas, such as around the old town of Market Harborough, has worked well to maintain ultra-safe ground for the Conservatives. Before the most recent boundary changes, Blaby, Rutland and Melton and Loughborough all benefited from such a mix as well as Harborough. Then with the creation of the all-suburban Charnwood, the suburban element in these other four seats was in each case reduced, to the Tories' disadvantage. The MP, Edward Garnier, was worried about the effects of the redistribution before the 1997 Election, but in fact the Liberal Democrat vote declined as well as his own, and Labour doubled its support to take a strong third place. If anything, he should have been more concerned in 2001, when there were signs that the voters had clarified the picture in Harborough and switched in significant numbers back from Labour to Lib Dem, although enough only to reduce Garnier's majority, to just over 5,000 on a 63% turnout. The Liberal Democrats won most of the county council wards within the Oadby and Wigston section of the seat on that day, but the Conservatives came back in the villages. The seat has the potential to become closer still, though, and Edward Garnier is right not to consider himself a shoo-in.

Social indices:			2001 Gen. Election:			
% Non-white	5.6		C	20,748	44.7	+2.9
% Prof/Man	34.0		LD	15,496	33.4	+3.9
% Non-manual	58.2		Lab	9,271	20.0	−5.2
£ Av prop val 2000	92 K		UKIP	912	2.0	
% Increase 97–00	39.5		C maj	5,252	11.3	
% Unemployed 2001	1.9		Turnout		63.3	−11.9
% Decrease 97–01	0.4		Elect	73,300		
% Fin hard/Rank	8.2	518				
% Pensioners	24.1					
% Prem mort/Rank	14	553				

Member of Parliament

Edward Garnier, a QC specialising in libel, elected here in 1992, was Shadow Attorney General (1999–2001). His vote for Clarke in 1997 underlined his strong support for the Maastricht Treaty, which he saw as in 'unashamed British national self-interest', and so his detachment from the Eurosceptic orthodoxy. Born in 1952 into an army family, and self-described as 'on the left wing of the party on social affairs' but 'rather more right wing on economics', he is drawn from a grander Tory tradition as the grandson of the eighth Baron Walsingham (and is linked through his wife to the Heathcote-Drummond-Willoughby family who traditionally represented the former Rutland and Stamford constituency), and was educated at Wellington and Jesus College, Oxford. A defender of the hunting and shooting lobby, he backed Portillo in 2001 and returned to the backbenches, his career temporarily becalmed.

HARLOW

One of the more predictable results of the 1997 Election was that Labour would gain Harlow easily. This was not primarily because of scandalous allegations against the colourful MP, Jerry Hayes, but rather because the Conservative tenure on this seat had always seemed aberrant, and liable to be confined to years of their national triumph.

The post-war Harlow New Town lies tucked in a once-rural corner of north-west Essex. Harlow rapidly grew from a population of around 5,000 at the end of the war to reach 80,000 by 1981; there was then a lull, but in recent years further expansion has taken place, of a different nature: new private estates on the edge of town, for example to the east in Potter Street ward. Like Basildon New Town, Harlow maintained a Labour council while having elected a Conservative MP in the three elections between 1983 and 1992. Labour won fairly easily in municipal contests in the various wards representing the New Town neighbourhoods: Little Parndon and Great Parndon, Passmores, Katherines with Sumner, Latton Bush, Tye Green, Brays Grove, Potter Street, Netteswell and Mark Hall. The Conservatives' two best wards are situated at opposite ends of the town, at Old Harlow in the far north-east and at the most affluent of the New Town neighbourhoods, Kingsmoor in the south-west, and they won Potter Street as well easily last time, and Great Parndon narrowly. This may be a sign that Labour's grip is shaky and shallow. In the last few years too the Liberal Democrats have arisen from a period of torpor and started to gain in local elections: in 2000, for example, in Mark Hall South and Netteswell East and West.

In the June 2001 General Election, too, Bill Rammell's majority was halved as both Conservative and Liberal Democrats increased their share. The Tories need to regain Harlow in order to form a government again, and in a community increasingly of new private as well as state housing and outlook who is to say that the era of volatility is over?

Social indices:			2001 Gen. Election:			
% Non-white	3.3		Lab	19,169	47.8	−6.3
% Prof/Man	28.2		C	13,941	34.8	+2.7
% Non-manual	53.9		LD	5,381	13.4	+4.0
£ Av prop val 2000	103 K		UKIP	1,223	3.0	+2.3
% Increase 97–00	47.7		SA	401	1.0	
% Unemployed 2001	2.4		Lab maj	5,228	13.0	
% Decrease 97–01	2.3		Turnout		59.8	−14.8
% Fin hard/Rank	24.4	207	Elect	67,074		
% Pensioners	21.8					
% Prem mort/Rank	26	411				

Member of Parliament

Bill Rammell, Labour's MP here since 1997, is an on-message loyalist rewarded in 2001 with the job of PPS to Tessa Jowell. A salesman's son, he was born in 1959, educated at Burnt Mill Comprehensive, Harlow, and Cardiff University, and worked primarily as a students' union manager at London University. He allowed himself the indulgence of one discordant bash in 1997 – abstaining over lone parent benefit cuts, but, as Labour's replacement for the evangelical Europhile Giles Radice, his next dissent is likely to come over any foot-dragging on UK accession to the common currency, outside of which he contends, Britain does not have an economic future. He also backs electoral reform.

HARROGATE AND KNARESBOROUGH

The former Chancellor of the Exchequer, Norman Lamont, sought a move to Harrogate and Knaresborough in 1997 in order to continue his parliamentary career after the abolition of his Kingston upon Thames seat. He was sadly disappointed. The Liberal Democrats achieved their third highest increase in vote share, 18.2%, and Phil Willis beat Lamont by over 6,000. He must have benefited too from one of the clearest examples of tactical voting, for Labour's share dropped from 13% to under nine: one of only 13 instances of any decline and their fifth worst showing anywhere. Clearly the voters of Harrogate and Knaresborough were very determined not to be represented by Mr Lamont. In 2001 with the added benefit of incumbency Phil Willis increased his share again, to 55%, one of the six highest figures registered in Britain for a non-Labour candidate. It seems as if Harrogate will join Bath and Cheltenham as large prosperous spas electing and re-electing Lib Dem MPs.

Harrogate is the largest spa town in the north of England, an elegant inland holiday resort 15 miles north of Leeds beyond Harewood House. Harrogate is larger than Leamington Spa and Tunbridge Wells, and almost rivals Bath and Cheltenham in the grandeur of its architecture and facilities. Like many spa towns, Harrogate had long been strongly Conservative with more than a hint of Liberalism, and although it is no longer fashionable to take the waters, it has developed into a major conference site, with a large new convention/concert centre having opened in December 1981. It is also a very popular and growing residential location, as new private houses have sprung up to join the Victorian mansions set around the Stray and Harrogate's many other green and flowery parks.

The seat takes in just a compact and predominantly urban area around Harrogate itself and the neighbouring Knaresborough, a prosperous town set in a bend of the River Nidd. Harrogate is known for one curious fact. It is the only place in the country to have had a Whig county councillor in living memory – Cecil Margolis of Harlow ward, who beat off Conservative, Liberal and Labour opposition in the 1981 Elections. Mr Margolis had stood for the Harrogate constituency in the October 1974 General Election, and polled 719 votes.

Social indices:			2001 Gen. Election:			
% Non-white	1.2		LD	23,445	55.6	+4.0
% Prof/Man	39.0		C	14,600	34.6	−3.8
% Non-manual	64.5		Lab	3,101	7.4	−1.4
£ Av prop val 2000	113 K		UKIP	761	1.8	
% Increase 97–00	44.7		PA	272	0.6	
% Unemployed 2001	1.3		LD maj	8,845	21.0	
% Decrease 97–01	1.5		Turnout		64.7	−8.4
% Fin hard/Rank	7.8	528	Elect	65,185		
% Pensioners	29.2					
% Prem mort/Rank	26	407				

Member of Parliament

Phil Willis, a white-haired, black-bushy-eyebrowed comprehensive school head-teacher of Irish Protestant descent, won here for the Liberal Democrats in 1997, by ending the Commons career of Norman Lamont, who had 'chicken-run' to Harrogate after failing to be selected in his changed Kingston constituency. Typecast as the Party's Education spokesman, he can sound like a fairly routine NUT activist on abolishing grammar schools, disliking Chris Woodhead during his tenure as Inspector of Schools, and opposing Tory plans for opted-out schools. A postman's son, born in 1941, he was educated at Burnley Grammar School, City of Leeds and Carnegie College, and Birmingham University, and spent 35 years at the chalk face. He opposes revision of the Commons oath for the benefit of Sinn Fein's MPs, and calls for the 30% 'No' minority in the Northern Ireland referendum on the 1998 Good Friday power-sharing agreement not to be forgotten. In common with 21 of his 52 Liberal Democrat MP colleagues, his political career has been built on his base as a councillor in the constituency.

HARROW EAST

The name of Harrow is probably associated most often by outsiders with the elite boys' school on the hill, attended by Winston Churchill and many other famous men, and bracketed with Eton in terms of privilege, history and social cachet. There is, however, another Harrow, down the hill, which is far from typified by that one institution. The outer north-west London borough of Harrow has a population of almost exactly 200,000. The eastern half is the less affluent, and its non-white population mainly of Indian origin has almost doubled to 30% in the last decade or so. It should not be assumed that the Asian vote, or indeed the Asian 'community', is homogeneous. The ethnic minority population of Harrow East is in the main part of the relatively successful and well-off bloc which spills over the border into Brent North. These are middle-class communities: Kenton and Wealdstone and Stanmore and Harrow Weald. Only the most ignorant of racists would fail to see the distinctions from poorer 'Asian' groups such as the Bangladeshis of Tower Hamlets.

Until 1997 both Harrow East and Brent North were regarded as safe Tory seats, and in 1992 Hugh Dykes had held East by over 11,000. Then disaster struck. Local issues, notably the threatened closure of Edgware hospital, reinforced the huge swing typical of all of outer London, and this corner of the capital's suburbia produced the very worst Conservative performances anywhere. Tony McNulty achieved a turnround of over 18% and Dykes lost by nearly 10,000. Later that very pro-European politician was to leave the Tories and join the Liberal Democrats. His successor as Tory candidate in 2001, Peter Wilding, could make no impact at all on Labour's lead: indeed technically McNulty secured a further wing of 3%, although a bigger movement was to be found in a 9% drop in turnout, and his majority passed into five figures. As in Brent North next door, this affluent middle-class seat with a large Asian minority now looks safe for Labour, as long as they remain in government.

One more interesting feature about Harrow East. In 1998, a typical recent year for which figures are available, more people entered university citing Harrow East as their home constituency than any other in England and Wales. This was due to three main factors: first, most of the top 20 seats in this list (see the table at the front of this book) were in Greater London, not only because of the tradition of education in the metropolitan centre but also because of its high numbers of mature students living in the capital; secondly, the Harrow East electorate is larger than average in size, for the university admissions figures are presented in numerical not percentage terms; and last but not least, a generally high priority is placed on education and qualifications in ethnically Asian households, a factor re-emphasised by the presence of Ealing Southall at second place on this particular list – an ordering which might, one could say, surprise the ignorant.

Social indices:			2001 Gen. Election:			
% Non-white	30.2		Lab	26,590	55.3	+2.8
% Prof/Man	37.7		C	15,466	32.2	−3.3
% Non-manual	67.3		LD	6,021	12.5	+4.3
£ Av prop val 2000	160 K		Lab maj	11,124	23.1	
% Increase 97–00	51.0		Turnout		58.9	−12.4
% Unemployed 2001	2.4		Elect	81,575		
% Decrease 97–01	2.1					
% Fin hard/Rank	8.5	505				
% Pensioners	23.9					
% Prem mort/Rank	21	468				

Member of Parliament

Tony McNulty, elected for Labour in 1997, is a local man. A Harrow councillor 1986–97 (and Council leader, 1995–97) and lecturer at the Polytechnic (then University) of North London, born in 1958 of Kilburn Irish parents, he was educated at Salvatorian (RC) College, Wealdstone, Stanmore Sixth Form College, and Liverpool and Virginia State Universities. His loyalism was reflected in his appointment as a PPS in 1997 to David Blunkett and Baroness Blackstone, and Assistant Whip in 1999. A tough municipal politician, more than at home in the Whips' Office, he has been described (by Liberal Democrat MP Ed Davey) as 'to charm what John Prescott is to sophistication'.

HARROW WEST

In a way, Gareth Thomas of Harrow West is the most unlikely – or at least unexpected – of all Labour MPs. In 1997 he overturned the largest Conservative lead, a numerical majority of 17,890, which reflected 32.7% of the total vote in 1992. He did not achieve quite the largest swing – that in neighbouring Harrow East was slightly larger, for example. Nevertheless it was an astonishing result. Labour had barely squeezed into second place five years before, polling 12,000 to the Tories' 30,000. Labour did even better than their average showing in Outer London, which was their best region anywhere in Britain. This section of outer north-west suburbia was affected by protests against the closure of the local Edgware hospital. Finally, a Referendum candidate took very nearly 2,000 votes, most of which would probably have gone to the Conservative defender, Robert Hughes.

There is much high-class outer London residential commuter housing in Harrow West. Harrow-on-the-Hill, with its famous public school, still cultivates the atmosphere of a prosperous village, rather like Mill Hill, Dulwich and Highgate elsewhere in London. Meanwhile Pinner and Hatch End are very similar in character to the next-door seat of Ruislip-Northwood, considering themselves to be a cut above mere suburbia. There is more middling social ground too, but less than 10% of the housing in either Harrow seat is owned by the council and over 70% of those living in Harrow West are employed in non-manual ('middle-class') jobs. It is true that over 20% of the population belong to non-white ethnic minorities, usually Labour-supporting groups, but in Harrow many of these are middle class, Indian in origin, with a greater than average propensity to vote Conservative – at least until 1997 when Labour formed a new government for the first time for 23 years.

This is part of 'Metroland', which grew extraordinarily rapidly in the inter-war period as London spread along new lines of communication to provide 'homes' (something more than houses) for commuters. The Middlesex county seat of Harrow, once held by Oswald Mosley, rose from 38,000 electors in 1924 to 168,594 at the time of the 1941 by-election; it was to be split into three seats after the war, then reduced to two in 1983. The West constituency had never even been close or considered marginal. It looks less like a Labour seat than just about any in Britain.

Given all the above, it might be expected that 1997 would turn out to be a flash in the pan. Not a bit of it: four years later not only did Thomas hold onto the seat, but he increased his majority substantially, defeating the former Conservative Research Department chief Danny Finkelstein with a further positive swing of over 5%. What can account for this continuing transformation in the politics of Harrow West? Incumbency plays a part, for other Labour MPs of the 1997 intake also held or strengthened their position. There is a regional element too, for elsewhere in north-west London Labour also did extraordinarily well in 2001, in Harrow East and most of all in Brent North. Finally, ethnicity may well play a part too, as in those two seats, with the middle-class Asian communities clearly switching from Conservative to Labour in large numbers. It looks now as if the hospital and Euro-referendum influences were relatively short-term and minor. Whether the other influences are lasting, only time can tell.

Social indices:			2001 Gen. Election:			
% Non-white	22.5		Lab	23,142	49.6	+8.1
% Prof/Man	46.1		C	16,986	36.4	−2.8
% Non-manual	73.2		LD	5,995	12.9	−2.6
£ Av prop val 2000	174 K		UKIP	525	1.1	
% Increase 97–00	53.3		Lab maj	6,156	13.2	
% Unemployed 2001	1.9		Turnout		63.5	−9.5
% Decrease 97–01	1.8		Elect	73,505		
% Fin hard/Rank	7.2	556				
% Pensioners	23.5					
% Prem mort/Rank	10	595				

Member of Parliament

Gareth R. Thomas (the 'R' being required to differentiate him from Gareth Thomas, MP for Clwyd West) was Labour's least expected new MP in 1997. Yet another Labour MP with teacher-councillor credentials, he was born (locally) in 1967, educated (locally) at Hatch End High School, then at Aberystwyth University and King's College, London, taught for four years at nearby Willesden High School, and was a local Harrow councillor for seven years. A loyalist constituency-active MP, who has taken an interest in environmental issues, he became PPS in 1999 to Charles Clarke (then a Home Office minister, but by 2001 in the Cabinet as Chairman of the Labour Party), and sought legislation to make voting compulsory in general elections – even though he had been returned in the 2001 Election with a five-fold increase in his own majority and on a turnout (63%) above the national average.

HARTLEPOOL

Few constituencies have in current times become more associated with their MP than Hartlepool with Peter Mandelson. The transplantation of this to some minds effete but by no means soft (in any sense, including the northern implication of dim) metropolitan southerner to a traditionally working-class steel and dock town in the far north of England was always a cause for query and even merriment, as in the hackneyed story of his alleged mistaking of mushy peas for guacamole. But when he was forced to resign from the Cabinet a second time in January 2001 a swarm of challengers emerged to attempt to finish off his extraordinary political career by ousting him from Parliament too. They too were a colourful bunch.

The Conservative, Gus Robinson, was a larger- and faster-than-life local businessman and boxing promoter, with origins, style and political sophistication in direct contrast with Mandelson's. Two independents rushed forward, including John Booth, the former colleague at the Labour Party's press office who was prevented by new electoral law from standing as Real Labour. Arthur Scargill, the leader and founder of the Socialist Labour Party, chose to contest Hartlepool himself, regarding Mandelson as uniquely worthy of that particular black spot (in 1997 the recipient had been the defecting Conservative MP Alan Howarth, parachuted by New Labour into Newport East in South Wales).

Many observers believed that Mandelson's majority would be slashed, and some that one of the bevy of opponents, perhaps the Liberal Democrat, might actually win. The campaign was conducted as a marginal, despite Labour's 17,500 majority in 1997. Although Mandelson kept out of the national limelight completely, the cameras were in evidence in Hartlepool. Yet on the night Mandelson's remarkable victory speech, full of personal defiant passion, was totally justified. Not only did he win by a mile with all his opponents crushed (Scargill and Booth obtained 3.5% between them, while Robinson was reduced to musing about whether the count had been fiddled), but he actually suffered no significant loss of vote share at all. He did substantially better than Tony Blair, a few miles away in Sedgefield. He – and perhaps Hartlepool too – had indeed been underestimated.

It might be concluded that it was all a matter of Labour's bedrock and unchallengeable strength in a northern heartland seat. Yet Hartlepool was held by the Conservatives from 1959 to 1964, and Labour had only won by 275 in their previous landslide and landmark year of 1945. Hartlepool had never been a homogeneous working-class seat, and there had at times been pockets of great prosperity as the large houses of the old west end physically still show. The long depression in a town of declining industries which had raised unemployment well above average had clearly abated: unemployment fell by 34% between 1997 and 2001. The markedly above-par showing in the north-east region, generally Labour's worst in England, can only suggest that Mandelson did produce an outstanding personal performance after all his travails. As that victory speech itself indicated, he is indeed a fighter not a quitter, and in constituency terms at least a winner not a loser.

Social indices:			2001 Gen. Election:			
% Non-white	0.7		Lab	22,506	59.1	−1.6
% Prof/Man	24.8		C	7,935	20.9	−0.5
% Non-manual	44.6		LD	5,717	15.0	+1.0
£ Av prop val 2000	50 K		SLP	912	2.4	
% Increase 97–00	22.6		Ind	557	1.5	
% Unemployed 2001	6.7		Ind	424	1.1	
% Decrease 97–01	3.4		Lab maj	14,571	38.3	
% Fin hard/Rank	30.6	126	Turnout		56.2	−9.4
% Pensioners	24.5		Elect	67,652		
% Prem mort/Rank	46	78				

Member of Parliament

Peter Mandelson, as a twice-sacked Cabinet Minister, first as Trade Secretary in 1998 after revelations about a large undisclosed loan from Geoffrey Robinson to buy a house, then as Northern Ireland Secretary early in 2001 following allegations that he had improperly intervened in the passport application of the Hinduja brothers, is the man who thus introduced the Second Going into British politics. Born in 1953, son of the advertising manager of the *Jewish Chronicle*, and educated at Hendon County Grammar School and St Catherine's College, Oxford, before his election in 1992 he was employed only in politics-related jobs, whether for unions, television or the Labour Party as communications chief 1985–90. With no hinterland beyond politics, he was the 'onlie begetter' of New Labour, a Blairite before Blair. As Labour's arch spinner he even spun his own familial recollections of his famous grandfather, Herbert Morrison, whom he actually rarely saw because Morrison objected to Mandelson's mother marrying a Jew, and because she resented her parents' loveless marriage and Morrison's remarriage after her mother's death. His first government post as Minister Without Portfolio in 1997 gave him responsibility for the Millennium Dome – with more Morrisonian recollections of the Dome of Discovery at the 1951 Festival of Britain. Like Morrison, he too was friendless in his party; as Ken Livingstone put it: 'formidable, even more loathed in the PLP than I was'. Entwined in the Blair–Brown rivalry as an acolyte of the Prime Minister, he has been seen as 'not half as good as he thinks he is, and not half as bad as everyone else thinks he is' (Neil Kinnock), and as 'a son-of-a-bitch, but a hell of an effective one' (George Galloway MP).

HARWICH

In 1997 the Referendum Party obtained their best result anywhere in Harwich, and in so doing presented Labour with one of their most unlikely gains – or so we all thought at the time. James Goldsmith's creation's candidate was Jeffrey Titford, a prominent local undertaker, with strong name recognition, and as some morbid observers pointed out, a member of one profession that all voters have to use. He obtained 4,923 votes, or 9.2%. Iain Sproat lost to Labour's Ivan Henderson by 1,216, or 2.3%.

However, this interpretation may have to be revised. Almost everyone assumed that Henderson would lose in 2001. Surely the high tide of New Labour had passed, and there was no longer the wreckage of an 18-year Conservative government to clear from the beach. The Referendum Party had died with its founder. Yet Ivan Henderson did win again, with an increased majority and a share of the vote improved by nearly 7%, one of their top 20 performances. The UK Independence Party did again do relatively well, its third best showing and just saving its deposit, but Tony Finnegan-Butler took fewer than half the number of votes that Titford had (with a name less likely to raise the spirits, perhaps). Harwich was undergoing a long-term movement towards Labour quite separate from the European issue. Possible explanations are variably convincing: the decline of the economy of seaside constituencies throughout Britain; the double incumbency of Henderson and his challenger Iain Sproat (Sproat had stood again in 2001, though no longer as an MP); and New Labour's classless and regionless appeal, confirmed by prudence and moderation in office (though Harwich is in Essex, where they notably lost in that Election). One clearer factor was a squeeze on the Liberal Democrats, who went down from an already modest 13% to just 8.5%: a loss of 3,000 votes, when Henderson won by 2,500. Not all of these defecting voters would have gone to Henderson, of course, and some must have stayed at home – but the fall in turnout was less than the national average here.

The Harwich constituency covers the north-eastern corner of Essex, and is centred on the seaside resorts of Clacton and the less brash Frinton-on-Sea and Walton-on-the-Naze as well as the east coast ferry port of Harwich. Harwich used to be a safe Conservative seat: even in 1966 Labour had been adrift by fully 6,640 votes. At the

1992 General Election, Iain Sproat obtained over half of all the votes cast, while the Liberal Democrats and Labour each received just under a quarter; this even split of the opposition allowed him to bask in a 17,000 majority. There are a number of Labour and Liberal Democrat wards, at least in local elections. Harwich is a hard-working and gritty port, and Labour can win most of its wards, along with the new private estate of Golf Green in Jaywick south of Clacton, and Ramsey inland from Harwich.

This is a very elderly seat. It ranks in the top half-dozen constituencies in terms of the proportion of pensioners, the only one on this particular list not on the south coast of England. The coastal wards of Clacton, and Walton and Frinton, all have between half and two-thirds of their households consisting solely of pensioners. Frinton is known for its restrictive local practices designed to keep the town sufficiently genteel. Elderly voters are the most hostile to European integration, and this may also have helped boost the anti-European vote in 1997 and 2001. They do turn out in greater numbers than younger voters. But it is now clear that they cannot be assumed to be reliably Conservative, and further predictions in Harwich would be hostages to fortune.

Social indices:			2001 Gen. Election:			
% Non-white	0.7		Lab	21,951	45.6	+6.9
% Prof/Man	27.9		C	19,355	40.2	+3.7
% Non-manual	52.9		LD	4,099	8.5	−4.6
£ Av prop val 2000	77 K		UKIP	2,463	5.1	
% Increase 97–00	45.8		Ind	247	0.5	
% Unemployed 2001	3.6		Lab maj	2,596	5.4	
% Decrease 97–01	2.9		Turnout		62.1	−8.6
% Fin hard/Rank	8.4	510	Elect	77,539		
% Pensioners	43.7					
% Prem mort/Rank	32	297				

Member of Parliament

Ivan Henderson, PPS to Home Office Minister Keith Bradley from 2001, a local dock worker who rose to become an RMT union organiser, is one of Labour's rare ex-manual worker MPs elected here in 1997 for a seat never previously held by Labour. A short man, with a down-turned mouth, born in 1958 and counting himself the first native-born MP for Harwich since Sir Anthony Deane in 1679, he attended the local comprehensive school named after his seventeenth-century predecessor, and has built his political career out of a defence of the local merchant marine industry. His union roots have not precluded his staunch loyalty to the Blairite credo, acknowledged by his promotion to PPS in 2001, and in December 2001 the about-to-defect rebel MP, Paul Marsden, claimed that he, as one of a group of MPs allegedly intimidating him, called him a 'f—ing traitor'. He tends to bowl loyalist questions, though tabled only five written ones in his first year.

HASTINGS AND RYE

There are some seats which are quite clearly changing in their economic and social nature and thus in their political preferences. Michael Jabez Foster became the first non-Tory MP in Hastings for nearly 100 years in 1997, and he almost exactly doubled his percentage majority in 2001. More strikingly still, his percentage share of the vote increased from 34 to 47. This was the best by a very considerable margin of all of the 640 candidates put forward by his party on 7 June 2001. Demographic and sociological transformations cannot work that quickly, and the problems of economic decline rarely do so. Another factor must have been at work. It is not hard to find it.

At the same time, another record was being set in the 1997–2001 comparisons. The Liberal Democrat share fell by 17.6%, clearly the worst of any of their 640 efforts. Tactical voting was taking place on a massive scale. It is difficult to avoid the conclusion that this was not a matter of voters just working out for themselves the best way to keep the Tories from regaining Hastings, for the Lib Dems had been only 600 votes from second place in 1997, and just over 3,000 off the lead itself. Had a deal been done between the parties, say involving Labour refraining from their best efforts in neighbouring Folkestone?

On the local Hastings Borough Council, Labour wins in wards with a strong working-class and council estate presence like Hollington, Ore, Broomgrove, and the quaintly named Wishing Tree, although the turnout here in the May 2000 contests was abysmal, usually under 20%. The Conservatives fight back in the faded resort of St Leonards. The constituency also includes the old Cinque Ports of Rye and Winchelsea and the modern beach resort of Camber Sands, as it forms the easternmost division in East Sussex, stretching to the Kent border. This terrain looks better for the Tories.

The Conservatives have not been over-popular in Hastings for some time. The recession struck the local tourist industry. There is a high proportion of elderly people adversely affected by the imposition of VAT on heating fuel. Young people living on social security wander aimlessly through the streets. The fishing industry has disappeared. Hastings does not wear a comfortable air of affluence. There is a major local issue surrounding the proposed road bypass, which promises new high-technology jobs to revivify the economy at the expense of despoiling green field sites, but poll suggestions that a majority of local residents are not convinced by the environmental argument are borne out by a lower than average Green vote in 2001. The lines are drawn as a major two-party battle in Hastings now, and whoever can offer the best hope of economic recovery is likely to win.

Social indices:			2001 Gen. Election:			
% Non-white	1.6		Lab	19,402	47.1	+12.7
% Prof/Man	32.8		C	15,094	36.6	+7.5
% Non-manual	56.6		LD	4,266	10.3	−17.6
£ Av prop val 2000	77 K		UKIP	911	2.2	+1.2
% Increase 97–00	38.8		Grn	721	1.7	
% Unemployed 2001	4.1		Ind	486	1.2	
% Decrease 97–01	3.6		MRLP	198	0.5	+0.2
% Fin hard/Rank	16.2	333	Ind	140	0.3	
% Pensioners	32.7		Lab maj	4,308	10.5	
% Prem mort/Rank	33	277	Turnout		58.4	−11.4
			Elect	70,632		

Member of Parliament

Michael Jabez Foster, PPS to the Law Officers, won this seat in 1997 as Labour's second least expected MP. A very local Labour MP as a native son of Hastings, born in 1946 and educated at Hastings Grammar School and Leicester University, he has long been active in both Hastings Borough Council and East Sussex County Council, contested the constituency three times previously, and was a local solicitor for nearly 20 years, specialising in employment law. In the Christian Socialist Movement (as a Methodist), he employs his biblical middle name only to distinguish himself from the anti-hunting Michael Foster, MP for Worcester, whose hate mail from hunting enthusiasts he otherwise received. He fluently campaigns on the serious social problems in Hastings, which were responsible for his election as its first non-Tory MP in 95 years. A keen supporter, against environmental lobbyists, of the proposed Hastings by-pass as a major stimulant to job creation, he was critical of the government's cancellation of the project in 2001, wondering how it 'could have overlooked the poverty of my constituents – the 28th poorest town in Britain'. Before becoming a PPS he had also criticised legal aid reforms.

HAVANT

Every national opinion poll published during the 2001 General Election campaign suggested that Labour was ahead by a double-figure percentage, and some by pollsters with massive reputations placed it above 20%. Such would project to a substantial increase in Mr Blair's majority, and attention was turned to Tory seats – and prominent personalities – vulnerable under such circumstances. In this category was Havant, and its intellectual member, David Willetts. He had held on by under 4,000 in 1997 after suffering a pro-Labour swing of 13%. His loss would be yet another major blow to the Tory leadership team, as well as an historic transformation in England's deep south.

If the Tories had indeed regressed further in 2001 Havant may well have fallen. It is right next door to a bloc of seats – Portsmouth North and Gosport, for example, which did swing further to Labour. Yet not only were the polls wrong – Labour only won nationally by 9% – but Willetts did better than his colleagues in nearby urban south Hampshire, resisting some tactical voting, benefiting from the decline in the anti-European party vote, and increasing his own share by 4%. He may now look forward to a further duration of tenure during which his frontbench career should flourish.

The population of the Borough of Havant, situated just north of Portsmouth, increased from 35,000 in 1951 to 109,000 in 1971. Until 1974 it was part of a Portsmouth seat, Langstone, which was of course greatly inflated by Havant's growth. Havant then earned a seat of its own. This is not an upper-middle-class seat, nor one which on the surface seems appropriate for the cerebrally-enhanced Willetts. There are post-war council estates in Labour wards like Barncroft, Battins, Bondfields and Warren Park. The Conservative portions are typified by modern private estates in wards like Stakes and Purbrook; and Hayling Island, lying flat between muddy, swampy Langstone and Chichester harbours and identified with retirement bungalows and holiday camps traditionally associated with visitors from places such as Reading. This is not the landscape of Tom Quad with its cathedral in Willetts' alma mater, Christ Church, Oxford. For nearly three decades this area safely returned Sir Ian Lloyd, the right-winger who was sometimes known as the 'Member for South Africa'. David Willetts may be a different kind of MP but he is still favourite for a similar tenure.

Social indices:			2001 Gen. Election:				
% Non-white	0.9		C	17,769	43.9	+4.2	
% Prof/Man	31.7		Lab	13,562	33.5	+1.5	
% Non-manual	53.5		LD	7,508	18.6	-3.8	
£ Av prop val 2000	104 K		Grn	793	2.0		
% Increase 97–00	38.1		UKIP	561	1.4		
% Unemployed 2001	2.5		Ind	244	0.6		
% Decrease 97–01	2.4		C maj	4,207	10.4		
% Fin hard/Rank	21.0	254	Turnout		57.6	-13.1	
% Pensioners	26.8		Elect	70,246			
% Prem mort/Rank	31	325					

Member of Parliament

David Willetts co-authored the book *Is Conservatism Dead?* (1997), and concluded it wasn't, so long as one meant 'civic conservatism', a.k.a. a further retreat of the State. Born in 1956 and educated at King Edward's School, Birmingham and Christ Church, Oxford, he has spent his entire working life as a policy worker for Tory ministers or at the Centre for Policy Studies, until elected here in 1992. Apart from his slip-up over Sir Geoffrey Johnson-Smith's 'wanting' advice on Neil Hamilton (when he was forced to resign as Paymaster General for apparently trying to influence the proceedings of the Standards and Privileges Committee), his rise has been effortless, as befits the professional politician, trimming as required. Otherwise 'massively clever', but without 'bottomless reserves of humour', he drew the short straw as drafter of the 2001 Conservative Election manifesto. A Lilley, then Hague, voter in 1997, he shadowed Education (1998–99) and Social Security (1999–2001) under Hague, voted for Portillo in 2001 and survived – with eight other Portillistas – in Iain Duncan Smith's Shadow Cabinet as spokesman on Work and Pensions.

HAYES AND HARLINGTON

If one travelled the streets of the west London marginal constituency of Hayes and Harlington during the days before the April 1992 Election, one would have thought that Labour was on target to make a vital gain. Every fourth house or so seemed to sport a poster for the Labour candidate John McDonnell. Very few proclaimed 'I love Dicks', the rather engaging slogan for the sitting Tory MP Terry Dicks. Yet Terry Dicks did win the election, albeit by just 53 votes, one of the slimmest margins in the election. Perhaps the voters' reluctance to admit openly to supporting the Conservatives is bred by the same phenomenon that helped to lead all the pre-election polls to show Labour doing better than they eventually did. Speaking to a pollster is free of charge; many people believed that they would be better off under a Conservative government because Labour would put taxes up. Some people may have given poll-takers the 'politically correct' line and then voted according to their own perceived interests in the privacy of the booth. It is also clear that Conservatives were disproportionately disinclined to talk to pollsters, just as they were to put up posters. This phenomenon was still apparent nationally in the 2001 Election campaign, though it had no bearing on the result in Hayes and Harlington. Indeed it is hard to imagine now that the seat was won by the Conservatives just nine years before. Neither its gritty and unglamorous appearance nor its recent election results betray this truth. In 2001 John McDonnell won by nearly 13,500 and it would now take a swing of over 20% for it to change hands again.

Hayes and Harlington is situated in the south-eastern corner of the borough of Hillingdon. Almost all of Heathrow Airport is in the seat, as are the communities of Yeading, Wood End and Harmondsworth. Nearly all the wards would have been close in the April 1992 photo-finish; Charville is probably the Conservatives' best ward, Barnhill, Botwell and Townfield (the heart of Hayes town) are the most solid for Labour; but all 23 councillors elected within the seat in May 1998 were Labour. The seat used to be almost all white, but the ethnic minority population virtually doubled in the 1980s, mainly due to an influx of Sikhs; it might be remembered that this seat is right next door to Ealing Southall. Hayes and Harlington is not posh. There are few professional and managerial workers or adults with higher educational qualifications. This seat was regularly Labour before the late MP Neville Sandelson defected to the SDP in the early 1980s, and it has now returned to that allegiance.

Social indices:			2001 Gen. Election:			
% Non-white	21.2		Lab	21,279	65.7	+3.7
% Prof/Man	25.1		C	7,813	24.1	−3.1
% Non-manual	51.9		LD	1,958	6.0	−1.4
£ Av prop val 2000	110 K		BNP	705	2.2	
% Increase 97–00	59.7		Ind	648	2.0	
% Unemployed 2001	2.4		Lab maj	13,466	41.6	
% Decrease 97–01	2.2		Turnout		56.3	−16.0
% Fin hard/Rank	14.2	367	Elect	57,561		
% Pensioners	20.2					
% Prem mort/Rank	34	263				

Member of Parliament

John McDonnell is the Labour MP to whom the term 'usual suspect' more than adequately applies. Elected in 1997, he was the most rebellious of that year's intake of 183 MPs – with 59 dissentient votes – and with only one MP (Jeremy Corbyn) more rebellious in the entire 418-strong PLP. He rebelled as soon as possible in the new Parliament in 2001 – over the EU Nice Treaty, the bombing of Afghanistan, and the Terrorism, Crime and Security Bill. A throwback to the days of the GLC when he actually fell out with Ken Livingstone over trimming on setting a rate, he was born in 1951, the son of a Liverpool-Irish docker-turned-bus-driver, and educated at Great Yarmouth Grammar School, Burnley Technical College, Brunel University and

Birkbeck College, London. Slight, dapper and good-looking with aquiline features, he has spent a lifetime as a political apparatchik either in Unions (NUM and TUC) or local government, as a full-time GLC councillor for Hayes and Harlington (1982–86), and, with no prospects for this unreconstructed Campaign Grouper at Westminster, he has climbed back onto Livingstone's resuscitated London bandwagon, advising the Mayor, and is assiduous in his defence of minorities such as the Irish in Britain and the Punjabis of his own constituency.

HAZEL GROVE

Sir Tom Arnold held on to the Hazel Grove seat with hairsbreadth majorities on four occasions, the last being in 1992, before retiring through ill health at the early age of 50. It came as no surprise that Andrew Stunell gained Hazel Grove for the Liberal Democrats in 1997, and gained it easily, racking up his party's third highest numerical majority among their 46 seats. Within an even richer harvest in 2001, Hazel Grove slipped slightly down the list of safety but stays in the top ten, and presumably among the last to fall should party fortunes decline to their more traditional levels.

This is a seat which has a long history of Liberal success, even in those eras of thinner pickings. In 1966 the seat of Cheadle, from which it was to be carved, was gained by Dr Michael Winstanley at the General Election. Cheadle was regained by the Tories in 1970, but when Cheadle was split in February 1974 Michael Winstanley correctly estimated that the most favourable parts to the Liberals were contained in Hazel Grove, which he duly won. Then came Tom Arnold's reign, or rather period as representative at Westminster, for the Liberal Democrats have consistently managed to win all six Stockport borough council wards within the constituency.

This seat in the south-eastern sector of the metropolitan borough of Stockport is not quite so well-off, or as suburban, as Cheadle in the south-west, not quite so 'naturally' Tory. As well as Hazel Grove itself, a strongly owner-occupied and middle-class commuting dormitory on the Buxton-to-Manchester rail line, and the more working-class ward of Great Moor further in towards Stockport (where the Liberals squeeze potential Labour support), there are the semi-rural towns of Marple, Romiley and Bredbury out towards the Pennine hills. Stunell should now be able to build on this very solid local base of support and appears to have a safe seat.

Social indices:			2001 Gen. Election:			
% Non-white	1.0		LD	20,020	52.0	−2.5
% Prof/Man	38.5		C	11,585	30.1	−0.4
% Non-manual	64.5		Lab	6,230	16.2	+4.3
£ Av prop val 2000	85 K		UKIP	643	1.7	+1.1
% Increase 97–00	26.4		LD maj	8,435	21.9	
% Unemployed 2001	1.6		Turnout		59.1	−18.4
% Decrease 97–01	0.9		Elect	65,107		
% Fin hard/Rank	11.7	418				
% Pensioners	26.6					
% Prem mort/Rank	25	417				

Member of Parliament

Andrew Stunell, Liberal Democrat Chief Whip from 2001 (and Deputy 1997–2001), won here in 1997 after narrowly missing victory in 1992. An architect, son of a civil engineer, born in the Surrey suburbs in 1942, he was educated at Surbiton Grammar School, Kingston Polytechnic and Manchester University, and worked as an architect for Runcorn New Town for 14 years. Environmentally concerned – in the Liberal mode – he has introduced a Bill to reduce 'unnecessary over-packaging' of retail products. With experience of a Lib-Con coalition on Cheshire County Council, he is no automatic endorser of the tacit packaging of the Liberals as a primarily anti-Tory Party, on which most of his colleagues' electoral success has been based.

HEMEL HEMPSTEAD

New Town seats in southern England were generally resistant to Labour's appeal in the 1980s and early 1990s: Harlow, Basildon, Welwyn-Hatfield, Stevenage and Crawley would be good examples. Then in 1997 the appeal of Tony Blair's party lured all of these seats into the fold, and along with them came Hemel Hempstead, the successor to the former West Hertfordshire division.

As the county of Hertfordshire has gained extra seats in successive boundary reviews, the seat based on the town of Hemel Hempstead has gradually been reduced to an urban core, with only a few semi-rural and village areas in addition, such as Flamstead and Markyate and the larger Kings Langley. Hemel Hempstead itself is a New Town, with a relatively high proportion of housing originally built by the public sector. In Dacorum borough elections there are a number of solid Labour wards, like Adeyfield East and West, Bennetts End, Chaulden/Shrubhill, Gadebridge and Grovehill.

Before 1997 this territory was outweighed by variety of other towns such as Tring and Harpenden. Yet it was not the boundary changes that ousted Robert Jones in that year, but rather the national decline in the Conservative vote. Labour's Tony McWalter won by over 3,500. Hemel Hempstead remains a relatively affluent town in a prosperous corner of south-eastern England, but this was not held against Labour in 2001; indeed much credit may well have been given to Tony Blair and especially Gordon Brown for maintaining financial stability, high employment and property values, which rose by 46% here during Labour's first term. More than in most places, the instrumental voters of Hemel appreciated the end of the association of the Labour Party with incompetent stewardship and financial crises. McWalter was returned with a slightly increased majority.

Social indices:

			2001 Gen. Election:			
% Non-white	3.2		Lab/Coop	21,389	46.7	+1.0
% Prof/Man	35.3		C	17,647	38.5	−0.6
% Non-manual	61.5		LD	5,877	12.8	+0.5
£ Av prop val 2000	126 K		UKIP	920	2.0	
% Increase 97–00	46.1		L/C maj	3,742	8.2	
% Unemployed 2001	1.5		Turnout		63.6	−13.5
% Decrease 97–01	1.0		Elect	72,086		
% Fin hard/Rank	13.1	395				
% Pensioners	23.2					
% Prem mort/Rank	13	557				

Member of Parliament

Tony McWalter, Labour's balding, red-faced victor here in 1997, cuts an eccentric dash as a Kantian philosopher, who prudently avoids discussing his hero on the doorsteps of Hemel Hempstead. Son of a painter and decorator, he was born in 1945 and educated at St Benedict's (RC), Ealing, and amassed five degrees from Aberystwyth and McMaster Universities, and University College, Oxford. An ex-polytechnic lecturer for 25 years, in philosophy and computing, his Catholicism is reflected in an interest in Northern Ireland, and his Kantian idealism in abstentions on lone parent and disability benefit cuts, and – in the new House elected in 2001 – against banning incitement to religious hatred (in the anti-terrorism legislation). In February 2002 he less than helpfully asked Tony Blair for 'a brief characterisation of the political philosophy which underlies his policies'.

HEMSWORTH

Hemsworth is a famous name, in electoral history at least. This is the seat which produced the largest Labour majority in so many general elections, remaining at over 30,000 in every contest between 1950 and 1974. This is where it was said that the Labour votes were weighed and not counted. The majority is not now so large as it was, due to boundary changes in 1983 which reduced its electorate, and the monolithic nature of the seat was weakened a little in the 1997 redistribution as well.

The constituency is based on the mining towns of Hemsworth, South Kirkby and South Elmsall, at the very heart of the former West Yorkshire coalfield. More widely known, perhaps, is Featherstone, a large mining village of 10,000 souls, with a famed community spirit – its Rugby League team has occasionally qualified to play teams from much larger towns in the Cup Final at Wembley. It is also a mighty Labour stronghold: in the May 1996 Wakefield borough elections, for example, the Labour candidate obtained 94% of the vote in a straight fight with a hapless Tory.

In 1997 a thoroughly anomalous ward was added: Wakefield South, which is by far the most Conservative part of the whole borough. It consists of suburbanised villages which are favoured residential areas for commuters to Wakefield, such as Crigglestone and Sandal. In May 2000 the Conservatives polled 65% in Wakefield South to Labour's 23%. It has nothing in common with the rest of the Hemsworth seat, which remains imbued with the culture and spirit of coal-mining even if that industry has essentially been destroyed. In 1981 more people were employed in mining in Hemsworth than in any other seat except for Dennis Skinner's Bolsover. This kind of tradition does not die quickly, and can more than absorb a pinprick from Wakefield South. In 2001 Jon Trickett retained the seat he had won in a by-election in 1996 (on the death of Derek Enright) by 15,000 votes.

Social indices:			2001 Gen. Election:				
% Non-white	0.7		Lab	23,036	65.4	−5.2	
% Prof/Man	26.3		C	7,400	21.0	+3.2	
% Non-manual	45.2		LD	3,990	11.3	+2.5	
£ Av prop val 2000	62 K		SLP	801	2.3		
% Increase 97–00	19.1		Lab maj	15,636	44.4		
% Unemployed 2001	3.4		Turnout		51.8	−16.1	
% Decrease 97–01	2.4		Elect	67,948			
% Fin hard/Rank	28.4	152					
% Pensioners	23.2						
% Prem mort/Rank	36	232					

Member of Parliament

Jon Trickett is a former Bennite Leeds councillor for 12 years who via leadership of the Council (1989–96) won this seat in 1996, and crowned his rightward trajectory by becoming PPS to Peter Mandelson (1997–98). A former plumber and builder for 12 years before becoming a full-time councillor for seven, he was born in 1950 and educated at Roundhay School, Leeds and studied politics at Hull and Leeds Universities. Given his leftist past, it was ironic that he was the first Labour candidate to be opposed by a Scargill Socialist whom he saw off, and then attacked Scargill for lacking the guts himself to face the humiliation of polling only 1,200 votes. For a former big city politician, his brief Westminster career as Mandelson's PPS comes as something of an anti-climax. In 2001 he joined the Public Accounts Committee, whilst also permitting himself a rebellious vote against the clause in the Terrorism, Crime and Security Bill banning incitement to religious hatred.

HENDON

The threatened closure of Edgware hospital did the Conservative government no favours at all in outer north-west London in 1997, suffering huge swings well above the national average. Edgware is in the Hendon seat, which Labour won in this new seat's first-ever contest by over 6,000 votes, defeating the veteran member Sir John Gorst, who had been in the House since 1970. His own efforts on behalf of the hospital had proved in vain, for his own cause at least.

The seat is divided into three quite distinct sections. In the north, on the edge of the city, are the middle-class suburbs of Edgware and Mill Hill. In the latter there is a touch of genuine wealth: expensive houses enjoying something of a rural village ambience around a famous public school. To the south, though, is the vast inter-war council estate of Burnt Oak, once known as Watling and studied by the pioneering sociologist Ruth Durant Glass. There is a very modern local authority development at

Grahame Park, built on the old Hendon airfield, and the Colindale ward is also predominantly working class. Both Burnt Oak and Colindale wards are strongly Labour.

In between are the two wards which truly justify the new seat's name: Hendon and West Hendon, politically closer, if not exactly 'in the centre'; the Liberal Democrats are weak here, their strength being confined to the Mill Hill ward, which they win in local elections. One of the reasons Labour has a significant presence in this seat is that over a fifth of its residents are non-white: 35% in West Hendon, 33% in Colindale. There is possibly an even stronger Jewish influence, although this is not as yet quantifiable in published census returns. Both Asian and Jewish communities are known for their commitment to education, and it should come as no surprise that Hendon constituency provided the third highest number of students entering university of all seats according to the latest available UCAS figure – and indeed the constituency is the site of several of London's leading tutorial colleges which do an excellent job of improving and imparting A level grades.

This is not inner-city territory, but it is 'London-half-way-out': a heterogeneous segment of the nation's big city, with mixed political characteristics to boot. As elsewhere in north-west London, New Labour further improved their position in 2001 in what remained a major party battle. Clearly they had the right formula to appeal here over the turn of the century.

Social indices:			2001 Gen. Election:			
% Non-white	22.1		Lab	21,432	52.5	+3.1
% Prof/Man	40.3		C	14,015	34.3	−2.7
% Non-manual	68.1		LD	4,724	11.6	+0.7
£ Av prop val 2000	171 K		UKIP	409	1.0	+0.5
% Increase 97–00	53.2		WRP	164	0.4	+0.1
% Unemployed 2001	3.2		Ind	107	0.3	
% Decrease 97–01	2.2		Lab maj	7,417	18.2	
% Fin hard/Rank	16.7	323	Turnout		52.2	−13.4
% Pensioners	24.7		Elect	78,212		
% Prem mort/Rank	20	483				

Member of Parliament

Andrew Dismore, a wire-rimmed-spectacled solicitor, was a surprise Labour winner in 1997. Born in 1954, a hotelier's son, educated at Bridlington Grammar School, Warwick University, the LSE and Guildford College of Law, he cut his political teeth as leader (1990–97) of the Labour minority on Westminster Council during the controversial Tory leadership of Dame Shirley Porter. An assiduous constituency MP with Greek Cypriot and Jewish minorities, he has sought legislation to ease religious restrictions on remarriage of Jewish women, rebelled on air traffic control privatisation, and allowed the expelled Ken Livingstone to canvass for him in 2001. Despite this he found himself on the Standards and Privileges Committee in 2001.

HENLEY

'One high-profile mane of blond hair replaces another in Henley' and 'Eurosceptic gain from Europhile' were trite ways to describe the only political change in the south Oxfordshire constituency safely passed on from Michael Ray Dibdin Heseltine to Alexander Boris de Pfeffer Johnson in 2001. True enough, the seat's solid Conservatism encourages personalisation of its successive members in order to find political differentiation and news value, even though this does a disservice to the subtler characteristics of Messrs Heseltine and Johnson and indeed of the Henley division itself. There are in fact some very un-Conservative parts of the seat.

Take Berinsfield, for example, the highly untypical and raw little overspill estate rather than village, outside Dorchester-on-Thames. In May 1999 the Tory candidate received just 25 votes there, or 3.7%, as the Liberal Democrats ousted a long-term Labour councillor. In those most recent local elections before the 2001 general contest, the Lib Dems also topped the poll in Benson, Chalgrove, Clifton Hampden, Crowmarsh, Forest Hill, Garsington (where the intellectual socialite lady Ottoline Morrell held court in the era of the Bloomsbury Group), Great Milton (site of Raymond Blanc's luxurious and possibly unsurpassed Manoir aux Quat' Saisons restaurant and hotel), Horspath (tucked behind the Cowley motor works), Watlington, Wheatley (last turn-off from the A40 before Oxford) and Woodcote.

Much more redolent of the constituency's political flavour are the ever-fashionable town of Henley-on-Thames, at the southern end of the seat, and Thame at its north end. Here too are Goring, beside the river; and Rotherfield Peppard, Nettlebed and Sonning Common, which are favoured by Reading's well-off commuters. Taking the constituency as a whole, it is one of the dozen with the fewest number of households in financial hardship. It ranks 627th out of the 641 seats in Britain on the index of premature mortality, poverty and avoidable deaths.

So it is possible to write about the seat rather than the MPs. Nevertheless, Boris did win easily enough in 2001, and should have a solid platform for a long and no doubt colourful parliamentary career. Despite all that local success, the Liberal Democrats only took 27% of the vote, fully 10% less than in the South Oxfordshire locals, and squeezed Labour hardly at all, as they garnered over 9,300 preferences: not bad, with no district or county councillors at all.

Social indices:			2001 Gen. Election:			
% Non-white	1.0		C	20,466	46.1	−0.3
% Prof/Man	44.0		LD	12,008	27.0	+2.3
% Non-manual	64.1		Lab	9,367	21.1	−1.6
£ Av prop val 2000	216 K		UKIP	1,413	3.2	
% Increase 97–00	71.9		Grn	1,147	2.6	+1.6
% Unemployed 2001	0.8		C maj	8,458	19.0	
% Decrease 97–01	0.8		Turnout		64.3	−13.3
% Fin hard/Rank	3.6	631	Elect	69,081		
% Pensioners	23.0					
% Prem mort/Rank	5	627				

Member of Parliament

Boris Johnson succeeded Michael Heseltine as MP here in 2001 – in his own words, the 'replacement of a snappy dresser with a man in stumblebum suits'. Defeated at Clwyd South in 1997 despite having gone to the trouble of learning Welsh for 'fish and chips', he was born in 1964, educated at Eton and Balliol College, Oxford, and worked as a journalist on the *Daily Telegraph* for 12 years before becoming editor of the *Spectator*, a post he retained after his election to the Commons. His deft self-presentation as a dishevelled young-fogeyish toff employing 1950s prep school argot, suggests acknowledgement of the fact that contemporary society accepts upper- and upper-middle-class mores only in the form of caricature. Nor indeed is his Englishness entirely pukka, with his paternal great-grandfather, Ali Kemal, having served as the last Interior Minister of the Turkish Empire before being murdered by Ataturk supporters. With journalistic outlets affording ample scope for humorous attitudinising, he has deplored the 'emotional correctness' of banning Rule Britannia from the Last Night of the Proms after the destruction of the World Trade Center; claimed that to describe the Muslim fundamentalist view of women as 'medieval' is an insult to the Middle Ages; urged low tax on Henley-brewed Brakspear's 'russet-hued nectar'; called for the speed limit to be raised to 80 mph; and described the Conservatives as 'a pragmatic, moderately Eurosceptic Party'. His own Euro-scepticism indeed permitted him, as one of only four of the 33-strong Tory intake of 2001, to back Kenneth Clarke for leader, claiming that 'with his boisterous, biffing, bonhomous temperament and his great spinnaker of a belly, he would provide a splendid contrast to the actorishness of Tony Blair'. Asked how William Hague was playing on the doorstep in the 2001 Election he enthused 'Huge, oh huge'!

HEREFORD

Almost unnoticed among the general impressions of Conservative failure and continued and indeed extended Liberal Democrat (and of course Labour) success in 2001 were around ten seats that the Lib Dems nearly lost to the Conservatives. Some of these had been marked down as vulnerable and their retention actually was seen as a cause for relief: Somerton/Frome, and Weston super Mare in Somerset, Devon West and North in foot-and-mouth country, Brecon/Radnor, Argyll/Bute and Southport where the long-serving MP retired. However in Hereford Paul Keetch suffered from none of these varying difficulties and yet still almost lost to the Tory Virginia Taylor. His share of the vote fell by fully 7%. Of the 37 defending Lib Dem MPs, only Peter Brand of the Isle of Wight did worse – and he was one of the two to be defeated.

When the Liberal Democrats reaped a haul of 46 seats in May 1997, their most since 1929, a number of seats finally fell in which they had been challenging closely for years. One of these was Hereford. They had trailed Sir Colin Shepherd by 3,000 in 1992, but reversed that result with double his majority. Hereford city itself has light industry and a surprisingly high proportion of council housing, especially in the south-western wards of Belmont and St Martins. The proportion of professional, managerial and white-collar workers is lower than the national average. This means that there was a substantial basic Labour vote for the Liberals to squeeze – Labour were themselves only 2,750 votes away from victory in the constituency in 1966. The Liberal Democrats have also achieved some of their greatest municipal successes here and they now hold most of the city seats on the Herefordshire unitary authority. However the all-out elections for that new body in May 2000 reveal the secret of Virginia Taylor's fine showing for the Tories. Across the seat as a whole the Lib Dems only polled 36%, to the combined 53% for Conservatives and Independents, who were still to be found contesting village seats successfully at the beginning of the twenty-first century.

The rural areas of southern Herefordshire have proved harder ground for the centrists. Here are Ross and the Wye valley, Abbey Dore and the Golden Valley, the Welsh border and the Black Mountains. This is an excellent stock-raising area (Hereford itself has the busiest municipal cattle market in England), and important for cereals, sugar-beet and fruit. The Hereford seat was Conservative from 1931, when the last Liberal member was defeated, to 1997. They are still very competitive, even at a time of national humiliation, and it remains to be seen whether the Welsh Marcher country will emulate the Scottish borders in their long-term preference for a centre alternative.

Social indices:			2001 Gen. Election:				
% Non-white	0.7		LD	18,244	40.9	−7.1	
% Prof/Man	29.2		C	17,276	38.7	+3.4	
% Non-manual	49.7		Lab	6,739	15.1	+2.6	
£ Av prop val 2000	90 K		UKIP	1,184	2.7		
% Increase 97–00	42.4		Grn	1,181	2.6		
% Unemployed 2001	2.3		LD maj	968	2.2		
% Decrease 97–01	1.9		Turnout		63.5	−11.8	
% Fin hard/Rank	14.8	356	Elect	70,305			
% Pensioners	27.7						
% Prem mort/Rank	21	464					

Member of Parliament

Paul Keetch, victor here in 1997, is in the Liberal tradition of local boy made good – born (1961) in Hereford, educated at Hereford High School and Sixth Form College, a former local councillor, with an ear close to the ground as an ex-PR man, defending Hereford cattle farmers and voting conservatively on hunting (in 2001 and 2002 votes backing his colleague Lembit Opik's 'Middle Way' of hunt-licensing), and a Defence spokesman from 1999, reflecting the importance of the local presence of the SAS HQ. A forceful, even an abrasive, speaker, he is a classic Liberal Democrat professional politician, right down to the statement that for him 'cider has always been a passion'.

HERTFORD AND STORTFORD

East Hertfordshire is a very Conservative part of England. Following the award of an 11th and extra seat to the county by the Commission which reported in 1995, there are now three safe Tory divisions fringing the Essex border: Broxbourne, Hertfordshire North East, and, between the two, Hertford and Stortford.

The seat consists of four towns and the countryside between. The towns, in order of size, are Bishops Stortford (with a population in 1991 of 28,000, up 22% over the past ten years), the county seat of Hertford (22,000), Ware (17,000) and Sawbridgeworth (8,000). These are not industrial or working class, but prosperous market towns which have developed as favoured office, service and residential centres. All vote Conservative at general election time, and indeed most other times too. Even in 2001 the new Tory candidate Mark Prisk, replacing Bowen Wells who had been in the Commons for 22 years, held on by 5,603 after none of the three main parties' shares of the vote changed significantly. The Liberal Democrats have some success locally in Ware and central Bishop's Stortford, and Labour win the Sele council estate in the north-western quadrant of Hertford and are competitive in the county town's Bengeo and Castle wards, but essentially this is Tory England, and will remain so.

The Conservative hold of the seat reflected the result in the mock elections in one of its finest and most long-standing institutions, Haileybury, the public school founded as a training college for the East India Company and later merged with the Imperial Service College attended by Rudyard Kipling. Haileybury may no longer tell the empire what to do, but the Hertford and Stortford seat certainly followed its lead in June 2001.

Social indices:			2001 Gen. Election:			
% Non-white	1.6		C	21,074	44.7	+0.6
% Prof/Man	43.2		Lab	15,471	32.8	+1.4
% Non-manual	68.0		LD	9,388	19.9	+2.2
£ Av prop val 2000	148 K		UKIP	1,243	2.6	+0.4
% Increase 97–00	58.2		C maj	5,603	11.9	
% Unemployed 2001	0.7		Turnout		62.8	–13.3
% Decrease 97–01	1.1		Elect	75,141		
% Fin hard/Rank	6.4	575				
% Pensioners	20.8					
% Prem mort/Rank	10	590				

Member of Parliament

Mark Prisk, a Cornish exile from a Tory-free county, was elected here in 2001 after having lost Wansdyke, then a Conservative-held seat, to Labour in 1997. Born in 1962, he attended Truro School and Reading University and worked as a chartered surveyor and ran his own business consultancy. Once listed by Julie Kilbride, then of the *Daily Telegraph*, as a One Nation Conservative, he backed Michael Portillo in all three of the leadership ballots in July 2001. As an MP for one of the home counties most submerged under concrete and bricks, he seeks to protect Hertfordshire's green belt from excessive development. He has a history of working against Euro-federalism, defending small businesses from late payment of accounts and the levying of VAT, and in the early 1980s founded the anti-CND organisation, Youth for Peace, through NATO. The absence of Conservative MPs in Wales (as well as Cornwall) ensured that he – as a rugby-playing Cornishman – was appointed to the Welsh

Affairs Select Committee in 2001, a not-inappropriate assignment given his past experience as a member of the Stanmore Choral Society.

HERTFORDSHIRE NORTH EAST

Although there were extensive boundary changes in Hertfordshire before the 1997 General Election, and an extra and new seat was granted to the county, Hertfordshire North East was a renamed rather than totally new constituency. Essentially it was based on the former Hertfordshire North, minus the town of Hitchin, plus some villages formerly in the Hertford and Stortford seat.

Herts North returned a Conservative MP with a majority of 16,500-plus over the Liberal Democrats in 1992, and five years later Oliver Heald hung on by 3,000, even though Labour increased their share from 21% to 36%. Four years after that, in 2001, there was little change in the absolute majority, but 7,000 fewer people voted. The elements of the old North Hertfordshire do also have some interesting history and competitive two-party politics. The largest town is Letchworth, the first garden city, founded by Ebenezer Howard in 1903. Howard believed that the garden city would be as great and significant an invention as the aeroplane, which first flew in the same year; he described both as 'harbingers of a new age'. He was wrong, and only one other garden city was built in England, also in Hertfordshire, at Welwyn. The legacy does survive in Letchworth's high proportion of non-private built housing, though much of it has now been sold off. Labour is well ahead in plebeian north-west Letchworth, although there are very attractive residential areas in the south of the town, including those around the Quaker St Christopher's school, a most unlikely alma mater for *Death Wish* film director Michael Winner, himself a vocal Conservative supporter until announcing a conversion to New Labour in 1997. Labour does not do so well outside Letchworth, in the small towns of Baldock and Royston and in the villages of the agricultural northern tip of the county.

Even more Conservative was the territory picked up from Hertford and Stortford (11,000 voters) and from Stevenage (4,000). The former includes such wealthy areas as Tewin and Thundridge, and the latter Watton at Stone, a village whose popularity with commuters is attested by that most rare of events: within recent memory a new railway station was opened to serve it. These two sections may well even have saved Heald's seat at the last two elections.

Social indices:			2001 Gen. Election:			
% Non-white	3.7		C	19,695	44.1	+2.4
% Prof/Man	38.6		Lab	16,251	36.4	+0.6
% Non-manual	60.1		LD	7,686	17.2	−1.0
£ Av prop val 2000	136 K		UKIP	1,013	2.3	
% Increase 97–00	51.7		C maj	3,444	7.7	
% Unemployed 2001	0.9		Turnout		64.9	−12.5
% Decrease 97–01	1.5		Elect	68,790		
% Fin hard/Rank	11.6	422				
% Pensioners	23.3					
% Prem mort/Rank	11	579				

Member of Parliament

Oliver Heald, a Tory Health spokesman from 2001, a Reading School and Cambridge (Pembroke)-educated employment law barrister, born in 1954, was elected in 1992, and is a discreet loyalist, who was soon on the career ladder as PPS to William Waldegrave and junior Social Security Minister 1995–97. Although citing Willie Whitelaw as his mentor, he nevertheless voted for Michael Howard for leader in 1997 and opposed a single European currency. A Whip (1997–2000) and a Home Office spokesman (2000–01) under William Hague, he reverted to his Positive Europe Group credentials in 2001 by voting for Kenneth Clarke – and still survived as one of 11 Clarke supporters on Iain Duncan Smith's frontbench team.

HERTFORDSHIRE SOUTH WEST

The parliamentary constituency of Hertfordshire South West is composed chiefly of the Three Rivers district – the rivers in question being the Chess, the Colne and the Grade. Three Rivers includes the affluent ultra-middle-class communities of Rickmansworth and Chorleywood, together with satellites like Croxley Green and the private estate of Moor Park. Indeed when figures for individual towns were for the last time released by the Census, in 1971, Chorleywood was the most middle class of any in England, with 78% working in non-manual occupations – and it will be more now.

In general elections all these are safely Tory, as are the towns of Berkhamsted and Tring, which are in Dacorum district, and situated in a fourth river valley, that of the Bulbourne. There are Labour voting areas in south-west Hertfordshire too, coming largely from the extensive (ex-)GLC overspill estate at South Oxhey, which fits in ill with its surroundings. The Liberal Democrats have a strong local vote in Croxley Green, and they were close behind Labour in third place in the 2001 General Election – this even division of the opposition certainly helped Richard Page to hold the seat comfortably even though his vote dropped by nearly 13,500 from 1992 to 2001. Some of the most affluent residential areas in the Home Counties are to be found in Hertfordshire South West, as at Moor Park – perhaps typically the home of a well-known public school (Merchant Taylors') – and a famed golf course set around a country house clubhouse. South Oxhey is a quite anomalous intrusion, rather like its fellow former GLC estate of Borehamwood in Hertsmere – and it does little to disturb the massive flow of Tory votes in the constituency in which it finds itself.

Social indices:			2001 Gen. Election:			
% Non-white	3.4		C	20,933	44.3	−1.7
% Prof/Man	45.8		Lab	12,752	27.0	−0.9
% Non-manual	69.6		LD	12,431	26.3	+4.0
£ Av prop val 2000	214 K		UKIP	847	1.8	
% Increase 97–00	53.9		PA	306	0.6	
% Unemployed 2001	1.1		C maj	8,181	17.3	
% Decrease 97–01	0.9		Turnout		64.4	−12.9
% Fin hard/Rank	7.1	557	Elect	73,367		
% Pensioners	25.1					
% Prem mort/Rank	12	577				

Member of Parliament

Richard Page, born in 1941 and educated at Hurstpierpoint and Luton Technical College, and one of the late Sir Julian Critchley's 'garagistes' as the owner of a car dealership, has been MP here since 1979, having previously snatched the Labour stronghold of Workington in a by-election in 1976. Self-designated as a mere 'spear-carrier in the great Conservative Party', he has been described as leading a political life of blameless obscurity. A champion of small businesses, he was briefly (1995–97) DTI Minister at the fag-end of the Major government, and was eventually made a DTI spokesman in 2001 by Hague, whom he backed in the 1997 leadership ballots, despite his own more Europhile record. Finally too old for further late promotions or even later revivals, with his leadership votes undisclosed in 2001, he returned to the backbenches at an age (60) where once there were consoling knighthoods.

HERTSMERE

Hertsmere contains the communities of Potters Bar, Borehamwood, Elstree, Bushey and Radlett. For some 20 years this area was represented by Cecil Parkinson, one of Mrs Thatcher's most favoured lieutenants, and a former Chairman of the Conservative Party, whose Cabinet career was interrupted from 1983 to 1987 by the Sara Keays scandal. Parkinson retired in 1992 and moved to the House of Lords, bequeathing a safe seat to James Clappison. The outcome of parliamentary contests here is based on a political battle between Conservative Potters Bar, in folklore the last outpost of London before the barbarian wastes of the North; and in the red corner Borehamwood, the 20,000-strong GLC 'out-estate', which has long provided a bloc of Labour support. But the Tories have always won, for they are also assisted by Radlett, an affluent commuter town straddling the A5 (the original home of the comfortable middle-class pop duo, Wham!, featuring George Michael), the solidly Conservative Elstree village and Bushey. Borehamwood looks like an isolated working-class outpost in south Hertfordshire. It can sustain six Labour wards on the local council, but despite an increase in their share of fully 16.5% in 1997 they could only cut Clappison's lead to just over 3,000. In 2001 the Referendum Party candidate disappeared, and Clappison increased his share by 3%, which is what they had got in 1997 (one partial coincidence, partial consequence); a Socialist Labour candidate arrived to take 1%, as Labour went down slightly (another).

Social indices:			2001 Gen. Election:			
% Non-white	4.2		C	19,855	47.8	+3.5
% Prof/Man	41.7		Lab	14,953	36.0	−2.2
% Non-manual	68.5		LD	6,300	15.2	+2.3
£ Av prop val 2000	171 K		SLP	397	1.0	
% Increase 97–00	44.5		C maj	4,902	11.8	
% Unemployed 2001	1.4		Turnout		60.3	−13.7
% Decrease 97–01	1.0		Elect	68,780		
% Fin hard/Rank	9.1	489				
% Pensioners	26.9					
% Prem mort/Rank	17	518				

Member of Parliament

James Clappison, elected here in 1992 in place of Cecil Parkinson and a man for all orthodoxies, adhered to the Thatcherite agenda in the 1980s, then bowled stooge questions at ministers in the Major government before joining it for the last two years as an Environment Minister. He sought to eject anti-Maastricht right-wingers from the 1922 Committee, and then served William Hague (for whom he had voted in 1997) variously, but eventually in the Treasury team. A pudgy-faced, boyish-looking farmer's son, he was born in 1956, and educated at St Peter's School, York and Queen's College, Oxford. Residually Yorkshire-accented, he assiduously nurses his vulnerable-looking constituency whose Jewish minority warms to his Zionism. Interestingly voting the big-hitting Europhile option of Kenneth Clarke in 2001, he survived to sit on Iain Duncan Smith's frontbench in the promoted post as Shadow Minister for Work – a somewhat Parkinsonian concept (C. Northcote, not Cecil).

HEXHAM

The fourth most vulnerable Conservative seat in Britain after the 1997 Election, Labour held genuine hopes of completing the annihilation of their main rivals in the north-eastern region when opinion polls suggested astonishingly during the 2001 campaign that they might increase their already huge majority. It was not to be. Those polls exaggerated their lead, partly because of 'shy' Tories not participating in the surveys, partly because of an underdog effect as British voters drew back from awarding an overall majority of 200-plus, and partly because of the low turnout, which affected Labour supporters more than others. It must be said, though, that a first ever Labour win in Hexham always seemed implausible; and also that despite the argument that holding an election during the foot-and-mouth outbreak might hinder voting, Hexham produced the second highest turnout in England, at nearly 71%.

Hexham is the second largest English constituency in area: it sprawls across 250,992 hectares, stretching from south of the River Tyne to the Scottish border, and including the vast forests of Wark and Kielder, as well as the most substantial section of Hadrian's Wall. Northumberland only merits three parliamentary seats by a strict application of the arithmetical rules, but it has been awarded four by successive Boundary Commissions because of exceptional geographical considerations, although the two giant rural seats in the county, Berwick and Hexham, are not noticeably smaller in electorate than the two compact industrial divisions, Blyth Valley and Wansbeck.

Hexham is exceptional in another way, too. It is the single surviving Conservative seat in the county. The other rural seat, Berwick, fell to the Liberals in 1973, and south-east Northumberland is a heavily populated, industrial Labour stronghold traditionally typified by coal-mining and shipbuilding. On the other hand Hexham seems almost to be designed to gather together Tory voters.

The upper Tyne valley is predominantly agricultural, with market centres at the prosperous small towns of Hexham and Corbridge, and further west up the Tyne valley at Haltwhistle. The only centre of Labour support is the industrial town of Prudhoe at the east end of the constituency. On the other hand Conservative votes pile up in the affluent residential Newcastle base of Ponteland-Darras Hall, where nearly all the houses are detached and owner-occupied.

Social indices:			2001 Gen. Election:			
% Non-white	0.6		C	18,917	44.6	+5.8
% Prof/Man	43.5		Lab	16,388	38.6	+0.4
% Non-manual	62.7		LD	6,380	15.0	−2.4
£ Av prop val 2000	112 K		UKIP	728	1.7	−0.8
% Increase 97–00	33.1		C maj	2,529	6.0	
% Unemployed 2001	2.2		Turnout		70.9	−6.6
% Decrease 97–01	1.1		Elect	59,807		
% Fin hard/Rank	8.4	509				
% Pensioners	27.8					
% Prem mort/Rank	21	466				

Member of Parliament

Peter Atkinson, an Opposition Whip from 1999 until February 2002, was elected in 1992. He is a journalist-turned-PR man for countryside interests – in his case the British Field Sports Society, and so, predictably, a leading opponent of gun control and anti-hunting legislation. Proximity, at least qualifying, him for the Scottish Affairs Select Committee, he was born in 1943, educated at Cheltenham College, and learnt his free-market Toryism on Wandsworth Council (1978–82). On the right, if not the hard right, his leadership votes were obscure in 1997 and 2001.

HEYWOOD AND MIDDLETON

This seat, contained wholly within the metropolitan borough of Rochdale, consisted until 1997 of the two towns mentioned in the constituency title. Now, though, a third element has been introduced: some 17,000 voters have been brought in from the Liberal Democrat fortress of Rochdale to boost Heywood and Middleton's electorate, which was considerably lower than the national norm.

The arrival of the wards of Castleton and Norden/Bamford add to the already considerable variety of Heywood and Middleton, but it remains a safe Labour seat. These are two outlying wards of differing political characteristics. Castleton, to the south of Rochdale's centre (and immediately east of Heywood), is middle income and strongly Liberal Democrat in both council and parliamentary elections. Norden and Bamford, on the other hand, is by far the most affluent ward in the town of Rochdale, the whole borough, and indeed the whole of the North West. Nearly half of all households have at least two cars, and over 94% of the housing is owner-occupied. It returns Tory councillors with large margins, although the electorate is likely to be sophisticated enough to have voted Liberal tactically in general elections, for Cyril Smith and Liz Lynne. This will no longer be possible, or necessary, and one may assume that the ex-Rochdale section of Heywood and Middleton will on balance usually favour the Conservatives over Labour.

This will not over-worry the incumbent party. Heywood and Middleton are both very divided. Middleton, for example, ranges from the affluent South ward, which is largely made up of the planned private estate of Alkrington Garden Village (home of the comic Bernard Manning), to West and Central, which are largely made up of the massive and troubled Langley council estate – considerably depopulated in the 1980s. South is usually Conservative in local elections, West always overwhelmingly Labour. In Heywood too there is a contrast between its usually Tory South ward, and a West ward characterised by the clutch of council tower blocks which form a notable landmark off the M66 motorway.

Overall, however, the Labour sections of this divided seat will continue to predominate, but its contrasts will make it an interesting seat to watch, and to represent.

Social indices:			2001 Gen. Election:			
% Non-white	2.0		Lab/Coop	22,377	57.7	–0.0
% Prof/Man	28.6		C	10,707	27.6	+4.6
% Non-manual	53.2		LD	4,329	11.2	–4.5
£ Av prop val 2000	55 K		Lib	1,021	2.6	+1.2
% Increase 97–00	16.1		Ind	345	0.9	
% Unemployed 2001	3.5		L/C maj	11,670	30.1	
% Decrease 97–01	2.0		Turnout		53.1	–15.3
% Fin hard/Rank	31.3	120	Elect	73,005		
% Pensioners	24.5					
% Prem mort/Rank	42	135				

Member of Parliament

Jim Dobbin, Labour's man here since 1997, and who has a dishevelled shaggily-bearded aspect, is an NHS microbiologist of 33 years' standing, born in 1941, a Fife miner's son, educated at Roman Catholic high schools in Cowdenbeath and Kirkcaldy, and at Napier College, Edinburgh. He was one of the few of the 1997 intake to vote against lone parent benefit cuts, and subsequently broke ranks on pensions, means testing of Incapacity Benefit, and air traffic control privatisation. As a former Rochdale councillor for 14 years (and briefly council leader 1996–97), he is inevitably antipathetic to the locally active Liberal Democrats, has sought the appointment of an Ex-Servicemen's Minister, and campaigned against cowboy builders.

HIGH PEAK

Although the Peak District was designated in 1951 as Britain's first National Park, and although the part of north-west Derbyshire therein includes some of its finest scenery, the High Peak constituency has been won by Labour three times since the war, although admittedly only when they have obtained an overall majority of landslide status, in 1966, 1997 and 2001. Who is to say that this is not to be a regular and continuing feature of British electoral politics? At the very least we can say that High Peak is now to be regarded as the kind of seat which will be won by whichever party comes first in the general election. In 2001 Tom Levitt led for Labour over the Conservatives by 9%, exactly the margin of difference nationally.

The reason why the beautiful High Peak is not safely Tory is that over 80% of its population live in five small towns. The mill-based communities of Glossop and New Mills look as if they belong in Lancashire or Yorkshire, and share the owner-occupied marginality of the more northern Pennines, as does Chapel-en-le-Frith, which is dominated by Ferodo (brake linings) and Whaley Bridge, increasingly popular with Manchester communities. The town of Buxton is starkly divided. In the western half of the town are to be found the sleepy mansions to which the Victorians retired to take the waters. But the centre of Britain's limestone quarrying industry lies in the white-scarred landscape around Buxton, and Buxton's east end, Fairfield, harbours a heavy and reliable Labour vote. The other Labour stronghold in the High Peak is at Gamesley, a windy Manchester overspill estate on a hill outside Glossop. The Conservatives' best chances lie in the villages of the seat, such as the touristy Castleton and affluent Hathersage, both in the Hope Valley, and among the hill farmers of the whitestone uplands around Tideswell; but the outcome is decided in the towns.

Social indices:			2001 Gen. Election:			
% Non-white	0.6		Lab	22,430	46.6	−4.2
% Prof/Man	36.2		C	17,941	37.3	+1.8
% Non-manual	55.1		LD	7,743	16.1	+4.9
£ Av prop val 2000	80 K		Lab maj	4,489	9.3	
% Increase 97–00	25.5		Turnout		65.2	−13.8
% Unemployed 2001	2.0		Elect	73,774		
% Decrease 97–01	1.0					
% Fin hard/Rank	14.9	355				
% Pensioners	24.2					
% Prem mort/Rank	26	397				

Member of Parliament

Tom Levitt, a schoolteacher (one of 49 in the PLP of 2001) who won at his second attempt here for Labour in 1997, has had his loyalism repaid by the post of PPS to Barbara Roche from 1999. A long-running Labour candidate and councillor, he was born in 1954, son of a university lecturer, and educated at Westwood High School, Leek and at Lancaster University. With his employment as a science teacher for 19 years, his routinely orthodox advocacy of comprehensive schooling (in which he had spent his entire life, both man and boy), and with his transition from soft-left unilateralist to New-Labour loyalist, he comes as a fairly standard issue Labour MP of the Blairite dispensation, as PPS to a minister with close links to Cherie Booth.

HITCHIN AND HARPENDEN

Like so many counties in the southern half of England, Hertfordshire enjoyed sufficient population growth to be awarded an extra constituency in the most recent parliamentary boundary review. In this case there is no doubt which the additional and new seat is. Indeed in many ways it stands out like a sore thumb. It is clearly an artificial creation, which has little internal cohesion, and which also breaks up several natural links between communities. The Boundary Commission themselves admitted that there are no real connections between the towns of Hitchin and Harpenden. Still, Hertfordshire deserved the allocation of an 11th seat and here it is.

Harpenden has been associated for parliamentary purposes in the past with Hemel Hempstead, until 1974, and more logically with St Albans from then till 1997. It is really tied economically much more closely to St Albans and to Luton in Bedfordshire than to anywhere else. Harpenden is one of the nation's most middle-class, affluent and Conservative towns. It houses some of the wealthiest of commuters to Luton, St Albans and, indeed, London. In the West Common area (SW Harpenden) it possesses one of the most opulent – maybe even ostentatious – residential neighbourhoods in the whole of Britain. The St Albans constituency Conservatives sadly rued the loss of Harpenden and its 21,000 voters. The MP Peter Lilley wisely abandoned the cathedral city and followed Harpenden into the new seat; Labour gained St Albans by over 4,000 while Lilley held on to his place, indeed briefly to become Deputy Leader of his party. Although relegated to the backbenches by 2001, Peter Lilley did stand, and win, again; his Labour opponent was the former Conservative MP for Hexham, Alan Amos, who had been forced to withdraw after a sexual scandal just before the 1992 Election.

Other wards from the St Albans City local authority area in this seat are Redbourn, Sandridge and Wheathampstead, all very comfortably off. These are in Harpenden's orbit, but Hitchin definitely is not. Formerly Hitchin was associated with Letchworth, Baldock and Royston in the North Hertfordshire constituency, a unit of considerable harmony. Hitchin is so close to Letchworth that their built-up areas almost run into each other. It may seem most strange to some locals that this connection is broken in favour of one with a town 15 miles to the south-west on the other side of Luton. However, some disruption was necessary to equalise electorates. Hitchin is a more mixed town socially and politically than Harpenden. It has a substantial Asian minority in Bearton ward, and Labour also wins at the council estate ward of Oughton. Nevertheless, the new division will remain safely Conservative, as Harpenden and the villages predominate. Perhaps the order of names in the seat's title should be reversed.

Social indices:			2001 Gen. Election:			
% Non-white	4.5		C	21,271	47.3	+1.5
% Prof/Man	47.4		Lab	14,608	32.5	–0.6
% Non-manual	70.0		LD	8,076	18.0	–2.1
£ Av prop val 2000	179 K		UKIP	606	1.3	
% Increase 97–00	56.2		Ind	363	0.8	
% Unemployed 2001	0.9		C maj	6,663	14.8	
% Decrease 97–01	1.3		Turnout		66.9	–11.1
% Fin hard/Rank	7.1	558	Elect	67,196		
% Pensioners	23.7					
% Prem mort/Rank	12	574				

Member of Parliament

Peter Lilley was elected here in 1997, after 14 years as an MP for St Albans. Initially (1997–98) William Hague's Shadow Chancellor, he is a one-time Gradgrind

Thatcherite who latterly appeared to trim in a One Nation direction. His defenders, however, say he was never as he seemed, merely playing to a right-wing gallery. Cerebral and diffident, he was born in 1943, attended Dulwich College and Clare College, Cambridge, and was an oil analyst and stockbroker before working in the Conservative Research Department for four years. A Treasury Minister under Margaret Thatcher (1987–90), he entered John Major's Cabinet at the DTI in 1990, and Social Security in 1992. He abortively ran for leader in 1997 and won the endorsement of 24 MPs out of 165. His ominous designation as 'Deputy Leader' in 1998 with a remit to muse on policy, sounded the death knell, and he was off the frontbench by 1999. A Portillo voter in 2001, he took to advocating legalisation of cannabis.

HOLBORN AND ST PANCRAS

In 2001 Frank Dobson's share of the vote in Holborn and St Pancras fell by over 11%, and in numerical terms by 8,000, a third of his total in 1997. Yet the Conservatives also lost both share and votes. Where had Labour's support gone? The answer lies, as the Americans say, every which way. The Liberal Democrats advanced by over 5% and took second place, shadowing their improvements in the northern half of the borough of Camden at Hampstead and Highgate, and even more at its next door seat of Hornsey and Wood Green. The Green Party, which had not put forward a candidate in 1997, saved its deposit by picking up 6%. Two left-wing socialists between them gathered over 4%. Finally, the turnout fell by 11% to less than half of the total number of voters registered.

The Holborn and St Pancras seat covers the southern half of the borough of Camden and contains many famous neighbourhoods in the capital city. Moving north from the centre of London it includes Holborn, fringing the City and sharing many of its financial interests; Bloomsbury, with its academic, literary and artistic tradition; King's Cross and St Pancras, great railway termini for the northern lines; Somers Town, Camden Town, Kentish Town, Chalk Farm and Primrose Hill. There are many distinguished names here, but this does not alter the fact that Holborn and St Pancras is a safe Labour seat, in which Frank Dobson still polled three times as many votes as his chief opponent in 2001.

Less than a quarter of the housing in the constituency is owner-occupied, and nearly half is still council-owned. The non-white population, less than the London average in 1981, doubled to 20% in the 1980s; this was largely accounted for by the arrival of the largest Bangladeshi settlement in London outside Tower Hamlets. Street life in this constituency can be rough, with a well-known centre of prostitution at Kings Cross and large numbers of homeless in Camden Town. There is some fine housing too, especially on the edge of Regent's Park and in enclaves like Primrose Hill, and as in Islington its proximity to the centre of London makes it attractive for young urban professionals who do not object to the great mix of inhabitants. These tend to be liberal in views, however, and the Conservatives cannot rely on any bloc of population in this inner north London seat.

Social indices:			2001 Gen. Election:			
% Non-white	20.7		Lab	16,770	53.9	−11.1
% Prof/Man	43.7		LD	5,595	18.0	+5.5
% Non-manual	64.3		C	5,258	16.9	−1.0
£ Av prop val 2000	277 K		Grn	1,875	6.0	
% Increase 97–00	56.5		SA	971	3.1	
% Unemployed 2001	6.9		SLP	359	1.2	
% Decrease 97–01	4.0		UKIP	301	1.0	
% Fin hard/Rank	35.6	87	Lab maj	11,175	35.9	
% Pensioners	22.4		Turnout		49.6	−10.7
% Prem mort/Rank	55	21	Elect	62,813		

Member of Parliament

Frank Dobson, one of Tony Blair's discarded Cabinet Ministers, and MP here since 1979, is a superficially cuddly, pugnacious, dirty-joke-telling Yorkshireman, and bearded Buster Merryweather lookalike. For two-and-a-half years as Health Secretary (1997–99) he said the NHS was getting better until forced by Blair to quit in order to stand against Ken Livingstone for Mayor of London in 2000 and be soundly beaten, after a selection contest in which his rivals (Livingstone and Glenda Jackson) were long denied the Labour Party membership list to which he had access. Thereafter fallen into a wounded silence, from which he emerged to call – as an atheist who had always bridled at Blair's churchiness – for repeal of the blasphemy laws in 2001, he was born in 1940, son of a railwayman, educated at Archbishop Holgate's Grammar School, York and LSE and worked as a civil servant for the CEGB, Electricity Council and Local Government Ombudsman, and ran Camden Council for a while in the 1970s. He lingers, somewhat beached, in the Commons, as one of eight discarded Cabinet Ministers, three of whom – himself excluded – are homosexual. In 2002 he led a revolt on faith schools.

HORNCHURCH

When the north-east London borough of Havering was divided into three seats in 1974, it was generally thought that there would be one safe Tory (Romford), one marginal (Upminster) and one safe Labour (Hornchurch). After much deviation from this prediction, in 2001 it finally appeared to fit the bill. From 1979 to 1997 all three seats were held by the Tories, as this predominantly white, mixed class but not wealthy, borough on the very fringe between London and Essex found Mrs Thatcher and her successor very much to its taste. Then in 1997 New Labour benefited from a very large swing throughout outer London to take all three Havering seats, as the Tories had lost both their momentum and their reputation for economic competence. At last in 2001 there was a differentiation in victory, if not in the direction of the electoral movement, as Romford fell to the Tories by a considerable margin, Upminster narrowly, and Labour's John Cryer just held Hornchurch.

Hornchurch is very far from being a posh or glamorous place. The seat has the highest proportion of junior non-manual (clerical, white-collar) workers of any of the 74 in Greater London. It has very few professionals or adults with higher educational qualifications such as degrees – less than half as many as the borough of Hackney, for example. It is the southern seat in the borough, the only one with a river frontage, set between Dagenham and Thurrock (two less-than-chic locations). The southern end of the constituency around Rainham and South Hornchurch is overshadowed by scenes of heavy industry, including the condemned Ford motor works, which has offered many locals employment but which was scheduled for closure in 2002. Nor are the other residential areas affluent – Elm Park, Hacton, Hylands, central Hornchurch. The seat has the look of being good Labour territory, and although it does not look safe it was at least held against the rightward swing of 2001. It will be among the most tightly contested seats in the country next time, but after that boundary changes are expected to split this seat asunder between a cross-borough safe Labour Dagenham and Rainham seat and a new competitive Hornchurch and Upminster.

Social indices:			2001 Gen. Election:			
% Non-white	3.7		Lab	16,514	46.4	–3.8
% Prof/Man	26.6		C	15,032	42.3	+5.0
% Non-manual	61.2		LD	2,928	8.2	+0.4
£ Av prop val 2000	111 K		UKIP	893	2.5	
% Increase 97–00	45.4		TW	190	0.5	–0.1
% Unemployed 2001	1.9		Lab maj	1,482	4.2	
% Decrease 97–01	1.7		Turnout		58.3	–14.0
% Fin hard/Rank	8.5	502	Elect	61,008		
% Pensioners	23.5					
% Prem mort/Rank	25	421				

Member of Parliament

John Cryer is a radical chip off two hard left blocks – his mother, Ann Cryer MP (for Keighley from 1997), and his late father Bob Cryer MP (for Keighley 1974–83 and Bradford South 1987–94). Elected here in 1997, he has disloyally turned up for most of the Campaign Group-led revolts against the government, on lone parent benefits, pensions, jury trials, air traffic control privatisation and Incapacity Benefits. A journalist, born in 1964, educated at Oakbank School, Keighley, Hatfield Polytechnic and the London College of Printing, he opposes a single European currency and PR. Very few new MPs joined Campaign in 1997; he was one of them, and by the end of that Parliament had voted against the government 21 times, the 22nd most dissentient Labour MP.

HORNSEY AND WOOD GREEN

A week after the June 2001 General Election the *Guardian* diary column got round to noticing that there had been apparently a huge swing away from Labour MP Barbara Roche in Hornsey and Wood Green, the western half of Haringey borough, which also includes Muswell Hill and Alexandra Palace. They were quick to ascribe this to her role as immigration minister and appeared to infer that the liberal-left intellectual voters of north Labour had punished her for the government's restrictive policies towards asylum speakers. This interpretation may fit the Guardian's prejudices, but it is less clear that it is supported by rational electoral analysis.

For a start, the fall in Roche's share of the vote, 12%, though unusually high was little more than that in nearby seats such as those of Glenda Jackson (Hampstead and Highgate) and Frank Dobson (Holborn and St Pancras), neither of whom had anything to do with immigration policy. Second, the beneficiaries in all three cases were the Liberal Democrats, who in Hornsey/Wood Green improved massively from 11% to 26%. To some extent this reflected local government advance, and it may be no coincidence that the Lib Dem candidate was Lynne Featherstone, who had been one of three who leapt forward to seize Muswell Hill ward from Labour in May 1998. It should be noted too that the Conservative vote went down proportionately even more than Roche's as well, and Lynne Featherstone's boost must have been at their expense too.

If the Liberal Democrats are to be seen as a left-wing party (as must also be the Greens, who saved one of their ten deposits here, and the Socialist Alliance and Socialist Labour, 3%), we need not alter the view that this part of North London has been swinging steadily to the left for some decades. Counting Labour (an arguable proposition these days), left-of-centre parties took 84% in Hornsey and Wood Green in 2001. Its predecessor, Hornsey, was never won by Labour, not even in 1945 or 1966. What accounts for this large and sustained move away from Conservatism in Hornsey and Wood Green?

It is impossible to quantify the several elements, but one is certainly social change. The seat has become very cosmopolitan, with not only a sizeable minority of Afro-Caribbeans and Asians as in many other parts of London but more unusually a large community of Cypriots, mainly Greek but with some Turkish – we are not far here from the so-called 'Green Lanes corridor' of Cypriot settlement. Another is the improvement in Labour's image since the days of the 1970s and early 1980s when the party was tarnished with the image of the 'loony left': Haringey Council proved so popular that Labour made 14 gains in 1994 and won 57 of the 59 seats. Finally, the white middle-class residents who live in this constituency, like their neighbours in the next-door seat of Hampstead and Highgate in Camden borough, are often intellectually inclined to the left: there are a lot of bedsit and flat dwellers here, and relatively few households with children. All this adds up to a seat which is socially, intellectually and politically well beyond the Conservatives' reach now.

Social indices:			2001 Gen. Election:			
% Non-white	20.0		Lab	21,967	49.9	−11.9
% Prof/Man	54.4		LD	11,353	25.8	+14.5
% Non-manual	75.0		C	6,921	15.7	−6.2
£ Av prop val 2000	210 K		Grn	2,228	5.1	+2.7
% Increase 97–00	65.1		SA	1,106	2.5	
% Unemployed 2001	4.2		SLP	294	0.7	−0.5
% Decrease 97–01	4.3		Ind	194	0.4	
% Fin hard/Rank	15.2	349	Lab maj	10,614	24.1	
% Pensioners	19.2		Turnout		58.0	−11.1
% Prem mort/Rank	30	335	Elect	75,967		

Member of Parliament

Barbara Roche, born Barbara Margolis in 1954, and educated at the Jewish Free School and Lady Margaret Hall, Oxford, had the exposed and sensitive job as Home Office Minister (1999–2001) responsible for immigration policy. Previously she rose quickly at the DTI (1997–99) and as Financial Secretary to the Treasury (1999). A small and square barrister, whose barrister husband is in the chambers of radical defence lawyer Michael Mansfield, she comes from a left background, having voted for Beckett (whose PPS she was), not Blair, in 1994. Dogged if charmless in recitation of her brief, her role on immigration and asylum was a key one in Labour's bid to out-flank the populism of Ann Widdecombe as Shadow Home Secretary. She suffered with a big swing to the Liberal Democrats, the second biggest against any Labour MP, and in June 2001 transferred to the Cabinet Office – either an inner sanctum or a cul-de-sac; her links to Cherie Blair may help to determine which.

HORSHAM

It is hard to imagine a more attractive seat from a Tory point of view than Horsham. This is the 11th safest Conservative seat in the country, and it is set in a county (West Sussex) still almost entirely comprised of safe Conservative divisions. The majority in 2001 approached 14,000, and that over the Liberal Democrats; nationally triumphant, Labour reached a fifth of the total vote and have no local councillors at all. The Liberal Democrats have not made a serious nuisance of themselves either, though they have local council representation in wards Riverside, Trafalgar and Roffey North. In a general election here there are no clouds on the blues' horizon.

The seat is centred on Horsham, a market town of some 23,000 people conveniently situated near Gatwick Airport and the M23, but spreads across a swathe of rich, rolling, wooded countryside which is quintessentially English. It takes in small towns and villages such as Billingshurst, Itchingfield, Nuthurst and Rusper. The prominent public schools of Christ's Hospital and Worth are within the borders. Average house values rose from £98,000 in 1997 to £163,000 by the most recent General Election. Only 4% of households are deemed to be in a state of financial hardship. If anything, the Tories might regret the concentration of such awesome electoral power in this Horsham seat, for in 2001 they lost Crawley next door while piling up their fifth largest lead here – not the most fortunate distribution of resources.

Social indices:			2001 Gen. Election:			
% Non-white	1.1		C	26,134	51.5	+0.7
% Prof/Man	42.3		LD	12,468	24.6	−0.2
% Non-manual	66.9		Lab	10,267	20.2	+1.5
£ Av prop val 2000	163 K		UKIP	1,472	2.9	+1.5
% Increase 97–00	65.8		Ind	429	0.8	
% Unemployed 2001	0.8		C maj	13,666	26.9	
% Decrease 97–01	0.7		Turnout		63.8	−12.0
% Fin hard/Rank	4.5	616	Elect	79,604		
% Pensioners	23.3					
% Prem mort/Rank	9	609				

Member of Parliament

Francis Maude, one of 18 offspring of MPs in the current House, as son of the late Angus Maude, right-wing Suez rebel and Thatcherite of the first hour, was elected here in 1997, having earlier been MP for North Warwickshire 1983–92. Born in 1953 and educated at Abingdon School and Corpus Christi College, Cambridge, a barrister and former director of his friend Archie Norman MP's ASDA Group and of Morgan Stanley, his Euroscepticism sits awkwardly with his signature of the Maastricht Treaty as a Treasury Minister in 1991. Not without prospects at one time as a dark horse, despite being uncharismatic and outclassed at the despatch box by Chancellor Brown, as Shadow Chancellor 1998–2000, and then moved to Shadow Foreign Secretary (2000–01), he foresaw a future homosexual Tory leader (his own homosexual brother having died of AIDS). He was a leader of Portillo's libertarian leadership bid in 2001, spurned Iain Duncan Smith's Shadow Cabinet for the backbenches, and teamed up with his friend Archie Norman to create a web site think tank called 'Xchange', designed to reconnect their party with the electorate.

HOUGHTON AND WASHINGTON EAST

Apart from the New Town of Washington, designated as late as 1964 and spreading across its windy hills a few miles west of Sunderland, the rest of this constituency consists of older communities on the former Durham coalfield. Houghton-le-Spring is only the largest of these. It also includes Hetton-le-Hole, Eppleton, Shiney Row, Herrington and other smaller villages. This terrain is more similar to Durham county seats like Sedgefield and Easington than to the metropolitan area of Tyne and Wear – even the parts of Washington included are not unlike Durham, for Newton Aycliffe and Peterlee are also New Towns within the county. Ryhope, formerly in Sunderland North constituency, is also included, and fits in well too, for rather than being an integral part of the newly designated city of Sunderland it too is a well-known former mining village, its closed colliery workings stretching out below the North Sea bed. Ryhope has a Labour tradition lasting almost the whole of the century too, and does not disturb the political balance of this least urbanised of all Tyne and Wear constituencies. In 2001 this was yet another seat where the turnout fell below 50%, although whether this was due to these traditional communities' lack of enthusiasm for New Labour's first government or a deeper disillusionment with the democratic process is dubious. It was more likely to be a question of an election which was nowhere near close either nationally or locally. However, this situation is unlikely to change next time – or as far as the Houghton and Washington East element is concerned, for the foreseeable future.

Social indices:			2001 Gen. Election:			
% Non-white	0.7		Lab	24,628	73.2	−3.2
% Prof/Man	22.1		C	4,810	14.3	+1.4
% Non-manual	47.6		LD	4,203	12.5	+4.8
£ Av prop val 2000	58 K		Lab maj	19,818	58.9	
% Increase 97–00	28.6		Turnout		49.5	−12.6
% Unemployed 2001	5.2		Elect	67,946		
% Decrease 97–01	1.4					
% Fin hard/Rank	32.4	111				
% Pensioners	23.6					
% Prem mort/Rank	47	63				

Member of Parliament

Labour's **Fraser Kemp**, with some facial resemblance to the Mekon, was elected in 1997 after a career as a party apparatchik par excellence, with 16 years as a Labour organiser including the masterminding of two big by-election victories at Mid Staffordshire and Dudley West in the early 1990s. A Durham miner's son, born in 1958, he attended Washington Comprehensive School. Tall, balding and convivial (seen by Paul Routledge as an 'inveterate lager-shifter'), he favours regional assemblies but not PR, which he rightly sees as destroying an inflated Labour majority. He sees the biggest betrayal of the working class as indulging in 'intellectual masturbation' and losing elections, and the arrival of this tough Geordie realist in the Whips' Office in 2001 seemed not only overdue but completely predictable.

HOVE

One of the most clear and symbolic demonstrations of the magnitude of Labour triumph on the first of May 1997 was their capture of Hove. The Hove constituency is an almost entirely residential area stretching back from the Regency squares and crescents on the seafront adjoining the twin (if larger) town of Brighton to sheltered hollows in the South Downs, with highly affluent housing in areas like Tongdean and around Hove Park. This used to be Brighton's more elegant and more staid western neighbour, with little of its robust, raffish or louche characteristics. Hove was thoroughly respectable. The Sussex county cricket ground is in Hove, whereas the racecourse (at which Pinky operated in Greene's Brighton Rock) is of course in Brighton. However in the last two decades or so many of the traits of Brighton seem to have spread, as multi-occupation, DSS claimants, the homeless and others on the fringes of society have become more visibly influential near the seafront.

Until the mid 1990s, Hove's politics had been predictable. The Liberal Des Wilson had failed to win it even in the 1973 by-election, at a time when seats such as Ripon and the Isle of Ely were falling. The only hint of industry is to be found at Portslade, near the eastern arm of Shoreham harbour, and until 1995 Labour's only wards were Portslade North and Portslade South. Then in the May local elections of that year the Conservatives lost control of Hove borough council (which was subsequently subsumed into a Brighton and Hove unitary authority) and Labour added ten more councillors to their six in Portslade. The Conservatives must still have felt the parliamentary seat was safe, with a 12,000 majority in 1992. But Labour's Ivor Caplin increased their share by 20%, and Robert Guy could not hold on. He lost by just under 4,000; it might be noted that the combined vote of the Referendum, Independent Conservative, and UK Independence candidates was 3,875. He also suffered from tactical voting, as the Liberal Democrats' vote was halved. Nevertheless, there seems to be a long-term movement towards Labour in this part of the south coast.

This was illustrated in 2001, when Hove seemed hardly to be fought as a marginal seat. The Conservatives could not afford to appoint a full-time agent. The Campaign on the ground was quiet, with no sense of a vital or close contest taking place. Sure enough, when the votes were counted, Ivor Caplin had just about maintained his majority, even though the minor party vote probably detracted more from his than from the Conservatives this time, and turnout dropped by 10%, which cannot have helped Labour. Hove must now, actually, be regarded as a naturally Labour seat these days.

Social indices:			2001 Gen. Election:			
% Non-white	3.2		Lab	19,253	45.9	+1.3
% Prof/Man	38.2		C	16,082	38.3	+1.9
% Non-manual	65.8		LD	3,823	9.1	−0.5
£ Av prop val 2000	118K		Grn	1,369	3.3	+1.9
% Increase 97–00	66.1		SA	531	1.3	
% Unemployed 2001	3.2		UKIP	358	0.9	+0.4
% Decrease 97–01	3.3		Lib	316	0.8	
% Fin hard/Rank	11.4	429	Ind	196	0.5	
% Pensioners	35.1		Ind	60	0.1	
% Prem mort/Rank	34	276	Lab maj	3,171	7.6	
			Turnout		59.2	−10.5
			Elect	70,889		

Member of Parliament

Ivor Caplin, one of Labour's winners in the three-seat Brighton conurbation in 1997, is a staunchly on-message Blairite MP. A former local councillor and Hove council leader, from a Jewish background, son of a chartered accountant, he was born locally in 1958, educated at King Edward's School, Witley and Brighton College of Technology, and worked in insurance for 20 years. Keen on sport (bemoaning the tribulations of groundless Brighton and Hove Albion Football Club) and animal welfare, his ultra-loyalty was recognised in his appointment as Margaret Beckett's PPS (1998–2001) and then as an Assistant Whip in 2001.

HUDDERSFIELD

Since 1983 the West Yorkshire textile town of Huddersfield has been united in a single compact constituency; or rather, most of it has. Decisively, the affluent western suburbs such as Lindley are in the Colne Valley seat, leaving the former Huddersfield East MP Barry Sheerman with the town centre, the large eastern council estates such as Deighton, most of the significant Asian and Afro-Caribbean minorities, and all of its safe Labour wards. Small wonder that Huddersfield has been a safe Labour seat, recording a majority over the Conservatives of 10,046 in 2001.

There is some Liberal Democrat activity in Kirklees borough elections. In May 2000, for example, the Lib Dems won Almondbury and Dalton wards, and came close in Paddock, but they can make no real impact in parliamentary contests, their share dropping to 15% last time. The Greens hold all three council seats in Newsome ward, but they could not reach the deposit threshold in 2001. Huddersfield is no more working class in socio-economic composition than Halifax or even Batley and Spen, but unlike those other West Yorkshire seats it has not dabbled with electing a Conservative MP, or come even close to dabbling. Huddersfield East had been solidly Labour since the war, and this end of the town seems to contrast itself with the western 'Nob Hill', once known as one of West Yorkshire's 'Millionaires Rows'.

Social indices:			2001 Gen. Election:			
% Non-white	17.1		Lab/Coop	18,840	53.2	−3.2
% Prof/Man	29.3		C	8,794	24.9	+3.9
% Non-manual	48.1		LD	5,300	15.0	−2.2
£ Av prop val 2000	56 K		Grn	1,254	3.5	+1.4
% Increase 97–00	15.3		UKIP	613	1.7	
% Unemployed 2001	5.3		SA	374	1.1	
% Decrease 97–01	2.5		SLP	208	0.6	
% Fin hard/Rank	36.9	76	L/C maj	10,046	28.4	
% Pensioners	26.9		Turnout		55.0	−12.7
% Prem mort/Rank	40	173	Elect	64,349		

Member of Parliament

Barry Sheerman, son of a clerk, born in 1940, educated at Hampton Grammar School and, after four years as a lab assistant, at the LSE, has been MP for Huddersfield since 1979, before which he was a Swansea-based politics lecturer for 13 years (as long indeed as had been Kingsley Amis whose phrase about over-expansion of the universities – 'more means worse' – drew from Richard Crossman the riposte that of course he'd think that after spending 13 years at Swansea). A Hattersley-linked frontbencher in the 1980s, who did not long survive his patron's retirement as Deputy Leader in 1992, he re-emerged in 1999 as Chairman of the Education Select Committee from which vantage point he made NUT-soothing assaults on HMI Chris Woodhead and populist attacks on Oxford's allegedly discriminating entrance procedures (claiming Oxford and Cambridge 'are not as good as they think they are'; whilst of him it has been said by a Tory former academic 'not as able as he thinks he is'). Unkindly dubbed 'an ageing crawler' (Matthew Parris, *The Times*), a Europhile Blairite loyalist, who has never strayed from centre-right affiliations in his party, his moving of the Loyal Address in June 2001 was considered less than Periclean.

HUNTINGDON

John Major, although generally regarded as a less-than-successful Prime Minister (yet he did, it should be remembered, serve seven years and win a general election against almost all predictions), was undoubtedly immensely liked and respected as a person. This was very apparent in the outstanding results accorded to him in his Huntingdon constituency: a majority of 36,000, far and away the highest anywhere in the UK in 1992, and 18,000, halved by boundary changes but still clearly the safest Tory victory, in 1997 with a well below average swing to Labour. Further evidence of the esteem in which Major is held in Huntingdon was shown by the 2001 Election result, when the Conservative vote fell by 7,000 or a share of 5.5%, while the Liberal Democrats moved up by over 9% to pip Labour's Takki Sulaiman for second place.

The low turnout in 2001, as well as Major's replacement by Jonathan Djanogly, has cut the majority, but it does not endanger the Conservative position. East Anglia is a desirable place to live, as the burgeoning number of its voters indicates; people do not come here to change the status quo. The new private estates of St Ives and St Neots and Godmanchester are among the relatively few places where John Major's dream of a classless but Conservative society seems plausible indeed.

Social indices:			2001 Gen. Election:			
% Non-white	2.6		C	24,507	49.9	−5.4
% Prof/Man	36.6		LD	11,715	23.9	+9.1
% Non-manual	56.0		Lab	11,211	22.8	−0.6
£ Av prop val 2000	99 K		UKIP	1,656	3.4	+2.8
% Increase 97–00	47.2		C maj	12,792	26.1	
% Unemployed 2001	1.1		Turnout		62.5	−12.4
% Decrease 97–01	1.2		Elect	78,604		
% Fin hard/Rank	9.7	471				
% Pensioners	19.1					
% Prem mort/Rank	11	585				

Member of Parliament

Here in the steps of Worcester Park man in 2001 came **Jonathan Djanogly** (pronounced Jan-og-lee), a right-wing opponent of the euro, who had unexpectedly beaten a pro-European barrister and Tory Reform Group member, David Platt, for the Conservative nomination. Dark and long-headed and from a wealthy Jewish family of (textile) manufacturers, he was born in 1965 and educated at University College School, Hampstead, Oxford Polytechnic and Guildford College of Law. A former Westminster councillor (1994–2001), he fought Oxford East in 1997. Thrustingly ambitious, he became a partner with the London solicitors' firm of Berwins in 1998, aged 33, and founded an audio-cassette business with his wife in 1994. He backed Iain Duncan Smith in all the ballots of the leadership election, joining 13 other new Tory MPs in writing to the *Telegraph* claiming he 'can unite the Party on Europe'. He takes an understandably nimbyish line on yet more housing developments in his despoiled seat of market towns once famous for returning Oliver Cromwell.

HYNDBURN

The Hyndburn constituency is one of Lancashire's classic Labour–Conservative marginals, and it is one of the four seats in the county which Labour gained from the Tories at the April 1992 General Election, probably largely influenced by the unpopularity of the poll tax in an area of small terraced owner-occupied houses. Like other seats in this category, such as Rossendale and Darwen, Pendle, and a couple of seats in each of Bolton and Bury, the huge Labour win of 1997 saw an historically untypical large Labour majority here, and Greg Pope's lead held up better in 2001 than in several of the others in the sub-region, but nevertheless it has a history of very close and sometimes surprising results. The seat is similar to the old Accrington division which existed before 1983. The political contests here have always been very keen. Labour did not lose Accrington between 1945 and 1979, but their majority was always narrow. It was widely predicted in 1983 that Hyndburn would be even closer. In its inaugural contest it certainly proved to be: after six counts the Conservative Kenneth Hargreaves was awarded victory late on the Friday afternoon. It was the last result to be declared in England. The majority was 21 votes, and in 1987 with the assistance of incumbency Hargreaves held on, but only by a couple of thousand.

Hyndburn is an east Lancashire seat made up of a number of small ex-textile towns: Accrington, Oswaldtwistle, Church, Rishton, Clayton-le-Moors and Great Harwood. Most of the wards are themselves marginal; these are tight-knit communities, with a large majority of owner-occupiers but also of those in working-class jobs. Everything seems to balance and to make for marginality. There is a plush Conservative residential area in the village of Baxendale; on the other hand over 40% of the population of Accrington Central ward is non-white, almost all of Pakistani origin. Despite Greg Pope's current majority of 8,000, the seat is truly competitive, as befits the geographical and spiritual centre of the most famous of the northern cricket leagues, the Lancashire League.

Social indices:			2001 Gen. Election:			
% Non-white	6.1		Lab	20,900	54.7	−0.9
% Prof/Man	27.4		C	12,681	33.2	+1.3
% Non-manual	47.6		LD	3,680	9.6	+1.0
£ Av prop val 2000	40 K		UKIP	982	2.6	
% Increase 97–00	17.8		Lab maj	8,219	21.5	
% Unemployed 2001	2.4		Turnout		57.6	−14.7
% Decrease 97–01	1.1		Elect	66,445		
% Fin hard/Rank	30.1	130				
% Pensioners	26.1					
% Prem mort/Rank	41	164				

Member of Parliament

Greg Pope was elected in 1992 and has followed a path of loyal semi-obscurity since his initial vote against the Maastricht Treaty on grounds of the social chapter opt-out. His campaigning for Tony Blair's Clause Four redraft earned him appointment as an Opposition Whip in 1995 and as a government Whip from 1997 to 2001. A former local government officer, he was born in 1960 and educated at St Mary's (RC)

College, Blackburn, and Hull University. A practising Catholic, his name appears on the ballot paper as 'Pope Gregory'. He was one of a score of government members removed from office in 2001 to make room for MPs from the 1997 intake, unluckily in his case given his relative youthfulness.

ILFORD NORTH

It is arguable that Labour won Ilford North for the first time ever in 1997, although they won seats so named in 1945 and October 1974. In the boundary changes which came into force in 1997, the Redbridge borough seat of Wanstead and Woodford was effectively abolished and its wards split up three ways. The largest section of that seat (but still a little less than half of the total) has been placed in a redrawn – some would say entirely new – Ilford North constituency. Ilford North had always been the more Conservative of the two Ilford seats; in fact Labour had only ever won the seat once since 1950, when Millie Miller broke the Conservative grip in October 1974. That triumph was short-lived, for Mrs Miller died just over three years later and Vivian Bendall won the subsequent by-election easily. He held on comfortably and had a majority of 9,000 in 1992. With the assistance of the ex-Wanstead and Woodford wards, this was increased to a notional 14,000 – but Linda Perham secured a phenomenal swing of 17% and won by over 3,000. This was almost a straight exchange of votes between Conservative and Labour. The Liberal Democrats were scarcely squeezed and the Referendum Party did not stand. In 2001 there was virtually no change in the major party shares of the vote here, unlike nearby Havering borough where the Conservatives made a substantial recovery. The UK Independence Party did make an appearance, but no significant impact.

This seat resembles the inner city much less than Ilford South. There is a much smaller percentage of non-white residents. The housing stock is more likely to consist of semi-detached rather than terraced streets. There is a Labour stronghold in the large peripheral ex-GLC estate of Hainault, the end of a tube line and almost in the heart of rural Essex. But Hainault is very untypical of Ilford North. Most of it is owner-occupied, lower-middle-class, historically Conservative territory like Barkingside, Aldborough and Fullwell. It is said that this is one of the most favoured residential areas for London taxi drivers. By gaining and retaining Ilford North, New Labour has demonstrated its ability to appeal to middle England, southern England, and suburban England.

Social indices:			2001 Gen. Election:			
% Non-white	12.9		Lab	18,428	45.8	−1.6
% Prof/Man	36.1		C	16,313	40.5	−0.2
% Non-manual	67.6		LD	4,717	11.7	+1.4
£ Av prop val 2000	135 K		UKIP	776	1.9	
% Increase 97–00	57.6		Lab maj	2,115	5.3	
% Unemployed 2001	2.5		Turnout		58.4	−13.2
% Decrease 97–01	2.1		Elect	68,893		
% Fin hard/Rank	10.3	455				
% Pensioners	27.8					
% Prem mort/Rank	24	434				

Member of Parliament

Linda Perham, a former local councillor, elected in 1997 as an MP representing Jewish and black-cab-driving voters, takes a strong line against racism and backs attempts, as with Sir George Young's 1998 bill, to regulate unlicensed and dangerous minicab drivers. Born in 1947, daughter of a gas board clerk, she was educated at Mary Datchelor Girls' School, Camberwell, Leicester University and Ealing Technical College, and worked as a librarian. She favours compulsory voting, is pro-Greek on Cyprus, and opposed to age discrimination.

ILFORD SOUTH

In 1992 Labour's Mike Gapes obtained one of the party's best results in the capital when he evicted Neil Thorne after a three-term tenure as Conservative MP for Ilford South. In 1997, after the extensive boundary changes affecting this part of north-east London, technically he had to gain his seat all over again.

Needless to say, in the circumstances of May 1997 Gapes had no difficulty in maintaining his place in Parliament. He required a positive swing of 2.5%; he achieved 16%, a huge figure but typical of the borough of Redbridge, and of Havering next door. In 2001 there was a further increase in the Labour share, which is now almost 60% (a higher figure incidentally than the Conservatives or Liberal Democrats obtained in any seat in Britain).

Ilford South had been a marginal seat for many years. Its representation has changed hands seven times since the war (including the 1945 Election). For 30 years two men alternated as MP: the Conservative was Albert Cooper, while Labour's man was Arnold Shaw. Neil Thorne gained it at the time of Mrs Thatcher's first triumph in 1979; his period of service scarcely outlasted hers.

Its political character reflects its mixed and balanced social characteristics. South contains the centre of Ilford, a major commercial and shopping centre for NE London, and the administrative headquarters of the borough of Redbridge, a rather artificial creation which stretches from the avenues of Woodford to the Barking/Dagenham border. The seat is heavily owner-occupied (less than one-twentieth is social housing), mainly of nineteenth-century terraces – the proportion of terraced housing, 64%, is among the highest in the country. Ilford South has attracted a large number of non-white residents in recent times, the proportion rising from 20% to 36% between 1981 and 1991, and it is believed that this figure will have risen substantially again when the 2001 census figures are available at constituency level. Loxford ward has a non-white majority, predominantly Asian. Labour does best in these wards, while the Conservatives fight back in Cranbrook, over towards the River Roding, and Wanstead. However, especially bearing in mind the social change affecting Ilford South, it is hard to imagine its reversion to marginal status.

Social indices:			2001 Gen. Election:			
% Non-white	35.5		Lab/Coop	24,619	59.6	+1.1
% Prof/Man	34.2		C	10,622	25.7	−4.4
% Non-manual	64.5		LD	4,647	11.3	+5.0
£ Av prop val 2000	106 K		UKIP	1,407	3.4	
% Increase 97–00	50.0		L/C maj	13,997	33.9	
% Unemployed 2001	4.8		Turnout		54.3	−15.1
% Decrease 97–01	3.1		Elect	76,025		
% Fin hard/Rank	14.1	372				
% Pensioners	21.3					
% Prem mort/Rank	28	375				

Member of Parliament

Mike Gapes, elected here in 1992, is one of Labour's many professional politicians, having worked previously for 15 years as a Labour Party apparatchik, mostly as a foreign policy specialist. A postman's son, born in 1952 and educated at Buckhurst Hill County High School and Fitzwilliam College, Cambridge, he is strongly pro-European in preference to Britain becoming 'an amusement park for American and Japanese tourists'. He was PPS to Northern Ireland Minister, Paul Murphy (1997–99) and was proud of 'being part of the British government's team negotiating the Good Friday Agreement'. A leading Labour friend of Israel, his 3,500 Jewish constituents are rather outnumbered by the third of local residents who are Hindus, Sikhs or Muslims. Once ambitious for more than life as a PPS – by 2001 to Lord Rooker – he has, if more estuarially-brogued, been likened to Nick Raynsford on steroids.

INVERNESS EAST, NAIRN AND LOCHABER

Few could dispute an assertion that general election contests in the northernmost bloc of constituencies in Scotland are consistently the most interesting in the UK. These vast seats (and this one is the second largest anywhere) are hard fought by candidates who have to project their individual merits as well as (or more than) the national party lines. Campaigning has to take place across great swathes of the most mountainous and difficult terrain in the United Kingdom. Great loyalty to long-established members is found alongside huge swings and the most unexpected results.

All the parties can clearly rely on substantial blocs of support. This seat is the heart of the hunting, shooting and fishing Highlands, packed with Conservative patriarchs and their estates. The Nationalists are aided by the Gaelic culture of the west coast and can count on some working-class support. Labour does best in the large public housing schemes in the city of Inverness, and among small farmers; and in the south of the seat in Lochaber is to be found Kinlochleven, the depressed former aluminium company town in the heart of some of the most beautiful scenery in Scotland. In 1992 the veteran Liberal, Sir Russell Johnston, had held on in Britain's tightest four-way marginal with a winning share of just 26.7%. In 1997 Labour's national strength was probably the decisive factor in enabling Labour's David Stewart to defeat Fergus Ewing, the holder of a famous name in SNP circles (he is the husband of the MSP for

Moray and son of Winnie, MEP for Highlands and Islands). The Liberal Democrats, deprived of Russell Johnston's incumbency, and the Conservatives, enduring national disaster, fell back to below 20%. Then in 2001 Stewart used the benefits of the necessary active incumbency to concentrate on local issues such as beef farming and oil rig construction to strengthen his grip, as the SNP fell back as they did across Scotland.

In February 2002 provisional boundary proposals suggested that by the next election Inverness will be reunited and paired with Badenoch to the south and east. For now though, it is still a vast and varied seat, with several distinct sections. Besides the city of Inverness itself, the large majority of which is in this division, it includes Nairn to the east, Speyside and a section of the Cairngorms, and spans the whole length of the Great Glen (including Loch Ness) to Fort William and beyond. The seat includes the nation's highest mountains and most famous monster/hoax. If anyone is able to spend the next campaign observing the election in this part of Scotland, they will again be rewarded by a fascinating and unpredictable tussle in most distinguished surroundings.

Social indices:			2001 Gen. Election:			
% Non-white	0.6		Lab	15,605	36.8	+2.9
% Prof/Man	32.1		SNP	10,889	25.6	−3.3
% Non-manual	53.0		LD	9,420	22.2	+4.7
% Unemployed 2001	2.9		C	5,653	13.3	−4.2
% Decrease 97–01	2.3		SSP	894	2.1	
% Fin hard/Rank	14.1	370	Lab maj	4,716	11.1	
% Prem mort/Rank	35	257	Turnout		63.2	−9.5
			Elect	67,139		

Member of Parliament

David Stewart, elected in 1997, third time lucky in the same seat, is a local man, born in 1956, educated at Inverness High School and Paisley College, who was a social worker or social work manager for 17 years with Inverness-based Highland Regional Council. His focus is local, on beef farming, oil-rig construction and EU Objective Funding. A loyalist, he also campaigns on behalf of diabetes. With only a third of the voters electing him in 1997 and the seat lost to the SNP in the 1999 Scottish Elections, he should have been vulnerable in 2001, especially after having to quit the Scottish Affairs Select Committee for leaking a report to Scottish Secretary Donald Dewar in 1999, but he doubled his majority in 2001 as the SNP suffered its post-devolution Westminster wilt. He was appointed in 2001 to the Work and Pensions Select Committee.

IPSWICH

The site of the first by-election of the 2001 Parliament, following the death of the 55-year-old Labour MP Jamie Cann in October of that year, the largest town in Suffolk already had one of the most curious and eventful electoral histories. Labour held Ipswich continuously from 1938 to 1970 – latterly the MP being Sir Dingle Foot, a former Liberal member (for Dundee, 1931–45) who was the elder brother of Michael. Then in 1970 Sir Dingle was beaten by just 13 votes by a Conservative with the unusual name of Ernle Money. Money retained the seat against the national swing in February 1974, when Labour were returned to power; his majority increased to 259. Then a popular local moderate Labour candidate, Ken Weetch, triumphed in October 1974 by a princely 1,733 margin. In 1979, when Mrs Thatcher was swept into office, Labour obtained their second best result anywhere in the country as Ipswich again swung against the tide to increase their majority to nearly 4,000. In 1983 Weetch held on to one of Labour's few seats in the southern half of England, and certainly their only seat in East Anglia – another fine performance. Ken Weetch seemed honoured in his own county. Some cheekily dubbed him – or maybe even his constituency – 'Ips-weetch'.

Then in 1987 Ipswich swung in an unusual manner once again, as Ken Weetch (to considerable surprise) was one of only half a dozen sitting Labour MPs defeated by the Conservatives. The new Tory member was Michael Irvine, himself the son of a former Labour MP (Sir Arthur Irvine, sometime of Liverpool Edge Hill). It has become clear that no one can count on a safe ride in Ipswich, and sure enough Irvine's position was unsure, and he lost after just one term. In 1992 Jamie Cann regained the seat for Labour, with a majority of just 265 – yet another three-figure margin. In 1997 even Ipswich did not buck the national landslide, and Cann won by 10,000, and in 2001 little changed except that the turnout fell by 15%, even more than the national average.

Labour tends to win wards with a high proportion of council-built housing, like Gainsborough and Priory Heath on the south-eastern edge of the town, and Chantry and Sprites to the south-west, and also in 'inner-city' wards in the centre such as Town and Bridge. The Conservatives fight back in favoured residential areas like Bixley and St Margaret's, and there are several marginal wards.

On 22 November 2001, the Labour candidate, the Suffolk county council leader Chris Mole, held Ipswich in a low-profile by-election overshadowed by war in Afghanistan. The turnout at 40% was higher than some dire predictions: more people did vote than attended the UEFA Cup football match between Ipswich Town (the 'Tractor Boys') and Inter Milan on the same day. No party could take much satisfaction. Labour's share dropped by 8% despite Tony Blair's international profile, which appeared to be reaping rewards at that moment. The Conservatives under their new leader Iain Duncan Smith also saw a drop in their share of 2%, from their already low base in June. The Liberal Democrats, although advancing by seven points, did not pull off one of their special by-election triumphs and failed to advance to second place.

Although currently looking like a safe seat for the first time since the 1960s, this county town on the River Orwell has shown before that it can behave in a very unpredictable manner, and should not be taken for granted by anyone.

Social indices:			2001 Gen. Election:			
% Non-white	4.7		Lab	19,952	51.3	−1.4
% Prof/Man	28.5		C	11,871	30.5	−0.6
% Non-manual	53.9		LD	5,904	15.2	+3.0
£ Av prop val 2000	75 K		UKIP	624	1.6	+1.2
% Increase 97–00	43.2		SA	305	0.8	
% Unemployed 2001	4.1		SLP	217	0.6	
% Decrease 97–01	2.3		Lab maj	8,081	20.8	
% Fin hard/Rank	20.6	266	Turnout		57.0	−15.2
% Pensioners	27.3		Elect.	68,198		
% Prem mort/Rank	29	359				

	22 November 2001 by-election:			
	Lab	11,881	43.4	−8.0
	C	7,794	28.4	−2.1
	LD	6,146	22.4	+7.2
	Oths	1,584	5.8	+2.9
	Lab maj	4,087	15.0	
	Turnout		40.2	−16.8
	Elect.	68,244		

Member of Parliament

Chris Mole became Ipswich's fifth Labour MP in 50 years at the November 2001 by-election following the death of Jamie Cann. Like Cann he came from a solid local base as Leader of the Labour–Liberal Democrat run Suffolk County Council from 1993, having lived in Ipswich for 20 years and been a county councillor from 1985. The product of a sanitised NEC-imposed shortlist of three, he allegedly caused some disappointment at Millbank in defeating two women for the nomination. Tall and lightly bearded and coming with a reputation as a Blairite Europhile, he fought a locally-focused campaign stressing the financial efficiency of his leadership of the county council. Born in 1958 and educated at Dulwich College and the University of Kent, he worked as a telecommunications research engineer from 1981 to 1998. His beard upped Labour's Commons total to 49 (where it had been 5 in 1970), and his public school education to 70 (16%) (where it had been 50 (15%) in 1970).

ISLE OF WIGHT

Because it is a county on its own, the Boundary Commission has consistently decided to retain the Isle of Wight as a single constituency, even though with over 106,000 voters it was by far the most populous in the United Kingdom at the last General Election, one-and-a-half times the English average electorate. Yet the islanders seem happy with such gross under-representation, as they have consistently opposed the detachment and merger of part of the island with territory on the mainland, such as the New Forest in Hampshire. They see the island as a separate entity with separate interests.

Although technically under-represented, the islanders do have the luxury of being able to say that they live in a marginal seat. In February 1974 Wight was hit by the political equivalent of a tidal wave as the Liberal Stephen Ross ousted a veteran Tory MP who had been involved in a financial scandal involving Bembridge Harbour.

Ross held on for 13 years by working hard and providing energetic constituency services, despite vigorous Tory challenges by candidates like Virginia Bottomley and Dudley Fishburn, who both subsequently entered Parliament in by-elections elsewhere. Ross also squeezed the Labour vote to a derisory minimum – they consistently recorded their worst performances anywhere in Britain. Then in 1987 Ross retired, and his successor as Liberal candidate was not able to hold the seat. The Conservative Barry Field never won comfortably, and he retired before the 1997 Election, when it came as no surprise that the Liberal Democrats regained the seat, by over 6,000 votes, despite a doubling of support for Labour.

In 2001 there was a fourth change of hands in less than 30 years as Andrew Turner regained the seat for the Tories, and Peter Brand was one of only two Lib Dem incumbents to be defeated, along with Jackie Ballard of Taunton. She had quite clearly been targeted by 'countryside' campaigners for her vocal opposition to fox hunting, but Dr Brand's below par performance was less expected and is less easily explicable. His support for euthanasia may have been somewhat tactless in a seat where at least 35% of the voters are pensioners. The Labour vote, far from being squeezed, increased again. The Liberal Democrats lost control of the Isle of Wight in local government in the 1998 elections for its new unitary authority, and their control there for several years may not have helped the MP. This constituency continues to rebuff being taken for granted. It remains to be seen who will take Wight on the night.

Social indices:			2001 Gen. Election:			
% Non-white	0.7		C	25,223	39.7	+5.7
% Prof/Man	31.9		LD	22,397	35.3	−7.5
% Non-manual	53.8		Lab	9,676	15.2	+2.1
£ Av prop val 2000	88 K		UKIP	2,106	3.3	+1.9
% Increase 97–00	48.4		Ind	1,423	2.2	
% Unemployed 2001	3.7		Grn	1,279	2.0	+1.3
% Decrease 97–01	3.2		Ind	1,164	1.8	
% Fin hard/Rank	9.2	483	SLP	214	0.3	
% Pensioners	35.0		C maj	2,826	4.5	
% Prem mort/Rank	25	414	Turnout		59.7	−12.2
			Elect	106,305		

Member of Parliament

Andrew Turner, a geography teacher who extricated himself from the chalk face to become a political apparatchik, first at Conservative Central Office and then as a special adviser on health service reforms and child support policy to Norman Fowler and John Moore, became one of the heroes of his party's 33-strong 2001 intake by ousting one of a pair of much-resented (in Tory eyes) Liberal Democrat MPs. His victim, Dr Peter Brand, had helpfully turned himself into a barn door target by speaking too frankly as a doctor about euthanasia in a seat with an ageing population. Son of a schoolteacher, Andrew Turner was born in 1953 and educated at Rugby, Keble College, Oxford, and Birmingham University, and latterly specialised as a consultant proselytising on behalf of the privatisation of state education, including vouchers and opted-out schools. Backing Iain Duncan Smith in all the leadership ballots, he has rejected regional assemblies as threatening rule of the Isle of Wight from Woking, and opposed a suggested tunnel to the island on both economic and environmental grounds, so seeking to eradicate his image as an 'overner' – Vectis argot for someone from the mainland three miles away at Portsmouth.

ISLINGTON NORTH

Islington North is, and long has been, a safe Labour seat in electoral terms. Yet the seat's history is more varied and interesting than these bare facts might imply. Labour's period of representation has not been unbroken here – though this is due more to the behaviour of politicians than of the local voters.

The inner north London borough of Islington was the scene of the first triumphs of the Social Democratic Party, and also of its first disaster. In 1981 and 1982 all three Labour MPs representing Islington defected to the SDP. Enough right-wing Labour councillors also defected to create the first SDP-controlled local authority. Then in May 1982 the municipal election results produced a devastating disappointment for the youthful party. Only one of their councillors retained his seat, facing a solid phalanx of 51 Labour members. The voters of Islington had decisively rejected the SDP council. Clearly the defecting MPs had as much to worry about as the councillors did. In 1983 Labour did indeed win both Islington seats reduced from three by the Boundary Commission, although Chris Smith only just did so in the South/Finsbury division both then and in 1987. Jeremy Corbyn won Islington North easily and has held it with large margins ever since, although in 2001 his lead was cut from 20,000 to 13,000 by a combination of two factors: a drastic drop in turnout, typical of inner city seats, to less than half of the voters on the roll; and revived Liberal Democrat activism, which saw their vote increase from 13% to 19%. They would still need a 22% swing to take this seat, though, which is most unlikely.

The seat includes a mixture of traditional working-class and gentrified neighbourhoods, with such well-known names as Highbury and the area around Arsenal FC, Tufnell Park, and the Blackstock Road area up to the edge of Finsbury Park, and Upper, but not Lower, Holloway. There is a significant Irish presence but the seat has scarcely more non-white residents than the London average. Having drastically redrawn the Islington seats in 1983, the Boundary Commission has since seen no need to make any further alterations. This is fairly fortunate for Islington, as both existing seats have electorates of around 60,000 compared with an England-wide average of nearly 70,000. The Commission have decided in this instance not to cross borough boundaries to equalise numbers, although they could have done so: Hackney, next door, is in a similar position. The borough is, therefore, over-represented. This is, and will remain, good news for the Labour Party and its four MPs in Hackney and Islington.

Social indices:			2001 Gen. Election:			
% Non-white	22.2		Lab	18,699	61.9	−7.4
% Prof/Man	43.8		LD	5,741	19.0	+5.4
% Non-manual	64.7		C	3,249	10.8	−2.2
£ Av prop val 2000	207 K		Grn	1,876	6.2	+2.0
% Increase 97–00	63.6		SLP	512	1.7	
% Unemployed 2001	7.6		Ind	139	0.5	
% Decrease 97–01	5.6		Lab maj	12,958	42.9	
% Fin hard/Rank	32.0	115	Turnout		48.8	−13.7
% Pensioners	19.2		Elect	61,970		
% Prem mort/Rank	47	74				

Member of Parliament

Jeremy Corbyn, MP here since 1983, was the most rebellious Labour MP in the 1997–2001 Parliament, with 64 dissenting votes, having been the third most rebellious Labour MP in the 1992 to 1997 Parliament with 72 rebellions. During the Blair government's first term he opposed everything: lone parent benefit cuts, university tuition fees, Murdoch's predatory pricing, incapacity benefit cuts, legal aid cuts, pensions unlinked to earnings, limited freedom of information, privatisation of air traffic control – and much more. At the start of the second term he voted for the dismissal of Stephen Byers' political adviser and against the bombing of Afghanistan, and rebelled serially against new anti-terrorism measures. A full-bearded, completely unreconstructed hard left-winger of compelling earnestness and unbendable conviction, with the image of a tortured Christ, his politics when not red are green – in two senses: as an apologist for any expression of radical Irish republicanism, and as a keen vegetarian environmentalist. A former union official for 12 years, eight of them with NUPE, born in 1949 and educated at Adams Grammar School, Newport (Shropshire) and (inconclusively) at North London Polytechnic, what is seemingly lacking in humour is made up for in intensity, in a life so absorbed by politics that he and his wife parted over her desire for the selective education of one of their children.

ISLINGTON SOUTH AND FINSBURY

Labour's Chris Smith has had his difficulties in winning Islington South in Finsbury, for the first time against SDP opposition in 1983, then holding on in 1987 – some even tipped him as in trouble against the Liberal Democrats in 2001. Many observers have pointed to the gentrification, even 'yuppification', of Islington. Parts of Barnsbury and Canonbury again became fashionable residential areas. Smart and chic shops, wine bars and restaurants opened up on the main thoroughfare of Upper Street and beyond. The temptation to connect these two features is evident.

Yet social change has not demonstrably been a key influence to Labour's difficulties in holding Islington South and Finsbury. In the main Islington South and Finsbury does remain a working-class, and Labour, fiefdom. There are wards with a high proportion of council tenants and non-white residents (mainly Afro-Caribbean), like Thornhill, which are overwhelmingly Labour at all levels. Islington South and Finsbury may have a slightly above average proportion of professional and managerial workers for London, but it has a very low share of the clerical and white-collar non-manual employees that market research firms call C1s. In other words, its social structure is loaded to the top and bottom of the scale.

A resident who exemplifies the top of the scale, Tony Blair, was elected Prime Minister in May 1997, while Islington South returned Chris Smith with a further increase of 11% in the Labour share. However, Labour does currently have severe difficulties in local government in Islington. There are, at the south end of the borough near the border with the City, wards with a high proportion of working-class council tenants and a relatively low number of non-white residents, like Bunhill and Clerkenwell, which have voted heavily Liberal Democrat in local elections in recent years (shades of Tower Hamlets). In 1998 the Lib Dem surge took most of the more gentrified areas too, including Canonbury and Barnsbury, and their candidates outpolled Labour's by 55% to 32% across the wards in the borough. In 2001 there was a swing of almost 8% from Labour to the Liberal Democrats, but it was based as much on the working-class elements of the seat as on the up-market shift which has received so much more attention. Smith, and New Labour, may look somewhat vulnerable to the Liberal Democrats, although it should be remembered that he held on by over 7,000 after all in 2001, but if the threat of rejection is further intensified, it will have come from all social strata in a most varied constituency.

Social indices:			2001 Gen. Election:			
% Non-white	15.4		Lab	15,217	53.9	−8.6
% Prof/Man	38.0		LD	7,937	28.1	+6.9
% Non-manual	59.5		C	3,860	13.7	+0.7
£ Av prop val 2000	274 K		SA	817	2.9	
% Increase 97–00	59.8		Ind	267	0.9	
% Unemployed 2001	6.3		Ind	108	0.4	
% Decrease 97–01	5.3		Lab maj	7,280	25.8	
% Fin hard/Rank	40.9	43	Turnout		47.4	−16.3
% Pensioners	23.5		Elect	59,515		
% Prem mort/Rank	47	64				

Member of Parliament

Chris Smith, dropped from Tony Blair's Cabinet in 2001, is a Labour politician with a doctorate on Wordsworth, elected in 1983 in a seat made marginal by Labour MP George Cunningham's defection to the SDP. Born in 1951, a civil servant's son, and educated at George Watson's College, Edinburgh and Pembroke College, Cambridge, he was given the job of Culture Secretary in 1997, before which he was best known as the first self-admitted homosexual MP (until 1997 when more followed suit). His stint as Culture Secretary was long enough for him to earn brickbats from the arts and media establishment, many members of which inhabit his modish constituency, as well as disappointing people interested in sport. With a thankless remit ranging over the BBC, the Millennium Dome, the Royal Opera House, Wembley Stadium, the National Lottery, and the Elgin Marbles, and too nice for politics, he faded from view in 2001, warning about making concessions to Murdoch, and denied – by a backbench revolt – even the consolation of a select committee chairmanship. He does not see how anyone who has read the Sermon on the Mount cannot end up a socialist.

ISLWYN

Just as the next-door seat of Blaenau Gwent, formerly Ebbw Vale, will always be associated with the great figures of its Labour MPs from 1929 to 1992, Aneurin Bevan and Michael Foot, Islwyn will be known for the shorter – but maybe even more influential – tenure in the Commons of the former party leader Neil Kinnock. This figure, possibly underrated during his superficially unsuccessful leadership, was elected to Bedwellty as a fiery radical in 1970, won the modified and renamed seat of Islwyn in 1983, and was almost immediately chosen as party leader to succeed Michael Foot. Neil Kinnock lost two general elections, the second in 1992 being ascribed in no small degree to his unpopular personality, but may in the long run have done much to make the Labour Party electable under his successors by modernising and moderating its image and essence. He stepped down after the 1992 Election, much disappointed, but was appointed to take up a role as a European Commissioner from January 1995, creating a by-election in Islwyn.

Anything but a comfortable Labour victory was hard to contemplate, for Islwyn is set in the heart of the south Wales valleys. It consists of former mining communities (the last pit in the constituency, Oakdale, closed in 1989); their names include Abercarn, Newbridge, Pontllanfraith, Blackwood, Cwmfelinfach, Crosskeys and Risca. This is singing country, full of rugby lovers – much after Neil Kinnock's heart. Don Touhig gratefully swapped a fruitless Labour candidature for Richmond and Barnes for that in the 1995 Islwyn contest, and duly won comfortably twice; but then in May 1999 there was a deep shock here, as Plaid Cymru actually took the constituency in the first Welsh Assembly election. This was largely due to mishandling by the New Labour leadership, as Alun Michael was imposed as Welsh leader in preference to Rhodri Morgan after Ron Davies's disgrace, but it shook the whole party in the valleys; Neil Kinnock's own view is unclear. In 2001 there were fears that the Nationalists might be able to produce some kind of action-replay, but this proved very wide of the mark, as they finished just about 50% behind Touhig, and actually third behind the Lib Dems too. A number of lessons had been learnt, including not to take Islwyn's support for granted, and in the end Labour may have come through a strengthening experience.

Social indices:			2001 Gen. Election:			
% Non-white	0.7		Lab/Coop	19,505	61.5	−12.6
% Welsh sp	3.4		LD	4,196	13.2	+4.8
% Prof/Man	22.5		PC	3,767	11.9	+5.6
% Non-manual	42.4		C	2,543	8.0	+0.2
£ Av prop val 2000	48 K		Ind	1,263	4.0	
% Increase 97–00	17.1		SLP	417	1.3	
% Unemployed 2001	3.7		L/C maj	15,309	48.3	
% Decrease 97–01	1.5		Turnout		61.9	−10.2
% Fin hard/Rank	28.8	149	Elect	51,230		
% Pensioners	25.1					
% Prem mort/Rank	33	279				

Member of Parliament

Don Touhig, a former Labour Whip (1999–2001), who was promoted to the Wales Office as a Junior Minister in 2001, and had, as one of the Blair government's loyal foot-soldiers, been earlier (1999) sacked but swiftly reappointed for leaking a Social Security committee report to Chancellor Gordon Brown whilst serving as his PPS (1997–99), was elected here in succession to Neil Kinnock in 1995. A small man of Irish jockey build, who spent 23 years on the local county council, he is one of three Welsh-Irish Catholics representing seats for Labour in Monmouthshire, an area where once the culture was uniformly that of Welsh Nonconformity, but where his work saving Catholic schools earned him a Papal knighthood. A miner's son, born in 1947 and educated at St Francis (RC) School, Pontypool, and East Monmouthshire College, he was a print manager and journalist, venturing out of south Wales only to hold the fort for Labour in hopeless Richmond in 1992. An instigator of legislation to protect 'whistleblowers' from victimisation, he backed Millbank's big battalions to ensure Alun Michael, not Rhodri Morgan, became Wales' First Minister. His appointment to the two-man post-devolution 'Wales' (not 'Welsh') Office in 2001, under Paul Murphy, meant the Principality was now being run – residually – by two natives of Pontypool, which some zealots would claim isn't even in Wales.

JARROW

The stereotype of the 1930s as a period of economic depression in Britain is now known to be an over-simplification. That decade also saw the greatest period of house-building in the country's history, and also the booming growth of new industries such as cars, chemicals and electricity in towns like Oxford, Slough and Luton. The pattern was very geographically varied, depending on the staple industry on which the local economy depended.

The south bank of the Tyne east of Newcastle achieved a kind of notoriety as the most depressed part of Britain in the inter-war slump years. As a result of the collapse of the Tyne shipbuilding industry, the male unemployment rate in the town of Jarrow rose to 70%, which accounts for the famous 'hunger march' to London in 1936. The unemployment rate was actually even higher in the next town on the Tyne, Hebburn, and both Jarrow and Hebburn are still Labour strongholds. The proportion of jobless on South Tyneside reached 20% again in the early 1980s, and at the time of the 2001 Election it was still one-and-a-half times the national average in the Jarrow constituency. Behind the battered river-front districts, large council developments like Jarrow's Primrose Estate still turn in heavy Labour margins. The third part of the constituency is the more mixed Boldon: West Boldon is an old colliery village, but East Boldon/Cleadon ward is a favoured private residential area which the Liberal Democrats pick up in South Tyneside borough contests. In the 2001 General Election the Lib Dems moved into second place in the seat as a whole ahead of the Tories, but remain over 17,000 and 50% of the vote behind Stephen Hepburn's rock solid share.

Jarrow will remain staunchly Labour. Its name remains a poignant and relevant reminder of the inequality and suffering associated with the blight of unemployment over 65 years after the famous Jarrow march.

Social indices:			2001 Gen. Election:				
% Non-white	0.9		Lab	22,777	66.1	+1.2	
% Prof/Man	25.7		LD	5,182	15.0	+4.0	
% Non-manual	50.7		C	5,056	14.7	-0.3	
£ Av prop val 2000	59 K		UKIP	716	2.1		
% Increase 97–00	14.2		Ind	391	1.1	-4.7	
% Unemployed 2001	5.9		SPGB	357	1.0	+0.0	
% Decrease 97–01	2.1		Lab maj	17,595	51.0		
% Fin hard/Rank	35.4	88	Turnout		54.6	-14.3	
% Pensioners	26.5		Elect	63,172			
% Prem mort/Rank	47	66					

Member of Parliament

Stephen Hepburn, a building worker turned local MP's researcher, followed his employer, Don Dixon, here as MP in 1997, having served on the local council for 12 years and obtained a conviction for assaulting a fellow councillor in 1995, in a row between Jarrow and South Shields factions on South Tyneside Council. Born in 1959, son of a shipyard worker, and educated at Springfield Comprehensive and Newcastle University, he did little to merit attention initially, tabling three written questions in his first year, but in late 2001 urged easier application of anti-social behaviour orders.

KEIGHLEY

Labour gained all nine Conservative constituencies in West Yorkshire in 1997, giving them a clean sweep of the 23 seats in the county. Some of these victories, such as Leeds NW, Shipley and Pudsey, were highly unexpected. Less of a surprise was one of Labour's front-line targets, Keighley, which Ann Cryer took by a comfortable 7,000 votes on a 10% swing. In 2001 Labour's dominance was confirmed as they held all these seats. In Keighley the majority was reduced to 4,000 and the turnout fell by 13% – but that they won at all was much to their gratification.

It might be thought that Keighley should be a Labour probable anyway; after all, they had held the seat so-named for most of the period from 1945 to 1983. Then, however, boundary changes brought in some new territory which tipped the constituency to the right. Keighley itself is a largely Labour town, with a sizeable ethnic minority population (especially in North ward, which is, however, the least strongly Labour of the three). Currently though, three other wards are joined with the three in Keighley. These include Worth Valley, a semi-rural seat with a chain of villages and small towns including the Brontës' Haworth, amongst the Pennine moors. Worth Valley is usually Conservative in local Bradford elections, except in a disastrous year. The other two Tory wards are mighty strongholds. Craven stretches over a fair spread of West Yorkshire countryside, including several small communities such as Silsden and Addingham. After Worth Valley it is the largest in acreage and least densely populated ward in Bradford, and between them they give the Keighley seat a semi-rural tone. The final ward is the best of all for the Conservatives: Ilkley, the spa town and affluent residential and commuting resort across its famous moor from Keighley, nestling on the slopes of the hills above the River Wharfe.

It is as hard to imagine Ilkley in a Labour seat as it is to contemplate the town of Keighley itself voting Conservative. It all adds up to a classically balanced marginal which will continue to be won by whichever party wins the general election as a whole.

Social indices:			2001 Gen. Election:				
% Non-white	7.5		Lab	20,888	48.2	−2.4	
% Prof/Man	34.7		C	16,883	39.0	+2.2	
% Non-manual	55.2		LD	4,722	10.9	+1.1	
£ Av prop val 2000	71 K		UKIP	840	1.9		
% Increase 97–00	20.1		Lab maj	4,005	9.2		
% Unemployed 2001	3.3		Turnout		63.4	−13.2	
% Decrease 97–01	1.1		Elect	68,349			
% Fin hard/Rank	20.3	272					
% Pensioners	27.4						
% Prem mort/Rank	29	363					

Member of Parliament

Ann Cryer, born in 1939 and so one of Blair's grannies, was elected in 1997 and with her newly elected son John (MP for Hornchurch), trod in the footsteps of her late husband Bob (MP for Keighley 1974–83 and for Bradford South 1987–94), the path of righteous rebellion against the government, on lone parent benefit cuts, university tuition fees, incapacity benefits, and privatisation of air traffic control. Her 16 rebellions during the 1997–2001 Parliament made her the most rebellious (jointly with Betty Williams) of the 65-strong 1997 intake of Labour women. Of 183 new Labour MPs in 1997, she (and her son, John) was among the mere six who immediately joined the hard left Campaign Group on reaching Westminster. Educated at secondary modern school in Darwen and at Bolton and Keighley technical colleges, after working as a Post Office clerk she became her husband's secretary, later writing an affectionate memoir of him. In 2001 she offended advocates of multiculturalism by calling for all immigrants to Britain to be obliged to learn English in order to avoid the joblessness awaiting non-English-speaking partners brought in to take part in arranged Muslim marriages – of which she, in any case, disapproved. She rebelled against the Terrorism, Crime and Security Bill in 2001.

KENSINGTON AND CHELSEA

It is a reasonable contention that if there was just one Conservative seat in the whole of Britain to survive a general election landslide, or one which would be least likely to be lost in a by-election, it would be Kensington and Chelsea. This is not because its majority is the highest in the land: that honour belonged in 2001 to the Richmond (Yorkshire) seat of the party leader, William Hague. It is more the utterly stubborn and recalcitrant nature of the Conservatism here. In May 1998, the wards in the Kensington and Chelsea constituency produced exactly the same results as they had in each election since 1982: Conservatives 24, Labour 2. The seat had some of the wards in the whole of Greater London with the highest share of the Conservative vote, all above 67%: Hans Town, Royal Hospital, Queen's Gate, North Stanley, Holland, Courtfield, Brompton, Abingdon. There was the one aberrant Labour ward of South Stanley, around the electric power-station, Chelsea Dock and the gasworks.

More typical of this elite seat are many of the famed institutions of London set among the many exclusive residential areas. Here are the Royal Hospital, the Chelsea Embankment, the Kings Road, the Natural History Museum, the Victoria and Albert Museum, Holland Park, the embassies of Kensington Palace Gardens, and Sloane Square. The well publicised myth of the 'Sloane Ranger' captures the essence of the more brusque variety of Kensington and Chelsea Conservatism, but in fact the voters are most likely to live in elegant tree-lined squares and select mews cottages tucked away behind larger dwellings.

Small wonder then that this is regarded as the single most attractive plum seat in the Commons for any Conservative; apart from its safety, its location is as convenient as any. In 1997 Alan Clark, the colourful character who became nationally well known through his brilliantly entertaining diaries, full of reminiscences of sex and snobbery, achieved and frustrated power and office, returned to Parliament after a five year gap to replace the disgraced Nicholas Scott; but his second coming was to last only two years before he was claimed by a brain tumour. First in the queue to succeed him in the 1999 by-election was Michael Portillo, who had famously and symbolically lost at Enfield Southgate in the Tory disaster of 1997, but was seen, not least by himself, as a future party leader. This hope too was dashed in the extraordinary events of summer 2001, and since it is unclear where Portillo's future career will lead, it is quite possible that this ultimate prize seat will become available yet again soon.

Social indices:			2001 Gen. Election:			
% Non-white	12.5		C	15,270	54.5	+0.8
% Prof/Man	62.9		Lab	6,499	23.2	−4.8
% Non-manual	79.9		LD	4,416	15.8	+0.5
£ Av prop val 2000	556 K		Grn	1,158	4.1	
% Increase 97–00	52.1		UKIP	416	1.5	+0.0
% Unemployed 2001	2.0		PA	179	0.6	
% Decrease 97–01	2.2		Ind	100	0.4	
% Fin hard/Rank	10.0	466	C maj	8,771	31.3	
% Pensioners	20.3		Turnout		45.2	−9.5
% Prem mort/Rank	29	369	Elect	62,007		

Member of Parliament

Michael Portillo, the failed leadership contender of 2001 (when in three ballots he won the support successively of 49, 50 and 53 MPs), was previously the emblematically unpopular, if dignified, Thatcherite victim of May 1997, when he surprisingly lost his seat at Southgate. Elected here at the November 1999 by-election in a revamped socially conscious form, including admission of his earlier homosexuality, he was born in 1953 and educated at Harrow County School for Boys and Peterhouse, Cambridge. As complete a party apparatchik as one could imagine, with eight years of

Central Office researching or ministerial advising before first entering the Commons in 1984, he was a Whip within two years, and in the Cabinet by 1992, at the Treasury, then Social Security, then Defence. A consummate professional politician, as demonstrated by first his advocacy, and then demolition, of the poll tax, and his rebranding in Opposition, his intended move from Shadow Chancellor (1999–2001) to Leader of the Opposition, though backed by 13 of Hague's Shadow Cabinet, foundered over suspicions about his apparently advanced opinions on homosexuality, drugs and, seemingly, all-women shortlists. Even his supporter, Alan Duncan, opined, 'He is a good man, he is a capable man, but he gives a lot of people the shivers'.

KETTERING

One of Labour's three super-marginal gains in Northamptonshire in 1997, Kettering, was regarded as their second most vulnerable seat in the UK in the 2001 campaign, with a majority of just 189 votes. Surely a lead this slender could not withstand any Conservative recovery at all, however small? And surely the Conservatives, free of office, could not but recover to some extent from their worst performance in at least one lifetime? Well, the Conservatives did recover, although indeed in a very small way; yet Kettering did not fall, and neither did Wellingborough or Northampton South. Labour were to be returned nationally with effectively the same overwhelming majority as four years before.

This is not the place to explain why Labour won a second landslide, but given a national swing to the Conservatives of 2% there is a need to account for the increase in their majority in Kettering, if only to 665. Labour proved efficient throughout the country in targeting their campaigning efforts to their critical marginals, in which their vote held up significantly better than average, and indeed often, as here, actually increased their share. The Liberal Democrats may not have tried as hard, and as here slightly declined. Turnout, which fell everywhere outside Northern Ireland, dropped by well under the average in Kettering and remained 8% above the national norm. Finally, Philip Sawford would have benefited from a personal incumbent vote, now denied to the Tories.

The constituency named Kettering was Labour from 1945 to 1983, and usually considered safe; but the situation was transformed in subsequent general elections as Labour's mainstay of Corby was removed and placed in a separate seat. In 1987 and 1992 in this (counter-?) revolutionised Kettering the Conservative Roger Freeman won with a majority of over 11,000. It took all of Labour's double-figure percentage swing for them to regain Kettering in 1997. Kettering itself has never been a solidly Labour town. Unlike Corby, whose economy was perilously based on the single industry of steel, Kettering has a variety of trades and light industries, including breakfast cereals, quality clothing and footwear, printing machinery and computer software. The seat also includes three of the small semi-industrial towns that are so common in central Northamptonshire: Burton Latimer, Desborough and Rothwell. Kettering's local authority district also takes in 23 villages around the Welland Valley, and the constituency is completed by some more rural and commuting villages from the Daventry district. That this epitome of middle England in the East

Midlands should now have been won twice by Labour is a sign of their current ability to appeal far outside their social and geographical heartlands, and as long as it is even close in Kettering it will not be a close contest for national government.

Social indices:			2001 Gen. Election:			
% Non-white	2.2		Lab	24,034	44.7	+1.4
% Prof/Man	32.2		C	23,369	43.5	+0.5
% Non-manual	54.6		LD	5,469	10.2	−0.5
£ Av prop val 2000	82 K		UKIP	880	1.6	
% Increase 97–00	43.7		Lab maj	665	1.2	
% Unemployed 2001	1.7		Turnout		67.4	−8.3
% Decrease 97–01	1.1		Elect	79,697		
% Fin hard/Rank	11.5	423				
% Pensioners	25.4					
% Prem mort/Rank	20	476				

Member of Parliament

Phil Sawford, a centre-parted-hair, periodic stooge questioner, whilst also being a Campaign Grouper, was Labour's most marginally elected MP in 1997. Local-born (1950), son of a building worker, and educated at Kettering Grammar School and then eventually at Ruskin College, reaching Leicester University in his early 30s to read sociology, he is a former Corby steelworker who became manager of a training organisation dealing mainly with the unemployed, and was leader of Kettering Council for six years before 1997. Despite a low Commons profile, he is one of the few MPs of the 1997 intake to emerge as a fairly frequent rebel – on pensions, Lords reform and air traffic control privatisation. He joined the Campaign Group by 1999, one of only 10 of the 183-strong 1997 intake to do so by that time. A local man very much made good, any or all of these assets – or the UKIP vote of 880 – could have explained his trebled but still perilously slight majority of 665 in 2001.

KILMARNOCK AND LOUDOUN

Here's the lowdown: this constituency produced one of the three best SNP results in industrial Scotland in 1997. Along with Glasgow Govan and Ochil, it saw the SNP share of the vote surpass 30%. Although the New Labour candidate Des Browne held on with a slightly increased majority of 7,000, the Nationalists' Alex Neil also improved by almost 4%. This advance was reflected in local elections too, where the SNP outpolled Labour in the unitary authority contests of 1999 within the seat, and in the inaugural Scottish Parliament election, also in that year, when Labour were only 7% ahead. This suggested that it would be wise to keep an eye open for a further interesting result here in the 2001 General Election, especially if Labour were to prove less popular after a spell of government than it was in 1997 – not an unreasonable assumption.

Yet apparently the attraction of the Nationalists declined the more distant the election, as it were, for in the Westminster battle not only did they not do as well as those for the East Ayrshire and Edinburgh bodies, but they did considerably more poorly than 1997. Admittedly they were deprived of their charismatic candidate from that year, the party leadership contender Alex Neil, but the 9% drop in their vote also reflected their national decline in these contests. Was Westminster still seen as relevant by Nationalist voters?

The seat consists of the proud and independent town of Kilmarnock (characterised as 'Graithnock' in the novels and short stories of its native son William McIlvanney), and some smaller communities such as Kilmaurs, Stewarton and the small textile towns of the upper Irvine valley: Galston, Newmills, Darvel. Though known for the production and bottling of whisky ('Johnnie Walker') this area has a variety of industries – and a rate of unemployment tha the rest of Scotland, although the rate fell by 25% between 1997 and 2001, perhaps another reason for Labour's share increase here (though their absolute vote declined as the turnout went down by over 15%). Its economic fortunes should play a major role in determining the result in Kilmarnock and Loudoun, or more likely a redrawn and rather alliterative Kilmarnock, Stewarton and Cumnock.

Social indices:			2001 Gen. Election:			
% Non-white	0.5		Lab	19,926	52.9	+3.1
% Prof/Man	29.8		SNP	9,592	25.5	−9.1
% Non-manual	48.6		C	3,943	10.5	−0.3
% Unemployed 2001	5.8		LD	3,177	8.4	+4.4
% Decrease 97–01	2.2		SSP	1,027	2.7	
% Fin hard/Rank	37.9	69	Lab maj	10,334	27.4	
% Prem mort/Rank	44	104	Turnout		61.7	−15.5
			Elect	61,049		

Member of Parliament

Desmond Browne was shoe-horned into this seat at the last minute in 1997 as a Donald Dewar-linked lawyer and Blairite replacement for retiring left-winger Willie McKelvey. Dewar's PPS (1998–99) and orthodox in his support for Labour's devolution settlement, he was born locally, in 1952, and educated at St Michael's (RC) Academy, Kilwinning, and at Glasgow University. His career at the Bar eclipsed by his move to Westminster, and rising 50, it was hard to see him making much advance on his small job as PPS to Northern Ireland Minister, Adam Ingram, until he replaced Ingram in his Junior Ministerial job in the Northern Ireland Office in 2001 – a second Catholic in a ministerial team of three.

KINGSTON AND SURBITON

One of the most remarkable results in the 2001 General Election occurred in Kingston and Surbiton. It had been the most surprising, and by far the closest, of the five Liberal Democrat gains in outer south-west London in 1997. Although they had taken control of Kingston borough council in 1994, few expected them to be able to translate that victory into parliamentary terms, and most observers considered the Conservative MP Richard Tracey safe, and cast their view towards neighbouring seats like Richmond Park and Twickenham. Tracey was estimated to have a notional 1992 majority of over 15,000. However, his support fell apart, the vote share dropping by no less than 16.5%, well above the national average, and even without squeezing Labour Edward Davey overtook Tracey to win by 56, the party's second lowest majority after the disputed Winchester result.

Many expected this to be a flash in the pan and doubted Davey's ability to hold the seat, particularly after the Liberal Democrats not only lost the borough of Kingston in May 1998 but ceased to be the largest party on the council. The Conservatives brought in a super-combative new candidate, the former Dover MP David Shaw, who had been brought up locally. A battle royal ensued. But the result was not even close as Davey won by an astonishing 15,676. His share of the vote had increased by over 23%, easily the best Lib Dem performance anywhere in another very good year for the party. Clearly tactical voting had played a large part, as the Labour support defected in droves, two thirds of it disappearing between 1997 and 2001 – perhaps the vigorous Lib Dem propaganda against the abrasive Shaw had an effect, plus the diversion of efforts into neighbouring Wimbledon, where Labour's share went up and the Liberal Democrat's down. Yet the Tory proportion itself fell by over 8%, so it was not just a question of tactics. It was a triumph for the 35-year-old Ed Davey, a name to be watched for the future, and contrastingly a disaster for David Shaw. Whoever would have thought that Surbiton, chosen as the fictional deep suburban setting for TV's sitcom *The Good Life*, could have seen a Conservative lose by such a vast margin. One suspects that Penelope Keith's character Margot Leadbetter would have done better.

Social indices:			2001 Gen. Election:			
% Non-white	8.0		LD	29,542	60.2	+23.5
% Prof/Man	43.8		C	13,866	28.2	−8.3
% Non-manual	71.2		Lab	4,302	8.8	−14.3
£ Av prop val 2000	170 K		Grn	572	1.2	
% Increase 97–00	68.9		UKIP	438	0.9	+0.1
% Unemployed 2001	1.5		SLP	319	0.6	
% Decrease 97–01	1.6		Ind	54	0.1	
% Fin hard/Rank	6.0	581	LD maj	15,676	31.9	
% Pensioners	25.1		Turnout		67.5	−7.8
% Prem mort/Rank	15	537	Elect	72,687		

Member of Parliament

Edward Davey, a Liberal Democrat Treasury spokesman, and co-originator of his Party's 1997 'penny on income tax to pay for education' policy, won the seat in 1997 to his great and justifiable surprise given the subsequent loss of his party's control of Kingston council a year later. A management consultant (1993–97) after four years as economics adviser to Liberal Democrat MPs, he was born in 1965, a solicitor's son, and educated at Nottingham High School, Jesus College, Oxford and Birkbeck College, London. Clean-cut and personable, if to some patronising, he appeared to face a hard fight against Conservative David Shaw, one of the more controversial partisan Thatcherite backbenchers during the 10 years (1987–97) he represented Dover, seeking a comeback in the town where he started his political career as a councillor. But such was Shaw's hard-right reputation that the Labour vote collapsed into Davey's arms, helping turn a 56-vote majority into one of 15,676. As Shadow Chief Secretary to the Treasury from 2001, he was well-placed to know how his party would be paying for all its generous spending commitments.

KINGSTON UPON HULL EAST

The east end of Hull contains the Humber city's main industrial area, several miles of commercial docks, and several square miles of council estates (although by the time of the 1991 Census almost half of all households were owner-occupied, now outnumbering the 40% in local authority accommodation). East is the safest of the three Labour seats in Hull, appropriately enough returning the former merchant seaman and renowned pugilist John Prescott to Parliament with a majority of over 15,000 in 2001, even on a turnout of just 46%. All the wards which make up the seat return a full slate of Labour councillors to the city council, now a unitary authority following the abolition of 'Humberside'. A typical stronghold would be the ward of Marfleet, which is by the river and includes the easternmost docks; six out of ten residents in Marfleet live in council-built housing, two-thirds do not have a car, and over one-tenth are single-parent families. Over 83% of the 16% who turned out in the May 1999 city elections voted Labour. On several occasions the Conservatives have not bothered (or been able) to put up candidates in local elections in Hull, where low turnouts are a symbol of the true lack of competition.

One might almost suggest that they might be advised not to contest Hull East at the next general election either, but that would be against precedence and principle, of course, and in any case the Tories would have to be seen to present an alternative to Labour's Deputy Prime Minister. Mr Prescott certainly has a fitting seat here in the solidly working-class east end of the industrial port and metropolis of Humberside, or rather of the East Riding of Yorkshire.

Social indices:			2001 Gen. Election:			
% Non-white	0.7		Lab	19,938	64.6	−6.7
% Prof/Man	18.9		LD	4,613	14.9	+5.1
% Non-manual	41.9		C	4,276	13.8	+0.1
£ Av prop val 2000	38 K		UKIP	1,218	3.9	
% Increase 97–00	14.3		SLP	830	2.7	
% Unemployed 2001	6.9		Lab maj	15,325	49.6	
% Decrease 97–01	1.6		Turnout		46.4	−12.5
% Fin hard/Rank	38.3	64	Elect	66,473		
% Pensioners	27.0					
% Prem mort/Rank	46	82				

Member of Parliament

John Prescott, Deputy Prime Minister, was elected MP for Hull East in 1970. Born in 1938, a railwayman's son who failed the 11-plus and so attended Ellesmere Port Secondary Modern School and went straight into the merchant navy at 17 for eight years, he entered Hull University via Ruskin College, Oxford, and spent two years as a seamen's union official before inheriting this safe seat. A frontbench spokesman for 18 years in Opposition before 1997 and a failed leadership contender in 1994, his job as Environment, Transport and the Regions supremo from 1997 to 2001 will be largely recalled for the non-arrival of an 'integrated transport system'. In the 2001 Election campaign he added to his portfolio of syntactical inexactitudes a distraction into pugilism at Rhyl, prompting the *Daily Telegraph* to reflect that 'if he had been Tony Blair his career would have been at an end', and that the incident revealed 'a boiling, brutish, ignorant nature'. Thereafter he was removed to the Cabinet Office, where allegedly all the progress-chasing ministers report not to him but to the Prime Minister, and where for his two Cabinet Office predecessors, Jack Cunningham and Mo Mowlam, the job had proved a final posting.

KINGSTON UPON HULL NORTH

Hull is a gritty predominantly working-class and industrial city; it does have jobs for middle-class workers but many of them live in suburban constituencies like Haltemprice and Howden or Beverley and Holderness. Of the three seats within the city boundaries North has the highest proportion of workers in professional, managerial and non-manual jobs, and one ward, Newland, actually elects a Liberal Democrat councillor on occasion. There is a bloc of what is for Hull almost elite housing around the university in wards such as Beverley and Stoneferry, and recently the Liberal Democrats have been starting to establish something of a cluster of support there, but they could only return two councillors in the 1999 Elections for the new Hull unitary authority, the sole opposition to the ruling Labour group. In the 2001 General Election the Liberal Democrats advanced to second place here as in many other northern working-class Labour strongholds, but as in almost all of the rest of these it was still a very distant second, although maybe a platform should the national government become unpopular.

Despite the middle-class enclave, North is a safe Labour seat, for it also contains the poorest council estates in wards such as Noddle Hill and Orchard Park, where over 80% of the housing was originally built by the city council. It may be safe, but it can hardly be called solid, for these wards break electoral records not just for high Labour shares of the vote but for low turnout. In Noddle Hill, for example, in May 1999, 13% of the electors went to the polls. Hull as a whole consistently turns in the lowest turnout of any city in the country in local elections, and all three seats produced general election participation rates of under 50% for the first time in 2001. This may still be more to do with the uncompetitive nature of its politics and its very working-class profile than apathy or alienation from the democratic process, but the latter factor can no longer be ruled out of consideration. In many ways this question is more important and interesting than that of who goes to Westminster as Hull's representatives: the electoral victor throughout the city in 2001 was abstentionism.

Social indices:			2001 Gen. Election:			
% Non-white	1.6		Lab	16,364	57.2	−8.7
% Prof/Man	24.9		LD	5,643	19.7	+5.1
% Non-manual	45.3		C	4,902	17.1	+2.1
£ Av prop val 2000	39 K		UKIP	655	2.3	
% Increase 97–00	11.5		SA	490	1.7	
% Unemployed 2001	7.0		LCA	478	1.7	
% Decrease 97–01	2.8		Ind	101	0.4	
% Fin hard/Rank	34.9	94	Lab maj	10,721	37.4	
% Pensioners	21.7		Turnout		45.4	−11.5
% Prem mort/Rank	35	242	Elect	63,022		

Member of Parliament

Kevin McNamara, the third-longest serving Labour MP, a former schoolteacher and college law lecturer, born in 1934 and educated at St Mary's (RC) College, Crosby, and Hull University, has been an MP here since winning the 1966 by-election that prompted Harold Wilson to hold a snap general election and win a 97-seat majority. A Liverpool Irishman, far too green to represent Labour's Northern Ireland policy in government as he had in opposition (1987–94), he left the frontbench in 1995, and failed in a move to change the Oath of Allegiance to let in the Sinn Fein MPs in 1998 and again in 2001 when he also sought to remove the bar to Catholic succession. Apart from a single-track preoccupation with Northern Ireland, he has rebelled on lone parent and disability benefit cuts, and earlier, in opposition, promoted bills to ban hunting and hare-coursing. In 2001 he voted serially against the anti-terrorism legislation.

KINGSTON UPON HULL WEST AND HESSLE

'It's a long way round whichever way you go'. Hull is rightly regarded as one of the least well-known of Britain's conurbations, the sort of place that people don't go to unless they have a good reason to visit, and not many have that; it is not on the way to anywhere, and few just pass through. It is nevertheless a proud and independent city, with a full range of civic institutions, a well-established university, and a range of industries in addition to its status as a leading east coast port. It is a regional centre of great economic and political influence.

It is also a Labour stronghold with three very safe seats – and its west end, unlike in many towns, is no exception. The Hull West seat contains much of the city centre and the fishing docks, and a variety of predominantly working-class residential areas (although noticeably less council housing than the other two Hull seats). There is some variety in the shape of the town of Hessle, bordering the city of Hull to the west, the northern terminus of the controversial Humber Bridge. Before 1997 Hessle was in the Conservative Beverley division, and a number of objections were raised at the local boundary inquiry by residents fearful of being swallowed up by the large (and 'socialist') neighbour. One sop to Hessle residents did come out of the inquiry process, though: the name of the small town was included in the constituency's title.

One curiosity in the 2001 General Election result here: whereas in the other two Hull seats the Liberal Democrats overtook the Conservatives to move into (a distant) second place, here the reverse happened. This would scarcely bother Labour's victorious Alan Johnson, although a turnout of 46% might and should.

Social indices:			2001 Gen. Election:			
% Non-white	1.4		Lab	16,880	58.4	−0.3
% Prof/Man	22.4		C	5,929	20.5	+2.4
% Non-manual	44.6		LD	4,364	15.1	−3.1
£ Av prop val 2000	44 K		UKIP	878	3.0	
% Increase 97–00	24.4		Ind	512	1.8	
% Unemployed 2001	7.3		SLP	353	1.2	
% Decrease 97–01	1.7		Lab maj	10,951	37.9	
% Fin hard/Rank	29.8	133	Turnout		45.8	−12.4
% Pensioners	28.4		Elect	63,077		
% Prem mort/Rank	43	123				

Member of Parliament

Alan Johnson, a former postman and eventually postman's union (CWU) leader, was elected here in 1997 after the last-minute exit-with-a-peerage of the sitting MP Stuart Randall. After a spell as PPS to Dawn Primarolo, he entered the government in 1999 as a DTI Minister responsible for the Post Office, moving up as Minister of State with responsibility for ACAS in 2001 – in both jobs poacher-turned-gamekeeper. A smooth, sharp-looking Londoner, born in 1950 and educated at Sloane Grammar School, Chelsea, he represents the acceptable face of marginalized union influence transmuted to Blairite specifications.

KINGSWOOD

Since first created as a seat in its own right in February 1974, Kingswood has been regarded as very marginal and until 1992 it was always won by whichever party won the general election itself: Labour in both 1974 contests, Conservative subsequently. However, in 1992 Labour's Roger Berry ousted the Conservative incumbent Rob Hayward with a better than average performance – a swing of nearly 6%, and subsequently Kingswood has veered well to the left of the norm among constituencies, having always seemed so close to average. After a further swing in their favour in 2001 Labour have a majority of 14,000 and the appearance of a seat which seems virtually safe.

Kingswood is an urban seat, and very much part of the Bristol conurbation. Most of its population is located just beyond the city's official local government limits, in the built-up area around Kingswood itself and Mangotsfield, but it also include two wards within Bristol, Frome Vale and Hillfields. Like the largest west country city as a whole, the seat has moved firmly away from the Conservatives for more than a decade now, and cannot for the time being be regarded as a marginal. However, the abolition of the county of Avon and its replacement by four unitary authorities on the former Somerset/Gloucestershire borders mean that further boundary changes are in the air in an area which has been much tinkered with over the past 30 years or so, and the Bristol city elements will be removed from a smaller Kingswood seat, which may in due course become closely fought once more.

Social indices:			2001 Gen. Election:			
% Non-white	1.7		Lab	28,903	54.9	+1.1
% Prof/Man	27.3		C	14,941	28.4	−1.6
% Non-manual	56.3		LD	7,747	14.7	+1.9
£ Av prop val 2000	95 K		UKIP	1,085	2.1	
% Increase 97–00	57.4		Lab maj	13,962	26.5	
% Unemployed 2001	1.4		Turnout		65.4	−12.3
% Decrease 97–01	1.9		Elect	80,531		
% Fin hard/Rank	10.3	458				
% Pensioners	26.6					
% Prem mort/Rank	19	492				

Member of Parliament

Dr Roger Berry, an academic economist originally elected in 1992, became virtuously identified with disability legislation, but has suffered from his equal keenness for left-Keynesian economics and a linked opposition to the deflationary economics of the Maastricht Treaty, seeing the European debate as the only place where the Labour left can raise the issues of tax, public spending and welfare. Born in 1948 and educated at Huddersfield New College and Bristol University, he taught economics at Bristol University and spent 12 years on the local Avon County Council. Disliking Labour's 'Welfare to Work' programme, he has restricted his disobedience to welfare issues in voting against lone parent benefit cuts and in 1999 leading the revolt on disability allowance cuts with his own amendment.

KIRKCALDY

The 'Lang Toun' of Kirkcaldy has a mile-long esplanade on the Firth of Forth, but the birthplace of Adam Smith and Robert Adam, and the childhood home of Gordon Brown (still a fan of the local football team, Raith Rovers, and likely to move to be MP for Kirkcaldy and Cowdenbeath after the boundary changes) is not really a seaside resort: it is an industrial, working-class town of solid Labour support. Even in 1955, the high-water mark of modern Conservatism in Scotland, when they won more than half the seats, they could get no closer than 7,500 votes behind Labour. Once a port for the Fife coalfield and a centre of the linoleum industry, Kirkcaldy has diversified its range of employment sources, although its rate of joblessness was still a little above the Scottish average in June 2001 (it stood seventh highest in the list of Scottish seats), and considerably higher than the British average (43rd).

There are other communities apart from Kirkcaldy itself, such as Burntisland and Kinghorn, which are tourist attractions on the Forth, but still vote Labour most years. The coastal strip extends to the north too, past a batch of villages named Wemyss to the little port of Buckhaven. All this is strongly Labour too. The Scottish Nationalists are a clear but distant second in Kirkcaldy now. One luminary may well be the Prime Minister fairly soon, which will be a source of pride to the local Labour faithful; while the Tories, who claim Adam Smith as one of their own, must think that he is rotating in his interment.

Social indices:			2001 Gen. Election:			
% Non-white	1.0		Lab/Coop	15,227	54.1	+0.5
% Prof/Man	28.5		SNP	6,264	22.2	−0.7
% Non-manual	51.1		C	3,013	10.7	−3.0
% Unemployed 2001	7.2		LD	2,849	10.1	+1.5
% Decrease 97–01	1.6		SSP	804	2.9	
% Fin hard/Rank	37.9	68	L/C maj	8,963	31.8	
% Prem mort/Rank	42	137	Turnout		54.6	−12.4
			Elect	51,559		

Member of Parliament

Dr Lewis Moonie, unlike the rest of the numberless ranks of Labour doctorates, actually has a real one – in medicine – albeit psychiatric medicine. Elected here in 1987 and a frontbench spokesman for eight years, he was dropped by Blair on the morrow of victory, but then oddly recalled as a Defence Minister in 2000. Born in 1947, son of a Tory accountant, he attended Grove Academy, Dundee, and St Andrew's and Edinburgh Universities. Barrel-shaped in the manner of Scots Labour MPs, he is, nonetheless, as a linguist and chess player, a good deal more cerebral than most and would no doubt have had an interesting professional line on why his predecessor as MP, Harry Gourlay, had recourse to a toupee.

KNOWSLEY NORTH AND SEFTON EAST

Although its geographical shape is far from absurd, this seat is a social and political monstrosity.

The borough of Knowsley, centred on Huyton and Kirkby east of Liverpool, proved an awkward case for the Boundary Commission which reported before the 1997 General Election. It was too big to have just one seat, but if it remained divided into two they would be unacceptably small. The existing Knowsley North was already reduced to less than 49,000 electors, following the depopulation of Cantril Farm and Kirkby through flight and demolition. The Commission decided that it was necessary to pair Knowsley with a neighbouring borough. St Helens was almost exactly the right size for two seats, and Liverpool for five, so that left Sefton, with its oversized Crosby seat. The outcome of the Commission's work has produced seats of fairly even electorates, but nevertheless created a storm of protest based on political and social animus and even fear.

Knowsley North was an impoverished and troubled Labour stronghold. One element of the newer seat under discussion consists of that seat less the town of Prescot, transferred into Knowsley South. This leaves the community of Kirkby, plus Knowsley Park and the ward still called Cantril Farm (where the turnout in the 2000 borough elections reached the dizzying heights of 15%). This is a council estate on the edge of Liverpool that developed a reputation for crime and drugs so horrific that it was renamed 'Stockbridge Village'. The image of Kirkby is scarcely any better. In the post-war years much of Liverpool's poorer population were resettled in council housing developments on the edge of the Merseyside conurbation. The best-known of these, and in some ways the most notorious, is Kirkby. Kirkby is not a New Town but a series of vast, depressing and impersonal council estates created in the 1950s. In 1951 the population was 3,000, in 1961 52,000. For many Britons, Kirkby was best known as the setting of the BBC TV police series of the 1960s, *Z Cars*. In the 1980s large parts of some of the worst estates, such as Tower Hill, were demolished. Kirkby was seen by many as an attempt at creating a community that failed. Small wonder that Knowsley North was the second safest Labour seat in England at the 1992 Election.

Now Knowsley North is paired with three wards formerly in middle-class Crosby, in an utterly divided seat. The wards of Park, Sudell and Molyneux together have an electorate of about 32,500, nearly half of the total of 71,000. It is likely that their proportion will increase. Most of these voters live in the town of Maghull, an expanding community of private housing (over 90% owner-occupied) popular with newly weds and the aspiring middle orders. The rest are scattered among smaller communities: Aintree, site of the Grand National, and some villages like Lunt and Ince Blundell on the fertile west Lancashire plain. These wards see close contests between Liberal Democrats and Conservatives locally, with Labour in third place overall.

Maghull residents fought hard not to be paired with Kirkby for electoral purposes, but the Commission's will prevailed. At least for the time being the monolithic nature of the Labour vote in Knowsley North easily outvotes Sefton East's somewhat more mixed pattern, and the regional swing to Labour which has made Crosby itself seem a safe seat nowadays suggests that this state of affairs is as permanent as can be foreseen.

Social indices:			2001 Gen. Election:			
% Non-white	0.9		Lab	25,035	66.7	−3.2
% Prof/Man	25.2		C	6,108	16.3	−1.0
% Non-manual	53.4		LD	5,173	13.8	+2.7
£ Av prop val 2000	62 K		SLP	574	1.5	−0.2
% Increase 97–00	16.2		Ind	356	0.9	
% Unemployed 2001	5.7		Ind	271	0.7	
% Decrease 97–01	3.0		Lab maj	18,927	50.4	
% Fin hard/Rank	28.2	157	Turnout		53.0	−17.1
% Pensioners	22.4		Elect	70,781		
% Prem mort/Rank	42	140				

Member of Parliament

George Howarth, one of 20 ministers or whips dropped by Tony Blair in 2001, was elected here in 1986 as a less photogenic replacement for the departed-for-TV, perma-tanned, prime-minister-who-never-was, Robert Kilroy-Silk. Inserted as part of the campaign to erode Militant influence on Merseyside, he reached the frontbench in 1990 and was a competent if colourless bottom ranking minister, at the Home Office (1997–99) where he resisted calls for the legalisation of cannabis, and in

Northern Ireland (1999–2001). A fitter-turned-TUC-official, he was born locally in 1949, son of a plumber, and attended Huyton Secondary School, Kirkby FE College, Liverpool Polytechnic and Salford University. Retorting when likened in appearance in the *Guardian* to a 'serial killer', that 'appearances are not always deceptive', his receding chin sports one of the PLP's 49 beards.

KNOWSLEY SOUTH

The second largest numerical majority for any party in 2001, 21,316, was recorded in Knowsley South, in Labour's interest. This was a remarkably high figure, given that the turnout was only 52% of the electorate. Knowsley South is essentially the successor to the Huyton constituency, which will for ever be associated with Harold Wilson, who won four general elections as leader of the Labour Party. Wilson enjoyed an excellent relationship with his seat. In 1964, the first election after he became leader of the party, he enjoyed a 10% swing and an increase in his majority from 6,000 to 19,000. When his first premiership came to an end in 1970, his lead at Huyton still increased. He did not suffer a serious negative swing in Huyton until 1979, after he had resigned the leadership; and he retired in 1983 after having represented this area in Parliament for nearly 40 years. It had started this period as a marginal; it ended as a very safe Labour seat.

This transformation was not entirely to Wilson's personal credit. Huyton and its smaller neighbour Roby were regarded 50 years ago as relatively upmarket residential areas, but the Conservative elements were swamped by overspill developments such as that of Kirkby in the 1950s. Kirkby is now in Knowsley North, not in this seat, but the tone of Knowsley South is given by the large council estates on the edge of the Liverpool conurbation like Page Moss, Woolfall Heath and Longview – the sort of places to which inner-city dwellers were decanted in the post-war slum clearances. The accent is determinedly Scouse, and the Conservative Party vote has declined rapidly here in recent years, as it has over the border in the city itself.

The borough of Knowsley is named not after a town, but after Knowsley Park, seat of leading local aristocrats, the Stanleys (Earls of Derby), although that is in Knowsley North. Knowsley South also includes Whiston and Halewood, the site of the Ford motor works, and now the cable-making town of Prescot, taken from Knowsley North. Merseyside is one of Labour's very strongest areas, and there is no prospect of a change in political allegiance here. They might as well weigh the votes as count them.

Social indices:			2001 Gen. Election:			
% Non-white	1.1		Lab	26,071	71.3	−5.9
% Prof/Man	23.5		LD	4,755	13.0	+4.7
% Non-manual	50.1		C	4,250	11.6	−1.0
£ Av prop val 2000	58 K		SLP	1,068	2.9	
% Increase 97–00	11.9		Ind	446	1.2	
% Unemployed 2001	7.2		Lab maj	21,316	58.3	
% Decrease 97–01	3.1		Turnout		51.8	−15.7
% Fin hard/Rank	35.6	85	Elect	70,681		
% Pensioners	22.8					
% Prem mort/Rank	45	92				

Member of Parliament

Eddie O'Hara, an unobtrusive MP here since 1990, long since (1993) retreated into the dignified non-partisan limbo of committee chairmanships, comes, Bootle-born in 1937, with good working-class credentials as the son of a horse-keeper at the local docks, if over-laid with education at Liverpool Collegiate School and Magdalen College, Oxford, and a teaching career taking him to Liverpool Polytechnic via several years as a classics master in two public schools. His passion for the Classics explains his partiality for Greek Cyprus and for most things Greek. As a Merseyside MP he defends local Pools interests against the National Lottery, and has translated Beatles songs into Latin.

LAGAN VALLEY

Lagan Valley may well be the seat both of the immediate past leader of the Ulster Unionist Party, and of the next leader. Until 1997 it had been held for 27 years by James (now Lord) Molyneaux, who quietly but cannily held his party together through external storms and internal dissension. Now however, diverse responses to the post-Good Friday Agreement political scene in Northern Ireland suggest that if the hard-liner Jeffrey Donaldson does succeed David Trimble, it will be as a result of a vehement and even violent splits in the province's largest party, which cast doubt on its future role and effectiveness.

The seat is to be found immediately to the south-west of Belfast. Lagan Valley is centred on the Lisburn District Council. The area is fairly compact and densely populated, and takes its name from the River Lagan, which eventually flows through the heart of Belfast into Belfast Lough. In addition to the substantial urban population of Lisburn, perhaps the surprise among five new cities created in the UK in 2002, there are a number of smaller communities, such as Hillsborough (site of the Anglo-Irish agreement of the mid-1980s), Moira and Glenavy. The M1 motorway bisects the constituency.

The political complexion of this predominantly Protestant seat is strongly Unionist. Back in the early 1980s the DUP improved its position and became very competitive in Lisburn, but they did not oppose James Molyneaux on the last three occasions he contested Lagan Valley, and since 1997 their candidates have had little room to do well against Jeffrey Donaldson. The Nationalist parties barely exceeded 10% of the vote between them, and it was Seamus Close of the middle-of-the-road Alliance Party who finished a very distant second in 2001. Donaldson, once the youngest member of the Northern Ireland Assembly, and still only 34 when first elected here, seems to have a safe seat for life. His broader political fate, and that of his party, is far more uncertain.

Social indices:		2001 Gen. Election:			
% Prof/Man	31.4	UUP	25,966	56.5	+1.1
% Non-manual	56.0	APNI	7,624	16.6	−0.6
% RC	13.7	DUP	6,164	13.4	−0.1
% Irish sp	2.4	SDLP	3,462	7.5	−0.2
% Unemployed 2001	2.3	SF	2,725	5.9	+3.4
% Decrease 97–01	1.8	UUP maj	18,342	39.9	
		Turnout		63.2	+1.0
		Elect	72,671		

Member of Parliament

Jeffrey Donaldson, elected here in 1997, is David Trimble's rival for the leadership of the Ulster Unionists as head of the anti-Agreement majority among the Party's reduced-to-six parliamentary group. Uncharacteristically cerebral and young (born in 1962) for a Unionist MP, most of whom were dismissed by Trimble as 'woodentops', he campaigned against the Good Friday Agreement in the 1998 referendum and was barred by Trimble as a candidate in the Northern Ireland Assembly elections. A former estate agent, educated at Kilheel High School and Castlereagh College, his mild and soporific manner conceal a steely ambition to be Trimble's replacement when power-sharing collapses, provided he is not outclassed by another non-woodentop, David Burnside.

LANCASHIRE WEST

West Lancashire is a starkly divided constituency. On the one hand it includes much of the fertile and prosperous west Lancashire plain centred on the town of Ormskirk. This is historically among the Conservative Party's best territory anywhere in the nation, with many overwhelmingly strong wards such as Aughton Park, Aughton Town Green and Bickerstaff. Interestingly, it is one of the centres of long-term Roman Catholic recusancy in England, with many ancient and prominent landowning Catholic families. On the other hand West Lancashire incorporates the New Town of Skelmersdale, which has one of the highest rates of unemployment in the country. Skelmersdale is even more strongly Labour than the rest of the constituency is Tory. In 2001 there was no doubt about which face of the division dominated. The Conservative Kenneth Hind had won each of the first two contests in this constituency, in 1983 and 1987, but it was always rather odd that Skelmersdale should have a Tory MP. This windy hilly town has never been one of the more successful New Towns. Besides the notorious joblessness, it has had difficulty attracting and keeping population, and a large number of houses remain empty. The attempt to sell them at knock-down prices – under £3,000 in some cases – has not worked well. Skelmersdale has played a major role in Labour's victories in West Lancashire since 1992, when Colin Pickthall beat Kenneth Hind by 2,000 votes. In 1997 the seat suddenly did not look marginal any more, as Pickthall increased his lead massively, to over 17,000, and won more than twice the votes of his Conservative rival. A key indicator has been that the town of Ormskirk itself has clearly given a majority of preferences to Labour over the Conservatives in the Lancashire county council elections coterminous with the last two general elections. In 2001 Pickthall's lead was apparently dramatically cut, to under 10,000, but this was much more due to a decline in turnout than a positive swing to the Tories, whose own vote slipped by more than 2,000. That abstentionism was higher in Skelmersdale than on the plain, as figures from the county council elections showed.

Social indices:			2001 Gen. Election:			
% Non-white	0.8		Lab	23,404	54.5	–5.9
% Prof/Man	35.4		C	13,761	32.0	+3.0
% Non-manual	55.7		LD	4,966	11.6	+4.4
£ Av prop val 2000	80 K		Ind	523	1.2	+0.5
% Increase 97–00	19.0		Ind	317	0.7	
% Unemployed 2001	3.7		Lab maj	9,643	22.4	
% Decrease 97–01	1.8		Turnout		59.0	–15.8
% Fin hard/Rank	20.8	259	Elect	72,858		
% Pensioners	22.4					
% Prem mort/Rank	29	365				

Member of Parliament

Colin Pickthall, Jack Straw's PPS since 1999 and a man with a rough-hewn piratically bearded visage, won this seat for Labour in 1992. A unilateralist Prescott-voting left-winger-turned-loyalist, he was born in 1944, attended Ulverston Grammar School and the Universities of Wales and Lancaster, and then taught in schools and higher education colleges for 25 years. An insulin-dependent diabetic, he has launched bills to ban hare coursing – famously practised in his constituency at the Waterloo Cup – backs the standard Labour teachers' opposition to league tables and selective schooling, and urges no foot-dragging on right-to-roam legislation.

LANCASTER AND WYRE

Before the 2001 Election Lancaster and Wyre looked like one of the two or three most vulnerable Labour seats in the whole of Britain. In the most recent local elections in the wards which make up the seat, the Conservatives had led by 14%, and in the June 1999 European elections if votes cast within the seat were totted up that advantage would have been over 20%. The seat had only been contested once, at the time of Labour's unprecedented 1997 landslide, and even then Hilton Dawson had only won by 1,295 votes, half the combined number polled by the anti-European parties. The Lancaster portion of the seat had only been won on rare occasion by Labour, and the Wyre section consisted of even more unpromising rural and suburban territory in an historically deeply Conservative part of Lancashire, the Fylde peninsula.

The boundaries of Lancaster and Wyre now reach almost to the Fylde coast, taking in the small towns of Preesall and Poulton-le-Fylde and villages such as Hambleton. The Lancaster division had an interesting history and some entertaining MPs: the adventurer and novelist Sir Fitzroy Maclean (1945–59), the homosexual-law crusader and multiple party-changer Humphry Berkeley (1959–66) and the redoubtable Dame Elaine Kellett-Bowman (1979–97). Hilton Dawson is the second ever Labour MP after Stanley Henig (1966–70). The 1966 Labour government lasted just four years, despite its overall majority of nearly 100, falling after a dismal display of incompetence involving clashes with and collapses before trade unionism, economic disasters ranging from inflation to devaluation, and internal divisions shoddily papered over by a leadership apparently battered from pillar to post. The contrast with the effective first term of New Labour under Messrs Blair and Brown was illustrated by Dawson's victory against the predictions and the odds, with a higher share of the vote on a turnout which held up rather better than the national average. The performance will have to be just as convincing in the party' unprecedented full second term for this unlikely seat to be held for a third time in a row.

Social indices:			2001 Gen. Election:			
% Non-white	1.4		Lab	22,556	43.1	+0.3
% Prof/Man	37.1		C	22,075	42.2	+1.6
% Non-manual	61.0		LD	5,383	10.3	−1.3
£ Av prop val 2000	75 K		Grn	1,595	3.0	+1.7
% Increase 97–00	23.3		UKIP	741	1.4	+0.2
% Unemployed 2001	2.2		Lab maj	481	0.9	
% Decrease 97–01	1.3		Turnout		66.3	−9.0
% Fin hard/Rank	7.9	526	Elect	78,964		
% Pensioners	30.6					
% Prem mort/Rank	28	372				

Member of Parliament

Hilton Dawson, elected in 1997, a local Lancaster councillor for ten years and child care-officer-turned-social services manager, born in 1953 and educated at Ashington Grammar School, and Warwick and Lancaster Universities, has rebelled against lone parent benefit cuts, a total ban on hand guns, and the Prime Minister's right to nominate life peers – a spattering of dissidence untypical of the on-message intake of 1997. He has a ponderous mode of speech.

LEEDS CENTRAL

The central and inner-city parts of Leeds have suffered from depopulation over the past decade or so in the same way (although not quite to the same extent) as the corresponding areas of the other large northern cities, Sheffield, Manchester and Liverpool. This necessitated the one boundary change in Leeds proposed by the 1995 Commission report. Central now takes in the innermost ward of the former Leeds South and Morley seat, Hunslet, in addition to its previous four wards.

This had no electoral effect. Central was already the safest of Labour's four Leeds seats, and Hunslet is one of the most working-class and strongly Labour wards in the whole city. The Central constituency covers the commercial area of the former woollen metropolis, the university buildings, and part of the city's relatively small black and Asian communities. Almost all of the old back-to-back housing for which Leeds was once famous has given way to modern redevelopment, some of it high-rise – the first ever residential tower block in Britain was built here, within the Richmond

Hill ward. The proportion of social housing is the highest in the city, although there is a majority of owner-occupiers in the tight-knit old terraced community of Beeston, home area of the poet Tony Harrison. Harrison celebrates traditional working-class life, and lifelong commitment to the Labour Party is very much in evidence in inner Leeds.

Tony Benn left the House of Commons in 2001 after a chequered career spanning over 50 years, but his name was assured of continuing, as in 1999 his son Hilary had entered the house in a by-election caused by the premature death of Derek Fatchett. The younger Benn won easily enough, but the turnout was only 19%, the lowest figure in Britain since the Second World War, which presaged the appalling participation rate throughout Britain in the 2001 General Election. In Leeds Central the figure was just 41% then, the fourth lowest in England – a figure which would deeply concern a true parliamentary democrat like Benn *père*.

Social indices:			2001 Gen. Election:			
% Non-white	8.4		Lab	18,277	66.9	−2.7
% Prof/Man	21.6		C	3,896	14.3	+0.5
% Non-manual	42.8		LD	3,607	13.2	+2.0
£ Av prop val 2000	48 K		UKIP	775	2.8	
% Increase 97–00	35.5		SA	751	2.8	+1.9
% Unemployed 2001	7.8		Lab maj	14,381	52.7	
% Decrease 97–01	3.2		Turnout		41.7	−13.0
% Fin hard/Rank	41.8	39	Elect	65,497		
% Pensioners	25.7					
% Prem mort/Rank	52	32				

Member of Parliament

Hilary Benn was elected at a 1999 by-election on the lowest turnout (19%) for half a century. The fifth member of his family to reach the Commons in four successive generations (and overlapping in the Commons for two years with his father, Tony), he represents Labour's only parliamentary dynasty, and one bettered by few on the Conservative benches. Born in 1953 and educated at Holland Park Comprehensive School (instead of his father's Westminster School, for which he had been entered) and Sussex University, he worked as a union (APEX then MSF) researcher for 22 years. A remarkable chip off his father's block in looks and mannerisms he may be, but ideologically he is, in his own words 'a Benn, but not a Bennite', having ditched his unilateralist and Eurosceptic past as a left-wing Ealing councillor for 20 years, for the Blairite road paved with realism and seats. He backed NATO's bombing of Serbia and favoured performance-related pay for teachers as former Education Secretary David Blunkett's political adviser (1997–99). Whimsically mocking the Fabians with 'What do we want? Gradual change. When do we want it? In due course', he acquired a walk-on part in 2001 as Junior Minister for International Development.

LEEDS EAST

The wards in the city of Leeds are very large. Not quite as large as those in Birmingham or Sheffield maybe, but populous enough to make minor adjustments between constituencies difficult, for the Commission do not violate ward boundaries. Typically a Leeds constituency will have just four wards, each of over 15,000 electors. The four which make up Leeds East are all different in character.

Seacroft has the highest proportion of council housing of any seat in the city, still over two-thirds council-owned in 1991, and consists of a series of vast, windy, almost all-white, working-class estates towards the eastern edge of the city, built in the 1930s and 1950s to house people moved from the city centre. It is overwhelmingly Labour. The Labour candidate received 74% of the vote in the local elections in May 2000. Halton ward, on the other hand, is an entirely different matter. There is virtually no council housing. Most of the middle-class Tory residential areas in Leeds are situated in the north of the city, but Halton is an exception, set along the A63 road near the eastern edge of the conurbation towards Garforth. In 2000 the Conservatives won the ward, as usual. A third different flavour, both socially and politically, is given by Burmantofts. This is an inner-city ward where old back-to-back housing has been cleared in favour of lower density development, some in the form of tower blocks. In the 1980s and early 1990s the Liberal Democrats took Burmantofts more often than not, but now it looks safely Labour. Finally, a fourth angle is provided by Harehills north-east of the city centre. Harehills still has much old terraced housing, and like neighbouring Chapeltown (in Leeds NE) it has been colonised by Leeds's Asian and black population – Harehills was 30% non-white in 1991. It seem to be heading in the other direction from Burmantofts. In 2000 the Liberal Democrats gained this ward from Labour. East's wards are individually interesting, but the overall result is less so. Labour wins easily. Leeds East will always be associated with its MP from 1955 to 1992, Labour's former Defence Secretary and heavyweight foreign expert Denis Healey, whom many thought was unlucky never to lead his party; he retired and gave way to the former city council leader George Mudie.

Social indices:			2001 Gen. Election:			
% Non-white	9.3		Lab	18,290	62.9	−4.5
% Prof/Man	24.2		C	5,647	19.4	+0.8
% Non-manual	49.1		LD	3,923	13.5	+3.2
£ Av prop val 2000	51 K		UKIP	634	2.2	
% Increase 97–00	18.5		SLP	419	1.4	
% Unemployed 2001	6.1		Ind	142	0.5	
% Decrease 97–01	3.9		Lab maj	12,643	43.5	
% Fin hard/Rank	39.8	55	Turnout		51.5	−11.3
% Pensioners	25.7		Elect	56,400		
% Prem mort/Rank	45	96				

Member of Parliament

George Mudie was elected in 1992, having been leader of Leeds city council for ten years. One of a score of Scots representing English seats for Labour, he was born in 1945, educated at Lawside Academy, Dundee (and later at Newbattle Abbey College, Midlothian), and worked as an engineer until becoming a NUPE official for 24 years. Very locally focused, and Old Labour, he rose quickly in the Whips' office from 1994, to Deputy Chief Whip by 1997, but was switched to Education as a Junior

Minister after refusing a posting to Northern Ireland, and dropped altogether a year later. He is one of Labour's small minority who vote against homosexual sex at 16, and as a former big city boss, dislikes regional government – which has nevertheless been arriving piecemeal (Ulster, Wales, Scotland, London) in much the same way as the Plymouth to Folkestone (Channel Tunnel) motorway was being constructed as an entirely random series of south coast bypasses.

LEEDS NORTH EAST

For years Leeds NE had been gradually moving away from its traditional status as a Tory stronghold, and in 1997 it fell to Labour for the first time. This was for 31 years the seat of Mrs Thatcher's guru and spiritual forebear and colleague, Sir Keith Joseph, but he saw his majority eroded, even in 1979, the year of Thatcherite take-over of the reins of government. His difficulty concerned social change. North East Leeds was held by many to be the best residential quadrant in the city, but gradually the parts of the wedge closest to the inner city changed in nature, as the older housing was taken over by students and other multi-occupiers, and members of the non-white communities. It needed a boundary change in 1983, which moved the centre of gravity of the seat further out towards the edge of the city, to keep NE in the 'safe Conservative' column. No such relief was provided by the Boundary Commissioners before 1997, for they left the lines unaltered.

The social and political mix of North East is also still moving in Labour's favour. There are still two very middle-class and affluent wards, but North, which is based on the modern owner-occupied housing developments of Alwoodley, on the far northern edge of the city, has usually been won by Liberal Democrats in Leeds city elections in recent years and Labour is competitive in the older classic residential area of Roundhay, near Leeds's biggest park. Moortown is one of the centres of the third largest Jewish community in Britain, after London and Manchester. When Jews stopped off at Leeds, having arrived at east coast ports a century or so ago, they settled in the Chapeltown/Harehills area. With success and affluence born of hard work and skills, they moved out into Leeds's northern middle-class area – Moortown, the Allertons, and beyond. Although there are many Jewish Conservatives (for whom voting for Sir Keith Joseph was logical enough), the Jewish vote has always been somewhat more Labour than average when controlling for class. Finally, the fourth and most southern ward, Chapel Allerton, contains much of the Chapeltown area which is still popular with those of immigrant stock. It is the most heavily non-white ward in the city, with a third of the population belonging to ethnic minority groups, approximately evenly black and Asian. Chapel Allerton is now strongly Labour, and indeed in May 2000 a 'Left Alliance' candidate was second there in the city elections

Labour did well in middle-class areas in general in 2001, and Leeds NE saw yet another swing in their direction. With a lead of 7,000, Fabian Hamilton should hold on even if the Conservative vote draws level with Labour nationally.

Social indices:			2001 Gen. Election:			
% Non-white	15.3		Lab	19,540	49.1	−0.0
% Prof/Man	44.6		C	12,451	31.3	−2.6
% Non-manual	68.2		LD	6,325	15.9	+2.0
£ Av prop val 2000	96 K		LA	770	1.9	
% Increase 97–00	38.5		UKIP	382	1.0	
% Unemployed 2001	3.6		SLP	173	0.4	−0.6
% Decrease 97–01	2.2		Ind	132	0.3	
% Fin hard/Rank	16.6	324	Lab maj	7,089	17.8	
% Pensioners	28.3		Turnout		62.0	−10.0
% Prem mort/Rank	25	415	Elect	64,123		

Member of Parliament

Fabian Hamilton was elected in 1997 after a bitter selection process involving the barring by Labour's NEC of the hard-left candidate Liz Davies. Black-bearded and sallow, born in 1955, son of a judge with the surname 'Uziell-Hamilton', and educated at Brentwood School and York University, his parliamentary career has been less eventful than his selection, with his Jewish background reflected in his concern for the Middle East peace process. Described by a fellow Leeds MP as 'a brilliant speaker, but a terrible businessman', he has worked in graphic design and computing, and served 11 years on Leeds council. In 2001 he uncharacteristically broke ranks to vote against the Terrorism, Crime and Security Bill.

LEEDS NORTH WEST

One of Labour's more unexpected gains in the 1997 General Election occurred in Leeds NW, not so much because of an unusually large increase in their vote share, but because they had to advance from third place in 1992, and clearly took votes from the previous runners-up, the Liberal Democrats, as well as the previous winners, the Conservatives. North Leeds is the major middle-class residential area in the West Yorkshire conurbation. A large proportion of the non-manual workers of Leeds live within the city limits, rather than commuting in from outside. This has meant that for many years Leeds was able to sustain two safe Conservative constituencies, North East and North West, while Sheffield had just one, and Manchester, Liverpool and Newcastle had been reduced to none at all. Now Leeds and Sheffield have joined that club, although Leeds NW was the hardest nut for Labour to crack.

Like NE, which was long the seat of Sir Keith Joseph, NW has been affected by the changing nature of its inner section, close to the city centre, but here too the Tory decline was delayed by boundary changes. North West used to include Kirkstall, named after the ruined abbey by the river Aire, but this Labour-inclined ward was moved into Leeds West in 1983. Another part of the old 'west end', Headingley, famed for its rugby league and cricket grounds, turned to Labour for the first time in the 1970s, as the large houses became multi-occupied and the middle classes moved further out. It is now a very weak ward for the Tories, heavily multi-occupied and favoured by students from the nearby university, which led to complaints even from the MP, Harold Best, a long-time local resident. However, the geographical and spiritual centre of the seat is no longer Headingley, as the seat also includes the more Conservative suburban wards of Cookridge and Weetwood out towards the edge of the city, and even extends well beyond the old boundaries to Otley and Wharfedale.

The Liberal Democrats have been advancing in Leeds council elections very recently, taking Weetwood and Headingley from Labour in 2000, but the Labour vote held up very well in the 2001 General Election. Indeed the Conservatives were the only major party to fall back in that year, and Leeds NW looks increasingly like yet another middle-class urban seat that has passed beyond their grasp.

Social indices:			2001 Gen. Election:			
% Non-white	5.9		Lab	17,794	41.9	+2.0
% Prof/Man	44.1		C	12,558	29.6	−2.5
% Non-manual	67.9		LD	11,431	26.9	+3.3
£ Av prop val 2000	97 K		UKIP	668	1.6	
% Increase 97–00	39.0		Lab maj	5,236	12.3	
% Unemployed 2001	2.1		Turnout		58.2	−12.4
% Decrease 97–01	1.6		Elect	72,945		
% Fin hard/Rank	12.8	400				
% Pensioners	27.5					
% Prem mort/Rank	21	473				

Member of Parliament

Harold Best, a bald and bearded electrician educated at a secondary modern and technical college, Leeds-born in 1937, was unexpectedly catapulted into Westminster in his 60th year in 1997, in a seat where he had been chairman of the local Labour Party for four years. Formerly a friend of the Marxist historian E.P. Thompson and a leading activist in CND, he subsequently confirmed his un-Blairite credentials by rebelling against lone parent benefit cuts, the predatory pricing of the Murdoch press, the Criminal Justice (Terrorism and Conspiracy) Bill, the Prime Minister's power to nominate life peers, and disability benefit cuts. In 2001 he rebelled against the proposed ban on incitement to religious hatred in the emergency Terrorism Bill. A sometime factionalist in the electricians' (ETU) union, he dislikes postal balloting, claiming it was used against him when he ran against Frank Chapple for the union leadership.

LEEDS WEST

Leeds West has seen two of the greatest reversals of fortune in recent British electoral history, within the last 20 years. It was held by Labour from the war up to the 1979 Election, Joe Dean's majority in that last year being nearly 10,000. Then in 1983 a thunderbolt struck. Coming from third place in the previous contest, the Liberal Michael Meadowcroft surprised nearly everyone (at least outside Leeds and outside the Liberal Party) by ousting Dean by over 2,000 votes. In fact this victory was based on one of the earliest and most thorough examples of 'community politics'. Moving from street to street, focusing on local problems, working from the bottom up and providing a concentrated, concerned and conscientious service, the Liberals had initially established a base in local politics and now reaped a rare parliamentary reward at the time of the ebb of Labour's fortunes.

Alas, it was to go all too sour: 1983 had proved a low-water mark for Labour, and in 1987 Meadowcroft was beaten after just one term by John Battle. Apparently his approach had been deemed to be more suitable for municipal than parliamentary purposes by the voters. Things went from bad to worse. Michael Meadowcroft never accepted the Liberals' alliance with the SDP, and helped to form a breakaway Liberal Party. He stood under their banner in Leeds West in 1992, splitting the centrist vote evenly with a Liberal Democrat – but neither secured even a tenth of the vote, and Battle's majority leapt from under 4,000 to nearly 14,000, over a Tory. West now seems safe for Labour than ever before, and Battle won by 15,000 from the Tory in 2001, but perhaps the tradition of community politics is not dead in Leeds West, for in that year the Green Party candidate David Blackburn increased his share of the vote from an unimpressive 2.2% in 1997 to 8.0%, which not only saved his deposit but represented his party's second best performance anywhere after Brighton Pavilion.

The seat consists of four wards near the river Aire in working-class west Leeds: Armley, Bramley, Kirkstall and Wortley, the centre of the Green activity, where Blackburn has been a councillor since 1998 and where the Greens received twice Labour's vote in 2000. West seems refreshingly open to small parties and new ideas, although under the present electoral system it is very hard to see David Blackburn or any other Green emulating Michael Meadowcroft and actually reaching the Commons.

Social indices:			2001 Gen. Election:			
% Non-white	3.9		Lab	19,943	62.1	−4.5
% Prof/Man	23.5		C	5,008	15.6	−1.9
% Non-manual	46.9		LD	3,350	10.4	+1.4
£ Av prop val 2000	51 K		Grn	2,573	8.0	+5.8
% Increase 97–00	26.1		UKIP	758	2.4	
% Unemployed 2001	4.4		Lib	462	1.4	−0.1
% Decrease 97–01	1.8		Lab maj	14,935	46.5	
% Fin hard/Rank	32.4	110	Turnout		50.0	−12.9
% Pensioners	25.7		Elect	64,218		
% Prem mort/Rank	40	185				

Member of Parliament

One of a clutch of former or ex-aspirant priests in Labour's ranks (see also David Cairns, Greenock and Chris Bryant, Rhondda), **John Battle**, a bearded former left-wing unilateralist and Gulf-War opponent, elected here in 1987, found himself as a Minister of State at the Foreign Office in a strange location for one whose diplomatic skills were somewhat disguised by an excitable, forceful and loquacious manner, and whose removal from office in the post-election reshuffle of 2001 came as no great surprise as the Foreign Office team was newly geared up with effortlessly smooth Europhiles. Born in 1951, the son of an electrician, and educated at Catholic schools and at Upholland (RC) Seminary, Liverpool and (later) at Leeds University, where he read English, he worked as a (Catholic) Leeds MEP's researcher, and then for Church Action on Poverty. He votes the Catholic ticket on abortion and had a certain interest in the dealings with Indonesia over East Timor. On being dropped in 2001 he joined other sacked ministers and never-to-be ministers on the International Development Select Committee.

LEICESTER EAST

The Leicester East MP and former Europe Minister Keith Vaz was the object shortly before the 2001 Election of multiple allegations regarding financial irregularities and his role in securing passports for the millionaire Hinduja brothers. Collapsing in a TV studio in spring 2001, he maintained a strikingly low profile both locally and nationally during the May/June campaign. Yet although his vote share slipped by 8%, this was scarcely a major collapse on the scale say of that of Labour's vote in St Helens South, where a defecting Conservative MP was selected (legitimately by the local membership), or Birmingham Perry Barr (where an Asian candidate was selected, also legitimately), still less than in Wyre Forest (where an independent anti-hospital closure campaigner swept away all opposition). Vaz was not reappointed to the ministerial team, but he held his seat very easily by over 13,000 votes, Labour's largest majority in Leicester. He had clearly maintained the faith and support of most of his local communities.

Leicester East is one of the most strongly Asian constituencies in Britain, with 38% of its population classing themselves as non-white in the 1991 Census – and Asians tend to turn out to vote in large numbers. There are several wards here which are majority non-white: Belgrave, Latimer and Rushey Mead along the A46 Fosse Way north of the city centre; Charnwood immediately east of the centre. Keith Vaz was the first member of the Commons of Asian origin for over 50 years, although he is a Catholic born in Aden while his Asian constituents have in the main migrated from India via East Africa, before the mass expulsions from Kenya and Uganda in the late 1960s and early 1970s. There are still middle-class (and/or white) wards in Leicester East: Evington, Thurncourt, Humberstone and West Humberstone. Whatever befalls Keith Vaz personally, with a five-figure majority Labour seem to have a safe seat now, and the proportion of Asian voters can only rise as their young population grow up.

Social indices:			2001 Gen. Election:			
% Non-white	38.0		Lab	23,402	57.6	–7.9
% Prof/Man	20.9		C	9,960	24.5	+0.5
% Non-manual	39.5		LD	4,989	12.3	+5.3
£ Av prop val 2000	54 K		SLP	837	2.1	+1.1
% Increase 97–00	24.1		BNP	772	1.9	
% Unemployed 2001	4.8		Ind	701	1.7	
% Decrease 97–01	1.2		Lab maj	13,442	33.1	
% Fin hard/Rank	38.0	67	Turnout		62.1	–7.3
% Pensioners	27.6		Elect	65,527		
% Prem mort/Rank	41	158				

Member of Parliament

Keith Vaz, who was dropped from the government in the post-election reshuffle of June 2001, had been the first Asian Minister in the Commons since the first ever – Lord Sinha in 1919. Elected in 1987 and self-presented as the Asian community's leading politician, he is in fact a public school (Latymer Upper) and Cambridge (Gonville and Caius)-educated solicitor-turned-barrister, born (1956) in Aden of Goan Catholic parents, and so shares with the rest of the albeit diverse British Asian community at least the colour of his skin. A smooth and skilled weaver amongst the orthodoxies as in his variable private and public utterances on Rushdie's *Satanic Verses*, his ministerial career had been delayed by allegations of involvement in in-fighting in local Leicester politics, but by 1999 he was first a Junior Minister in the Lord Chancellor's department and then, in the same year, Minister for Europe. But thereafter he was soon engulfed in a rich stew of allegations relating to donations from businessmen to the Labour Party, his ownership of properties, his intervention in the passport application by the billionaire Hinduja brothers and the added claims that he had not fully co-operated with the parliamentary watchdog's enquiry into his affairs. Under the weight of these pressures his ministerial career collapsed, notwithstanding his patron, Lord Chancellor Irvine's, view of him as 'the most incredible networker I have ever seen'.

LEICESTER SOUTH

It is hard to remember now that in 1983 Leicester South produced the closest result in the whole election, and the last to be declared on the first night. It was a bitter blow for Labour, on a night of many such knock-backs as Mrs Thatcher was on her way to victory by 140-plus seats. Their sitting member Jim Marshall lost to the Conservative Derek Spencer by just seven votes. In 2001 Marshall was back, returned by over 13,000 with substantially more than half of the votes cast, at a time when Labour obtained their second successive overall majority of over 160. The two elections seem a century apart, although in fact the transformation occurred within only two decades.

One can see how the Conservatives used to be able to win this seat. South contains the best residential areas in Leicester itself, especially in the Knighton area. Mansions line the A6 as it leaves Leicester on its way south-east towards Market Harborough. The former Leicester South East, which was abolished in 1974, was safely Conservative. There is also another owner-occupied Conservative ward in the south-west of the city, at Aylestone. More mixed are the almost all-white council estate wards Eyres Monsell and Saffron Lane, and Castle, which includes Leicester University. However, there are also true Labour strongholds. South contains most of the city centre, and a sizeable proportion of Leicester's huge (80,000 strong) Asian community. This old textile town has become known since the Second World War as one of the centres of immigration to Britain.

After the first wave from the Asian subcontinent in the 1950s and 1960s, there was a particular boost when General Idi Amin expelled the Ugandan Asians in 1972. Many found their way from East Africa to Leicester, and settled in the privately rented and owner-occupied terraces around the centre of the town. Spinney Hill ward reported itself to be 82% non-white at the 1991 Census and voted 89% for Labour in the city council elections of the same year. Crown Hills was 76% non-white, Wycliffe just over 50%. There is also a prominent Afro-Caribbean community in the seat, particularly in the Highfields area. In the last couple of general elections these innermost wards have counteracted the influence of the leafy suburbs, and South now looks pretty much safe for Labour.

Social indices:			2001 Gen. Election:			
% Non-white	32.3		Lab	22,958	54.5	–3.5
% Prof/Man	31.3		C	9,715	23.1	–0.7
% Non-manual	49.8		LD	7,243	17.2	+3.4
£ Av prop val 2000	64 K		Grn	1,217	2.9	
% Increase 97–00	30.3		SLP	676	1.6	+0.3
% Unemployed 2001	6.0		UKIP	333	0.8	
% Decrease 97–01	1.6		Lab maj	13,243	31.4	
% Fin hard/Rank	36.9	75	Turnout		58.0	–9.1
% Pensioners	23.9		Elect	72,671		
% Prem mort/Rank	38	203				

Member of Parliament

Jim Marshall, a rough-hewn former polytechnic lecturer, elected interruptedly here since 1974 (he was out from 1983–87) rose quickly in four years as a Leicester city councillor to become its leader before election as a local MP. Born in 1941 and educated at Sheffield City Grammar School and Leeds University, he was dropped by Smith as a frontbencher on Northern Ireland in 1992, voted for Beckett not Blair in 1994, and rebelled 24 times against the Whips in the 1992–97 Parliament, often over Europe. He rebelled against the government on student fees, Incapacity Benefits, legal aid cuts and freedom of information, between 1997 and 2000, and rebelled serially against the Terrorism, Crime and Security Bill in 2001. Scurrilously tabloid-linked to Clare Short in 1997, passé and quiet, he was out-gunned in Leicester by Ministerial neighbours, Keith Vaz and Patricia Hewitt during the Blair government's first term, and by Patricia Hewitt on her own thereafter.

LEICESTER WEST

Leicester West is essentially the white working-class seat in the East Midland city. It has the fewest non-white residents by far. It also has the highest proportion of council-built housing. These facts are not unconnected, for Asians have preferred to live together in owner-occupied or privately rented houses rather than being dispersed among council estates. Thus in Leicester West we find wards like North Braunstone (still with 77% council housing at the time of the 1991 Census, and only 3% non-white) and Mowmacre (57% and 3% respectively).

West was for a long time the safest Labour seat in the city, now it is the least, although after the last two landslides none of them are vulnerable. In 1983 it was the only constituency that Labour held; in 2001 it had the smallest of the three majorities. How did this happen? Like many other East Midland working-class districts, West showed favour to Mrs Thatcher's policies and government. It does not have the solid Labour voting blocs of East and South, although the white areas in those seats are of higher status. Greville Janner's majority slipped to a mere 1,200 in 1987, Patricia Hewitt won last time by a comfortable 9,500-plus. The age of Thatcherism had passed on and away and West now supports a different kind of conservatism, Blairite – and Brownite – New Labour.

Social indices:			2001 Gen. Election:			
% Non-white	15.3		Lab	18,014	54.2	–1.0
% Prof/Man	22.8		C	8,375	25.2	+1.5
% Non-manual	41.8		LD	5,085	15.3	+1.1
£ Av prop val 2000	50 K		Grn	1,074	3.2	+1.8
% Increase 97–00	28.6		SLP	350	1.1	–0.1
% Unemployed 2001	6.2		SA	321	1.0	+0.2
% Decrease 97–01	1.7		Lab maj	9,639	29.0	
% Fin hard/Rank	37.2	73	Turnout		50.9	–12.5
% Pensioners	25.8		Elect	65,267		
% Prem mort/Rank	44	108				

Member of Parliament

Patricia Hewitt, the first (with Charles Clarke) of the 1997 intake to reach the frontbench in 1998 (as Economic Secretary to the Treasury), she was also (with Clarke) the first to enter the Cabinet – as Trade and Industry Secretary in 2001, having been a Minister of State at the DTI from 1999 to 2001. For a swifter Cabinet entry one has to recall Peter Shore in 1967 (after three years as an MP) and Harold Wilson in 1947, after two years. Born in 1948 into the Australian political establishment (as daughter of Sir Lennox Hewitt, leading civil servant in the Prime Minister's Office and later head of QANTAS), she attended the Church of England Girls' School, Canberra, ANU and Newnham College, Cambridge, then rose through a series of politics-related jobs as head of the NCCL, aide to Neil Kinnock (co-drafting his famous 1985 Militant-bashing conference oration), and deputy head of the think-tank IPPR, before increasing her disposable income with three years at Andersen Consulting. Highly able, small, intense and possessing a charmless self-confidence, with a somewhat patronising, deliberately articulated mode of speech, she has inspired in one Labour MP the sentiment that he would prefer Norman Tebbit as a desert island cohabitee. The last of a metropolitan coterie of Labour women to reach the Commons – Harman, Jowell, Hodge – she has now outstripped them all.

LEICESTERSHIRE NORTH WEST

A glance at the boundaries of North West Leicestershire might indicate an attempt to create a Labour seat in rural Leicestershire. From that party's point of view, the better parts of both Bosworth and Loughborough – both Conservative gains in the 1970s, after long periods in Labour's hands – were gathered together in 1983 in this new constituency based on the declining Leicestershire coalfield. In fact the Boundary Commission did not act in a politically partisan manner, of course. They simply based the extra seat they awarded to the county on the local government district of the same name which now forms the whole of the seat. For all their hopes, NW Leicestershire for a long time proved a disappointment for Labour. In 1983 the Conservatives won by nearly 7,000 votes; in 1987 by nearly 8,000. It hardly seemed marginal. Then in 1992 the swing to Labour in this seat almost matched that in the city of Leicester: 6%. This slashed David Ashby's majority to under a thousand. In 1997, after David Ashby had departed under a small cloud, Labour finally triumphed, with one of the largest majorities of any gain, 13,219.

The biggest town is Coalville, named after what was for so long its staple industry; the market town of Ashby-de-la-Zouch is more Conservative, but it still voted in a Labour county councillor on the same day as the 2001 General Election. The villages and smaller communities of the constituency tend to vote according to whether their original dependence was on mining or on agriculture. Overall this is a more working-class seat than average, and it is likely that Labour will be able to match the three terms that the Tories won here between 1983 and 1992.

Social indices:			2001 Gen. Election:			
% Non-white	0.8		Lab/Coop	23,431	52.1	−4.3
% Prof/Man	30.4		C	15,274	33.9	+3.0
% Non-manual	49.1		LD	4,651	10.3	+1.7
£ Av prop val 2000	74 K		UKIP	1,021	2.3	
% Increase 97–00	30.7		Ind	632	1.4	
% Unemployed 2001	1.7		Lab maj	8,157	18.1	
% Decrease 97–01	1.3		Turnout		65.8	−14.2
% Fin hard/Rank	13.3	391	Elect	68,414		
% Pensioners	24.9					
% Prem mort/Rank	22	457				

Member of Parliament

David Taylor, Labour victor here in 1997, is a local man, born in 1946 at Ashby-de-la-Zouch, educated at Ashby Boys' Grammar School and Leicester Polytechnic, and a former local councillor and computer manager at the nearby Leicestershire county council offices for 20 years. Claiming to be a traditional mushy-peas rather than an avocado Labourite, he has salted his inconspicuous loyalism with vocal defence of small businesses buried by red tape, and has coped with the threat to his Leicestershire skies from the local East Midlands Airport, by rebelling against air traffic control privatisation. He echoed Gordon Brown's anti-elitist assault on public schools in 2000, and in 2001 resisted the Terrorism, Crime and Security Bill.

LEIGH

As one travels west from Manchester towards Liverpool, from the Borough of Salford to the borough of Wigan, the scenery flattens into a plain, and the traditional economic base changes from the textiles of the Pennines to coal. However, the Lancashire coalfield has declined throughout the century and as the pits closed smaller-unit light industries have been established here, in Leigh and in the smaller towns of the plain, such as Atherton, Hindley and Golborne. This is the terrain which makes up the Leigh parliamentary constituency. In 2001 Labour's new candidate Andy Burnham, replacing the quiet veteran Lawrence Cunliffe, over 40 years his senior, and obtained a majority of over 16,000, even though fewer than half of the voters on the electoral roll actually stirred themselves to vote, a decline of over 15%, and a lower level than those of the other Wigan borough seats.

There is a strong anti-Tory culture here, probably based on the history of coal-mining; it should also be remembered that this is a very working-class seat, with a high proportion of skilled manual workers. This is traditional Labour heartland support. The seat is over 99% white; there is one of the lowest proportions of one-parent families of any of Labour's strongholds in the North West – only neighbouring Wigan and Makerfield have lower. The Labour Party has lost its old-fashioned strength among stable communities outside the inner cities, but that very disappointing turnout must cast doubt on the level of its enthusiasm.

Social indices:			2001 Gen. Election:			
% Non-white	0.8		Lab	22,783	64.5	−4.4
% Prof/Man	25.5		C	6,421	18.2	+2.6
% Non-manual	45.6		LD	4,524	12.8	+1.6
£ Av prop val 2000	48 K		SLP	820	2.3	
% Increase 97–00	15.3		UKIP	750	2.1	
% Unemployed 2001	3.1		Lab maj	16,362	46.4	
% Decrease 97–01	1.6		Turnout		49.7	−16.0
% Fin hard/Rank	23.9	211	Elect	71,054		
% Pensioners	24.0					
% Prem mort/Rank	39	194				

Member of Parliament

Elected in 2001, **Andy Burnham**, former political adviser to former Culture Secretary Chris Smith, inherited this safe seat by way of a late selection process in March, involving an NEC-imposed shortlist. Born, son of a telephone engineer, in 1970, and raised locally in Culcheth, he attended St Aelred's (RC) High School, Newton-le-Willows and Fitzwilliam College, Cambridge. He worked from 1994 as adviser to Labour's Health spokesmen – including Tessa Jowell – was Labour campaign organiser in the North West in the 1997 Election, and worked for Chris Smith from 1998 to 2001. Working for Smith enabled him to claim credit for targeting National Lottery money to local former coalfield areas in the form of free TV licences for the old, and grants for new sports facilities. Coming with Chris Smith's strong endorsement, he arrived not a moment too soon, as Smith's writ ran out with his sacking from the Cabinet in the post-election reshuffle. He joined the Health Select Committee as the start, presumably, of another apparatchik's effortless rise.

LEOMINSTER

Looked at one way, Leominster was a Conservative gain from Labour at the 2001 General Election. How so, when the latter party had only taken 17% of the vote in

1997? The answer lies in the defection to Labour in June 1998 of the moderate pro-European Tory elected that year, Peter Temple-Morris. He did not seek to contest this or any other seat in 2001, as Shaun Woodward so controversially did, but quietly moved up to the Lords, leaving the Tories to regain Leominster with little fuss or national publicity, with an increased majority, while Labour again polled 17%. It was all very civilised compared with the rows in St Helens South.

Leominster is a very different part of England from St Helens, of course (it would be hard to imagine a greater contrast in one small country). Essentially the northern half of the old county of Herefordshire, the Leominster constituency has itself had a remarkable political history. First, the Conservatives have beaten the Liberals by less than 3,000 votes on no fewer than seven occasions since 1918. Second, Labour have at various times polled some of their worst showings in the whole of Britain here, reaching a low of 1,932 or 3.8% in 1983. Finally, Leominster was at the last published Census the most rural seat in England, with over 60% of residents living in enumeration districts classed as rural, and over an eighth of all workers employed on the land, compared with just 2% nationally. All this suggests the possibility of a continuing Conservative–Liberal Democrat dogfight, especially after the latter party's surprise victory in the economically similar south Shropshire seat of Ludlow in 2001, yet in fact Leominster has produced easy Tory victories ever since 1979.

The seat is a mixture of small towns and numerous villages. No community is larger than Leominster itself (often pronounced 'Lemster'), at just under 10,000. There are also Kington, and Bromyard and Ledbury over towards the Malvern Hills, and the tiny spa of Tenbury Wells, and the half-timbered Weobley. Local politics are run on individual and often independent lines. Despite its history of close contests, the Liberal Democrats seem to have missed their opportunity in Leominster. Unless this trend is reversed, Leominster's competitive electoral record will become more and more a piece of history. Elections may have become less interesting in Leominster, even though politics recently took an unusual turn.

Social indices:			2001 Gen. Election:			
% Non-white	0.4		C	22,879	49.0	+3.7
% Prof/Man	37.2		LD	12,512	26.8	−1.0
% Non-manual	54.4		Lab	7,872	16.8	−0.6
£ Av prop val 2000	108 K		Grn	1,690	3.6	+1.5
% Increase 97–00	42.6		UKIP	1,590	3.4	+2.2
% Unemployed 2001	1.6		Ind	186	0.4	
% Decrease 97–01	1.4		C maj	10,367	22.2	
% Fin hard/Rank	6.3	577	Turnout		68.0	−8.6
% Pensioners	30.0		Elect	68,695		
% Prem mort/Rank	15	541				

Member of Parliament

In the steps of floor-crossing Peter Temple-Morris comes another – and maybe this time more loyal – son of a Tory MP, **Bill Wiggin**, son of Sir Jerry Wiggin (MP for Weston-Super-Mare 1969–97). Born in 1966, and one of the few Old Etonians chosen as new candidates in safe Conservative seats, his educational trajectory after Eton was deviantly to read economics at Bangor rather than Range-Rover crashing at Cirencester. But thereafter he resumed a more conventional path as successively a coffee buyer, a bullion trader, and a merchant banker, eventually with Commerzbank, responsible for foreign exchange option hedging strategy. Scion of a Herefordshire gentleman-farming family, he was quickly on the attack over the mishandling of the foot-and-mouth crisis and in defence of country sports, but his election – and that of Boris Johnson (Henley), David Cameron (Witney) and Hugo Swire (East Devon) – was insufficient to sustain his party's rump of Old Etonians, which dwindled in 2001 to 14.

LEWES

The apparently calm East Sussex seat of Lewes offers the nation's strongest evidence of rewards for hyper-activity in British politics. Not only did the extraordinary level of activity and self-publicity generated by the Liberal Democrat Norman Baker see off the moderate and civilised Tory MP, Tim Rathbone, in 1997, but his record question-asking and continual appearances in the local press guaranteed return in 2001 with a majority increased near sevenfold. He browbeat his opponents into submission, and one might almost say the same of the electorate.

Besides Lewes itself, a market and administrative centre with a medieval castle reflecting its historical importance, the seat includes the seaside resort of Seaford and the rather depressed ferry port of Newhaven, as well as a swathe of inland country behind the Brighton to Eastbourne coast. It stretches east to include the Polegate suburb of Eastbourne, and includes a number of places with artistic connections, such as Glyndebourne and some of the country retreats of the Bloomsbury group. In the East Sussex county elections which took place on the same day as the last general election, the Lib Dems won in Lewes itself, in Newhaven, and in the Blatchington division of Seaford. They also won Polegate, which has also been in a seat with a Liberal Democrat MP in living memory (David Bellotti, 1990–92). Mr Baker's energy seems unlikely to flag and he looks assured of a continued lively career making an impact both in the Commons and locally.

Social indices:			2001 Gen. Election:				
% Non-white	1.0		LD	25,588	56.3	+13.1
% Prof/Man	42.0		C	15,878	34.9	−5.6
% Non-manual	64.6		Lab	3,317	7.3	−3.3
£ Av prop val 2000	125 K		UKIP	650	1.4	+0.9
% Increase 97–00	52.3		LD maj	9,710	21.4	
% Unemployed 2001	1.8		Turnout		68.5	−7.9
% Decrease 97–01	1.5		Elect	66,332		
% Fin hard/Rank	7.7	532				
% Pensioners	36.3					
% Prem mort/Rank	20	480				

Member of Parliament

Norman Baker, a Home Affairs spokesman and the first Liberal (Democrat) MP in Sussex since the party won Chichester in 1923, won here in 1997 and quickly established a reputation as a blunderbuss-style targeter of corruption and malpractice. Of somewhat reptilian visage, with a cynical glint in his eye, and a populist political animal to his fingertips, he rose locally as a councillor and bag-carrier for the Lib Dem MP-for-Eastbourne-for-2-years, David Bellotti. Residually Scots-accented, he was born in Aberdeen in 1957 and educated at Royal Liberty School, Romford and at Royal Holloway College, London and worked disparately as a language teacher, railway station manager, and off-licence and record chain shop manager. Predictably loathed by local Tories for his constituency-wide ubiquity and regular sympathetic local press coverage, they disliked him less following his role in Peter Mandelson's political assassination as tabler of the question that exposed the Minister's alleged involvement in the Hinduja brothers' passport bid. The consummate constituency MP, living over his party's shop in the High Street, nothing escapes his attention, from bad rail services and local floods to the Middle East where, he noted in late 2001, rare American pressure on Israel caused it to 'start throwing toys out of its pram'. Only if familiarity breeds contempt will he not remain MP for Lewes for as long as he likes.

LEWISHAM DEPTFORD

Labour have put up a series of shaky performances in south London's inner-city river-front constituencies in the last two decades. Bermondsey fell to the Liberal Simon Hughes in a by-election just before the 1983 General Election and has never returned to the fold. Greenwich fell to the SDP in a by-election just before the 1987 General Election and was only just won back in 1992. Woolwich MP John Cartwright defected to the SDP in 1981 and held on through the next two General Elections. However, this apparent weakness (in traditional Labour seats) has never spread to the northernmost seat in the borough of Lewisham, Deptford. Labour's hold on Deptford has never looked even remotely challenged, and in 2001 Joan Ruddock commenced her third term with a majority of 15,000, securing 65% of the total vote. This is an inner-city seat. In the last published census almost a third of the population here classified themselves as non-white, the vast majority of them as black Afro-Caribbeans – one of the highest proportions of black residents anywhere in Britain, in fact. There are middle-class workers here (parts of the seat are surprisingly close to the City), but the cultural predominance is far from patrician. The most northern wards are the strongest for Labour, those in the communities of New Cross and Deptford itself. The seat extends to include Brockley, Ladywell and Honor Oak Park.

All wards are normally Labour and this is the one constituency in Lewisham which has never been marginal. Both Conservatives and Liberal Democrats make little impact in Deptford. However, the Green Party did come second in a number of the wards here in the borough elections of 1998, doing particularly well in Drake, and saved their deposit in 2001; and the Socialist Alliance almost did so, in the person of

Ian Page, who had come close to winning a council seat in Pepys three years earlier – indeed these parties, generally regarded as minor, came closer to challenging Labour locally than the main opposition organisations did.

Social indices:			2001 Gen. Election:			
% Non-white	32.1		Lab	18,915	65.0	–10.0
% Prof/Man	34.9		C	3,622	12.4	–3.1
% Non-manual	61.3		LD	3,409	11.7	–3.1
£ Av prop val 2000	117 K		Grn	1,901	6.5	
% Increase 97–00	71.7		SA	1,260	4.3	
% Unemployed 2001	7.6		Lab maj	15,293	52.5	
% Decrease 97–01	5.4		Turnout		46.3	–11.6
% Fin hard/Rank	36.3	79	Elect	62,869		
% Pensioners	18.0					
% Prem mort/Rank	44	102				

Member of Parliament

Joan Ruddock, a woman with a calm smile set in a bland white face, and one of Tony Blair's earliest dropped ministers, had spent a year (1997–98) as 'Minister for Women' (and an unpaid minister at that – the officially sanctioned payroll having been completed before her slightly late appointment was made). Born in 1943, the daughter of a working-class Tory, and educated at Pontypool Grammar School for Girls and Imperial College, London, her political career was assisted by her friendship with the Kinnocks (for whom she curbed her criticism of the Gulf War in 1991 in order to keep in step) and her leadership of CND (1981–85), a past she has recently tended to airbrush ('that was then and now is now … I have moved on') in favour of a new interest in environmental degradation and organic farming. A neat, icily attractive, carefully presented woman, she shares her life with Frank Doran, Labour MP for Aberdeen Central, another discarded left-wing frontbencher. 'Fluent and flinty' (Quentin Letts), her central preoccupation with the condition of women was asserted in her call in 2001 for women to play a role in the post-Taliban government of Afghanistan.

LEWISHAM EAST

The south-east London borough of Lewisham has done Labour proud in the last ten years. In 1992 they already held Deptford, and they gained both West and East from the Tories, to win all three seats in the borough. Both the gains required larger than average swings, and the more difficult of two hard nuts to crack was Lewisham East. In 1987 the tiny but high-flying Tory MP Colin Moynihan had won with a majority of nearly 5,000 votes. Bridget Prentice pulled off one of Labour's best wins anywhere with a swing of no less than 6.7%. To some extent this marked a return to the normal for Lewisham East. Before Moynihan gained it in 1983, it had been held by Labour's Roland Moyle for most of the preceding 20 years. Under its current boundaries the Tories have only won the seat twice, on both occasions when they have been returned with an overall majority in the Commons in three figures.

Labour now win very easily in Lewisham East, by nearly 9,000 votes in 2001 on a very poor turnout of just over half the registered electors. Here are to be found the large council estates of Grove Park and Downham, the latter of whose local Liberal Democrat success in borough elections is not rewarded in parliamentary elections. The Conservatives' best ward is St Mildred (Lee), the base of their solitary councillor(s) after the May 1994 and 1998 Lewisham borough elections, and they are also quite strong in Blackheath, on the Greenwich border. Despite the fact that East includes the only two wards in the whole of the borough of Lewisham not to elect Labour councillors it now looks very like a safe seat, although distinctly the least strong of the three.

Social indices:			2001 Gen. Election:			
% Non-white	14.7		Lab	16,116	53.6	−4.7
% Prof/Man	37.8		C	7,157	23.8	−2.1
% Non-manual	64.4		LD	4,937	16.4	+5.3
£ Av prop val 2000	137 K		BNP	1,005	3.3	
% Increase 97–00	62.1		SA	464	1.5	
% Unemployed 2001	5.1		UKIP	361	1.2	
% Decrease 97–01	3.4		Lab maj	8,959	29.8	
% Fin hard/Rank	24.3	209	Turnout		51.5	−14.9
% Pensioners	26.9		Elect	58,302		
% Prem mort/Rank	40	184				

Member of Parliament

Bridget Prentice, a Blair-discarded Whip (1995–98) who was demoted to the ranks of PPS to fellow Scot Brian Wilson (1998–99) and the Lord Chancellor (1999–2001), was the more loyal half of a political couple though she has since divorced from husband, Gordon Prentice, who entered the House at the same time in 1992. Scots-born in 1952, a joiner's daughter, and Catholic-educated before attending Glasgow University, she taught in Catholic schools – including the Blairs' London Oratory. As a Whip she helped quell the big rebellion on lone parent benefits, keeping most of the uneasy sisters in line, and as the Lord Chancellor's PPS she backed curbs on jury trials in the face of backbench civil libertarian resistance.

LEWISHAM WEST

Lewisham is a borough which can be described as 'Middle London'. It stretches from Deptford, decidedly of the inner city, to the borders of Bromley and Beckenham, in outer suburban south-east London. It also enjoys a cross-section of social characteristics. Lewisham West, for example, has just under 55% owner-occupied housing and just over 25% council tenancies. These figures are close to the Greater London average, as is the non-white proportion, 19% (although, untypically, most of these are Afro-Caribbeans – there are very few Asians in Lewisham). Small wonder then that Lewisham West was historically a classic critical marginal. It has changed hands between parties seven times since (and including) 1945. Most recently, it formed one of Labour's nine gains in London in the General Election of 1992. Then in

1997 it shared London's intense desire for a change in government – indeed it surpassed the average in this respect, for the Tory vote fell by 19%, the highest figure in the capital.

There is clearly a long-term swing against the Conservatives, as they won no seats at all here in the London borough elections of 1998, not even Catford or Horniman, Sydenham or Perry Hill, where they traditionally had a good chance. In 2001 there was yet another strengthening of the Labour position and it does not look at all like there will be an eighth change of hands in the foreseeable future, even after the Bromley borough boundary is crossed to take in Penge for the next but one election.

Social indices:			2001 Gen. Election:			
% Non-white	18.6		Lab	18,816	61.1	–0.9
% Prof/Man	36.4		C	6,896	22.4	–1.5
% Non-manual	64.8		LD	4,146	13.5	+3.7
£ Av prop val 2000	115 K		UKIP	485	1.6	
% Increase 97–00	60.4		Ind	472	1.5	
% Unemployed 2001	6.2		Lab maj	11,920	38.7	
% Decrease 97–01	3.7		Turnout		50.6	–13.4
% Fin hard/Rank	27.4	166	Elect	60,947		
% Pensioners	24.1					
% Prem mort/Rank	35	260				

Member of Parliament

Jim Dowd, elected in 1992 and a Whip 1993–2001, with an interlude (1995–97) as a Northern Ireland spokesman in Opposition, though London-raised comes from a half-Irish, half-German background. Born in Germany in 1951, and educated at a Catford comprehensive and at the London Nautical School, he was employed as a telecommunications engineer for 15 years while doubling-up for 20 years as a Lewisham councillor, where he learnt the habits of discipline now expected of Labour's large parliamentary majority, as someone who spent only one of his nine years as an MP off the frontbench, until dropped, and shunted onto the Health Select Committee in 2001.

LEYTON AND WANSTEAD

In the boundary changes which came into effect at the 1997 Election, the Commission decided to broach the border between the north-east London boroughs of Waltham Forest and Redbridge in two separate places. The result was to abolish and break up the Wanstead and Woodford constituency in Redbridge, a Tory stronghold and Winston Churchill's final seat. Two wards in the south-west corner of that seat, Wanstead and Snaresbrook, are now linked with Leyton from Waltham Forest.

Leyton has had an interesting electoral history. It was regarded as safely Labour until 1965, when the Foreign Secretary, Patrick Gordon Walker (who had lost his seat at Smethwick after an allegedly racist Tory campaign the previous year) attempted to re-enter Parliament at a by-election. The voters, perhaps feeling that the candidate was being imposed on them or smuggled in, rejected him – his second defeat in a year.

He did manage to win Leyton in Labour's landslide of 1966, and hold the seat for eight years, but his successor also had a chequered parliamentary career. Bryan Magee, an academic philosopher and the host of sophisticated TV shows, always seemed a slightly odd choice to represent an essentially inner East End seat, and he defected to the SDP a few months after their creation. He did not do too well in 1983, when Harry Cohen again recaptured Leyton for Labour.

Waltham Forest borough elections within this seats are tightly contested between Liberal Democrat and Labour. The Liberal Democrats win in wards such as Cann Hall and Leyton, Labour in Leytonstone and Cathall, which is over 40% non-white and has the highest proportion of council tenants in the borough: seemingly an odd combination, but in fact the ethnic minority population of Waltham Forest is evenly divided between Afro-Caribbeans and Asians. Meanwhile the two Redbridge wards, Snaresbrook and Wanstead, are Labour-Conservative marginals. In the seat as a whole, in parliamentary elections, the Tories and Lib Dems are left to fight it out for second, way behind Harry Cohen, who takes about three times as many votes for Labour.

Social indices:			2001 Gen. Election:			
% Non-white	31.6		Lab	19,558	58.0	−2.8
% Prof/Man	41.7		C	6,654	19.7	−2.5
% Non-manual	66.4		LD	5,389	16.0	+0.9
£ Av prop val 2000	114 K		Grn	1,030	3.1	
% Increase 97–00	57.6		SA	709	2.1	
% Unemployed 2001	4.9		UKIP	378	1.1	
% Decrease 97–01	4.9		Lab maj	12,904	38.3	
% Fin hard/Rank	24.7	203	Turnout		54.8	−8.5
% Pensioners	21.6		Elect	61,549		
% Prem mort/Rank	34	265				

Member of Parliament

Harry Cohen, elected here in 1983 in the wake of Bryan Magee's defection to the SDP, is a de-bearded, toned-down version of his formerly high-decibelled, but still Cockney-accented self, and lacking – it has been suggested – the sourness of his hard-left colleagues. A pro-Palestinian Jew who opposed the Gulf War and criticises Israel, he rebelled 36 times against the Whips in the 1992–97 Parliament. Born in 1949, son of a cab driver, he attended secondary modern schools and East Ham Technical College, before training as an accountant. A short and chirpy Cockney sparrow with the style of a market trader, despite his retained Campaign Group membership his rebellions against the Blair government have been modest: on freedom of information, military action against Iraq, and curbs on jury trials, with him settling instead for specialist scrutiny on the Defence Select Committee (1997–2001). The hard-left Socialist Alliance ran against him in 2001 over his non-rebellious record.

LICHFIELD

This seat is named after Dr Samuel Johnson's birthplace, but by no means dominated by the city of the triple-spired cathedral. Lichfield itself is a smallish but prosperous and growing community – it is unusual to find a place where the greatest population increase in the 1980s occurred in the Central ward, but this was indeed the case here, as new private estates spread, for example in the Boley Park area. The voters in the new developments are open to persuasion, but seem to favour the Conservatives on balance most years, according to local election evidence, all we have at the micro-psephological level. The constituency also includes villages like Armitage and King's Bromley, and Bagots and Yoxall wards from East Staffordshire district; and 5,500 in Alrewas and Whittington once in a constituency called Staffordshire South East. This rural territory is very Conservative. There is one other inclusion, untypical not only of this seat but of almost anywhere in Britain: the Little Aston ward, right on the edge of the West Midlands conurbation near Streetly at the edge of Sutton Park, where over 73% of the massive mansion households have at least two cars: a figure higher not only than anywhere else in Staffordshire, but also than anywhere in the West Midlands – or even in the county of Surrey. Little Aston voted 90% Conservative in May 1999. A contrast is provided by 24,000 electors from Burntwood, prior to 1997 attached to Cannock in a solidly Labour seat.

In the very pro-Labour circumstances of 1997, Lichfield looked extremely marginal, posting a Tory majority of just 238, but Michael Fabricant was still able to hold on, unlike half of his colleagues. Although Lichfield Cathedral is dedicated to St Chad, there was no Florida-style multiple recount in 2001, as the Conservatives secured a swing from Labour of 5%, well above the national average, and even more superior to their performance in marginal seats. Fabricant seems likely to add his particular brand of colour to the Commons benches for quite some time to come.

Social indices:			2001 Gen. Election:			
% Non-white	0.9		C	20,480	49.1	+6.2
% Prof/Man	38.0		Lab	16,054	38.5	–3.9
% Non-manual	59.1		LD	4,462	10.7	–0.6
£ Av prop val 2000	93 K		UKIP	684	1.6	
% Increase 97–00	34.1		C maj	4,426	10.6	
% Unemployed 2001	1.8		Turnout		65.3	–12.1
% Decrease 97–01	0.8		Elect	63,794		
% Fin hard/Rank	9.5	477				
% Pensioners	20.4					
% Prem mort/Rank	17	512				

Member of Parliament

Michael Fabricant, elected in 1992 for an earlier version of this seat, is the son of a Brighton rabbi, born in 1950, educated at Brighton and Hove Grammar School and at four universities, including Sussex and Southern California. A fluent, red-faced, forcefully articulated former electronics engineer who was once (according to Simon Hoggart) 'well-known as a disc jockey in several parts of Hove', he is famous essentially for his wig. Orthodoxly Eurosceptic, but with a light-weight persona as a self-parodying Commons performer, he is among the Tory minority who vote for homosexual sex at 16, is in a minority of one in wanting the Lichfield diocese to become a third Anglican archdiocese, and is in favour of the UK joining NAFTA instead of the EU.

LINCOLN

The fine old city of Lincoln would make a most aesthetically and technically satisfying location for a documentary on recent British political and electoral history. The results in the last few general elections have been fairly reflective of the state of play nationally, although since 1987 the numbers cast for the centre parties have been decidedly low – and thereby hangs a tale.

Behind the façade of a political 'weathervane' lies an unusual and instructive recent history. Lincoln remained Labour from 1945 right through till 1973, when the sitting MP Dick Taverne resigned from the party and fought a triumphant by-election as an independent Democratic Labour candidate opposed to Labour's leftward drift. This assured Lincoln a place in social democratic history, and Taverne held his seat in the first General Election of 1974, though not in the second – he was beaten by Margaret Jackson, later as Margaret Beckett, MP for Derby South, Deputy and Acting Labour leader at the time. Throughout the 1970s the Democratic Labour group remained active in local Lincoln politics. Even in 1979 it may be surmised that the votes cast for a Democratic Labour candidate let in the Conservative Kenneth Carlisle for the first Tory victory in Lincoln for nearly 50 years.

In the 1980s, though, the centre's hopes faded. Lincoln may have seen almost the beginning of the Long March of social democracy, but the storm blew out as the SDP Alliance's vote dipped below 20% in 1987 and the Liberal Democrats could hardly muster much more than one-eighth of the total vote in 2001. The heady days of centre triumph seem well and truly over. Lincoln's Taverne House social club was set up in 1973 as a social centre for the Democratic Labour Party. The decline of that movement can be summed up by its closure due to lack of support in 1987. It reopened as a night club called the Rack and Ruin.

As with the national battle, two-party politics have made a comeback in Lincoln. Labour have recovered firm control of the city council, and indeed Lincoln's appearance is still reminiscent of a Labour seat. Thousands of tourists visit Lincoln's magnificent cathedral and castle set on a dominant limestone ridge above the river Witham, and the quaint streets of the old town on the hill between. Yet the view from the top of the ridge is of heavy manufacturing industry and terraced housing below to the south, and there are sprawling council estates behind the cathedral to the north – one, St Giles, even became notorious for minor riots in the early 1990s. The only ward in which the Conservatives have managed to return any councillors in recent years is the aptly named Birchwood, where new private estates have advanced into the birch trees, nearly doubling in population in the 1980s. Ironically Birchwood's growth may have helped to wrest the seat from the Tories, for the boundary changes which came into force in 1997 were very damaging for them, removing a number of middle-class suburbs beyond the city's boundaries around North Hykeham. In 2001 there was virtually no movement between the parties, although all lost as the turnout dropped

15% to just 56%. Gillian Merron maintained a comfortable 8,400 lead. Given the nature of Tony Blair's 'New Labour' Party, though, this may not seem to many to be anything other than the final quashing of social democracy in Lincoln.

Social indices:			2001 Gen. Election:			
% Non-white	1.2		Lab	20,003	53.9	−1.0
% Prof/Man	27.7		C	11,583	31.2	+0.2
% Non-manual	49.6		LD	4,703	12.7	+1.8
£ Av prop val 2000	49 K		UKIP	836	2.3	
% Increase 97–00	17.7		Lab maj	8,420	22.7	
% Unemployed 2001	4.1		Turnout		56.0	−15.1
% Decrease 97–01	4.0		Elect	66,299		
% Fin hard/Rank	26.0	190				
% Pensioners	27.1					
% Prem mort/Rank	41	154				

Member of Parliament

Gillian Merron, Labour's quiet victor here in 1997, comes from a background as a union (UNISON) organiser, picked from an all-women short list, and as a loyalist was made a PPS in 1998, to Defence Ministers, and by 2001 to Northern Ireland Secretary John Reid. Born in 1959 and educated at Wanstead High School and Lancaster University, the pursuer of modishly apolitical issues relating to Commons' working hours and football, she generally focuses on constituency concerns such as the near bottom-ranked local university, and is elusive about details concerning her family or family of origin, though by 2001 the *Jewish Chronicle* was listing her as one of 13 Jewish Labour MPs.

LINLITHGOW

Since he is (among many other things) a staunch anti-devolutionist and fierce opponent of Scottish separatism, it is not surprising that Tam Dalyell, the Father of the House of Commons since 2001, has had a lot of trouble with the SNP in his constituency; nor that he has thus far always emerged from the struggle triumphant. When he first won his seat, then called West Lothian, in a by-election in 1962, he had to fend off a challenge from William Wolfe, who was to be a long-time chairman of the Scottish National Party. This was the first of seven contests in which Dalyell vanquished Wolfe. Then in 1983 boundary changes reduced the swollen electorate of West Lothian considerably, as the New Town of Livingston was removed to form the basis of its own constituency. The old name for the county of West Lothian was Linlithgowshire, and since 1983 a seat has once again been based on Linlithgow, the ancient burgh near the Forth. Dalyell has gone on to win Linlithgow five times, again usually with the SNP in second place, to bring his number of victories to 12, more than any other current MP.

Linlithgow itself is a mixed town in which all four main parties can poll respectably in a reasonable year. The other electoral divisions are working class, with a majority of council tenants, and see sharp contests between Labour and SNP. This is the old shale-mining area around Whitburn, Bathgate, Armadale and Blackburn. The mining was replaced by newer industries such as the former British Leyland motor works at Bathgate but its legacy remains in the ugly slag heaps, or 'pit bings', which dominate the otherwise flat countryside, giving it a unique aspect. This territory lines the M9 motorway as it passes between Edinburgh and Glasgow. In 2001, just before the General Election, the area suffered a new economic threat with the announced closure of the Motorola factory at Bathgate. The SNP are the only serious challengers here, finishing only 9% behind in the Scottish Parliament election, 3% behind in the European elections, and actually receiving more votes in the 1999 unitary authority elections than Labour, but Linlithgow seems to prefer Tam Dalyell to represent it at Westminster.

Social indices:			2001 Gen. Election:			
% Non-white	0.5		Lab	17,207	54.4	+0.2
% Prof/Man	26.9		SNP	8,078	25.5	−1.3
% Non-manual	49.1		C	2,836	9.0	−3.6
% Unemployed 2001	3.9		LD	2,628	8.3	+2.4
% Decrease 97–01	0.7		SSP	695	2.2	
% Fin hard/Rank	38.7	59	Ind	211	0.7	
% Prem mort/Rank	42	148	Lab maj	9,129	28.8	
			Turnout		58.0	−15.9
			Elect	54,599		

Member of Parliament

Tam Dalyell (not a.k.a. Sir Tam Dalyell, tenth baronet, of the Binns, Linlithgow) was first elected in 1962, and so became Father of the House on the retirement of Sir Edward Heath in 2001. A ponderously articulated eccentric who perceptively admits that to be effective you don't have to mind being a bore, he is known for his dogged campaigns, all worthy of display on his regimental standard: Belgrano, Lockerbie, Westland, the Gulf War, and the West Lothian question – which beats Schleswig-Holstein as the one nobody bothers answering. Rebelling against the Blair government on student fees, Incapacity benefits, legal aid cuts, freedom of information and air traffic control privatisation, his 29 dissident votes made him the ninth most rebellious Labour MP in the 1997–2001 Parliament. In the new House elected in 2001 – notwithstanding his new status as Father of the House – he rebelled in favour of sacking Stephen Byers' political adviser, against the bombing of Afghanistan, and – serially – against the anti-terrorism legislation. Born in 1932, the grandson and great-grandson of Bengal governors, he is one of Labour's two Old Etonians, followed in both cases by Trinity, Cambridge, wears ankle-length trousers and walks with a shuffling gait. Of the four baronets elected to the 2001 Commons, his was the oldest.

LIVERPOOL GARSTON

While many parts of the land returned Conservatives with increasing enthusiasm through the 1980s, others turned more and more against that government, rejecting its philosophy and prescriptions. Even when they last won a general election in 1992, the Conservatives won few seats in Scotland, and in Wales. They also did appallingly in the city of Liverpool, winning no seats at all – nor coming anywhere near to it. Garston used to be the classic Labour/Conservative marginal in Liverpool, swinging with the national tide in 1974 and 1979, and resisting the Liberal municipal success more completely than any other area of the city. It was indeed safely Conservative before 1974, even in 1966, although this was partly due to a strong Orange-Protestant working-class vote. But Garston does not look like a Tory constituency, or even a marginal, now. Maria Eagle joined her twin sister Angela (member for Wallasey) with a majority of 18,000 in 1997 and Labour are certain to hold Garston for the foreseeable future as well. That this is so is due to the special circumstances of Liverpool, for the seat contains most of the city's most attractive residential areas. Garston is composed of the south-eastern sector of Liverpool, and it includes two very different types of neighbourhood. Allerton and Woolton are two of the most middle-class, owner-occupied districts of the city; in fact Woolton was the last of the 33 wards in the city to return any Conservative councillors at all, and that as long ago as 1994; they managed just 13% to the Lib Dems' 73% in 2000. These two wards are joined by one other of the same ilk, Grassendale, which contains big houses in private gated estates down near the Mersey, like Cressington Park. It too is now won by the Liberal Democrats at local level.

On the other hand, Garston also includes the massive peripheral council estate of Speke near the renamed John Lennon airport, the terraced centre of Garston itself (in St Mary's ward), and the largely abandoned ultra-modern horror of Netherley, where the tower blocks were demolished scarcely more than a decade after being built, having been identified as one of the most alarming of the slums in Liverpool, reminiscent of some of the worst blights of United States cities, and a nightmarish vision of urban squalor. It is highly symbolic that in this most divided of constituencies the electoral predominance should now so clearly be given to the politics associated with the poverty of Speke and Netherley rather than to those traditionally associated with the affluence of Woolton. Nor does there seem to be a way back in Garston, or in Liverpool, for the party which governed Britain for 18 years.

Social indices:			2001 Gen. Election:			
% Non-white	2.5		Lab	20,043	61.4	+0.1
% Prof/Man	30.8		LD	7,549	23.1	+4.1
% Non-manual	56.5		C	5,059	15.5	−0.2
£ Av prop val 2000	72 K		Lab maj	12,494	38.3	
% Increase 97–00	23.7		Turnout		50.2	−15.0
% Unemployed 2001	5.8		Elect	65,094		
% Decrease 97–01	3.2					
% Fin hard/Rank	28.2	155				
% Pensioners	28.9					
% Prem mort/Rank	45	94				

Member of Parliament

Maria Eagle, with a similarly monotonously piping voice as, but more humorous-seeming and heterosexual than, her twin sister Angela, won here in 1997. A solicitor in Liverpool, she was born, a printer's daughter, in 1961, and educated at Formby High School and Pembroke College, Oxford, and has become identified with legislation to ban mink fur farming. Herself the product of all-women shortlists, she wants changes to the Sex Discrimination Act to allow their reintroduction to alter the Labour Party's 'traditional male culture'. In 2001 she joined her sister in the Junior Ministerial ranks of the government, in her case at Work and Pensions.

LIVERPOOL RIVERSIDE

Liverpool is a city of art and music and sport and humour. It was once a great centre of commerce too, a proud and active port. Now, largely through a vicious circle of labour unrest, economic blight and under-investment, ill-served by local and central government alike, it is by most indicators the most depressed community in England. Most of the inhabitants bear up well, even in resentment; as the local saying goes, 'If you didn't laugh you'd cry'. The Riverside constituency is the heart of the city, stretching along active, decayed and redeveloped dockland from the Bootle boundary as far as Aigburth. At the time of the 2001 Election its male unemployment rate was 14%, the third highest in Britain after Birmingham's two city centre seats. It contains some of the poorest and most deprived urban areas in Britain, and some of the most dramatically depopulated. The northern wards, Vauxhall and Everton, are almost all white, but have suffered from some of the worst unemployment and housing conditions in the city. Much of the housing has been demolished, leaving an urban wasteland, with great open spaces but a couple of miles from the city centre. The population of these two wards halved, from 26,000 to 13,000, between 1981 and 1991. There are some optimistic signs, like the cooperative housing venture of the Eldonians, but in general the figures bear out the story: under 10% of owner-occupation, over 85% of households without access to a car.

This area has a varied political history. West of the Scotland Road, towards the docks, lay the original Irish Catholic ghetto which sent T.P. O'Connor to Westminster as an Irish Nationalist for no less than 44 years. Up the hill in Everton lay the heart of Orange Protestant reaction – Protestant councillors were elected as late as the 1970s. Both areas now rank as among Labour's strongest in the whole country in general elections, and in the city in local elections, although that is not saying much when they could win only half a dozen wards against the Liberal Democrat tide in May 2000, for example. South of Liverpool's fine city centre and Chinatown (Abercromby ward), in Liverpool 8 postal district, lie the multi-racial wards of Granby, Arundel and Dingle, the 'Toxteth' which produced the most serious riots of the summer of 1981 – it should be noted that those riots were less connected with race than elsewhere, for some Liverpudlians can demonstrate a disrespect for authority, and for the police, untypical of largely conformist England.

This remains one of the very strongest Labour seats in England, of course, but a far more striking record lies in the turnout level, which in 2001 plummeted to 34%, the lowest of any of the 659 constituencies and the lowest in any constituency in a general election within living memory. The true victor here was the near despair of non-participation in the democratic process itself, and it is hard to see what will motivate the disconnected voters of Liverpool Riverside in a future which seems to hold so little for so many.

Social indices:			2001 Gen. Election:				
% Non-white	10.4		Lab/Coop	18,201	71.4	+0.9	
% Prof/Man	31.8		LD	4,251	16.7	+3.4	
% Non-manual	51.8		C	2,142	8.4	−1.1	
£ Av prop val 2000	59 K		SA	909	3.6	+1.5	
% Increase 97–00	43.0		L/C maj	13,950	54.7		
% Unemployed 2001	10.3		Turnout		34.1	−17.9	
% Decrease 97–01	5.5		Elect	74,827			
% Fin hard/Rank	40.9	45					
% Pensioners	26.2						
% Prem mort/Rank	61	9					

Member of Parliament

Louise Ellman, elected here in 1997 after selection from an all-women shortlist, is virtually a one-club politician as a persistent advocate of public-private partnerships of the sort she trailed when leader for 16 years of Lancashire county council. One of 13 Labour MPs listed as Jewish by the *Jewish Chronicle,* a severe-seeming persistent critic of Arab activities in the Middle East, she was born Louise Rosenberg in 1945 and educated at Manchester High School for Girls and Hull and York Universities, and originally lectured in further education before becoming a full-time local politician.

LIVERPOOL WALTON

It is extremely hard to believe now that the Tories actually held the seat of Liverpool Walton until 1964, when it was gained by Eric Heffer from Sir Kenneth Thompson. Under Heffer, a staunch and nationally prominent left-winger who died in 1991, Walton became a mighty Labour stronghold, and at the 2001 General Election his successor Peter Kilfoyle recorded a majority of 18,000 over the Liberal Democrats. The Conservatives were third with the humiliating total of 1,726 votes. Kilfoyle amassed 78% of the vote, not only Labour's highest share, but the highest of any of the 3,318 candidates putting themselves forward for election to the Commons that day. However, far more people did not bother to vote than supported Kilfoyle, or indeed voted at all.

It is true that in 1983 Walton had expanded to take in most of the abolished Kirkdale seat; but after all that division too had been a gain from the Tories in 1964. Walton's history does not simply involve a long swing to the left in this most socialist of cities, though. The Liberal Democrats have built up great strength on Liverpool City Council over the years, as the effective opposition to a Labour Party often disastrously divided by internal disputes, and they won the local elections in most wards in this seat in May 2000. Nobody could accuse the city council politics of Liverpool of being dull, for all its status as a Labour stronghold in Westminster terms.

Walton is the northernmost of the Liverpool seats. It contains a variety of housing types in the wards of Warbreck, Melrose, County, Fazakerley, Breckfield and the footballing ward of Anfield, which contains the Goodison Park ground of Everton as well as the world-famous home of Liverpool FC.

Liverpool's representation was again reduced before the 1997 Election, this time from six seats to five. It is salutary to remember that when Walton was gained by Labour, only just over 30 years ago, the city had nine Members of Parliament (in the 1959–64 House six of them were Tories!). The relative and absolute decline of the population of Liverpool has almost halved its representation, the nature of which has simultaneously been utterly transformed: few would bet against a complete slate of Labour MPs being returned for the foreseeable future, but it is harder to know when more than half of the electors here will again be persuaded to visit the polling stations on general election day.

Social indices:			2001 Gen. Election:			
% Non-white	1.3		Lab	22,143	77.8	–0.6
% Prof/Man	18.4		LD	4,147	14.6	+3.4
% Non-manual	44.9		C	1,726	6.1	–0.3
£ Av prop val 2000	35 K		UKIP	442	1.6	
% Increase 97–00	18.8		Lab maj	17,996	63.2	
% Unemployed 2001	8.7		Turnout		43.0	–16.6
% Decrease 97–01	4.3		Elect	66,237		
% Fin hard/Rank	40.7	47				
% Pensioners	25.6					
% Prem mort/Rank	51	42				

Member of Parliament

Peter Kilfoyle is one of the few of Blair's ministers to have voluntarily resigned rather than be required to quit. Elected here in the wake of Eric Heffer's death in 1991, he is an old-style Labour machine politician, whose name was made as the North West Regional organiser who cleared out the Militant infiltration of Liverpool. Born into the working class in 1946, he attended Catholic schools and Durham University from which he dropped out to do manual work for five years, until training as a teacher at Christ's College, Liverpool. A rough-hewn, beefy, Scouse-accented extrovert, his resignation in 1999 as a Defence Minister over Old Labour concern for neglect of the heartlands, was heralded in 1996 when he ridiculed the Mandelson–Liddle tract, the *Blair Revolution*, as 'condescending' and 'trite'. His own book *Left Behind*, published in 2000, savaged Mandelson. In 2001 he rebelled against the Terrorism, Crime and Security Bill and in 2002 crticised dispatch of troops to fight in Afghanistan.

LIVERPOOL WAVERTREE

The Liberal Democrats control Liverpool City Council with a very large overall majority. In May 2000, for example, they won 26 of the 35 available seats (and

'Liberals' won two more), to Labour's six, with one Independent. The votes cast in their favour within the city boundaries added up to 54.5% of the whole, more than twice Labour's total. Labour was clearly not trusted to run Liverpool, whose voters had not forgotten the regime led by the Militant Derek Hatton and his allies in the 1980s. Indeed the great strength of the Liberal alternative goes way back to the early successes in the 1960s of such founding fathers as Cyril Carr of Church ward, Wavertree constituency. Yet with the single exception of David Alton, successively MP for Edge Hill and Mossley Hill between 1979 and 1997, the Lib Dems and their predecessors have never even come close to making a parliamentary breakthrough, and this remained the case in 2001.

Wavertree would be their best bet. It includes 25,000 of the former Mossley Hill voters in Picton and Church wards. That section is outnumbered by the 47,000 or so previously in Broadgreen, which Labour's Jane Kennedy won in 1992. However, Wavertree is an old name for the seat of their first breakthroughs, revived in 1997 after a 14-year gap. It is of fairly middle-class composition (for Liverpool) – and the Liverpool middle class have long been accustomed to voting Liberal, not Conservative, to try to keep Labour out of power in Town Hall and Westminster alike; this has spread to most of the working-class wards away from the innermost city too now. Yet in 2001 the Liberal Democrat candidate Christopher Newby, a Broadgreen councillor, could only poll 24% to Jane Kennedy's 63%. Clearly they want him and his colleagues in the municipal buildings, not the Commons, or perhaps more appositely Tony Blair is not associated with the recent history of the local Labour Party in Liverpool. It is the clearest example of ticket splitting in British politics, massive and sustained.

Social indices:			2001 Gen. Election:			
% Non-white	3.7		Lab	20,155	62.7	−1.7
% Prof/Man	32.1		LD	7,836	24.4	+2.8
% Non-manual	58.5		C	3,091	9.6	−1.1
£ Av prop val 2000	52 K		SLP	359	1.1	
% Increase 97–00	17.1		SA	349	1.1	
% Unemployed 2001	6.9		UKIP	348	1.1	
% Decrease 97–01	4.2		Lab maj	12,319	38.3	
% Fin hard/Rank	25.0	200	Turnout		44.3	−18.6
% Pensioners	25.9		Elect	72,555		
% Prem mort/Rank	45	98				

Member of Parliament

Jane Kennedy, a Minister of State in the Northern Ireland Office from 2001, after two years as a Junior Minister in the Lord Chancellor's Department and five years a Whip, was first elected in 1992, as a replacement for the expelled Militant-linked Terry Fields, and as the first woman MP in Liverpool since Bessie Braddock (1945–70). Part of the Labour clean-up team to rid Liverpool of Militant, she was born in 1958, attended Haughton Comprehensive School and, inconclusively, Liverpool University, spent nine years as a child care officer and rose politically as a NUPE/UNISON organiser. Attractive in a slightly androgynous way, and a Zionist, she joined the Lord Chancellor's team as the only non-lawyer.

LIVERPOOL WEST DERBY

West Derby is essentially Liverpool's council estate seat, situated on the north-eastern edge of the city and containing estates like Norris Green in Pirrie ward, an inter-war development, and post-war Gillmoss and Dovecot. It is arguable that the description above is no longer valid, as under half of the housing in West Derby is now rented from the local authority, but despite council house sales the ambience of the council estate environment is still pervasive – and certainly still bears very strongly on the political preferences of the neighbourhood. In 2001 Robert Wareing, having beaten off a more serious threat to his continued tenure in the Commons, an internal party reselection challenge, polled two-thirds of the vote here to his nearest challenger's 15%.

There are owner-occupied areas in the seat too, in West Derby village and in Sandfield Park and the new developments around Croxteth Hall. This is the setting of that most intelligent, convincing and socially aware of soap operas, *Brookside*, which has seemingly addressed every conceivable social issue in its 20 years on the air. Even Croxteth ward has stopped voting Conservative now, and it is astonishing to think that West Derby was Conservative right up to 1964; the MP in 1945 was Sir David Maxwell-Fyfe. Housing redevelopment and the destruction of the Orange Protestant vote put paid to Tory chances. The only threat to Labour's continued hold on West Derby in recent years was the defection of the MP Eric Ogden to the SDP in the early 1980s; but like the two other Liverpool Labour defectors, Richard Crawshaw (Toxteth) and James Dunn (Kirkdale), Ogden was not re-elected in 1983.

Almost unnoticed elsewhere, second place in West Derby in 2001, as in 1997, was actually taken not by the Tories or the Liberal Democrats, but by what must be regarded as a fringe candidate, Stephen Radford of the Liberal Party, a city councillor and member of the Gay Christian Movement. Nevertheless, he received fewer than one in six votes in the latest Westminster contest, a sharp contrast with his performance in securing council re-election for Tuebrook ward just a year before in May 2000, when the result was as follows: Liberal 2,215, Labour 247, Lib Dem 83, Conservative 64.

Social indices:			2001 Gen. Election:			
% Non-white	1.3		Lab	20,454	66.2	–5.0
% Prof/Man	20.1		Lib	4,601	14.9	+5.3
% Non-manual	47.0		LD	3,366	10.9	+1.9
£ Av prop val 2000	48 K		C	2,486	8.0	–0.6
% Increase 97–00	20.2		Lab maj	15,853	51.3	
% Unemployed 2001	8.4		Turnout		45.5	–15.9
% Decrease 97–01	4.8		Elect	67,921		
% Fin hard/Rank	37.8	71				
% Pensioners	25.9					
% Prem mort/Rank	52	38				

Member of Parliament

Robert (Bob) Wareing, once mocked for his resemblance to Charlie Drake, is the least Blairite of Liverpool's politically-sanitised MPs as a Campaign Group member, and was the only Labour MP who failed to be automatically re-selected in 1999/2000. Of Dickensian cherubic looks, he was originally elected in 1983 as a left-wing replacement for right-winger Eric Ogden, but was himself to become a target of hard-left Militant. Born locally in 1930, and educated at Alsop High School, Bolton College of Education and, extramurally, London University, he was initially a clerk before becoming a further education lecturer. Out of step with the Blair government in his support for Serbia, he was suspended for non-registration of a Serbian business connection, and has rebelled liberally on lone parent benefit cuts, military action against Iraq, classifying freedom-fighting exiles as terrorists, the Prime Minister's powers to nominate life peers, the bombing of Serbia and Kosovo, disability benefit cuts, and air traffic control privatisation. With 22 rebellions in the 1997–2001 Parliament he was Labour's 20th most dissenting MP. After June 2001 he rebelled against the Terrorism, Crime and Security Bill.

LIVINGSTON

Before the reorganisation of local government in Scotland in the late 1990s, which abolished the unwieldy regions in favour of unitary authorities, Livingston was the only New Town in the Lothian region; East Kilbride, Cumbernauld and Irvine were all in Strathclyde, and Glenrothes in Fife. Although it is considerably closer to Edinburgh than to Glasgow, it has drawn its population from both of Central Scotland's big cities. Like many of the government-designated New Towns in both England and Scotland, it suffers a high degree of social dislocation – unemployment, welfare cases, mental illness. Despite the variety of architecture, the housing appears low cost and of indifferent quality. Despite the attempted variety of 'neighbour-hoods', Livingston seems a soulless and depressing place.

The New Town formed the basis for its own constituency when it was carved out of Midlothian and West Lothian in 1983. As such it offered a sanctum for Robin Cook, whose Edinburgh Central seat had been merged with Edinburgh North in a new Central which the Tories did indeed win that year. It has never been completely reliable, though, sharing the volatility of other New Towns south of the border. Both the Alliance and the Conservatives came within 5,000 votes of Cook in Livingston in 1983, but that was a disastrous year for Labour. Since then the SNP has emerged as the greatest threat, advancing strongly in 1992 as they did in most parts of working-class central Scotland.

The SNP obtained over 40% of the vote in the 1999 unitary contests here, and Cook can be thankful that the seat contains other communities besides the disrupted neighbourhoods of the New Town, where the SNP do best, exploiting multiple alienation. Labour still wins easily in the Calders and the more stable ex-coalfield towns and villages like Broxburn and Uphall. Robin Cook must contunie to look over his shoulder at the Nationalists, though, and much will depend on the overall strength of the two contending parties at the time of the next general election.

Social indices:			2001 Gen. Election:			
% Non-white	1.3		Lab	19,108	53.0	−1.9
% Prof/Man	26.8		SNP	8,492	23.6	−3.9
% Non-manual	51.8		LD	3,969	11.0	+4.3
% Unemployed 2001	3.3		C	2,995	8.3	−1.1
% Decrease 97–01	0.6		SSP	1,110	3.1	
% Fin hard/Rank	32.2	113	UKIP	359	1.0	
% Prem mort/Rank	41	166	Lab maj	10,616	29.5	
			Turnout		55.6	−15.5
			Elect	64,850		

Member of Parliament

Robin Cook, after being Foreign Secretary for four years – initially an 'ethical' one, and confirming that the Special Relationship was in the safe hands of a former unilateralist, was unwillingly reshuffled in 2001 from Palmerstonian grandeur to the Leadership of the Commons – a post in which he had been preceded by two women as a way of maintaining a 5-women quota in the Cabinet, and where he seemed likely to hit the headlines for little more than proposing a 12 o'clock venue for Prime Minister's Questions, so depriving the viewers of the 3 pm weekly event of the sight of the also marginalised Deputy Prime Minister seated alongside the PM, desperately trying to stay awake after a good lunch. Born in 1946 and educated at Aberdeen Grammar School, Royal High School, Edinburgh and Edinburgh University, he was elected (for Edinburgh Central, 1974–83) at the age of 28, advanced as a soft left-winger who opposed devolution and, under Blair, initially resisted the Clause Four rewrite. A resistantly-bearded man without limitless charm, but for his highly public and messy dropping of his wife, he might have had the eventual option of being Prime Minister of Scotland (a.k.a. First Minister of the Scottish Executive), a rare distinction even if performed by three people in two-and-a-half years after 1999.

LLANELLI

In the first elections for the newly established Welsh Assembly, in May 1999, Plaid Cymru broke out of their traditional Welsh-speaking heartlands in the west to make dramatic inroads in the southern valleys, which caused great consternation in the Labour Party establishment. Neil Kinnock's old seat of Islwyn fell, and the mighty citadel of the Rhondda, and thirdly Llanelli. All had been believed to be rock solid, part of the core of support as old as Labour itself. By the time of the General Election of 2001, though, things had moved on. Rhodri Morgan was a popular and independent standard bearer for Labour in Wales. Plaid Cymru could not be seen as so relevant to Westminster politics, nor to have much influence in the UK Parliament as a whole. Indeed in Rhondda and Islwyn they had flattered to please, and their vote fell way back out of serious contention in 2001. In Llanelli, however, it held up better, improving from 19% to 31% and reducing Denzil Davies's majority from 16,000 to 6,000.

Why did the Plaid vote advance more here? The answer lies in the dualistic culture of the Llanelli constituency. Llanelli became known by the early twentieth century as

Britain's greatest tinplate manufacturing centre. Here was the western end of the great anthracite coalfield. In recent years other industries have had to be attracted to supplement and replace these staples. This is a predominantly working-class seat, which includes Burry Port, Kidwelly and the brewing village of Felinfoel as well as Llanelli itself. Here too can be found many of the cultural characteristics of the industrial valleys – a famous rugby union team, singing, Nonconformist chapels. But it is also a Welsh-speaking district, where around half the population are bilingual. In that sense at least it does belong with the west, rather than with the English-influenced Glamorgan counties. Right next door in Carmarthen East and Dinefwr, Plaid Cymru made their only gain in the 2001 Election, from Labour. They may call themselves the 'Party of Wales' in English, and deny their commitment to full independence for Wales in an attempt to broaden their appeal, yet Plaid Cymru have still not broken those linguistic links – with both their embedded strengths and weaknesses.

Social indices:			2001 Gen. Election:			
% Non-white	0.5		Lab	17,586	48.6	−9.3
% Welsh sp	46.5		PC	11,183	30.9	+11.9
% Prof/Man	27.3		C	3,442	9.5	−2.6
% Non-manual	48.0		LD	3,065	8.5	−0.7
£ Av prop val 2000	42 K		Grn	515	1.4	
% Increase 97–00	21.4		SLP	407	1.1	−0.7
% Unemployed 2001	4.5		Lab maj	6,403	17.7	
% Decrease 97–01	2.8		Turnout		62.3	−8.4
% Fin hard/Rank	22.0	243	Elect	58,148		
% Pensioners	31.5					
% Prem mort/Rank	37	226				

Member of Parliament

Denzil Davies, Labour MP, first elected here in 1970 (replacing Jim Griffiths who had himself held the seat for 36 years) is a Euro- and devo-sceptic Labour veteran out of step with the younger generation of Welsh Labour MPs. Born in 1938, and educated at Queen Elizabeth's Grammar School, Carmarthen and Pembroke College, Oxford, he was a Treasury Minister from 1975 to 1979 but reverted to practice at the Bar once his frontbench career (as Defence spokesman) aborted under Kinnock in 1988. His political incorrectness on Europe and devolution, which he saw as 'the unbundling of the British state', is matched by his wife Ann Carlton's dismissive view of all-women shortlists, and he votes against homosexual sex at 16. In the 1997–2001 Parliament he was Labour's 13th most rebellious MP, with 25 dissenting votes, often against European legislation. In the new House elected in 2001 he rebelled against the EU Nice Treaty, and – serially – against the anti-terrorism legislation. Only Alan Williams (Swansea West) has sat longer for a Welsh constituency.

LONDONDERRY EAST

The Democratic Unionist Party, associated by most throughout the UK with the name of Paisley, made great strides in the 2001 General Election, gaining three seats from their Ulster Unionist rivals and returning five members altogether compared with two in 1997. This was largely due to Protestant and unionist frustration with the peace process consequent on the Good Friday Agreement of 1998, as the majority community felt that more concessions had been made on their behalf by such as the UUP leader David Trimble than by the Nationalists or Republicans on the other side of the sectarian divide. Strangford, vacated by Ulster Unionist deputy leader John Taylor, fell to the DUP, and two sitting members of Trimble's party were defeated: Cecil Walker of Belfast North and William Ross of East Londonderry.

Despite its name (which some feel is a concession to Protestant feeling) Londonderry East contains none of the city of Derry, which is to be found in the Foyle constituency. It is instead predominantly rural and an important agricultural area. It now contains just two complete district council areas, Limavady and Coleraine; 12 wards from the district of Magherafelt including the town of that name itself, were transferred to Mid Ulster in major boundary changes in the rural west of Northern Ireland in 1997, amounting to a loss of about 19,000 voters in all.

In the west the seat backs into the Sperrin mountains, but the northern coast, fringing Lough Foyle and the Atlantic, is much more fertile. The main urban centres are Coleraine and Limavady, but there are numerous small market towns such as Kilrea and Dungiven. Coleraine is the site of the New University of Ulster. There is also a tourist industry based on the north coast and Portrush in particular.

Londonderry East is predominantly unionist but it harbours pockets of intense Nationalist feeling. In 2001 the SDLP polled 21% of the vote here and Sinn Fein a further 16%. The winner, though, was Gregory Campbell, a long-time Derry city politician 17 years William Ross's junior, and an altogether more articulate and abrasive representative of the hardline unionist cause. Politics in Northern Ireland continued to polarise, 'agreement' or no.

Social indices:		2001 Gen. Election:			
% Prof/Man	28.8	DUP	12,813	32.1	+6.5
% Non-manual	50.3	UUP	10,912	27.4	−8.2
% RC	33.3	SDLP	8,298	20.8	−0.9
% Irish sp	4.6	SF	6,221	15.6	+6.5
% Unemployed 2001	6.3	APNI	1,625	4.1	−2.3
% Decrease 97–01	3.5	DUP maj	1,901	4.8	
		Turnout		66.1	+1.4
		Elect	60,276		

Member of Parliament

Greg Campbell, a former civil servant turned self-employed businessman, won this seat for Paisley's DUP from the Ulster Unionist Willie Ross in 2001, an unexpected result given Ross's own hard-line stance on power-sharing with Republicans without IRA decommissioning. Born in 1953 and educated at Londonderry Technical College and Magee College, he personally represents the impoverished wing of working-class Unionists who 'enjoyed none of the benefits of the so-called Unionist ascendancy'. Elected to the Northern Ireland Assembly for this seat in 1998 and one of his party's two representatives on the Northern Ireland Executive as Minister for Regional Development, he condemns the British government's continual appeasing of the

Catholics as leaving the Protestant community 'angry, disillusioned, discriminated against and marginalized, not only since the Belfast Agreement but for decades before'. He joined the DUP aged 18 in 1971 and appropriately saw his victory here 30 years on as a 'No Surrender' message.

LOUGHBOROUGH

Loughborough: Labour 1945–79; Conservative majority 17,648 in 1987; Labour majority in 2001 6,378. What can account for these transformations? Above all else, boundary changes. Certainly the fortunes of the major parties have ebbed and flowed, but in this case the more powerful determinant of the destiny of a seat have been the policies and whims of the parliamentary Boundary Commission.

Almost the only part of the constituency which has remained constantly present since the war is the town of Loughborough itself. Up to 1979 the seat was completed by the bulk of the Leicestershire coalfield, territory which has since 1983 been included in the North West Leicestershire division. This was the keystone of Labour's victories in Loughborough from 1945 to 1974. The area which replaced the coalfield had very different characteristics. The valley of the Soar, north of Leicester, contains many large suburban villages which stretch to the boundary of the city itself. All are solidly Conservative, and form part of the white middle-class Leicester commuting belt. They were the bedrock of Stephen Dorrell's easy victories from 1983 to 1992. Then, though, the Boundary Commission intervened again, taking most of the Soar Valley section out of Loughborough, and placing Birstall and other such communities in the brand new Charnwood division. Almost exactly 20,000 voters were removed. Only Barrow-upon-Soar and Quorndon (famed for its hunt) remain from the terrain added in 1983. In compensation the seat took the town of Shepshed from North West Leicestershire, leaving it as a fairly compact core centred firmly on Loughborough itself, with just a small area of Wolds villages.

This is very bad news for the Conservatives. The Soar Valley section was so strongly Tory that Dorrell's 11,000 majority in 1992 would have been trimmed by at least 7,000 votes if the new boundaries had been in place. Shepshed is fairly evenly divided between the main parties. The town of Loughborough has a number of Labour wards; this industrial engineering town contains numerous old terraces and council estates, and a sizeable non-white minority. There is a comfortable middle-class area in the south-west of the town in Outwoods and Nanpantan wards, but overall Loughborough is quite capable of rejecting the Conservatives even in a general election. Even with a slightly smaller swing than the national average, it was an easy picking for Labour in 1997, and like so many new MPs then Andy Reed improved his position after his first term, but it would still be close to being dead even in a dead even year.

Social indices:			2001 Gen. Election:			
% Non-white	7.2		Lab/Coop	22,016	49.7	+1.2
% Prof/Man	32.7		C	15,638	35.3	−2.4
% Non-manual	52.9		LD	5,667	12.8	+1.0
£ Av prop val 2000	80 K		UKIP	933	2.1	
% Increase 97–00	26.0		L/C maj	6,378	14.4	
% Unemployed 2001	2.9		Turnout		63.2	−12.8
% Decrease 97–01	0.6		Elect	70,077		
% Fin hard/Rank	17.9	308				
% Pensioners	23.0					
% Prem mort/Rank	16	534				

Member of Parliament

Andy Reed, a short, eager loyalist, rewarded as a PPS in 2000 (and by 2001 to Margaret Beckett), was elected in 1997 and dismissed by *Red Pepper* as 'well-presented and good with the media, (but) no politics whatsoever', and seen as resembling one of those cherubs puffing the breeze from the corners of ancient maps. As local as local gets, born in 1946, he was schooled at secondary schools in Birstall in the Leicester suburbs, attended Leicester Polytechnic and worked for Leicester-shire County Council variously on urban regeneration, economic development, employment and European affairs for nine years. He is churchy, plays rugby, likes the internet, poses stooge questions and backs East Midlands regionalism.

LOUTH AND HORNCASTLE

This seat effectively covers the north-eastern quadrant of the county of Lincolnshire. A popular impression of Lincolnshire is that it is composed entirely of flat fields growing vegetables and flowers under a huge sky. But this is belied by the Wolds, a green hilly landscape of mixed and wealthy farming. The windswept and rather untidy towns of the Fens are far away in spirit and in appearance from the affluent and elegant Louth, with its towering church spires. (In the nineteenth century Louth was known as the 'nest of rooks' because it was full of absentee black-coated clergymen hiding from their rural parishes, which became infected with Primitive Methodism.) This is one of two Lincolnshire seats, along with South Holland and the Deepings, which ranks among the 20 most rural in Britain, and the ten such in England. The seat also includes the northern part of Lincolnshire's resort coast, with towns such as Mablethorpe, Sutton-on-Sea and Chapel St Leonards, although Skegness and Ingoldmells were moved in the latest boundary changes in 1997 to another seat, Boston and Skegness. The same changes removed the country market town of Horncastle from its association with Gainsborough, which had lasted for three elections, and reunited it with much of the country it was formerly linked with. At the same time the name of the seat under discussion has been changed from East Lindsey to Louth and Horncastle.

The Liberal Democrats had challenged strongly in parts of this seat in the 1980s, but have fallen back in recent years, and it was Labour who doubled their vote and moved forward into second place in 1997. This clarified, there was some tactical voting in 2001 as Labour advanced by a further 2%, while the Lib Dems fell back by about 4%, neither in line with national or regional trends. Labour were ahead in Mablethorpe and Louth South in the Lincolnshire county elections on the same day, the Liberal Democrats nowhere. Sir Peter Tapsell still won fairly easily though, to take his place as the oldest of the 166 Conservative MPs returned, and Louth and Horncastle can be characterised as a safe Conservative seat.

Social indices:			2001 Gen. Election:			
% Non-white	0.5		C	21,543	48.5	+5.0
% Prof/Man	31.7		Lab	13,989	31.5	+1.8
% Non-manual	50.2		LD	8,928	20.1	−4.4
£ Av prop val 2000	64 K		C maj	7,554	17.0	
% Increase 97–00	29.3		Turnout		62.1	−10.5
% Unemployed 2001	2.5		Elect	71,556		
% Decrease 97–01	1.8					
% Fin hard/Rank	7.5	543				
% Pensioners	32.4					
% Prem mort/Rank	34	267				

Member of Parliament

Sir Peter Tapsell emerged from the 2001 Election as the lone Conservative survivor from the 1950s, when he was elected in 1959 at Nottingham West as one of the beneficiaries of Harold Macmillan's 'You Never Had It So Good' landslide. Losing the seat back to Labour in 1964, he then migrated to Lincolnshire where he has been an MP since 1966. A stockbroker educated at Tonbridge and Merton College, Oxford, he was born in 1930, the son of a Malayan rubber planter. A Eurosceptic, but from a deviant One Nation Keynesian as well as Germanophobic perspective, he backed Heseltine against Thatcher, having opposed her on the poll tax. One of the last Tories to wear three-piece suits, a ponderous speaker with a patrician lisp and with a face permanently tanned – it has been suggested – by the furnace of his tremendous self-esteem, he is one of the last of the grandees and claimed that had he run for, and been elected, Speaker in 2000 he would have 'looked great in tights' (because) 'I have very good legs; all the women in my life have commented on this'.

LUDLOW

One of the least tipped gains in the 2001 General Election, when only 20 seats changed hands in Britain (27 in the UK – the turnover in Northern Ireland was much higher, relatively), was at Ludlow, consequent in a small part on the second last-minute retirement of a sitting Conservative MP in 14 years. In 1987 Eric Cockeram had been forced out after dealing in BT shares, but in 2001 Christopher Gill left Ludlow, and his party, voluntarily to pursue his anti-European and right-wing causes untrammelled by both the party Whip and a seat in the Commons. The beneficiary was the young Liberal Democrat Matthew Green, coming apparently from nowhere in a seat in which his party had made little impact before: under 30% in the 1997 General Election, 26% in the May 1999 local elections (mostly losing to

Independents, in one of their rare surviving bastions in England), 14% in the June 1999 European elections. The trend had scarcely been encouraging.

The Ludlow constituency covers most of the southern half of Shropshire. Ancient small towns like Church Stretton, Bishop's Castle, Clun and Ludlow itself seem deep in the countryside. These were already parliamentary borough constituencies when their eighteenth-century politics were studied and anatomised by the famed historian Lewis Namier. The status of this terrain as a border area is emphasised by the presence of great castles like that at Ludlow, which dominates one of the most perfectly preserved medieval towns in Britain, now known also as a small-scale culinary paradise, with several nationally renowned restaurants. The countryside of South Shropshire, overlooked by the hills of the Long Mynd and Wenlock Edge, is remote and relatively little visited despite its attractiveness. There is another section to the constituency, around Bridgnorth. This is much more in the orbit of the West Midlands conurbation, but it also is predominantly Conservative and Independent in local politics, with little Liberal Democrat tradition of success.

Apart from the disappearance of the incumbent in a fit of indignation against his own party, another clue to Green's surprise victory is given by the Labour vote, which declined far more than the Tory share, as there was an obvious move to tactical voting across the constituency. One feels that if Matthew Green can provide a stable and steady level of constituency service, he could build up a personal vote which would enable him to hold Ludlow for a lengthy period: this seat clearly values independence and individuality in its politicians.

Social indices:			2001 Gen. Election:			
% Non-white	0.5		LD	18,620	43.2	+13.5
% Prof/Man	37.9		C	16,990	39.4	−3.0
% Non-manual	54.8		Lab	5,785	13.4	−12.0
£ Av prop val 2000	108 K		Grn	871	2.0	+0.3
% Increase 97–00	40.3		UKIP	858	2.0	+1.2
% Unemployed 2001	1.6		LD maj	1,630	3.8	
% Decrease 97–01	1.0		Turnout		68.4	−7.2
% Fin hard/Rank	7.6	537	Elect	63,053		
% Pensioners	28.0					
% Prem mort/Rank	15	536				

Member of Parliament

Matthew Green, the youngest Liberal Democrat MP, unexpectedly captured Ludlow from the Conservatives in 2001, aided by the late desertion of the seat by the disaffected Europhobic MP Christopher Gill, and a non-local replacement. A former sales manager with a timber firm for 15 years, but latterly running his own PR company, he was born in 1970 in Shropshire and educated at Priory School Shrewsbury and Birmingham University. Classically handsome and burly, and the first Liberal MP for Ludlow since 1886, his focus is routinely local – complaining about foot-and-mouth, poor rural roads and schools, and health authority boundaries incorporating Shropshire with other counties – but accompanied by an abrasive style and a reliance on tactical Labour votes. A spokesman on youth affairs in 2002 he sought legislation on votes at 16.

LUTON NORTH

The two Luton seats produced almost identical results in 2001, with Labour slightly increasing their share of the vote to just over 55%, 25% ahead of the Conservatives, but they are not as alike as peas in a pod. North is now entirely contained within the borough. There is less industry and fewer non-white voters here than in Luton South. There is plenty of new private housing, most specifically on the northern edge of the built-up area in Bramingham ward, which increased in population from 7,000 to 12,000 in the 1980s. North also contains Luton's safest Tory ward, Icknield, which harbours the town's classiest housing along the A6 towards Bedford (though many managerial workers live outside Luton, in dormitory towns like Harpenden, in Dunstable and in wealthy villages like Studham).

Labour can fight back, in the council estates of Lewsey and Sundon Park and Leagrave; as one drives through the seat on the M1, tower blocks are prominent only a few yards away. Many of the former Vauxhall car factory employees and other skilled manual workers live in the northern section of Luton, and their votes may be counted as volatile and very much 'up for grabs'. With the basis of Luton's modern economy shattered by the General Motors decision to close down all motor production in their former British headquarters, Luton's future is in an unclear and transitional state. This could be a seat which will again be characterised by large swings, and as such much attended to by the major political parties. It could move either way, to the safe Labour expression of long-term decline, or, more optimistically and perhaps more likely, to the volatile instrumentalism of a varied employment base in prosperous southern England, well connected to all forms of transport, and suited to renewal through inward investment.

Social indices:			2001 Gen. Election:			
% Non-white	17.4		Lab	22,187	56.7	+2.1
% Prof/Man	28.2		C	12,210	31.2	–3.1
% Non-manual	53.0		LD	3,795	9.7	+0.6
£ Av prop val 2000	77 K		UKIP	934	2.4	+0.9
% Increase 97–00	42.0		Lab maj	9,977	25.5	
% Unemployed 2001	2.7		Turnout		59.3	–14.0
% Decrease 97–01	2.1		Elect	65,998		
% Fin hard/Rank	19.3	284				
% Pensioners	18.3					
% Prem mort/Rank	29	370				

Member of Parliament

Kelvin Hopkins, bald and trim-bearded, won here in 1997 and promptly joined the Campaign Group, one of only 10 of the 183-strong 1997 intake to do so. A former UNISON/NALGO research officer, he was born in 1941 and educated at Queen Elizabeth Grammar School, Barnet, and Nottingham University. He has turned up for all the major rebellions, on lone parent benefit cuts, student grants, Murdoch predatory pricing, freedom of information, the Prime Minister's right to nominate life peers, jury trial curbs, legal aid reform, pensions, disability benefit cuts and air traffic control privatisation – the full Campaign Group diet of dissidence. In fact he was the

1997–2001 Parliament's seventh most dissentient Labour MP, with 32 rebellions against the Whips.

LUTON SOUTH

Luton South contains most of the institutions associated in the public mind with this rather unglamorous town: the ruins of the Vauxhall motor works, the airport which is so popular with European holiday package operators, the huge Arndale shopping centre. The Conservatives did really well to hold this functional heart of Luton in the 1992 General Election. The odds seemed stacked against them. Labour could rely on the council estate of Farley ward, and even more on the majority non-white (mainly Asian) wards of Dallow and Biscot, in the 'inner city' terraces north and west of the town centre. Even in more middle-class wards – Putteridge, Crawley and Stopsley – the locally active Liberal Democrats topped the poll. Yet in 1992 the then PPS to John Major, Graham Bright, held on with a majority of 799 over Labour with the Lib Dems securing only 10% of the vote. They have not come close again. In 1997 Margaret Moran took Luton South by over 11,000 votes on a swing of 12%, Graham Bright losing his seat as John Major was losing the country.

Since the Second World War, Luton has been one of the most politically marginal towns in the country. Its most famous MP was the 'Radio Doctor', Charles Hill (1950–63), who stood, rather quaintly, as a 'Liberal and Conservative', but voted with the Tories in the House. But Labour could win the old unified seat of Luton, and did in a 1963 by-election, 1964 and 1966. When the town was divided into two seats in 1974 they won both. In 1997 and 2001 they did so again, in elections overshadowed by the closure of the Vauxhall plant complex. Not surprisingly, perhaps, turnout dropped by 13% in 2001 as all major parties lost votes, and Luton's future is cloudy.

Social indices:			2001 Gen. Election:			
% Non-white	20.9		Lab	21,719	55.2	+0.3
% Prof/Man	28.0		C	11,586	29.4	−1.9
% Non-manual	52.2		LD	4,292	10.9	+1.3
£ Av prop val 2000	78 K		Grn	798	2.0	+1.3
% Increase 97–00	45.0		UKIP	578	1.5	+0.7
% Unemployed 2001	4.0		SA	271	0.7	
% Decrease 97–01	2.3		WRP	107	0.3	
% Fin hard/Rank	26.1	189	Lab maj	10,133	25.8	
% Pensioners	20.6		Turnout		57.0	−13.4
% Prem mort/Rank	40	180	Elect	68,985		

Member of Parliament

Margaret Moran, gor-blimey-accented, and sorter-out of the hard left as leader of Lewisham Council, won this seat in 1997 after selection from an all-women shortlist. The daughter of Irish immigrants, she was born in 1955 and educated at St Ursula's Convent School, Greenwich, St Mary's (RC) College of Education, Twickenham, and Birmingham University, and formerly ran a 'Housing for Women' housing association. Locally focused in a traditionally marginal seat, she has been a PPS since

December 1997, and by 2001 to Home Office Minister, Baroness Morgan of Huyton, and favours computer-based 'teledemocracy' to increase electoral participation rates among women and ethnic minorities. She also worries about disease, domestic violence and bad housing in her local Asian community.

MACCLESFIELD

Nicholas Winterton only just retained Macclesfield for the Conservatives in a by-election held during the mid-term unpopularity of the Heath government in 1971 – his majority was just 1,079. However, following that narrow squeak he has been re-elected eight times, on each occasion with a thumping majority. From where does this ardent enthusiast derive such strong support?

The east Cheshire town of Macclesfield itself comprises about half the constituency. This former silk manufacturing centre has expanded greatly since the war, with the growth of new private estates pleasantly set on the edge of the Cheshire plain just beneath the Peak District foothills. There is still terraced and even working-class housing in central and south Macclesfield, and there are council estates at Weston in the west and Hurdsfield in the north-east, but more typical are the thousands of post-war private houses in estates like Tytherington and Bollinsbrook in the north and north-west of the town. Winterton takes great pride in being a 'good constituency MP', in championing and boosting all Macclesfield's causes, and in representing all voters, whether supporters or not.

However, his majority really piles up in the other part of the seat. This is the affluent Cheshire commuter belt for Manchester, including Disley, Poynton, Bollington and Prestbury. In the last named, which locally has the reputation of being the 'richest village in England', Rolls-Royces abound and the detached homes with external (mock) gas lamps and trim lawns are reminiscent of a wealthy American neighbourhood. In 2001 very little happened in Macclesfield. Turnout dropped by 13%. There were only three candidates, representing the main trio of parties, and their shares of the vote scarcely deviated from four years before. Given that Winterton's style seems to suit the taste of the electorate in this outermost orbit of Cheshire commuterland, there is no reason why he should not carry on as before; all centuries seem to come the same to him.

Social indices:			2001 Gen. Election:				
% Non-white	0.9		C	22,284	48.9	−0.7
% Prof/Man	44.7		Lab	15,084	33.1	−0.6
% Non-manual	64.0		LD	8,217	18.0	+1.3
£ Av prop val 2000	111 K		C maj	7,200	15.8	
% Increase 97–00	28.3		Turnout		62.3	−12.9
% Unemployed 2001	1.3		Elect	73,123		
% Decrease 97–01	1.2					
% Fin hard/Rank	12.3	409				
% Pensioners	24.1					
% Prem mort/Rank	19	488				

Member of Parliament

Nicholas Winterton, first elected here in 1971, became in 2001 the fourth longest-serving Conservative MP, outdistanced only by Sir Peter Tapsell, Sir Patrick Cormack and Kenneth Clarke. Unlike them he has never reached the frontbench, and in trying to reach the Speaker's chair in 2000 polled only 116 votes, the fourth lowest total in a field of 12. Non-knighted because loathed by the Whips – who tipped him out of the Health Select Committee Chairmanship in 1992 – to himself he is 'a man of independent view', to some a man of integrity, to others a shallow populist. Born in 1938 and educated at Rugby, he worked for 20 years for his father-in-law's plant hire firm. Pink-faced, flared-nostrilled, pugnacious, opinionated and a foghorn-voiced staccato speaker, he is Eurosceptic (the second most rebellious Tory on Maastricht) and homophobic (aggressively heckling Tory MP Eleanor Laing's homophile speech in 1998), but not an orthodox free-market Tory, favouring import controls to protect British manufacturing, and opposing Heseltine's pit closures. He backs the Turks in Cyprus, votes with a hardline rump against power-sharing in Northern Ireland, and opposes stupid names for pubs.

MAIDENHEAD

When the humorous writer John O'Farrell, who has made part of his living reminiscing in a hangdog manner about the angst of being a Labour supporter through long years of opposition, decided to stand for his beloved party in his home town in 2001, he clearly expected the contest to be easily cast as a David versus Goliath struggle, with the Conservative incumbent Theresa May standing as a colossus warding off his puny challenge. His witty and engaging BBC2 video diary of the campaign did follow that script. There was, however, to be a fly in the ointment in the form of the Liberal Democrats' Kathryn Newbound, who almost spoilt the story by nearly winning. O'Farrell apparently missed this possibility, as did almost all of those observing from outside the Maidenhead seat.

It was fair enough to depict Maidenhead as affluent, comfortable and largely typified by Maidenhead town, whose 37,000 or so voters make up rather over half the voters. The rest come from traditionally Conservative semi-rural wards, some of which are previously in the Wokingham unitary authority. The seat borders the Thames for some miles, taking in Cookham, Charvil, Sonning and Twyford, and reaching to the west almost to the Reading suburbs. However, many pundits did not notice that in the 2000 local elections a year before the general election, the Lib Dems piled up only 1% fewer votes than the Conservatives within the seat, winning wards in Maidenhead town like Cox Green, Furze Platt and Kathryn Newbound's own Pinkneys Green. The Liberal Democrat advance was not primarily a matter of squeezing the O'Farrell vote, but it moved substantially directly from the Tories. This is not a healthy trend for Theresa May, for the Tories, and far more people will know that Maidenhead will seriously be worth watching, and that Labour will be a sideshow, next time.

Social indices:			2001 Gen. Election:			
% Non-white	5.1		C	19,506	45.0	−4.8
% Prof/Man	49.2		LD	16,222	37.4	+11.2
% Non-manual	70.4		Lab	6,577	15.2	−2.9
£ Av prop val 2000	221 K		UKIP	741	1.7	+1.2
% Increase 97–00	66.2		MRLP	272	0.6	
% Unemployed 2001	1.0		C maj	3,284	7.6	
% Decrease 97–01	0.8		Turnout		63.6	−12.0
% Fin hard/Rank	5.6	595	Elect	68,130		
% Pensioners	21.6					
% Prem mort/Rank	12	564				

Member of Parliament

Theresa May, though only elected in 1997, was quickly onto the frontbench and even into the Shadow Cabinet as Education spokesman (1999–2001), because of the very low female numbers on the Conservative benches. A former banker who adapted quickly to the Commons as a combative and fluent performer, she was born in 1956 and educated at Wheatley Park Comprehensive School, Oxfordshire, and St Hugh's College, Oxford, where she obtained a degree in geography. As Tory spokesman on women's issues she opposed Health spokesman Liam Fox's call in January 2001 for a 'huge restriction, if not abolition' of the current abortion law. She backed Portillo in 2001 and was given the Transport, Local Government and the Regions spokesmanship. She favours some sort of discrimination to ensure more women MPs.

MAIDSTONE AND THE WEALD

Ann Widdecombe may have been disappointed to find that virtually none of her colleagues in the Commons would back her bid to become Conservative Party leader in succession to William Hague after the hammering of June 2001, but she could take solace in her undoubted popularity in her constituency, where her share of the vote had just increased by 5% and her majority increased into five figures, even as over 8,000 fewer people expressed a preference.

For quite some years now, the Boundary Commission has not been able to devise a scheme which enables the whole of Kent's county town, Maidstone, to be brought together in one constituency. In the general elections from 1983 to 1992 the seat named Maidstone included a number of villages in the agricultural area surrounding the town – places like the picturesque Leeds Castle. Yet significant chunks of the town itself, such as East ward and North ward, were excluded and placed in the higgledy-piggledy and artificially created seat of Mid Kent. Now a new arrangement has been sculpted by the imaginative commissioners. East and North are brought back into the Maidstone seat, and much rural territory to the east of the town has been transferred to the new Faversham/Mid Kent. Yet rather than obtain a compact solution, the Commission have for reasons of numeric equality taken out a different section of the town of Maidstone, the working-class council estate wedge to the south-east including Shepway and Park Wood. To complete the rather confused picture, the seat also now extends through the hills of the Weald all the way to the

Sussex border, taking in the eastern end of the borough and constituency of Tunbridge Wells. It is named Maidstone and the Weald (though it only includes part of the latter – and, indeed, the former). It does include Benenden, the site of the prestigious girls' school, Sissinghurst, with its castle and gardens, and the attractive Wealden towns of Cranbrook and Hawkhurst. It would take a political earthquake to shake Miss Widdecombe's mighty grip on this seat, even with its mixed name and constitution.

Social indices:			2001 Gen. Election:			
% Non-white	1.8		C	22,621	49.6	+5.5
% Prof/Man	38.3		Lab	12,303	27.0	+0.8
% Non-manual	63.0		LD	9,064	19.9	−2.5
£ Av prop val 2000	125 K		UKIP	978	2.1	+1.5
% Increase 97–00	50.3		Ind	611	1.3	
% Unemployed 2001	1.4		C maj	10,318	22.6	
% Decrease 97–01	1.6		Turnout		61.6	−12.4
% Fin hard/Rank	6.8	563	Elect	74,002		
% Pensioners	24.6					
% Prem mort/Rank	15	538				

Member of Parliament

Ann Widdecombe, Shadow Home Secretary under William Hague (1999–2001) and MP here since 1987, was strangely trailed as a potential Tory leader, despite serious difficulties for the marketing men required to promote an untelegenic, shrill-voiced, churchy spinster, who has described TV as 'filth'. Born in 1947 and educated at a convent in Bath and at Birmingham University and at Lady Margaret Hall, Oxford, she worked previously as a university administrator and was a minister at Social Security, then Employment, then the Home Office between 1990 and 1997. Her political breakthrough from joke to heroine came in 1998 with her character assassination of the unpopular Michael Howard, under whom she had served at the Home Office but whose leadership hopes she effectively crushed. She left Canterbury for Rome over female ordination and prompted eight fellow Shadow Cabinet members to admit their dope-sodden pasts in order to scotch her emotive call for on-the-spot fines for cannabis possession in 2000. In the tiny Tory minority against fox hunting, she was an Ancram, then Clarke, voter in 2001, and then retreated to the backbenches under Iain Duncan Smith.

MAKERFIELD

Before 1983 there was a parliamentary constituency called Ince. It was a name which had the advantage of brevity, but the drawback of obscurity. Not many people living far away from the old Lancashire coalfield around Wigan had heard of the small town of Ince-in-Makerfield, one of the humbler places to have a seat named after them. In 1983 this privilege was forcibly withdrawn as the boundary changes moved Ince to be gobbled up by its large neighbour Wigan. The new seat of Makerfield was created, more than half of it previously contained in the Ince division. Now, another set of boundary changes have taken Ince out of Wigan again, and placed it back in the Makerfield constituency. However, the seat has not been retitled.

This is fair enough, for the largest town in the seat is not Ince, but Ashton-in-Makerfield. This is a seat of small towns, mostly with very strong working-class traditions, including that of voting Labour. Like its neighbouring seats of Leigh and Wigan, this is old-fashioned country. There are virtually no members of ethnic minorities: the seat was 99.4% white in the last published Census. The proportion of one-parent families is well below the national average, and nothing like the rate it is in the big cities. Other parties than Labour scarcely exist, and often fail to provide candidates in local elections, in the small towns of Ashton, Ince, Abram and Winstanley. Worsley Mesnes is really part of Wigan itself. The one place where there is a substantial middle-class population, and where the Tories get within shouting distance in local elections, is the town of Orrell, west of Wigan towards Skelmersdale, as proud of its outstanding rugby union team as its big neighbour is of its dominant rugby league side. Possibly the location of the 15-player code club is not coincidental: in the north of England it is widely regarded as a middle-class game.

Orrell is an anomaly in Makerfield though, and Ian McCartney was returned with a massive 17,750 majority in 2001, even after the turnout fell by 16%, well above the average as in many monolithically working-class seats. The people of Makerfield would not endorse any other party but Labour, but they might come out for no party at all.

Social indices:			2001 Gen. Election:			
% Non-white	0.6		Lab	23,879	68.5	−5.1
% Prof/Man	24.5		C	6,129	17.6	+2.2
% Non-manual	47.9		LD	3,990	11.4	+3.1
£ Av prop val 2000	54 K		SA	858	2.5	
% Increase 97–00	26.8		Lab maj	17,750	50.9	
% Unemployed 2001	2.7		Turnout		50.9	−15.9
% Decrease 97–01	2.1		Elect	68,457		
% Fin hard/Rank	20.1	277				
% Pensioners	21.2					
% Prem mort/Rank	37	213				

Member of Parliament

Ian McCartney, possessor, at five feet, of the Commons' lowest profile, and with no neck, a Scottish accent – it has been said – so thick you can slice it like haggis, and likened to a chubby, macho Glaswegian mouse, was elected here in 1987. Son of Hugh McCartney, a Labour MP from 1970 to 1987, he was born in 1951, educated at Lenzie Academy, Langside College, Glasgow and the Merchant Navy Training College, Gravesend. He operates as a pugnacious, working-class, Tory-bashing Scot under the patronage of John Prescott. A laterally-sliding Minister of State since 1997, he has served successively at the DTI (1997–99), Cabinet Office (1999–2001) and from 2001 as Minister of Pensions. He piloted the minimum wage legislation in 1998, but John Prescott's backing was insufficient to land him a Cabinet post in the wake of Peter Mandelson's resignation from the DTI in 1999.

MALDON AND CHELMSFORD EAST

This is a very safe Conservative seat. The district of Maldon is staunchly Tory, containing as it does just two small towns (Maldon and Burnham-on-Crouch) and the commuting area of Heybridge/Ingatestone in addition to numerous villages set on the flattish land between the estuaries. Nor are the Chelmsford wards hostile: they do not reach into the county town itself, but consist of rural territory to its south and east and the suburban communities of Great Baddow and Galleywood on Chelmsford's southern edge. The town centre is all in the Chelmsford West seat.

Chelmsford is noted for the success of the Liberal Democrats in local elections, but this is concentrated more in the town than in the surrounding countryside, and in any case was little in evidence in the 2001 General Election when the Conservatives won by nearly 8,500 and Labour finished second. Essex, as befits one of the three most populous shire counties, did not act as a single unit in 2001. Some seats notably moved towards the Conservatives, such as Castle Point and Billericay where Labour dropped back and Southend West where the Liberal Democrat challenge faded, while Harwich saw a further improvement for Labour after their great leap forward in 1997. However, Maldon and Chelmsford East took a middle line, and no significant swing of any kind was recorded.

Social indices:			2001 Gen. Election:			
% Non-white	1.1		C	21,719	49.2	+0.6
% Prof/Man	39.3		Lab	13,257	30.1	+1.3
% Non-manual	64.3		LD	7,002	15.9	−3.5
£ Av prop val 2000	123 K		UKIP	1,135	2.6	+0.7
% Increase 97–00	50.8		Grn	987	2.2	+0.9
% Unemployed 2001	1.4		C maj	8,462	19.2	
% Decrease 97–01	1.8		Turnout		63.7	−12.4
% Fin hard/Rank	4.8	608	Elect	69,201		
% Pensioners	23.7					
% Prem mort/Rank	17	520				

Member of Parliament

John Whittingdale, Shadow DTI Secretary under Iain Duncan Smith after two years (1999–2001) as William Hague's PPS and two as a Whip, was first elected in 1992. A former political secretary of Margaret Thatcher (1988–92), he rebelled against Maastricht too little for her but too much for John Major. Born in 1959 and educated at Winchester (the only MP left from that place and where he was seen as a bit of a Widmerpool) and at University College, London, he worked almost exclusively as a party staffer for ten years before reaching the Commons, and after voting for Lilley, then Redwood, then Hague, sought to get Margaret Thatcher to block the Clarke-Redwood pact in the final round of the leadership election in 1997. His Thatcherism, like that of Portillo (whose friend he is), is modulated by the realism of the professional politician.

MANCHESTER BLACKLEY

Very few people would be able to guess which parliamentary seat in England has the cheapest housing. According to the property research company Experian, though, it is Manchester Blackley, with an average value in 2000 of £30,838. This would contrast with the mean in Kensington and Chelsea at the same time (£555,835), or if more realistically we wish to stay within Greater Manchester, Altrincham and Sale West (£153,764). It is not that the housing quality is the poorest in Blackley; it is a function, as one would expect in a market society and economy, of supply and demand. There is simply more owner-occupied housing to be had in Blackley, where at least half of the properties come into this category, than, say in Manchester Central, where the few owners in the heart of the city tend to have more desirable homes such as fashionable developments in newly converted warehouses. This is why even lower values on average are to be found in the Welsh valleys (Rhondda). It is still a surprise though that nowhere as 'affordable' as Blackley is to be found in Liverpool, Sheffield or Newcastle.

Blackley (pronounced 'Blakely') is north Manchester. It is something of a mixed constituency still. Wards such as Crumpsall and Moston were once predominantly middle-class residential areas, abutting Heaton Park and the Broughton Park neighbourhood of Salford, by tradition that borough's most affluent, but by 2000 they were solidly Labour and the Conservatives did not even put up a candidate in Moston in the city elections. Also on the northern edge of the city are two wards which have long been overwhelmingly Labour, because of their historic majority of housing in local authority ownership: Charlestown and Blackley itself. Then there is the other section of Blackley. This is the northern inner city, strongly Labour: the nineteenth-century terraces of Lightbowne, still resolutely almost all-white. Harpurhey's old housing stock, on the other hand, has been mainly cleared out and replaced with bleak modern council redevelopment. For 1997 there arrived from the Manchester Central division a different kind of inner-city ward, Cheetham. Cheetham Hill was once one of England's few true Jewish ghettos, a point of entry for poor immigrants from eastern Europe around the turn of this century. Some of the distinctive names of long-defunct businesses can still be seen above the tattered shops of Cheetham Hill, but the Jewish community has gone. Now 35% of the population is non-white, mainly Asian, as Cheetham Hill continues to act as a multicultural reception area. It stretches into the city centre as far as the grim fortress of Strangeways Prison.

The Liberal Democrats finish second in all seven of the wards in this seat in Manchester council elections, but in the 2001 General Election they maintained a wretched 11% and third place. The only serious alternative to voting Labour was not voting at all. That was a very seriously tempting prospect, and 55% of the electorate took it.

Social indices:			2001 Gen. Election:			
% Non-white	9.4		Lab	18,285	68.9	−1.1
% Prof/Man	23.0		C	3,821	14.4	−0.8
% Non-manual	43.2		LD	3,015	11.4	+0.4
£ Av prop val 2000	31 K		SLP	485	1.8	
% Increase 97–00	15.3		SA	461	1.7	
% Unemployed 2001	6.5		Ind	456	1.7	
% Decrease 97–01	3.0		Lab maj	14,464	54.5	
% Fin hard/Rank	44.0	29	Turnout		44.9	−12.6
% Pensioners	27.9		Elect	59,111		
% Prem mort/Rank	60	10				

Member of Parliament

Graham Stringer, a tall, burly, poker-faced former leader of Manchester Council (1984–96), is a recycled hard left-winger-turned-New-Labour Minister, who, after a two-year spell in the Cabinet Office, appropriately – given his hard mien – entered the Whips' Office. Elected here in 1997, he was Manchester-born in 1950, son of a railway clerk, and educated at Merton Brook High School and Sheffield University. An energetic defender of Manchester commercial interests when Council leader, he backs elected mayors but opposes regional government as a threat to the big city power he enjoyed. An effective ward heeler and local party manager, he vigorously backs expansion of Manchester airport to the dismay of the nearby Cheshire gin-and-Jag-belt. He takes a lot of interest in sport.

MANCHESTER CENTRAL

The fine buildings of Manchester's commercial centre still hint at its claim that it was once the second city of the British Empire, the nerve centre of the world's trade in cotton and other textiles. However, the centre is surrounded on all sides by a belt of impoverished inner-city residential areas: to the east Miles Platting, Bradford, Clayton, Newton Heath, and Ancoats, which so shocked Friedrich Engels in the 1840s; to the south Ardwick; and to the south-west the troubled communities of Hulme and Moss Side. All these neighbourhoods are situated in the Central division of Manchester; and all are solidly Labour. Indeed Manchester Central is by many definitions one of the poorest seats in Britain.

Manchester Central's unemployment rate at the time of the 2001 General Election was only surpassed in the north-west by Liverpool Riverside, with nearly 14% of employment-age men out of work. The proportion of single young adults aged 15–24 with a dependent child or children was the highest anywhere in England, at over 9% at the time of the last published census. Manchester Central ranked third in 1998 in the Britain-wide list of claimants of Income Support and sixth of those in receipt of Incapacity Benefit. Although some publicity has recently been given to the return of residents, including affluent professionals, to the heart of the city, these number a few thousand only, and are highly untypical of most living here. Central demonstrates most of the problems of inner-city blight which have afflicted post-war Britain. It includes the sites of some of the most notorious housing redevelopments in any city:

the 'Bison'-built 'Fort' Beswick, now demolished; the planning disaster at Hulme, depopulated and largely occupied by squatters; and, arriving from Stretford in the boundary changes, Moss Side. Moss Side is one of the most lawless places in the land, where drug dealing is rife and related shootings far from uncommon. There is a large Afro-Caribbean minority population.

Not surprisingly, Tony Lloyd, the former Stretford MP, achieved 69% of the vote in 2001, and a numerical majority of nearly 14,000, even in a seat with an appalling turnout of a little under 40%.

Social indices:			2001 Gen. Election:			
% Non-white	19.2		Lab	17,812	68.7	−2.3
% Prof/Man	26.5		LD	4,070	15.7	+3.4
% Non-manual	44.6		C	2,328	9.0	−2.8
£ Av prop val 2000	65 K		Grn	1,018	3.9	
% Increase 97–00	72.2		SLP	484	1.9	−0.5
% Unemployed 2001	10.2		PA	216	0.8	
% Decrease 97–01	4.7		Lab maj	13,742	53.0	
% Fin hard/Rank	51.2	14	Turnout		39.1	−13.4
% Pensioners	23.9		Elect	66,268		
% Prem mort/Rank	61	7				

Member of Parliament

Tony Lloyd, one of Blair's dropped jobbing ministers in 1999, narrowly missed defeating Clive Soley by six votes as PLP Chairman in 2000, and was beaten again in 2001 by Jean Corston. Mancunian-brogued, and of somewhat lugubrious countenance, he was first elected in 1983 and soon set up as a routine North West/Mancunian regionalist. Born in 1950, a printer's son, educated at Stretford Grammar School and Nottingham University, a former accountant and lecturer, and a Prescott voter in 1994, he performed weakly under questioning on Sierra Leone as a Foreign Office Minister in the Foreign Affairs Select Committee and lost his ministerial job in the second annual reshuffle in 1999.

MANCHESTER GORTON

Gorton is situated south-east of Manchester's city centre, geographically clustered around a notable local landmark, Belle Vue's zoological park and funfair. The constituency includes Longsight, the south-eastern part of Manchester's belt of inner-city desolation, which is strongly Labour and over 40% non-white, as it is the core of the city's Asian community. Levenshulme, a little further out from the centre, is a Liberal Democrat target ward and contains only 3% council housing. Rusholme and Fallowfield also contain many owner-occupiers, and were once part of Manchester's southern middle-class area (which accounts for the location of Manchester Grammar School, independent now and still one of the most successful day schools in the country). Now, though, these wards have declined in social status as the more affluent Mancunians have fled southwards and out to Cheshire. Gorton itself has a recent tradition of Liberal Democrat activism, and a Gorton North ward city councillor Jackie Pearcey closed the gap in second place in her second attempt here in the 2001 General Election, increasing her share of the vote again while Labour's veteran Gerald Kaufman slipped a little. Their problems, though, were that Kaufman still obtained over nearly three times the number of her votes, and that they could not positively inspire as many electors even as in 1997, as turnout dropped to under 43%, the seventh lowest figure in the UK.

Social indices:			2001 Gen. Election:			
% Non-white	20.1		Lab	17,099	62.8	−2.5
% Prof/Man	27.2		LD	5,795	21.3	+3.8
% Non-manual	47.7		C	2,705	9.9	−1.8
£ Av prop val 2000	38 K		Grn	835	3.1	+1.2
% Increase 97–00	32.5		UKIP	462	1.7	
% Unemployed 2001	8.0		SLP	333	1.2	−0.2
% Decrease 97–01	4.1		Lab maj	11,304	41.5	
% Fin hard/Rank	36.8	78	Turnout		42.7	−13.8
% Pensioners	23.5		Elect	63,834		
% Prem mort/Rank	56	18				

Member of Parliament

Gerald Kaufman, tall, bald, waspish, exotically-suited and a once-prominent right-wing factionalist, was elected in 1970, having risen politically as one of Harold Wilson's kitchen cabinet, in his case as the less high-profile equivalent of Alistair Campbell. Born into a Leeds Jewish family in 1930 and educated at Leeds Grammar School (where he recalls anti-Semitic bullying) and Queen's College, Oxford, he presided over the Culture Select Committee from 1997. Denied Cabinet office by his parliamentary career coinciding with the long years of the Thatcher hegemony, he shadowed pretty well everything in Opposition, but now rests content with ponderous and caustic adjudication on chattering class concerns such as Covent Garden and the BBC. He has been described by Brian Sedgemore as 'a man with a tongue so sharp that it hurts just to see his mouth open'.

MANCHESTER WITHINGTON

There are few better examples in England of long-term political and electoral change than Manchester Withington. This is a seat which was retained by the Conservatives in 1966 when Labour won the General Election with a majority of 100 seats. In 1992 the Tories won the General Election, but Withington, its boundaries drawn if anything more favourably to the right than in 1966, gave Labour a majority of 9,735 after a swing of over 7%. By 2001 the Conservatives had slipped to third, nearly 40% behind Labour and overtaken by the more locally active and successful Liberal Democrats, in the person of two-time candidate Yasmin Zalzala. This particular part of Manchester's southern side had been moving leftwards for decades. Withington had always included the classic middle-class wards of Didsbury (the strongest Tory ward in the city, and the only one in most of the council elections of the 1990s, but now held by the Lib Dems), Barlow Moor and Withington itself. It also now covers

Chorlton-cum-Hardy, once regarded as second only to Didsbury in its favour for the Conservative Party. Yet as time passed the Tory grip became shakier. The big houses were being multi-occupied, broken up, or were slipping down the scale of social status. Council estates had been established as Old Moat and Burnage in the inter-war years.

In the end, though, it was not just demographic change which has done for the Conservatives in south Manchester. Manchester's seats have all swung to Labour; the city clearly gave the thumbs down to the governments of 1979 to 1997. Part of this was due to the nature of Withington's still substantial middle-class vote – it has a higher proportion of professional and managerial workers than Altrincham and Sale West, the only Conservative seat left in Greater Manchester after 2001. But these are people who choose to live in the city, with its high-spending left-wing administration; there are a disproportionate number of teachers, university lecturers, and doctors here (the seat contains the famous Christie Hospital and Holt Radium Institute). They represent the intellectual middle class, not the bourgeoisie. As such the Tory Party of the 1980s and subsequently has been perceived as working against both their tastes and their interests.

Social indices:			2001 Gen. Election:			
% Non-white	10.6		Lab	19,239	54.9	–6.7
% Prof/Man	46.2		LD	7,715	22.0	+8.4
% Non-manual	67.1		C	5,349	15.3	–4.1
£ Av prop val 2000	103 K		Grn	1,539	4.4	
% Increase 97–00	60.9		SA	1,208	3.4	+2.6
% Unemployed 2001	4.1		Lab maj	11,524	32.9	
% Decrease 97–01	4.4		Turnout		51.9	–14.7
% Fin hard/Rank	19.2	286	Elect	67,480		
% Pensioners	25.6					
% Prem mort/Rank	45	91				

Member of Parliament

Keith Bradley, Minister of State at the Home Office from 2001, following spells as a Junior Social Security Minister (1997–98) and Deputy Chief Whip (1998–2001), having discarded both a beard and a routinely municipal left-wing past on Manchester city council, was elected here in 1987, and as a frontbencher (1991–97) specialised in Social Security policy. Born in 1950 and educated at Bishop Vesey's Grammar School, Sutton Coldfield, Manchester Polytechnic and York University, he worked previously as an NHS bureaucrat. As number two in the Whips' office, he did not require reminding that in February 1997 he said Labour was 'completely opposed to the privatisation of the National Air Traffic Control Services'.

MANSFIELD

The Nottinghamshire constituency of Mansfield produced arguably the Labour Party's best single result in the 1992 General Election. Alan Meale's share of the vote increased by no less than 17%, from 37% to 54%. His majority, which in 1987 was a paltry 56, the lowest of any Labour seat in Britain, rose to a princely 11,724. What had appeared to be one of the nation's most super-marginal divisions now looked very like a truly safe Labour seat. What on earth happened between 1987 and 1992?

That question is probably phrased incorrectly. Dramatic changes in the political history of Mansfield began before 1987; and perhaps we should ask what under earth, as all is wrapped up with the mining industry.

Mansfield is at the centre and heart of the Nottinghamshire coalfield. This means that it has long been one of the most important centres of mining in the country, as Nottinghamshire grew (absolutely, then relatively) to rival Yorkshire as the nation's biggest field. This meant that it used to be a solidly Labour seat, regarded as safe before 1983. Then events occurred thick and fast in Mansfield and the coalfield, with political repercussions. Nottinghamshire miners had had a tradition of non-militancy, and in 1984 they resented Arthur Scargill's decision to call a national strike without a national ballot. Many Notts miners worked through the strike, despite the attentions and abuse of flying pickets, often from Yorkshire. The bitterness continued after the year-long strike was over, as many Notts men continued to belong to the breakaway Union of Democratic Mineworkers, not the NUM. Don Concannon, the Mansfield MP, consistently supported the working miners and then the UDM, but when he announced his retirement following a serious car crash the Mansfield Labour Party nominated a left-wing pro-NUM candidate, Alan Meale. A further swing to the Conservatives was registered in 1987, which on top of the poor performance in Labour's duff year of 1983 reduced the Labour majority to double figures. The 1,580 votes cast for a 'Moderate Labour' candidate did not help Meale either.

Then the tide changed as it became clear that their activities in 1984–85 would not save many Nottinghamshire miners from redundancy, as the government closed pits in their county too, including the ring of collieries surrounding Mansfield. Many felt betrayed by the Conservatives, and to some it seemed that Scargill's cause might have been justified after all. Even in Nottinghamshire, the coal industry seems to have little future as the century draws to an end, and the turns and twists of the history of this most passion-arousing of manual industries continue to dominate the politics of Mansfield. In 1997 the wheel turned full circle as Meale increased his majority to over 20,000, truly Concannon-like.

There is a sizeable middle-class residential area in the south of the town around Berry Hill, but in essence this is the archetype of a working-class community, or series of communities: Ravensdale and Mansfield Woodhouse, Forest Town and the Garibaldi estate, Pleasley Hill and Cumberlands. Many miners, ex-miners and their dependants must have voted Conservative in 1987; it seems unlikely that they will do so again in the foreseeable future. Protest against Labour, who have not in any way reversed the decline of the coal industry, is more likely to take the form of abstentionism. In 2001 turnout dropped by 15%, and Meale's vote by over 9,000.

Social indices:

			2001 Gen. Election:			
% Non-white	1.2		Lab	21,050	57.1	−7.3
% Prof/Man	25.6		C	10,012	27.2	+6.0
% Non-manual	46.5		LD	5,790	15.7	+4.7
£ Av prop val 2000	52 K		Lab maj	11,038	30.0	
% Increase 97–00	23.9		Turnout		55.2	−15.5
% Unemployed 2001	4.3		Elect	66,748		
% Decrease 97–01	2.4					
% Fin hard/Rank	22.3	237				
% Pensioners	24.8					
% Prem mort/Rank	34	274				

Member of Parliament

Alan Meale, one of Tony Blair's sacked ministers, had risen precariously as a Prescott-backed Junior Minister in Prescott's department, who made his name previously as an animal (especially badger) protection buff and before all that as a hard-left Campaign Group supporter before winning the seat in 1987. He was born in 1949 in County Durham and Catholic-school-educated before, eventually, acquiring a degree in creative writing from Sheffield Polytechnic. Strabismic and Zapata-moustached, and initially for 11 years a manual worker, his trajectory from hard-left grouper to pipe-smoking animal welfarist did not help him when he became embroiled, as a backer of Greek Cyprus, with a Cypriot businessman, for though exonerated of wrong-doing he lost his job in the 1999 reshuffle.

MEDWAY

Nobody can say that a stark and clear choice was not presented to the voters of the Medway division of Kent in June 2001. In the red corner: Bob Marshall-Andrews the self-proclaimed least favourite backbencher of Tony Blair, independent and unruly. His opponent: a young Conservative by the name of Mark Reckless. Result: a rough and tumble of a fight, followed by a Reckless defeat. This area has long seen close and significant political struggles, and there can have been less cause than in most places for apathy or complacency; yet even here over 40% of registered electors ducked out of making a judgment at the end.

Before 1983 Rochester and Chatham used to be one of those rare seats in Kent that Labour might hope to win in a good year. But the boundary changes of that year worked against them here. Rochester and Chatham were separated from each other, and each half lumped in with some Conservative rural terrain. Chatham was submerged first in a ragbag of a seat called Mid Kent which extended through villages and countryside to take in part of Maidstone, and is now in Chatham and Aylestone which similarly dilutes its influence. Rochester is only part of the seat of Medway, invented in 1983 and unchanged in the boundary review of the 1990s.

The Medway seat consists of Rochester and Strood, together with some 20,000 further voters on the north side of the river. The city of Rochester attracts tourism because of its early castle and cathedral in the old town in the loop of the Medway, and also because of its association with Charles Dickens. Yet Rochester was just as inclined to vote Labour as its less glamorous twin town of Chatham. However, it is countered by the Conservative villages and suburbs in the flatlands across the Medway. This territory includes that caravan site of a seaside resort, Allhallows-on-Sea, the Hoo peninsula and the Isle of Grain with its British Gas terminal and container port on the site of the old BP oil refinery, as well as the marshes also known for Dickensian connections.

Rochester and Chatham was a natural and long-respected unit. In 1959, 1964, 1970, October 1974 and 1979 it was gained by the party which won the General Election as a classic marginal, swinging with the tide. It seems as if Medway may have similar characteristics. In 1997 Labour won the General Election with a lead throughout Britain of 12%; and they won Medway by 12% as well. In 2001 Marshall-Andrews won by between 9% and 10%, recording almost exactly the lead Labour did in the Britain as a whole. Medway looks like one of the most electorally typical seats in England, except that the Liberal Democrats did less than half as well as average.

Social indices:			2001 Gen. Election:			
% Non-white	4.6		Lab	18,914	49.0	+0.1
% Prof/Man	26.8		C	15,134	39.2	+2.3
% Non-manual	51.4		LD	3,604	9.3	–0.8
£ Av prop val 2000	90 K		UKIP	958	2.5	+1.6
% Increase 97–00	50.8		Lab maj	3,780	9.8	
% Unemployed 2001	3.1		Turnout		59.5	–13.0
% Decrease 97–01	2.7		Elect	64,930		
% Fin hard/Rank	12.0	414				
% Pensioners	22.0					
% Prem mort/Rank	31	319				

Member of Parliament

Robert (Bob) Marshall-Andrews QC, double-barrelled by the combination of his parents' surnames, was born in 1944, son of a working-class Tory printer, attended Mill Hill (as a scholarship boy) and Bristol University, and comes with a raffish bucolic look and with all the devil-may-care individualism of the successful barrister, and a partly buried futuristic holiday home in Pembrokeshire. Elected in 1997, and with a whiff of radical chic, he joined the Campaign Group and took a rebellious road against the Blair government – leading a revolt on the Prime Minister's right to nominate life peers, and predictably for a barrister, opposing jury trial curbs. He has also turned up for pretty well all the disobedience: on bombing Kosovo, disability benefit cuts, pensions linked to average earnings, air traffic control sell-off, freedom of information, and so on. By the end of the 1997–2001 Parliament he was running seventh in a strong field of rebels with 32 dissident votes to his credit. In 2001 he voted against the bombing of Afghanistan and the emergency anti-terrorism legislation. Meanwhile, at the 1999 Party Conference, Tribune Rally, another joker, Steve Pound, auctioning a Harrods hamper for £1,250 enquired, 'Where's Marshall-Andrews? That's only an hour's work for him'.

MEIRIONNYDD NANT CONWY

In the USA 'ethnic minority' districts are created by law (the Voting Rights Act) to provide guaranteed representation for blacks and Hispanics. The nearest thing to this in Britain is the Welsh-speaking seat of Meirionnydd Nant Conwy. In 1983 the Boundary Commission originally proposed uniting Merioneth, as the seat was then known, with much of the Tory-held English-speaking Conway on the north coast. This caused a storm of protest, not least because it would have eliminated one of the two seats that Plaid Cymru then held. After an inquiry, the Commission decided to expand Merioneth only slightly, taking just the sparsely populated mountainous southern part of Aberconwy district, to become the clumsily named Meirionnydd Nant Conwy. This arrangement was retained without revision by the latest (1995) Commission report. The seat has an electorate of just 33,000, making it the smallest in Wales and less than half the average-size seat for the United Kingdom. This over-representation is justified not by reference to language or party of course, but by the mountainous and difficult terrain of Snowdonia, much of which is covered by this seat. The upshot, though, is a guaranteed seat for Plaid Cymru, who unlike most small parties are favoured not hindered by the electoral system as currently arranged.

All four Plaid Cymru MPs sit for seats where a majority of inhabitants can speak Welsh and many do as a first language. In 1992 the former parliamentary leader Dafydd Elis Thomas, who stood well to the left of the political spectrum, gave up the Meirionnydd constituency he had held for 18 years, even though he was only 45 years old. The seat passed safely on to a new candidate, Elfyn Llwyd, who did indeed manage a positive swing to increase the Plaid majority. In 2001 Llwyd maintained his position, while Plaid's position was weakened where long-serving MPs retired in Caernarfon and Ynys Mon, in the latter case fatally. This means that Meirionnydd is now the safest of their four.

Like its neighbouring seat of Caernarvon, Merioneth passed through a long pre-war Liberal stage and a post-war period of Labour support. This is not good ground for the Tories. There are holiday resorts like Barmouth and Harlech, with its medieval castle; however, the Conservatives have slipped back to third place. But the largest centre of population is the unique slate-mining town of Blaenau Ffestiniog, high in the hills, which has suffered from economic depression since many quarries closed. Slate tips hang over the town, which has the functional character of a single-industry community. It has some of the lowest property prices anywhere in Britain. Blaenau Ffestiniog was once solidly Labour, but Plaid Cymru now get most of the votes there.

The Nationalists have clearly garnered most of the former Labour and Liberal support, and there seems no reason why Elfyn Llwyd should not continue to represent his select band of electors for the foreseeable future: at least, until a Boundary Commission decides to right the over-representation of this particular part of Wales, or indeed of Wales in general.

Social indices:			2001 Gen. Election:			
% Non-white	0.5		PC	10,459	49.6	−1.1
% Welsh sp	65.0		Lab	4,775	22.7	−0.4
% Prof/Man	33.0		C	3,962	18.8	+2.8
% Non-manual	50.2		LD	1,872	8.9	+1.9
£ Av prop val 2000	59 K		PC maj	5,684	27.0	
% Increase 97–00	27.3		Turnout		63.5	−12.5
% Unemployed 2001	3.9		Elect	33,175		
% Decrease 97–01	1.9					
% Fin hard/Rank	6.6	569				
% Pensioners	31.7					
% Prem mort/Rank	31	323				

Member of Parliament

Elfyn Llwyd, Plaid Cymru's MP here since 1992, and its Commons leader since 1999, is something of a paradox: a genial small town solicitor with an unzealous, unpartisan manner, who nonetheless as a student changed his surname from Hughes to the rare Welsh name of 'Llwyd', and who believes that 'the Welsh speaker is a second-class citizen in his own country', a scarcely credible notion in the densely Welsh-speaking part of Wales he inhabits. Born into a Nationalist family in 1951, he attended Llanrwst Grammar School, Ysgol Dyffryn Aberconwy, Llanrwst, Aberystwyth University and Chester Law College. Like his Plaid colleagues, he votes a leftist ticket on non-Nationalist issues such as defence, Iraq, the homosexual age of consent, and jury trials. There are shades of Lloyd George Liberalism here, as befits one who served his legal apprenticeship under Lloyd George's nephew in Portmadoc. But his call for all Welsh Court lawyers to be bilingual could smack of restrictive practice.

MERIDEN

There are very few seats which Labour won in 1966 but not in 2001 (there are many where the reverse is the case). One is Uxbridge in outer west London; another is Meriden in the West Midlands.

Meriden is a constituency with a complex electoral history. Labour won the constituency when it was first contested in 1955, the Conservatives came out first in 1959, Labour in 1964 and 1966, the Tories again in the 1968 by-election and 1970. The boundary changes of the early 1970s were felt to favour Labour, as was the construction of the vast tower-block Birmingham overspill estate of Chelmsley Wood, and John Tomlinson won Meriden for Labour in both 1974 Elections. Then a 9% swing gave Tory Iain Mills a 4,000 majority in 1979 – the fifth time the seat had changed hands in under 25 years – but in 1997, despite a swing close to the national average, Labour could not take the seat. Iain Mills had died shortly before the election, and it was Caroline Spelman who held on by the narrow margin of 582 votes. In 2001 she increased her lead sevenfold, which is not saying as much as it sounds.

This is in some ways surprising, for further boundary changes in 1983 pared down the electorate as the northern half, around Coleshill and Atherstone, was placed in the new North Warwickshire division. It might be thought that the space-age towers of

Chelmsley Wood should never again be in a Tory seat, yet this is what has happened. The overspill estate does indeed create four Labour wards (Chelmsley Wood, Kingshurst, Fordbridge and Smith's Wood), with a combined population of just over 40,000, wedged in between the Birmingham city boundary and the M6 motorway; this housing was still 50% council rented in 1991. However it is still outvoted by the more rural and suburban wards of the Meriden constituency, which curls round the town of Solihull to take in the northern, eastern and southern quadrants of the borough, some of which were previously in the very Conservative Solihull constituency. This includes some of the most attractive – and expensive – residential areas in the Solihull borough and indeed in the whole of the West Midlands, exemplified by Lady Byron Lane in Knowle, a 'millionaire's row' whose inclusion in the same seat as Chelmsley Wood is one of the most bizarre effects of the Commission's work. Other Conservative areas in the constituency include Dorridge, Hockley Heath, Bickenhill, Hampton in Arden, Balsall Common (certainly not to be confused with Balsall Heath, a red light area of Birmingham), Castle Bromwich and the small town of Meriden itself.

Overall this must be considered one of the most divided and disparate constituencies in Britain, and it should be noted that it is currently the Conservative-held seat with the highest proportion of electors living in financial hardship according to the Experian index, over 25% (although this is only makes it no.196 in the country). In addition to Chelmsley Wood and the affluent suburban villages, it also includes the National Exhibition Centre, Birmingham International Station, and the airport. This is geographically the heart of England, but it must now be regarded as a seat which has deviated to the right of centre, and if Labour could not win in 1997, it is hard to imagine them ever doing so again.

Social indices:			2001 Gen. Election:			
% Non-white	2.7		C	21,246	47.7	+5.7
% Prof/Man	33.2		Lab	17,462	39.2	−1.8
% Non-manual	59.6		LD	4,941	11.1	−1.9
£ Av prop val 2000	124 K		UKIP	910	2.0	
% Increase 97–00	32.9		C maj	3,784	8.5	
% Unemployed 2001	3.2		Turnout		59.9	−11.9
% Decrease 97–01	2.1		Elect	74,439		
% Fin hard/Rank	25.4	196				
% Pensioners	20.6					
% Prem mort/Rank	23	448				

Member of Parliament

Caroline Spelman, one of four women members of Iain Duncan Smith's Shadow Cabinet – in her case with responsibility for International Development and Women's Issues – was elected in 1997, and swiftly became a Whip and then by 1999 a Health spokesman. Born in 1958, educated at Hertfordshire and Essex Girls' Grammar School and Queen Mary College, London, she was director of her family's food and biotechnology company and a persuasive, personable former spokesman for European beet-growers. As one of only five new Tory women MPs in 1997, and one of only 14 altogether, she joined the Central Office team in 2000 to promote more women candidates, but with scant success given the mere nine women selected in the 75 most winnable Labour and Liberal Democrat seats, and with only one of those elected in 2001.

MERTHYR TYDFIL AND RHYMNEY

Merthyr Tydfil was the first great boom town of the south Wales industrial revolution. At the end of the eighteenth century it became one of the leading iron and coal working towns in the world. In 1801 it was the largest town in Wales, a hurly-burly melting pot of recent immigrants, where fortunes were to be made very rapidly among much poverty. Through the nineteenth century the names of Dowlais, Cyfarthfa and many other works made Merthyr one of the most famous industrial towns in Britain. But its growth stopped early, and it has been losing population for over a century. The pits and steelworks are silent now, and new forms of employment have had to be sought out in the scarred environment at the head of the vale.

By 1983 the Merthyr constituency's electorate had fallen to under 40,000, and the Boundary Commission had to look elsewhere to make up the numbers. It found them in the neighbouring Upper Rhymney valley to the east, taking voters from Michael Foot's Ebbw Vale and Neil Kinnock's Bedwellty. Merthyr is a town of history, and it might be worth recalling that it has given the Labour Party a couple of shocks over the years. In 1970 the octogenarian MP S.O. Davies was not reselected by the party on grounds of age. He stood as an Independent and won easily. On his death in 1972 the Welsh Nationalists ran his successor Ted Rowlands close in the by-election. They have never won a south Welsh valleys industrial seat, although they have threatened on a number of occasions in by-elections. In 1999 Plaid Cymru obtained 27% in the inaugural Cardiff Assembly elections, cutting Labour's lead in the constituency to only 4,000. However, although they moved up from fourth to second in 2001, more than doubling their share, they would need a further 24% swing actually to oust the new MP Dai Havard. The Merthyr Tydfil/Rhymney seat looks invulnerable. The first Labour parliamentary leader, James Keir Hardie, sat for Merthyr between 1900 and his death in 1915. His tradition has not been forgotten here in the cradle of valley industrialism.

Social indices:			2001 Gen. Election:			
% Non-white	0.7		Lab	19,574	61.8	−14.9
% Welsh sp	7.1		PC	4,651	14.7	+8.7
% Prof/Man	21.7		LD	2,385	7.5	+0.1
% Non-manual	42.3		C	2,272	7.2	+0.8
£ Av prop val 2000	39 K		Ind	1,936	6.1	
% Increase 97–00	22.1		SLP	692	2.2	
% Unemployed 2001	5.2		PA	174	0.5	
% Decrease 97–01	3.4		Lab maj	14,923	47.1	
% Fin hard/Rank	38.3	63	Turnout		57.2	−12.1
% Pensioners	26.5		Elect	55,368		
% Prem mort/Rank	45	99				

Member of Parliament

Dai Havard became MP here in 2001, a seat which had seen only two MPs in 67 years (S.O. Davies 1934–72 and Ted Rowlands 1972–2001). Unlike his predecessors, a local boy, born at the southern end of Merthyr Vale at Treharris in 1950 into a family that had switched from Liberal to Labour during the Boer War (the earliest possible date there was for joining the Labour Party), he attended Treharris Secondary Modern School, Quaker's Yard Technical School and eventually Warwick University. A bald, trim-bearded miner's son, he came to the Commons as one of a clutch of Union organisers – in his case running MSF in Wales for 12 years and quickly speaking up for retaining Labour's link with the unions. His selection for Merthyr having earned Claire Short's displeasure for being conducted in a 'men-only' bar, he had earlier pioneered postal balloting of his union members to give greater legitimacy to selections for the Welsh Assembly and the Welsh Labour leadership. Likening himself to Merthyr's first Labour MP, Keir Hardie (1900–15) as 'a socialist and trade unionist', he undoubtedly endorses the hopeless-sounding sentiment expressed by Edward VIII on his visit to the dereliction of Dowlais in 1936 that 'something must be done'; the same phrase as employed by Ted Rowlands MP in his book on Merthyr, a town where over half the households were again economically inactive by 2001.

MIDDLESBROUGH

Beware embedded errors. Just as the Press Association reported that Labour had won the 1997 General Election with an overall majority of 179, counting the Speaker as a Labour MP (a crass solecism given the impartiality of the chair of the House, her election on non-party lines, and the fact that the Speaker does not vote in divisions), it may become widely repeated that the Socialist Alliance produced their best performance in Middlesbrough in the 2001 General Election with over 10% of the vote, while the Liberal Democrats produced easily their worst anywhere, with under 2%, and lost their only deposit in England. Any knowledgeable observer can see that these two votes were transposed – but as that category did not include any of the national newspapers reporting the full results or even the House of Commons library, the myth has taken root.

Middlesbrough constituency still does not take in the whole of the town, which is too large for one seat and not large enough for two of its own. Seven of its southern wards remain in a seat formerly called Langbaurgh and now Middlesbrough South and East Cleveland (which presumably improves most people's chances of identifying where it is). That seat is a hotly contested marginal. The Middlesbrough division itself is rock-solid for Labour. Although there are one or two middle-class wards in addition to Kader in the south-western section of the seat (Acklam and Kirby), mostly the ground is hopeless for the Conservative Party. There are massive and very poor council estates east of the town centre, like those in Thorntree ward, which still had 76% council tenants in 1991, and 14.5% single parents of children under 16, and 77% with no car. Less than 1% of the residents of Thorntree are non-white, as is the case in other council estate wards like Pallister and Berwick Hills; but 36% of the inhabitants of the inner-city terraces of Westbourne ward come from ethnic minority groups. All these areas are very heavily Labour, although turnout has sunk to very low depths: under 18% in Thorntree for example in the May 1999 local elections, and under 50% in the seat as a whole in 2001.

Middlesbrough is predominantly a working-class, deprived town, and the parts of it included in this division maintained a male unemployment rate of 13%, the eighth highest of any constituency, at the time of the 2001 General Election. Between 1997 and 2000 house values scarcely rose at all, and in fact performed worst of any seat within England and Wales. Wise Conservative campaigners in Middlesbrough will devote their energies to trying to regain the Middlesbrough South and East Cleveland constituency.

Social indices:			2001 Gen. Election:			
% Non-white	5.8		Lab	22,783	67.6	−3.9
% Prof/Man	24.4		C	6,453	19.1	+2.0
% Non-manual	46.2		LD	3,512	10.4	+1.9
£ Av prop val 2000	38 K		SA	577	1.7	
% Increase 97–00	0.2		SLP	392	1.2	
% Unemployed 2001	9.1		Lab maj	16,330	48.4	
% Decrease 97–01	3.5		Turnout		49.8	−15.2
% Fin hard/Rank	36.9	77	Elect	67,659		
% Pensioners	24.3					
% Prem mort/Rank	53	26				

Member of Parliament

Stuart Bell, bizarrely 'our conduit to the Almighty' (Paul Flynn MP) as Second Church Estates Commissioner, and this notwithstanding authorship of a steamy novel entitled *Paris 69*, was elected here in 1983. A right-wing pro-European Francophile and DTI spokesman dropped from the frontbench on the morrow of victory in 1997, he got the church job as a consolation prize. A County Durham miner's son who eventually became a barrister, he was born in 1938 and educated at Hookergate Grammar School and (eventually) Gray's Inn. By politically-incorrectly taking the accused parents' side against the social workers and doctors in the Cleveland child sex abuse scandal, he memorably offended important Labour client groups in the local government and social work lobbies, later keenly backing the dismantling of Cleveland county council. Nor does he like PR or homosexual sex at 16.

MIDDLESBROUGH SOUTH AND EAST CLEVELAND

An unwieldy name to replace an unpronounceable one: this is not actually a new constituency, but very similar to the Langbaurgh seat which existed between 1983 and 1997. Langbaurgh (the most usual attempt at this word was to say Lang-barf) was a critical marginal, changing hands twice in the period 1991–92. Middlesbrough South and East Cleveland – the order of the names is illogical and breaks the Commission's own rules, as well as being unconscionably long – also counts as a marginal, although in the circumstances of Labour's last two triumphs they have won it at a canter.

Langbaurgh was held by Richard Holt, described in a previous edition of this *Almanac* as 'a jolly northern partisan partial to "unhealthy" food', in 1987 with a majority of just over 2,000. In the by-election in November 1991 caused by his death after a heart attack, Labour's Ashok Kumar captured the seat, although the relatively small swing and majority (again 2,000) may well have been partially due to a reaction against an Asian candidate in a 99% white seat. Certainly the normally very accurate Harris/ITN exit poll suggested a majority of around 6,000 – the gap being accounted for largely by those not wishing to admit they had voted Conservative. In any case, Dr Kumar's hold on the seat was short-lived indeed. In April 1992 his by-election opponent Michael Bates reversed the result, winning by 1,564. Whatever Ashok Kumar's race, though, he has come to be regarded with great favour here. Not only did he regain the seat with a regionally typical swing in 1997, but he did decidedly better than average for Labour MPs in the North East in 2001, as his share actually increased as his colleagues' went down by 4%.

The name of the seat, clumsy though it is, does describe it reasonably accurately. The Cleveland hills overlook industrial Tyneside. They are in themselves largely rural still, and their villages usually return Conservative majorities. Yet it was the ironstone discovered here that led to the boom of Middlesbrough as a steel town in the nineteenth century. The unpopular county of Cleveland was recommended for abolition by the Banham Commission after 20 years of existence since 1974, so the name becomes available for half a constituency's title, reduced to referring once again just to the Cleveland hills.

Both halves of the seat are usually closely fought between the major parties. East Cleveland includes the Labour Loftus and Lockwood/Skinningrove areas, a number of marginal wards, and the very Conservative seaside resort of Saltburn. East Cleveland supplies about 40,000 of the electors in this seat. The other 31,000 come from seven very varied wards in the southern part of the town of Middlesbrough. Wards such as Park End and Easterside are part of Middlesbrough's rock-hard Labour council estate belt – Park End voted 82% Labour in the 1999 council elections, for example.

Other areas are middle class – Marton, Nunthorpe, and the new private estates of Newham ward. Why did we say that the name 'Middlesbrough South and East Cleveland' breaks the Boundary Commission's own rules? For reasons which seem to convince only themselves, the Commission say they place the compass point after the name in a borough seat (Stockton North and South, say) and before in a county seat (North Durham, North Cornwall). The distinction between borough and county seats means very little anyway, but surely this one must be one or the other. In fact it is designated as a county seat, so the Commission should by their own logic have called it South Middlesbrough and East Cleveland – if they did have to use five words.

Social indices:			2001 Gen. Election:			
% Non-white	0.7		Lab	24,321	55.3	+0.6
% Prof/Man	33.2		C	14,970	34.0	−0.9
% Non-manual	55.6		LD	4,700	10.7	+3.2
£ Av prop val 2000	64 K		Lab maj	9,351	21.3	
% Increase 97–00	14.5		Turnout		61.5	−14.5
% Unemployed 2001	5.3		Elect	71,485		
% Fin hard/Rank	17.5	312				
% Pensioners	24.3					
% Prem mort/Rank	39	188				

Member of Parliament

Dr Ashok Kumar, one of Labour's 12 non-white MPs (but in his case in a 99% white seat), an agnostic of Sikh origin, was born in Uttar Pradesh, India, in 1956, and educated at Rykneld School, Derby, and Aston University, where he obtained a doctorate in fluid dynamics. A research scientist at British Steel before winning a by-election here in 1991 (and losing in 1992), he has had to fight off contraction of the local Corus-run steel works. Round-faced and pleasant-looking, he is one of many to have made the transition from the soft-left orthodoxies of the 1980s to the modernising Blairite nostrums of the 1990s, though in 2002 he opposed 'faith schools' as liable to foment Muslim fundamentalism.

MIDLOTHIAN

The only interesting political contests in Midlothian (at least nowadays – it was the site of a famous campaign by Gladstone in the nineteenth century) occur when the Scottish Nationalists enjoy one of their periodic revivals. In 1974, the Labour majority was reduced to 4,000 – and that in a much larger seat than the current one, which contained most of Livingston New Town. In 1999 the SNP received 30% of the vote in the Scottish Parliament (constituency section) elections. This was not maintained in 2001. On most occasions Midlothian is simply a safe Labour seat.

This historic county south of Edinburgh is composed mainly of working-class industrial communities with a preponderance of council housing, many with a background of coal-mining. Examples are Loanhead, Bonnyrigg and Lasswade, Dalkeith, Easthouses, Gorebridge and Newtongrange. Midlothian is a homogeneous seat, characterised by small-town and working-class values. The SNP advanced from 10% to 22%, and from fourth to second, in 1992, and improved again to 25% in 1997. This fell back to 21%, though, last time – well under half of that of the new Labour MP David Hamilton, and Labour look safe in Midlothian unless the SNP manage to conquer literally dozens of their central Scotland strongholds next time.

Social indices:			2001 Gen. Election:			
% Non-white	0.5		Lab	15,145	52.7	−0.8
% Prof/Man	24.8		SNP	6,131	21.3	−4.2
% Non-manual	51.9		LD	3,686	12.8	+3.7
% Unemployed 2001	2.1		C	2,748	9.6	−1.3
% Decrease 97–01	1.9		SSP	837	2.9	
% Fin hard/Rank	33.0	106	PA	177	0.6	
% Prem mort/Rank	44	110	Lab maj	9,014	31.4	
			Turnout		59.1	−15.1
			Elect	48,625		

Member of Parliament

In replacing retiring miner Eric Clarke, Labour came up in 2001 – unbelievably – with another miner, **David Hamilton**, notwithstanding the ending of the local mining industry with the closure in 1997 of Monktonhall Colliery, a pit whose rescue by a private consortium he had secured in 1983. Born in 1950, and educated at Dalkeith High School, he was a miner for 20 years until being unfairly dismissed during the 1984/5 strike, when he was Co-ordinating Chairman of 22 strike centres involving 3,500 miners in the Lothian coalfield. A local councillor since 1995, he has worked latterly in voluntary sector jobs involving the raising of EU funding for Midlothian, and the renovation of local council houses. His CV resonates here, if not in Islington, as the sole coalminer (in place of two retiring) in Labour's 38-strong 2001 intake. Moreover, he joined the first rebellion, in June 2001, against the staffing of select committees with docile loyalists.

MILTON KEYNES NORTH EAST

When in a rare interim adjustment between reviews the Boundary Commission created a second seat for the north Buckinghamshire New City of Milton Keynes, in January 1989, most observers thought that the lines had been drawn in a way which would see the Tories defending on two fronts. In Milton Keynes SW, the more urban of the two new divisions, Labour was clearly going to be the main challenger. In North East, however, local election results and some confident private predictions suggested that the Liberal Democrats had the better opportunity of the opposition parties. This analysis – which almost indicated that there might be a pact of mutual candidate withdrawal mirroring a national plan – was proved false by the first ever general election result in Milton Keynes NE, in April 1992, when Labour finished second in that seat too, and in 1997 doubly false as Labour increased their share by over 15% to pull off an improbable victory. A third blow in 2001 should finally have finished off any such theory: White not only successfully defended his 240 majority, but increased it to 1,800, and his share, while the Liberal Democrats were stuck in third on 17%.

This is not to say that the Lib Dems don't do well in local elections. In May 2000, for example, they polled 49% in the wards within this seat, while Labour and Conservative were stuck on 22% apiece. They won all the wards within the seat, consisting of parts of the northern tip of Bucks such as the village wards of Lavendon and Olney, where a traditional pancake race is run every Shrove Tuesday, the old borough of Newport Pagnell, and some affluent commuting (and golfing) territory at Woburn Sands, and also include New Town wards as at Linford, Bradwell and Pineham, precisely the areas in which Milton Keynes most rapidly grew in recent years. Clearly the two-party battle in general elections means that the Lib Dems cannot approach, still less sustain, the credibility to overcome the 'wasted vote' argument. North East is the better of the two Milton Keynes divisions for the Tories. North East is more middle class than South West, and has far lower a proportion of council housing. It will still be hard for Labour's MP Brian White to defend his majority in anything other than landslide conditions.

Social indices:			2001 Gen. Election:			
% Non-white	5.4		Lab	19,761	42.0	+2.5
% Prof/Man	39.2		C	17,932	38.1	−0.9
% Non-manual	64.7		LD	8,375	17.8	+0.4
£ Av prop val 2000	97 K		UKIP	1,026	2.2	
% Increase 97–00	37.8		Lab maj	1,829	3.9	
% Unemployed 2001	1.6		Turnout		62.4	−10.4
% Decrease 97–01	1.3		Elect	75,526		
% Fin hard/Rank	9.6	474				
% Pensioners	16.7					
% Prem mort/Rank	10	591				

Member of Parliament

Brian White, a beaky-nosed, bearded, cadaverous Ulsterman (one of the few in Mainland politics; see also Mawhinney and Opik), paradoxically is a computer man with a local interest in something a little more arcane, namely the printing of Acts of Parliament on vellum, which is solely done at a printing works in his constituency. A Milton Keynes councillor for ten years, born in 1957, and educated at Methodist College, Belfast, his CV is all 'information technology'. As he puts it, 'I spent 20 years in information technology as an assistant analyst designing systems', and he had one or two things to say about the Millennium Bug.

MILTON KEYNES SOUTH WEST

Milton Keynes is unique. There have officially been New Towns in the United Kingdom since the work of the Reith Committee in the late 1940s, but only one New City. Designated in 1967, long after the bulk of communities created or expanded by the New Town movement, Milton Keynes was the most ambitious venture of all. It was intended to provide homes and jobs for 250,000 people by the early 1990s; actually in 2001 the population of the borough was 210,000, up nearly 40,000 in the previous decade. Clearly the impact of such massive development on the north Buckinghamshire landscape has been dramatic; there are countless views, both positive and negative, about the variegated modern architecture of the numerous residential areas, the road system with its endless roundabouts and rather sinister numbering system; the gigantic indoor shopping centres and multi-screen cinema of central Milton Keynes, to which many people go but where nobody lives; the concrete cows in one of the few remaining fields. There is no denying that the local economy, society and politics have been transformed – how successfully is a matter of opinion.

For parliamentary purposes Milton Keynes was split into two between the 1987 and 1992 Elections, a rare example of an adjustment by the Boundary Commission between their regular reviews, and one which has obviated the need for any further change. The South West division was always going to be the better for Labour, and it has turned out to be a successful hunting ground for them; the Conservatives won in 1992 when John Major pulled off his surprise General Election victory, but Phyllis Starkey gained it by 10,000 in 1997 and held on by 7,000 in 2001, a fair example of the response to Labour's first term – the drop in majority was as much due to the reduced turnout as a small move back towards the Conservatives. It is the more compact of the two constituencies, and contains the long-established communities of Bletchley and Fenny Stratford, and, some miles away to the north, Wolverton and Stony Stratford; the Loughton valley between the two; and some of the more original architecture of the New City development, such as Coffee Hall in Woughton ward. The parts of the New City in this seat are less inclined to the Conservatives than those further east and north, although the newest ward of all, Loughton Park, which has almost entirely been developed since the 1980s, has always consisted entirely of private housing and has not usually favoured Labour. Historically, Labour's strongest ward is Wolverton, an old railway town which provided their only county councillor in Buckinghamshire in their disastrous year of 1977.

Social indices:			2001 Gen. Election:			
% Non-white	6.2		Lab	22,484	49.5	−4.2
% Prof/Man	29.1		C	15,506	34.2	+0.7
% Non-manual	54.7		LD	4,828	10.6	−1.3
£ Av prop val 2000	88 K		Grn	957	2.1	
% Increase 97–00	45.4		UKIP	848	1.9	
% Unemployed 2001	2.0		LCA	500	1.1	
% Decrease 97–01	1.6		SA	261	0.6	
% Fin hard/Rank	20.4	269	Lab maj	6,978	15.4	
% Pensioners	17.7		Turnout		59.2	−12.2
% Prem mort/Rank	31	310	Elect	76,607		

Member of Parliament

Phyllis Starkey, by 2001 a Foreign Office PPS and one of Labour's more academic women from the 1997 intake, with a look about her more north Oxford than Milton Keynes, is a staunch loyalist on everything where loyalty counts, notably defending the government on television during the first big revolt against lone parent benefit cuts in 1997. A somewhat swivel-eyed, intense research scientist, born in 1947 and educated cerebrally at Perse Girls' School, Cambridge, Lady Margaret Hall, Oxford, and Clare College, Cambridge, where she acquired a doctorate in biochemistry, she was – as former leader of Oxford city council – among the most experienced of Labour's municipal realists in the new intake. Her original features are a staunchly anti-Zionist preference for the Palestinian cause, and a desire to regulate the nightclub bouncing profession.

MITCHAM AND MORDEN

A question for a psephological trivia quiz: which was the last seat gained by the Conservative Party in a parliamentary by-election? The answer is Mitcham and Morden, in the south London borough of Merton. This occurred in June 1982, and it was the first by-election gain by any governing party for over 20 years. As might be expected, it was achieved in rather extraordinary circumstances. Bruce Douglas-Mann was one of 29 MPs who defected from their parties to the new Social Democratic Party after its foundation in 1981. Unlike the other 28, Douglas-Mann nobly decided to resign from Parliament in order to seek a fresh mandate from the electors of Mitcham and Morden, who had elected him as a Labour candidate since 1974. These electors preferred, however, to choose the Tory Angela Rumbold, by a 4,000 majority over Douglas-Mann, with Labour third; she increased her majority in 1983, and Labour regained second place.

When this seat was created before the February 1974 Election it seemed likely to be a Labour-inclined marginal, and it was only the unique circumstances of the 1982 by-election – a sitting SDP defector, the unpopularity of London Labour at the time, the Falklands War – which allowed the Conservatives in. However, Mrs Rumbold, now Dame Angela, was one of the more obvious likely casualties of Labour's revival, and in 1997 she went down by nearly 14,000 to Siobhain McDonagh. It was scarcely a contest, as Labour even won the other seat in the borough of Merton, Wimbledon, against all odds and expectations.

Set in the valley of the river Wandle, Mitcham and Morden covers the southern part of the borough, which has been controlled by Labour since 1990. Almost all of Mitcham and Morden's wards now vote Labour in local elections. The seat includes some down-market neighbourhoods, from the terraces of Colliers Wood at the inner end of the division towards Tooting Broadway through the ill-starred Phipps Bridge estate, to take in part of the vast St Helier council estate near the boundary with the borough of Sutton. The Conservatives do best in Lower Morden and around Mitcham Common, but there are some seats which are swinging steadily in the long-term towards Labour, and this is one of them. In 2001 Siobhain McDonagh further increased her vote, to reach a mighty 60%, while the Conservatives slipped back nearly another 6%. The former National Front leader John Tyndall, a prominent figure on the far Right in the 1970s, surfaced to take just 642 votes for the BNP.

Social indices:			2001 Gen. Election:			
% Non-white	19.9		Lab	22,936	60.4	+2.1
% Prof/Man	29.0		C	9,151	24.1	−5.6
% Non-manual	60.0		LD	3,820	10.1	+2.5
£ Av prop val 2000	115 K		Grn	926	2.4	+1.6
% Increase 97–00	58.1		BNP	642	1.7	+0.6
% Unemployed 2001	3.3		UKIP	486	1.3	+1.0
% Decrease 97–01	3.1		Lab maj	13,785	36.3	
% Fin hard/Rank	20.2	276	Turnout		57.8	−15.5
% Pensioners	24.0		Elect	65,671		
% Prem mort/Rank	31	315				

Member of Parliament

Siobhain McDonagh, elected here in 1997 at her third attempt, performed her part in the Blairite revolution by savaging Arthur Scargill for his opposition to the Clause Four redraft. Locally born in 1960 into an Irish Catholic building-worker's family, and educated at Holy Cross Secondary Modern, Colliers Wood, and at Essex University, her sister Margaret was General Secretary of the Labour Party 1998–2001, and her parliamentary aide, David Cairns, was elected MP for Greenock in 2001, following her campaign to lift the ban on ex-RC priests sitting as MPs. A Merton councillor for 15 years who worked in the housing sector, she registers her on-message support in the press whether praising Alastair Campbell or damning Ken Livingstone for his negative impact on Labour's support in London.

MOLE VALLEY

In all of the 659 constituencies in the United Kingdom, the seat with the lowest unemployment figures at the time of the General Election of 7 June 2001 was Mole Valley, with 173 men claiming, and 53 women, just 0.5% of the workforce.

Where is Mole Valley, a stranger may ask? The most romantic answer is: the Surrey hills. It is indeed true that this seat includes the attractions of Leith Hill, the highest point in south-eastern England, which reaches 1,000 feet with the assistance of a monumental tower; and of Box Hill, to which Londoners have been travelling for relaxation and restoration for well over a century. However, there are few voting residents on the hills, of course, and the most recent Boundary Commission made an attempt to change the constituency's name to reflect the two main population centres: Dorking and Leatherhead. The Mole Valley District Council objected, and strangers will still have to ask.

In the boundary changes before the 1997 Election the very Conservative neighbourhood of Ashtead was moved to Epsom and Ewell, but the even more Conservative (and more populous) villages of Send, Effingham, the Clandons and the Horsleys came in from Guildford. The geographical centre of gravity of the seat has been moved a few miles to the west, but the political centre of gravity remains exactly where it was before: well to the right.

Since its creation in 1983, Mole Valley has provided a safe haven for a former Home Secretary and Conservative Party Chairman, Kenneth Baker, who had had two previous seats, Acton and St Marylebone, and since 1997 for Sir Paul Beresford, who had one – Croydon Central – where he was beaten for the Conservative nomination by David Congdon, whose seat had been abolished. This proved a blessing in disguise, for Labour gained Croydon Central, while remaining a very distant third in Mole Valley.

Social indices:			2001 Gen. Election:			
% Non-white	1.1		C	23,790	50.5	+2.5
% Prof/Man	47.4		LD	13,637	29.0	−0.3
% Non-manual	70.1		Lab	7,837	16.6	+1.9
£ Av prop val 2000	237 K		UKIP	1,333	2.8	+2.0
% Increase 97–00	61.1		PA	475	1.0	
% Unemployed 2001	0.5		C maj	10,153	21.6	
% Decrease 97–01	0.9		Turnout		69.5	−9.4
% Fin hard/Rank	4.4	623	Elect	67,770		
% Pensioners	27.7					
% Prem mort/Rank	7	617				

Member of Parliament

Sir Paul Beresford, MP here since 1997 when he fled an abolished Croydon seat, a New Zealand dentist, acquired his parliamentary seat and knighthood as a reward for converting Wandsworth council – as its leader 1983–92 – into a Thatcherite Kingdom of Heaven on Earth, by pioneering the privatisation of local government services, his lasting memorial being a council still in Conservative control and providing from its ranks many subsequent aspiring Tory candidates in target seats. Born in 1946 and educated at schools in Nelson, New Zealand and at Otago and London Universities, he practised dentistry on Park Lane until 1994, having been elected as MP for Croydon Central in 1992. Converting badly from Wandsworth Town Hall to the Commons, he was unimpressive as a Junior Environment Minister 1994–97 and disappeared onto the backbenches under Hague's leadership, after – oddly – backing Clarke as leader.

MONMOUTH

There was for a long time a dispute about whether Monmouthshire was in Wales or England. The coal-mining valleys of Ebbw Vale and Abertillery and Pontypool clearly do belong to the culture and tradition of south Wales. However, the Monmouth constituency itself shows why there was ever cause for debate. Only 2% of the population can speak Welsh. Plaid Cymru obtain a derisory vote – 1,068 votes or 2.4% in 2001, their worst in the 40 Welsh seats. The soft and fertile green farmland of the Usk and Wye valleys is of a type found only on the English borders. Finally, Monmouth has generally shown a most un-Welsh favour to the Conservative Party: although they do not hold any seats in Wales at present, it is now clearly their best chance of a gain, having finished only 384 votes short in 2001 – and having shown that they can do it by winning it in the Welsh Assembly elections in May 1999, the sole Conservative victory in the constituency section for either devolved national body.

The affluent and comfortable small country towns of Monmouth and Abergavenny near the Black Mountains seem more typical of English rural areas. The smaller communities such as Usk and Raglan are even more Conservative. This part of the land is steeped in Anglo-Norman history and culture, such as Raglan Castle and Tintern Abbey. Labour's strongest point lies at the side of another mighty Norman castle, Chepstow. Even Chepstow isn't very Welsh, though: it is situated on the Wye border with Gloucestershire and at the end of the Severn road bridge. Four wards are included from the Cwmbran area, but these are situated in Croesyceiliog and Llanyrafon, which have a higher than average proportion of owner-occupiers for that ex-New Town.

It would now only take a swing of less than 0.5% back to the Conservatives for them to retake Monmouth. They could do this while still losing a general election by yet another landslide.

Social indices:		2001 Gen. Election:			
% Non-white	0.6	Lab	19,021	42.8	−5.0
% Welsh sp	2.2	C	18,637	41.9	+2.7
% Prof/Man	42.5	LD	5,080	11.4	+1.9
% Non-manual	61.5	PC	1,068	2.4	+1.3
£ Av prop val 2000	97 K	UKIP	656	1.5	
% Increase 97–00	33.5	Lab maj	384	0.9	
% Unemployed 2001	2.1	Turnout		71.5	−9.3
% Decrease 97–01	1.6	Elect	62,202		
% Fin hard/Rank	8.2 519				
% Pensioners	28.9				
% Prem mort/Rank	17 515				

Member of Parliament

Huw Edwards, a polytechnic lecturer who welcomed the conversion of the polytechnics into universities (and vice-versa), was first elected here in 1991, lost the seat in 1992 and regained it in 1997. He was born in 1953 into the London Welsh community, son of a London-based Welsh Congregational Minister, educated at Eastfields High School, Mitcham, Manchester Polytechnic and York University. A fan of Frank Field's record in the field of low pay, as a social policy specialist, he operates quietly between the hammer of the Tory countryside and farming lobby and the Labour votes dependent on the Llanwern steelworks whose contraction he vigorously denounced in February 2001. Only Labour's second MP in Monmouth, his near squeak in 2001 might well recall Michael Foot's agent introducing Foot as the (1935) candidate with the astute declaration: 'Well, here we are in bloody old Tory Usk'.

MONTGOMERYSHIRE

Montgomeryshire is the site of the longest-standing Liberal tradition in British politics. With the single exception of 1979, it has been won by the Liberals (however named) for well over a century, since mid-Victorian times. Among the MPs have been party leader (1945–56) Clement Davies and Emlyn Hooson (in the House 1962–79). Few were amazed when the controversial Tory Delwyn Williams turned out to be a one-term wonder, as Alex Carlile won the Montgomery seat back in 1983; in 1997 Lembit Opik had no trouble taking over the seat with a majority of over 6,000 (this in a seat with a very small electorate), and it would be astonishing if the Lib Dems were to suffer a second reverse next time. This is truly Liberal country.

Country, indeed. Montgomeryshire has another claim to fame. It had for many years held the record as the seat with the highest proportion of the employed population engaged in agriculture, although it has been surpassed by Galloway and Upper Nithsdale in Scotland. It is still a seat of farmers, though. Some rear sheep, up in the hills; but Montgomeryshire is not in general wild countryside, but fertile, rolling land near the English boundary. There is one notable exception to the rural rule. Here is the smallest of the designated New Towns in Britain, the appropriately named Newtown (it has actually existed for centuries). Newtown has more than doubled in population since the war, but it is still only 10,000 altogether. The only other community of over 2,000 is Welshpool.

In 2001 Lembit Opik further strengthened his grip on his adopted seat, as the Labour vote (which fell back in Wales as a whole that year) dropped from 19 to 11%, while the Nationalists remained very weak. Mr Opik has clearly maintained a weather eye on his rural base while becoming nationally better known as a highly presentable and reasonable-sounding spokesman for his party.

Social indices:			2001 Gen. Election:			
% Non-white	0.5		LD	14,319	49.4	+3.5
% Welsh sp	23.3		C	8,085	27.9	+1.8
% Prof/Man	34.5		Lab	3,443	11.9	−7.3
% Non-manual	51.7		PC	1,969	6.8	+1.8
£ Av prop val 2000	70 K		UKIP	786	2.7	
% Increase 97–00	28.1		PA	210	0.7	
% Unemployed 2001	1.9		Ind	171	0.6	
% Decrease 97–01	0.5		LD maj	6,234	21.5	
% Fin hard/Rank	8.2	514	Turnout		65.5	−9.4
% Pensioners	27.9		Elect	44,243		
% Prem mort/Rank	27	386				

Member of Parliament

Lembit Opik, Ulster-born of Estonian parents, in 1997 inherited this most traditional of Liberal seats, lost only once since the nineteenth century, and broke his back hang-gliding in 1998. A tall, thin man with an engagingly lopsided smile, and a pin-ball expert, he was born in 1965, the son of an astronomer, educated at Royal Belfast Academical Institution and Bristol University, and worked for Proctor & Gamble in Newcastle for nine years before taking to the Montgomeryshire hills. He is essentially a two-club politician: predicting the wipe-out of the planet by oncoming rogue asteroids, and urging a 'Middle Way' between banning fox hunting and permitting its unlicensed continuance, preferably before the asteroids arrive. His nuanced line on hunting made a good deal of sense in a party few of whose seats are not rural in character, and in a vote in March 2002 169 MPs – including 17 of the 53 Liberal Democrats – backed the 'Middle Way' of hunt licensing. The Commons' only Lutheran, albeit residually Ulster-brogued, he has observed that his Scrabble-evoking name rearranged spells 'I kil to be MP'. His Ulster origins qualify him for the thankless task of Northern Ireland spokesman.

MORAY

In 2001 the Labour Party and the Liberal Democrats advanced in Moray, while the Tories and the SNP fell back. Although the Nationalists still won, their majority was cut back from the best part of 6,000 to a decidedly more vulnerable 1,744. The reason for this was clear: the transfer from the Westminster to the Scottish Parliament of the popular MP Margaret Ewing, a member of the well-known Nationalist dynasty (daughter-in-law of Winnie, who was MP here in the 1970s), who had held the seat since 1987. She has been replaced by the 31-year-old Angus Robertson, who will have to establish himself in his own right in this independently minded seat in north-east Scotland.

It is sometimes said that the SNP presents whichever political face is most attractive to the voters of a neighbourhood: left-wing in industrial west and central Scotland, right-wing 'tartan Tories' in the rural east and north. Both Ewings offer living proof that this cannot be entirely justified, for both have now been elected for both industrial and rural seats – Winnie won the historic 1967 Hamilton by-election from Labour, and held the seat till 1970, while Margaret formerly sat in the Commons for a term (October 1974–79) for East Dunbartonshire, as Mrs Bain.

There is no doubt that Moray is part of rural Scotland. The largest community is the cathedral town of Elgin, Labour's strongest area by far. There are a large number of small burghs: the port of Buckie (good for the Nationalists), Forres (site of the only Conservative victory in the Moray unitary authority elections of 1999), Dufftown, Cullen, Rothes, Aberlour and Lossiemouth, where Ramsay MacDonald was born. The rolling farmland of Speyside also cuts through the heart of this seat, with its Scotch whisky distilleries; there is one electoral division attractively named Glenlivet, which includes the polling districts of Knockando East and West.

Social indices:			2001 Gen. Election:			
% Non-white	0.5		SNP	10,076	30.3	−11.2
% Prof/Man	22.9		Lab	8,332	25.1	+5.2
% Non-manual	40.9		C	7,677	23.1	−4.5
% Unemployed 2001	2.9		LD	5,224	15.7	+6.8
% Decrease 97–01	2.1		SSP	821	2.5	
% Fin hard/Rank	20.1	278	Ind	802	2.4	
% Prem mort/Rank	36	234	UKIP	291	0.9	
			SNP maj	1,744	5.2	
			Turnout		57.3	−10.9
			Elect	58,008		

Member of Parliament

Angus Robertson, a half-German Scottish Nationalist, was elected in 2001 as the replacement for Margaret Ewing who had left to concentrate on the Scottish Parliament. He was born (in London) in 1969, educated at Broughton High School, Edinburgh and at Aberdeen University, where he studied politics and international relations. A former journalist, who worked latterly as European policy adviser to the SNP group in the Scottish Parliament (to which he failed to get elected as candidate for Midlothian in 1999), he was – in minor party fashion – immediately on arrival at the Commons appointed Foreign Affairs spokesman, and proceeded to laud EU expansion, but with independent Scottish membership alongside states such as Germany, from which his mother came after the War. He is concerned about the Inverness-to-Gatwick air link – understandably as it is his means of getting to work.

MORECAMBE AND LUNESDALE

Labour won a large number of seats for the first time ever in the May 1997 General Election, and a disproportionate number of these are based on seaside resorts – to take just a selection: Hove, Brighton Pavilion, Hastings and Rye, Thanet North, Harwich, Scarborough and Whitby, and both Blackpool divisions. To these can be added Morecambe and Lunesdale. Back in 1966 Labour were not even within 10,000 votes in the Morecambe seat (then paired with Lonsdale rather than Lunesdale). They pulled off an increase in share of vote of over 19% in 1997, and won by the astonishing (for here) margin of 5,965 votes. In 2001 there was no swing at all between Labour and Conservative, and the Liberal Democrats were further squeezed to less than a tenth of the vote.

Morecambe and Lunesdale also includes the seaside resort of Morecambe, with its wide variety of characteristics from the quiet and elegant northern suburb of Bare to the more plebeian amusement-arcade land to the south; Heysham, with its ferry terminal and nuclear power-station, between them producing a formidably gritty and functional shorescape; and a sliver of countryside wedged between the Lune and the Morecambe Bay coast, all the way to the Cumbria border. The latter element is very Conservative, including a number of villages, and small seaside resorts like Bolton-le-Sands. The only exception is the Labour-voting railway town of Carnforth, rather ironically the place of origin of Cecil Parkinson. However, the long-term movement away from the Conservatives in coastal areas means that the former Chairman's party is now longer favourite in Morecambe and Lunesdale.

Social indices:			2001 Gen. Election:				
% Non-white	0.6		Lab	20,646	49.6	+0.7	
% Prof/Man	31.1		C	15,554	37.3	+0.6	
% Non-manual	54.0		LD	3,817	9.2	-2.2	
£ Av prop val 2000	56 K		UKIP	935	2.2		
% Increase 97–00	17.9		Grn	703	1.7		
% Unemployed 2001	4.0		Lab maj	5,092	12.2		
% Decrease 97–01	1.9		Turnout		60.7	-11.7	
% Fin hard/Rank	11.6	421	Elect	68,607			
% Pensioners	32.8						
% Prem mort/Rank	35	239					

Member of Parliament

Geraldine Smith is one of Labour's less conspicuous as well as least expected MPs. Formerly a postal clerk, she was born, a seaman's daughter, in 1961 and locally educated at Morecambe High School and Morecambe and Lancaster College. An all-women shortlist beneficiary, locally focused in her campaigning against seaside town decline (a decline from which, ironically, Labour has benefited right round the coast), she has salted her record only with politically incorrect votes against homosexual law reform.

MORLEY AND ROTHWELL

Whereas some metropolitan boroughs are so drawn as to exclude parts of their suburbs or built up area, Leeds has expanded to include previously independent local government units, as a result of which it has a higher population (680,000) and consequently parliamentary constituency allocation than any other single borough except Birmingham (counting London still as 33 separate entities). Technically Pudsey is a Leeds city seat, and this one too. In fact, although there is no longer any reference in its title, Morley and Rothwell does include one ward from within the historic boundaries of Leeds, the peripheral council estate of Middleton, on its southern edge, where the writer ('Billy Liar') Keith Waterhouse grew up. This seat is the successor to the former Leeds South and Morley which existed before 1997 and more tenuously to the Leeds South of pre-1983. If that lineage is accepted, the new MP Colin Challen, who replaced the retiring John Gunnell in 2001, has quite some acts to follow. The two previous MPs for this seat and its Leeds South predecessor were Merlyn Rees (1963–92), Home Secretary in James Callaghan's government, and Hugh Gaitskell, Leader of the Labour Party from 1955 to 1963.

Gradually the depopulation of the Leeds inner city has forced the boundaries outwards, and Morley and Rothwell is in general not be quite so safe as its predecessors. Morley North almost returned a Tory councillor in May 2000, and Rothwell was won by a Lib Dem, a year before the General Election; but in the big event Challen won easily as only the Liberal Democrat (slightly) increased their share, and the main move was to non-participation, which accounted for 46% of the electorate.

Social indices:			2001 Gen. Election:				
% Non-white	1.1		Lab	21,919	57.0	−1.5	
% Prof/Man	25.2		C	9,829	25.6	−0.8	
% Non-manual	52.7		LD	5,446	14.2	+3.1	
£ Av prop val 2000	65 K		UKIP	1,248	3.2		
% Increase 97–00	27.3		Lab maj	12,090	31.4		
% Unemployed 2001	2.3		Turnout		53.5	−13.6	
% Decrease 97–01	1.5		Elect	71,815			
% Fin hard/Rank	20.9	256					
% Pensioners	24.8						
% Prem mort/Rank	30	339					

Member of Parliament

Colin Challen, Labour's replacement in 2001 for the prematurely aged retiring MP John Gunnell, was born in 1953 and educated at Norton Secondary School, Malton Grammar School and Hull University, and worked as a self-employed printer and publisher after earlier stints as a Labour Party organiser, a postman and a supplier-accountant in the RAF, and was for eight years a Hull city councillor. Author of a book on Tory Party 'secret funding', as a keen member of the League Against Cruel Sports he also supported the banning of Anne Mallalieu's pro-hunting fringe meeting at the Brighton Labour Party conference in 2000. Big, burly and bearded, he backs the EU from a point midway between Europhiles and Europhobes, anxious for its aid for his backward region.

MOTHERWELL AND WISHAW

Not a single one of the 659 parliamentary constituencies is boring, but some hold public interest more than others. The page for the seat of Motherwell and Wishaw was that accessed least of any on the *Daily Telegraph* Election 2001 website, written by the authors of this Almanac. It is probably our fault.

It is true that little dramatic was expected to happen in that most recent election campaign, or did. This is yet another of the solidly Labour industrial central Scottish constituencies, with a working-class and council housing majority. The economy of this area in the Clyde valley south-east of Glasgow has traditionally been dominated by steel. It has been literally and figuratively overshadowed by the vast and threatened Ravenscraig steelworks, and its hopes of prosperity have risen and fallen with those of the Scottish steel industry.

There is only one ward in the constituency with a significant Conservative vote, Ladywell, with a majority of owner-occupied housing catering for the small middle-class sections of Motherwell. More typical would be the residential ward nearest to the Ravenscraig works, Craigneuk, where 86% of the housing was still in local authority ownership at the time of the last published Census, and 70% of households did not possess a car, and where the Tories polled just 69 votes (4%) in the North Lanarkshire unitary elections in 1999. This is an old-fashioned and relatively unchanging society – for example, 96% of the population was born in Scotland, just about the highest of any constituency. This is no reason for the rest of the United Kingdom to lack curiosity about it, or not to care about the fate of its electorate.

Social indices:			2001 Gen. Election:			
% Non-white	0.7		Lab	16,681	56.2	−1.2
% Prof/Man	28.4		SNP	5,725	19.3	−3.2
% Non-manual	51.8		C	3,155	10.6	−0.4
% Unemployed 2001	6.3		LD	2,791	9.4	+3.0
% Decrease 97–01	2.0		SSP	1,260	4.2	
% Fin hard/Rank	48.6	20	SLP	61	0.2	−2.0
% Prem mort/Rank	53	25	Lab maj	10,956	36.9	
			Turnout		56.6	−13.5
			Elect	52,418		

Member of Parliament

Frank Roy, a local-born and locally Catholic-educated steel worker with a minimal mouth-encircling beard, who worked as a barman while studying at Glasgow Caledonian University after being made redundant, and then as bag-carrier for Labour

MP Helen Liddell, was elected here in 1997. His profile was low until he was criticised in 2000 for betting on the election of the Glaswegian Speaker Michael Martin, and then provoking the odder tribal spat over advising Irish PM Ahern not to visit Motherwell to open a shrine to the victims of the Irish potato famine, in case it caused sectarian strife. As PPS to Scottish Secretary Helen Liddell and ex-PPS to Northern Ireland Secretary John Reid, both of whom are Catholics, it was unclear if this was a ruse to reassure working-class Protestants who might fall for the SNP's Orange blandishments. But by then resigning as a PPS, he might also have reassured Ulster Catholics; sophisticated Caledonian footwork, if true.

NEATH

In 2001 the Welsh Nationalists, Plaid Cymru, more than doubled their share of the vote in Neath, and the well-established Labour MP Peter Hain suffered a drop of 13%. Technically this added up to a conventional swing from Labour of over 11%, one of their worst performances in the UK. In a way, though, this just shows how misleading the attempt to reduce the story of an election result to a single figure is, for Hain still took over three times the Nationalist vote, and the drop in turnout by 7,000 voters did not figure in the swing percentage at all.

Neath is one of those many industrial South Wales valley constituencies which run in north/south strips along the dips in the ridged and folded landscape. It includes most of the Neath and Dulais valleys, and some of the Upper Swansea valley too. At the southern end of the seat is the medium-sized town of Neath itself. The lower reaches of the valleys are almost entirely given over to industry – at one time coal, later aluminium and engineering; many of the hillsides have been afforested for timber. Neath has been safely Labour since 1922, and that did not change even though Labour slipped a little and the Plaid improved in 2001.

The Nationalists have never been truly strong in this predominantly English-speaking constituency, and although there are some middle-class residential areas in and around Neath, which is a proud town with a strong rugby- and cricket-playing tradition – up the hill in Cimla, for example, and in the suburb of Bryn-coch – the Conservatives can't even win these areas in local elections, and finished fourth behind the Liberal Democrats in 2001.

Social indices:			2001 Gen. Election:			
% Non-white	0.7		Lab	21,253	60.7	−12.8
% Welsh sp	26.0		PC	6,437	18.4	+10.3
% Prof/Man	26.2		LD	3,335	9.5	+3.2
% Non-manual	47.1		C	3,310	9.5	+0.8
£ Av prop val 2000	48 K		SA	483	1.4	
% Increase 97–00	22.2		PA	202	0.6	
% Unemployed 2001	4.3		Lab maj	14,816	42.3	
% Decrease 97–01	1.7		Turnout		62.4	−11.9
% Fin hard/Rank	19.5	283	Elect	56,107		
% Pensioners	28.8					
% Prem mort/Rank	41	167				

Member of Parliament

Peter Hain, as Minister of State at the Foreign Office, wrote a highly prescient Fabian booklet in January 2001 entitled *The End of Foreign Policy*, for that is precisely what it was for him, as he was reshuffled immediately (allegedly for excessive candour on Zimbabwe, Iraq and American missile defence) to the DTI as Energy Minister, if only to return in June as Minister for Europe, despite an earlier record of Euroscepticism. He is a successful graft onto the Labour stem of a radical Liberal who made his name as an anti-Springbok campaigner and South African-framed alleged bank robber. Elected here in 1991 notwithstanding his earlier rugby-cancelling activities, for which he was dubbed 'Hain the Pain', he is one of the Blair government's outspoken residual Keynesians, of the sort who might at least theoretically justify a change of gear on public spending. Born in 1950, educated in Pretoria until his radical anti-Apartheid parents moved to England, and then at Emanuel School, Wandsworth and Sussex University, he has handsome good looks and, like a good many politicians, something of a solitary nature.

NEWARK

It is conventional wisdom that candidates' personalities and records count for relatively little in British general elections, due to the strength of the party system and the need to choose a government and prime minister. Some MPs, especially Liberal Democrats, do seem to strengthen their position through assiduous constituency work, and in recent years it has become apparent that party leadership brings an immediate increase in majority. The Conservative defector Shaun Woodward obtained a smaller majority at St Helens South in 2001 than a local candidate would have, but he still won. However, it is rare to be able to suggest that an official party representative has actually been responsible for losing a seat. Nevertheless, the poor performance of Labour's Fiona Jones in Newark does raise such questions.

Let us start soberly with the statistics. Only five Labour incumbents lost to the Conservatives in 2001, three in the Essex sub-region; elsewhere in the East Midlands and in Nottinghamshire (in Gedling and Broxtowe), those defending victories in 1997 actually improved their position. But in Newark Labour lost 8% of their share and suffered a negative swing of over 7% to the Conservative victor Patrick Mercer.

Fiona Jones had been the last of the new Labour intake to make her maiden speech, but this may have indicated only humility. Then she and her agent were arrested on electoral expense charges, convicted and disqualified; they were acquitted on appeal and reinstated, but the palaver must have had a negative effect, even if unfair. She was also involved in internal party splits, which led to the departure of prominent Newark town Labour politicians such as Gill Dawn, the former council leader, who contested Newark North as an Independent in the county elections on the same day as the 2001 General Election. All in all, it came as little surprise when the Conservatives, who had already taken a large lead in district and Euro elections here in 1999, made a rare gain on their generally disastrous day.

The town of Newark-on-Trent itself, once known as the Key to the North, earned a reputation for cropping up in English history, as the site of the death of King John for example, and most notably as a Royalist base in the Civil War. But despite its castle, old market square, fine town houses and streets named 'gates' as in York, Newark's residential areas are more typified by large council estates at the north and south ends of the town. Its private housing is not outstanding either, yet the town of Newark has consistently given the Conservatives a majority in general elections. More Conservative still are the tiny cathedral city of Southwell and commuter villages like Collingham and Winthorpe. The seat also includes some territory that was formerly in Bassetlaw before 1983: the market town of East Retford, marginal in politics, and large villages like Tuxford. All of these add up to a homogeneous seat, with two market towns each of around 20,000 souls and their surrounding rural communities. The A1 trunk road, once called the Great North Road, passes through the heart of the constituency for over 20 miles, effectively binding it together.

Patrick Mercer has four years at least to carve his own distinctive mark on the constituency, and it will be interesting to see if it differs again from the regional and national norm when it is his turn to be put to the test.

Social indices:			2001 Gen. Election:			
% Non-white	0.9		C	20,983	46.5	+7.1
% Prof/Man	31.3		Lab	16,910	37.5	−7.8
% Non-manual	52.5		LD	5,970	13.2	+1.8
£ Av prop val 2000	75 K		Ind	822	1.8	
% Increase 97–00	32.5		SA	462	1.0	
% Unemployed 2001	2.9		C maj	4,073	9.0	
% Decrease 97–01	1.8		Turnout		63.5	−11.0
% Fin hard/Rank	14.1	371	Elect	71,089		
% Pensioners	26.4					
% Prem mort/Rank	33	290				

Member of Parliament

Patrick Mercer, one of the eight Conservatives who recaptured seats from Labour or Liberal Democrats in 2001, was born in 1956, educated at King's School Chester, and at Exeter College, Oxford, and spent 25 years in the Army (serving nine tours of duty in Northern Ireland) before working freelance on BBC Radio after 1999. As son of a former Bishop of Exeter, a suitably churchy occupant for a constituency containing the seat (at Southwell) of a diocese, he was assisted in his capture of Newark by the dissension in local Labour ranks and the troubled career of Labour MP Fiona Jones who had been damaged by allegations (against which she successfully appealed) of election overspending. A Duncan Smith voter in all the leadership ballots in July 2001, he inevitably specialises in defence matters as a member of the Defence Select Committee and has ridiculed the 'safety culture' concerns about the deleterious effect on soldiers' hearing caused by barking dogs.

NEWBURY

On 6 May 1993 the west Berkshire constituency of Newbury dealt a terrific blow to John Major's government – and a fatal one to Norman Lamont's Chancellorship of the Exchequer. The occasion was a by-election caused by the untimely death of Judith Chaplin, formerly the political secretary to Prime Minister Major and MP for less than a year. She had held Newbury by over 12,000 votes in April 1992; but in the now-famous by-election the Conservative candidate (unkindly characterised as 'Mr Blobby') was trounced by the Liberal Democrats' David Rendel with a well-nigh unbelievable majority of 22,055. This represented a swing of 28.4% from Conservative to Lib Dem on a turnout of over 71% – one of the largest changes of mood in British electoral history, and one which presaged a series of electoral disasters for the Conservatives from which they had not significantly recovered even by 2001. It was therefore a surprise in that most recent general election that Rendel, by then planted for over eight years, had trouble in holding Newbury against a Conservative Party whose resurgence was so limited that its leader had resigned by breakfast-time the next day.

About half of the acreage of Berkshire is to be found in the constituency, which covers the western part of the county, stretching from the edge of Reading across the Downs and along the A4 to the borders with Oxfordshire, Hampshire and Wiltshire. Newbury is the only town of any size, and even its connection with industry has declined since the sixteenth century, when a man named Jack of Newbury was reported to have been operating a very early woollen weaving factory. Thatcham, also in the valley of the river Kennet, is another centre of population (and the Lib Dems' strongest area of all in 1993), but most of the seat's electorate is to be found in small towns like Hungerford (scene of the Michael Ryan massacre) and in villages and rural areas. Lambourn is the centre of the Downland racehorse training, and there is a well-known course at Newbury itself.

The reason that Rendel won by only the equivalent of a short head in 2001 is not due to any recovery in the Labour vote, crushingly squeezed in 1993 and 1997; it was still the second lowest in the General Election after Winchester, where similar circumstances had pertained. Rather it was a re-assertion of the natural embedded Conservatism of this area, suppressed for one general election after a dramatic by-election, a not uncommon phenomenon. The result shadowed very closely the local elections in West Berkshire unitary authority in May 2000. The impact of the by-election has now effectively faded enough to give warning of a photo-finish the next time a parliamentary race is run.

Social indices:				2001 Gen. Election:			
% Non-white	1.3			LD	24,507	48.2	−4.7
% Prof/Man	39.6			C	22,092	43.5	+5.6
% Non-manual	62.9			Lab	3,523	6.9	+1.4
£ Av prop val 2000	160 K			UKIP	685	1.3	+0.8
% Increase 97–00	71.3			LD maj	2,415	4.8	
% Unemployed 2001	0.8			Turnout		67.3	−9.4
% Decrease 97–01	0.8			Elect	75,490		
% Fin hard/Rank	5.2	603					
% Pensioners	22.0						
% Prem mort/Rank	16	526					

Member of Parliament

David Rendel, the Liberal Democrats' only Old Etonian MP until the third Viscount Thurso arrived from Caithness in 2001, has been MP here since winning the by-election on a routinely massive 28% swing in 1993 at his third attempt. Born in 1949 and educated, after Eton, at Magdalen College, Oxford, he was previously an operational analyst with Shell and Esso. Parachuted into Newbury in 1984 to plan long-term for a seizure of a seat with an ailing Tory MP, his great-uncle had been Liberal MP for Montgomeryshire in the 1880s, with one of his daughters married to one of Gladstone's sons. Rather foolishly, given his very clipped upper-class mien (but noting that 'two of our last four leaders have been Old Etonians'), he ran for the Liberal leadership in 1999, polled very badly and was thereafter marginalised by Charles Kennedy, having been misinterpreted as disparaging the new leader's talented performances on chat shows, which might explain why by 2001 he was spokesman on higher education. Against the environmentalists he pitched conventionally for the Newbury by-pass and opposed the Greenham women.

NEWCASTLE UNDER LYME

The Borough of Newcastle under Lyme, to the west of Stoke-on-Trent and commonly considered to be part of the Potteries, is a region of great variety. There are communities shaped by coal-mining at Silverdale, Chesterton and Knutton; good residential areas in Westlands, Seabridge, Thistleberry and parts of Porthill and Wolstanton; and spice is added by Keele University and its denizens. Small wonder that Frank Bealey, Jean Blondel and W.P. McCann of Keele decided to analyse Newcastle under Lyme at book length in 1965 in *Constituency Politics.*

Yet despite these diverse characteristics, Newcastle under Lyme has remained loyal to Labour since the war. At the 1983 General Election, Labour's nadir in that period, John Golding, a well-known right-wing activist on the NEC, still held a majority of nearly 3,000 – a good result in a seat nearly as middle class as average, although the Potteries as a sub-region have a long and solid Labour tradition. Golding dropped something of a parliamentary bombshell in 1985 when he announced at the age of 54 that he was seeking the general secretaryship of his own union, the Post Office Engineers. He duly won this post, and was replaced as Labour candidate by his wife Llin, a notable and stalwart local moderate, and herself the daughter of an MP (Ness Edwards, Caerphilly 1939–68). Yet despite Labour's lead in the national polls at the time, Mrs Golding only held the seat by 800 votes in 1986 against a surprisingly strong Liberal Alliance challenge. This only goes to prove that the centre should never be underestimated in by-elections, but this has not been replicated in national contests, and in 2001 the Lib Dems obtained only 15% here, as the Golding dynasty finally relinquished their 30-year hold on the 'other' Newcastle, as Llin was replaced by Paul Farrelly.

Social indices:			2001 Gen. Election:				
% Non-white	1.3		Lab	20,650	53.4	−3.1	
% Prof/Man	28.1		C	10,664	27.6	+6.1	
% Non-manual	48.5		LD	5,993	15.5	+1.5	
£ Av prop val 2000	59 K		Ind	773	2.0		
% Increase 97–00	21.9		UKIP	594	1.5		
% Unemployed 2001	2.5		Lab maj	9,986	25.8		
% Decrease 97–01	1.1		Turnout		58.8	−14.8	
% Fin hard/Rank	22.7	231	Elect	65,739			
% Pensioners	27.6						
% Prem mort/Rank	35	245					

Member of Parliament

Paul Farrelly in 2001 became the sixth consecutive Labour MP for this seat since 1922, and the first to be locally born, in 1962. The City Editor of the *Observer*, he was educated at Wolstanton Grammar School and St Edmund Hall, Oxford, and became a Reuters correspondent and corporate financer at Barclays de Zoete Wedd, joining *The Observer* in 1997 after two years at the *Independent on Sunday*. A campaigner on NHS provision in North Staffordshire, he recalls his Irish immigrant father's early death from strokes following loss of his job after the Tory privatisation of British Gas. Albeit with strong local roots, he is also an example of a metropolitan parachutee, selected for a safe Labour seat by an OMOV system usually favouring local councillors. With his son John bearing the redolent second name of 'Josiah', recalling Newcastle's first Labour MP, Colonel Josiah Wedgwood, elected as a Liberal in 1910 and whose switch to Labour began the long run of Labour MPs in 1922, in June 2001 he was one of only four of Labour's 38-strong intake to rebel against the Whips' attempt to pack the select committees.

NEWCASTLE UPON TYNE CENTRAL

Newcastle Central is a somewhat odd – or at least oddly named – seat, which wrong-footed many casual observers when it returned a Conservative MP at the 1983 General Election. Many would still be surprised that a seat named Newcastle upon Tyne Central could ever have been held by the Tories, even though they lost it in 1987 and now for a variety of reasons it seems to have passed well beyond recapture. The fact is that the Central that was created in 1983 bore very little resemblance either to an inner city seat or to the previous division which was so named, which was based on the impoverished core of the city and which is now incorporated in Tyne Bridge. Central now surrounds Town Moor, the large stretch of open land just north of the city centre. As in most cities, the housing on the edge of the main park tends to be desirable and upmarket, so it is scarcely surprising that Central is now the Conservatives' best seat in Newcastle. But it is a little unusual that the seat entitled 'Central' should no longer include much of the commercial and shopping centre of the city, which is in the Tyne Bridge seat (which crosses the river to include part of Gateshead). The current Newcastle Central is geographically in the centre of the city, but not socially or politically so.

This does not mean that the Conservatives can hold out much hope of actually winning it again in the foreseeable future. Piers Merchant benefited from Labour's disastrous performance in 1983, when the Tories were returned to government with an overall majority of over 140 seats, and even then only won by 2,000. Jim Cousins reversed this result in 1987, and had increased his majority to over 11,500 in 1997. The Conservatives find it difficult to compete even the most middle-class parts of the seat in local elections: Jesmond and Moorside have much pleasant but multi-occupied housing, with a large student population and atmosphere: both of Newcastle's universities are located in this area. Jesmond and South Gosforth at the affluent northern end of the city show Liberal Democrat tendencies in Newcastle city elections, and Stephen Psallidas advanced to just pip the Tories for second place in the 2001 General Election. Although socially disparate, Newcastle's regional swing to the left has made Central safe for Labour.

Social indices:			2001 Gen. Election:			
% Non-white	6.2		Lab	19,169	55.0	−4.2
% Prof/Man	45.0		LD	7,564	21.7	+6.7
% Non-manual	65.8		C	7,414	21.3	−2.2
£ Av prop val 2000	88 K		SLP	723	2.1	
% Increase 97–00	25.6		Lab maj	11,605	33.3	
% Unemployed 2001	4.7		Turnout		51.3	−14.8
% Decrease 97–01	3.1		Elect	67,970		
% Fin hard/Rank	23.8	212				
% Pensioners	28.4					
% Prem mort/Rank	44	113				

Member of Parliament

Jim Cousins, a bearded replica of the late John Osborne, and with a related right to look back in anger at his dismissal after three years from the frontbench in 1995 for going AWOL with Ann Clwyd among the Kurds, was elected here in 1987. He was born in 1944, educated at City of London School, New College, Oxford and LSE and worked as a lecturer and contract researcher with trade unions. Cerebral and aloof, and a Beckett not Blair supporter in 1994, he had resisted the Gulf War in 1990 and after his dismissal in 1995 has been an assiduous questioner and vocal north-east regionalist. He voted against the government on predatory pricing of the Murdoch press and on Incapacity Benefit cuts. Unlucky to have been denied office, he was appointed to the Treasury Select Committee in 1997.

NEWCASTLE UPON TYNE EAST AND WALLSEND

This might sound like a merger of the two former divisions of Newcastle East and Wallsend, both Labour strongholds before the 1997 boundary changes. Does this betoken a net loss for Labour in north Tyneside? In fact the change less radical than the name implies, and Tyne and Wear was retained the 13 seats it possessed before the last redistribution. The Newcastle East seat was somewhat undersized so the Boundary Commission added two wards from the North Tyneside borough, totalling

17,000 voters. These are Northumberland and Wallsend, which just happened to be the eponymous town of a constituency. The bulk of the old Wallsend seat remains, but it has had to be renamed North Tyneside (or Tyneside North).

These revisions did not damage Labour's position here, which is very strong. There is one leafy and attractive ward which the Tories usually won in happier times, (Jesmond) Dene, but it is now very strongly Liberal Democrat – the Lib Dems moved forward by 9% into second place in the seat as a whole in the 2001 General Election. All the others are strongly Labour now: they include Byker, home of the famous 'Byker Wall', a dramatic working-class modern housing development, and Walker and Walkergate down by the river, with a history of shipbuilding. All these wards have a large majority of council-built housing, though like most of Tyneside there is only a tiny non-white population. The additions are immediately to the east of the Newcastle city boundaries, and share many of the economic, historical and indeed political characteristics of the bulk of the East constituency. The name has become more clumsy, but the boundary changes are logical enough. The MP here, Nick Brown, was Secretary of State for Agriculture during the foot-and-mouth crisis in early 2001, but a less rural constituency would be hard to imagine.

Social indices:			2001 Gen. Election:			
% Non-white	2.1		Lab	20,642	63.1	–8.1
% Prof/Man	25.1		LD	6,419	19.6	+9.0
% Non-manual	49.5		C	3,873	11.8	–2.1
£ Av prop val 2000	55 K		Grn	651	2.0	
% Increase 97–00	23.3		Ind	563	1.7	
% Unemployed 2001	6.1		SLP	420	1.3	–0.3
% Decrease 97–01	3.4		CPGB	126	0.4	–0.0
% Fin hard/Rank	34.9	93	Lab maj	14,223	43.5	
% Pensioners	28.3		Turnout		53.2	–12.6
% Prem mort/Rank	48	56	Elect	61,494		

Member of Parliament

Lugubrious-looking **Nick Brown**, Minister of State for Work from 2001, but previously (1998–2001) Agriculture Minister, cut a somewhat hapless figure trudging round the farmsteads of England mired in foot and mouth disease. A Beckett not Blair supporter, and one of Gordon Brown's backers in his unlaunched leadership bid, he was sidelined from Chief Whip (1997–98) to Agriculture in Blair's first reshuffle in 1998. Born in 1950, son of an electricity board clerk, and educated at a secondary modern and at a technical school in Tunbridge Wells, and at Newcastle University, he worked in advertising at Proctor & Gamble and (for five years) as a researcher and adviser to the GMB, until elected to replace SDP-defecting MP Mike Thomas in 1983. He is one of half a dozen Labour MPs whose homosexuality has been acknowledged. As Chief Whip he applied the thumbscrews to a clutch of MPs accused of dissidence or alleged malefactions, but in 2001 suffered a humiliation of his own by becoming a sacked Cabinet Minister who accepts demotion to a non-Cabinet post, a distinction he shared after 2001 with Harriet Harman.

NEWCASTLE UPON TYNE NORTH

Newcastle North has had a somewhat unusual history since its inception in its present form in 1983 (this seat has nothing at all in common with the constituency named Newcastle North before that time, and is in fact based on the Newcastle West division which was abolished in that year). In its first contest it produced a genuinely three-way marginal result. Less than 8% separated the Liberal Alliance in third place (29.9%) and the Labour victor, Bob Brown (37.6%). In between the Conservatives (32.5%) also staked a claim to be regarded as serious contenders. Then in 1987, despite another landslide Tory victory at national level, they dropped back severely in Newcastle North, while the Alliance, though suffering disappointment in the election nationally, actually increased their share of the vote. It looked like Newcastle North could be classed as one of those rare seats where the centre could mount a real challenge to Labour. Then in 1992 the Liberal bubble burst. Their share plummeted from 33% to 19%, the almost equal beneficiaries being Labour, whose majority increased to 9,000, and the Conservatives, who moved forward into second place. There was a further 12% swing to Labour in 1997, bringing Doug Henderson's majority to over 19,000. It does not look like a three-way marginal now.

This is a mixed constituency, varying between peripheral owner-occupied suburbia and peripheral council estates. The seat sweeps around the western edge of the city, including Woolsington, the site of Newcastle Airport, through Labour Denton and Lemington and the more Tory Westerhope, to reach the Tyne at Newburn. The Liberal Democrats still do very well in local council elections in the far north of the seat, in Castle and Grange wards beyond the old county boundaries in Gosforth and beyond, in commuterised villages like Brunswick. In 2000 they obtained 37% overall in the city elections here, but in the General Election the next year they did only half as well and still came third. The Lib Dems form a credible opposition to Labour on the council (unlike the Conservatives who have had no councillors at all elected in Newcastle since 1992), but are not in the running for national government.

Social indices:			2001 Gen. Election:			
% Non-white	1.8		Lab	21,874	60.1	−2.0
% Prof/Man	29.7		C	7,424	20.4	+1.0
% Non-manual	57.8		LD	7,070	19.4	+4.9
£ Av prop val 2000	66 K		Lab maj	14,450	39.7	
% Increase 97–00	17.0		Turnout		57.5	−11.7
% Unemployed 2001	3.3		Elect	63,208		
% Decrease 97–01	2.8					
% Fin hard/Rank	26.4	184				
% Pensioners	26.9					
% Prem mort/Rank	34	271				

Member of Parliament

Doug Henderson, elected here in 1987, was an Opposition spokesman from 1988 and covered Foreign Affairs and Defence as a middle rank minister until being dropped in 1999. One of a score of itinerant Scots in English Labour seats, he rose as a

GMB union official, originally as a Scottish organiser but eventually in the union's Newcastle stronghold. Wiry and ex-moustachioed and unflatteringly dubbed in *The Times* as amongst those who were 'too talentless even to be nearly-men', the son of a railwayman, he was born in 1949, and attended Waid Academy, Fife, and Strathclyde University. A slight union apparatchik raised to a slight ministerial career, he has had more time for his jogging hobby after 1999, and to attack the decision to send combat troops to Afghanistan in 2002.

NEW FOREST EAST

The very name of this constituency must have struck despair into the hearts and souls of Liberal Democrat and Labour parties when it was created by the Boundary Commission which reported in 1995. One New Forest was bad enough (1992, Conservative majority: 20,405); the prospect of two must have been appalling.

In the eventuality, the pill has been sweetened, not only by the immense success that both those parties have enjoyed in 1997 and 2001, but also by the fact that one of the New Forest seats, East, no longer looks like a rock solid Tory certainty. In 2001 Julian Lewis's majority was just 3,829 over the Liberal Democrats, with a substantial Labour share of over 20% which could in theory still be squeezed should the left of centre gang up on the incumbent.

At least half of the area of the ancient Forest is indeed included in the East constituency, together with familiar names to tourists such as those of the small towns of Brockenhurst and Lyndhurst in the heart of the woods. However, the vast bulk of the population is actually sited in the 'Waterside' parishes, on the west shore of Southampton Water. Here we have Totton, which attained a population of 26,000 in the 1991 Census; Marchwood, which nearly doubled to 5,000; Hythe and Dibden (19,000); and Fawley with its vast oil refinery (13,500). Each of these is more populous than any of the older communities in the Forest itself, and although the seat contains beauty spots such as Bucklers Hard and Beaulieu Abbey, its overall impression is much more gritty, being typified and dominated by the towers and flares at Fawley, where many of its constituents work.

Social indices:			2001 Gen. Election:			
% Non-white	0.8		C	17,902	42.4	−0.5
% Prof/Man	33.4		LD	14,073	33.4	+1.1
% Non-manual	59.5		Lab	9,141	21.7	−3.1
£ Av prop val 2000	132 K		UKIP	1,062	2.5	
% Increase 97–00	61.6		C maj	3,829	9.1	
% Unemployed 2001	1.0		Turnout		63.2	−11.5
% Decrease 97–01	1.1		Elect	66,767		
% Fin hard/Rank	5.4	597				
% Pensioners	24.9					
% Prem mort/Rank	17	508				

Member of Parliament

Dr Julian Lewis, elected here in 1997, voted for Redwood, then abstained, in the Hague-Clarke run-off, and in 2001 backed the winner and became a Whip. A tall, thin man with a set smile and extremely precise diction, he was born in 1951, son of a Jewish tailor, and educated at Dynevor Grammar School and Balliol College, Oxford, and with a doctorate in strategic studies from St Anthony's College, Oxford, he quit as Deputy Director of the Conservative Research Department in 1996 in order to campaign against Europe. In 2001 he promised 'never to vote for a single European foreign policy, a single European defence policy, or a single European currency instead of the pound'. Previously his preoccupation was with Cold War threats to Western security from left-wingers in the Parliamentary Labour Party, copiously listed in his 'Who's Left' dossier of 1992, which named 207 Labour MPs as supporters of '17 prominent left-wing causes'.

NEW FOREST WEST

The New Forest West constituency contains 64,000 of the 75,000 electors of the former New Forest seat which existed before the 1997 Election, so it can truly be regarded as its successor. Nearly half of the actual woodland that gives this district its name is in fact in the neighbouring seat of New Forest East, but trees (and ponies) do not have votes and the bulk of that division's electors were formerly in Romsey and Waterside.

New Forest West includes the unofficial 'capital' of the forest, Ringwood; the port of Lymington from which ferries sail to Yarmouth on the Isle of Wight; and, larger in population than either of these, the rather suburban sprawl of New Milton, which is just inland from Christchurch Bay and economically looks westwards to the Bournemouth 'conurbation'. It also extends northwards from Ringwood up the valley of the River Avon to Fordingbridge. There are of course forest villages too; the New Forest is one of England's oldest 'playgrounds', a place enjoyed by medieval kings who relished hunting (except possibly William Rufus who was killed by an arrow here), and more recently by a much wider range of tourists, who seek both wooded, heathland scenery and an attractive coastline.

On its first contest in 1997, West was one of only 34 seats which gave their Conservative MP a five-figure majority, and this despite over 7% of the total vote being shared between Referendum and UK Independence Parties. By 2001 the European issue had been considerable, but one suspects temporarily, defused by the promise of a referendum on entry to the Euro common currency sometime during the next parliament, and the specifically anti-federalist vote halved, while the right-wing Conservative MP Desmond Swayne benefited: his share increased by 5% to become the second highest anywhere after that of his then leader William Hague in Richmond (Yorkshire), with a numerical majority of over 13,000, one of the ten highest Conservative margins.

Social indices:			2001 Gen. Election:			
% Non-white	0.5		C	24,575	55.7	+5.2
% Prof/Man	38.9		LD	11,384	25.8	−2.0
% Non-manual	61.6		Lab	6,481	14.7	+0.4
£ Av prop val 2000	156 K		UKIP	1,647	3.7	+0.6
% Increase 97–00	51.8		C maj	13,191	29.9	
% Unemployed 2001	1.1		Turnout		65.0	−9.8
% Decrease 97–01	1.6		Elect	67,806		
% Fin hard/Rank	4.8	611				
% Pensioners	40.8					
% Prem mort/Rank	15	535				

Member of Parliament

Desmond Swayne, made a Health spokesman in February 2001, a Defence spokesman in September, after voting for Iain Duncan Smith, and then a Whip in February 2002, attracts a good deal of Labour mockery for his sub-Wintertonesque right-wing bombast delivered in the style of one of Harry Enfield's caricatures. With his low hairline once eliciting werewolf howls, he allegedly stood over a King's Cross beggar until he had eaten a tuna-filled baguette he had given him and then told him to go home because he could no longer be hungry. Born in 1956 and educated at Bedford School and St Andrew's University, he was a public school master for seven years and then a computer systems manager with a bank. His reference to St Bernard of Clairvaux's problem about not working alongside a woman without wishing to make love, did not go down well with feminist MPs. Nor was everyone happy with the thought of him, with (brief) responsibility for Defence having a finger too close potentially to a nuclear button.

NEWPORT EAST

In 1997 the Yorkshire miners' leader Arthur Scargill stood for Parliament for the first time at the age of 59 – but not in any of his broad acres strongholds, and not for Labour. He contested Newport East, never a mining area, although in south Wales. Why did he do this ? He wished to make a point on behalf of the Socialist Labour Party he had himself founded against Labour's last-minute selection of Alan Howarth, the former Conservative MP for Stratford on Avon who had defected during the course of the 1992–97 Parliament. Scargill obtained 1,951 votes; Howarth received 21,481.

Newport is the third largest town, and from March 2002 the third city, in Wales, a port which has served the eastern valleys since industry came to south Wales. The previously unified Newport was safely Labour, but in 1983 it was divided along the line of the river Usk, which flows through the centre of the town, and each half was diluted with rural territory from the Monmouth seat. This gave the Conservatives hope, and indeed they won the West division in its inaugural contest in 1983; but that was a terrible year for Labour, and now both the Newport seats look beyond the Tories' grasp. In the eastern division can be found the vast Llanwern steelworks, Newport's largest single employer, offering about 4,500 jobs. Labour can rely on the support of threatened steelworkers and others living in the peripheral eastern council estates such as Ringland and Alway. The rest of Newport East of the Usk is more mixed, but Labour does tend to win in wards like St Julian's and Victoria, which includes a fair number of Newport's small non-white communities. The Conservative vote is stronger in the outlying wards around Magor and Langstone, and along the coast almost as far as Chepstow.

It is true that Howarth only increased the Labour vote by 2.7% in 1997, 5% less than his colleague Paul Flynn in West. This is almost exactly the share that Scargill received. However, he had been rewarded with a safe seat, and this must have acted as an incentive for future defectors to New Labour like Shaun Woodward, who himself moved from Witney to St Helens South in 2001.

Howarth's own performances continue to be less than scintillating. In 2001 his vote slipped by 4,000, mainly because of a massive reduction in turnout of over 17%, the highest in Wales, but also after a drop in vote share, mainly to the advantage of the Liberal Democrat. Among those losing their deposits were Liz Screen of Socialist Labour and Madoc Batcup of Plaid Cymru.

Social indices:			2001 Gen. Election:			
% Non-white	2.9		Lab	17,120	54.7	−2.9
% Welsh sp	2.0		C	7,246	23.2	+1.8
% Prof/Man	27.4		LD	4,394	14.0	+3.6
% Non-manual	50.3		PC	1,519	4.9	+2.9
£ Av prop val 2000	68 K		SLP	420	1.3	−3.9
% Increase 97–00	32.7		UKIP	410	1.3	
% Unemployed 2001	3.9		CPGB	173	0.6	
% Decrease 97–01	1.8		Lab maj	9,874	31.6	
% Fin hard/Rank	20.5	267	Turnout		55.7	−17.3
% Pensioners	23.9		Elect	56,118		
% Prem mort/Rank	38	204				

Member of Parliament

Alan Howarth, Labour MP here since being airlifted in at the last minute in 1997, is the first of the small batch of Conservative MPs who did a Sir Shortly Floorcross in reverse by showing it was perfectly possible for public-school and Oxbridge-educated Tory MPs to go Labour. A former Thatcherite education minister (1989–92), he was elected for Stratford-upon-Avon in 1983 after a short Central Office career, but as a liberal on social policy trailed his anxieties in the *Guardian* and crossed the floor in 1995. Born in 1944, son of Tom Howarth, sometime High Master of St Paul's School, he was educated at Rugby and King's, Cambridge. A tall, introverted man of austere look, he now has the luckless task of watching the near dismantling of the huge Llanwern steelworks, without even the incongruous consolation of being Arts minister, a job from which he was dropped after three years in 2001, leaving him in the lonely limbo that is the ultimate fate of all floor-crossers.

NEWPORT WEST

In its very first campaign, in 1983, Newport West was won by the Conservatives: the first victory for that party in Newport since 1945. The reasons for this apparently surprising result are multiple. Newport had been split by the Boundary Commission whose report was enacted earlier that year. The more Conservative middle-class residential wards within Newport itself are mainly situated west of the river, most notably at Allt-yr-yn, and also at Graig. As well as this, a number of rural and commuter communities previously in the Monmouth seat were included in a Newport division for the first time. These all harbour Conservative voters too, though not enough to win the unitary authority seats in 1999 – Marshfield, Bassaleg, and Rogerstone – and the former Roman town of Caerleon set in its bend of the river Usk has turned to the Liberal Democrats in recent years.

Labour fought back to gain Newport West in 1987, and by 2001 Paul Flynn's majority was over 9,000. The seat now scarcely looks marginal at all. It must be remembered that 1983 was a very poor year indeed for Labour, as they slipped to just 28% of the national vote. In a better year they would always be favourites to win Newport West, despite the Tory elements mentioned above. There are many neighbourhoods favourable to Labour too: the large peripheral council estate of Bettws is in the seat, as are the town centre and dockland areas, with their terraced housing and the bulk of Newport's Asian and Afro-Caribbean population: Pillgwenlly ward is about one-fifth non-white, and the Newport Alliance Party finished a clear second in the first unitary council elections in May 1999. There are few constituencies in Wales which have a significant ethnic minority vote; Newport West only has 3.5%, but this is exceeded only in three Cardiff seats.

Newport has only a tiny Welsh-speaking population and Plaid Cymru only polled 2,510 votes in West in 1997 even after quadrupling their share. The Conservatives closed the gap in 2001 by over 5,000, but their best performance in this constituency remains their first.

Social indices:			2001 Gen. Election:			
% Non-white	3.5		Lab	18,489	52.7	−7.8
% Welsh sp	2.4		C	9,185	26.2	+1.8
% Prof/Man	36.2		LD	4,095	11.7	+2.0
% Non-manual	59.0		PC	2,510	7.2	+5.5
£ Av prop val 2000	72 K		UKIP	506	1.4	+0.6
% Increase 97–00	33.6		BNP	278	0.8	
% Unemployed 2001	4.8		Lab maj	9,304	26.5	
% Decrease 97–01	1.9		Turnout		58.7	−15.9
% Fin hard/Rank	23.6	217	Elect	59,742		
% Pensioners	26.4					
% Prem mort/Rank	35	246				

Member of Parliament

Paul Flynn, a fluent, deep-voiced, bearded garden gnome replica and – at least verbally – awkward squaddie, resisted 'Old Labour vote-rigging and New Labour control freakery' over the election of Alun Michael as Labour's Welsh Assembly leader and voted against the government on Murdoch's predatory pricing, the prime minister's power to nominate life peers, incapacity and disability benefit cuts, jury trial curbs, and air traffic control privatisation. Born in 1935, a postman's son, and like a growing number of Welsh Labour MPs, of part Irish parentage (see also Paul Murphy, Don Touhig and Kevin Brennan – though unlike any of them, Flynn is Welsh-speaking), he attended St Illtyd's (RC) College, Cardiff and Cardiff University, worked as an industrial chemist in the steel industry and was elected here in 1983. He campaigns against bull bars on vehicles and against endowment mortgages, and for the decriminalisation of soft drugs and euthanasia. He rose politically as researcher for ex-MEP, now MP, Llew Smith, the PLP's most rebellious Welsh MP.

NEWRY AND ARMAGH

In 2001, as in 1997, three SDLP MPs were returned to Westminster. One of these was from an urban Catholic-majority seat, Foyle (the city of Derry). Two were from rural areas, the neighbouring border seats of South Down and Newry and Armagh. Originally the Boundary Commission proposed merging the more Nationalist parts of both these seats in a border seat of Newry and Mourne before the 1997 Election, but after an inquiry the status quo was restored, at least as far as Newry and Armagh was concerned. Both rural SDLP seats were thus preserved.

This seat includes the south Armagh 'bandit country' where for many years the British army patrolled only in the air, and the city (from 2002) of Newry, also long a no-go area for foot patrols. The more unionist northern section includes the cathedral city of Armagh, the ecclesiastical capital of Ireland. The seat is predominantly agricultural, with a major apple-growing industry. Much of the countryside is very scenic, but this superficial impression conceals the fact that this predominantly Nationalist constituency has seen some of the most violent incidents of the troubles.

The Newry and Armagh seat always looked ripe for a Nationalist victory, but in 1983 the Catholic vote was heavily split between SDLP and Provisional Sinn Fein candidates, and it was not until the opportunity afforded by the unionists' decision to resign and seek approval of their opposition to the Anglo-Irish agreement in by-elections in 1986 that Seamus Mallon was able to defeat Jim Nicholson. In 2001 Mallon's position was considerably weakened by the rise in Sinn Fein support typical in the province, part of a continuing trend: since 1992 the SF share has risen from 12.5 to 30.9%, and when Mallon, who is a senior citizen, retires, the more hardline Nationalist Party must now be the favourite to take over here.

Social indices:		2001 Gen. Election:			
% Prof/Man	30.8	SDLP	20,784	37.4	−5.6
% Non-manual	50.4	SF	17,209	30.9	+9.9
% RC	61.8	DUP	10,795	19.4	
% Irish sp	15.7	UUP	6,833	12.3	−21.5
% Unemployed 2001	6.1	SDLP maj	3,575	6.4	
% Decrease 97–01	4.2	Turnout		76.8	+1.4
		Elect	72,466		

Member of Parliament

Seamus Mallon, the details man as Deputy Leader of the SDLP to John Hume's broad-brush leader, has about him the tortured air of a long-suffering advocate of a cause – constitutional nationalism – whose time has not yet come, but who is borne along on the expectation of its eventual arrival. Like Hume a former schoolteacher, he was born in 1936 and educated at Christian Brothers Abbey Grammar School, Newry and St Joseph's Education College, Belfast, was elected in 1983 and tenuously served as Deputy Leader to David Trimble in the Northern Ireland power-sharing executive (until 2001 when he retired). His role in the SDLP was once to counterbalance the more green stance of John Hume, but both have aged and wilted under the pressure on the Catholic electorate of a Sinn Fein – to which he has always been more hostile than Hume – now purporting to have exchanged violence for voting. His party, with three MPs in 2001, became the smallest of the four Ulster parties at Westminster.

NORFOLK MID

In Labour's massive triumph in 1997, they took one seat in rural Norfolk, NW, and nearly seized a couple more: SW and Mid. Meanwhile the Liberal Democrats came close in North. During the 2001 Election campaign, as all opinion polls suggested an even greater Labour lead, further gains were mooted. In the end, though, while the Lib Dems did notch up their target, Labour did rather badly in the largest East Anglian county. They lost North West, one of only five Conservative gains at their expense, and went backwards sharply in Gillian Shephard's South West and here in Norfolk Mid. They could scarcely blame the election-wide drop in turnout, which was well below average here, as over 70% went to the polls – this happened in only seven other English seats, including neighbouring Norfolk North.

In 1974 Norfolk lost a parliamentary seat when Central Norfolk was abolished, sending Ian Gilmour off in search of a new constituency. In 1983 Norfolk regained its eight-strong delegation, and again there is a seat which almost surrounds Norwich, and touches neither the sea nor Norfolk's boundary with any other county. Mid Norfolk is now its name. The seat includes part of the Broads, and a few small towns, such as East Dereham, Aylsham and Acle, spread across the interior of this big county. Most of the urban wards voted Labour in the last municipal elections before 2001, in May 1999, but in 2001 the vast swathe of villages in this open countryside must have turned out in goodly numbers to stave off the prospect of yet further Tory losses, offering Mr Blair even more of an alarming elective dictatorship.

Social indices:			2001 Gen. Election:			
% Non-white	0.5		C	23,519	44.8	+5.2
% Prof/Man	32.4		Lab	18,957	36.1	−1.2
% Non-manual	55.2		LD	7,621	14.5	−0.5
£ Av prop val 2000	90 K		UKIP	1,333	2.5	
% Increase 97–00	45.4		Grn	1,118	2.1	−0.1
% Unemployed 2001	1.6		C maj	4,562	8.7	
% Decrease 97–01	1.7		Turnout		70.1	−6.1
% Fin hard/Rank	4.5	617	Elect	74,911		
% Pensioners	27.9					
% Prem mort/Rank	10	587				

Member of Parliament

Keith Simpson, a Conservative Whip (2000–2001) and earlier a Defence spokesman, was elected in 1997 as one of the handful of Clarke supporters in that intake of Tory MPs, despite his own concealed doubts over the single currency. A burly, moustached, jovial man with the aspect of a Mace grocer, he was born in 1949, educated at Thorpe Grammar School Norfolk, Hull University and King's College, London, lectured at Sandhurst and Shrivenham and authored books on 'the Old Contemptibles' and the Waffen SS, with a look about him appropriately more of the former than of the latter. Voting for Portillo in 2001, he returned to the backbenches under Iain Duncan Smith.

NORFOLK NORTH

Privately, top Liberal Democrat Party strategists nominated North Norfolk as one of their very best chances of a further gain in the 2001 General Election, following their dramatic advance to 46 seats in 1997. This did indeed come to pass. Their success was based on a number of factors. There was a large Labour vote to squeeze – 25%, or 14,000, in 1997. Tactically these voters were persuaded to turn to the Liberal Democrat Norman Lamb to oust the one-term Conservative MP David Prior. In return, Labour concentrated on trying to hold their own marginal next door, Norfolk NW, where the Lib Dems sank even further to just 8%. Armies of Liberal Democrat activists swarmed over the ground, and key speakers harangued the electorate. This is all called targeting, and the Lib Dems, and Norman Lamb, hit the bullseye on 7 June.

This is still rather odd, as there is something of a Labour tradition here. North Norfolk had the rare distinction of being an agricultural seat electing a Labour MP from 1945 to 1970. Like South and South West Norfolk, there was a history of organised agricultural trade unionism and a rural working-class Labour vote, itself very unusual in England. Then in 1970 the President of the National Union of Agricultural Workers, Bert Hazell, was ousted as MP for North Norfolk by Ralph Howell. The constituency does, though, not look like a Labour area. It contains a peaceful and genteel section of the Norfolk coast around the holiday resorts of Sheringham, Cromer and the Runtons, and Wells-next-the-Sea; small inland towns like Holt, North Walsham and Fakenham; and dozens of villages. It also includes the greater part of the Norfolk Broads, such as those around Horning and Hoveton.

Now that Norman Lamb has taken his place as one of the pack of 52 Liberal Democrat MPs, further vigilance and constant activity will be needed to maintain his position, but this can bring electoral rewards, as that other Lib Dem Norman, Baker of Lewes, can demonstrate most effectively. That East Sussex seat was not traditional Liberal territory either. But all traditions have to start somewhere, and hard work usually brings rewards.

Social indices:			2001 Gen. Election:			
% Non-white	0.5		LD	23,978	42.7	+8.4
% Prof/Man	27.6		C	23,495	41.8	+5.3
% Non-manual	47.3		Lab	7,490	13.3	−11.7
£ Av prop val 2000	89 K		Grn	649	1.2	
% Increase 97–00	44.7		UKIP	608	1.1	
% Unemployed 2001	2.1		LD maj	483	0.9	
% Decrease 97–01	1.8		Turnout		70.2	−6.1
% Fin hard/Rank	5.6	593	Elect	80,061		
% Pensioners	36.0					
% Prem mort/Rank	21	471				

Member of Parliament

The Liberal Democrats' **Norman Lamb** was elected here – at his third attempt – in 2001, amid rumours (denied by him) of a tacit Lib-Lab pact covering this seat and neighbouring NW Norfolk. A solicitor specialising in employment law, he was born in 1957, the son of a University of East Anglia academic climatologist, and educated at Wymondham College, Leicester University and City of London Polytechnic. Keen on a decentralised version of the EU, fresh-faced and boyish-looking, he quickly slotted into the role of a Liberal Democrat constituency MP, bemoaning the collapse of public services and rural infrastructure. He is East Anglia's first Liberal MP since 1951, and this constituency's first since Noel Buxton quit the Liberals for Labour – in this seat – in 1922.

NORFOLK NORTH WEST

In 1812 Spencer Perceval became the only British Prime Minister ever to have been assassinated. He was killed by a man named Bellingham. In 1997 the Conservative MP for Norfolk North West, Henry Bellingham, lost his seat to Labour by just 1,339 votes; and a significant role in this reverse, which might have spelled the death of Bellingham's political career (although he was later resurrected), was the 2,923 votes polled for the Referendum Party by a candidate called Percival – a distant descendant of the murdered Prime Minister. Such are the minor ironies thrown up by each general election campaign.

Labour had been helped in Norfolk North West once the situation returned to normal after that unique defection of a Tory MP (Christopher Brocklebank-Fowler) to the SDP in the early 1980s, which for several elections boosted the SDP vote and depressed that of Labour. The seat is similar to the former King's Lynn, which existed before 1974, and elected Labour MPs during their periods of government of 1945–51 and 1964–70. They lost it to Brocklebank-Fowler in that last year by just 33. Lynn is an industrial town, as well as a port which was once the third most important in the country. The prosperous town houses in the centre of Lynn still give evidence of its affluent past, but now it has taken in much overspill population from London. Like other East Anglian ports (Lowestoft and Great Yarmouth), King's Lynn usually gives a majority of its votes to Labour, at least in local elections. However its influence is counterbalanced elsewhere in the constituency. Here we find the holiday resort of

Hunstanton, the orbit of royal influence around Sandringham, and the wind-blown agricultural villages of west Norfolk, truly part of the Fens, and where cereals and sugar-beet form the basis of a rural economy.

Norfolk North West is a classic marginal, and it changed hands again in 2001. The Conservatives only gained five seats from Labour that year, a most disappointing harvest, but North West was probably the most likely and predictable of these. Labour lost control of King's Lynn and West Norfolk council in May 1999. In the European elections of June 1999 within the seat, the Conservatives received 17% more votes than Labour. North West Norfolk was one of only three Labour-held seats with more than 2,000 voters employed in agriculture, at a time when countryside issues were expected to reflect particularly badly on the government. The former MP, Henry Bellingham, stayed on to contest the seat again. He was not opposed by a Referendum candidate or a Percival, increased his share by 7%, and returned to the Commons after a four-year gap by nearly 3,500 votes.

Social indices:			2001 Gen. Election:			
% Non-white	0.8		C	24,846	48.5	+7.0
% Prof/Man	27.8		Lab	21,361	41.7	−2.1
% Non-manual	47.6		LD	4,292	8.4	−1.2
£ Av prop val 2000	72 K		UKIP	704	1.4	
% Increase 97–00	31.4		C maj	3,485	6.8	
% Unemployed 2001	2.3		Turnout		66.2	−8.6
% Decrease 97–01	2.6		Elect	77,387		
% Fin hard/Rank	12.9	397				
% Pensioners	36.0					
% Prem mort/Rank	26	410				

Member of Parliament

Henry Bellingham was one of seven former Conservative MPs who returned to the Commons in 2001 – in his case for his former constituency, lost in 1997. A former friend of Diana, Princess of Wales and one-time PPS to Malcolm Rifkind, he was first elected in 1983 and established a reputation as an advocate of restored monarchies in Libya, Yugoslavia and Romania, as a defender of small businesses, and as a critic of concessions to the Irish Republic. In 2001 he was appointed to the Northern Ireland Select Committee. An Eton-and-Magdalene educated landowner, barrister and Member of Lloyd's, a member of Whites and Pratts, owning a stud and opposed to gun control and right-to-roam legislation, he cuts a rare patrician dash in a Tory Party long-suburbanised. Declining to reveal for whom he had voted in the 2001 leadership ballots, he nonetheless asked Press Gallery journalist Michael Brown how he had voted – not realising that Brown had been defeated, like him, in 1997. He was however more open in acknowledging both his descent from John Bellingham, assassin of Prime Minister Spencer Perceval in 1812, and that as such he might have married above his station, his wife Emma being a descendant of another Prime Minister, Lord North. He is one of 14 Old Etonian Conservative MPs, the lowest number ever.

NORFOLK SOUTH

In 1997 South seemed to be the only really safe Conservative seat left in the county of Norfolk, as John Macgregor won by a relatively comfortable looking 7,378 votes; the second highest majority was Gillian Shepherd's 2,464 next door in South West. However, this was not an unusually strong Conservative performance. In fact Macgregor's vote fell by over 12%, almost exactly the Norfolk average. The only reason why he held on with apparent ease was that the Liberal Democrats also fell back in second place, and Labour's advance to a close third.

South Norfolk is based on the small towns of Diss and Wymondham, Harleston and Loddon, and numerous villages extending to the Suffolk border. As in many other rural Norfolk seats, Labour had a strong presence here in general elections through the 1950s and 1960s, and this tradition has not entirely died, which is actually to the Conservatives' advantage. Their share of the vote in 2001, at just of 42%, was actually their lowest in rural Norfolk, but the opposition was evenly divided, unlike in North, say. The Liberal Democrats are clearly the strongest force in local elections here. The results in the May 1999 South Norfolk council elections produced the following distribution of councillors: Liberal Democrat 27, Conservative 16, Labour 2, Independent 2. In the General Election, the two conflicting oppositional forces almost cancelled each other out, and Richard Bacon held on by nearly 7,000 over his squabbling rivals.

Social indices:			2001 Gen. Election:			
% Non-white	0.5		C	23,589	42.2	+2.0
% Prof/Man	34.3		LD	16,696	29.9	+1.6
% Non-manual	56.9		Lab	13,719	24.5	−1.5
£ Av prop val 2000	94 K		Grn	1,069	1.9	+1.1
% Increase 97–00	46.6		UKIP	856	1.5	+0.9
% Unemployed 2001	1.4		C maj	6,893	12.3	
% Decrease 97–01	1.7		Turnout		67.6	−10.8
% Fin hard/Rank	4.7	612	Elect	82,710		
% Pensioners	28.0					
% Prem mort/Rank	1	635				

Member of Parliament

Richard Bacon replaced the retiring John MacGregor for the Conservatives here in 2001. Formerly a merchant banker with Barclays de Zoete Wedd, and a financial journalist with Euromoney Publications, he became a partner in the Brunswick Group, a financial communications consultancy. He lists himself as hostile to devolution and PR, and in favour of 'retaining control of tax and spending in the UK', and of setting by ability in schools. Born in 1962 and educated at King's School, Worcester and the LSE, he fought Vauxhall in 1997, and campaigned against devolved London government. An adviser of the right-wing libertarian MP Richard Shepherd, he backed David Davis, then Iain Duncan Smith, in the leadership ballots in 2001.

NORFOLK SOUTH WEST

The constituency of South West Norfolk has one of the most extraordinary and interesting post-war electoral histories in the United Kingdom. Indeed the academic political writer R.W. Johnson found it possible to contribute an article about this one seat to the journal *Parliamentary Affairs* in 1972. The facts are remarkable. Seven times between 1945 and 1966 the majority of the winning candidate in South West Norfolk was less than 1,000. Four times the seat swung against the national trend. There is a saying – 'Norfolk do different'. In politics, at least, South West Norfolk certainly did.

Sidney Dye won the seat for Labour by 53 votes in 1945, held it by 260 in 1950, but lost it to the Conservative D.G. Bullard by 442 the next year. Dye regained it – by 193 – in 1955, but on his death in 1958 the new Labour candidate A.V. Hilton increased the majority in the by-election (held on 25 March 1959) to a princely 1,354. In the General Election of the same year, though, Hilton's lead was reduced to 78, and in 1964 Paul Hawkins gained the seat for the Tories (against the tide) by 123. Hawkins then held it continuously for 23 years – by 775 in 1966 and steadily increasing his majority to its final level of nearly 15,000. South West Norfolk is a clearer example than any other of the fading of rural radicalism in Norfolk, for its boundaries did not alter between 1950 and 1983.

Then, however, Thetford and a large part of the lonely heath of Breckland came in from South Norfolk. Much of East Anglia resembles an armed camp, and this district is no exception. There is a large battle area forbidden to the general public north of Thetford, and big airfields adorn the flat countryside. Over 6% of those in employment are in the armed services, the highest figure in Norfolk and exceeded only by Huntingdon and Bury St Edmunds in East Anglia. The little towns of Swaffham and Watton, and Downham Market, offer some Labour support, while the Thetford overspill estates offer solid backing; or certainly they did in 1997, as Labour advanced by 11% and cut Gillian Shepherd's majority to less than 2,500.

In 2001 there were rumours that Labour would actually take SW Norfolk, but in the event the Conservatives produced one of their very best results, Gillian Shephard increasing her share by fully 10%, a figure exceeded only by Andrew Rosindell in his extraordinary victory at Romford, undoubtedly his party's best performance, and in Tatton, which scarcely counts because of Martin Bell's departure. The advance in South West came roughly equally at the expense of Labour, the Liberal Democrats and the anti-Europeans, a spread which can only redound the more to Gillian Shephard's own credit.

Social indices:

% Non-white	1.1	
% Prof/Man	25.2	
% Non-manual	42.9	
£ Av prop val 2000	78 K	
% Increase 97–00	41.7	
% Unemployed 2001	1.6	
% Decrease 97–01	1.8	
% Fin hard/Rank	10.5	452
% Pensioners	28.0	
% Prem mort/Rank	22	453

2001 Gen. Election:

C	27,633	52.2	+10.2
Lab	18,267	34.5	−3.3
LD	5,681	10.7	−3.2
UKIP	1,368	2.6	
C maj	9,366	17.7	
Turnout		63.1	−10.2
Elect	83,903		

Member of Parliament

Gillian Shephard, who rose as part of Major's East Anglian mafia to be the senior woman in the Conservative government, lingered on the frontbench in Opposition for two years but, with age and Europhilia telling against her, left for the backbenches in 1999. In 2001 she failed to return to prominence when losing by 66 votes to 79 to Sir Michael Spicer in the 1922 Committee chairmanship election. As an ex-teacher, married to a comprehensive school headmaster, she was less right wing than she sounded on vouchers and selectivity as Education Secretary. Tiny, direct and classless, born in 1940, and educated at North Walsham Girls' School and St Hilda's College, Oxford, she came from a background of livestock dealing, and as Minister of Agriculture (1993–94) luckily moved on before the BSE crisis struck. As Education Secretary (1995–97) she could often sound like a shrill schoolmistress, which after 2001 she seemed likely to have to be in her new role as 'head of candidate development' at Central Office, charged with persuading the blue-rinsed matrons of Virginia Water to allow the election of women as Conservative MPs.

NORMANTON

Normanton is not one of the better-known constituency names. It is doubtful if many people who live far from this part of West Yorkshire could identify where it might be. It is not on any major routes, so people tend not to pass through it on the way to another destination. The population base is stable, with considerably fewer people than average changing their address in the year previous to the Census being taken ('migrants'). Normanton may be relatively obscure, but it has every bit as much a right to return a member of parliament as the cities of London and Westminster or Hampstead and Highgate.

The seat is wrapped around the city of Wakefield like a kidney, from Normanton and Sharlston to the east, to Stanley north of Wakefield, Ossett to the west, and finally Horbury to the south-west. Horbury is a relative newcomer, replacing Rothwell in 1997. All of these are small towns. Normanton itself has only 19,000 inhabitants, Ossett 15,000, Horbury 14,000.

Essentially the Normanton constituency is safe for Labour without being overwhelmingly so. Their best ward is Normanton and Sharlston, where the economy was forged by coal-mining. The other parts of the seat, where textiles used to be the main industry, are much more marginal, and the Tories actually managed to win the Stanley/Wrenthorpe ward, where there has been some new private housing development, in May 1992 (though not since). Horbury (which has come in from the Wakefield division) is better for the Conservatives than Rothwell (which has been joined with Morley). Nevertheless, these minor boundary changes did not shake Labour's grip; in 2001 Bill O'Brien, Labour's third oldest MP, won again, by nearly 10,000.

Social indices:			2001 Gen. Election:				
% Non-white	0.9		Lab	19,152	56.1	−4.5	
% Prof/Man	28.7		C	9,215	27.0	+3.4	
% Non-manual	52.6		LD	4,990	14.6	+2.2	
£ Av prop val 2000	61 K		SLP	798	2.3		
% Increase 97–00	15.8		Lab maj	9,937	29.1		
% Unemployed 2001	2.2		Turnout		52.2	−16.1	
% Decrease 97–01	1.8		Elect	65,392			
% Fin hard/Rank	17.1	315					
% Pensioners	23.4						
% Prem mort/Rank	33	286					

Member of Parliament

Bill O'Brien, a former miner and MP here since 1983, was extensively pencilled-in as the leading candidate for a last-minute kicking upstairs to make way for the Treasury adviser, Ed Balls, one half of a golden New Labour couple as husband of Junior Minister Yvette Cooper, who sits for the next-door seat of Pontefract and Castleford. The man of whom it was said by Michael Heseltine that Labour economic policy in Opposition was not 'Brown's but balls', waited, however, in vain for Bill O'Brien to create a vacancy. The fourth oldest MP, born in 1929, Catholic-educated and (extramurally) at Leeds University, he was a coal-face worker for nearly 40 years before exchanging the pithead baths for a Commons seat. An anti-Scargill moderate, he served as a statutory Catholic Northern Ireland spokesman in Opposition, and is in the tiny Labour minority which votes against homosexual sex at 16.

NORTHAMPTON NORTH

Northamptonshire proved to be one of Labour's very best counties in both 1997 and 2001. They had won no seats at all in the three General Elections from 1983 to 1992. Then in 1997 they gained five of the six, missing only Daventry. Three of these were highly unexpected and narrow: Kettering, Wellingborough and Northampton South. Two were high on Labour's hit list and won by five-figure majorities, Corby and Northampton North – in the latter case by exactly 10,000. What is more, in 2001 all five were held, the three super-marginals with positive swings and increased shares of the vote and majorities, and Northampton North with no swing of any note and a lead reduced only because the turnout fell by 14%, which affected all parties equally. Overall, the Labour share in the county fell by only 1.3%, and it contributed fully to their second successive landslide.

Northampton was one of the last places to be designated as a New Town, in 1968; like most New Towns in the southern half of England, the subsequent arrival of overspill population and of swathes of modern local authority housing did not seem to push the politics of Northampton further towards Labour. Of course Northampton was no greenfield site awaiting an entirely new community, but already a major county town of over 100,000 people. But it was held by Reginald Paget for Labour from 1945 to 1974. How did Northampton come to have two Conservative MPs from 1979 to 1997?

Paget was something of an eccentric, a fox hunting pro-hanging Labour MP on the far right of his party. Northampton seems to go in for controversial MPs, for the Labour member for the North division after 1974's split into two seats was Maureen Colquhoun. She got into hot water with her local party and achieved notoriety for her professed lesbianism. There is some evidence that the 8% swing which defeated her in North was partly due to personal unpopularity.

Northampton's gain of a second seat was due to New Town growth, and North is the seat which contains most of it as it sprawls north-east towards Wellingborough, north of the river Nene. Here we have hyper-modern neighbourhoods like Lumbertubs, Thorplands and Links, swallowing up old villages and farmlands. These nests of oddly shaped little boxes do tend to give Labour a majority; but North also includes some of the better residential areas of Northampton, in Parklands and Headlands, and out in Welford to the north-west. Only the older council estate of Dallington – Kings Heath really can be counted as a Labour stronghold. The Boundary Commission's proposals for Northampton for the election after next have already been published and subjected to an enquiry, and given that the Conservative Party's rather imaginative suggestion to create three Northampton seats with the Labour vote concentrated in a Central division was rejected, there is little in the way of a threat even on a far horizon in Northampton North.

Social indices:			2001 Gen. Election:			
% Non-white	5.9		Lab	20,507	49.4	−3.3
% Prof/Man	26.1		C	12,614	30.4	−3.0
% Non-manual	51.8		LD	7,363	17.7	+5.0
£ Av prop val 2000	67 K		UKIP	596	1.4	+0.5
% Increase 97–00	33.5		SA	414	1.0	
% Unemployed 2001	3.2		Lab maj	7,893	19.0	
% Decrease 97–01	1.6		Turnout		56.0	−14.2
% Fin hard/Rank	28.0	160	Elect	74,124		
% Pensioners	23.9					
% Prem mort/Rank	30	334				

Member of Parliament

Sally Keeble, one of Labour's 29 public-school-and-Oxbridge educated MPs, in her case at Cheltenham Ladies College and St Hughes College, Oxford, and a pageboy-bobbed mandarin's daughter (her father, Sir Curtis Keeble, having been British ambassador in Moscow), was elected in 1997. A former journalist who worked as Labour Party press officer, and in PR for ILEA and the GMB union, she was born in

1951, short and flat dumbed-down-to-classlessly-voiced, after establishing a reputation as an effective leader of Southwark Council in the early 1990s, was picked from an all-women shortlist, and criticised Joe Ashton for being found in a Thai sauna in her constituency. As PPS to Hilary Armstrong after 1999, in less on-message mode, she backs an elected House of Lords. Promoted to the government in 2001 as Junior Minister in the Local Government and the Regions Ministry, the team of which she formed part was likened in aspect to a geography department in a former polytechnic.

NORTHAMPTON SOUTH

Shortly before the 2001 General Election campaign, the Labour MP for Northampton South Tony Clarke was reported as suggesting that his Conservative opponent Shailesh Vara was the 'wrong kind of Asian' to regain this ultra-marginal seat. This was a clumsy, not a malevolent, comment, and referred to the fact that Vara's background was Ugandan-Indian and Hindu rather than Pakistani and Muslim (like most of the small minority population in Northampton South), showing a sensitivity to and recognition of the varieties of Asian nationality and culture not always grasped. It was certainly a brave and open-minded move by the Conservatives to select an ethnic minority candidate in one of their most hopeful target marginals, and there is no evidence that Vara's race or religion had anything to do with his defeat. He did as well – or as badly – as his white counterparts in the other key marginals in the county.

One of the most unexpected results of the 1997 Election had been Labour's first ever victory in Northampton South, as the Conservative Deputy Speaker Michael Morris went down to Tony Clarke by 744 votes on a swing of 13.4%. Labour never quite managed to win Northampton South soon after its creation in 1974, when Northampton was first divided into two seats. They lost to the Conservative Michael Morris by 179 votes in February 1974 and by 141 votes in October. On both occasions the Labour candidate was the unfortunate John Dilks, who had also lost to the Independent Social Democrat Dick Taverne in the 1973 Lincoln by-election, and who has never to this day entered Parliament.

In the 1983 boundary changes the undersized constituency took in 13 villages from the rural South Northants district and Daventry constituency, despite a rearguard action by the Labour Party at the local inquiry. These villages, like Roade and Kislingbury, are safely Conservative, and house many affluent commuters to the county town. The urban part of the Northampton South division does contain Labour wards like Castle in the town centre and in the old council estate of Delapre, but also high-quality residential areas such as Weston Favell. Michael Morris increased his majority to 17,000 by 1992.

Most of Northampton's continued population growth since the 1980s has been in the South constituency, notably in the Nene Valley amd the Hunsburies, territory which is scheduled for removal as Northamptonshire gains an extra seat in forthcoming boundary changes – but not until after the next election. Another close contest is expected before then, and if Shailesh Vara is reselected, he will again have a very good chance of entering the Commons.

Social indices:			2001 Gen. Election:			
% Non-white	5.2		Lab	21,882	42.9	+0.5
% Prof/Man	32.9		C	20,997	41.1	+0.0
% Non-manual	58.8		LD	6,355	12.5	+1.4
£ Av prop val 2000	92 K		UKIP	1,237	2.4	+0.4
% Increase 97–00	49.1		Ind	362	0.7	
% Unemployed 2001	2.4		PA	196	0.4	
% Decrease 97–01	1.3		Lab maj	885	1.7	
% Fin hard/Rank	12.4	408	Turnout		59.8	−12.1
% Pensioners	23.0		Elect	85,271		
% Prem mort/Rank	30	345				

Member of Parliament

Tony Clarke's unexpected victory here in 1997 sent Michael Morris, the Conservative MP of 23 years, scuttling off to the Lords with the splendidly Cromwellian title of Lord Naseby. Clarke, a classic product of OMOV, local born in 1963, educated locally at Lings Upper School, a bearded local councillor and a social work trainer, made few headlines until wading waist deep in political incorrectness by referring to his Conservative Asian challenger, Shailesh Vara, a City-based solicitor, as 'exactly the right kind of candidate against us we'd want', as an Asian in a seat where some of the voters 'have shown themselves in the past to be quite racist in their voting', and who was in any case the 'wrong sort' of Asian as a Ugandan-born Hindu in a seat where the ethnic vote is Muslim Bangladeshi or Pakistani. Such nuanced playing of the race card in the only Tory target seat with a non-white candidate saw Tony Clarke re-elected by an undisturbed, if slight, majority.

NORTHAVON

One of the earliest and most unexpected Liberal Democrat gains of the night of the May 1997 General Election came at Northavon, which gave the first inkling that a party which polled fewer votes than in 1992 was about to increase the number of its seats from 18 to 46. Sir John Cope lost a majority of nearly 11,000 in a seat which although in the south-western quadrant of England, is far from the centre of the traditional Liberal Celtic fringe territory.

First, a word about the name of this seat. It must always be remembered in understanding the thinking behind the boundaries of the United Kingdom's parliamentary constituencies that the Boundary Commission were bound according to their terms of reference to work on the local government administrative lines pertaining in 1991. Subsequently there have been major reforms in local government throughout much of the country, but these could not be taken into account. For example, the county of Avon, unpopular since its creation in 1974, has now been abolished. But the Boundary Commission of 1995 calculated the number of seats to which it was entitled: ten, very nearly 11 (its electorate was 10.48 times the national quota/average in 1991) and drew their lines within the doomed county. Thus Northavon's now anachronistic name and its *raison d'être*.

Northavon was created in 1983, but it was very similar to the former South Gloucestershire division; indeed all of its constituent parts are included in the new unitary authority of South Gloucestershire. A perhaps surprising proportion of Northavon's electorate also live not in villages but in growing residential areas, although there are no large towns. Most prominent are Yate (1991 Census population 19,400), Thornbury (12,400), Winterbourne (9,100), Dodington (8,500), and Almondsbury (7,100). These are dominated by modern medium-cost private housing, and young families – the constituency's proportion of pensioners (13%) is reminiscent of 'New Town' demographics and is one of the lowest in Britain. Older-fashioned places include Chipping Sodbury and the famous country seat at Badminton. There is plenty of countryside in Northavon, but mostly it looks to Bristol as an economic and social magnet. This was the justification for its original inclusion in Avon, although many residents always preferred to think of themselves as identifying with traditional South Gloucestershire.

Webb has worked hard to build up a personal local following to hold this seat, and he has become a prominent frontbench spokesman in the Commons, all by the age of 35 in 2001, when these efforts were repaid as he was returned with a majority of nearly 10,000, one of his party's largest, though admittedly inflated by an above average turnout of 71% in a larger seat than the electoral quota. This means that boundary changes are in the offing, and Northavon will survive for only one more election before being subsumed in new seats called (not very pithily) Yate and Thornbury, and Filton and Bradley Stoke.

Social indices:			2001 Gen. Election:			
% Non-white	0.9		LD	29,217	52.4	+10.0
% Prof/Man	37.0		C	19,340	34.7	−4.3
% Non-manual	63.8		Lab	6,450	11.6	−4.1
£ Av prop val 2000	107 K		UKIP	751	1.3	
% Increase 97–00	46.9		LD maj	9,877	17.7	
% Unemployed 2001	1.0		Turnout		70.7	−8.5
% Decrease 97–01	1.0		Elect	78,841		
% Fin hard/Rank	4.4	619				
% Pensioners	19.0					
% Prem mort/Rank	3	630				

Member of Parliament

Steve Webb, surprisingly elected in 1997, and initially keen to be addressed by his recently-acquired Bath University professorial rank, is a social policy expert, notably on pensions, qualifying him for immediate appointment in 1997 as his party's Social Security spokesman, and in 2001 – under a new dispensation – 'Work and Pensions'. Rather exaggeratedly billed (by the *Evening Standard*) as making David Willetts 'look like a thicko', he was, as his voice betrays, Birmingham-born in 1965, attended Dartmouth High School, Birmingham and Hertford College, Oxford, and worked at the Institute for Fiscal Studies for nine years, and at Bath University for two. It was his Liberal Democrat-tabled amendment on lone parent benefit cuts that sparked Labour's first big backbench revolt in 1997. He backed Simon Hughes for leader in 1999, and lives a little dangerously for a Liberal Democrat MP with a hunting seat by voting for an outright ban and not his colleague Lembit Opik's 'Middle Way', but his urban voters more than match the Duke of Beaufort's distinctively-clad retinue.

NORWICH NORTH

For many years the city of Norwich was remarkably loyal to the Labour Party. Even in 1979, when the Conservatives won the General Election easily, Labour retained both Norwich parliamentary seats and won 39 of the 48 seats on the city council. Their grip on the Town Hall continued to be unassailable in the 1990s. There were two reasons for this strong showing. One is that Norwich has historically had a very high proportion of council housing: over 50% within the city council area in 1981, and still over 37% in 1991 after a decade of council house sales and purely private building. The other is that a considerable part of the owner-occupied middle-class Tory-voting districts of Norwich actually lies outside the city boundaries in other districts such as Broadland and South Norfolk. The electoral balance in Norwich North was dramatically altered in 1983 when about 30,000 voters from the northern suburbs came in to a newly-drawn division which was half inside the city and half outside.

From being the safest Labour seat in East Anglia, the base of Health Secretary David Ennals, it became a marginal, which the Tory Patrick Thompson won by nearly 6,000 in 1983 and by nigh-on 8,000 in 1987. These results, coming in years when the Conservatives won the general elections with overall majorities above a hundred seats, always flattered them. Not all of the suburban territory in Sprowston, Thorpe St Andrew and Hellesdon was affluent, even if it was mainly composed of private housing; and the wards within the city were strongly Labour: one can see the serried rows of council-constructed houses from Mousehold Heath, once the scene of Robert Ket's famous rebellion in 1549. Labour proved much more competitive in Norwich in 1992, securing a swing of over 7% in North, and reducing Thompson's majority to a razor-thin 266, in an general election which itself produced an uncomfortably narrow victory for John Major.

The two disparate halves of the constituency still battle it out for political victory around Mousehold Heath, but in 2001 as in 1997 the result was a very clear win for Labour's Ian Gibson. This only reflects Labour's national lead, though, and the result was not very different from that in England as a whole. If the Conservatives are to form a government again under the present electoral system (which they support), they will have to take Norwich North and places like it.

Social indices:			2001 Gen. Election:			
% Non-white	1.0		Lab	21,624	47.4	−2.3
% Prof/Man	25.7		C	15,761	34.6	+2.1
% Non-manual	52.7		LD	6,750	14.8	+2.2
£ Av prop val 2000	74 K		Grn	797	1.7	
% Increase 97–00	38.6		UKIP	471	1.0	
% Unemployed 2001	2.6		Ind	211	0.5	
% Decrease 97–01	2.3		Lab maj	5,863	12.9	
% Fin hard/Rank	16.8	319	Turnout		60.9	−15.0
% Pensioners	26.9		Elect	74,911		
% Prem mort/Rank	19	485				

Member of Parliament

Dr Ian Gibson, one of a score of Scots representing Labour in English seats in exchange for the four English north of the border, won here at his second attempt in 1997. With a high forehead assisted by substantial hair loss, fading good looks and an ironical air, a recycled ex-Trotskyist from the International Socialists/Socialist Workers' Party, he was born in 1938, educated at Dumfries Academy and at Edinburgh, Indiana and Washington Universities, and was a biologist at the University of East Anglia for 32 years. Entering the Commons at 58, a specialist in biotechnological research, and a spokesman on most things scientific, he takes a pragmatic line on various of the new orthodoxies, such as hostility to genetically modified organisms, and support for all-women shortlists, and has only rebelled selectively – on lone parent and disability benefit cuts. In 2001, as chairman of the Science and Technology Select Committee, he called on ministers to 'come clean' on whether their children had received the MMR vaccine.

NORWICH SOUTH

Through much of the medieval period Norwich was the second city of England. Since that time it has been overtaken by many others in population, but it remains an important provincial centre. The fine cathedral, many other churches, and town houses of the historic centre bear witness to its time as a wool-trading town and rich commercial metropolis. Norwich South contains the city centre, the cathedral close, and also the University of East Anglia on the south-western edge of Norwich. It used to be a classic marginal, swinging with the tide and won by whichever party won the general election as a whole, as it did in 1964, 1970 and 1974. Then in 1983 major boundary changes brought in wards from the former safe Labour Norwich North, which altered South's political character.

The redistribution couldn't save Labour's John Garrett in the Conservative landslide year of 1983, when Labour's manifesto was described (by one of their own prominent members, Gerald Kaufman) as 'the longest suicide note in history'. But Norwich did not turn its back on Labour so decisively – or permanently, perhaps – as so much of the rest of England, and Garrett was able to regain South narrowly in 1987, when it became Labour's only seat in East Anglia. In 1992 he increased his majority to over 6,000. In 1997 Charles Clarke took over with a standard (i.e. unprecedented) swing, and won by 14,000. South now looks like a safe seat in parliamentary terms, but increasingly an eye should be kept on the Liberal Democrats, who received easily the most votes in the 11 wards within the seat in the city council elections of 2000, 10% more than Labour, and won nine of them. They were still third in the 2001 General Election, but their candidate has now twice in succession increased their share. He is Andrew Aalders-Dunthorne, and there is a fair chance that if he should break through and win he will be the first in the alphabetical list of MPs.

Social indices:			2001 Gen. Election:			
% Non-white	1.9		Lab	19,367	45.5	−6.2
% Prof/Man	34.8		C	10,551	24.8	+1.1
% Non-manual	57.1		LD	9,640	22.6	+4.0
£ Av prop val 2000	80 K		Grn	1,434	3.4	+1.9
% Increase 97–00	43.8		LCA	620	1.5	−0.1
% Unemployed 2001	3.9		SA	507	1.2	
% Decrease 97–01	3.4		UKIP	473	1.1	
% Fin hard/Rank	25.9	191	Lab maj	8,816	20.7	
% Pensioners	28.9		Turnout		64.7	−7.8
% Prem mort/Rank	27	388	Elect	65,792		

Member of Parliament

Charles Clarke, reaching the Cabinet in 2001 as the first (with Patricia Hewitt) of the 1997 intake of MPs to do so, is an apparatchik (as ex-head of Neil Kinnock's office for 11 years, 1981–92), who was born into the mandarinate (as the son of Sir Richard Clarke, head of the Ministry of Technology in the Wilson years). Resistantly-bearded, and jug-handled-eared, he joined the government in 1998 as a Junior Minister at Education, moving to the Home Office in 1999. Born in 1950, and educated at Highgate and King's College, Cambridge, his Cabinet post as 'Minister Without Portfolio and Party Chair' offended traditionalists for whom the party chairmanship was not in the gift of Downing Street, but a rolling office filled annually by obscure but elected members of the NEC. (Who, for example remembers George Brinham of the woodworkers' union, who was chairman when Hugh Gaitskell made his 'fight, fight, and fight again' speech in 1960 and who was subsequently bludgeoned to death?) Not that Clarke is entirely orthodox, having criticised – if not voted against – lone parent benefit curbs in 1997, and admitted, as Party Chairman, that some aspects of the NHS were worse than when Labour came to power. Not one to finesse a point, he described Iain Duncan Smith's frontbench team as 'nutters'.

NOTTINGHAM EAST

Fewer than half of the 203,000 registered electors in the East Midlands city of Nottingham voted on 7 June 2001. Not only was this a shocking statistic in absolute terms, but the relative drop since 1997 was 16%, well above average, and the comparison with other large communities in the region such as Leicester, Northampton and Derby was also very unfavourable. Why did this disturbing development have such force – if that's the right word for abstentionism – in Nottingham? The middle-class residential areas are to be found outside the city boundaries in Gedling, Broxtowe and Rushcliffe, where the turnouts were above average and nearly 20% higher than within the city limits. In the first two of these there was a real chance of a change of hand, which has not been true of East, say, for nine years. But at least there have been Conservatives in Nottingham in recent memory, which is not true a few miles down the A52 in Derby South; yet the participation there was 56%, here over 10% less. Something of the mystery remains.

Of all the seats that Labour gained from the Tories at the 1992 General Election, none proved so easy as Nottingham East – at least in the sense that the winning margin there was the largest of all Labour gains in Britain. John Heppell ousted the Member since 1983, Michael Knowles, by the extremely wide margin of 7,680 votes. The seat had suffered from problems with candidates and the Nottinghamshire reaction against Labour associated with the miners strike in the 1980s, though, and that decade should be seen as an aberration. It has been safely Labour since 1992.

Nottingham East consists of a long strip of wards on the edge of the city. These neighbourhoods are of varying natures. In the southern half are to be found inner-city areas, with council estates and a considerable portion of Nottingham's large non-white (both Asian and Afro-Caribbean) communities. These are concentrated in the wards of Manvers, Forest, the site of the annual Goose Fair, Radford and St Ann's, a former near-slum which has been heavily and ambitiously redeveloped since the war. In the north the streets become hilly and tree-lined, near the border with the middle-class Tory suburb of Carlton in the Gedling constituency; here are wards such as Mapperley and Greenwood.

There may – and should – be more interest at the next general election in how healthy the democratic process is in Nottingham as measured by electoral participation, than actually in who wins the seat. It is the sort of prize that may turn to dust and ashes if the voters are not interested in the outcome.

Social indices:			2001 Gen. Election:			
% Non-white	15.7		Lab	17,530	59.0	–3.3
% Prof/Man	30.9		C	7,210	24.3	+0.8
% Non-manual	50.3		LD	3,874	13.0	+2.9
£ Av prop val 2000	52 K		SA	1,117	3.8	
% Increase 97–00	10.7		Lab maj	10,320	34.7	
% Unemployed 2001	6.9		Turnout		45.5	–15.1
% Decrease 97–01	5.2		Elect	65,339		
% Fin hard/Rank	38.5	61				
% Pensioners	24.7					
% Prem mort/Rank	49	49				

Member of Parliament

Bearded **John Heppell**, PPS to John Prescott 1998–2001 (and previously to Lord Richard, 1997–98) was promoted to the Whips Office in 2001. Despite his background as a fitter and workshop supervisor with British Railways, he appeared to have made little headway with his former boss on an 'integrated transport policy'. Elected here in 1992, Geordie-accented, he was born, son of a miner, in 1948, and educated at Rutherford Grammar School and Ashington Technical College, and was initially a fitter with the NCB. Selected for the seat as a local county councillor after a prolonged dispute involving rival Asian contenders, he backed Margaret Beckett for leader, not Tony Blair, in 1994, but became something of an on-message performer after 1997, not withstanding his backing for republicanism. One of the PLP's dwindled minority of 51 (12%) former manual workers, on behalf of his Asian constituents he backs calls for a Kashmir plebiscite, but no longer do his knuckles bear the inscriptions 'love' and 'hate'.

NOTTINGHAM NORTH

Nottingham is an industrial East Midlands city of some 260,000 people, whose economy was traditionally more than usually dominated by three major employers – Raleigh cycles, Player's cigarettes and Boots the Chemists. It is the home of two popular universities, some excellent breweries, and in general it is characterised by good value and a relatively low cost of living. It has a substantial non-white minority, consisting of both Asian and Afro-Caribbean communities, and most of the middle-class suburban residential areas are defined in constituencies other than the three bearing the name of the city – a recipe for good Labour ground.

North-west Nottingham is undoubtedly the most working-class and strongly Labour part of the city. In this North constituency are to be found the large peripheral council estates, in Strelley, Aspley and Bilborough wards, and also the old working-class community of Bulwell, where Kenneth Clarke's family originated. Despite everything – the large council-estate majority, the fact that 70% of the electorate still worked in manual working-class jobs, the long Labour tradition, the presence of an incumbent MP of nearly 25 years' service, William Whitlock – the Tories won the redrawn Nottingham North on its inaugural contest in 1983. It was just about Labour's worst and most surprising result of that miserable election. Labour's Graham Allen regained Nottingham North in 1987, although only by 1,665 votes; this was the year when most Nottinghamshire results were affected by the miners' strike of 1984–85.

As in the case of other seats in the city and county, Labour has benefited from a large positive swing in North since then, but the turnout has plummeted from 75% in 1992 to 47% in 2001, one of the greatest drops in the country. This cannot be simply due to the end of its brief marginal status in the elections of the 1980s, or pacific contentment with the demi-paradise created in north Nottingham by Blairite New Labour, but rather a deep-seated malaise whereby more working-class, younger, and council tenant voters do not connect with the electoral apparatus that so fascinate some of us. It might also be noted that according to recent UCAS figures, there were fewer students entering university from home addresses in this constituency than any other in England, just 115 in 1998 – this contrasts with the highest number in that year, 940 in Harrow East. Very few natives enjoy at any time in their lives the pleasures and advantages of higher education, even in a city known for its attractions of the student world.

Social indices:			2001 Gen. Election:			
% Non-white	5.1		Lab	19,392	64.5	−1.2
% Prof/Man	17.4		C	7,152	23.8	+3.5
% Non-manual	38.9		LD	3,177	10.6	+2.6
£ Av prop val 2000	46 K		SLP	321	1.1	
% Increase 97–00	19.2		Lab maj	12,240	40.7	
% Unemployed 2001	5.6		Turnout		46.7	−16.3
% Decrease 97–01	3.7		Elect	64,281		
% Fin hard/Rank	43.9	31				
% Pensioners	27.2					
% Prem mort/Rank	45	97				

Member of Parliament

Graham Allen, elected here in 1992, one of the tallest MPs, and one of a number of de-moustachioed Labour ones (in Blairite facially-correct mode), was No.4 in the Whips' office until dropped after the 2001 Election. Suited, as the owner of a rather flat Nottingham-accented brogue, to the silence of the Whips' Office, his origins were as a party staffer, previously at Labour's headquarters or at the GLC. Born in 1953 and educated at Forest Fields Grammar School, Nottingham, City of London Polytechnic and Leeds University, he came originally with a taste for institutional tinkering in the direction of the 'separation of powers', as a Whip settled for their more realistic 'fusion', but after being dropped in 2001 reverted to his earlier interest in recognising what he now termed Blair's 'presidential power' by formally adopting a US-style constitution. He disliked the bulldozing through Parliament of the Terrorism, Crime and Security Bill of November 2001.

NOTTINGHAM SOUTH

Nottingham South consists of at least three very different neighbourhoods. The first is based on the city centre. This includes the industrial and working-class Meadows area between the hilly 'downtown' and the River Trent, the heavily non-white Lenton ward near the old Raleigh cycle factory, and, anomalously, the old west end of the city, the Park estate, which is spaciously laid out in crescents and 'circuses', and is still almost all white, even though Caribbeans and Asians dominate the terraces on the other side of the Derby Road. Even Park ward is Labour though, as it includes most of the city centre as well as the classy old estate.

The Conservative vote in the Nottingham South constituency is to be found on the city's western edge, around the rolling green campus of the University of Nottingham. Here are the mansions of Wollaton, Nottingham's most favoured residential area, and Abbey and Robin Hood wards. The Nottingham West division was abolished back in 1983, leaving its MP Michael English without a seat.

The third element of the seat really is southern, on the other side of the Trent. The largest element here is provided by the massive post-war peripheral council estate of Clifton. There has been much buying of council houses by their occupiers in Nottingham in the last ten or 15 years, and less than half of the property in Clifton is still local-authority owned; but the estate remains safely Labour in local elections at least.

Nottingham South is essentially a Labour seat, but it was held by the Conservatives until 1992. This was basically because of Labour's poor showing at both national and regional level in 1983 and 1987; in 1992 Alan Simpson managed to claim Labour's inheritance in South, ousting Martin Brandon-Bravo by over 3,000 votes with a 5% swing. Labour won all seats in Nottinghamshire but one (Rushcliffe) in 1997, with an average increase in vote share of 10%. The improvement in South was lower than that, and this is still distinctly the least strong of what are three safe Labour seats in Nottingham.

Social indices:

% Non-white	11.9				
% Prof/Man	32.0				
% Non-manual	52.5				
£ Av prop val 2000	80 K				
% Increase 97–00	37.4				
% Unemployed 2001	4.8				
% Decrease 97–01	3.1				
% Fin hard/Rank	28.0	158			
% Pensioners	27.3				
% Prem mort/Rank	41	157			

2001 Gen. Election:

Lab	19,949	54.5	–0.8
C	9,960	27.2	–0.5
LD	6,064	16.6	+3.7
UKIP	632	1.7	
Lab maj	9,989	27.3	
Turnout		50.1	–16.9
Elect	73,049		

Member of Parliament

Alan Simpson, MP here since 1992, is one of the hardest left-wing critics of the Blair government, as the fourth most dissenting MP in the 1997 to 2001 Parliament (with 38 rebellious votes), having previously been the eighth most rebellious backbencher in Opposition between 1992 and 1997. Merseyside-born in 1948 and educated at Bootle Grammar School and Nottingham Polytechnic, he worked in the voluntary sector in Nottingham, eventually in racial equality, and was a local county councillor for eight years. A leading member of the Campaign Group, he is a man for all rebellions, from 1997 on lone parent benefit cuts, university tuition fees, military action against Iraq, the bombing of Kosovo, Incapacity Benefit cuts, legal aid cuts, jury trial curbs, pensions linked to earnings, freedom of information, privatising of air traffic control, and – after the 2001 Election – the bombing of Afghanistan and the anti-terrorism measures. An intense, sardonic, vegetarian footballer, who favours alternative and complementary medicine and home energy conservation, and is hostile to GM crops, he predicts that international capitalism will provoke mass migration and war, and has correspondingly low expectations of ministerial advancement, it being anyway axiomatic that a ministerially ambitious member of the Campaign Group is an oxymoron.

NUNEATON

In the 1992 General Election Labour gained Nuneaton from the Conservatives. At first sight this might be construed as a considerable achievement, as a swing of 6.5% was registered, larger than the national or regional average for all constituencies and much larger than average for targeted marginals. Yet in fact this was largely a result of a return to Nuneaton's traditional political loyalties. The question was more one of how Labour had ever managed to lose the seat in the first place. A little history may be in order here.

Nuneaton is essentially a working-class and industrial town, an important railway centre and the metropolis for the old Warwickshire coalfield. It was for many decades a Labour stronghold. Before 1983 the Conservatives had last won it in 1931, when they won the vast majority of the seats in the country, and then only by 2,000 votes. When the Boundary Commission announced plans to remove the town of Bedworth and replace it with three rural wards, the left-wing MP Les Huckfield decided to seek nomination for a safe seat at Wigan. Some felt that it was inappropriate for a captain to abandon a sinking ship in this manner.

Huckfield failed to be adopted for Wigan in the end, but it would have done him no good to stay at Nuneaton (except that it might have salvaged his reputation) for his old seat was submerged beneath the true-blue Tory flood in Labour's disastrous year of 1983 – indeed they almost fell to third behind the SDP. In 1987 Stevens's majority increased a little as both Conservatives and Labour benefited from a steep decline in Alliance support. The centre vote fell by another 8% in 1992 and all of it, and more, went to Labour's candidate Bill Olner as the party re-established control over the representation of Nuneaton. There was a typical national swing against the Conservative government in 1997, but in 2001 Olner's majority was halved by a small swing to the Tories and a larger swing to abstentions.

The town has consistently voted in Labour-controlled councils, though, and most of its wards are safe for that party: the old terraced central wards of Abbey and Chilvers Coton with a significant Asian minority; the council estates at Attleborough and Stockingford; and Camp Hill near the slagheaps of old mineworkings. The Tories can on occasion win wards in affluent north-east Nuneaton (St Nicholas and Weddington) and in Whitestone to the east of the town, and they have chances too in the three rural wards of Wolvey, Fosse and Earl Craven. But it is reasonable to expect them to be outvoted in any but an abnormally bad year for Labour, and it may well come to be seen that the Thatcherite elections of the 1980s were a historical aberration, in Nuneaton at least.

Social indices:			2001 Gen. Election:			
% Non-white	3.5		Lab	22,577	52.1	−4.1
% Prof/Man	28.5		C	15,042	34.7	+3.8
% Non-manual	49.3		LD	4,820	11.1	+2.3
£ Av prop val 2000	67 K		UKIP	873	2.0	+1.6
% Increase 97–00	27.3		Lab maj	7,535	17.4	
% Unemployed 2001	2.0		Turnout		60.1	−14.2
% Decrease 97–01	1.8		Elect	72,101		
% Fin hard/Rank	21.0	255				
% Pensioners	22.6					
% Prem mort/Rank	28	379				

Member of Parliament

Bill Olner, one of the dwindling band of Labour proletarians, was elected here in 1992 after 35 years as a machinist at Rolls Royce in Coventry. Born locally in 1942 and educated at Atherstone Secondary Modern and North Warwickshire Technical College, he sat on Nuneaton Council for 21 years and ran it for five, and is predictably locally-focused. A Commons doughnutter in Opposition, seated behind Tony Blair at question time so as to be in the TV frame despite efforts by the Whips to replace him by more photogenic women, he has post-1997 been displaced anyway by the hordes of ministerial parliamentary private secretaries. He has retreated to the dignified obscurity of the Chairmen's Panel.

OCHIL

The Ochil hills straddle the border between Scotland's former Central and Tayside regions (artificial creations which have now been abolished in local government reorganisation north of the border). They reach their highest peak at Ben Cleuch (2,364 feet); though hardly lofty by the standards of the Highlands, they still form an impressive backdrop to the local landscape here between the rivers Forth and Tay. Despite being named after a range of rural hills, Ochil is not a Conservative constituency.

In the 1999 Scottish Parliament elections Labour won in Ochil, but only by 3% from the Scottish Nationalists, who had a long and strong tradition in this area and felt that they could go one better in the Westminster general election two years later. The Scottish Nationalists won the former Clackmannan and East Stirlingshire when the broadcaster and journalist George Reid defeated Dick Douglas in February 1974, to register one of their seven victories. In October of the same year Reid increased his majority to over 7,000, but this proved the high-water mark of SNP success in the 1970s. In 1979 Martin O'Neill regained the seat for Labour, and he won the somewhat modified Clackmannan division easily enough thereafter.

Ochil's main component is the district and old county of Clackmannan, an industrial and working-class part of central Scotland, its small towns (Alva, Tillicoultry, Alloa, Dollar) in the main dominated by council housing and shaped by a history of coal-mining, now long gone. It no longer contains any electors from the East Stirlingshire area, having donated several thousand around Carron and parts of Stenhousemuir to the two Falkirk seats, both of which were a little small. However, Clackmannan was smaller still, and Ochil spreads both some miles to the east to take in the little town of Kinross by Loch Leven, formerly in the rural and Conservative seat of Perth and Kinross, and also to the west to take in the Airthrey electoral division formerly in Stirling.

George Reid, the former Clackmannan/East Stirlings MP, fought Ochil against Martin O'Neill in its first contest in 1997, and obtained the SNP's second best result against Labour in industrial Scotland (after Glasgow Govan), increasing their share of the vote (from 1992 notional figures) by 8% and losing by less than 5,000. After the 1999 close shave, O'Neill was under genuine pressure in 2001, but he held his share almost exactly while the Nationalists slipped a little and failed to close the gap at all. Especially given forthcoming boundary changes linking it with Strathearn from their Perth seat, Ochil is still one of the SNP's best hopes should Labour's popularity slip in central Scotland, but it remains to be seen whether their energies will permanently be diverted towards Edinburgh.

Social indices:			2001 Gen. Election:			
% Non-white	0.9		Lab	16,004	45.3	+0.3
% Prof/Man	30.0		SNP	10,655	30.2	−4.2
% Non-manual	50.4		C	4,235	12.0	−2.6
% Unemployed 2001	3.7		LD	3,253	9.2	+4.0
% Decrease 97–01	2.0		SSP	751	2.1	
% Fin hard/Rank	29.9	131	MRLP	405	1.1	
% Prem mort/Rank	41	170	Lab maj	5,349	15.2	
			Turnout		61.3	−16.1
			Elect	57,554		

Member of Parliament

Martin O'Neill, one of the generation of ambitious MPs for whom victory came too late in 1997, Labour's most senior backbench Scottish MP, as chairman of the Trade and Industry Select Committee, was dropped as a frontbencher in 1995 on grounds of age. Burly and affable, he was born in 1945 and educated at Trinity Academy, Edinburgh and, after five years as an insurance office clerk, attended Heriot-Watt University and became a teacher. His time came in the Kinnock years as the Defence spokesman who braved the minefield involved in coaxing Labour away from unilateralism, and masking his disappointment at not being a minister, has proved a hands-on loyalist, managing to deflect blame for major industrial closures of car plants and steelworks away from ministers.

OGMORE

Ogmore-by-Sea is a small resort on the soft Glamorgan coast near Porthcawl. However, Ogmore is in fact a mining valley seat, named after Ogmore Vale and Ogmore Forest between Maesteg and Pontypridd. It does not reach the Bristol Channel, at Ogmore-by-Sea or anywhere else. Rather it is resolutely industrial, set in the hills which once were coal-rich. It contains famous names from the history of South Wales, such as Maesteg; the dramatic terraces clinging to the sides of the blind Garw valley such as Pontycymmer and Blaengarw at the head of the valley, with its amazing cricket ground carved out of the mountainside by unemployed miners; and Price Town in the Ogmore valley, just over the top from the Rhondda.

Ogmore went into the 2001 General Election as one of Labour's dozen safest seats. They obtained 74% of the vote in 1997, with a majority of over 24,000. Most outside observers expected the veteran MP Sir Ray Powell to retire, as indeed they had four years before, perhaps to give way to a much younger candidate more wedded to the New Labour establishment, but once again he was determined to stay on in the Commons. His result was relatively poor, losing 12% of that huge share, while all three of the other parties competing improved, all moving up from single figures to double: a unique result, if one which does not of course in any way threaten Labour's iron grip on the constituency – it merely slipped down the list of safety to 46th. This position was disrupted in February 2002 by the by-election which had been caused by the death of 73-year-old Sir Ray Powell in early December 2001: after a further drop in the Labour share of 20%, Ogmore was temporarily placed at number 166.

There is no effective opposition, in general elections at least. This is by most measures the most working-class constituency in Wales. The percentage of professional, managerial and technical workers is the lowest in the principality, lower even than Rhondda or Blaenau Gwent. Combined with the tradition of Labour support in the South Wales valleys, which is a hundred years old, this makes Ogmore's result a foregone conclusion. The communities are traditional and close-knit: this seat has the lowest proportion of households made up of one person living alone of any in Wales (which itself has a lower average than Great Britain as a whole). The proportion of single-parent families is no higher than average. This is the kind of constituency where any kind of deviancy is discouraged. One such example of deviant behaviour would be to vote other than for the Labour Party in a general election.

Social indices:			2001 Gen. Election:			
% Non-white	0.5		Lab	18,833	62.0	−11.9
% Welsh sp	8.4		PC	4,259	14.0	+7.0
% Prof/Man	20.1		LD	3,878	12.8	+3.6
% Non-manual	38.2		C	3,383	11.1	+1.4
£ Av prop val 2000	47 K		Lab maj	14,574	48.0	
% Increase 97–00	12.6		Turnout		58.2	−14.9
% Unemployed 2001	3.7		Elect.	52,185		
% Decrease 97–01	1.7					
% Fin hard/Rank	28.0	159	14 February 2002 by-election:			
% Pensioners	24.0		Lab	9,548	52.0	−10.0
% Prem mort/Rank	40	171	PC	3,827	20.8	+6.8
			LD	1,608	8.8	−4.0
			C	1,377	7.5	−3.6
			Soc Lab	1,152	6.3	+6.3
			Oths	864	4.7	+4.7
			Lab maj	5,721	31.2	
			Turnout		35.2	−23.0
			Elect.	52,209		

Member of Parliament

Huw Irranca-Davies held the seat for Labour at the by-election in February 2002. His hyphenated name incorporating his wife's Sardinian surname, he is in fact the nephew of the late Ifor Davies, Labour MP for Gower from 1959 to 1982. Gowerton-born in 1963 and educated at Gowerton Comprehensive before attending Crewe and Alsager College of Education, in 2001 he fought the Brecon and Radnorshire seat whose Labour vote is clustered nearby at Ystradgynlais at the head of the Swansea valley. A business studies lecturer at the Swansea Institute of Higher Education, he was billed in the by-election as a 'lecturer in tourism' – not inappropriately given the conversion of the ex-mining valleys of Glamorgan into industrial archaeological theme parks. A clean-cut and personable member of the New Labour orthodoxy, he arrived in Ogmore by way of a sanitised Millbank shortlist which excluded left-wing *Tribune* editor Mark Seddon, but received campaign support from the left-wing icon Dennis Skinner in a successful bid to close down a

Welsh Nationalist challenge seeking to fan protest over uncompensated miners, and steelworkers' alleged resentment of Tony Blair's backing for an Indian tycoon's purchase of the Romanian steel industry.

OLD BEXLEY AND SIDCUP

The area covered by the constituency of Old Bexley and Sidcup was represented for over 51 years from 1950 to 2001 by a man who became the Father of the House of Commons (that is, the member with the longest continuous service), the former Conservative Party leader and Prime Minister Sir Edward Heath. From 1950 to February 1974 his seat was called Bexley, and from then until 1983 he represented Sidcup. In the 1983 boundary changes the constituency was unchanged but renamed Old Bexley and Sidcup. In the 1995 report from the Boundary Commission the name was not altered but the seat was considerably expanded.

This section of outer south-east London has the highest proportion of owner-occupiers anywhere in the capital, and almost the highest throughout the United Kingdom. It also has almost the lowest number of non-white residents. This is deeply suburban Kentish London, a far cry from the cosmopolitan central city.

After 14 terms in Parliament, Sir Edward finally retired a month short of his 85th birthday, and for a while it looked as if his seat would have to be regarded as a genuine two-party marginal, and no certain inheritance at all for Derek Conway, chosen as his replacement as Tory candidate. This was not because of some huge personal vote built up over all those decades – indeed the eventual result found no trace of any such thing – but rather the opinion polls which suggested that further increased favour for Labour, especially in Greater London, would bring this constituency within their range. After all, Sir Edward himself had only held on by 3,569 in 1997. In fact, the polls were inaccurate predictors, and there was no overall swing to Labour in London, or in Old Bexley and Sidcup. Derek Conway probably has little to fear from other parties, but it is fairly safe to say he will not represent this area as long as his predecessor. If he were to, he would go on until he's 99 years old.

Social indices:			2001 Gen. Election:			
% Non-white	4.0		C	19,130	45.4	+3.4
% Prof/Man	34.0		Lab	15,785	37.5	+2.4
% Non-manual	67.5		LD	5,792	13.7	−2.4
£ Av prop val 2000	130 K		UKIP	1,426	3.4	+2.4
% Increase 97–00	51.6		C maj	3,345	7.9	
% Unemployed 2001	1.3		Turnout		62.1	−13.4
% Decrease 97–01	2.3		Elect	67,841		
% Fin hard/Rank	6.7	568				
% Pensioners	25.3					
% Prem mort/Rank	9	601				

Member of Parliament

In 2001 Sir Edward Heath's successor here was **Derek Conway**, MP for Shrewsbury for 14 years until unexpectedly losing in 1997, and one of a score of Conservative casualties of that year who sought their way back in 2001. Like Ted Heath a meritocrat of humble origins, he was born in Newcastle on Tyne in 1953, raised on a council estate, and educated at secondary modern school, technical college and polytechnic. He fought his way up via politics, contesting his first parliamentary seat (Durham) aged 21 in 1974, and then led the Tories on Tyne and Wear County Council. A Eurosceptic-turned-Whip under John Major, he was active in the TA and worked variously for charities, ranging from Action Research for the Crippled Child to the Cat Protection League, of which he became chief executive in 1998. Though he rebelled under Margaret Thatcher against signing the Single European Act in 1985, and initially backed Eurosceptic David Davis for leader in 2001, he was one of only four of the 33-strong Tory intake of 2001 to vote for Kenneth Clarke with whose Europhile views he disagreed but whom he thought the party would be mad not to elect.

OLDHAM EAST AND SADDLEWORTH

There could scarcely have been a more competitive, multi-sided, passionate, even vitriolic campaign and contest anywhere in Britain in May-June 2001 than in Oldham East and Saddleworth. Not only was this seat a rare three-way marginal which had been held by Conservatives, Liberal Democrats and Labour, all in the previous six years, but it was the seat most afflicted with a highly publicised bout of inter-racial violence, actually in the month running up to the general election. This was either caused, or exploited (or both) according to the deeply polarised assessments, by the activity of the British National Party, who despite the major party battle for honours here received over 5,000 votes, 11% of the total.

The riots were centred on Glodwick, in the inner south-east of Oldham, and its neighbouring all-white residential areas such as the council estate at Fitton Hill. Among the rival claims were those of 'no-go areas' for white people in the former and Asians in the latter. Although not entirely true, this reflected a genuine hostility and conflict which had been building up for some years, and which shocked local communities and the nation, through widespread and in part sensationalist press coverage, peaking in May 2001.

The resentments of predominantly white working-class residents, blaming Asians for perceived preferential treatment, produced a wave of support for the racist far right party unprecedented in general elections. It was paralleled in Oldham West and in Burnley, but initially these seats received less attention not only because they had not been the epicentre of rioting before the election, but also because they were not marginal seats. This one most certainly is. On the death of Conservative MP Geoffrey Dickens in 1995, it was taken by the Liberal Democrats' Chris Davies, with the Tories falling back to third. Then in 1997 Labour's candidate in the by-election, Phil Woolas, an ardent supporter of the current leadership, moved up to take the seat, and in the smoke and sound of election night many missed that he had only held on by under 3,000 votes with a share of just 38%. This seat remains a multi-sided battle, well worth keeping an eye on for a number of reasons, not all due to the health of democracy locally.

Not all of this seat is affected by riots, or indeed within the town of Oldham itself. The three wards within Oldham have quite a different history and tradition from the bulk of the seat. Two of them, St James and St Mary's, have voted Labour by overwhelming margins, though for different reasons. St James is strongly influenced by council estates, and is almost all white. St Mary's on the other hand is over 30% non-white, includes part of the Glodwick community, and counts as part of Oldham's inner-city belt of deprived and decayed housing.

The remainder includes Saddleworth, a composite name for a number of village communities like Delph, Diggle, Dobcross and Uppermill, now much favoured by commuters and well-off residents who enjoy the flavour of the country life in the hills. Crompton, Milnrow and Lees are also small 'Lancashire' towns which are willing to elect Liberal Democrat councillors.

That the BNP received 11% when the troubles were concentrated in just about 30% of the seat suggests that within Oldham itself they must have polled considerably more than 11%, perhaps a quarter of all votes cast; and who knows how many electors were so disaffected as not to vote at all? Even in so high-profile a contest, with such a variety of options, nearly 40% abstained. It's all very disturbed, and disturbing.

Social indices:			2001 Gen. Election:			
% Non-white	5.2		Lab	17,537	38.6	–3.1
% Prof/Man	31.7		LD	14,811	32.6	–2.8
% Non-manual	53.3		C	7,304	16.1	–3.6
£ Av prop val 2000	58 K		BNP	5,091	11.2	
% Increase 97–00	20.4		UKIP	677	1.5	
% Unemployed 2001	3.0		Lab maj	2,726	6.0	
% Decrease 97–01	1.1		Turnout		61.0	–13.0
% Fin hard/Rank	24.4	206	Elect	74,511		
% Pensioners	23.2					
% Prem mort/Rank	43	129				

Member of Parliament

Phil Woolas, who reached the frontbench as an Assistant Whip in 2001, was elected here for Labour in 1997 after failing to take the precursor seat in a dirty Mandelson-run by-election campaign in 1995, which saw the victory of a Liberal Democrat candidate smeared by Labour as soft on drugs and higher taxes. An ex-GMBU Communications Director (1991–97) and TV producer, born in 1959 and educated at Nelson Grammar School and Manchester University, with ambition-driven flexibility he has endorsed sundry orthodoxies and currently has a personal interest in resisting any national Lib-Labbery. Once pro-Troops Out, he now votes against attempts to change the Oath to enable the Sinn Fein MPs to take their seats. A consummate political animal, former PPS to Lord (Gus) Macdonald (1999–2001), he is one of a clutch of ex-NUS Presidents all risen or rising on Labour's benches – Jack Straw, Charles Clarke, Jim Murphy, Lorna Fitzsimmons. He urges faster integration of the Muslim community with the white population to curb local racism.

OLDHAM WEST AND ROYTON

The far right have historically proved electoral failures in Britain. The destruction of the Weimar Republic in Germany in the early 1930s was accompanied and ensured by the success of the Nazi Party, which obtained over 40% of the popular vote, and also of the Communists. In both France and Italy since the Second World War neo-fascists have returned substantial blocs of national assembly members. Yet in this country no overtly racist or fascist group has ever returned an MP, no more than a handful of local councillors, and usually the fate has been one of lost deposits, disorganisation, division, and essentially a failure to connect with the aims or views of any significant section of any community. In 2001, however, the British National Party, with a clear racist platform, saved five deposits in England and obtained over 10% in three seats. It did best of all in Oldham West and Royton, where its national leader Nick Griffin took 16%, one-sixth of the votes cast – and beat the Liberal Democrats into third place. He, like his almost equally successful colleague in Oldham East and Saddleworth, took the platform for the count wearing a gag as a result of the returning officer's bar on inflammatory speeches, but he had most certainly made a strong point of a kind.

This constituency covers an area harbouring very divided communities, with distressingly little mutual understanding or sympathy.

There is a large Asian population in the inner city, mostly Muslim and including one of the largest Bangladeshi communities in the North. Much of the heart of Oldham is beset with serious problems sustained by poverty. Coldhurst ward, which covers most of the town centre, is 37% non-white, and most of the white residents live in bleak council developments. Werneth was once the grand west end of Oldham, but its large mansions are decayed or demolished, and it too is heavily Asian. The town's prosperity was based on huge textile mills, almost all gone or converted, although some of the most dramatic scenery of the Lancashire cotton age can still be glimpsed as one sweeps down from the Pennines on the M62. William Cobbett was MP at one time, in 1832 when cotton was king. The vacuum left by that industry has not been entirely filled, and the unemployment rate is higher than average, though not dramatically so. There are owner-occupied and lower-middle-class areas too, particularly in south Royton and east Chadderton, but the Conservative vote declined by almost as much as Labour's did in 2001 and they were very nearly beaten for second by the BNP. With turnout sinking to 57% as well, the political picture here reflects a long-term reality of deep disharmony, needing only a catalyst to spark conflagration. It is not adequate to blame outside agitators. The problems, and solutions, lie with the communities of the borough of Oldham.

Social indices:			2001 Gen. Election:			
% Non-white	13.7		Lab	20,441	51.2	–7.6
% Prof/Man	25.3		C	7,076	17.7	–5.7
% Non-manual	47.0		BNP	6,552	16.4	
£ Av prop val 2000	45 K		LD	4,975	12.4	+0.6
% Increase 97–00	10.2		Grn	918	2.3	
% Unemployed 2001	4.4		Lab maj	13,365	33.4	
% Decrease 97–01	0.9		Turnout		57.6	–8.5
% Fin hard/Rank	33.7	103	Elect	69,409		
% Pensioners	25.8					
% Prem mort/Rank	44	107				

Member of Parliament

Michael Meacher, Environment Minister since 1997, elected originally for an Oldham seat in 1970, was, after the 2001 Election, with his DEFRA boss Margaret Beckett, one of only two ministerial survivors of the pre-1979 Callaghan government. Originally a hard left-winger who ran for the Labour Deputy Leadership against Roy Hattersley in 1983 as Tony Benn's Vicar on Earth, he was born in 1939, educated at Berkhamsted School, New College, Oxford and the LSE, and lectured in social administration at York University. Included in 1997 in the government, but not of Cabinet rank, as a constantly elected member of the Shadow Cabinet, he had backed Prescott, not Blair, in 1994. Cerebral, earnest and humourless, his career has been dogged by accusations of pretentiousness in exaggerating his father's humble origins, and of affluence, as in exposés of the number of his properties. Although he started rowing back from the Bennite left as long ago as 1984 when he opposed Scargill's unballoted miners' strike, not even the advocacy of Lord Hattersley has secured him a Cabinet post.

ORKNEY AND SHETLAND

The Highlands and Islands of northern Scotland demonstrate some of the most unusual and independent political preferences in the UK. This takes a multiplicity of forms. Before the 1983 General Election, the four northernmost constituencies in Britain had MPs of four different parties; this has been modified by defections and mergers since, but the seats remain individual in the extreme, and politics truly local. The Orkney and Shetland division is most definitely one of a kind.

For a start, its independence from Scotland should be stressed. In 1987 the SNP left this seat alone uncontested, and the Orkney and Shetland Movement candidate, John Goodlad (General Secretary of the Shetland Fishermen's Association), collected over 14% of the vote – by far the best showing until 2001 by anyone outside the 'main' parties in that election. The OSM did not run again in 1992, and the SNP has reappeared, but they could not match its 1987 showing. Some think that if Scotland ever became independent, Orkney and Shetland would secede from Scotland! It might be borne in mind how remote these chains of islands are. The capital of Shetland, Lerwick, is 204 miles north of Aberdeen – and just 234 miles west of Bergen in Norway. Shetland remained in Norwegian hands until the fifteenth century.

The party which has become utterly associated with Orkney and Shetland has now won 15 general elections in a row there, by far their best run in the UK. For ten of those the Liberal candidate was Jo Grimond, leader of his party from 1956 to 1967 and much responsible for modernising the image of the Liberals and revivifying the party after their darkest period just after the Second World War. No other party could approach Grimond's vote, but when he announced his retirement in 1983 it remained to be seen whether his support could be transferred to another Liberal, or whether it was largely personal. The success first of Jim Wallace (who gave this seat up in 2001 to concentrate full time on the Scottish parliament, where he is Lib Dem leader and Deputy First Minister in the ruling coalition) and now of Alistair Carmichael, has shown that Liberalism can convincingly survive a popular and senior MP's departure. It is true that Carmichael's share in 2001 was 10% less than Wallace's in 1997, but no single other party has more than 20% of the vote share, and it is hard to see exactly where a challenge might come from (apart perhaps from an Orkney and Shetland movement, not heard from in 15 years).

Orkney and Shetland's electoral politics have remained stable through times of great change. There was a population boom in the 1970s due to the development of the North Sea oil industry, including the Sullom Voe terminal in Shetland and Flotta in Orkney (opened in 1977). Although the numbers have now stabilised, and there are still only 32,000 electors, there is no practical chance that the Boundary Commission would extend this seat's boundaries. Apart from its great physical size, and poor internal communications, it would be impossible to claim that any territory on the mainland shared common ties and interests. It is likely that this most distant of all constituencies will continue to send a Liberal Democrat all the way to Westminster.

Social indices:			2001 Gen. Election:			
% Non-white	0.5		LD	6,919	41.3	−10.6
% Prof/Man	30.3		Lab	3,444	20.6	+2.3
% Non-manual	47.4		C	3,121	18.7	+6.4
% Unemployed 2001	2.0		SNP	2,473	14.8	+2.1
% Decrease 97–01	1.3		SSP	776	4.6	
% Fin hard/Rank	9.1	488	LD maj	3,475	20.8	
% Prem mort/Rank	31	318	Turnout		52.4	−11.6
			Elect	31,909		

Member of Parliament

Alistair Carmichael followed the Scottish deputy Prime Minister Jim Wallace as the Liberal Democrat's MP for this 50-year long stronghold – the only Liberal seat which has been successfully transferred twice to new incumbents since the war (Grimond–Wallace–Carmichael). A chubby-faced, bucolic-looking solicitor, born in 1965 and educated at Islay High School and Aberdeen University, he fits well this traditional rural, small-town and island seat, as an island hill farmer's son, married to a vet and who, as a solicitor and former deputy procurator fiscal, can more than reassure on the law and order flank. Also a Kirk elder, he departed from his classic Liberal Democrat MP's defence of constituency interests only to deliver a pro-Arab-sounding party conference speech in 2001 after the terrorist attacks in New York.

ORPINGTON

In March 1962 a new political phenomenon emerged: 'Orpington man', the symbol of the rebellion of traditional Tory voters against the government of Harold Macmillan (whose own seat of Bromley was right next to Orpington). The Liberal Eric Lubbock beat the Conservatives' Peter Goldman after a massive swing. This type of by-election outcome has since become familiar – indeed, in recent years, the norm. At the time, though, it rocked the political landscape, and contributed to the downfall of Macmillan himself the next year. Orpington is one of the most famous landmarks in electoral history.

Lubbock held on through two by-elections before he was defeated by the Conservative right-winger Ivor Stanbrook in 1970, and although the Liberal Democrats reduced the Tory majority to under 3,000 in 1997, at least they held the seat, which is more than they did in half of those they were defending.

Orpington man (and woman, of course) may have been sleeping for the past 40 years but he or she have not passed on and away. In 2001 the Liberal Democrats very nearly took the seat, as Chris Maines, Bromley borough councillor for Orpington Central ward, cut Horam's majority to 269, his party's nearest miss of a gain (Taunton was lost to the Tories by a smaller margin). This photo-finish had been foreshadowed by the local elections of May 1998, when the Lib Dems were just ahead of the Conservatives and won 12 seats within the constituency to the Conservatives' six. Given that Labour won three too, in St Mary Cray and St Paul's Cray, and that their vote was squeezed from 17% in 1997 to 11% in 2001, Horam can count himself lucky to have survived to continue his long and multi-faceted career in the Commons, for one more term at least.

The Orpington constituency is situated on the very fringes of rural Kent. It now includes more rural wards, Biggin Hill (the site of a famous Battle of Britain aerodrome controversially proposed as a private airfield for business users) and Darwin; Orpington now covers more than half of the acreage of the giant borough of Bromley. This is one of the few places within the Greater London boundaries where farming takes place and open country can be seen. As a whole though, the seat is not rural but suburban, and maybe a mirror in outer south-east London of the Liberal Democrat success in the outer south-west sector of the metropolis. This is a dark reflection on the Tories' continued chances here.

Social indices:			2001 Gen. Election:			
% Non-white	2.7		C	22,334	43.9	+3.3
% Prof/Man	38.4		LD	22,065	43.3	+7.7
% Non-manual	69.5		Lab	5,517	10.8	−7.0
£ Av prop val 2000	162 K		UKIP	996	2.0	+1.1
% Increase 97–00	50.3		C maj	269	0.5	
% Unemployed 2001	1.6		Turnout		68.4	−8.0
% Decrease 97–01	1.4		Elect	74,423		
% Fin hard/Rank	7.7	533				
% Pensioners	25.2					
% Prem mort/Rank	13	561				

Member of Parliament

John Horam, a man-for-all-parties, was elected here for the Conservatives in 1992, having earlier been Labour, then SDP, MP for Gateshead West (1970–83). After the 2001 Election he was the only survivor of the Gadarene rush of some 30 Labour MPs into the SDP in 1981, and the only one to engineer survival as a Tory. Owner of an economics consultancy, he was born in 1939 and educated at Silcoates School, Wakefield and at St Catherine's College, Cambridge. Dubbed 'a dirty double rat' by Dennis Skinner, and by Simon Hoggart as making 'the Vicar of Bray look like Bedgellert the Faithful Hound', in embracing Conservatism he opted for it in its most Thatcherite monetarist form. Short and chubby and balding with a birdlike tuft, and disliking the above references to his political serial monogamy, in 2001 he came perilously close to experiencing from the wrong end another Liberal revival in Orpington. Rewarded for his defection to the Tories with junior posts (at Public Service and Health) in the Major government between 1995 and 1997, he disappeared from the frontbench under Hague, and nailed the lid down on his career in 2001 by voting for Kenneth Clarke.

OXFORD EAST

This is not the Oxford of dreaming spires, tourism and privileged ease, but the 11 wards of the city east of the rivers Thames and Cherwell, now joined by South ward. East has to all intents and purposes now become a safe Labour seat. The long-term swing to Labour in the city of Oxford is an exceptional phenomenon, and one which needs explanation.

It is true that east Oxford has been the better half of the city for the Labour Party since the arrival of the motor industry in the inter-war years. Here Rover's Cowley complex – formerly Pressed Steel and Morris Motors – straddles the eastern bypass, literally miles from the university-dominated centre of the city. Here too are peripheral council estates: post-war prefabricated Barton; Wood Farm; Rose Hill; Northway in New Marston; and Blackbird Leys, the sprawling 1960s development which by the 1990s had achieved national notoriety (somewhat exaggerated) as a centre of riotous unrest and illegal car theft and racing ('twocking' and 'hotting' respectively, in the argot). Further in, just across Magdalen Bridge from the city centre, lies St Clement's, which looks like Oxford's nearest thing to an inner-city area but is influenced by counter-culture radicals – St Clement's re-elected a Green city councillor in a four-way contest in May 2000 and re-elected a Green county councillor on the same day as the 2001 General Election. There are strong and on occasion successful Green challenges in other wards too, such as South and East. There is terraced housing off the Cowley Road, and a concentration of Asians in East and St Clement's wards (about 20% of the population in each case); these wards have swung far to the left since the days when they were the homes of deferentially Tory or Liberal college servants.

However, demographic change is not the only reason for the swing of Oxford to the left in both city and national politics. Many of those employed are in the public sector, including education and health, two services which are held to be served ill by the long-established Conservative government. A high proportion of the voters are intellectuals and graduates, which skews their preferences to the left compared with their 'expected' occupational class position. The Labour Party in Oxford East has been exceptionally strong and well organised over the last decade. It is hard to imagine circumstances under which this side of Oxford will again elect a Conservative MP. Nowadays the main challenge at both city, and since 2001, parliamentary level comes not from the Tories, or even the Greens, but from the Liberal Democrats, who took the wards of Headington, Iffley, Old Marston/Risinghurst, Quarry and Temple Cowley in May 2000 and advanced to second with an 8% swing from Andrew Smith in 2001. It is arguable at a time when Mr Smith is an utterly solid member of New Labour's financial team in the Cabinet that this reflects a continuing leftward trend across the river.

Social indices:			2001 Gen. Election:			
% Non-white	9.7		Lab	19,681	49.4	−7.4
% Prof/Man	37.2		LD	9,337	23.4	+8.7
% Non-manual	57.4		C	7,446	18.7	−3.3
£ Av prop val 2000	142 K		Grn	1,501	3.8	+1.7
% Increase 97–00	54.4		SA	708	1.8	
% Unemployed 2001	2.4		UKIP	570	1.4	+0.9
% Decrease 97–01	2.0		SLP	274	0.7	
% Fin hard/Rank	17.0	316	PA	254	0.6	
% Pensioners	25.4		Ind	77	0.2	+0.1
% Prem mort/Rank	33	292	Lab maj	10,344	26.0	
			Turnout		53.5	−15.5
			Elect	74,421		

Member of Parliament

Andrew Smith, Chief Secretary to the Treasury from 1999, and previously Employment Minister (1997–99), has been MP here since 1987 when his victory was seen as the start of Labour's fight back in the South from which it had virtually been eliminated in 1983. Alleged sufferer from a charisma-bypass and with a much remarked-upon monotonous slowly-articulated turkey-voice, he was born in 1951, son of an aircraft worker, and educated at Reading Grammar School and St John's College, Oxford, and worked for the Oxford and Swindon Co-op for eight years before 1987, and was an Oxford City councillor 1976–87. Previously piloter of the Welfare to Work strategy, as Chief Secretary he loyally mirrors the Chancellor's 'prudence', and negotiated a hugely profitable mobile phone strategic partnership. Though a Brown protégé he does share his Oxford college, St John's, with Tony Blair.

OXFORD WEST AND ABINGDON

As quite widely predicted, the sophisticated constituency of Oxford West and Abingdon elected a Liberal Democrat, Evan Harris, to Parliament for the first time in 1997. The defeat of the Conservatives was probably helped considerably by tactical voting on the part of potential Labour supporters (the Labour vote only went up by

4%, compared with a national average of 9%). Nevertheless, the main problem was the serious haemorrhaging of Conservative support in this part of the world. They could not win a single ward in this seat in the local elections of May 2000 or June 2001, and in fact had had no success of any kind within Oxford city since 1992.

The five wards, basically those west of the rivers Cherwell and Thames, contain the whole of the historic walled city of Oxford, the bulk of the university, the main shopping centre and the town and county halls. The seat also includes the well-known intellectual and professional residential areas of north Oxford. It encompasses too the traditionally working-class enclaves of Jericho and Osney in west ward, now heavily gentrified, and the volatile student vote of the university-dominated Central ward, which has elected Conservative, Labour and SDP-Alliance councillors since its creation in 1979 and is now a Liberal Democrat– Green marginal! The academic vote is fairly consistently ranged against the Conservatives nowadays, though: Oxford University dons denied Mrs Thatcher an honorary degree in 1985 in protest against education cuts and her broader policies. Oxford as a city has been moving to the left, with its reliance on public sector employment and intellectual disdain for modern Conservatism. The Tories will have to rely on the territory outside the city to get back to the Commons again.

There are problems there too. Abingdon itself and the owner-occupied sprawl between the two towns around Radley and Kennington have a tradition of voting Liberal in local elections, although they have probably favoured the Conservatives in the national contests which that party has won. They cannot be trusted in harder times for the Tories. The same seems to be true now of the seat as a whole, especially as the practice of tactical voting seems to becoming ever more firmly entrenched.

Social indices:			2001 Gen. Election:			
% Non-white	3.8		LD	24,670	47.8	+4.9
% Prof/Man	42.8		C	15,485	30.0	−2.6
% Non-manual	64.6		Lab	9,114	17.7	−2.5
£ Av prop val 2000	166 K		Grn	1,423	2.8	+1.6
% Increase 97–00	54.6		UKIP	451	0.9	+0.5
% Unemployed 2001	1.0		Ind	332	0.6	
% Decrease 97–01	0.8		Ind	93	0.2	
% Fin hard/Rank	5.4	598	LD maj	9,185	17.8	
% Pensioners	22.8		Turnout		64.5	−12.6
% Prem mort/Rank	8	611	Elect	79,915		

Member of Parliament

Dr Evan Harris, who has been Liberal Democrat higher education spokesman, was elected here in 1997, in a seat where the education scarcely gets any higher. A former hospital doctor at the Radcliffe, and son of a medical professor, he was born in 1965 and educated at the Blue Coat School, Liverpool and Wadham College, Oxford. The only Liberal Democrat MP from a Jewish family, sallow-skinned in a Levantine sort of way and handsome, if with a rather staring gaze, he is strongly in favour of legalising homosexual sex at 16 to make medical advice more accessible to young men, and in February 2001 introduced a bill to legalise human embryo cloning. In

2001 and 2002 he voted for the more conservative 'hunt licensing' option – not banning – of hunting. One of only two medics on the Liberal Democrat benches after 2001, he reverted to being spokesman on Health, as he had been 1997–99.

PAISLEY NORTH

Paisley is Scotland's fifth largest town, and for long formed a single seat on its own. Since 1983, though, it has been divided down the middle and each half joined by urban areas outside Paisley itself. In the case of Paisley North, it is the town of Renfrew which was added, and, for the 1997 Election, Linwood, the site of the troubled car plant (and allegedly the power base of former Renfrewshire West MP Tommy Graham, who was expelled from the party after the deeply unsavoury ructions during which the Paisley South member Gordon McMaster committed suicide in 1997). Both Renfrew and Linwood are strongly Labour, and although the Abercorn section of Paisley includes a couple of Tory-inclined wards, including the very middle-class Ralston/Oldhall neighbourhood, this is essentially a very safe Labour seat. North includes the ferocious and fearsome Ferguslie Park neighbourhood, which has some of the most powerful statistical indicators of social deprivation in Britain, and lost more than half of its population between 1981 and 1991.

Tragically, both Labour MPs for Paisley constituencies died in late 1990, Allen Adams of North at the early age of 44. Both the resulting by-elections were held on the same day, 29 November – the day after John Major had become Prime Minister. The main challenge came from the SNP, but it was comfortably resisted by the Labour candidate, who held on, hoping to continue Allen Adams's work – she is Irene, his widow, who has since won by large margins three times.

Paisley politics have been very rough in recent years, but the abrasiveness and abrasions have mainly taken place within the dominant party. Both Paisley seats will expand to take in extra territory, in this case North Renfrewshire, and further internecine party strife is not impossible,

Social indices:			2001 Gen. Election:			
% Non-white	0.8		Lab	15,058	55.5	–4.0
% Prof/Man	25.5		SNP	5,737	21.1	–0.8
% Non-manual	51.8		LD	2,709	10.0	+3.0
% Unemployed 2001	5.0		C	2,404	8.9	–0.7
% Decrease 97–01	2.1		SSP	982	3.6	
% Fin hard/Rank	47.1	22	PA	263	1.0	–0.6
% Prem mort/Rank	53	30	Lab maj	9,321	34.3	
			Turnout		56.6	–12.1
			Elect	47,994		

Member of Parliament

Irene Adams, elected here in 1990 in succession to her late husband Allen Adams, is identified as a strong devolutionist with the more Nationalist wing of the Labour Party in Scotland, and with factional in-fighting in the Labour Party in Renfrewshire, one alleged by-product of which was the suicide of her Paisley South friend and colleague in 1997 following a feud with Tommy Graham, MP for Renfrewshire West until 2001. She was born locally in 1947 and educated at Stanely Green High School, Paisley and worked as her husband's secretary. She backed Prescott, not Blair, for leader in 1994, and has bravely challenged local drug gangs. As a Scottish MP with a post-devolution depleted postbag, and so time on her hands, she has joined the panel of Commons Chairmen.

PAISLEY SOUTH

Shortly after he had easily retained Paisley South for Labour in the 1997 General Election, the MP Gordon McMaster committed suicide amid claims that he was being smeared by rival Labour politicians. His death unleashed not only a plethora of allegations of misconduct within the local party, but also unwelcome publicity for Paisley as 'the town called malice', with a serious problem of drug gangs. There followed in November of that year a very awkward by-election for Labour, in which they were patently relieved to hold off an SNP challenge by just 2,731 votes, representing an 11% swing to the SNP (on a 43% turnout). The voters were clearly rather disillusioned. By 2001 however, the new MP, the high-flying Douglas Alexander, had so ensconced himself that South was an even safer seat than Paisley North, which is saying something, and it should not stand in his career path, at least until the Scottish seats are reduced in number: as with Paisley North, South expands to join parts of Renfrewshire in the forthcoming boundary changes.

The southern half of Paisley is now paired with the smaller town of Johnstone a few miles to the west for parliamentary purposes. Paisley's main industries have been thread mills, cars and engineering, but all have suffered economic insecurity in recent decades. This was once H.H. Asquith's seat (1920–24), and the Liberals nearly won Paisley in the 1961 by-election and in 1964 – but their vote has been much reduced in recent years, and they finished third in both the by-election and the 2001 General Election.

Social indices:			2001 Gen. Election:			
% Non-white	0.5		Lab	17,830	58.4	+0.9
% Prof/Man	28.5		SNP	5,920	19.4	−4.0
% Non-manual	53.1		LD	3,178	10.4	+1.0
% Unemployed 2001	4.7		C	2,301	7.5	−1.1
% Decrease 97–01	2.4		SSP	835	2.7	+2.3
% Fin hard/Rank	46.1	24	PA	346	1.1	
% Prem mort/Rank	52	36	Ind	126	0.4	
			Lab maj	11,910	39.0	
			Turnout		57.2	−11.9
			Elect	53,351		

Member of Parliament

Douglas Alexander, a protégé of Gordon Brown and involved with him at Millbank in running the 2001 Election campaign, was elected here at a by-election following the suicide of Gordon McMaster MP in 1997. Accused by Diane Abbott MP of 'reciting the line of the day from Millbank', his Commons profile has been a good deal lower than his sister Wendy's in the Scottish Parliament where she serves as a Labour Minister. Born, a son of the manse, in 1967 and educated at Park Mains High School, Erskine, at Lester B. Pearson College, Vancouver and Edinburgh and Pennsylvania Universities, he was a solicitor in a law firm with links to the Labour Party, and served Gordon Brown as a researcher. In 2001 his connections assured him a Junior Ministerial post at the DTI, responsible for e-commerce and competitiveness.

PENDLE

The Pendle constituency takes its name from the distinctive mountain whose mass overshadows the small towns of north-east Lancashire. The seat was created in 1983. Then it incorporated the whole of the former Nelson and Colne seat, together with Barnoldswick and Earby, which used to be in Yorkshire (and are still regarded as being so by many of their residents).

Nelson and Colne was one of the great marginal Lancashire seats, with a dramatic history of switches of party allegiance, and Pendle has proved to be of the same ilk. Nelson and Colne was held narrowly for many years by Sydney Silverman, justly renowned for his part in the abolition of capital punishment. After his death in 1968 it alternated between Labour and Tory, and Pendle has continued that tradition. The seat is composed of a group of small towns which owe their origins to the Pennine textile industry of the nineteenth century.

Their political preferences are very varied. 'Red' Nelson has long been known for its favour of Labour, and this has been reinforced in recent years by the arrival of a large population of Pakistani origin; the central Nelson ward of Whitefield is more than half non-white, and it is a Labour stronghold like the neighbouring wards of Bradley and Walverden. Colne has proved good ground for the Liberal Democrats at local level and developed a reputation as being something of a northern haven for the 'hippy' culture in the 1960s and 1970s. Reedley and Barrowford are desirable residential and commuting bases and strongly favour the Conservatives. Earby and Barnoldswick are competed for by all three major parties in Pendle local elections. There are also some rural wards which, though sparsely populated, helped to tip the seat to the Conservative John Lee in Mrs Thatcher's two triumphal years in 1983 and 1987; 1992 and 1997, however, proved very different.

At the turn of the 1990s Pendle was frequently quoted as a – maybe the – prime example of a marginal seat where the Conservatives would be hurt by the introduction of the poll tax. It is full of low-cost owner-occupied terraced housing which was low-rated under the old system – indeed its proportion of terraced housing at the time of the last published figures, 64.4%, was the highest in the whole of the North West. The demands on individuals of the community charge were far more onerous in most cases. John Lee himself recognised the dangers and campaigned against the poll tax after leaving the government (he was eventually to leave the party as well) in 1989. His efforts were in vain; Labour's Gordon Prentice reversed his 2,000 majority as Pendle formed one of the four Labour gains in Lancashire.

Although Labour increased the majority to 11,000 in 1997, this area has demonstrated often enough before that its loyalties should never be taken for granted, and in 2001 there was an unusually large swing back to the Conservatives and, in a seat in proximity to racially troubled Burnley, the BNP very nearly saved their deposit. Although the absolute level of unemployment was not among the highest in the country, it was one of only two seats of the 659 where the numbers did not fall between June 1997 and June 2001 (the other was Bosworth in Leicestershire). The Tories are in range of regaining Pendle in 2005 or 2006.

Social indices:			2001 Gen. Election:			
% Non-white	10.3		Lab	17,729	44.6	−8.7
% Prof/Man	27.5		C	13,454	33.9	+3.6
% Non-manual	45.8		LD	5,479	13.8	+2.2
£ Av prop val 2000	43 K		BNP	1,976	5.0	
% Increase 97–00	9.7		UKIP	1,094	2.8	
% Unemployed 2001	3.5		Lab maj	4,275	10.8	
% Increase 97–01	+0.0		Turnout		63.2	−11.4
% Fin hard/Rank	31.7	119	Elect	62,870		
% Pensioners	26.9					
% Prem mort/Rank	37	218				

Member of Parliament

Gordon Prentice, once part of a model husband-and-wife team of Hammersmith-councillors (in his case council leader)-turned MPs in 1992, has parted both domestically and politically from his wife, Bridget (who became PPS to the Lord Chancellor). Despite seven years as a Labour Party staffer and seven months as PPS to Gavin Strang, he quit in December 1997 in order to vote against lone parent benefit cuts, and to follow that up with a string of rebellious votes on freedom of information, the prime minister's right to nominate life peers, pensions linked to average earnings, disability benefit cuts and air traffic control privatisation. By the end of the 1997–2001 Parliament he had rebelled 25 times and was ranked 13th in the table of dissidents. He promptly rebelled after the 2001 Election against the ban on incitement to religious hatred in the Terrorism, Crime and Security Bill. Born in 1951 and educated at George Heriot's School, Edinburgh and Glasgow University, an apparatchik oddly transformed into a sardonic rebel, he has sprayed mocking comments all over the Dome, Lib-Labbery (understandable because the Liberals are his local opponents – and in the shape of the sectarian oddball, Tony Greaves) and Tony Blair personally, at one point observing that 'we cling on to his every word'. He is also very concerned about the right to roam and banning hunting, and blamed the farmers for spreading foot-and-mouth.

PENRITH AND THE BORDER

There may well be no coincidence that the seat in England which suffered the most in the great foot-and-mouth epidemic of 2001 – according to DEFRA figures, 602 cases up to 12 July 2001, more than four times as many as the next worst affected seat, Dumfries – also saw one of the highest increases in the Conservative share of the vote. Portraying themselves as the party friendly to the countryside and its folk, here amid the empty fields and mass animal graveyards, the Tories increased their share by 7%, and Penrith and the Border is now the second safest Conservative seat in Britain. The farming and tourist industries here had little reason to celebrate Labour's four years – or certainly not their fourth year – in government as a time of plenty, although it was the Liberal Democrats who suffered the most from a haemorrhage in their support.

Penrith and the Border was long associated with William Whitelaw, for a long time the loyal lieutenant of Edward Heath, who was (fairly narrowly) beaten by Margaret Thatcher in the final ballot for the Conservative leadership in 1975, who served as deputy leader under her, and who was granted a hereditary peerage (the first for some 20 years) shortly after the General Election of 1983. The controversial timing of this honour tested the patience of the electorate of Penrith and the Border, which was thereby called on to visit the polling stations for the second time in seven weeks; and the new Tory candidate David Maclean held on by only 552 votes over the Liberal Alliance. This proved a one-off shot across the bows of the newly returned government, though, and Maclean re-established a majority of Whitelaw-like proportions in 1987 and 1992. Even in 1997 he had little trouble: Penrith and the Border was one of those seats where the local Liberal Democrats were unable to persuade Labour voters to support them tactically, and the Labour candidate doubled her share while the Lib Dems fell back. Perhaps it was just too big.

Penrith and the Border is the largest seat physically in England, by some way surpassing the acreage of another border seat, Hexham. As this vast size implies, it is sparsely populated. The only towns of any size are Penrith itself, Wigton (lauded by its native son Melvyn Bragg in *Speak for England*) and Appleby. It stretches from the Solway Firth to the Yorkshire Dales, from the Scottish border at Gretna Green to Helvellyn in the heart of the Lakes. The Liberal Democrats and Labour seem lost among all these acres.

Social indices:			2001 Gen. Election:			
% Non-white	0.3		C	24,302	54.9	+7.3
% Prof/Man	35.4		LD	9,625	21.8	–4.9
% Non-manual	53.7		Lab	8,177	18.5	–3.1
£ Av prop val 2000	82 K		UKIP	938	2.1	
% Increase 97–00	25.3		LCA	870	2.0	
% Unemployed 2001	1.6		Ind	337	0.8	
% Decrease 97–01	0.9		C maj	14,677	33.2	
% Fin hard/Rank	6.8	562	Turnout		65.3	–8.3
% Pensioners	27.1		Elect	67,776		
% Prem mort/Rank	25	420				

Member of Parliament

David Maclean, Conservative Chief Whip from 2001, is one of a number of ambitious Scots Tories who, in order to pursue their political ambitions, had to depart what was eventually the Tory-free zone north of 'the border' featured in the name of his seat. Replacing Willie Whitelaw at a by-election in 1983, he rose from Whip to minister of state in ten years, in which he refused an offer of a Cabinet post – Agriculture – in order to stay with Michael Howard at the Home Office, but immediately disappeared from the frontbench in Opposition in 1997 after backing the unsuccessful Howard leadership candidacy. A pin-striped abrasive right-winger with an emphatic style of oratory, born in 1953, a tenant farmer's son, and educated at Fortrose Academy and Aberdeen University, and formerly working for Securicor, he has taken to specialising in wrecking private members' bills, notably politically-correct ones on subjects such as fur farming, aided by his new frontbench colleague Eric Forth. He backed David Davis, then Iain Duncan Smith, in 2001. He claims most of the beggars in London are Scottish and he always gives them something – a piece of his mind.

PERTH

The Perth seat still includes much rolling countryside as well as the eponymous town: in 2002 it passed through Glencarse and Bridge of Earn to the environs of the small towns of Auchterarder and Crieff, although these Strathearn elements join Ochil in the provisional boundary changes. The battle here is between Conservatives and Scottish Nationalists, and often a very close battle it has been too. The last Conservative MP was the colourful Sir Nicholas Fairbairn, who (against many expectations) managed to hold on in Kinross and West Perthshire and subsequently Perth and Kinross since October 1974, when his initial majority was just 53. In his final contest in 1992 he beat the SNP by just over 2,000. There had been other tight battles in between, and there were more to come in the new Perth. Sir Nicholas died in early 1995 and the loss of the Perth and Kinross seat to the SNP's Roseanna Cunningham in the by-election which followed, on 25 May, was seen as inevitable at a time of great government unpopularity. That phrase clearly still applied at the 1997 General Election, but Ms Cunningham won Perth by only 3,000 and the Conservatives, who had sunk to third in 1995, came back quite strongly – in the circumstances. This is still a conservative, if not currently Conservative, corner of North Britain. In 2001 Roseanna Cunningham had moved on to represent this area in the Edinburgh Parliament set up in 1999, and it was time for another super-close finish in Perth.

The main SNP dynasty is the Ewing family. No, this is not borrowed from American soap dramas of the 1980s. Annabelle Ewing, the new MP, is the daughter of Winnie, and sister-in-law of Margaret, both former representatives at Westminster. Her winning percentage of 29.7 was the lowest in any of the 659 in the UK in 2001, owing not only to the gap of 48 votes over the Conservative Elizabeth Smith, but also to a majority of less than 2,000 over Labour's Marion Dingwall. The Liberal Democrat was a woman too, Vicki Harris, so this is also the only seat where females occupied the first four positions.

Like most Scottish towns, Perth itself does have working-class council estates, such as those in its western Letham and Tulloch sections, which provide the heart of the Labour vote. But in the main this is a prosperous part of Lowland Scotland. Perth has many neighbourhoods with solid and large houses built in its distinctive dark gritstone, and there is still little unemployment, just 2.7% in June 2001. Outside the town the main agricultural bases are livestock and fruit-growing; the soil is of relatively high quality and well-watered. It may yet prove again fertile ground for the

Conservatives, and the proposed replacement of Strathearn with areas of acreage in Atholl from the abolished Tayside North maintains the tight political balance.

Social indices:			2001 Gen. Election:			
% Non-white	0.7		SNP	11,237	29.7	−6.7
% Prof/Man	33.5		C	11,189	29.6	+0.3
% Non-manual	55.6		Lab	9,638	25.5	+0.7
% Unemployed 2001	2.7		LD	4,853	12.8	+4.8
% Decrease 97–01	2.1		SSP	899	2.4	
% Fin hard/Rank	20.3	271	SNP maj	48	0.1	
% Prem mort/Rank	43	117	Turnout		61.5	−12.4
			Elect	61,497		

Member of Parliament

With the departure of the abrasive Anglophobic republican Roseanna Cunningham for the Edinburgh Parliament, the SNP picked a famous name to defend this seat: **Annabelle Ewing**, daughter of Winnie, and near repeater of her mother's historic by-election win at Hamilton in 1967, when she ran Labour perilously close in the 1999 Hamilton South by-election. She in turn, victor here by a menacing margin of 48 votes, like her mother a solicitor, was born in 1960, attended Craigholme School, Glasgow and Glasgow University, has enjoyed a life immersed in Scottish Nationalism, and emerged with mother, brother (Fergus) and sister-in-law (Margaret) as part of a political dynasty, if – to her chagrin – the only member of it stuck at Westminster. Sporting a somewhat severe short-back-and-sides haircut, she has admitted that she does not feel British at all.

PETERBOROUGH

The Peterborough constituency has a distinguished history as the site of ultra-close general election battles, and may well have such a future as well, as Labour's Helen Brinton saw her majority fall to less than 3,000 (or 7%) in 2001. It should be remembered that Labour were 9% ahead nationally then, and should the Conservatives ever come near to forming a government again, Peterborough and the controversial Ms Brinton (now Clark) would fall.

In 1966 Peterborough produced jointly the closest contest of any parliamentary division in post-war elections (together with Carmarthen in February 1974). The sitting Conservative MP, Sir Harmar Nicholls, defeated Labour's Michael Ward by just three votes. Seven recounts were necessary. Then in 1968 this cathedral city on the edge of the Fens was designated as one of the last New Towns. The population rose from 76,000 (1961) to 115,000 (1981) largely through the acceptance of London overspill. The seat is still growing, although the development is very much concentrated in the private sector nowadays, and new hi-tech and high-skill industries have been brought in. The electrification of the main east coast railway line has brought the city to within an hour's commuting distance of London.

All this cannot have helped Labour to regain the seat in 1997. On the other hand, large council-built estates as in Ravensthorpe ward provide a solid base for a Labour vote that reached 50% in 1997 and was still 45% in 2001, and Central ward is now over 50% non-white. These figures indicate that the Lib Dems are weak in Peterborough, although their improvement last time, which was not based on significant local government success, weakened Helen Brinton's position – perhaps it represented a reduction in tactical voting now the Conservatives were out of office. Peterborough will remain a two-way fight to be watched closely at the next general election.

Social indices:			2001 Gen. Election:			
% Non-white	10.3		Lab	17,975	45.1	−5.2
% Prof/Man	29.0		C	15,121	38.0	+2.8
% Non-manual	54.9		LD	5,761	14.5	+3.8
£ Av prop val 2000	58 K		UKIP	955	2.4	+1.7
% Increase 97–00	23.0		Lab maj	2,854	7.2	
% Unemployed 2001	3.4		Turnout		61.3	−12.1
% Decrease 97–01	2.8		Elect	64,918		
% Fin hard/Rank	25.1	199				
% Pensioners	22.8					
% Prem mort/Rank	30	344				

Member of Parliament

Helen Clark (formerly Brinton), one of the big 1997 new intake of 65 women Labour MPs, experienced a good deal of adverse press publicity, some of which concerning her domestic life, over which she successfully took legal action. Harshly dubbed by the *Guardian* 'an alien life force designed by Millbank to stay on message for a thousand years without new batteries', originally emerging from an all-women shortlist and self-confessedly 'totally without ideological baggage', she is a former teacher, born in 1947, and educated at Spondon Park Grammar School, Derby and Bristol University. Now reflecting the contemporary Labour activists' concern for animal welfare, in the early 1990s she backed Bryan Gould's Keynesian 'Full Employment Forum'. She suffered an adverse swing of 4% in June 2001 and remarried in August.

PLYMOUTH DEVONPORT

Plymouth Devonport is one of the most famous constituency names. It seems to attract MPs of high public profile and national renown. Michael Foot was the Labour MP from 1945 to 1955, when he was ousted by Dame Joan Vickers, who represented Devonport in the Conservative interest for nearly 20 years until in 1974 she herself was beaten by a Labour candidate – Dr David Owen. Owen, who had been member for the neighbouring Sutton seat since 1966, did very well to hold Devonport for Labour in 1979, by 1,001 votes against the national tide. Next this former Labour Foreign Secretary became a founding member (1981) and leader (1983) of the Social Democratic Party. Twice he held Devonport with some ease. Then his colourful political career took a new turn. Refusing to accept the vote of his SDP members to merge with the Liberals, Owen again went his own way – as the undisputed leader of a

Social Democratic Party that was so identified with him that many dubbed it 'Owenite'.

Although the 'continuing' SDP destructively split the centre vote in by-elections early in the 1987 Parliament, especially at Richmond (Yorkshire) when William Hague entered the Commons, it never built up a national campaigning base and Owen was forced to wind it up in 1990. Rather than fight Devonport again, he retired, took a seat in the Lords, and undertook projects of international importance. His departure after nearly 20 years led to another remarkable result in his old constituency.

Labour increased their share of the vote by no less than 20%, to win by over 7,000 votes from the Tories. Clearly most of Owen's support had come from people who were basically Labour sympathisers, and Devonport is essentially a Labour seat. It includes not only the naval base and docks, but great swathes of council-built housing located on the hills of Plymouth's northern fringe, in wards like Budshead and Southway. This is all working-class territory, and even given the armed service presence, which normally skews a constituency to the right, Labour should now be safe here. The Owenite aberration is a distant memory. Patterns had returned to normal by 1997, as an average national swing of 12.6% pushed David Jamieson's majority up to a massive 19,000 – the highest in a Plymouth seat since the Second World War. Turnout fell to a modern low of 56% in 2001.

Social indices:			2001 Gen. Election:			
% Non-white	0.8		Lab	24,322	58.3	−2.6
% Prof/Man	17.7		C	11,289	27.1	+2.9
% Non-manual	38.2		LD	4,513	10.8	+0.1
£ Av prop val 2000	57 K		UKIP	958	2.3	+1.4
% Increase 97–00	19.7		SA	334	0.8	
% Unemployed 2001	2.9		SLP	303	0.7	
% Decrease 97–01	3.7		Lab maj	13,033	31.2	
% Fin hard/Rank	28.5	151	Turnout		56.6	−13.1
% Pensioners	23.1		Elect	73,666		
% Prem mort/Rank	37	223				

Member of Parliament

David Jamieson, a Junior Transport Minister from 2001 after four years in the Whips' office, elected here for Labour in the wake of David Owen in 1992, was for 22 years a school teacher, eventually in Plymouth, born in 1947 and educated at Tudor Grange Grammar School, Solihull and St Peter's Teacher Training College, Birmingham. A defender of local defence interests, he also piloted a bill in 1995 on regulation of activity centres following the drowning of Plymouth schoolchildren off Lyme Regis and engaged in a good deal of name calling with Plymouth Tory MP Gary Streeter over the latter's SDP Tory-baiting past, before falling silent as a Whip in 1997. His reaching the bottom of the ministerial ladder in 2001 came dangerously late for one in his 55th year.

PLYMOUTH SUTTON

Beware! This seat was not the successor to the constituency of the same name which was contested at the 1992 Election, and resulted in a fairly easy win for the Conservative Gary Streeter. It is largely composed of the former marginal Plymouth Drake, held by Dame Janet Fookes by just 2,013 votes over Labour in April 1992.

Most of the old Plymouth Sutton was situated east of the river Plym in Plympton and Plymstock. This area, including some 40,000 electors, has now been transferred to form the base of the new South West Devon seat. The remaining three wards west of the Plym have been divided between the two Plymouth constituencies that survive.

The two wards of Efford and Mount Gould were added to the six in Drake to create this seat – which most confusingly was named Sutton rather than Drake. It was even harder for the Conservatives to defend, as both Efford and Mount Gould are essentially Labour wards, at least in local elections. Labour obtained a swing of just over 10% in 1997 and won the first contest in the metamorphosed Sutton by over 9,000 votes. In 2001 Linda Gilroy held on comfortably as the party shares were very much a case of 'as you were', but municipal contests are interesting and very closely fought, as seems only proper in the home seat of the University of Plymouth's renowned, invaluable, and widely respected Local Government Elections Centre.

The Conservatives' strongest ward is Compton, north of the centre, where they polled 63% in the all-out unitary authority elections of May 2000. Labour fights back in St Peter's, but most wards here are marginal, some with split representation in 2000: Efford, Mount Gould, and Sutton ward, which includes the heart of the city and the Hoe. Ironically Sutton ward was in the Drake constituency at the time of the last three elections; there really does seem no accounting for the logic of the naming of parliamentary constituencies in the city of Plymouth.

Social indices:			2001 Gen. Election:			
% Non-white	1.2		Lab/Coop	19,827	50.7	+0.6
% Prof/Man	28.4		C	12,310	31.5	+1.2
% Non-manual	50.9		LD	5,605	14.3	+0.5
£ Av prop val 2000	59 K		UKIP	970	2.5	+1.4
% Increase 97–00	22.9		SLP	361	0.9	
% Unemployed 2001	4.5		L/C maj	7,517	19.2	
% Decrease 97–01	6.3		Turnout		57.1	–10.3
% Fin hard/Rank	21.9	246	Elect	68,438		
% Pensioners	28.2					
% Prem mort/Rank	40	177				

Member of Parliament

Linda Gilroy, Labour victor here in 1997 after selection from an all-women shortlist, was Scots-born in 1949 and educated at Stirling High School, Edinburgh and Strathclyde Universities. Originally working for Age Concern in Scotland she was latterly South West Regional Manager of the Gas Consumer Council, and operates in the House as an inevitable defender of Plymouth's defence interests, as a bowler of planted questions, and as an instigator of legislation to regulate fireworks. Her reward for such diligence was to become PPS to Nick Raynsford in 2001.

PONTEFRACT AND CASTLEFORD

As one travels eastwards from Leeds, the Pennine countryside gradually flattens into a plain, and the traditional base of the economy changes from textiles to coal. Great rivers like the Aire and the Ouse water the low-lying land, and have been tapped by massive power stations which tower over the landscape. This is scenery dominated by heavy industry, by the production of power and energy. One travels too from the city of Leeds into the city of Wakefield, where there are no Tory seats. Wakefield is a Labour powerhouse in every sense.

Pontefract and Castleford used to be one of the strongest coal-mining constituencies in West Yorkshire, but the collieries have closed down, and productive industry is better signified by the huge Ferrybridge power station near Knottingley, the third town in the constituency besides those named in the title. This constituency is still a mighty Labour stronghold, though. Castleford, with 30,000 electors, holds the largest influence in the constituency. Knottingley is smaller but just as nearly as monolithic. Pontefract is a historic town with a notable castle, and does have some Tory votes in its southern ward; but Labour's core strength in this seat was epitomised by Yvette Cooper's 25,700 majority in 1997. Less than half of those on the register turned out in 2001 though, and like many of her New Labour colleagues, the verdict on Ms Cooper's first term was marked by the perception of a conspicuous lack of both enthusiasm and alternatives.

Social indices:			2001 Gen. Election:			
% Non-white	0.7		Lab	21,890	69.7	−6.0
% Prof/Man	18.8		C	5,512	17.6	+4.0
% Non-manual	38.6		LD	2,315	7.4	+0.0
£ Av prop val 2000	54 K		UKIP	739	2.4	
% Increase 97–00	13.5		SLP	605	1.9	
% Unemployed 2001	4.1		SA	330	1.1	
% Decrease 97–01	2.0		Lab maj	16,378	52.2	
% Fin hard/Rank	30.2	129	Turnout		49.7	−16.7
% Pensioners	24.5		Elect	63,181		
% Prem mort/Rank	41	155				

Member of Parliament

Yvette Cooper, one of Labour's 1997-vintage *jeunesse d'orée*, was elected following her airlifting here, after the last-minute ennoblement of Sir Geoffrey Lofthouse. Dubbed the 'dazzling star of the Blairite nomenklatura', a former staffer for Gordon Brown in Opposition, and wife of Brown's adviser Ed Balls, she duly joined the government as a Junior Health Minister in 1999 after the birth of her first child. Born in 1969 and educated at Eggars Comprehensive School, Alton, Balliol College, Oxford, Harvard and the LSE, with elfin good looks as well as brains, and her career tucked in around babies – with maternity leave arranged for her second one in 2001 – she has been the object of flattering if un-PC plaudits from sadly retired Tory Knights of the Shire such as Sir Peter Emery.

PONTYPRIDD

In the 2001 General Election Plaid Cymru, the 'Party of Wales', did relatively well, compared with the Scottish Nationalists. Across Wales they improved from exactly 10% to 14.3% of the vote, moving ahead of the Liberal Democrats; the SNP dropped 2% to 20% north of the English border. Plaid Cymru maintained their level of four seats, winning one and losing one; the SNP, with high hopes of gains, actaully dropped one to five. One of the reasons for the Plaid's modest advance was an improvement in the south Welsh industrial working-class valleys: although they did not win any seats here, as they had in the May 1999 Welsh Assembly elections (Rhondda, Islwyn, Llanelli) they did advance to second place in 11 of the 13 predominantly ex-mining 'valley' constituencies – making up a potentially useful team, as it were.

Pontypridd is one of these, although all the collieries have closed. It is composed mainly of the Taff and Ely valleys north-west of Cardiff between Rhondda and Caerphilly. As well as 'Ponty' itself the communities include Rhydyfelin, Tonyrefail, Treforest (with its industrial estate offering many post-mining jobs) and Taff's Well. Towns which do not fit so closely into the history of the coal valleys include Llantwit Fardre, Llantrisant, the site of the Royal Mint and of many other largish non-traditional employers, and the two more middle-class areas, Creigiau, a new private estate, and Pentyrch, just on the other side of the M4 motorway from the affluent private Cardiff suburb of Radyr. As befits a seat on the edge of the old coalfield rather than at its heart, it is not quite so monolithic a Labour stronghold as Rhondda, say, or Blaenau Gwent or Cynon Valley. All three main opposition parties to Labour obtained over 10% in 2001. The Liberal Democrats made a modest but clear advance from fourth to second place in 1997, but it should be noticed that their candidate's name was Howells, just as was that of the Labour man, and they fell back to fourth again last time. The occupational make-up of the seat is only a little more working class than the British average. However, despite all the above, Labour's Kim Howells still won by almost 18,000 even on a turnout of just 58%.

Social indices:			2001 Gen. Election:			
% Non-white	1.2		Lab	22,963	59.9	−3.9
% Welsh sp	10.0		PC	5,279	13.8	+7.3
% Prof/Man	31.2		C	5,096	13.3	+0.4
% Non-manual	55.0		LD	4,152	10.8	−2.6
£ Av prop val 2000	61 K		UKIP	603	1.6	
% Increase 97–00	27.1		PA	216	0.6	
% Unemployed 2001	2.4		Lab maj	17,684	46.2	
% Decrease 97–01	2.1		Turnout		58.0	−13.5
% Fin hard/Rank	18.1	303	Elect	66,105		
% Pensioners	22.7					
% Prem mort/Rank	32	307				

Member of Parliament

Dr Kim Howells, a laterally-moving Junior Minister successively at Education (1997–98), DTI (1998–2001) and Culture (Tourism, from 2001), was elected at a by-election in 1989, having travelled the full distance from the time when he was first unknown as the student radical who sought to recreate the 1968 occupation of the Sorbonne at Hornsey College of Art, through three years in the Communist Party as recently as 1978–82, to his pronouncing the end of the 'S' (for socialism) word in 1996, for which apostasy he probably owes his ministerial car at the dangerously advanced age of 55. Born in 1946, son of a communist lorry driver, he attended Mountain Ash Grammar School, Hornsey College of Art, Cambridgeshire College of Arts and Technology and Warwick University, and worked originally, if briefly, as a miner, and steel worker, but then as a Swansea University researcher, freelance broadcaster, and research officer for the South Wales NUM. A gregarious, extravert boyo, and a former opponent of devolution which he later came to endorse, having 'trotted from Trotsky, via canapés with Kinnock, to Beaujolais with Blair' (Alex Carlile, former Liberal MP), he remained in 2001 a bottom-ranked minister after four years, dangerously admitting he was 'always amazed when anyone gives me a job'. His populist dismissal in 2001 of the Royal Family as 'a bit bonkers', may well have done him no harm amongst the Blairite nomenklatura.

POOLE

The first Conservative MP to be returned on election night, 7 June 2001 was Robert Syms of Poole: this after over 100 Labour members and several Liberal Democrats had already been declared. The ever-optimistic, or rather ever-spinning, studio Tory spokesmen claimed that the less urban areas declare later, but on that night, as four years earlier, they were whistling in the dark, and not only did the Conservative tally never catch up, but they managed to crawl to a total of only one more seat in 2001 than in 1997. Poole is therefore doubly untypical: not only a Conservative hold, but a Tory constituency which can only be described as fully urban. How has it survived the cull of Tory seats in the towns and cities?

Poole has often been regarded as a suburb of Bournemouth, and indeed there are several attractive residential areas which are suitable for use as commuting bases, including Sandbanks, home of celebrities and of some of the highest property values outside fashionable areas of London, and Branksome Park with its million-pound houses in piney woods near the border with Bournemouth West. Yet it is also very much an independent town, successful and expanding, and declared a growth area in the Strategic Plan for the South East. It has already attracted a variety of new modern industry and new population. It had reached 131,500 inhabitants by 1991 and is too populous to stand as a single seat, five of its wards being included in Dorset Mid and Poole North, gained by the Liberal Democrats in 2001.

Poole too has shown a strong tendency to support the Liberal Democrats in borough and county council elections – for example, in May 1995 the Conservatives only received 34% of the vote in the borough elections; the Liberal Democrats polled over 38% and controlled the council. In 2000, though, the Conservatives re-took the lead and as yet there is no sign of this pattern being replicated in general elections, as even in 2001 the Conservatives held on by over 7,000, as Labour advanced ahead of the Lib Dems into second place. Opposition to Syms is now almost equally divided. Poole remains affluent, even booming. Between 1997 and 2000 housing prices rose by 63% to an average of £160,000. Unemployment, already much lower than average, recorded one of the seven biggest falls in England between 1997 and 2001. In all these circumstances the Conservatives should continue to hold on indefinitely.

Social indices:			2001 Gen. Election:			
% Non-white	1.0		C	17,710	45.1	+3.0
% Prof/Man	33.2		Lab	10,544	26.9	+5.3
% Non-manual	58.4		LD	10,011	25.5	−5.3
£ Av prop val 2000	160 K		UKIP	968	2.5	+1.4
% Increase 97–00	63.0		C maj	7,166	18.3	
% Unemployed 2001	1.4		Turnout		60.7	−10.2
% Decrease 97–01	2.4		Elect	64,644		
% Fin hard/Rank	8.9	492				
% Pensioners	34.8					
% Prem mort/Rank	28	374				

Member of Parliament

Robert Syms, an Environment spokesman (1999–2001), was elected in 1997, a right-wing Eurosceptic and owner of a Chippenham-based family building and plant hire firm, who rose politically as leader of North Wiltshire District Council and as a county councillor for 12 years. With something of a boxer's visage, born in 1956 and educated at Colston's School, Bristol, a Portillo-supporter who *faute de mieux* backed Lilley in 1997, he favours first-past-the-post over PR. His Wiltshire roots could explain his job as PPS to Devizes MP Michael Ancram, as Party Chairman, but he backed Portillo not Ancram in 2001 and returned to the backbenches.

POPLAR AND CANNING TOWN

The Conservatives did poorly out of the most recent (1997) boundary redistribution, especially in London. The changes made by the Commission in Newham and Tower Hamlets proved no exception. The Tories' hopes of gaining a seat here in the East End could not have been more effectively dashed.

It might be thought that the very idea of the Conservative Party winning a seat here in the heart of the old docklands is fanciful; but this would be to ignore the history of the Newham South constituency. In 1987 the Conservatives secured an extraordinary 9% swing, and slashed Nigel Spearing's majority for Labour to 2,766. In 1992 the Tory performance in the seat again exceeded their average and Spearing's majority was further reduced, to 2,502. This seat was the site of the redevelopment of the old docklands, with the construction of the London City airport and the new housing estates of Beckton, which must have helped the Conservatives. The other reason for their showing was possibly the reaction of the white working-class voters living in troubled neighbourhoods like Canning Town and Plaistow against Labour's perceived favour for ethnic minorities. Only 25% of the population of the seat were non-white, less than any other seat in the inner East End. Now, however, Newham South has been abolished, and its constituent wards split three ways. The Tories' chances are also blown apart.

The largest section of Newham South was placed together with the bulk of the former Bow and Poplar in the seat which crosses the river Lea, the boundary between the boroughs of Newham and Tower Hamlets. The resulting seat, Poplar and Canning Town, will in all probability always be won by Labour with a large majority, but it is possible to envisage all kinds of unfortunate problems and incidents along the way.

This new seat covers a number of places with racial tensions as severe as any in Britain. The Poplar section includes the Isle of Dogs, whose Millwall ward was the site of the election of the British National Party's Derek Beackon in a 1993 by-election. The victory of an openly racist far-right party in an area where the arrival of indigent Bangladeshis has caused much resentment, overtly on the issue of housing allocation, caused a storm of protest and concern. After a massive campaign Labour ousted Derek Beackon in the May 1994 local elections, but the BNP did well in other wards within the new seat and remain active. There are also serious racial divisions in the Canning Town district of Newham. In 1997 the British National Party leader at the time John Tyndall polled over 7% of the vote in this new constituency and they held their deposit again in 2001. Whoever represents Poplar and Canning Town is likely to have a complex and challenging task.

Social indices:			2001 Gen. Election:			
% Non-white	27.9		Lab	20,862	61.2	−2.0
% Prof/Man	26.3		C	6,758	19.8	+4.8
% Non-manual	49.5		LD	3,795	11.1	+0.8
£ Av prop val 2000	183 K		BNP	1,743	5.1	−2.2
% Increase 97–00	110.2		SA	950	2.8	
% Unemployed 2001	9.2		Lab maj	14,104	41.4	
% Decrease 97–01	2.9		Turnout		45.4	−13.1
% Fin hard/Rank	60.2	5	Elect	75,173		
% Pensioners	21.2					
% Prem mort/Rank	54	24				

Member of Parliament

Jim Fitzpatrick, PPS to Alan Milburn (1999–2001), and as a former member of the Socialist Workers' Party, sharing with Milburn a left-wing past, was elected here in 1997. A neatly-coiffured, long-nosed, poker-faced Scot, born in 1952 and Catholic-educated at Holy Cross School and Holyrood Secondary School, Glasgow, he was a fireman or Fire Brigade Union official for 23 years. Chairman of the London Labour Party since 1991, he rebelled against student grant abolition in 1998, and backed the Livingstone–Kiley plan for the tube, but not that seriously or he would not have become an Assistant Whip in 2001.

PORTSMOUTH NORTH

The anti-paedophile hysteria, inflamed by the national tabloid press, which gripped the working-class north Portsmouth estate of Paulsgrove in August 2000, presented one of the least appealing spectacles during the first term of New Labour government. But would it lead to a right-wing electoral backlash in the 2001 General Election, which might oust the Labour MP, Syd Rapson, even though he had reflected local sentiment? Not a bit of it. The demonstrators would probably fail to connect their actions with party politics, and in 2001 Rapson actually increased his majority after a further swing. Paulsgrove had re-elected a Labour councillor easily in May 2000, although on a turnout of only 18%.

Portsmouth North had been one of the first spectacular Labour gains on the night of the 1997 General Election. The overturning of a 9,000 Tory majority with a swing of 13.5% indicated the likelihood of Labour's greatest ever landslide. This surprised almost all observers (although not the national bookmakers), but Portsmouth does in fact have something of a Labour tradition, although admittedly one which had been dormant for two decades. From 1966 to 1979 the locally popular Labour moderate Frank Judd (later a Director of Oxfam) held on to Portsmouth West, and its successor Portsmouth North, by hair-raisingly small margins. He finally lost in 1979, by 2,000 votes, to Peter Griffiths, a Conservative who had obtained notoriety in 1964 when he ousted Patrick Gordon Walker at Smethwick after an allegedly racist campaign. He only represented Smethwick for two years but, assisted by boundary changes, Griffiths held on for the 18 years of the Tory government.

There are Labour wards, as at Nelson (on Portsea Island) and at Paulsgrove in the far north-west of the constituency, off the island and under the Downs. But the Conservatives reply strongly in Drayton and Farlington, north-east towards Havant, and Hilsea, and usually Copnor and Cosham. Britain's premier naval port was never traditionally safe ground for Labour, despite its relatively crowded, fairly working-class character, and very mixed standard of housing. Now however, Rapson and his party seem more entrenched than Frank Judd ever was.

Social indices:			2001 Gen. Election:			
% Non-white	1.6		Lab	18,676	50.7	+3.5
% Prof/Man	26.6		C	13,542	36.7	−0.9
% Non-manual	49.2		LD	3,795	10.3	−0.3
£ Av prop val 2000	81 K		UKIP	559	1.5	+0.9
% Increase 97–00	40.0		Ind	294	0.8	
% Unemployed 2001	2.0		Lab maj	5,134	13.9	
% Decrease 97–01	2.8		Turnout		57.4	−12.8
% Fin hard/Rank	20.7	262	Elect	64,256		
% Pensioners	26.6					
% Prem mort/Rank	31	328				

Member of Parliament

Syd Rapson won here for Labour in 1997, after 18 years on Portsmouth City Council. A bald and portly aircraft fitter and AEU convenor, he was born in 1942 and raised by his grandparents, and educated at Southsea Modern and Paulsgrove Secondary Modern schools and Portsmouth Dockyard College. An inevitable defender of his city's defence interests as the first local man ever to represent Portsmouth for Labour, he judged it prudent in 2000 to go along with a local populist wave of hysteria against paedophiles on the Paulsgrove estate, where he himself was born.

PORTSMOUTH SOUTH

In 1997 Mike Hancock regained Portsmouth South, which he had represented for three years in the 1980s as an SDP MP, now as a Liberal Democrat. This must have come as a great relief, given his previous near misses. There were a number of constituencies in which the 1992 General Election result was almost exactly a replay of that five years before in 1987. However, very few of them were in critical marginal seats, and few can have been as heartbreaking for the loser as Portsmouth South. In 1987 David Martin (ironically the man who had failed to hold a vacant Yeovil against Paddy Ashdown in 1983) ousted Mike Hancock, who had gained Portsmouth South in a by-election in 1984. Martin won by just 205 votes. In 1992 Hancock was again a candidate; this time Martin increased his margin of victory to a princely 242.

Clearly Hancock, and the Liberal Democrats, have a genuine and long-lasting appeal in this tight-knit seat on Portsea Island. Mike Hancock had been a councillor on Portsmouth City Council since 1971, and on Hampshire County Council since 1973, dominating Fratton ward in both cases (for example, 71% of the vote in a four-way county contest in 1993). With a power base such as this, he would surely have beaten David Martin, an incomer from Devon, but for the fact that both 1987 and 1992 were seen as contests between the Conservatives and Labour at national level.

Hancock regained South by a comfortable (for this seat) majority of 4,000 in 1997, although it was mainly due to the collapse of the Conservative vote in favour of Labour. In 2001 however he needed no such help, nor even tactical voting: he increased his share by 5% at the equal expense of other parties. Almost single-handedly Hancock has transformed the politics of this compact, crowded seat which is one of the most densely populated outside the big cities – Fratton and Havelock wards actually have over 100 residents per hectare, which is almost unknown outside London. Space is at a premium here in Central Portsmouth and its resort area, Southsea, on the peninsula almost entirely bounded by Portsmouth Harbour, Langstone Harbour, and Spithead. It is an ideal setting for the Liberal Democrats', and Mike Hancock's, brand of community politics.

Social indices:			2001 Gen. Election:			
% Non-white	3.5		LD	17,490	44.6	+5.1
% Prof/Man	31.2		C	11,396	29.1	−2.1
% Non-manual	53.0		Lab	9,361	23.9	−1.4
£ Av prop val 2000	85 K		SA	647	1.6	
% Increase 97–00	50.0		UKIP	321	0.8	+0.5
% Unemployed 2001	3.2		LD maj	6,094	15.5	
% Decrease 97–01	4.0		Turnout		50.9	−13.3
% Fin hard/Rank	23.8	213	Elect	77,095		
% Pensioners	29.0					
% Prem mort/Rank	39	198				

Member of Parliament

Mike Hancock recaptured this seat in 1997 having held it for three years earlier for the SDP after a 1984 by-election. A former Labour-then-SDP-then-Lib Dem Portsmouth councillor for 24 years, and on Hampshire County Council, which he led

1993–97, he brings to his party rare working-class origins as a former engineering worker and AEU shop steward. A heavily-bearded and shaggy-haired ex-Salvationist and a sailor's son, born in 1946 and educated at Copnor and Portsea School, he is a campaigner for animal welfare and for the disabled (as a former Mencap district officer). Now largely retreated to the non-partisan world of the Chairmen's Panel, with Bob Russell he is the only Liberal Democrat MP to have started his political career – as a councillor – in the Labour Party.

PRESELI PEMBROKESHIRE

Before 1983 Pembrokeshire formed a single constituency. It had a rather curious electoral record, returning among its MPs Major Gwilym Lloyd George, the son of David, endorsed by both Liberals and Conservatives in 1945, and his successor, the increasingly eccentric Labour member Desmond Donnelly, who eventually stood as a 'Democrat' in 1970 and split the vote, allowing the Tories in for a period which was to last for 22 years until Labour's Nick Ainger regained the seat in 1992. For eight of those years Nicholas Edwards (MP 1970–87) was Secretary of State for Wales in Mrs Thatcher's government.

Nowadays the whole of South Pembrokeshire, with over 30,000 electors, has been joined with the western part of Carmarthen. What is left is the northern part of the county, named after the Preseli hills at its heart. The main towns are Haverfordwest, Fishguard and the oil refining port of Milford Haven. It also includes the tiny cathedral city of St David's and a dramatic coastline, plus the islands of Ramsey, Skomer and Skokholm. Nick Ainger chose to contest the Carmarthen West and South Pembrokeshire seat, leaving a new Labour candidate Jackie Lawrence to fight here. In 1997 she won easily, by almost 9,000, but the marginal balance of this mixed division became more clear after Labour's relatively poor performance in Wales in 2001, when the Conservatives cut her lead to under 3,000 and Plaid Cymru almost exactly doubled their share. In an even year Preseli Pembrokeshire would return to the Tories, and there must be a good chance of at least a more even year in 2005 or 2006. It could be very close.

Social indices:			2001 Gen. Election:			
% Non-white	0.7		Lab	15,206	41.3	−6.9
% Welsh sp	24.4		C	12,260	33.3	+5.6
% Prof/Man	34.0		PC	4,658	12.7	+6.3
% Non-manual	52.6		LD	3,882	10.6	−2.5
£ Av prop val 2000	63 K		SLP	452	1.2	
% Increase 97–00	29.7		UKIP	319	0.9	
% Unemployed 2001	4.1		Lab maj	2,946	8.0	
% Decrease 97–01	3.7		Turnout		67.8	−10.7
% Fin hard/Rank	9.7	473	Elect	54,283		
% Pensioners	26.9					
% Prem mort/Rank	34	269				

Member of Parliament

Jackie Lawrence won here for Labour in 1997, helped in her selection from an all-women shortlist by having been researcher for Pembroke MP Nick Ainger. Birmingham-born in 1948 and educated at Upperthorpe School, Darlington, she arrived in Pembrokeshire in the 1970s and learned Welsh to help her children cope with bilingualism at school. A pitcher of planted questions and fully signed up to the contemporary orthodoxies on devolution and hunting, she has done little to trouble the scorers.

PRESTON

The turnout of 29% in the Preston by-election of November 2000 caused by the death of Audrey Wise was not just a matter of the alternative attractions of Christmas shopping. It presaged the dramatic national fall of June 2001 – to '50.00%' here, according to the officially published election results; and Mark Hendrick won again with a comfortable margin but a reduced numerical majority from 1997.

Before 1983 the seats called Preston North and Preston South were among the most marginal in the country. The smallest majority at the 1979 General Election was gained by the Conservative Robert Atkins at Preston North – just 29 votes. Labour's Stan Thorne won Preston South, traditionally rather better for his party, by 621 votes. Yet since Preston has been united as a single constituency, Labour has had no difficulty whatever, and won by over 18,000 votes in 1997.

This apparent mystery is explained by the fact that prior to 1983 both Preston seats included Conservative suburban territory. North contained the very middle-class community of Fulwood, now in the Ribble Valley constituency, while South crossed the river Ribble to take in Walton-le-Dale, which was then switched to South Ribble. Preston itself is strongly inclined to Labour. It is an old cotton town, the home of Richard Arkwright of spinning jenny fame. It has a large Asian community in the inner parts of the town, especially around Deepdale (the home of Preston North End football club), terraced working-class streets, council estates like the Labour fortress of Ribbleton, and only one regularly Conservative ward, Ashton. It was also one of the main centres of Irish Catholic immigration in the nineteenth century. In March 2002 it was the only English community among five new cities created for the Queen's Golden Jubilee.

Social indices:			2001 Gen. Election:			
% Non-white	12.3		Lab/Coop	20,540	57.0	−3.8
% Prof/Man	23.2		C	8,272	23.0	+1.0
% Non-manual	45.6		LD	4,746	13.2	−1.5
£ Av prop val 2000	47 K		Ind	1,241	3.4	
% Increase 97–00	17.4		Grn	1,019	2.8	
% Unemployed 2001	4.3		Ind	223	0.6	
% Decrease 97–01	2.4		L/C maj	12,268	34.0	
% Fin hard/Rank	32.9	107	Turnout		50.0	−15.9
% Pensioners	25.1		Elect	72,077		
% Prem mort/Rank	50	45				

Member of Parliament

Mark Hendrick replaced the late Audrey Wise here in the 2000 by-election, having beaten her left-wing daughter, Val, to the nomination. Half-Somali, he was born in Salford in 1958, and educated at Salford Grammar Technical School, Openshaw Technical College, Manchester and Liverpool Polytechnics and Manchester University, qualifying in electrical engineering and computer science, and then working for the Science and Engineering Research Council. He was a Salford City Councillor for eight years, and MEP for Central Lancashire (including Preston) from 1994 to 1999. Though a moderate New Labour figure, he reportedly declined NEC advice to seek a seat in the Midlands and so failed to secure a high enough placing on the local list for the European Parliament election in 1999. His election brought the total of Labour's ethnic minority non-white MPs to 10, increased by 2001 to 12.

PUDSEY

Labour increased their share of the vote in the Pudsey constituency by 19% between 1992 and 1997, a remarkable figure but not the highest anywhere – there were nine greater figures recorded. What was really out of the ordinary was that this advance came more at the expense of the Liberal Democrats than the defending Tories. Pudsey had at one time been thought to be a Lib Dem target, but their vote fell from 26% to 14% in 1997, and Labour leapt forward to seize the seat by over 6,000. In 2001 there was almost no movement at all in the shares of vote of the three main parties, even as turnout fell by 11%: abstentionism clearly affected all parties equally.

The Pudsey constituency is situated between the two largest towns in West Yorkshire, Leeds and Bradford. It consists of three units: Pudsey itself, the Leeds suburb of Horsforth, and Aireborough, which is a composite ward made up of the towns of Guiseley, Yeadon and Rawdon in the Aire valley. Although technically within the city of Leeds now, Pudsey retains a hard-headed independence and community of interest which justifies its existence in its present form as a constituency.

Much of the housing in the division is made up of neat Pennine stone terraces dating from the period before the First World War, and of unpretentious inter-war semis. However, an untutored impression of its appearance can mislead: this is a comfortable middle-class seat in the main. Over three-quarters of the housing is owner-occupied. Well over 50% of employment is in non-manual occupations. Jobseekers are among the lowest quartile in the UK. There are hardly any non-white residents. Horsforth is an expensive dormitory for Leeds. It is scarcely surprising that the Conservatives held Pudsey from 1922 to 1997.

Yet just as they have now won two national landslides, it is Labour who now rules in the home constituency of Yorkshire cricket (Sir Len Hutton, Brian Close, Ray Illingworth) and fish and chips (Harry Ramsden).

Social indices:			2001 Gen. Election:			
% Non-white	2.1		Lab	21,717	48.1	−0.0
% Prof/Man	35.1		C	16,091	35.6	−0.7
% Non-manual	60.1		LD	6,423	14.2	+0.2
£ Av prop val 2000	80 K		UKIP	944	2.1	
% Increase 97–00	27.3		Lab maj	5,626	12.5	
% Unemployed 2001	1.6		Turnout		63.3	−11.1
% Decrease 97–01	0.6		Elect	71,405		
% Fin hard/Rank	14.0	375				
% Pensioners	25.4					
% Prem mort/Rank	18	495				

Member of Parliament

Paul Truswell, a Leeds City councillor for 15 years, unexpectedly won this seat in 1997 after 75 years of Conservative occupation. Born in 1955, son of a steelworker, and educated at Firth Park Comprehensive School, Sheffield and Leeds University, he worked successively as journalist and local government officer before 1997, since when he has been conspicuous only for piloting through a bill to make off licence staff liable for sales to under-age customers, following the death of a local 14-year-old boy who had been run over after drinking three cans of lager. His bill also made it unlawful for adults to buy drink and hand it to children outside.

PUTNEY

One of the most bitter results – and certainly televised counts – of the 1997 General Election came at Putney, where most media attention was paid to the sitting MP, the former minister and 'personality' David Mellor arguing with the founder and leader of the Referendum Party, Sir James Goldsmith. In fact the winner by 3,000 votes was the Labour candidate, Tony Colman, who thus broke an apparent two-decade trend towards the Tories in this part of south-west London.

In some ways Putney is socially similar to its neighbour to the west, Richmond and Barnes. It is well over 70% middle class, with a strong academic and intellectual presence, and a reputation for progressive politics. Comfortably set between the greenery of Barnes Common, Putney Heath, Wimbledon Common and Richmond Park, there is considerable affluence in the constituency, and a lower than average non-white population for Greater London. Yet unlike Richmond, it is not the Liberal Democrats but Labour who benefit from the still-substantial anti-Tory vote – indeed the Lib Dems captured little over one-eighth of the votes cast in the last general election.

The reason for this lies partly in Putney's political geography. The Labour strength is concentrated in the division's council estates: the model cottage estate at Roehampton was one of the earliest local authority housing developments in Britain, and since the war it has been joined by the large development on the other (west) side of Roehampton Lane, which with its tower blocks and landscaped layout seems to be strongly influenced by the architectural and social ideas of Le Corbusier. Other early examples of the tower block concept are to be found at Wimbledon Parkside.

Together with garnering middle-class support, these neighbourhoods enabled the one-time Arts Minister Hugh Jenkins to hold Putney for Labour from 1964 to 1979. Then he lost the seat to David Mellor, who benefited from the low tax policies of the Tory-controlled borough of Wandsworth and from social, economic and demographic change.

It is a sign of the successful appeal of the reformed Labour Party under Tony Blair that despite these handicaps they could win Putney in 1997, and it wasn't Goldsmith's doing; he actually did little better than average for candidates of his party and polled only about half as many votes as the Labour majority. With Goldsmith's departure from the scene, there was no Conservative improvement in 2001. However, should the bases of Labour support crumble, principally their delivery of successful economic policy between 1997 and 2001, Putney could very easily return to the Conservative ranks.

Social indices:			2001 Gen. Election:			
% Non-white	12.0		Lab	15,911	46.5	+0.8
% Prof/Man	49.5		C	13,140	38.4	−0.5
% Non-manual	71.8		LD	4,671	13.6	+2.9
£ Av prop val 2000	245 K		UKIP	347	1.0	+0.5
% Increase 97–00	65.7		PA	185	0.5	
% Unemployed 2001	2.6		Lab maj	2,771	8.1	
% Decrease 97–01	2.6		Turnout		56.5	−16.6
% Fin hard/Rank	20.6	265	Elect	60,643		
% Pensioners	25.2					
% Prem mort/Rank	36	230				

Member of Parliament

Tony Colman, an unusual Labour figure as a former company director-turned-council-leader, won this seat in 1997. Previously for six years leader of Merton Council and before that a chief executive, then director, at Burton's Group plc, he was born in 1943 and attended Paston Grammar School, North Walsham and Magdalene College, Cambridge. Variously described as 'prissy', 'dapper' and 'camp', with a record of complaint about the local Tory flagship, Wandsworth Council, he also claims credit for the reduction by a half of sleep-disrupting night flights into Heathrow over Putney. He was PPS to Northern Ireland Minister Adam Ingram (1998–2000) until his age, which he increasingly looked, caused him to make way.

RAYLEIGH

Rayleigh is a relatively new constituency name, introduced for the first time by the Boundary Commission which reported in the spring of 1995. That Commission increased the allocation of parliamentary seats to the county of Essex by one. However it would be a mistake to assume that Rayleigh is the extra, new constituency. In fact this seat is essentially the former Rochford division, minus a little over 10,000 voters in Rochford itself, Great Wakering, and out to Foulness Island which have been added to the existing Southend East. The seat now called Rayleigh was in fact less altered (except in name) than many other Essex seats. Rather, the constituency with the best claim to be regarded as the additional one in the county is Essex North.

Rayleigh is very Conservative indeed. It consists of a number of suburban communities north-west of Southend-on-Sea, most of which have grown rapidly through private housing development since the Second World War. As well as Rayleigh itself, these include Hockley and Hawkwell, and Hullbridge up towards the Crouch. On the other (north) bank of the Crouch is a place which typifies this area's growth: South Woodham Ferrers. This community more than doubled its population in the 1980s, and according to the 1991 Census one of its two wards, South Woodham Ferrers Collingwood East and West (yes, that is one ward name) increased from 200 in 1981 to 7,546 in 1991 – a rise of 3,673%! All of this development is owner-occupied, of course. There was never much council housing in this part of Essex and the Rayleigh seat has probably the highest proportion of owner-occupiers anywhere in Britain, along perhaps with the neighbouring Castle Point, both of the order of 90%.

The Rayleigh seat is not upper class. The proportion of residents with higher academic or professional qualifications is lower than the national average, as is that of those in higher management. Nevertheless, the Conservative majority in Rochford even in 2001 was 8,290 over Labour, even after another small drop in the Conservative percentage majority among votes cast, and a larger decline in the total number of votes, as turnout dropped to 61%.

Social indices:			2001 Gen. Election:			
% Non-white	1.2		C	21,434	50.1	+0.4
% Prof/Man	35.5		Lab	13,144	30.7	+1.8
% Non-manual	65.7		LD	6,614	15.5	–4.3
£ Av prop val 2000	115 K		UKIP	1,581	3.7	
% Increase 97–00	46.8		C maj	8,290	19.4	
% Unemployed 2001	1.4		Turnout		61.0	–13.6
% Decrease 97–01	1.4		Elect	70,073		
% Fin hard/Rank	3.8	629				
% Pensioners	22.0					
% Prem mort/Rank	10	594				

Member of Parliament

Mark Francois, former Director of the lobbyist firm Market Access, chubby-faced and Essex-reared, was born in 1965, attended Nicholas School, Basildon, Bristol University and King's College, London. Battle-hardened, he served for four years on Basildon Council in the early 1990s, fought Ken Livingstone at Brent East in 1997, and narrowly missed selection for the Kensington and Chelsea by-election fought by Michael Portillo in 1999, and for East Devon in 2000. A combative questioner who cuts an abrasive dash with estuarial speech in the manner of David Amess, Basildon's MP before he relocated to a higher class of whelk stall in Southend, he expressed his Euroscepticism in backing Iain Duncan Smith in the 2001 leadership ballots.

READING EAST

Reading has on several occasions seen notable examples of the Boundary Commission's willingness to cross local boundaries to create new constituencies of appropriate size. Both of Reading's seats (currently defined as East and West) include external territory as well as wards from the town itself. Reading East's now consists of four close-in and high-density suburban wards within the unitary authority of Wokingham: Bulmershe, Loddon, South Lake and Whitegates, essentially the wards which make up Woodley.

This dilution of the urban core made it harder for Labour to win Reading seats, and they can only do so when they win a general election with a large majority, as in 1997 and 2001. Even in 1997, even with a swing of nigh on 14% in East, their majority only reached 3,795, but Reading notably swung further to Labour in 2001, although this was less marked in the East than in the West division. The economy was clearly the main cause of this endorsement. Unemployment in June 2001 stood at 1.5%, down 46% on 1997 and lower than in all but around 100 seats. Property values had risen by no less than 71% in the same period, from an average value of £88,500 to £152,000, a rate of increase surpassed in only 16 seats, 11 of these within Greater London. This actually caused great difficulties in housing those in essential but low-paid jobs, such as nurses and firefighters, and raised the threat of a labour shortage in the Reading area.

Not, it seems a Labour shortage though. In May 2000 the Conservatives won only one ward (Thames) in the whole seat, as the Liberal Democrats took all the Woodley areas contested and Labour easily cleaned up in inner Reading. Barring a massive local economic downturn, Jane Griffiths has sunny prospects at the next general election too.

Social indices:			2001 Gen. Election:			
% Non-white	9.8		Lab	19,531	44.8	+2.1
% Prof/Man	42.0		C	13,943	32.0	−3.2
% Non-manual	65.6		LD	8,078	18.5	−0.0
£ Av prop val 2000	152 K		Grn	1,053	2.4	
% Increase 97–00	71.5		UKIP	525	1.2	+0.7
% Unemployed 2001	1.5		SA	394	0.9	
% Decrease 97–01	1.3		Ind	94	0.2	
% Fin hard/Rank	10.0	465	Lab maj	5,588	12.8	
% Pensioners	20.1		Turnout		58.4	−11.7
% Prem mort/Rank	18	506	Elect	74,637		

Member of Parliament

Jane Griffiths, a former Caversham-based BBC translator with expertise in Russian and Japanese, was surprisingly elected here for Labour in 1997. Born in 1954 and educated at Cedars Grammar School, Leighton Buzzard and Durham University, she rose politically as a Reading councillor (1989–99). Tall and sallow-skinned, she has protested at male Tory MPs' sexism, whilst at the same time campaigning for more action to combat prostate and testicular cancer by getting Reading councillors and footballers to stand in the street in their underpants. She has also called for a discouragement of new jobs in the overheated Thames Valley in order to ease pressure on housing, and for marital rights for homosexual couples.

READING WEST

Labour did even better in Reading West than its neighbour to the east in 2001. Martin Salter increased his party's share by no less than 8% since 1997, the eighth highest Labour advance in Britain, to make a total of 24.5% since 1992, converting a Conservative majority of over 12,500 into a Labour win by nearly 9,000. He was probably helped by some tactical voting as the Liberal Democrat vote has plummeted, in a way it certainly has not in the nearby seat of Newbury, but essentially he has improved Labour's share in his own right. This is a result of a combination of economic boom conditions, as in Reading East, and his own independence from the government, which has distinguished him from almost all of his huge fellow intake of 1997, most notably in his courageous resistance to air traffic control privatisation.

Reading is an industrial centre, noted for many years for beer, biscuits and bulbs, and later for Metal Box, but nowadays much more for high-technology and corporate headquarters. It is a railway junction, and conveniently situated for the M4 and Heathrow airport, but also a university town. It is in many ways a microcosm of England: it is scarcely surprising that several sociological surveys, and the BBC's controversial 1970s documentary series *The Family*, have been set in this British version of 'Middletown'.

There is a fair selection of council estates in the Reading West division, such as that at Southcote on the old A4 road and Whitley at the southern edge of the town (transferred from Reading East in time for the last election). The 'inner city' terraces, with their sizeable non-white population, are mainly now in the East division – in Abbey, Redlands and Katesgrove wards, though Battle remains in West. But there are swathes of middle-class owner-occupied housing too, of all ages and statures. Reading West also continues to take in tracts of land outside the town itself, including the smart Thames-side villages at Pangbourne and Purley, as well as Theale and Calcot by the Kennet. With this presence of thousands of electors from outside the town, Reading West, like East, must be viewed as a potential Tory regain in circumstances other than those recently pertaining. Salter has shown signs of building a personal vote though, and with a 53% share in 2001 he will be very hard to shift. He seems to represent the best of modern Labour, new in the sense of fresh, without being sycophantic and faceless.

Social indices:			2001 Gen. Election:			
% Non-white	6.1		Lab	22,300	53.1	+8.0
% Prof/Man	33.4		C	13,451	32.0	−6.9
% Non-manual	60.2		LD	5,387	12.8	+0.1
£ Av prop val 2000	124 K		UKIP	848	2.0	+1.5
% Increase 97–00	66.7		Lab maj	8,849	21.1	
% Unemployed 2001	1.5		Turnout		58.6	−11.5
% Decrease 97–01	1.3		Elect	71,688		
% Fin hard/Rank	13.3	388				
% Pensioners	20.9					
% Prem mort/Rank	24	435				

Member of Parliament

Martin Salter, elected here in 1997, a former regional manager of a housing association, has moved from Blairite loyalism to rebellious votes against air traffic control privatisation, whilst also heading up a campaign of resistance against bank branch closures. An estuarially-brogued former Reading Councillor (and deputy leader), he was born in 1954 and educated at Hampton Grammar School and Sussex University, and now resists overcrowding of jobs and housing in the booming Thames corridor. He sought partial renationalisation of the railways after the Paddington train crash in 1999 when it was erroneously thought there were many victims from Reading.

REDCAR

The retirement of the popular figure of Mo Mowlam not only from the Cabinet but from the Commons itself in 2001 was followed by a decline in the Labour majority in Redcar from 21,000 to 13,000. This should not be held in any way against her successor Vera Baird, though, for the swing from Labour to Conservatives was regionally high in the north-east of England – it was even greater in Tony Blair's own Sedgefield seat – and half of it was caused by the nationally typical 13% fall in turnout.

Redcar itself is untypical of the seat that bears its name, for it is a seaside resort on the North Sea, and its wards are the only ones that have regularly elected Conservative councillors (including in the elections for the unitary authority of Redcar and Cleveland in 1999). The constituency is in fact safely Labour, its political tone given much more by heavy industrial south Teesside. Historically the main employers here have been the ICI chemical complex at Wilton and British Steel's works near South Bank. It is a stark and functional landscape, and the very atmosphere here seems polluted and unhealthy, and indeed the medical statistics suggest that this is indeed the case; the premature mortality rate is 19% higher than the average constituency. The Labour majority comes from unglamorous, purpose-built communities like Dormanstown, Eston, and Grangetown, a community whose best-known product is the 'blue' comedian Roy 'Chubby' Brown, a favourite among live working-class audiences (his material is not deemed suitable for TV). It would be very hard to argue that there is anything left-wing about Brown's form of comedy, but Grangetown gave 73% of its votes to Labour in the 1999 local elections (on a 26% turnout).

Many will miss Mo Mowlam's distinctive style, but we should not write off her replacement's chances of making a mark too, and Redcar constituency will be very unlikely to stand in her way.

Social indices:			2001 Gen. Election:			
% Non-white	0.8		Lab	23,026	60.3	−7.1
% Prof/Man	23.0		C	9,583	25.1	+2.0
% Non-manual	47.0		LD	4,817	12.6	+3.1
£ Av prop val 2000	50 K		SLP	772	2.0	
% Increase 97–00	10.5		Lab maj	13,443	35.2	
% Unemployed 2001	7.0		Turnout		57.7	−13.3
% Decrease 97–01	2.8		Elect	66,179		
% Fin hard/Rank	26.9	175				
% Pensioners	24.3					
% Prem mort/Rank	43	124				

Member of Parliament

Vera Baird QC was elected here in 2001, one of four women in Labour's 38-strong intake. Cropped red-headed, born in 1952, daughter of a maintenance painter, and educated at Chadderton Grammar School and Newcastle Polytechnic and the OU, she was called to the Bar (Gray's Inn) in 1975 and took silk in 2000. A feminist who has written books entitled *Rape in Court* and *Defending Battered Women Who Kill*, she works in the Chambers of the radical barrister Michael Mansfield, with Patrick Roche, husband of Labour MP and minister Barbara Roche, among her colleagues. Making an unusual career move at the age of almost 50, she seemed a long-shot for the first female Attorney or Solicitor General, if her Bar experience defending striking miners, Wapping trade unionists, Greenham women, and 'Stop the City' rioters, could be ignored, but she was pipped to that particular post by the resurrected Harriet Harman.

REDDITCH

Redditch was designated as a New Town as late as 1964, and grew in population from 34,000 in 1961 to 77,000 in 1991. Much of this consisted of West Midlands overspill. Many of the accents here are redolent of metropolitan West Midlands or 'Brum' rather than of the rural Worcestershire burr, and there is an ethnic minority community in Central and Batchley, untypical of the situation in, say, Bromsgrove or Wyre Forest. Labour won most of the county council divisions contested simultaneously with the General Election in June 2001 (a useful guide to the breakdown of the voting in the national battle, except that the Liberal Democrats often do better in the more local elections), such as Batchley in the north-west of the town, where most of the housing was originally built by the local council, and Matchborough, Lodge Park and Winyates, but most of these saw narrow margins. The Conservatives fight back in the west of Redditch, and in the two rural wards which survive, Feckenham and Inkberrow. Overall, this is a tightly contested and well balanced constituency.

Jacqui Smith held Redditch for Labour with a majority of under 2,500 in 2001. Her 7% lead over the Conservatives approaches Labour's national performance, but in an even year, should there ever be such a thing again, they would probably lose here. Indeed it would be possible for the Tories to win Redditch and still lose the general election. They need to gain not only this seat, 29th on their target list of Labour marginals, but many more difficult to overturn. This is a measure of the mountain they have to climb to form a new government.

Social indices:			2001 Gen. Election:			
% Non-white	3.6		Lab	16,899	45.6	−4.2
% Prof/Man	30.8		C	14,415	38.9	+2.8
% Non-manual	53.1		LD	3,808	10.3	−0.7
£ Av prop val 2000	88 K		UKIP	1,259	3.4	
% Increase 97–00	36.5		Grn	651	1.8	
% Unemployed 2001	2.6		Lab maj	2,484	6.7	
% Decrease 97–01	2.0		Turnout		59.2	−14.3
% Fin hard/Rank	24.5	205	Elect	62,543		
% Pensioners	19.0					
% Prem mort/Rank	16	523				

Member of Parliament

Jacqui Smith, a Minister of State for Health from 2001, and earlier a Junior Education Minister (responsible for schools) 1999–2001, was elected here in 1997, following selection from an all-women shortlist. With a fairly standard Labour pedigree as a teacher for 11 years and local councillor for eight, she had the additional experience as researcher for Terry Davis MP, who had represented the area in the 1970s. A teacher's daughter, born in 1962 in London, as reflected in her speech, she was educated at Perrins High School, Malvern and Hertford College, Oxford. A wholly on-message Blairite, she is one of a handful of the 1997 intake of women to have babies since becoming an MP, followed, in her case, a year later by deployment of her combative demeanour as a minister. Of the 35 new Labour women MPs elected in 2001 who had been selected from all-women shortlists, she was one of five who by 2001 were in government posts. In December 2001 she refused to say whether she had had her baby vaccinated with the MMR vaccine, following the Prime Minister's similar response to the question.

REGENT'S PARK AND KENSINGTON NORTH

As far as the Conservative Party is concerned, the outcome of the redistribution of parliamentary constituencies in the London boroughs of Westminster and Kensington/Chelsea before 1997 was a case of 'woe, woe and thrice woe'. At the 1992 Election, there were four seats in these two boroughs, all of them won by the Conservatives. Now there are three seats, and one of them is safely Labour. This adds up to an overall loss of three to the Tories, just in this part of central London alone.

The four Westminster and Kensington and Chelsea constituencies which were contested in 1992 were all very small, and clearly some major adjustments had to be made. All sides would accept that a pairing of boroughs was necessary. However, the choice of pairing made by the Commission and the subsequent detailed internal arrangements could scarcely have worked out better for Labour. It is possible that Kensington/Chelsea could have been linked with its neighbouring borough to the west, Hammersmith and Fulham. Rather, a cross-border seat uniting North Kensington with the bulk of the Westminster North seat has been created. Rather illogically (since Regent's Park is not entirely within its boundaries) it is called Regent's Park and Kensington North. In 2001 Karen Buck retained it by over two to one from the Conservatives. The problem for the Conservatives is not so much with the Westminster North section. The difficulties are caused by North Kensington.

Kensington was a starkly divided seat, one of the most politically polarised in Britain. The wards in the south of the seat are all Conservative, often massively so. They are now placed in the Kensington and Chelsea constituency. The five wards north of Notting Hill Gate, on either side of Ladbroke Grove, are all strongly Labour. These are all included in Regent's Park and Kensington North. North Kensington is sometimes known as 'Notting Hill', and is widely reckoned to be one of the centres of London's Afro-Caribbean community. It is the site of the carnival at the end of August, but in fact less than a quarter of the population here is non-white, and there are many Moroccans who are not on the voting register. The whole area does have housing and crime problems, many poor residents, and presents a striking contrast with the opulence of South Kensington.

There is similar territory in north Westminster too: the wards of Queen's Park, Harrow Road and Westbourne are strongly Labour, and counteract the political influence of the mixed Little Venice and Maida Vale and the strongly Conservative St John's Wood. There is some logic in pairing the socially and economically similar north Kensington and north Paddington areas; but it provides a huge slice of good fortune for the Labour Party. The only development on the horizon lies in the next round of boundary changes, not due to come into force until after the next general election, so scarcely an immediate problem; but the Commission's proposals are already known, and they involve a recreation of the Kensington seat. The loss of the north Kensington wards might be thought to threaten Labour's position here, but in fact it is proposed that they will be replaced by different but still solid wards from the southern edge of the borough of Brent, uniting Queens Park and Kilburn. Labour can cope with the concept of a new seat of Regent's Park and Brent South.

Social indices:			2001 Gen. Election:			
% Non-white	25.2		Lab	20,247	54.6	−5.3
% Prof/Man	43.7		C	9,981	26.9	−2.0
% Non-manual	65.3		LD	4,669	12.6	+4.1
£ Av prop val 2000	296 K		Grn	1,268	3.4	
% Increase 97–00	47.7		SA	459	1.2	
% Unemployed 2001	5.5		UKIP	354	1.0	
% Decrease 97–01	3.3		Ind	74	0.2	
% Fin hard/Rank	28.4	154	Lab maj	10,266	27.7	
% Pensioners	22.0		Turnout		48.8	−15.4
% Prem mort/Rank	48	58	Elect	75,886		

Member of Parliament

Karen Buck, a Labour Party staffer for ten years before winning this seat in 1997, and one of a clutch of new Labour MPs who as Westminster councillors publicised the 'homes for votes' affair under the Conservative leadership of Dame Shirley Porter, has made less of a mark in the Commons than might have been expected, and certainly less than fellow former Westminster councillors, Andrew Dismore and Peter Bradley, but she refused an offer of appointment as a Whip, preferring to devote her efforts to her constituents. Born in 1958 and educated at Chelmsford County High School for Girls and the LSE, her career appeared to peak before 1997 in another respect: she was the last woman to be picked from an all-women shortlist, her selection being the cause of a complaint which led in 1996 to the suspension of the practice.

REIGATE

Although to some the very name of Reigate summons up the image of the Surrey 'gin and Jag' belt, in fact this seat is somewhat less socially and even politically monolithic than most of the others in the county. Some of the rare Labour-supporting local authority and county council wards in Surrey are to be found in the largish town of Reigate, in the (former) council estates in the east and south of the town, and in Redhill, its busy commercially oriented neighbour. Over 50,000 people live in the Reigate–Redhill mini-conurbation, establishing a large enough community to sustain substantial working-class neighbourhoods.

Both the Liberal Democrats and Labour seem capable of registering a five-figure vote in this constituency, and it was Labour who did so in their very strong years of 1997 and 2001. It is difficult to avoid the suspicion that the Liberal Democrats did not try to win this seat very hard, with much better prospects elsewhere in Surrey, notably in Guildford. Certainly their campaign was relatively less visible on the ground.

But let us not over-egg the pudding. This is still a very safe Conservative seat; there are very affluent and desirable residential neighbourhoods, for example in north-west Reigate up against the shoulder of the North Downs, in Banstead, in exclusive Kingswood, and there are a number of places like Tadworth where the village atmosphere is not quite extinguished.

The safety of this seat was demonstrated in 1997 when the sitting MP, Sir George Gardiner, was effectively deselected by the Conservatives, but stood under the banner of the Referendum Party. He obtained the fourth best share for this party, 7%, but although it is likely that he must have taken support from the official Conservative, Crispin Blunt, the latter still won by nearly 8,000, and, having overcome this initial obstacle, seems destined for a long career in the Commons.

Social indices:			2001 Gen. Election:			
% Non-white	2.8		C	18,875	47.8	+4.0
% Prof/Man	47.0		Lab	10,850	27.5	−0.3
% Non-manual	70.8		LD	8,330	21.1	+1.1
£ Av prop val 2000	183 K		UKIP	1,062	2.7	+2.1
% Increase 97–00	54.4		Ind	357	0.9	
% Unemployed 2001	0.6		C maj	8,025	20.3	
% Decrease 97–01	1.3		Turnout		60.7	−13.7
% Fin hard/Rank	5.8	584	Elect	65,023		
% Pensioners	27.4					
% Prem mort/Rank	22	455				

Member of Parliament

Crispin Blunt won Reigate in 1997 as replacement for the expelled Sir George Gardiner. Son of a general, and a former captain (for 11 years) in the Royal Hussars, he was born in 1960 and educated at the military public school, Wellington, as a prelude to nearby Sandhurst, and Durham University. A former adviser both as Defence and Foreign Minister of Sir Malcolm Rifkind (1993–97), he followed Rifkind's journey from pro-European to Eurosceptic, favouring 'a Europe of nation states' and opposing the Amsterdam Treaty. Seen by some as patronising, he lives up to his names as both 'crisp' and 'blunt', though the nickname of 'Crippen' is said to be a joke. One of 11 former serving officers on the Conservative benches after 2001, he voted for Michael Ancram's traditionalist centre-right option in the leadership ballots.

RENFREWSHIRE WEST

There are a number of desirable private residential areas in western Renfrewshire, all of which would vote Conservative heavily if they were in England and some have done so anyway: these include Bridge of Weir and Kilmacolm in the Gryffe valley, and the expanding semi-rural ward of Houston. This is pleasant country inland from the Firth of Clyde and just outside the west-central Scottish industrial conurbation which includes Glasgow and Paisley.

It is hard to underestimate the sheer unpopularity of the 'English' Conservative Party in Scotland, though, and they finish third in West Renfrewshire behind the SNP and a long way behind Labour. The town of Erskine, at the south end of the Clyde bridge named after it, splits its support between Labour and the Nationalists; but the seat is really decided in the tough working-class shipbuilding town of Port Glasgow, on the lower reaches of the Clyde adjoining Greenock. Port Glasgow was previously associated with Greenock in a constituency with a Labour majority of 15,000. That seat could easily afford to lose Port Glasgow, and it tipped the balance this division, which had elected a Conservative as Renfrew West and Inverclyde in 1983.

The main alarums here in recent years have concerned the antics and activities of its MP from 1987 to 2001, Tommy Graham, elected for Labour three times but expelled during the last Parliament for his involvement in the extremely unpleasant intra-Labour Party disputes which contributed to the suicide of Paisley South MP

Gordon McMaster in 1997. Graham continued to sit as Independent Labour but did not contest the 2001 General Election, when Jim Sheridan took over for the official party with the same percentage of the vote as Graham had four years before.

This seat is likely to be abolished and split between Paisley seats before the next election.

Social indices:			2001 Gen. Election:			
% Non-white	0.6		Lab	15,720	46.9	+0.4
% Prof/Man	36.2		SNP	7,145	21.3	−5.2
% Non-manual	60.9		C	5,522	16.5	−2.1
% Unemployed 2001	3.6		LD	4,185	12.5	+4.8
% Decrease 97–01	0.8		SSP	925	2.8	
% Fin hard/Rank	28.9	143	Lab maj	8,575	25.6	
% Prem mort/Rank	43	130	Turnout		63.3	−12.7
			Elect	52,889		

Member of Parliament

Jim Sheridan replaced the disgraced and expelled Labour MP, Tommy Graham, as MP here in 2001. As one of the few manual workers in Labour's 38-strong intake, his background could scarcely be more proletarian. Born in 1952 into a Catholic family, he attended St Pius Secondary School, Glasgow, and worked from the age of 15 as a print-room assistant with Beaverbrook Newspapers for three years, a semi-skilled painter for six years, a machine operator for five, and a material handler at Pilkington Optronics for 15 years, until 1999 when he became a full-time Renfrewshire District Councillor. He has also been actively involved in the TGWU as a convenor and on national committees. At the time of his selection to replace Tommy Graham, he was also – conveniently – chairman of the local Constituency Labour Party. In a PLP of 412 MPs with a mere 51 drawn from manual occupations, his CV is redolent of an age long gone, and his seat provisionally (2002) earmarked for abolition.

RHONDDA

Writing in 1997, it was almost impossible to imagine Rhondda as anything other than a mighty Labour stronghold. Yet just two years later, in the inaugural contest within the seat for the Welsh Assembly to sit in Cardiff, Plaid Cymru's Geraint Davies beat the Labour candidate Wayne David by over 2,000 votes. What is more, for the 2001 General Election Labour selected a true outsider, Chris Bryant: born in England, gay, ordained in the Church of England, a public schoolboy; as the campaign battle lines were drawn it seemed almost now to be a shock if he were elected.

Yet the strength of Labour support and the broad mindedness of the valley community voters was too easily underestimated, and in the event Bryant won by 16,000 votes, losing 7% since 1997 but far more importantly and tellingly keeping 68%. It was the Welsh Assembly election which was aberrant, not Chris Bryant's candidature. This true citadel of the valleys was unbroached.

The Labour majority in the Rhondda constituency in 1997 had been 24,931; the party achieved 74.5% of the vote. The two Rhonddas – Fach and Fawr – are the archetypes of the popular image of the South Wales mining valleys. The names of the communities strung like beads along the valley bottom, or clinging to the steep sides of the hills, are as famous as their chapels and male voice choirs: Treherbert, Treorchy, Tonypandy, Ton Pentre, Tylorstown, Ferndale and Mardy, which was a Communist citadel in the 1930s and had one of the last pits to close in the Rhondda. The Communists came second in a general election in a Rhondda seat as recently as 1966.

But it is for Labour voting that the Rhondda is best known. Before 1974 it enjoyed two seats, one in each valley. There is an unbroken tradition of Labour MPs here right back to the election of the Lib-Lab W. Abraham (known as Mabon) in 1885. Although mining has vanished from the Rhondda valleys, the proud little owner-occupied communities of terraced houses retain much of their traditional proletarian spirit. There are scarcely any council houses in the Rhondda. One exception is the windy, bleak, troubled post-war estate of Penrhys, on the top of the hill between the two valleys; Penrhys has been notably less successful as a harmonious unit than the older settlements.

It will be interesting to see how the Welsh Nationalists do in the next Assembly elections here in 2003. Was their victory an expression of the suitability of Plaid Cymru for a specifically Welsh devolutionary body or was it rooted more narrowly in time, due to the Labour leadership's imposition of Alun Michael as their prospective First Secretary? In any case, whatever happens it seems as if Rhondda's MP will be the superficially surprising figure of Chris Bryant for a long time to come.

Social indices:			2001 Gen. Election:			
% Non-white	0.6		Lab	23,230	68.3	−6.1
% Welsh sp	8.2		PC	7,183	21.1	+7.8
% Prof/Man	20.8		C	1,557	4.6	+0.8
% Non-manual	41.1		LD	1,525	4.5	−1.2
£ Av prop val 2000	27 K		Ind	507	1.5	
% Increase 97–00	8.1		Lab maj	16,047	47.2	
% Unemployed 2001	4.0		Turnout		60.7	−10.8
% Decrease 97–01	3.6		Elect	56,059		
% Fin hard/Rank	33.6	105				
% Pensioners	28.8					
% Prem mort/Rank	46	77				

Member of Parliament

Chris Bryant, elected in 2001, was an unusual replacement for Labour's retiring Allan Rogers here in Labour's oldest seat. A former Anglican priest, born (1962) into a Conservative family, he attended public school (Cheltenham) and Oxford (Mansfield College), and joined the Labour Party aged 24. He served as a curate in High Wycombe for three years, was a Labour agent for Frank Dobson in Holborn and St Pancras, and latterly worked as the BBC's Head of European Affairs. Tall, pallid, straight-faced, and openly homosexual, he is a former Chairman of the Christian Socialist Movement and author of various books on Christian socialism, Stafford Cripps, John Smith and Glenda Jackson. As a former Whip on Hackney Council, responsible for expelling Labour councillors, so costing Labour control, he backs PR as a means of avoiding corrupt one-party councils. The first Anglican priest to renounce his orders to qualify to sit in the Commons, he favours disestablishment of the Church of England.

RIBBLE VALLEY

Even the safest of seats can no longer be relied on if a by-election arises. Ribble Valley in rural north Lancashire produced the 13th largest Conservative percentage majority in Britain in 1987. Then in November 1990, the new Prime Minister John Major asked its MP, David Waddington (then Home Secretary) to become Leader of the House of Lords. The subsequent by-election in March 1991 turned out to be a Liberal Democrat triumph, as Mike Carr overturned Waddington's 19,500 majority to win by nearly 5,000 on a 25% swing. In previous eras it would have been quite remarkable; now we have become used to such cataclysmic shifts of opinion. The Conservatives did not defend a single by-election seat successfully from February 1989 to July 1997.

It must of course also be pointed out that we are used to the recapture of by-election losses at the subsequent general election. Ribble Valley, like all other six that the Conservatives lost between 1987 and 1992, returned to the fold. Nigel Evans beat Mike Carr in the April 1992 re-run by 6,542 votes. He now probably has a safe seat, for in 1997 he actually increased his majority slightly, one of the very few constituencies in which his party did; but the impact of the by-election might not have worked itself out until 2001, when there was a further swing of over 5% from the Liberal Democrats to the Conservative, while Labour also improved by 5%.

Ribble Valley could after all almost have been drawn as a Conservative banker when it was created in 1983. It consists of comfortable small towns like Clitheroe, Longridge and Whalley; the affluent Preston suburb of Fulwood; and a swathe of villages, from the affluent and suburbanised environs of Burnley and Blackburn (like Mellor and Wilpshire) across beautiful countryside to the haunting Forest of Bowland. There is little Labour strength here, and what presence there was has been weakened by tactical voting in favour of the Liberal Democrats. Nor was there much long-term Liberal strength in evidence before the opportunity provided by – and seized on – in the 1991 by-election.

Social indices:			2001 Gen. Election:			
% Non-white	1.7		C	25,308	51.5	+4.8
% Prof/Man	42.8		LD	14,070	28.6	−6.4
% Non-manual	62.8		Lab	9,793	19.9	+4.2
£ Av prop val 2000	80 K		C maj	11,238	22.9	
% Increase 97–00	21.5		Turnout		66.2	−12.6
% Unemployed 2001	1.0		Elect	74,319		
% Decrease 97–01	0.7					
% Fin hard/Rank	7.4	547				
% Pensioners	25.6					
% Prem mort/Rank	31	322				

Member of Parliament

Nigel Evans, an itinerant Welsh newsagent and tobacconist, won here in 1992, his fourth parliamentary contest, having lost the safe seat to the Liberal Democrats at the 1991 poll-tax dominated by-election. Born in 1957 and educated at Dynevor School, Swansea and Swansea University, with a family newsagent's business, somewhat unavoidably – given his party's Welsh wipe-out – he became in 1997 frontbench spokesman for Welsh affairs, remaining there typecast as one of the few Welsh-born (but not Welsh-seat-representing) Tory MPs. A gimlet-eyed, partisan, professional politician, he signed up for all the passing orthodoxies, whether 'Walkerite' (in Wales), Thatcherite or Majorite, and loyally backed the Maastricht legislation. In Opposition he dismissed Welsh devolution as 'a turbo-charged county council', and has taken to voting for 16 as the homosexual age of consent, and backed the libertarian Portillo candidacy in the 2001 leadership ballots.

RICHMOND (YORKS)

William Hague may not only have lost the 2001 General Election with no significant improvement at all in his party's position, but he resigned as Conservative leader by breakfast the very next day. One small compensation was that his own performance in his constituency of Richmond, North Yorkshire was outstanding. He improved on his own share of the vote four years before, when he was still Welsh Secretary, by over 10%, to give him a lead over his local Labour rival of 16,319, by some margin the largest Tory majority. He received 37% of the vote, which also promoted Richmond to be technically the safest seat. Whether it will be he who has the easy task of defending this huge lead is not as yet clear.

Yorkshire is vast, and diverse. Even the county of North Yorkshire alone contains four of the largest-area parliamentary constituencies in England (Richmond, Ryedale, Skipton and Ripon, and Vale of York). Here in Richmond is to be found some of the finest unspoilt scenery in the country, the remoter northern half of the Yorkshire Dales National Park, around the beautiful valleys of Swaledale and Wensleydale. This deeply Conservative farming country is so far removed from the industry of the cities of South and West Yorkshire that one can see why some Yorkshire folk think that their homeland could be a state in itself.

The politics of the county of Yorkshire are as varied as the scenery, and as the economy. The huge seat of Richmond, in the far north-west of the county, contains no large towns. Northallerton is the county town of North Yorkshire, and Richmond is an ancient stronghold at the foot of Swaledale. Another centre of population is provided by the army camp at Catterick. But there are hundreds of villages, often little more than hamlets, among the hilly sheep and dairy farms made famous by James Herriot's Yorkshire vet novels.

This idyllic appearance was blighted by recurrent foot and mouth in 2001, which savaged the economy of the Dales through its impact on both farming and tourism. With luck this will prove a temporary if brutal setback, but no one is predicting that the damage done in that fateful year to William Hague's political career will ever be righted, for all his personal strengths and popularity here in his Yorkshire base.

Social indices:			2001 Gen. Election:			
% Non-white	0.7		C	25,951	58.9	+10.1
% Prof/Man	34.8		Lab	9,632	21.9	−5.9
% Non-manual	42.1		LD	7,890	17.9	−0.5
£ Av prop val 2000	92 K		MRLP	561	1.3	
% Increase 97–00	24.5		C maj	16,319	37.1	
% Unemployed 2001	1.7		Turnout		67.4	−6.0
% Decrease 97–01	0.9		Elect	65,360		
% Fin hard/Rank	7.6	535				
% Pensioners	24.4					
% Prem mort/Rank	17	511				

Member of Parliament

William Hague resigned as Conservative leader in 2001 after four years and an electoral humiliation, in which his party made a net gain of one seat, from 165 to 166, the single seat effectively being that at Tatton, lost in 1997 to an Independent who did not contest it again in 2001. Born in 1961, son of a Yorkshire soft drinks manufacturer, he was educated at Wath-on-Dearne Comprehensive School, Magdalen College, Oxford and INSEAD Business School, Paris, and worked for eight years as a management consultant with McKinsey's. In 1989 he won the Richmond by-election, was PPS to Chancellor Norman Lamont by 1990, a Social Security Minister by 1993, and in the Cabinet, albeit at the Welsh Office, by 1995. In 1997 he beat Kenneth Clarke for the leadership in a third ballot run-off by the vote of 92 MPs to 70. Four years on, a career launched with a collar-length-haired 16-year-old schoolboy's sub-Churchillian conference speech of 1977, foundered as an electorally-routed 40-year-old with premature baldness undisguised by a Grade One haircut, and a nasally accented Northern voice mocked by Southern members of his own party. The personal mistake was that of the ambitious politico seeking the leadership too soon; the political error was to target the party's core electorate of ageing xenophobes without bidding for the millions of lost middle-class managers; the historical misfortune was to be running against a Labour government installed on Tory terrain and with a booming economy. His career representing the failure of hope over inexperience, and the first Conservative leader in 80 years to be denied the premiership, in premature retirement he took up the piano.

RICHMOND PARK

Affluence – indeed wealth – and Conservatism do not necessarily go together. Property values in Richmond Park constituency were at the turn of the twenty-first century the fourth highest in the country, with an average of £303,000. It was also in the list of the five seats with the highest proportion of professional and managerial workers. It had the 570th highest number of electors in households in financial hardship. It is now in all practical respects a safe Liberal Democrat seat.

The Liberal Democrats finally gained the seat based on Richmond, Surrey, in 1997. This was actually something of a surprise, for after many close contests it seemed as if the Boundary Commission had just created a safe seat for Jeremy Hanley in the redrawn and renamed Richmond Park.

When Jeremy Hanley first contested Richmond and Barnes in 1983 he won by just 74 votes. For some years the Conservatives had been on the slide, facing some of the most active Liberalism anywhere in the South East with a moribund organisation and some alleged complacency. In 1986 the Liberals swept to power in the borough of Richmond-upon-Thames, winning 49 seats to the Conservatives' three and others' none. They have kept the combined opposition total below 20 ever since. Small wonder that for over a decade Richmond and Barnes was a top-priority target seat for the Liberals in their various guises.

Richmond and Barnes was a very intellectual constituency. Over a third of adults possessed higher educational qualifications (such as degrees) in 1991 compared with a national average of 13%. It was also extremely middle class. Less than two out of ten of those in work had a manual job. The Liberal Democrats strength in the borough made them favourites to win another contest in Richmond and Barnes. Then in time for 1997 came the boundary changes. Richmond and Barnes (less East Twickenham ward, which was on the 'Middlesex' side of the river and has been returned to its seat of origin, Twickenham) was merged with the northern part of Kingston. This effectively abolished Norman Lamont's seat, but it also assisted Jeremy Hanley considerably.

The new territory included the extremely Conservative Coombe and Kingston Hill wards, with their private roads and mansions set around golf courses. It would have added about 5,000 to Hanley's majority if it had been incorporated back in 1992. A word about the new name of the seat. The Commission originally proposed calling it Richmond and Barnes, but this would not acknowledge the arrival of some 26,000 new voters from north Kingston and made it sound like a takeover not a merger. The seat also includes the neighbourhoods of East Sheen, Mortlake, Palewell, Ham and Petersham as well as Coombe and northern New Malden and Kingston. Some bright spark spotted that one thing that all these places had in common was that they bordered on Richmond Park, the largest open space in the capital. While it might be argued that those who live in the park, like deer and Princess Alexandra, do not cast many votes, nevertheless it is at least a positive and unifying feature. Would that many other seats were so pithily named.

In 1997 it clearly looked as if Twickenham was a more realistic target for the Liberal Democrats than Richmond Park, but in the Tories' disastrous year in Outer London they lost not only Twickenham and Richmond Park, but also Kingston/Surbiton, Sutton/Cheam and Carshalton/Wallington, a great swathe of former Surrey. There was initial speculation as to how many of these would be lost, but in fact all five were held with increased majorities, as the Conservatives failed to revive even in opposition and the local MPs all developed and publicised their active service record, and one would now bet that all five will once again be Liberal Democrat after the next general election.

Social indices:			2001 Gen. Election:			
% Non-white	7.0		LD	23,444	47.7	+3.0
% Prof/Man	57.8		C	18,480	37.6	−1.9
% Non-manual	78.9		Lab	5,541	11.3	−1.3
£ Av prop val 2000	303 K		Grn	1,223	2.5	
% Increase 97–00	59.1		UKIP	348	0.7	
% Unemployed 2001	1.5		Ind	115	0.2	
% Decrease 97–01	1.5		LD maj	4,964	10.1	
% Fin hard/Rank	6.6	570	Turnout		67.6	−11.8
% Pensioners	25.2		Elect	72,663		
% Prem mort/Rank	14	552				

Member of Parliament

Dr Jenny Tonge, a former GP and local councillor, won the seat at her second attempt in 1997. A pleasant-looking woman with a sultry voice – if seen by her defeated Conservative opponent Sir Jeremy Hanley as an old bruiser – she endeavours to square up to the brusque and bullying Clare Short as International Development spokesman, and takes a practical GP's liberal line on matters relating to teenage contraception and soft drugs. Born in 1941, the daughter of a Liberal-voting teacher, and educated at Dudley Girls High School and University College Hospital Medical School, she sits on her party's social democratic wing as an advocate of more taxation and assiduously pursues constituency interests such as supermarket siting, unsafe mini-cabs, hospital run-downs and incessant aircraft noise, notwithstanding in the latter case her own advantageous deafness in one ear. She gave sisterly backing to Jackie Ballard in the Liberal Democrat leadership ballot in 1999, but unlike Ballard exhibits the political canniness which explains why she is still an MP and Ballard is not.

ROCHDALE

The Liberal Democrats did very well in the 1997 General Election, winning 46 seats – the highest number for a 'centre' party since 1929. Only three of their sitting MPs were defeated, and two of these (Chris Davies and Diana Maddock) were by-election victors. The only one to lose who had been elected in 1992 was Liz Lynne of Rochdale, who could not hold on against the resurgent Labour Party.

For 20 years the politics of the industrial ex-textile Greater Manchester town of Rochdale was dominated by its gigantic MP, and it came as a surprise to many who did not know the constituency thoroughly that he was able to hand it on at the 1992 General Election to a very different Liberal Democrat figure, Liz Lynne.

In autumn 1972 the massive Cyril Smith caused a political earthquake when he seized Rochdale from the Labour Party in a by-election. A series of landslides to the Liberals followed, the abortive third-party revival of the early 1970s. The Liberal tide ebbed, but Cyril Smith remained, representing Rochdale in the Commons like a rock in the ocean of major-party MPs. His majority rose and fell, but always remained respectably in four figures. In 1987 it dropped to 2,779 as Labour recovered from their 1983 disaster, and when he announced his retirement (not for the first time, but on this occasion he really meant it) it was widely predicted that Labour would resume their place after Smith's distinctive tenure. This proved an underestimation of Liz Lynne, an actress who had contested Harwich in Essex in 1987, for she held on by 1,839. Rochdale had become a Liberal town, in local as well as national elections.

The Conservatives have been thoroughly squeezed as they have languished in third place in the last ten parliamentary contests in Rochdale. Many of those inclined to the right now vote routinely for the Liberals in both council and general elections. Indeed there is some suggestion that Rochdale is starkly divided on left–right grounds, and that this is connected to some extent with the presence of a (largely Pakistani) Asian community in the town, amounting to about 15% of the whole population. Certainly Labour do best in those areas of high ethnic concentration, such as the inner wards of Central/Falinge and Smallbridge/Wardleworth – although it is true that these are also the poorest wards with plenty of council housing and working-class white residents. The Liberal Democrats fight back in almost all-white wards like Spotland, west of the town centre, and Balderstone, with its large council estate presence.

Liz Lynne moved on after her 1997 defeat, and in some ways the new Liberal Democrat candidate Paul Rowen did well after two such strong personalities to lose only 5% of vote share in 2001, and this entirely to the Tories' advantage. Lorna Fitzsimons did not strengthen Labour's position, and should the government's second term run into serious difficulty so may she.

Social indices:			2001 Gen. Election:			
% Non-white	14.9		Lab	19,406	49.2	−0.2
% Prof/Man	29.1		LD	13,751	34.9	−5.1
% Non-manual	49.3		C	5,274	13.4	+4.6
£ Av prop val 2000	55 K		Grn	728	1.8	
% Increase 97–00	23.2		Ind	253	0.6	+0.2
% Unemployed 2001	4.5		Lab maj	5,655	14.3	
% Decrease 97–01	2.3		Turnout		56.7	−13.5
% Fin hard/Rank	34.9	92	Elect	69,506		
% Pensioners	24.5					
% Prem mort/Rank	48	57				

Member of Parliament

Lorna Fitzsimons, a loud, locally-accented, fast-talking, pint-sized (5 feet no inches) ex-student leader who claims to 'embody New Labour' and was once dubbed by the Trotskyist Labour Briefing as 'a power-mad parasite', ousted the Liberal Democrats here in 1997 at the age of 29. A mill-worker's daughter, born in 1967, she was locally-educated at Wardle High School and Rochdale College of Art, and Loughborough College of Art and Design. Rigorously on-message, defending first lone parent benefit cuts as one of the 'hard choices', and then endorsing (amidst a barrage of cat-calls) student grant abolition, she slowed down the launch of her career by a somewhat raunchy tabloid interview. But by 2001 she was a PPS – albeit to the Leader of the House, Robin Cook, whose star it could be said was not firmly in the ascendant. Working with Cook meant working with his deputy – another ex-NUS leader – Stephen Twigg.

ROCHFORD AND SOUTHEND EAST

This is a slightly oddly named seat, for it contains the whole of Sir Teddy Taylor's former Southend East constituency, which makes up by far the bulk of the division. The Rochford element is only a small fraction of the seat which used to bear that name, most of which is now in Rayleigh, amounting to just over 10,000 voters. One would have thought that 'Southend East and Rochford' would have been a far more suitable name, and indeed Rochford is quite fortunate to receive a mention at all.

Southend East is in general the more working-class end of the town, and Labour made a rare strong showing in the 1980 by-election which brought Teddy Taylor back to the Commons, holding his lead to a mere 430 votes. However most of its wards are still strongly Conservative: the party can usually rely on the support of the four coastal wards, which are, working from the centre to the east, Milton, Southchurch, Thorpe and Shoebury(ness). In recent years Labour has usually won the two inland wards of Victoria and St Luke's, but in May 2000 both of these were gained by the Conservatives on turnouts of around 20%.

Effectively Southend East has expanded to its east and north to take in the communities of Rochford and Great Wakering, and the sparsely populated flatlands between the river Roach and the mouth of the Thames, which include Foulness Island, the site of the once-proposed Maplin Airport. Although this territory makes the seat much larger in area and a county constituency, it has little impact electorally. In 1997 Teddy Taylor did rather better than average for a Conservative in Essex, and must have been helped by the absence of a Referendum candidate due to his Euroscepticism; but he would have won in any case, as his majority surpassed 4,000. In 2001 he increased the gap to 7,000. One exceptional feature was the low Lib Dem vote, just over 7%; possibly the local effort was diverted into Southend West, a long-term target in which all their local council success has taken place – but they slipped to third there too. They don't get out of single figures in Castle Point, Harwich or Basildon either. South Essex is clearly not liberally inclined at present.

Social indices:			2001 Gen. Election:			
% Non-white	2.6		C	20,058	53.6	+4.8
% Prof/Man	32.1		Lab	13,024	34.8	–4.9
% Non-manual	61.5		LD	2,780	7.4	–2.0
£ Av prop val 2000	82 K		Grn	990	2.6	
% Increase 97–00	34.0		Lib	600	1.6	–0.7
% Unemployed 2001	4.1		C maj	7,034	18.8	
% Decrease 97–01	4.5		Turnout		53.5	–10.5
% Fin hard/Rank	17.6	311	Elect	69,991		
% Pensioners	30.3					
% Prem mort/Rank	35	256				

Member of Parliament

Following the 2001 Election **Sir Teddy Taylor** had served as a Conservative MP for 37 years, with a short break of ten months in 1979–80. An energetic, populist Glaswegian who won Glasgow Cathcart in 1964 and lost it after 15 years in 1979 (when the seat swung to Labour against the pro-Tory trend of that year), he switched, as all Scots Tories must, to England in order to resume his career at Southend in 1980. Stocky and bald and from a lower-middle-class background, born in 1937 and educated at Glasgow High School and Glasgow University, his one-club political career was determined in 1971 when he quit his Scottish Office Junior Ministerial job over Edward Heath's decision to apply for Common Market membership, since when he has been in the van of every Europhobic revolt, until losing the Whip in 1994. Like many of his anti-EU ilk an unclubbable loner, he is however seen as 'nutty but nice' in his old-fashioned suit, redolent of a character from a 1950s Ealing comedy. He accompanies his Europhobia with across-the-board right-wing sentiments on hanging, homosexuality, abortion and immigration, but is in the small Conservative minority opposing fox hunting. Needless to say, unlike the hapless Tories left behind in Scotland and having to live with it, he opposes devolution as a root-and-branch Unionist.

ROMFORD

There can be little doubt where the very best Conservative result occurred in their deeply disappointing 2001 General Election: Romford. This seat is in the outer East End London borough of Havering, on the very fringe of Essex (and considered by most residents as still part of that distinctive county, well beyond London postcodes and an awful long way in every sense from, say, Richmond Park). The Tory candidate was very much a local man, Andrew Rosindell, who had already done outstandingly well to win Chase Cross ward and build up his share of the vote from 21% in 1986 to 81% (one of the very highest figures in the 32 London boroughs) in 1998. In the parliamentary battle here in 2001 not only did Rosindell produce one of only eight Conservative gains anywhere, but the party's share went up by 11.4%, top of the list among the 643 constituencies they contested – and with a majority of 6,000, Rosindell now finds himself well over half way up the list of safety of Conservative seats, 94th out of 166.

On what was this extraordinary improvement based? Conservative associations and candidates everywhere else, and of course the central party, would love to know if it could be replicated, for an advance of this magnitude is necessary for the Tories to form another government. This may not be so easy. Rosindell is clearly a candidate of dynamic energy, long and well planted in his locality and skilled in connecting with the concerns of the local Romford community in a way far more typical of the Liberal Democrats in recent times. Also the area is particularly open to a staunch right-wing appeal: it should be noted that the Conservatives did very well too to regain Upminster, and Havering was easily the borough in which they improved most in London, and they did exceptionally well in several Essex seats too. Party membership in this sub-region has been replenished rather than aged. Romford marks a beacon, an aim for Conservatives to aspire to across the land: but to say that it will be easy to emulate would be to underrate the personal efforts of Rosindell and his colleagues here.

Romford constituency covers the north-western part of Havering, but it is also the true heart of that borough; at least it contains the small and quaintly named community of Havering-atte-Bower, and Havering Park. In 1997 all three seats in the borough were won by Labour, benefiting from both a national and regional swing, and of the three the capture of Romford represented the greatest achievement and the greatest surprise.

This is owner-occupied (80%), white (96.5%), and suburban. There are relatively few inhabitants from the top or bottom end of the social scale; it has an unusually high proportion of skilled manual workers for a seat which is technically part of Greater London. There are some up-market residential areas like Gidea Park, and no large council estates, current or former. Romford town centre is a major shopping hub (although threatened by out-of-town malls such as the giant Thurrock Lakeside development), and in general the seat is prosperous without being affluent.

Despite his lengthy service in Chase Cross ward, and two previous candidatures for Parliament in other seats, Andrew Rosindell was only 35 years of age when elected and seems to have a safe seat already. It will be very interesting to see if his style continues to produce deviant results now he has 60,000 constituents rather than 5,000.

Social indices:			2001 Gen. Election:			
% Non-white	3.5		C	18,931	53.0	+11.4
% Prof/Man	29.6		Lab	12,954	36.3	–6.9
% Non-manual	63.3		LD	2,869	8.0	+0.1
£ Av prop val 2000	115 K		UKIP	533	1.5	
% Increase 97–00	45.9		BNP	414	1.2	–0.1
% Unemployed 2001	1.9		C maj	5,977	16.7	
% Decrease 97–01	1.4		Turnout		59.6	–11.1
% Fin hard/Rank	9.7	472	Elect	59,893		
% Pensioners	24.2					
% Prem mort/Rank	18	507				

Member of Parliament

Andrew Rosindell recaptured this seat in 2001 on the biggest pro-Tory swing (9.1%) of the election. Son of a tailor and rooted in the Essex suburbs where he was Romford-born in 1966, he attended Marshall's Park Secondary School in Romford and worked for most of the time before 1997 as a freelance journalist and researcher for the right-wing MP for Ilford North, Vivian Bendall, and thereafter ran Bill Cash's anti-EU European Foundation. Hyperactive, he joined the Conservatives at 14, became a Havering councillor at 24, and fought two general elections in Glasgow and Thurrock in 1992 and 1997, on both occasions accompanied by his Union-Jack-coated Staffordshire bull terrier, Spike. A caricature of Essex-man, with a distinct facial resemblance to a young Alf Garnett, he covered the full gamut of right-wing prejudices on hanging, flogging, sexual offenders, abortion, South African sanctions, Europe and immigration, though it was on the latter that he was obliged to retract in 2001 when as a Duncan Smith supporter (in all the ballots) he was asked to quit the Monday Club and Conservative Way Forward in order not to damage his campaign. Early in 2002 the BBC evaded his call for re-instating the National Anthem at the nightly close-down of television, on the grounds that TV no longer closed down.

ROMSEY

After the tragic death of the Conservative MP Michael Colvin and his wife in a house fire in February 2000, the Liberal Democrats won the subsequent by-election in May after a remarkable squeeze on the Labour vote, which was pared down to just 3.75%. This level of tactical voting could only have been created by a positive campaign, rather than just not trying very hard (and it is interesting to see that this Labour – Lib Dem cooperation had continued nearly three years after the Conservatives had been removed from office, and while the Liberal Democrats were in national opposition); it could hardly be sustained in the circumstances of the 2001 General Election. Indeed Labour did slide up to 8% in Romsey then, still one of their poorest results in Britain, but Sandra Gidley held the seat with only a slightly reduced majority. So far in the M3 corridor through the historic county of Hampshire, Romsey looks more like Eastleigh, where the Liberal Democrats have retained a seat won in an initial by-election, than Christchurch, which returned to become a safe Tory seat.

The population of Hampshire grew faster than that of any other county between 1976 and 1991, the last two dates at which the entitlement to parliamentary constituencies has been assessed, surpassing 1.5 million in the latter year. As a result, it is the only county to which the 1995 Boundary Commission awarded two extra seats, a rise from 15 to 17. One of the seats which was undoubtedly new is Romsey. It contains territory which appears to have been cobbled together to make up the numbers; it consists of wards which came from four previous seats, but which formed a majority in none of those.

The largest single element in the new seat is centred on the town after which it is named. About 30,000 electors come from the former Romsey and Waterside division, though the Waterside portion of that seat was more populous (over 50,000 electors) and now forms the basis of the New Forest East constituency. The Romsey seat now extends further north up the Test Valley to take in more attractive villages, several with rolling rustic names: the wards of Dun Valley, Harewood, Kings Somborne and Michelmersh, Nether Wallop and Broughton, Over Wallop, and Stockbridge. These add up to around 10,000 voters who formerly were included in North West Hampshire, centred on Andover.

The two other sources reduced the electorates in two other constituencies. Chandler's Ford and Hiltingbury (13,000 voters) came in from Eastleigh, where they couldn't save the Tories in the 1994 by-election; Hiltingbury is noted for the abysmal performances of local Labour candidates (5% of the vote in May 2000, for example). Finally, and most oddly of all, the safest Conservative ward in Southampton, Bassett, was transferred along with its 11,500 electors from Southampton Test. This is a wholly urban area, totally part of the city, and it is hard to see what it has in common with, say, Over Wallop (which is midway between Andover and Salisbury). Its loss had a negative impact on the Conservatives' chances in the formerly super-marginal Southampton Test. However, although Romsey looked almost to be drawn to corral Conservatives into an ultra-safe seat, things just haven't worked out that way, a demonstration of the unpredictability engendered by the intervention of by-elections.

Social indices:			2001 Gen. Election:			
% Non-white	2.0		LD	22,756	47.0	+17.5
% Prof/Man	43.9		C	20,386	42.1	−3.9
% Non-manual	66.7		Lab	3,986	8.2	−10.3
£ Av prop val 2000	156 K		UKIP	730	1.5	−2.0
% Increase 97–00	59.6		LCA	601	1.2	
% Unemployed 2001	0.7		LD maj	2,370	4.9	
% Decrease 97–01	1.1		Turnout		68.7	−8.3
% Fin hard/Rank	6.2	579	Elect	70,584		
% Pensioners	24.2					
% Prem mort/Rank	−5	639				

Member of Parliament

Sandra Gidley, a standard Lib Dem by-election landslide phenomenon, appeared here in May 2000 when she converted the 51st safest Conservative seat into the Liberal Democrats' 47th seat, the achievement being the more remarkable for taking a constituency off the Tories in opposition. A typical local councillor made good, she is the personification of ordinariness, born in 1957, a supermarket pharmacy manager, married to an electronics engineer, who likes 'a tough game of badminton'. She was educated at Eggars Grammar School, Alton, at schools in Holland and Germany, and at Bath University, worked as a pharmacist for 21 years, and became a Health spokesman in 2001. Her capture and retention of the seat confirmed the 'M3 rule' of electoral politics: that any by-election within half an hour's drive of the London to Southampton M3 motorway is – as at Newbury, Christchurch, Eastleigh, Winchester, and now Romsey – the Liberal Democrats' for the taking.

ROSSENDALE AND DARWEN

This area has a long tradition of marginality. Before the 1983 boundary changes the Rossendale seat was a compact unit, with good internal lines of communication along a group of east Lancashire Pennine valleys. From Rawtenstall at their heart these ran west to Haslingden, east to Bacup, south to Ramsbottom, north towards Burnley. Rather as in South Wales, distinct communities lay along the valleys like beads on a chain, places like Waterfoot and Stacksteads, Crawshawbooth and Lumb and Love Clough. These industrial communities were once divided between church and chapel, largely Conservative and Liberal respectively, but they have now come to be very closely contested between Labour and Conservative – there are virtually no safe wards, and each community is a microcosm of political as well as economic and social competition. In 1983 the boundaries were enlarged to stretch across some miles of uninhabited moorland to take in the town of Darwen, also created by the textile revolution but now gentrifying as a favoured residential area, especially in the ultra-middle-class Turton.

Labour won four seats from the Conservatives in the county of Lancashire in 1992, and the closest of these gains was Rossendale and Darwen. Janet Anderson ousted the sitting Conservative David Trippier by just 120 votes. It is not surprising that the margin was so close, as it was the stiffest of the four tasks; Trippier had led by very nearly 5,000 in 1987. As in the neighbouring seats of Pendle and Hyndburn, the poll tax played a significant role in assisting Labour to achieve the swing required; the seat contains much terraced housing which had been low-rated under the old system of property taxation. People here felt their pockets and purses squeezed by the government's new policy, and they determined to repay the Conservatives in the voting booths.

The seat had therefore already been gained before Labour's great sweep of 1997. Janet Anderson's majority increased to 11,000 then, but it was more than halved in 2001 as both the Conservatives and the Liberal Democrats advanced, and also the turnout fell by over 14%. The three main parties' share of the vote in Rossendale and Darwen is now not too far from their national average, and it must therefore still be considered a critical marginal.

Social indices:			2001 Gen. Election:			
% Non-white	1.6		Lab	20,251	49.0	−4.7
% Prof/Man	30.9		C	15,028	36.3	+4.1
% Non-manual	51.9		LD	6,079	14.7	+4.1
£ Av prop val 2000	53 K		Lab maj	5,223	12.6	
% Increase 97–00	23.2		Turnout		58.8	−14.6
% Unemployed 2001	2.4		Elect	70,280		
% Decrease 97–01	0.5					
% Fin hard/Rank	23.6	216				
% Pensioners	24.0					
% Prem mort/Rank	38	207				

Member of Parliament

Janet Anderson, a former Whip who rose to be a Junior Minister at Culture, Media and Sport (1998–2001), is a professional politician with as solid a Labour pedigree as could be wished; as a granddaughter and great-granddaughter of Durham miners, daughter of a Labour Party agent, and herself a former PA to Barbara Castle (1974–81) and Jack Straw (1981–87). Born in 1949 and educated at Trowbridge Girls' High School, Kingswood Grammar School, Bristol and Central London Poly-technic, she was elected in 1992 in the next seat to Castle's and Straw's Blackburn, and was soon being run against the left Keynesian Peter Hain as secretary of the Tribune Group when it mattered who controlled it. Her somewhat risqué press interview as Labour spokesman on women, in which she predicted women becoming 'more promiscuous under Labour' may however have retarded this feminist apparatchik's ministerial progress. What just might have terminated it in 2001 was her pre-election commitment that the Blairs would help the foot-and-mouth-damaged tourist industry by holidaying in Britain. They did and she was sacked.

ROSS, SKYE AND INVERNESS WEST

When an MP becomes leader of their party during a parliament, they usually find a dividend in the form of a significantly improved position in their own constituency at the subsequent general election. Ironically this happened to William Hague a couple of hours before he resigned the leadership of the Conservative Party on 8 June 2001, but it was also a benefit for the Liberal Democrat Charles Kennedy, whose party improved to 52 seats, their best since the 1920s – so he had no reason at all to reassess his position. The improvement from 39% to 54% in Ross, Skye and Inverness West was his party's third best, after the extraordinary Kingston/Surbiton result and Romsey, distorted by a year 2000 by-election. This was very much one in the eye for those who had extrapolated from an unprofessional opinion poll throughout the Highlands to suggest that Kennedy's seat was vulnerable as he was leading the national campaign. Nobody aware of the electoral practice in seats such as this would have entertained such an idea.

In the 1995 boundary changes, Charles Kennedy's former Ross, Cromarty and Skye seat lost some acreage and about 10,000 electors in the form of Easter Ross to the expanded Caithness and Sutherland. In return it picked up a similar number of voters in wards of Inverness west of the Caledonian canal, but this is a more compact area. Despite these changes, though, this constituency remained the largest in area of any in the United Kingdom. Not surprisingly, it contains some of the most spectacular scenery in the nation. It stretches all the way from Cromarty and the fertile Black Isle on the east coast to the stark grandeur of the Wester Ross wilderness and the sea-loch-pocked west coast. Since 1983 it has included the island of Skye, which boasts the most dramatic landscape of any Scottish island, with its rounded Red Cuillin mountains and razor-backed Black Cuillins.

Yet in all its near two million acres this seat houses only 56,000 electors, which makes canvassing and campaigning a personal business. This division, however named, has never paid very much attention to national political trends. As recently as 1970 there was a Liberal MP in Ross and Cromarty, Alasdair Mackenzie, but his vote proved to be a product of loyalty to the man, not the party. The Liberal vote collapsed in the 1970s, the Tories regained the seat, and the SDP were granted the Alliance nomination in 1983. The result was to many the most surprising of any in that election. The Conservative Energy Minister Hamish Gray was defeated by a 24-year-old fighting his first parliamentary campaign, Charles Kennedy, for a party fighting its first general election, the SDP. Much has moved on in every sense from then, but Charles Kennedy is still MP for these many acres, and will in all probability be for even more if proposals are confirmed for the replacement of Inverness West with his home base of Lochaber, around Fort William and Ben Nevis.

Social indices:			2001 Gen. Election:			
% Non-white	0.5		LD	18,832	54.1	+15.4
% Prof/Man	30.0		Lab	5,880	16.9	−11.8
% Non-manual	50.4		SNP	4,901	14.1	−5.5
% Unemployed 2001	4.2		C	3,096	8.9	−2.0
% Decrease 97–01	3.1		Grn	699	2.0	+1.2
% Fin hard/Rank	15.6	342	SSP	683	2.0	
% Prem mort/Rank	41	168	UKIP	456	1.3	
			Ind	265	0.8	
			LD maj	12,952	37.2	
			Turnout		61.6	−10.2
			Elect	56,522		

Member of Parliament

Charles Kennedy, an MP at 23 (in 1983) and his party's leader at 39 (in 1999), will, at the age of 78 (in 2031) have overtaken Lloyd George's record of 55 years an MP. Suffering, as all leaders of his party tend to, from not being taken seriously, he comes anyway with a reputation for not taking himself seriously. Victor in the leadership race over fellow bachelor (but more tortured) Simon Hughes, he is seen as less pro-Labour than Paddy Ashdown, but as with all Liberal Democrats, he has to weave between left and right, and to be nominally 'anti-Labour' is no bad thing with Europhile, but anti-Labour, disillusioned Conservative votes to secure. Born in 1959, a crofter's son of Catholic origins, he attended Lochaber High School, Fort William and Glasgow and Indiana Universities. Unlike most of his rural seat colleagues, he votes the full abolition line on hunting.

ROTHERHAM

Like Sheffield, Doncaster and Barnsley, the Metropolitan Borough of Rotherham is a Labour stronghold in South Yorkshire. As in Barnsley, the Conservatives find it very difficult to establish even a significant minority of seats on the Rotherham Council, and the three constituencies assigned to the borough by the Boundary Commission are all completely safe for the Labour Party. This is a land of heavy industry, where coal and steel have both been major sources of employment, and where both have suffered severe or terminal pressures and decline. The gritty communities bear the impress of function rather than beauty or elegance.

The town of Rotherham itself used to be ringed by coal-mines, but almost all have been closed in the last couple of decades. Moreover it has also lost its most famous and dramatic industrial scene, provided by the great British Steel works along the road south-west to Sheffield by the river Don. Now this terrain resembles an urban desert, the desecration of its economy relieved only by the huge out-of-town shopping centre of Meadowhall. Rotherham has been a Labour seat since a by-election in 1933 ended an anomalous two-year period of Conservative representation. There is a pleasant middle-class residential area in south-east Rotherham, which sustains one occasionally Tory ward, Broom, but far more typical are the council estates of wards such as Herringthorpe and Greasbrough and the terraces of Boston and Central, where there is a small Asian community. All these elect Labour councillors – and indeed MPs – with scarcely any competition.

There was another by-election in Rotherham, in 1994, caused by the untimely death of Jimmy Boyce, who had been MP for less than two years after succeeding Stan Crowther at the 1992 General Election. It is not always easy for any party to defend a seat in a by-election, and Denis MacShane held Rotherham with a reduced majority of 7,000 over the Liberal Democrats on a much smaller turnout in May 1994. Having overcome this hurdle, MacShane has had and can expect even easier a ride for the foreseeable future in a town which, as much as any other in England, is a symbol of the decline and death of some of our most traditional industries.

Social indices:			2001 Gen. Election:			
% Non-white	5.0		Lab	18,759	63.9	−7.4
% Prof/Man	25.9		C	5,682	19.4	+5.1
% Non-manual	49.2		LD	3,117	10.6	+0.2
£ Av prop val 2000	49 K		UKIP	730	2.5	
% Increase 97–00	19.2		Grn	577	2.0	
% Unemployed 2001	5.3		SA	352	1.2	
% Decrease 97–01	4.7		Ind	137	0.5	
% Fin hard/Rank	36.1	80	Lab maj	13,077	44.5	
% Pensioners	24.9		Turnout		50.7	−12.2
% Prem mort/Rank	39	191	Elect	57,931		

Member of Parliament

Denis MacShane, a metropolitan journalist dropped into this dying coal and steel seat for the by-election in 1994, and finally, brought to the frontbench as a Junior Foreign Office Minister in 2001, is misleadingly self-described as 'a Eurosceptic who is profoundly pro-European'. In fact he is one of the Labour Party's most committed Europhiles, as befits a former Geneva-based trade union organiser, married to a French Vietnamese wife, and the son of a Polish emigré, born Josef Denis Matyjaszek in 1948 (his current surname being that of his mother). One of Labour's 30 public-school-and-Oxbridge-educated MPs, he attended St Benedict's (RC) School, Ealing and Merton College, Oxford, and London University where he acquired a doctorate in economics. Something of a loner, of whom it has been cruelly said (by David Aaronovitch of the *Independent*) that 'nobody likes a smart-arse, so he always speaks in tones of mingled pity and condescension', in November 2001 it was revealed that he had guided the hand of the Muslim Labour MP, Khalid Mahmood, in crafting an article for the *Observer* expressing the support of British Muslims for the onslaught in Afghanistan on Osama bin Laden and the Taliban.

ROTHER VALLEY

Rather as the Don Valley surrounds Doncaster, the Rother Valley seat has traditionally wrapped itself around Rotherham like a red blanket. It consists of the south-eastern sector of the Metropolitan Borough of Rotherham, with a large number of small communities, mostly created by the coal-mining of the South Yorkshire field: places such as Maltby, Dinnington, Kiveton Park and Thurcroft. Some of the pits here were opened relatively recently, after the First World War, and remained among the last to survive in the British industry: Maltby would be such an example. Other villages are more rural and agricultural, but nevertheless there is no bloc of Conservative support which can win a single ward at local election level, or secure more than 22% of the vote across the constituency in the 2001 General Election.

There is something of a 'neighbourhood effect', whereby middle-class owner occupiers (say) in predominantly Labour areas are less likely to vote Conservative than people of the same economic characteristics who are situated in a solidly Tory suburb. South Yorkshire is decidedly not Conservative country, and the party's lack of local activity reflects a kind of demoralisation, a certainty that they will never win the semi-rural Rother Valley, even with the diminution and indeed perhaps permanent extinction of deep coal-mining. The industrial – and Labour – tradition lives on beyond the grave of the collieries.

Social indices:			2001 Gen. Election:			
% Non-white	0.7		Lab	22,851	62.1	−5.5
% Prof/Man	27.0		C	7,969	21.7	+5.0
% Non-manual	50.8		LD	4,603	12.5	+0.9
£ Av prop val 2000	54 K		UKIP	1,380	3.7	
% Increase 97–00	18.1		Lab maj	14,882	40.4	
% Unemployed 2001	3.4		Turnout		53.2	−14.1
% Decrease 97–01	2.7		Elect	69,174		
% Fin hard/Rank	18.9	290				
% Pensioners	21.9					
% Prem mort/Rank	32	304				

Member of Parliament

Kevin Barron, a one-time Scargillite miner, elected here in 1993, progressively distanced himself from his former mentor to the extent of losing his NUM sponsorship, and co-running the campaign backing Blair's Clause Four redraft in 1995. Born in 1946, son of a power station worker, he attended Maltby Secondary Modern School and Ruskin College, Oxford, and worked at Maltby colliery for 21 years until 1983. Once rising as PPS to Neil Kinnock (1985–88), his career levelled out as a Health spokesman dropped on the morrow of victory in 1997, having earlier failed in a bid to become Chief Whip. Known now as a campaigner against tobacco advertising, even he has loyally accepted delays in implementing a ban on Formula One. Helplessly too, he otherwise understandably bemoans a dead coalfield.

ROXBURGH AND BERWICKSHIRE

In 1983, the leader of the Liberal Party at the time, David Steel, found that his Roxburgh, Selkirk and Peebles constituency, which he had first won at a by-election in 1965, was split in two. He chose to stand for the western of the two new seats, named Tweeddale, Ettrick and Lauderdale; but far from creating additional problems for the Liberals in the Scottish borders, that redistribution actually granted them an extra seat, for Steel was joined in 1983 by Archy Kirkwood, who has won Roxburgh and Berwickshire ever since.

This was originally something of a surprise, for Roxburgh and Berwickshire seemed such a tempting creation to the sitting Conservative MP for Aberdeen South, Iain Sproat, that he abandoned that constituency in favour of adoption here in the east Borders. This proved one of the greatest misjudgements of modern electoral history as Sproat lost to Kirkwood by 3,000 votes, while the Tories held Aberdeen South easily in 1983. (It did not stop Sproat returning to the Commons for a still more southern seat, Harwich in Essex, in 1992, becoming Sports Minister and losing again, to Labour in 1997.) Now Roxburgh and Berwickshire actually looks the safer of the two Liberal Democrat Scottish Border seats, as Kirkwood's majority exceeded Sir

David Steel's in 1992, and easily that of his successor Michael Moore in 1997 and 2001.

Roxburgh includes the largest town in the Borders, Hawick, and the smaller Kelso and Jedburgh with their ancient abbeys. This is good farming country, as well as including many tourist attractions and being known as a mecca for fishing and rugby. The towns have traditionally been the centres of the tweed and knitwear industry. Local elections are often not fought on party lines, and the personal vote of candidates is considerable. That said, Archy Kirkwood must be a strong favourite for re-election for a sixth term, probably in a relatively unchanged Berwick, Roxburgh and Selkirk. The appeal of the Conservative Party has faded dramatically even only just north of the border in recent years.

Social indices:			2001 Gen. Election:			
% Non-white	0.2		LD	14,044	48.8	+2.3
% Prof/Man	25.1		C	6,533	22.7	−1.2
% Non-manual	42.7		Lab	4,498	15.6	+0.7
% Unemployed 2001	3.0		SNP	2,806	9.7	−1.6
% Decrease 97–01	0.3		SSP	463	1.6	
% Fin hard/Rank	26.8	179	UKIP	453	1.6	+1.0
% Prem mort/Rank	33	283	LD maj	7,511	26.1	
			Turnout		61.2	−12.7
			Elect	47,059		

Member of Parliament

Archy Kirkwood, unusually for a Liberal Democrat MP from a Labour-voting working-class background, and who initially himself had Labour affiliations, was first elected here in 1983. Son of a railwayman, born in 1946 and educated at Cranhill Senior Secondary School, Glasgow and Heriot-Watt University, he worked as a solicitor at Hawick in David Steel's Borders constituency until inheriting this part of it. A specialist on social security policy, now retreated into the non-partisan realm of select committee chairmanship (by 2001 Work and Pensions), he was for five years (1992–97) his party's Chief Whip, having spent most of his time before that shadowing Health and Social Security. Somewhat cadaverous-looking, he votes with the countryside lobby against fox hunting bans.

RUGBY AND KENILWORTH

One of the more unlikely Labour gains of the 1997 Election, this seat was seized by Andy King by just 495 votes from the MP for 14 years, James Pawsey. It is not a surprise that the town of Rugby should be represented by a Labour member – this has happened before. It certainly is that Kenilworth ever should be.

Rugby and Kenilworth is one of the more illogically drawn seats in England. The two towns after which the division are named have little in common, and their shared parliamentary representation dates only from 1983. Kenilworth, part of the borough of Warwick, looks much more to Leamington Spa, Warwick, and indeed Coventry than it does to Rugby, a town much further away in terms of both mileage and spirit. Nor are their political preferences similar.

When Rugby formed a constituency on its own it had one of the most peculiar of electoral histories. First of all, it elected the eccentric 'rustic sage' W.J. 'Bill' Brown as an Independent during the war, in 1942, and again in 1945 against official Labour and Conservative opposition. It then developed as a major-party marginal with the habit of swinging against the national tide – towards the Conservatives in 1964, towards Labour in 1970, and towards the Conservatives again in October 1974. Finally in 1979 it came resoundingly into line, as James Pawsey beat the sitting Labour MP William Price with an 8% swing.

On its own, though, Labour is still competitive in the town of Rugby, despite its encapsulation of the spirit of the nineteenth-century public school (William Webb Ellis and rugby union, Dr Thomas Arnold the famous headmaster, Tom Brown and his famous schooldays), Rugby is actually a heavy engineering centre and a largely working-class town. There are still several wards where Labour wins large majorities: the rather aptly named Benn, with its terraced housing and large ethnic minority population in the town centre, and the wards in the north of the town, industrial Newbold and New Bilton. The Tories fight back in the southern half of Rugby and in the affluent villages in rural Warwickshire which are also included in the borough. However, Kenilworth is one of the most attractive commuting bases for Coventry, little over five miles away. While its sophisticated electorate has often returned local Liberal councillors, it remains one of Britain's most affluent and middle-class towns. It is indeed a sign of the deep disillusionment with the long stewardship of the Conservatives that Rugby and Kenilworth joined 144 other constituencies as Labour gains in 1997.

As in neighbouring Warwick and Leamington, as in several East Midlands seats such as Kettering and Wellingborough, Labour actually improved their position in this very close marginal in 2001. It was not critical. They could have lost Rugby and Kenilworth and been returned with another vast overall majority. But voters felt that the government was worthy of a second term, not so much a second chance as to carry on with what was seen as good work, and so was Andy King.

Social indices:			2001 Gen. Election:			
% Non-white	4.5		Lab	24,221	45.0	+2.0
% Prof/Man	36.9		C	21,344	39.7	−2.6
% Non-manual	60.5		LD	7,444	13.8	−0.4
£ Av prop val 2000	98 K		UKIP	787	1.5	
% Increase 97–00	41.1		Lab maj	2,877	5.3	
% Unemployed 2001	2.0		Turnout		67.4	−9.7
% Decrease 97–01	1.1		Elect	79,764		
% Fin hard/Rank	11.8	417				
% Pensioners	25.6					
% Prem mort/Rank	24	437				

Member of Parliament

Andy King, a Catholic Scotsman was dropped in here, after eight years as a local county councillor, in May 1997. A motor mechanic and postal worker-turned-social work manager, he was born in 1948, son of a labourer, and educated at St John the

Baptist School, Uddington, Lancashire, Coatbridge Technical College, Missionary Institute London, Stevenage College, Nene College, Northampton, and Hatfield Polytechnic. Very unobtrusive as an MP, his unexpected arrival in 1997 ought to have been followed by his expected exit in 2001.

RUISLIP-NORTHWOOD

The Ruislip-Northwood constituency is situated on the very north-western edge of London. It is a desirable residential area which shares many of the characteristics of the neighbouring seat of South West Hertfordshire over the county boundary. It is strongly Conservative by current standards. In 2001 John Wilkinson obtained a majority of 7,500, and this in a seat of only 60,000 electors, almost 10,000 below the average for England, in a disastrous year for his party.

The nature of the residential areas in Ruislip-Northwood range from the solidly middle class to wealthy and exclusive neighbourhoods and private estates, these latter being concentrated in Eastcote, Ruislip and Northwood wards (although the Merchant Taylors' School and the Moor Park estate, associated with Northwood, are actually just over the border in Hertfordshire). Most wards voted in Conservatives easily even in the May 1994 local elections, and Ruislip-Northwood remains an epitome of suburbia, and one of the safest Conservative seats in Greater London.

For some decades now this part of London, like the capital as a whole, has been over-represented – that is, its seats have been smaller than average, and fewer votes are needed to elect an MP. In the next boundary review, not due to be enforced until two elections hence, Hillingdon will lose its entitlement to three full seats, and it was proposed that this northern seat will cross the borough boundary to take in Pinner from Harrow West. Northwood and Pinner would be a solidly Conservative seat, and the parts of Ruislip taken into Uxbridge would assist the Tories there, but the loss of Pinner will make the Conservatives' chances of regaining Harrow West, which they think should rightfully be theirs, much harder. So they were not pleased, and contested the north London recommendations vigorously.

Social indices:			2001 Gen. Election:				
% Non-white	7.4		C	18,115	48.8	−1.5	
% Prof/Man	41.3		Lab	10,578	28.5	−4.4	
% Non-manual	69.7		LD	7,177	19.3	+3.1	
£ Av prop val 2000	168 K		Grn	724	1.9		
% Increase 97–00	52.6		BNP	547	1.5		
% Unemployed 2001	1.3		C maj	7,537	20.3		
% Decrease 97–01	1.2		Turnout		61.1	−13.1	
% Fin hard/Rank	5.2	601	Elect	60,788			
% Pensioners	26.9						
% Prem mort/Rank	19	491					

Member of Parliament

John Wilkinson, one of the Conservatives' 14 Old Etonian MPs, was first elected here in 1979, though had been an MP for Bradford North from 1970 to 1974.

Pink-faced and boyish-looking notwithstanding his age (he was born in 1940), he was educated at Eton where his father was a master, Cranwell, and Churchill College, Cambridge, and served in the RAF for five years, whence his expertise in defence-related matters and his preference for American over European links. A Europhile-turned-Eurosceptic, he was one of eight Tories to lose the Whip over rebel-voting on Europe in 1994. Threatened in his local party for this dissidence, he nevertheless also called for an elected House of Lords and backed an elected London Assembly, again opposing the official Party line, and has been described as 'intense and unyielding' and 'decent but somewhat obscure'. He voted for the most right-wing leadership option of Redwood in 1997, even following him into the final round pact with Kenneth Clarke, but backed the more unorthodox Portillo ticket in 2001.

RUNNYMEDE AND WEYBRIDGE

This was the most heavily altered of Surrey's 11 constituencies before the 1997 Election, as the entirely new name implies. In fact it is based on the old seat of Chertsey and Walton, but fairly loosely. About 25,000 voters from that seat, in Walton-on-Thames and Hersham, were transferred to a division now to be called Esher and Walton. In exchange about the same number were brought in from Surrey North West; these live in the communities of Egham, Englefield Green, Hythe, Thorpe and Virginia Water. A new MP, Philip Hammond, won the new Runnymede and Weybridge constituency with a majority of very nearly 10,000 in 1997. There was almost no change at all in the pattern of party preference among those who voted in June 2001, but only 56% did so, the lowest turnout in Surrey, and below even the English and UK average. There is a theory that the non-voters in 2001 were 'Old Labour' – but in Runnymede and Weybridge, where the fall was 15% or 9,000 souls, this could hardly be predominantly or even disproportionately so.

The borough of Runnymede, in north-west Surrey, is named after the meadows by the Thames where Magna Carta was signed in 1215. The 'great charter' was not actually the guarantee of democratic popular liberties that so many admirers, especially American, believe, but rather an enforced set of concessions squeezed by warring and rebellious barons out of the underestimated King John (who was probably more likely to look after the interests of the common people than they were). However, there is no reason to believe that elections in the Runnymede and Weybridge seat will be anything other than strictly democratic, although it is true that the party most associated with the British aristocracy will emerge victorious.

Part of Windsor Great Park is within this constituency, but more votes are cast in some elite areas where new money is very evident. St George's Hill, Weybridge, belies its past as a haunt of the primitive communist Diggers of the 1640s to rank as probably the best known of the private estates of the super-rich, with its multi-million pound houses widely spaced and jealously guarded. Almost as exclusive and ostentatious is the Wentworth estate around the golf club near Virginia Water, most of which is in Surrey. The rest of the constituency is less grand, ranging from the merely very affluent (Oatlands Park) through the comfortable middle class (Addlestone, New Haw) to the more mixed and slightly seedy (Chertsey town).

The chances of Digger, communist, or any other kind of revolution are minimal in Runnymede and Weybridge.

Social indices:			2001 Gen. Election:			
% Non-white	2.8		C	20,646	48.7	+0.1
% Prof/Man	43.1		Lab	12,286	29.0	−0.5
% Non-manual	66.9		LD	6,924	16.3	+0.0
£ Av prop val 2000	226 K		UKIP	1,332	3.1	+1.9
% Increase 97–00	64.3		Grn	1,238	2.9	
% Unemployed 2001	0.7		C maj	8,360	19.7	
% Decrease 97–01	1.0		Turnout		56.1	−15.3
% Fin hard/Rank	5.7	589	Elect	75,569		
% Pensioners	25.7					
% Prem mort/Rank	13	559				

Member of Parliament

Philip Hammond, a DTI spokesman from 2001 and previously (1998–2001) a Health spokesman, was elected in 1997. A somewhat cadaverous-looking management consultant and small manufacturer of medical equipment, he was Essex-born in 1955 and attended Shenfield School, Brentwood, and University College, Oxford. Relatively unpartisan, he has been rather mercilessly mocked as resembling a 'Moss-Bros "suits-you-sir" sales assistant' (Matthew Parris) and admits to being a non-golfer in a seat littered with golfing facilities. In 1997 he voted for Lilley, then Hague; in 2001 for Portillo.

RUSHCLIFFE

This seems to be just the right seat for Kenneth Clarke. It is strongly associated with his home town, the realistic, down to earth, somewhat gritty, land of good value, what you see is what you get Nottingham. But its also is solidly Conservative, consisting as it does of the suburbs and rural areas of south Nottinghamshire in which the more respectable and successful, enterprising and law-abiding, educated yet conventional members of society live. It is not flashy or trendy, nor reactionary or insular. It has sustained the reliably unmodernised politics of Mr Clarke for over 30 years.

Rushcliffe is the southernmost constituency in Nottinghamshire. There is no town called Rushcliffe – the seat was named after the local authority district with which it was identical at the time of the wave of boundary changes in the county in 1983; it should be noted that it bears little resemblance to the seat of the same name which existed before 1974, which was actually the predecessor of the current Broxtowe.

The largest community in Rushcliffe is West Bridgford, the 70% middle-class commuter suburb which lies across Trent Bridge from the centre of Nottingham. The Nottingham Forest football ground, the Test cricket ground, and the Notts County Council headquarters all lie technically in West Bridgford, which indicates that it can really be counted as an integral part of Greater Nottingham (although most residents would resist incorporation with all vigour). The rest of Rushcliffe is more rural, but it includes a handful of prosperous small towns or overgrown villages: Bingham,

Radcliffe-on-Trent, Keyworth, East Leake, Ruddington. These are all popular with affluent commuters to Nottingham and beyond, and are all very Conservative. There are also about 50 villages of a similar political persuasion. The only Labour-inclined community is the anomalous Cotgrave, where the first coal-mine south of the Trent was sunk as recently as the 1960s, and which lasted barely 30 years. Its closure has added to the social and economic problems which have afflicted Cotgrave for over a decade.

The seat is 79% owner-occupied, 98% white and in 1997 it was the only seat in the county of Nottinghamshire which resisted the Labour advance. The Conservatives will have to extend their appeal to different types of seat if Ken Clarke's party is to regain the office to which it became accustomed in the twentieth century.

Social indices:			2001 Gen. Election:			
% Non-white	2.3		C	25,869	47.5	+3.1
% Prof/Man	45.0		Lab	18,512	34.0	−2.2
% Non-manual	68.4		LD	7,395	13.6	−0.7
£ Av prop val 2000	113 K		UKIP	1,434	2.6	+2.0
% Increase 97–00	46.2		Grn	1,236	2.3	
% Unemployed 2001	1.5		C maj	7,357	13.5	
% Decrease 97–01	1.5		Turnout		66.5	−12.4
% Fin hard/Rank	5.1	604	Elect	81,839		
% Pensioners	25.0					
% Prem mort/Rank	15	545				

Member of Parliament

Kenneth Clarke, MP for Rushcliffe since 1970 when he recaptured the seat lost to Labour in 1966, has twice been passed over for the Conservative leadership, in 1997 and 2001. On the second occasion he carried a plurality – 59 – of the Tory MPs (against Iain Duncan Smith's 54 and Michael Portillo's 53) but lost when the matter was thrown, for the first time under new rules introduced by William Hague, to the membership by a margin of six (61%) to four (39%), because of the gap between his own Europhilia and the Euroscepticism of the Tory grass roots. From a working-class Tory background, born in 1940, son of a pit electrician who became a jewellery shop owner, but grandson of a communist tool-room engineer at Raleighs, he attended Nottingham High School and Gonville and Caius College, Cambridge and chose the Bar as a route into Tory politics. A Commons frontbencher of unparalleled longevity – continuously for 25 years from 1972 to 1997 – he occupied four Cabinet posts at Health, Education, Home Office, and Treasury, between 1988 and 1997. A breezy, opinionated, big hitter with a paunch, with paucity of detail masked by vast self-confidence, and recalled as a successful Chancellor who was famously ignorant of economics, he earned a reputation for not suffering fools gladly, which – as his 2001 campaign manager conceded – was 'a serious deficiency in a party full of them'. With his goose over-cooked by the introduction of the rank and file membership into leadership elections, his second return in 2001 to Rushcliffe-les-deux-Eglises seemed likely to be definitive as he joined R.A. Butler and Denis Healey in the ranks of Best Prime Ministers We Never Had.

RUTLAND AND MELTON

The smallest of the historic counties of England, Rutland lost its administrative independence when it was absorbed into Leicestershire in 1974, but regained it as a England's smallest unitary authority, calling itself Rutland County Council, in the late 1990s. It was long associated with another county for parliamentary purposes, in the shape of the constituency of Rutland and Stamford (Lincolnshire), and this has not changed. In 1983 the new county boundaries were recognised in the constituency boundaries as Rutland (still a local government district) was tied to Melton Mowbray. Melton made room for Rutland by losing most of the suburban Soar valley north of Leicester to Loughborough, and in 1995 the Boundary Commission removed the remaining suburban element (Thurmaston, Syston, East Gosford, Queniborough and Six Hills) between the rivers Soar and Wreake, leaving Rutland and Melton as an much more rural seat. It even picked up about 9,000 village voters from Harborough to make up partially for the 22,000 lost to the new Charnwood.

This is a constituency of fox hunting, pork pies and Stilton cheese, and of notable independent schools (Uppingham was intensely treated in Stephen Fry's schooldays – and nights – autobiography *Moab is my Washpot* and Oakham's headmaster is to move on to Eton). It is still one of the most solidly Conservative in its region, as Alan Duncan held on by nearly 9,000 in 2001 over Labour, who had leapfrogged past the Liberal Democrats into second place four years earlier.

Social indices:			2001 Gen. Election:			
% Non-white	1.0		C	22,621	48.1	+2.3
% Prof/Man	35.7		Lab	14,009	29.8	+0.8
% Non-manual	53.9		LD	8,386	17.8	−1.4
£ Av prop val 2000	109 K		UKIP	1,223	2.6	+1.0
% Increase 97–00	43.7		Grn	817	1.7	
% Unemployed 2001	1.0		C maj	8,612	18.3	
% Decrease 97–01	0.5		Turnout		65.0	−10.1
% Fin hard/Rank	8.0	523	Elect	72,448		
% Pensioners	24.4					
% Prem mort/Rank	14	548				

Member of Parliament

Alan Duncan, a Foreign Affairs spokesman from 2001, and previously a DTI and Health spokesman under William Hague, and Hague's political aide 1997–98, was elected in 1992. Small, slim and expensively dressed – 'a Bonsai Heseltine' (Matthew Parris) – who spun for William Hague and by one of Shirley Porter's Georgian terraced council houses via a neighbour's discount in desirable Gayfere Street (the fuss over which caused him to resign in 1994 as Brian Mawhinney's PPS), he was born in 1957, educated at Merchant Taylor's, Northwood and St John's College, Oxford, and worked as an oil trader, at one time for the subsequently tax-evading Clinton-pardoned fugitive, Marc Rich. A Hague voter in 1997, and a Portillo voter in 2001, a right-wing libertarian who urges a minimalist state and has called for drug decriminalisation, he is prominent among the Tory minority consistently voting to legalise homosexual sex at 16. He broke ranks during the 2001 Election to say he would 'never' support the euro, 'a socialist project dressed up in business language'.

RYEDALE

The Liberals always picked up seats in the mid-term of unpopular governments, both Tory and Labour. In their current guise as Liberal Democrats they still do. Sometimes they hold on to these for many years, as in the case of Alan Beith's seat, and David Chidgey's, and Simon Hughes's. They can even pass on such seats once the original victor has retired (as in the case of David Steel's Tweeddale). On other occasions the triumph is short-lived, the constituency returns to its former allegiance, and the by-election victor unfortunately returns to relative obscurity after a brief spell in the Commons. Such a fate befell David Austick (who won Ripon in 1973 and lost it for good in 1974), Graham Tope (Sutton and Cheam, 1972) and in more recent elections, Chris Davies (Oldham East and Saddleworth) and Diana Maddock (Christchurch). In 1987 the most spectacular example was that of Elizabeth Shields.

Mrs Shields had overturned a 16,000 Tory majority in the Ryedale by-election of May 1986, caused by the death of John Spence, to become the Alliance's only female MP at the time. She won by 4,940 votes, a large turn-round or 'swing' in this vast, mainly rural North Yorkshire, seat. Then in the general election the next year the Conservatives replaced their by-election candidate, a merchant banker from London, with a locally rooted man, John Greenway. Mr Greenway regained Ryedale with a majority of fully 9,740 votes, and the discomfited Elizabeth Shields lost her seat by one of the largest margins of all (officially endorsed) sitting members in recent times. In 1992 she stood again, but this time John Greenway won by over 18,000. It had all been a flash in the pan.

This is scarcely surprising, really, given Ryedale's rock-hard inherent Conservatism. The seat stretched over a substantial chunk of the broad acres of Yorkshire, from the northern suburbs of York past Malton-Norton and Pickering to reach the cost at Filey, some 40 miles from the county town. The Liberal Democrat candidate in the last two elections has been Keith Orrell, not a local but the former opposition leader on South Tyneside council (representing Cleadon and East Boldon ward), and he has cut the majority below 5,000, garnering a respectable 36% in 2001; but this was at a time when the highest number of third-party representatives were elected to Westminster for 62 years. It was emphatically not by-election circumstances.

Social indices:			2001 Gen. Election:			
% Non-white	0.4		C	20,711	47.2	+3.4
% Prof/Man	30.6		LD	15,836	36.1	+2.7
% Non-manual	50.7		Lab	6,470	14.7	−3.2
£ Av prop val 2000	93 K		UKIP	882	2.0	+0.1
% Increase 97–00	35.2		C maj	4,875	11.1	
% Unemployed 2001	1.7		Turnout		66.0	−8.8
% Decrease 97–01	0.9		Elect	66,543		
% Fin hard/Rank	7.5	541				
% Pensioners	31.3					
% Prem mort/Rank	17	510				

Member of Parliament

John Greenway, a Conservative Sport and Tourism spokesman, is a former policeman-turned-insurance broker who spent five years in the Metropolitan Police and was elected in 1987, when he retrieved the seat from a Liberal by-election winner. Mildly strabismic, and cold-eyed in a way not untypical of officers of the watch, and regarded as a somewhat discursive and moderately cerebral speaker, he voices the policeman's desire to hang police murderers. Born in 1946, he is the son of a chemical process worker, and was educated at Sir John Deane's Grammar School, Northwich and Hendon Police College. Although, interestingly, a backer of Kenneth Clarke for leader in 1997, as a Yorkshire neighbour of William Hague he was brought onto the frontbench as a Home Affairs (1997–2000) and Sport (2000–) spokesman, retaining the latter job even after again backing Clarke in all the ballots in 2001.

SAFFRON WALDEN

Saffron Walden constituency covers the most rural and pleasant scenery in Essex, its north-western quadrant. It is the largest seat in area in the county and the only one which reaches the list of the country's 100 most agricultural seats. It includes the small towns of Saffron Walden (population 14,000), Halstead (10,000) and Great Dunmow (5,000) and over a hundred villages. The peace is disturbed by the presence of Stansted Airport. In general, however, the ambience is far gentler than that in the rest of busy, bustling, hard-driving Essex. The politics reflect that atmosphere too.

The Saffron Walden seat has a long history of liberal and moderate Toryism. This was for many decades the seat of R.A. Butler, whose grave is in Saffron Walden churchyard. On his retirement in 1965 'Rab' was replaced by another civilised Conservative, Peter Kirk. His untimely death caused another by-election, in 1977, which brought in yet another Tory from the same tradition (which would become known as 'wet', perhaps), Sir Alan Haselhurst. Those two by-elections passed without incident, largely because they took place at times of Labour government and Liberal quiescence. If there were to be a by-election in Saffron Walden nowadays there might well be an upset, probably to the benefit of the Liberal Democrats, who do well in local elections; but in general elections matters tend to proceed as normal with very little in the way of swings between all three parties. The 1987 result was virtually a carbon copy of 1983, and nothing much changed in 1992 either. Even in 1997 Haselhurst's majority was less affected than most, as the Liberal Democrats lost votes too although they remained in second place. Once again, there was no significant change in 2001 as the Liberal Democrat Elfreda Tealby-Watson trailed Haselhurst by 12,000. Like the local Tories, the air of timelessness survives.

Social indices:			2001 Gen. Election:			
% Non-white	0.8		C	24,485	48.9	+3.6
% Prof/Man	40.6		LD	12,481	24.9	−1.9
% Non-manual	61.2		Lab	11,305	22.6	+1.1
£ Av prop val 2000	155 K		UKIP	1,769	3.5	+2.4
% Increase 97–00	57.3		C maj	12,004	24.0	
% Unemployed 2001	0.8		Turnout		65.2	−11.8
% Decrease 97–01	1.3		Elect	76,724		
% Fin hard/Rank	3.2	636				
% Pensioners	23.4					
% Prem mort/Rank	4	628				

Member of Parliament

Sir Alan Haselhurst, one of his party's senior MPs with 28 years' (interrupted) service, was elected here in 1977 after four earlier years as MP for Middleton and Prestwich (1970–74). Marginalised by his rejection of Thatcherism as a traditional One Nation Europhile, rebelling over the poll tax and eye and dental test charges, and describing Margaret Thatcher as 'domineering and over-riding', he opted after 1992 for the decent obscurity of Commons chairmanships, becoming in 1997 Deputy Speaker to Betty Boothroyd. He was, however, passed over for the Speakership, polling only 140 votes and rivalled by another Tory, Sir George Young, despite expectations of Buggins' turn and the tradition of partisan alternation, when the job went in 2000 to Labour's Michael Martin. Slight and trim, he was born in 1937, attended King Edward VI Grammar School, Birmingham, Cheltenham College and Oriel College, Oxford, and originally an executive in one of Peter Walker's companies, as the 63-year-old Deputy Speaker and Chairman of Ways and Means, he was heading inexorably for a fairly early peerage.

ST ALBANS

The seat in Britain which most closely replicated the national voting percentages in 2001 was St Albans, where Labour's Kerry Pollard held on with 42%, the Conservatives trailed with 33%, and the Liberal Democrats picked up 21%. This was an excellent indicator of the decline of the Tories in the last two elections, for Labour had previously won the Hertfordshire cathedral city seat of St Albans only once before 1997, in 1945.

The (at the time) Cabinet Minister Peter Lilley abandoned the bulk of his St Albans constituency before the 1997 Election, and in this respect at least he proved to have good judgment, for Labour seized the seat after a swing of approximately 15%. Although Lilley had a lead of 16,400 over the Liberal Democrats in 1992, much of this has depended on the contribution of Harpenden and other wards outside St Albans itself. Harpenden is a massively Conservative affluent commuting base, and now forms half the base of the 11th and extra constituency Hertfordshire was given in the 1997 boundary changes – Hitchin and Harpenden. Its departure, and that of the other northern semi-rural wards of Redbourn and Sandridge, was a grievous blow to the St Albans Conservative Party.

The centre of gravity of the St Albans division was shifted to the south. About 29,000 electors north of the city, mainly in Harpenden, were lost. In return came about 18,000 voters from the south. Most of these were previously in the Watford seat, these living in the Park Street and St Stephen's wards, which are semi-rural and include the communities of Bricket Wood and Chiswell Green.

The old and historic community of St Albans itself has some Labour wards, such as the 'social housing' areas of Sopwell and Batchwood, and the central St Peter's, and many Liberal Democrat wards – the Marshalswicks, Clarence and Cunningham. The city has developed a tradition of voting Liberal in local elections, but the Lib Dems sunk to third in the 1997 Election, finishing a poor third, as Kerry Pollard leapt to first in an unexpected gain for Labour in Hertfordshire's most ancient community. Despite the departure of Harpenden, this remains a very affluent and middle-class part of south-eastern England. St Albans is the only current Labour seat among the 50 with the fewest electors in financial hardship according to the Experian/national statistics rankings. As such it is both a striking testament to Labour's broad appeal in 1997 and 2001, and a potent indicator of potential vulnerability should it contract.

Social indices:			2001 Gen. Election:			
% Non-white	6.5		Lab	19,889	45.4	+3.4
% Prof/Man	48.0		C	15,423	35.2	+2.0
% Non-manual	70.5		LD	7,847	17.9	−3.1
£ Av prop val 2000	190 K		UKIP	602	1.4	
% Increase 97–00	59.1		Lab maj	4,466	10.2	
% Unemployed 2001	0.7		Turnout		66.3	−11.2
% Decrease 97–01	1.1		Elect	66,040		
% Fin hard/Rank	5.4	599				
% Pensioners	22.9					
% Prem mort/Rank	14	550				

Member of Parliament

Kerry Pollard, elected in 1997 as only the second-ever Labour MP for St Albans – the 1945 landslide having produced the first – in 2001 became the first to win it twice. Rare among the big 1997 intake as a fairly regular backbench rebel, he voted against the government on student grant abolition, criminal justice, NATO bombing of Kosovo, Incapacity Benefit cuts, and pensions linked to earnings. A Catholic, white trim-bearded, black-eyebrowed, former local councillor, he was born in 1944, son of a publican, educated at Thornleigh Grammar School and Thornleigh College, Bolton, and worked for over 30 years as an engineer with British Gas. In January 1999 he voted against 16 as the homosexual age of consent, called in March 2001 for rail re-nationalisation, and in November 2001 rebelled against the bombing of Afghanistan. He opposes voluntary euthanasia.

ST HELENS NORTH

Although it is technically within the county of Merseyside (which has had no administrative status since Mrs Thatcher abolished the GLC and the six metropolitan counties in 1986), St Helens is a proud and independent town. It is in no way a suburb of Liverpool, and although its big neighbour to the west is only about a dozen miles away the accent is quite different, unpermeated by the twang of Scouse. Indeed, some Liverpudlians call people from St Helens 'woollybacks', implying a rural naïvety. In fact St Helens is an industrial town, dominated by the world-famous Pilkington's glass works but also shaped by other manufacturing and by the coal reserves which lay beneath the Lancashire plain.

St Helens North contains just the northern edge of the town itself, the wards around the A580 East Lancs Road. Most of its population lives in previously independent communities such as Billinge, Haydock (the site of Haydock Park racecourse), Rainford and Newton-le-Willows. North is very slightly the more affluent and less working class of the two constituencies. The only two regularly Tory wards in the borough elections are here: the north-west St Helens ward of Windle, named after a brook that flows through one of the most attractive residential areas of St Helens; and the community of Rainford with its new private estates, a popular commuting area for both St Helens and Liverpool. Newton-le-Willows, an old railway town, has often elected Liberal Democrats in municipal contests, but that party performs poorly in general elections in both St Helens seats. The rest of the seat is solidly Labour at all levels of government.

The MP, the former local council leader Dave Watts, avoided the attention given to his new colleague in St Helens South in 2001 and his share of the votes cast dropped by only 4% since 1997 (compared with 19% in South), although the number of Labour votes cast decreased by fully 9,000 due to a drop in turnout to a wretched 53%. There seems no reason why Mr Watts should retire to make way for another local or other candidate, and this seat will remain Labour in all foreseeable circumstances.

Social indices:			2001 Gen. Election:			
% Non-white	0.5		Lab	22,977	61.1	−3.8
% Prof/Man	28.5		C	7,076	18.8	+1.5
% Non-manual	51.5		LD	6,609	17.6	+4.8
£ Av prop val 2000	57 K		SLP	939	2.5	+0.8
% Increase 97–00	18.1		Lab maj	15,901	42.3	
% Unemployed 2001	3.9		Turnout		53.3	−15.7
% Decrease 97–01	1.9		Elect	70,545		
% Fin hard/Rank	20.6	264				
% Pensioners	24.6					
% Prem mort/Rank	36	228				

Member of Parliament

Dave Watts, PPS to John Spellar from 1999, is a low-flying 1997 entrant off the local St Helens council, where he was a councillor for 18 years and which he led for four years, still locally-focused on regionally-necessary EU grants and resentful of the rate support disparity between (Tory) Westminster Council and St Helens. Born in 1951, son of a storekeeper, and educated at Seel Road Secondary Modern School in Huyton, he worked for his predecessor John Evans MP for four years and before that was a shop steward at a United Biscuits factory. He backs first-past-the-post voting and the Greeks in Cyprus.

ST HELENS SOUTH

Probably more press attention was focused on St Helens South than any other constituency in the United Kingdom in the May–June 2001 General Election campaign. Yet this was not a marginal seat – far from it. In 1997 Labour's Gerry Bermingham had won the seat with no national publicity or external interest by 24,000 votes. The reason for all the fuss was his last-minute withdrawal, and his replacement, after local members chose from a shortlist vetted by the central party in London, which eliminated the strongest local contenders, to the man elected as Conservative MP for Witney in Oxfordshire four years before, the defector Shaun Woodward. Noting the wealth of Mr Woodward's wife, a Sainsbury heiress, and their mansion in the South with its accoutrements contrasting with the everyday lot of St Helens voters, the new Labour candidate was pursued by a swarm of press, photographers, men dressed as butlers, and a number of opponents vying to defeat, or at least embarrass, him in the election. These included the Socialist Alliance, Socialist Labour, and two independents in addition to the parties contesting most English seats. In the end Shaun Woodward won, but he was severely damaged, in electoral terms most individually by the Liberal Democrats, who improved by 10%. The two Socialists took 12% between them, and the turnout dropped by 15%, some of whom must have been disillusioned traditional Labour supporters. All in all Woodward received 19% less of the vote share than Bermingham had. In absolute terms the official Labour tally fell from over 30,000 to under 17,000. It was Labour's second worst performance after Wyre Forest, but that had been a less humiliating experience, as Dr Richard Taylor's triumph there was not based on a personalised attack. The story in St Helens South had proved self-fulfilling.

This was not a very suitable seat for Woodward, although he would probably have had grave trouble anywhere. St Helens is a tough working-class town. The bulk of St Helens is contained within its South division. It is overshadowed by the factories of Pilkington's, one of the world's leading glass makers, and its ancillary industries. This was once a coal-mining area too, and miners' welfares can still be seen in places like the eastern ward of Parr and Hardshaw, a Labour stronghold whose voting practices are reminiscent of coalfield seats. Unlike many urban centres in England there are virtually no ethnic minority residents here: both St Helens seats are over 99% white. The tone and accent are Lancashire, not Merseyside; possibly the closest town in social and political character to St Helens is Wigan. Also like Wigan, the most popular and successful sport is rugby league, that epitome of muscular northern manual working-class culture; St Helens is one of the largest towns not to have a Football League soccer club.

It is a town of fixed and traditional tastes, and these clearly do not yet include Shaun Woodward. But they do encompass loyalty to the Labour Party, and it must be remembered that he actually did receive more than twice as many votes as anyone else, and nearly 50% of all those cast. At the same time, the circumstances of his first campaign here will never be forgotten.

Social indices:			2001 Gen. Election:			
% Non-white	0.9		Lab	16,799	49.7	−18.9
% Prof/Man	25.9		LD	7,814	23.1	+9.7
% Non-manual	48.8		C	4,675	13.8	−1.1
£ Av prop val 2000	55 K		SA	2,325	6.9	
% Increase 97–00	25.9		SLP	1,504	4.4	
% Unemployed 2001	5.3		UKIP	336	1.0	
% Decrease 97–01	1.9		Ind	271	0.8	
% Fin hard/Rank	26.6	180	Ind	80	0.2	
% Pensioners	23.6		Lab maj	8,985	26.6	
% Prem mort/Rank	43	132	Turnout		51.9	−14.6
			Elect	65,122		

Member of Parliament

Shaun Woodward, the floor-crossing Conservative who switched to Labour over Tory homophobia and Europhobia in December 1999, was awkwardly dropped in here by Millbank on a shortlist excluding strong local contenders at the start of the 2001 Election campaign, courtesy of the last-minute exit of the sitting MP, Gerry Bermingham. Born in 1958 and educated at Bristol Grammar School and Jesus College, Cambridge, he married a Sainsbury heiress and worked at Central Office and the BBC before being elected as Tory MP for Witney in 1997. With his sudden switching to Labour after two-and-a-half years as a partisan Labour-baiting MP seeming less convincing than the slower transitions of fellow Tory deserters Alan Howarth and Peter Temple-Morris, the choice of St Helens for his new career as a Labour MP had a certain symmetry; for it was here between 1945 and 1958 that the Labour MP was Sir Hartley Shawcross, whose eventual desertion of Labour was to earn him the soubriquet 'Sir Shortly Floorcross'. Following Reg Prentice (who crossed from Labour to Conservative) and Alan Howarth (from Conservative to Labour) he is only the third post-war MP to effect a seamless switch – without interruption of Commons membership – from a safe seat of one party to a safe seat of another, although unlike Prentice and Howarth he was not (at least in 2001) rewarded with a ministerial post.

ST IVES

The Liberal Democrats have often been accused of trying to be all things to all voters, and of trimming their policies to suit the tastes of the region in which they are campaigning. They would probably say that this includes a healthy degree of local awareness, listening to the community. It is likely to cause difficulties only if ever they were to approach the responsibilities of government. Certainly in the very south-western tip of England, their first term MP Andrew George strengthened his position substantially in 2001, increasing his vote share by 7% to notch up more than half of all cast, having shown scepticism of the European Union's fisheries policy.

This constituency in south-west Cornwall, incorporating the Scilly Isles, had produced one of the most interesting and dramatic contests of the 1997 General Election. The Conservatives were in trouble in St Ives throughout the previous Parliament. David Harris had only won by 1,645 in 1992, and there had been accusations of some electoral irregularities in the treatment of proxy votes for those in residential homes for the elderly. David Harris announced his retirement, although he later sought nomination for other seats. Fishermen in the constituency railed bitterly against the EEC's policies which allow excessive foreign competition and against 'quota-hopping'. With the great general unpopularity of the government, it came as no surprise that the Liberal Democrat Andrew George went one better than his performance in 1992 and defeated the new Tory candidate William Rogers by no less than 7,170 votes. The Referendum candidate obtained 3,714 votes, or a share of 6.9%, their fifth best anywhere, and the UK Independence Party added over 500 more; by 2001 the anti-European element had been at least temporarily weakened, and a sole UKIP candidate received less than half of the combined 1997 support.

Land's End and Lizard Point, and the towns of Penzance, St Ives, Helston and St Just are all in the seat, along with the Goonhilly Downs with their distinctive satellite communications aerial dishes. This now looks life a safe Liberal Democrat seat, and the nearest the Conservatives can get to Land's End lies in their seat on the other side of the Tamar and of Plymouth, at South West Devon, about 80 miles away.

Social indices:			2001 Gen. Election:			
% Non-white	0.6		LD	25,413	51.6	+7.1
% Prof/Man	30.6		C	15,360	31.2	+0.0
% Non-manual	50.4		Lab	6,567	13.3	−1.9
£ Av prop val 2000	89 K		UKIP	1,926	3.9	+2.9
% Increase 97–00	43.8		LD maj	10,053	20.4	
% Unemployed 2001	3.7		Turnout		66.3	−8.9
% Decrease 97–01	3.5		Elect	74,256		
% Fin hard/Rank	12.1	413				
% Pensioners	31.4					
% Prem mort/Rank	27	384				

Member of Parliament

Andrew George, elected in 1997, is the first Liberal MP for St Ives since Walter Runciman defected to the National Liberals in 1932. Mildly strabismic, locally-born (1958) at Mullion and educated at Helston Grammar School, he attended Sussex University and (for a year) University College, Oxford, and is appropriately his party's Fisheries spokesman as MP for the fading, once-great fishing port of Newlyn. Representing a relatively urban seat he can afford votes for outright hunting bans, but otherwise operates as a critic of the Common Fisheries Policy and – a one-time member of Mebyon Kernow – a campaigner for all things Cornish. Of the Liberal Democrats' four Cornish MPs, he sounds, and is, the most convincing.

SALFORD

Between the wars over 200,000 people lived in Salford, widely regarded as Manchester's twin city. Its urban depopulation has been as dramatic as any in this country. By the time of the 1981 Census Salford had shrunk to 98,000 and in 1983 its two tiny parliamentary constituencies were reduced to one, which was called Salford

East because it omitted one western ward, Weaste and Seedley, which was placed in the Eccles division. By 1991 Salford had shed further thousands of inhabitants, now boasting scarcely over 80,000 souls, and in the most recent round of boundary changes Weaste and Seedley have been returned, and the seat renamed plain Salford. In 2001 the number of votes cast was further reduced, not just by a reduction of nearly 5,000 in the electoral register in the last four years, but because only 41% of these actually voted, a total of little over 22,000 in all.

This is a very working-class and strongly Labour constituency. In some parts of the seat slum clearance and piecemeal and unplanned abandonment of housing neighbourhoods have given rise to clusters of tower blocks and low density desolation as bleak as any in Manchester's devastated inner-city belt. Central wards such as Ordsall, Blackfriars, Langworthy and Pendleton vote massively for Labour (and it might be noted that there are very few voters from ethnic minority groups in Salford). Salford still penetrates almost into the centre of Manchester; its boundary is the river Irwell, just behind the great shopping street of Deansgate. There are still terraces of Victorian housing, similar to the fictional one which has become legendary on TV as 'Coronation Street' – it is not coincidental that Granada TV's headquarters and studios are in this constituency at Quay Street.

Some trees do grow in Salford, in Broughton Park (Kersal ward) in the north-east, near Manchester's affluent northern suburb of Prestwich, and to a lesser extent in Claremont ward around Irlams o' th' Height. Only ever capable of winning Kersal ward in local elections (in a good year), the Conservatives could scrape together fewer than 3,500 votes in 1997, and the Liberal Democrats barely nudge past them, as Labour's Hazel Blears won almost by default. She will need her renowned sense of humour as she continues to represent one of England's most depressed areas.

Social indices:			2001 Gen. Election:			
% Non-white	3.3		Lab	14,649	65.1	−3.9
% Prof/Man	26.3		LD	3,637	16.2	+5.9
% Non-manual	47.9		C	3,446	15.3	−2.1
£ Av prop val 2000	49 K		SA	414	1.8	
% Increase 97–00	34.0		Ind	216	1.0	
% Unemployed 2001	4.4		Ind	152	0.7	
% Decrease 97–01	3.1		Lab maj	11,012	48.9	
% Fin hard/Rank	39.1	57	Turnout		41.6	−14.9
% Pensioners	28.0		Elect	54,152		
% Prem mort/Rank	59	12				

Member of Parliament

Hazel Blears, elected here in 1997, in 2001 became one of 21 MPs of the 183-strong intake of 1997 to achieve a government post – in her case as a Junior Health Minister. A small, impish-looking solicitor previously employed with Manchester City Council, she came with a left-wing reputation as a unilateralist and opponent of the Clause Four redraft, but had performed as a loyalist bowler of stooge questions and for a while was Alan Millburn's PPS (1997–99). Born in 1956, the daughter of a maintenance fitter, and educated at Wardley Grammar School, Eccles Sixth Form

College, Trent Polytechnic and Chester College of Law, and a Salford City Councillor for eight years, one of her helpful questions in February 2001 implicated former Tory MP Timothy Kirkhope in the Hinduja brothers affair, in order to take the heat off Peter Mandelson and Keith Vaz.

SALISBURY

The one unchanged seat in Wiltshire after the sweeping boundary changes which affected the county in time for the 1997 Election is Salisbury. This is not too surprising, as this is south Wiltshire, at the other end of the county from the rapid population growth around Swindon, and separated from it by the sometimes wild and lonely extent of the Salisbury Plain. This is far from the M4 corridor, and far from a New Town ambience too.

The ancient city of Salisbury is far too small to have a seat of its own, despite the grandeur of its cathedral (the tallest church spire in England) and close (in which resides in luxury the former Conservative Prime Minister Edward Heath). It has to take in territory extending to the towns of Amesbury and Wilton, and west to Tisbury, and also to the large army camps on the Plain, like Bulford and Durrington; this seat has one of the highest proportions of servicemen of all, over 8%. Stonehenge lies within the seat, plus dozens of villages: it is as rural as any in Wiltshire. It is all a far cry from the days before the great Reform Act of 1832, when the deserted Old Sarum, just outside the modern Salisbury, returned two MPs.

In the most recent era, Wiltshire has proved a great disappointment for the Liberal Democrats in parliamentary terms. Although they have achieved considerable success in parliamentary terms in Somerset on one border with the county, and Hampshire on another, and indeed in the Newbury seat in west Berkshire, the rural parts of this county remain a blue island on the map. In 2001 in Salisbury the Lib Dem candidate Yvonne Emmerson-Peirce fell a further 6% behind Robert Key. A substantial working-class Labour vote exists in the seat, in council estate areas of Salisbury like Bemerton and in the army camps on the Plain (though the turnout among servicemen is notoriously low) – they got 45% in 1966, and retained nearly 18% in 1997 and 2001. This loyalty helps to deny the Liberal Democrats any chance of even getting close to the sitting Conservative MP, but tactical voting would not be sufficient to take it. Not only is Liberal Democrat local government success far less of a solid platform in Wiltshire than in other counties such as Somerset, but they have not had the benefit of a by-election in the county (such as those which acted as catalyst in Newbury, Romsey, Eastleigh, Christchurch and in a way Winchester) for almost 40 years, just about the exact extent of their modern revival. On such contingencies constituency politics often depend.

Social indices:				2001 Gen. Election:			
% Non-white	0.9			C	24,527	46.6	+3.7
% Prof/Man	32.5			LD	15,824	30.1	–2.1
% Non-manual	53.7			Lab	9,199	17.5	–0.1
£ Av prop val 2000	143 K			UKIP	1,958	3.7	–2.0
% Increase 97–00	66.9			Grn	1,095	2.1	+1.0
% Unemployed 2001	0.9			C maj	8,703	16.5	
% Decrease 97–01	1.5			Turnout		65.3	–8.4
% Fin hard/Rank	8.7	500		Elect	80,538		
% Pensioners	27.2						
% Prem mort/Rank	22	454					

Member of Parliament

Robert Key, a DTI spokesman under Iain Duncan Smith from 2001, is a churchy man for a churchy seat as son of a former Bishop of Truro. Elected in 1983 – in succession to another bishop's son, Michael Hamilton – he was born in 1945, educated at Sherborne and Clare College, Cambridge and taught economics at Harrow for 14 years before becoming MP. More genial than his similarly well-upholstered and double-chinned constituent Sir Edward Heath (for whom he was briefly PPS), he has trimmed from One Nation Europhilia to a degree of scepticism and backed Peter Lilley, then William Hague, for leader in 1997. A Junior Minister from 1990 (at Environment, then National Heritage), John Major dropped him as a Transport Minister in 1994. A voter for lowering the homosexual age of consent to 16, he was less politically correct on the matter of women in the armed forces as a Defence spokesman (1997–2001). He backed Portillo in 2001.

SCARBOROUGH AND WHITBY

The dramatic coast from Scarborough to Whitby, and the North Yorkshire Moors behind it, look like natural Conservative territory. Scarborough is the major Yorkshire seaside resort, and along with tourism, agriculture forms the main basis of the economy here, along with some fishing from the old port of Whitby at the northern end of the seat. However, just as on the south coast (Hove, Hastings, Thanet North) and on the west coast (Blackpool, Morecambe, Crosby) Labour showed that they were strong enough to win here for the first time ever in 1997, and to hold on with no diminution of strength in 2001.

This was indeed a safe Tory seat, held from 1945 to 1992 by two knights of the shires, but the SDP had high hopes here in 1983 when the Alliance first fought a general election, while Labour have for many years enjoyed considerable strength in the town of Scarborough, heading the poll in almost all of its eight wards in May 1999. In 1997 Lawrie Quinn advanced by 16%, well above the national and regional average, probably benefiting from some Liberal Democrat tactical voting, and also from the economic decline and demographic change which have affected so many seaside areas. Four years later in a re-run of the previous contest, both Quinn and his Tory predecessor as MP, John Sykes, increased their share as the Lib Dems were squeezed to a single figure percentage, one of their worst performances in England. The Tories will need a swing of 4% to regain Scarborough and Whitby.

Social indices:			2001 Gen. Election:			
% Non-white	0.6		Lab	22,426	47.2	+1.6
% Prof/Man	31.1		C	18,841	39.6	+3.4
% Non-manual	53.5		LD	3,977	8.4	−5.8
£ Av prop val 2000	66 K		Grn	1,049	2.2	
% Increase 97–00	20.8		UKIP	970	2.0	
% Unemployed 2001	4.0		PA	260	0.5	
% Decrease 97–01	1.6		Lab maj	3,585	7.5	
% Fin hard/Rank	13.8	382	Turnout		63.2	−8.4
% Pensioners	32.1		Elect	75,213		
% Prem mort/Rank	29	357				

Member of Parliament

Lawrie Quinn, a pink-cheeked, red-nosed railwayman – latterly an engineer with Railtrack – unnecessarily, as it turned out in 2001, kept his job open following his unexpected victory here in 1997, where he was washed in on Labour's high tide in the downwardly-mobile seaside towns. An engine driver's son, born in 1956 and educated at Harraby School, Carlisle and Hatfield Polytechnic, he has performed as a campaigner for local interests and a bowler of loyalist questions, straying latterly as a vocal critic of the proposed American National Missile Defence system because of the local Fylingdales tracking station, but insufficiently to preclude being appointed PPS to junior DTI Minister Douglas Alexander in 2001.

SCUNTHORPE

Scunthorpe has finally got a seat of its own. Or rather a seat which has just the town's name in its title. Until February 1974 Scunthorpe was the dominant element in a seat named solely after the tiny market town of Brigg, eight miles away. For the next three elections the two had equal representation in the title of 'Brigg and Scunthorpe'. Finally, in 1983 this ill-matched marriage was broken (Brigg is Conservative and rural in outlook; Scunthorpe a generally Labour town created by heavy industry); Brigg was now placed happily in a Conservative seat together with Cleethorpes. Scunthorpe still couldn't get its name even at the front of a constituency title, though. It was still paired with a few parishes from the rural borough of Glanford (whose headquarters, ironically, are in Brigg) – in a seat named Glanford and Scunthorpe. By 2001, though, those rural elements had been pared down, the electorate reduced to a rather spindly 59,000, and there is now a seat called just plain Scunthorpe.

Scunthorpe has now recovered from an aberration in its electoral history. Even when the seat it dominated was called Brigg, it could ensure Labour representation; the area remained solidly in their hands from 1935 to 1979. Then Brigg and Scunthorpe was lost as Mrs Thatcher came to power, although by just 486 votes; and after the favourable boundary changes for Labour it was only their disastrous national showing of 1983 that kept Glanford and Scunthorpe Tory, this time by 637. In 1987, though, Elliot Morley regained the seat, and has since increased his majority over twentyfold from 512 to 10,372 in 2001.

It seems appropriate that Scunthorpe should now have a Labour MP. This is an industrial landscape. Scunthorpe, set on a bluff above the valley of the river Trent, is dominated by its massive steelworks, alive or dead. Its very existence was brought about in the nineteenth century by the local reserves of ironstone, and it boomed like other steel towns such as Middlesbrough and Corby. Almost all of the wards are very heavily Labour: Ashby Grange and Lincoln Gardens, Park and Riddings, Brumby and Frodingham and Crosby Town, where there is a significant Asian population. The middle-class Tory minority is concentrated in a small enclave around Central Park in Kingsway ward, as well as beyond the town boundaries. Property values are stagnant, their minimal 7% increase between 1997 and 2000, higher only than Middlesbrough. Average house prices in the latter year were just £42,000, compared with £107,000 in, say, Slough. The constituency of Scunthorpe will now remain Labour in all but the most exceptional of circumstances.

Social indices:			2001 Gen. Election:			
% Non-white	2.5		Lab	20,096	59.8	−0.6
% Prof/Man	22.3		C	9,724	28.9	+2.6
% Non-manual	41.4		LD	3,156	9.4	+1.0
£ Av prop val 2000	42 K		UKIP	347	1.0	
% Increase 97–00	7.4		Ind	302	0.9	
% Unemployed 2001	4.4		Lab maj	10,372	30.8	
% Decrease 97–01	1.9		Turnout		56.3	−12.5
% Fin hard/Rank	27.7	163	Elect	59,689		
% Pensioners	24.6					
% Prem mort/Rank	39	187				

Member of Parliament

Elliot Morley is one of the Labour government's most typecast ministers as a Junior Agriculture Minister since 1997 and before that an Agriculture spokesman for eight years. First elected in 1987, a burly, ex-bearded, pink-cheeked, light-voiced former schoolteacher, born in 1952 and educated at St Margaret's Church of England High School, Liverpool and Hull College of Education, he spent the Opposition years calling for bans to protect animal welfare (of hunted whales, foxes, mink and stags, of battery hens, tethered sows, and crated veal calves) and then in government had to justify foot-dragging in implementing bans, and dealing as Fisheries Minister with the further contraction of the UK industry at the behest of the Common Fisheries Policy. But he welcomes the EU's redefinition of animals as 'sentient beings'.

SEDGEFIELD

For nine years there was no constituency called Sedgefield. In 1974 the Boundary Commission abolished it, and with it ended the parliamentary career of its Labour MP, David Reed. In 1983 the Commissioners changed their mind, breathed life into the seat again, and created a safe harbour for a young man who rapidly rose into a – indeed the – leading position in his party and then his country: Tony Blair.

Sedgefield is south-eastern County Durham. It almost completely surrounds the town of Darlington, taking in all the rural wards of Darlington Borough. There are Conservative voters here, and in the small town of Sedgefield itself (population

5,000) with its racecourse and Shrove Tuesday football match. But these areas are easily swamped by the solid Labour vote on the former coalfield, in big villages like Chilton, Ferryhill and Trimdon, the site of Blair's constituency residence, *Myrobella*. All the pits which gave rise to these communities are now long closed, and attempts have been made to establish new light industries. In 1997 the Spennymoor area was replaced by the New Town of Great Aycliffe – this being the result of a swap with Bishop Auckland constituency. This did not weaken Blair's grip on the Sedgefield seat, for all three County Durham New Towns are solidly Labour, unlike their counterparts in the south of England.

In 2001 the Prime Minister did not do as well in Sedgefield as average for a Labour candidate in that general election, as his share of the vote fell back from a mighty 71% to just under 65%. There were inevitably mutterings that he had not been seen as much in his constituency, but this seems an inevitable function of government, and in fact the result is little worse than the regional norm – the North-East was one of Labour's worst areas, not least because turnout fell by over 10%, as here. While it is tempting to point out that Blair individually did not do as well as William Hague, Charles Kennedy, Peter Mandelson or Gordon Brown, such mischievous thoughts will not weaken the PM's secure hold on this constituency. Tony Blair's first parliamentary contest was in Beaconsfield in Buckinghamshire, in the 1982 by-election. Sedgefield could hardly provide a more contrasting or a more favourable prospect.

Social indices:			2001 Gen. Election:			
% Non-white	0.5		Lab	26,110	64.9	−6.3
% Prof/Man	29.0		C	8,397	20.9	+3.1
% Non-manual	47.7		LD	3,624	9.0	+2.5
£ Av prop val 2000	57 K		UKIP	974	2.4	
% Increase 97–00	20.1		SLP	518	1.3	+0.3
% Unemployed 2001	4.2		Ind	375	0.9	
% Decrease 97–01	0.8		WFLOE	260	0.6	
% Fin hard/Rank	29.5	137	Lab maj	17,713	44.0	
% Pensioners	25.4		Turnout		62.0	−10.6
% Prem mort/Rank	41	156	Elect	64,925		

Member of Parliament

Tony Blair, elected in 1983, became leader of the Labour Party in 1994, dropped Clause Four, and achieved in 1997 Labour's biggest ever landslide of 418 seats, by taking the Party into the Conservative southern heartlands. Claiming to come 'with no ideological baggage' but born in 1953 into a Conservative-voting family and educated at Fettes and St John's College, Oxford – where he was apolitical – he rose in Labour politics in his twenties as an employment law barrister, and as a frontbencher coined an eye-catching sound-bite, 'tough on crime, tough on the causes of crime', simultaneously reassuring to *Guardian* and to *Mail* readers. If Labour's 1997 victory was based largely on a rejection of the Conservatives and on perceptions of a Labour Party sanitised and unified mostly under Smith and Kinnock, it also owed something to Blair's classless appeal to middle England in contrast to his predecessors' more limited regional personas. With no 'big idea' emerging to clinch the second term denied Attlee and Wilson, reliance was placed on perceptions of Labour's economic competence, and of a Conservative Party still stuck with the image that sunk it in 1997, salted by a dose of focus-group-driven populism and a hope, no doubt, that the foot and mouth epidemic would somehow disable the hecklers from the WI. In a curious repeat of the 1997 landslide, the 2001 standstill election produced 412 Labour MPs, with Labour polling 25% of the electorate and 41% not voting at all. It was a remarkable achievement.

SELBY

The countryside south of York around Selby is so flat that it is more prone to major flooding than anywhere else in Britain. Selby itself was an inland port on the Ouse, and the big rivers of the plain are now tapped by massive power stations like those at Drax near the A1(M) trunk road. There is another industry on, or rather under, the Selby flatlands – the most recent, and modern, and presumably last coalfield to be exploited in the country, where high technology has been used to mine deep and concealed seams. These pits, at places like Wistow and Riccall and Stillingfleet, are among the last few operating in a once proud national industry. However, unlike in other parts of the country, the arrival of mining in the Selby area has not brought a political transformation. The seat remained Conservative until 1997. Many miners commute from other constituencies, and even those who have migrated can safely be absorbed. The other sources of employment in Selby are known for their Conservatism – farming, and brewing, which is centred on the town of Tadcaster.

There always was a Labour vote in the towns (Selby, Tadcaster and Sherburn-in-Elmet) and the University of York is situated in the constituency, at Heslington just outside the city boundaries. But only in a quite exceptional year like 1997 could Labour gain the Selby seat, as John Grogan increased their share by 10% to defeat the former (1983–92) West Lancashire MP, Kenneth Hind. After Labour's successful first term in office Grogan again held his 45% share in 2001 and won a second unexpected victory. In an even year though, the Tories would be strong favourites to regain the constituency. This is still essentially rural Britain, not traditional Labour country. Even if Selby should house the last coal-mines in Britain, ironically it is likely then to be a Conservative seat.

Social indices:			2001 Gen. Election:			
% Non-white	0.5		Lab	22,652	45.1	−0.8
% Prof/Man	34.4		C	20,514	40.8	+1.7
% Non-manual	56.2		LD	5,569	11.1	−1.0
£ Av prop val 2000	80 K		Grn	902	1.8	
% Increase 97–00	28.7		UKIP	635	1.3	+0.3
% Unemployed 2001	2.0		Lab maj	2,138	4.3	
% Decrease 97–01	1.7		Turnout		64.5	−10.4
% Fin hard/Rank	9.6	475	Elect	77,924		
% Pensioners	22.9					
% Prem mort/Rank	20	482				

Member of Parliament

John Grogan, third-time-lucky in the same seat in 1997, is Yorkshire-born (1961) of Irish origins, educated at St Michael's (RC) College, Leeds and St John's College, Oxford, where he ran the Students' (not to be confused with the Oxford) Union and then worked as a Labour Party staffer, mostly with Leeds City Council. He operates as a locally-focused MP, with threatened brewing, coal and farming interests to defend, and in February 2001 had a train crash named after his constituency.

SEVENOAKS

West Kent is socially and politically very similar to Surrey, just over the county boundary. The Sevenoaks constituency has the highest proportion of professional and managerial workers of any seat in Kent, the largest amount of detached houses, and the smallest proportion of social housing tenants (less than 5%). Not surprisingly, it is one of the two safest Conservative seats in the county too.

Sevenoaks is close enough to London to fall within the middle-class commuting zone, and the affluent villages around places like Westerham and Eynsford are scarcely dependent on agriculture. The only significant Labour vote is in Swanley, which is rather close to Dartford, but they could not do better than a distant second in 2001. The Liberal Democrats pose only a little more of a threat in municipal contests, winning in Crockenhill and Eynsford and the (ironically named) Sevenoaks Wildernesse ward – that final 'e' gives the game away; but are not as active as elsewhere in the country – and county – and again finished in third place with a slightly reduced vote in the last general election. This really is true-blue south-eastern England, a fitting site for Winston Churchill's Chartwell, the country seat of a man who was a patriotic, even Nationalist Prime Minister in the wartime 1940s and the stable if staid 1950s.

Social indices:			2001 Gen. Election:			
% Non-white	1.2		C	21,052	49.4	+4.0
% Prof/Man	41.9		Lab	10,898	25.6	+1.0
% Non-manual	67.9		LD	9,214	21.6	-2.5
£ Av prop val 2000	188 K		UKIP	1,155	2.7	
% Increase 97–00	52.1		Ind	295	0.7	+0.2
% Unemployed 2001	1.1		C maj	10,154	23.8	
% Decrease 97–01	1.6		Turnout		63.9	-11.5
% Fin hard/Rank	5.7	588	Elect	66,648		
% Pensioners	24.3					
% Prem mort/Rank	15	546				

Member of Parliament

Michael Fallon was a rising hard-right Thatcherite Whip (1988–90) and Education Minister (from 1990) until he lost his seat at Darlington in 1992. Elected here in 1997, brought back onto the frontbench by William Hague as a DTI, then Treasury, spokesman, he was dropped in 1999. A surgeon's son, born in 1952, he was educated at Epsom College and St Andrew's University, famous for its 'Mafia' gathered at the feet of the free market economist, Dr Madsen Pirie. Co-author of the 1985 'No Turning Back' manifesto calling for the sell-off of the NHS and schools, he combines a theological espousal of the market with a frosty unclubbable manner, which appeared to ensure that, notwithstanding nine earlier years spent as a party staffer, and despite voting the Iain Duncan Smith ticket in 2001, he remained on the backbenches.

SHEFFIELD ATTERCLIFFE

The east side of Sheffield still offers one of the most stark and dramatic industrial vistas in Britain. Whereas a few years ago heavy industry and steelworks packed the valley of the Don as it flowed not so quietly towards Rotherham, dominating the scene by day and night as the great blast furnaces burned, now a scene of industrial – or rather post-industrial – desolation strikes the observer. The furnaces are extinguished, most of the great buildings demolished, leaving flattened ground and rubble, the legacy of a fatal recession in the steel trade. It may represent a sudden transformation for the sightseer; but this is as nothing to the effect on the economic life of the local residents of east Sheffield. If anything, they have come out better than might be expected, and a new and very different image cast by Sheffield as one skirts its eastern fringes on the M1 motorway is given by the giant (and highly successful) Meadowhall out-of-town hyper-shopping centre. In its own way this is just as impressive, and just as large a source of employment, as the old British Steel works at Tinsley on the Rotherham border.

Attercliffe is south-east Sheffield, taking in part of Meadowhall and the Don valley ex-steelworks. It is one of Sheffield's four super-safe Labour seats, but it is not by any means typified by inner-city characteristics. There is a higher proportion of semi-detached housing than anywhere else in Sheffield (49%) and most of it is owner-occupied, not 'social housing'. One of Sheffield's few ethnic minority areas, in this case Pakistani, is to be found at Darnall, but the other three wards (Handsworth, Birley and Mosbrough) are virtually all white. In fact Mosbrough has seen a private housing boom over the last decade or so, growing so much that it is very clearly Sheffield's most populous ward: signs may be seen here for 'Mosbrough townships', almost a New Town layout and a symbol of new growth not death and decay. We are at the furthest edge of the city from the crowded centre here. This is low-cost housing, though, and it is being taken up by working-class residents, particularly the skilled manual workers or C2s – who, contrary to the myths spread by advertising agents and other marketers dabbling in politics, are neither the critical 'swing group' nor concentrated in marginal seats. In fact they are concentrated in safe Labour seats – like Sheffield Attercliffe.

As elsewhere in Sheffield the Liberal Democrats have done well at Labour's expense in recent May city council elections, taking 42.5% within the bounds of the constituency in 1999 and winning in Birley and Darnall, but they failed to win these wards in 2000 and did not manage even to improve from third place in the 2001 General Election. They still pose no immediate threat to the dominant party in the majority of seats in Sheffield.

Social indices:			2001 Gen. Election:			
% Non-white	4.4		Lab	24,287	67.8	+2.5
% Prof/Man	23.1		C	5,443	15.2	−0.9
% Non-manual	48.1		LD	5,092	14.2	−1.5
£ Av prop val 2000	52 K		UKIP	1,002	2.8	
% Increase 97–00	16.6		Lab maj	18,844	52.6	
% Unemployed 2001	3.9		Turnout		52.4	−12.3
% Decrease 97–01	2.3		Elect	68,386		
% Fin hard/Rank	27.6	164				
% Pensioners	28.5					
% Prem mort/Rank	33	278				

Member of Parliament

Clive Betts, elected here in 1992, would appear to be a man of underfulfilled promise as a big city (Sheffield) council leader whose Westminster career languished in the Whips Office for five years until petering out in 2001. Born in 1950 and educated at King Edward VII School, Sheffield, and Pembroke College, Cambridge, he was a local government economist before running Sheffield City Council for five years following David Blunkett's reign, winning the approval of those who vaunt his Sheffield-promoted 'New Realism' of public–private partnerships, though seen by others as an unfashionably big spender. Gargoyle-featured and uncharismatic, as a backbencher he predictably focused on local government finance, but as a Whip was pleased to be responsible for the Minimum Wage Bill.

SHEFFIELD BRIGHTSIDE

Brightside, north-east Sheffield, is the steel city's peripheral council estate, or in fashionable parlance social housing, constituency. Over half of the housing was still owned by the local authority at the time of the 1991 Census despite council house sales and a lack of new building – this was the highest figure in Sheffield and indeed in the entire Yorkshire/Humberside region. Brightside is also the most working class of Sheffield's six seats and the most strongly Labour, by a small margin from Attercliffe. On most measures of social deprivation it ranks just behind Central – unemployment is twice the national average, single-parent households among the young (16–24 age group) more than twice the norm. The seat also sent the second fewest number of students into higher education, according to Leeds University analysis of UCAS figures for 1998, and Sheffield Attercliffe was third in this particular list. As in the case of the constituency with even fewer entrants to higher education, Nottingham North, Sheffield's own university has a high academic and social reputation – but it is indeed very much on the other side of the city, in the middle-class, and Tor-turned-Liberal Democrat, Hallam division.

Most of the constituency – Firth Park and Parson Cross, Southey Green and Shiregreen and Nethershire – was constructed in the inter-war years, and consists of semi-detached council houses very unlike the massive tower blocks found in the centre of the city. One thing it does have in common with the rest of the city, though: the estates sprawl and climb over Sheffield's many hills, offering dramatic vistas which dispel the dreary nature of the accommodation. It is easy, literally, to see why Sheffield has been the most loyal of England's major cities to the Labour Party since 1918.

Labour's David Blunkett received 77% of the vote in the 2001 General Election, a figure exceeded in only two English constituencies, Liverpool Walton and Bootle, and he actually increased his vote by over 3%, unlike other very safe Labour seats and despite a drop in turnout to less than 47%. The Liberal Democrats, who have been active in leading the opposition to Labour in local Sheffield politics in recent years, collapsed back into third with less than a tenth of the (not very many) votes cast.

Social indices:			2001 Gen. Election:			
% Non-white	5.0		Lab	19,650	76.9	+3.4
% Prof/Man	16.6		C	2,601	10.2	+1.8
% Non-manual	37.3		LD	2,238	8.8	−5.9
£ Av prop val 2000	36 K		SA	361	1.4	
% Increase 97–00	9.2		SLP	354	1.4	−0.0
% Unemployed 2001	6.8		UKIP	348	1.4	
% Decrease 97–01	4.3		Lab maj	17,049	66.7	
% Fin hard/Rank	48.8	17	Turnout		46.7	−10.8
% Pensioners	28.5		Elect	54,711		
% Prem mort/Rank	46	86				

Member of Parliament

David Blunkett, Home Secretary from 2001, only the third blind MP and the first blind Cabinet Minister, was first elected here in 1987 after seven years running Sheffield Council, to which he was elected at the age of 22. Born blind in 1947 and educated at blind schools and, eventually, at Sheffield University, he taught for 13 years at Barnsley College of Technology. Resistantly-bearded, he was elected, as the first non-MP since Harold Laski, to the constituency section of Labour's NEC in 1983, and proceeded to weave a middle way between the hard left and the Militant-baiters. As Education spokesman 1994–97 and Secretary of State for Education 1997–2001, he has also manoeuvred through the deadening orthodoxies of the teachers' unions and the elegant jargon of the educational establishment, routinely employing the verb 'to deliver' as if education was something tipped off the back of a truck. His transfer to the Home Office saw a determined temperament well deployed during the passage of stark anti-terrorism legislation in 2001. With a history of resistance to a lowered homosexual age of consent, he was by 2001 voting politically correctly in favour.

SHEFFIELD CENTRAL

Sheffield was heavily bombed in the war, and owing to this and slum clearance programmes the face of the city centre has been transformed by the massive new developments of commerce and working-class accommodation. Often these rise above the city in soaring towers, on occasion displaying greater architectural originality and interest than most, and made more impressive by the hilly setting of this switchback city. Hyde Park, a great wall of flats within a few hundred yards of Park Square itself, was a good example. Thought by many to be unfit for human habitation, it was pressed into service as temporary housing for the 1992 World Student Games, which took place – and lost money – in Sheffield. This development has now been demolished and replaced by low-rise individual houses.

The central Sheffield seat, called Park before 1983, has of course long been an ultra-safe Labour seat, though the Liberal Democrat candidate Ali Qadar, councillor for Nether Edge ward since 1996, polled nearly 20% in 2001, the best Liberal Democrat showing against a Labour MP in the city. Much of Central consists of high-rise buildings or council house estates such as those in Castle and Manor wards, south-east of the centre, but there are also older terraces in places like Sharrow, Netherthorpe and Burngreave which afford homes for Sheffield's small non-white population. The ethnic minority proportion reaches 15% in Central, by far the highest in a city which for all its poverty has fewer racial tensions than most large British conurbations.

Sheffield Central is truly an inner-city constituency. As well as its fair share of problems such as unemployment (23% in 1991, by far the highest in Yorkshire, and among the top ten in England) and poor housing, it harbours many of Sheffield's famous and vibrant landmarks and institutions: the University (it has the third highest proportion of students in Yorkshire after Sheffield Hallam and Leeds North West), the Crucible Theatre (host also to the world snooker championship each year), Sheffield United football ground, the town hall (the heart of the 'Socialist Republic of South Yorkshire'), the spectacularly set artificial ski run, some of the abandoned steel works in the valley of the Don, and, marking new initiative and enterprise among the ruins, the centre of the recently constructed tram network. Sheffield is a city of much charm and attraction as well as grit, and its proud civic (and Labour) tradition is centred here in its heart.

Social indices:			2001 Gen. Election:			
% Non-white	14.5		Lab	18,477	61.4	−2.2
% Prof/Man	35.4		LD	5,933	19.7	+2.5
% Non-manual	53.3		C	3,289	10.9	−1.0
£ Av prop val 2000	60 K		Grn	1,008	3.4	+0.7
% Increase 97–00	28.2		SA	754	2.5	+1.2
% Unemployed 2001	8.2		SLP	289	1.0	
% Decrease 97–01	5.0		UKIP	257	0.9	
% Fin hard/Rank	35.0	91	WRP	62	0.2	+0.0
% Pensioners	27.3		Lab maj	12,544	41.7	
% Prem mort/Rank	46	85	Turnout		48.5	−4.6
			Elect	62,018		

Member of Parliament

Dick Caborn, a laterally-sliding Minister of State (from Environment to DTI to Sport), was elected here in 1983 (after a term – 1979–84 – as MEP for Sheffield) as a semi-hard left-wing replacement for one of Labour's 'faceless Freds', the somnolent right-winger, Fred Mulley. With only two years as an Opposition spokesman before

1997, he owes his ministerial career to John Prescott, having run his leadership campaign in 1994. Equally he owes to the Prescott connection his reshuffling sideways out of Prescott's Environment department in 1999, as the Prime Minister sought to intrude more Blairite figures throughout the government. A trim-bearded, stooped, blunt Yorkshireman and one of Labour's former proles, as an engineering worker and shop steward. He was born in 1943 and attended Hurlfield Comprehensive School, FE college and Sheffield Polytechnic. His own backing for regional government was reflected in his ministerial responsibility for setting up regional development agencies in 1999. As Sports Minister he denied press reports of his going to Wimbledon and saying he wasn't keen on tennis (as distinct from playing tennis), but in any case saw his remit as looking 'at the whole structure of sport (to) use it much more on the agenda of social inclusion'.

SHEFFIELD HALLAM

Sheffield Hallam must be one of the most sophisticated constituencies in the country. In the 1997 General Election records were broken here. In particular, the Liberal Democrats, in gaining the seat for the first time from the Conservatives, recorded their highest rise of share of vote anywhere: 20.6%. One of the reasons for this must be tactical voting, for Hallam also witnessed the fourth worst Labour change anywhere, a drop of 5%. The only other seat where this pattern was even nearly repeated was also in Yorkshire, and also a Liberal Democrat gain, Harrogate and Knaresborough.

Many people regard Sheffield as the archetype of an industrial and working-class city. Such an impression is encouraged by the most common travellers' views of the city, from the M1 as it passes the east end of the town with its huge Meadowhall shopping centre on the site of a deceased steelworks, or from the city centre with its tower blocks climbing from the myriad of hills. However, as is the case of many British towns, there is a sharp divide between the west end of Sheffield, historically upwind of industry, dirt and smoke, and the classic east end areas. In Sheffield the middle-class residential area which serves England's third-largest city is situated almost entirely within the city boundaries. The Hallam division was held by the Conservatives up to and including 1992 (their last seat in South Yorkshire), and has one of the highest proportions of professionally qualified people of any constituency in Britain.

South-western Sheffield, from the bohemian university area of Broomhill through Ecclesall and Fulwood out to the fringe of the Peak District at Dore and Totley, is a leafy neighbourhood of outstanding residential quality. There are many dark-stone mansions standing solidly among the wooded hills, and only some of them are now broken up into flats and bedsits. Further out can be found modern semis and detached houses in great numbers as Sheffield's professional and managerial groupings gather together in as concentrated a pattern of residential segregation as may be found in Britain. Nearly 80% of those in work here are in middle-class occupations.

The Conservatives were uncomfortably aware of the destruction of their last 'middle-class' seats in places like Liverpool and Manchester, where Withington was held in 1966 but is easily won by Labour now. The way to finish off the Tories in Sheffield was to vote for the party which had already come to dominate the council representation in Hallam, the Liberal Democrats; and the well-educated Labour supporters living here took the hint in a major way, as Richard Allan ousted Sir Irvine Patnick by over 8,000 votes. This gain was consolidated in 2001, as Allan increased his absolute and percentage lead, after a further slight drop in Labour's share and the highest turnout in the city by almost 10%: all very middle-class behaviour.

Social indices:			2001 Gen. Election:			
% Non-white	3.1		LD	21,203	55.4	+4.1
% Prof/Man	59.3		C	11,856	31.0	−2.1
% Non-manual	80.1		Lab	4,758	12.4	−1.1
£ Av prop val 2000	119 K		UKIP	429	1.1	
% Increase 97–00	42.4		LD maj	9,347	24.4	
% Unemployed 2001	2.1		Turnout		63.4	−8.9
% Decrease 97–01	1.8		Elect	60,288		
% Fin hard/Rank	4.4	622				
% Pensioners	28.9					
% Prem mort/Rank	2	638				

Member of Parliament

Richard Allan, a Liberal Democrat Education spokesman (with responsibility for computers), was elected in 1997. Tufted-haired and fastidiously minimally-bearded, he came with a public-school (Oundle) and Cambridge (Pembroke) education and a penchant for information technology, for which he became his party's spokesman in 2001, and which had previously provided him with employment in the NHS. Classless-seeming, although an obvious beneficiary of the 1997 anti-Tory tactical voting landslide, as a Liberal MP in Sheffield he has to live with his party's local antipathy to Labour with whom they vie for control of the city council.

SHEFFIELD HEELEY

Heeley is south Sheffield. In the past it has been the one Sheffield seat which changed hands with the political tide, and could be regarded as a Con–Lab marginal. But the last time this happened was in February 1974. Then its boundaries were altered in Labour's favour in the early 1970s, and again in the early 1980s when the ultra-Labour Park ward was picked up from the constituency which previously bore that name. The seat is now safely Labour. Much of the southern edge of Sheffield is composed of newish housing schemes, like those in the spectacular Gleadless valley, where tower blocks climb up the steep sides of the hills. There is one middle-class area, unsurprisingly over in the south-west towards Hallam constituency, in Beauchief ward.

Beauchief is now usually won by Liberal Democrat candidates for the city council, and in May 2000 that party's local activism enabled them to take all the others here too (Heeley itself, Park, Intake and Norton), and altogether in the last local elections before the 2001 parliamentary contest they took 58% of the vote within the Heeley constituency, 23% ahead of Labour. In one of the most dramatic examples of ticket splitting in Britain, though, their share plummeted by 35% when confronted with the task of choosing a Westminster government, while Labour's went up by 22% – not rally a swing, but rather a differentiation. In parliamentary terms this remains a very safe Labour seat. However, if the national Labour government should ever become as unpopular as Sheffield City Council, it is clear to which party the voters will turn in Sheffield, and in Heeley.

Social indices:			2001 Gen. Election:			
% Non-white	2.4		Lab	19,452	57.0	–3.7
% Prof/Man	24.7		LD	7,748	22.7	+1.4
% Non-manual	50.2		C	4,864	14.2	–1.4
£ Av prop val 2000	53 K		Grn	774	2.3	
% Increase 97–00	17.2		SLP	667	2.0	
% Unemployed 2001	4.9		UKIP	634	1.9	
% Decrease 97–01	3.3		Lab maj	11,704	34.3	
% Fin hard/Rank	31.9	117	Turnout		54.4	–10.6
% Pensioners	30.9		Elect	62,758		
% Prem mort/Rank	35	251				

Member of Parliament

In place of the left-wing engineer Bill Michie came in 2001 **Meg Munn**, one of only four women selected to fight Labour-held seats where the MP had retired. A local girl made good, she was Sheffield-born in 1959 and raised in the constituency, joining the Party aged 16, and attending Rowlinson Comprehensive School and York and Nottingham Universities. A social worker, she was until 2000 Assistant Director of Children's Services in York. A Nottingham city councillor for four years (1987–91), strapping and with a pleasant toothy smile in the wholesome manner of a Girl Guide Commissioner, rarely for Labour candidates these days (in a party which may have a religiose leader but where most activists are hostile to religion) she lists her membership of the Methodist Church. Fluent in French and German, she is keenly pro-European, both in principle and for the Objective One funding from which her area benefits.

SHEFFIELD HILLSBOROUGH

Before the 1997 General Election, a leading Liberal Democrat national campaigner predicted that his party would take two seats in Sheffield, Hallam from the Conservatives, and Hillsborough from Labour; he was emphatically correct about the former, and emphatically wrong about the latter.

The constituency of Hillsborough, north-west Sheffield, was a safe Labour seat until 1983. Then the expansion of Sheffield's city boundaries in the early 1980s turned Hillsborough into one of the nation's very few Labour–Liberal marginals. The new additions, a mixture of housing types and including some semi-rural acreage, usually elect Liberals at local election level, and have shown some inclination to do so in parliamentary contests. Chapeltown, Ecclesfield, High Green and Stocksbridge were previously in Penistone constituency, where the Liberals failed to make much of an impact. However, in the first contest in the redrawn Hillsborough in 1983 the

Liberal candidate finished in a very strong second place, cutting Martin Flannery's majority down to a bare 1,500 votes. In 1987 there was a considerable degree of tactical voting, as the Conservatives dropped back a further 10% in third place and both Labour and Liberals increased their share – Labour slightly more, so that Flannery's lead stretched to just over 3,000.

Labour's new candidate, Helen Jackson, again doubled the majority in 1992, indicating that Hillsborough might after all be vulnerable only in one of Labour's very bad years. The Liberal Democrats could not be written off, however. In May 2000, for example, as part of their vigorous thrust in the city of Sheffield, they won every single ward within the Hillsborough constituency, Stocksbridge, Hillsborough and Walkley as well as their long-term strongholds of Chapel Green and South Wortley. The Hillsborough ward community is old-established and vigorous (although it does not include the famous and tragic ground of the Sheffield Wednesday Football Club, which is in the Labour ward of Owlerton in the neighbouring Brightside seat). However, the constituency which bears its name is the most detached of the Sheffield seats from the city itself, spreading way beyond the historic boundaries through suburbs and fields as far as the independent town of Stocksbridge, with its working steel works. The ward of South Wortley alone covers as much acreage as the whole of the city on pre-1970s boundaries, and the Hillsborough seat as now constituted takes in well over half of Sheffield's total area. It is justly designated a county seat.

The difference between the politics of Sheffield city council and Parliament was demonstrated starkly in 2001 when Helen Jackson was returned with over 34% more votes than her Lib Dem challenger. The Liberal Democrats took 63% in the city contests of 2000, 23% 13 months later in the general election. Hillsborough might not be happy about Labour's municipal stewardship, but Tony Blair's New Labour seemed fine for government.

Social indices:			2001 Gen. Election:			
% Non-white	1.0		Lab	24,170	56.8	–0.0
% Prof/Man	29.2		LD	9,601	22.6	–3.3
% Non-manual	54.7		C	7,801	18.3	+3.8
£ Av prop val 2000	61 K		UKIP	964	2.3	
% Increase 97–00	26.0		Lab maj	14,569	34.3	
% Unemployed 2001	2.6		Turnout		56.6	–14.4
% Decrease 97–01	2.5		Elect	75,097		
% Fin hard/Rank	15.3	347				
% Pensioners	24.8					
% Prem mort/Rank	24	430				

Member of Parliament

Helen Jackson, elected here in 1992, and PPS to Northern Ireland Secretaries Mo Mowlam (1997–99), Peter Mandelson (1999–2001) and John Reid (2001–), is a reconstructed left-winger adapted to the compromises of office. The sister of the one-time Labour MP Chris Price, she was born in 1939, was public-school (Berkhamsted) and Oxford (St Hilda's)-educated, and was a teacher for 19 years before becoming a full-time Sheffield City Councillor, where she resisted paying the poll tax until the last moment. Voting for Gould as leader in 1992 and Beckett in 1994, she voted pre-1997 with the hard left on defence cuts, opposed the US in Central America, and campaigned assiduously against privatised Yorkshire Water. As a loyal PPS she now presents a straight bat in defending the Blair government.

SHERWOOD

In 1983 Sherwood became an entirely new, extra, 11th constituency in Nottinghamshire. It was not based on a local authority district like the other ten, but it included elements of Ashfield, Gedling and Newark. It did, though, have a common economic base to tie it together. Coal was – and to a certain extent still is – king here, and the new seat rose straight into the top five in the national list of divisions dominated by employment in mining. This made it all the more amazing that Sherwood was won in 1983 and 1987 by a Conservative farmer, Andrew Stewart. The political world had to contend with a startling new phenomenon: the Tory mining seat.

The area taken from Newark constituency is effectively the Dukeries coalfield which was opened up in the 1920s, transforming a district previously known for its large aristocratic estates in the remnants of Sherwood Forest. This was one of the most prosperous coalfields in the country, until the threat and practice of pit closures finally came to this part of east Nottinghamshire as well. Ollerton, Edwinstowe, Bilsthorpe, Blidworth and Clipstone always formed the Labour strength in the old Newark seat, and did not blend in easily with the rural part of the seat or with the rather Conservative market town of Newark-on-Trent itself. Similarly, Calverton, a modern mining village, was removed from the Gedling (Carlton) constituency, and Hucknall (Ashfield) is an old-established mining town in the Leen valley which was opened up in the nineteenth century.

There were also some agricultural villages and one very affluent residential area south of Mansfield, Ravenshead. But all the same Sherwood seemed to have been drawn to provide an extra-safe Labour seat in Nottinghamshire. Yet in the year 1983 no ostensible Labour stronghold was safe, or sacred. Since then the Dukeries coalfield has had a tempestuous time: working through the coal strike, beleaguered by flying Yorkshire pickets, deaths outside Ollerton Colliery, and the UDM breakaway. Labour were in no position to retake Sherwood in 1987, and Stewart increased his majority to 4,500. Then the government started to threaten pit closures even in this modern coalfield, and many miners felt betrayed by the Conservatives. Blidworth was the first to go, then there was a fatal accident at Bilsthorpe, which was placed on the list of the doomed along with Clipstone, and a merger was proposed between Ollerton and Thoresby Colliery near Edwinstowe. One began to wonder if any of the pits really had a future. In 1992 there was a swing of over 6% to Labour in Sherwood, and Labour's Paddy Tipping replaced Stewart with a majority of nearly 3,000, and in 1997 he enjoyed the standard large swing in Nottinghamshire to increase this to a mighty 17,000. Even after a 5% swing back towards them in 2001, it seems very likely that the Conservatives' happy sojourn in the forest has come to a decisive end.

Social indices:

% Non-white	0.9	
% Prof/Man	28.5	
% Non-manual	48.7	
£ Av prop val 2000	75 K	
% Increase 97–00	40.9	
% Unemployed 2001	3.0	
% Decrease 97–01	1.8	
% Fin hard/Rank	16.7	322
% Pensioners	23.1	
% Prem mort/Rank	28	380

2001 Gen. Election:

Lab	24,900	54.2	–4.3
C	15,527	33.8	+5.1
LD	5,473	11.9	+3.3
Lab maj	9,373	20.4	
Turnout		60.7	–14.9
Elect	75,670		

Member of Parliament

Paddy Tipping, elected here in 1992, was deputy to Margaret Beckett as Leader of the House from 1999 until dropped from the government in 2001. Dubbed (by Matthew Parris) as 'so unimportant that New Labour's style police have not even bothered to remove his beard', and as having a name that 'sounds like an alternative Saturday night sport for canal-side skinheads bored with queer-bashing', he is a former Nottinghamshire County Councillor and a social worker. Born in 1949, he was educated at Hipperholme Grammar School, Halifax and Nottingham University. A voter in 1994 for Beckett, not Blair, he has resisted coal industry decline even under Labour, and can also be construed as a bit of a nuisance as a keen 'Right to Roamer'. Even his on-message ministerial defence of Labour's House of Lords reforms provoked a backbench revolt against prime ministerial patronage in 1999.

SHIPLEY

The youngest MP elected at the 1997 General Election was Christopher Leslie, who at the age of 24 obtained a signal triumph in defeating the influential senior Tory, the chairman of the 1922 Committee, Sir Marcus Fox. This was the first Labour victory in Shipley since 1945, although it had been won by them several times in the inter-war years; but since then there have been pro-Tory boundary changes, and also this has become an affluent suburban and semi-rural constituency, a considerable change from the industrial origins of the towns here.

The seat always included the rather Conservative small towns of Bingley and Baildon, noted for hills and mills, and the division's eponymous town. Shipley was always starkly divided between its west ward, the home of successful West Yorkshire business people and professionals – it might have been the model for 'T' Top' in John Braine's *Room at the Top*, for Braine certainly spent many years in Shipley; and the industrial east ward, which includes among other communities Titus Salt's planned nineteenth-century village of Saltaire. Shipley East is the only ward in the seat that regularly votes in Labour councillors. These three towns are supplemented by two large wards stretching across the moors in differing directions. To the south-west, Bingley Rural takes in the small and very Conservative villages of Denholme, Cullingworth and Wilsden. To the north-east, across Rombalds Moor (named after a giant who was reputed to stalk it) the constituency was given a salient into Wharfedale to take in Burley and Menston. This ward – also named Rombalds – is amongst the most heavily Tory in West Yorkshire.

Although Christopher Leslie held on again, narrowly, in 2001 by slightly increasing his own share, Shipley is still basically inclined to the Conservatives, and it would only take a further 2% swing for them to regain it; and if that were to happen it might be another 50 years before Labour mastered this area again – assuming, rashly, that there will be no major reform of the electoral system in that time.

Social indices:			2001 Gen. Election:			
% Non-white	3.3		Lab	20,243	44.0	+0.6
% Prof/Man	39.2		C	18,815	40.9	+3.1
% Non-manual	64.5		LD	4,996	10.9	–4.2
£ Av prop val 2000	79 K		Grn	1,386	3.0	
% Increase 97–00	22.9		UKIP	580	1.3	
% Unemployed 2001	2.5		Lab maj	1,428	3.1	
% Decrease 97–01	1.2		Turnout		66.1	–10.2
% Fin hard/Rank	13.7	383	Elect	69,577		
% Pensioners	27.0					
% Prem mort/Rank	28	373				

Member of Parliament

Chris Leslie, Labour's fluent and personable youngest MP and the Baby of the House until the arrival of David Lammy in 2000, came in on the 1997 landslide and within a year was the first of the intake to become a PPS, in his case to Lord Falconer (1998–2001). Initially seen by Tory detractors as having 'a slavish desire to ingratiate himself with his masters', he was born in 1972, educated at Bingley Grammar School and Leeds University, and previously worked in the brief time available between University and Westminster for Bradford Labour Party and for a Bradford councillor. In 2001 he joined by then a total of 21 MPs of the 1997 183-strong intake on the government frontbench as Junior Minister at the Cabinet Office – the youngest minister, still not yet 30.

SHREWSBURY AND ATCHAM

On 10 December 2001 Labour's overall majority went down by two, as Paul Marsden announced his defection to the Liberal Democrats after a bitter and well-publicised dispute with the party Whips and leadership over their policy towards Afghanistan and their alleged rough treatment of his dissenting opinions. He became the 53rd Liberal Democrat MP, although the switch was merely symbolic in such a one-party state as Britain in the first years of the new millennium.

When Labour's 29-year-old candidate Paul Marsden had gained Shrewsbury and Atcham in 1997 he was breaking a very long and distinguished Conservative tradition in this constituency. Shropshire politics remained dominated by the landed and wealthy long after the introduction of universal enfranchisement. The second Earl of Plymouth and the first Viscount Bridgeman both represented county constituencies in their commoner days. The previous (sixth) Earl Harrowby represented Shrewsbury, and when he (once) lost the seat it was to a Liberal multi-millionaire. The Conservative MP from 1945 was Sir John Langford-Holt. When he retired in 1983, local Conservatives rejected the overtures of Warren Hawksley, who wanted to migrate from the neighbouring, marginal Wrekin division (which he did indeed lose, in 1987) and instead brought in Derek Conway from Newcastle upon Tyne. Mr Conway was selected at 29, the same age as Langford-Holt when he inherited the seat, and for over a decade it seems as if he could rely on as long a leasehold on this desirable property.

The constituency is dominated by Shropshire's county town, with its famous public school and agricultural show, and its English and Welsh Bridges and other medieval echoes. The constituency name was altered in 1983 to give recognition to the local government borough of Shrewsbury and Atcham, and indeed the seat does run west to the Welsh border. It is in the rural areas, as well as in the wealthier neighbourhoods of Shrewsbury such as Kingsland, that Conservative support is strongest. The town itself has several Labour wards in its central and eastern sectors, and in the Shrewsbury and Atcham borough elections of May 1999 they won the former Liberal Democrat strongholds south of Shrewsbury, in Meole Brace and Bayston Hill. Labour were only third in 1992, but even then they did manage to secure 26%, and with a nationally average swing of 11% directly from the Tories, Marsden could just surpass Conway by 1,670 votes, with the Liberal Democrats retaining the support of about a quarter of the electorate.

Much depended on how that third bloc might split in 2001, and fragment it did, as the Liberal Democrat vote fell from 14,000 to 6,000. Labour's share increased by nearly twice as much as the Tories' did, and Marsden, benefiting from his own incumbency as well as the government's lack of unpopularity, doubled his majority. Marsden will presumably try to defend this seat as a Liberal Democrat: unlike defectors to the larger parties a transfer to a safe seat is not a possibility. Nor should his chances be written off. He may be seen as a brave and independently-minded politician, able to exploit the benefits of incumbency, and by 2005 or so the New Labour appeal may have dissipated for many others as well as Marsden himself. Nor should it be forgotten that before the 2001 Election, when the Lib Dem share was halved by tactical voting and a non-targeted campaign, this had not been a particularly weak seat for them: they finished second in 1992. The Welsh Marches are not a bad region either, as Shrewsbury/Atcham borders both Ludlow and Montgomeryshire. It could be a fascinating three-way fight.

Social indices:			2001 Gen. Election:			
% Non-white	1.0		Lab	22,253	44.6	+7.6
% Prof/Man	33.7		C	18,674	37.4	+3.4
% Non-manual	56.0		LD	6,173	12.4	−12.6
£ Av prop val 2000	88 K		UKIP	1,620	3.2	+2.4
% Increase 97–00	38.4		Grn	931	1.9	
% Unemployed 2001	1.9		Ind	258	0.5	
% Decrease 97–01	1.1		Lab maj	3,579	7.2	
% Fin hard/Rank	10.2	461	Turnout		66.6	−8.7
% Pensioners	26.4		Elect	74,964		
% Prem mort/Rank	22	451				

Member of Parliament

Paul Marsden, a birdlike-visaged 'quality assurance manager' with the sort of modishly wire-rimmed spectacles designed to make the wearer look cerebral, was born in 1968, educated at Helsby High School and Teesside Polytechnic, unexpectedly won this seat in 1997, spent four years without making headlines other than wobbling over the fuel tax protests and whether or not to fight the seat again, but in the event did so. Then, in the aftermath of the terrorist attack on the World Trade Center in New York, he voted for the sacking of Stephen Byers' press aide for wanting to 'bury' some bad news in the coverage of the disaster, called for a vote on and led a revolt against the bombing of Afghanistan, released the transcript of his acrimonious confrontation with the Chief Whip in which he was accused of being an 'appeaser', wrote a rude letter to Tony Blair, accused 'thugs' from the Whips' Office of intimidating him in a Commons bar, and joined the Liberal Democrats as their 53rd MP and the first Labour MP to defect since the SDP exodus of 1981, amongst which were numbered James Dunn and John Roper, whose names liveth for evermore. But at the time, December 2001, the loss of an MP to the Opposition was the first fly in the Blairite ointment.

SHROPSHIRE NORTH

The Conservatives only held the one seat in Shropshire in 2001, having lost Ludlow that year to follow Shrewsbury/Atcham and The Wrekin in 1997, but they did at least strengthen their position substantially here in North Shropshire as the first term MP Owen Paterson increased his share of the vote by fully 8%, while the Liberal Democrats (whose efforts in the county seemed concentrated in the southern division of Ludlow) fell back by the same figure. Labour had approached to within 2,250 in 1997, but it no longer looks like a marginal.

This seat is very much set on the Welsh border. Remnants of Wat's Dyke and Offa's Dyke offer reminders of the time when this was Mercia's – and England's – front line against Celtic raids. There are wards called Llanyblodwel and Llanymynech. The population is scattered among half a dozen or so small towns and many villages, many deeply rural in character. The biggest of the towns is Oswestry (population 14,000); others include Market Drayton, Whitchurch, Wem and Ellesmere on its lake. In local elections this is one of the few parts of England where Independents still rule. There are many unopposed contests, including those allowing a handful of Labour councillors from the towns, and from the area bordering Wrexham's old coalfield. However, turnout was rather above average in 2001 and 1997 may well have been the high-water mark of Labour's achievement in north Shropshire.

Social indices:			2001 Gen. Election:			
% Non-white	0.5		C	22,631	48.6	+8.4
% Prof/Man	31.7		Lab	16,390	35.2	−0.7
% Non-manual	51.0		LD	5,945	12.8	−7.6
£ Av prop val 2000	82 K		UKIP	1,165	2.5	
% Increase 97–00	34.7		Ind	389	0.8	
% Unemployed 2001	2.6		C maj	6,241	13.4	
% Decrease 97–01	0.8		Turnout		63.1	−9.6
% Fin hard/Rank	11.2	435	Elect	73,716		
% Pensioners	27.4					
% Prem mort/Rank	25	422				

Member of Parliament

Owen Paterson, PPS to Iain Duncan Smith from 2001 having backed him in all the leadership ballots, and a toff amidst the suburban dross of contemporary Tory MPs, was elected in 1997 as the charming-if-abrasively partisan, Radley and Cambridge (Corpus Christi)-educated, son-in-law of Viscount Ridley. Born in 1956, he previously worked with his family's British Leather Company from 1979, and was by 1993 its managing director. As a pugnacious right-winger who backed Redwood in 1997, he campaigns against all legislation affecting the countryside, whether beef bans, high fuel duty, hunting bans, and beleaguered hauliers, and monumentally filibustered a bill to ban fur farming. Good-looking and oozing savoir faire, he also dismissed Welsh devolution as involving 'a coachload of superannuated county councillors'. He was a Whip 2000–01.

SITTINGBOURNE AND SHEPPEY

'Sittingbourne and Sheppey' was chosen by the Boundary Commission for this seat on its creation before the 1997 Election, although a more logical and indeed shorter name would have been 'Swale'.

The Swale is the channel which divides the flat Isle of Sheppey from the mainland, and the local district council is named after it; the three main population centres in the Swale district are Faversham (now removed for parliamentary purposes), Sittingbourne and Sheppey, together with some villages in the orchard-strewn countryside between. Sittingbourne, sited on the A2 trunk road, has a population of nearly 40,000 and is clearly the largest element in the constituency. It is usually mainly Conservative, at least in general elections, but it does have Liberal Democrat wards like Milton Regis. The whole constituency is diverse in character. The Isle of Sheppey is no holiday paradise. Besides its rather eerie and Dickensian marshland, and low-lying fields, it has industrial and working-class districts which give Labour strong support in council elections, particularly in the port of Sheerness with its history of troubled industrial relations.

This area has by no means been safely Conservative, historically. The Faversham seat on which it is based was actually held by Labour, very narrowly, throughout the period from 1945 to 1970. After that, though, the growth of owner-occupied housing and the long-term swing away from Labour in the south-east took it beyond their grasp. In 1992 Roger Moate won his seventh election in Faversham, with a majority of 16,000 over evenly-divided opposition. However, in Labour's golden year of 1997, Derek Wyatt recaptured the success of the pre-1970 Faversham days and Sir Roger Moate joined the list of 17 Tory knights who were defeated. The margin was under 2,000, though, and Sittingbourne/Sheppey was regarded as a prime target for the Tories to regain in June 2001. It was a further heavy blow for them both locally and nationally that no seat in Kent was regained, and that in several the New Labour incumbent increased his majority, as here. The figures suggest that Derek Wyatt managed to persuade some more Liberal Democrat supporters to switch, although simple change of party share figures must be seen in a context of a 15% reduction in turnout. Given that Labour was probably the party which suffered most from abstentions, one suspects that in a closer national contest Wyatt might even be able to pull out some extra voters who stayed at home in 2001; but then, if it is closer he is in deep trouble anyway.

Social indices:			2001 Gen. Election:			
% Non-white	1.1		Lab	17,340	45.8	+5.2
% Prof/Man	26.6		C	13,831	36.5	+0.2
% Non-manual	50.0		LD	5,353	14.1	−4.2
£ Av prop val 2000	82 K		Ind	673	1.8	
% Increase 97–00	44.8		UKIP	661	1.7	+0.7
% Unemployed 2001	3.3		Lab maj	3,509	9.3	
% Decrease 97–01	2.8		Turnout		57.5	−14.8
% Fin hard/Rank	15.5	343	Elect	65,825		
% Pensioners	23.4					
% Prem mort/Rank	29	360				

Member of Parliament

Derek Wyatt, Labour's 13th least expected winner in 1997, and described as 'on the butch wing of the Culture, Media and Sports Select Committee', is a big shambling man with a nose broken by rugby (some of it international). Born in 1949, son of an accountant, and educated elongatedly at Westcliff County High School, Colchester Royal Grammar School, St Luke's College, Exeter, St Catherine's College, Oxford, and the Open University, he comes from a background in satellite (BSkyB) television, and as an MP has majored in computing, and particularly the internet and e-mail (setting up an all-party group), overlain with a populist concern for sport. A bemoaner of North Kent's 'necklace of poverty', he rebelled on predatory newspaper pricing and against the Freedom of Information Bill's exclusion of policy advice, and favours the return of the Elgin Marbles. Dubbed 'Parliament's internet visionary', his computer company, The World Internet Forum, went into liquidation in March 2001.

SKIPTON AND RIPON

The Skipton and Ripon seat consists of the countryside which most people would consider to be the heart of the Yorkshire Dales – Settle, Skipton, Ripon and Wharfedale. These southern dales are more accessible to the great population centres of industrial Lancashire and West Yorkshire, and as a result villages like Grassington and Burnsall have a softer, more commercial air than the more rugged communities further north. Here are tourist targets like Bolton Priory, Fountains Abbey and Malham Tarn. There are some old textile mills in Skipton, but the constituency's economy is heavily dependent upon tourism and farming. this made life exceptionally hard here during the severe and protracted foot and mouth outbreak of 2001. It also shapes, and probably in that crisis year reinforced, its preferred political flavour: strong conservatism.

In 1983 Skipton and Ripon brought together major parts of two old seats, both formerly in the West Riding. Skipton lost the small ex-mill towns of Barnoldswick and Earby, which are now in Lancashire, as well as Sedbergh and Dentdale, which are now in Cumbria. Barnoldswick and Earby were Labour's only source of any strength at all in the Skipton seat, which was considered something of a Liberal–Conservative marginal (though the Conservatives always won). In October 1974 the dynamic Liberal candidate Claire Brooks lost at Skipton by only 590 votes. To the east, the Ripon constituency lost the Conservative towns of Ilkley and Otley in Lower Wharfedale, for they were then in the metropolitan county of West Yorkshire. Ripon too was a seat with a Liberal tradition in recent years, for the bookseller David Austick won it in their boom year of 1973 at the same time as Clement Freud won the Isle of Ely. However, Austick could hold Ripon for less than a year, and by 1979 the Conservative former academic Keith Hampson had increased his majority to 16,000 there.

The Liberals initially felt that they had a chance in this huge seat in the south-west of North Yorkshire. It was after all a combination of two seats which offered them some of their brightest hopes of the 1970s. But the Liberal challenge declined rapidly in the late 1970s and 1980s, and their time of opportunity here in the southern dales seems to have passed by. In 1997 and 2001 they actually lost ground and David Curry retained a five-figure lead – princely compared with those of most of his colleagues in those years.

Social indices:			2001 Gen. Election:			
% Non-white	0.7		C	25,736	52.4	+5.8
% Prof/Man	39.3		LD	12,806	26.1	+0.9
% Non-manual	57.7		Lab	8,543	17.4	−5.0
£ Av prop val 2000	96 K		UKIP	2,041	4.2	
% Increase 97–00	27.9		C maj	12,930	26.3	
% Unemployed 2001	1.4		Turnout		65.3	−10.1
% Decrease 97–01	0.7		Elect	75,201		
% Fin hard/Rank	8.7	496				
% Pensioners	29.0					
% Prem mort/Rank	20	479				

Member of Parliament

David Curry, a One Nation Clarke-backing Europhile casualty of the Conservatives' Eurosceptic orthodoxy, spent four months as William Hague's Agriculture spokesman until quitting over the 'not-for-a-decade' commitment against the single currency in November 1997. Elected in 1987 after two terms as an MEP, he served as an Environment (mostly housing) or Agriculture Minister from 1989 to 1997. A duck-voiced, short-tongued ex-journalist, born in 1944 into a family of teachers, and educated at Ripon Grammar School, Corpus Christi College, Oxford and Harvard University, he is in the Conservative minority prone to vote for lowering the homosexual age of consent to 16. In April 1996 he had been given added and thankless responsibility as 'Minister for the South West' for stopping Cornwall going Liberal or Labour – which it duly did in its entirety in 1997.

SLEAFORD AND NORTH HYKEHAM

The Boundary Commission does not have a consistent policy with regard to the nomenclature of parliamentary constituencies. Very often these are decided after local inquiries taken by Assistant Commissioners who are barristers appointed to review the recommendations for a single county. These are independent operators who listen to a variety of opinion at the inquiry stage. Local communities like to be mentioned in the title of the division. Thus the Assistant Commissioner advised that the proposed seat of Mid Lincolnshire should be renamed Sleaford and North Hykeham. Many communities are not so lucky. Let us bear in mind that the following towns, many of which did have a seat named after them at one time, do not figure in current constituency titles: Barnstaple, Kidderminster, Margate, Dorking, Oswestry, Ilkeston, Belper, Northallerton, Accrington, Chester-le-Street, Nelson and Colne, Whitby, Port Talbot, Aberdare, Arbroath, Larne, Ballymena and Enniskillen. This is just a selection. Yet we must get used to referring to quite a mouthful: the Honourable Member for Sleaford and North Hykeham.

It is hard to cavil at the recognition of Sleaford, an old market town which has long formed the centre of an extensive area of farming villages. However it really is a surprise that North Hykeham is so honoured. This is really a suburban area of Lincoln, straggling along the A46 Fosse Way south of the cathedral city. It does have some 9,000 electors, but retains the character not so much of an overgrown village as of a peripheral housing estate. If all places of such size were included, constituency titles would generally be impossibly unwieldy.

Whatever one's view of its name, the inclusion of North Hykeham in the seat is indeed significant – but not for this division! This is a relatively new seat, fought for the first time in 1997, made up principally of voters from the old Grantham constituency, which lost its eponymous town to Grantham and Stamford. Thirteen-and-a-half thousand voters came from the marginal Lincoln – yes, the North Hykeham wards and the similar Skellingthorpe and Waddington West. This is Conservative territory, and was vital for that party's 2,000 majority in the Lincoln city seat. It was sadly missed, as Labour seized the pared-down Lincoln, while Douglas Hogg held the fresh creation by over 5,000. Thus we can see some of the more subtle effects of the Boundary Commission's work: a safe new and extra Tory seat has been created in Lincolnshire, but at the same time a vital marginal, Lincoln, has been shifted over to Labour: net result in an even year: a Labour gain of one seat. 2001 was not an even year, of course, but the Conservatives will be out of business, politically speaking, if one never comes along again.

Social indices:			2001 Gen. Election:			
% Non-white	0.7		C	24,190	49.7	+5.7
% Prof/Man	31.8		Lab	15,568	32.0	−2.3
% Non-manual	51.1		LD	7,894	16.2	+1.0
£ Av prop val 2000	73 K		UKIP	1,067	2.2	
% Increase 97–00	31.7		C maj	8,622	17.7	
% Unemployed 2001	1.7		Turnout		65.3	−9.1
% Decrease 97–01	1.3		Elect	74,561		
% Fin hard/Rank	6.2	578				
% Pensioners	27.3					
% Prem mort/Rank	21	472				

Member of Parliament

Douglas Hogg QC, a chip off the old block as a mix of first-rate brains and an immature personality, is the eldest son of Lord Hailsham (Quintin Hogg) and became, on his father's death in 2001, the third Viscount Hailsham, with (under the Blairite dispensation) no interruption to his Commons career. Elected here in 1997 but first in 1979 for Mrs Thatcher's native heath of Grantham, and although a frontbencher from 1983, he was not of her ilk nor equally of Hague's, and so in 1997 backed Clarke and then retreated to the Inns of Court. Spit-roasted as Agriculture Minister (1995–97) by the BSE crisis, a slight and lisping loner, he has been variously seen as 'one of the rudest men in British politics, if not the entire world' (Simon Hoggart, the *Guardian*), and 'like his father an amalgam of cleverness and foolishness, (he) confronted Britain's democratic masses with pinched self-righteousness and irritability' (Hywel Williams). He was born in 1945 and followed his father via Eton and Christ Church to Lincoln's Inn, and is the fourth Hogg in five generations to sit in the Commons. His leadership votes in 2001 were unrevealed.

SLOUGH

For many years Slough was united with Eton in a constituency which had a strong claim to be the most quaintly drawn in England. Notable left-wing MPs such as the peace campaigner Fenner Brockway (1950–64) and Joan Lestor (1966–83) had the privilege of representing the small town of Eton, which is dominated by the most famous boys' school in the world. It was said to be a tradition for Labour MPs to be bombarded with flour bags on their annual visits to the school. Then in 1983 the anomaly was ended – the seat of Slough became coterminous with its local borough boundaries, and Eton was swapped for two peripheral council estates, Wexham and Britwell.

It is truly ironic that at the very moment when the seat became just plain 'Slough' the Conservatives gained it. John Watts defeated Joan Lestor by 3,000 votes in 1983 and held on twice. This requires some explanation, since for many people Slough evokes the image of one of the few unsightly 'red' enclaves in Home Counties true-blue suburbia. They are thinking of the vast inter-war industrial estates along the Great West Road which inspired John Betjeman to implore 'Come, friendly bombs, and fall on Slough' in the 1930s; of large council-housing estates; and of the large

Asian population (the constituency is now 28% non-white) concentrated near the centre of the town. In fact Slough has always possessed Conservative wards too. The strongest is the middle-class residential area of Upton, just east of the town centre, but more Tory votes come from the western and eastern ends of the borough, where the sizeable semi-independent communities of Burnham and Langley have leaned to the right in most recent elections. It is possible too that quite a few members of the Asian community voted Labour in local elections (Slough has remained solidly Labour-controlled), but for the incumbent MP John Watts at general election time.

Slough went Labour (probably for some considerable time) by fully 13,000 votes on an above national average swing of over 13% in 1997, and Fiona Mactaggart benefited from a further swing in 2001. This was probably due to three main factors. Labour did very well in most of Berkshire – see for example the Reading seats, or even Wokingham – due to the rapidly growing economy and prosperity of the sub-region: property prices rose by 53% between 1997 and 2000 during Labour's first term. Fiona Mactaggart has proved a high-profile MP both locally and in the media. And many members of the large Asian community have probably brought their parliamentary voting more in line with that for the local council, now that both are Labour-controlled, and look like remaining so for the foreseeable future.

Social indices:			2001 Gen. Election:			
% Non-white	28.1		Lab	22,718	58.3	+1.6
% Prof/Man	29.8		C	10,210	26.2	−3.1
% Non-manual	54.6		LD	4,109	10.5	+3.2
£ Av prop val 2000	107 K		Ind	859	2.2	
% Increase 97–00	53.0		UKIP	738	1.9	
% Unemployed 2001	3.1		Ind	364	0.9	
% Decrease 97–01	1.6		Lab maj	12,508	32.1	
% Fin hard/Rank	26.9	176	Turnout		53.8	−14.1
% Pensioners	21.3		Elect	72,429		
% Prem mort/Rank	38	206				

Member of Parliament

Fiona Mactaggart, appointed leader of Labour's Campaign Team in the wake of the lifeless landslide of June 2001, after being PPS to Culture Secretary Chris Smith (1997–2001), was elected in 1997 after selection from an all-women shortlist which squashed the parliamentary hopes of Labour's 1992 candidate Eddie Lopez. An anglicised Scot, the maternal granddaughter of a Conservative MP (Sir Herbert Williams who was an MP variously between 1924 and 1955), and daughter of a right-wing millionaire property developer and third baronet, she was born in 1953 and educated at Cheltenham Ladies College and King's College, London, and worked as a primary school teacher and lecturer in education. Big, strapping and extrovert and with a background as a councillor (1986–90) in the highly polarised Wandsworth Council, she campaigns on local health and immigration issues, and is mildly Eurosceptic. A millionairess in her own right and a sufferer from multiple sclerosis, whilst never casting a vote against the government she has attacked anaemic New Labour for its 'vanilla politics'.

SOLIHULL

Solihull used to be one of the two safest Conservative seats in Great Britain, returning a majority of over 32,000 in 1979 when Mrs Thatcher came to power, for example. In the very different national circumstances of 2001 it is scarcely surprising that this was nowhere near matched, at 9,407, but it is still one of the 45 safest. Ironically one of the seats much nearer the top of the list is another affluent suburb of Birmingham, Sutton Coldfield; but Solihull is the proud possessor of a metropolitan borough bearing its name (which also includes Meriden constituency), while Sutton Coldfield has rather reluctantly been incorporated in the city of Birmingham for local government purposes.

Solihull does contain the world-renowned Land Rover motor works, and the territory north of the railway line is somewhat less fashionable – Elmdon and Lyndon wards. But Shirley and Silhill, St Alphege and Olton, are all safely Conservative. Solihull is largely a creation of the twentieth century: until 1932 it did not even have urban district status, with a scattered population of just 25,000, and in its modern form it would scarcely be recognisable to the poet W.H. Auden, who grew up here on Lode Lane. Over 85% of the housing in the seat is owner-occupied and, almost uniquely for a large town, the percentage of non-manual workers approaches 70%. Why is Solihull quite so Conservative? Perhaps it is because so many of the middle-class commuters to Birmingham are concentrated in restricted areas, here and in Sutton Coldfield, whereas in London such people are spread much more widely in the West End, outer London and the Home Counties, and even further afield such as in Brighton and Oxford. Yet Birmingham is the nation's second largest city, and generates much prosperity and affluence. Another point is that Solihull is 97% white, but the cosmopolitan racial mixture of the West Midlands is a pervasive factor in the politics of the West Midlands conurbation. The white middle classes and skilled workers are particularly prone to the appeal of the Conservative Party as one which seeks to maintain law and order, protect property and control immigration.

The Conservative percentage of the vote in Solihull has been stuck at 45% for the last two elections, and its position on the list of safety would fall considerably if voters could decide which of their two main rivals have the best chance of challenging them: the race for second place here in both 1997 and 2001 ended in a photo-finish on 25%. The electoral position here seems to have reached a position of stasis, and as long as that is the case Conservatives like John Taylor will continue to represent Solihull without a real threat of defeat.

Social indices:			2001 Gen. Election:			
% Non-white	3.1		C	21,935	45.4	+0.8
% Prof/Man	41.6		LD	12,528	26.0	+0.7
% Non-manual	69.6		Lab	12,373	25.6	+1.3
£ Av prop val 2000	130 K		UKIP	1,061	2.2	
% Increase 97–00	41.7		PA	374	0.8	−0.3
% Unemployed 2001	1.5		C maj	9,407	19.5	
% Decrease 97–01	1.1		Turnout		62.6	−12.1
% Fin hard/Rank	5.3	600	Elect	77,094		
% Pensioners	26.5					
% Prem mort/Rank	8	614				

Member of Parliament

John Taylor, has been MP here since 1983. An affable pudgy-faced solicitor, born in 1941 and educated at Bromsgrove School and a law college, he rose without trace through a series of junior posts since first entering the government Whips Office in 1988. With a reputation as a Groucho Marx impersonator, he is also numbered amongst the Tory minority that votes to ban fox hunting. He initially backed Michael Howard for leader in 1997, but then switched ideologically-incongruously to Kenneth Clarke, whose PPS he had been. In 2001 he backed the orthodox Ancram candidacy. Earlier in the year he had tried to ban the 'suburban nightmare' of *cyprus leylandii* hedges.

SOMERTON AND FROME

Somerton and Frome was a new seat in 1983, carved out of the two previous divisions in eastern Somerset, Wells and Yeovil. The first two contests in the new constituency in the 1980s saw fairly easy Tory victories, with a majority of 9,500 in 1987. With a new candidate in 1992, though, and the Western regional swing to the Liberal Democrats, the Somerset county councillor (for Frome North) David Heath slashed the lead to under 4,500. The small semi-industrial towns which typify the constituency all elected Liberal Democrats in their landslide win in the 1993 county council elections: Frome, Castle Cary, Langport, Wincanton and Somerton itself (which only has a population of 2,000 and must be considered lucky to be mentioned in the seat's title).

It came as no great surprise when in 1997 two parliamentary gains in Somerset followed the years of local government success: Taunton and Somerton and Frome. Indeed, the margin of David Heath's victory might perplex – only 130, at a time when his party were making gains in less traditionally strong areas like Sheffield Hallam and Oxford West by several thousands. The reason was probably the rise in the Labour share in third place here, while Heath actually lost a few votes. His position remained insecure after his initial election, as fox hunting and other 'countryside' issues led the Conservatives to target the Liberal Democrats defending constituencies in the county (Jackie Ballard was indeed defeated in Taunton). What is more, local elections did not go so well, and when the votes cast in Mendip and South Somerset wards within the Somerton and Frome seat in May 1999 were added up, the Conservative total almost exactly matched that of the Lib Dems. The Conservatives received 26% more votes in the European elections of June 1999, although this was on a pro-Tory issue with a very low turnout.

Over 70% of electors did vote in the 2001 General Election, which was true in only eight of England's 529 seats, and this may have helped Heath to hold on narrowly again, by another three-figure margin (668) with a 4% increase in vote share, presumably largely at Labour's expense. Heath's number of votes increased, which was very untypical of 2001, so it is hard to argue that he didn't deserve to win; but it took a very hard fight indeed to do so, pulling out all the stops.

Social indices:			2001 Gen. Election:			
% Non-white	0.4		LD	22,983	43.6	+4.1
% Prof/Man	35.3		C	22,315	42.4	+3.1
% Non-manual	53.2		Lab	6,113	11.6	–4.7
£ Av prop val 2000	111 K		UKIP	919	1.7	+1.2
% Increase 97–00	56.5		Lib	354	0.7	
% Unemployed 2001	1.3		LD maj	668	1.3	
% Decrease 97–01	1.7		Turnout		70.3	–7.3
% Fin hard/Rank	7.2	555	Elect	74,991		
% Pensioners	27.6					
% Prem mort/Rank	12	566				

Member of Parliament

David Heath was elected here in 1997. A black-bearded, bear-like optician from Frome who served on Somerset County Council for 12 years (1985–97) and led it for four (1985–89), he was born in 1954 and educated as a scholarship boy at Millfield School and at St John's College, Oxford (as a contemporary of Tony Blair). Sensitive to a rural economy in crisis, he votes very cautiously on gun control and on hunting, backing 'licensing' of hunts and abstaining on outright abolition, a prudent sensitivity to the local presence of the kennels of the Blackmore Vale Hunt, and one ignored to her cost by his defeated Taunton neighbour, Jackie Ballard. Sounding cautious as well on the euro doubtless helped ease his majority upwards to 668 in a constituency most of whose fields were proclaiming their Tory loyalties in June 2001. Formerly a Foreign Affairs and then Agriculture spokesman, his 'Work and Pensions' remit in 2001 did not look like promotion. His seat contains what should be a Liberal shrine at Mells, where Asquith's grandson, the second Earl of Oxford and Asquith (in his 86th year) resides in the Manor House, and Asquith's daughter Lady Violet Bonham-Carter, mother-in-law of Jo Grimond, lies in the churchyard.

SOUTHAMPTON ITCHEN

Southampton Itchen has always been one of Labour's strongest constituencies in the south of England outside London. During the pit of the party's popularity in Mrs Thatcher's heyday, the Tories did win it twice (1983 and 1987), but before then it had been the seat of the first Labour Speaker, Horace King (1955–71), and it returned to its traditional loyalty with a majority of 14,000 in 1997. Of course in the context of that year this now seems nothing unusual, even in the southern region, with similar majorities in places like Basildon, Kingswood, Oxford East and, indeed, next door at Southampton Test. Labour's John Denham held his position in 2001, but the turnout fell by fully 16%, to its lowest level ever in the seat, by some margin: just 54%.

The Southampton constituencies are named after the two rivers which flow into Southampton Water. Itchen is really the eastern half of the city, containing the mainly twentieth-century portion of Southampton beyond the River Itchen, but also the heart of the city centre in Bargate ward on the western bank. It has shown itself very much open to modernisation in recent years, with its Ocean Village development with its fashionable housing and leisure developments on the Itchen, and Southampton FC's brand new stadium, purpose-built but nevertheless returned to previously blighted land within the St Mary's district which had given it its name back in the nineteenth century. Test, on the other hand, is in every way west. Both the constituencies were for many elections considered extremely marginal, replicating the national social and demographic, and electoral averages very closely.

Itchen is slightly the more working class of the Southampton seats, and it had the higher percentage of non-white residents in 1992, but it is still far from suffering great poverty or high unemployment. There is not too glaring an economic gap between council estates like Thornhill in Bitterne ward and the private housing of Bitterne Park and Harefield. Most of the wards are marginal in an even year; one prominent exception is Bargate, where the Asian population is concentrated. Both Southampton seats now look, rather like the country, like Labour bankers, in every sense of that word, including that used in crossword puzzles.

Social indices:			2001 Gen. Election:			
% Non-white	4.2		Lab	22,553	54.5	−0.3
% Prof/Man	25.0		C	11,330	27.4	−1.0
% Non-manual	51.8		LD	6,195	15.0	+3.3
£ Av prop val 2000	89 K		UKIP	829	2.0	+1.7
% Increase 97–00	54.9		SA	241	0.6	+0.4
% Unemployed 2001	2.8		SLP	225	0.5	−0.6
% Decrease 97–01	2.8		Lab maj	11,223	27.1	
% Fin hard/Rank	23.5	220	Turnout		54.0	−16.1
% Pensioners	26.0		Elect	76,603		
% Prem mort/Rank	37	211				

Member of Parliament

John Denham, since 1997 a laterally-moving Minister of State (for Social Security, then Health, then from 2001 at the Home Office), was elected third-time-lucky here in 1992, a former Southampton-based city and county councillor. A one-time unilateralist opponent of Trident and Cruise and proponent of 'extra-parliamentary action' to achieve a 'democratic socialist society', by 1994 he was apologizing at a party conference fringe meeting for the factionalism of the 1980s, and as part of Labour's 'Southern strategy' to revive electorally in the south of England, urging the party to acknowledge that nowadays 'ten times as many people sell insurance as dig coal'. Born in 1953 and educated at Woodroffe Comprehensive, Lyme Regis and Southampton University, he worked originally for a raft of voluntary sector organisations (War on Want, Friends of the Earth, the British Youth Council), and was quickly onto the frontbench by 1995 and into government in 1997 as a pensions specialist, where his suit and switched-on rictus make him a model Blairite minister.

SOUTHAMPTON TEST

Hampshire is the only county which received two extra seats in the Boundary Commission review of parliamentary constituencies before the 1997 Election. Two safe new Tory seats, then? Well no, not exactly. It is true that both of the additional divisions created, one in the north of the county and one in the south, are very Conservative. But changes elsewhere went a considerable way to cancelling this out. Specifically, the critical marginal seat of Southampton Test was tipped over to the Labour side by small but significant boundary changes.

At first sight it would seem that the damage done to the Tories' chances in Southampton Test was minimal. One ward, St Luke's, was gained from the other Southampton seat, Itchen; one ward, Bassett, was lost to the new Romsey division. Yet this may well be enough to be decisive, should the Conservatives ever recover enough to challenge for an overall majority in the Commons. The new acquisition, St Luke's, is usually a Labour ward, consisting largely of 'inner-urban' terraced housing, with about a sixth of its population non-white. However, it is the loss of Bassett which is the more serious blow. Bassett, in Southampton's leafy northernmost suburbs, is by any criterion the most Conservative ward in the city: 75% of its households have access to a car and 29% have two or more. In a typical general election Bassett might have added about 3,000 to the Conservative vote compared with Labour. Clearly this would not tip the balance in 2001, for example, when they lost by 11,000, but in 1992 when they last held on narrowly, Test had played its part, but James Hill had only won by 585.

Southampton Test has long been one of the classic British marginal seats, changing hands in 1955, 1966, 1970, 1974, 1979 and 1997. It is also very similar in social and economic make-up to the nation's average. It is not surprising that the level of political contest and consciousness is keen, or that party membership is among the highest in the country.

Southampton is a great seaport, but more of a Merchant Navy and ferry base than a military zone, and it has little of the Royal Navy Conservatism of Portsmouth and Gosport. Test is West, as far as Southampton is concerned. The wards tend not to be quite as homogeneous and marginal as in Itchen. Having lost Bassett the best Conservative ward is Shirley, in the pleasant green residential area west of the Common near the distinguished King Edward VI Grammar School. However, Labour can more than fight back now in Redbridge, a large council estate ward on the edge of the city towards Totton, and Coxford and Millbrook give Labour an advantage too in all but disastrous years like those of the 1980s.

Test has been a very accurate 'weather-vane' marginal, swinging with the national tide. However, with a combination of the Hampshire boundary changes and the national swing since 1997 it now looks like a safe Labour seat, and indeed one which they could win even if they lost a general election. 'As goes Test, so goes the nation' no longer applies.

Social indices:			2001 Gen. Election:			
% Non-white	5.5		Lab	21,824	52.5	−1.7
% Prof/Man	32.5		C	10,617	25.5	−2.5
% Non-manual	55.3		LD	7,522	18.1	+4.4
£ Av prop val 2000	84 K		UKIP	792	1.9	+1.5
% Increase 97–00	48.7		SA	442	1.1	
% Unemployed 2001	2.6		SLP	378	0.9	
% Decrease 97–01	3.5		Lab maj	11,207	27.0	
% Fin hard/Rank	23.6	218	Turnout		56.3	−15.6
% Pensioners	25.9		Elect	73,893		
% Prem mort/Rank	38	201				

Member of Parliament

Dr Alan Whitehead, who reached the frontbench as Junior Minister for Local Government and the Regions in 2001, is the former leader of Southampton City Council and ex-Professor of Public Policy at Southampton Institute, and was third time lucky here in 1997, when on the one last avalanche principle, he replaced a 585 Tory majority with his own 13,684 majority. An airbrushed ex-left-winger who attacked as 'electoralism' Denis Healey's call at the 1983 party conference for Labour to become a mainstream party again, he came, with beard reduced to moustache, more mundanely to extol the merits of regional government, and to intone the mantra of an 'integrated transport policy' (having sought to build a light railway in Southampton), and in 1999 joined fellow intellectual Baroness Blackstone as her PPS. Born in 1950 and educated at Isleworth Grammar School and Southampton University, acquiring a PhD in politics, he ran the British Institute of Industrial Therapy but plausibly mocks the Liberal Democrats as 'a franchise party', with whoever controls the local photocopier deciding the local policy.

SOUTHEND WEST

Like another Essex seat, Chelmsford, Southend West was long a target for the Liberals, but seems to have slipped away. For years the Liberal Democrats and their predecessors have been able to match the Tory share of the vote in local elections in the wards which comprise Southend West, but Paul Channon had a majority of almost 12,000 in 1992, and even in 1997, when the Conservative vote in Essex collapsed (down no less than 16% here), the Labour vote, far from being squeezed, nearly doubled to over 22%. It looked as if Southend West electors were bearing the national Labour–Conservative contest in mind as well as that in their own neck of the woods. The new Tory candidate David Amess, having moved from Basildon, kept his seat in Parliament despite getting less than 40% of the total vote. In 2001 the picture continued to get blacker for the Liberal Democrats as they lost another 8% and were pipped for second place by Labour, although just by 53 votes. This split of his opponents' support was so even that David Amess could not have wished for an easier run.

Southend is a large town of some 150,000 residents, situated on the south-east Essex coast – or rather on the mouth of the Thames. It has long been known as a premier (and close) holiday resort for Londoners, especially Eastenders. The western side is, as so often, the more desirable in terms of residential areas. Here we have Leigh-on-Sea and Westcliff-on-Sea, and Chalkwell, and inland Prittlewell and the newer housing at Eastwood. All these wards are marginal in Southend borough elections, and the Lib Dems always win the compact central ward of Westborough. In May 2000, however, the Tories took five of the other six within the seat, gaining most of them from the Lib Dems. The Conservatives now have very much tightened their grip on Southend West at all levels. Having been in the Channon family for over 80 years, it may well be in the Amess family for twenty.

Social indices:			2001 Gen. Election:			
% Non-white	2.3		C	17,313	46.3	+7.6
% Prof/Man	37.2		Lab	9,372	25.1	+2.3
% Non-manual	66.4		LD	9,319	24.9	−8.2
£ Av prop val 2000	92 K		UKIP	1,371	3.7	+2.3
% Increase 97–00	36.2		C maj	7,941	21.2	
% Unemployed 2001	2.5		Turnout		58.3	−11.7
% Decrease 97–01	3.4		Elect	64,116		
% Fin hard/Rank	8.4	506				
% Pensioners	33.1					
% Prem mort/Rank	13	558				

Member of Parliament

David Amess, first elected in 1983 as the original Basildon man whose retention of the seat in 1992 heralded the Conservatives' unexpected re-election, chicken-ran to this safer seat, in justifiable expectation of Labour seizing Basildon in 1997. Born into the East End Catholic working class in 1952, he attended St Bonaventure's Grammar School, Newham, and Bournemouth College of Technology, and worked largely in agencies specialising in book keeping and temping. A clearly articulated if almost self-parodying partisan right-winger, though somewhat toned-down from his earlier Basildonian incarnation, he was Portillo's PPS for ten years, votes the Catholic line on embryo research and abortion, is in the small Conservative minority opposed to fox hunting, and brings to Southend his more compatible whelk stall Cockney brogue in place of the upper-class Etonian drawl of his Guinness dynasty predecessor, Paul Channon.

SOUTH HOLLAND AND THE DEEPINGS

This rather unwieldy name is attached to a constituency which in effect covers the south-eastern corner of Lincolnshire. The former Parts of Holland were so named because of the similarity of the terrain here to the country across the North Sea, and indeed much of the land here is low and flat, drained Fens, situated mainly between the Rivers Nene and Welland, and fringing the Wash. Agriculture and related industries predominate here, particularly vegetable production, and there are vast fields of flowers around the largest town, Spalding. Other communities above village-size in South Holland include Holbeach and Long Sutton. A number of Dutch families have done well – Van den Bergh and Geest are two well-known names. In appearance the countryside is very un-English, with its unchanging views and vast open skies. However the political party which finds the ground here most fertile is English enough – the Conservative Party.

South Holland and the Deepings was a new seat in 1997. About 26,000 of its voters came from the former Holland with Boston, the seat of the veteran independently minded backbencher Sir Richard Body. However a majority of the electorate was previously in Quentin Davies's Stamford and Spalding, itself split almost exactly in half by the last Boundary Commission. This portion includes the small area of South Kesteven added on to Holland – Market Deeping, West Deeping and Deeping St Nicholas – which have been dignified by inclusion in the constituency's title. Both of the seats which donated territory to South Holland and the Deepings were very strongly Tory with Labour in second place; the Liberal Democrats are, surprisingly, extremely weak in so rural an area.

Not surprisingly, the Lib Dems have made little impact in South Holland and the Deepings either and in 2001 John Hayes increased his majority over Labour to over 11,000. It is the safest Tory seat in the county of Lincolnshire.

Social indices:			2001 Gen. Election:			
% Non-white	0.6		C	25,611	55.4	+6.2
% Prof/Man	27.7		Lab	14,512	31.4	−1.9
% Non-manual	46.7		LD	4,761	10.3	−5.3
£ Av prop val 2000	74 K		UKIP	1,318	2.9	
% Increase 97–00	35.1		C maj	11,099	24.0	
% Unemployed 2001	1.3		Turnout		62.5	−9.4
% Decrease 97–01	0.8		Elect	73,880		
% Fin hard/Rank	7.3	548				
% Pensioners	28.2					
% Prem mort/Rank	30	348				

Member of Parliament

John Hayes was elected in 1997 and joined the Agriculture Select Committee as MP for the second most agricultural seat in England. A Redwood, then Hague, supporter in 1997, he opposes devolution and English regionalism, the euro, PR and as a meritocratic working-class grammar school boy (born in 1958 and educated at Colfe's, Lewisham) who got to Nottingham University, defends grammar schools and was an education spokesman 2000–01. With lop-sided facial features redolent of Asa Briggs, he was formerly a computer company sales director but, fairly presciently for a computer buff, observed in 1999 that 'information' does not equal 'wisdom'. Having dubbed calls for breast-feeding in the Commons as 'politically correct clap-trap', in 2001 he prominently backed Iain Duncan Smith and became No.3 in the Opposition Whips' Office.

SOUTHPORT

The genteel resort of Southport, 20 miles north of Liverpool, should by all indicators be a Tory citadel. Besides its characteristics as an up-market seaside town, less working-class in nature and appeal than the bustling Blackpool further up the coast, and noted more for its flower show than its funfair, Southport is a desirable commuting base for the more affluent Merseyside commuters. It could not be more different from the other end of the Borough of Sefton, or further from the poverty and unemployment of Bootle. Yet Southport, like so much of Merseyside county, of all classes, has long shared a predilection for the Liberal centre, and in 1987 it joined Liverpool Mossley Hill in returning a Liberal Alliance MP. The Conservatives recaptured Southport in 1992, but in 1997 the veteran Lib Dem candidate Ronnie Fearn returned at the age of 66 in triumphant fashion, and in 2001 he was able to hand over to another local and municipally-rooted, and more intellectually-inclined, candidate, philosophy teacher and Sefton LD leader John Pugh.

The fights between centre and right are likely to remain close and tough in Southport, in parliamentary and local elections alike. Essentially the Liberal Democrats do best inland, in the terraces of modest housing east of the promenade and the broad main street, Lord Street, in wards like Norwood and Kew; while the Conservatives are ahead on the seafront, especially in the top residential areas of Ainsdale, Hillside, and Birkdale, near the championship golf course, which are especially suitable for commuting.

The Conservative victory in 1992 can probably best be explained by the fact that in that year it looked as if Labour could and indeed would form a government. The relatively well-off voters of Southport did not mind Ronnie Fearn in Westminster, but they did not want Neil Kinnock in Downing Street. By 1997 though, even 'sandgrounders' (residents of Southport) did not mind the possibility of letting in Tony Blair, and they definitely did want to cause John Major to remove. John Pugh had a serious fight on his hands against hard-working and ambitious Conservative and Labour candidates in 2001, and may need some time to build up to Ronnie Fearn's popularity levels in Southport.

Social indices:			2001 Gen. Election:			
% Non-white	1.2		LD	18,011	43.8	−4.3
% Prof/Man	38.1		C	15,004	36.5	+0.5
% Non-manual	63.7		Lab	6,816	16.6	+4.4
£ Av prop val 2000	77 K		Lib	767	1.9	+1.1
% Increase 97–00	20.8		UKIP	555	1.3	
% Unemployed 2001	3.3		LD maj	3,007	7.3	
% Decrease 97–01	1.9		Turnout		58.1	−13.9
% Fin hard/Rank	7.8	529	Elect	70,785		
% Pensioners	34.5					
% Prem mort/Rank	35	243				

Member of Parliament

Dr John Pugh, a public school master with a doctorate in Logic from Durham University, was elected here in 2001 in succession to the retiring Liberal Democrat MP Ronnie Fearn, so confirming (as in five other Liberal Democrat-held constituencies in 2001) that his party is now capable of transferring seats to new incumbents where once it was thought to be dependent on the irreplaceable personal appeal of the sitting MP. Head of Philosophy at Merchant Taylor's School, Crosby, he was born in 1950, and educated at Prescot Grammar School, Maidstone Grammar School and at Durham and Manchester Universities, accumulating five degrees in the process. Cadaverous of features, with a high forehead compensating for a slight chin, he rose politically as a local Sefton Borough councillor, becoming Council Leader in 2000. He has called for more police and attacked the application of 'consumer–producer' terminology to the NHS, and by his election spared the voters a reversion of the constituency to the Conservatives in the shape of an undertaker who was a member of the George Formby Society.

SOUTH RIBBLE

The Conservatives declined from holding nine seats in Lancashire in 1992 to just two in 2001. One of these losses can be put down to boundary changes in 1997, as the county's allocation was reduced by a seat – but the other six were Labour gains. One of these was South Ribble, where there was a direct swing from the Conservatives of 12% in 1997, even higher than the county average, and no significant movement between the main parties in 2001 compared with a swing of 2.3% in Lancashire as a whole. That was nowhere near enough to take even one seat back in the county, but in South Ribble their showing didn't even represent a start.

As the name implies, this seat hugs the south bank of the river Ribble, over the water from Preston. It should not be confused with Ribble Valley, which is a much more rural division further inland, and which is still Tory. South Ribble contains the town of Leyland, with a population of about 20,000, and the suburban parishes of Penwortham and Longton, south-west of Preston, which are even more populous – amounting to around 30,000 souls. There are a number of other communities too, such as Farington and Much Hoole, along with some villages on the flat Lancashire plain: Hesketh-with-Becconsall, North Meols, Rufford and Tarleton.

South Ribble is effectively of highly marginal status. The Conservatives won the first two contests here (1983, 1987) fairly easily, but then in 1992 Robert Atkins saw his majority cut to under 6,000, and Labour have taken the seat in their last two landslide victories, though by less than 4,000 in 2001 when the turnout fell by 15%. South Ribble is a mixed and interesting seat. The plain villages are very Conservative indeed, while South Ribble borough council elections tend to produce photo-finishes between Labour and Conservative, as in May 1999 (21 Labour and 18 Conservative): Penwortham and Longton were formerly in the massively Tory South Fylde, but Leyland is an industrial town – it gave its name to the trucks and to the car manufacturer which used to be 'British Leyland'. New industries and population have been attracted too. This is the site of the grandiosely named Central Lancashire New Town, a project which has faded away now but which did bring new industrial estates like that at Moss Side, Leyland, and new housing estates, although the population has not increased in the manner of Milton Keynes. It is not clear what if any political impact the New Town development had. In the South and Midlands New Towns have been poor ground for Labour in recent decades, but not so in the North: Skelmersdale undoubtedly has led West Lancashire into Labour hands since 1992.

The Conservatives must recover this seat if they are even going to come close to forming a government again. They need a swing of just over 4%, which should be within their capacity; indeed, they could take South Ribble and still lose the next election.

Social indices:			2001 Gen. Election:			
% Non-white	1.0		Lab	21,386	46.4	−0.5
% Prof/Man	33.2		C	17,594	38.1	+0.5
% Non-manual	59.8		LD	7,150	15.5	+4.9
£ Av prop val 2000	72 K		Lab maj	3,792	8.2	
% Increase 97–00	25.3		Turnout		62.5	−14.6
% Unemployed 2001	1.5		Elect	73,794		
% Decrease 97–01	1.0					
% Fin hard/Rank	8.7	493				
% Pensioners	23.3					
% Prem mort/Rank	27	385				

Member of Parliament

David Borrow is a Labour backbencher emblematic of the 1997 intake: a public sector employee (local government officer) and local (Preston) councillor, diligent over local concerns – in his case the aerospace industry, loyal to the government and one of a small number of Labour MPs to declare his homosexuality. Born in 1952 and educated at Mirfield Grammar School and Lanchester Polytechnic, less typically he came with a history of factional in-fighting on Preston Council where he was temporarily ousted from the leadership by the hard left Valerie Wise.

SOUTH SHIELDS

South Shields is many towns in one. It has in its time been a shipbuilding metropolis at the mouth of the Tyne, an active coal-mining community and a holiday resort on the North Sea. With the decline of all these industries it has turned to a still more varied economy with a large number of light industrial estates. There is even an attempt to market South Tyneside for tourism as 'Catherine Cookson Country'.

Its politics, however, are not so varied. Labour utterly dominates the local council, being capable of winning almost every ward, although the most middle-class, West Park, has clearly rejected them since 1994. Oddly, the Conservatives have a long tradition of not contesting municipal elections in South Shields. For many years they have stood as Progressives, an anti-Labour label also used in South Yorkshire and elsewhere, and still in some use here. In the 2001 General Election standing under their national name the Conservatives only managed to muster 5,000 votes and a share of under 17%; the Liberal Democrats nearly doubled their share and finished only 13 votes behind in third place, while Labour did four times as well as both of them. South Shields is overall a working-class seat, with a level of male unemployment of 12% in June 2001, which placed it in ninth place of all 529 English constituencies and nearly three times the national average. There are only one-tenth the national proportion of detached houses – two in a hundred rather than 20. There is even a small but rather exotic ethnic minority community: there have been Bangladeshis in South Shields for a few years, and Yemenis for decades.

In 2001, at almost the same time as Shaun Woodward was selected at St Helens South, the head of No.10's Policy Unit David Miliband was chosen as Labour candidate here, after a very late decision by David Clark (who had been in Tony Blair's first Cabinet only four years before) to retire. There was no fuss at all, not so much because of the glare of attention focused on Mr Woodward, but because David Miliband, although a Londoner and a policy 'wonk' with no previous connection with South Shields, was a clear long-term (if only 35) member and servant of the party, clearly too with no servants of his own.

Social indices:			2001 Gen. Election:			
% Non-white	2.1		Lab	19,230	63.2	−8.3
% Prof/Man	24.4		C	5,140	16.9	+2.3
% Non-manual	47.8		LD	5,127	16.8	+8.0
£ Av prop val 2000	52 K		UKIP	689	2.3	
% Increase 97–00	9.5		Ind	262	0.9	
% Unemployed 2001	9.0		Lab maj	14,090	46.3	
% Decrease 97–01	2.4		Turnout		49.3	−13.3
% Fin hard/Rank	40.6	48	Elect	61,802		
% Pensioners	28.9					
% Prem mort/Rank	47	73				

Member of Parliament

David Miliband was neatly inserted here via an NEC-imposed shortlist during the first week of the 2001 campaign in succession to the obligingly late-retiring-for-a-peerage discarded minister, David Clark. From the core of the Blairite inner circle, he had run the Downing Street Policy Unit since 1997 and before that headed Blair's office in Opposition. Co-author of the 1997 manifesto, if seen as stronger on ideas than presentation, he was born in 1965 and educated at Haverstock Comprehensive, Corpus Christi, Oxford and MIT. Ideologically somewhat displaced from his family of origin, his father, the late Marxist academic Ralph Miliband, would doubtless have been as concerned about David's book *Re-inventing the Left*, as he was oddly surprised at the lack of socialism from Labour governments, as recounted in his own book, *Parliamentary Socialism*. Tall, dark and very boyish looking, he recounted in his maiden speech how his predecessor-but-two as MP for South Shields – James Chuter Ede – had as Home Secretary in the Attlee government initially refused his Polish-born Jewish grandfather, Samuel Miliband, the right of continued residence in Britain. Saying of his Marxist father, Ralph, that 'people are products of their time', he is certainly a product of his, with a ministerial career seemingly inevitable.

SOUTHWARK NORTH AND BERMONDSEY

The electoral history and indeed current landscape of this seat are both extraordinary. This is one of the poorest of London's inner-city constituencies. It includes such run-down neighbourhoods, dominated by massive public housing developments, as the Elephant and Castle, the Old Kent Road, the Borough, and the ex-docklands neighbourhoods of Bermondsey and Rotherhithe. A seat that less evokes the rural beauty of, say, Ross, Skye and Inverness West or Tweeddale, Ettrick and Lauderdale could scarcely be imagined.

Yet this is not a Labour seat but the site of the Liberal Democrats' one and only true inner-city stronghold. Simon Hughes won in 2001 with a majority of nearly 10,000. In 1997 he had held on against the Labour surge, although with a reduced lead since 1992 of 3,387, despite a false report on TV on election night that he had been beaten. The restoration of his accustomed comfortable lead was perhaps due both to the increased familiarity of New Labour now it had served a term in government and to their selection of Kingsley Abrams, who is black. This part of inner London has not been renowned for its tolerance of minority candidates.

Simon Hughes's success is based on a mixture of history and energetic current activity. The Liberals were undoubtedly helped to win the 1983 Bermondsey by-election, caused by the resignation of the Labour right-winger Robert Mellish, by the ructions in the local Labour Party and the selection of Peter Tatchell as official Labour candidate. Independent Labour candidate John O'Grady, leader of Southwark Borough Council for 14 years until he was ousted in a far left take-over, bitterly opposed Tatchell and sections of the right-wing press portrayed him as a gay Australian draft-dodger. The traditional working-class electorate soon worked out that the man to vote for to keep Tatchell and the left out was the Liberal, Simon Hughes. He won by a mile.

Since then, however, Hughes has not faced Tatchell (who was not again selected by Labour, anywhere); he has held on, consolidated by his own efforts and also by the growing success of local Liberal candidates in northern Southwark borough elections. This is one of the inner-city boroughs where there have been controversial Labour administrations, and by 1998 the Lib Dems (as they now were) held 27 council seats to Labour's 33; in 1982 they had held none. They now led in all the wards within Southwark and Bermondsey. Here many residents see local Labour as incompetent and left-wing. Less than one-fifth of residents are non-white, and the largest single group of these are of African origin; many are not eligible to vote, and many more do not choose to do so (the overall turnout in 2001 was 50%). The old docklands still harbour traditional views distrustful of minorities of all kinds. It might also be noted that there has also been some owner-occupied modern residential development in the old Surrey Docks which has increased the population of the Dockyard ward by over 50% since 1981. It too is safely Liberal Democrat.

New Labour showed in 1997 that they can perform somewhat more effectively here than at municipal level (even with the council leader Jeremy Fraser as their candidate), but if they couldn't dislodge Hughes while leaping into office, it seems unlikely that they will do so after years of government.

Social indices:			2001 Gen. Election:			
% Non-white	18.2		LD	20,991	56.9	+8.3
% Prof/Man	31.4		Lab	11,359	30.8	−9.5
% Non-manual	56.7		C	2,800	7.6	+0.6
£ Av prop val 2000	198 K		Grn	752	2.0	
% Increase 97–00	99.0		NF	612	1.7	
% Unemployed 2001	7.2		UKIP	271	0.7	
% Decrease 97–01	4.2		Ind	77	0.2	
% Fin hard/Rank	55.1	9	LD maj	9,632	26.1	
% Pensioners	24.2		Turnout		50.1	−12.1
% Prem mort/Rank	56	15	Elect	73,527		

Member of Parliament

Simon Hughes, Liberal victor over another bachelor, Labour's controversial-because-openly homosexual Peter Tatchell, in the 1983 by-election, and then 16 years on defeated by another bachelor, Charles Kennedy, in his party's 1999 leadership race, has skilfully retained this inner-city working-class seat for almost 20 years against Labour, without recourse to the crude populism of Cyril Smith in Rochdale (a town in any case of much greater identity than a collection of high-rise council flats in inner London). A barrister, son of a brewer, born in 1951 and educated at Christ's College, Brecon, Selwyn College, Cambridge and the Inns of Court School of Law, clean-cut and well-scrubbed, he is variously likened to a self-righteous prep school master, or to a vicar who'd let you beat him at table tennis. Having shadowed most of the domestic portfolios (Health, Environment, Education) from 1999 he led on Home Affairs.

SPELTHORNE

Spelthorne is a very distinctive part of Surrey; indeed many of residents would say it is not in – or of – that county at all. This is that area north of the Thames, historically in Middlesex, whose residents preferred not to be included in Greater London when that county was abolished in 1965. Surrey seemed better to suit their tastes and self-image, although probably most would have favoured no change at all – for these are, in general, very conservative people. They are very Conservative, too. David Wilshire secured a majority of nigh on 20,000 in the 1992 General Election, and withstood a typically huge outer London swing of 14.5% in 1997.

The main communities in a thoroughly built-up area are Staines, Sunbury-on-Thames, Ashford and Shepperton. Jammed between London's great western reservoirs and Heathrow Airport, Spelthorne might not seem to be a very attractive residential area. Indeed, there are few of the large detached houses, private roads and leafy suburbs and prosperous villages associated with Surrey. There are one or two working-class areas, most notably Stanwell, which was the only county council ward to give Labour a majority on the same day as the 2001 General Election, and the proportion of professional and managerial workers is clearly the lowest in the county. Spelthorne is 97% white, and differs very much in ethnic composition from the neighbourhoods in Hounslow borough on the other side of the airport, from which many of its residents, and its MP differentiate themselves vigorously. It is the only one of the 11 Surrey seats where Labour could finish second in 1992, but it still didn't rank as a viable target in 1997, or in 2001 when there was no significant swing between parties. David Wilshire should remain safe for the foreseeable future in Spelthorne.

Social indices:			2001 Gen. Election:			
% Non-white	3.4		C	18,851	45.1	+0.2
% Prof/Man	35.1		Lab	15,589	37.3	–0.9
% Non-manual	65.1		LD	6,156	14.7	+1.6
£ Av prop val 2000	148 K		UKIP	1,198	2.9	+2.0
% Increase 97–00	56.9		C maj	3,262	7.8	
% Unemployed 2001	1.0		Turnout		60.8	–12.8
% Decrease 97–01	1.4		Elect	68,731		
% Fin hard/Rank	4.9	606				
% Pensioners	23.6					
% Prem mort/Rank	14	555				

Member of Parliament

David Wilshire, a man with a somewhat variegated repertoire, elected in 1987, is a hardline right-winger on Northern Ireland backing the successful Paisleyite candidate in the September 2000 Antrim South by-election. He was a last ditch defender of the poll tax, and backed Redwood in leadership ballots (but did not disclose his final vote) in 1997. He takes the liberal line on embryo research and capital punishment but not on hippy new age travellers, whom he would like to send to a mid-Atlantic island on a one-way ticket. Born in 1943, he attended the Methodist public school, Kingswood, and Fitzwilliam College, Cambridge, ran a sports and camping business, and was a waste-cutting leader of Wansdyke District Council for six years. He stated in his 2001 Election address that he would 'never vote to scrap the pound', and voted for David Davis in the first two leadership ballots.

STAFFORD

It was all too familiar a story for the Conservative Party on the night of 7 June 2001. Attempting to recapture a seat on which they could historically rely. which had fallen for the first time in well over a generation to Labour in the unprecedented landslide of 1997, they not only failed to secure a recapture but fell back even further relatively. They had not lost Stafford in Labour's previous great victory of 1966, nor in the by-election in 1984 while they were in government. Just as nationally Labour's position was scarcely weakened in 2001, David Kidney held on in Stafford with a majority reduced only because the turnout fell by over 10%.

The town of Stafford itself has a variety of industry and an historic centre ringed by hideous major road development. There are strongly Labour wards such as Highfields by the railway tracks to the south of the town, and in Coton, Common, and Holmcroft in the north-east. The Conservatives fight back in comfortable suburbs like Weeping Cross. However, Stafford is not large enough to form the basis of an urban constituency of its own, and the Tories counter in the countryside.

The rural element in the mix was weakened somewhat in 1997 by the boundary changes which created the new seat of Stone, to which the former Stafford MP Bill Cash wisely migrated, but Labour would have gained the constituency in any case in 1997, and held it in 2001. The Tories must hope that the electorate will turn against the Labour government for them to obtain the 6% swing now needed to regain Stafford. If they do so narrowly, Labour will be on the verge of losing their overall majority, but no more than that. To be sure of forming a government themselves, the Tories must look to replace Kidney's 5,000 majority with one of their own of a similar magnitude.

Social indices:			2001 Gen. Election:			
% Non-white	2.1		Lab	21,285	48.0	+0.4
% Prof/Man	35.6		C	16,253	36.6	−2.6
% Non-manual	58.4		LD	4,205	9.5	−1.1
£ Av prop val 2000	81 K		UKIP	2,315	5.2	
% Increase 97–00	27.8		Ind	308	0.7	
% Unemployed 2001	2.6		Lab maj	5,032	11.3	
% Decrease 97–01	0.5		Turnout		65.3	−11.3
% Fin hard/Rank	12.9	398	Elect	67,934		
% Pensioners	23.3					
% Prem mort/Rank	22	461				

Member of Parliament

David Kidney, Labour victor here in 1997, is a local solicitor and former Stafford councillor (for ten years), born in 1955, son of a clerk, and educated at Longton High School, City of Stoke Sixth Form College and Bristol University. A loyalist to the extent of endorsing the party's *volte face* between Opposition and Office on air traffic control privatisation, he campaigns on local issues, such as the post-water-privatisation running of small sewage works and the state of the services on the West Coast main line bisecting his constituency. He has shown concern about air travel-induced deep vein thrombosis.

STAFFORDSHIRE MOORLANDS

The redrawing of the constituency boundary of Staffordshire Moorlands in 1997 marked a tragic story for its Conservative defenders. Originally the Boundary Commission's proposals carried little threat, simply suggesting the removal of two rural wards, Checkley and Forsbrook, to the new Stone division. Then at the public inquiry disaster struck. The problem was caused by the community of Kidsgrove, which the Commission proposed to split, leaving half in Stoke North and moving half to Newcastle under Lyme. Nothing to do with Staffordshire Moorlands, one might think. However, the Assistant Commissioner who took the inquiry was convinced that Kidsgrove must remain united, and that the only place to put it was in Staffordshire Moorlands; it is true that the area was in the former Leek seat, Moorlands' predecessor before 1983. Kidsgrove is solid Labour territory, and the problem was that if its 19,000 voters were all to be put in Moorlands, then more rural (and hence Tory) wards would have to be moved out. These were Alton, home of the Towers, one of the most popular theme and entertainment parks in Britain; Kingsley, and the small town of Cheadle (not to be confused with the other Cheadle in Cheshire, which has a parliamentary constituency named after it). Altogether, with Checkley and Forsbrook, this adds up to 21,500 largely Conservative voters placed in the new Stone division. To cap it all, Stoke North was now underpopulated; and has been given 5,500 voters from the affluent commuting suburbs of Endon, Brown Edge and Stanley – previously in Staffordshire Moorlands.

Moorlands is the northernmost seat in the county, bordering Cheshire and Derbyshire's Peak District. Some of the finest countryside in the Midlands is situated here – much of Dovedale and many other Peak District dales, such as the Manifold Valley. It stretches as far as the little market town of Longnor, high in the hills near Buxton in Derbyshire's High Peak constituency. The rugged hill farmers of the high moors and the dairy farms of the gentler slopes produce a solid Conservative vote. But the main town, Leek, remains marginal, true to its industrial background – in some ways it looks and behaves like the southernmost Pennine textile town. The terrain becomes more Labour as one moves towards the Potteries: Biddulph resembles Kidsgrove and shares a common ex-mining tradition. With the arrival of Kidsgrove the industrial element of the Moorlands seat has been massively strengthened at the expense of the uplands, and Charlotte Atkins has had little trouble winning the first two contests in the redrawn constituency. The Conservatives feel most hard done by.

Social indices:			2001 Gen. Election:			
% Non-white	0.4		Lab	20,904	49.0	−3.2
% Prof/Man	27.9		C	15,066	35.3	+2.8
% Non-manual	46.7		LD	5,928	13.9	+1.8
£ Av prop val 2000	62 K		UKIP	760	1.8	
% Increase 97–00	30.9		Lab maj	5,838	13.7	
% Unemployed 2001	2.0		Turnout		63.9	−13.4
% Decrease 97–01	1.1		Elect	66,760		
% Fin hard/Rank	15.6	341				
% Pensioners	23.3					
% Prem mort/Rank	30	342				

Member of Parliament

Charlotte Atkins, daughter of former left-wing Preston MP, Ron Atkins, was elected here in 1997. Born in 1950 and educated at Colchester High School and the LSE, she rose in Labour politics via the trade union route as a researcher and parliamentary officer. Her own left-wing past safely airbrushed, she was co-author in 1981 with Chris Mullin of the innocuous-sounding *How to select and reselect your MP*, which was actually the left-wing activists' manual for tipping right-wing MPs out of the party and into the SDP. But by 1990 she was the NEC-imposed candidate in the Eastbourne by-election and in the 1990s a leading activist in the orthodox pursuit of feminisation via all-women shortlists. A Wandsworth councillor (1982–86), in the front row of the famous 1997 'Blair's Babes' photograph, she has been less obtrusive since. On-line as well as on-message, she has advocated sacking 'computer-phobic-schoolteachers' and in 2001 she was made PPS to Baroness Symons, a Trade Minister.

STAFFORDSHIRE SOUTH

This constituency is in fact the former Staffordshire South West, represented since its creation in 1974 by Patrick Cormack and renamed in 1983. Before 1974 this growing area formed part of the Cannock division, and it was largely responsible for the defeat of Labour's Jennie Lee there in 1970. At its inception, Staffordshire South West was one of the very few seats in the country to be composed entirely of rural district councils. Yet this might be misleading. Although there are no large towns, the voters come almost entirely not from an agricultural background, but from the newish suburban communities fringing the western edge of the West Midlands conurbation – in order of size, Wombourne (13,400), Perton on the edge of Wolverhampton, which doubled its population to 11,000 in the 1980s, Great Wyrley, Codsall and Brewood.

This is very good ground for the Conservatives, and contrasts sharply with the inner-city areas only a few miles to the east. Over 80% of the housing is owner-occupied, mostly built since the war. It is this element, and the new West Midlands middle class spawned by the affluence of the 1950s and 1960s, that gives this constituency its powerful Conservatism. Only 1% of the population is of Afro-Caribbean or Asian origin, yet the politics of South Staffordshire are effectively influenced by the racial mix of the inner conurbation. This is one of the 'snow-white' areas that moved to the right in response to immigration. It is scarcely more middle class than the national average, and has less than a third of the proportion of professionals of, say, Birmingham Edgbaston. It is also a very young seat, with among the most youthful age profiles of any seat in the West Midlands.

In 2001 Labour cut Cormack's majority to its lowest ever, but this was still a relatively comfortable 6,881. In fact the Conservative share increased slightly, but all the parties' number of votes fell because turnout dropped to an unprecedentedly poor 60% – in this seat it had never before been below 70%. We can get a clue about where party support came from. The Staffordshire county elections took place on the same day, and Labour managed to return two councillors in this district, for Essington and Great Wyrley. The Conservatives won all the others fairly easily, and the Liberal Democrats could finish (a distant) second only in Wombourne.

Social indices:			2001 Gen. Election:			
% Non-white	1.1		C	21,295	50.5	+0.5
% Prof/Man	34.9		Lab	14,414	34.2	−0.5
% Non-manual	61.3		LD	4,891	11.6	+0.3
£ Av prop val 2000	91 K		UKIP	1,580	3.7	
% Increase 97–00	29.7		C maj	6,881	16.3	
% Unemployed 2001	2.3		Turnout		60.3	−13.9
% Decrease 97–01	1.0		Elect	69,925		
% Fin hard/Rank	10.6	449				
% Pensioners	23.3					
% Prem mort/Rank	10	597				

Member of Parliament

Sir Patrick Cormack, who under William Hague attained the distinction of being Deputy Shadow Leader of the House of Commons from 1997 to 2000, was first elected in 1970 (when he despatched Nye Bevan's widow, Jennie Lee, to the House of Lords), and has the gratifying knowledge that after the 2001 Election only one other Tory – Sir Peter Tapsell – had served longer as a Conservative Member of (as he daintily pronounces it) 'Parl-i-a-ment'. An orotund and rather splendidly Trollopian figure, who has fashioned a fruity-voiced, disdainful persona out of a Grimsby (born in 1939) childhood and a Hull University education, he has been dubbed variously as 'a man of such majesty that even colleagues do not always appreciate how majestic he is' (Matthew Parris), and as one 'whose frock-coated presence has lent tone to many a St Margaret's memorial service' (Sir Julian Critchley). He has nonetheless a record as a 'One Nation' rebel against Thatcher on the poll tax, benefit cuts, GLC abolition, and eye and dental check charges, even if he voted first for Lilley in 1997, and only thereafter for Clarke. In 2001 he voted for Clarke in all the ballots and joined him on the backbenches, the better to peruse the passing scene, having been foiled in his attempt in 2000 to do so from the Speaker's chair by receiving only 130 votes.

STALYBRIDGE AND HYDE

In essence the Stalybridge and Hyde constituency consists of the south-eastern or Cheshire part of the metropolitan borough of Tameside. It is in fact the only one of Tameside's three seats which is wholly within the borough: the Denton and Reddish division includes wards from Stockport borough, and Ashton-under-Lyne now crosses the border with Oldham. Before 1997 there were minor boundary changes in Stalybridge and Hyde which moved the geographical centre of the seat north-east. The town of Dukinfield was all within the constituency before, but the Dukinfield ward has now been transferred to Denton/Reddish; the rather confusingly named 'Dukinfield Stalybridge' ward was retained. To compensate for the loss of Dukinfield ward Mossley came in from Ashton. Mossley was once an independent urban district within Lancashire, so in a sense this is the first crossing of an ancient county boundary within this seat; but in fact Mossley more or less straddles the river Tame, just as it flows down from the heights of the Pennines to the east. Mossley is physically the last, or perhaps first (depending on whether one looks from the Lancashire or the Yorkshire end of the valley), of the ex-textile towns that have populated the Tame valley since the Industrial Revolution.

These changes had a politically neutral effect. Both Dukinfield and Mossley wards are fairly strongly inclined to Labour (although Mossley has strong Independent candidates in Tameside borough elections, who won in May 1999 and 2000 for example) and both are about the same size. In any case Stalybridge and Hyde has become a safe Labour seat, which has not fallen to the Tories since before the Second World War. It was marginal in the 1950s, when Fred Blackburn held on narrowly three times (majority 298 in 1951, 155 in 1955); but like many Northern urban seats it has swung away from the Tories in recent decades and Tom Pendry could hold it by over 4,000 even in Labour's terrible year of 1983.

This is a more working-class seat than average, and it has a higher percentage in employment in manufacturing industry than any other constituency in the North West. It has a high proportion too of skilled manual workers, the famed C2s, who contrary to popular view are to be found in their largest numbers not in marginal seats but in safe Labour divisions such as this. There are Tory voters, in Hyde Werneth and in the hilly and semi-rural Stalybridge South, with its desirable residential areas looking down on the valley. Except for Mossley, all other wards are consistently Labour: the old terraced town centres of Hyde and Stalybridge, and the huge bleak windy post-war Manchester overspill housing estate of Hattersley, split between Hyde Godley and Longdendale wards. Hattersley is another reason for the long-term movement to Labour, but it has stopped growing and their position is still improving here. Stalybridge and Hyde is no Jekyll and Hyde, but a very reliable parliamentary performer.

Social indices:			2001 Gen. Election:			
% Non-white	3.1		Lab	17,781	55.5	−3.4
% Prof/Man	27.9		C	8,922	27.8	+3.3
% Non-manual	50.0		LD	4,327	13.5	+1.5
£ Av prop val 2000	60 K		UKIP	1,016	3.2	
% Increase 97–00	24.5		Lab maj	8,859	27.6	
% Unemployed 2001	2.9		Turnout		48.4	−17.4
% Decrease 97–01	1.8		Elect	66,265		
% Fin hard/Rank	27.1	172				
% Pensioners	24.1					
% Prem mort/Rank	40	172				

Member of Parliament

James Purnell, a Downing Street insider, inherited this safe seat in 2001, having been selected from an NEC-devised shortlist following the late retirement of the departing-with-a-peerage veteran MP Tom Pendry. Born in 1970, he was educated at the Royal Grammar School, Guildford, and at Balliol College, Oxford, after which he immediately went to work for Tony Blair, then Shadow Employment spokesman, leaving after three years to work at the think tank, IPPR, and at the BBC as Head of Corporate Planning, and returning to work at 10 Downing Street from 1997 to 2001. With a reputation as an anti-left factionalist earned from his involvement in blocking the Leeds North East candidacy of his fellow Islington councillor Liz Davies in 1995, he recalled in his maiden speech in 2001 that Stalybridge was the site of Hugh Gaitskell's 1952 attack on the Bevanites as 'fellow travellers', in order to register his own opposition to any 'talk of counter-insurrections or coups' in the Labour Party. Coy about disclosing his schooling at an independent school in Guildford, he is happier in attributing that town's capture by the Liberal Democrats in 2001 to the support of affluent Europhiles rather than the less affluent Eurosceptics on which the party relies in its south-western heartland. In 2001 he was parked on the obscure Work and Pensions Select Committee while awaiting a presumably inevitable call to the frontbench.

STEVENAGE

Stevenage has produced a series of spectacular and often unexpected results in General Elections for nearly 20 years now. That in 1997 needs to be explained with reference to recent history: since 1987 Labour had advanced by no less than 29% in two general elections, and the Liberal Democrats lost 25% compared with the SDP candidate of that year. Meanwhile the Tory MP Tim Wood saw his own vote drop by 11%, allowing New Labour's style guru Barbara Follett to regain the seat by a hearty 11,582 votes. It still surprises many that Stevenage, based on the first New Town to be designated in Britain, should be held by the Tories at all.

Their success began in 1979, when Shirley Williams, the Labour MP for Hertford and Stevenage was ousted by Bowen Wells. This was a shock in its own right, as Mrs Williams was a Cabinet Minister in James Callaghan's defeated government, but it has to be said that there were very significant – and very Conservative – elements in that seat as well as the town of Stevenage. By 1983 Hertford, Ware and the rural district around them had been removed, and Stevenage for the first time had a seat almost of its very own. Most people seemed to think that Labour would be very likely to win the new Stevenage, including, apparently, the sitting MP Bowen Wells, who migrated to another Hertfordshire seat (Hertford and Stortford). However, 1983 marked a low ebb for Labour, and indeed they sank to a poor third behind the new force of the Social Democratic Party. Shirley Williams had been one of the founding leaders of the SDP, but she did not contest Stevenage in 1983; she was defending Crosby, which she had won in a by-election in 1981. If she had been available, she probably would have been returned to the Commons in 1983, rather than losing in Crosby – for Ben Stoneham, a less-well-known SDP candidate, held Timothy Wood's majority to just 1,755 that year.

The SDP and the Alliance were still in existence in 1987, and came second again in Stevenage, although the Tory majority increased to 5,000 plus. However the party had died by 1992, and it is clear that their vote could not be transferred en bloc to the Liberal Democrats. Rather, much of it returned to Labour as we have seen, and having disposed of the SDP problem Labour could now set their sights clearly on the Tory defenders. Their change of image appealed to Stevenage voters, and they may well now see Stevenage as a safe seat for the first time – but one can never be sure, here in the oldest New Town. In 2001 Barbara Follett, no longer quite a pin-up girl of New Labour, lost over 6,000 voters as abstentionism and Liberal Democracy became more fashionable, but the Conservatives improved not at all and still do not look like recapturing Stevenage.

Social indices:			2001 Gen. Election:			
% Non-white	3.5		Lab	22,025	51.9	−3.5
% Prof/Man	35.8		C	13,459	31.7	−1.1
% Non-manual	62.1		LD	6,027	14.2	+5.3
£ Av prop val 2000	105 K		SA	449	1.1	
% Increase 97–00	48.7		Ind	320	0.8	
% Unemployed 2001	1.9		PA	173	0.4	+0.0
% Decrease 97–01	2.3		Lab maj	8,566	20.2	
% Fin hard/Rank	16.0	336	Turnout		61.3	−15.5
% Pensioners	20.8		Elect	69,203		
% Prem mort/Rank	17	509				

Member of Parliament

Barbara Follett, a Blairite fallen from grace along with, and largely because of, her millionaire husband Ken (author of airport-bookstall bestsellers), who criticised Tony Blair's 'control-freakery' and has described him as 'petulant', was elected in 1997. She was born in 1942 and educated in Addis Ababa and Cape Town, and eventually at the LSE. Originator, as style and colour coordination consultant to Labour MPs, of the verb 'to Follett', she also boosted the feminisation of the PLP by setting up Emily's List to push female candidates, with her husband promoted acquisition of the Excalibur computer used for instant rebuttal during the 1997 campaign, and staged £1,000-a-head fundraising dinners – until excluded from the inner circle. It is hard to believe that this brightly-coloured, shoulder-padded, pushing-60 going on 18-year-old with three husbands before Ken (one of them murdered by the South African security forces) has sunk with so little trace as an MP. It was the view, expressed in late 2001, of an earlier Labour MP for Stevenage, Shirley Williams, that Labour's women MPs had power-dressed themselves into oblivion.

STIRLING

There was once a great battle at Bannockburn, which is situated in the Stirling constituency; and in its own way, thankfully somewhat less bloody, that parliamentary seat has seen two terrific close-fought contests in 1987 and 1992. The eventual winner on each occasion was the controversial right-wing figure of Michael Forsyth, sometime Scottish Tory Party chairman, and later Secretary of State – but he held on by just 548 votes in 1987 and by 703 in 1992. He was probably only able to squeeze in the second time because of the general slight recovery of Conservative fortunes north of the border following the replacement of the highly unpopular Margaret Thatcher as national party leader; yet this is somewhat ironic, for there are few more enthusiastic Thatcherites than Michael Forsyth. In 1997 all three Cabinet ministers with seats in Scotland were defeated fairly easily, although the swings against them were rather less than those suffered by their English counterparts. In 2001 Forsyth's success in holding Stirling as long as he did was put into context as the Tories slipped another 8%, although Labour fell back substantially too and rather unusually the gainers were those in third, fourth and even fifth place, as the SNP enjoyed a vote share increase rare for that year, the Lib Dems improved from a very low base, and the Scottish Socialist Party made their first appearance.

Stirling's former, and possibly future, marginal status was guaranteed by its social and geographical balance. Apart from the Viewforth area, Stirling itself is inclined to Labour as are most Scottish towns. However, this is far from a compact urban seat. It spreads well up into the lochs and hills, to take in the holiday area of the Trossachs, including Callander, the model for the fictional Tannochbrae of *Dr Finlay's Casebook*, past the 3,852 foot peak of Ben More as far as Killin, at the western end of Loch Tay. All this has usually been Conservative territory. So too are some of the affluent small towns in the north-east of the constituency, such as Dunblane with its little cathedral, an idyllic spot whose peace was shattered by the school shootings in 1995.

Without the high profile Michael Forsyth, and having suffered negative boundary changes in 1997, the Conservatives failed to command even a quarter of the vote in Stirling in 2001 and do not look like winners again in the near future.

Social indices:			2001 Gen. Election:			
% Non-white	0.7		Lab	15,175	42.2	−5.2
% Prof/Man	39.1		C	8,901	24.8	−7.7
% Non-manual	60.8		SNP	5,877	16.4	+3.0
% Unemployed 2001	3.5		LD	4,208	11.7	+5.5
% Decrease 97–01	2.0		SSP	1,012	2.8	
% Fin hard/Rank	17.2	314	Grn	757	2.1	
% Prem mort/Rank	43	116	Lab maj	6,274	17.5	
			Turnout		67.7	−14.2
			Elect	53,097		

Member of Parliament

Anne McGuire was elected in 1997 after selection from an all-women shortlist, and swiftly rewarded for her role on Labour's Scottish Executive in pulling the Labour Party in Scotland into step with the Blairite leadership, by being made PPS to Donald Dewar in December 1997 after loyally backing the controversial lone parent benefit cuts, and in 1998 being promoted into the government as an Assistant Whip, becoming a full Whip in 2001. A railway signalman's daughter from Labour's West of Scotland Catholic core, she was born in 1949, educated at Our Lady of St Francis Secondary School, Glasgow and Glasgow University, and worked for Community Service Volunteers and the Scottish Council for Voluntary Organisations.

STOCKPORT

The borough of Stockport lies close up against Manchester's southern borders, although historically it was located in Cheshire rather than Lancashire. Two of the three seats located entirely within the borough are middle-class suburban commuter belt territory (Cheadle and Hazel Grove) and both now held by the Liberal Democrats; but the heart of the borough, the town after which it is named, is thoroughly industrial, very much a product of the Industrial Revolution, with a strong working-class element, and in the last ten years it has become safely Labour.

The north west of England proved fruitful ground for Labour in the 1992 General Election. They gained eight seats from the incumbent Conservative government, a most satisfactory regional quota. However, only one of these was in Greater Manchester – four were in Lancashire, two in Cheshire, and one in Merseyside. The solitary contribution from the metropolitan area with the most constituencies in the region was Stockport.

This was the first time that Labour had won the Stockport seat since its creation in 1983. They had been competitive in both of the two small seats that the town had enjoyed before 1983, but in the major redistribution of that year the more Labour elements both of North (Reddish) and South (Brinnington) were removed to the new Denton and Reddish division. This left a truncated Stockport, based on its western middle-class wards of Heaton Moor and Heaton Mersey (ex-North) and Davenport (ex-South). There were Labour wards too, around the town centre, such as Edgeley near the railway station; but matters were made even worse for them by the candidature of a sitting Stockport (South) MP, Tom McNally as an SDP defector in 1983. Thus that year Tony Favell won for the Tories really quite easily, by 5,800.

Gradually, though, the regional swing and Labour's gradual recovery from the pit into which they had sunk in 1983 improved their position; and another element which helped was the decline and dissolution of the SDP. Anne Coffey's position in Stockport in 1997 was considerably helped by the return of Brinnington in boundary changes. Brinnington is a massive hilltop post-war council estate, which votes 80% for Labour in a good year in council elections, and together with a swing which was even larger than the regional norm Ms Coffey now had a very safe seat, with a majority of 19,000, a level previously unknown in Stockport. Turnout dropped to 53% in 2001, and the Labour majority to 11,000, but the unified central Stockport is by no means a marginal constituency.

Social indices:			2001 Gen. Election:			
% Non-white	3.2		Lab	20,731	58.6	−4.3
% Prof/Man	35.6		C	9,162	25.9	+3.6
% Non-manual	58.4		LD	5,490	15.5	+4.9
£ Av prop val 2000	70 K		Lab maj	11,569	32.7	
% Increase 97–00	23.9		Turnout		53.3	−18.3
% Unemployed 2001	2.7		Elect	66,397		
% Decrease 97–01	2.2					
% Fin hard/Rank	21.1	252				
% Pensioners	24.6					
% Prem mort/Rank	42	147				

Member of Parliament

Ann Coffey, PPS originally to Tony Blair (1997–98) and then to Alistair Darling (from 1998), has risen swiftly since her election in 1992, as a Whip in 1995 and Health spokesman in 1996. A Scots-born (1946) social worker for 21 years, educated peripatetically at Nairn Academy, Bodmin Grammar School, Bushey Grammar School (her father was in the RAF) and at South Bank Polytechnic and Manchester University, she spent eight years on Stockport Council. Her promotion in 1995 was presaged by her membership of the New Clause Four Campaign, and followed in 1996 by her backing of tougher discipline for Labour MPs.

STOCKTON NORTH

Much of the interest of the Stockton North constituency lies in its share of Stockton's electoral history. Both Labour members in the town defected to the SDP in the early 1980s. The one who represented the lineal antecedent of Stockton North was William Rodgers, possibly the least well known of the 'Gang of Four' original leaders of the party, but a man who put a formidable amount of work into the organisation of the party and the Alliance, and indeed into the thought which lay behind it. But he lost Stockton North in 1983, indeed finishing third in a tight three-way contest.

That Rodgers had effectively split the traditional Labour vote in 1983 was made clear when in his absence in 1987 (fighting Milton Keynes) Frank Cook increased his majority from 1,870 to 8,801. The illusion of a marginal had been dispelled, and it came as no surprise when Cook increased his lead to five-figure proportions in 1992 and doubled it to over 20,000 in 1997. Stockton North does indeed physically look like a Labour stronghold. It includes Billingham, where the massive ICI chemical plant dominates an industrial skyline, and home town of Jamie Bell, the young actor and dancer who played *Billy Elliott*. The centre of Stockton and the council estates to the north-west are traditionally Labour, and the Tories only surpass 30% of the vote through some middle-class pockets of support in areas such as Glebe, Whitton and the village of Wolviston. In most other wards they achieve a derisory vote, often in double figures, in contests for Stockton's unitary authority.

Delving further back into history, beyond the era of William Rodgers, Stockton on Tees was Harold Macmillan's constituency from 1924 to 1945 (except for a two-year break from 1929). Eventually the elderly Macmillan decided to take the name of his earldom from the town, but even he could only win Stockton in disastrous years for Labour, and after the war he moved down to a very different kind of urban seat – Bromley in Kent. Macmillan remembered Stockton for its experience of poverty and unemployment, for its gritty charm, rather than for its loyalty to the Conservative Party. With a male unemployment rate in June 2001 of 9%, more than twice the national average, and a Labour lead of 14,500, much of this still applies.

Social indices:			2001 Gen. Election:			
% Non-white	0.9		Lab	22,470	63.4	−3.4
% Prof/Man	24.5		C	7,823	22.1	+3.3
% Non-manual	46.9		LD	4,208	11.9	+1.0
£ Av prop val 2000	55 K		Grn	926	2.6	
% Increase 97–00	27.3		Lab maj	14,647	41.3	
% Unemployed 2001	6.8		Turnout		54.3	−14.7
% Decrease 97–01	3.7		Elect	65,192		
% Fin hard/Rank	28.8	146				
% Pensioners	23.7					
% Prem mort/Rank	48	60				

Member of Parliament

Frank Cook, as a long-time local critic, replaced SDP defector Bill Rogers as Labour MP for Stockton in 1983. Originally a Campaign Grouper who voted for Heffer and Meacher as a leadership team in 1983, he has since mellowed into a maverick who, as a leading figure in the Commons shooting club, politically-incorrectly votes against gun control even post-Dunblane (which he blamed on 'police negligence'), has an interest in defence issues dating from his time in the Parachute Regiment, and is concerned about civil and military nuclear power. Small and pink-faced, he was born in 1935, educated at Corby School, Sunderland and De la Salle (RC) College, Manchester, worked initially as a schoolteacher, and then as an engineering industry project manager. A Catholic who prefers to see himself as 'an MP who is a Catholic and not a Roman Catholic who is an MP', he reflects his church's opinion on abortion. In December 2001 he angered Dunblane parents by calling for the handgun ban to be lifted to allow Commonwealth Games competitors to train.

STOCKTON SOUTH

In 1997 Labour gained Stockton South very easily (along with the other urban Tory seat in the North East, Tynemouth) with a huge swing of nearly 16%. However, this figure must be placed in the context of its strange recent electoral history. The Stockton South seat produced a superficially odd result in the 1992 General Election. Although the Conservatives saw their national majority in the Commons slashed from nearly 100 to just 21, the Tory majority in this constituency went up from 774 to 3,369. There are three factors which need to be considered in seeking an explanation for this aberrant result.

The first lies in the electoral background of the Stockton South division. In its inaugural contest in 1983 it was one of only half a dozen in the country won by the SDP. The victor was Ian Wrigglesworth, who had been elected under the Labour banner to represent Thornaby, which was in effect renamed as Stockton South. It has to be said that Wrigglesworth was fortunate to hold on in 1983. He won then by only 103 votes, and that over a candidate who had been more or less disowned by his party. Thomas Finnegan, selected by the Conservatives shortly after the 1983 campaign opened, was unmasked as a former National Front candidate after nominations had closed. Leading ministers like Nigel Lawson and Sir Keith Joseph (both Jewish) openly snubbed the hapless Finnegan, and all his public meetings were cancelled. He was clearly a source of much embarrassment to his party leadership, but all the same he nearly won. This might perhaps give a clue that Stockton South always was basically (if marginally) a Conservative seat.

The second factor concerns, doubly, incumbency. In 1987 Wrigglesworth could command a considerable personal vote based on his 13-year tenure as MP for the area, but a 27-year-old barrister, Tim Devlin, only had to harness the natural Tory vote to record one of under a dozen Conservative gains in that general election. It was a close three-way contest, with less than 3,000 votes covering all the candidates. In 1992, though, in Wrigglesworth's absence the centre party's vote collapsed, dropping from

34% to 15%. Meanwhile Devlin was now the incumbent, which must have helped him to produce his increased majority.

The third element which has helped the Conservatives here is that not only is the seat mainly middle-class and owner-occupied, but that it has been getting more so. Long-established Conservative wards include those in the west end of the town of Stockton, like Hartburn and Bishopsgarth. Although once in Yorkshire, and Richmond constituency, the desirable residential areas of Eaglescliffe and Egglescliffe, Yarm and Preston are also in the seat. New development is still taking place. Yarm grew in the 1980s, and even more spectacularly so did Ingleby Barwick ward, whose population mushroomed 177.7% in the decade before the 1991 Census.

However, there are Labour wards too, of course, such as Thornaby's neighbourhood of Stainsby (whose distaff side was sung about by Chris Rea), and strongholds at Parkfield, Victoria and Village, and it now seems as if the impact of the SDP and their subsequent good luck has finally been neutralised. There was little change recorded in 2001, apart from a 14% turnout drop. Although nowhere near as strongly Labour as Stockton North, this constituency will probably remain in the same hands next time.

Social indices:			2001 Gen. Election:			
% Non-white	2.4		Lab	23,414	53.0	−2.3
% Prof/Man	34.2		C	14,328	32.4	−0.6
% Non-manual	59.7		LD	6,012	13.6	+4.5
£ Av prop val 2000	65 K		SA	455	1.0	
% Increase 97–00	19.2		Lab maj	9,086	20.6	
% Unemployed 2001	4.6		Turnout		62.2	−13.9
% Decrease 97–01	2.3		Elect	71,026		
% Fin hard/Rank	15.5	344				
% Pensioners	20.9					
% Prem mort/Rank	34	272				

Member of Parliament

Dari Taylor, a PPS to Defence ministers from 2001,Welsh-born (1944) daughter of the late Dan Jones, MP for Burnley (1959–83), won this seat in 1997, following selection from an all-women shortlist which the local Labour Party had initially resisted. A Sunderland councillor for 11 years (1986–97), she was educated at Ynyshir Girls' School, Rhondda, and Nottingham University, and worked as an FE lecturer and as an education officer with the GMB. A feminist campaigner for women in the armed forces, she damned Tory MP Desmond Swayne for his 'utterly offensive and shameful' quotation from St Bernard of Clairvaux about the impossibility of being with a woman and not having intercourse with her.

STOKE-ON-TRENT CENTRAL

Stoke-on-Trent used to have a strong claim to have been consistently the most favourable city in England to the Labour Party, but for a raft of reasons that assertion could now longer be sustained. Stoke has returned a full slate of three Labour members to Parliament ever since 1945, which is a unique record. However,

Liverpool polled a higher Labour percentage for the first time in 1997, and Sunderland is now a city. Hull and Manchester's Labour figures were also higher in 2001. In municipal elections it passed out of Labour's control only once, in the dark days of the late 1960s, and only one (Trentham Park) of the city's 20 wards regularly returned Conservative victors until the 1990s. Yet in May 2000 Labour won only four of the 20, losing out not only to Conservative (four) and Liberal Democrat (four) but also, and in a way more ominously to Independents (eight, all they contested). In the June 2001 General Election Labour lost between 5% and 9% in each of the three Stoke constituencies, while independents saved two deposits and nearly a third (in South, where the BNP also stood and received a four-figure vote). There were racial disturbances, mirroring those in Bradford, Burnley and Oldham, in the summer of the same year. Labour won all the Stoke seats clearly, but their dominance was not unchallenged.

There is no substantial middle-class residential neighbourhood within the city, nothing to provide the basis for a solid Tory vote – or seat. Why is this? Partly it is a function of the fact that the city of Stoke-on-Trent is made up of many small, semi-independent communities, more even than the 'Five Towns' of Arnold Bennett. As in the Black Country, each town in the Potteries is a working-class and industrial unit. The industries of the district are in general long-established: all stages of pottery production, of course, and an old coalfield. Stoke-on-Trent still bears its industrial scars more clearly than most British cities. There are relatively few tower blocks, more Victorian houses, often still blackened by the once ferocious grime. It looks the part of the Labour stronghold.

The Central of its three constituencies is made up of the administrative headquarters of Stoke itself, the shopping centre of Hanley, the poorest 'inner-city' ward of Shelton, which includes Etruria, and much of Stoke's tiny ethnic minority population (4%, mainly Pakistani, in 1991). There are also the eastern peripheral council estate wards of Abbey and Brookhouse (both Independent in 2000), and Berryhill (still strongly Labour). Shelton was won by the Tories in the local elections in May 2000 and Hanley Green and Stoke West by the Liberal Democrats. Whether all this is a temporary and localised loss of faith in Labour, or whether the displaced Etonian MP will have further cause for concern remains to be seen, here in the heart of the Potteries.

Social indices:			2001 Gen. Election:			
% Non-white	4.2		Lab	17,170	60.7	−5.6
% Prof/Man	19.6		C	5,325	18.8	+2.1
% Non-manual	38.0		LD	4,148	14.7	+2.7
£ Av prop val 2000	37 K		Ind	1,657	5.9	
% Increase 97–00	10.6		Lab maj	11,845	41.9	
% Unemployed 2001	4.5		Turnout		47.4	−15.4
% Decrease 97–01	2.2		Elect	59,750		
% Fin hard/Rank	30.7	125				
% Pensioners	26.5					
% Prem mort/Rank	50	44				

Member of Parliament

Mark Fisher, dropped in the Blair government's first reshuffle in 1998 as Arts Minister, is one of Labour's more exotic blooms, as the son of the former Tory MP Sir Nigel Fisher (1950–83), and as one the PLP's two Old Etonians. A Friar Tuck look-alike with shiny bald pate, though preferring comparison with Humpty Dumpty, he was born in 1944 and after Eton attended Trinity College, Cambridge. Such a background making it prudent to act left, he duly joined the Campaign Group on election in 1983. His patrician voice and film industry interests made him an ideal choice for Arts spokesman from 1987, but his interest in freedom of information involved him in a clash with Lord Chancellor Irvine, Jack Straw and Peter Mandelson in 1998, just prior to his ministerial exit. Subsequently he rebelled on Incapacity Benefit cuts, legal aid curbs, pensions, and freedom of information, and in 2001 he both spoke and voted against David Blunkett's emergency anti-terrorism measures. The tenth in a line of Old Etonian Labour MPs (William Pethick-Lawrence, John Oldfield, Oliver Baldwin, John Strachey, Hugh Dalton, Reginald Paget, Dick Mitchison, Ben Whittaker and Tam Dalyell), he is the sporter, with just a hint of Simon Callow camp, of one of the Commons' most mellifluous upper-middle-class brogues.

STOKE-ON-TRENT NORTH

The northern part of Stoke-on-Trent is made up in the main of two of Bennett's 'Five Towns', Burslem and Tunstall. This is solidly working-class territory, which in most past years produced a full slate of Labour councillors in annual city council elections, but since 1998 other groups, principally an organised slate of Independents, have seriously eroded this position. One of the first onto the city council was Lee Wanger, elected for Tunstall North in 1998, who received over 11% of the vote in the 2001 General Election, one of a surprisingly large number of Independents and minor party candidates to do well in what was in many ways a very quiet set of election results.

Let us not exaggerate this impact. It has never been a marginal seat, and Labour have almost always won by a majority substantially into five figures since the war. The Election of 2001 was no exception, as Joan Walley retained a lead of 12,000, as the Tory vote slipped slightly. Stoke North is just as safe as the other two seats in the Potteries city, despite some fairly major boundary changes before the 1997 Election which transferred the working-class town of Kidsgrove into Staffordshire Moorlands in return for two very different wards from that same constituency: Brown Edge, and Endon and Stanley. While these are not far physically from Stoke's north-eastern border on the road towards Leek, they are in fact Conservative and middle-class suburbs, with an opposing political, social and cultural slant to the rest of North.

Stoke North, and Joan Walley, absorbed this unfamiliar new territory easily; after all there are only some 5,500 electors – Stoke does not command an extensive commuter belt. The transfer added to the Tories' problems in Staffordshire Moorlands, now in Labour's hands, but the Boundary Commission said that there was no protest from within Stoke North's old borders about the arrival of Brown Edge, Endon and Stanley. It is scarcely surprising.

Social indices:			2001 Gen. Election:			
% Non-white	2.8		Lab	17,460	58.0	−7.2
% Prof/Man	17.4		C	5,676	18.8	−1.3
% Non-manual	35.5		LD	3,580	11.9	+1.2
£ Av prop val 2000	44 K		Ind	3,399	11.3	
% Increase 97–00	32.3		Lab maj	11,784	39.1	
% Unemployed 2001	3.3		Turnout		51.9	−13.6
% Decrease 97–01	1.4		Elect	57,998		
% Fin hard/Rank	28.9	144				
% Pensioners	27.3					
% Prem mort/Rank	44	103				

Member of Parliament

Joan Walley came in here in 1987 as a left-wing replacement for the deselected right-wing Labour MP John Forrester, and briefly joined the Campaign Group, until opposing Benn and Heffer's challenge to Kinnock and Hattersley in 1988. A Gould voter in 1992 and a Prescott voter in 1994, she was dropped from the frontbench by Tony Blair in 1995 after seven years covering Environment and Transport. Pleasant-looking if pedestrian, she was born in 1949 and educated at Biddulph Grammar School and Hull University, spent four years as an eventually surcharged Lambeth councillor, worked variously in local government or for NACRO, and became (as a member of the Environmental Audit Select Committee from 1997) preoccupied with green causes, notably GM food. In 2000 she rebelled on linking pensions to average earnings.

STOKE-ON-TRENT SOUTH

The third Labour constituency in Stoke, the South division covers the two southernmost towns of the Potteries, Longton and Fenton, and the peripheral areas of Blurton, Meir Park (formerly mainly council estate, now partially sold off) and Weston Coyney. It appears the least monolithic of the three. Whereas the Labour MPs in North and Central obtained comfortable five-figure majorities in 1992, that in South was only 6,909, scarcely more than it had been in 1987. In 2001 George Stevenson's share fell by 8% to barely over half, while the BNP's candidature foreshadowed the rumour of a march which led to the racially-charged riot of mid-July, following disturbances in Lancashire and Yorkshire. Labour won none of the seven wards within the seat in the unitary authority elections of May 2000, as the Tories took three, the Liberal Democrats two and the Independents (who also did very well in the General Election) two.

The reasons for this (minor) deviationism are fairly clear. South does harbour a higher level of Conservative support than the other Stoke seats. The area around Trentham Park in the extreme south-west of the city – an unsurprising compass point, given the prevailing winds in Britain – is the most attractive middle-class residential sector. Meanwhile, although the ethnic minorities in Stoke are very small, they are not well integrated and the town has been suggested to be on a list of possible areas for exploitation by the far right. Unemployment in Stoke is about 50% higher than the national average, its trend in South between June 1997 and June 2001 was the third least positive of all UK seats, and there is a feeling that Labour has neglected, and maybe failed, this long-term stronghold.

Social indices:			2001 Gen. Election:			
% Non-white	2.3		Lab	19,366	53.8	−8.2
% Prof/Man	20.7		C	8,877	24.6	+2.3
% Non-manual	39.0		LD	4,724	13.1	+2.9
£ Av prop val 2000	49 K		Ind	1,703	4.7	
% Increase 97–00	21.2		BNP	1,358	3.8	+2.5
% Unemployed 2001	3.9		Lab maj	10,489	29.1	
% Decrease 97–01	0.1		Turnout		51.4	−14.6
% Fin hard/Rank	24.7	204	Elect	70,032		
% Pensioners	25.0					
% Prem mort/Rank	39	195				

Member of Parliament

George Stevenson, Labour MP here since 1992, came with impeccable if increasingly rare working-class credentials as a former bus driver, pottery worker and miner, and miner's son. Born in the Yorkshire coalfield in 1938, he was educated at Queensbury Road Secondary Modern, Stoke, and reached the Commons after 14 years on Stoke City Council and ten years in the European Parliament. Dark and stocky, he protests at defective rail transport, and has rebelled on linking pensions to average earnings, disability benefit cuts and air traffic control privatisation. Less parochially he opposes self-regulation of solicitors by the Law Society, and attacks the Chinese occupation of Tibet, as secure a business as Labour's occupation since 1935 of Stoke South.

STONE

Staffordshire gained a 12th seat in the most recent round of boundary changes before the 1997 Election, and this unquestionably is it. The Stone division is constructed from fairly equal portions of three previous constituencies. These three seats had much in common. All returned a Conservative MP in 1992, but two were gained by Labour in 1997, and the other one nearly fell. Ironically, though, Stone remained more comfortably in Tory hands – it had gathered together some of the most favourable parts of each of its donor seats, to their disadvantage.

Slightly the largest section of the three is that which was formerly in Mid Staffordshire (25,500 electors). This was the northernmost part of that rather artificial constituency, which was itself generated by the population growth in the central part of the county and brought into existence only in 1983. The area contains the town of Stone itself, which gave Labour a narrow majority in the historic 1990 by-election (we know this from exit polls) but which almost certainly votes predominantly Conservative in general elections, as well as several villages, which are reliably Tory.

The smallest donation was still fairly substantial: 18,000 voters from the rural, western part of the Stafford division. There are a couple of communities which just about class as large villages rather than small towns, Gnosall and Eccleshall, but no major population centres. The Conservative Party in Stafford has missed these voters keenly. Even more serious for the Tories though was the loss of 21,500 predominantly Conservative voters in Staffordshire Moorlands, as the area of Cheadle and Checkley is transferred to Stone. This Churnet Valley area also includes the popular day-trip attraction of Alton Towers, and is one of the most Conservative parts of the Moorlands seat, which has now become a safe Labour seat (having gained Kidsgrove from Stoke-on-Trent North).

In theory three sitting MPs had a claim on Stone, but the man selected was the rebellious anti-European right-winger Bill Cash, member for Stafford since 1984. Possibly benefiting from the absence of Referendum or UK Independence opponents, Cash held off Labour by nearly 4,000 in 1997 and just over 6,000 in 2001, and it looks as if he still has a safe seat – at least in electoral terms, for no one knows where the complex and bitter Euro-politics of the Conservative Party will lead.

Social indices:			2001 Gen. Election:			
% Non-white	0.5		C	22,395	49.1	+2.2
% Prof/Man	37.6		Lab	16,359	35.8	−3.8
% Non-manual	58.0		LD	6,888	15.1	+3.0
£ Av prop val 2000	84 K		C maj	6,036	13.2	
% Increase 97–00	27.5		Turnout		66.3	−11.5
% Unemployed 2001	1.4		Elect	68,847		
% Decrease 97–01	0.6					
% Fin hard/Rank	6.3	576				
% Pensioners	24.9					
% Prem mort/Rank	29	356				

Member of Parliament

Bill Cash, a single-track obsessive as his party's leading Maastricht Eurosceptic and Germanophobic scourge of the federasts, was elected MP for Stafford in 1984 and for this seat in 1997. Voting against Maastricht 47 times, he toned down from outright defiance to abstention in the run-up to gaining reselection in the much changed map of Staffordshire seats before 1997. An immensely tall and earnest solicitor wrapped in a conspicuous pin stripe, and an outsider as a Catholic (born in 1940, educated at Stonyhurst and Lincoln College, Oxford) with a Quaker father (killed in action near Caen in 1944), and a sense that 'we were definitely not part of the Establishment', he backed Redwood, then Hague, in 1997, and Duncan Smith in all the ballots in 2001. For this latter choice he was surprisingly rewarded with the appointment of Shadow Attorney General, his first job after 17 years as an MP, at the age of 61, and without actually being a barrister.

STOURBRIDGE

Stourbridge is a prosperous and independent town within the borough of Dudley on the very border between the West Midlands conurbation and the Worcestershire countryside. Before 1997 it had not been represented by a Labour MP since being joined with its socially and politically similar neighbour to the east, Halesowen, in 1974. Now that fruitful partnership for the Tories has been dissolved, as Halesowen is linked with parts of Sandwell. Stourbridge has finally gained a seat of its own – or at least one named after it.

Its 40,000 voters are not enough to merit a whole constituency, but are topped up by one ward each from the old Dudley East and West divisions. That from East, Quarry Bank and Cradley, usually votes Labour in Dudley borough elections; but Amblecote, previously in West, has seen extensive new private housing development in the 1980s, which tilted it to the Tories. Amblecote is the most populous ward in the whole metropolitan borough, having grown by over 50% since 1981 due to housing infilling on previously industrial land. The Stourbridge section of the seat includes some Labour territory, such as the Lye and Wollescote ward with its ex-council estates, but there are also Conservative bankers like Pedmore and Stourbridge East. In an even year between the two main parties the Stourbridge seat would be very close, but the 11% swing recorded in 1997 gave Labour all the seats in Dudley, this one nearly as comfortably as the others. In 2001 the Conservatives recovered only a couple of points, and still need another 5% swing to take Stourbridge in 2005 or 2006. It must be considered a marginal vital to the destination of the responsibility of UK government.

Social indices:			2001 Gen. Election:			
% Non-white	3.2		Lab	18,823	47.1	–0.0
% Prof/Man	31.5		C	15,011	37.6	+1.8
% Non-manual	55.9		LD	4,833	12.1	–2.2
£ Av prop val 2000	70 K		UKIP	763	1.9	
% Increase 97–00	17.8		SLP	494	1.2	
% Unemployed 2001	3.4		Lab maj	3,812	9.5	
% Decrease 97–01	0.9		Turnout		61.8	–14.7
% Fin hard/Rank	18.2	302	Elect	64,610		
% Pensioners	22.7					
% Prem mort/Rank	21	470				

Member of Parliament

Debra Shipley, elected in 1997 after selection from an all-women shortlist, is one of the 'Blair's Babes' who took to producing babes of her own after the election, if discreet about all aspects of her family relationships. Born in 1957, the daughter of a factory worker, and educated at Kidderminster High School, Oxford Polytechnic and London University, she previously worked on 'course development' at the University of Central England. As an MP she has majored in the contemporary orthodoxies of child abuse, with her Protection of Children Act in 1999 establishing a blacklist of child abusers, and environmental pollution, raising in February 2001 the issue of radiation from mobile phone masts and drawing from Tory MP Michael Fabricant the opinion that such masts had the equivalent effect of a 50-watt light bulb.

STRANGFORD

The last Northern Irish Boundary Commission's original proposals involved the abolition of the constituency of Strangford, which would have been very inconvenient for the then senior Ulster Unionist MP John Taylor. However, after a public inquiry the seat was reprieved, and still exists in only slightly modified form. The area around Dundonald in the outer eastern suburbs of Belfast came in from North Down; a few thousand electors arrived from Lagan Valley around Carryduff; some more around Derrybot from South Down. In return, the Donaghadee area was lost to North Down.

The core of the constituency, however, was unaltered. Its focus remains the Ards peninsula and Strangford Lough. It is a mixture of thinly-populated rural territory and fairly desirable commuting areas within reach of Belfast, such as Comber and Newtownards, where there is also significant industry. Employment is also provided by agriculture, fishing and tourism.

The population is very heavily Protestant and unionist, and the representation of Strangford at Westminster is decided by the contest between the main unionist parties. In 1997 (in a kind of mirror image of the advance of Sinn Fein in Nationalist areas) the more extreme DUP advanced by about 10% in Strangford, and Taylor's majority was cut to its smallest yet, less than 6,000. When John Taylor announced his retirement before the 2001 General Election, it was clear that his party would struggle to hold this seat, and his 1997 opponent Iris Robinson, wife of the Belfast East MP, did indeed take it with another 12% increase in the DUP share. If anything, in the polarised atmosphere of that time, with the Good Friday Agreement under extreme pressure as the Protestant community felt that their many concessions had produced little response from Republicans, the surprise was that the Ulster Unionists kept Mrs Robinson's majority to just 1,000. Clearly the answer lies in the Alliance Party's share of the vote, which was halved between 1997 and 2001.

Social indices:		2001 Gen. Election:			
% Prof/Man	29.3	DUP	18,532	42.8	+12.6
% Non-manual	55.3	UUP	17,422	40.3	−4.0
% RC	12.4	APNI	2,902	6.7	−6.4
% Irish sp	2.1	SDLP	2,646	6.1	−0.6
% Unemployed 2001	3.3	SF	930	2.2	+0.9
% Decrease 97–01	2.0	Ind	822	1.9	
		DUP maj	1,110	2.6	
		Turnout		59.9	+0.5
		Elect	72,192		

Member of Parliament

Iris Robinson's victory over the Ulster Unionists here in 2001 boosted the DUP's Westminster representation to five, only one seat fewer than the UUP's six, and provided the Commons with its fifth husband-and-wife team, her husband Peter, Deputy Leader of the DUP, having sat for East Belfast since 1979. Born in 1949 in Belfast and educated at Knockbreda Intermediate School and Castlereagh Technical College, her life has been one immersed in politics, paralleling her husband as a local (Castlereagh) councillor, a Northern Ireland Assembly member, and now as an MP –

so prompting her Ulster Unionist Party rival David McNarry to speculate about the salaries being accumulated in the Robinson household. Her pitch is the conventional Paisleyite one of a loyalist people betrayed and let down by David Trimble's Ulster Unionists. With an intensity matching her husband's, she sees herself as neither 'polished nor professional' but as 'an uncomplicated working-class girl', and indeed owed her victory in 2001 to the polarisation of the loyalist and Republican communities around their hard proletarian cores.

STRATFORD-ON-AVON

It might be thought that Stratford-on-Avon would prove one of the most civilised of English constituencies. Famed throughout the world as the home of the most favoured of all playwrights, Stratford welcomes all kinds of sophisticates as well as the more humble types of tourist. Yet in some ways South Warwickshire is deep and mysterious countryside, where dark rumours abound. It is said that the last witch-lynching in Britain took place here, as late as the 1940s. There were surprising newspaper reports in the 1970s that the little town of Southam harboured the British headquarters of the Ku Klux Klan.

This is the only truly rural constituency in Warwickshire, extending from the plain of the Avon around Stratford up the scarp of Edgehill into the Cotswold hills. Not far from Stratford can be found remote villages and strong rural working-class accents. Primitive or sophisticated, town or country, this constituency is strongly Conservative, with the Liberal Democrats notching their sole second place in the county in 2001. Apart from Stratford itself, the towns are too small to be independent of their agricultural hinterland. Southam, Bidford-on-Avon and Alcester are all around the 5,000 mark. In the north around Wootton Wawen can be found the comfortable home of long-distance commuters to Birmingham.

Some distinguished – and controversial – figures have represented Stratford-on-Avon. It was the seat of John Profumo, the disgraced War Secretary, and after the by-election caused by his resignation in 1963, of Angus Maude, Mrs Thatcher's first Paymaster-General. Then in October 1995 the member since 1983, Alan Howarth, gave up the Tory whip and crossed the floor. For nearly two years Stratford entertained the phenomenon of a Labour MP. But this appears to have had no permanent effect. In 2001 the former minister John Maples held the seat with the 20th highest numerical Tory majority.

Social indices:			2001 Gen. Election:			
% Non-white	0.7		C	27,606	50.3	+2.0
% Prof/Man	38.9		LD	15,804	28.8	+3.2
% Non-manual	60.6		Lab	9,164	16.7	−3.9
£ Av prop val 2000	141 K		UKIP	1,184	2.2	+1.3
% Increase 97–00	49.4		Grn	1,156	2.1	
% Unemployed 2001	1.1		C maj	11,802	21.5	
% Decrease 97–01	1.0		Turnout		64.4	−11.8
% Fin hard/Rank	5.7	587	Elect	85,241		
% Pensioners	26.5					
% Prem mort/Rank	16	533				

Member of Parliament

John Maples, first elected for Lewisham West (1983–92) was returned here in 1997 as a replacement for the floor-crossing Alan Howarth. A Europhile wet who trimmed rightwards, but insufficiently, he was dropped from William Hague's frontbench in 2000, after three years as successively Shadow Health, Defence and Foreign Secretaries, his earlier ministerial career under John Major (as a Junior Treasury Minister) having ended with his defeat in the 1992 Election. Born in 1943, educated at Marlborough, Downing College, Cambridge and the Inns of Court, and with a lawyer-turned-PR-man's ability smoothly if uncharismatically to argue a brief, and dubbed 'so smooth he could make a good wine waiter' (the *Observer*), he nevertheless as Deputy Party Chairman in 1994 blurted out the awful truth about the unpopularity of the Major government in a leaked memo. He backed Hague in 1997 and Clarke in 2001, having attributed the second Tory defeat to giving up the centre ground and confusing the electorate's Euroscepticism with being anti-European.

STRATHKELVIN AND BEARSDEN

There are no Conservative seats left within the city of Glasgow; the Tories' last bastion, Hillhead, in the heart of the West End, fell to Roy Jenkins in the 1982 by-election. As in cities south of the border, there are large middle-class blocs outside the city boundaries, such as Eastwood, but if one were to ask a Glaswegian where the heart of 'posh' suburbia was to be found, the answer would most likely be – Bearsden. Nor is this perception far out. With 90% owner-occupiers and 82% non-manual workers even back in 1981, Bearsden ranks as the most middle-class town in the whole of Britain.

How, then, did Bearsden come to have a Labour MP (even if he was, admittedly, a brain surgeon by profession)? It could be argued that it is outvoted by Strathkelvin, principally the towns of Bishopbriggs and Kirkintilloch, both of which are normally Labour in local elections. However, Bearsden does itself have tendencies of disloyalty to the Tories. Several of the local wards elect Liberal Democrats; and Bearsden's experience is one more example of the fact that Scots from backgrounds which would generate solid Conservatism in England cannot be relied on for their support.

In 2001 Sam Galbraith retired through ill health, but his successor John Lyons had no difficulty retaining the seat, all the more easily because the opposition was split almost evenly between three parties. The Liberal Democrats did well to move up from fourth to second, almost doubling their share to produce their best result ever in Strathkelvin and Bearsden. Almost unnoticed, they were the only party of the 'big four' to increase their proportion of the Scottish vote, and they overtook the Conservatives north of the border for the first time for the best part of a century. Major boundary changes are not proposed, but the seat is likely to leap up the alphabetic lists under the even less pithy name of Bearsden, Bishopbriggs and Kirkintilloch West.

Social indices:			2001 Gen. Election:			
% Non-white	2.3		Lab	19,250	46.4	−6.5
% Prof/Man	43.7		LD	7,533	18.2	+8.4
% Non-manual	70.3		SNP	6,675	16.1	−0.2
% Unemployed 2001	2.5		C	6,635	16.0	−4.1
% Decrease 97–01	1.7		SSP	1,393	3.4	
% Fin hard/Rank	17.4	313	Lab maj	11,717	28.2	
% Prem mort/Rank	31	313	Turnout		66.1	−12.8
			Elect	62,729		

Member of Parliament

John Lyons was elected here in 2001 in place of the ailing Sam Galbraith after serving for 12 years as the Scottish organiser of UNISON (previously NUPE) and for 18 years previously working as a mechanical engineer. Of Labour's 38 new MPs in 2001, six were former high-ranking union officials, emerging from a selection process in which separate unions agreed not to rival each other in selected seats. Glasgow-born in 1949, he was educated at Woodside Secondary School and eventually at Stirling University. With a light workload as a post-devolution MP, he joined five other new Scottish MPs on the Scottish Affairs Select Committee and could look forward to a fairly quiet life, given that the Boundary Commissioners in 2002 appeared not to be threatening this seat. Meanwhile he is not without some facial resemblance to Nicholas Parsons.

STREATHAM

Labour did not win the Streatham constituency in 1966. They did not even win it in their landslide year of 1945. But they did win Streatham in 1992, and in 1997 Keith Hill increased his majority to over 18,000. That says much about the change in the social nature of this part of south London, although boundary changes have also contributed to Labour's advance.

It is true that in 1983 the Streatham seat was expanded to include the Town Hall ward, which contains a large part of central Brixton and is strongly Labour. Previously it had consisted of the most middle-class part of the long thin borough of Lambeth, the south-western corner. Here, at Streatham South and Streatham Wells, can be found genuine outer London suburbia – a far cry from the Thames frontage in Vauxhall constituency. However, boundary changes did not take place between 1983 and 1987, when Labour increased their share of the vote by 7.7% and closed down the Conservative lead from nearly 6,000 to 2,400; nor between 1987 and 1992, when Keith Hill benefited from a further swing of nearly 6% to beat Sir William Shelton (an MP for 22 years) by over 2,000. Social and political factors must account for those large movements in the same direction.

There can be no doubt that Streatham has become less of a conventional suburban seat in recent decades. By the time of the 1991 Census, over a quarter of its population was from the non-white ethnic groups, mainly Afro-Caribbean; it is within the orbit of the large concentration of London's black communities in central Lambeth, often generically (and not too accurately) described as 'Brixton'. Black voters are the most committed of any ethnic group to the Labour Party (although less likely than average to register or to turn out to vote). Second, the late 1980s saw the unravelling of a period of exceptional unpopularity for Labour in Lambeth, following the far-left regimes of such as 'Red Ted' Knight at the beginning of the decade. The party had almost certainly suffered from this in the 1983 Election, a performance from which they were to recover.

Having won Streatham once, Labour had every chance of repeating their success, especially as further boundary changes have now added more of the 'Brixton' area in the shape of the Tulse Hill and St Martin's wards. These were previously in the Norwood division, which was split asunder as Lambeth and Southwark between them lost a seat. Tulse Hill actually includes most of Railton Road, the so-called 'front line' in the riots of 1981; St Martin's is situated further up the hill and contains the railway station and shopping centre named Tulse Hill. This is bearing more and more of the marks of an inner-city constituency. Further evidence for this was provided in 2001, when fewer than half of registered voters turned out. This factor, together with the 7% taken by Greens and Socialist Alliance, was typical of high-density urban areas in the general election of that year.

Social indices:			2001 Gen. Election:			
% Non-white	28.0		Lab	21,041	56.9	−5.9
% Prof/Man	45.8		LD	6,771	18.3	+4.8
% Non-manual	68.5		C	6,639	17.9	−3.8
£ Av prop val 2000	165 K		Grn	1,641	4.4	
% Increase 97–00	69.4		SA	906	2.4	
% Unemployed 2001	7.0		Lab maj	14,270	38.6	
% Decrease 97–01	4.3		Turnout		48.7	−11.6
% Fin hard/Rank	22.9	228	Elect	76,021		
% Pensioners	20.7					
% Prem mort/Rank	45	94				

Member of Parliament

Keith Hill, Deputy Chief Whip from 2001 after a year as Minister for London and originally a union and Party apparatchik, won Streatham in 1992 as its first ever Labour MP, after 16 years as political officer with the NUR, two years in the Labour Party's international department, and originally eight years teaching politics at Leicester and Strathclyde Universities, during which time he was briefly an academic expert in 'segmented pluralism' in Belgium, a prelude to his later knowledge of Tory-induced segmented pluralism on the railways. Born in 1943, a printer's son, and educated at City of Leicester Boys' Grammar School and Corpus Christi College, Oxford, given ageism he was lucky to be made a Whip in 1998, assisted by a gregarious and youthful manner belying his 55 years. With the largest rictus in the business and with an effortlessly fluent high camp style at the despatch box, making him one of the government's insufficiently sung heroes (despite his unintentionally ambiguous dubbing of motor cycling enthusiast Hazel Blears MP, as 'Blears the Bike'), he once enquired of a constituent who had complained at how Streatham had gone down hill, 'Why else do you think you've got a Labour MP?'

STRETFORD AND URMSTON

This is a seat of two distinct halves, in the western Greater Manchester borough of Trafford. The first element consists essentially of the communities of Urmston, Flixton and Davyhulme (which lost ownership of – or even mention in – a constituency title in 1997, which is very unusual). This is really the north-western end of the 'Cheshire' belt which girdles southern Manchester and houses so many of that city's commuters and middle-class workers. This territory is 80% owner-occupied, almost all white and clearly Conservative. Winston Churchill (junior)'s old Davyhulme seat also included the anomalous Bucklow ward, which was dominated by Partington, a large council estate built to serve the massive ICI chemical works at Carrington. But the real disaster for the Tories occurred in the half of the seat at the Stretford end, as it were.

The Stretford portion is now strongly Labour. Clifford ward was 45% non-white in the last published Census; Stretford's ethnic minority population includes large numbers of Asians as well as Afro-Caribbeans. Talbot ward is also essentially part of Manchester's inner city. In effect the old Stretford seat which existed before the 1983 changes has been recreated, one which Winston Churchill held narrowly through the 1970s, but which has suffered from the decline of its inner residential areas and a pro-Labour regional swing in the intervening years. In 1997 and 2001 the ex-Stretford parts overpowered the ex-Davyhulme wards, and the former Trafford council leader Beverley Hughes won last time by over 13,000, maintaining that numerical majority even though the turnout fell by nearly 15%.

Social indices:			2001 Gen. Election:			
% Non-white	9.2		Lab	23,804	61.1	+2.6
% Prof/Man	28.6		C	10,565	27.1	–3.4
% Non-manual	56.4		LD	3,891	10.0	+1.8
£ Av prop val 2000	67 K		Ind	713	1.8	
% Increase 97–00	24.5		Lab maj	13,239	34.0	
% Unemployed 2001	3.5		Turnout		55.0	–14.7
% Decrease 97–01	2.1		Elect	70,924		
% Fin hard/Rank	18.0	306				
% Pensioners	24.9					
% Prem mort/Rank	37	216				

Member of Parliament

Beverley Hughes, a Home Office Minister from 2001, after two years as an Environment Minister and one as PPS to the equally worthy Environment Minister Hilary Armstrong (1998–99), was elected in 1997, with a 'bog-standard' (as Alistair Campbell might say) Labour MP's background of local councillor (Trafford, which she led for two years) and lecturer (in social work, having earlier been a probation officer). Born in 1959 and educated at Ellesmere Port Grammar School and Manchester University, she was one of the first of Labour's 1997 65-strong intake of women MPs to be given a job. Making few headlines as a ministerial advocate of executive mayors, she did seem a little overstretched, defending David Blunkett's emergency anti-terrorism measures in late 2001.

STROUD

Many observers felt that Labour must be at their most vulnerable in the seat of Stroud in 2001. For example the internationally respected weekly, *The Economist* focused on it as a critically marginal rural seat, which Labour might lose due to their perceived anti-rural bias, typified by the strident demonstrations of the Countryside Alliance against the government. This analysis was misguided on almost every count. Stroud was not a critical marginal. Labour could have lost it and retained a very satisfactory overall majority of 130. It was scarcely a rural seat, with less than 5% employed in agriculturally-related pursuits. Finally, far from losing it, the sitting MP David Drew increased his majority, on a relatively high turnout of 70%, as the Liberal Democrats and Green Party both lost vote share while the Tories remained static and Labour increased by nearly 5%. A better example of the New Labour government's ability to allay doubts about its intentions and ability to deliver its promises could scarcely be wished.

At first sight Labour's victory in Stroud was one of their most spectacular gains in 1997, but in fact the anti-Tory swing was no higher than the national par. This just shows the extent of the movement to Labour, although they did win the seat in 1945. They also seem to have been helped by tactical voting on the part of Liberal Democrats, who polled 33% in the county council elections on the same day, but only 15% (a drop from 21 in 1992) in the general.

The constituency of Stroud is situated south of Gloucester. Much of it is physically part of the Cotswold range of hills, although the countryside slopes down to the vale of the Severn around Berkeley. If, compared with a neighbouring seat like that itself named Cotswold, there is more industry here, there are still beauty spots in an area containing Laurie Lee's Slad. One or two dramatic industrial valleys prove striking sights: Chalford and the Golden Valley, and the Dursley and Cam district, where Labour can win local elections in a good year. Labour also win locally in Stroud itself, and they clearly outpolled the Conservatives in the Stonehouse, Cam and Dursley ward and the two Stroud electoral divisions in the coterminous June 2001 county elections.

Apart from producing one of this book's co-authors, Stroud has one claim to fame which it would not wish; in recent years it has unfortunately developed the reputation of having one of the highest incidences of meningitis in Britain. Environmental considerations loom large here: Green Party candidates have been elected to the district council from both Stroud and Nailsworth wards in recent years, but they disappointed here in the 2001 General Election, doing much worse than in inner-city seats. Stroud may not truly be rural, but it is not metropolitan either.

Social indices:			2001 Gen. Election:			
% Non-white	0.6		Lab/Coop	25,685	46.6	+3.9
% Prof/Man	36.4		C	20,646	37.4	−0.5
% Non-manual	56.5		LD	6,036	10.9	−4.5
£ Av prop val 2000	106 K		Grn	1,913	3.5	−0.5
% Increase 97–00	54.4		UKIP	895	1.6	
% Unemployed 2001	1.9		L/C maj	5,039	9.1	
% Decrease 97–01	1.0		Turnout		69.9	−10.5
% Fin hard/Rank	7.5	542	Elect	78,878		
% Pensioners	27.1					
% Prem mort/Rank	11	586				

Member of Parliament

David Drew, residually Gloucestershire-burred and elected in 1997, was a local councillor for eight years and, variously a teacher or polytechnic lecturer for 21, and in 2001 achieved what had eluded his sole Labour predecessor in this seat, Ben Parkin (1945–50), the local Wycliffe College schoolmaster, by winning Stroud in two consecutive elections. Born in 1952, the son of a company accountant, and educated at Kingsfield School, Kingswood, Bristol and at Nottingham and Birmingham Universities and at Bristol Polytechnic, he has campaigned for a Rural Affairs ministry as MP for a seat with both a vocal countryside lobby and Green Party activity, and supports the restoration of the local Severn–Thames Stroudwater Navigation canal, blocked and disused since the 1940s. Otherwise he either votes against or abstains on legalising homosexual sex at 16, and co-signed a Eurosceptic letter to the *Guardian* in January 2002.

SUFFOLK CENTRAL AND IPSWICH NORTH

The Liberal Democrats have a reputation for strength in the rural areas of Britain, but the county of Suffolk is an exception. They finished third in all of the seven seats here in 1997 and 2001, and in four cases, including Suffolk Central and Ipswich North, they slipped back from second place in 1992, ceding the runner-up position to Labour in 1997 and further losing ground, presumably because of the squeeze on the third-placed party in what had become tight two-way marginals, last time.

Labour, on the other hand, did very well in 1997. They strengthened their grip on the county town, Ipswich, gained Waveney (Lowestoft), and ran the Conservatives fairly close (for the first time ever) in the more rural seats. In Central they increased their share by 15% and cut Michael Lord's majority to 3,500. In 2001 that numerical majority actually slipped a little further, but that was due to a decline in turnout of 12%; however, Suffolk Central and Ipswich North is scarcely a one-party state even yet.

In extensive boundary changes before the 1997 Election, the seat gained a substantial portion from Suffolk Coastal, in fact its western or least coastal bit, which includes Framlingham with its majestic castle, Earl Soham, Wickham Market and the sprawling Ipswich suburb of Kesgrave. These joined the territory which was already in Central, a swathe of villages in Suffolk's fertile and gently rolling heart, golden with corn and dark green with oak trees in the summer. The only town in this section is the tiny Eye, population 1,774, which actually had a parliamentary seat named after it until 1983.

Four wards of north-west Ipswich are included somewhat awkwardly in the seat. These consist of two Labour peripheral council estate wards, Whitton and White House, and two Conservative middle-class residential areas, Broom Hill and Castle Hill. They cancel each other out, politically. However, after many representations, in 1995 the Boundary Commission finally decided to acknowledge their presence in the name of the seat, at the cost of creating one of the most unwieldy titles anywhere in the land.

Social indices:			2001 Gen. Election:			
% Non-white	1.8		C	20,924	44.4	+1.8
% Prof/Man	31.9		Lab	17,455	37.1	+1.2
% Non-manual	54.0		LD	7,593	16.1	−4.5
£ Av prop val 2000	99 K		UKIP	1,132	2.4	
% Increase 97–00	46.4		C maj	3,469	7.4	
% Unemployed 2001	1.9		Turnout		63.5	−11.7
% Decrease 97–01	1.4		Elect	74,200		
% Fin hard/Rank	8.1	521				
% Pensioners	27.4					
% Prem mort/Rank	12	570				

Member of Parliament

Sir Michael Lord, a bald, pleasant and rare arboriculturalist of right-wing, free-market hue, and first elected on the high Thatcherite tide of 1983, was the 16th most rebellious Tory MP on the Maastricht Bill with 35 dissentient votes in 1992–93. Born in 1938, a schoolmaster's son, and educated at William Hulme's Grammar School, Manchester, and Christ's College, Cambridge, he worked previously in his own tree-selling business, seeks more tax incentives for forestry, but has fallen silent since 1997 as one of the Speaker's three deputies, in his case as Deputy Chairman of Ways and Means. He ran for Speaker in 2000 but polled only 146 votes. An advocate of capital punishment – if not as a means of controlling the Commons – he has dismissed abolitionists' arguments as 'lies, damned lies and statistics'.

SUFFOLK COASTAL

During the 2001 General Election campaign, as opinion polls suggested a national Labour lead of up to 20% (compared with 11% in 1997), attention turned to seats which might even be gained by the party in government, including several in rural Suffolk, including Coastal. As it happens these were all held by the Conservatives, but with similar majorities to 1997, and it is clear that they cannot be regarded as beyond Labour's grasp, especially should turnout levels return to the high figures recorded prior to that election. That gap between opinion poll figures and the actual result was partially accounted for by Labour voters staying at home, knowing that overall victory was certain.

In the parliamentary boundary changes which came into force at the 1997 Election, the Suffolk Coastal seat became even more coastal. About 20,000 voters from the westernmost part of the seat – that is, the most inland – were transferred to the Suffolk Central and Ipswich North division. Also, some 10,000 electors were annexed as the seat's northern border moves further up the North Sea shore, taken a few more miles from Waveney. The Coastal seat now covers almost the whole of the Suffolk sea frontage, apart only from the area around Lowestoft which is still in Waveney. There is now a thinner strip of hinterland behind the coast.

Suffolk Coastal, like all the other seats in the county, saw a strong Labour advance at the 1997 General Election, as John Gummer's majority was slashed from (a notional) 16,700 to just 3,250. There are Labour wards in the towns in the consti-tuency. Felixstowe, the largest, is a bustling (private) port and an active seaside resort. Woodbridge is a lively town a few miles up the River Deben. Leiston also has a population of over 5,000 and is the nearest town to the Sizewell nuclear power plant. Aldeburgh is smaller than these, an elegant mecca for music lovers – the Snape Maltings lie just inland. It is joined by its quaint neighbour, Southwold, and another town of about 5,000 souls, Halesworth. That such territory should ever rank among Labour's targets shows just how far the Conservatives have declined in the last decade.

Social indices:			2001 Gen. Election:			
% Non-white	2.4		C	21,847	43.3	+4.8
% Prof/Man	31.9		Lab	17,521	34.8	+2.0
% Non-manual	52.3		LD	9,192	18.2	–3.2
£ Av prop val 2000	103 K		UKIP	1,847	3.7	
% Increase 97–00	55.2		C maj	4,326	8.6	
% Unemployed 2001	1.6		Turnout		66.4	–9.4
% Decrease 97–01	2.0		Elect	75,963		
% Fin hard/Rank	6.7	566				
% Pensioners	31.9					
% Prem mort/Rank	6	621				

Member of Parliament

John Selwyn Gummer was first elected at Lewisham West in 1970, sporting in those days the only Tory beard in a House where all the beards could be numbered on a very few chins. Beaten in 1974 he returned clean-shaven in 1979 as MP for Eye – a seat since superfluously abolished and resprayed as 'Suffolk Coastal'. Slight and high-pitched, it was said of him, allegedly by John Major, that he 'would be considered one of the best politicians of his generation if only he were one stone heavier, one foot taller, and his voice one octave lower'. Continuously in government from 1981 to 1997, tackling all his jobs – latterly in Cabinet as Minister of Agriculture (1989–93), then Environment Secretary (1993–97) – with 'well-scrubbed enthusiasm' (the *Independent*), and with precisely articulated speech, he is churchy, as the son of an ex-Baptist Church of England canon, and as a bolter to Rome over women priests, but will be better remembered for force-feeding his daughter Cordelia a burger in order to show how safe beef was. Born in 1939 and educated at King's School Rochester and

Selwyn College, Cambridge, where he met and networked with the Tory Cambridge Mafia of Clarke, Brittan, Lamont, Howard, *et al.*, he worked in publishing and embarked on a political career inevitably stamped by the Europhilia of his origins in the Heath years. A Clarke voter in 1997 and 2001, by 2001 he and Kenneth Clarke were the last members of Margaret Thatcher's cabinets remaining in the Commons.

SUFFOLK SOUTH

After it was generally acknowledged that he had a good campaign as the Tories' Agriculture spokesman during the foot and mouth crisis of 2001, Tim Yeo of Suffolk South was returned in the General Election of June that year with the largest majority of any Tory seat in the county. That is not actually saying very much, as he beat Labour by just over 5,000. He benefited from a modest 4% increase in the Conservative vote, which was in line with the county average, and turnout fell by 11%, close to the national norm. There are few individual rewards in constituency contests for established candidates.

Most of Suffolk South is archetypal Tory rural England: here we have the so-called Constable country along the Stour near East and West Bergholt (though Flatford Mill is actually on the Essex bank of the river). The former wool towns of Lavenham and Long Melford, their huge churches betokening an affluent past, look exactly what they often have been – the sites of film sets. There are many other highly attractive villages too, their houses sporting thatched roofs and colour-washed flanks, which are not as well-known even as the county has become more popular with long-distance London commuters and weekenders. The largest community is that of Sudbury and its satellite, Great Cornard, both of which have Labour wards based on council estates built to accommodate London overspill after the Second World War. The other centre of Labour strength in the constituency, Haverhill, was however moved into Suffolk West before 1997. Hadleigh is the only other town.

There is a substantial non-Conservative vote in Suffolk South – Labour took 30% of the total cast in 2001 and the Liberal Democrats 25%. It is unlikely, though, that there will be a unification of an anti-Tory movement, certainly while that party remains out of office, and the most likely projection is of an increased lead for Tim Yeo again next time.

Social indices:			2001 Gen. Election:				
% Non-white	0.8		C	18,748	41.4	+4.1	
% Prof/Man	36.3		Lab	13,667	30.2	+0.9	
% Non-manual	57.2		LD	11,296	24.9	−2.8	
£ Av prop val 2000	107 K		UKIP	1,582	3.5		
% Increase 97–00	45.0		C maj	5,081	11.2		
% Unemployed 2001	1.6		Turnout		66.2	−11.0	
% Decrease 97–01	1.5		Elect	68,408			
% Fin hard/Rank	7.9	527					
% Pensioners	27.3						
% Prem mort/Rank	2	633					

Member of Parliament

Tim Yeo, who moved from being Shadow Agriculture Minister under William Hague
to being Shadow Culture Secretary under Iain Duncan Smith in 2001, has been MP
here since the seat's creation in 1983 when he replaced the sitting MP Keith Stainton.
Born in 1945, a doctor's son, and educated at Charterhouse and Emmanuel College,
Cambridge, he worked for Peter Walker before running the Spastics Society, and rose
as an MP under the patronage of Douglas Hurd, whom he backed for leader in 1990.
Since then he has redefined One Nation Toryism as not 'excessively pro-European or
left-wing' and trimmed in the direction of William Hague's right-wing Euroscepticism, backing him rather than Clarke in 1997, and Portillo in 2001. A
pink-faced, plummy-voiced charmer, he is still recalled as the first of John Major's
Back-to-Basics casualties, exposed in 1994 for earlier fathering two illegitimate
children, for which he was forced to resign as an Environment Minister and fend off a
deselection threat, but managed – luckily – to retain his seat in the electoral rout of
1997. His family celebrated his 50th birthday with a banner declaiming '50 but
frisky'; whilst Simon Hoggart (the *Guardian*) calculated that 'the average adult
British woman is four times more likely to have a love child by Tory Agriculture
Spokesman, Tim Yeo, than to contract CJD through beef on the bone'.

SUFFOLK WEST

It should first of all be explained that despite appearances to the contrary, Suffolk
West is not in fact the wholly new and extra seat awarded to the county in the
boundary changes enacted during the life of the 1992–97 Parliament. It bears a new
name; we have previously known a Suffolk Central and South and even Coastal, but
none titled West. However, the bulk of this seat is made up of voters from the former
Bury St Edmunds, over 46,000 of them; and they represent the majority of that Bury
St Edmunds seat. In effect, Suffolk West is merely a heavily modified Bury St
Edmunds constituency, which has lost the town that gave it its name; now Bury has
been joined with new terrain to the east, but it is the seat now named after that town
which really was the brand new division in 1997.

The ex-Bury St Edmunds territory includes a variety of neighbourhoods. The
Forest Heath district in the north-west corner of the county has a strong armed
services presence, like many other areas of East Anglia; Mildenhall is here, and
Lakenheath. Indeed the old Bury seat had the highest proportion employed in the
services of any constituency in the eastern region. This does not betoken left-wing
preferences. In the far west of the county, actually in a curiously shaped salient into
Cambridgeshire, lies the town of Newmarket, surrounded by gleaming stud-farms
behind high hedges and walls. As befits the home of the Jockey Club, Newmarket is
staunchly Tory. To the south-west lies a bloc taken not from Bury St Edmunds but
from Suffolk South, to reduce the inflated electorate of that seat. This is also mainly
rural, but does include the town of Haverhill which doubled in size due to the
construction of council estates for London overspill in the 1950s and 1960s. This is
the only concentration of Labour votes in Suffolk West.

In 2001 Labour slipped back from their peak four years before, when they fell only 1,867 votes short of taking this seat. The Tories held their vote; Labour lost just over 2,000, probably because of a very poor turnout of under 60%. They lost every county electoral division within the Forest Heath division in the Suffolk elections which took place on the same day, although they came close in Mildenhall, but they won both Haverhill wards easily and polled steadily in the rural areas. That they should ever have made the new Suffolk West look like a marginal is an eloquent testament to the truly broad appeal of Tony Blair and New Labour.

Social indices:			2001 Gen. Election:			
% Non-white	3.9		C	20,201	47.6	+6.7
% Prof/Man	25.3		Lab	15,906	37.5	+0.4
% Non-manual	44.0		LD	5,017	11.8	−2.2
£ Av prop val 2000	91 K		UKIP	1,321	3.1	
% Increase 97–00	43.7		C maj	4,295	10.1	
% Unemployed 2001	1.1		Turnout		59.6	−11.9
% Decrease 97–01	1.3		Elect	71,220		
% Fin hard/Rank	14.6	360				
% Pensioners	22.7					
% Prem mort/Rank	14	547				

Member of Parliament

Richard Spring narrowly won here in 1997, having held Bury St Edmunds previously for five years. A former stockbroker, who married into the Suffolk landowning aristocracy, he was born in South Africa in 1946 and educated at Rondesbosch School, Capetown, Capetown University and Magdalene College, Cambridge. After voting in 1997 for Lilley and then Hague, he reached the frontbench as a Culture spokesman in 1998, switching to Foreign Affairs in 2000 despite his still-recalled tabloid exposure in 1995 for a three-in-a-bed incident during which he allegedly made indiscreet remarks about the physical attributes of Norma Major and Michael Portillo, which cost him his job as PPS to Sir Patrick Mayhew. Self-dubbed a 'centre-right-wing Tory', he has campaigned against drug abuse and the treble-counting of Labour government spending plans, and for tax breaks for his local racing industry. In 2001 he voted for the narrowly-defeated Portillo option, but retained his Foreign Office spokesmanship under Iain Duncan Smith.

SUNDERLAND NORTH

Wearside is one of the most depressed industrial areas in Britain, with male unemployment rates in both Sunderland constituencies within the top 50 in England in June 2001, and particularly severe amongst the young. Sunderland's economy was heavily based on the now-defunct Durham coalfield, for which it was the major port, and on shipbuilding – in the nineteenth century Sunderland claimed to be the world's largest shipbuilding town. All this is gone now. A wide range of newer employers have been attracted to Wearside – among those that come to mind are Nissan, Rolls-Royce, Corning (Pyrex), Nike, Dewhirst, Vaux, Grove-Coles and Philips – this has not compensated fully for the decline of the traditional base. Sunderland is now very much a Labour town.

There are still Tory wards in Sunderland North, along the coast north of the town centre: Fulwell, which includes Seaburn, and St Peter's, which includes Roker. This is the resort of Sunderland, with a new multi-million pound leisure complex at Seaburn and some serviceable beaches. But this littoral strip is easily outvoted by the town's central terraces and by the massive council estate developments inland, at Castletown, Hylton Castle, Southwick and Town End Farm. This north-western corner of Sunderland is one of the most extensive tracts of solidly working-class residential development in England, and is overwhelmingly Labour in its preferences.

Rather overshadowed by its neighbour to the South, which was the first to declare on election night 1997, North produced an almost identical swing and result – and it too spelt disaster for the Conservatives, and a change of government after 18 years. In 2001 the Sunderland seats were again among the very first to declare, but this time the story they told was of a dramatically reduced turnout, particularly among traditional Labour voters – just 49% here, down 10% on four years before. This was not just because the result both locally and nationally was a foregone conclusion, although that played a large part, but because of a deeper and more serious failure to connect the democratic act of voting with issues relevant to the ordinary people of Sunderland – and of the rest of Britain.

Social indices:			2001 Gen. Election:				
% Non-white	1.0		Lab	18,685	62.7	−5.6	
% Prof/Man	22.0		C	5,331	17.9	+1.2	
% Non-manual	46.7		LD	3,599	12.1	+1.7	
£ Av prop val 2000	48 K		Ind	1,518	5.1		
% Increase 97–00	13.9		BNP	687	2.3		
% Unemployed 2001	6.3		Lab maj	13,354	44.8		
% Decrease 97–01	2.5		Turnout		49.0	−10.0	
% Fin hard/Rank	36.1	81	Elect	60,846			
% Pensioners	26.7						
% Prem mort/Rank	46	84					

Member of Parliament

Bill Etherington, elected in 1992, is one of the dwindling band of former miners or NUM-sponsored MPs, by 2001 reduced to 11. Born in 1941 and regionally-accented, he was educated at Monkwearmouth Grammar School and extra-murally at Durham University, and was a fitter at Dawson Colliery for 20 years. A lesser member of the hard-left Campaign Group, he turns up for most of the rebellions against the government, notably lone parent benefit cuts, student grants, criminal justice, the Prime Minister's power to nominate life peers, Incapacity Benefit cuts, and jury trial curbs – but not regularly enough to figure in the top 25 most rebellious Labour MPs in the 1997–2001 House, nearly all Campaign Groupers.

SUNDERLAND SOUTH

It took just 46 minutes from the closure of the polls on the first of May 1997, to the beginning of the Returning Officer's declaration of the result in Sunderland South – as far as we know, an all-time record. The swing of over 10% to Labour confirmed the media exit polls, and signalled the commencement of the avalanche of ill-fortune which buried John Major's Tory government.

It has become a matter of pride for Sunderland South to be the first constituency to declare, and it happened again in 2001, but this time the massive national Labour victory was expected, although not on a turnout of less than 60% (less than 50% in this seat). This led to a reduction in Chris Mullin's majority to under 14,000, as the abstentionism was at its greatest among working-class Labour supporters, unenthused by the government's first term – and by all positive alternatives placed before them – and not motivated by the prospect of a close result.

Sunderland is a great North Eastern Labour stronghold, suffering still from the decline of its staple industries of coal and shipbuilding. Yet there was a time (1953–64) when its South division was held by the Conservatives, although always narrowly. It is true that there was a substantial middle-class residential area here, south-west of the town centre. However, Tyne and Wear has been moving surely towards Labour for many years, and in 1983 the Tory bloc was to some extent broken up by the Boundary Commissioners; only St Michael's and Hendon wards remain in their hands now, the latter marginally.

South is now every bit as safe for Labour as North. It too has its massive council estates inland, at Thorney Close and Pennywell and Grindon and now at South Hylton, transferred in the most recent boundary changes from North. The line between the two Sunderland constituencies does not in general follow the Wear, for North encroaches to its south in most of the town but, with the acquisition of South Hylton, Sunderland South does now reach at least a stretch of the river on which the town stands. At the southern end of the seat the old mining village of Ryhope has been lost, moved into Houghton and Washington East; there is still a former colliery community in South at Silksworth, and the change makes very little net difference. Sunderland South is no longer a marginal, and is unlikely to be so again even should prosperity return to Wearside.

Social indices:			2001 Gen. Election:			
% Non-white	1.5		Lab	19,921	63.9	−4.2
% Prof/Man	28.2		C	6,254	20.1	+1.2
% Non-manual	52.3		LD	3,675	11.8	+0.2
£ Av prop val 2000	54 K		BNP	576	1.8	
% Increase 97–00	11.6		UKIP	470	1.5	−0.0
% Unemployed 2001	7.1		MRLP	291	0.9	
% Decrease 97–01	3.5		Lab maj	13,667	43.8	
% Fin hard/Rank	34.9	95	Turnout		48.3	−10.5
% Pensioners	25.9		Elect	64,577		
% Prem mort/Rank	43	115				

Member of Parliament

Chris Mullin, elected here in 1987, is a sometime Bennite factionalist latterly transformed into a Blairite minister before a chosen reversion to the backbenches and a clearer conscience in 2001. As the only Campaign Group member to vote for Blair as leader in 1994 he was eventually rewarded in 1999 with a junior job as an Environment Minister with responsibility for defending the partial privatisation of air traffic control in the face of repeated backbench revolts, but from which embarrassment he was rescued early in 2001 by consignment to the obscurity of a post at International Development. All this was some way on from his identity as a campaigner against miscarriages of justice involving Irish Republicans, and his authorship of the radical activists' manual, *How to Select and Reselect Your MP*, which was devised to push 30 right-wing Labour MPs out of the Party, in order to be replaced by people like him. During the Blair government's first term he organised a revolt against the predatory pricing of Murdoch's newspapers, but otherwise repaid the confidence of the Whips in his chairmanship of the Home Affairs Select Committee (1997–99 and from 2001). Tall, lean and ascetic, of donnish aspect, with a Vietnamese wife, he was born of half-Irish parentage in 1947, and educated privately at St Joseph's (RC) College, Ipswich and at Hull University, where he read the *Daily Telegraph*.

SURREY EAST

As the name implies, this is the easternmost section of the county, up against the Kent border. It includes the small towns of Caterham and Warlingham, in their folded valleys not too far from the edge of Greater London in the form of the borough of Croydon. Further out are to be found Oxted and Lingfield, and a number of affluent villages like Godstow on the A25. The order of the parties varies little whichever part of the seat one analyses: Labour third, Liberal Democrat second, Conservative first and foremost.

In 1997, after the addition of Horley, next to Gatwick Airport, with its additional 14,700 voters, despite a drop in his share of the vote of 10%, Peter Ainsworth was able to retain Surrey East with a majority of over 15,000 – the third largest of any Conservative seat, just behind one at the other end of the county, Surrey Heath. In 2001 both of these seats slipped down that list a little, due to a slight increase in the Liberal Democrat share and a bigger decrease in turnout, but this is an even more affluent county than ever. In 2001 unemployment in Surrey East was 0.6%, the 654th highest – that is sixth lowest – in the United Kingdom (the two lowest of all, Mole Valley and Surrey Heath, are also in the county). Average property prices in 2000 were £171,000, up 50% since 1997, the year of the last general election. Rich and getting richer, it is scarcely surprising that Surrey's east end resembles that of London very little socially or politically: here we are likely to continue to see predominant Conservatism with a substantial touch of Liberal Democracy.

Social indices:			2001 Gen. Election:			
% Non-white	2.0		C	24,706	52.5	+2.4
% Prof/Man	42.1		LD	11,503	24.4	+2.0
% Non-manual	67.9		Lab	8,994	19.1	−2.1
£ Av prop val 2000	171 K		UKIP	1,846	3.9	+2.9
% Increase 97–00	50.2		C maj	13,203	28.1	
% Unemployed 2001	0.6		Turnout		62.7	−12.3
% Decrease 97–01	1.2		Elect	75,049		
% Fin hard/Rank	3.5	633				
% Pensioners	25.1					
% Prem mort/Rank	15	540				

Member of Parliament

Peter Ainsworth, shadowing DEFRA – the new Environment and Farming ministry – from 2001, was elected in 1992. With handsome good looks honed in central casting, and the smooth manner of a merchant banker (Warburgs), he was born in 1956, educated at Bradfield and Lincoln College,, Oxford and, with the M23 ploughed straight through his constituency, is understandably worried about the environment which he sought to protect in his bill defending hedgerows from agri-business interests. A former Wandsworth councillor (1986–94), he cuts a more centrist dash than the deregulatory privatisers typical of that genre. A Tory Whip from 1996, he backed Hague in 1997, shadowed Culture, Media and Sport from 1998, and voted adventurously for Portillo in 2001.

SURREY HEATH

There is indeed heathland in the north-western corner of Surrey; one passes through it as one leaves London on the M3 motorway, soldiers exercise on it near Chobham and Bisley, and in places one can forget that this is actually in the heart of the Home Counties. In fact, though, this constituency is thoroughly urban, or at least suburban, as far as its electorate is concerned. The seat is based on the communities of Camberley and Frimley, with ballast provided by smaller places such as Bagshot and Windlesham, site of some of the most expensive houses in the country, the property of such as Arab sheikhs. This sandy-soiled territory is very heavily owner-occupied, middle class, white, highly affluent and materialistic (more than half the households have at least two cars). There is a strong military presence. There is functionally no unemployment (the second lowest rate in the whole of the UK in the June 2001 figures by constituency). All this adds up to a perfect recipe for conservatism, and Conservatism. Yet it is not quite so monolithic as may be thought.

In 2001 Nick Hawkins's majority was actually reduced by over 5,000, partly because of a very low turnout of under 60%, 15% down on 1997, but also he narrowly failed to obtain an absolute majority of the votes cast as the Liberal Democrats improved to over a quarter of the vote. This was still less than the 32% obtained in the May 1999 local elections, which gave them seven seats on Surrey Heath council, in Bagshot, Mytchett and Frimley Green; Labour also managed over a fifth of the vote and returned seven councillors, in the more working-class parts of Camberley like Old Dean. Surrey Heath might always be Conservative, but it is not all Conservative.

Social indices:			2001 Gen. Election:			
% Non-white	2.4		C	22,401	49.7	−1.9
% Prof/Man	43.0		LD	11,582	25.7	+3.9
% Non-manual	67.6		Lab	9,640	21.4	+0.3
£ Av prop val 2000	185 K		UKIP	1,479	3.3	+2.1
% Increase 97–00	54.6		C maj	10,819	24.0	
% Unemployed 2001	0.5		Turnout		59.5	−14.7
% Decrease 97–01	0.6		Elect	75,858		
% Fin hard/Rank	2.7	640				
% Pensioners	18.4					
% Prem mort/Rank	7	616				

Member of Parliament

Nick Hawkins, an International Development spokesman from 2001, was the most accomplished chicken-runner in 1997 when he migrated from one of the Conservatives' most marginal seats (Blackpool South) to this, their second safest seat that year. A barrister-turned-corporate-legal-adviser, blessed with nonpatrican features and a blunt, partisan manner, born in 1957, son of a research physicist, and educated at Bedford Modern School and Lincoln College,, Oxford, he was first elected in 1992. He wobbled against pit closures under the Major government, but was otherwise loyalist on Maastricht and keen on rail privatisation. A Hague supporter in 1997, he joined the frontbench in 1999 first as a Legal Affairs, and then Home Affairs, spokesman. His high volume, pugnacious call for the party-fund- raising Lord Chancellor's scalp in March 2001 was dismissively wafted away by Labour minister David Lock (who was himself to be wafted away at the General Election). He backed the most adventurous, Portillo, option in the 2001 leadership ballots.

SURREY SOUTH WEST

Outer Surrey, towards the Sussex and Hampshire borders, contains some of the most pleasant countryside and residential areas in southern England. The three main towns within the Surrey South West constituency are Godalming, Haslemere and Farnham, after which a very similar seat was named before the 1983 boundary changes. Here too are to be found a number of villages, and landmarks like the Devil's Punchbowl near Hindhead; the countryside is rather sandy, and there is heathland punctuated by the occasional unexpected feature such as the large ponds at Frensham. This is not close-in London commuting territory, although only a small proportion of workers are employed in agriculture. It is a 'rural Home Counties' seat, but one with an exceptionally vulnerable Conservative MP.

The Liberal Democrats remain very active and successful in local politics (the relevant borough council is named Waverley where the Lib Dems returned 24 councillors to the Conservatives' 31 in 1999), and have now thrice pressed Virginia Bottomley close in Surrey South West: once in her initial contest, the by-election in 1984 caused by the death of Harold Macmillan's son Maurice, again in 1997 when this seat recorded the closest result in Surrey, and in 2001 when they did best yet, reducing the Tory majority to three figures – although this was no longer their best performance as they actually won Guildford. They will undoubtedly be pressing hard to make it two in Surrey next time.

Social indices:			2001 Gen. Election:			
% Non-white	1.3		C	22,462	45.3	+0.7
% Prof/Man	46.1		LD	21,601	43.6	+3.8
% Non-manual	67.6		Lab	4,321	8.7	−0.7
£ Av prop val 2000	205 K		UKIP	1,208	2.4	+1.7
% Increase 97–00	57.2		C maj	861	1.7	
% Unemployed 2001	0.7		Turnout		66.9	−11.1
% Decrease 97–01	0.8		Elect	74,127		
% Fin hard/Rank	4.4	620				
% Pensioners	27.7					
% Prem mort/Rank	8	612				

Member of Parliament

Virginia Bottomley, faded pearl of the Surrey hills, was first elected here in 1984 following the death of Viscount Macmillan, son of Harold. Born in 1948 into the high-minded public-serving upper-middle-class elite that produced her uncle, Douglas Jay, her cousin Peter, and her father John Garnett, ex-Director of the Industrial Society, she attended Putney High School for Girls and Essex University and worked as a psychiatric social worker. A tall, blonde, lisping English rose variously likened to a young Barbara Woodhouse, an Angela Brazil heroine and Mary Poppins on crack, her exposed statistics-sodden defensive performance as Health Secretary towards the fag-end of the Major government was deemed sufficiently voter-hostile for her to be relegated to the margins as National Heritage Secretary, and thence ('voluntarily' according to Hague) to the backbenches after voting for Kenneth Clarke for leader in 1997. Her leadership preferences in 2001 were not readily disclosed, whereas those of her husband Peter – an Ancram supporter – were. In 2002 she announced her intention to resign.

SUSSEX MID

Although it looks as if it covers a fairly substantial area on the map, a good three-quarters of the electorate of the Mid Sussex constituency is concentrated in just four towns. These are the old market towns of East Grinstead and Cuckfield, and the newer residential developments at Haywards Heath and Burgess Hill, which owe their existence to commuting facilitated by the main London to Brighton railway: the morning rush-hour train is scheduled to take 44 minutes from Haywards Heath to London Victoria, and 50 minutes from Burgess Hill.

The political balance of the Mid Sussex division is very Conservative. The electorate is affluent and middle class in the main, and the percentage unemployed is among the lowest in Britain, just 0.7% in June 2001. There are no substantial ethnic minority communities. There is an extraordinarily low proportion of council housing, less than 5% across the seat as a whole back in the 1991 Census, one of the lowest figures in England, and probably even lower now given the changes in tenure arrangements over the last decade or so. It exceeded 10% only in one ward, Haywards Heath Bentswood, which happens to be the only ward that Labour wins easily. The Liberal Democrats were the leaders in Burgess Hill and East Grinstead in the West Sussex county elections which took place on the same day as the 2001 General Election, but the Conservatives stormed back in the villages, and despite a substantial drop of 13% in the turnout Nicholas Soames held on by nearly 7,000.

Social indices:			2001 Gen. Election:			
% Non-white	1.5		C	21,150	46.2	+2.7
% Prof/Man	43.6		LD	14,252	31.1	+0.5
% Non-manual	69.2		Lab	8,693	19.0	+0.3
£ Av prop val 2000	154 K		UKIP	1,126	2.5	+1.3
% Increase 97–00	59.5		MRLP	601	1.3	
% Unemployed 2001	0.7		C maj	6,898	15.1	
% Decrease 97–01	0.8		Turnout		64.9	−12.9
% Fin hard/Rank	3.9	628	Elect	70,632		
% Pensioners	24.3					
% Prem mort/Rank	8	615				

Member of Parliament

Nicholas Soames, a former Defence (1994–97) and Agriculture (1992–94) Minister, has been an MP since 1983, first as Jorrocks-among-the-Gatwick-baggage-handlers as member for Crawley, and since 1997 as member for the more up-market but commuter-strewn Mid Sussex seat. He weighs in at 18 stone-reduced-to-16, six foot three inches, as a loud Bunteresque food mountain. Born in 1948, educated at Eton, but then, with seven 'O' levels, at Mons Officer Cadet School (rather than Sandhurst), he is the last remnant, and that in the female line, of the great Spencer-Churchill dynasty which gave the House his grandfather, Sir Winston, his uncle Randolph, and his now-departed cousin, Winston, and is the only MP each generation of whose family has sat in the House of Commons since the eighteenth century. Out of time and out of place, he was out of synch with William Hague on Europe, and on the 'balls-aching nonsense' of McKinseyite management clap-trap, such as MP-bonding sessions at Eastbourne. Elevating snobbery to a fine art, he has shouted requests to ex-ship's steward John Prescott for a gin and tonic, dismissed ex-MP Tim Sainsbury as his grocer, and told Dennis Skinner to get in some gulls eggs and his wife out of curlers in case he called in while shooting in Derbyshire. He shot his first stag at 14, compared his baby daughter to a 'fair-sized salmon', and was given a colouring book for his 40th birthday. By 2001 there were only 13 other Old Etonian Tory MPs, with his only scaled-down rival amongst them in these stakes the somewhat ersatz Boris Johnson. A One Nation Europhile Clarke voter in 1997, he opted for the more ritzy Portillo candidacy in 2001 and refused a job as a Defence spokesman.

SUTTON AND CHEAM

The Liberal Democrats (and their linear predecessors) have now won Sutton and Cheam in two different periods. The first was short lived, following a by-election in one of their periods of short-term success (1972) which flattered only to please – it was lost at the next general election (February 1974) and the Liberals, as they then were, failed to make a permanent or major breakthrough winning only 14 seats throughout the country. The latest success is current and looks more long-lasting and large-scale. Paul Burstow has now won Sutton and Cheam in two general elections, in which the Liberal Democrats have successively taken 46 and 52 seats: a much more tangible achievement. It is a fulfilling time to be a Lib Dem.

They took a linked group of five Tory seats in outer south-west London in 1997, ousting Lady Olga Maitland here by 2,000 votes, but this was the only one they had ever held before, albeit very briefly. Sutton and Cheam has a place in the annals of by-election history – but not a very prominent one. It was one of the clutch of victories that constituted the Liberal false dawn of the early 1970s. Some of those triumphs were repeated as seats were held in subsequent general elections – Rochdale in six of them, for example. But that other gain in 1972, Graham Tope's in South London suburbia, was reversed scarcely over a year later, in February 1974.

Graham (now Lord) Tope is still a member of a phenomenally successful (electorally speaking) Liberal Democrat local council in the borough of Sutton. However, he never really looked like getting back into the Commons, and passed the mantle on to other candidates. In 1992 Paul Burstow, a local councillor for Rosehill ward, could not get within 10,000 votes of Lady Olga, but in the very different national circumstances five years later the positions were reversed, and like his four colleagues in the neighbouring boroughs of Richmond and Kingston he increased his majority in 2001, disappointing Lady Olga again. He is set for a much longer tenure as MP than Graham Tope enjoyed.

Social indices:			2001 Gen. Election:			
% Non-white	6.2		LD	19,382	48.8	+6.5
% Prof/Man	42.1		C	15,078	38.0	+0.1
% Non-manual	71.2		Lab	5,263	13.2	−2.2
£ Av prop val 2000	140 K		LD maj	4,304	10.8	
% Increase 97–00	56.8		Turnout		62.4	−12.6
% Unemployed 2001	1.3		Elect	63,648		
% Decrease 97–01	1.5					
% Fin hard/Rank	7.3	550				
% Pensioners	25.5					
% Prem mort/Rank	18	499				

Member of Parliament

Paul Burstow, Liberal Democrat apparatchik and victor here in 1997, is a tall, small-nosed bespectacled successor to the similarly featured Graham Tope who won the seat for the Liberals in 1972. Local-boy-made-good in the manner of many Liberals, he was born in 1962, educated locally at Glastonbury High School and Carshalton College of Further Education and at South Bank Polytechnic, and served on Sutton Council for ten years and worked as a party staffer on local council campaigning. Classlessly-accented and fluent, a Social Services spokesman since 1999 on the old, he cuts a competent dash in the House, and in 2001 effortlessly doubled his majority in a re-run against the Serbo-Scottish aristocrat, Lady Olga Maitland, who had obeyed Central Office instructions and stayed to fight again in her old infantry trench rather than chicken-run elsewhere.

SUTTON COLDFIELD

The former Conservative Party chairman Sir Norman Fowler was often amused to disparage the BBC's ludicrous projections of by-election swings into seats in the House of Commons by quoting the one which left him as the only Tory MP in Parliament. This indicates just how safe Sutton Coldfield is, his seat from 1974 for 27 years, although in 2001 it recorded not the greatest but the 28th highest percentage majority of any Conservative seat. This drop was possibly a result of Sir Norman's decision to leave Parliament, presumably to spend more time with his family, and perhaps with his directorships, but it might be pointed out that there was a small but noticeable swing to Labour in the other super-safe Conservative suburban seat in Greater Birmingham too, Solihull.

Sutton Coldfield is an ultra-middle-class suburb of Birmingham, taken into that city's boundaries in the local government reforms of 1974. There its three wards, New Hall, Vesey and Four Oaks, form an anomalous solid true-blue phalanx even in a time of Conservative unpopularity. There is virtually no council-built housing, and 97% of its inhabitants are white. Three-quarters of employees who live in Sutton Coldfield work in non-manual occupations, mostly in a professional and managerial capacity. The constituency is set in leafy surroundings around Sutton Park, which is so large that it gives a pleasant semi-rural ambience. Four Oaks Park in particular harbours stately mansions in their own grounds. The strength and depth of this seat's Conservatism can be fully explained. Sutton Coldfield is the goal of many aspiring West Midlanders, and offers the material ultimate in what has been accused of being an over-materialist part of Britain.

Social indices:			2001 Gen. Election:				
% Non-white	3.0		C	21,909	50.4	−1.8	
% Prof/Man	45.8		Lab	11,805	27.2	+3.3	
% Non-manual	73.0		LD	8,268	19.0	−0.3	
£ Av prop val 2000	123 K		UKIP	1,186	2.7		
% Increase 97–00	35.1		Ind	284	0.7		
% Unemployed 2001	2.2		C maj	10,104	23.3		
% Decrease 97–01	0.7		Turnout		60.5	−12.5	
% Fin hard/Rank	6.2	580	Elect	71,856			
% Pensioners	25.9						
% Prem mort/Rank	9	607					

Member of Parliament

Andrew Mitchell, a merchant banker with Lazards, one of seven former Conservative MPs who returned in 2001, was previously (1987–97) MP for Gedling. Son of Sir David Mitchell, MP (1964–97) and a descendant of other eighteenth-century MPs, he was born in 1956, and educated at Rugby, Sandhurst and Jesus

College, Cambridge and worked first in his family's wine-importing business (El Vino's) before moving to merchant banking. Swiftly rising by 1988 as PPS to William Waldegrave and John Wakeham, he was a Whip by 1992 and a junior Social Security Minister by 1995. He made headlines as the first Tory Whip on the Members' Interests' Committee, opposed by a sit-in by Labour MP Dale Campbell-Savours protesting against Mitchell's mobilising of the Committee's Conservative majority in favour of avoiding a full enquiry into sleaze allegations against Neil Hamilton – a dispute defused by his move from the Committee to a ministerial post. Smooth and 'almost crazy with ambition' (Gyles Brandreth), he nonetheless trimmed in the wrong direction in 2001, moving from backing the eliminated Eurosceptic David Davies to voting for Kenneth Clarke. Thence to the obscurity of the Work and Pensions Select Committee.

SWANSEA EAST

Swansea is the second city of Wales, boasting a population of over 180,000, and possessing two full parliamentary seats. It is the economic and commercial centre for a major portion of west Wales, and an industrial powerhouse in its own right. It has also for four decades now been a Labour stronghold, returning two Labour MPs at each general election since 1964.

The north and east sides of Swansea form the city's working-class and industrial heartland. Here are the docks, the steel, tinplate and copper works, and most of the social housing – concentrated in solidly Labour wards like Morriston and Llansamlet and Penderry. In boundary changes in 1983 East lost its share of the city centre, and its borders have not been altered in more recent reviews. In 1997 Labour's Donald Anderson increased his already substantial majority over the Conservatives to a massive 25,569. There is not a single Tory ward within East's boundaries on Swansea City Council, and indeed they did not contest several wards in the 1999 unitary authority elections. Effectively Swansea East sees unopposed Labour returns in general elections too; the Conservative, Liberal and Plaid Cymru challenges can only be regarded as purely nominal, each securing a fraction over one-tenth of the vote in 2001, although Anderson's numerical majority was reduced by over 9,000 due to a drop in turnout from 67% to a wretched 52%.

Social indices:			2001 Gen. Election:			
% Non-white	1.1		Lab	19,612	65.2	−10.2
% Welsh sp	10.5		PC	3,464	11.5	+8.1
% Prof/Man	21.6		LD	3,064	10.2	+1.3
% Non-manual	46.6		C	3,026	10.1	+0.8
£ Av prop val 2000	44 K		Grn	463	1.5	
% Increase 97–00	14.1		UKIP	443	1.5	
% Unemployed 2001	4.8		Lab maj	16,148	53.7	
% Decrease 97–01	1.8		Turnout		52.5	−14.9
% Fin hard/Rank	23.6	219	Elect	57,273		
% Pensioners	24.7					
% Prem mort/Rank	42	149				

Member of Parliament

Donald Anderson, a tall, bald and arthritic, earnest *eminence grise* as Chairman of the Foreign Affairs Select Committee, who, courtesy of a large backbench revolt, survived the Whips' attempt to drop him from the post in 2001 in order to find a job for the sacked Cabinet Minister, Chris Smith, was first elected for Monmouth (1966–70) and for this seat in 1974. A non-practising barrister, born in 1939, son of a fitter, educated at Swansea Grammar School, Swansea University and the Inner Temple, he was initially a diplomat. Formerly for nine years an Opposition spokesman on Foreign or Legal Affairs, until discarded by Blair in 1995, he brings to questions such as pornography, drink and Sunday trading a steely Methodist eye, and is a former voter against lowering the homosexual age of consent, reduced in recent votes to mere abstention. In March 2001 he disapproved of former Labour MP Leo Abse's posthumous 'outing' of the late Viscount Tonypandy, ex-Speaker George Thomas, whose fumblings in Soho cinemas had been gratuitously recounted by the amateur psychoanalyst.

SWANSEA WEST

Swansea has been known as a great industrial centre at the mouth of the Tawe since the eighteenth century. But it also has its leafy suburbs, its university college, and a fine new city centre rebuilt after the extensive bomb destruction of 1941. All these are in Swansea West, which was also historically the city's marginal seat – at least until 1983, when boundary changes moved the Conservative seaside resort of Mumbles into the Gower constituency, which has subsequently and consequently become the more vulnerable seat.

There are however still several middle-class and potentially Conservative-inclined wards within Swansea West. These include the affluent suburb of Sketty; the Mayals ward out towards the Mumbles; and further in towards the centre, Uplands, which has an intellectual ambience due to university influence and contains the birthplace of Dylan Thomas (and later residence of Kingsley Amis) on Cwmdonkin Drive. These areas are outvoted, though, by Labour wards like Cockett, Townhill with its 70% share of council tenants, and the city's central neighbourhoods. Killay was solidly Liberal Democrat in the May 1999 Swansea unitary authority elections and indeed in the June 2001 General Election both the Lib Dems and Plaid Cymru made modest advances in third and fourth places while Labour and the Conservatives fell back. With a drop in vote share of over 7%, taking him back to less than half, and with fewer votes cast altogther, the veteran Alan Williams, second most senior of all MPs in length of tenure, saw his majority slip back into four figures.

Social indices:			2001 Gen. Election:			
% Non-white	3.1		Lab	15,644	48.7	−7.5
% Welsh sp	9.2		C	6,094	19.0	−1.5
% Prof/Man	36.6		LD	5,313	16.6	+2.0
% Non-manual	59.3		PC	3,404	10.6	+4.0
£ Av prop val 2000	65 K		UKIP	653	2.0	
% Increase 97–00	24.1		Grn	626	2.0	
% Unemployed 2001	5.3		SA	366	1.1	
% Decrease 97–01	2.1		Lab maj	9,550	29.8	
% Fin hard/Rank	22.2	239	Turnout		56.2	−12.7
% Pensioners	30.1		Elect	57,074		
% Prem mort/Rank	36	227				

Member of Parliament

Alan Williams, elected in 1964, is the last survivor of Labour's election-winning intake of that year, when he won the seat back from the Conservatives, and is now the second longest continuously serving MP. He is the only member of Harold Wilson's 1964–70 government remaining in the Commons, having served as a Junior Minister for Economic Affairs (1967–69) and for Technology (1964–70). A Junior Minister again under Wilson and Callaghan between 1974 and 1979, and Opposition spokesman under Wilson, Foot and Kinnock, he joined the Public Accounts Committee in 1989 and remained thereafter to build a reputation notably as a critic of Royal Household expenditure. A miner's son, he was born in 1930, educated at Cardiff High School, Cardiff College of Technology and University College, Oxford, and was a lecturer in economics at the Welsh College of Advanced Technology before becoming an MP. Out of step with Blairite orthodoxy on Europe and devolution, he is seen by ageist younger Welsh Labour MPs as part of the 'Alzheimer's Tendency' along with MPs Ted Rowlands, who retired in 2001, and Denzil Davies. Sardonically he has noted that four of the departments in which he served were subsequently abolished.

SWINDON NORTH

There is considerable economic growth creating wealth and jobs along the M4 west of London, in towns such as Reading and Swindon, which probably accounts for the further swings to Labour both recorded in the 2001 General Election, and also for continued housing and population growth, all of which has made Swindon the closest to a boom town in Britain around the turn of the century.

Even by the 1992 Election, it was clear that there would have to be major boundary changes in the Swindon area in north-east Wiltshire. The seat of Swindon itself had 90,000 electors, over 20,000 in excess of the average in England. What is more, a considerable part of the built-up area of 'Greater Swindon', in the Thamesdown District, was excluded from the Swindon constituency and placed in with more rural terrain in Devizes, which had also reached the 90,000 mark. In fact, Wiltshire was entitled to more than six seats, when it still had only five. It is arguable that it is Swindon North that is the extra seat awarded by the Boundary Commission. (Actually they called it North Swindon, as it is technically a county not a borough seat, but everyone will ignore that.)

Swindon North takes in most of the wards of the former Swindon seat north of a line roughly drawn along the railway track, together with the northern wards of Thamesdown formerly in Devizes: (Stratton) St Margaret, St Philip, Highworth, Blunsdon, and Covingham. Some of these are still fairly rural and independent, but mostly they are part of Swindon's built-up area and great post-war growth. The small town of Cricklade was also taken from the North Wiltshire division. Although this territory was all in safe Conservative hands before the boundary changes, it is by no means hopeless for Labour, who win Highworth, Covingham and St Philip in local elections. What is more, the northern half of the old marginal Swindon seat was undoubtedly the better for Labour, with strongholds like Gorse Hill and Moredon, and the majority council housing ward of Whitworth. Overall, Swindon North, although annexing the more rural territory of the two new Swindon seats, formed their better chance of a gain.

As it happened, Labour won both Swindon seats fairly easily in the 1997 landslide, but North will be slightly the harder for the Conservatives to 'regain', although this seems an unlikely prospect after 2001, when Michael Wills increased his majority to over 8,000; and the continuing growth in population will give Wiltshire yet another seat in the election after next, when the extraneous territory outside the Thamesdown unitary authority, such as the anomalous Cricklade, will be removed.

Social indices:			2001 Gen. Election:			
% Non-white	1.9		Lab	22,371	52.9	+3.1
% Prof/Man	27.9		C	14,266	33.7	−0.1
% Non-manual	53.7		LD	4,891	11.6	−1.4
£ Av prop val 2000	101 K		UKIP	800	1.9	
% Increase 97–00	58.7		Lab maj	8,105	19.1	
% Unemployed 2001	1.7		Turnout		61.0	−12.6
% Decrease 97–01	1.0		Elect	69,335		
% Fin hard/Rank	15.5	345				
% Pensioners	22.5					
% Prem mort/Rank	22	452				

Member of Parliament

Michael Wills was only the third of the 183-strong Labour intake of 1997 to be given a job – as Junior Minister at the DTI (1999), Education (1999–2001) and in the Lord Chancellor's department (from 2001). He had been elected after an acrimonious selection contest in which he as a metropolitan Blairite was pitted against the local AEEU convenor Jim D'Avila, and which, with other defeats for its nominated candidates elsewhere, led to AEEU withdrawal of funds from Labour. A quiet, tall, smooth and beaky former diplomat (for four years) and television producer (at LWT for 17 years with Peter Mandelson on his staff), he was born in 1952 and educated at public school (Haberdashers' Aske's) and Cambridge (Clare College). Appointed in 1998 by Chancellor Brown as a former adviser, to proselytise on behalf of a single European currency, and backing Brown's view of Britain as 'the first multicultural, multinational state', he was in 2000, as Education Minister for IT, given added ministerial responsibility – as someone of Austrian Jewish and New Zealand Irish Catholic parentage – for 'patriotism' and 'national identity'.

SWINDON SOUTH

Swindon presents an anomaly in the social and political geography of southern England. Set in the heart of a group of shires which are true-blue in parliamentary terms, with a strong centrist presence in municipal politics, it is a town which more often than not returned a Labour MP in the years from 1945 to 1997, when it was split into two constituencies; and although the single Swindon was narrowly gained by the Conservatives in 1983, both Swindon North and South are now quite strongly Labour, and getting more so, and a rare and growing outpost in its predominantly rural environment. What accounts for its presence in Wiltshire?

The answer takes us back to the arrival of the Great Western Railway in 1835, followed shortly by one of the largest locomotive works in the world. Swindon had become an industrial town. It has always since remained one of Britain's great railway junctions. But its industrial character has been reinforced by modern developments following the 1952 Town Development Act, which brought Plessey, Burmah Oil and countless other employers. Swindon is well situated for a boom town, just off the M4 within easy reach of London by road. Along with industrial estates have come housing estates, which has meant that Swindon has expanded outwards in every direction. In the 1980s this growth was concentrated to the south-west in the wards of Toothill and Freshbrook (itself newly created in that decade). The population of the area covered by these two wards increased from 8,000 to 25,000 between 1981 and 1991. It is no wonder that Swindon was granted a second parliamentary seat by the 1995 Boundary Commission.

The Swindon South constituency took in most of the former marginal Swindon division, and added a small amount of territory formerly in Devizes. This is very slightly the more Conservative of the two Swindon prospects now. Not only is the ex-Devizes section fairly rural, rather than suburban, consisting of the village wards of Chiseldon and Ridgeway and the old small town of Wroughton, but the better residential areas of Swindon itself are in the seat: the new owner-occupied housing of Toothill, and the older ward of Lawns, traditionally the best residential area of the town, and the most Conservative. There are also Labour strongholds, such as the council estate ward of Park and Central, where there are old terraces near the town centre and station. More relevantly perhaps, Swindon with its aspects of a 'New Town' having overtaken the old industrial base, seems to have proved an ideal receptor of the appeal of 'New Labour', and after a further increase of nearly 5% in her share in 2001, Julia Drown now had an overall majority of votes cast, as did Michael Wills in North.

Social indices:			2001 Gen. Election:			
% Non-white	4.1		Lab	22,260	51.3	+4.5
% Prof/Man	33.7		C	14,919	34.4	−1.4
% Non-manual	60.1		LD	5,165	11.9	−2.5
£ Av prop val 2000	98 K		UKIP	713	1.6	
% Increase 97–00	57.9		Ind	327	0.8	
% Unemployed 2001	2.2		Lab maj	7,341	16.9	
% Decrease 97–01	1.4		Turnout		61.0	−11.8
% Fin hard/Rank	16.5	326	Elect	71,080		
% Pensioners	20.6					
% Prem mort/Rank	26	402				

Member of Parliament

Julia Drown was elected here in 1997 and promptly placed on the Health Select Committee, having previously worked as a public service accountant in the NHS, most recently at the Radcliffe Infirmary in Oxford. Fluent and déclassé in speech, daughter of a picture restorer and a nurse, and London-born in 1962, she attended Hampstead Comprehensive and University College, Oxford, and as a health service campaigner loyally defends government initiatives such as prescription charge increases below the rate of inflation, even prepared to rebut charges of hospital failings in television audience-participation shouting-matches such as 'Kilroy'. Along with scores of Labour Mps, she makes up for any radical deficit by vigorously opposing fox hunting, declaring it as barbaric as the outlawed practices of bear-baiting, cock-fighting and dog-fighting. One of a handful of the 1997 intake to have a baby since her election, she also sought unsuccessfully to be allowed to breast-feed at will in the Palace of Westminster, leading Tory Gillian Shepherd to wonder about schoolteachers breast-feeding in class or barristers in court.

TAMWORTH

Tamworth was one of the fastest-growing towns in England in the second half of the twentieth century, even though it has never been a designated New Town. It rose from a population of 23,000 in 1951 to 69,000 in 1991, and it now has claimed a constituency name, if not quite a constituency, of its own. The seat is very similar to the old Staffordshire South East which existed from 1983 to 1997; it still needed about 16,000 rural electors to bring its electorate up close to the quota; Tamworth is still not quite big enough to fill up a whole constituency.

The developments in Tamworth have been of both council housing and, more recently, of private estates. Most of the new residents come from the West Midlands conurbation, as the predominant accent testifies. Tamworth now looks very different from its former self, with tower blocks rising immediately above the historic town centre, and burgeoning sprawl in many directions. It was at one time part of the large and marginal Lichfield and Tamworth division, of which Lichfield was considered the more Conservative half. On the split of that seat in 1983, Labour was reckoned to have a good chance in Staffordshire South East, but it was not to be; in that disastrous year David Lightbown won the seat's inaugural contest by nearly 11,000 votes for the Conservatives.

In 1987 he retained almost exactly the same majority, but over the SDP. The highly unusual advance by the SDP into second place occasioned comment at the time, as it fitted neither a local nor a regional pattern. The suggestion that a substantial bloc of votes may have been misplaced at the count (no recount was requested or necessary seeing as the Tories had clearly won) was reinforced by an apparently huge swing from the centre to Labour in 1992 – the Liberal Democrat vote was down from the SDP's reported 27% in 1987 to less than 10%.

Sir David Lightbown died in 1996, and Brian Jenkins won the Staffordshire South East seat on a 22% by-election swing. He repeated this performance in Tamworth in a General Election the next year, this time beating Lady Lightbown, the former member's widow. After 2001, with a lead of 11%, he is in a very similar position to the government. If they should fall, most likely he would too.

Social indices:			2001 Gen. Election:			
% Non-white	1.2		Lab	19,722	49.0	–2.8
% Prof/Man	29.0		C	15,124	37.6	+0.8
% Non-manual	52.2		LD	4,721	11.7	+3.7
£ Av prop val 2000	78 K		UKIP	683	1.7	+1.0
% Increase 97–00	32.8		Lab maj	4,598	11.4	
% Unemployed 2001	2.7		Turnout		57.8	–16.4
% Decrease 97–01	0.8		Elect	69,596		
% Fin hard/Rank	20.1	279				
% Pensioners	18.6					
% Prem mort/Rank	27	383				

Member of Parliament

Brian Jenkins hit the headlines by winning the Staffordshire South East by-election by miles on a 22% swing in 1996, and then sank without trace under the huge Blairite intake of 1997 as an inconspicuous backbencher of impeccably loyalist credentials. The archetypal local (FE) lecturer and councillor, he was born in 1942, son of a miner, and educated at Kingsbury High School, Tamworth and Coventry College, and later in his 30s at Coleg Harlech, the LSE and Wolverhampton Polytechnic, and rose from initial occupations as an instrument mechanic at the CEGB and an engineer at Jaguar Cars. He has campaigned against the Birmingham Northern Relief Road opposed by Labour in Opposition, but sanctioned in office. His role as PPS to Joyce Quin from 1997 ended with her sacking in 2001. A faltering speaker, in November 2001 he fumbled a question about imprisoned British 'train' (meaning 'plane') spotters in Greece.

TATTON

The Cheshire constituency of Tatton, named after a large area of uninhabited land, Tatton Park, which lies at its geographical heart, produced a unique result in the 1997 General Election. The sitting Conservative MP (since 1983), Neil Hamilton, was embattled by allegations of sleaze, of taking cash for questions on behalf of the Harrod's store owner Mohamed Al-Fayed. He was opposed by the BBC war correspondent Martin Bell, standing as an Independent, as the Labour and Liberal Democrat candidates withdrew (although eight minor candidates did not). Bell won a famous victory, ousting Hamilton by 11,000 votes, but he did promise to serve just one term as an Independent, which meant that Tatton did return to conventional party politics next time, in 2001.

The basic political structure of this seat is uniform; and the colour of that uniform is deep, true blue. Here is the prosperous market town of Knutsford (Mrs Gaskell's 'Cranford'). Even more upmarket is Wilmslow, where many ICI managerial workers reside, and a favoured relocation base for corporate headquarters in the North West. Finally there is the exclusive commuting base of Alderley Edge, one of the most desirable and Conservative communities in the north of England. Following the single aberrant term of the would-be dragon-slaying knight in a white suit, Martin Bell, who moved on to a less successful cause and campaign at Brentwood and Ongar in Essex, Tatton's traditional loyalties elected 30-year-old George Osborne, who should have a very long and secure run here, as long as he resists temptations and stays out of mischief.

Social indices:			2001 Gen. Election:			
% Non-white	1.2		C	19,860	48.1	+10.7
% Prof/Man	47.9		Lab	11,249	27.3	
% Non-manual	69.3		LD	7,685	18.6	
£ Av prop val 2000	136 K		UKIP	769	1.9	
% Increase 97–00	33.2		Ind	734	1.8	
% Unemployed 2001	1.3		Ind	505	1.2	
% Decrease 97–01	1.1		Ind	322	0.8	
% Fin hard/Rank	10.4	454	Ind	154	0.4	
% Pensioners	27.0		C maj	8,611	20.9	
% Prem mort/Rank	23	439	Turnout		63.5	−12.9
			Elect	64,954		

Member of Parliament

With the retreat of the Man in the White Suit, Martin Bell, Tory expectations of recapturing one of their safest seats were realised by **George Osborne**. With a patrician air mistaken for that of an Etonian, the son of the 17th baronet Sir Peter Osborne (albeit a wallpaper manufacturer) and son-in-law of Lord (formerly David) Howell (MP 1966–97), he was born in 1971 and educated at St Paul's School, Magdalen College, Oxford, and Davidson College, USA. The complete political apparatchik, he was William Hague's political secretary and speech writer from 1997, coaching him for his Commons exchanges with Tony Blair, and working previously in the Conservative Research Department, as a political adviser at the Ministry of Agriculture and at No.10 under John Major. A Eurosceptic on the socially liberal wing of the party, he voted for Michael Portillo in the July 2001 leadership ballots and joined him on the backbenches. He is the youngest Conservative MP, and in the constituency which effectively accounts for the Tories' net gain of one seat in 2001, from 165 to 166.

TAUNTON

One of only two sitting Liberal Democrat MPs to lose in the June 2001 General Election, Jackie Ballard of Taunton paid in general for her rather abrasive, uncompromising style, and in particular for her strident anti-fox hunting stance in a semi-rural constituency. Clearly the object of a targeted campaign by the Conservatives, she pointed out herself that the turnout was much higher in areas such as Dulverton in Exmoor, where turnout exceeded 70% (we can tell this from Somerset county council election returns from the same day), than in areas of natural support for her, where hunting was of much less relevance, like the working-class estates of Taunton, where it barely surpassed 50%. Given that she lost by only 235 votes, this was clearly a factor. However, it might be pointed out as well that she did not benefit either from further tactical voting by Labour supporters – the Labour share actually increased in 2001. The disappearance of Referendum and BNP candidates who had contested Taunton in 1997 cannot have helped either. Finally, Jackie Ballard would be wrong to take the Liberal Democrat loss entirely personally: in the local council elections of 1999 her Lib Dem colleagues also fell 4% behind their Conservative opponents.

This seat consists of the Taunton Deane borough (where the Liberal Democrats lost overall control in 1999) together with four wards of the West Somerset district, which stretches through the little town of Dulverton on the river Exe across Exmoor to the Devon border. Taunton Deane also includes Wellington (where Jeffrey Archer went to school) as well as the county town itself, which has its share of light industry and council estates, particularly in its eastern wards. Much will depend next time on whether the next Liberal Democrat candidate (after her defeat Jackie Ballard moved to Iran) can persuade the urban voters in Taunton and Wellington to abandon Labour – and also to come out and vote at all.

Social indices:			2001 Gen. Election:			
% Non-white	0.7		C	23,033	41.7	+3.0
% Prof/Man	35.1		LD	22,798	41.3	–1.4
% Non-manual	58.3		Lab	8,254	14.9	+1.4
£ Av prop val 2000	97 K		UKIP	1,140	2.1	
% Increase 97–00	43.9		C maj	235	0.4	
% Unemployed 2001	1.8		Turnout		67.6	–8.8
% Decrease 97–01	2.4		Elect	81,651		
% Fin hard/Rank	10.6	448				
% Pensioners	30.1					
% Prem mort/Rank	23	441				

Member of Parliament

Adrian Flook became one of his party's heroes by being one of only two Conservative candidates in 2001 to wrest seats back from the Liberal Democrats in the Tories' one-time southern heartland. In recapturing Taunton he was assisted by the one-term Liberal Democrat MP, Jackie Ballard, who, against all the normal rules of her party, had confronted rather than balanced local interests, by taking on the pro-hunting lobby, and whilst no enthusiastic supporter of hunting himself, benefited from this abrasive misjudgement. A Bristol wine merchant's son, he was born in 1963, educated at King Edward's School, Bath, and Mansfield College, Oxford, and previously worked as a merchant banker, as a director of his family's firm and a financial PR consultant. A councillor in his party's emblematic right-wing borough of Wandsworth, and blooded in the ultra-safe Labour seat of Pontefract in 1997, he voted for the more pragmatic Eurosceptic choice of Portillo in the July 2001 leadership ballots. With boundary commissioners proposing to reduce his seat – at the next election-but-one – to its more urban core, his tenure is far from secure. Meanwhile in late 2001 he announced that he was looking for a wife.

TAYSIDE NORTH

The difficulties met by the SNP in defending the four Westminster seats vacated by MPs transferring to the Scottish Parliament in 2001 (one was lost to the Conservatives in Galloway and Upper Nithsdale, and two were held very narrowly) were ascribed by some observers to the resentment by electors who felt that were presented with a 'second team' of candidates, the most able and highly regarded being reserved for that Edinburgh Assembly. This was in no sense the case at North Tayside, where the newly elected party leader John Swinney's replacement was something of a celebrity, and an engaging and determined competitor, the musician Pete Wishart, of the band Runrig. He was very much in the 'first XI', and did just as well as Swinney had.

This large predominantly rural constituency consists of the northern parts of the old counties of Perthshire and Angus. The largest built-up areas are in the latter section: Forfar and Brechin, the small cathedral city which came in from Angus East in 1997. There are, however, many other famous placenames to be found within the seat. Here are the small towns of Kirriemuir and Blairgowrie, Rattray and Coupar Angus, and the picturesque Pitlochry and Aberfeldy. There are Shakespearian connections too – Glamis and Birnam. The terrain rises into the southern fringe of the Highlands: it includes Blair Atholl castle and the Pass of Killiecrankie, the lochs Tay, Tummel and Rannoch, tall mountains such as Ben Lawers and Carn Mairg, and glens such as Glen Garry and Glenshee. At election times, though, there have been genuine and tight contests to represent all this soft and rugged beauty.

Much of the terrain was in the vast Kinross and West Perthshire seat that was vacated for Sir Alec Douglas-Home when he returned to the Commons to take his place as Prime Minister in 1963. That seat remained loyal to Sir Alec until his retirement in 1974, but only elected his replacement Nicholas Fairbairn by 53 votes in October of that year. In 1992 Tayside North returned Bill Walker with a majority of just under 4,000 – hardly princely, but the fourth highest Tory lead north of the border. Tayside North is a Conservative–SNP marginal, like its neighbour Perth. Like Perth, it has recently been gained by the Nationalists, but not in a by-election. In 1997 John Swinney increased the SNP share by 6%, while Walker lost over 10%; and in 2001 there was no relative change between the two leading parties although Labour, Liberal Democrats and abstentions all increased their numbers. That may well have been the last contest in Tayside North, suggested for abolition in the 2002 Scottish Boundary Commission proposals, its vast area transferred to Perth and to Angus.

Social indices:			2001 Gen. Election:			
% Non-white	0.6		SNP	15,441	40.1	−4.8
% Prof/Man	30.3		C	12,158	31.6	−4.2
% Non-manual	49.5		Lab	5,715	14.8	+3.6
% Unemployed 2001	2.6		LD	4,363	11.3	+3.2
% Decrease 97–01	1.5		SSP	620	1.6	
% Fin hard/Rank	18.4	297	Ind	220	0.6	
% Prem mort/Rank	30	332	SNP maj	3,283	8.5	
			Turnout		62.5	−11.8
			Elect	61,645		

Member of Parliament

With the retreat of the less than charismatic bank-managerial SNP leader, John Swinney, to the Scottish Parliament, the Nationalists substituted the dour-looking, oblong-headed **Pete(r) Wishart** here in 2001. Somewhat unconventional as SNP candidates go in not being a regulation Scots lawyer or – as likely – a Scots teacher (although trained as one), he is a self-employed pop musician originally with the group Runrig, and has been Director of Scotland Against Drugs and Fast Forward Positive Lifestyles. Also highly atypical in his petty bourgeois party as a self-described former socialist with Fife coalfield roots, he was born in 1962 and educated at Queen Anne High School, Dunfermline, and Moray House College of Education, where he was a Labour activist until the home rule issue pushed him into campaigns against nuclear dumping and tolls on the Skye bridge, and eventually – though not until 1997 – into the SNP. In truly bizarre fringe party tradition he has moved from rock musician to novice MP to Chief Whip, in as little time as it takes to say 'the settled will of the Scottish people'.

TEIGNBRIDGE

The Liberal Democrats held all their three seats in Devon in 2001, against almost all predictions, and added a fourth. The Conservative MP for Teignbridge Patrick Nicholls had had a chequered career which had included a conviction for drunken driving after having been reported to the police by a taxi-driver whom he had hired but then rejected after a disagreement about the fare – at the 1990 Conservative Party conference in Bournemouth – and twice removed from a government or party post, the second time for describing the French as a nation of collaborators and the Germans as having caused both World Wars in a newspaper in 1994. Yet his defeat by the Liberal Democrat's persistent Richard Younger-Ross was not due to this history. He retained his percentage from 1997. More it was a matter of the Liberal Democrats squeezing the Labour and perhaps Green vote, while the UK Independence candidate, who was Viscount Exmouth, substantially increased the anti-European share, which was very rare in 2001, when that issue had been considerably defused, at least for the time being.

The south Devon seat of Teignbridge covers the coast between the rivers Dart and Exe (between Torbay and Exmouth) and its hinterland. It is centred on the river Teign, which enters the English Channel at the resort of Teignmouth. A little further up that river is the division's largest town, Newton Abbot. It also includes another seaside and retirement community, Dawlish, and, inland, some of the prettiest scenery in Britain, near the eastern scarp of Dartmoor, around Moretonhampstead and Bovey Tracey.

Younger-Ross and his enthusiastic team pulled out all the stops in 2001, and there was a palpable aura of inevitable defeat about the Tory campaign. If this level of energy is maintained now he has been elected, regional and national precedent suggests that incumbency services have every chance of turning this into a safe Liberal Democrat seat.

Social indices:			2001 Gen. Election:			
% Non-white	0.5		LD	26,343	44.4	+5.7
% Prof/Man	35.4		C	23,332	39.3	+0.1
% Non-manual	57.9		Lab	7,366	12.4	−5.6
£ Av prop val 2000	97 K		UKIP	2,269	3.8	+1.3
% Increase 97–00	44.9		LD maj	3,011	5.1	
% Unemployed 2001	1.9		Turnout		69.3	−7.7
% Decrease 97–01	1.8		Elect	85,533		
% Fin hard/Rank	7.5	539				
% Pensioners	34.7					
% Prem mort/Rank	23	445				

Member of Parliament

Richard Younger-Ross was third-time-lucky in capturing this seat for the Liberal Democrats in 1997, so compensating for the loss of the nearby Taunton seat back to the Conservatives. Born in Surrey suburbia in 1953, he was educated at Walton-on-Thames Secondary School, Ewell Technical College and Oxford Polytechnic, and worked as an architect after spells helping to run his father's insurance brokerage, and the family's shop at Shepperton Film Studios. With his victory over an especially abrasive Conservative MP in the shape of Patrick Nicholls a prize for persistent ward-heeling over ten years in the small towns and lanes of South Devon, his double-barrelled name implies less high birth than a decision to link his wife's (Younger) name with his own (Ross) – in the manner of the Labour MP John Austin-Walker, who reverted to the name of Austin when he fell out with his wife. Unlike his Liberal Democrat colleagues in more rural West and North Devon he voted to ban hunting on 2002.

TELFORD

Shropshire was one of the many English shire counties to receive an extra seat in the redistribution recommended by the latest Boundary Commission, which reported in 1995 and came into effect at the 1997 General Election. Its population growth had been centred on Telford New Town, which as the Commission pointed out, forms the main growth point for the whole of the West Midlands region. Telford formed the core of The Wrekin seat, which by 1992 exceeded 90,000 electors, making it one of the half dozen most populous seats in the United Kingdom. Telford also provides

Labour's strongest support in Shropshire, and indeed The Wrekin was won ten times by Labour from their first success in 1923 to 1992; but it was never truly safe, because electors from rural Shropshire were always included with the industrial communities. Now all that has changed and for the first time there is a safe Labour seat in Shropshire.

The Commission broke the old Wrekin division into two, and attempted to include as much of the New Town area as possible in the brand-new Telford constituency. This also has the effect of concentrating the Labour vote there. In 2001 David Wright polled twice the number of votes of his Conservative opponent, and it is hard to imagine his defeat in any foreseeable circumstances. It is fitting in many ways that this seat should finally inherit the mantle of a Labour banker, for it was industrial before Telford was constituted a New Town – long before, in fact, as the name of the seat implies. This is one of the birthplaces of the world's first industrial revolution: the forge of Abraham Darby's works at Coalbrookdale, where iron was smelted with coke in the first decade after 1700. A mile away is another famous eighteenth-century achievement, Thomas Telford's iron bridge of 1779 over the gorge of the Severn, which forms the heart of Britain's most extensive industrial museum. As time passed other industrial towns joined Coalbrookdale, Ironbridge and Coalport: Dawley, Wellington and the coal-mining community of Oakengates. This produced a substantial built-up area, scarred by productive industry, which was unified by the establishment of Telford New Town in the 1960s. Most of this old working-class territory is included in the new Telford seat, although enough remains in The Wrekin division (Wellington and Donnington for example) to form the basis for Labour's wins there in 1997 and 2001.

Social indices:			2001 Gen. Election:			
% Non-white	3.1		Lab	16,854	54.6	−3.2
% Prof/Man	23.6		C	8,471	27.4	+0.0
% Non-manual	43.6		LD	3,983	12.9	+1.1
£ Av prop val 2000	59 K		UKIP	1,098	3.6	
% Increase 97–00	27.9		SA	469	1.5	
% Unemployed 2001	3.4		Lab maj	8,383	27.2	
% Decrease 97–01	0.8		Turnout		51.9	−13.7
% Fin hard/Rank	30.8	122	Elect	59,486		
% Pensioners	17.9					
% Prem mort/Rank	29	353				

Member of Parliament

Dave Wright, a locally-based local government officer, replaced Tony Blair's retiring-for-a-peerage PPS, Bruce Grocott, here in 2001, after a late (March 2001) selection contest involving non-local aspirants, including Whitehall and Westminster political advisers. Self-described as a 'specialist in the development of housing strategies and public–private partnerships', he is preoccupied with the routine dereliction of municipal housing estates and the proliferation of agency work and the casualisation of the workforce that involves. Locally-born in 1966, educated at Wrockwardine Wood Comprehensive, Telford, and at Wolverhampton Polytechnic, he was a councillor on Wrekin District for eight years and on Oakegates Council for ten, whilst working for another (Sandwell Metropolitan) council, and presiding as chairman over the neighbouring Wrekin CLP. Scarcely do they come more local or municipal than this classic beneficiary of OMOV.

TEWKESBURY

The large east Gloucestershire seat of Cirencester and Tewkesbury had to be split up after the 1992 General Election, when its electorate reached 88,000, and the overall population growth in the county justified a sixth and additional seat. Most of the population and acreage of that seat is now to be found, however, in the new Cotswold constituency. The Tewkesbury seat is a much more compact but still growing entity, consisting of about 38,000 voters from the old Cirencester and Tewkesbury, plus 18,000 from the former West Gloucestershire and just over 14,000 from Cheltenham.

Much of this territory actually consists of suburbs of both Gloucester and Cheltenham (which more or less run into each other as both have grown in recent decades) rather than rural villages in pretty Cotswold country. There are some of the latter, and the seat contains charming spots like Winchcombe near Sudeley Castle, Cleeve Hill with its racehorse gallops above Cheltenham course, Dumbleton with its estate village, and the eponymous town of Tewkesbury, low-lying near the confluence of the Severn and Avon rivers but boasting its medieval abbey. Yet the largest communities in the division are Bishop's Cleeve, the centre of major modern developments immediately to the north of Cheltenham and Churchdown, basically a suburb of Gloucester which like Brockworth and Innsworth has come in from West Gloucestershire. It is this territory, well within the urban orbit of the Gloucester–Cheltenham 'conurbation', which above anywhere else has caused the electoral growth which created Gloucestershire's additional seat, and which gives it its political character.

Whether at the urban or rural end of the spectrum, however, all parts of the Tewkesbury constituency are Conservative in general elections. In the first two contests in Tewkesbury in 1997 and 2001 the Tories held on relatively easily, both times with a 46% share as the Liberal Democrats and Labour have almost split the opposing vote equally with 26% to 28% each, with Labour just nudging ahead in the latter year. In some parts of the land tactical voting is the norm now, usually to the disadvantage of the Conservatives. This phenomenon has not yet reached Tewkesbury.

Social indices:			2001 Gen. Election:				
% Non-white	0.8		C	20,830	46.1	+0.3
% Prof/Man	35.4		Lab	12,167	26.9	+0.7
% Non-manual	62.0		LD	11,863	26.2	−1.8
£ Av prop val 2000	109 K		Ind	335	0.7	
% Increase 97–00	43.1		C maj	8,663	19.2	
% Unemployed 2001	1.5		Turnout		64.3	−12.2
% Decrease 97–01	0.8		Elect	70,276		
% Fin hard/Rank	10.8	445				
% Pensioners	26.4					
% Prem mort/Rank	12	569				

Member of Parliament

Laurence Robertson, a hard right-winger surprisingly brought onto the frontbench as a Whip in 2001, was elected here in 1997 with a rare-for-the-Tories northern-accented voice, a Redwood-backing, hard-line Eurosceptic adversary of a single currency, anti-devolutionist, and a voter – with a small knot of Tory MPs – against power-sharing in Northern Ireland. Although a PR-man who was previously a work study engineer and industrial consultant, he is one of the very few Tory MPs of proletarian origin as the son of a mine worker (colliery electrician), born in 1958, and educated at secondary modern school after failing the 11-plus, before eventually transferring to Farnworth Grammar School. He defends the racing industry (based locally at Cheltenham Race Course), and criticised Hague for sacking Redwood in 2000. He resurfaced amid accusations of racism in 2001, endorsing the retiring MP John Townend's opinion that the British were becoming 'a mongrel race', and warning himself of the dangers of 'cramming' members of different ethnic groups into 'a crowded island'. Told to sign a retraction or leave the Party, he subsequently voted for Iain Duncan Smith in the leadership ballots and was rehabilitated as a Whip.

THANET NORTH

At one time the Isle of Thanet had just one seat of its own, but since 1974 it has been divided into two (along varying axes), an arrangement which was not disturbed by the round of boundary changes before the 1997 Election. Both Thanet constituencies, North and South, are diluted with territory from outside the Thanet district proper. In the case of North this comes in the highly Tory form of Herne Bay and Reculver, along the coast to the west. The parts of the Isle of Thanet itself which are included consist of a built-up strip of resorts: Cliftonville, Margate, Westgate-on-Sea and Birchington. This is traditionally the Londoner's day trip/bank holiday playground, the site of family away days and of now mythologised battles between Mods and Rockers. The various towns have somewhat distinct reputations: Margate is held to be raffish and more working class, and has recently become associated with one of its most famed daughters, the artist Tracey Emin, while Cliftonville is seen as more upmarket and even snooty.

Little of this can be seen in the voting patterns. Thanet North, unlike its neighbour South, remained loyal to the Conservatives in 1997 and 2001, although Roger Gale's majority was dramatically cut from more than 18,000 to less than 3,000 in the former year before doubling again in the latter. Labour clearly came first in the county council ward of Margate Central, but the failed to overcome the heavy odds stacked against them in Thanet North as a whole. Over 29% of the population here – and 39% of the eligible voters, and more than that of those who actually vote – are pensioners, compared with a national average of 19%. Unlike Thanet South this part of the most south-eastern tip of Britain still stands true-blue Conservative and is likely to remain so.

Social indices:			2001 Gen. Election:			
% Non-white	1.1		C	21,050	50.3	+6.2
% Prof/Man	30.0		Lab	14,400	34.4	−4.0
% Non-manual	53.8		LD	4,603	11.0	−0.4
£ Av prop val 2000	78 K		UKIP	980	2.3	+1.4
% Increase 97–00	38.0		Ind	440	1.1	
% Unemployed 2001	4.5		NF	395	0.9	
% Decrease 97–01	3.1		C maj	6,650	15.9	
% Fin hard/Rank	14.3	365	Turnout		59.3	−9.5
% Pensioners	39.0		Elect	70,581		
% Prem mort/Rank	37	215				

Member of Parliament

Roger Gale, conspicuous primarily as one of the small group of Conservative MPs who regularly vote for fox hunting bans, was first elected in 1983 having lost Birmingham Northfield to Labour at a 1982 by-election. A former radio and TV producer-turned-PR consultant, he was born in 1943, and educated at Hardye's School, Dorchester, and the Guildhall School of Speech and Drama. A campaigner against press excesses, he has targeted Murdoch for an attack on his private life, and the *Guardian* for its assault on Jonathan Aitken's links with Al-Fayed. He backed Hague for leader in 1997 and David Davis in 2001.

THANET SOUTH

Many constituency results in June 2001 demonstrated the limited but real incumbency effect which assists sitting MPs in UK politics, but few more clearly than the two in Thanet. In Thanet North the Conservative Roger Gale doubled his majority as he increased his share by over 6% and his lead by over 10%; while right next door in Thanet South Stephen Ladyman, who had gained the seat for Labour in 1997, effectively held his share and suffered a net swing of less than 1%. If he had only performed as well as his party in its twin seat, he would have been evicted from the Commons.

One of the most dramatic of all the unexpected results of the 1997 Election had taken place in Thanet South, where the former Cabinet Minister Jonathan Aitken was defeated after Labour increased their vote by a massive 18%, wiping out his majority of over 11,000. There may have been tactical voting too, as the Liberal Democrats plummeted from 18 to 11% of the total vote. All in all, South seemed determined to rid itself of Aitken, who ended up serving a jail sentence for perjury following court cases around corruption allegations. It was thought at the time that this breath of scandal, which had already ended his Cabinet career in 1995, might have helped to account for the size of the swing in 1997, but it is unlikely to have played a role in the continued exceptional Labour performance in 2001.

The Isle of Thanet is not a real island, cut off from the mainland of Britain by a continuous channel of water, like that other Kentish isle, Sheppey. Some have said that this particular isle at the north-eastern tip of Kent is defined by a state of mind: unadventurous, old-fashioned, patriotic, and most certainly conservative. Thanet

South is not quite as dominated by tourism and retirement homes as Thanet North. In addition to the thoroughly respectable resorts of St Peter's, Eastcliff and Westcliff, and Broadstairs where Edward Heath grew up, it also has the more plebeian Ramsgate, still a working ferry port, and there are Labour council-estate wards inland at Newington and Northwood. It also stretches south to take in the old and graceful Cinque Port of Sandwich, which has the only Open championship golf course in the south of England. The percentage of pensioners is slightly lower than that of Thanet North (which is among the top ten in the whole of Britain). All this made it easier for Labour to win it than its northern partner – but not much. Now it has been won, though, its results seem to be deviating further, and may continue to do so.

Social indices:			2001 Gen. Election:			
% Non-white	1.0		Lab	18,002	45.7	−0.5
% Prof/Man	30.5		C	16,210	41.1	+1.3
% Non-manual	53.6		LD	3,706	9.4	−2.3
£ Av prop val 2000	85 K		Ind	770	2.0	
% Increase 97–00	46.4		UKIP	501	1.3	−0.1
% Unemployed 2001	4.0		NF	242	0.6	
% Decrease 97–01	3.4		Lab maj	1,792	4.5	
% Fin hard/Rank	13.9	379	Turnout		64.2	−7.5
% Pensioners	34.6		Elect	61,462		
% Prem mort/Rank	30	347				

Member of Parliament

Dr Stephen Ladyman was elected as the 20th least expected Labour MP in 1997 in an area never previously lost by the Conservatives. A computer manager formerly with the locally-based Pfizer drugs company, he was born in 1952 and Catholic-educated at Our Lady of Walsingham School, Liverpool, Birkenhead Institute, Liverpool Polytechnic and Strathclyde University, where he obtained a doctorate in physics. He backs the EU for its regional funding for the declining seaside towns, and gave up his lucrative Pfizer share options on becoming an MP, claiming he'd rather be that than a millionaire. In 2001 he was appointed PPS to Defence Minister Adam Ingram.

THURROCK

Famously, Labour failed to capture the marginal Basildon seat, supposedly the spiritual home of 'Essex Man', at the April 1992 General Election. They did however regain a seat which has every bit as much a claim to be a classic critical constituency in that county, and maybe more typical than the New Town of Basildon: Thurrock.

The loss of Thurrock in 1987, Labour's last remaining seat in Essex after their reverses in Harlow and Basildon, illustrated their decline in this part of south-east England better than any other. As late as 1974 Labour could command a 20,000 majority in this Thames-side division, but after three large negative swings the Labour MP Dr Oonagh McDonald was ousted by the Tory Timothy Janman, who turned out to be a tiny strident extremist in the mould of Peter Bruinvels, the former Leicester East MP.

The borough of Thurrock does not look like Conservative terrain. It stretches along the north bank of the Thames east of London from the Dartford tunnel and Thurrock–Dartford bridge past Purfleet with its power station through Grays and the dockland of Tilbury almost to Canvey Island. The north-eastern part of the borough is now in the Basildon constituency, leaving Thurrock as a predominantly working-class constituency, with a larger than average proportion of council housing. Here are to be found London's outermost docks, for Tilbury is the main container port for the capital. Labour's best areas are Tilbury, the Chadwell St Mary council estate, West Thurrock/Purfleet, Aveley and South Ockendon/Belhus. The Conservatives can fight back in Little Thurrock and much of Grays, but Labour control Thurrock easily at local council level. Their recapture of the parliamentary seat in 1992 was still a notable achievement, and in the different atmosphere of 1997 they achieved a huge swing which took Andrew Mackinlay's majority back almost to the 1974 level. Its most recent spin imparted by the modernisation of the Labour Party, the wheel had turned full circle. It was reduced to almost exactly 10,000 in 2001 by a 5% net swing to the Conservatives and by an unusually large 17% drop in turnout to less than half of the total registered electorate.

Despite its reputation as a backwoods, almost all-white, right-wing working-class area, Thurrock does in several ways very much look to the future of Britain. Its Lakeside shopping centre is one of the largest and most successful in Europe, employing thousands and attracting millions of out-of-town shoppers a year. There is a very large development of modern private housing at Chafford Hundred west of Grays, which has been energetically marketed. The electorate increased by 5,000 in the four years before 2001. Money is being poured into the redevelopment of this north bank of the Thames, and its image is rightly changing.

Social indices:			2001 Gen. Election:			
% Non-white	2.7		Lab	21,121	56.5	−6.8
% Prof/Man	21.7		C	11,124	29.8	+3.0
% Non-manual	50.3		LD	3,846	10.3	+2.2
£ Av prop val 2000	79 K		UKIP	1,271	3.4	+1.6
% Increase 97–00	47.6		Lab maj	9,997	26.8	
% Unemployed 2001	3.4		Turnout		48.8	−17.1
% Decrease 97–01	2.8		Elect	76,524		
% Fin hard/Rank	22.3	238				
% Pensioners	23.7					
% Prem mort/Rank	35	241				

Member of Parliament

Andrew Mackinlay, a short, chirpy, Cockney sparrow, perched on the frontbench below the gangway, started out on the right but, outflanked there by the Blairites, has become a populist critic of backbench sycophancy and the bowling of patsy soft-ball questions, and yet is never found in any of the major rebellions against the government – making him a Dennis Skinner-type-turn but with its teeth drawn. He had some backing in the PLP chairmanship's election of 2000, though not that much, because he polled only 77 votes. Born in 1949 and educated at the Salesian (RC)

College, Chertsey, he worked initially as a clerk with Surrey County Council and then for ten years as a NALGO official. A Beckett, not Blair, voter in 1994, he fought four parliamentary contests before winning here in 1992, and has made a mark with his (unsuccessful) campaign to secure pardons for executed First World War deserters.

TIVERTON AND HONITON

This constituency name suggests a merger between two long-standing parliamentary constituencies. In fact the seat is predominantly based on the former Tiverton division, with just 8,500 or so voters around the town of Honiton itself transferred from its former eponymous seat in 1997, the bulk of which remains intact under the name of Devon East. There are two elements to the Tiverton and Honiton seat, aptly characterised by its name. These can be summed up as Mid Devon and East Devon, and not only because those are the titles of the two local authority districts currently in the area. Mid Devon, based on Tiverton, is rolling farmland punctuated by small market towns. Tiverton is the largest, with a population of 17,000, and its Westexe South ward actually returned Mid Devon's only Labour councillor in the May 1999 Elections. Cullompton and Crediton each have about 6,000 residents. Smaller still – indeed only enlarged villages – are Uffculme and Willand in the Culm Valley, and Silverton on the Exe. Politics here are local, independent and secretive. The Liberal Democrats pursue the Conservatives closely in national contests. This is inland Devon, and its age structure is very different from the coast. There are fewer incomers and retirees, and relatively little dependence on tourism.

East Devon is in general somewhat different in nature: a much older demographic profile, as the coastline attracts visitors and those who come to stay. It is more Conservative: Honiton used to be the Tories' safest seat in Devon. The contrast between Mid and East should not be over-emphasised, though. It is after all the inland part of East Devon which is included in this constituency, and it is nowhere near as elderly as the coast itself. Tiverton and Honiton is now an entirely inland seat.

The Conservative MP Angela Browning must have been relieved to hold on here in her party's disastrous year of 1997, and she only did so because her share of the vote declined by a little less than the national average, while Labour in third place, rather than being squeezed, strengthened their position slightly. In 2001, though, the Labour vote remained static as there was a substantial movement directly from Liberal Democrat (down 3%) to Conservative (up 6%) and next time it will only rank No.17 on the Lib Dem target list of Tory seats.

Social indices:			2001 Gen. Election:			
% Non-white	0.4		C	26,258	47.1	+5.7
% Prof/Man	37.2		LD	19,974	35.8	−2.7
% Non-manual	57.8		Lab	6,647	11.9	−0.9
£ Av prop val 2000	103 K		UKIP	1,281	2.3	
% Increase 97–00	54.2		Grn	1,030	1.8	+1.0
% Unemployed 2001	1.5		Lib	594	1.1	−0.0
% Decrease 97–01	1.1		C maj	6,284	11.3	
% Fin hard/Rank	8.5	503	Turnout		69.2	−8.9
% Pensioners	30.1		Elect	80,646		
% Prem mort/Rank	16	530				

Member of Parliament

Angela Browning was 1994–98 and 1999–2001 one of the Conservatives' female frontbenchers, *faute de mieux* given paucity of numbers. First elected in 1992, and with beaky angular features, she presents herself as a somewhat defensively strident Redwood campaign-managing Eurosceptic. Born in 1946, daughter of a Reading University lab technician, educated – ordinarily – at Westwood Girls' Grammar School, Reading and at technology colleges in Reading and Bournemouth, she formerly worked as a sales manager and management consultant. A Junior Agriculture Minister under John Major (1994–97), she quit the Opposition frontbench in 1998 to look after her disabled son but then returned in 1999 to unanticipated prominence as Shadow Leader of the Commons. She backed Iain Duncan Smith in all the ballots in 2001 but then left for the backbenches.

TONBRIDGE AND MALLING

In the boundary changes necessitated by the award of an extra seat to the county of Kent which came into force at the 1997 General Election, the centre of gravity of the Tonbridge and Malling constituency was shifted westwards. It lost around 26,000 voters from its east end to the new Chatham and Aylesford division. In exchange it gained some 11,000 to the west from Sevenoaks: this includes the town of Eden bridge, and the affluent farming country around Hever Castle and Pinehurst Place. This achieved the required amount of slimming down of the electorate. The political balance of the seat was not altered. In 2001 Sir John Stanley achieved the second highest majority of any of the nine remaining Conservative MPs in the 'Garden of England': over 8,000, reduced from five figures only because of the 11% drop in turnout.

Tonbridge is an ancient town with the remnants of a motte and bailey castle, in countryside long known for mineral extraction, orchards and hop fields, as the multiplicity of outhouses, mostly converted, attests; the urban areas' employment sources in paper and packaging mills, distribution, light and general industry and services have been supplemented more recently by high-technology centres such as that at Kings Hill. The primary eponymous town is also known as an educational centre, not only of the leading independent Tonbridge School but of Judd School at the other end of the town, alma mater of one of this volume's authors.

Tonbridge and Malling is a very healthy constituency, not just for the Conservatives, but for its residents in general: the premature mortality rate as calculated in Health Inequalities and Policy in Britain (1999) places it just 20 seats down the list of 641 British constituencies, with only 73% of the average number of avoidable deaths.

Social indices:			2001 Gen. Election:			
% Non-white	0.9		C	20,956	49.4	+1.4
% Prof/Man	41.0		Lab	12,706	29.9	+2.7
% Non-manual	64.4		LD	7,605	17.9	−1.3
£ Av prop val 2000	176 K		UKIP	1,169	2.8	+1.7
% Increase 97–00	48.8		C maj	8,250	19.4	
% Unemployed 2001	1.2		Turnout		64.4	−11.6
% Decrease 97–01	1.6		Elect	65,939		
% Fin hard/Rank	7.8	531				
% Pensioners	24.6					
% Prem mort/Rank	7	620				

Member of Parliament

Sir John Stanley is a man whose heyday was all in the long-gone years of the Thatcher hegemony, as Margaret Thatcher's former PPS and seller-off of council houses, serving her as a middle rank Minister at Housing, Defence and Northern Ireland, until leaving office (dropped by her) in 1988 with a reputation for abrasiveness. Born in 1942 and educated at Repton and Lincoln College, Oxford, and formerly with Rio Tinto Zinc, he was first elected here in 1974, making him (jointly with other February 1974 entrants) the fifth senior Tory MP in length of service. Seen as somewhat wooden and humourless, following his exit from government he criticised his patroness's poll tax, in 1997 – despite hostility to Euro-federalism – backed Kenneth Clarke for leader, and later as a Foreign Affairs Select Committee member from 1992, praised Tony Blair's resolution in Kosovo. His leadership votes in 2001 went undisclosed.

TOOTING

Tooting always resisted the blandishments of the Conservative Party in a way that the other two constituencies in the borough of Wandsworth have not. While Battersea and Putney elected Conservative MPs in the Thatcher era, and swung further to the Conservatives even in 1992, the Labour majority in Tooting, having reached a precarious 1,400 in 1987, jumped to over 4,000 in that year. What accounts for this apparent deviation from the local trend?

One should, perhaps, start with the ethnic make-up of the Tooting constituency. The two wards which never were tempted to vote in Conservatives even when offered the juicy bribe of a minimal poll or council tax bill in 1990 and 1994 were Graveney and Tooting itself. Each was around 37% non-white at the time of the last published census. A third ward, Furzedown near Tooting Bec Common, split its representation in 1994 and 1998; it is 30% non-white. Overall the Tooting division has risen from

21% to over 26% ethnic minority population in the 1980s, at a time when the proportion in Battersea, uniquely, actually fell. Also, while the percentage of owner-occupiers has risen over the decade and that of council tenants fallen, this has been in line with the national average rather than far exceeding it as in the rest of Wandsworth. In short, Tooting has not gentrified and moved up the social scale as much as Battersea and Putney have.

There has been some gentrification, as young professionals have spotted bargains in the housing market, and there are some solidly Conservative wards, like Springfield and Nightingale, which are situated 'between the Commons' (Wandsworth and Clapham that is). But more typical are the bustling, cosmopolitan, multi-ethnic areas around Tooting Bec and Tooting Broadway. It would seem that Labour has passed its lowest point in Tooting, and in 1997, when the re-modelled party was recapturing Battersea and Putney, an even bigger swing in Tooting increased Tom Cox's majority to a very safe 15,000, reduced to 10,000 mainly by the Britain-wide turnout fall in 2001.

Social indices:			2001 Gen. Election:			
% Non-white	26.3		Lab	20,332	54.1	−5.6
% Prof/Man	46.9		C	9,932	26.4	−0.7
% Non-manual	70.9		LD	5,583	14.9	+5.5
£ Av prop val 2000	210 K		Grn	1,744	4.6	+3.5
% Increase 97–00	71.9		Lab maj	10,400	27.7	
% Unemployed 2001	3.8		Turnout		54.9	−14.3
% Decrease 97–01	4.3		Elect	68,447		
% Fin hard/Rank	14.7	358				
% Pensioners	20.1					
% Prem mort/Rank	40	175				

Member of Parliament

Tom Cox, long pencilled in as a potential candidate for an eve-of-campaign elevation-to-the-peerage to make way for a parachutee from the Blairite nomenklatura, is one of Labour's longest runners – first elected in 1970, a period exceeded by only three Labour MPs. A former power station worker, and before that a Bevin boy, he was born in 1930 and educated (as far as he is prepared to reveal) at an LCC council school and (in some form) at the LSE. Apart from being a Whip between 1974 and 1979, he has performed as a loud-voiced backbench campaigner against local kerb crawlers, backed the Greeks against the Turks in Cyprus and, when it mattered, kept the Tories out of at least one of the three parliamentary seats in their 1980s yuppified flagship borough of Wandsworth.

TORBAY

Probably no seat was more widely or frequently mis-predicted before the 2001 General Election results were announced. Adrian Sanders had only ousted the Conservative MP in 1997 by 12 votes, and since that time the Liberal Democrat-run unitary authority council had suffered a shattering and comprehensive reversal in the all-out elections of May 2000, when they were very nearly 'all out', retaining only four councillors to face 32 Tories. But just as Liberal Democrat-run councils have traditionally not necessarily led to Lib Dem MPs, the reverse clearly applies, as Sanders increased his own majority more than 50-fold, to a very robust 6,708. It was one of the earliest marginals declared on the night, and all around the country Tory activists watching were suddenly dispirited, given the expectations of a gain which had been built up.

The bustling seaside resorts of Torbay are perhaps on balance too plebeian to justify the title of the Devon Riviera, but there can be no doubt that Torquay and Paignton still form one of the most popular and famous of goals for those holiday-makers who choose to stay in Britain. The vast numbers of hotels, guest houses and bed and breakfast establishments lining the hilly streets attest to that, even if not all of them do the best of business nowadays.

Politically Torbay was long regarded as an epitome of England's deep south, but the Conservative dominance was subjected to a series of strong Liberal Democrat challenges. The Liberal Democrats won in recent contests in Torbay at all other levels than parliamentary. They took control of the unitary borough council. In the European elections of June 1994 the Liberal Democrat candidate Adrian Sanders would in all probability have won in the Devon and East Plymouth constituency but for the existence of a 'Literal Democrat' who took 10,000 votes – he lost to the Conservative by a margin of a few hundred. The same Adrian Sanders was the candidate when Rupert Allason was defeated in that nail-biting contest in 1997, so it might be said that justice was finally done. No predictions will be offered for the next contests at local authority, European or parliamentary level.

Social indices:			2001 Gen. Election:			
% Non-white	0.8		LD	24,015	50.5	+10.9
% Prof/Man	32.6		C	17,307	36.4	−3.2
% Non-manual	56.5		Lab	4,484	9.4	−5.4
£ Av prop val 2000	86 K		UKIP	1,512	3.2	−0.5
% Increase 97–00	37.8		Ind	251	0.5	
% Unemployed 2001	4.7		LD maj	6,708	14.1	
% Decrease 97–01	2.4		Turnout		65.7	−8.1
% Fin hard/Rank	12.1	412	Elect	72,409		
% Pensioners	36.3					
% Prem mort/Rank	30	346				

Member of Parliament

Adrian Sanders, an insulin-dependent diabetic, narrowly won here in 1997, locally born (1959) and educated (Torquay Grammar School) and who worked as a Party apparatchik (for Paddy Ashdown), fought the seat in 1992, and in 1994 lost the Devon Euro seat because of a spoiling 'Literal Democrat' candidate siphoning-off 10,000 votes. A Housing spokesman, he campaigns for diabetes and for the deprived south-west peninsula, and has been dubbed – for the benefit of older listeners – 'Sanders of the Riviera'. His extraordinary success in retaining the seat in 2001 owed a good deal to the inadequacy of his Tory opponent whom – after being charged with a firearms offence for brandishing an air rifle in a confrontation with an alleged vandal in the run-up to the election – he dubbed 'Wyatt Twerp'.

TORFAEN

Torfaen is the constituency that covers the furthest east of the series of great South Welsh industrial valleys. The base of its economy has changed more than most. Mining is no longer active here, as elsewhere, but light and varied industry has been attracted to provide alternative employment. The most unusual and distinctive feature of Torfaen is that it includes most of the only New Town in South Wales, Cwmbran, which is by far the largest centre of population in the valley, housing over 40,000 people.

However, the name with which this valley constituency has been most associated with is that of Pontypool. When the 1983 Boundary Commission originally suggested that the town of Pontypool itself should be detached to join parts of Islwyn, the neighbouring constituency, the sitting Pontypool MP led a storm of protest. The Commission changed its mind, and the Torfaen valley has been saved as a parliamentary unit, little different from the old Pontypool seat.

Torfaen is a Labour stronghold. To its east, the ex-mining valleys give way to rural border country, where Conservatives are still competitive. But here we are still in working-class country with powerful and long Labour traditions. The old Pontypool seat was one of those which remained true to Labour even in 1931. From 1935 to 1946 Roy Jenkins's father was Labour MP for Pontypool, and the future SDP founder-leader went to school in the constituency at Abersychan Grammar School. The growth of Cwmbran has not weakened Labour's position, either. Unlike English New Towns with their volatile swings and notable lack of loyalty to Labour, Cwmbran follows rather the Scottish model. Due to Cwmbran, Torfaen has the highest proportion of council-built, and as we are now encouraged to deem it, social housing of any seat in Wales.

Paul Murphy won his fourth election in Torfaen in 2001, although his majority over the Tories fell to 16,000 from 24,000 as turnout fell by 14% and the Labour proportion of those cast by 7%. This is almost an entirely English-speaking seat, situated as far east as it is, and in 1997 Plaid Cymru had suffered the humiliation of finishing fifth behind the Referendum Party, but in a generally good year for them in 2001 they more than tripled their share from that abyss of a base, and managed to save their deposit, which was more than they could do in five other seats even then.

Social indices:			2001 Gen. Election:			
% Non-white	0.7		Lab	21,883	62.1	−7.0
% Welsh sp	2.4		C	5,603	15.9	+3.6
% Prof/Man	24.7		LD	3,936	11.2	−1.0
% Non-manual	45.7		PC	2,720	7.7	+5.3
£ Av prop val 2000	55 K		UKIP	657	1.9	
% Increase 97–00	28.6		SA	443	1.3	
% Unemployed 2001	3.7		Lab maj	16,280	46.2	
% Decrease 97–01	2.0		Turnout		57.7	−14.0
% Fin hard/Rank	29.5	138	Elect	61,110		
% Pensioners	24.4					
% Prem mort/Rank	40	182				

Member of Parliament

Paul Murphy, Secretary of State for Wales, was first elected here in 1987 as a rather lacklustre-seeming replacement for the exotic amateur psychoanalyst Leo Abse, but reached the frontbench as early as 1988. With his Cabinet seat earned by his role as a negotiator of the Good Friday Agreement, as the statutory Catholic minister in the Northern Ireland Office, he was born in 1948, son of a Welsh-Irish Catholic miner and educated at West Monmouth School, Pontypool and Oriel College, Oxford, and was a further education college lecturer in Ebbw Vale for 16 years. Safe but uncharismatic, his lugubrious countenance is well suited to the run down of his area's main single source of employment, the Llanwern steelworks.

TORRIDGE AND WEST DEVON

This is this seat's correct name, even though it is often to be found listed under 'Devon West and Torridge'.

Torridge and West Devon is a vast seat, by far the largest in the county and one of the half-dozen biggest in England. It stretches from rugged Hartland Point and the picturesque village of Clovelly, and Westward Ho! and the old shipbuilding port of Appledore, all at its northern end, through Bideford, and small market towns like Okehampton and Holsworthy and Torrington, to take in much of Dartmoor, including the bleak Princetown with its fearsome prison. The south-easternmost community is Chagford, on the boundary with Teignbridge. There is some dependence on tourism on the coast, but most of the seat is inland: only two seats in England boast a higher proportion of workers employed in agriculture, fishing and forestry. All in all this is economically, historically and regionally good ground for the Liberal Democrats, but their eventual victory in 1997 came about after a complicated series of events.

In 1992 the Tory MP Emma Nicholson had been re-elected with a majority of 3,600 over the Liberal Democrats, but during the course of the subsequent Parliament she decided she could not continue as a government supporter, and crossed the floor to join her erstwhile opponents. Unlike a defector to Labour, Alan Howarth, she did not seek another term, either in this seat or another. This left the field clear for John Burnett, who had contested the seat before, in 1987, to defeat the new Conservative candidate Ian Liddell-Grainger. Burnett must have thought he had a good chance of holding Torridge and West Devon for some time to come; certainly many others did, but they had reckoned without the return of foot and mouth disease in early 2001, which affected Devon more than almost anywhere else in England, and this constituency more than almost anywhere in Devon. The Tory candidate Geoffrey Cox fought a vigorous campaign, mobilising on the basis of countryside issues and the grievances of farmers and those in the tourist trade, against a government based in London which seemed deficient in sympathy and even competence. The Liberal Democrats were not in government of course, but the Conservatives claimed the role of chief Opposition. In the end Burnett, who had worked hard for four years to avoid seeming a catspaw of (or even sympathetic to) Labour, held on with a reduced majority. He must hope, like his constituents, that the worst is past.

Social indices:			2001 Gen. Election:			
% Non-white	0.4		LD	23,474	42.2	+0.3
% Prof/Man	35.6		C	22,280	40.0	+1.5
% Non-manual	52.2		Lab	5,959	10.7	−1.7
£ Av prop val 2000	92 K		UKIP	2,674	4.8	+1.7
% Increase 97–00	40.9		Grn	1,297	2.3	
% Unemployed 2001	2.8		LD maj	1,194	2.1	
% Decrease 97–01	1.7		Turnout		70.5	−7.4
% Fin hard/Rank	8.2	517	Elect	78,976		
% Pensioners	30.6					
% Prem mort/Rank	24	431				

Member of Parliament

John Burnett, elected in 1997, and a Home Affairs spokesman from 2001, is arguably the Liberal Democrat MP most reassuring to Conservative voters, as an opponent of gun control, hunting bans and homosexual sex at 16. Born in 1945, his pedigree is also familiar – Ampleforth, Dartmouth, the Royal Marines, local solicitor based at Okehampton, and a beef farmer (only 'Ampleforth' among that checklist might trouble the more resistant of the Reformed tradition). With plenty of accompanying savoir faire and an affable, doggy-like visage, it could be said this constituency already has a Conservative MP, in a Barbour – but sporting a yellow rosette, and luckily blamed for nothing, whether the failings of Tory or Labour governments, and so able to survive the foot-and-mouth crisis in his constituency.

TOTNES

The Conservatives lost two seats to the Liberal Democrats in Devon in 1997, and nearly lost three more – Teignbridge, Tiverton/Honiton, and Totnes. All were held by a margin of less than 2,000 votes, and in Totnes it was just 877. In 2001, though, these seats went three different ways. Tiverton/Honiton was not widely regarded as a likely Lib Dem gain. Teignbridge was gained, by a clear margin of 3,000. Totnes was very vigorously contested – some thought too much so, as the dynamic high-profile Liberal Democrat candidate Rachel Oliver was accused of playing on Anthony Steen's age (he was 61) after she referred to his appearance in an interview. Things got rough, and the experienced Conservative MP prevailed, by an unexpectedly large margin. It should be remembered though that Ms Oliver, though much maligned afterwards for her forward conduct of the campaign, did actually increase the Liberal Democrat share by over 2%. Anthony Steen's went up by 8%, but in 1997 there had been a Local Conservative taking well over 2,000 votes as well as two anti-European candidates. Perhaps the effective gap she had to make up was larger than it had seemed.

The south Devon district of South Hams enjoys some of the most attractive scenery in England, but it is scarcely developed for tourism and in no way ruined by commercial exploitation. Sea creeks penetrate deep inland along the wooded valleys of the Dart, the Avon, and the Erme. There are also grand cliffs and headlands, with names familiar to those used to sailing up the English Channel: Bolt Tail, Bolt Head, Prawle Point, Start Point. The small towns are among the most elegant and stylish in Britain – the sophisticated yachting centres of Salcombe and Dartmouth, and the medieval town of Totnes further up the Dart.

The Totnes seat includes all of the South Hams described in the paragraph above except for the Erme valley; it extends to the edge of Torbay to take in the fishing port and resort of Brixham, with yet another headland at Berry Head, and also Blatchcombe; and the section taken from Teignbridge. This is the south-eastern edge of Dartmoor, including Haytor and the small towns of Buckfastleigh and Ashburton, bypassed by the traffic speeding down the A38 towards Cornwall. After the publicity given to the bitter election campaign of June 2001, all those involved will probably hope for a quiet spell of some years bypassed by national politics in this southernmost Devon constituency.

Social indices:			2001 Gen. Election:			
% Non-white	0.4		C	21,914	44.5	+8.0
% Prof/Man	36.1		LD	18,317	37.2	+2.3
% Non-manual	56.3		Lab	6,005	12.2	−4.2
£ Av prop val 2000	114 K		UKIP	3,010	6.1	+4.3
% Increase 97–00	42.1		C maj	3,597	7.3	
% Unemployed 2001	2.7		Turnout		67.9	−8.4
% Decrease 97–01	1.6		Elect	72,548		
% Fin hard/Rank	8.4	508				
% Pensioners	35.5					
% Prem mort/Rank	13	560				

Member of Parliament

Anthony Steen, a rare Tory MP (one of 11) dating back to the Heath leadership, was first elected (for Liverpool Wavertree) in 1974 and transferred here (as South Hams) in 1983, defeating the local incumbent Tory MP Ray Mawby for the nomination. An environmental critic of excessive housing sprawl in Devon, who despite Euro-scepticism, backed Clarke in 1997 and 2001, he was born in 1939, educated at Westminster School and – originally a barrister – was a Lloyd's underwriter for 26 years. One of the few Tory MPs with a Jewish background, a loather of smoking, tall and with a shock of white hair, and a fanatical cyclist, he cuts a slightly mad-professor figure. Never risen above being PPS to Peter Brooke briefly (1992–94), he advises small airlines, using one of them to fly down from London to the constituency, whilst nevertheless describing his 2001 hopeful Liberal Democrat challenger, Rachel Oliver, as a 'blow-in from London'. In what was a bitterly fought confrontation he accused her of ageism for challenging him, as 'a white-haired old man' to a race up steep Fore Street in Totnes. With the seat high on the Liberal Democrats' list of expected gains given the small 877 Tory majority in 1997, by quadrupling the majority in 2001 he must have felt he deserved the knighthood he would inevitably have acquired had the Conservatives not lost office in 1997.

TOTTENHAM

Haringey is a long, thin London borough, stretching all the way from the edge of upper-crust Hampstead Heath in the west to the industrial and working-class valley of the river Lea in the east. It is a far cry, socially and politically, from Highgate to Tottenham. Tottenham is a very cosmopolitan constituency. Nearly 40% of the population is non-white, belonging to diverse ethnic groups but being mostly Afro-Caribbean – only two seats (Brent South and Vauxhall) have a higher proportion than Tottenham's 24.8%. In addition to this, there is a large number of Cypriots: the seat includes a ward named Green Lanes, after the long road which forms the spine of London's largest Cypriot community.

Tottenham has been regarded as a safe Labour seat for many years, although in the 1959 Parliament the Labour MP Alan Brown defected to the Conservatives. However, he was beaten easily in 1964 by Norman Atkinson, a leading Tribunite who was for some years elected Treasurer of the national Labour Party. Atkinson fought off another kind of challenge in 1983, when boundary changes brought half of the abolished seat of Wood Green into the Tottenham constituency, and he had to win a selection contest against the Labour MP there, Reg Race (who briefly re-emerged in 2001 as the replacement for Tony Benn beaten by the Lib Dems in Chesterfield). Atkinson was himself dropped in 1987, as the local party controversially selected Bernie Grant, the black leader of Haringey Council, who had entered the demonology of the right following remarks he made after the Broadwater Farm riots of autumn 1985, when a policeman was hacked to death. The Labour majority was reduced to just over 4,000, its lowest figure since the war. Could even Tottenham be vulnerable, with Bernie Grant as candidate?

The answer was given in the 1992 and 1997 General Elections. It was a resounding 'no'. Last time Mr Grant was the beneficiary of a 13% swing and increased his majority to a most satisfactory 20,000. There were two reasons for this. First, ten years of incumbency had shown Bernie Grant to be far from the ogre he had been portrayed to be. To some extent the result was a re-establishment of Labour's natural position in Tottenham after the aberration of 1987. There was another factor too: Labour had done outstandingly well in recent years in the borough of Haringey. The western seat, Hornsey and Wood Green was easily gained on a 6% swing in 1992 and by 1997 it too had a 20,000 Labour majority.

Bernie Grant died in 2000, and in the June by-election he was succeeded without fuss by a very different kind of candidate, who became the youngest member of the Commons, David Lammy. In 2001 Labour's share dropped dramatically in

Hornsey/Wood Green, but not in Tottenham, and Lammy should have no problems with a base for a long and potentially high-flying career.

Social indices:			2001 Gen. Election:			
% Non-white	38.3		Lab	21,317	67.5	−1.8
% Prof/Man	30.2		C	4,401	13.9	−1.8
% Non-manual	52.4		LD	3,008	9.5	−1.3
£ Av prop val 2000	111 K		Grn	1,443	4.6	+1.8
% Increase 97–00	64.4		SA	1,162	3.7	
% Unemployed 2001	8.9		Ind	270	0.9	
% Decrease 97–01	6.5		Lab maj	16,916	53.5	
% Fin hard/Rank	34.1	99	Turnout		48.2	−8.8
% Pensioners	18.6		Elect	65,567		
% Prem mort/Rank	45	95				

Member of Parliament

David Lammy, a high-flying Blairite barrister, by being elected at the June 2000 by-election in place of the late Bernie Grant, ensured that Labour's tally of black and Asian MPs remained at nine, having beaten Grant's white widow for the nomination. Like Grant from a Guyanese background, he was born in July 1972 (making him the new Baby of the House in place of Christopher Leslie, born in June 1972) and educated at King's School, Peterborough, London University and Harvard Law School, and was once frisked by a policeman at the High Court on the assumption he was the accused. As early as 2001 he was PPS to Education Secretary Estelle Morris.

TRURO AND ST AUSTELL

The boundaries of Cornwall's five parliamentary constituencies did not need to be altered one iota by the Boundary Commission in their 1995 review, but they did make one change: the name of the long-established Truro constituency was altered to add mention of its largest town – and indeed the largest town in the whole county – St Austell. This decision does make the constituency name unwieldy – only Ayr, Hove, and York were shorter. Yet it can scarcely be begrudged. St Austell and its hinterland, the old china clay mining belt of central Cornwall, form the political as well as demographic heart of the seat. It is and has been for a while a Liberal (Democrat) stronghold, underwriting one of the party's safest bets.

In October 1974 an abrasive and rough-hewn but warm and independent Cornishman gained the Truro division from a rather inactive Conservative MP; and David Penhaligon was to build the seat into a personal fiefdom before his untimely death at the age of 42 at the end of 1986 in a car crash on an icy road in his constituency. A huge sympathy vote swept a 24-year-old, Matthew Taylor, to Westminster in the March 1987 by-election. Some doubted whether he could fill Penhaligon's shoes, and in the general election of the same year his majority was cut back ominously to under 5,000. However, given a full term to establish himself in his own right, and benefiting from a surge which was to give the Lib Dems control of traditionally Independent Cornwall County Council from 1993, he now seems perfectly secure. In the last General Election in 2001 his lead over the Tories fell from 12,000 to 8,000, but this was not due to any reduction in his share, still over 48% – rather the very strong anti-European minor party vote had been halved to the Tory benefit, and turnout fell by 10%. The huge heaps of waste which survive from the china clay mining present one of England's weirdest landscapes, now seen by many more people after the phenomenal success as a tourist attraction of the Eden Project biomes. Matthew Taylor now seems comfortably at home in this strange terrain, and with this renamed seat's distinctive Cornish political tendencies.

Social indices:			2001 Gen. Election:			
% Non-white	0.5		LD	24,296	48.3	–0.2
% Prof/Man	32.6		C	16,231	32.3	+5.8
% Non-manual	55.3		Lab	6,889	13.7	–1.6
£ Av prop val 2000	97 K		UKIP	1,664	3.3	+2.3
% Increase 97–00	47.5		MK	1,137	2.3	+1.5
% Unemployed 2001	2.8		Ind	78	0.2	
% Decrease 97–01	2.7		LD maj	8,065	16.0	
% Fin hard/Rank	8.0	525	Turnout		63.5	–10.4
% Pensioners	31.4		Elect	79,219		
% Prem mort/Rank	26	399				

Member of Parliament

Matthew Taylor, Liberal Democrat Treasury spokesman from 1999, was elected here at the March 1987 by-election in succession to the car crash victim, stage Cornishman David Penhaligon, whose parliamentary aide he had been. A tall, monotonous-voiced, cold-stare-visaged, articulate backer of Ashdown and Kennedy-style Lib-Labbery, the adopted son of a television scriptwriter, he was born in 1963 and educated at University College School, Hampstead and Lady Margaret Hall, Oxford, one of ten Lib Dem MPs with a public school and Oxbridge background. Inevitably a campaigner on 'more for Cornwall', he rather over-egged the pudding by entirely mis-predicting a swamping influx of two million solar-eclipse-seeking trippers in 1999, his dire predictions arguably emptying the boarding houses, but made a more sensible prediction a year later in acting as Charles Kennedy's leadership campaign manager, and getting as his reward the Treasury spokesmanship. An opponent of a complete ban on hand guns, he nevertheless votes for complete abolition of hunting.

TUNBRIDGE WELLS

A mild shock as well as mild amusement was caused on local election night in May 1994 when it was announced that the Conservatives had lost overall control of Tunbridge Wells Council. It was hardly an earth-shattering result: this was only one of many Tory local election reverses which had been building up cumulatively in a long series of mid-term protest votes against a government which had been in office for 15 years by then. The party actually retained power on Tunbridge Wells Borough Council on the chair's casting vote. Yet it is a sign of the image of Tunbridge Wells as a true-blue bastion of conservatism and Conservatism that the May 1994 result made headlines. The popular view is that this has always been the home of the irate correspondent to the letter pages of right-wing newspapers, 'Disgusted of Tunbridge Wells'.

In fact there is no reason why Tunbridge Wells should not share the disaffection with the Conservative government that led to so few councils remaining in Tory control up and down the country. True, the constituency contains a prosperous spa town and a swathe of affluent countryside stretching along the Sussex border, including part of the Weald. Yet in recent years spa towns have not been safe territory for the Conservatives elsewhere in the country: note the chastening experiences of Chris Patten in Bath and John Taylor in Cheltenham in 1992, and Norman Lamont in Harrogate in 1997. Quaint and even opulent rural villages have been electing Liberal Democrat councillors throughout southern England for years. Tunbridge Wells has no reason to be seen as immune from the centrist challenge in mid-term elections. It is not exceptional. It should be remembered too that what would be exceptional would be for the Lib Dems to transfer their municipal success to win the parliamentary seat, from a position of being 9,730 votes behind in June 2001, when Tunbridge Wells was actually the safest Conservative constituency in Kent. That really would make sensational news.

In addition to Tunbridge Wells itself and its satellite town of Southborough, the seat still contains its Wealden hinterland in 'hurst' country, taking in such places as Lamberhurst, Speldhurst and Goudhurst. In the 1997 boundary changes, though, it lost some other 'hursts' (Anglo-Saxon for wooded hills and their settlements): Sissinghurst, Sandhurst and Hawkhurst. These were transferred to Maidstone and the Weald in the general shake-up caused by the granting of a 17th and extra seat to Kent by the latest Parliamentary Boundary Commission, and coincided with the replacement as MP of Sir Patrick Mayhew, a true gentleman (and now Lord Mayhew of Twysden near Kilndown on the Weald) by the supermarket chief Archie Norman.

Social indices:			2001 Gen. Election:			
% Non-white	1.3		C	19,643	48.9	+3.7
% Prof/Man	40.8		LD	9,913	24.7	−5.0
% Non-manual	65.3		Lab	9,332	23.2	+2.8
£ Av prop val 2000	160 K		UKIP	1,313	3.3	+2.7
% Increase 97–00	66.8		C maj	9,730	24.2	
% Unemployed 2001	1.2		Turnout		62.3	−11.8
% Decrease 97–01	1.4		Elect	64,534		
% Fin hard/Rank	7.4	546				
% Pensioners	26.3					
% Prem mort/Rank	12	576				

Member of Parliament

Archie Norman, self-described as 'definitely a businessman in politics, not a politician in business', was elected in 1997 whilst still Chairman of ASDA, spent a year making himself disliked as Deputy Party Chairman, imposing reforms seemingly designed to root out from Central Office over-50-year-old smokers with untidy desks, and calling for more gay, black and female candidates, and then was brought onto the frontbench as a spokesman, by 2000 leading on the Environment. A very unpractised Commons debater who owed his rapid rise to having shared with William Hague a McKinsey past, and seen as an unclubbable cold fish, he was born in 1954 and educated at Charterhouse, Emmanuel College, Cambridge and Harvard Business School. His enforced bonding for MPs at Eastbourne was boycotted by Heath, Heseltine and Soames. A leading Portillo backer in 2001 who, by early 2002, was evoking 'One Nation' Toryism, he has ascribed the second landslide defeat to the party's obligation to its 'recidivist element', and has hinted at leaving politics if the party fails to change.

TWEEDDALE, ETTRICK AND LAUDERDALE

For some years after its creation in 1983, Tweeddale, Ettrick and Lauderdale appeared to be that very rare thing, a safe Liberal seat. It was the successor to Roxburgh, Selkirk and Peebles, which the young David Steel had won in a by-election in 1965 and gradually made more secure, despite his liberal policies on such matters as abortion and homosexual law reform and his opposition to the 1969 South African rugby tour. After his elevation to the Liberal leadership in 1976 Steel needed to worry no more about the marginality of his constituency in the western Borders. In 1979 he won by over 10,000 votes, and he held the redrawn and renamed – and smaller – Tweeddale, Ettrick and Lauderdale by nearly as large a lead in 1983. At that election Steel polled over 58% of the vote, a landslide in Borders terms. A decade later, though, in the 1990s, the seat looked once again like a marginal.

David Steel resigned as party leader in 1988, while still under 50 years of age but apparently jaded by the Liberals' electoral disappointments and the acrimonious breakup of the Alliance. He was knighted the next year, and sat on the backbenches as an 'elder statesman' of the centre. His vote had slipped by over 8% in 1987, and in 1992 it fell by another 10% – from 58% to 40% in nine years. Steel's majority over the Tories slumped to 2,500 in 1992, and it seemed as if he was back to the tough early days trying to hold the seat.

Not entirely surprisingly, he decided to retire, and in 1997 his successor as Liberal Democrat candidate Michael Moore only held on after another 9% slump (making 27% in exactly ten years) with a smaller majority still, 1,489, now over Labour, who were helped by the arrival in the boundary changes of Penicuik from Midlothian, far from the English border. More typical of the seat are the textile and market towns of Galashiels, Selkirk and Peebles, and the numerous farms and villages of this substantial section of the Scottish border country. Churchgoing is still strong here, as are other conservative traditions; while at the same time a healthy individualism is encouraged. The 2001 General Election saw a fascinating battle with a somewhat unexpected result, as Moore pushed the Lib Dem vote up again, by fully 11%. This was not at the expense of the nationally governing party, but rather of both the Conservatives and the SNP, both of whom fell back substantially not only from 1997 but also from the Scottish Parliament results here in 1999. It almost looked as if there was a local tactical vote to prevent Labour from winning here for the first time ever and for the last, perhaps, as this seat is almost certainly doomed, mostly becoming part of a forthcoming four-way marginal, proposed to be called Peebles, Clydesdale and Annandale.

Social indices:			2001 Gen. Election:			
% Non-white	0.4		LD	14,035	42.3	+11.0
% Prof/Man	33.3		Lab	8,878	26.7	−0.7
% Non-manual	56.9		C	5,118	15.4	−6.7
% Unemployed 2001	2.0		SNP	4,108	12.4	−4.7
% Decrease 97–01	0.8		SSP	695	2.1	
% Fin hard/Rank	20.4	268	Lib	383	1.2	+0.2
% Prem mort/Rank	25	427	LD maj	5,157	15.5	
			Turnout		63.9	−12.7
			Elect	51,966		

Member of Parliament

Michael Moore, alternately a Transport and Scotland spokesman and the political son and heir of David Steel, who installed him here after his own 32-year stint, was elected in 1997, one son of the manse in the steps of another. A keen devolutionist who helped broker the Scottish Lab-Lib coalition in 1999 despite having Labour – which he comfortably saw off on a 6% Labour to Lib Dem swing in 2001 – as his own local opponent, tall, boyish-looking and Ulster-born in 1965, he was educated at fee-paying Strathallan School, Jedburgh Grammar School and Edinburgh University, and worked as an accountant for six years. Notwithstanding his former profession, his role as an assiduous constituency MP involves defence of the local textile industry.

TWICKENHAM

The phenomenally successful local election activity of the Liberal Democrats (or rather, their predecessors) which started in Richmond spread over the river into the Twickenham sector of the borough of Richmond-upon-Thames in the early 1980s. With the boundary changes turning Richmond and Barnes into the rather more Conservative Richmond Park, the Lib Dems decided to make their number one target in the area the seat on the Middlesex shore, Twickenham. As it happens, in the rout which afflicted the Conservatives in 1997 they won Richmond Park as well, and indeed three other seats in outer south-west London. It was Twickenham which saw their biggest majority though, and it was regarded as the safest of the five in the 2001 campaign. Vincent Cable, an informed, intelligent and senior national spokesman and an energetic self-publicist locally, backed by a supercharged local machine, duly increased his majority to over 7,500, although this was somewhat overshadowed by Edward Davey's astonishing increase next door in Kingston and Surbiton.

The Liberal Democrats still hold the vast majority of council seats within the Twickenham constituency, although they have not quite been able to repeat the clean sweep they achieved in May 1986. Since 1998 the Conservatives have held all the seats in Central and South Twickenham, and West Twickenham has now been won twice by Labour. One would think that a suburb whose name is known as the home of English rugby union (a game dominated by Establishment conservatism) would be safely Tory, and indeed it was, until the outburst of municipal Liberal activism and success. It is still true of course that many residents must split their vote, returning Lib Dem councillors while preferring a Conservative national government to deal with matters such as tax and defence. Toby Jessel was an active constituency MP, helping to save Kneller Hall from closure, for example. This was not enough to save him when the burghers of Twickenham lost faith in John Major's national government, though, and Vincent Cable was well able to build up his own incumbency factor.

There was only one minor boundary change before the 1997 Election: the return of the anomalous East Twickenham ward, which had been associated with Richmond across the Thames since 1983. In addition to the four Twickenham town wards, the seat includes the communities of Whitton, Teddington and the various Hamptons. In August 2001 it was revealed that a higher proportion of residents in the borough of Richmond upon Thames earned over £60,000 a year than in any other local authority in Britain, and that borough very definitely includes Twickenham; although slightly less wealthy than the 'Surrey' bank of the river property prices are still among the 15 highest in the land, with an average in 2000 of £227,000. This is a very comfortable, desirable place to live.

Social indices:			2001 Gen. Election:			
% Non-white	5.6		LD	24,344	48.7	+3.6
% Prof/Man	53.2		C	16,689	33.4	−4.3
% Non-manual	76.2		Lab	6,903	13.8	−1.8
£ Av prop val 2000	227 K		Grn	1,423	2.8	
% Increase 97–00	60.7		UKIP	579	1.2	
% Unemployed 2001	1.2		LD maj	7,655	15.3	
% Decrease 97–01	1.4		Turnout		67.4	−12.0
% Fin hard/Rank	7.3	552	Elect	74,135		
% Pensioners	24.6					
% Prem mort/Rank	12	567				

Member of Parliament

Dr Vincent Cable, second-time-lucky victor here in 1997, reached the Liberal Democrats via the Labour Party and the SDP, having earlier fought elections under both labels, and worked for John Smith when he was Labour's Trade Secretary in 1979. Born in 1943, he attended Nunthorpe Grammar School, York, Fitzwilliam College, Cambridge, and Glasgow University where he obtained an economics doctorate, and worked variously as an academic and overseas development executive, and eventually in the oil industry, latterly as Chief Economist with Shell. His party's Trade and Industry spokesman from 1999, his effortless fluency is salted with a hint of abrasiveness, and his rational acceptance of Lib-Lab tactical voting with initial reservations about the impact on business of a minimum wage increase. Nor is he averse to highlighting worry about the migration of pupils (many of them Afro-Caribbean) from poorer boroughs into schools in his own affluent borough of Richmond-upon-Thames. He has sought to curb age discrimination, and to promote intercountry adoptions.

TYNE BRIDGE

When the Tyne Bridge seat was first created in 1983 it caused some controversy, for it was the first time that a constituency had crossed the natural barrier of the River Tyne and the borough boundaries to combine the inner-city and central portions of both Newcastle and Gateshead. In many ways, though, it was a logical creation. The south bank of the Tyne, the Teams, Bensham, Dunston and Bede wards of Gateshead, are socially and economically similar to the inner city of Newcastle and wards such as Benwell and Scotswood west of the city centre.

This is by most measures the most blighted constituency in Tyne and Wear, which has struggled economically for decades. Its male unemployment rate of 10% in 2001 was the highest by some way; the percentage of council housing, though falling due to sales and changes in tenure status, was also higher than any other North-Eastern seat; and Tyne Bridge boasted the fewest detached houses (1.3%). Much of the housing stock consists of blocks of grim-looking flats erected in post-war slum clearance schemes. The western inner city is more depressed than neighbourhoods like Byker to the east, with less of a community spirit. There are very real problems for the extremely poor Asian ethnic minority communities like Bangladeshis in Newcastle's West End, mostly in Elswick ward, where they have been subject to racial abuse and persecution on a scandalous scale.

Given the multiple deprivations suffered by Tyne Bridge, it would be surprising if Labour were not consistently elected with large majorities. This has indeed been the case, even in a by-election in 1985 when Dave Clelland was elected to replace the late Harry Cowans. In 2001 Tyne Bridge was the tenth safest Labour seat in Britain, as they polled 70% to the Conservatives' 13%. There can be only one winner in elections here in central Gateshead and central Newcastle. The conflicts here in the sore heart of the Tyneside conurbation lie in the inhabitants' battles against intimidating circumstances and gloom-ridden prospects.

Social indices:			2001 Gen. Election:			
% Non-white	4.0		Lab	18,345	70.5	−6.3
% Prof/Man	19.6		C	3,456	13.3	+2.2
% Non-manual	42.3		LD	3,213	12.3	+4.4
£ Av prop val 2000	43 K		SLP	533	2.0	
% Increase 97–00	28.3		SA	485	1.9	+0.4
% Unemployed 2001	7.7		Lab maj	14,889	57.2	
% Decrease 97–01	4.6		Turnout		44.2	−12.9
% Fin hard/Rank	42.3	38	Elect	58,900		
% Pensioners	25.3					
% Prem mort/Rank	57	13				

Member of Parliament

David Clelland, an Assistant Whip from 1995 to 2001 – in Opposition and in government is one of Labour's shrinking group of working-class trade unionists, formerly an electrical fitter and AEEU shop steward at NEI in Gateshead where he was eventually made redundant after 21 years. Born in 1943, he attended Kelvin Grove Boys' School, Gateshead and local technical colleges. Elected in 1985, he owed his selection for the seat to his leadership of Gateshead Council and his family's friendship with the deceased MP Harry Cowans. A short and cheery pipe-smoking Geordie, he has been an assiduous representative of North East regional concerns, and notably of his local armaments factory. But in 2001, in order to make room in the Whips' Office for nine of the 1997 intake, he was dropped.

TYNEMOUTH

The only Conservative constituency in Tyne and Wear, Tynemouth in North Tyneside, fell to Labour in the 1997 landslide. Only once before had it ever been won by Labour, in their post-war triumph of 1945. For many years until 1974 Tynemouth was represented by Dame Irene Ward, who became known as the 'Mother of the House of Commons' (she first entered Parliament in 1931). Her successor as Tory MP, Neville Trotter, could still win by over 9,500 votes in 1983, a solid performance in a region which has traditionally been hostile to Conservatism, but the writing was on the wall. Trotter retired in 1997, and Labour's Alan Campbell defeated his successor by over 11,000, and won again with virtually no weakening in his position in 2001, despite a year of decidedly disappointing North Tyneside borough election results in May 2000, when the Conservatives received more votes and returned more councillors (seven to two) in the wards which make up the seat. Having overcome this municipal glitch, it now looks like a safe Labour seat.

Tynemouth certainly has its share of heavy industry and Labour supporters. Squeezed into the south-eastern corner of the old Northumberland county in the angle created by the River Tyne and the North Sea, it is a split constituency. Along the river bank the economy has been shaped by the struggling shipyards and docks with their council estates behind them – Chirton, Collingwood, parts of North Shields. This is the strongly Labour section of the seat. But as one turns the corner at the mouth of the Tyne and heads northward, one enters a different kind of territory. Here are the seaside resorts and middle-class residential areas on the rocky North Sea coast: Tynemouth, Cullercoats, Whitley Bay, Seaton Sluice. The owner-occupied estates behind Whitley Bay, around Monkseaton, bare and treeless as they are, house many Conservative commuters to Newcastle. There is even a 'North/South divide' within the Tynemouth constituency.

Social indices:			2001 Gen. Election:			
% Non-white	1.3		Lab	23,364	53.2	−2.1
% Prof/Man	37.5		C	14,686	33.5	+0.1
% Non-manual	63.8		LD	5,108	11.6	+2.8
£ Av prop val 2000	68 K		UKIP	745	1.7	+0.8
% Increase 97–00	13.4		Lab maj	8,678	19.8	
% Unemployed 2001	4.0		Turnout		67.4	−9.8
% Decrease 97–01	2.6		Elect	65,184		
% Fin hard/Rank	15.7	339				
% Pensioners	29.7					
% Prem mort/Rank	35	249				

Member of Parliament

Alan Campbell won the seat for Labour in 1997, a local schoolteacher in Whitley Bay and then nearby in Ashington for a total of 17 years, born in 1957, educated at Blackfyne Secondary School, Consett and at Lancaster and Leeds Universities and at Newcastle Polytechnic. No great troubler of the scorers, he has focused on local concerns such as one-armed bandits in working men's clubs, and on the importance of European funding, and expressed reservations about moves towards PR voting. In 2001 he was lifted from one level of unobtrusiveness to another, becoming PPS to Cabinet Office Minister, Lord Macdonald.

TYNESIDE NORTH

The seat named North Tyneside by the Boundary Commission (and which is renamed Tyneside North by most observers and reference books) does not include the whole of Tyne and Wear north of the former river, nor does it include more than half of the metropolitan borough of North Tyneside. It is in fact in essence the former Wallsend constituency which existed up to 1997, with relatively minor alterations which include the loss of Wallsend ward itself.

Hadrian's Wall really did reach its eastern end on the Tyne at Wallsend, the site of a substantial Roman fort. Now, however, to equalise electorates Wallsend itself, and the neighbouring ward of Northumberland, have been added to the Newcastle East constituency, which was undersized; at the other, eastern end of the river frontage, one ward has been taken from Tynemouth. This is Riverside; which includes part of North Shields and part of the notorious Meadow Well estate, which achieved national prominence due to an outbreak of lawlessness early last decade. Most of the Tyneside North seat is inland and away from the banks of the river. Here are to be found an admixture of former mining villages, new private estates, and large council developments. The best known of the latter is probably the grim fort-like redoubt known as Killingworth Township, perhaps the most stark and dramatic of all the North Eastern housing redevelopments created by post-war reconstruction. Longbenton ward still had two-thirds of its housing stock in local authority hands by the time of the 1991 Census. Mining has only relatively recently left villages like Backworth and Dudley, and like much of the division they retain a great loyalty to the Labour Party.

There are some middle-class voters in the more commuterised of the villages, such as Wideopen and Seaton Burn along the A1, but the Tories polled less than a quarter of the vote in the old Wallsend and are unlikely ever to do any better in this renamed division. They managed just 14% in 2001. Nor in such a working-class seat does there seem to be much of an alternative appeal to the left: Socialist Labour and Socialist Alliance candidates both stood, but polled less than one in a hundred of the votes cast. The most common form of protest against the government, or maybe wider than that, was abstention: 42% on the roll did not vote.

Social indices:			2001 Gen. Election:			
% Non-white	0.7		Lab	26,127	69.5	−3.2
% Prof/Man	22.0		C	5,459	14.5	+0.9
% Non-manual	48.0		LD	4,649	12.4	+1.8
£ Av prop val 2000	57 K		UKIP	770	2.0	
% Increase 97–00	20.7		SA	324	0.9	
% Unemployed 2001	5.2		SLP	240	0.6	
% Decrease 97–01	3.0		Lab maj	20,668	55.0	
% Fin hard/Rank	32.3	112	Turnout		57.9	−10.0
% Pensioners	27.0		Elect	64,914		
% Prem mort/Rank	42	141				

Member of Parliament

Stephen Byers, Transport, Local Government and Regions Secretary from 2001, enjoyed a meteoric rise after his election in 1992, assisted no doubt by the airbrushing – contemporaneously with Mandelson – of his moustache in 1995. A sometime Bennite and a local (Newcastle) polytechnic lecturer, he was born in 1953, son of an RAF technician, and attended Chester City Grammar School, Chester College of Further Education and Liverpool Polytechnic, and rose politically through 12 years on the local North Tyneside council. A Gould, not Smith, voter in 1992, he moved significantly in a Blairite direction in provocatively calling during the 1996 TUC Congress for looser Labour links with the unions, and as DTI Secretary (1998–2001) managed to deflect blame for major car and steelworks closures onto duplicitous foreigners. But as Schools Standards Minister in 1998 he failed the Dan Quayle test when answering '54' to the question 'What is 7 times 8?'. In 2001 his career further wobbled with the exposure of his spin doctor's attempt to bury bad news in the wake of the terrorist attacks on the World Trade Center, his pushing into receivership of Railtrack, reports of the calamitous condition of the railways, and again in February 2002 with the messy sacking of squabbling aides. Here was no ministry in which an ambitious man should tarry.

TYRONE WEST

In the most recent round of boundary changes, which came into force in time for the 1997 UK General Election, Northern Ireland was awarded an 18th and additional seat. This was not the Commission's original intent. Their first plan had been radically to redraw the existing 17 constituencies, but this would have involved the reduction of Belfast's four seats to three, which would have caused problems for prominent Unionist politicians such as Martin Smyth and the DUP's Peter Robinson. The Strangford seat of the Ulster Unionist MP John Taylor would also have disappeared. There would have been problems too for Nationalist politicians, as the seats of Seamus Mallon and Eddie McGrady, both of the SDLP, would have crashed together. Given so much disruption, it was only to be expected that there would be vociferous objections. After a series of public inquiries an 18-seat scheme was suggested, which would not threaten the tenure of any sitting members.

The new name is West Tyrone, but it is arguable whether that seat actually has the best claim to be the additional division. It consists of the whole of two local government districts, Omagh and Strabane. Omagh was previously in Mid Ulster – and so was half of Strabane. This means that three-quarters of the electors of West Tyrone were previously in the Mid Ulster seat (the other quarter around the town of Strabane itself coming from Foyle). What is more, most of the former Mid Ulster is now in West Tyrone. There is therefore a case that the seat which now bears the name of Mid Ulster was the new one, made up of minor parts of three former constituencies.

Despite the circumstances described in the first paragraph, West Tyrone did see an incumbent defeated in 2001, as Willie Thompson, an anti-agreement Ulster unionist was ousted in favour of Sinn Fein's Pat Doherty. West Tyrone has a Catholic and Nationalist majority, as might be expected in a predominantly rural seat in the west of Northern Ireland. Strabane has long been known as a Republican stronghold which has suffered great economic difficulties and massively high unemployment. However, as in the case of the Fermanagh and South Tyrone and Mid Ulster (both former and new) seats, a Protestant Unionist could win if the SDLP and Sinn Fein stand against each other and split the Nationalist vote almost equally in this potential plum. This is precisely what happened in 1997, as both the SDLP and Sinn Fein polled between 14,000 and 15,000, letting the Ulster Unionist William Thompson in although he only took 34.6% of the vote.

In 2001, however, a resurgent as well as insurgent Sinn Fein felt they had an excellent chance of taking a clear majority of the Catholic vote, and thus gaining the seat, until the relatively late entry of a strong SDLP candidate, the popular grandmother Brid Rodgers, born in the Republic and regarded as a very successful Northern Ireland Executive minister. After a campaign marred by accusations of intimidation and impersonation, which resulted in a massive turnout of 80%, second highest in the UK (casting grave doubt on the theory that it is areas of low turnout where society shows a lack of democratic good health and harmony) Doherty did take almost 60% of the anti-unionist vote and won, yet another example in that most vigorously contested general election in Northern Ireland of a victory for a more extreme over a more moderate stance.

Social indices:		2001 Gen. Election:			
% Prof/Man	31.6	SF	19,814	40.8	+10.0
% Non-manual	48.9	UUP	14,774	30.4	–4.1
% RC	63.2	SDLP	13,942	28.7	–3.3
% Irish sp	11.1	SF maj	5,040	10.4	
% Unemployed 2001	7.9	Turnout		79.9	+0.4
% Decrease 97–01	4.0	Elect	60,739		

Member of Parliament

Pat Doherty, a sometime site engineer, Glasgow-born son of a migrant Donegal man and brother of one of the IRA's Balcombe Street gang who served a long prison term, captured this seat in 2001 from its unlikely one-term Ulster Unionist incumbent, Willie Thompson, whose 1997 win on 35% of the poll came courtesy of a split Republican vote. But even Doherty's 2001 win was a surprise, given the assumed popularity of the SDLP candidate, the Northern Ireland Agriculture Minister, Mrs Brid Rogers. A vice-president of Sinn Fein since 1988, he rose politically as the electoral face of hard-line republicanism, organising to eclipse the SDLP electoral machine, as in his own capture of the West Tyrone seat in the Northern Ireland Assembly election in 1998. Seen variously as cutting a 'grandfatherly figure' (*Belfast Telegraph*), or as resembling 'a shambolic science teacher' (the *Scotsman*), and as being 'genial, apparently completely open, and smiles readily' (the *Independent*), one place he will not be seen is on the floor of the House of Commons – so making such judgments difficult to verify. He also likes building stone walls.

ULSTER MID

Or more properly Mid Ulster, as named by the Boundary Commission; and even this is dubious, as 'Ulster' is a term which should strictly be used for nine counties which include three in the Republic (Monaghan, Cavan and Donegal). This is the west-central rural seat in Northern Ireland, and it has one of the most dramatic and turbulent electoral histories in the whole of the United Kingdom.

Like its neighbour, Fermanagh and South Tyrone, Mid Ulster's contests have been marked by abstentionism, absenteeism, disqualification, vote splits between rival factions and controversial by-elections. Mid Ulster had had an anti-unionist majority for many years, but after the disqualification of the Sinn Feiner Tom Mitchell as a convicted felon in 1955 the Catholic vote divided to let in the unionist George Forrest. On his death in 1969 the seat was won by the 21-year-old Bernadette Devlin (later McAliskey) as a Nationalist Unity candidate. But she lost it to the OUP's John Dunlop on another split vote in February 1974, and he benefited from further Catholic schisms till 1983. He did not stand again that year, and the unionist standard passed to the Paisleyite DUP, who had recently increased their strength in the area. The split between more moderate and more extreme nationalism allowed the Reverend William McCrea to hold Mid Ulster from 1983 to 1997.

In the extensive boundary changes which come into force in 1997, Mid Ulster's lines were substantially shifted while the essential political situation remains the same. The Omagh district has been lost to the new and additional West Tyrone division, while 20,000 voters are taken in from East Londonderry, in the Magherafelt district, and 9,000 around Coalisland from the Fermanagh and South Tyrone constituency. This new territory also includes some Nationalist strongholds, and in 1997 Sinn Fein advanced very strongly and Martin McGuinness re-established the Republican hold here, strengthening it further as he advanced by another 11% in 2001. The DUP and SDLP fell back almost equally, the former due to relative abstentions, presumably, as one cannot imagine voters shifting from DUP to Sinn Fein.

It might be noted that the turnout was still recorded as 81.3%, the highest of any of the 659 constituencies. There is clearly not a correlation between turnout and support for the democratic institutions of government, since more than half of those who did vote supported a party and a man opposed to the very existence of the United Kingdom, and of the sovereignty of its assembly at Westminster, where McGuinness will not take the oath of allegiance and therefore not officially take his seat. Those pontificating about the causes and implications of the massive turnout drop across the sea in Britain should at least think about that.

Social indices:		2001 Gen. Election:			
% Prof/Man	31.1	SF	25,502	51.1	+11.0
% Non-manual	48.5	DUP	15,549	31.1	−5.2
% RC	60.4	SDLP	8,376	16.8	−5.3
% Irish sp	18.6	WP	509	1.0	+0.5
% Unemployed 2001	3.9	SF maj	9,953	19.9	
% Decrease 97–01	5.2	Turnout		81.3	−4.8
		Elect	61,390		

Member of Parliament

Martin McGuinness, dubbed by his Protestant near-namesake, the former unionist MP Ken Maginnis, 'the Godfather of Godfathers', with IRA command in Derry at the time of Bloody Sunday in 1972, unexpectedly won this seat in 1997 on the highest turnout of any UK constituency (86%), feeding traditional unionist suspicion of the time-honoured Republican 'vote-early-vote-often' principle, and the mobilisation of the graveyard vote. A curly-haired, ascetic and supposedly strong church-goer from a devout Catholic rather than a Republican family (an uncle having been Catholic Bishop of Nottingham, and one of McGuinness's names being 'Pacelli' – the surname of Pope Pius XII), born in 1950 in Derry's Bogside, he failed the 11-plus and attended the Christian Brothers' Brow of the Hill Technical College, Derry, leaving at 15 to work as a shop assistant and later a butcher's apprentice. Endeavouring with Sinn Fein President, Gerry Adams, to demonstrate that 'the war is over', he took office as Education Minister in the Northern Ireland Power-Sharing Executive in 1999 but was denied integration at Westminster by the refusal of MPs to back attempts to allow the Sinn Fein MPs to evade the Oath of Allegiance. With his new-found access to the pork barrel as a high-spending minister likely to boost his party's electoral fortunes, and liking to be compared in appearance to Art Garfunkel, he is – as with all 50-year-old ex-terrorists, higher up the learning curve.

UPMINSTER

The Conservatives only regained half a dozen seats from Labour in 2001, a harvest thin enough to lead to a cacophony of breast-beating and another change of party leader, but two of these were in Havering. Most publicity went to Andrew Rosindell's excellent performance in Romford, but Keith Darvill was also removed in the next constituency.

The constituency of Upminster is a long, thin strip of the eastern edge of Havering borough, which means the eastern edge of London too. It is the terminus of the District underground line. It has another distinct characteristic too. It has the highest proportion of white residents of any of London: over 97.5%. In administrative terms, it is on the border with Essex. In the hearts and minds of its residents Upminster is very much part of that county.

The seat is starkly divided between its northern and southern parts. In the north is the huge council development of Harold Hill, which has a population of 30,000 and sustains three wards which are safely Labour in local elections. In the south is the middle-class Cranham and the leafy and affluent Emerson Park, with professional and even wealthy residents. Thus Upminster contains the most upmarket and downmarket parts of Havering.

The outcome in political terms, however, is much the same as that in Romford and Hornchurch. All swung strongly to the right from the 1970s to 1992, and all were gained by Labour after huge swings in 1997. In Upminster Keith Darvill increased the Labour share by over 16%, but this was still enough only to win by 2,770. Nevertheless, Labour held 30 seats which were more vulnerable to the Tories in 2001, and lost none with bigger margins. The result was somewhat unexpected. Council and European elections in 1998–99 had not been particularly ominous, and the 59-year-old Angela Watkinson could not claim Rosindell's remarkable electoral achievements in borough elections over the previous decade. It seems to have been a matter of sub-regional swing, plus a touch of a coat-tail effect.

Social indices:			2001 Gen. Election:			
% Non-white	2.3		C	15,410	45.5	+6.0
% Prof/Man	33.0		Lab	14,169	41.9	–4.3
% Non-manual	64.5		LD	3,183	9.4	–0.1
£ Av prop val 2000	135 K		UKIP	1,089	3.2	
% Increase 97–00	42.8		C maj	1,241	3.7	
% Unemployed 2001	2.0		Turnout		59.6	–12.7
% Decrease 97–01	2.0		Elect	56,829		
% Fin hard/Rank	15.0	353				
% Pensioners	28.5					
% Prem mort/Rank	24	438				

Member of Parliament

Angela Watkinson, the only woman among 33 new Conservative MPs in 2001, whose election no more than compensated for the retirement of Teresa Gorman, came late to the fray as the oldest Tory newcomer at the age of 59. Born in 1941 in Leytonstone, she attended Wanstead County High School (and later took a public administration course), married a policeman, worked for six years as a bank clerk, raised a family of three children for 12 years, resumed work as a secretary in a special school for 12 years, and worked finally as a local government official for seven years. A Conservative Party member from the age of 24, she was elected to Havering Council in 1994. The product, with Romford's Andrew Rosindell, of a Tory mini-revival in the working-class Essex suburbs, despite Upminster being only the party's 52nd target seat, she was soon, as a Duncan Smith supporter, obliged to renounce her Monday Club membership in order that his campaign not be damaged by association with the Club's policy of favouring voluntary repatriation of immigrants. She had also in 1998 subscribed to Bill Cash's anti-EU European Foundation.

UPPER BANN

It is a sign of the divisive political turmoil besetting Northern Ireland at the time of the June 2001 General Election – not only sectarian but intra-community – that the leader of the largest party and First Minister of the devolved Power-Sharing Executive, David Trimble, almost lost his own seat. The threat came not from a Nationalist or Republican bent on extracting the six counties in the north-east of Ireland from the United Kingdom, but from the Paisleyite Democratic Unionist Party arguing that he had made too many concessions in the 'peace process'. Their candidate David Simpson received 29.5%, 18% more than the DUP had in 1997, a huge swing by any standard. Trimble's place in the Commons, like that as First Minister, and like that as leader of his party, hung by a thread.

Upper Bann lies in the heart of Northern Ireland, having no sea coast and not touching the border with the Republic. It lies to the south of Lough Neagh, the province's great lake, and it is named after the river Bann, which flows into the lake. The constituency covers the Craigavon district council area and almost half the Banbridge district.

The seat is mainly rural with a strong dependence on agriculture, but it also contains some sizeable towns. Lurgan and Portadown were the twin urban centres on which the new city of Craigavon was founded, but its centre just did not grow to meet expectations. Both towns have their own industries and have direct access to Northern Ireland's M1, which runs through the centre of the constituency. Banbridge is an important market town on the dual carriageway and main route to the border and Dublin. There is an important tourist attraction in the excellent coarse fishing on the river Bann.

In its brief life (it was created in 1983) Upper Bann has elected two prominent MPs. It has seen two by-elections, too. The first was created by the simultaneous resignation of all 15 unionist members in 1986 in protest at the Hillsborough Agreement. The second was altogether more tragic, the result of the death at scarcely 50 years of age of Harold McCusker, a much-respected leading figure in the OUP, and possibly a future leader of his party. The 1990 by-election saw the more or less inevitable success and succession of the OUP candidate, David Trimble, who went on to become leader in 1995. What is follows at constituency and all other levels would have been almost impossible to predict, as are future convolutions in the political path taken by Northern Ireland.

Social indices:		2001 Gen. Election:			
% Prof/Man	25.7	UUP	17,095	33.5	−10.1
% Non-manual	46.5	DUP	15,037	29.5	+18.0
% RC	38.5	SF	10,770	21.1	+9.0
% Irish sp	7.4	SDLP	7,607	14.9	−9.3
% Unemployed 2001	4.0	WP	527	1.0	−0.1
% Decrease 97–01	1.7	UUP maj	2,058	4.0	
		Turnout		70.3	+2.4
		Elect	72,574		

Member of Parliament

David Trimble, leader of the Ulster Unionists and First Minister of the tenuous Northern Ireland Power-Sharing Executive set up in 1998, was first elected in 1990. Like many leaders, a man who has moved towards the centre from more radical origins, he stands in a virtual minority of two (himself and Sylvia Hermon) amongst his six-strong parliamentary group, the rest of whom can no longer be dubbed 'the Woodentops', (as he had described the more slow-witted UUP MPs, who died or retired before 2001), with at least two of his anti-Agreement Commons colleagues – Donaldson and Burnside – posing threats to his UUP leadership. A deft performer in a culture of pedestrian black-and-whiters, a 'giant among pygmies' (according to the *Observer*), he was born in 1944 into a family of classic Protestant siege mentality (with a County Cavan policeman father who was obliged to relocate to Belfast following Partition, and with other family links back to the siege of Derry in 1689), educated at Bangor Grammar School and Queen's University, Belfast where he read law and became a law lecturer. Carrot-haired, with a pink, Ulster-Scots face and a hurried short-stepped gait, though influenced by IRA-defector Sean O'Callaghan's view that 'the war is over', he knows he could go the way of all Ulster Unionist flesh, by emulating the fate of his power-sharing predecessor Brian Faulkner. Twelve of the 18 Northern Ireland MPs are also MLAs (Members of the Northern Ireland Assembly); the missing ones – apart from the SDLP's John Hume – all Unionists, four of whom are not in the Assembly because he can't trust them to support him.

UXBRIDGE

The first by-election of the 1997 Parliament took place in Uxbridge on the last day of July that year, caused by the sudden death of Sir Michael Shersby one week after the General Election. He had only held the seat by 724 votes, but Labour made a tactical error in dispensing with their candidate, a local councillor David Williams, and parachuting in a New Labour favourite from Hammersmith/Fulham. The Conservatives on the other hand selected a well known Uxbridge department store owner, John Randall, who increased their majority to 3,000. It was the first Tory win in a by-election since 1989.

There was no overall control in the outer West London borough of Hillingdon after the photo-finish all-out elections of May 1998, but the Conservative candidates within Uxbridge wards were 17% ahead of Labour. Although there were predictions that Randall would be in trouble in the 2001 General Election, when his individual characteristics would be less prominent than in the by-election, and although Greater London was the Tories' weakest region in England (the only one in which their share went down between 1997 and 2001) he actually held on with an increased majority. Clearly his personal vote had become stronger still with incumbency.

In parliamentary terms, there was a time in the 1960s and 1970s when the borough's three constituencies seemed to consist of one safe Labour seat (Hayes and Harlington), one safe Conservative (Ruislip-Northwood), and one marginal (Uxbridge). Yet all three were held by the Tories from 1983 to 1997, and if Labour couldn't win Uxbridge in the July 1997 by-election, when they were standing at 60% in the national opinion polls, it seems doubtful under what circumstances they could.

There are two gaps to be explained. One is that between local and national elections. The other is between the present and the past: Uxbridge was held by Labour from 1945 to 1959 and from 1966 to 1970. It has become common in Britain in recent decades for voters to take the opportunity of protesting at government performance by rejecting its local candidates in mid-term elections. The question of change through time needs a more specific answer. Uxbridge is a suburban seat on the edge of London with a relatively small percentage of non-white residents for the capital. Such seats moved rapidly away from Labour during the years of that party's drift to the left and consequent internal strife in the late 1970s and early 1980s. Uxbridge's owner-occupation rate also increased rapidly due to council house sales, to reach 70% in 1991. Not much has been moving in Labour's direction here; how many seats are there which Labour did win in 1966 but not in 1997? (The answer is: Bedfordshire South West, Meriden – and Uxbridge.)

There are a variety of neighbourhoods within the wards which make up Uxbridge. Labour does best in Yiewsley, Uxbridge South and Colham. The Conservatives' strongest wards are West Drayton near Heathrow airport, Uxbridge North, and especially Ickenham north of the A40, which closely resembles the Ruislip-Northwood constituency in social and political nature. The three wards from the community of Hillingdon are closely balanced, one each won by the three main parties in 1998.

Social indices:			2001 Gen. Election:			
% Non-white	8.3		C	15,751	47.1	+3.6
% Prof/Man	33.8		Lab	13,653	40.9	–1.0
% Non-manual	60.7		LD	3,426	10.3	–0.6
£ Av prop val 2000	139 K		UKIP	588	1.8	
% Increase 97–00	57.0		C maj	2,098	6.3	
% Unemployed 2001	1.5		Turnout		57.6	–14.7
% Decrease 97–01	2.0		Elect	58,066		
% Fin hard/Rank	9.9	468				
% Pensioners	22.6					
% Prem mort/Rank	20	474				

Member of Parliament

John Randall, a collector's item as a Tory MP with a beard who votes against fox hunting, has a degree in Serbo-Croat and likes bird-watching in Cuba, and was elected at a by-election in 1997, soon after the huge Labour landslide, when as a local department store owner he saw off a Labour candidate dubbed an intruder for coming from 12 miles away in Hammersmith. Variously compared to Forrest Gump and a garden gnome, he was born in 1955, educated at Merchant Taylors', Northwood and the School of Slavonic and East European Studies, London and inherited the managing directorship of Randall's, his family's Uxbridge store, in 1988. Unpretentious and not overly partisan, he was sympathetic towards the Serbs in the Kosovo conflict and likes reading Russian novels on the tube journey (18 stops) in from Uxbridge. His leadership votes in 2001 went unrevealed.

VALE OF CLWYD

In the major boundary changes in north-east Wales consequent upon the 1995 Boundary Commission's award of an extra constituency to the former county of

Clwyd, two seats were created, both largely based on the former Clwyd North West. That division returned Rod Richards with the largest Conservative majority in Wales, over 6,000, in 1992. However, in 1997 the Tories managed to lose both Clwyd West, based on Colwyn Bay and Abergele, and this then new seat of Vale of Clwyd.

Vale of Clwyd is compactly situated, as the name implies, on the low-lying land around the river Clwyd as it flows into the Irish Sea. The battle is well and truly joined in the scrap between the major parties. The constituency includes the eastern part of the old Clwyd North West, around the coastal resort of Rhyl with its open flat sands and amusement arcades, within its troubled west and south-western sectors of its working-class Labour voting concentration; and the inland territory which includes the tiny cathedral city of St Asaph and Rhuddlan, with its Norman castle. From Delyn came Rhyl's eastern neighbour, Prestatyn, another flat seaside town, with about 12,000 electors – not its most strongly Labour element, though. From Clwyd South West, a safeish Labour seat, came about 8,000 voters a little further up the river, mainly in and around the old county town of Denbigh – not its most Labour part either. Overall this should add up to an even fight in an even year.

Now for a paragraph for the man who was Deputy Prime Minister during the 2001 Election: John Prescott's birthplace Prestatyn is in this seat. So is the town of Rhyl, location of Prescott's famous punch of an egg-throwing protester, the media highlight of the 2001 national election campaign, and in all probability the only thing from it which will be retained in popular memory. Like everything else which happened during the four weeks immediately before the election, there is no evidence that it affected the ultimate result.

In the circumstances of 1997, when the Tories lost every seat they were defending in Wales, Chris Ruane had won Vale of Clwyd by nearly two to one. It was closer in 2001, as Labour slipped back as almost everywhere else in Wales, but Labour must be expected to start as favourites here next time too. Both the Liberal Democrats and Plaid Cymru are very weak in this Vale.

Social indices:			2001 Gen. Election:			
% Non-white	0.7		Lab	16,179	50.0	−2.7
% Welsh sp	21.0		C	10,418	32.2	+2.4
% Prof/Man	32.9		LD	3,058	9.5	+0.7
% Non-manual	55.8		PC	2,300	7.1	+1.2
£ Av prop val 2000	55 K		UKIP	391	1.2	+0.5
% Increase 97–00	18.1		Lab maj	5,761	17.8	
% Unemployed 2001	3.8		Turnout		63.1	−11.5
% Decrease 97–01	1.9		Elect	51,247		
% Fin hard/Rank	11.0	439				
% Pensioners	34.1					
% Prem mort/Rank	39	200				

Member of Parliament

Chris Ruane, a bland-looking, oval-faced, locally born-and-bred Catholic primary school teacher, won the seat in 1997. Born in 1958, son of a labourer, educated at Blessed Edward Jones High School, Rhyl, Aberystwyth and Liverpool Universities and at South Wales Polytechnic, he returned in 1982 to teach for 15 years, until elected in 1997, at the Rhyl primary school he had attended in the 1960s, and served eight years on Rhyl Council. Reliant on notes when speaking, he extols cycling, has attacked local environmental pollution, backed Welsh devolution as promising the 'last Quango in Powys', and been a member of the Welsh Affairs Select Committee from 1999.

VALE OF GLAMORGAN

In June 2001 Labour MP John Smith held on to his seat, the Vale of Glamorgan, with a majority of 4,700 – almost exactly half that he had enjoyed in 1997, but still secure against a swing of up to 5% next time. However, this had not always been a Labour seat. The closest result of any recorded in the 1992 General Election was that of the Vale of Glamorgan. The Conservative Walter Sweeney regained the seat, which had been lost to Labour in a by-election in May 1989, by just 19 votes. It is often pointed out that the Tories recaptured all seven of their by-election losses of the 1987–92 Parliament, but this one was a little close for comfort. It would have taken only ten of the Vale's 66,000 voters to change their minds for the Conservatives to lose it again at the 1997 Election, and in fact over 5,000 switched to Labour (net).

The Vale does have the elements of a genuine marginal, not just one made to appear so by the mischance of the death of the long-serving Tory MP Sir Raymond Gower in 1989. The seat's largest town is Barry, a working port with several solidly Labour wards. Despite the existence of a Conservative-voting neighbourhood in the holiday resort of west Barry, such as Baruc ward, the town does not look as if it should be in a Conservative seat; yet it was for decades, since 1951, apart from the three-year aberration between 1989 and 1992. The Conservative strength lies elsewhere, in the soft and affluent farming country and commuting villages of the hinterland, in the heart of the Vale itself. Here are overwhelmingly Tory wards, based on villages like Peterson-super-Ely, Wenvoe with its TV mast and Rhoose near Cardiff Airport. The largest community is the comfortable, even slightly twee, market town of Cowbridge, just off the A48 trunk road along which the traffic thunders on its way to Cardiff.

The Vale versus Barry; it seems on recent evidence to be a fairly even contest most of the time, and if the Conservatives win another general election they will have to regain the seat, Barry and all.

Social indices:			2001 Gen. Election:			
% Non-white	1.3		Lab	20,524	45.4	−8.5
% Welsh sp	6.8		C	15,824	35.0	+0.7
% Prof/Man	35.0		LD	5,521	12.2	+3.0
% Non-manual	60.2		PC	2,867	6.3	+3.8
£ Av prop val 2000	77 K		UKIP	448	1.0	
% Increase 97–00	14.1		Lab maj	4,700	10.4	
% Unemployed 2001	3.6		Turnout		67.4	−12.8
% Decrease 97–01	1.9		Elect	67,071		
% Fin hard/Rank	10.2	463				
% Pensioners	24.3					
% Prem mort/Rank	26	406				

Member of Parliament

John Smith was elected in 1997, having held the seat after a by-election from 1989 to 1992. Harshly dubbed (by Simon Hoggart) as a 'low-tech flying fortress loaded with 10,000 lbs of sycophancy', he is an orthodox loyalist with an air-brushed CND past whose by-election victory in 1989 symbolised Labour's climb-back to electoral credibility under the Kinnock leadership. Born in 1951 of Welsh-Irish parents but with the commonest name in the English language, and educated at Penarth County School and (later) Cardiff University, he was initially a building worker, RAF cook, and joiner before lecturing in business studies, and was a local councillor for 12 years. Safe rather than inspired and ex-moustachioed, he has served as a PPS to Roy Hattersley (1990–92) and John Reid (1997–99) until making way for younger orthodox foot soldiers.

VALE OF YORK

In some cases the creation of a new safe seat actually hurts the party which apparently benefits. In several counties, for example, in the most recent boundary review before the 1997 Election, an additional Conservative constituency has drawn so much Tory support from several other seats that their own majorities have been reduced, or even eliminated. This would seem to be the case in Lincolnshire, for example, and Leicestershire, and perhaps Hampshire too. In North Yorkshire, though, the same did not happen. The eighth and extra division justly awarded to the county due to its population growth is the Vale of York. It is indeed a solid Tory 'gain', won by nearly 10,000 even after a swing to Labour of over 15% in 1997. It does take true-blue voters from four other Conservative seats. Yet the Tory strength here in the heart of North Yorkshire is so great that most of those constituencies have easily withstood the impact of their lost legions.

The most generous of the donor seats was Ryedale, which gave up its south-western corner, stretching from the country around Easingwold in the heart of the Vale itself through to the suburbs of York, such as Haxby and the Rowntree chocolate firm's turn of the century 'model village' of New Earswick. Second, there were around 20,000 voters from the Richmond constituency, to the north of the Ryedale portion, centred on the market and horse-racing town of Thirsk. Then there were over 10,000 from the rural wards of the former Harrogate seat, directly to the west of York itself. Finally 6,000 electors around the small town of Boroughbridge (north-west of the city) came in from Skipton and Ripon.

Virtually all of this is Conservative territory, with the Liberal Democrats distantly second even in places where they can win local elections, but slipping to third in the inaugural general election. As the name implies, the countryside is flatter than elsewhere in the 'broad acre' county of Yorkshire, although not entirely so: there are some rolling hills. The economy is dominated by fertile farmland, and prosperous small market and commuting towns, and many villages. This will remain good ground for the Conservative Anne McIntosh, who increased her share by 7% in 2001 as the seat moved into the safest 20 on the Conservative list.

Social indices:			2001 Gen. Election:			
% Non-white	0.5		C	25,033	51.6	+6.9
% Prof/Man	36.2		Lab	12,516	25.8	−0.6
% Non-manual	57.2		LD	9,799	20.2	−3.6
£ Av prop val 2000	99 K		UKIP	1,142	2.4	
% Increase 97–00	33.3		C maj	12,517	25.8	
% Unemployed 2001	1.2		Turnout		66.1	−9.9
% Decrease 97–01	0.8		Elect	73,335		
% Fin hard/Rank	8.0	524				
% Pensioners	25.1					
% Prem mort/Rank	17	513				

Member of Parliament

Anne McIntosh, a spokesman on Culture, Media and Sport from 2001, was elected in 1997 having been an MEP for North Essex and South Suffolk (or thereabouts) since 1989 and, as such, not in synch with her party's current Europhobia – indeed with a record of having called (in 1991) for a federal Europe with a single currency, foreign and defence policy and with European law taking precedence over national law (which as a barrister working in European Community Law made sense at least personally). Since 1997 she has buried – indeed reversed – much of this, attacking the Social Chapter and comparing euro banknotes to Marks and Spencer vouchers. As a Scot, born in 1954 and educated at Harrogate College and Edinburgh University, her apostasy has also seen her oppose devolution, which for Euro-federalists should be all of a piece. Though a Clarke voter in 1997 and 2001, one could be forgiven for seeing in her pinch-faced, austere and intense expression a certain inner conflict. She was one of ten Clarke supporters to be appointed to Iain Duncan Smith's shadow team in 2001.

VAUXHALL

The north end of the borough of Lambeth is part of London's true inner city. Rather as in the neighbouring borough to the east, Southwark, the well-publicised problems of the local Labour Party who have run the council have been exploited by the Liberal Democrats, and in May 1994 when Labour lost their overall majority the Lib Dems took the five northern wards of (let's take it from the top) Bishop's, Prince's, Oval, Stockwell and Vassall, and made an inroad in winning one seat in Larkhall. In the two Clapham wards (Town and Park) the Conservatives pressed Labour hard in 1994, and the only wards where Labour won easily were Ferndale near the centre of Brixton and Angell. In 1998 Labour did better, but the Liberal Democrats still provided the candidate topping the poll in four of those wards and took over from the Tories in second place in Clapham Park.

However, Labour's municipal difficulties do not seem to be translated into parliamentary problems in Vauxhall, at least as long as an attractive image is presented. Thus Labour managed to hold the seat with an increased majority at the 1989 by-election caused by the retirement of Stuart Holland, with a carefully-managed campaign and the centrally-imposed candidature of Kate Hoey. In 2001

Hoey secured 59% of the vote, while the Liberal Democrats remained consigned to (a distant) second place. Clearly the people of Vauxhall wish to punish Labour's Lambeth Council leaders, but not the party in that institution just across the river from Bishop's ward, the House of Commons.

This seems logical enough. Although there is some gentrification in an area so close to Westminster and the heart of London, although the seat contains distinguished landmarks like County Hall, the South Bank arts complex, Lambeth Palace, the Waterloo stations and the Oval cricket ground, this is actually poor inner-city terrain in the main. Here are dangerous council estates like Stockwell Park, and the terraced streets north of Brixton which have seen drug-related murders. Over a third of the population comes from ethnic minority groups and half still live in social housing. Labour's national image, and that of Kate Hoey, are sufficiently distanced from that of the scandal-ridden Lambeth regime to retain Vauxhall's general election loyalties.

Social indices:			2001 Gen. Election:			
% Non-white	34.3		Lab	19,738	59.1	−4.7
% Prof/Man	40.9		LD	6,720	20.1	+4.1
% Non-manual	62.2		C	4,489	13.4	−1.8
£ Av prop val 2000	210 K		Grn	1,485	4.4	+2.2
% Increase 97–00	73.6		SA	853	2.6	
% Unemployed 2001	7.3		Ind	107	0.3	
% Decrease 97–01	5.5		Lab maj	13,018	39.0	
% Fin hard/Rank	46.4	23	Turnout		44.8	−10.7
% Pensioners	18.8		Elect	74,474		
% Prem mort/Rank	56	17				

Member of Parliament

Kate Hoey joined the ranks of the disgruntled sacked when she lost her job as Sports Minister in 2001. Once one of Labour's tousled-haired, shoulder-padded, feminising shock troops of the 1980s, and elected here in 1989, she had combined her career as Sports Minister (1999–2001) with politically incorrect views in favour of fox hunting, gun ownership and football terracing, as oddly unsympathetic to 'women's ministries or female issues', and as a unionist in Irish politics – a fairly off-message attitudinal set. Bearing the stamp of her Ulster background with a metallic if modulating nasal brogue, she was born in 1946 into a farming family, attended Belfast Royal Academy, Ulster College of Physical Education and City of London College, and worked as a further education lecturer and eventually as 'educational adviser' to Arsenal, Spurs and Chelsea football clubs. Like many Blair ministers she has an airbrushed left-wing past, in her case as a member of the Trotskyist International Marxist Group, in which incarnation she gave NUS President Jack Straw some trouble back in the late 1960s. Briefly by proxy drawn into the halcyon electoral days of 1997, it was her partner Tom Stoddart who helped coax Martin Bell to stand as a Labour-backed 'Independent' in Tatton. Her misfortune was to hold office in a ministry – Media and Sport – of such cultural centrality to populist New Labour that it was the only one to suffer a clean sweep of ministers in 2001. But she nudged herself towards the exit by getting it wrong (apparently) on what to do with Wembley Stadium – the contemporary cultural equivalent of debate about the restoration of the West front of Wells Cathedral.

WAKEFIELD

The Boundary Commission which reported in 1995 linked the West Yorkshire borough of Wakefield with Kirklees not Leeds. The cross-borough seat is Wakefield itself.

Wakefield has lost the outlying town of Horbury to Normanton constituency and the Wakefield South ward to Hemsworth. Horbury was fairly evenly divided between Labour and Conservative, but South ward, centred on the suburban villages of Crigglestone and Sandal, is by far the strongest for the Tories in the whole borough. However, the redistribution did not boost David Hinchliffe's majority in its own right, as the two Kirklees wards which arrived from Dewsbury, Kirkburton and Denby Dale, are between them if anything more Tory than Wakefield South, at least in general elections. These are small, owner-occupied, all-white communities in semi-moorland some miles to the south-west of Wakefield. The acreage of the seat almost doubled, and it is far less compactly set around the city itself. In 2001 Hinchliffe lost 7% from his vote share, and probably missed out on the votes of most of the nearly 15% who did not vote compared with 1997, but still won by 8,000.

Wakefield was the capital of the old West Riding, and of the metropolitan county of West Yorkshire until its abolition in 1986. It is a cathedral city and a historic market centre, with some fine buildings. Yet in the end its political preferences are shaped more by the fact that it is also the focus of a heavy industrial belt and a former major coalfield. It has been held by Labour since 1932, when Arthur Greenwood, who had been Minister of Health in Labour's second government (1929–31) returned to the Commons after the disaster of 1931. Another MP for Wakefield (1964–87) was Walter Harrison, the party's tough 'sergeant-major' (Deputy Chief Whip). Harrison nearly lost Wakefield in his last contest in 1983, but that was an exceptionally bad year for Labour, and 70-plus years of continuous victory should not be broken next time.

Social indices:			2001 Gen. Election:			
% Non-white	3.1		Lab	20,592	49.9	–7.5
% Prof/Man	33.5		C	12,638	30.6	+2.2
% Non-manual	54.1		LD	5,097	12.4	+1.2
£ Av prop val 2000	67 K		Grn	1,075	2.6	
% Increase 97–00	21.5		UKIP	677	1.6	
% Unemployed 2001	3.5		SLP	634	1.5	
% Decrease 97–01	1.8		SA	541	1.3	
% Fin hard/Rank	20.7	260	Lab maj	7,954	19.3	
% Pensioners	23.9		Turnout		54.5	–14.5
% Prem mort/Rank	32	301	Elect	75,750		

Member of Parliament

David Hinchliffe, a dogged and earnest former social worker (for 19 years) and Health Select Committee chairman from 1997, first elected here in 1987, is a local man off Wakefield Council (1971–88), a railwayman's son, born in 1948, educated at Cathedral Secondary Modern School, Wakefield, Wakefield Technical College, Leeds Polytechnic and Bradford University. Bearded and no Blairite, he voted for Prescott in 1994 and quit the frontbench in 1995 after shadowing Social Services and Community Care for three years, partly because of his opposition to New Labour 'modernising'.

WALLASEY

Labour's victory in the north-east Wirral seat of Wallasey at the 1997 General Election by a margin of 19,000 votes was one of the clearest examples of the long-term shift to the left by residents of both banks of the river Mersey. Labour had gained Wallasey for the first time ever in 1992 – they did not win it in 1945 or 1966, their previous two years of landslide victory nationally. They had come close, sure enough; they cut the controversial former Transport Minister Ernest Marples's majority to just 589 in 1966, and got within 2,000 votes of victory in October 1974. By 1987, however, when the Conservatives actually won the election with an overall majority of over 100 seats, Labour reduced the majority of the Foreign Office Minister of State, Lynda Chalker, to 279 votes. The red shift was occurring, and the writing was on the wall.

In 1992 Labour's young candidate Angela Eagle had little apparent difficulty in beating Lynda Chalker by almost 4,000 votes – one of the party's more comfortable gains. Their support is strongest at the two ends of the seat. Seacombe ward is just across the docks to the north of Birkenhead town centre, and shares many of the qualities of the true Merseyside inner-city district, suffering from the economic blight of the decline of the shipbuilding and related industries. On the other hand, Leasowe ward is dominated by its isolated council estate at the north end of the Wirral peninsula. The Conservatives fight back in Wallasey ward itself, and Moreton, Liscard, and New Brighton are winnable in good years. There are some of these still: 2000 was a recent example. Nevertheless, even though June 2001 was not quite as overwhelmingly successful for Angela Eagle as 1997, she still won by over 12,000 after a 16% turnout drop. As its name implies, New Brighton was founded as a seaside resort, which once boasted a tower higher than Blackpool's, but now the tower is gone and New Brighton has lost its popularity as the Mersey has silted up. It seems like a reflection of the economic decline of the constituency as a whole.

Social indices:			2001 Gen. Election:			
% Non-white	0.9		Lab	22,718	60.8	−3.8
% Prof/Man	28.0		C	10,442	28.0	+4.1
% Non-manual	53.0		LD	4,186	11.2	+2.9
£ Av prop val 2000	49 K		Lab maj	12,276	32.9	
% Increase 97–00	18.8		Turnout		57.6	−16.0
% Unemployed 2001	5.9		Elect	64,889		
% Decrease 97–01	4.3					
% Fin hard/Rank	20.8	257				
% Pensioners	28.6					
% Prem mort/Rank	47	69				

Member of Parliament

Angela Eagle, a laterally moving Junior Minister from 1997, first at Environment (1997–98), then Social Security (1998–2001) and Work and Pensions (from 2001), elected in 1992, is half of the first set of parliamentary twins, unless there were others – though not of course female – in Simon de Montfort's Parliament or the Witenagemot. The only disclosed lesbian MP, a printer's daughter, she was born in 1961, attended Formby High School and St John's College, Oxford, and worked for the public sector union COHSE for eight years, first as a researcher and finally as its parliamentary liaison officer. A Beckett-voter in 1994 and now situated at the leftward end of the Blairite spectrum, albeit as a replacement for a Militant-supporting candidate in Wallasey in 1992, she is blessed with a sometimes acidic manner and piping voice, and plays chess and cricket.

WALSALL NORTH

In terms of net percentage change in the main parties' vote no seat in the United Kingdom saw less movement between 1997 and 2001 than Walsall North. Both Labour and Conservative increased by 1.50% (yes, that is the same to 100th of 1%). Nor was their any significant development among other parties. However, turnout did fall by over 15% or well over 10,000 voters. Abstentions affected all parties, effectively equally.

Walsall North and Walsall South seem to march hand-in-hand when it comes to results in general elections. As in the previous three contests, in 2001 Labour's majority was within a thousand or so of each other: between 9,000 and 10,000. Yet they are actually rather different seats, with different sources of support. North is the more working-class constituency, but South has a much larger non-white population – over 20% of its residents come from ethnic minority groups. Walsall North, by contrast, is 94% white. Its proportion of local authority-built housing – still over four in ten in 1991 – is the second highest of any seat in the West Midlands county. These last two facts are not coincidental, for non-whites, especially Asians, prefer to avoid the council estates, where they are not always welcomed.

Labour have on occasion come close to losing Walsall North in general elections despite its class and housing make-up, and actually did lose it in a 1976 by-election following the disgrace of the disappearing former Cabinet Minister John Stonehouse.

David Winnick recaptured it in 1979, and has now built up his majority to a comfortable level, although the seat is not quite monolithic. The Liberal Democrats have had some success in the western wards of Short Heath and Willenhall North, but they do not do well in national elections. In 2000 the Conservatives won both wards in the community of Bloxwich, but as with the changes in vote share of the two largest parties in 2001, the relationship between them was nearly exact too: the Tories had almost precisely half the number that Labour did.

Social indices:			2001 Gen. Election:			
% Non-white	6.0		Lab	18,779	58.1	+1.5
% Prof/Man	18.1		C	9,388	29.1	+1.5
% Non-manual	38.1		LD	2,923	9.0	−0.3
£ Av prop val 2000	52 K		UKIP	812	2.5	
% Increase 97–00	16.5		SA	410	1.3	
% Unemployed 2001	5.4		Lab maj	9,391	29.1	
% Decrease 97–01	2.7		Turnout		48.9	−15.1
% Fin hard/Rank	40.3	50	Elect	66,020		
% Pensioners	22.8					
% Prem mort/Rank	45	90				

Member of Parliament

David Winnick, one of Labour's lone-operating awkward squaddies, was first elected here in 1979, but much earlier (1966–70) sat for Croydon South. He was born in 1933, educated somewhat erratically during the Second World War, and worked variously as a clerk, an advertising manager for *Tribune*, and in the UK Immigration Advisory Service. Admitting that he is 'unclubbable', and dubbed by John Major as having 'about as much charm as a puff adder', he was the 23rd most rebellious Labour MP between 1992 and 1997 with 25 dissenting votes, was vocal in opposition to Blair's dropping of Clause Four, and opposed the Blair government on lone parent benefit cuts, predatory pricing of the Murdoch press, disability benefit cuts, air traffic control privatisation, and freedom of information. In the new House elected in 2001 he rebelled against regular health checks for Incapacity Benefit claimants, and against the Terrorism, Crime and Security Bill. An opponent of PR and ageism, and of standard left-wing supporters of Milosevic and Saddam Hussein, he is also a Jew who supports the creation of a Palestinian state.

WALSALL SOUTH

While Walsall North is a homogeneous white working-class seat on the edge of the West Midlands built-up area, Walsall South is sharply divided internally. Several wards are reminiscent of the inner city. The non-white population is a substantial 20%, about half of these being of Indian origin and a quarter Pakistani. These residents are concentrated in three wards, Palfrey, Pleck and St Matthew's in the centre and inner south parts of Walsall. Rather unusually, these wards have not always been reliably Labour in local elections, such as those in May 2000, when Mohammed Yaqub won the last named for the Conservatives – but it should be remembered that the local Labour Party has under-performed in Walsall Borough elections in recent years. The party can rely only on the two wards in the community of Darlaston, a classic gritty small Black Country town.

On the other hand there is also a very solid Conservative bloc indeed, particularly in the Paddock ward along the main road from the centre of Walsall towards Birmingham. This is one of the best residential areas in the whole of the West Midlands by most standards of measurement, including the electoral: in May 2000, Paddock voted 81% Conservative in a straight fight with Labour. More marginal is the physically detached neighbourhood of Pheasey, which on a map looks as if it should more logically form part of the Birmingham city ward of Oscott.

Bruce George has done well to hold Walsall South through Labour's many and long dark days, and after nearly 30 years should remain favourite to hold on if he stands again even in Walsall, whose loyalty to Labour can never be taken for granted, especially after a further small swing in 2001.

Social indices:			2001 Gen. Election:			
% Non-white	20.2		Lab	20,574	59.0	+1.1
% Prof/Man	25.1		C	10,643	30.5	−1.2
% Non-manual	46.9		LD	2,365	6.8	+0.5
£ Av prop val 2000	62 K		UKIP	974	2.8	
% Increase 97–00	14.3		SA	343	1.0	
% Unemployed 2001	5.9		Lab maj	9,931	28.5	
% Decrease 97–01	2.9		Turnout		55.7	−11.6
% Fin hard/Rank	34.1	100	Elect	62,657		
% Pensioners	25.0					
% Prem mort/Rank	43	119				

Member of Parliament

Bruce George, a large, bald, pot-bellied and, in his own words, 'anglicised Welshman', won this seat in 1974, and has enjoyed a parliamentary career of mind-numbing repetitiveness as a backbench Defence specialist, finally heading the appropriate select committee from 1997, and claiming never to have been offered, nor sought, a frontbench job. A policeman's son, born in 1942, he attended Mountain Ash Grammar School and Swansea and Warwick Universities and has been a polytechnic and an Open University lecturer. In trouble locally over his pro-NATO stance when the Labour Party was in thrall to left-wing activists, the later sanitising of the party has allowed him to emerge as a sage exponent of the current orthodoxies. Of rather lone disposition, and a sider with the Turks rather than the Greeks on Cyprus, he votes against homosexual sex at 16.

WALTHAMSTOW

Labour regained Walthamstow from the Conservatives by 3,000 votes at the 1992 Election, and retained a massive 15,000 majority in 2001 consolidating a tremendous performance in 1997, but this part of north-east London, half way out to the edge of the conurbation, has given Labour a number of shocks in recent decades.

Walthamstow was the scene of two of the disastrous by-election results which befell Harold Wilson's 1966–70 government. At that time Walthamstow was divided into East and West constituencies. Both seats were lost to the Tories following the death of their Labour members, West in 1967 and East in 1969. The loss of Walthamstow West was an especial blow. Not only did it require an 18% swing, but West had been the seat of Labour Party leader Clement Attlee from 1950 until his retirement in 1955. Labour went into the 1970 election holding neither of the Walthamstow seats. They then found a saviour in the form of Eric Deakins. First he won back West, defeating the Tory by-election victor Fred Silvester in 1970. Then as the Boundary Commission produced a unified Walthamstow seat in 1974, the East MP since 1967 Michael McNair-Wilson wisely moved to Newbury, as Deakins won easily. Then in 1987 Eric Deakins was in turn ousted by the Conservative Hugo Summerson.

The Conservatives' occasional successes in Walthamstow seem unlikely if one merely considers the statistics of the seat. None of the wards came anywhere near electing a Tory councillor in the last borough elections in May 1998, polling just 15% in the wards within the constituency. The seat is working class, consisting mainly of elderly housing stock, and three out of every ten residents are from an ethnic minority group. For explanations of the Conservative success in 1987 one has to look to political rather than social causation.

The Conservatives under Mrs Thatcher won with an overall majority of over 100 seats that year, and did particularly well as one moved north and east from London, where her brand of Conservatism appeared to appeal to the (white) working-class as well as middle-class electorate. The SDP also did quite well in Walthamstow in 1987, polling a quarter of the vote, and it is interesting that the 11% advance achieved by Labour's Neil Gerrard in taking the seat in 1992 matched the decline in the centre's share; the Conservative lost little ground themselves. Finally, from the 1990s the Labour Party in Waltham Forest, and nationally, was moving back to the political centre after a period when it was associated by many with far-left and minority causes. This change was typified by New Labour and personified by Tony Blair, both proving very much to the taste of Walthamstow electors in 1997 and 2001.

Social indices:			2001 Gen. Election:			
% Non-manual	29.1		Lab	21,402	62.2	−1.0
% Prof/Man	32.3		C	6,221	18.1	−2.2
% Non-manual	60.1		LD	5,024	14.6	+0.9
£ Av prop val 2000	97 K		Ind	806	2.3	
% Increase 97–00	66.7		BNP	389	1.1	
% Unemployed 2001	5.9		UKIP	298	0.9	
% Decrease 97–01	3.5		PA	289	0.8	
% Fin hard/Rank	26.9	177	Lab maj	15,181	44.1	
% Pensioners	22.8		Turnout		53.5	−9.3
% Prem mort/Rank	38	202	Elect	64,403		

Member of Parliament

Neil Gerrard was elected in 1992, fresh from being leader of Waltham Forest Council where huge rate rises had delivered the Walthamstow seat to the Conservatives against the trend in 1987. He defied the Labour Whip 26 times during the 1992 Parliament and resigned as Dawn Primarolo's PPS in order to abstain over lone parent benefit cuts, and voted against the threatened use of force against Iraq, pensions linked to earnings, Incapacity Benefit cuts and jury trial curbs, ending the 1997–2001 Parliament with 24 rebellious votes and 18th among the list of Labour rebels. Of gnarled, coarse-featured, broken-nosed visage, he was born in 1942, son of a primary schoolteacher, educated at Manchester Grammar School and Wadham College, Oxford, and previously worked as a schoolteacher, then FE lecturer in computing. He calls for the Palestinians' 'right to return', an anti-AIDS strategy, and defence of asylum-seekers' rights.

WANSBECK

The Wansbeck constituency is based on the former Morpeth seat which existed before 1983, but it is more appropriately named now. Morpeth is an old market town on the A1 Great North Road, and it now houses many affluent commuters to Newcastle. As such it is far from a Labour stronghold, and socially it is unlike the tough working-class communities of the former Northumberland coalfield nearby, which give the constituency its political tone. The seat now takes its title from the river Wansbeck, and from the local authority district of the same name.

Labour won Morpeth in every General Election since the Second World War with great comfort. The Labour preferences were determined by the presence of the large mining town of Ashington, home of the footballing Charlton brothers, and industrial Newbiggin by the coast, where retired pit ponies used to graze by the sea. In the 1983 boundary changes another rough-hewn community created by mining, Bedlington, came in from Blyth to replace some villages lost to Berwick.

Wansbeck is basically an even safer seat for Labour than Morpeth was. In the late 1960s the career of Morpeth MP Will Owen was clouded by (unproven) allegations that he had passed information on to the Soviet Union. But his successors George Grant, John 'Geordie' Thompson and Denis Murphy have sat quietly in the Commons since 1970, among the battery of Labour MPs from North Eastern 'mining' seats. Some of the centrist strength in neighbouring Blyth Valley seemed to infect Wansbeck in Labour's disastrous year of 1983, but even then they retained a lead of nearly 8,000, and in 1997 the Liberal Democrats increased their vote slightly and moved back into second place. This was not just a flash in the pan, but based on significant local government success: in May 1999 the Lib Dems took 37% of the vote within the seat to Labour's 41%, and took 20 seats on Wansbeck Council to Labour's 25, having won none at all four years before. In 2001, Denis Murphy held the seat with an 8% lower Labour vote than in 1997, and the Liberal Democrat Alan Thompson increased by almost as much. With a nationally average reduction in turnout Murphy's majority went down by over 9,000, although it is still safe, for the time being, despite the dramatic changes in local government.

Social indices:			2001 Gen. Election:			
% Non-white	0.5		Lab	21,617	57.8	−7.7
% Prof/Man	28.4		LD	8,516	22.8	+6.8
% Non-manual	48.9		C	4,774	12.8	−1.2
£ Av prop val 2000	59 K		Ind	1,076	2.9	
% Increase 97–00	19.3		Grn	954	2.5	+0.4
% Unemployed 2001	4.8		UKIP	482	1.3	
% Decrease 97–01	2.4		Lab maj	13,101	35.0	
% Fin hard/Rank	26.4	186	Turnout		59.4	−12.3
% Pensioners	28.1		Elect	62,989		
% Prem mort/Rank	40	183				

Member of Parliament

Denis Murphy was a novelty in Labour's 183-strong 1997 intake as the sole mine worker (in his case a pit electrician), having worked for nearly 30 years at the local Ashington-Ellington pit as an electrician until made redundant in 1994. Born in 1948 and educated at St Cuthbert's Grammar School, Newcastle and Northumberland College, a local councillor for seven years, eventually council leader, he has inevitably attacked the decline of the mining industry – including the closure of his own pit in 1999, and less-inevitably rebelled against disability benefit spending cuts. His virtual silence in the Commons is symbolic of the demise of an industry that gave Labour its first MPs, reduced in 2001 to an 11-man rump.

WANSDYKE

Labour's Dan Norris won the Wansdyke seat in 1997, the first time his party had gained it in its 14-year history. The increase in their share of the vote was nearly 17%, well above average, and the Liberal Democrats declined by 7%, so there is evidence of tactical voting designed to oust the Conservative government. In 2001 Norris held on with a slightly increased majority, and the percentages polled by the three main parties then made Wansdyke one of the closest constituencies in the country to the national average.

If Northavon was the new, some would say 'artificial' name for South Gloucestershire after the creation of the county of Avon, Wansdyke was effectively the successor seat to the old North Somerset constituency. It is named after the ancient ditch that traverses this part of the English countryside, and centres on the town of Keynsham, situated between Bristol and Bath, and Midsomer Norton and Radstock, which despite their rustic names are isolated Labour towns which once formed the heart of the defunct Somerset coalfield. Labour's gain in 1997 was preceded by a good set of results for their candidates for the new unitary authority of Bath and North East Somerset two years previously. Then they not only won Midsomer Norton and Radstock wards easily, but also Keynsham South, North and West, Paulton, Peasedown St John and even villages like Tisbury and Farmborough. These areas, in the main situated on or near the old coalfield, have suffered economically since its demise back in the 1960s, and clearly showed a determination to change the national administration in 1997. However, there are also still affluent commuting areas for

Bristol and Bath such as Chew Magna, Chew Stoke and Compton Dando, and the Tories were very disappointed not to recapture Wansdyke after a single aberrant term – and almost devastated to have got no closer at all.

Social indices:			2001 Gen. Election:			
% Non-white	0.6		Lab	22,706	46.3	+2.2
% Prof/Man	34.6		C	17,593	35.9	+0.6
% Non-manual	59.3		LD	7,135	14.5	−2.3
£ Av prop val 2000	110 K		Grn	958	2.0	
% Increase 97–00	48.4		UKIP	655	1.3	+0.5
% Unemployed 2001	0.8		Lab maj	5,113	10.4	
% Decrease 97–01	1.5		Turnout		69.3	−9.9
% Fin hard/Rank	6.9	561	Elect	70,728		
% Pensioners	25.0					
% Prem mort/Rank	10	596				

Member of Parliament

Dan Norris, an Assistant Whip from 2001, was elected in 1997 in his second attempt to win the seat. An orthodox loyalist, born in 1960, son of a social worker, and educated at Chipping Sodbury Comprehensive and Sussex University, as a former social worker concerned about child abuse, he was well-placed to ride the populist wave when paedophilia hit the headlines, and to make a show of interest in another matter of New-Labour-modish-concern, by riding (investigatively) with the local hunt in the run-up to a fox hunting vote. He is the first Labour MP in the former Somerset coalfield seat (as 'Frome') to win it twice consecutively, it previously being captured only in 1929 and 1945.

WANTAGE

It is quite rare for a party to win a parliamentary seat in England with less than 40% of the vote, given the fact that most contests are in effect at the maximum between three parties, but the Conservatives did so in Wantage in both 1997 and 2001. What is more, Wantage would not even be called a marginal, as Robert Jackson has won by clearly over 5,000 on each occasion. This was only possible because Labour and the Liberal Democrats split the opposition equally, each polling just over 28% last time.

Essentially the constituency covers the south-western quarter of the presently constituted county of Oxfordshire, between Oxford and Swindon. The main towns are Didcot and Wallingford from the South Oxfordshire district and Faringdon and Wantage from the Vale of White Horse. Didcot, which has a famous place as a junction in railway mythology, and a massive power station, is still a Labour town despite its growth as a relatively inexpensive commuting base. Wallingford votes in Liberal Democrat representatives on the local and county councils. Wantage had an early SDP recruit, Alec Spurway, as its county councillor back in 1981, and also now keeps faith with the Liberal Democrats, along with its sizeable and much more modern satellite, Grove. The Lib Dems control the Vale of White Horse at district council level. The Tories are much more competitive in the large villages that make up the balance of this seat – places like Marcham and Drayton, Shrivenham, Harwell (near the Atomic Energy Research Establishment), and many more, but if either Labour or the Lib Dems could establish which of them is the more effective challenger, and establish the pattern of tactical voting which has become part of political praxis in so many other seats, Jackson would be very vulnerable.

Social indices:			2001 Gen. Election:			
% Non-white	1.1		C	19,475	39.6	−0.2
% Prof/Man	39.7		Lab	13,875	28.2	−0.7
% Non-manual	60.3		LD	13,776	28.0	+1.5
£ Av prop val 2000	146 K		Grn	1,062	2.2	+1.0
% Increase 97–00	61.5		UKIP	941	1.9	+1.1
% Unemployed 2001	0.7		C maj	5,600	11.4	
% Decrease 97–01	0.9		Turnout		64.5	−13.7
% Fin hard/Rank	4.1	625	Elect	76,129		
% Pensioners	22.6					
% Prem mort/Rank	7	619				

Member of Parliament

Robert Jackson was elected in 1983 after serving a term as MEP for the area including the Wantage constituency. Son of a copper miner, born in 1946 in Bulawayo, and educated at Falcon College, Rhodesia, and St Edmund Hall, Oxford, he worked variously as an Oxford don (All Souls) and political advisor, for example to Lord Soames, as an EEC Commissioner and as last Governor of Rhodesia. A tall, bespectacled figure of donnish mien, his brief Junior Ministerial career (1989–93) involved him angering the universities by calling for the abolition of student grants and effectively the privatisation of higher education. Even if these are ideas whose time has come or is coming, his eclipse as a Clarke-voting Europhile in 1997 and 2001 was complete. In October 2001 he welcomed the new Tory leadership's relegating of Europe as 'the big issue', but in a Europhile speech.

WARLEY

What, only one Warley? There used to be two. The borough of Sandwell was over-represented with four seats when its electorate justified scarcely more than three, and it might be thought that the two Warley seats, East and West, have simply been merged. In fact the solution adopted by the Boundary Commission in 1997 is more complex than that. The Warley West seat has effectively been broken up, with three wards linked with Halesowen in a cross-border Dudley/Sandwell Halesowen and Rowley Regis seat. Two wards have been moved into West Bromwich West. Just one ward, Langley, is placed together with the whole of Warley East in the new Warley division. It is therefore in effect a little-altered but renamed Warley East.

Warley East was based on the old Smethwick constituency, which came to national prominence in 1964 when Labour's Patrick Gordon Walker was defeated against the national swing by Conservative Peter Griffiths, who was accused of adopting a racist campaign. The bearded, booming-voiced actor Andrew Faulds won

Smethwick back in 1966, and remained in Parliament for 31 years, although his majority fell as low as 3,400 in 1983. In 1997 he was succeeded by the former Warley West MP John Spellar.

As its history suggests, Warley possesses both a large non-white community and a substantial Tory vote. It is a starkly divided seat. In its northern and eastern sections it includes the strongly Labour St Paul's, Soho/Victoria and Smethwick wards, which abut the heavily Asian Soho and Handsworth neighbourhoods of west Birmingham. These three wards are all about 50% non-white. On the other hand, to the south is a more Tory area around Old Warley and Warley Abbey, with its parks and comfortable private housing. This is the kind of 'snow-white' region near to a concentration of people of immigrant stock which is keenly aware of the racial question. Old Warley is just across the border from Birmingham's middle-class Harborne and Quinton districts, in the Edgbaston constituency.

However, Labour has won this seat (however named) for three and a half decades now and look safe enough in Warley whenever the next general election comes along.

Social indices:			2001 Gen. Election:			
% Non-white	23.2		Lab	19,007	60.5	−3.3
% Prof/Man	20.8		C	7,157	22.8	−1.3
% Non-manual	42.1		LD	3,315	10.6	+0.8
£ Av prop val 2000	55 K		SLP	1,936	6.2	
% Increase 97–00	25.4		Lab maj	11,850	37.7	
% Unemployed 2001	6.1		Turnout		54.1	−11.0
% Decrease 97–01	2.4		Elect	58,071		
% Fin hard/Rank	42.6	36				
% Pensioners	28.3					
% Prem mort/Rank	44	101				

Member of Parliament

John Spellar, Minister of State for Defence, was elected for the precursor seat of Warley West in 1992 having briefly held Birmingham Northfield in 1982–83. Born in 1947, he had a public-school (Dulwich) and Oxford (St Edmund Hall) education but is scarcely typical of the genre, as a short, London-brogued, ginger-bearded, pugnacious former EETPU right-wing apparatchik and fixer, who campaigned to purge left-wingers from Labour's NEC and to weight local selection committees to save right-wing MPs and oust left-wing ones. Effortlessly irascible-seeming, in 1997 he was appointed to the MOD as part of the Blair government's most right-wing ministerial team, moving in 2001 to become Minister of Transport – a bed of nails of no assistance to any political careerist. He has opposed all-women shortlists and homosexuals in the forces.

WARRINGTON NORTH

It was in Warrington in July 1981 that the Social Democratic Party launched its first parliamentary election campaign. Their standard bearer in the Warrington by-election was Roy Jenkins, later to be chosen as the first leader of the party. Although Labour's candidate Doug Hoyle held on to the seat by 1,759 votes, Jenkins came close enough to prove that the SDP would be a force to be reckoned with in the years to come. Although Roy Jenkins moved on to fight, win, and eventually lose Glasgow Hillhead, while Doug Hoyle sat in the Commons representing a Warrington constituency for 16 years, one feels that the name of Warrington will always be most associated with Jenkins's finest hour and the (short-lived) dawn of hope for the SDP.

Warrington North is the successor to the seat fought between Jenkins and Hoyle, and it has never seen another close contest. Its boundaries are much modified from those in operation in 1981: that Warrington seat comprised a tiny core of the town, which had spread far beyond its administrative boundaries long before it was named as a latter-day New Town in 1968. Many of these neighbourhoods – Great Sankey and Penketh as well as those designated for the Development Corporation – were in the Newton constituency before 1983. Now the whole of Greater Warrington is included in one borough, which is effectively divided in two for parliamentary purposes. Most of the New Town housing is in Warrington North, which included the whole of the town north of the Mersey until the most recent boundary changes, which took the central Howley and Whitecross ward into South for the 1997 Election.

This is a strongly Labour 'inner-city' area, with terraced housing and a small ethnic minority community, but its loss caused no problems for Labour, who increased their lead over the Tories to 19,500 in 1997. Technically there was a small swing to Labour in 2001, but of much more importance was the drop in turnout, which was unusually severe at 17%. Nowadays the centrist challenge is long gone and the Liberal Democrats are very weak in Warrington North.

Social indices:			2001 Gen. Election:			
% Non-white	1.3		Lab	24,026	61.7	−0.4
% Prof/Man	31.0		C	8,870	22.8	−1.2
% Non-manual	55.0		LD	5,232	13.4	+3.1
£ Av prop val 2000	72 K		UKIP	782	2.0	
% Increase 97–00	34.3		Lab maj	15,156	39.0	
% Unemployed 2001	2.9		Turnout		53.7	−16.8
% Decrease 97–01	1.3		Elect	72,445		
% Fin hard/Rank	20.2	275				
% Pensioners	22.2					
% Prem mort/Rank	41	160				

Member of Parliament

Helen Jones was elected here in 1997, having been surprisingly selected from an NEC-imposed all-women shortlist, with herself the only local name, as a last-minute replacement for the winkled-out-with-a-peerage Doug Hoyle, in a seat thought to be earmarked for the rising Blairite star, Yvette Cooper. Born in 1954 and educated at the Ursuline Convent, Chester, Chester College and at University College, London, Manchester Metropolitan University and Liverpool University, she worked variously as a schoolteacher, as 'Justice and Peace Officer' for the Liverpool Catholic Archdiocese and eventually a solicitor. With a forthright, emphatic mode of delivery, she reflected the feminisation of the PLP in her attack on FCO mandarin Sir David

Gore-Booth's use of the term 'company wife', but whimsically noted that the word 'socialism' did not feature in her 1997 Election address. Her long record of local activism had not, by 2001, been reflected in preferment at Westminster.

WARRINGTON SOUTH

South is much the more interesting of the two Warrington seats, at least in so far as it has been a critical marginal while North is safe Labour. In 1992 Labour gained South for the first time, managing a swing of just over 3% which enabled Mike Hall to oust the sitting Conservative Christopher Butler by a mere 191 votes. Boundary changes led Hall to opt for the neighbouring Weaver Vale seat in 1997, but South was comfortably won by Helen Southworth with a five-figure majority. In 2001, that lead was cut to 7,000 and it is conceivable that it will be close again. Indeed it must be, should the Conservatives seek to restore the overall majority status they enjoyed between 1979 and 1997.

The majority of Warrington's middle-class population is situated south of the Manchester Ship Canal, in suburbs like Stockton Heath, Appleton, Grappenhall and Lymm, which have always been in Cheshire (unlike the town centre, which was in Lancashire until the early 1970s). The Liberal Democrats are very competitive in this area in local elections – indeed they received the highest percentage of any party in the May 2000 local elections throughout the constituency – but it forms the core of the Tory strength in the constituency in general elections. A more even battle between the two major parties is to be found west of Warrington, in Great Sankey and Penketh, which have seen the growth of private housing estates in recent decades. On the Labour side are the wards of Latchford and Westy, which are set on a kind of island between the Ship Canal and the Mersey. Again, the picture varies considerably between local and national contests, with the Lib Dems far stronger in the former: in June 2001 General Election they only took 16%, compared with 42% the year before for Warrington unitary authority.

Social indices:			2001 Gen. Election:			
% Non-white	1.4		Lab	22,409	49.3	−2.9
% Prof/Man	36.5		C	15,022	33.0	+0.5
% Non-manual	60.7		LD	7,419	16.3	+3.2
£ Av prop val 2000	91 K		UKIP	637	1.4	
% Increase 97–00	32.6		Lab maj	7,387	16.3	
% Unemployed 2001	2.1		Turnout		61.2	−15.0
% Decrease 97–01	1.2		Elect	74,283		
% Fin hard/Rank	11.5	424				
% Pensioners	22.9					
% Prem mort/Rank	32	308				

Member of Parliament

Helen Southworth, a loyalist elected here in 1997 after selection from an all-women shortlist, is a former voluntary sector worker, latterly with Age Concern, who campaigns on the disabled, in-town shopping centres, regional government, women entrepreneurs and violence against women, and opposed the transfer of the synchrotron from her constituency to Oxfordshire. Born in 1956, she was educated at Larkhill Convent, Preston, and Lancaster University. In one of the photographs of Tony Blair surrounded by his Babes on the steps of Church House, Westminster in May 1997, she was the one right next to him, inadvertently sticking her tongue out, but she was nevertheless by 2001 PPS to Paul Boateng, at the Treasury.

WARWICK AND LEAMINGTON

Warwick and Leamington might be thought to be an archetypal safe Tory seat. This was Sir Anthony Eden's constituency for 34 years; Royal Leamington Spa is the most well known of the Midland inland watering-holes. In 1987 Sir Dudley Smith's majority was nigh on 14,000, and that over the SDP. Yet all is not at all as it seems. In 1997 Labour won the seat for the first time, as the 70-year-old incumbent Sir Dudley Smith was ousted by James Plaskitt. This was not a total surprise in the circumstances of that landslide election, and they were probably helped by two new factors. The Referendum and UK Independence candidates probably hurt Smith, but only a little as they polled less than 2,000 votes between them (and not all of those would have gone to the Conservatives otherwise). More important was a drop in Liberal Democrat support of over 5%, probably indicating tactical voting against the government.

In 2001 though, neither of these applied, and yet Plaskitt strengthened his position – in fact, he almost doubled his majority. The special factor this time was probably incumbency – or rather double incumbency, for in addition to Labour benefiting from Plaskitt's new status and opportunities as MP for the last four years, the Conservatives had lost any personal vote that Dudley Smith had built up over the previous 30 years.

Both Warwick and Leamington have substantial blocs of Labour support. Warwick has a large council estate in the west of the town, while south Leamington harbours one of the largest Asian communities in any small town in the Midlands, concentrated in the Willes and Brunswick wards. Leamington is also an industrial town – Automotive Products long the best-known of its employers. Its spa and tourist functions have been more or less dormant of recent years, and its politics seem likely to continue to belie the elegant impression given by the fine streets laid out in a gridiron pattern in the centre and north of the town.

That all said, the Conservatives must have high hopes of regaining Warwick and Leamington. Besides the two major towns of the constituency, there are a number of villages, such as Radford Semele and Cubbington, Leek Wootton, Lapworth, where the Tories usually have a massive lead over Labour – even in Barford, where a pub is named after a local man, Joseph Arch, the founder of agricultural trade unionism. Also, a few thousand voters are included from Stratford-on-Avon district: these reside in the wealthy commuting villages of Henley-in-Arden and Tanworth, and will further boost the Conservative position in the rural areas. Their residents must get used to being represented by a Labour MP.

Social indices:			2001 Gen. Election:			
% Non-white	6.3		Lab	26,108	48.8	+4.3
% Prof/Man	40.1		C	20,155	37.6	−1.2
% Non-manual	62.7		LD	5,964	11.1	−0.7
£ Av prop val 2000	130 K		SA	664	1.2	
% Increase 97–00	50.4		UKIP	648	1.2	+0.7
% Unemployed 2001	2.1		Lab maj	5,953	11.1	
% Decrease 97–01	0.9		Turnout		65.8	−9.9
% Fin hard/Rank	14.5	361	Elect	81,405		
% Pensioners	26.2					
% Prem mort/Rank	28	377				

Member of Parliament

James Plaskitt, who won the seat in 1997, has lived a parliamentary life of relative obscurity, rising in 2001 to oppose compulsory voting, and as a loyalist has stepped out of line only minimally in order to dub the Dome 'a white elephant'. Mustachioed and backing PR, he was born in 1954, son of a Methodist pastor and teacher, educated at Pilgrim School, Bedford, and University College, Oxford, and initially taught politics at Brunel and Oxford Universities and then worked as a business consultant. His surprisingly successful defence of the seat in 2001 denied the Commons a new Conservative MP in the shape of David Campbell Bannerman, the descendant of one Prime Minister, in a seat once occupied by another (Sir Anthony Eden).

WARWICKSHIRE NORTH

Warwickshire was once one of the most populous counties in England. But with the removal of the city of Coventry and the great West Midlands conurbation centred on Birmingham, Warwickshire was left as a highly truncated rump which only possesses five parliamentary constituencies. Its current electorate entitles it to a sixth, but the Boundary Commission's allocations will not be put into force until the election after next, at the earliest. Two of the five Warwickshire seats changed hands in the 1992 Election results, an unusually high proportion – these were Labour gains at Warwickshire North and Nuneaton – and two more in 1997 (Rugby/Kenilworth and Warwick/Leamington), leaving only Stratford in Conservative hands. All four Labour seats were retained in 2001.

Warwickshire North was created in 1983. It was always considered a good bet for Labour though, and it might be noted that they only lost it in two 'Thatcher' general elections when the Tories romped home with an overall majority of over 100 seats. In a more even year Labour might be expected to win. In a very good year like 2001 it looked like a safe seat, with a majority of over 9,500. It is one of the few semi-rural seats in England of which this can be said.

One of the reasons for Labour's strength here lies in the old industrial communities scattered around the former Warwickshire coalfield, even though they are in the main no larger than villages: Baddesley Ensor, Arley, Polesworth, Dordon, Hurley, Kingsbury, Newton Regis, Hartshill on the edge of Nuneaton, and the larger town of Atherstone, on the A5. There are Conservative agricultural villages and larger commuting bases such as Coleshill, Water Orton and Curdworth, but much of this terrain is more like the ex-coal-mining districts of Derbyshire and Nottinghamshire in political behaviour (and some of them turned their backs on Labour in 1983 and 1987 too).

The other boon for Labour is Bedworth, separated from Nuneaton in 1983. It can have come as no surprise when the Tory MP Francis Maude lost Warwickshire North in 1992; it had never been securely his. Maude was regarded as one of the abler Tories of the younger generation in the House, but unlike his father (Sir Angus, who held Stratford for 20 years) he could not rely on a safe and long-term parliamentary base in the county of Warwickshire: he moved on to Horsham in West Sussex from 1997. One other personal point. Mike O'Brien's Conservative opponent in 2001 was the former England international high jumper Geoff Parsons. Not only will he need to find a better constituency in which his political ambition might vault, but whoever takes on Labour in North Warwickshire may need a pole to assist them to soar to victory.

Social indices:			2001 Gen. Election:			
% Non-white	2.0		Lab	24,023	54.1	−4.3
% Prof/Man	26.8		C	14,384	32.4	+1.2
% Non-manual	48.0		LD	5,052	11.4	+3.9
£ Av prop val 2000	76 K		UKIP	950	2.1	+1.2
% Increase 97–00	28.5		Lab maj	9,639	21.7	
% Unemployed 2001	2.0		Turnout		60.2	−14.6
% Decrease 97–01	1.6		Elect	73,828		
% Fin hard/Rank	14.2	368				
% Pensioners	22.2					
% Prem mort/Rank	26	412				

Member of Parliament

Mike O'Brien, Junior Minister at the Home Office from 1997 to 2001, was first elected in 1992, and has been dubbed (by the *Telegraph*) as 'so quiet it is easy to assume he is harmless', yet by insisting he had received a phone call from Peter Mandelson in the Hinduja brothers passport affair, secured the latter's second resignation in January 2001 and – arguably – his own exit from the government after the 2001 Election. A dapper solicitor of Irish good looks, born in 1954, son of a railway worker, he attended the Blessed Edward Oldcombe (RC) School, Worcester, Worcester Technical College and North Staffs Polytechnic. He was relieved in 1999 of the hornet's nest of Immigration Control, swapping it for the political football of the this-year-next-year-sometime-never banning of hunting. He rejects the metropolitan conventional wisdom of legalising cannabis – concerned about the prospect of 'putting a bunch of middle-aged, chilled-out cannabis smokers on our roads'.

WATFORD

Labour gained five seats in Hertfordshire in 1997, having had no representatives in the county since 1983, and held them all in 2001. These confirmed and consolidated advances covered all types of community in the county, from old to new. Watford is the best example in Hertfordshire of a predominantly nineteenth-century industrial town. The oldest major community in the county (also a gain in 1997) is St Albans, the Roman town of Verulamium and an important medieval centre. Hertfordshire is also a county which has boomed in the twentieth century, as the foundation of the four New Towns of Stevenage, Hemel Hempstead, Welwyn Garden City and Hatfield made it the nation's fastest growing shire in the 1960s and 1970s. The three constituencies covering the New Towns completed Labour's quintet of gains.

Watford is unique in the county, and long was in political terms too. For years after the last war it was the safest, and on occasion the only, Labour seat in the county. As the New Towns grew, though, Watford ceased to be the largest town in Herts, or its Labour citadel. In 1979 the Labour MP Raphael Tuck retired and his successor as candidate Tony Banks (later to become a prominent Newham MP) was defeated by Tristan Garel-Jones for the Tories. Then in 1983 extraneous territory outside the town was added, and Garel-Jones held on fairly easily until his retirement in 1997.

Watford town is mixed and politically competitive. In local elections the most recent results, for example in May 2000, have shown all three main parties securing a similar share of the vote. There is a non-white minority of about one-tenth of Watford's population, spread fairly widely around the town but most numerous (25%) in the central Vicarage ward. There are large council-housing minorities in wards such as Leggatts, Holywell and Meriden. On the other hand the Conservative vote is more concentrated in the excellent residential area around Cassiobury Park and along the A411 in the north-west of the town – Park and Nascot wards. The Tories also do well in the suburban terrain outside the borough of Watford, and in a nationally even year they might just be able to nose ahead again in this constituency; certainly more close and critical contests can be expected in this key marginal.

In 2001 Watford's result was as close to the national average as that of any constituency – Labour was a couple of percentage points stronger, and the Liberal Democrats weaker by the same amount – but it is very unlikely under the first-past-the-post electoral system that seat results will cluster around the national norm, as tactical voting considerations squeeze the third party in a two-party marginal. Only the Liberal Democrat local government strength kept their vote as high as 17% in 2001.

Social indices:			2001 Gen. Election:			
% Non-white	8.8		Lab	20,992	45.3	−0.0
% Prof/Man	37.8		C	15,437	33.3	−1.5
% Non-manual	64.4		LD	8,088	17.4	+0.7
£ Av prop val 2000	130 K		Grn	900	1.9	
% Increase 97–00	52.4		UKIP	535	1.2	
% Unemployed 2001	1.7		SA	420	0.9	
% Decrease 97–01	1.3		Lab maj	5,555	12.0	
% Fin hard/Rank	10.9	440	Turnout		61.2	−13.4
% Pensioners	22.4		Elect	75,724		
% Prem mort/Rank	18	501				

Member of Parliament

Claire Ward, youngest woman MP, was elected here in 1997. A trainee solicitor when elected, she was born in 1972, daughter of a shipwright-turned-housing-association manager, and educated at Loreto (RC) College, St Albans, Hatfield Polytechnic (which became the University of Hertfordshire whilst she was there), Brunel University and the London College of Law. Short, chubby-faced and pretty, though taken to be a Blairite loyalist, as youth representative on the NEC 1991–95, she signed a Tribune appeal in 1999 urging Labour return to its 'democratic socialist' roots. Youth-centred, she urges a strategy to curb smoking by the young, calls for votes at 16, opposes a lower minimum wage for the young, and admits to sometimes not admitting she is a Labour MP when with people she doesn't know. She attacked Keith Vaz over feuding in the Leicester Labour Party, and claimed he obstructed an NEC investigation into the matter in 1994. Suitably, given her views on smoking, she became PPS to Health Minister John Hutton in 2001.

WAVENEY

One cannot find a more easterly point in East Anglia or indeed the whole of Great Britain than Ness Point, which is situated in the parliamentary constituency of Waveney. This northernmost seat in Suffolk is named after the River Waveney, which forms the border with Norfolk in this area, and consists largely of Lowestoft, the second largest town in the county, and the smaller towns of Beccles and Bungay.

Labour regained this seat with a very comfortable 12,000 majority in 1997. Its predecessor seat, more comprehensibly named Lowestoft (how many non-locals know where 'Waveney' is without looking it up?), was held by Labour from 1945 to 1959, and posed problems even for its well-known Tory MP from 1959 to 1987, James Prior. His majority was reduced to 358 in 1966 and 2,000 in October 1974. In 1992 Prior's agent and successor David Porter won by 6,700 after a 4% swing to Labour, and that in a big seat where nearly 70,000 votes were cast; it was reduced by boundary changes in 1997 taking 10,000 voters around Halesworth and Southwold into Suffolk Coastal, and after a reduction in turnout in 2001 less than 47,000 votes were cast altogether. Just over half of these were for the Labour candidate, Bob Blizzard, who looks as if he now has a safe seat here.

The reason for the strength of the Labour Party in a Suffolk coastal seat lies in Lowestoft's economy. The town has a long-established fishing industry and its port, as well as handling a general cargo business, is also a base for servicing off-shore exploration installations. Lowestoft is also home to a variety of industries including food-processing, shipbuilding and engineering. It has a large number of working-class wards with a significant minority of 'social' accommodation, and returns Labour majorities in local elections. Beccles also has its share of industry, most notably printing, and sent a Labour councillor to the county administration in the simultaneous elections of 1997 and 2001.

The Conservatives have done badly in many coastal areas in the last two general elections, in all corners of Britain (one thinks of their losses in St Ives, Thanet South, Morecambe and Tynemouth for example) and now no longer hold this easternmost seat, just as they do not hold the most southerly, westerly or northerly.

Social indices:			2001 Gen. Election:			
% Non-white	0.7		Lab	23,914	50.7	−5.3
% Prof/Man	27.1		C	15,361	32.6	−1.9
% Non-manual	47.5		LD	5,370	11.4	+2.4
£ Av prop val 2000	63 K		UKIP	1,097	2.3	
% Increase 97–00	29.6		Grn	983	2.1	
% Unemployed 2001	4.6		SA	442	0.9	
% Decrease 97–01	3.8		Lab maj	8,553	18.1	
% Fin hard/Rank	15.6	340	Turnout		61.6	−13.6
% Pensioners	31.2		Elect	76,585		
% Prem mort/Rank	30	333				

Member of Parliament

Bob Blizzard was elected in 1997 as a standard product of the Labour landslide: a 40-something schoolteacher (for 24 years) and local councillor (for ten years), in his case council leader. A burly, vigorous speaker, he was born in 1950, attended Culford School, Bury St Edmunds, and Birmingham University and taught English for 25 years. An assiduous campaigner on local issues such as poor transport and fishing, he loyally defends government policy across a broad front, and deplores the damaging impact on English-brewed beer of bootlegging from the continent. His ultra-loyalty was acknowledged in his entry to the ranks of PPS – to Baroness Hayman (MAFF) 1999–2001 and Nick Brown (Work and Pensions) from 2001. He dislikes litter.

WEALDEN

The Sussex Weald is a largely agricultural and heavily wooded district of soft southern English scenery. Indeed this neck of the woods has entered the hearts and imagination of generations of children, for it includes Ashdown Forest, used by A.A. Milne (who lived in the village of Hartfield) as the setting for the adventures of Winnie the Pooh and his mythical friends. People travel to the area to play Pooh-sticks on the original Pooh Bridge. This is the countryside of the constituency of Wealden, and the Conservative predominance is such that the other parties must be as gloomy as Eeyore at the prospect of challenging it.

The Wealden seat has existed since 1983; basically it consists of the former East Grinstead without the town of that name, which is in West Sussex county and Mid Sussex constituency. There are no large towns in Wealden; the largest are Crowborough (18,500), Hailsham (17,500), Uckfield (11,500) and Forest Row (5,000). There are no Labour wards at all, although at national level the cross-class and cross-region appeal of Mr Blair's party has enabled them to advance over the last two general elections to the giddy heights of 20%. There are some Liberal Democrats on the local council, but that has remained Tory-controlled even throughout and beyond 18 years of Conservative government. It would indeed take a very blustery political day for the Conservative hegemony to be blown loose in Wealden.

Social indices:			2001 Gen. Election:			
% Non-white	0.9		C	26,279	49.8	+0.0
% Prof/Man	41.6		LD	12,507	23.7	−2.0
% Non-manual	65.0		Lab	10,705	20.3	+3.1
£ Av prop val 2000	156 K		UKIP	1,539	2.9	+2.0
% Increase 97–00	62.5		Grn	1,273	2.4	
% Unemployed 2001	0.8		Ind	453	0.9	
% Decrease 97–01	0.9		C maj	13,772	26.1	
% Fin hard/Rank	4.7	613	Turnout		63.5	−10.8
% Pensioners	28.5		Elect	83,066		
% Prem mort/Rank	11	581				

Member of Parliament

Charles Hendry, one of seven former MPs returning to the Commons in 2001, replaced the veteran Sir Geoffrey Johnson-Smith. Previously (1992–97) MP for High Peak, he migrated to the lower peaks of the Weald for his fourth parliamentary contest in a different seat, having earlier fought Clackmannan (1983) and Mansfield (1987). A pink and plump-faced son of a stockbroker, he was born in 1959 and educated at Rugby and Edinburgh University and worked in PR at Ogilvy and Mather before joining the inside track of special advisers, in his case to Social Security Secretary Tony Newton, but more important were his links with William Hague, as his former PPS and as his Chief of Staff from 1997 to 1998. In 1994 he was one of 44 Tory MPs voting to lower the homosexual age of consent to 16, though he married in 1995 'to quell the rumours' as he put it. With links to the socially-conscious One Nation tradition, he has shown tendencies to trim, as over Maastricht. In 2001 he initially voted for Michael Ancram, then kept his counsel, but was still made a Whip by Iain Duncan Smith. He shows signs of seeking to emulate his Liberal Democrat neighbour Norman Baker as a press-visible constituency MP.

WEAVER VALE

Sometimes when a county gains an extra seat in parliamentary boundary changes it is not apparent which is the newcomer, as several seats are almost equally changed. In the case of Cheshire in the latest review which took effect in 1997, this is not the case. Weaver Vale was an entirely new name for a new seat which is not based on any one previously existing division. Instead it gathered together territory and electors from four Cheshire divisions: Eddisbury, Warrington South, Tatton and Halton. It is set fairly compactly towards the west-centre of the county (at its 'heart', as it were), but it really is an artificial creation which has several disparate and discordant elements. It has very Labour terrain as well as very Tory areas, as one would expect given that it drew from two Labour and two Conservative seats.

Actually it is not quite as simple as that. In fact, essentially three of the consistent areas are Labour-inclined, and only one Conservative – the arrival of an anomalous Labour part of a Tory seat is the decisive factor tipping the balance of Weaver Vale to the left. There is nothing unusual about the part of Eddisbury which is included (23,000 voters). This is essentially the one Conservative element in Weaver Vale. Eddisbury was and is a safe Tory seat, and this part is not exceptional. It includes the small towns of Frodsham and Helsby, associated villages in north-west Cheshire, and the affluent Hartford neighbourhood near Northwich, home of some long-distance commuters to London.

It might be thought that the ex-Tatton section of the new seat (14,000 electors) would be Conservative too. After all, Tatton is traditionally one of the Tory strongholds in the county, although of course Neil Hamilton was defeated by the Independent Martin Bell in the unique circumstances of 1997. In fact all of the five wards donated by Tatton to Weaver Vale were won by Labour in most local elections. This is the Northwich–Witton–Winnington area, a working-class and industrial group of communities founded on salt-mining and still heavily dependent on employers in the chemical industry such as ICI. This was always an aberrant part of Tatton. Over 16,000 Labour-inclined voters came from Warrington South. This chunk of territory does include a pleasant village in Daresbury, but is mainly composed of the eastern sprawl of Runcorn New Town, which includes recently developed wards such as Murdishaw. The Conservative Party hardly operates in Runcorn, which is unfortunate for their chances in Weaver Vale as the final donor constituency is the over-whelmingly Labour Halton, its gift two more wards of the eastern half of Runcorn.

Essentially Weaver Vale consists of two Labour ends (east Runcorn and Northwich) and a rural Conservative centre. Like a barbell, the ends carry more weight and Weaver Vale elected the former Warrington South MP Mike Hall by a margin of around two to one in its first two contests in 1997 and 2001.

Social indices:			2001 Gen. Election:			
% Non-white	0.8		Lab	20,611	52.5	−3.9
% Prof/Man	32.3		C	10,974	27.9	−0.6
% Non-manual	53.8		LD	5,643	14.4	+2.1
£ Av prop val 2000	84 K		Ind	1,484	3.8	
% Increase 97–00	25.6		UKIP	559	1.4	
% Unemployed 2001	3.8		Lab maj	9,637	24.5	
% Decrease 97–01	2.2		Turnout		57.6	−15.6
% Fin hard/Rank	22.4	235	Elect	68,236		
% Pensioners	22.6					
% Prem mort/Rank	31	324				

Member of Parliament

Mike Hall was elected in 1992 for Warrington South, where his experience as leader of Warrington Council (1985–92) led him as an MP to advocate strengthened unitary local government. Born in 1952, son of a maintenance engineer, he attended St Damian's (RC) Secondary Modern, Ashton-under-Lyne, Padiham College of Higher Education, and Manchester University, and taught for 15 years. A voter against the third reading of the Maastricht Bill in 1993 and a Prescott, not Blair, voter in 1994, he introduced legislation to curb puppy-farming in 1997, whilst PPS to Ann Taylor, Leader of the Commons. After a three-year stint as an Assistant Whip (1998–2001) his parliamentary career went into reverse, as he reverted to bag-carrier as PPS to Alan Milburn, Health Secretary.

WELLINGBOROUGH

Wellingborough was held by Labour for all but five years between 1945 and 1969 – throughout the Tory 1950s, in fact. However Peter Fry then gained it at a by-election and held it until 1997, when they only just crept back in by 187 votes, after a slightly smaller than average swing. As in the case of the other top Conservative targets in Northamptonshire – and indeed elsewhere in Britain – in 2001, Kettering and Northampton South, the Labour sitting MP improved his position. Paul Stinchcombe's majority was multiplied by a factor of more than ten. That is not saying too much though – it is still barely over 2,500. In any year but that of a Labour landslide, Wellingborough will return to the Tories.

The seat is compactly based on the towns of Wellingborough, Rushden and Higham Ferrers. There is a substantial non-white presence in central Wellingborough, but the seat has clearly moved to the right over the last three decades. The traditional industries of shoemaking, tanning, and iron foundry work have been joined by many new light industries and services, rail and road links have both improved recently, and new population and prosperity has been brought to an old East Midlands industrial area.

The homogeneous nature of this seat was demonstrated in the Northamptonshire county council results of the contests on the same day as the 2001 General Election. Almost all of the county divisions within the seat were also close, the Tories nudging ahead only in Finedon, Redwell, Rushden South and Higham Ferrers. It is interesting to note that the turnout was higher in the Conservative areas, suggesting both that the middle-class vote was less affected by the abstentionism so evident in 2001, and that Labour would have done even better if the turnout had not slumped. If the rejection of participation is part of a long-term trend, this is good news for the Tories, both here and nationally. If it was a blip caused by the foregone conclusion of the 2001 Election on the other hand, their chances of regaining Wellingborough – and power – are further reduced.

Social indices:			2001 Gen. Election:			
% Non-white	5.4		Lab	23,867	46.8	+2.6
% Prof/Man	27.6		C	21,512	42.2	−1.6
% Non-manual	50.6		LD	4,763	9.3	−0.0
£ Av prop val 2000	71 K		UKIP	864	1.7	−0.4
% Increase 97–00	47.0		Lab maj	2,355	4.6	
% Unemployed 2001	2.6		Turnout		65.9	−9.2
% Decrease 97–01	0.8		Elect	77,389		
% Fin hard/Rank	18.5	294				
% Pensioners	24.2					
% Prem mort/Rank	21	469				

Member of Parliament

Paul Stinchcombe, elected in 1997, although a barrister reared in the Lord Chancellor's chambers, is not averse to criticising cuts in the legal aid budget and civil rights infringements in anti-terrorism legislation, and is a thoughtful critic in other areas, such as excessive greenfield site housing and harsher asylum laws. Born in 1962, son of a local government officer, he was educated at High Wycombe Royal Grammar School, Trinity College, Cambridge and Harvard Law School, and has spent his time on Select Committees, first Home Affairs, then Environment and Rural Affairs from 1998.

WELLS

As the Liberal Democrats successively advanced to their best tally of seats since the 1920s, it was something of a surprise that they failed to win Wells in 1997 and 2001, situated as it is in one of their strongest counties, Somerset. Liberal (Democrat) candidates achieved a strong second place in the last six general elections in the Mendips in the Wells constituency – five times in the person of Alan Butt Philip between 1974 and 1992. It looks good territory for the alternative to the two main parties: the core of the seat lies in the historic communities of Wells and Glastonbury; Wells with its magnificent cathedral and Bishop's Palace, Glastonbury with its abbey and its Tor, a mound with mystical prehistoric associations. The streets of Glastonbury are full of New Age shops and travellers reminiscent of 1960s hippies, though it is doubtful if many of them are local voters. This is the countryside of Camelot, with its mythical Arthurian connotations. The Mendip hills stand above the flat plain of the Somerset Levels.

There is also industry here: Street is an old (Clark's) shoe-making town; and there is the tourism of Cheddar and the seaside resort of Burnham-on-Sea, probably the most Conservative parts of the seat. The Liberal Democrats won nearly half the seats on Mendip Council in 1995, and ten of the 11 county council seats in that district in 1993. Then things began to go wrong, and it looks as if they will not add Wells MP David Heathcoat-Amory to their impressive list of scalps. One of the reasons why they failed to win the seat by 528 votes in 1997 was the performance of a well-known and charismatic Labour candidate, Michael Eavis, the local farmer who runs the annual music festival at Pilton near Glastonbury, which attracts tens of thousands of people. His share rose by 7.5%, the highest of any Labour candidate in Somerset. His relative success means that the Liberal Democrats were still bogged down in the mire in the Wells constituency.

Then in 1999 their results in Mendip district marked a sharp decline, as the Tories became the largest party on the council. In the 2001 General Election Labour, minus Eavis, declined but it was Heathcoat-Amory who increased his share, and indeed absolute number of votes (the turnout held up better than average in a hard-fought seat). The Lib Dems fell back on Somerset county council on the same day, and lost Taunton constituency. They had retreated from their high-water mark, in the levels and elsewhere.

Social indices:			2001 Gen. Election:			
% Non-white	0.5		C	22,462	43.8	+4.4
% Prof/Man	35.6		LD	19,666	38.3	–0.1
% Non-manual	56.5		Lab	7,915	15.4	–2.7
£ Av prop val 2000	104 K		UKIP	1,104	2.2	
% Increase 97–00	50.8		WRP	167	0.3	
% Unemployed 2001	2.1		C maj	2,796	5.4	
% Decrease 97–01	1.6		Turnout		69.2	–8.9
% Fin hard/Rank	8.4	507	Elect	74,189		
% Pensioners	31.0					
% Prem mort/Rank	25	428				

Member of Parliament

David Heathcoat-Amory, elected for Wells in 1983 and a minister from 1989 to 1996, resigned in 1996 as Paymaster General in the Major government to oppose the single currency but was reinstated to the frontbench under William Hague as Shadow Chief Secretary (1997–2000) and Shadow Trade Secretary (2000–01). A diffident, somewhat uncharismatic accountant, farmer and sometime Lloyd's underwriter, he was born (1949) into a rich West Country family (which included his great uncle, Derick Heathcoat-Amory, Chancellor of the Exchequer under Macmillan) and was educated at Eton and Christ Church, Oxford. With his Thatcherite convictions reflected in his initial hesitation between Howard and Redwood in 1997, he had nonetheless earlier expressed doubts on the poll tax. He led the hunting-down of Labour's Paymaster General, Geoffrey Robinson in 1997–98, and in 2001 backed the unorthodox Portillo candidacy and retreated again to the backbenches.

WELWYN HATFIELD

Labour successfully defended all their five seats in Hertfordshire in 2001, all gains four years before, as they confirmed the position of the nationally dominant Blair–Brown government. The nearest to a loss by some way though, was Welwyn Hatfield. In most cases where a new Labour MP had evicted a sitting Tory, they benefited in 2001 from the double incumbency effect, replacing their predecessor's personal vote with their own. One wonders in this case whether the circumstances of the 1997 contest, and the nature of the previous Conservative MP, had actually negated this by creating an anti-vote then.

The abrasive David Evans made some very rude comments about his Labour opponent Melanie Johnson during the 1997 Election campaign, relating to her status (and that of her children) not being formally married, but she took sweet revenge when she beat him by a comfortable 5,500 votes on the day itself. In 2001 the Election passed very quietly, and the new Conservative candidate Grant Shapps increased his party's share by 4%. With her's dropping by the same amount, and a 15% decline in turnout, Melanie Johnson saw her majority slip to 1,196.

The county of Hertfordshire is in many ways the epitome of modern England. Its population has shown the highest percentage increase over the past 50 years. Alone of all counties, it boasts two garden cities and four New Towns, all examples of the twentieth century's ideas of planned urban units. In a sense the constituency of Welwyn Hatfield contains two New Towns and one garden city, for Hatfield is a Reith Committee New Town, and Welwyn Garden City also became a government-sponsored New Town after the war, although it began life as Ebenezer Howard's second privately-financed garden city, following Letchworth, in 1920.

How do these test-tube communities vote? Like many New Towns, Welwyn and Hatfield have by tradition been both marginal and volatile. In local elections Labour can hold a lead in Hatfield and in the New Town estates of eastern Welwyn Garden City. But west of the railway tracks, in Welwyn's leafy inter-war garden city itself, the Conservatives are strong in Handside and Sherrards wards. It is a divided town, west versus east on classical lines. The smaller communities which make up the constituency are all very Tory areas, such as Old Welwyn and Brookmans Park. The Conservatives must regain this seat if they are to make any inroads at all into Labour's majority at the next election.

Social indices:			2001 Gen. Election:			
% Non-white	3.1		Lab	18,484	43.2	−3.9
% Prof/Man	38.3		C	17,288	40.4	+3.9
% Non-manual	63.8		LD	6,021	14.1	+0.5
£ Av prop val 2000	148 K		UKIP	798	1.9	
% Increase 97–00	38.0		PA	230	0.5	+0.0
% Unemployed 2001	1.2		Lab maj	1,196	2.8	
% Decrease 97–01	1.1		Turnout		63.9	−14.7
% Fin hard/Rank	16.0	335	Elect	67,004		
% Pensioners	25.9					
% Prem mort/Rank	21	467				

Member of Parliament

Melanie Johnson, elected in 1997 after selection form an all-women shortlist, and a heroine following the description of her by her Tory MP opponent David Evans as 'a single girl, lives with her boyfriend, three bastard children, never done a proper job', has a slight CV as a loyalist backbencher heckled by some of her more left-wing sisters for defending university tuition fees. Born in 1955, daughter of a civil engineer, she attended Clifton High School for Girls, Bristol, University College, London and (inconclusively) King's College, Cambridge, and worked as a member relations officer for the Co-op before spending four years as a schools inspector. To

Quentin Letts (late of the *Daily Telegraph*) 'as prim-lipped as a supermarket manageress', she became Economic Secretary to the Treasury from 1999 to 2001, and an under-secretary at the DTI in 2001, but took leave of absence to have treatment for breast cancer.

WENTWORTH

The constituency which covers those parts of the metropolitan borough of Rotherham to the north and east of its eponymous town revives the name of Wentworth, after the country house and park which is now an adult education centre. This countrified and aristocratic territory in the far north-western corner of the seat is, however, untypical of the gritty, working-class, and industrial character of the division as a whole. The former Wentworth seat which existed before 1950 (on somewhat different boundaries) was one of Labour's safest redoubts in the whole of Britain – it gave them a majority of over 17,000 even in their black year of 1931, when they won only 50 seats nationwide. The current division, revived in 1983, comes essentially into the same category.

The seat is constituted of electors formerly in Rother Valley, such as those in Rawmarsh and Wickersley and Bramley, together with some from the old Dearne Valley, which had to be split up between Barnsley, Doncaster and Rotherham constituencies after those metropolitan boroughs were formed in the 1960s. This latter segment includes towns such as Swinton and Wath-upon-Dearne, which still bear a backward and impoverished look, and Brampton, the colliery village for Cortonwood pit, the threatened closure of which figured prominently at the start of the great coal strike of 1984–85. Coal once dominated the economy here; its decline as a source of employment has done the same thing. Both effects help to ensure that Wentworth will remain one of Labour's very safest seats, in the heart of their rock-solid South Yorkshire belt. Their vote increased by less than average in 1997, but that was largely because they already held about 70% of the total share, and fell back by a little more than average in 2001, but that was due to the turnout plummeting to 53%.

Social indices:			2001 Gen. Election:			
% Non-white	0.4		Lab	22,798	67.5	–4.8
% Prof/Man	23.6		C	6,349	18.8	+3.8
% Non-manual	45.2		LD	3,652	10.8	+1.6
£ Av prop val 2000	55 K		UKIP	979	2.9	
% Increase 97–00	26.7		Lab maj	16,449	48.7	
% Unemployed 2001	4.3		Turnout		52.8	–12.6
% Decrease 97–01	3.5		Elect	64,033		
% Fin hard/Rank	26.3	188				
% Pensioners	24.9					
% Prem mort/Rank	37	224				

Member of Parliament

John Healey, a sharp-nosed TUC apparatchik, a campaigns and communications director for three years and earlier in similar jobs in the private and union (MSF) sectors, was elected in 1997 after a last-minute selection in a seat supposedly pencilled in for ex-Tory MP Alan Howarth, or the Blairite favourite Yvette Cooper. Born in 1960, son of a prison service PE official, with a perhaps incongruous public school (St Peter's, York) and Cambridge (Christ's College) education – one of 30 Labour MPs to be so educated, he had risen by 1999 as PPS to Gordon Brown after having performed as a loyal proponent of the minimum wage, introduced his own bill on improving employee rights and called for medals for Suez Canal Zone veterans. In 2001 he reached the frontbench as Junior Education Minister responsible for 'adult skills and lifelong learning', one of 21 of the 1997 intake to serve as ministers in the second Blair government.

WEST BROMWICH EAST

Labour has always held West Bromwich East since its creation in 1974, but it has often been a struggle. Peter Snape won by less than a thousand votes twice, reaching a low of a 296 majority in Labour's dark days of 1983. It looks now as if the worst is over for Labour in West Bromwich East, though. Snape increased his lead to nearly 3,000 in 1992, and over 13,000 in 1997, handing over safely enough to Tom Watson in 2001 as only just over half the electorate voted.

This seat was a genuine marginal for two decades, even if the Tories never won it. There is a substantial middle-class and owner-occupied bloc in the north-east of the seat, in neighbourhoods fringing Sandwell Park like Charlemont, and spreading east beyond the Tame valley to Great Barr and Newton wards. One complication is that the Liberal Democrats have been strong in some of these wards in Sandwell borough elections for many years – in 2000, for example, the Liberal Democrats polled 31% within this seat but the centre has never performed well in general elections in this constituency. In 2001 only 14% chose the Lib Dem candidate. Presumably the middle-class voters of Charlemont, Great Barr and Newton have returned to their ancestral Tory loyalties when selecting a national government with responsibilities for taxation, defence, public expenditure and so on. Not that it has done them any good in West Bromwich East. Labour fights back in the other parts of the seat, in the Friar Park council estate and in central West Bromwich. This is a gritty, industrial, working-class area at the heart of the Black Country. Some of the wards still have council-house majorities; where they do not, as at West Bromwich Central, there is a large non-white population, mainly of Indian (Sikh and Hindu) origin. East now looks solidly safe for Labour.

Social indices:			2001 Gen. Election:			
% Non-white	14.6		Lab	18,250	55.9	−1.3
% Prof/Man	20.9		C	8,487	26.0	+1.6
% Non-manual	42.8		LD	4,507	13.8	−1.1
£ Av prop val 2000	56 K		UKIP	835	2.6	
% Increase 97–00	15.0		SLP	585	1.8	
% Unemployed 2001	5.8		Lab maj	9,763	29.9	
% Decrease 97–01	2.2		Turnout		53.4	−12.1
% Fin hard/Rank	39.8	56	Elect	61,198		
% Pensioners	26.5					
% Prem mort/Rank	44	112				

Member of Parliament

Tom Watson inherited this seat from Peter Snape in 2001. A stocky, affable union and party apparatchik who was for the last four years before becoming an MP the National Political Organiser of the AEEU, he was born in 1967 into a politically active family, attended Kidderminster Secondary School, and King Charles I High School, Kidderminster and Hull University. His political originality comes in his role as founder-editor of the Liberal Democrat targeting quarterly magazine *Liberal Demolition*. An Old-Labour style right-wing union fixer, he dislikes the presence of ex-SDP-ers Roger Liddle and Andrew Adonis in the No.10 Policy Unit, defends the union block vote, and backs his union's opposition to PR. He has also called for Jeffery Archer to be stripped of his peerage, and backed the introduction of ID cards. His dislike of the Liberal Democrats was enhanced by their support for the candidacy of the Labour-ousting Independent MP Dr Richard Taylor in Wyre Forest, i.e. Kidderminster, his native heath.

WEST BROMWICH WEST

In 1997 the electoral politics of West Bromwich West were distorted by the fact that its MP was the Speaker of the House of Commons at the time, Betty Boothroyd, which meant that she did not contest it actively or on party lines (she had been its Labour MP from 1973 to 1992) and was not opposed by Conservative or Liberal Democrat candidates. This situation changed on her retirement in 2000. First there was a by-election that November, which was won with relatively little fuss by Labour's Adrian Bailey on a turnout of just 27.6%. This proved a precursor of the General Election eight months later, when even more unexpectedly only 20% more voters went to the polls. Two features in an otherwise unexceptional result were the very low percentage for the Liberal Democrats, one of their five worst showings in England, and the fact that they were pressed for third by the BNP, who almost saved their deposit – their candidate John Salvage actually did better than his party leader Nick Griffin had in the by-election the previous year.

   This seat was created in 1974 as a successor to the old Wednesbury, the seat of the eccentric former Labour Cabinet Minister John Stonehouse, who among other things switched to the English National Party and engineered his own disappearance in Australia. West Bromwich West lies in the centre of the Black Country, and consists of a chain of old industrial communities known for their variety of engineering and metalworking industries: Wednesbury, Tipton, Great Bridge, and (joining from the splintered Warley West in 1997) Oldbury and Tividale.

There are more Conservative pockets, such as Wednesbury North, but essentially this is not a favoured residential area. There are virtually no professional workers, very few in managerial jobs, and both skilled and unskilled manual categories reach proportions some 50% higher than average. The proportion of voters living in housing originally built by the local authority is the highest anywhere in the West Midlands. The seat is socially, economically and politically similar to neighbouring Wolverhampton South East and Dudley North.

Social indices:			2001 Gen. Election:			
% Non-white	11.1		Lab/Coop	19,352	60.8	
% Prof/Man	15.9		C	7,997	25.1	
% Non-manual	37.5		LD	2,168	6.8	
£ Av prop val 2000	49 K		BNP	1,428	4.5	
% Increase 97–00	16.6		UKIP	499	1.6	
% Unemployed 2001	6.3		SLP	396	1.2	
% Decrease 97–01	1.9		L/C maj	11,355	35.7	
% Fin hard/Rank	43.4	33	Turnout		47.7	–6.7
% Pensioners	25.5		Elect	66,777		
% Prem mort/Rank	45	100				

Member of Parliament

Adrian Bailey, a member of the Northern Ireland Select Committee from 2001, was elected at the December 2000 by-election as Labour's replacement for the departed Speaker, Betty Boothroyd. A bearded political organiser for the Co-operative Party (1982–2000), and before that a Cheshire County Council librarian for 11 years, he was born in 1945 and educated at Cheltenham Grammar School, Exeter University and Loughborough College of Librarianship. An allegedly uncharismatic deputy leader of the local Sandwell Council, and with three earlier parliamentary contests in hopeless Tory-held seats on his CV, his selection was said to worry Millbank beardists, with (by 2001) some 48 PLP beards – apart from his own – compared to only five Liberal Democrat, one Tory and Gerry Adams.

WESTBURY

The small towns of west Wiltshire contain a surprising degree of industry, and most of them are far from picturesque. Westbury is actually only the third largest of the four main towns in the constituency which bears its name – why on earth not call it West Wiltshire, especially as Chippenham was renamed as North Wiltshire in 1983 even though that town was clearly the biggest in the division and is three times the size of Westbury? The other towns are the hilly Bradford-on-Avon, which for long depended on a large tyre factory; the military centre of Warminster, which is also the UFO sighting capital of the United Kingdom; and the largest of all, Wiltshire's county town of Trowbridge, which started as a weaving centre but has diversified into foodstuffs and brewing. A fifth town, Melksham, was transferred into the Devizes division in the most recent round of parliamentary boundary changes in 1997.

Melksham was the most inclined to Labour of any part of a constituency in which that party has consistently finished third in recent general elections. Most of the rest sees a (somewhat unequal) fight between Conservative and Liberal Democrat, which the Tories won by 5,000 even in 2001, despite the Liberal triumph in winning over 50 seats nationally and retaining Somerton and Frome just over the county boundary. Bradford-on-Avon's physical attractions mean that it is more Conservative than most of the other towns. It is set in a ring of hills, near the beautiful Limpley Stoke valley, and is suitable for commuters to Bath and Bristol. Warminster, in the Upper Wylye valley, is in that part of Wiltshire which resembles a large armed encampment; this also tends to influence it to the right. The Conservatives can rely most strongly on the rural parts of the seat, from Holt in the north to Mere in the south.

Swings in the Westbury constituency have been low in recent elections, and it would take a political earthquake to unseat the Conservatives from this county seat in the lee of Longleat House, even though the aristocratic MP from 1992 David Faber (grandson of Harold Macmillan) gave up at the age of 39 and was replaced by Andrew Murrison.

Social indices:			2001 Gen. Election:			
% Non-white	1.2		C	21,299	42.1	+1.5
% Prof/Man	32.5		LD	16,005	31.6	+1.7
% Non-manual	54.0		Lab	10,847	21.4	+0.3
£ Av prop val 2000	104 K		UKIP	1,261	2.5	+1.1
% Increase 97–00	49.2		Grn	1,216	2.4	
% Unemployed 2001	1.5		C maj	5,294	10.5	
% Decrease 97–01	1.9		Turnout		66.7	−9.7
% Fin hard/Rank	9.5	478	Elect	75,911		
% Pensioners	27.5					
% Prem mort/Rank	16	525				

Member of Parliament

Dr Andrew Murrison, a Fareham-based Royal Navy surgeon for 15 years before reverting to being a locum GP, was selected here in 2000 in place of the unusually-early-retiring Old Etonian scion of the Macmillan-Cavendish dynasty, David Faber, who vacated the seat after only nine years at the age of 39. With an open personable manner characteristic of the Senior Service, he was born in 1961 and educated at Harwich High School, RNC Dartmouth and (on a Navy scholarship) at Bristol University Medical School and later at Hughes Hall, Cambridge. A Bow Grouper and former assistant to the Clarke-supporting Sir Peter Lloyd, MP for Fareham, his selection for this safe seat without a previous general election candidacy would not have been unassisted by his work at Central Office as assistant to the candidate-screener-in-chief, Lord Freeman, in 1999–2000. Whilst routinely hostile to a European super-state he nonetheless voted the pragmatic and ambiguous Portillo ticket in the July leadership ballots in 2001.

WESTERN ISLES

Western Isles is in many ways the most individual of all 659 parliamentary constituencies. It has the smallest electorate, by far, with just 21,807 voters at the last election. It is the only seat in Scotland which has a majority of Gaelic-speakers, 68% in the last published census figures. Amazingly, it has the highest proportion of detached houses of any seat in Britain (also 68%) – not stockbroker mansions but the small farms and crofts found uniquely in the Highlands. This is probably the only part of the United Kingdom where the Sabbath is still almost universally observed or enforced. What is more, its electoral record is unique.

Social conservative values remain strong in the tight-knit communities of the Outer Hebrides, where poverty and the hostile elements have long had to be combated by stern faith, but these certainly do not include loyalty to the Conservative Party, which has performed miserably here for the whole of living memory. Crofters traditionally voted Labour, and returned the same MP, Malcolm Macmillan, from 1935 to 1970. Then Donald Stewart won the seat for the SNP, and for the first four years of his 17-year tenure he was the only representative of his party in the Commons. Yet politics prove time and time again to be more based on individuals in the Western Isles than anywhere else in Britain. On Stewart's retirement in 1987, there was another massive swing, as Labour's Calum MacDonald took advantage of a drop of 26.5% in the SNP vote to regain the seat for his party. He has held it in three more elections, although in 2001 his share slipped by 10%, and he won by barely over 1,000, as the SNP advanced: this was the reverse of their pattern elsewhere, and indicates once again that the Western Isles results cannot be taken for granted.

The boundary of the Western Isles division is unchanged yet again in the latest review. What other territory could possibly be included to help equalise electorates? Nowhere else is quite like this. The seat includes the Outer Hebridean islands of Lewis and Harris, Benbecula, North and South Uist and the smaller inhabited members of the chain like Barra and Vatersay. It stretches 130 miles from north to south. These bare treeless islands still rely on fishing and farming, and whisky and tweeds, rather than enjoying a boom based on oil like Orkney and Shetland. Only five Scottish seats have a higher proportion of owner-occupiers, but this is far from a middle-class seat: the proportion of non-manual workers is among the lowest in Scotland. There is likely to be one change in the constituency though, as the Gaelic culture is reflected in the name of – wait for it – Na h-Eileannan An Iar.

The contest here will always bear little resemblance to what goes on elsewhere in Britain. Calum MacDonald will be re-elected only if it is perceived locally that he is doing a good job. Here in these wind-blown outposts politics is an intense, inward-looking business, unrelated to national developments – even the national currents of Scotland, never mind Westminster, 600 miles and a sea crossing away.

Social indices:			2001 Gen. Election:			
% Non-white	0.4		Lab	5,924	45.0	−10.6
% Prof/Man	26.5		SNP	4,850	36.9	+3.5
% Non-manual	44.4		C	1,250	9.5	+2.8
% Gaelic sp	68.4		LD	849	6.5	+3.4
% Unemployed 2001	4.8		SSP	286	2.2	
% Decrease 97–01	3.6		Lab maj	1,074	8.2	
% Fin hard/Rank	15.1	352	Turnout		60.3	−9.7
% Prem mort/Rank	47	71	Elect	21,807		

Member of Parliament

Calum MacDonald, elected in 1987 as a native son of Lewis, was born in 1956 and educated at Nicolson Institute, Stornoway and Edinburgh University, and at the University of California, Los Angeles, where he taught political philosophy for three years. An insulin-dependent diabetic, with a characteristic strong Hebridean accent which, as with North Welsh-speakers, can make English sound very much like a second language, he became a minister in Donald Dewar's Scottish Office (1997–99), having been Dewar's PPS, until devolution left it hollowed out and him redundant. A keen Europhile, who rebelled to vote as one of only five Labour MPs with the Tories for Maastricht in May 1993, he also favours close links with the Liberal Democrats, but reflects conservative Hebridean – whether Catholic or Protestant – views on abortion, embryo experimentation, and Sabbatarianism. Neither his devolutionary zeal nor Euro-federalism appears to insulate him from a strong nationalist threat.

WEST HAM

In 1997 the inner East London boroughs of Tower Hamlets and Newham between them lost a parliamentary seat: their constituencies all had electorates unacceptably below the national average, and the total allocation for the two boroughs dropped from five to four. Tony Banks's seat, Newham North West, only had 46,000 voters in 1992, compared with the English norm of 69,000. What happened is that the former Newham North West was supplemented by three wards from the abolished Newham South: Bemersyde, Hudsons and Plaistow. This effectively united the pre-Newham borough of West Ham. Before 1974 West Ham had two seats of its own, which indicates the level of population loss in the area.

There have been other major changes in the last two or three decades too. Newham is one of the most heavily non-white boroughs in London, and it has rapidly become more so in the last 20 years. Now over a fifth of the population of West Ham is Afro-Caribbean, and over a fifth Asian. This is one of the reasons why it is the most solidly Labour-supporting of all London boroughs. In May 1998 its wards elected a clean slate of 60 Labour councillors, the one borough in London which could thus be described as a one-party state. None of the wards were even close, and distant second places were shared between a wide variety of labels, including Socialist Labour, the BNP, and 'Democrat'. West Ham contains many communities associated with the inner East End for many years: Stratford, Upton, Plashet, Forest Gate. Its football club has been a symbol for Eastenders, its narrow terraces reflecting the tight-knit housing neighbourhoods. As the bifurcation of the capital and its suburbs has continued, Labour has strengthened its grip in seats like West Ham while losing ground further out in places such as Romford. The Tories are hammered in West Ham.

Social indices:			2001 Gen. Election:			
% Non-white	43.1		Lab	20,449	69.9	−3.0
% Prof/Man	27.8		C	4,804	16.4	+1.4
% Non-manual	52.8		LD	2,166	7.4	+0.0
£ Av prop val 2000	92 K		Grn	1,197	4.1	
% Increase 97–00	69.8		UKIP	657	2.2	
% Unemployed 2001	7.9		Lab maj	15,645	53.4	
% Decrease 97–01	5.7		Turnout		48.9	−10.1
% Fin hard/Rank	38.3	65	Elect	59,828		
% Pensioners						
% Prem mort/Rank	47	65				

Member of Parliament

Tony Banks, one of only three ministers drawn from the Campaign Group in 1997, lasted for two years as Sports Minister before being replaced, ostensibly in order for him to campaign for the UK's bid to host the football world cup. A loquacious, rent-a-quote, cheeky chappy elected in 1983, his surprising appointment to the government had reflected his transition from the role of left-wing factionalist in Livingstone's 1980s GLC where his 12 years as a councillor culminated in chairing the body as it sank after Margaret Thatcher's direct hit, to self-deprecating jester in the Blairite 1990s. Born in 1943 and educated at Archbishop Tenison's Grammar School, Kennington, and York University, he worked successively for two unions (as Head of Research at the AUEW and as Assistant General Secretary of the Association of Broadcasting Staffs), and has been dubbed oxymoronically (by Ian Aitken) 'the left's most effective comedian'. With his street credibility enhanced after a mugging by black youths in his constituency, he is also a stickler for animal welfare, opposing Mayor Livingstone's expulsion of the pigeon-feeders from Trafalgar Square, the 'cruel and wanton' slaughter of animals in the foot and mouth epidemic, craving hunting bans and oddly – given the surrounding Afghan medieval tribal carnage of late 2001 – condemning the plight of the animals in Kabul Zoo.

WESTMORLAND AND LONSDALE

The former county of Westmorland used to form one complete constituency of its own. Then in 1974 it lost its independence in local government when it was incorporated in the new county of Cumbria, and in 1983 it was associated in parliamentary terms with Lonsdale – once the 'detached' part of Lancashire across Morecambe Bay from the main body of the county – and with the Sedbergh area formerly in Yorkshire.

Although no longer drawn along historic boundaries this Westmorland and Lonsdale seat still possesses a homogeneous, rural and Conservative character. With 15% of the insured male population employed on the land, it is fitting that the MP for over 30 years until 1997 was Michael Jopling, who was for some years Secretary of

State for Agriculture in Mrs Thatcher's Cabinet. Another source of Conservatism lies in the tourist industry which is economically so vital here in the southern Lake District. England's largest lake, Windermere, is within the bounds, as are Coniston Water and Grasmere with its Wordsworthian associations. The attractions of the profound beauty of Westmorland have engaged many poets and artists, and many of its inhabitants have found strong reason to resist radical change, political or otherwise. The formidable writer of children's stories, Beatrix Potter, who settled here at Sawrey, numbered active commitment to the Conservative Party among her many interests, even in the days before full female suffrage.

This seat could well be in the process of becoming a marginal. The Liberal Democrats have turned in some useful performances in local elections in the south Lakeland area, winning seven of their ten seats on Cumbria County Council here in June 2001. They cut the Tory lead to 3,000 in the 2001 General Election, as Labour's vote, predominantly found in the largest town, Kendal, with its light industry and working-class housing estates was clearly squeezed on tactical grounds. More than one of Cumbria's seats offer a rebuke to the simplistic theory that physical beauty necessarily guarantees a Conservative Member of Parliament, and it may be that one day soon Westmorland and Lonsdale will join them.

Social indices:			2001 Gen. Election:			
% Non-white	0.4		C	22,486	46.9	+4.7
% Prof/Man	34.4		LD	19,339	40.4	+7.0
% Non-manual	55.3		Lab	5,234	10.9	−9.7
£ Av prop val 2000	102 K		UKIP	552	1.2	
% Increase 97–00	28.0		Ind	292	0.6	
% Unemployed 2001	0.9		C maj	3,147	6.6	
% Decrease 97–01	1.0		Turnout		67.8	−6.5
% Fin hard/Rank	6.5	574	Elect	70,637		
% Pensioners	31.9					
% Prem mort/Rank	20	484				

Member of Parliament

Tim Collins, elected here in 1997, is the apparatchik's apparatchik – a professional politician to his bootstraps, parachuted into this traditional safe seat hundreds of miles from London, where since leaving university he worked uninterruptedly for the Conservative Party. An Essex dairy farmer's son, he was born in 1964 and attended the minor public school, Chigwell, and King's College, London. At 22 he joined Central Office in the Research Department (1986–89), advised Michael Howard initially on the poll tax and then against the minimum wage (1989–92), was John Major's Press Secretary in the 1992 Election (and claimed much credit for the result), became Director of Communications at Central Office 1992–95, joined the No.10 Policy Unit in 1995, and spent the two years up to the 1997 Election as media consultant to the Party Chairman, Brian Mawhinney. Flat, classlessly-spoken, with the obsessive politico's beady-eyed partisan glint, and allegedly devoid of much cultural hinterland, as Deputy Party Chairman under William Hague from 1999 to 2001 he helped draft Hague's racially controversial 'foreign land' speech in early

2001, but warned Election candidates against making their Election addresses more Eurosceptic. After the July 2001 leadership election – where he initially backed Michael Ancram he became Shadow Minister for the Cabinet Office opposite John Prescott.

WESTON-SUPER-MARE

Although anomalously pressed for over two decades into the unpopular county of Avon, Weston-super-Mare has always really been part of Somerset. This may account for the fact that like all of the seats in that county, Weston was targeted by the Liberal Democrats in the 1997 campaign; and unlike two of those they were successful as Brian Cotter took advantage of a ten point drop in the Conservative share to win by 1,200.

Weston is a largish town of over 60,000 people and can quite adequately form the basis of a fairly compact constituency. Although Weston has traditionally shown all the political traits of an area dependent on tourism (the extensive rows of guesthouses, the fashionable residential areas in the hilly north of the town, the non-unionised and casual workers in the service and summer industries), the seat's Conservative majority slipped in consecutive elections – to just under 8,000 with less than 50% of the total share in 1987, and to 5,342 in 1992. The writing was on the wall, and it was underlined by the intervention of a Referendum candidate, who actually polled about twice the number of votes that Cotter won by in 1997.

In 2001 Cotter was under great pressure. His party appeared to have peaked in Somerset, however defined, and in the last local elections Tory candidates had led by over 10% within the seat. In the 1999 European elections, the Liberal Democrats had picked up an abysmal 14.5% across the seat, although this was in the context of an election fought on the regional list system and on one of their weakest issues. Brian Cotter had himself made less of an impact that some other new Lib Dem MPs. Finally, the Labour vote was not squeezed further, but actually increased slightly in share in 2001. Given all this, his victory even though by a margin of just 338, their narrowest successful defence, was a tribute to the party's continued national revival.

Social indices:			2001 Gen. Election:			
% Non-white	0.9		LD	18,424	39.5	−0.6
% Prof/Man	33.8		C	18,086	38.7	+1.0
% Non-manual	57.6		Lab	9,235	19.8	+1.9
£ Av prop val 2000	85 K		UKIP	650	1.4	
% Increase 97–00	41.1		Ind	206	0.4	
% Unemployed 2001	2.0		Ind	79	0.2	
% Decrease 97–01	2.6		LD maj	338	0.7	
% Fin hard/Rank	11.3	430	Turnout		62.8	−10.9
% Pensioners	33.1		Elect	74,343		
% Prem mort/Rank	26	405				

Member of Parliament

Brian Cotter, a small plastics manufacturer born in 1938 and educated at the Benedictine public schools, St Benedict's Ealing, and Downside, won the seat in 1997 at his second attempt. An oval-faced, beaky, de Gaulle-without-the-height look-alike, with thinning hair draped across a balding pate, he has hit few headlines as his party's spokesman on small businesses, for which he is typecast as the owner of a local small plastics manufacturing company, and as an internet buff. With no hunting in his largely urban constituency he votes the politically correct ticket of a complete ban, leaving his rural colleagues further down the south-west peninsula to vote the Countryside Alliance ticket.

WIGAN

Wigan is one of the stereotypes of a northern industrial town of old music-hall jokes, and George Orwell chose it as the site of one of his most famous investigations into working-class and industrial poverty in the 1930s, in *The Road to Wigan Pier*. But Wigan now has a modern town centre, and a variety of industries which have relieved its historic dependence on coal-mining. It has an excellent wooded residential district in the north of the town and relatively few urban problems. It is a lively cultural centre, especially noted in the 1980s for its popular disco music. Wigan's most popular sport is rugby league, and their team has been close to invincible in major national competitions for years. Even the notorious Pier itself is now developed as a tourist centre, identified by brown English Heritage road signs. Many people now find Wigan an attractive place to visit and live in.

This does not mean that it is not a Labour stronghold still; far from it. In September 1999 following the death of Roger Stott, Labour's Neil Turner held the seat with more than three times the votes cast for the second placed candidate, though nobody got many votes, as turnout in the by-election plunged to 25%. Not much more than twice as many voted in 2001, when the national government was being chosen. There is one occasionally Tory ward within the town, Swinley along the A49 road as it wends out of Wigan to the north. The Liberal Democrats usually pick up the Beech Hill ward in local elections, but seem utterly incapable of translating this into general election success; indeed in May 2000 the Lib Dem parliamentary candidate Trevor Beswick lost his council seat to Labour there. All the other wards are working-class parts of Wigan: Norley, unopposed in 2000, Newtown and Whelley. This is inner Wigan, but it is dissimilar in many ways to much of modern inner-city Britain. There is no significant non-white population as in other 'Lancashire' towns like Blackburn and Bolton. There have been no significant riots as in Oldham and Burnley. There is no higher than the average proportion of single-parent families. This may not be a Conservative community, but in many ways it is conservative. The history and traditions of Labour support here have proved deeper than the coal seams which played so much of a role in starting them; those seams are exhausted, but the strength of Labour's resources is not.

Social indices:			2001 Gen. Election:				
% Non-white	0.8		Lab	20,739	61.7	−6.8	
% Prof/Man	27.6		C	6,996	20.8	+3.9	
% Non-manual	49.8		LD	4,970	14.8	+4.8	
£ Av prop val 2000	57 K		SA	886	2.6		
% Increase 97–00	19.3		Lab maj	13,743	40.9		
% Unemployed 2001	3.4		Turnout		52.5	−15.3	
% Decrease 97–01	3.0		Elect	64,040			
% Fin hard/Rank	25.2	197					
% Pensioners	24.5						
% Prem mort/Rank	35	250					

Member of Parliament

Neil Turner was elected at a by-election in 1999. Whilst no model Blairite, given his beard and reservations about elected mayors, he is otherwise a very safe pair of municipal hands, with 25 years service on Wigan Council, and a conventional advocate of public–private partnerships. By 2001 PPS to Iain McCartney, Work and Pensions Minister, born in 1945 and educated at Carlisle Grammar School, he was formerly a quantity surveyor. Surveying the (small) quantity of electors who bothered to vote in his by-election, he favours various measures – including electronic voting from home – to boost turnout. In March 2001 he scored something of a first by returning a constituent's letter with spelling mistakes ringed, an elitist practice no longer common even in schools.

WILTSHIRE NORTH

This seat, in its former (but very similar) incarnation as Chippenham, has had a history of marginality. In 1966, for example, the Conservatives held on by only 694 votes. Yet this was not, as might at first be thought, against a strong Labour challenge in that year when they won the General Election with a majority of 100 seats. It was over the Liberals, who at that time had relatively few target seats as promising as Chippenham. In 1964 they had come close as well – the majority then was just over 1,500. Suddenly, though, it all went wrong for the Liberals and their successors. In 1970 the MP Daniel Awdry, who had struggled every time before, increased his majority to over 10,000. Since then it has never been really close. In 1983 the name of the seat was changed, but even in 1997 the new candidate James Gray held on by nearly 3,500 at a time when so many West England seats were falling to the Lib Dems. In 2001 there were many well-publicised tips of a Conservative defeat again, but this was very much a case of the media looking after its own, as the Liberal Democrat hopeful this time was Hugh Pym, formerly of ITN, now of the BBC. He did not even get as close as his party had four years before.

The relative decline of the centrists in North Wiltshire requires explanation. Such is provided by a close consideration of the electoral history of the Chippenham seat. The Liberal surge was started, as so often, by a by-election. In the autumn of 1962 a by-election was caused by the elevation to the peerage of the former Education Secretary Sir David Eccles, a victim of the 'Night of the Long Knives'. Eccles had held Chippenham safely, but the Conservatives were lucky to hold the seat in the by-election with a mere 37% of the vote against resurgent Liberal and Labour parties who split the opposition mid-term protest vote. As is common, the opportunity provided by a fortuitous by-election affects the results in the seat for some elections to come, before things return to 'normal'. This is what happened in Chippenham/North Wiltshire.

The name change in 1983 was a little odd, as Chippenham itself is a growing town of some 25,000 souls, the third largest in the county (1991 Census); certainly it is much bigger than Westbury, after which the West Wiltshire seat is so strangely named. The other population centres are Corsham, Wootton Bassett, Lyneham and Malmesbury. The Lib Dems are still the largest party on the district council which has almost the same borders. Yet one still feels that they need another by-election actually to win North Wiltshire at parliamentary level, and if stabs in the back have not been outlawed from ministerial politics, nights of long knives no longer put people into the Lords. By-elections are, nowadays, avoided like the plague they can bring to the defending party.

Social indices:			2001 Gen. Election:			
% Non-white	1.2		C	24,090	45.5	+1.7
% Prof/Man	33.4		LD	20,212	38.2	+0.4
% Non-manual	53.4		Lab	7,556	14.3	+0.0
£ Av prop val 2000	126 K		UKIP	1,090	2.1	+1.4
% Increase 97–00	56.5		C maj	3,878	7.3	
% Unemployed 2001	0.9		Turnout		66.6	–8.5
% Decrease 97–01	1.1		Elect	79,524		
% Fin hard/Rank	8.6	501				
% Pensioners	23.6					
% Prem mort/Rank	12	568				

Member of Parliament

James Gray, a Defence spokesman by 2001, elected here in 1992, is an itinerant Scots Tory, if of the impeccably anglicised genre, as distinct from the more Caledonian-brogued Sir Teddy Taylor and Eric Forth. Born in 1954 into the Scots Presbyterian establishment (an elite than which there scarcely comes any more ponderous), his father was Minister of Dunblane Cathedral and Moderator of the General Assembly of the Church of Scotland, and he attended fee-paying Glasgow High School, Glasgow University and Christ Church, Oxford. Phobic on devolution and fox hunting bans, a futures broker-turned-political consultant, his tall, good-looking, statesmanlike mien and urbanely modulated voice, suggest at least middle rank placing in a Conservative administration of the 1950s. A Hague voter in 1997, he eventually reached the frontbench as an Education spokesman and Whip in 2000. In 2001 his leadership votes went unrevealed.

WIMBLEDON

Wimbledon is best known nationally and internationally as the home of the (ultra-conservative) English lawn tennis establishment, evoking memories of strawberries and cream and the ivied walls of the All-England Club. Parts of this seat contain some of the most affluent and desirable residential territory and property in the whole of Greater London. Around the Common and Wimbledon Park are large detached houses reminiscent of outer Surrey. This is the so-called Wimbledon 'Village', with an attractive elevated position.

It thus produced one of the very greatest shocks of the 1997 Election when Roger Casale won the seat for Labour by 3,000 votes after a massive 19.5% increase in vote share. At first sight this seems inexplicable. The SW20 postal code minority of this seat (most of it is SW19) was also solidly Conservative – Cottenham Park, Raynes Park. All these neighbourhoods are leafy, middle class and high income. Over 70% of Wimbledon's employed population work in white-collar, non-manual occupations. Average property prices were £250,527 in 2000, according to the research company Experian, which was not only one of the highest ten figures of any constituency, but represented a 74% increase since the general election year of 1997, the fourth greatest rise of any seat.

However, there is another side to the seat: down the hill, across the railway track, in the valley of the river Wandle, terraced housing spreads out towards Haydons Road station and South Wimbledon tube station. This area, mainly in Abbey and Trinity wards, looks as if it could be in many 'half-way out' London seats, like Tooting or Norwood, both consistently held by Labour even in 1983. There are significant non-white minorities, multi-occupied residences, and pockets of elderly working-class people. This section provided a solid base for Labour to mount a challenge, but the stunning gain can be explained only in terms appeal of Tony Blair's New Labour Party to middle-class voters in the south of England, and especially in outer London, in 1997. There is no doubt that they continued to do well in the next four years, as the housing value statistics testify, and in 2001 Casale further increased his vote by 3%. This was the same figure by which the Lib Dem share fell. There was in all probability an arrangement made concerning the neighbouring seat of Kingston and Surbiton, where the Labour vote collapsed and Edward Davey pulled off his astonishing victory. Davey appears safe now, but one suspects that the government will have to continue to deliver prosperity for Roger Casale to be in the same happy position.

Social indices:			2001 Gen. Election:			
% Non-white	12.5		Lab	18,806	45.7	+3.0
% Prof/Man	51.6		C	15,062	36.6	+0.1
% Non-manual	77.1		LD	5,341	13.0	−3.6
£ Av prop val 2000	251 K		Grn	1,007	2.4	+1.5
% Increase 97–00	74.0		Ind	479	1.2	
% Unemployed 2001	1.3		UKIP	414	1.0	
% Decrease 97–01	1.9		Lab maj	3,744	9.1	
% Fin hard/Rank	5.8	585	Turnout		64.3	−11.2
% Pensioners	24.2		Elect	63,930		
% Prem mort/Rank	13	563				

Member of Parliament

Roger Casale, a Europhile lecturer at a former polytechnic (Greenwich), elected here in 1997, routinely suffered Conservative mockery and derision every time he rose to speak, on the 'shurely shome mishtake' principle of having the effrontery to be a Labour MP in Wimbledon, and with a public-school (Hurstpierpoint) and Oxford (Brasenose) pedigree to boot. His increased majority on a pro-Labour swing in 2001 would thus have caused some gloom in Tory suburbia. Born in 1960, son of a Wimbledon schoolteacher, his loyalist interventions have something of an unpractised air, notably when he thanked the government for 'wiring up children (in a school in Wimbledon) to computers'. But he has been an effective ward heeler, and no-one has ever won Wimbledon twice for Labour before.

WINCHESTER

The Winchester constituency seemed set on breaking records in 1997. First, in the General Election on 1 May, Mark Oaten was declared the victor on behalf of the Liberal Democrats by just two votes, the lowest margin anywhere since before the Second World War. The declaration did not come until 6.30 pm on Friday evening, 2 May, long after all the others were in. Then, after a court case in which it was agreed that 55 ballot papers had wrongly been excluded due to a lack of franking by electoral officers (and which if counted would have put Oaten two votes behind his Tory opponent, the former MP Gerry Malone), a re-run of the election was ordered. This was a first since before the First World War. However, the by-election, which took place on 20 November, was not exactly close. Oaten increased his majority over Malone approximately 11,000 fold, to 21,900.

Voters traditionally dislike being forced into by-elections soon after a general election, if they feel them to be unnecessary. Malone was portrayed as a bad loser, and with the Conservatives still lower in the national polls than in May, and an invisible campaign by Labour, which resulted in them polling their lowest vote in living memory, less than 1,000 votes, Oaten leapt from having the lowest majority of any Liberal Democrat to having comfortably the highest.

Winchester is a city associated with the Establishment, with comfort and privilege. It has a renowned cathedral, and it is the centre of one of the most esteemed and well-endowed Church of England dioceses; in the Middle Ages there were suggestions that Winchester should be the seat of a third English archbishop. Winchester College is a major public school with a social status second only to Eton, and an academic reputation second to none. It is also known to be among the most prosperous of constituencies according to many statistical indices – certainly its unemployment rate has historically been among the lowest in the United Kingdom. Less than half of the electorate of the constituency is in the city itself, the rest being spread across comfortable villages and small towns in the inland heart of Hampshire.

Oaten was able to capitalise on his unusual by-election triumph to hold Winchester in 2001 with a majority roughly half way between those he notched or piled up in 1997. We shall have to wait for another full term before the effects of that amazing year are fully worked out, but in polling over 32,000 votes in 2001, on the highest turnout in Britain (though not the UK) in one of the largest electorates, he has an enormous base of support – in fact the highest total of any MP by a considerable margin.

Social indices:			2001 Gen. Election:			
% Non-white	1.0		LD	32,282	54.6	+12.5
% Prof/Man	44.1		C	22,648	38.3	−3.8
% Non-manual	64.5		Lab	3,498	5.9	−4.6
£ Av prop val 2000	182 K		UKIP	664	1.1	+0.4
% Increase 97–00	59.4		WR	66	0.1	
% Unemployed 2001	0.9		LD maj	9,634	16.3	
% Decrease 97–01	1.0		Turnout		72.3	−6.4
% Fin hard/Rank	7.0	559	Elect	81,852		
% Pensioners	26.7					
% Prem mort/Rank	9	604				

Member of Parliament

Mark Oaten, a close collaborator of Charles Kennedy as first (1999–2001) his PPS and then (from 2001) as Chairman of the Party, comes of the generation (born in 1964) to be impressed by the new Social Democratic Party in 1981, which he duly joined, becoming an SDP councillor in 1986 in Watford before you could say 'Gadarene rush' – eventually leading the Liberal Democrat group. Educated at Queen's Secondary Modern School, Watford, and at Hatfield Polytechnic, his experience as a PR man equips him for the task of holding a safe Tory seat as a Liberal Democrat, hence his lack of support for hunting bans and backing of important local army interests on Japanese compensation for POWs, and making good deductions of pay of ex-POWs in German and Italian camps. Tall and street-wise looking, he also naturally sought legislation to stop candidates calling themselves 'Literal Democrats' in order to allow bona fide Liberal Democrats like him to win by majorities of 20,000 at the 1997 by-election, rather than by two votes, as at the earlier general election.

WINDSOR

Windsor is full of institutions which are bywords for wealth, privilege, and the higher reaches of the English Establishment. Not only does it include the mighty Windsor Castle, frequent residence of Her Majesty although suffering from a serious fire in 1993, and the whole of the Royal Great Park, it also includes Eton, dominated by perhaps the most famous private school in the world, which has alone produced 19 prime ministers. Average property prices of £227,000 in 2000 are exceeded by those in only three seats outside London, and there are residential areas associated with extreme comfort: Sunningdale and Sunninghill; Ascot with its renowned racecourse and mansions along private roads on the Crown Estates; Old Windsor, site of Elton John's mansion, with its regularly acquired then auctioned collections of luxury ephemera; and Bray by the Thames, location of Michel Roux (Snr)'s luxury restaurant, the Waterside Inn, and residence of stars of the magnitude of Michael Parkinson and Rolf Harris.

Given this rich mix of splendour and ostentation, one might think that Windsor rates among the Tories' very safest seats, and indeed the Liberal Democrats, who increased their share of the vote by no less than 8% in the old Windsor and Maidenhead in 1992, failed to increase their share in this new cut-down Windsor division either 1997 or 2001, despite winning most of the councillors in Windsor and its suburb of Clewer in the most recent unitary local elections in May 2000. It should be remembered, though, that former Windsor and Maidenhead voters make up less than half of the new Windsor constituency. Labour won the single ward of south-east Slough brought in to make up the numbers, Foxborough, on the same day as the 2001 General Election, and as in other Berkshire seats did well then to increase their share to a rather surprising five-figure vote, a 24% share (and they also, odd as it sounds, hold Eton West). The single most prolific source of electors, though, is the 'non-Bracknell' section of the former East Berkshire, which had a 28,000 Tory majority in 1992. This mink-lined territory should continue comfortably to suppress any rebelliousness on the part of the Windsor – or Eton – townspeople.

Social indices:			2001 Gen. Election:			
% Non-white	4.7		C	19,900	47.3	−0.9
% Prof/Man	44.2		LD	11,011	26.1	−2.5
% Non-manual	67.0		Lab	10,137	24.1	+5.8
£ Av prop val 2000	227 K		UKIP	1,062	2.5	+1.9
% Increase 97–00	67.2		C maj	8,889	21.1	
% Unemployed 2001	1.1		Turnout		60.9	−12.6
% Decrease 97–01	0.7		Elect	69,136		
% Fin hard/Rank	5.6	592				
% Pensioners	22.4					
% Prem mort/Rank	10	600				

Member of Parliament

Michael Trend, son of Harold Wilson's Cabinet Secretary, Sir Burke Trend, was elected MP here in 1992. A tall, heavily-built, former journalist, eventually on the *Daily Telegraph*, he was born in 1952, and attended Westminster School and Oriel College, Oxford. A restrained Establishment figure and a churchy Tory of traditional mien, he was, as Deputy Party Chairman under Brian Mawhinney, involved in the controversy over Michael Ashcroft's donations to the Party, sought to hold together Europhile and Eurosceptic wings, and was only moderately Eurosceptic as a Foreign Affairs spokesman 1998–99. Switching to a spokesmanship on Social Security in 1999, he was dropped in 2000. A Hague voter in 1997, his choice in the leadership ballots of 2001 was undisclosed. A church organist, he has objected to the BBC's dropping of televised church services at Christmas, and has – inevitably – a good deal to say about aircraft noise over Windsor.

WIRRAL SOUTH

A very late harbinger of the Tory disaster in the General Election of May 1997 occurred in February of that year, when Ben Chapman seized the Wirral South vacancy caused by the death of the MP Barry Porter with a majority of nearly 8,000. Often in previous parliaments such defeats had been reversed, but three months later Chapman won again with a barely reduced lead. He completed the hat-trick in 2001.

There are four parliamentary constituencies in the Wirral section of Merseyside. These are now all held by Labour. Traditionally the Conservative strength is concentrated in the west and south of the peninsula. Wirral South is essentially middle-class residential territory, and Barry Porter had held a fairly comfortable 8,000 margin over Labour in 1992. Labour's support is at its strongest in the heart of chemical-land on the Mersey, at Bromborough and the planned Lever nineteenth-century company town of Port Sunlight. The Liberal Democrats usually win Eastham ward at local level, but do poorly in general elections as in the rest of the Wirral; and in May 1997 they could only manage 10% of the vote in Wirral South. The Conservatives are stronger inland, in Bebington and Clatterbridge wards and most of all in Heswall, the most prosperous community in the whole of the Wirral (90% owner-occupied, with over 44% of households owning at least two cars), still holding 72% there in May 2000. Like other middle-class redoubts and refuges in Merseyside (Hoylake/West Kirby, Formby, Blundellsands) Heswall now finds itself in the unusual position of being represented by a Labour MP.

Social indices:			2001 Gen. Election:			
% Non-white	0.9		Lab	18,890	47.4	–3.5
% Prof/Man	38.3		C	13,841	34.8	–1.6
% Non-manual	64.8		LD	7,087	17.8	+7.4
£ Av prop val 2000	87 K		Lab maj	5,049	12.7	
% Increase 97–00	25.1		Turnout		65.6	–15.4
% Unemployed 2001	2.6		Elect	60,653		
% Decrease 97–01	2.3					
% Fin hard/Rank	11.3	431				
% Pensioners	27.6					
% Prem mort/Rank	22	463				

Member of Parliament

Ben Chapman is a product of one of Labour's stupendous by-election victories, subsequently fallen like the rest into backbench obscurity, his moment of triumph having come in February 1997 within weeks of Labour's general election landslide. A pleasant-looking man, born in 1940 and educated at Appleby Grammar School, who rose through the ranks of the civil service to become a commercial attaché in the diplomatic service, serving in Ghana, Tanzania and China, he was cynically picked as Labour candidate for his business-friendly image – 'Ben Chapman Means Business', and seen by his Conservative opponent as 'a blank piece of paper on which a script can be written'. His orthodox temperament was acknowledged in his prompt appointment as Dick Caborn's PPS in 1997. As a symbol of middle-class disaffection with the Conservatives in 1997, his fate in 2001 was instructive: a majority down from 7,000 to 5,000 on a 1% pro-Tory swing – the national result, and implying slight electoral scepticism.

WIRRAL WEST

The safest Conservative seat in the whole of Merseyside in 1992 was Wirral West. When it fell to Labour (taking with it the former Cabinet Minister David Hunt) in 1997 it signalled the end of Tory representation in that metropolitan county. Whether they will regain any seats is a moot point, for the region has been swinging strongly away from them for some decades, and in 2001 this continued here, as in Crosby over the Mersey, as Stephen Hesford increased his majority to 4,000.

The north-west corner of the Wirral peninsula is predominantly taken up by middle-class residential areas. Most typical are the seaside towns of Hoylake and West Kirby, whose popular appeal as resorts are limited by the mudbanks off the Wirral, and the absence of the sea, but which serve as affluent commuter bases for Liverpool and Birkenhead. Much the same applies to the wards of Royden and Thurstaston, on the bank of the Dee estuary. Overall the Conservatives were 17% ahead of Labour in local elections within the seat in May 2000, but this could not be translated into a regain 13 months later, perhaps because the turnout in 2001, though lower than usual at 65%, was still much higher than the 26% recorded in the Wirral borough battles.

The constituency also includes the wards of Upton and Prenton on the edge of Birkenhead, both of which contain parts of the Woodchurch council estate, as well as a mixture of private housing of mainly post-war vintage. Parts of Woodchurch are very depressed in nature, and offer a solid basis for Labour support in this constituency, but not enough to win it on its own. The 1997/2001 success must have involved, too, the conversion of middle-class and even wealthy voters to the sanitised appeal of New Labour. If they do not blot their copybook in their second term, Tony Blair's party may win yet again in Wirral West.

Social indices:			2001 Gen. Election:			
% Non-white	0.7		Lab	19,105	47.2	+2.3
% Prof/Man	42.4		C	15,070	37.2	−1.8
% Non-manual	67.4		LD	6,300	15.6	+2.9
£ Av prop val 2000	83 K		Lab maj	4,035	10.0	
% Increase 97–00	20.6		Turnout		65.0	−12.0
% Unemployed 2001	3.1		Elect	62,294		
% Decrease 97–01	2.4					
% Fin hard/Rank	11.0	438				
% Pensioners	30.4					
% Prem mort/Rank	25	425				

Member of Parliament

Stephen Hesford, a Gray's Inn barrister who happens to be a Labour MP rather than vice versa, elected in 1997, is an unobtrusive, loyal Labour backbencher, whose opposition to grammar schools led to unfounded allegations of his using private schools for his own children. He was born in 1951, son of a small businessman but grandson of a miner, and educated at Urmston Grammar School, Bradford University, Central London Polytechnic and the Inns of Court School of Law.

WITNEY

This was one of those seats whose contest in 2001 was notable more for who did not compete than who did. The sitting MP, Shaun Woodward, had been elected as a Conservative with a 7,000 majority over Labour in 1997, but in December 1999 he defected from the party to join the governing party, citing the Tories' drift to the right, particularly on social issues, and denying charges of careerism. During the 2001 campaign he was to be found in the gritty northern town of St Helens, into which he had been parachuted at the last minute by a less-than-fully democratic process. There was never a chance that he would stay and fight Witney, either in a by-election or a general election, as many critics demanded, and the Conservatives duly took it again as David Cameron quietly inherited it with an increased share and majority.

The Witney seat is based on the West Oxfordshire local government district. Witney itself is a growing industrial and residential town, 20 miles west of Oxford. Its population increased by 30% to nearly 19,000 between the 1981 and 1991 Censuses. The renowned blanket works has been joined by new factories on industrial estates. Other urban centres include the old mill town of Chipping Norton on the edge of the Cotswolds, Carterton near RAF Brize Norton, Eynsham, Charlbury (a hilly and picturesque little town which was, counter-intuitively, held by the Labour group leader in the May 2001 county elections) and Woodstock, site of Blenheim Palace. Taking into account the smaller villages which make up the electorate, the constituency overall should remain Conservative, with the opposition conveniently divided between Liberal Democrat and Labour.

Social indices:			2001 Gen. Election:			
% Non-white	1.0		C	22,153	45.0	+2.0
% Prof/Man	34.8		Lab	14,180	28.8	−1.8
% Non-manual	56.2		LD	10,000	20.3	+0.5
£ Av prop val 2000	154 K		Grn	1,100	2.2	+1.1
% Increase 97–00	52.2		Ind	1,003	2.0	
% Unemployed 2001	0.5		UKIP	767	1.6	+0.2
% Decrease 97–01	0.8		C maj	7,973	16.2	
% Fin hard/Rank	5.2	602	Turnout		65.9	−10.8
% Pensioners	23.1		Elect	74,624		
% Prem mort/Rank	2	632				

Member of Parliament

David Cameron replaced the floor-crossing Shaun Woodward as MP here in 2001, one party apparatchik (for six years) in place of another, and like Woodward with additional experience of the media, as Head of Corporate Affairs at Carlton Television (for seven years). Sporter of a now-rare cut glass pedigree, he is the great-great-grandson and great grandson on his mother's side of the former Tory MP for Newbury W.G. Mount (1885–1900) and W.A. Mount (1900–06, 1910–22), born in 1956, and educated at Eton and Brasenose College, Oxford, from whence straight into Conservative Central Office, where he helped draft legislation he now sees as excessive, for Michael Howard, Norman Lamont and Michael Portillo – whose pragmatic ticket he backed in the leadership ballots in July 2001. In 1997 he had fought and lost Stafford, where he opposed the single currency and further European integration. One of the smallest number (14) of Old Etonian Conservative MPs ever, he gently mocks the arriviste pretensions of his still Oxfordshire-based turncoat predecessor, Shaun Woodward, with whom he had worked on the Tory 1992 Election team – claiming that 'from the hill behind my cottage I can almost see some of the glittering spires of his great house'.

WOKING

The number of those claiming unemployment benefit in Woking constituency, already small in 1997, fell by 60% to become the fifth lowest in the country in June 2001, at barely over 0.5%. Average property values rose by 68%, one of the highest figures in the land, over much the same period. This prosperity probably produced a politically neutral effect, as reinforcement of the natural Conservatism of affluent Surrey was balanced by the feel-good factor under the Labour government.

Woking is the largest town in Surrey (with a borough population of 84,000 in the 1991 Census) – or at least it is if one includes, like the borough and constituency of Woking, surrounding communities such as Byfleet and Sheerwater. The main threat to the Tories here in national and (more relevantly) local elections comes from the very active Liberal Democrats. Woking is large enough to have working-class terraces (Old Woking) and council estates (Sheerwater). There are extensive developments of medium-cost private housing: one ward, Goldsworth Park, grew rapidly as late as the 1980s. The Central and Maybury ward is 33% non-white, three times as high as any other in the whole of the county of Surrey, and Labour polled 72% there in a three-way local contest in May 1999. The Conservatives are far from in control of Woking Borough Council. Yet there are also very affluent wards (Horsell East and Woodham, Pyrford, Mayford and Sutton), and the overall tone used to be very Conservative when it came to general elections. Then in 1997 the new candidate Humfrey Malins, replacing Sir Cranley Onslow, suffered what was possibly the greatest genuine drop in share of the vote since 1992, 20.7%. That would be to discount the three anomalous cases of West Bromwich West (where the Tories did not oppose the Speaker), Tatton (Neil Hamilton versus Martin Bell) and Gordon (where there were extensive boundary changes and the estimators of notional results for 1992 appear to have been in error).

The main reason for Malins's great loss of support in Woking seems to have been the intervention of an Independent Conservative, who saved his deposit with over 3,900 votes, in addition to the 2,700 taken by Referendum and UK Independence candidates. However, he was saved by the fact that it was Labour, in third place, whose vote share went up, not the perennial Liberal Democrat Philip Goldenberg. In 2001 Malins essentially recovered the 8% which had gone to the Independent Conservative, and is now much closer to the absolute safety of a 50% share.

Social indices:			2001 Gen. Election:			
% Non-white	5.1		C	19,747	46.0	+7.6
% Prof/Man	42.5		LD	12,988	30.3	+3.0
% Non-manual	67.6		Lab	8,714	20.3	−0.7
£ Av prop val 2000	181 K		UKIP	1,461	3.4	+2.4
% Increase 97–00	68.1		C maj	6,759	15.8	
% Unemployed 2001	0.6		Turnout		60.3	−12.4
% Decrease 97–01	0.9		Elect	71,163		
% Fin hard/Rank	7.5	540				
% Pensioners	22.3					
% Prem mort/Rank	6	624				

Member of Parliament

Humfrey Malins was returned as MP for this seat in 1997, having earlier been MP for Croydon North West (1983–92). A solicitor-risen-to-Recorder, born in 1945, son of an Anglican parson, he attended the churchy minor public school, St John's, Leatherhead, and Brasenose College, Oxford. A socially-conscious One Nation Tory, he relocated rightwards to vote for Hague in 1997, and as founder of the Immigration Advisory Service, seeks to address the problem without recourse to a Dutch auction on asylum seeker expulsion, and is also concerned at the link between drug dependence and crime. Retreated into the non-partisan role of Commons Chairman, he backed Clarke in all three ballots in 2001 and was appointed to a Home Affairs spokesmanship.

WOKINGHAM

This division remains anchored by the town of Wokingham itself, but the centre of gravity, geographically speaking at least, has been moved from due east of Reading to curl round the south of the county town much more than it did previously. The two largest communities are Wokingham itself and the modern, expanding community of Earley, which has grown very rapidly since the 1980s, to match the population of Wokingham at 28,000. One ward alone, Redhatch, increased from 5,900 in 1981 to 14,900 at the time of the 1991 Census. As this all occurred in the Thatcher years it consists entirely of private owner-occupied stock, of course – the bedrock of the Tory dream of the property-owning democracy.

Indeed Wokingham constituency holds a number of social, demographic and economic records.

This is the seat with the lowest proportion of pensioners, only 16% of the electorate according to the Age Concern rankings. It also has the lowest proportion of premature deaths of any of the 641 seats in Britain, at an average of 65% of the whole, which if one thinks about it represents a different trend entirely. This is, though, closely connected with yet another extreme statistic: this is the seat with the lowest number of electors in financial hardship, as defined by the Experian index of deprivation. Problems here are those of affluence: property values are so high that it is very difficult to attract lower-paid but essential workers like firefighters, nurses, and teachers: in August 2001 Holt School in Wokingham was featured in the national media as it lost a remarkably high proportion of staff who could not afford to live in the area. That this is an area of labour shortage is proved by one other ranking: the constituency had the fourth lowest unemployment of the 659 at the time of the last General Election in June 2001.

How did all this pan out politically? John Redwood held the seat, but he was placed under more pressure than might be expected by the Liberal Democrat Royce Longton, who cut his majority to less than 6,000, and by the well-publicise celebrity Labour candidate Matthew Syed: the Commonwealth table tennis champion and first athlete to be selected for the UK team for the Sydney Olympics, with a first in PPE from Balliol College, Oxford, and a true local, growing up in Earley, son of an Indian doctor and attending the local comprehensive school. Those who think that no-one has better credentials for a better New Labour leader, after fighting a different seat in future, cannot be far wrong.

Social indices:			2001 Gen. Election:			
% Non-white	3.1		C	20,216	46.1	−4.0
% Prof/Man	48.7		LD	14,222	32.4	+1.1
% Non-manual	72.9		Lab	7,633	17.4	+0.6
£ Av prop val 2000	176 K		UKIP	897	2.0	
% Increase 97–00	62.8		MRLP	880	2.0	+0.3
% Unemployed 2001	0.6		C maj	5,994	13.7	
% Decrease 97–01	0.5		Turnout		64.1	−11.7
% Fin hard/Rank	2.6	641	Elect	68,430		
% Pensioners	22.3					
% Prem mort/Rank	−5	641				

Member of Parliament

John Redwood, Welsh Secretary (1993–95) and twice Tory leadership challenger (1995 and 1997), was discarded by William Hague in 2000 after three years shadowing Trade and Industry, and then Environment, having forged in 1997 an anti-Hague pact, likened to the Molotov–Ribbentrop arrangement of 1939, with Kenneth Clarke. Seen by his former campaign aide (Hywel Williams) as 'the original non-team player' and 'the Thames Valley Malvolio' with 'suburban prejudices allied to a fine mind', he was born in 1951, the only child of an accounts clerk, attended Kent College, Canterbury and Magdalen College and St Anthony's College, Oxford, and acquired a Fellowship of All Soul's. Initially a Rothschild's banker, he headed Margaret Thatcher's No.10 Policy Unit from 1983 to 1985. With his relationship with Hague already troubled by his pact with Clarke in 1997, it cannot have helped for it to have been revealed that he saw Hague as a man of 'trainspotting vacuity overlaid by the gloss of management theory'. Routinely described as 'half-human, half-Vulcan' he is also something of a pragmatic professional politician, as evidenced in his arrangement with Clarke who had earlier claimed Redwood's brand of 'extreme right-wing simplistic ideology' would keep the Party out of power for a thousand years. He voted for Iain Duncan Smith in the final ballot in 2001, but stayed on the backbenches.

WOLVERHAMPTON NORTH EAST

By tradition, the industrial Black Country town of Wolverhampton, north-west of Birmingham, had three safe parliamentary seats, two Labour and one Conservative. However, doubt had already arisen about the safe Labour status of Wolverhampton North East, despite its council housing majority, when the veteran MP Renee Short's majority was cut to a paper-thin 214 in 1983. On her retirement (perhaps stimulated by a threat of deselection) the trenchant Tory Maureen Hicks was able to make one of only half a dozen gains for her party, admittedly by a margin (204) even smaller than Renee Short's. This predominantly white and strongly working-class part of the West Midlands, with its higher than average proportion of skilled and semi-skilled industrial workers, council house tenants, and council house buyers, clearly had responded to Mrs Thatcher's political appeal. North East had become a marginal.

In 1992 all three Wolverhampton seats swung heavily back towards Labour, and North East looks on paper like one of their easier gains. Ken Purchase, who had failed to hold the seat in 1987, beat Maureen Hicks by nearly 4,000; in fact, she managed to hold the Tory vote steady, while the Liberal Democrat share was more than halved. After the Labour landslides of 1997 and 2001 they now outvote the Tories by two to one, while the Liberal Democrats still do worse than almost anywhere else in the country. There is still Conservative strength, at its greatest at the north end of the seat, in Bushbury. There has been some new private residential development in Oxley. Mixed wards include Fallings Park and the two in the semi-independent town of Wednesfield, a couple of miles to the north-east of Wolverhampton – it is not to be confused with Wednesbury, which is in the West Bromwich West constituency. All of these areas were won by Tories in the May 2000 local elections, and although there was no swing in 2001 there is potential for this parliamentary seat to be close again should (when?) the government slips up. Labour's strongest wards are Heath Town, and most convincingly of all, the Low Hill council estate. Only about a tenth of the population of North East is non-white, and nearly half of these are of Afro-Caribbean origin; there are relatively few Asians.

Social indices:			2001 Gen. Election:			
% Non-white	11.8		Lab/Coop	18,984	60.3	+1.0
% Prof/Man	19.5		C	9,019	28.6	+0.7
% Non-manual	40.3		LD	2,494	7.9	+2.5
£ Av prop val 2000	51 K		UKIP	997	3.1	
% Increase 97–00	16.4		L/C maj	9,965	31.7	
% Unemployed 2001	6.2		Turnout		52.1	−15.1
% Decrease 97–01	1.8		Elect	60,486		
% Fin hard/Rank	41.1	42				
% Pensioners	23.9					
% Prem mort/Rank	42	152				

Member of Parliament

Ken Purchase, elected in 1992, combines being PPS to Robin Cook (from 1997) with regular visits to Bahrain on whose behalf he proselytises despite its questionable record on human rights. A toolmaker-turned-adviser to worker-controlled co-operatives, he was born in 1939, attended Springfield Secondary Modern School, Wolverhampton and Wolverhampton Polytechnic, spent 20 years on Wolverhampton Council, in 1994 voted for Beckett not Blair, and in 1999, unusually for a PPS, claimed that DTI Secretaries Mandelson and Byers had pressed Foreign Secretary Robin Cook to agree to supplying Hawk jets to Indonesia.

WOLVERHAMPTON SOUTH EAST

South East is the safest of the three Labour seats in Wolverhampton. The Labour vote held up much better than in Wolverhampton North East in the 1980s, and it never looked like following its neighbour into Tory hands. The class make-up of the two seats is similar, but South East has older housing, not being on the edge of the West Midlands conurbation, and a much higher proportion of non-white residents.

This is the most recent of the three constituencies to be designated as a Wolverhampton seat. In the mid-1960s the county borough of Wolverhampton was expanded to include the town of Bilston, which had formed the basis of its own seat in association with the other once independent towns of Coseley and Sedgley, now in Dudley North. In 1974 the Parliamentary Boundary Commission caught up with this development and created a Wolverhampton South East division which has essentially remained the same ever since.

Besides Bilston itself, South East includes the working-class East Park ward of Wolverhampton, and Ettingshall and Blakenall south of the town centre. All the wards are held by Labour at local level. Blakenall has some pleasant housing, as for example at Goldthorn Park, but is also over 50% non-white (mainly residents of Indian origin). About a quarter of the population of South East is non-white, although with fewer registered voters, but this contributes to its status as a safe Labour seat.

It looks the part. The borough of Wolverhampton is dominated by a mixture of industries, many of them heavy, and some struggling: the unemployment rate here was nearly twice the national average in 1991. This seat is set among some of the most scarred and polluted townscape in Britain. The train journey from Wolverhampton to Birmingham takes the traveller through a stark panorama created by the Industrial Revolution.

Social indices:			2001 Gen. Election:				
% Non-white	23.2		Lab/Coop	18,409	67.4	+3.7	
% Prof/Man	17.0		C	5,945	21.8	+1.6	
% Non-manual	36.8		LD	2,389	8.8	−0.7	
£ Av prop val 2000	46 K		NF	554	2.0		
% Increase 97–00	17.8		L/C maj	12,464	45.7		
% Unemployed 2001	7.4		Turnout		50.6	−13.5	
% Decrease 97–01	1.3		Elect	53,931			
% Fin hard/Rank	50.7	15					
% Pensioners	25.9						
% Prem mort/Rank	46	81					

Member of Parliament

Dennis Turner, Clare Short's PPS from 1997 and previously a Whip for four years, elected in 1987, is one of Labour's dwindling rump of proles, in his case a burly Black Countryman who as a beer-and-betting, chips-and-mushy-peas specialist is bothered about full pint measures disregarding the head, and as chairman of the Commons Catering Committee was credited with getting chips onto a Commons menu that had come (according to Joe Ashton) to resemble that of a Kensington wine bar. Born in 1942 and educated at Stonefield Secondary Modern School, Bilston, and Bilston FE College and, variously, a local town or county councillor for 20 years, he was initially a steelworker, then transport manager, and finally chairman of a redundant steelworkers' co-operative involved in leisure provision. His Commons catering role led him to call for a 'really lovely party' to celebrate the rescue of the Rover car plant at Longbridge in 2000.

WOLVERHAMPTON SOUTH WEST

Wolverhampton South West will for ever be associated with Enoch Powell. Powell represented this seat from 1950 to February 1974, but then refused to contest the General Election as the Tory candidate, voted Labour himself, and called on his anti-Common Market supporters to do the same. In October of the same year he returned to Parliament after having migrated to South Down in Northern Ireland, and to the Ulster Unionist Party.

South West was traditionally the safe Conservative seat in Wolverhampton, although Powell clearly had a personal vote and personal influence as well. Ironically, considering that Enoch Powell is probably best known for his strictures about race (although this was only one of his many interests), South West also includes some of the heaviest concentrations of non-white residents in the town – over 20% in 1991. These have settled in the town centre, in St Peter's ward, and in Graiseley. Both of these are strong Labour wards, but the rest of Wolverhampton South West is a solidly middle-class peripheral residential district on the edge of the West Midlands conurbation. Tettenhall in the north-west, Penn in the south-west and Merry Hill between them, are strongly Conservative and mainly modern. Park is the old west end of the town, and traditionally the educational centre, containing the girls' and boys' grammar schools, the latter most recently famed for its national award-winning History website, activehistory.co.uk.

One wonders what Enoch Powell thought when Labour gained his old seat for the first time in 1997. This was one of the most prominent results on the night, not only because of its symbolic Powellian value for Labour, but because it was one of the first critical marginals to declare. The MP of 23 years, Powell's successor Nicholas Budgen, lost on a 10% swing to New Labour new candidate Jenny Jones. There were changes and departures between 1997 and 2001. Enoch Powell died, and Jenny Jones announced that she intended to serve one term only. Replacing her, suffering only a 2% erosion of vote share, was not a 'Blair Babe' in any sense, but Rob Marris. As long as he can hold this affluent seat to the far west not only of Wolverhampton but of the whole West Midlands conurbation, Labour will form the government of the United Kingdom. This is surely the definition of a most critical marginal.

Social indices:			2001 Gen. Election:			
% Non-white	21.2		Lab	19,735	48.3	−2.1
% Prof/Man	37.1		C	16,248	39.7	−0.2
% Non-manual	58.6		LD	3,425	8.4	+0.2
£ Av prop val 2000	77 K		Grn	805	2.0	
% Increase 97–00	25.9		UKIP	684	1.7	
% Unemployed 2001	5.7		Lab maj	3,487	8.5	
% Decrease 97–01	1.1		Turnout		60.9	−11.6
% Fin hard/Rank	24.4	208	Elect	67,171		
% Pensioners	28.5					
% Prem mort/Rank	34	268				

Member of Parliament

Rob Marris, elected in place of the one-term retiring Labour MP Jenny Jones, is a solicitor, born in 1955, educated at St Edward's School, Oxford, and at the University of British Columbia and Birmingham Polytechnic. As a student in Canada he worked as a bus driver and trucker, is a member of Greenpeace and describes himself as 'well-versed in matters Canadian', which should help when confronting the problem of the lumbering industry in Wolverhampton. Whilst opposing the takeover of a local real-ale-brewing brewery, he has acknowledged being not as big a beer-drinker as his colleague Dennis Turner in Wolverhampton South East. In June 2001 he was one of only four Labour MPs to rebel against the Whips' attempt to remove Gwyneth Dunwoody and Donald Anderson from Select Committee chairmanships.

WOODSPRING

The Woodspring seat – or at least its name – is a rather curious memorial to a strange piece of local government history. The county of Avon was created in 1974 and lasted for just over 20 years. The Boundary Commission, working in its glacial way, caught up with this development in 1983, redrawing former Somerset (and Gloucestershire) boundaries to fit this creation. Woodspring looked very much like the extra constituency assembled from the odd bits left over as the seats of Weston and North Somerset were converted into the new Weston and Wansdyke. There is no town called Woodspring, and the name was taken from the local government district, itself created in 1974 – although that unit has now itself been abolished by the Local Government Commission. The parliamentary constituency remains, a product of a short-lived and unloved conception.

The Woodspring division includes the expanding towns of Clevedon (1991 population 21,000) and Nailsea (16,000), the Gordano Valley, and Portishead on the coast (11,000). It extends as far as Long Ashton and Failand, set in wooded 'country club' land just over the Clifton bridge from the most fashionable part of Bristol itself – it is here that the golf clubs and school sports clubs catering for Bristol's affluent classes can mostly be found. It is all very much on the 'right side' of Bristol.

Woodspring is the safest Conservative seat within several dozens of miles. Clevedon and Portishead are seaside resorts of faded elegance, but decidedly upmarket from the larger, more bustling and more plebeian Weston a few miles down the coast. For 1997 the seat lost 12 rural wards and about 18,000 voters to Wansdyke, around the Chew Valley mainly, but picked up Wrington (with its fine church tower reputedly Gilbert Scott's model for the monumental Victoria Tower at the Houses of Parliament) and Yatton (8,000) from Weston.

In 2001 the Tory majority increased slightly, as Labour's advance into second place was entirely achieved at the Liberal Democrats's expense. This is actually one of the most affluent seats in the whole country, never mind the south-west region: it has the third fewest electors in financial hardship after Wokingham and Surrey Heath, and the second lowest rate of premature mortality and avoidable deaths (just 65% of average). The link between health and poverty is crystal clear.

Social indices:			2001 Gen. Election:			
% Non-white	0.7		C	21,297	43.7	−0.8
% Prof/Man	42.3		Lab	12,499	25.6	+4.9
% Non-manual	69.9		LD	11,816	24.2	−6.1
£ Av prop val 2000	122 K		Ind	1,412	2.9	
% Increase 97–00	52.3		Grn	1,282	2.6	+1.4
% Unemployed 2001	0.9		UKIP	452	0.9	
% Decrease 97–01	0.9		C maj	8,798	18.0	
% Fin hard/Rank	2.8	639	Turnout		68.7	−9.9
% Pensioners	25.6		Elect	71,023		
% Prem mort/Rank	5	640				

Member of Parliament

Dr Liam Fox, a Whip (1994–96) and Junior Foreign Office Minister at the end (1996–97) of the Major government and Shadow Health Secretary from 1999, is a Scottish-born (1961) GP, educated at St Bride's (RC) High School, East Kilbride and Glasgow University, who relocated to England after losing at Roxburgh and Berwickshire in 1987, and won Woodspring in 1992. A self-confessed child of Thatcher, because 'Thatcherism is the only Conservatism that people of my age have ever known', he voted for Howard then Hague in 1997, and as an ex-pat Scot was given the job of opposing Scottish devolution from the safety of the Bristol green belt. With his Catholicism reflected in his call for policy on abortion to be devolved to the Scottish Parliament (where it was more likely to be restrictive) and his later urging of January 2001 for 'huge restriction, if not abolition, of the current abortion law', he nevertheless voted for the permissive Portillo candidacy in 2001, and was one of nine Portillistas appointed to Iain Duncan Smith's Shadow Cabinet.

WORCESTER

Labour won Worcester for the first time ever in 1997, and although this was mainly a product of their biggest ever victory nationally, the reason was also partly to do with boundary changes.

The reason why the Conservatives had always been able to hold this seat in the past was largely to do with the fact that it always contained electors outside the county town and cathedral city itself. Back in 1945 and 1966 it included the spa and salt-mining town of Droitwich, and although it was transferred in 1983 to the new Mid Worcestershire, there remained a number of villages with rolling Worcestershire names like Drakes Broughton and Inkberrow, Pinvin and Upton Snodsbury. These, all very Conservative and amounting to an electorate of over 10,000, departed in 1997, mainly to the new Mid Worcs. This left the city of Worcester on its own, which Labour had little difficulty in winning by over 7,000. The result was in effect repeated in 2001 on a 12% lower turnout.

Labour has some very strong areas in Worcester itself, including a number of wards with a strong council estate presence in the east beyond Shrub Hill station: Nunnery, Holy Trinity, St Barnabas and St Martin's. In the 2001 General Election it is likely that Labour were also ahead in the central All Saints and St Nicholas wards, with their terraced houses and small Pakistani community. St Clement's, across the Severn from the racecourse, is marginal. The Conservatives win in Bedwardine, across the river from the cathedral and containing the New Road cricket ground, St Peter in the south of the town with its new private estates, and Claines and St Stephen at the north end of Worcester. We can tell much about the detailed electoral geography of the city from the local ward results, particularly those of June 2001 on the same day as the last general election. Pared down to its urban core, Worcester is a better prospect for Labour than it has ever been. The Boundary Commission have created similar 'doughnut' constituencies elsewhere, as at Worcester's fellow cathedral city of Lincoln; and in almost all cases this means bad news for the Conservative Party.

Social indices:			2001 Gen. Election:			
% Non-white	2.1		Lab	21,478	48.6	−1.5
% Prof/Man	32.3		C	15,712	35.5	−0.2
% Non-manual	57.0		LD	5,578	12.6	+0.1
£ Av prop val 2000	88 K		UKIP	1,442	3.3	+1.5
% Increase 97–00	46.9		Lab maj	5,766	13.0	
% Unemployed 2001	2.2		Turnout		62.0	−12.5
% Decrease 97–01	1.5		Elect	71,255		
% Fin hard/Rank	14.0	374				
% Pensioners	24.5					
% Prem mort/Rank	30	336				

Member of Parliament

Michael Foster, victor for Labour here in 1997, is a very tall, standard on-message loyalist recruited from the chalk-face (as an accountancy lecturer) before which he was a management accountant with Jaguar Cars. Born in 1963, son of a car worker, he attended Great Wyrley High School, Walsall, Wolverhampton Polytechnic, and the University of Central England, and is defined by his, albeit fleetingly articulated, assault on fox hunting which set the ball rolling for the permanent booting-around of an issue seen by the focus group analysts as a good mobiliser of populist urban sentiment against the toff-sodden shires. For his PC pains and on-message loyalism he became PPS to Higher Education Minister Margaret Hodge in 2001.

WORCESTERSHIRE MID

Like many counties in the southern half of England, Hereford and Worcester enjoyed sufficient population growth in the 1980s to deserve the award of an extra parliamentary constituency in the 1997 boundary changes, just as it had in the previous review in 1983. Just as in that previous review the new and extra seat – the eighth in the county in this case – has been created in the heart of the county with portions sliced off from a number of seats. What is more, just as in 1983 the new seat has been named Mid Worcestershire; but it must be stressed that the division which now bears that name is not the successor to that which was called Mid Worcestershire from 1983 to 1997 and bears rather little resemblance to it.

The bulk of the former Mid Worcs was based on the town of Redditch, which has now been given its own seat, taking with it some 58,000 of the electorate of 84,000 (which was far too large to be maintained). The minority section, around the spa and salt-mining town of Droitwich and its surrounding villages, did go into the new Mid Worcs; but a larger donation (over 28,000 voters) came from the former South Worcestershire, centred on the town of Evesham and the lush fruit-growing countryside around. Finally some other euphonious villages, like Upton Snodsbury and Drakes Broughton, were detached from Worcester, which is now reduced to its urban core.

All of this territory, predominantly rural but with some small towns, is inclined to the Conservatives. In May 1999 Labour could win the local (Wychavon) council wards of Droitwich West, Evesham East and Evesham West, but their support is too confined, and Peter Luff, cannily transplanting himself from Worcester, beat them by a comfortable 9,500 in the new seat's first contest, and 10,500 in its second.

Social indices:			2001 Gen. Election:			
% Non-white	0.5		C	22,937	51.1	+3.7
% Prof/Man	35.9		Lab	12,310	27.4	−1.5
% Non-manual	56.3		LD	8,420	18.8	+0.1
£ Av prop val 2000	119 K		UKIP	1,230	2.7	+1.5
% Increase 97–00	54.6		C maj	10,627	23.7	
% Unemployed 2001	1.4		Turnout		62.4	−12.0
% Decrease 97–01	0.8		Elect	71,985		
% Fin hard/Rank	9.3	482				
% Pensioners	24.5					
% Prem mort/Rank	20	481				

Member of Parliament

Peter Luff, a Whip from 2000, as MP for Worcester 1992–97 wisely migrated here to evade the high Labour tide of 1997. A PR man with additional interests in his family's printing business, he is a protégé of Peter Walker from whom he inherited the Worcester seat in 1992. A Tory Reform Group Europhile, he nonetheless rejects the other half of the Euro-federalists' agenda, namely the break-up of the old nation states via regional devolution. Born in 1955 and educated at Windsor Grammar School and Corpus Christi College, Cambridge, he has latterly emerged as the Conservative component of the 3-party trio (the others being Labour's Kate Hoey and the Liberals' Lembit Opik) proposing a 'middle way' to restrict but not ban hunting. A Clarke voter in 1997, his preferences were less readily revealed in 2001.

WORCESTERSHIRE WEST

The county of Hereford and Worcester was still used as a basic unit by the Parliamentary Boundary Commission which reported in 1995, despite the fact that by that time changes in local government structure seemed imminent, which threatened the end of its two decades of life. There were sweeping changes in the constituency lines occasioned by the grant of an extra seat, and these included the demise of a South Worcestershire division and the creation of one called West Worcestershire.

There is a strong resemblance between the two. Most of South Worcestershire's electors are now in West Worcestershire, although nearly 30,000 around Evesham and Broadway were transferred into the newly minted Mid Worcestershire seat. The 50,000 plus voters from the old South who have gone into West are joined by 11,000 from Leominster: this is the area around Martley, Broadheath and Hallow. It is this salient, to the north-west of Malvern, that persuaded the Commission to change the name of the seat to West Worcestershire.

It is predominantly rural, with rolling farmland and fruit-growing country, which is poor ground for Labour and has little in the way of a long tradition of local Liberalism, as exists in Herefordshire further west. The largest town is Great Malvern, a spa and inland holiday resort, the home of Elgar, whose music is held by many to capture the very spirit of 'Englishness'. Malvern seems the essence of comfortable Tory England like the constituency as a whole. The seat also includes the small town of Pershore, surrounded by orchards, and the area around Bredon Hill, which like the Malvern Hills forms a landmark that can be seen for many miles around.

The Tory grip on this green and pleasant part of England has weakened to a surprising extent, as Sir Michael Spicer's majority was reduced to less than 4,000 in 1997 by the Liberal Democrats, who apparently managed to persuade some thousands of potential Labour voters to support them as the best way of removing Mr Major's government – Labour's increase in vote share was their 612th best; and it fell again slightly in 2001 as the Conservatives only slightly improved.

Social indices:			2001 Gen. Election:			
% Non-white	0.6		C	20,597	46.0	+0.9
% Prof/Man	41.5		LD	15,223	34.0	−3.3
% Non-manual	62.0		Lab	6,275	14.0	−1.7
£ Av prop val 2000	126 K		UKIP	1,574	3.5	
% Increase 97–00	46.7		Grn	1,138	2.5	+0.5
% Unemployed 2001	1.3		C maj	5,374	12.0	
% Decrease 97–01	1.2		Turnout		67.1	−9.1
% Fin hard/Rank	8.2	520	Elect	66,769		
% Pensioners	24.5					
% Prem mort/Rank	11	578				

Member of Parliament

Sir Michael Spicer, as the most right-wing candidate, was elected Chairman of the 1922 Committee in June 2001, by 79 votes to Gillian Shepherd's 66. First elected (for Worcestershire South) in 1974, and a sometime protégé of Cecil Parkinson, he rose and fell with his patron (as a minister from 1984 to 1990, and as a Party Vice-Chairman 1981–84), discarding his originally 'wet' credentials for free-market zealotry and dropping his earlier Europhilia to become one of the leading Maastricht rebels in 1992–93, with 37 votes against the government, and seeing the single currency as a harbinger of a single state. Slight and breezy, a brigadier's son, born in 1943 and educated at the soldiers' school, Wellington College, and at Emmanuel College, Cambridge, dropped by Major in 1990 over the ERM, he led Michael Howard's leadership campaign in 1997, and in 1999 made John Prescott look very foolish by flooring him with a question on the proposed EU withholding tax, about which the Deputy Prime Minister clearly had not been briefed even to be informed of its existence.

WORKINGTON

Workington is the safest of Labour's four seats in Cumbria – indeed, the only one of which they can be absolutely sure in a general election, even after their share fell by 9% in 2001, relatively a very bad year for them in the county: the new candidate Tony Cunningham (no relation of Jack next door in Copeland) retained a majority nearly 11,000, considerably higher than his namesake's. Yet Workington has had a Conservative MP far more recently than Copeland or Carlisle.

Workington was the apparently super-solid Labour seat (indeed, one of the 50 or so to survive the disaster of the 1931 General Election) which created a shock by electing a Conservative, Richard Page, in the 1976 by-election caused by the elevation of the former Agriculture Minister Fred Peart to the House of Lords. This was a mid-term reverse caused by national governmental unpopularity, a familiar enough event more recently, which said little about Workington's preferences when a genuine choice of government was at stake; and Dale Campbell-Savours reversed his own and his party's defeat three years earlier at the 1979 General Election.

At first sight, Workington seems an odd division to return a Labour MP with a five-figure majority. Much of the acreage lies in the Lake District National Park, from Cockermouth to the busy tourist resort of Keswick by Derwentwater. Other renowned lakes such as Buttermere and Crummock Water are also included. In fact, though, this rural part of the constituency is comfortably outvoted by the coastal belt of west Cumbrian industry – Workington itself with its council estates and grimy steelworks, Maryport, now trying to attract tourism to its defunct dockland, and the other small, depressed communities of this declining and remote part of far north-west England.

Social indices:

			2001 Gen. Election:			
% Non-white	0.3		Lab	23,209	55.5	−8.7
% Prof/Man	27.8		C	12,359	29.6	+5.1
% Non-manual	45.4		LD	5,214	12.5	+4.4
£ Av prop val 2000	67 K		LCA	1,040	2.5	
% Increase 97–00	25.2		Lab maj	10,850	25.9	
% Unemployed 2001	4.1		Turnout		63.4	−11.7
% Decrease 97–01	2.9		Elect	65,965		
% Fin hard/Rank	21.8	248				
% Pensioners	27.2					
% Prem mort/Rank	36	229				

Member of Parliament

Alongside the unrelated Jack Cunningham in next-door Copeland, Labour selected the bearded schoolteacher **Tony Cunningham** as replacement for the retiring Dale Campbell-Savours in 2001. A local boy, born in Workington in 1952 and educated at Workington Grammar School and Liverpool University, he was a teacher for 18 years (11 of which in Maryport), sat as the local (Cumbria and North Lancashire) MEP from 1994 to 99, and latterly ran a human rights organisation. A Labour spokesman on Third World issues in the European Parliament, and who wrote a report on landmines in 1995, he was leader of the local Allerdale Borough Council 1992–94, and Mayor of Workington in 1990–91. Labour MPs do not come any more local than such classic products of the OMOV selection system – a reversion almost to the time when municipal figures were elevated to the Commons as if to the aldermanic bench.

WORSLEY

The town of Worsley itself is widely known in the North West as a desirable residential area. It is conveniently situated near the M62 motorway, which crosses northern England from Liverpool almost to Hull. In addition to Worsley itself, the ward includes the owner-occupied and well-off communities of Roe Green, Egerton Park, Broad Oak and Hazelhurst. Many successful businesspeople have chosen to make their homes here. One famous resident is the Manchester United football star Ryan Giggs, who spent much of his childhood growing up in a much poorer, inner part of Salford borough. It is only logical that he should have moved out to the top neighbourhood for some miles around, in the north-west sector of Greater Manchester.

The tone of the first paragraph would suggest that the Worsley constituency might be safely Conservative. This could not be further from the truth. The fact is that Worsley is highly untypical of the constituency which bears its name. Almost every other ward in the seat is a Labour banker. Here are to be found the social housing estate of Little Hulton, the working-class town of Walkden with its two wards (Walkden alone is twice the size of Worsley), and three wards from the borough of Wigan, a name famed for Labour loyalties: Bedford-Astley, Tyldesley East, and a newcomer in the 1995 boundary changes, Hindsford. Hindsford includes the western half of Tyldesley and the eastern part of the town of Atherton, and was a rare win for the Liberal Democrats in May 2000.

This territory, elsewhere, might not be solidly Labour. In Tyldesley East, for example, a third of households own a second car. These wards are predominantly owner-occupied and nearly all white. Nevertheless these wards of Wigan borough share a very anti-Tory political culture. So much so, in fact, that in May 2000 the Conservative Party did not put up a candidate in Tyldesley East.

Terry Lewis's majority was reduced to 12,000 on an exceptionally low 51% turnout in 2001, and Labour should be able to hold that level comfortably.

Social indices:			2001 Gen. Election:			
% Non-white	1.2		Lab	20,193	57.1	−5.1
% Prof/Man	30.8		C	8,406	23.8	−0.5
% Non-manual	55.2		LD	6,188	17.5	+3.9
£ Av prop val 2000	63 K		SLP	576	1.6	
% Increase 97–00	18.6		Lab maj	11,787	33.3	
% Unemployed 2001	3.0		Turnout		51.0	−16.8
% Decrease 97–01	1.2		Elect	69,300		
% Fin hard/Rank	22.5	234				
% Pensioners	24.3					
% Prem mort/Rank	40	179				

Member of Parliament

Terry Lewis, MP since 1983, is a Campaign Group left-winger who was excelled in his defiance of the Labour whip by only five other MPs in the 1992–97 House, but who has ranked less highly as a rebel against the Blair government. Born in 1935 and Catholic-educated at Our Lady of Mount Carmel Secondary Modern, Salford, and previously a power station engineer, he has resisted the Blair government on lone parent benefit cuts, student grants, predatory pricing of the Murdoch press, the prime ministerial power to nominate life peers, pensions linked to earnings, Incapacity Benefit cuts, and air traffic control privatisation and, after the 2001 Election, on the emergency Terrorism, Crime and Security Bill. Prurient on pornography and tobacco, he once called out to Ann Widdecombe, 'Make it quick; your broomstick's been clamped!'

WORTHING EAST AND SHOREHAM

This seat includes the four easternmost wards of Worthing borough, Broadwater, Gaisford, Offington and Selden, together with the local authority district of Adur, which includes the towns of Shoreham and Southwick, and Lancing and Sompting. Adur used to be a desert for the Conservatives, as the Liberal Democrats dominated the council in the 1980s and early 1990s, and Labour took the lion's share of the wards in 1999. The Tories put things right in May 2000 and held on well in the 2001 General Election, while Labour demonstrated that their local government performance was no fluke by moving up to second place ahead of the Lib Dems, who produced one of their worst results anywhere, as they dropped by 8% in a seat where they had been challenging strongly enough in 1997 to restrict Tim Loughton's majority to 5,000. Both in local government and parliamentary politics their bubble has well and truly burst here, which is not at all nationally typical. One factor may have been the replacement as candidate of their long-term Adur council leader Martin King.

Worthing is known as a seaside and retirement resort, whereas there is light industry in the Adur section and a working port based on Shoreham harbour. Whereas Worthing West has the highest proportion of pensioners in the electorate of any seat, things are a little different in this constituency which ranks 27th in that regard. Effectively the two seats of Shoreham and Worthing were mingled together in boundary changes in 1997, but the result is still that of two safe Tory seats.

Social indices:			2001 Gen. Election:			
% Non-white	1.4		C	18,608	43.2	+2.7
% Prof/Man	33.8		Lab	12,469	29.0	+5.0
% Non-manual	59.6		LD	9,876	22.9	−7.6
£ Av prop val 2000	108 K		UKIP	1,195	2.8	+1.0
% Increase 97–00	56.0		LCA	920	2.1	
% Unemployed 2001	1.3		C maj	6,139	14.3	
% Decrease 97–01	1.7		Turnout		59.9	−13.0
% Fin hard/Rank	9.9	470	Elect	71,890		
% Pensioners	33.8					
% Prem mort/Rank	22	459				

Member of Parliament

Tim Loughton, an Environment spokesman (2000–01), who backed Portillo in 2001 and became a Health spokesman, was elected in 1997. A right-wing partisan pursuer of Geoffrey Robinson and critic of Labour's treatment of General Pinochet, he was born in 1962, educated at Priory School, Lewes, Warwick University and Clare College, Cambridge, and worked for Fleming Asset Management. He boasts a record of vocal opposition to a single currency, as in May 2001 when he urged its resistance 'at all costs' as 'the last step in the jigsaw of a European super-state'. He scored an own goal in March 2001 with an injudicious headlined reference to William Hague, for whom he had campaigned in the 1997 leadership ballots, as a 'baldy with a funny accent'.

WORTHING WEST

The West Sussex seaside town of Worthing is associated in many people's minds with one thing: the extreme age of its inhabitants. In the list of seats ranked on the basis of research conducted by Age Concern and Sheffield University in the year 2000, Worthing West was top, with over 45% of its electorate of pensionable age, forming an estimated 50% of actual voters due to the greater propensity of senior citizens to apply their democratic rights. In the circumstances of 2001, when the national turnout fell dramatically, this figure may have been even higher: perhaps even a majority of votes were cast by pensioners – although the overall turnout figure in the seat was no higher than the national average, at just under 60%.

Comparatively elderly voting was associated in political terms with strong Conservatism – Worthing has never been considered remotely marginal at parliamentary level. As a self-contained town of some 94,000 people it did have light industry, a service economy, financial service centres and other diversity which sustains a more nationally typical age and family structure. However, in Worthing West the 1997 Boundary Commission created a seat which manages to bring together the part of Worthing with the most retirees, the western half of its seafront, the wards of Marine, Heene and Goring; and some equally elderly communities brought in from Shoreham: Rustington, East Preston/Kingston and Ferring. 'Grey power' really will decide the outcome of contests in Worthing West.

This is likely to benefit the Conservatives. West is a more reliable seat for them than its partner to the east, Worthing East and Shoreham, which has a history of Labour and Liberal Democrat strength, at least at local level. While it is true that in the 1990s the Lib Dems gained (unlikely as it may sound) control of Worthing Council, they never cracked the Conservative coastal strongholds such as Goring-by-Sea; and the ex-Shoreham communities such as Rustington came from Arun district, not the more Liberal Democrat Adur. Worthing West, as well as being be the most elderly, may as a result be the most female of all the constituencies in the United Kingdom. The 'Golden Girls' of England's deep south coast by the true-blue English Channel seem certain to influence Worthing West in the Conservative interest, and that of its quirky MP, Peter Bottomley.

Social indices:			2001 Gen. Election:			
% Non-white	1.2		C	20,508	47.5	+1.3
% Prof/Man	36.7		LD	11,471	26.5	−4.6
% Non-manual	64.4		Lab	9,270	21.5	+5.2
£ Av prop val 2000	114 K		UKIP	1,960	4.5	+2.5
% Increase 97–00	51.4		C maj	9,037	20.9	
% Unemployed 2001	1.1		Turnout		59.7	−12.5
% Decrease 97–01	1.8		Elect	72,419		
% Fin hard/Rank	8.3	513				
% Pensioners	45.1					
% Prem mort/Rank	27	389				

Member of Parliament

Peter Bottomley prudently chicken-ran here in 1997 from Labour-threatened Eltham (which he had represented, originally as Woolwich West, since 1975). His short ministerial career (1984–90) is recalled for his outspoken attacks on drink-driving. A Europhile wet, he was born in 1944, son of a diplomat, was educated at Westminster School and Trinity College, Cambridge and worked in advertising. Seen (by Craig Brown) as exhibiting a 'twinge of loopiness', he cycles round London, smiles a good deal, and is well-supplied with the self-absorption of the politician with a mission, if with objectives not always immediately clear. He backed Hague in 1997 and the orthodox Ancram candidacy in 2001, and took up the defence of the beleaguered Parliamentary Standards Watchdog, Elizabeth Filkin. Though he regards his wife, Virginia, as a more successful politician than he, he now sits on a majority of 9,037, she on one of 861.

THE WREKIN

The great cone-shaped peak of The Wrekin dominates the mid-Shropshire countryside. But the seat named after the hill is no longer quite the same as the classic marginal which has changed hands between Labour and Conservative seven times in the last 50 years (in 1945, 1955, 1966, 1970, 1974, 1979, and 1987). In time for 1997 Shropshire was awarded a fifth and additional constituency as a result of population growth. The bulk of Telford New Town, the main source of Labour's strength in The Wrekin over recent decades, was hived off into a seat of its own (Telford). The remainder of the old Wrekin seat was joined by voters from Ludlow and North Shropshire to form a much less industrial and working-class division.

There is still quite an amount of 'New Town' and old industrial territory in The Wrekin, in areas like Donnington, Wellington and the fast growing Leegomery ward; but the boundaries seem almost designed to put Labour wards into the Telford constituency, and there is a lot of rural and small town (and Conservative) country around places such as Shifnal and Newport. This is no longer a compact urban seat but a fairly extensive slice of mid-Shropshire including villages like Lilleshall, where international sportspeople train. In most years all this would be expected to favour the Conservatives, but in the exceptional circumstances of 1997 Labour's Peter Bradley could defeat the former East Leicester MP Peter Bruinvels by 3,000 votes. Given its rural nature, and the noise made by the Countryside Alliance and others against the Blair government, most pundits predicted a Tory gain for Jacob Rees-Mogg, the son of the former editor of *The Times*, in 2001. Once again The Wrekin surprised them, as Bradley held on with a slightly increased majority. He – or rather the government – will have to do remarkably well again to make it three in a row on such unlikely ground.

Social indices:			2001 Gen. Election:			
% Non-white	4.4		Lab	19,532	47.1	+0.1
% Prof/Man	29.2		C	15,945	38.4	−1.8
% Non-manual	52.5		LD	4,738	11.4	−1.4
£ Av prop val 2000	82 K		UKIP	1,275	3.1	
% Increase 97–00	33.5		Lab maj	3,587	8.6	
% Unemployed 2001	2.2		Turnout		63.0	−13.5
% Decrease 97–01	0.3		Elect	65,837		
% Fin hard/Rank	17.9	307				
% Pensioners	23.9					
% Prem mort/Rank	30	349				

Member of Parliament

Peter Bradley, elected in 1997 as one of three new Labour MPs to have launched careers as Westminster City councillors in opposition to Shirley Porter's alleged homes-for-votes affair, has sought to maintain a high profile as befits a metropolitan PR man unexpectedly re-located to rural Shropshire. Born in 1953 and educated at Abingdon School and Sussex University, he has led calls for a Rural Affairs ministry and also spent time targeting the Belize-based Tory Party Treasurer, Michael Ashcroft. He is also concerned about MPs moonlighting, calculating in January 2002 that 155 of them have outside earnings. His re-election in 2001 denied the Commons the eccentric persona of the Woosterish young fogey, Jacob Rees-Mogg, whose election would have sustained the Conservatives' 1997 complement of 15 Old Etonians, reduced in his absence to 14.

WREXHAM

Wrexham was once the mining capital of North Wales, surrounded by a coalfield which reached public notice with the Gresford colliery disaster of 1934, in which hundreds of men were killed. The town is still ringed by large villages full of chapels which were once completely dependent upon mineral extractive industry: as well as Gresford, places like Llay, Brymbo and Rhosllanerchrugog. Now, however, the whole area is being transformed by economic diversification and development, as new investment is flowing in to create a wide variety of manufacturing employment. There is a vast industrial estate spreading over several square miles in the countryside to the east of Wrexham. The local council proclaimed that it is a boom area. Unemployment was below the Welsh average at 3.2% in June 2001, down 36.5% since 1997.

Wrexham used to be a genuine Labour stronghold, with a majority of over 17,000 in 1966, for example. In 1983 it lost some of its hinterland, though, as the new Clwyd South West seat was created, and this, combined with the defection to the SDP of its MP Tom Ellis and the fact that it was just about the worst year in Labour's history anyway, reduced the new member John Marek's majority to just 424 votes, by far their tightest squeak in over 50 years. The Liberals did very well in 1983 too, but they slipped back sharply in 1987 and Marek's majority increased tenfold. He retired in 2001 to devote his attentions to the Welsh Assembly, but Ian Lucas held Wrexham easily by 9,000 votes or 30% of the total. There are Conservative parts of Wrexham, such as the newish all-private housing estate of Borras Park in the north-east of the town, but they are outvoted by the working-class areas, such as the council estates of Caia Park in its south-eastern quadrant.

Whatever Wrexham's economic future holds, it is hard to imagine another close contest such as that of 1983, when several unique factors coincided.

Social indices:			2001 Gen. Election:			
% Non-white	1.0		Lab	15,934	53.0	−3.1
% Welsh sp	10.0		C	6,746	22.5	−1.4
% Prof/Man	29.6		LD	5,153	17.1	+3.9
% Non-manual	50.1		PC	1,783	5.9	+2.7
£ Av prop val 2000	70 K		UKIP	432	1.4	
% Increase 97–00	29.3		Lab maj	9,188	30.6	
% Unemployed 2001	3.2		Turnout		59.5	−12.2
% Decrease 97–01	1.8		Elect	50,465		
% Fin hard/Rank	18.6	293				
% Pensioners	25.9					
% Prem mort/Rank	35	240				

Member of Parliament

Ian Lucas, Labour's fresh-faced replacement here for Welsh-Assembly-departed John Marek, is a solicitor, born in 1960, raised in a council house, the grandson of a Durham miner, educated at Greenwell Comprehensive, Gateshead, Newcastle Royal Grammar School, New College, Oxford, and Chester Law College. Sometime Chairman of Wrexham CLP, his legal business is currently Oswestry-based and has acted on behalf of Trevor Rees-Jones, the bodyguard who survived the Princess of Wales' fatal car crash and whom he advised over publication of his version of the events in the face of opposition from Mohamed Al-Fayed. Self-described as 'a High Street solicitor ... patient and polite ... determined, persistent and persuasive', his political rise has been based on his local activism in Wrexham CLP and his performance in 1997 in North Shropshire when he cut the Tory majority from 13,000 to 2,000.

WYCOMBE

The town of High Wycombe itself has light industrial estates, many working-class voters, and a notable non-white community, which includes both Afro-Caribbeans and Asians and totals well over one-tenth of the population. It is also one of those places which has in the last ten years or so developed a reputation for violence and lawlessness late at night, in its case made all the more ugly by racial overtones. At the 1992 Election the Wycombe constituency delivered to the Tory MP Ray Whitney a majority of over 17,000 votes over the Liberal Democrat candidate, and even in 1997 after a 14% increase in the share of the Labour vote they still could not dislodge him; but the seat must now be regarded as a marginal and it gave Whitney's replacement, the *Daily Telegraph* journalist Paul Goodman, several frights before he took his Commons place in 2001.

About half of the electorate of this seat live outside High Wycombe itself, in affluent Marlow by the Thames and in many true-blue villages in the low Chiltern hills. In 1997 and 2001, when the Labour vote held steady at a substantial 35%, High Wycombe itself would have given them a lead: we can tell this from the county council election results on the same day, which provided all five of Labour's seats in Buckinghamshire in the latter year. This is not so surprising, despite the seat's solidly Conservative history, when one considers the modern industry at places like Cressex in the south-west of the town, and the dramatic urban scene which can be viewed from the M40 motorway as it sweeps in switchback fashion to the east of the town on its way between Oxford and London. Like so many medium-sized communities in south-east England, High Wycombe has opened its preferences and tastes up in the climate of a New Labour Party and indeed a New Labour administration. The highest proportion of ethnic minority residents are to be found in the (curiously rural-sounding) High Wycombe central wards of Oakridge and Tinkers Wood (33% non-white in 1981), and Bowerdean and Daws Hill (23%). These produced mixed results in the 1999 district results, but were taken by Labour in 2001 on a general election turnout.

Social indices:			2001 Gen. Election:			
% Non-white	12.6		C	19,064	42.4	+2.5
% Prof/Man	37.4		Lab	15,896	35.3	−0.1
% Non-manual	60.0		LD	7,658	17.0	−1.5
£ Av prop val 2000	153 K		UKIP	1,059	2.4	
% Increase 97–00	49.4		Grn	1,057	2.4	+1.0
% Unemployed 2001	1.9		Ind	240	0.5	
% Decrease 97–01	0.8		C maj	3,168	7.0	
% Fin hard/Rank	10.8	444	Turnout		60.2	−10.9
% Pensioners	19.6		Elect	74,647		
% Prem mort/Rank	18	498				

Member of Parliament

Paul Goodman, *Daily Telegraph* journalist and Eurosceptic, replaced the retiring Europhile MP, Sir Ray Whitney as Conservative MP in 2001. Born in 1959 and educated at the minor public school, Cranleigh, and at York University, he cites as an 'achievement' 'playing my part in ensuring that the *Daily Telegraph* is the main newspaper holding this Labour government properly to account'. One of William Hague's speechwriters, and a former Chairman of the Federation of Conservative Students, he has changed from backing immediate legalisation of drugs to favouring gradual decriminalisation. A novice candidate in this safe Tory seat, he spent, despite Jewish parentage, two years as a novice monk and a further year as home affairs editor on the *Catholic Herald*. In his maiden speech he invoked – with the Victorian Prime Minister's Hughenden House in his constituency – Disraeli's One Nation ideal, and voted in the first two leadership ballots for David Davis, and in the third for Iain Duncan Smith.

WYRE FOREST

In the last two general elections there has been one seat which has bucked all other trends and distinguished itself by electing a truly Independent MP, on a single issue of overwhelming import in the campaign, and shocking at least one major party out of any complacency they may have developed. In 1997 it was Tatton, where Martin Bell ran on an anti-corruption ticket and toppled the Conservative Neil Hamilton to provide one of the undoubted highlights of election night. Yet Dr Richard Taylor's achievement in 2001 in Wyre Forest was in several ways even greater. Unlike Martin Bell, he did not benefit from the withdrawal and tacit support of both main national parties opposing the sitting MP, but only of the Liberal Democrats, with relatively slender resources and polling only 8% in 1997. He was up against a perfectly respectable Junior Minister, David Lock, in a successful government in the process of being re-elected with another massive majority. He won by 17,630 votes, polling a share of 58%, higher than any candidate in Britain other than an official Labour standard bearer in a safe seat, and garnering more votes than anybody at all except for Mark Oaten in Winchester.

The issue which had given rise to this astonishing and complete triumph struck a resounding chord in an electorate which almost always names the National Health

Service as the most important political issue facing the country and their own families, linked with powerful local interest: closure of hospital provision in Kidderminster, the main town of the constituency, and its suggested transfer to Worcester. The pressure group set up to oppose this, Health Concern, had already proved its power and popularity by winning almost every seat it contested on the local council in 1999 and 2000. parliamentary elections are normally a different matter though, but Richard Taylor and his 28,487 voters thought and proved otherwise.

Where is Wyre Forest? Well, it is not in Lancashire and it has nothing to do with the Wyre constituency which existed from 1983 to 1997 or the present Lancaster and Wyre seat. It does in fact comprise the north-western corner of the geographical county of Worcestershire. There has been a seat named Wyre Forest since 1983, but it is in fact very similar to the previous seat of Kidderminster, which is easily the largest town, and a place of which most people have heard. The Wyre Forest seat contains three main towns of varying sizes and a number of villages. Kidderminster is best known as a centre of the carpet manufacturing industry; the second town, Stourport-on-Severn, is a canal centre; and the smallest, Bewdley, set quaintly also on the Severn, will always be associated in political terms with its member in the inter-war years, Stanley Baldwin. The Conservatives did hold the seat until David Lock seized it in the Labour landslide in 1997, and he would have been expecting a tough fight to hold it against a Tory regain at the end of his first term, before he was inundated by the hospital protection tide sweeping down the upper Severn. It is too early to tell what will happen at the next general election. Dr Taylor may prove to serve one term only, as Martin Bell did, in which case Wyre Forest will return to being a major party marginal; or if he considers his work is not done, the immediate circumstances of the next election will be decisive.

Social indices:			2001 Gen. Election:			
% Non-white	0.9		Ind	28,487	58.1	
% Prof/Man	32.7		Lab	10,857	22.1	−26.6
% Non-manual	51.4		C	9,350	19.1	−17.1
£ Av prop val 2000	81 K		UKIP	368	0.8	+0.2
% Increase 97–00	28.7		Ind maj	17,630	35.9	
% Unemployed 2001	2.3		Turnout		68.0	−7.4
% Decrease 97–01	1.2		Elect	72,152		
% Fin hard/Rank	14.8	357				
% Pensioners	24.3					
% Prem mort/Rank	26	408				

Member of Parliament

Dr Richard Taylor's election in this seat in 2001 was the election's most eccentric result: with a 66-year-old retired hospital consultant winning as an Independent protesting about the running down, by the unelected local health authority of Kidderminster Hospital. Dubbed by the sitting Labour MP David Lock, a single issue meddler, he has more of a local base than the outgoing Independent MP Martin Bell, with his 'Kidderminster Hospital and Health Concern' organisation having captured half the seats on the local council and running it after May 2000 in alliance with

Conservative and Liberal Democrat support. He has also sought to broaden his appeal to one against 'unelected quangos and civil servants' in general. Self-described as a 'political mess' having voted for all the parties in his time, he was born in 1934, the son of a Manchester cotton spinner, was educated at the Leys School, Cambridge, Clare College, Cambridge, and Westminster Hospital Medical School, and served in London hospitals and in the RAF before spending 23 years as a consultant at Kidderminster Hospital until retiring in 1995. Tall, and with the consultant's manner – both kindly and patronising, and with a tendency to rely on notes for his Commons interventions, his political attitudes – comprising Euroscepticism, and support for fox hunting and private schools – seem not to imply great radicalism. Duly included on the Health Select Committee, he was in 2001 the 17th oldest MP and one – as he points out – of the Commons' 39 old age pensioners.

WYTHENSHAWE AND SALE EAST

In general, the parliamentary boundary changes in Greater Manchester before the 1997 Election marked a disaster for the Conservatives, and one which was largely caused by being outmanoeuvred by the opposition parties in the local inquiries. One particularly notable example of this concerns the partisan history (before it was ever contested) of the constituency of Wythenshawe and Sale East.

The city of Manchester continued to shrink in the 1980s, and it was clear that it could not justify its allocation of five full seats. The border with one of the neighbouring boroughs would have to be crossed, to give Manchester four-and-a-bit constituencies. In their original proposals, the Commission suggested breaking up the undersized Manchester Wythenshawe division, and placing two of its wards in a new Altrincham. The Conservatives would have been happy with this, as Altrincham could easily have absorbed Baguley and Woodhouse Park. Then at the inquiry, which took place from 8–10 November 1993, the Assistant Commissioner was persuaded that Wythenshawe was a community which should not be broken up, due to its strong internal ties. The recommendations were reversed: the Wythenshawe seat was retained as a whole, and three Sale wards were added to it. It was effectively a take-over. Labour won the new seat comfortably. The Conservatives organised a storm of protest at the revised plans, including some people who thought that the city of Manchester might be invading their territory for local government purposes, but to no avail – their request for a second inquiry was not granted.

A parliamentary boundary review does not actually mean that the city boundaries will be changed for municipal purposes. However, it is true that the old Wythenshawe constituency extended far to the south on land annexed in the inter-war years on which both Manchester (Ringway) Airport and the massive overspill council estate of Wythenshawe were built. It was always fair to describe it as a 'council estate' seat, 76% of the housing being in local authority ownership in 1981 and 58% still in 1991 after a decade of sales. The Wythenshawe development was one of the largest in Europe, growing to a population of roughly 60,000 in the 1930s. It is awkwardly situated on the edge of the city, six to eight miles from Piccadilly, but it has not suffered quite so severely from inadequate services, high unemployment and the other extreme social and economic deprivations as its counterparts in Liverpool and

Glasgow have. Yet it is resolutely and remorselessly working class, and a solid area of Labour support. The former Wythenshawe seat did contain areas outside the estate itself, north of the A650 road: Brooklands is a good residential area, and Northenden mixed. Before 1964 this kind of area was enough to give the Conservatives victory, but the estate, and its growth, ultimately controlled the destiny of the seat. Its control of this new seat was scarcely dented by the arrival of three 'Sale East' wards: Priory from Davyhulme, and from Altrincham/Sale another Brooklands (bordering the Manchester city ward of the same name) and Sale Moor. The original Commission proposals would have removed a Labour seat in this area. The final report saved it, and in knock-on changes to the north destroyed Winston Churchill's Davyhulme. The Conservative Party were unsurprisingly furious and sad about the blows to their chances here in south-west Greater Manchester.

Social indices:			2001 Gen. Election:			
% Non-white	2.7		Lab	21,032	60.0	+1.9
% Prof/Man	27.8		C	8,424	24.0	−1.1
% Non-manual	51.9		LD	4,320	12.3	−0.1
£ Av prop val 2000	74 K		Grn	869	2.5	
% Increase 97–00	24.5		SLP	410	1.2	−0.9
% Unemployed 2001	4.1		Lab maj	12,608	36.0	
% Decrease 97–01	2.8		Turnout		48.6	−14.7
% Fin hard/Rank	39.9	53	Elect	72,127		
% Pensioners	29.7					
% Prem mort/Rank	48	55				

Member of Parliament

Paul Goggins, an ex-bearded Catholic social worker, was elected in 1997. PPS to Home Secretary David Blunkett from 2001, and previously to John Denham (1998–2000), born in 1953, he was educated at St Bede's (RC) Grammar School, Manchester, Ushaw (RC) College, Durham and Manchester Polytechnic. Originally a child care social worker with the Liverpool Catholic Archdiocese, he ran a children's home in Wigan for eight years, was Project Director for the (Methodist-run) NCH Action for Children for five years, and followed fellow Catholic and Labour MP John Battle as Director of Church Action on Poverty for eight years, doubling-up in the latter post as a Salford City councillor. A stalwart of the Christian Socialist Movement at a time when most Labour activists are embarrassed about, if not hostile to, religion, he has appeared on BBC Radio Four's *Thought for the Day*, to declare that 'the heart of religion is a concern for justice'. Impeccably loyal, he backed lone parent benefit cuts without being able to tell left-winger John McDonnell where they were promised in Labour's manifesto, and backs expansion of Manchester Airport against the local opposition from Cheshire's stockbroker belt NIMBY voters.

YEOVIL

Just as the General Election of 2001 showed that becoming a party leader can reap rewards in terms of constituency performance (Charles Kennedy in Ross/Skye/

Inverness West, William Hague in Richmond), it also was clear that the seat of a former number one can swing against his party, as the successors found of John Major in Huntingdon, Ieuan Wyn Jones in Ynys Mon and Paddy Ashdown in Yeovil.

The south Somerset seat of Yeovil may have been Conservative from its creation in 1918 to 1983, but it had become a Liberal Democrat stronghold over the next four elections, dominated by its MP, the popular leader of the party Paddy Ashdown. Ashdown, a former Marine and diplomat, had built up a great head of steam after several years of local campaigning, and seized the opportunity presented by John Peyton's retirement to gain the seat in 1983. He did not look back. Consolidating his position in the Yeovil seat by local and national energy and enthusiasm, he increased his majority in 1987, and again in 1992 and 1997 – now boosted too by nine years' publicity as national leader of his party.

In 2001, though, David Laws found his lead over the Tories reduced to a bare 8%, compared with Ashdown's last margin of 21%, and the Liberal Democrat majority fell from over 11,000 to under 4,000. Some of this was due to the collapse of the Referendum Party's anti-European vote, but some of it was Ashdown's personal support too, based on his own established and widely attested hard work locally over 20 years since his move to the Old Post Office in the idyllic village of Norton-sub-Hamdon as well as his national prominence. Things could be worse for Laws though. The party remains solidly in the lead in local elections at both South Somerset district and county level within the seat, in Yeovil town itself, and in the countryside and smaller towns of Chard, Crewkerne and Ilminster, all within striking distance of the Dorset border. The largest employer in Yeovil is Westland Helicopters, who have a number of plants in and around the town. A political row involving Westland nearly brought down the mighty Margaret Thatcher in 1986. Paddy Ashdown never managed that – her own party did – but he deserves much of the credit for giving the Liberal Democrats the greatly enhanced credibility they take with them into the new century.

Social indices:			2001 Gen. Election:			
% Non-white	0.6		LD	21,266	44.2	−4.6
% Prof/Man	30.1		C	17,338	36.0	+8.4
% Non-manual	51.7		Lab	7,077	14.7	−0.2
£ Av prop val 2000	94 K		UKIP	1,131	2.3	
% Increase 97–00	52.2		Grn	786	1.6	+0.3
% Unemployed 2001	1.5		Lib	534	1.1	
% Decrease 97–01	1.4		LD maj	3,928	8.2	
% Fin hard/Rank	12.7	403	Turnout		63.4	−9.5
% Pensioners	29.2		Elect	75,977		
% Prem mort/Rank	17	516				

Member of Parliament

David Laws, successor to Sir Paddy Ashdown here in 2001, was drawn from the Liberal Democrats' inner sanctum as a merchant banker (first with J.P. Morgan for five years and then as Managing Director at Barclay's de Zoete Wedd from 1992 to 1994) who turned party apparatchik, working as the Party's economic adviser

(1994–97), and as Director of Policy and Research (1997–99). Born in 1965, he enjoyed something of a gilded youth, educated at the Catholic public school, St George's College, Weybridge (where he won the *Observer* Mace Debating Competition) and King's College, Cambridge, where he obtained a double first in economics. An incisive questioner of Treasury ministers after 2001, he had earlier provided the advice enabling Treasury spokesman Malcolm Bruce to discover a 'black hole' in Chancellor Brown's spending plans and was appointed to the Treasury Select Committee in 2001. One of seven Liberal Democrat MPs to have inherited Lib Dem seats in 2001, in his case – as in others – a lot of the inherited majority was lost in the process.

YNYS MON

Everyone would agree that Labour had another great result in the 2001 General Election, enjoying a unprecedented second crushing victory in succession with an overall majority of over 160. Yet in fact they only made two gains, one from the Conservatives in Dorset South and one in Ynys Mon, where the Plaid Cymru leader Ieuan Wyn Jones had retired. His replacement Eilian Williams failed to hold the island the English (and many Welsh) call Anglesey, and Albert Owen became probably the most unexpected new Labour MP: almost no-one outside the area had predicted a nationalist loss. In retrospect this was missing an obvious possibility, for we can now see that the nationalists did badly almost everywhere where they gave up a Westminster seat for one in a devolved body, whether in Scotland or Wales. This was partly because these small parties, like the Liberal Democrats, rely more on personal votes than the big two; and partly because nationalist voters were most likely to see Westminster as less relevant now an assembly had come into being.

When the Boundary Commission renamed the Anglesey constituency Ynys Mon in 1983, it moved from near the beginning almost to the end of the alphabetical list of seats, but it has remained an insular parliamentary unit on its own. The decision to change the name to the Welsh form seemed logical enough at the time, for 62% of the population do speak Welsh, many employing it as their preferred language. It appeared even more logical after 1987, when Ieuan Wyn Jones was elected Plaid Cymru MP for Ynys Mon.

He won in somewhat unusual circumstances. The Conservative member of eight years' standing, Keith Best, had fraudulently entered multiple applications for the British Telecom share offer, and had been forced to withdraw as candidate at the 11th hour. It now seems likely that this might have proved critical, for Plaid Cymru won fairly easily (by over 4,000 votes) in 1987, but the Conservatives improved their performance in 1992 against the regional trend and cut Ieuan Wyn Jones's majority down to a slender 1,100. 1997 produced the same winner, but a modified result, as Labour took second place from the Conservatives after increasing their vote by nearly 10%. They were clearly the best placed to inherit the seat on Ieuan Wyn Jones's 2001 departure.

Ynys Mon will remain an individual and possibly unpredictable constituency, especially if Labour should become less popular after a second term of government.

One thing is certain – it may be the last of the Welsh seats in alphabetical order, but it is very far from the least, in terms of electoral interest at any rate.

Social indices:			2001 Gen. Election:			
% Non-white	0.5		Lab	11,906	35.0	+1.8
% Welsh sp	62.0		PC	11,106	32.6	−6.8
% Prof/Man	32.1		C	7,653	22.5	+1.0
% Non-manual	51.1		LD	2,772	8.1	+4.3
£ Av prop val 2000	60 K		UKIP	359	1.1	
% Increase 97–00	15.1		Ind	222	0.7	
% Unemployed 2001	6.2		Lab maj	800	2.4	
% Decrease 97–01	2.3		Turnout		64.0	−11.4
% Fin hard/Rank	10.8	443	Elect	53,117		
% Pensioners	28.2					
% Prem mort/Rank	37	225				

Member of Parliament

Albert Owen recaptured this seat from the nationalists for Labour in 2001, a matter of weeks after the death of Labour's last Anglesey MP, Cledwyn Hughes (1950–79). One of only two MPs registering Labour gains in the election, he was born in 1959, educated locally at Holyhead County Comprehensive School, Coleg Harlech, and York University, and served as a merchant seaman for 17 years until becoming a welfare rights officer in 1992 and manager of Holyhead's Advice, Information and Training Centre for Anglesey County Council from 1997 to 2001. Aided in his election campaign by Anglesey-born Glenys Kinnock and by Cledwyn Hughes' widow, by Plaid Cymru's resources being too thinly spread as they sought to capture the neighbouring Conwy seat, by the unpopularity of the outgoing Plaid MP Ieuan Wyn Jones, and by dissension over his chosen successor, his defeat of the Plaid here compensated for the loss of Carmarthen East to the nationalists. His immediate rebellion in June 2001 against the Labour Whips' attempt to pack Select Committees took some shine off his achievement, without precluding his own assignment to the Welsh Affairs Committee.

YORK, CITY OF

Before the 1992 General Election York was the Conservatives' most marginal seat. On that day, though, it was not even close. Labour needed a swing of around one-tenth of 1% to capture York, but achieved 50 times that – 5%. Conal Gregory, the Market Research Society's representative in Parliament, suffered an even greater disaster than his polling clients, and lost to Labour's Hugh Bayley by 6,342 votes – the second heaviest defeat of a sitting Tory MP (after Michael Knowles of Nottingham East). There was some local muttering about defeatism in the Tory ranks, and a lack of energy in the defence of so vulnerable a seat, especially at a time when the pollsters were bruiting gloomier news for the government than the eventual outcome nationally would bring.

Bayley's majority leapt in 1997 to over 20,000, by far the highest York has seen. In 2001, though, his share dropped by nearly 8%, a much worse than average result, although it could easily be absorbed. Most of this slack was taken up by the Liberal Democrat candidate Andrew Waller. Although the Liberal Democrats do very well in local elections in York, for example taking 40% and clearly finishing first in the unitary authority in 1999, they have tended to be squeezed out of national contests by the tight two-party situation. There is just a hint of evidence that this may be changing, but Labour will need to be much more unpopular nationally before this constituency seems competitive again.

York is a city of great interest and diversity. It is of course famed for its cathedral-Minster and its medieval walls, which attract a vast throng of visitors. The central ward, Guildhall, is full of elegant town houses and twee shops, but that didn't stop it voting Labour every May in the 1990s. York is also a notable railway centre, and a manufacturing metropolis for engineering, leather and chemicals, and chocolate, cocoa and confectionery. The Rowntree Quaker tradition may have something to do with the radical tinge to York's modern politics, and even with the local Liberal vote, but for a long time Liberalism was dormant in York, and the most recent local government success is probably a phenomenon of much more recent origin.

Social indices:			2001 Gen. Election:			
% Non-white	1.1		Lab	25,072	52.3	−7.7
% Prof/Man	30.8		C	11,293	23.5	−1.2
% Non-manual	52.4		LD	8,519	17.8	+6.6
£ Av prop val 2000	82 K		Grn	1,465	3.1	+1.5
% Increase 97–00	31.8		SA	674	1.4	
% Unemployed 2001	3.0		UKIP	576	1.2	+0.7
% Decrease 97–01	2.4		MRLP	381	0.8	
% Fin hard/Rank	15.9	337	Lab maj	13,779	28.7	
% Pensioners	27.7		Turnout		59.7	−13.9
% Prem mort/Rank	33	288	Elect	80,431		

Member of Parliament

Hugh Bayley, as Junior Social Security Minister (1999–2001), was a successfully niche-marketed-if-unobtrusive politician with an academic background in health economics, and a former PPS to Frank Dobson (1997–99). Elected for York at his second attempt in 1992, he was born in 1952, son of an architect, and before attending Bristol and York Universities, was part of an oddly numerous group of Labour MPs educated at Haileybury – including Clement Attlee, Christopher Mayhew, Geoffrey de Freitas, and (currently) Barry Gardiner. Before doing research into care of the old at York University, he was a NALGO officer, and a TV producer specialising in the Third World. Ex-bearded, and married to a wife of Caribbean origin, he is concerned about flooding in York, living as he does on the banks of the River Ouse. Retired at 49, he graced the International Development Select Committee with two other dropped ministers from the 2001 reshuffle.

YORKSHIRE EAST

In 1974 the county of Humberside came into existence for the purposes of the administration of local government. This was not popular with the citizens of either the East Riding of Yorkshire, or of north Lincolnshire, both of whom maintained the proud traditions of their historic counties. North of the estuary (which actually served to divide rather than unite 'Humberside' folk) the desire and determination to keep a Yorkshire identity was emphasised in many ways, including the renaming of the District of North Wolds as the Borough of East Yorkshire. In 1995 the parliamentary Boundary Commission seized the opportunity to redraw the constituency lines in this area to produce a seat with exactly the same borders and name as East Yorkshire – although common press usage inevitably places the compass point after the name of the county. Following the abolition of Humberside, local government has now been reorganised into unitary authorities in this part of Britain, effectively subsuming the East Yorkshire borough within a larger East Riding, but this seat has not yet been affected.

Most of East Yorkshire consists of most of the former Bridlington division (47,000 voters), together with just over 21,000 from the northern tip of the abolished Boothferry seat. There are two main kinds of terrain. One is the coast, stretching from the largest town of Bridlington, a seaside resort and port of note, to the great cliffs of Flamborough Head, falling short of Filey. Inland are the rolling Wolds, with their fine mixed agricultural land, and the market towns of Driffield, Market Weighton and Pocklington. There is also a centre of population at Stamford Bridge, the site of the other famous battle of 1066. However, the political warfare in this seat will scarcely be as keen.

Labour can win local elections consistently only in Bridlington Old Town and South, and have a few votes in the second largest metropolis, Driffield. The Lib Dems have little tradition of local activism either on the coast or on the Wolds. The new seat of East Yorkshire, proudly bearing its much fought-for name, elected the former Bridlington MP John Townend by just over 3,000 votes from Labour in 1997. Townend's retirement was not without controversy in 2001, as he bowed out with controversial remarks concerning Britain's multi-cultural society (the word mongrel slipped out) and although widely disowned he was not suspended or expelled from the party, partly on the grounds that he was departing from Parliament anyway. No effect of the manner of his going could be discerned as Greg Knight became one of seven Tory victims of the 1997 landslide to return to the Commons.

Social indices:			2001 Gen. Election:			
% Non-white	0.4		C	19,861	45.9	+3.2
% Prof/Man	31.5		Lab	15,179	35.0	−0.8
% Non-manual	49.7		LD	6,300	14.5	−4.0
£ Av prop val 2000	66 K		UKIP	1,661	3.8	
% Increase 97–00	24.8		Ind	313	0.7	
% Unemployed 2001	3.9		C maj	4,682	10.8	
% Decrease 97–01	1.0		Turnout		59.9	−10.7
% Fin hard/Rank	10.6	451	Elect	72,342		
% Pensioners	30.8					
% Prem mort/Rank	29	368				

Member of Parliament

Greg Knight Deputy Shadow Leader of the House from 2001, was originally MP for Derby North, when he entered on the Thatcherite flood of 1983 and left on the Blairite flood of 1997. Risen through the Whips Office, eventually serving as Deputy Chief Whip 1993–96, he left few footprints, and served only briefly as a DTI Minister (1996–97). A solicitor, born in 1949, and educated at Alderman Newton's Grammar School, Leicester and Guildford College of Law, a beefy ex-bearded bachelor, he has backed anti-hunting and animal welfare bills and written books of parliamentary anecdotes. In April 2001 he lived up to his 'Silent Knight' reputation in prudently staying out of the controversy over his predecessor John Townend's allegedly racist remarks. His re-election to the Commons in June 2001 also showed a certain deftness. When he was defeated in 1997 he had been an MP for almost 14 years, a span very close to the post-1970 MPs' average tenure of 12 years 11 months or – approximately – three parliamentary terms. But with skills and intelligence acquired in seven years as a Whip, latterly quelling the Europhobes for John Major, he ignored the Central Office diktat against would-be retreads chicken-running, in his case to safe seats in Yorkshire, and gave his career a rare second wind, even walking back onto the frontbench after casting leadership ballots first for Eurosceptic David Davis, then for Europhile Kenneth Clarke. Such are the political arts.

Maps

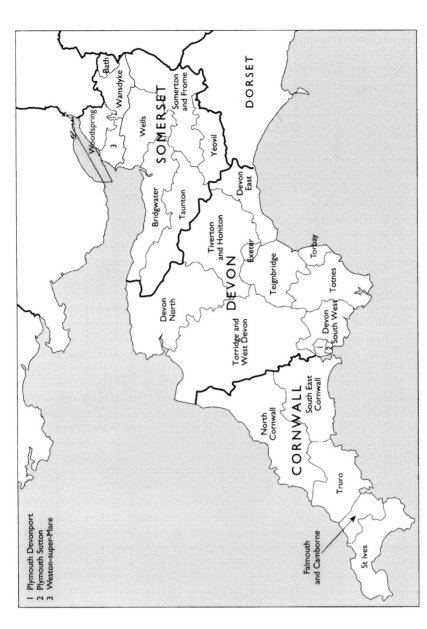

1 Plymouth Devonport
2 Plymouth Sutton
3 Weston-super-Mare

Woodspring
Bath
Wansdyke
SOMERSET
Wells
Somerton and Frome
Bridgwater
Taunton
Yeovil
Devon East
Tiverton and Honiton
Exeter
Teignbridge
Torbay
Totnes
DEVON
Devon North
Torridge and West Devon
Devon South West
DORSET
North Cornwall
South East Cornwall
CORNWALL
Truro
Falmouth and Camborne
St Ives

Map 1   South West England

Map 2   Wessex

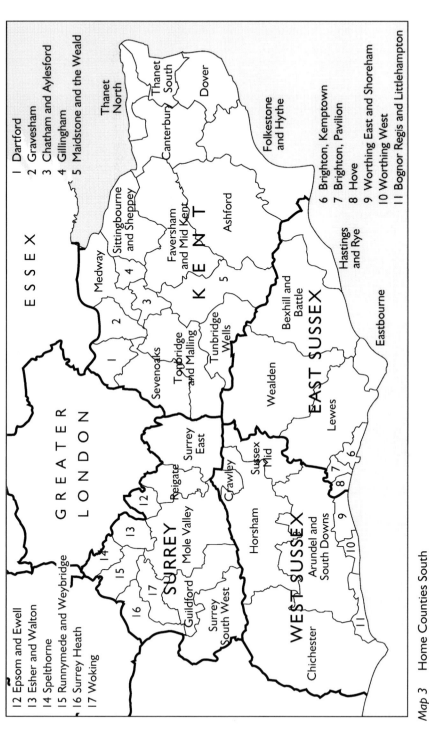

1 Dartford
2 Gravesham
3 Chatham and Aylesford
4 Gillingham
5 Maidstone and the Weald

6 Brighton, Kemptown
7 Brighton, Pavilion
8 Hove
9 Worthing East and Shoreham
10 Worthing West
11 Bognor Regis and Littlehampton

12 Epsom and Ewell
13 Esher and Walton
14 Spelthorne
15 Runnymede and Weybridge
16 Surrey Heath
17 Woking

Map 3   Home Counties South

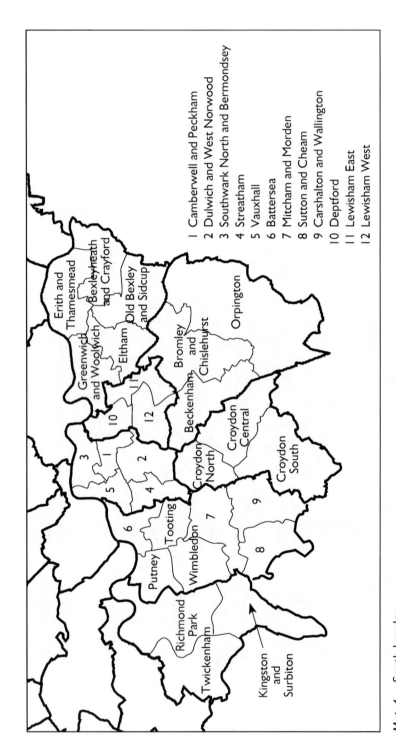

1 Camberwell and Peckham
2 Dulwich and West Norwood
3 Southwark North and Bermondsey
4 Streatham
5 Vauxhall
6 Battersea
7 Mitcham and Morden
8 Sutton and Cheam
9 Carshalton and Wallington
10 Deptford
11 Lewisham East
12 Lewisham West

Erith and Thamesmead
Bexleyheath and Crayford
Greenwich and Woolwich
Eltham
Old Bexley and Sidcup
Bromley and Chislehurst
Orpington
Beckenham
Croydon Central
Croydon North
Croydon South
Putney
Tooting
Wimbledon
Richmond Park
Twickenham
Kingston and Surbiton

Map 4   South London

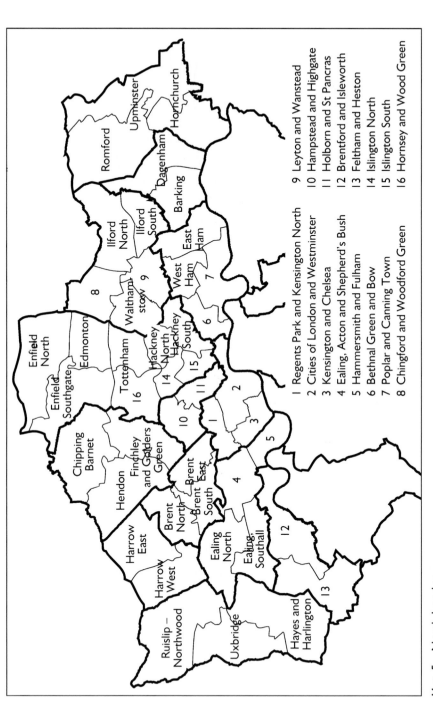

1 Regents Park and Kensington North
2 Cities of London and Westminster
3 Kensington and Chelsea
4 Ealing, Acton and Shepherd's Bush
5 Hammersmith and Fulham
6 Bethnal Green and Bow
7 Poplar and Canning Town
8 Chingford and Woodford Green
9 Leyton and Wanstead
10 Hampstead and Highgate
11 Holborn and St Pancras
12 Brentford and Isleworth
13 Feltham and Heston
14 Islington North
15 Islington South
16 Hornsey and Wood Green

Map 5   North London

1 Oxford West and Abingdon
2 Oxford East
3 Milton Keynes South West
4 Bedford
5 Luton North
6 Hertfordshire South West
7 Reading West
8 Reading East

Map 6　Home Counties North

Map 7 East Anglia

Map 8   Welsh Marches and Warwickshire

1 Sparkbrook and Small Heath
2 Halesowen and Rowley Regis
3 West Bromwich East
4 West Bromwich West
5 Wolverhampton North East
6 Wolverhampton South East
7 Wolverhampton South West

Map 9 West Midlands

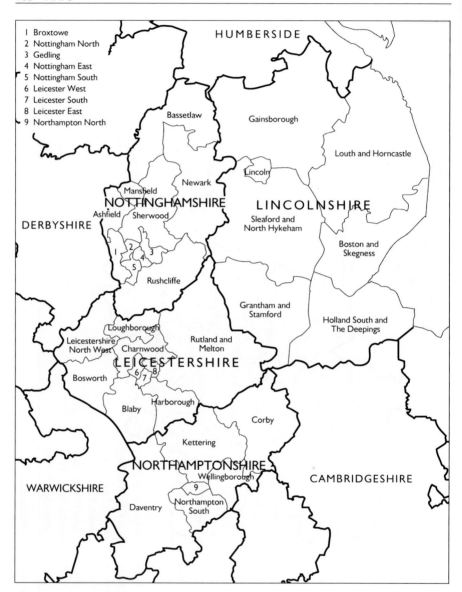

1 Broxtowe
2 Nottingham North
3 Gedling
4 Nottingham East
5 Nottingham South
6 Leicester West
7 Leicester South
8 Leicester East
9 Northampton North

HUMBERSIDE

Bassetlaw

Gainsborough

Louth and Horncastle

Lincoln

Newark

Mansfield

NOTTINGHAMSHIRE

LINCOLNSHIRE

Ashfield   Sherwood

DERBYSHIRE

Sleaford and
North Hykeham

Boston and
Skegness

1 2
4 3
5

Rushcliffe

Grantham and
Stamford

Holland South and
The Deepings

Loughborough

Leicestershire
North West   Charnwood

Rutland and
Melton

LEICESTERSHIRE

Bosworth

6 8
7

Blaby

Harborough

Corby

Kettering

NORTHAMPTONSHIRE

Wellingborough

CAMBRIDGESHIRE

WARWICKSHIRE

9

Daventry   Northampton
South

Map 10   East Midlands

1 Stoke-on-Trent North
2 Stoke-on-Trent Central
3 Stoke-on-Trent South
4 Newcastle under Lyme

Map 11   North Midlands

1   Manchester, Central
2   Manchester, Gorton
3   Manchester, Withington
4   Manchester, Blackley
5   Wythenshawe and Sale East
6   Oldham West and Royton

Map 12   Greater Manchester

1 Liverpool, Walton
2 Liverpool, West Derby
3 Liverpool, Riverside
4 Liverpool, Wavertree
5 Liverpool, Garston
6 Knowsley South
7 Knowsley North and Sefton East
8 Bootle
9 Crosby
10 Southport
11 Blackpool South
12 Blackpool North and Fleetwood

Morecambe
and Lunesdale

Lancaster and Wyre

Ribble Valley

Pendle

L A N C A S H I R E

12

Burnley

Fylde

11

Hyndburn

Preston

Blackburn

Ribble South

Rossendale
and Darwen

Chorley

10

Lancashire
West

G R E A T E R
M A N C H E S T E R

9

M E R S E Y S I D E 7

8

14

14 St Helens North
15 St Helens South
16 Wirral South
17 Wirral West
18 Birkenhead
19 Wallasey

15

6

3

4

19

5

17 18

16

C H E S H I R E

Map 13   Lancashire and Merseyside

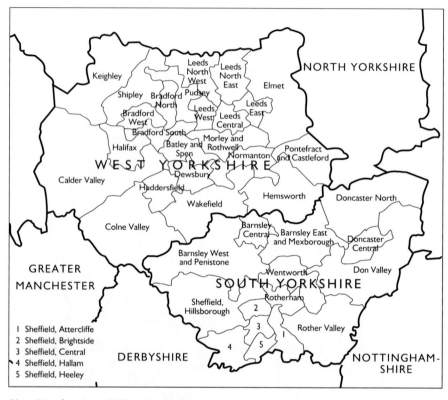

Map 14 South and West Yorkshire

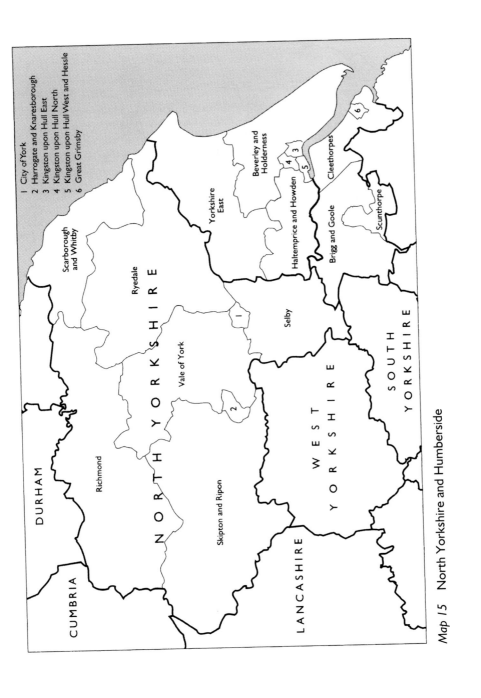

Map 15 North Yorkshire and Humberside

1 City of York
2 Harrogate and Knaresborough
3 Kingston upon Hull East
4 Kingston upon Hull North
5 Kingston upon Hull West and Hessle
6 Great Grimsby

CUMBRIA

DURHAM

Richmond

NORTH YORKSHIRE

Scarborough
and Whitby

Ryedale

Skipton and Ripon

Vale of York

Yorkshire
East

Beverley and
Holderness

LANCASHIRE

WEST
YORKSHIRE

Selby

Haltemprice and Howden

Brigg and Goole

SOUTH
YORKSHIRE

Cleethorpes

Scunthorpe

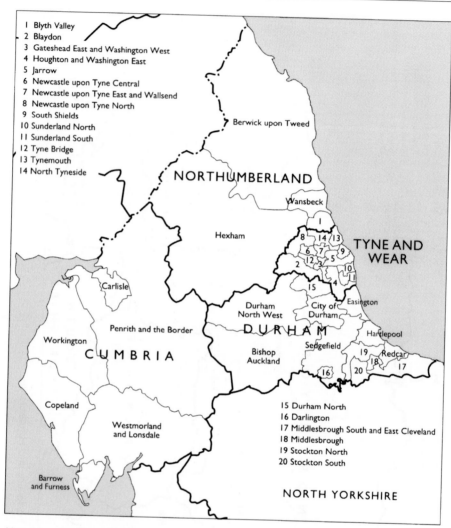

1 Blyth Valley
2 Blaydon
3 Gateshead East and Washington West
4 Houghton and Washington East
5 Jarrow
6 Newcastle upon Tyne Central
7 Newcastle upon Tyne East and Wallsend
8 Newcastle upon Tyne North
9 South Shields
10 Sunderland North
11 Sunderland South
12 Tyne Bridge
13 Tynemouth
14 North Tyneside

Berwick upon Tweed

NORTHUMBERLAND

Wansbeck

Hexham

1
8 14 13
6 7   9
2 12 5
      10
   4
15

TYNE AND
WEAR

Carlisle

Durham
North West

City of
Durham

Easington

DURHAM

Hartlepool

Penrith and the Border

Workington

CUMBRIA

Bishop
Auckland

Sedgefield

19   Redcar
   18
20   17

Copeland

Westmorland
and Lonsdale

15 Durham North
16 Darlington
17 Middlesbrough South and East Cleveland
18 Middlesbrough
19 Stockton North
20 Stockton South

16

Barrow
and Furness

NORTH YORKSHIRE

Map 16   Northern England

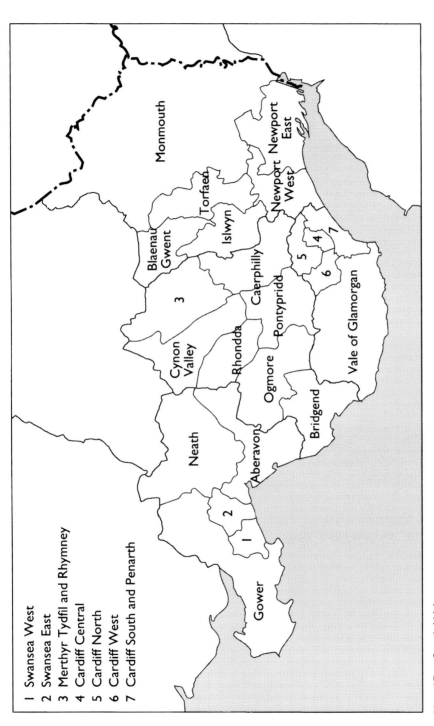

1 Swansea West
2 Swansea East
3 Merthyr Tydfil and Rhymney
4 Cardiff Central
5 Cardiff North
6 Cardiff West
7 Cardiff South and Penarth

Gower

Neath

Cynon
Valley

Blaenau
Gwent

Monmouth

Torfaen

Islwyn

Newport
East

Newport
West

Caerphilly

Rhondda

Pontypridd

Ogmore

Aberavon

Bridgend

Vale of Glamorgan

Map 17   South Wales

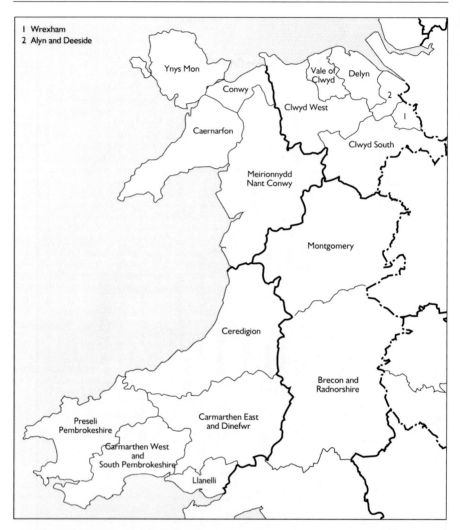

Map 18 Mid and North Wales

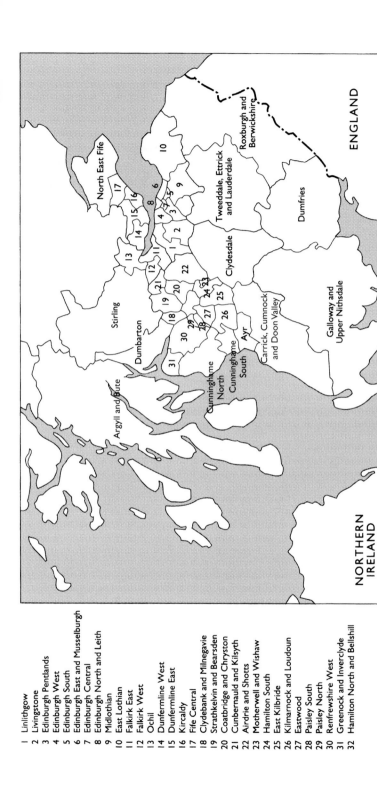

1 Linlithgow
2 Livingstone
3 Edinburgh Pentlands
4 Edinburgh West
5 Edinburgh South
6 Edinburgh East and Musselburgh
7 Edinburgh Central
8 Edinburgh North and Leith
9 Midlothian
10 East Lothian
11 Falkirk East
12 Falkirk West
13 Ochil
14 Dunfermline West
15 Dunfermline East
16 Kircaldy
17 Fife Central
18 Clydebank and Milngavie
19 Strathkelvin and Bearsden
20 Coatbridge and Chryston
21 Cumbernauld and Kilsyth
22 Airdrie and Shotts
23 Motherwell and Wishaw
24 Hamilton South
25 East Kilbride
26 Kilmarnock and Loudoun
27 Eastwood
28 Paisley South
29 Paisley North
30 Renfrewshire West
31 Greenock and Inverclyde
32 Hamilton North and Bellshill

Map 19 Southern Scotland

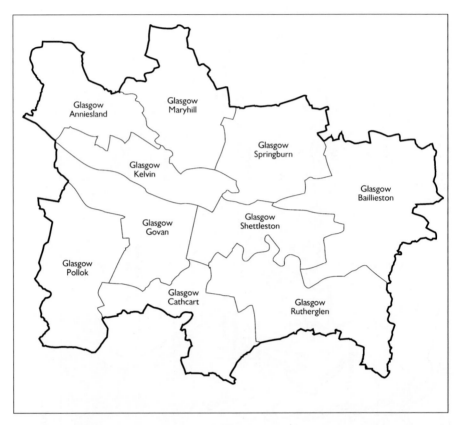

Map 20 **Glasgow**

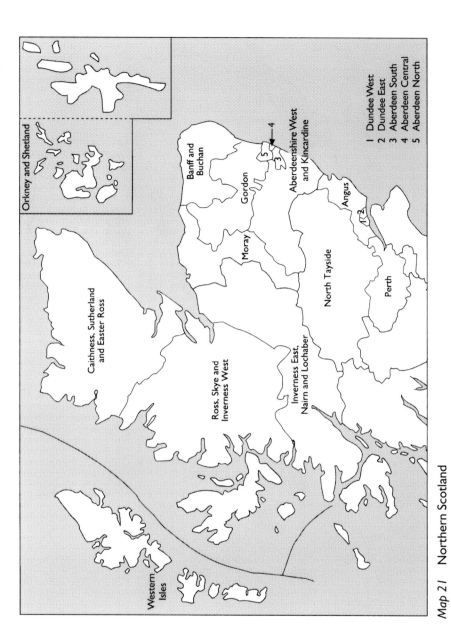

Map 21 Northern Scotland

Orkney and Shetland

Caithness, Sutherland and Easter Ross

Ross, Skye and Inverness West

Inverness East, Nairn and Lochaber

Western Isles

Banff and Buchan

Gordon

Moray

Aberdeenshire West and Kincardine

Angus

North Tayside

Perth

1   Dundee West
2   Dundee East
3   Aberdeen South
4   Aberdeen Central
5   Aberdeen North

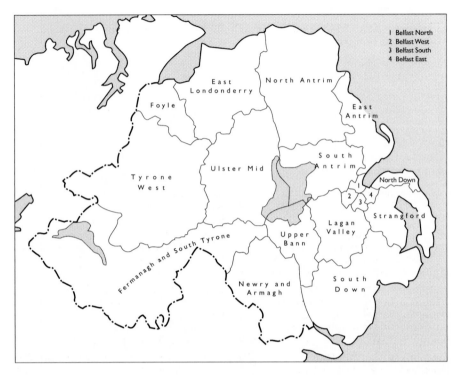

Map 22   Northern Ireland

Index of Members of Parliament